EF
3.91 v.5
1e

AMERICAN DECADES

PRIMARY SOURCES

1940-1949

AMERICAN DECADES
PRIMARY SOURCES
1940-1949

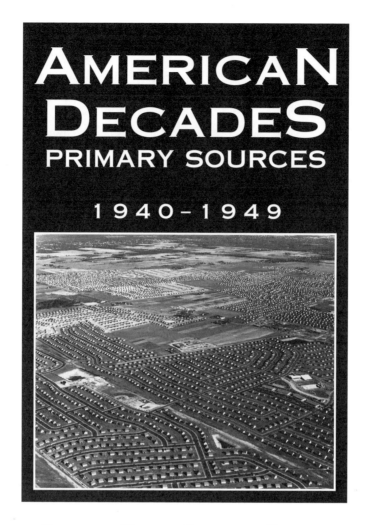

CYNTHIA ROSE, PROJECT EDITOR

GALE®

THOMSON
GALE

Detroit • New York • San Diego • San Francisco • Cleveland • New Haven, Conn. • Waterville, Maine • London • Munich

American Decades Primary Sources, 1940–1949

Project Editor
Cynthia Rose

Editorial
Jason M. Everett, Rachel J. Kain, Pamela A. Dear, Andrew C. Claps, Thomas Carson, Kathleen Droste, Christy Justice, Lynn U. Koch, Michael D. Lesniak, Nancy Matuszak, John F. McCoy, Michael Reade, Rebecca Parks, Mark Mikula, Polly A. Rapp, Mark Springer

Data Capture
Civie A. Green, Beverly Jendrowski, Gwendolyn S. Tucker

Permissions
Margaret Abendroth, Margaret A. Chamberlain, Lori Hines, Jacqueline Key, Mari Masalin-Cooper, William Sampson, Shalice Shah-Caldwell, Kim Smilay, Sheila Spencer, Ann Taylor

Indexing Services
Lynne Maday, John Magee

Imaging and Multimedia
Dean Dauphinais, Leitha Etheridge-Sims, Mary K. Grimes, Lezlie Light, Daniel W. Newell, David G. Oblender, Christine O'Bryan, Kelly A. Quin, Luke A. Rademacher, Denay Wilding, Robyn V. Young

Product Design
Michelle DiMercurio

Composition and Electronic Prepress
Evi Seoud

Manufacturing
Rita Wimberley

For permission to use material from this product, submit your request via Web at http://gale-edit.com/permissions, or you may download our Permissions Request form and submit your request by fax or mail to:

Permissions Department
The Gale Group, Inc.
27500 Drake Rd.
Farmington Hills, MI 48331-3535
Permissions Hotline:
248-699-8006 or 800-877-4253, ext. 8006
Fax: 248-699-8074 or 800-762-4058

Cover photographs reproduced by permission of Bettmann/Corbis (Chrysler Corporation's Tank Arsenal Factory, center; Tuskegee airmen, spine), The Granger Collection, New York (Duke Ellington, left), and UPI/Corbis-Bettmann (Aerial view of Levittown, New York, background; President Harry S. Truman, right).

LIBRARY OF CONGRESS CATALOGING-IN-PUBLICATION DATA

American decades primary sources / edited by Cynthia Rose.
   v. cm.
Includes bibliographical references and index.
Contents: [1] 1900-1909 — [2] 1910-1919 — [3] 1920-1929 — [4] 1930-1939 — [5] 1940-1949 — [6] 1950-1959 — [7] 1960-1969 — [8] 1970-1979 — [9] 1980-1989 — [10] 1990-1999.
   ISBN 0-7876-6587-8 (set : hardcover : alk. paper) — ISBN 0-7876-6588-6 (v. 1 : hardcover : alk. paper) — ISBN 0-7876-6589-4 (v. 2 : hardcover : alk. paper) — ISBN 0-7876-6590-8 (v. 3 : hardcover : alk. paper) — ISBN 0-7876-6591-6 (v. 4 : hardcover : alk. paper) — ISBN 0-7876-6592-4 (v. 5 : hardcover : alk. paper) — ISBN 0-7876-6593-2 (v. 6 : hardcover : alk. paper) — ISBN 0-7876-6594-0 (v. 7 : hardcover : alk. paper) — ISBN 0-7876-6595-9 (v. 8 : hardcover : alk. paper) — ISBN 0-7876-6596-7 (v. 9 : hardcover : alk. paper) — ISBN 0-7876-6597-5 (v. 10 : hardcover : alk. paper)
   1. United States—Civilization—20th century—Sources. I. Rose, Cynthia.
E169.1.A471977 2004
973.91—dc21

2002008155

CONTENTS

Entries are arranged in chronological order by date of primary source. For entries with one primary source, the entry title is the primary source title. Entries with more than one primary source have an overall entry title, followed by the titles of the primary sources.

Fashion and Design

Government and Politics

Law and Justice

Lifestyles and Social Trends

ADVISORS AND CONTRIBUTORS

Advisors

CARL A. ANTONUCCI, JR. has spent the past ten years as a reference librarian at various colleges and universities. Currently director of library services at Capital Community College, he holds two master's degrees and is a doctoral candidate at Providence College. His particularly enjoys researching Rhode Island political history during the 1960s and 1970s.

KATHY ARSENAULT is the dean of library at the University of South Florida, St. Petersburg's Poynter Library. She holds a master's degree in Library Science. She has written numerous book reviews for *Library Journal*, and has published articles in such publications as the *Journal of the Florida Medical Association*, and *Collection Management*.

JAMES RETTIG holds two master's degrees. He has written numerous articles and has edited *Distinguished Classics of Reference Publishing* (1992). University librarian at the University of Richmond, he is the recipient of three American Library Association awards: the Isadore Gibert Mudge Citation (1988), the G.K. Hall Award for Library Literature (1993), and the Louis Shores-Oryx Press Award (1995).

HILDA K. WEISBURG is the head library media specialist at Morristown High School Library and specializes in building school library media programs. She has several publications to her credit, including: *The School Librarians Workshop*, *Puzzles, Patterns, and*

Problem Solving: Creative Connections to Critical Thinking, and *Learning, Linking & Critical Thinking: Information Strategies for the K-12 Library Media Curriculum*.

Contributors

PETER J. CAPRIOGLIO is a professor emeritus at Middlesex Community College, where he taught social sciences for thirty years prior to his retirement. He has a master's in sociology, and he is currently at work on a book entitled, *The Glory of God's Religions: A Beginner's Guide to Exploring the Beauty of the World's Faiths*.

Chapter: Religion.

PAUL G. CONNORS has a strong interest in Great Lakes maritime history, and has contributed the article "Beaver Island Ice Walkers" to *Michigan History*. He earned a doctorate in American history from Loyola University in Chicago. He has worked for the Michigan Legislative Service Bureau as a research analyst since 1996.

Essay: Using Primary Sources. *Chronologies:* Selected Events Outside the United States; Government and Politics, Sports Chapters. *General Resources:* General, Government and Politics, Sports.

CHRISTOPHER CUMO is a staff writer for *The Adjunct Advocate Magazine*. Formerly an adjunct professor of history at Walsh University, he has written two books, *A History of the Ohio Agricultural Experiment Station, 1882–1997* and *Seeds of Change*, and has contributed to numerous scholarly journals. He holds a doctorate in history from the University of Akron.

Chapter Chronology, General Resources: Business and the Economy, Education, Medicine and Health, Science and Technology.

JENNIFER HELLER holds bachelor's degrees in Religious Studies and English Education, as well as a master's in Curriculum and Instruction, all from the University of Kansas. She has been an adjunct associate professor at Johnson County Community College in Kansas since 1998. She is currently at work on a dissertation on contemporary women's religious literature.

Chapter Chronology, General Resources: Religion.

DAVID M. HOLFORD has worked as an adjunct instructor at Ohio University, Park College, and Columbus State Community College; education curator for the Ohio Historical Society; and held editorial positions at Glencoe/McGraw Hill and Holt, Rinehard, and Winston. He holds a doctorate in history from Ohio State University. A freelance writer/editor since 1996, he has published *Herbert Hoover* (1999) and *Abraham Lincoln and the Emancipation Proclamation* (2002).

Chapter Chronology, General Resources: Lifestyles and Social Trends, The Media.

JONATHAN KOLKEY is the author of *The New Right, 1960–1968* and *Germany on the March: A Reinterpretation of War and Domestic Politics Over the Past Two Centuries*. He earned a Ph.D. in history from UCLA. Currently an instructor at West Los Angeles College, he is at work on *The Decision For War*, a comprehensive historical study of the politics and decision-making process behind war. Dr. Kolkey lives in Playa Del Rey, California.

Chapter: Business and Economy.

JACQUELINE LESHKEVICH joined the Michigan Legislative Service Bureau as a science research analyst in 2000. She earned her B.S. in Biochemistry from Northern Michigan University and a master's degree, also in Biochemistry, from Michigan Technological University. A contributor to such publications as *Nature Biotechnology* and *Plant Cell*, she is also an amateur astronomer.

Chapter: Science and Technology.

SCOTT A. MERRIMAN currently works as a part-time instructor at the University of Kentucky and is finishing his doctoral dissertation on Espionage and Sedition Acts in the Sixth Court of Appeals. He has contributed to *The History Highway* and *History.edu*, among others. Scott is a resident of Lexington, Kentucky.

Chapter: Law and Justice.

JOSEPH R. PHELAN is a scholar in residence at Strayer University in Washington, D.C. Previously he served as director for the Office of the Bicentennial of the U.S. Constitution at the National Endowment for the Humanities and has taught at the University of Toronto, the Catholic University of America, and the Art Gallery of Ontario. He earned a doctorate from the University of Toronto.

Chapter: The Arts, Fashion and Design.

NADINE FRANCE MARTINE PINÈDE serves as program coordinator for Grantmakers Without Borders. She holds a doctorate in History, Philosophy, and Policy Studies in Education and an M.A. in Philanthropic Studies from Indiana University, as well as an M.A. in English and Modern Languages from St. John's College and a B.A. in Literature and Social Criticism from Harvard University. She has contributed articles to such publications as *The New York Times* and *Radcliffe Quarterly*.

Chapter: Education.

DAN PROSTERMAN is an adjunct professor of history at St. Francis College, as well as an adjunct lecturer at Pace University. He holds an M.A. in history at New York University and is working on his doctoral dissertation on the subject of anti-Communism in New York City during the Great Depression and World War II.

Chapter: The Media.

LORNA BIDDLE RINEAR is the editor and co-author of *The Complete Idiot's Guide to Women's History*. A Ph.D. candidate at Rutger's University, she holds a B.A. from Wellesley College and a master's degree from Boston College. She resides in Bellingham, Massachusetts.

Chapter Chronology, General Resources: The Arts, Fashion and Design.

MARY HERTZ SCARBROUGH earned both her B.A. in English and German and her J.D. from the University of South Dakota. Prior to becoming a freelance writer in 1996, she worked as a law clerk in the Federal District Court for the District of South Dakota and as legal counsel for the Immigration and Naturalization Service. She lives in Storm Lake, Iowa.

Chapter Chronology, General Resources: Law and Justice.

AMY H. STURGIS has written numerous articles and book chapters, in addition to the books *Presidents from Washington Through Monroe, 1789–1825: Debating* *the Issues in Pro and Con Primary Documents* and *Presidents Hayes Through McKinley, 1877–1901: Debating the Issues in Pro and Con Primary Documents* (forthcoming). She holds a Ph.D. from Vanderbilt University. She is an adjunct instructor at Belmont University in Nashville, Tennessee.

Chapter: Government and Politics, Lifestyles and Social Trends.

WILLIAM J. THOMPSON has been a history instructor at the Community College of Baltimore County, Catonsville, since 1996. He received both his bachelor's and master's degrees in history from the University of Maryland, Baltimore County. He has written for the *Encyclopedia of African-American Civil Rights*, the *Washington Post*, and the *Baltimore Sun*.

Chapter: Sports.

SUSAN P. WALTON is a librarian, freelance writer, editor, and researcher. Her primary interest is the history of science and medicine. Her writings have appeared in *The New York Times*, *International Wildlife*, *Health*, and others.

Chapter: Medicine and Health.

ACKNOWLEDGMENTS

Following is a list of the copyright holders who have granted us permission to reproduce material in this volume of American Decades Primary Sources. *Every effort has been made to trace copyright, but if omissions have been made, please let us know.*

Copyrighted material in *American Decades Primary Sources, 1940–1949*, was reproduced from the following periodicals: *American Journal of Obstetrics and Gynecology*, v. 42, August 1941, pp. 193–206, for "Original Communications: The Diagnostic Value of Vaginal Smears in Carcinoma of the Uterus" by George N. Papanicolaou and Herbert F. Traut. Copyright 1941 by C. V. Mosby Company. Reproduced by permission of Elsevier. —*The Antioch Review*, Summer, 1945. Reproduced by permission. —*Atlantic Monthly*, v. 176, 1945. Reproduced by permission. —*Chemical and Engineering News*, v. 24, April 25, 1946 for "Analogies between Antibodies and Simpler Chemical Substances" by Linus Pauling. Published 1946 American Chemical Society. Reproduced by permission of the American Chemical Society. —*Christian Century*, June 15, 1949. Reproduced by permission. —*Collier's*, June 23, 1945; v. 120, September 27, 1947; v. 123, February 19, 1949. —*Holiday*, 1954. Reproduced by permission. —*Life*, v. 12, February 16, 1942; v. 19, 1945; v. 27, August 8, 1949. © 1942, 1945, 1949 Time Inc. Reproduced by permission. —*The New York Times*, March 10, 1940; December 16, 1941; June 30, 1942; October 29, 1942; November 9, 1942; March 28, 1943; August 25, 1943; July 19, 1946; October 10, 1946; November 10, 1946; December 4, 1947; December 12, 1948; January 10, 1949. Copyright © 1940, 1941, 1942, 1943, 1946, 1947, 1948, 1949 by The New York Times Company. Reproduced by permission. —*The New Yorker*, August 31, 1946. —*Roswell Daily Record*, July 8, 1947. Reproduced by permission. —*Sat-urday Evening Post*, v. 214, December 6, 1941; v. 216, February 19, 1944; v. 220, September 20, 1947; September 6, 1958. Reproduced by permission. —*Scripps-Howard Wirecopy*, January 10, 1944. Reproduced by permission of Scripps Howard Foundation. —*Time*, v. XLIII, May 8, 1944; December 7, 1946; December 14, 1946; September 15, 1947. © 1944, 1946, 1947 Time Inc. Reproduced by permission. —*The Wall Street Journal*, August 31, 1943. Reproduced by permission.

Copyrighted material in *American Decades Primary Sources, 1940–1949*, was reproduced from the following books: Aiken, Howard. From "The Harvard News Release," in *Makin' Numbers*. The MIT Press, 1999. Copyright © 1999 by The MIT Press. All rights reserved. Reproduced by permission. —Barr, Alfred H., Jr. From "Introduction," in *What is Modern Painting?* Museum of Modern Art, 1943. Copyright © 1943 by The Museum of Modern Art. All rights reserved. Reproduced by permission. —Benedict, Ruth. From "Foreword to the 1945 Edition," in *Race: Science and Politics*. The Viking Press, 1940. Copyright 1940, 1943, 1945 by Ruth Benedict, renewed © 1968, 1971, 1973 by Robert G. Freeman. Reproduced by permission of Viking Penguin, a division of Penguin Putnam Inc. —Coffin, Robert P. Tristram. From "America was Schoolmasters," in *Primer for America*. The MacMillan Company, 1943. Copyright © 1943 by The Macmillan Company; copyright renewed © 1971 by Margaret Coffin Halvosa, Mary Alice Westcott, Robert P. Tristram Coffin, Jr., and Richard N. Coffin. All rights reserved. Reproduced by permission of Scribner, an imprint of Simon & Schuster Adult Publishing Group. — Cohen, Felix S. From "Indian Self-Government, 1949," in *Red Power: The American Indians' Fight for Freedom*. Yale University Press, 1949. All rights reserved. Reproduced by permission of Yale University Press. — Deutsch, Albert. From "New York's Isle of Despair," in *The Shame of the States*. Harcourt, Brace and Company, 1948. Copyright © 1948 by Albert Deutsch. All rights reserved. —Fermi, Enrico. From "Feasibility of a Chain Reaction," in *Collected Papers, Volume 2, 1939–54*. The University of Chicago Press, 1962. Copyright © 1962 by The University of Chicago Press. All rights reserved. Reproduced by permission. —From "Jewish-Christian Relations, The World Council of Churches. World Council of Churches Documents," in *The First Assembly of the World Council of Churches, Official Report*. The World Council of Churches, 1948. Reproduced by permission. —From "Superman vs. The Atom Man," Episode L851, in *The Superman Radio Scripts: Volume I: Superman vs. the Atom Man*. Published by Billboard Books, an imprint of Watson-Guptill Publications, 2001. © DC Comics. All rights reserved. Reproduced by permission. —Goodson, Martia Graham. From "The United Negro College Fund," in *Chronicles of Faith: The Autobiography of Frederick D. Patterson*. University of Alabama Press, 1991. Copyright © 1991 by The University of Alabama Press. All rights reserved. Reproduced by permission. —Hayek, Friedrich A. From "Planning and the Rule of Law," in *The Road to Serfdom*. University of Chicago Press, 1944. Copyright © 1944 by University of Chicago Press, renewed 1972 by Friedrich A. Hayek. All rights reserved. Reproduced by permission of the publisher and the author. —Heller, Peter. From "Sugar Ray Robinson," in *"In This Corner . . . !"* Simon and Schuster, 1973. Copyright © 1973 by Peter Heller. All rights reserved. Reproduced by permission of the author. —Hillway, Tyrus. From "The Eight Year Study," in *American Education*. Houghton Mifflin Company, 1964. Copyright © 1964 by Tyrus Hillway. All rights reserved. Reproduced by permission. —Huxley, Julian. From "Preface," in *Evolution: The Modern Synthesis*. Harper & Brothers, Publishers, 1942. Copyright © 1942 by Julian Huxley, renewed 1970. All rights reserved. Reproduced by permission of the author's estate. —Inada, Lawson Fusao, Patricia Wakida and William Hohri. From "A Teacher at Topaz: Eleanor Gerard Sekerak," in *Only What We Could Carry*. Heyday Books, 2000. Copyright © 2000 by Heyday Books. Reproduced by permission. —Irons, Peter. From "Here Comes Jehovah!" in *The Courage of Their Convictions*. Penguin Books, 1988. Copyright © 1988 by Peter Irons. All rights reserved. Reproduced by permission of The Frce Press, an imprint of Simon & Schuster Adult Publishing Group. —Kinsey, Alfred C., Wardell B. Pomeroy and Clyde E. Martin. From "Historical Introduction," "In-cidence Data In Present Study," "Homosexual Outlet," and "Animal Contacts," in *Sexual Behavior In The Human Male*. W.B. Saunders Company, 1948. Copyright © by W.B. Saunders Company. All rights reserved. Reproduced by permission of The Kinsey Institute for Research in Sex, Gender, and Reproduction, Inc. —Lane, Rose Wilder. "The Third Attempt," in *The Discovery of Freedom: Man's Struggle Against Authority*. Fox & Wilkes, 1943. Copyright © 1943 by Fox & Wilkes. All rights reserved. Reproduced by permission. —Liebman, Joshua Loth. In *Peace of Mind*. Simon and Schuster, 1946. Copyright © 1946 by Simon and Schuster. All rights reserved. Reproduced by permission. —Macleish, Archibald. From "The Irresponsibles," in *The Irresponsibles: A Declaration*. Duell, Sloan, and Pearce, 1940. Copyright © 1940 by Archibald Macleish. All rights reserved. Reproduced by permission. —Meyer, Ray with Ray Sons. From "Chapter 4," in *Coach*. Contemporary Books, Inc., 1987. Copyright © 1987 by Ray Meyer and Ray Sons. All rights reserved. —Murrow, Edward R. From "Can They Take It?" in *Reporting World War II: Part One; American Journalism 1938–1944*. The Library of America, 1995. Copyright © 1941 by Edward R. Murrow. All rights reserved. Reproduced by permission. —Peale, Norman Vincent. From "Chapter 1," in *A Guide to Confident Living*. Prentice Hall, Inc., 1948. Copyright © 1948 by Prentice Hall, Inc. All rights reserved. Reproduced by permission of Simon & Schuster Adult Publishing Group. —Rand, Ayn. From *The Fountainhead*. Bobbs-Merrill Company, 1943. Copyright 1943 by The Bobbs-Merrill Company, renewed 1968 by Ayn Rand. Reproduced by permission. —Robinson, Sugar Ray with Dave Anderson. From "Edna Mae," and "Marriage and Mike Jacobs," in *Sugar Ray: The Sugar Ray Robinson Story*. Viking Press, 1970. Copyright © 1969, 1970 by Sugar Ray Robinson. Reproduced by permission of Viking Penguin, a division of Penguin Group (USA) Inc. —Schrodinger, Erwin. From "Epilogue: On Determinism and Free Will," in *What Is Life? and Other Scientific Essays*. Doubleday & Company, Inc., 1956. Copyright © 1956 by Doubleday & Company, Inc. All rights reserved. Reproduced by permission of Cambridge University Press and the author. —Terkel, Studs. From "Don McFadden," in *The Good War*. Pantheon Books, 1984. Copyright © 1984 by Studs Terkel. All rights reserved. Reproduced by permission of Donadio & Olson, Inc. —Tireman, L. S. and Mary Watson. From "Nambe Children at Work," in *A Community School in a Spanish-Speaking Village*. University of New Mexico Press, 1948. Copyright © 1948 by The University of New Mexico Press, renewed 1976 by Dorothy Tireman-Capes and Marjor Tireman-Delzell. All rights reserved. Reproduced by permission. —Veeck, Bill with Ed Linn. From "Chapter 1: A Can of Beer a Slice of Cake—and Thou Eddie Gaedel," and "Chapter

11: It Only Takes One Leg to Walk Away," in *Veeck—As in Wreck: The Autobiography of Bill Veeck*. Putnam, 1962. Copyright © 1962 by Mary Frances Veeck and Edward Linn. All rights reserved. Reproduced by permission. —Von Neumann, John. From *The General and Logical Theory of Automata*, a lecture delivered on September 20, 1948 at the Hixton Symposium at the California Institute of Technology. Copyright © 1948 by John Von Neumann. Reprinted with permission. —Wakatsuki Houston, Jeanne, and James D. Houston. From "Outings, Explorations," in *Farewell To Manzanar*. Houghton Mifflin Company, 1973. Copyright © by James D. Houston. Reproduced by permission. —Ward, Mary Jane. In *The Snake Pit*. Random House, 1946. Copyright © 1946 by Mary Jane Ward. All rights reserved. Reproduced by permission of Random House, Inc. —Warshow, Robert. From "The Gangster as Tragic Hero," in *The Immediate Experience*. Doubleday & Company, Inc., 1964. Copyright © 1964 by Doubleday & Company, Inc. All rights reserved. Reproduced by permission of the author. —Webster, Paul Francis and Duke Ellington. Song lyrics from *I Got It Bad (And That Ain't Good)*, 1941. Copyright © 1941 Webster Music Company/EMI Robbins Music, copyright renewed. All rights reserved. Reproduced by permission of Webster Music Company. —Williams, Ted and John Underwood. From *My Turn At Bat: The Story of My Life*. Simon and Schuster, 1969. Copyright © 1969, 1988 by Ted Williams and John Underwood. All rights reserved. Reproduced by permission of Simon & Schuster Adult Publishing Group and JCA Literary Agency. —Woodworth, R.S. From "Heredity and Environment: A Critical Survey of Recently Published Material on Twins and Foster Children," in *Heredity and Environment: A Critical Survey of Recently Published Material on Twins and Foster Children*. Social Science Research Council, 1941. Copyright © 1941 by Social Science Research Council. All rights reserved. Reproduced by permission. —Wright, Frank Lloyd. From "Taliesin Square-Paper Number 10," in *Frank Lloyd Wright Collected Writings*. Edited by Bruce Brooks Pfeiffer. New York: Rizzoli, 1992. Copyright © 1946, 1994, 2003 The Frank Lloyd Wright Foundation, Scottsdale. Reproduced by permission of the Frank Lloyd Wright Foundation.

Copyrighted material in American Decades Primary Sources, 1940–1949, was reproduced from the following web sites: From "291. Declaration of Purpose," Schiller Institute. Online at http://www.schillerinstitute.org/health/hill_burton.html (February 7, 2002). Reproduced by permission of the author. —Johnson-Noga, Aleene. From "Foreword," "Suggested Beauty Routine," and "Additional Beauty Routine." Online at http://www.aagpbl.org/history/hist_cs.html#beauty. (February 20, 2002). © All-American Girls Professional Baseball League (AAGPBL). Reproduced by permission of the AAGPBL Players Association, Inc. —From "This Month in Physics History—November 17–December 23, 1947: Invention of the First Transistor." Online at http://www.aps.org/apsnews/1100/110004.html (April 9, 2002). Reproduced by permission of the author. —Letter from Niels Bohr to Heisenburg, 1941. Niels Bohr Archive. Online at: http://www.nbi.dk/NBA/papers/docs/doltra.htm (April 18, 2002). Reproduced by permission of The Niels Bohr Archive. —Scher, Linda. From South Carolina Voices: Lessons from The Holocaust, South Carolina Council on The Holocaust, 1995. Online at: http://library.thinkquest.org/12663/survivors/witness.html (February 8, 2002). Reproduced by permission. —United Nations. From "Charter of the United Nations Preamble, June 26, 1945." Online at http://www.unhchr.ch/html/menu3/b/ch-cont.htm (February 8, 2002). Reproduced by permission. —United Nations. From "Universal Declaration of Human Rights, written at the United Nations in 1948," in The Avalon Project, Universal Declaration of Human Rights. Online at http://www.un.org/Overview/rights.html (February 8, 2002). Reproduced by permission.

ABOUT THE SET

American Decades Primary Sources is a ten-volume collection of more than two thousand primary sources on twentieth-century American history and culture. Each volume comprises about two hundred primary sources in 160–170 entries. Primary sources are enhanced by informative context, with illustrative images and sidebars—many of which are primary sources in their own right—adding perspective and a deeper understanding of both the primary sources and the milieu from which they originated.

Designed for students and teachers at the high school and undergraduate levels, as well as researchers and history buffs, *American Decades Primary Sources* meets the growing demand for primary source material.

Conceived as both a stand-alone reference and a companion to the popular *American Decades* set, *American Decades Primary Sources* is organized in the same subject-specific chapters for compatibility and ease of use.

Primary Sources

To provide fresh insights into the key events and figures of the century, thirty historians and four advisors selected unique primary sources far beyond the typical speeches, government documents, and literary works. Screenplays, scrapbooks, sports box scores, patent applications, college course outlines, military codes of conduct, environmental sculptures, and CD liner notes are but a sampling of the more than seventy-five types of primary sources included.

Diversity is shown not only in the wide range of primary source types, but in the range of subjects and opin-

ions, and the frequent combination of primary sources in entries. Multiple perspectives in religious, political, artistic, and scientific thought demonstrate the commitment of *American Decades Primary Sources* to diversity, in addition to the inclusion of considerable content displaying ethnic, racial, and gender diversity. *American Decades Primary Sources* presents a variety of perspectives on issues and events, encouraging the reader to consider subjects more fully and critically.

American Decades Primary Sources' innovative approach often presents related primary sources in an entry. The primary sources act as contextual material for each other—creating a unique opportunity to understand each and its place in history, as well as their relation to one another. These may be point-counterpoint arguments, a variety of diverse opinions, or direct responses to another primary source. One example is President Franklin Delano Roosevelt's letter to clergy at the height of the Great Depression, with responses by a diverse group of religious leaders from across the country.

Multiple primary sources created by particularly significant individuals—Dr. Martin Luther King, Jr., for example—reside in *American Decades Primary Sources*. Multiple primary sources on particularly significant subjects are often presented in more than one chapter of a volume, or in more than one decade, providing opportunities to see the significance and impact of an event or figure from many angles and historical perspectives. For example, seven primary sources on the controversial Scopes "monkey" trial are found in five chapters of the

1920s volume. Primary sources on evolutionary theory may be found in earlier and later volumes, allowing the reader to see and analyze the development of thought across time.

Entry Organization

Contextual material uses standardized rubrics that will soon become familiar to the reader, making the entries more accessible and allowing for easy comparison. Introduction and Significance essays—brief and focused—cover the historical background, contributing factors, importance, and impact of the primary source, encouraging the reader to think critically—not only about the primary source, but also about the way history is constructed. Key Facts and a Synopsis provide quick access and recognition of the primary sources, and the Further Resources are a stepping-stone to additional study.

Additional Features

Subject chronologies and thorough tables of contents (listing titles, authors, and dates) begin each chapter. The main table of contents assembles this information conveniently at the front of the book. An essay on using primary sources, a chronology of selected events outside the United States during the twentieth century, substantial general and subject resources, and primary source-type and general indexes enrich *American Decades Primary Sources*.

The ten volumes of *American Decades Primary Sources* provide a vast array of primary sources integrated with supporting content and user-friendly features.

This value-laden set gives the reader an unparalleled opportunity to travel into the past, to relive important events, to encounter key figures, and to gain a deep and full understanding of America in the twentieth century.

Acknowledgments

A number of people contributed to the successful completion of this project. The editor wishes to acknowledge them with thanks: Eugenia Bradley, Luann Brennan, Neva Carter, Katrina Coach, Pamela S. Dear, Nikita L. Greene, Madeline Harris, Alesia James, Cynthia Jones, Pamela M. Kalte, Arlene Ann Kevonian, Frances L. Monroe, Charles B. Montney, Katherine H. Nemeh, James E. Person, Tyra Y. Phillips, Elizabeth Pilette, Noah Schusterbauer, Andrew Specht, Susan Strickland, Karissa Walker, Tracey Watson, and Jennifer M. York.

Contact Us

The editors of *American Decades Primary Sources* welcome your comments, suggestions, and questions. Please direct all correspondence to:

Editor, *American Decades Primary Sources*
The Gale Group, Inc.
27500 Drake Road
Farmington Hills, MI 48331–3535
(800) 877–4253

For email inquiries, please visit the Gale website at www.gale.com, and click on the Contact Us tab.

ABOUT THE VOLUME

The United States of the 1940s marked the beginnings of significant social and political change. Men were shipped off to fight in World War II, and women entered the workforce in larger numbers than ever before to "hold down the homefront," earning a taste of what it meant to be independent. African Americans fought beside their white counterparts in the war and returned home unwilling to accept the inequality under which they'd lived for so long. The United States ushered in the nuclear age with the atomic bombings of Hiroshima and Nagasaki, but also solidified its role as an international leader by helping to rebuild Europe and Japan under the Marshall Plan. The Soviet Union—once an ally—became a feared enemy, and Americans looked for communists in their midst while the U.S. government shifted its policies from world war to Cold War. But while the government prepared to fight the communists, the public enjoyed the offerings of the first supermarkets. The following documents are just a sampling of the offerings available in this volume.

Highlights of Primary Sources, 1940–1949

- *The Life of John Brown, No. 17,* painting by Jacob Lawrence
- Linus Pauling's research notebooks
- Photographs of supermarkets in the 1940s
- World War II editorial cartoons by Dr. Seuss
- "Richard Wright's Blues," review of Wright's novel, *Black Boy,* by Ralph Ellison

- *Farewell to Manzanar* and "A Teacher at Topaz" memoirs of teachers in Japanese-American internment camps
- Text facsimile of "Greenlight" letter from President Franklin D. Roosevelt to Major League Baseball commissioner Kenesaw Mountain Landis in 1942
- Interviews with Holocaust Survivors
- Photographs of Eames Chairs by Ray and Charles Eames
- Testimony of J. Edgar Hoover before the House Un-American Activities Committee (HUAC)
- World War II ration stamp booklets issued by the U.S. government
- *The Common Sense Book of Baby and Child Care,* by Dr. Benjamin Spock

Volume Structure and Content

Front matter

- Table of Contents—lists primary sources, authors, and dates of origin, by chapter and chronologically within chapters.
- About the Set, About the Volume, About the Entry essays—guide the reader through the set and promote ease of use.
- Highlights of Primary Sources—a quick look at a dozen or so primary sources gives the reader a feel for the decade and the volume's contents.

- Using Primary Sources—provides a crash course in reading and interpreting primary sources.
- Chronology of Selected World Events Outside the United States—lends additional context in which to place the decade's primary sources.

Chapters:

- The Arts
- Business and the Economy
- Education
- Fashion and Design
- Government and Politics
- Law and Justice
- Lifestyles and Social Trends
- The Media
- Medicine and Health
- Religion
- Science and Technology
- Sports

Chapter structure

- Chapter table of contents—lists primary sources, authors, and dates of origin chronologically, showing each source's place in the decade.
- Chapter chronology—highlights the decade's important events in the chapter's subject.
- Primary sources—displays sources surrounded by contextual material.

Back matter

- General Resources—promotes further inquiry with books, periodicals, websites, and audio and visual media, all organized into general and subject-specific sections.
- General Index—provides comprehensive access to primary sources, people, events, and subjects, and cross-referencing to enhance comparison and analysis.
- Primary Source Type Index—locates primary sources by category, giving readers an opportunity to easily analyze sources across genres.

ABOUT THE ENTRY

The primary source is the centerpiece and main focus of each entry in *American Decades Primary Sources.* In keeping with the philosophy that much of the benefit from using primary sources derives from the reader's own process of inquiry, the contextual material surrounding each entry provides access and ease of use, as well as giving the reader a springboard for delving into the primary source. Rubrics identify each section and enable the reader to navigate entries with ease.

Entry structure

- Key Facts—essential information pertaining to the primary source, including full title, author, source type, source citation, and notes about the author.

- Introduction—historical background and contributing factors for the primary source.

- Significance—importance and impact of the primary source, at the time and since.

- Primary Source—in text, text facsimile, or image format; full or excerpted.

- Synopsis—encapsulated introduction to the primary source.

- Further Resources—books, periodicals, websites, and audio and visual material.

Navigating an Entry

Entry elements are numbered and reproduced here, with an explanation of the data contained in these elements explained immediately thereafter according to the corresponding numeral.

Entry Title, Primary Source Type

•1• "Ego"
•2• Magazine article

•1• **ENTRY TITLE** The entry title is the primary source title for entries with one primary source. Entry titles appear as catchwords at the top outer margin of each page.

•2• **PRIMARY SOURCE TYPE** The type of primary source is listed just below the title. When assigning source types, great weight was given to how the author of the primary source categorized it. If a primary source comprised more than one type—for example, an article about art in the United States that included paintings, or a scientific essay that included graphs and photographs—each primary source type included in the entry appears below the title.

Composite Entry Title

•3• Debate Over *The Birth of a Nation*

•1• "Capitalizing Race Hatred"
•2• Editorial

•1• **"Reply to the *New York Globe*"**

•2• **Letter**

•3• **COMPOSITE ENTRY TITLE** An overarching entry title is used for entries with more than one primary source, with the primary source titles and types below.

Key Facts

•4• **By:** Norman Mailer

•5• **Date:** March 19, 1971

•6• **Source:** Mailer, Norman. "Ego." *Life* 70, March 19, 1971, 30, 32–36.

•7• **About the Author:** Norman Mailer (1923–) was born in Long Branch, New Jersey. After graduating from Harvard and military service in World War II (1939–1945), Mailer began writing, publishing his first book, the bestselling novel *The Naked and the Dead,* in 1948. Mailer has written over thirty books, including novels, plays, political commentary, and essay collections, as well as numerous magazine articles. He won the Pulitzer Prize in 1969 and 1979. ■

•4• **AUTHOR OR ORIGINATOR** The name of the author or originator of the primary source begins the Key Facts section.

•5• **DATE OF ORIGIN** The date of origin of the primary source appears in this field, and may differ from the date of publication in the source citation below it; for example, speeches are often given before they are published.

•6• **SOURCE CITATION** The source citation is a full bibliographic citation, giving original publication data as well as reprint and/or online availability (usually both the deep-link and home-page URLs).

•7• **ABOUT THE AUTHOR** A brief bio of the author or originator of the primary source gives birth and death dates and a quick overview of the person's life. This rubric has been customized in some cases. If the primary source is the autobiography of an artist, the term "author" appears; however, if the primary source is a work of art, the term "artist" is used, showing the person's direct relationship to the primary source. Terms like "inventor" and "designer" are used similarly. For primary sources created by a group, "organization" may have been used instead of "author." If an author is anonymous or unknown, a brief "About the Publication" sketch may appear.

Introduction and Significance Essays

•8• **Introduction**

. . . As images from the Vietnam War (1964–1975) flashed onto television screens across the United States in the late 1960s, however, some reporters took a more active role in questioning the pronouncements of public officials. The broad cul-tural changes of the 1960s, including a sweeping suspicion of authority figures by younger people, also encouraged a more restive spirit in the reporting corps. By the end of the decade, the phrase "Gonzo Journalism" was coined to describe the new breed of reporter: young, rebellious, and unafraid to get personally involved in the story at hand. . . .

•8• **INTRODUCTION** The introduction is a brief essay on the contributing factors and historical context of the primary source. Intended to promote understanding and jump-start the reader's curiosity, this section may also describe an artist's approach, the nature of a scientific problem, or the struggles of a sports figure. If more than one primary source is included in the entry, the introduction and significance address each one, and often the relationship between them.

•9• **Significance**

Critics of the new style of journalism maintained that the emphasis on personalities and celebrity did not necessarily lead to better reporting. As political reporting seemed to focus more on personalities and images and less on substantive issues, some observers feared that the American public was ill-served by the new style of journalism. Others argued that the media had also encouraged political apathy among the public by superficial reporting. . . .

•9• **SIGNIFICANCE** The significance discusses the importance and impact of the primary source. This section may touch on how it was regarded at the time and since, its place in history, any awards given, related developments, and so on.

Primary Source Header, Synopsis, Primary Source

•10• **Primary Source**

The Boys on the Bus [excerpt]

•11• **SYNOPSIS:** A boisterous account of Senator George McGovern's ultimately unsuccessful 1972 presidential bid, Crouse's work popularized the term "pack journalism," describing the herd mentality that gripped reporters focusing endlessly on the same topic. In later years, political advisors would become more adept at "spinning" news stories to their candidates' advantage, but the essential dynamics of pack journalism remain in place.

•12• The feverish atmosphere was halfway between a high school bus trip to Washington and a gambler's jet junket to Las Vegas, where small-time Mafiosi were lured into betting away their restaurants. There was giddy camaraderie mixed with fear and low-grade hysteria. To file a story late, or to make one glaring factual error, was to chance losing everything—one's job, one's expense account, one's drinking buddies, one's mad-dash existence, and the methedrine buzz that comes from knowing stories that the public would not know for hours and secrets that the public would never know. Therefore reporters channeled their gambling instincts into late-night poker games and private bets on the outcome of the elections. When it came to writing a story, they were as cautious as diamond-cutters. . . .

•10• **PRIMARY SOURCE HEADER** The primary source header signals the beginning of the primary source, and "[excerpt]" is attached if the source does not appear in full.

•11• **SYNOPSIS** The synopsis gives a brief overview of the primary source.

•12• **PRIMARY SOURCE** The primary source may appear excerpted or in full, and may appear as text, text facsimile (photographic reproduction of the original text), image, or graphic display (such as a table, chart, or graph).

Text Primary Sources

The majority of primary sources are reproduced as plain text. The font and leading of the primary sources are distinct from that of the context—to provide a visual clue to the change, as well as to facilitate ease of reading. Often, the original formatting of the text was preserved in order to more accurately represent the original (screenplays, for example). In order to respect the integrity of the primary sources, content some readers may consider sensitive was retained where it was deemed to be integral to the source. Text facsimile formatting was used sparingly and where the original provided additional value (for example, Aaron Copland's typing and handwritten notes on "Notes for a Cowboy Ballet").

Narrative Break

•13• I told him I'd rest and then fix him something to eat when he got home. I could hear someone enter his office then, and Medgar laughed at something that was said. "I've got to go, honey. See you tonight. I love you." "All right," I said. "Take care." Those were our last words to each other.

■ ■ ■

Medgar had told me that President Kennedy was speaking on civil rights that night, and I made a mental note of the time. We ate alone, the children and I. It had become a habit now to set only four places for supper. Medgar's chair stared at us, and the children, who had heard

about the President's address to the nation, planned to watch it with me. There was something on later that they all wanted to see, and they begged to be allowed to wait up for Medgar to return home. School was out, and I knew that Van would fall asleep anyway, so I agreed.

•13• **NARRATIVE BREAK** A narrative break appears where there is a significant amount of elided material, beyond what ellipses would indicate (for example, excerpts from a nonfiction work's introduction and second chapter, or sections of dialogue from two acts of a play).

Image Primary Sources

Primary source images (whether photographs, text facsimiles, or graphic displays) are bordered with a distinctive double rule. The Primary Source header and Synopsis appear under the image, with the image reduced in size to accommodate the synopsis. For multipart images, the synopsis appears only under the first part of the image; subsequent parts have brief captions.

•14• "Art: U.S. Scene": *The Tornado* by John Steuart Curry (2 OF 4)

•14• **PRIMARY SOURCE IMAGE HEADER** The primary source image header assists the reader in tracking the images in a series. Also, the primary source header listed here indicates a primary source with both text and image components. The text of the *Time* magazine article "Art: U.S. Scene," appears with four of the paintings from the article. Under each painting, the title of the article appears first, followed by a colon, then the title of the painting. The header for the text component has a similar structure, with the term "magazine article" after the colon. Inclusion of images or graphic elements from primary sources, and their designation in the entry as main primary sources, is discretionary.

Further Resources

•15• **Further Resources**

BOOKS
Dixon, Phil. *The Negro Baseball Leagues, 1867–1955: A Photographic History.* Mattituck, N.Y.: Amereon House, 1992.

PERIODICALS
"Steven Spielberg: The Director Says It's Good-Bye to Spaceships and Hello to Relationships." *American Film* 13, no. 8, June 1988, 12–16.

WEBSITES
Architecture and Interior Design for 20th Century America, 1935–1955. American Memory digital primary source collection, Library of Congress. Available online at http://memory.loc.gov/ammem/gschtml/gotthome

.html; website home page: http://memory.loc.gov /ammem/ammemhome.html (accessed March 27, 2003).

AUDIO AND VISUAL MEDIA

E.T.: The Extra-Terrestrial. Original release, 1982, Universal. Directed by Steven Spielberg. Widescreen Collector's Edition DVD, 2002, Universal Studios.

•15• FURTHER RESOURCES A brief list of resources provides a stepping stone to further study. If it's known that a resource contains additional primary source material specifically related to the entry, a brief note in italics appears at the end of the citation. For websites, both the deep link and home page usually appear.

USING PRIMARY SOURCES

The philosopher R.G. Collingwood once said, "Every new generation must rewrite history in its own way." What Collingwood meant is that new events alter our perceptions of the past and necessitate that each generation interpret the past in a different light. For example, since September 11, 2001, and the "War on Terrorism," the collapse of the Soviet Union seemingly is no longer as historically important as the rise of Islamic fundamentalism, which was once only a minor concern. Seen from this viewpoint, history is not a rigid set of boring facts, but a fascinating, ever-changing field of study. Much of this fascination rests on the fact that historical interpretation is based on the reading of primary sources. To historians and students alike, primary sources are ambiguous objects because their underlying meanings are often not crystal clear. To learn a primary document's meaning(s), students must identify its main subject and recreate the historical context in which the document was created. In addition, students must compare the document with other primary sources from the same historical time and place. Further, students must cross-examine the primary source by asking of it a series of probing investigative questions.

To properly analyze a primary source, it is important that students become "active" rather than "casual" readers. As in reading a chemistry or algebra textbook, historical documents require students to analyze them carefully and extract specific information. In other words, history requires students to read "beyond the text" and focus on what the primary source tells us about the person or group and the era in which they lived. Unlike chemistry and algebra, however, historical primary sources have the additional benefit of being part of a larger, interesting story full of drama, suspense, and hidden agendas. In order to detect and identify key historical themes, students need to keep in mind a set of questions. For example, Who created the primary source? Why did the person create it? What is the subject? What problem is being addressed? Who was the intended audience? How was the primary source received and how was it used? What are the most important characteristics of this person or group for understanding the primary source? For example, what were the authors' biases? What was their social class? Their race? Their gender? Their occupation? Once these questions have been answered reasonably, the primary source can be used as a piece of historical evidence to interpret history.

In each *American Decades Primary Sources* volume, students will study examples of the following categories of primary sources:

- Firsthand accounts of historic events by witnesses and participants. This category includes diary entries, letters, newspaper articles, oral-history interviews, memoirs, and legal testimony.

- Documents representing the official views of the nation's leaders or of their political opponents. These include court decisions, policy statements, political speeches, party platforms, petitions, legislative debates, press releases, and federal and state laws.

- Government statistics and reports on such topics as birth, employment, marriage, death, and taxation.

- Advertisers' images and jingles. Although designed to persuade consumers to purchase commodities or to adopt specific attitudes, advertisements can also be valuable sources of information about popular beliefs and concerns.

- Works of art, including paintings, symphonies, play scripts, photographs, murals, novels, and poems.

- The products of mass culture: cartoons, comic books, movies, radio scripts, and popular songs.

- Material artifacts. These are everyday objects that survived from the period in question. Examples include household appliances and furnishings, recipes, and clothing.

- Secondary sources. In some cases, secondary sources may be treated as primary sources. For example, from 1836 to 1920, public schools across America purchased 122 million copies of a series of textbooks called the McGuffey Reader. Although current textbooks have more instructional value, the Reader is an invaluable primary source. It provides important insights into the unifying morals and cultural values that shaped the worldview of several generations of Americans, who differed in ethnicity, race, class, and religion.

Each of the above-mentioned categories of primary sources reveals different types of historical information. A politician's diary, memoirs, or collection of letters, for example, often provide students with the politicians' unguarded, private thoughts and emotions concerning daily life and public events. Though these documents may be a truer reflection of the person's character and aspirations, students must keep in mind that when people write about themselves, they tend to put themselves at the center of the historical event or cast themselves in the best possible light. On the other hand, the politician's public speeches may be more cautious, less controversial, and limited to advancing his or her political party's goals or platform.

Like personal diaries, advertisements reveal other types of historical information. What information does the WAVES poster on this page reveal?

John Phillip Faller, a prolific commercial artist known for his *Saturday Evening Post* covers, designed this recruitment poster in 1944. It was one of over three hundred posters he produced for the U.S. Navy while enrolled in that service during World War II. The purpose of the poster was to encourage women to enlist in the WAVES (Women Accepted for Volunteer Emergency Service), a women's auxiliary to the Navy established in

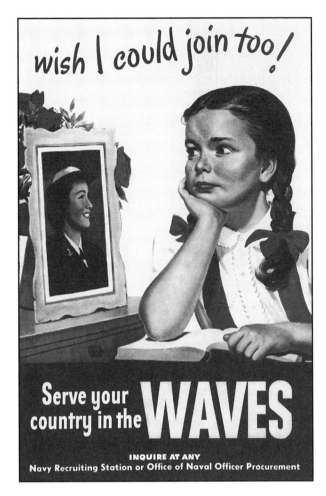

1942. It depicts a schoolgirl gazing admiringly at a photograph of a proud, happy WAVE (perhaps an older sister), thus portraying the military service as an appropriate and admirable aspiration for women during wartime. However, what type of military service? Does the poster encourage women to enlist in military combat like World War II male recruitment posters? Does it reflect gender bias? What does this poster reveal about how the military and society in general feel about women in the military? Does the poster reflect current military and societal attitudes toward women in the military? How many women joined the WAVES? What type of duties did they perform?

Like personal diaries, photographs reveal other types of historical information. What information does the next photograph reveal?

Today, we take electricity for granted. However, in 1935, although 90 percent of city dwellers in America had electricity, only 10 percent of rural Americans did. Private utility companies refused to string electric lines

THE LIBRARY OF CONGRESS.

to isolated farms, arguing that the endeavor was too expensive and that most farmers were too poor to afford it anyway. As part of the Second New Deal, President Franklin Delano Roosevelt issued an executive order creating the Rural Electrification Administration (REA). The REA lent money at low interest rates to utility companies to bring electricity to rural America. By 1950, 90 percent of rural America had electricity. This photograph depicts a 1930s tenant farmer's house in Greene County, Georgia. Specifically, it shows a brand-new electric meter on the wall. The picture presents a host of questions: What was rural life like without electricity? How did electricity impact the lives of rural Americans, particularly rural Georgians? How many rural Georgians did not have electricity in the 1930s? Did Georgia have more electricity-connected farms than other Southern states? What was the poverty rate in rural Georgia, particularly among rural African Americans? Did rural electricity help lift farmers out of poverty?

Like personal diaries, official documents reveal other types of historical information. What information does the next document, a memo, reveal?

From the perspective of the early twenty-first century, in a democratic society, integration of the armed services seems to have been inevitable. For much of American history, however, African Americans were prevented from joining the military, and when they did enlist they were segregated into black units. In 1940, of the nearly 170,000-man Navy, only 4,007, or 2.3 percent, were African American personnel. The vast majority of these men worked in the mess halls as stewards—or, as labeled by the black press, "seagoing bellhops." In this official document, the chairman of the General Board refers to compliance with a directive that would enlist African Americans into positions of "unlimited general service." Who issued the directive? What was the motivation behind the new directive? Who were the members of the General Board? How much authority did they wield? Why did the Navy restrict African Americans to the "messman branch"? Notice the use of the term "colored race." Why was this term used and what did it imply? What did the board conclude? When did the Navy become integrated? Who was primarily responsible for integrating the Navy?

CONFIDENTIAL

DOD Dir. 5200.10, June 29, 1960
NND by *FB*   date *Oct. 5, 1961*

DOWNGRADED AT 3 YEAR INTERVALS;
DECLASSIFIED AFTER 12 YEARS
DOD DIR 5200.10 NARS-NT

G.B. No. 421
(Serial No. 201)
SECRET   Feb 3, 1942

SECRET

From: Chairman General Board.
To: Secretary of the Navy.

Subject: Enlistment of men of colored race to other than
             Messman branch.

Ref: (a) SecNav let. (SC)P14-4/MM (03200A)/Gen of
             Jan 16, 1942.

        1.   The General Board, complying with the directive
contained in reference (a), has given careful attention to the
problem of enlisting in the Navy, men of the colored race
in other than the messman branch.

        2.   The General Board has endeavored to examine the
problem placed before it in a realistic manner.

A.   Should negroes be enlisted for **unlimited** general service?

        (a) Enlistment for general service implies that the
individual may be sent anywhere, - to any ship or station where
he is needed. Men on board ship live in particularly close
association; in their messes, one man sits beside another; their
hammocks or bunks are close together; in their common tasks they
work side by side; and in particular tasks such as those of a
gun's crew, they form a closely knit, highly coordinated team.
How many white men would choose, of their own accord, that their
closest associates in sleeping quarters, at mess, and in a gun's
crew should be of another race? How many would accept such
conditions, if required to do so, without resentment and just
as a matter of course? The General Board believes that the
answer is "Few, if any," and further believes that if the issue were
forced, there would be a lowering of contentment, teamwork
and discipline in the service.

        (b) One of the tennets of the recruiting service
is that each recruit for general service is potentially a leading
petty officer. It is true that some men never do become petty
officers, and that when recruiting white men, it is not possible
to establish which will be found worthy of and secure promotion
and which will not. If negroes are recruited for general service,
it can be said at once that few will obtain advancement to petty
officers. With every desire to be fair, officers and leading
petty officers in general will not recommend negroes for promotion
to positions of authority over white men.

DOWNGRADED AND
DECLASSIFIED   - 1 -   CONFIDENTIAL

The General Board is convinced that the enlistment of negroes for unlimited general service is unadvisable.

B.   Should negroes be enlisted in general service but detailed in special ratings or for special ships or units?

(a) The ratings now in use in the naval service cover every phase of naval activity, and no new ratings are deemed necessary merely to promote the enlistment of negroes.

(b) At first thought, it might appear that assignment of negroes to certain vessels, and in particular to small vessels of the patrol type, would be feasible. In this connection, the following table is of interest:

Type of Ship	Total Crew	Men in Pay Grades 1 to 4	Men in Pay Grades 5 to 7 (Non-rated)
Battleship	1892	666	1226
Light Cruiser (10,000 ton)	988	365	623
Destroyer (1630 ton)	206	109	97
Submarine	54	47	7
Patrol Boat (180 foot)	55	36	19
Patrol Boat (110 foot)	20	15	5

NOTE: Pay grades 1 to 4 include Chief Petty Officers and Petty Officers, 1st, 2nd and 3rd Class; also Firemen, 1st Class and a few other ratings requiring length of service and experience equal to that required for qualification of Petty Officers, 3rd class. Pay grades 5 to 7 include all other non-rated men and recruits.

There are no negro officers and so few negro petty officers in the Navy at present that any vessels to which negroes might be assigned must have white officers and white petty officers. Examination of the table shows the small number of men in other than petty officer ratings that might be assigned to patrol vessels and indicates to the General Board that such assignments would not be happy ones. The assignment of negroes to the larger ships, where well over one-half of the crews are non-rated men, with mixture of whites and negroes, would inevitably lead to discontent on the part of one or the other, resulting in clashes and lowering of the efficiency of the vessels and of the Navy.

- 2 -

The material collected in these volumes of *American Decades Primary Sources* are significant because they will introduce students to a wide variety of historical sources that were created by those who participated in or witnessed the historical event. These primary sources not only vividly describe historical events, but also reveal the subjective perceptions and biases of their authors. Students should read these documents "actively," and with the contextual assistance of the introductory material, history will become relevant and entertaining.

—Paul G. Connors

CHRONOLOGY OF SELECTED WORLD EVENTS OUTSIDE THE UNITED STATES, 1940–1949

1940

- Max Beckmann paints *Circus Caravan.*
- T.S. Eliot's long poem *East Coker,* the second part of his *Four Quartets,* is published.
- Graham Greene's novel *The Power and the Glory* is published.
- Carl Jung's *Psychology and Religion* is published.
- Arthur Koestler's novel *Darkness at Noon* is published.
- Igor Stravinsky composes his *Symphony in C Major.*
- Dylan Thomas's *Portrait of the Artist as a Young Dog,* a collection of largely autobiographical short stories, is published.
- On January 14, Japanese premier Gen. Abe Nobuyuki resigns. Adm. Yonai Mitsumasa forms a new cabinet.
- On January 27, in Rangoon, Burma, a riot breaks out between Hindus and Muslims.
- On February 9, the Irish Supreme Court upholds a law authorizing the internment without trial of suspected members of the Irish Republican Army.
- On February 12, the Dominican Republic announces a contract to resettle one hundred thousand European refugees.
- On February 16, the British destroyer *Cossack* attacks the German ship *Altmark,* liberating some three hundred English prisoners. Norway protests the attack, which violated Norwegian territorial waters.
- On February 18, President José Félix Estigarribia of Paraguay announces he is assuming dictatorial powers.
- On February 21, in the small Polish village of Auschwitz, construction begins on a German concentration camp.
- On February 22, in Tibet, a six-year-old boy is crowned the fourteenth Dalai Lama.

- On February 28, in Egypt, the twenty-eight-hundred-year-old sarcophagus of Pharaoh Psusennes is opened, revealing treasures that rival those found in the tomb of Tutankhamen.
- On March 1, Italian laws restricting the professional practices of Jews go into effect.
- On March 12, defeated in the Soviet-Finnish war, the Finns sign a treaty ceding the Karelian Isthmus and the Rybachi Peninsula to the Soviet Union and granting it lease rights to the Hango Peninsula in return for their continued independence.
- On March 18, at a meeting on the Italian side of the Brenner Pass, Benito Mussolini informs Adolf Hitler that Italy will enter the war against Britain and France.
- On March 19, U.S. ambassador to Canada James Cromwell declares in an official address that Hitler is bent on the destruction of American social and economic order.
- On March 20, French premier Edouard Daladier resigns; the next day Paul Renaud forms a new cabinet and creates a war council in expectation of a German invasion.
- On March 26, the Mexican government announces the expropriation of 1.5 million acres of land held by three American corporations.
- On March 30, Wang Ching-wei establishes a Chinese government under the supervision of occupying Japanese troops.
- On April 9, Germany invades Denmark and Norway. Belgium refuses to allow the British to move their troops through the Low Countries.
- On April 10, King Haakon VII of Norway repudiates the puppet government of Norwegian Nazi Vidkun Quisling.

- On April 18, in India, the All-India National Congress calls for civil disobedience against British rule.

- On May 10, Germany invades Belgium and Holland, beginning its "blitzkrieg" (lightning war) through the Low Countries into France. Neville Chamberlain resigns as British prime minister and is succeeded by Winston Churchill.

- On May 13, Churchill announces to the House of Commons, "I have nothing to offer but blood, toil, tears, and sweat."

- On May 14, the Dutch army surrenders to Germany. Authorities report that one hundred thousand Dutch troops, more than one-fourth of their army, have been killed in the fighting. The official capitulation papers are signed the next morning.

- From May 17 to May 18, German troops take Brussels and Antwerp in Belgium.

- On May 20, the German army takes Amiens, France.

- On May 26, German troops take Calais.

- On May 27, the British begin to evacuate Dunkirk, France. England is left practically disarmed by the defeat, but in the House of Commons on June 4 Churchill declares, "We shall defend our island whatever the cost may be, we shall fight on the beaches, we shall fight on the landing grounds, we shall fight in the fields and in the streets . . . we shall never surrender."

- On May 28, King Leopold III of Belgium surrenders his country to the Germans.

- On May 30, Reich commissioner Arthur Seyss-Inquart assumes office as civil administrator of the occupied Netherlands.

- On June 3, German planes bomb Paris.

- On June 7, King Haakon VII and his Norwegian government go into exile in London.

- On June 9, an armistice is signed in Norway.

- On June 10, Italy declares war on Britain and France. The next day its planes bomb British bases on Malta and in Aden, while the British hit Italian air bases in Libya and Italian East Africa.

- On June 11, President Getúlio Vargas of Brazil reasserts his country's neutrality.

- On June 12, the heaviest single Japanese bombing attack on Chungking, China, kills 1,500 people and leaves 150,000 homeless. Between May 18 and August 14, Japanese planes drop 2,500 tons of bombs on the city, killing more than 2,000 civilians and injuring nearly 3,500.

- On June 14, the German army enters Paris; Hitler orders a three-day celebration of the victory. The French government relocates to Bordeaux.

- On June 15, The Soviet Union occupies the small Baltic nation of Lithuania; two days later it takes over neighboring Estonia and Latvia, demanding that all three countries put themselves under Soviet protection.

- On June 16, Italian planes bomb British bases in Egypt.

- On June 17, French premier Reynaud resigns and is replaced by World War I hero Marshal Philippe Pétain, who calls for surrender to the Germans.

- On June 18, German planes raid the east coast of England. In a radio broadcast from London, Gen. Charles de Gaulle of France calls on his countrymen to rally behind him as he continues to oppose Germany from exile.

- On June 22, the French government signs an armistice with the Nazis in the Compiégne Forest, where Germany surrendered to the Allies in World War I. Germany occupies three-fifths of France, leaving the southern portion as a so-called Free Zone. De Gaulle announces the formation of the French National Committee in London to continue fighting alongside the British Empire.

- On June 24, France and Italy sign an armistice.

- On June 26, Turkey declares itself a nonbelligerent.

- On June 28, the Soviet Union occupies Bessarabia and northern Bucovina, in Romania.

- On June 30, the Germans occupy the Channel Islands.

- On July 2, the French government establishes itself at Vichy. On July 10, it replaces the Third Republic with a new constitution creating an authoritarian government and investing full power on the chief of the French state, Pétain.

- On July 6, Hitler makes peace overtures to Britain.

- On July 10, German aircraft bomb South Wales.

- On July 14, Fulgencio Batista defeats Ramon Grau San Martin for the presidency of Cuba.

- On July 16, Hitler issues Directive 16, ordering the invasion of Great Britain. During the Battle of Britain, which lasts from early August to November, the British lose 827 aircraft, but they shoot down 2,409 German planes.

- On July 21, the Soviet Union annexes Latvia, Lithuania, and Estonia.

- On July 22, Prince Konoye Fumimaro of Japan forms a new government. At the second Pan-American conference, U.S. secretary of state Cordell Hull proposes a collective trusteeship of European possessions in the New World; the proposal is adopted on July 28.

- On July 25, the United States places severe restrictions on the export of scrap metal, petroleum, and petroleum products, and it bans the export of aviation fuel and lubricating oil outside the Western Hemisphere; the measure is aimed chiefly at Japan, which relies heavily on American oil.

- On August 2, Italian troops invade British Somaliland, occupying the capital, Berbera; on August 19 British forces are evacuated.

- On August 6, Germany orders the expulsion of all Jews from Kraków, Poland.

- On August 15, the Minseito Party, the last remaining political party in Japan, dissolves itself, making the nation an authoritarian state.

- On August 17, Germany announces a "total" naval blockade of the British Isles.

- On August 20, reflecting on the conduct of the Royal Air Force (RAF) in the Battle of Britain, Churchill declares, "Never in the field of human conflict was so much owed by so many to so few."

- On August 24, the first German bombing of London occurs.

- On August 25, the RAF bombs Berlin, an event Luftwaffe head Hermann Göring had assured Hitler could never happen.
- From September 7 to September 15, the London Blitz, massive German bombardment of London, occurs.
- On September 13, Italian troops invade Egypt from Libya.
- On September 22, Vichy France accedes to a Japanese ultimatum demanding bases in northern Indochina near the Chinese border.
- On September 25, after meeting heavy resistance from Vichy French forces, British and Free French forces led by General de Gaulle abandon an invasion of Dakar, in French West Africa.
- On September 27, Germany, Italy, and Japan sign the Tripartite Pact in Berlin, committing themselves to providing each other with military assistance in case of attack by any nation not already at war against them.
- On October 1, military delegations from several Latin American nations visit Washington, D.C., for consultations.
- On October 2, all Jews in occupied France are required to register with police.
- On October 7, German troops move into Romania.
- On October 12, Hitler postpones "Operation Sealion," a German invasion of Britain, until spring 1941.
- On October 18, Vichy France bars Jews from positions in government, the teaching profession, the armed forces, the press, film, and radio. On October 30 Pétain announces a policy of collaboration with Germany.
- On October 28, Italian troops invade Greece.
- On November 8, Italian troops begin retreating from Greece.
- On November 11, British fighter planes cripple much of the Italian fleet in an engagement at Taranto.
- On November 14, the English automotive center of Coventry is carpet-bombed by 449 German aircraft. The attack creates a firestorm that kills more than 550 people and destroys the city's fourteenth-century cathedral.
- On November 20, Hungary joins the Axis.
- From November 23 to November 24, Romania and Slovakia sign the Tripartite Pact with the Axis.
- On November 24, Slovakia joins the Axis.
- From November 26 to November 27, the RAF conducts heavy night raids on Cologne.
- On November 30, Japan formally recognizes the puppet government of Wang Ching-wei in China.
- From December 9 to December 11, the British crush the Italians at Sidi Barrani, Egypt, wiping out four divisions and taking more than twenty thousand prisoners.
- On December 17, in North Africa the British take Sidi Omar and Sollum from the Italians.
- On December 25, the Germans suspend bombing of London until December 27.
- On December 29, the Germans drop incendiary bombs on the center of London, causing the worst damage to the city since the fire of 1666.

1941

- Bertolt Brecht's play *Mother Courage and Her Children* premieres in Zurich.
- Benjamin Britten composes his opera *Paul Bunyan.*
- Noel Coward's play *Blithe Spirit* premieres in London.
- T.S. Eliot's long poem *The Dry Salvages,* the third part of his *Four Quartets,* is published.
- Erich Fromm's *Escape From Freedom,* an analysis of fascism, is published.
- Franz Werfel's novel *The Song of Bernadette* is published.
- On January 10, Germany and the Soviet Union announce what the German government calls the largest grain deal in history.
- On January 21, the British suppress publication of the communist newspaper *Daily Worker.*
- On January 22, Tobruk, Libya, falls to British and Free French forces.
- On January 26, British forces invade Somaliland.
- On January 28, the Free French announce the capture of Murzuk, in southern Libya.
- On February 2, three days of riots between soldiers and anti-British demonstrators come to an end in Johannesburg, South Africa.
- On February 6, British forces capture Bengasi, in eastern Libya.
- On February 9, British warships shell Genoa, Italy.
- On February 10, Great Britain breaks off diplomatic relations with Romania because German troops have been deployed there.
- On February 12, Gen. Erwin Rommel arrives in Tripoli to take command of German and Italian forces in Libya.
- On February 24, in a speech to the Japanese Diet, Foreign Minister Matsuoka Yosuke demands the cession of Oceania to Japan.
- On March 1, Bulgaria joins the Axis.
- On March 3, the Soviet Union denounces Bulgaria for allying itself with the Axis powers.
- On March 5, Nazis in Amsterdam sentence eighteen Dutch resistance fighters to death.
- On March 7, the British recapture Somaliland.
- On March 25, Yugoslavia joins the Axis; anti-Nazi riots erupt in Belgrade, and on March 27 the pro-Axis government is overthrown in a military coup.
- From March 28 to March 29, the British navy destroys much of the remaining Italian fleet off Cape Matapan, Greece.
- On April 3, Italian and German troops force the British to evacuate Bengasi, Libya.
- On April 4, the German army invades the Balkan Peninsula; it then crosses into Yugoslavia and Greece on April 6.
- On April 10, the Danish envoy to Washington, D.C., announces an agreement to provide American protection for Greenland; the government of Nazi-occupied Denmark declares the agreement void on April 12.

- On April 13, the Soviet Union and Japan sign a neutrality pact.

- On April 17, the Yugoslavian army surrenders to the Axis.

- On April 19, the British land troops in Iraq to protect the oil fields after the Baghdad government has displayed an increasingly pro-Axis bias. Military exchanges between the British and Iraqis follow.

- On April 27, German forces occupy Athens.

- On May 5, following the British conquest of Ethiopia, Emperor Haile Selassie returns to assume the throne lost in the Italian conquest of 1936.

- On May 8, Nazi air raids flatten Hull, England.

- On May 9, the RAF conducts devastating air raids on Hamburg and Bremen.

- On May 10, Rudolf Hess, Hitler's personal deputy, parachutes into Scotland.

- From May 10 to May 11, Nazi bombers blitz London, damaging the House of Commons, Westminster Abbey, and Big Ben.

- On May 16, the RAF bombs German airfields in Syria.

- On May 20, the Germans launch an invasion of Crete, completing their conquest of the island on June 1.

- On May 21, the U.S. ship *Robin Moor* is torpedoed and sunk by a German U-boat off the coast of Brazil.

- On May 24, the British battle cruiser *Hood* is sunk by the German battleship *Bismarck* between Greenland and Iceland.

- On May 27, the British navy sinks the *Bismarck* off the French coast.

- On May 31, British forces enter Baghdad, and the Iraqi government agrees to an armistice.

- On June 8, British and Free French troops invade Syria, taking Damascus on June 21.

- On June 18, Germany and Turkey sign a ten-year friendship treaty.

- On June 22, Germany and Italy declare war on the Soviet Union, as Germany launches a massive attack on three fronts. Turkey declares its neutrality. Britain assures the Soviets of aid, as does the United States, as President Franklin D. Roosevelt declares on June 25 that the neutrality act does not apply to Russia.

- On June 26, Finland joins the Axis attack on the Soviet Union; German troops are already within fifty miles of Minsk, which falls to them on June 30.

- On June 27, Hungary declares war on the Soviet Union.

- On July 1, the Germans capture Riga, the capital of Lithuania; the next day the Nazis capture 160,000 Russian troops near Bialystok.

- On July 3, Soviet premier Joseph Stalin announces a "scorched earth" defense; two days later German mechanized troops reach the Dnieper River, three hundred miles from Moscow.

- On July 7, the United States occupies Iceland with naval and marine forces; the Icelandic parliament approves the occupation on July 10.

- On July 8, the Nazi advance into Russia stalls. An estimated nine million men are engaged in the war between Germany and Russia.

- On July 18, Japanese premier Konoye forms a new cabinet, which includes four generals and three admirals.

- On July 19, Bolivia announces the uncovering of an Axis plot and ousts the German diplomatic minister.

- On July 23, Vichy France accedes to Tokyo's demand for military bases in Indochina.

- On July 24, German troops advance to the outskirts of Leningrad and Smolensk. Japanese troops arrive in southern Indochina.

- On July 25, the United States and Great Britain freeze all Japanese assets; Japan retaliates the next day by freezing American and British assets.

- On July 31, Japan formally apologizes for sinking the American gunboat *Tutuila* in Chungking, China, on July 30.

- On August 1, President Roosevelt places an embargo on the export of all motor fuel oils outside the Western Hemisphere except to the British Empire.

- On August 8, Vichy military observers estimate the casualties from the first forty-eight days of the German invasion of the Soviet Union to be 1.5 million Axis troops and 2 million Russians.

- On August 19, German troops lay siege to Odessa.

- On August 21, in Paris two communists are executed, and thousands more so-called communists and anarchists are arrested as the Germans crack down on the Resistance. By month's end eleven more suspected Resistance members are executed, and in Paris alone thousands of Jews are deported to Nazi concentration camps.

- On August 25, responding to increasing Axis infiltration, Soviet and British troops invade Iran.

- On August 28, the Vichy regime executes three more suspected Resistance fighters; on August 29 they will execute eight more men.

- On August 29, German troops occupy Tallinn, Estonia.

- On September 4, German U-boats attack the U.S. destroyer *Greer,* en route to Iceland; the *Greer* counterattacks with depth charges.

- On September 5, German artillery begins shelling Leningrad.

- On September 10, German authorities in Oslo place the city under martial law after several strikes break out; on September 12, they begin mass arrests of trade unionists.

- On September 11, President Roosevelt authorizes American ships to protect themselves by shooting first if they feel threatened by Axis warships; the next day Berlin announces that it will take appropriate countermeasures.

- On September 14, the first Russian-based RAF wing arrives in the Soviet Union. In Zagreb, Yugoslavia, the central telephone exchange is bombed, and Axis authorities arrest and execute fifty Resistance fighters.

- On September 16, under pressure from the Allies, ailing Reza Shah Pahlevi of Iran abdicates in favor of his twenty-one-year-old son, Mohammed Reza Pahlevi.

- On September 18, Stalin orders the conscription of all Soviet workers between the ages of sixteen and fifty for after-hours military training.

- On September 21, German troops enter Kiev and reach the Sea of Azov, cutting off the Crimea.

- On September 28, German authorities announce the arrest of Czech premier Alois Elias on charges that he had plotted high treason with the Czech government in exile in London. Many other arrests and executions follow, and on October 5, German radio reports 159 executions and 900 arrests so far.

- On October 2, Hitler announces a final drive against Moscow.

- On October 15, the Germans capture Kalinin, one hundred miles northwest of Moscow. Soviet troops begin their final evacuation of Odessa.

- On October 16, Axis troops capture Odessa. In Japan, Premier Konoye resigns. On October 18, Lt. Gen. Tojo Hideki forms a new cabinet, making himself premier, minister of war, and home minister.

- On October 17, the U.S. destroyer *Kearny* is torpedoed and damaged off the coast of Greenland.

- On October 19, the Germans lay siege to Moscow.

- On October 21, in reprisal for the slaying of a German officer, fifty French citizens are executed in Nantes, and the Germans warn they will execute fifty more if the killers of the officer are not turned over by October 23.

- On October 22, the Nazis seize one hundred people in Bordeaux after the killing of another German officer; fifty are killed immediately and fifty are held hostage, as in Nantes. Because of an international outcry, execution of the Nantes and Bordeaux hostages is first postponed and then suspended indefinitely on October 30.

- On October 22, in Zagreb, Yugoslavia, newspapers report the execution of two hundred citizens in reprisal for an attack on two German officers.

- On October 30, the U.S. destroyer *Reuben James* is sunk off the coast of Iceland.

- On November 6, the United States announces $1 billion in lend-lease aid to the Soviet Union.

- On November 9, in Vienna Nazi authorities announce the execution of twenty Czechs.

- On November 17, special envoy Kurusu Saburo delivers Japanese premier Tojo's ultimatum to President Roosevelt. Tojo demands American withdrawal from China and the lifting of the U.S. economic embargo in return for peace in the Pacific.

- On November 18, Britain begins an invasion of Libya that drives Rommel's forces back to the point at which he began his invasion of Egypt.

- On November 19, the United States and Mexico sign trade and financial agreements designed to stabilize currency and resolve nationalization claims.

- On November 24, the United States dispatches troops to Dutch Guiana to help Dutch troops protect its bauxite mines.

- On November 28, reports from Shanghai indicate that transports carrying some thirty thousand Japanese troops are moving southward from China toward Haiphong in Indochina.

- On November 30, in an inflammatory speech, Japanese premier Tojo declares that Anglo-American exploitation of Asia must be purged.

- On December 2, in Trieste, sixty people go on trial on various charges, including espionage and involvement in a 1938 plot to assassinate Mussolini; on December 14, nine are sentenced to death, and others receive long prison terms.

- On December 6, the Soviet army begins a counteroffensive along the Moscow front.

- On December 7, in a surprise attack, Japanese planes bomb U.S. naval and air bases at Pearl Harbor, Hawaii, destroying two battleships and four other capital vessels. Japanese air forces simultaneously attack U.S. bases in the Philippines, Guam, and Wake Island, and British bases in Hong Kong and Singapore, while also invading Malaya and Thailand by land and sea. A Japanese declaration of war on the United States is delivered after the attack.

- On December 8, the United States, Great Britain, the Free French government, and the Dutch government in exile in London declare war on Japan, as do Canada, Costa Rica, Honduras, San Salvador, Guatemala, Haiti, and the Dominican Republic. Thailand capitulates to the Japanese.

- On December 11, Germany and Italy declare war on the United States; the U.S. Congress unanimously responds by declaring war on Germany and Italy—as do Cuba, Costa Rica, Nicaragua, Guatemala, and the Dominican Republic; Mexico severs relations with both nations.

- On December 13, Japanese forces take Guam.

- On December 14, Turkey and Ireland declare neutrality in the U.S./Japanese war.

- On December 16, a Japanese submarine shells the Hawaiian port of Kahului, one hundred miles southwest of Honolulu.

- On December 22, Prime Minister Churchill and other British officials visit Washington, D.C., to establish a combined American-British military command for the war.

- On December 23, Japanese forces complete their invasion of Wake Island.

- On December 25, the British garrison at Hong Kong surrenders to the Japanese.

- On December 30, Mohandas K. Gandhi resigns from the All-India National Congress Party because it has abandoned civil disobedience.

1942

- Albert Camus's novel *The Stranger* is published.

- T.S. Eliot's *Little Gidding,* the fourth part of his *Four Quartets,* is published.

- Dmitry Shostakovich composes his Seventh Symphony, his homage to Leningrad.

- On January 1, in Washington, D.C., twenty-six Allied nations, including the United States, Great Britain, the Soviet Union, and China, sign a pact agreeing not to make separate peace with Germany.

- On January 2, the Japanese take Manila.

- From January 14 to January 15, the RAF conducts heavy bombing raids on port facilities at Hamburg and Rotterdam, beginning a long series of air attacks on port and factory cities in Germany and occupied Europe.

- From January 15 to January 28, foreign ministers of the Western Hemisphere nations, including the United States, meet in Rio de Janeiro. With the exception of Argentina and Chile, they sever diplomatic relations with Axis nations and agree to collective-security arrangements.

- On January 17, the Japanese invade Burma.

- On January 20, leading Nazi officials meet in Wannsee, near Berlin, to plan a "final solution" to the "Jewish problem."

- On January 21, in North Africa, Rommel begins a counteroffensive that drives the British back into Egypt within two weeks.

- On January 26, the first U.S. troops arrive on British soil.

- On January 29, the Soviet Union, Great Britain, and Iran conclude a treaty providing for wartime occupation of Iran. The Soviets station troops in the northern section of the country, the British in the south, to guard Iranian oil reserves and vital supply lines from the Persian Gulf to the Soviet Union.

- On February 15, Japan occupies Singapore and Malaya.

- On March 3, the RAF bombs the Renault works outside Paris, destroying the factory, which has been manufacturing tanks and aircraft engines for the Germans.

- On March 7, the Japanese complete their invasion of Java.

- On March 23, British envoy Sir Stafford Cripps arrives in India to offer postwar dominion status; the terms of the offer are rejected by the Indian Congress on April 11. The British respond by imprisoning Indian Nationalists.

- On March 28, the RAF bombs Lübeck, Germany, inflicting heavy damage in the important Baltic port.

- On April 2, Dr. William Temple, archbishop of York, becomes archbishop of Canterbury.

- On April 18, "Doolittle's Raiders," a squadron of U.S. Army Air Corps bombers led by Brig. Gen. James H. Doolittle, raid Tokyo and other Japanese cities.

- From April 23 to April 26, the RAF bombing of the Baltic port of Rostock is the heaviest on any city since the beginning of the war. The Germans begin reprisal raids on British cities.

- On May 1, the Japanese take Mandalay, forcing the British to begin withdrawal from Burma to India.

- From May 4 to May 9, American and Japanese naval forces trade blows in the Coral Sea.

- On May 6, U.S. forces surrender the Philippines to the Japanese.

- On May 7, the Allies take Bizerte and Tunis.

- On May 26, Great Britain and the Soviet Union sign a twenty-year alliance. Rommel begins a new offensive in the western Sahara.

- On May 27, Reinhard Heydrich, second in command of the Gestapo, is shot in Czechoslovakia; he dies on June 3. In retaliation, the Nazis kill thousands of Czechs, including everyone in the town of Lidice.

- On May 30, more than one thousand Allied bombers level Cologne, the major railway center of western Germany.

- On June 3, Japanese aircraft attack a U.S. naval base in the Aleutian Islands. A few days later, they land troops on Attu and Kiska, in the western Aleutians.

- From June 4 to June 6, the United States cripples the Japanese fleet at the battle of Midway.

- From June 9 to June 28, Rommel's victories in North Africa force the British to retreat to El Alamein, east of Alexandria, Egypt.

- On June 18, the United States declares war on Bulgaria.

- On June 25, Maj. Gen. Dwight D. Eisenhower is appointed commander in chief of Allied military forces.

- From July 1 to July 9, Rommel's troops attack El Alamein, attempting to reach and gain control of the Suez Canal, but they are turned back by British forces.

- From July 16 to July 17, during the Rafle du Vel' d'Hiver (Roundup of the Winter Velodrome), more than twelve thousand Jews are arrested and held in a Paris sports arena for deportation to Germany and the occupied countries of Eastern Europe.

- From July 26 to July 29, the Allies conduct one of their most successful bombing raids on Hamburg.

- On August 7, the United States lands troops on Guadalcanal, where the Japanese have been building an airstrip since early July; from November 12 to November 15, American naval forces score a costly victory in a major sea battle for control of this strategically important island in the Solomon Islands, but the Japanese fight on until February 1943.

- From August 12 to August 15, Churchill, Stalin, and American representative Averell Harriman meet in Moscow to discuss the progress of the war against Germany.

- On August 25, German troops reach the outskirts of Stalingrad.

- On August 27, British scientists announce the discovery of penicillin.

- On September 14, the German siege of Stalingrad begins.

- On October 5, Prof. Gilbert Murray helps to found Oxfam to help relieve starvation in occupied Europe.

- From October 23 to October 26, the British Eighth Army, under the leadership of Lt. Gen. Bernard L. Montgomery, defeats Rommel's forces at El Alamein.

- On November 8, Allied troops under Gen. Dwight D. Eisenhower land in French North Africa to support the British offensive in Egypt. The United States and Vichy France break off diplomatic relations. In a speech in Munich, Hitler incorrectly announces that Stalingrad is "firmly in German hands."

- From November 9 to November 11, German troops occupy the so-called Free Zone of France.

- On November 11, the Allies take Algiers and Oran in Algeria, and also Casablanca and Rabat in Morocco.
- On November 13, Tobruk, Libya, is retaken by the British.
- From November 19 to November 22, a Soviet offensive lifts the siege of Stalingrad, but heavy fighting in the area continues until February 1943.
- On November 20, the British retake Benghazi, Libya.

1943

- Aram Khachaturian composes his *Ode to Stalin.*
- Harold Laski's political study *Reflections on the Revolution of Our Time* is published.
- Thomas Mann's novel *Joseph the Provider* is published.
- Jacques Maritain's *Christianity and Democracy* is published.
- Henri Michaux's *Exorcismes,* a collection of war poems, is published.
- Henry Moore sculpts his *Madonna and Child.*
- Sean O'Casey's play *Red Roses for Me* premieres in Dublin.
- Sergey Prokofiev composes his opera *War and Peace.*
- Jean-Paul Sartre's philosophical work *Being and Nothingness* is published.
- Dmitry Shostakovich composes his Eighth Symphony.
- The Aqua-Lung is invented.
- Hitler suppresses publication of the *Frankfurter Zeitung.*
- From January 14 to January 27, Churchill and Roosevelt confer with the joint chiefs of staff at Casablanca, Morocco, and demand unconditional surrender by the Axis powers.
- On January 22, American and Australian forces overrun the last pockets of Japanese troops in New Guinea.
- On January 23, the British Eighth Army takes Tripoli, Libya.
- On January 31, on the outskirts of Stalingrad, the Germans under Gen. Friedrich Paulus capitulate. Stalin announces the capture of more than 45,000 prisoners, including thirteen generals, and the deaths of 146,700 Germans. The remaining German troops in the area, including eight more generals, surrender on February 2.
- On February 9, the last Japanese forces retreat from Guadalcanal.
- On February 20, at the Kasserine Pass in Tunisia, Allied troops are forced to retreat by Rommel's Afrika Korps. On February 25, Allied troops retake the pass.
- From March 2 to March 4, the Japanese are defeated by the United States in the battle of the Bismarck Sea, losing a convoy of twenty-two ships and more than fifty aircraft.
- On April 20, the Nazis massacre Jews in the Warsaw ghetto.
- From May 7 to May 9, after the Allies take Tunis and Bizerte, the German forces in Tunisia surrender unconditionally.
- On May 11, American forces land on Attu in the Aleutian Islands. They complete their invasion of the island on June 2, and the Japanese abandon Kiska without a fight by July 27.
- On May 22, Moscow announces it has dissolved the Third Communist International (Comintern), formed in 1919.

- On June 3, French generals de Gaulle and Henri Giraud form the French Committee of National Liberation (CFLN) to coordinate the Free French war effort.
- On June 4, a military coup in Argentina is staged by generals Arturo Rawson and Pedro Ramirez.
- On July 10, the Allies invade Sicily, overcoming the last remaining forces on the island at Messina on August 17.
- On July 19, Allied forces bomb Rome for the first time.
- On July 25, Mussolini resigns. Italian king Victor Emmanuel III asks Marshal Pietro Badoglio to form a new government.
- On August 1, the Japanese grant independence to Burma, which declares war on the United States and Great Britain.
- From August 14 to August 24, Allied representatives meet in Quebec to plan a war strategy.
- On September 8, Eisenhower announces the unconditional surrender of Italy to the Allies. Stalin permits the reopening of many Soviet churches.
- On September 9, Allied troops land near Salerno, Italy.
- On September 10, Germany announces the occupation of Rome and northern Italy.
- On September 12, German commandos led by Capt. Otto Skorzeny rescue Mussolini from house arrest in San Grasso and take him to northern Italy, where he forms a new Fascist government.
- On September 30, the Allies occupy Naples, Italy.
- On October 13, the Italian government led by Badoglio declares war on Germany.
- On October 14, the Japanese declare the Philippines independent.
- From October 19 to October 30, the Allies confer in Moscow and agree that Germany will be stripped of all territory acquired since 1938.
- On November 1, American forces land at Bougainville in the Solomon Islands.
- On November 6, the Russians retake Kiev.
- On November 19, Sir Oswald Mosley, a British Fascist leader imprisoned since May 1940 as a security risk, is released on the grounds of failing health.
- From November 22 to November 26, Churchill, Roosevelt, and Chinese Nationalist leader Chiang Kai-shek meet at Cairo, Egypt, to plan a postwar Asian policy.
- From November 28 to December 1, Stalin, Churchill, and Roosevelt meet in Teheran, Iran, to discuss war strategy and plan the structure of the postwar world.

1944

- Béla Bartók composes his Sonata for Solo Violin Concerto.
- Max Beckmann paints his *Self-Portrait in Black.*
- Paul Hindemith composes his opera *Herodias.*
- Max Horkheimer and Theodor Adorno's *Dialectic of Enlightenment,* a study of Western Marxism and authoritarianism, is published.
- Aldous Huxley's novel *Time Must Have a Stop* is published.

- Somerset Maugham's novel *The Razor's Edge* is published.

- Henry Moore sculpts the first version of his *Family Group*.

- Jean-Paul Sartre's play *No Exit* premieres in Paris.

- On January 11, Moroccan nationalists demand independence from France.

- On January 22, Allied troops land at Anzio, Italy, in an attempt to outflank German defense positions in central Italy. Progress is slow, as they meet stubborn resistance.

- On January 27, the German siege of Leningrad ends.

- On January 30, at Brazzaville, in the Congo, African leaders discuss the postwar decolonization of Africa.

- From February 24 to February 25, President Ramirez of Argentina is overthrown in a coup led by Gen. Edelmiro Farrell.

- On March 4, American planes bomb Berlin.

- On March 6, in a daylight raid American bombers drop 2,000 tons of bombs on Berlin.

- On March 15, the Soviet Union officially replaces "The Internationale" with "Hymn of the Soviet Union" as its national anthem.

- On June 4, Allied forces enter Rome.

- On June 6, Allied forces establish beachheads in Normandy, France, and begin the liberation of Western Europe. The operation, code-named "Overlord," involves more than four thousand ships, three thousand planes, and four million troops. The day becomes known as D-Day.

- On June 13, the Germans begin attacking Britain with their V-1 rockets, launching more than seven thousand against England by August 24.

- On June 15, American long-range Superfortress aircraft begin bombing operations against the Japanese home islands.

- On July 1, the Allies confer in Bretton Woods, New Hampshire, hoping to establish a stable postwar economic system.

- On July 3, the Soviets announce their recapture of Minsk.

- On July 18, Tojo resigns as Japanese prime minister.

- On July 20, at Hitler's East Prussian headquarters, a bombing assassination attempt fails. Plotters are executed during the night, including Col. Claus von Stauffenberg, chief of staff of the Home Army.

- On August 12, Allied troops take Florence, Italy.

- From August 21 to August 29, in Washington, D.C., at the Dumbarton Oaks conference, the Allies begin discussions on the formation of the United Nations (UN).

- On August 25, Allied troops liberate Paris.

- On September 4, Allied troops liberate Brussels.

- On September 8, the Germans begin V-2 rocket attacks on England.

- On September 12, Romania signs an armistice with the Allies.

- From September 17 to September 28, Allied efforts to secure Rhine bridges and outflank the Germans at Eindhoven and Arnhem fail.

- On September 19, Finland signs an armistice with the Allies.

- On September 29, the Soviet Union invades Yugoslavia.

- From October 9 to October 20, Churchill and Stalin confer in Moscow.

- On October 20, American forces led by Gen. Douglas MacArthur land in the Philippines.

- From October 23 to October 26, during the Battle of Leyte Gulf, the largest naval battle of World War II, American forces destroy the remainder of the Japanese fleet.

- On December 16, German general Karl von Rundstedt launches an unsuccessful German offensive in the Ardennes. This "Battle of the Bulge" is the last major German military offensive of World War II.

1945

- Martin Buber's theological study *For the Sake of Heaven* is published.

- Carlo Levi's autobiographical work *Christ Stopped at Eboli* is published.

- Jean Giraudoux's play *The Madwoman of Chaillot* premieres in Paris.

- George Orwell's novel *Animal Farm* is published.

- Karl Popper's *The Open Society and Its Enemies,* a study of authoritarianism, is published.

- Jean Renoir's movie *The Southerner* is released.

- Roberto Rossellini's movie *Open City,* filmed in postwar Rome, is released.

- Dmitry Shostakovich composes his Ninth Symphony.

- Igor Stravinsky composes his *Symphony in Three Movements.*

- Evelyn Waugh's novel *Brideshead Revisited* is published.

- In France, women gain the right to vote.

- In January, part one of Sergey Eisenstein's movie *Ivan the Terrible* is released and achieves instant success, earning Eisenstein a Stalin Prize. Completed in February 1946, part two, however, is denounced by the Central Committee of the Communist Party for its unflattering portrayal of Ivan and his bodyguard and is promptly banned. It is not publicly released until 1958.

- On January 1, in Egypt elections boycotted by the nationalist Wafd result in the election of Ahmed Maher Pasha as premier.

- On January 18, the Soviets announce the liberation of Warsaw.

- On January 20, the provisional Hungarian government of Gen. Bela Miklos signs an agreement of unconditional surrender to the Allies.

- On January 22, British troops retake Monywa, in Burma, reopening the land route to China.

- On January 26, Soviet troops reach the Prussian coast at Elbing, severing East Prussia from the rest of Germany.

- On January 27, the Red Army liberates Auschwitz.

- On January 29, Soviet troops cross the 1939 border between Poland and Germany, entering the province of Pomerania in northeastern Germany. By February 2, they control most of East Prussia.

- On January 31, Soviet troops cross the Oder River, coming within fifty miles of Berlin.

- From February 4 to February 11, Roosevelt, Churchill, Stalin, and other Allied leaders confer at Yalta, in the Crimea, on issues of postwar international organization. They agree to divide Germany into separate Allied occupation zones.

- On February 13, the Soviets capture Budapest after a fifty-day seige.

- On February 14, the Allies firebomb Dresden, Germany.

- On February 19, U.S. Marines land at Iwo Jima, 750 miles south of Tokyo. The island falls to the Americans on March 17, at a cost of four thousand American and twenty thousand Japanese lives.

- On February 21, the Inter-American Conference convenes in Mexico City to discuss economic issues such as conversion to a peacetime economy.

- On February 24, U.S. troops drive the last Japanese forces from Manila, the Phillippines. After announcing the Egyptian declaration of war on Germany and Japan, Premier Ahmed Maher Pasha is assassinated in Cairo.

- On March 6, U.S. troops capture Cologne, Germany.

- On March 7, the American First Army crosses the Rhine at Remagen, Germany.

- On March 9, American Superfortress bombers drop more than 2,300 tons of incendiary bombs on Tokyo.

- On March 19, the Soviet Union formally denounces a 1925 nonaggression treaty with Turkey and demands diplomatic revisions.

- On March 30, the Soviets capture Danzig, Poland.

- On April 1, American forces invade Okinawa, 360 miles south of Tokyo.

- From April 9 to April 13, the Red Army enters Vienna.

- On April 12, President Roosevelt dies at Warm Springs, Georgia. He is succeeded by Vice President Harry S. Truman. American troops liberate Buchenwald concentration camp.

- On April 21, Soviet troops reach the outskirts of Berlin.

- On April 25, advancing armies of the United States and the Soviet Union meet at Torgau, on the Elbe River in Germany. The UN conference opens in San Francisco. The delegates complete the UN charter on June 26.

- On April 28, in Como, Italy, Mussolini is executed by Italian partisans.

- On April 29, the U.S. Seventh Army enters Munich and liberates the concentration camp at Dachau. German troops in Italy surrender to the Allies.

- On April 30, Hitler commits suicide at his bunker in Berlin.

- On May 2, the Germans surrender Berlin to the Soviets.

- On May 8, German military authorities formally surrender to the Allies, ending World War II in Europe. The day becomes known as V-E Day.

- On May 19, demonstrations erupt in Lebanon and Syria following the landing of French troops sent to reestablish colonial control.

- On May 22, Yonabaru, the key Japanese position on Okinawa, is taken by American forces. The Japanese surrender the island on June 21, at a cost of thirteen thousand American and one hundred thousand Japanese lives.

- On May 23, French authorities report 1,300 casualties in a nationalist uprising staged by Berber tribesmen in Algeria.

- On May 29, French artillery shells Damascus after street fighting breaks out between Syrians and French troops.

- From June 3 to June 25, French troops are withdrawn from Beirut and Damascus, as France requests UN mediation.

- On June 11, the Liberal Party, led by Prime Minister Mackenzie King, wins in the Canadian elections, but King loses his seat in the House of Commons.

- On July 5, the United States completes the reoccupation of the Philippines, at a cost of nearly twelve thousand men.

- On July 16, the United States successfully detonates the first atomic bomb at Alamagordo Air Force Base in New Mexico.

- From July 17 to July 26, Truman, Stalin, Churchill, and other Allied representatives meet in Potsdam, a suburb of Berlin, and issue the Potsdam Declaration, demanding unconditional surrender from Japan.

- On July 26, elections in Britain result in a Labour Party landslide; Clement Attlee succeeds Churchill as prime minister.

- On August 6, the U.S. Superfortress bomber *Enola Gay* drops an atomic bomb on the Japanese city of Hiroshima, killing more than fifty thousand people and leveling four square miles of the city.

- On August 8, the Soviet Union declares war on Japan and attacks Japanese forces in Manchuria the next day.

- On August 9, the United States detonates an atomic bomb on the Japanese city of Nagasaki, killing more than forty thousand people and destroying a third of the city.

- On August 10, the Japanese Supreme Council votes to accept the surrender terms of the Potsdam Declaration.

- On August 14, the Soviet government concludes a treaty with the Chinese Nationalist government of Chiang Kai-shek.

- On August 15, the Allies accept the unconditional surrender of the Japanese; the day is known as V-J Day. The French sentence Pétain to death as a Nazi collaborator; the sentence is later commuted to life imprisonment.

- On August 28, U.S. troops land on the home islands of Japan to supervise the disarmament of the Japanese military.

- On September 2, in ceremonies aboard the U.S.S. *Missouri,* moored in Tokyo Bay, the Japanese formally surrender to the Allies, ending World War II.

- In Hanoi, Vietnamese nationalist leader Ho Chi Minh declares Vietnamese independence, using a copy of the American Declaration of Independence supplied by the Office of Strategic Services.

- On September 20, the All-India Congress Committee, led by Gandhi and Jawaharlal Nehru, convenes. It rejects British proposals for national autonomy and calls for the removal of Britain from India.

- From October 11 to October 12, Gen. Eduardo Avalos seizes control in Argentina. His government is overthrown on October 17 by Col. Juan Perón.
- On October 21, elections for the French Constituent Assembly result in significant gains for the communists.
- On November 10, the United States, Great Britain, and the Soviet Union recognize the communist government of Albania, led by Col. Enver Hoxha.
- On November 13, the Constituent Assembly of France unanimously elects Charles de Gaulle as head of the French government.
- On November 18, Antonio de Oliveira Salazar's National Union Party wins the Portuguese elections, which are boycotted by the opposition.
- On November 20, in Nuremberg, the trials of top Nazi leaders for crimes against humanity begin.
- On December 14, the U.S. government sends Gen. George C. Marshall as envoy to China to mediate in the civil war between the communists and nationalists.
- On December 15, the Allied Control Commission abolishes Shintoism as the state religion of Japan.
- On December 27, Allied foreign ministers, meeting in Moscow, call for the establishment of a provisional democratic government in Korea. Soviet forces occupy Korea north of the thirty-eighth parallel, while U.S. troops occupy the southern portion of the country.

1946

- Simone de Beauvoir's novel *All Men Are Mortal* is published.
- Benjamin Britten composes his opera *The Rape of Lucretia.*
- Marcel Carné's movie *Les Portes de la Nuit* is released.
- Ernest Cassirer's *The Myth of the State,* a study of political science, is published.
- André Gide's *Journal, 1939–42* is published.
- David Lean's movie *Great Expectations* is released.
- Michael Polanyi's *Science, Faith and Society,* an analysis of scientific method and medicine, is published.
- Bertrand Russell's *A History of Western Philosophy* is published.
- Dylan Thomas's *Deaths and Entrances,* a collection of poems, is published.
- Women gain the right to vote in Italy.
- On February 24, Perón, leader of a Fascistic political movement, is elected president of Argentina.
- On March 2, British troops complete their evacuation of Iran, but Soviet troops remain, violating the Anglo-Russian treaty of 1942. Following diplomatic pressure from the United States and Great Britain, the Soviet Union withdraws its troops by May 9.
- On March 5, in a speech at Westminster College in Fulton, Missouri, Churchill warns that, in Europe, "an iron curtain [of communism] has descended across the continent."

- On March 22, Great Britain recognizes the independence of Transjordan, which came under British mandate after World War I.
- On April 18, the League of Nations conducts its final assembly in Geneva, turning over its assets to the UN.
- On June 3, Italians vote to replace their monarchy with a republic.
- On July 1 and July 25, the United States conducts atomic bomb tests at Bikini Atoll in the Pacific Ocean.
- On July 4, the United States grants independence to the Philippines.
- On September 8, Bulgarian voters reject their monarchy in favor of a republic; on September 15, Bulgaria is declared a people's republic.
- On October 13, French voters approve a new constitution, which establishes the Fourth Republic.
- On October 16, at Nuremberg, as a result of their convictions for war crimes, ten leading Nazis are executed. Nazi chief Hermann Göring, scheduled to hang with the others, commits suicide two hours before the executions.
- On November 10, French Communists score significant electoral gains, resulting in political deadlock in the French Assembly.
- On November 22, French authorities, seeking the surrender of Vietnamese nationalists, bombard the cities of Haiphong and Hanoi, killing six thousand.
- On December 16, Socialists led by Léon Blum form a new French government.

1947

- Benjamin Britten composes his opera *Albert Herring.*
- Albert Camus's novel *The Plague* is published.
- Charlie Chaplin's movie *Monsieur Verdoux* is released.
- Anne Frank's *The Diary of a Young Girl* is published.
- Erich Fromm's *Man for Himself,* a psychological study of ethics, is published.
- Alberto Giacometti sculpts *Man Pointing.*
- Le Corbusier begins the Unité d'habitation, an apartment complex intended to function as a self-sufficient community, in Marseilles.
- H.R. Trevor-Roper's historical work *The Last Days of Hitler* is published.
- On January 1, the British and Americans join their German occupation zones into a single economic unit.
- On January 29, American envoys, led by General Marshall, abandon efforts to negotiate an end to the Chinese civil war.
- On February 10, the Allies sign formal peace treaties with Italy, Bulgaria, Romania, Hungary, and Finland, officially ending the hostilities of World War II.
- On March 3, Martial law is declared in Palestine after increased incidences of Zionist attacks against British personnel.
- On March 4, France and England sign a fifty-year military alliance.

- On March 12, speaking to a joint session of the U.S. Congress, President Truman requests $500 million in military and economic assistance for the governments of Greece and Turkey.

- On April 29, the Constituent Assembly of India outlaws untouchability, affirming equal rights for all, regardless of race, religion, caste, or sex.

- On May 3, a new Japanese constitution, drafted by the United States, goes into effect.

- In June, France is paralyzed by a series of strikes.

- On June 27, Soviet, British, and French representatives meet in Paris to discuss American proposals for economic assistance to Europe. Talks break down on July 2 when Soviet foreign commissar Vyacheslav Molotov denounces the Americans' "Marshall Plan" as politically motivated and refuses to participate in the reconstruction program.

- On August 15, India and Pakistan become independent nations, ending nearly 350 years of British colonial rule on the Indian subcontinent.

- On September 2, nineteen Western Hemisphere nations, including the United States, sign the Rio Pact, committing themselves to collective defense against aggression.

- On October 5, the Soviet Union announces that, during a secret meeting in Warsaw in September, the Communist parties of the Soviet Union, Bulgaria, Czechoslovakia, France, Hungary, Italy, Poland, Romania, and Yugoslavia created the Communist Information Bureau (Cominform) to coordinate the activities of European Communist parties and trade unions.

- On October 26, India annexes Kashmir, provoking war with Pakistan; on December 30, the conflict will be referred for settlement to the UN.

- On December 30, after King Michael of Romania abdicates, the Romanian parliament abolishes the monarchy and proclaims the nation a people's republic.

1948

- The first volume of Winston Churchill's memoir, *The Second World War,* is published.

- Graham Greene's novel *The Heart of the Matter* is published.

- Aldous Huxley's novel *Ape and Essence* is published.

- Laurence Olivier stars in a screen version of *Hamlet.*

- Vittorio de Sica's movie *The Bicycle Thieves* is released.

- Belgium grants the right to vote to women.

- On January 1, the Benelux Customs Union is established.

- On January 4, Burma becomes an independent nation.

- On January 20, Gandhi is assassinated.

- On February 4, Ceylon becomes independent.

- On February 25, communists seize control of the Czechoslovakian government. Czech nationalist Jan Masaryk dies on March 10 after falling from a window. Reported as a suicide, his death arouses suspicion in the West.

- On March 1, British and American authorities establish a central bank to serve their occupation zones of Germany.

- On March 17, France, the United Kingdom, and the Benelux countries sign the Brussels Pact, a fifty-year military alliance.

- On April 3, the U.S. Congress appropriates $6 billion for the Marshall Plan to aid Western European reconstruction.

- On May 1, North Korea proclaims itself a people's republic and adopts a Soviet-style constitution.

- On May 14, the state of Israel is declared, as the British mandate in Palestine comes to an end. At midnight, troops from Egypt, the Transjordan, Syria, Lebanon, and Iraq invade Palestine; the UN effects a truce on July 15.

- On May 26, the United Party loses control of the South African House of Assembly after running on a platform that included a gradual increase in the rights of native Africans. The victorious Nationalist Party and its coalition partner, the Afrikaner Party, advocate a policy of strict apartheid.

- On June 18, France merges its German occupation zone with the Anglo-American zone, forming a single West German political unit.

- On June 20, a new currency, the deutsche mark, is established for West Germany.

- On June 24, Soviet authorities halt all surface traffic from West Germany into Berlin, blockading the city. Western authorities respond with an airlift to supply the western sections of Berlin with vital necessities.

- On June 28, the Soviet Union expels Yugoslavia from the Cominform, signaling hostile relations between the two communist governments.

- On July 25, Britain ends the rationing of bread.

- In August, Soviet scientists who disagree with the environmental evolutionary theories of geneticist T.D. Lysenko are purged from the Russian scientific establishment.

- On August 15, South Korea formally proclaims itself the Democratic Republic of Korea.

- On August 22, in Amsterdam, 147 Protestant and Orthodox denominations from forty-four countries found the World Council of Churches.

- On November 12, an American military tribunal finds Tojo and six other Japanese defendants guilty of war crimes and sentences them to death. They are executed on December 23.

- On December 27, Cardinal József Mindszenty is arrested by the communist government of Hungary on charges that he furnished Western powers with information about Soviet-Hungarian relations and urged Western intervention in Hungary. On February 8, 1949, he is sentenced to life imprisonment for high treason.

1949

- Simone de Beauvoir's feminist work *The Second Sex* is published.

- T.S. Eliot's play *The Cocktail Party* premieres in Edinburgh.

- George Orwell's novel *1984* is published.

- Paul Tillich's theological study *The Shaking of the Foundations* is published.

- From January 20 to January 23, representatives of nineteen Middle Eastern, Far Eastern, and Australasian nations meet in New Delhi to discuss Asian affairs. They issue a statement critical of Dutch efforts to prevent the Netherlands East Indies from becoming the independent nation of Indonesia.

- On January 25, the Soviet Union and communist countries of Eastern Europe announce that they have established the Council for Mutual Economic Assistance.

- On March 8, France agrees to recognize the independence of Vietnam within the French Union and to reinstall Vietnamese emperor Bao Dai.

- On April 4, twelve nations, including the United States and the Brussels Pact nations, form the North Atlantic Treaty Organization (NATO), committing themselves to mutual military assistance.

- On April 18, the Republic of Ireland is officially proclaimed.

- On May 5, ten Western European states form the Council of Europe to promote peace and foster European cooperation.

- On May 11, Israel is admitted to the UN.

- On May 12, Soviet authorities, announcing they have completed road and rail "repairs," end the Berlin blockade.

- On June 29, American occupation forces are withdrawn from Korea. South Africa signals a hardening of apartheid restrictions by banning mixed marriages and automatic citizenship for immigrants from Commonwealth countries.

- On August 5, the United States terminates all military and economic assistance to the Nationalist Chinese government of Chiang Kai-shek.

- On August 14, the conservative Christian Democratic Party, led by Konrad Adenauer, garners 31 percent of the vote in the first postwar parliamentary election in the new Federal Republic of Germany (West Germany).

- On September 23, American, British, and Canadian officials announce that the Soviet Union has successfully detonated an atomic bomb.

- On October 1, the communist People's Republic of China is proclaimed.

- On October 7, the eastern, Soviet-occupied zone of Germany declares itself the German Democratic Republic.

- On October 24, in New York, the permanent headquarters of the UN is dedicated.

- On November 8, Cambodia becomes an independent nation within the French Union.

- On November 26, India adopts a federal constitution and opts to remain within the British Commonwealth.

- On December 16, the British Parliament further restricts the powers of the House of Lords.

- On December 27, led by President Sukarno, the United States of Indonesia becomes an independent nation.

1

THE ARTS

JOSEPH R. PHELAN

Entries are arranged in chronological order by date of primary source. For entries with one primary source, the entry title is the same as the primary source title. Entries with more than one primary source have an overall entry title, followed by the titles of the primary sources.

Important Events in the Arts, 1940–1949

1940

• On February 29, *Gone with the Wind* wins the Academy Award for best motion picture.

• On June 12, American artists vote to withdraw from the Venice Art Exhibit because of the war.

• On October 22, Piet Mondrian arrives in New York, in exile from the war in Europe.

• On October 31, the Hollywood film industry pledges facilities to produce army training films.

• On November 14, the American Academy of Arts and Letters gives the Howells Medal for Fiction to Ellen Glasgow for the most distinguished work of the past five years.

MOVIES: *Fantasia,* Walt Disney feature-length animation; *The Grapes of Wrath,* starring Henry Fonda, directed by John Ford; *The Great Dictator,* directed by and starring Charlie Chaplin; *Knute Rockne, All-American,* starring Ronald Reagan; *The Philadelphia Story,* starring Katharine Hepburn, Cary Grant, and Jimmy Stewart; *Rebecca,* starring Laurence Olivier, directed by Alfred Hitchcock.

FICTION: Walter von Tilburg Clark, *The Ox-Bow Incident*; William Faulkner, *The Hamlet*; Ernest Hemingway, *For Whom the Bell Tolls*; Richard Llewellyn, *How Green Was My Valley*; Carson McCullers, *The Heart is a Lonely Hunter*; Upton Sinclair, *World's End*; Thomas Wolfe, *You Can't Go Home Again* (published posthumously); Richard Wright, *Native Son.*

POPULAR SONGS: "Along the Santa Fe Trail," Glenn Miller and his Orchestra with Ray Eberly; "Boog-it," Cab Calloway and his Orchestra; "Can't Get Indiana off My Mind," Kate Smith; "Devil May Care," Bing Crosby; "Dream Valley," Sammy Kaye and his Orchestra; "I Can't Love You Any More," Benny Goodman with Helen Forrest; "Java Jive," The Ink Spots; "Just to Ease My Worried Mind," Roy Acuff; "Love Lies," Tommy Dorsey and his Orchestra with Frank Sinatra; "Strange Fruit," Billie Holliday.

1941

• On January 31, the NAACP awards the Joel Springarn medal to Richard Wright.

• On February 27, *Rebecca* wins the Academy Award for best motion picture.

• On March 6, Gutzon Borglum, sculptor of the presidential busts on Mount Rushmore, dies; his son, Lincoln, vows to complete his father's work.

• On March 17, President Roosevelt opens the National Gallery of Art in Washington, D.C.

• On March 28, Cary Grant announces that he will donate his salary from his upcoming movie to British war relief.

• On June 6, the American Writers' Congress presents the Randolph Bourne Memorial Award for "distinguished service to the cause and culture of peace" to Theodore Dreiser. The following day, they select Richard Wright's *Native Son* as the best novel published since 1939.

• A subcommittee of the Senate Interstate Commerce Committee conducts hearings to determine whether or not Hollywood movies promote American military intervention in World War II.

MOVIES: *Buck Privates,* starring Abbott and Costello; *Citizen Kane,* directed by and starring Orson Welles; *Dumbo,* Walt Disney film; *High Sierra,* starring Humphrey Bogart; *How Green Was My Valley,* directed by John Ford, starring Donald Crisp; *The Maltese Falcon,* directed by John Huston, starring Humphrey Bogart; *Meet John Doe,* directed by Frank Capra; *Sergeant York,* starring Gary Cooper.

FICTION: A. J. Cronin, *The Keys of the Kingdom*; Edna Ferber, *Saratoga Trunk*; F. Scott Fitzgerald, *The Last Tycoon* (published posthumously); Ellen Glasgow, *In This Our Life.*

POPULAR SONGS "Boogie Woogie Bugle Boy," The Andrews Sisters; "Everything Happens to Me," Tommy Dorsey with Frank Sinatra; "Frenesi," Artie Shaw and his Orchestra; "Hawaiian Sunset," Sammy Kaye with Marty McKenna; "I Wonder Why You Said Goodbye," Ernest Tubb; "Jump For Joy," Duke Ellington with Herb Jeffries; "This Love of Mine," Tommy Dorsey with Frank Sinatra; "'Til Reveille," Bing Crosby; "When My Blue Moon Turns Gold Again," Gene Autry.

1942

• On January 16, Carole Lombard dies in a plane crash while returning from a war bond rally.

• On February 8, Mark Rothko holds his first solo exhibition at the Artists' Gallery in New York.

• On February 27, *How Green was My Valley* wins the Academy Award for best motion picture.

• On March 12, Italian singer Ezio Pinza is held by U.S. government as an enemy alien.

• On March 30, actor Lew Ayres is placed in a detention camp for conscientious objectors after refusing to serve in the military. After weeks of detention, he will join the Army as a non-combatant.

• On May 2, Aaron Copland's *Lincoln Portrait* premieres.

• On July 4, *This Is the Army,* a soldier revue with a cast of three hundred army men, opens at a Broadway theater in New York.

• On July 8, James Petrillo, president of the American Federation of Musicians, announces a ban on recording because of a dispute with American Society of Composers, Authors and Publishers (ASCAP).

• On August 12, Clark Gable enlists in the Army.

• On September 23, a Dial Press poll names Carl Sandburg the "greatest living American writer" Ernest Hemingway and Willa Cather finish second and third.

• On October 26, Agnes de Mille's ballet, *Rodeo,* premieres in New York, danced by the Ballets Russes de Monte Carlo and featuring a score composed by Aaron Copland.

• On November 18, Thornton Wilder's *The Skin of Our Teeth* opens in New York.

• On December 7, the Metropolitan Museum of Art opens its Artists for Victory exhibit.

MOVIES: *Casablanca,* starring Humphrey Bogart, Ingrid Bergman, and Paul Henreid; *The Magnificent Ambersons,* directed by Orson Welles; *Mrs. Miniver,* starring Greer Garson and Walter Pidgeon, directed by William Wyler; *Pride of the Yankees,* starring Gary Cooper; *Road to Morocco,* starring Bob Hope, Bing Crosby, and Dorothy Lamour; *This Gun for Hire,* starring Alan Ladd and Veronica Lake; *Wake Island,* starring William Bendix; *Woman of the Year,* starring Katharine Hepburn and Spencer Tracy; *Yankee Doodle Dandy,* starring James Cagney.

FICTION: Pearl S. Buck, *Dragon Seed*; William Faulkner, *Go Down, Moses*; Zora Neale Hurston, *Dust Tracks on the Road*; Upton Sinclair, *Dragon's Teeth*; Eudora Welty, *The Robber Bridegroom*; Franz Werfel, *The Song of Bernadette*.

POPULAR SONGS: "All I Need Is You," Dinah Shore; "Der Fuehrer's Face," Spike Jones and his Band; "I Had the Craziest Dream," Harry James with Helen Forrest; "I'll Always Be Glad to Take You Back," Ernest Tubb; "I'll Be Around," The Mills Brothers; "It Won't Be Long," Roy Acuff; "Lover Man," Billie Holliday; "Praise the Lord and Pass the Ammunition," Kay Kyser and his Orchestra; "Private Buckeroo," Gene Autry; "Take Me," Tommy Dorsey with Frank Sinatra; "White Christmas," Bing Crosby.

1943

• On January 7, Marian Anderson sings at Constitution Hall, having wrested an agreement from the Daughters of the American Revolution that the organization's racial segregation policy will not be in force.

• On March 4, *Mrs. Miniver* wins the Academy Award for best motion picture.

• On March 14, Aaron Copland's *Fanfare for the Common Man* debuts with the Cincinnati Symphony Orchestra.

• On March 30, *Oklahoma!* opens in New York.

• On May 17, the Council on Books announces plans to ship 35 million pocket-sized books to overseas servicemen.

• On November 9, Jackson Pollock's first solo show opens at the Art of This Century Gallery.

• On December 7, *Carmen Jones,* a musical comedy by Oscar Hammerstein II, based on Georges Bizet's *Carmen,* opens in New York with an all-African American cast.

• On December 9, Frank Sinatra is declared 4-F, unable to fight in World War II because of a punctured eardrum.

• On December 18, W.E.B. DuBois becomes the first African American elected to the National Institute of Arts and Letters.

• On December 24, the *Motion Picture Herald* reports that Betty Grable is the number one box office draw in America.

MOVIES: *Guadalcanal Diary,* starring William Bendix; *Mission to Moscow,* starring Walter Huston; *The North Star,* written by Lillian Hellman; *The Outlaw,* starring Jane Russell; *Since You Went Away,* starring Claudette Colbert and Jennifer Jones; *Song of Bernadette,* starring Jennifer Jones; *Stormy Weather,* starring Lena Horne; *Tender Comrade,* starring Ginger Rogers, screenplay by Dalton Trumbo; *Watch on the Rhine,* starring Paul Lukas and Bette Davis.

FICTION: Sholem Asch, *The Apostle*; Louis Bromfield, *Mrs. Parkington*; Erskine Caldwell, *Georgia Boy*; John Dos Passos, *Number One*; Arthur Koestler, *Arrival and Departure*; William Saroyan, *The Human Comedy*; Betty Smith, *A Tree Grows in Brooklyn*; Wallace Stegner, *The Big Rock Candy Mountain*; Robert Penn Warren, *At Heaven's Gate.*

POPULAR SONGS: "Comin' in on a Wing and a Prayer," The Song Spinners; "Don't Sweetheart Me," Lawrence Welk and his Orchestra with Wayne Marsh; "G.I. Jive," Louis Jordan and his Tympany Five; "I'll Be Home for Christmas," Bing Crosby; "Rusty Dusty Blues," Count Basie and his Orchestra with Jimmy Rushing; "That Ain't Right," The King Cole Trio; "Travelin' Light," Billie Holiday.

1944

• On March 2, *Casablanca* wins the Academy Award for best motion picture.

• On March 20, the Boston Board of Retail Merchants bans the sale of Lillian Smith's interracial love story, *Strange Fruit.* The book is later banned from the mails by the U.S. Postal Service.

• On May 2, the Museum of Modern Art purchases its first works by Jackson Pollock (*The She-Wolf*) and Robert Motherwell (*Pancho Villa Dead and Alive*).

• On August 7, the Justice Department files suit ordering motion-picture producers to end theater ownership and restore competition.

• On December 15, Glenn Miller dies in a plane crash, traveling from London to Paris.

• On December 16, Boston police arrest a bookseller for selling Erskine Caldwell's *Tragic Ground.* A judge later rules that the book is not obscene.

MOVIES: *Double Indemnity,* directed by Billy Wilder; *The Fighting Seabees,* starring John Wayne; *Gaslight,* starring Ingrid Bergman; *Hail the Conquering Hero,* directed by Preston Sturges; *Laura,* starring Gene Tierney and Dana Andrews; *Lifeboat,* directed by Alfred Hitchcock; *Meet Me in St. Louis,* starring Judy Garland and Margaret O'Brien; *Since You Went Away,* starring Claudette Colbert and Joseph Cotten; *Thirty Seconds Over Tokyo,* starring Van Johnson, screenplay by Dalton Trumbo; *To Have and Have Not,* starring Humphrey Bogart and Lauren Bacall.

FICTION: Saul Bellow, *Dangling Man*; Erskine Caldwell, *Tragic Ground*; Isak Dinesen, *Winter Tales*; Howard Fast, *Freedom Road*; John Hersey, *A Bell for Adano*; Charles Jackson, *The Lost Weekend*; D.H. Lawrence, *The First Lady Chatterley*; Katherine Anne Porter, *The Leaning Tower and Other Stories*; Lillian Smith, *Strange Fruit.*

POPULAR SONGS: "Ac-cent-tchu-ate the Positive," The Andrews Sisters; "Be-bop," Dizzy Gillespie; "G.I. Blues," Floyd Tillman; "Good, Good, Good," Xavier Cougat and his Orchestra; "Groovin' High," Dizzy Gillespie; "I'm Making Believe," Ella Fitzgerald; "Sentimental Journey," Les Brown and his Orchestra with Doris Day; "That Ole Devil Called Love," Billie Holiday; "You Always Hurt the One You Love," The Mills Brothers.

1945

• On March 31, Tennessee Williams's *The Glass Menagerie* opens on Broadway.

• On May 5, Ezra Pound is arrested by U.S. armed forces in Genoa on charges that he made treasonous radio broadcasts from Italy during the war.

• On October 11, the Daughters of the American Revolution refuse African American pianist Hazel Scott the use of Constitution Hall; the following day President Harry Truman condemns the organization for its racism.

• On October 30, Martha Graham's modern dance, *Appalachian Spring,* debuts in Washington, D.C., with music composed by Aaron Copland.

MOVIES: *Anchors Aweigh,* starring Frank Sinatra and Gene Kelly; *The Lost Weekend,* starring Ray Milland and Jane Wyman; *Mildred Pierce,* starring Joan Crawford; *They Were Expendable,* directed by John Ford and starring John Wayne; *A Tree Grows in Brooklyn,* directed by Elia Kazan.

FICTION: John Steinbeck, *Cannery Row*; Irving Stone, *The Immortal Wife*; Jessamyn West, *The Friendly Persuasion*; Richard Wright, *Black Boy.*

POPULAR SONGS: "Beulah's Boogie," Lionel Hampton and his Orchestra; "Choo Choo Ch'Boogie," Louis Jordan and his Tympany Five; "Gotta Be This or That," Benny Goodman and his Orchestra; "Homesick—That's All," Frank Sinatra; "I Think I'll Go Home and Cry," Roy Acuff; "I'll Be Back," Gene Autry; "I'm Tired," Private Cecil Grant; "Let It Snow! Let It Snow! Let It Snow!," Vaughn Monroe and his Orchestra; "Till the End of Time," Perry Como; "Waitin' for the Train to Come In," Peggy Lee.

1946

• On March 7, *Lost Weekend* wins the Academy Award for best motion picture.

• On March 13, Bennett Cerf agrees to include twelve Ezra Pound poems in the new edition of *An Anthology of Famous English and American Poetry* after first announcing that none would be included.

• On March 30, critic Robert Coates uses the term "Abstract Expressionism" to describe the New York modernists.

• On October 9, *The Iceman Cometh,* Eugene O'Neill's first production in twelve years, opens in New York.

• On December 11, Hank Williams cuts his first single, "Calling You," with a flip side of "Never Again (Will I Knock on Your Door)," for the New York-based independent label, Sterling.

• On December 13, Walt Disney's *Song of the South* is called "an insult to the Negro" by the National Negro Congress.

MOVIES: *The Best Years of Our Lives,* directed by William Wyler; *The Big Sleep,* starring Humphrey Bogart and Lauren Bacall; *It's a Wonderful Life,* directed by Frank Capra, starring Jimmy Stewart; *The Postman Always Rings Twice,* starring John Garfield and Lana Turner; *The Razor's Edge,* starring Tyrone Power; *The Yearling,* starring Gregory Peck and Jane Wyman.

FICTION: Carson McCullers, *The Member of the Wedding*; J.D. Salinger, *The Catcher in the Rye*; Robert Penn Warren, *All the King's Men*; Eudora Welty, *Delta Wedding*; William Carlos Williams, *The Build Up*; Edmund Wilson, *Memoirs of Hecate County.*

POPULAR SONGS: "All Alone in the World," Eddy Arnold; "Atomic Power," The Buchanan Brothers; "The Christmas Song," Nat King Cole; "Coax Me a Little Bit," The Andrews Sisters; "The Frim Fram Sauce," Ella Fitzgerald and Louis Armstrong; "Kentucky Waltz," Bill Monroe; "Laughing on the Outside," Dinah Shore; "Long Time Gone," Tex Ritter; "Rainbow at Midnight," Ernest Tubb; "Route 66!," The King Cole Trio; "Something Old, Something New," Frank Sinatra.

1947

• On March 13, *The Best Years of Our Lives* wins the Academy Award for best motion picture.

• On May 7, *The Mother of Us All,* an opera by Virgil Thomson and Gertrude Stein based on the life of Susan B. Anthony, debuts at Columbia University.

• On September 29, *Annie Get Your Gun* is banned in Memphis because of its racially integrated cast.

• In October, the House Committee on Un-American Activities (HUAC) launches an extensive investigation into Communist activities in the movie industry. Friendly witnesses appear before the committee, testifying to the left-wing sympathies of several prominent persons. When called to testify, ten of those named, known as the "Hollywood Ten," refused to answer the committee's questions. They were convicted of contempt of Congress and blacklisted by Hollywood studios.

• On October 22, the motion picture *Forever Amber* opens in New York. Francis Cardinal Spellman and the Catholic Legion of Decency condemn it, but it brings in a record first-day gross of more than twenty-five thousand dollars.

• On December 3, the Screen Directors' Guild bars communists from holding office.

• On December 3, Tennessee Williams's *A Streetcar Named Desire* opens on Broadway.

MOVIES: *Forever Amber,* directed by Otto Preminger, starring Linda Darnell; *Gentleman's Agreement,* directed by Elia Kazan, starring Gregory Peck; *The Ghost and Mrs. Muir,* starring Gene Tierney and Rex Harrison; *Miracle on 34th Street,* starring Edmund Gwenn and Natalie Wood; *The Secret Life of Walter Mitty,* starring Danny Kaye.

FICTION: John Horne Burns, *The Gallery*; John Gunther, *Inside U.S.A*; Chester Himes, *Lonely Crusade*; Laura Hobson, *Gentleman's Agreement*; James Michener, *Tales of the South Pacific*; John Steinbeck, *The Pearl*; Lionel Trilling, *The Middle of the Journey.*

POPULAR SONGS: "Anniversary Song," Tex Beneke and the Glenn Miller Orchestra; "Christmas Dreaming," Frank Sinatra; "Footprints in the Snow," Bill Monroe; "Heartaches," Ted Weems and his Orchestra; "Here Comes Santa Claus," Gene Autry; "I Want to Cry," Dinah Washington; "I've Only Myself to Blame," Doris Day; "Move It On Over," Hank Williams; "Near You," The Andrews Sisters; "Open the Door, Richard," Count Basie and his Orchestra; "Peg O' My Heart," The Harmonicats; "Wedding Bells," Hank Williams.

1948

- On January 15, the Screen Actors' Guild bars communists from holding office.

- On March 20, *Gentleman's Agreement* wins the Academy Award for best motion picture.

- On March 27, following imprisonment on a narcotics charge, blues singer Billie Holiday performs at New York's Carnegie Hall.

- On August 7, Hank Williams joins the country-music radio program *Louisiana Hayride.*

- On October 6, the Museum of Modern Art purchases its first work by Willem de Kooning (*Painting*).

- On October 25, the Supreme Court upholds a New York obscenity ban on Edmund Wilson's *Memoirs of Hecate County.*

- On November 29, the Metropolitan Opera season opens with Verdi's *Otello.* It is the first time a Met production is shown on television.

- On December 30, *Kiss Me, Kate,* with songs by Cole Porter, opens in New York.

MOVIES: *Joan of Arc,* starring Ingrid Bergman; *Key Largo,* starring Humphrey Bogart and Lauren Bacall; *The Red Shoes,* directed by Michael Powell and Emeric Pressburger; *The Snake Pit,* starring Olivia de Havilland; *The Treasure of the Sierra Madre,* directed by John Huston, starring Humphrey Bogart.

FICTION: Erskine Caldwell, *This Very Earth*; Truman Capote, *Other Voices, Other Rooms*; John Dos Passos, *The Grand Design*; William Faulkner, *Intruder in the Dust*; Norman Mailer, *The Naked and the Dead*; Thomas Mann, *Doctor Faustus*; Carl Sandburg, *Remembrance Rock*; Irwin Shaw, *The Young Lions*; Elizabeth Spencer, *Fire in the Morning*; Gore Vidal, *City and the Pillar.*

POPULAR SONGS: "Am I Asking Too Much?," Dinah Washington; "Black Coffee," Sarah Vaughan; "Blue Christmas," Ernest Tubb; "Bouquet of Roses," Eddy Arnold; "The Deck of Cards," Tex Ritter; "Faraway Places," Bing Crosby and the Ken Darby Choir; "Gloria," The Mills Brothers; "Honky Tonkin'," Hank Williams; "The Huckle Buck,"

Frank Sinatra; "Mansion on the Hill," Hank Williams; "Oklahoma Waltz," Patti Page; "The Pretty Mama Blues," Ivory Joe Hunter.

1949

- On February 10, Arthur Miller's *Death of a Salesman,* directed by Elia Kazan, opens on Broadway.

- On February 19, Ezra Pound receives the Bollingen Prize for the *Pisan Cantos.*

- On March 24, *Hamlet* wins the Academy Award for best motion picture.

- In April, Paul Robeson is misquoted by the Associated Press as saying that African Americans would not fight a foreign war to defend their nation. This comment provokes an investigation of African American loyalty by the House Committee on Un-American Activities.

- On June 4, Hank Williams's "Lovesick Blues" hits number one on the hillbilly chart of *Billboard* magazine.

- On June 11, Hank Williams joins the country-music radio program *Grand Ole Opry.*

- On August 9, *Life* magazine asks the question, "Jackson Pollock: Is He the Greatest Living Painter in the United States?"

- On August 19, the Library of Congress discontinues all prizes for art, music, and literature on the recommendation of Congress after Ezra Pound was awarded the Bollingen Prize.

- On September 4, anti-communist demonstrators picket a concert by Paul Robeson; 150 persons are injured in a violent clash between protestors and concert-goers after the show.

MOVIES: *Adam's Rib,* starring Spencer Tracy and Katharine Hepburn; *The Heiress,* starring Olivia De Havilland and Montgomery Clift; *Letter to Three Wives,* directed by Joseph L. Mankiewicz; *Sands of Iwo Jima,* starring John Wayne; *She Wore a Yellow Ribbon,* directed by John Huston, starring John Wayne.

FICTION: Nelson Algren, *The Man With the Golden Arm*; Paul Bowles, *The Sheltering Sky*; Truman Capote, *A Tree of Night and Other Stories*; William Faulkner, *Knight's Gambit*; Shirley Jackson, *The Lottery*; John P. Marquand, *The Point of No Return*; Eudora Welty, *The Golden Apples.*

POPULAR SONGS: "Baby, It's Cold Outside," Dinah Shore and Buddy Clark; "Bali Ha'i," Perry Como; "Boogie Chillin'," John Lee Hooker; "Cabaret," Rosemary Clooney; "Careless Hands," Mel Torme; "A Dreamer's Holiday," Perry Como; "He Calls Me Crazy," Billie Holiday; "I'm So Lonesome I Could Cry," Hank Williams; "Land of Love," Nat King Cole; "Smokey Mountain Boogie," Tennessee Ernie Ford.

"The Aims of Music for Films"

Newspaper article

By: Aaron Copland

Date: March 10, 1940

Source: Copland, Aaron. "The Aims of Music for Films."
The New York Times, March 10, 1940.

About the Author: Aaron Copland (1900–1990) was a composer, performer, and teacher. He began his formal musical education at the age of fourteen by taking private piano lessons. He studied in Paris with Nadia Boulanger, the first of many Americans to do so. His best-known symphonic works incorporate American popular song types, such as hymns, cowboy tunes, Mexican dances, Latin American rhythms, and folk tunes. ∎

Introduction

The ease with which Aaron Copland could move from popular to serious music, his ability to incorporate folk and jazz in his symphonic compositions, and his endless energy and wit made him an especially welcome visitor in the Hollywood of the late 1930s and 1940s. During this period, which is often called the golden age, Hollywood was eager to attract superior talent, even if it didn't quite know what to do with it.

Copland, a superior talent, was eager to try composing movie music. He worked on many commercial films during a ten-year period, including *Of Mice and Men* (1939), *Our Town* (1940), *The North Star* (1943), *The Red Pony* (1948), and *The Heiress* (1949), which won him an Academy Award for best film score.

Copland also liked to reflect on his experiences as a creative artist in various venues. Throughout this period, he was delivering lectures at Columbia University and the New School for Social Research on his experiences in Hollywood. The article he wrote for *The New York Times,* written just after he finished his first scoring job in Hollywood, illustrated his efforts to educate the public about movie music. Copland knew from firsthand experience that audience expectations were the bottom line for the Hollywood producers. He also knew that an article like his could influence that expectation.

In his article, he argued that the better the movie the better the music it deserved. He said that movie music quality could be improved if audiences became aware of the film music, which they took for granted. He explained how a score should heighten the effect on the screen, rather than overwhelm it. He said that the key to movie music was the emotional link it provided between the audience and the characters.

Significance

Copland was one of the most industrious, intelligent, and articulate composers of the twentieth century. Above all, he spoke with the authority of a creative artist. He spent a lifetime trying to remind a performer-oriented musical culture that it owed its existence as well as its future to the composer. He was devoted to the music of the twentieth century and to the notion that classical music needed to renew itself through a dialogue with living contemporary music and by interacting in every possible way with the popular audience. In all these ways, Copland was the model of the composer as educator, a role which his greatest protégé, Leonard Bernstein, took to even greater heights in the 1950s and 1960s.

Movie music has come a long way since Copland wrote his scores for Hollywood. Before Copland, there were two kinds of Hollywood composers, European émigrés and homegrown hacks. The first contributed nothing distinctly American to films, and in a way that was their appeal to Hollywood producers. The second contributed something American but were not as refined.

After Copland led the way, there was a string of serious, quality American composers who successfully worked in Hollywood. The great movie scores would probably not have been developed without the work of Copland; many of these were written by Elmer Bernstein, Leonard Bernstein, Alex North, Bernard Herrmann, and John Williams, who are among the most well-known and popular composers of the 20th century.

Copland was the tireless advocate of quality in music, and what he wrought has had a lasting influence on the quality of Hollywood movies. In fact, movie music has become so popular that people listen to it independently of the movies for which it was written. One could say that if there is a viable popular music it is movie music.

Primary Source

"The Aims of Music for Films"

> **SYNOPSIS:** Copland reflects on his experience writing film scores for Hollywood movies in this *The New York Times* article.

There is an old tradition that the better a motion picture score is, the less attention it attracts.

Aaron Copland (right) was the model of the composer as educator, a role which his greatest protégé, Leonard Bernstein, took to even greater heights in the 1950s and 1960s. They are pictured here together in Bernardsville, New Jersey, August 1945. THE LIBRARY OF CONGRESS.

This is one of the oldest superstitions in Hollywood and leaves me rather in the position of the king in the old fable who flattered himself on his finery when really he had nothing on at all. For I cannot bring myself to believe that the moment one becomes aware of the "background music" in a motion picture it has already ceased to fulfill its function.

Perhaps it is professional pride that influences my opinion, for I should not like to think that the six long weeks spent scoring *Of Mice and Men* were actually devoted to the composition of a sort of musical vacuum. But even in the disinterested capacity of private citizen and habitual moviegoer I am obliged to differ with those critics who believe a musical score should be screened and not heard. To any one who does not believe that the addition of music heightens the emotional impact and dramatic interest of a motion picture I suggest a visit to a studio

projection room when a film is being shown before its score has been dubbed in. One reel of flat silences and interminable pauses is usually enough.

Seriously, I think the principal reason so few people are consciously aware of the music they hear from the screen is that audiences have not yet been fully informed on the subject. Only a few years ago most filmgoers were not conscious of the importance of direction, either, yet today there are several Hollywood directors whose names have a greater drawing power at the box office than those of many stars.

It is common knowledge that the United States is the world center of musical activity. There are 2,000,000 concertgoers annually, in addition to the millions of radio and phonograph fans. It seems curious that little or no effort is made in Hollywood to interest this vast audience in the elaborate musical backgrounds of the major films. On the Continent producers have found it to their advantage to exploit the scores of such composers as Prokofieff, Shostakovich and Honegger, and it seems to me that Hollywood might profit by this example. If the composers of the better motion picture scores were featured as an additional attraction to the merits of the film the public would soon become aware of the part played by music in their movies.

If the scores of motion pictures are to gain more attention, however, they must be worthy of it. At a practical estimate, 90 per cent of the films produced in Hollywood are getting just about the kind of music they deserve, no better and no worse. It is the other 10 per cent—the cream of the cinematic crop—with which the hope of better movie music lies. If the superior films are given scores of comparable originality and distinction, a higher type of music will in time be instilled throughout the product of the entire industry.

From a technical, almost mechanical, standpoint there is no doubt that the usual Hollywood scores are perfection itself. Their artistic weaknesses have been pointed out so often that they hardly bear repeating, but perhaps their most annoying fault is their stubborn similarity. No matter what the period of a picture is, or its setting and story, the average musical background is intrinsically the same, usually in the lush tradition of the late nineteenth century.

The other day I saw a picture that had as its setting medieval Europe. There was one scene in a cathedral, and the accompanying music was a most authentic fifteenth century motet. But the next shot was of the heroine, and the score immediately shifted to a reflection of the sweetest of Strauss waltzes, thus projecting the audience four centuries forward in as many seconds.

Certainly, one does not require that the musical background of a modern motion picture adhere literally to the period in which it is set; we do not expect the score of *Elizabeth and Essex,* for instance, to consist of *Greensleeves* played on the virginals, any more than we expect the picture itself to be a documentary transcription of Tudor history. But inconsistency, in music as in costumes or sets, can destroy quicker than anything else the illusion of a motion picture.

Of Mice and Men gave me my first opportunity to understand the problems and possibilities of composing for a major film. There is a tradition that composers are invariably frustrated in Hollywood and never allowed to do just what they want, but here, at least, is one exception. Maybe I was lucky; there are definite advantages in writing for an independent producer like Hal Roach. There is no musical director to act as middleman between the composer and studio bosses and who is therefore reluctant to approve any experimental innovations. Lewis Milestone, the director, expressed his confidence in the composer he had chosen by issuing no advance instructions. I appreciated that.

It is generally difficult for a composer who theretofore had written only for the concert stage to come to Hollywood and remember that he is not still the center of attraction. But if the film for which he has been engaged is genuinely good, it is not long before he becomes excited at the project of helping the picture as a whole convey its message. He quickly forgets himself in his enthusiasm for the immediate assignment and is immensely gratified whenever his work is singled out. One of my most cherished memories is the fact that Lewis Milestone added four seconds to *Of Mice and Men* for the sake of the score. For a panoramic scene in which five barley wagons make their way across a field I had composed a melody which needed about four seconds more to play itself out. I put the problem to Mr. Milestone and without hesitation he added the necessary footage to the sequence.

In composing the score of *Of Mice and Men,* however I succeeded, the primary purpose was to write music which somehow suggested the background of the film, the daily life on a California ranch. To do this, I occasionally employed music of a folk-song character, though using no direct quotations, simple tunes that might have been whistled by George and Lenny. The temper of the music varied, of course, with every scene, but always I tried to keep away from the overlush harmonies that are so common on the screen and usually defeat their own purpose by overemphasis. As a matter of fact, what you do not do is often as important as what you do do in scoring a motion picture.

On the whole, though, the score, as any score, is designed to strengthen and underline the emotional content of the entire picture. The best explanation, I think, of just what is the purpose of music in the film has been given by Virgil Thomson. It is his conception that the score of a motion picture supplies a bit of human warmth to the black-and-white, two-dimensional figures on the screen, giving them a communicable sympathy that they otherwise would not have, bridging the gap between the screen and the audience. The quickest way to a person's brain is through his eye but even in the movies the quickest way to his heart and feelings is still through the ear.

Further Resources

BOOKS

Copland, Aaron. *Copland on Music.* Garden City, N.Y.: Doubleday, 1960.

————. *What to Listen for in Music.* New York: McGraw-Hill, 1988.

Pollack, Howard. *Aaron Copland: Life and Work of an Uncommon Man.* New York: Henry Holt, 1998.

WEBSITES

"The Aaron Copland Collection." Library of Congress. Available online at http://memory.loc.gov/ammem/achtml/achome .html; website home page http://www.loc.gov (accessed February 26, 2003).

"The Irresponsibles"
Speech

By: Archibald MacLeish

Date: 1940

Source: MacLeish, Archibald. *The Irresponsibles: A Declaration.* New York: Duell, Sloan, and Pearce, 1940, 24–34.

About the Author: Archibald MacLeish (1892–1982), a poet, playwright, and public intellectual, was born in Illinois and educated at Yale University and Harvard Law School. MacLeish was a distinguished poet, an influential journalist, Librarian of Congress during the Roosevelt administration, a Pulitzer Prize-winning Broadway playwright, and a professor of poetry at Harvard. ■

Introduction

Archibald MacLeish belonged to the generation of modernist poets that included his fellow Americans Ezra Pound and T. S. Eliot. Both Pound and Eliot rejected large aspects of the American way of life and moved to Europe. MacLeish, however, was always able to combine a modernist approach to literature with a clear understanding of the importance of the civil and religious liberties and democratic way of life protected by the U.S. Constitution. This balanced method surely had its basis in his education in civil and constitutional law he received as a student at Harvard Law School under his mentor Felix Frankfurter.

In 1939, Frankfurter, after being nominated as a Supreme Court justice, urged Franklin D. Roosevelt (served 1933–1945) to nominate MacLeish, "a scholarly man of letters," for the post of the librarian of Congress. Some senators opposed MacLeish's confirmation because of his alleged pro-communist tendencies. The American Library Association also opposed him because he was neither a librarian nor a library administrator.

Archibald MacLeish was appointed Librarian of Congress by President Roosevelt. **THE LIBRARY OF CONGRESS.**

Nevertheless, the Senate confirmed him by a vote of sixty-eight to eight, with twenty-five senators abstaining. He became the ninth librarian of Congress on October 2, 1939, and served in the post until 1944.

President Roosevelt turned to MacLeish to mobilize American writers and intellectuals in the 1940s. "The Irresponsibles" is one of a series of speeches that MacLeish made on the theme of the responsibility of American writers. MacLeish draws a vivid picture of the silence of the intellectuals during the 1930s when Adolf Hitler in Germany, Joseph Stalin in Russia, and Francisco Franco in Spain were liquidating all opposition to their tyrannical governments, including intellectuals and writers.

Significance

The situation of writers and intellectuals in the United States during the Great Depression was the subject of much controversy and criticism. What was the proper role and responsibility of the artist and the intellectual in such a world crisis? Many writers supported the general goals of the American Communist Party, especially when they coincided with the fight against fascism, while others—notably Charles Beard—opposed the United States' entering World War II (1939–1945). Although suspicious of the leadership tactics and the loyalty of the leaders of the Communist Party, MacLeish frequently made common cause with them.

By the time of the attack on Pearl Harbor and the American entrance into World War II, the need for cultural leadership was obvious. If there was a growing consensus on the need for writers and artists to intelligently support the war effort at home and abroad, it is due in large part to MacLeish's efforts. An advocate of the involvement of writers and scholars in war, MacLeish used his position as Librarian of Congress to speak out on behalf of liberal democracy. He urged librarians to "become active and not passive agents of the democratic process," and criticized his fellow intellectuals for their failure to defend American culture against the threat of totalitarianism.

After the death of President Roosevelt in 1945, MacLeish returned to private life as the Boylston Professor of Rhetoric at Harvard University, where he began teaching what was to become a legendary poetry course. He continued to write poetry and drama, including *JB*, a contemporary adaptation of the *Book of Job* for which he won the Pulitzer Prize, and *Scratch*, an adaptation of *The Devil and Daniel Webster*. He is considered to be a model twentieth-century American public intellectual.

Primary Source

"The Irresponsibles" [excerpt]

SYNOPSIS: "The Irresponsibles" is one of several speeches MacLeish gave as the librarian of Congress during the period before the United States entered World War II. In the following speech, he attempts to mobilize writers and intellectuals to support Roosevelt administration policy.

They [writers and intellectuals] are silent in our time because there are no voices which accept responsibility for speaking. Even the unimaginable indecencies of propaganda—even the corruption of the word itself in Germany and Russia and in Spain and elsewhere—even the open triumph of the lie, produced no answer such as Voltaire in his generation would have given. And for this reason—that the man who could have been Voltaire, who could have been Las Casas, does not live: the man of intellectual *office*, the man of intellectual *calling*, the man who *professes* letters—professes an obligation as a servant of the mind to defend the mind's integrity against every physical power—professes an obligation to defend the labors of the mind and the structures it has created and the means by which it lives, not only privately and safely in his study, not only strictly and securely in the controversies of the learned press, but publicly and at the public risk and

danger of his life. He does not exist because the man of letters no longer exists. And the man of letters no longer exists because he has been driven from our world and from our time by the division of his kingdom. The single responsibility, the wholeness of function of the man of letters, has been replaced by the divided function, the mutual antagonism, the isolated irresponsibility of two figures, each free of obligation, each separated from a portion of his duty—the scholar and the writer.

Why this substitution has come about—whether because the methods of scientific inquiry, carried over into the humanities, destroyed the loyalties and habits of the mind or for some other reason, I leave to wiser men to say. The point is that there has been a substitution. The country of the man of letters has been divided between his heirs. The country that was once the past and present—the past made useful to the reasons of the present, the present understood against the knowledge of the past—the country that was once the past and present brought together in the mind, is now divided into past on one side, present on the other.

Past is the scholar's country: present is the writer's. The writer sees the present on the faces of the world and leaves the past to rot in its own rubbish. The scholar digs his ivory cellar in the ruins of the past and lets the present sicken as it will. A few exceptions noted here and there—men like Thomas Mann—the gulf between these countries is complete. And the historical novels fashionable at the moment, the vulgarizations of science, the digests of philosophy only define its depth as a plank across a chasm makes the chasm deeper. That it should be necessary to throw such flimsy flights from one side to the other of the learned world shows how deeply and disastrously the split was made.

That scholarship suffers or that writing suffers by the change is not asserted. Scholarship may be more scientific: writing may be purer. Indeed there are many who believe, and I among them, that the time we live in has produced more first-rate writers than any but the very greatest ages, and there are scholars of a scholarship as hard, as honest, as devoted as any we have known. But excellence of scholarship and writing are not now in question. What matters now is the defense of culture—the defense truly, and in the most literal terms, of civilization as men have known it for the last two thousand years. And there the substitution for the man of letters of the scholar and the writer, however pure the scholarship, however excellent the writing, is a tragic and immeasurable loss. For neither the modern scholar nor the modern writer admits responsibility for the defense. They assert on the contrary, each in his particular way, an irresponsibility as complete as it is singular.

The irresponsibility of the scholar is the irresponsibility of the scientist upon whose laboratory insulation he has patterned all his work. The scholar has made himself as indifferent to values, as careless of significance, as bored with meanings as the chemist. He is a refugee from consequences, an exile from the responsibilities of moral choice. He has taught himself to say with the physicist—and with some others whom history remembers—"What is truth?" He has taught himself with the biologist to refrain from judgments of better or worse. His words of praise are the laboratory words—objectivity—detachment—dispassion. His pride is to be scientific, neuter, skeptical, detached—superior to final judgment or absolute belief. In his capacity as scholar the modern scholar does not occupy the present. In his capacity as scholar he loves the word—but only the word which entails no judgments, involves no decisions, accomplishes no actions. Where the man of letters of other centuries domesticated the past within the rustling of the present, making it stand among us like the meaning of a statue among trees, the modern scholar in his capacity as scholar leaves the present and returns across the past where all the men are marble. Where the man of letters of other centuries quarried his learning from the past to build the present the modern scholar quarries his learning from the past to dig the quarries.

It is not for nothing that the modern scholar invented the Ph.D. thesis as his principal contribution to literary form. The Ph.D. thesis is the perfect image of his world. It is work done for the sake of doing work—perfectly conscientious, perfectly laborious, perfectly irresponsible. The modern scholar at his best and worst is both these things—perfectly conscientious, laborious and competent: perfectly irresponsible for the saving of his world. He remembers how in the Civil Wars in England the scholars, devoted only to their proper tasks, founded the Royal Society. He remembers how through other wars and other dangers the scholars kept the lamp of learning lighted. He does not consider that the scholars then did other things as well as trim the lamp wicks. He does not consider either that the dangers change and can be greater. He has his work to do. He has his book to finish. He hopes the war will not destroy the manuscripts he works with. He is the pure, the per-

fect type of irresponsibility—the man who acts as though the fire could not burn him because he has no business with the fire. He knows because he cannot help but know, reading his papers, talking to his friends—he knows this fire has consumed the books, the spirit, everything he lives by, flesh itself—in other countries. He knows this but he will not know. It's not his business. Whose business is it then? He will not answer even that. He has his work to do. He has his book to finish. . . .

The writer's irresponsibility is of a different kind. Where the modern scholar escapes from the adult judgments of the mind by taking the disinterested man of science as his model, the modern writer escapes by imitation of the artist. He practices his writing as a painter does his painting. He thinks as artist—which is to say he thinks without responsibility to anything but truth of feeling. He observes as artist—which is to say that he observes with honesty and truthfulness and without comment. His devotion, as with every honest painter, is devotion to the thing observed, the actual thing, the thing without its consequences or its antecedents, naked of judgment, stripped of causes and effects. The invisible world, the intellectual world, the world of the relation of ideas, the world of judgments, of values, the world in which truth is good and lies are evil—this world has no existence to the honest artist or to the honest writer who takes the artist for his model. His duty is to strip all this away—to strip away the moral preference, the intellectual association.

He sees the world as a god sees it—without morality, without care, without judgment. People look like this. People act like that. He shows them looking, acting. It is not his business why they look so, why they act so. It is enough that he should "make them happen." This is the whole test, the whole criterion, of the work of the writer-artist—to show things as they "really happen": to write with such skill, such penetration of the physical presence of the world, that the action seen, the action described, will "really happen" on his page. If he concerns himself with motive at all he concerns himself with the "real" motive, meaning the discreditable motive which the actor conceals from himself. His most searching purpose is to find, not the truth of human action, but the low-down, the discreditable explanation which excuses him from care. The suggestion that there are things in the world—ideas, conceptions, ways of thinking—which the writer-artist should defend from attack: the suggestion above all that he was under obligation to defend the inherited culture, would strike him as ridiculous.

Artists do not save the world. They practice art. They practice it as Goya practiced it among the cannon in Madrid. And if this war is not Napoleon in Spain but something even worse than that? They practice art. Or they put the art aside and take a rifle and go out and fight. But not *as artists*. The artist does not fight. The artist's obligations are obligations to his art. His responsibility—his one responsibility—is to his art. He has no other. Not even when his art itself, his chance to practice it, his need to live where it is practiced, may be in danger. The writer-artist will write a bloody story about the expense of blood. He will present the face of agony as it has rarely been presented. But not even then will he take the weapon of his words and carry it to the barricades of intellectual warfare, to the storming of belief, the fortifying of conviction where alone this fighting can be won.

There are examples in history of civilizations made impotent by excess of culture. No one, I think, will say of us that we lost our intellectual liberties on this account. But it may well be said, and said with equally ironic emphasis, that the men of thought, the men of learning in this country were deceived and rendered impotent by the best they knew. To the scholar impartiality, objectivity, detachment were ideal qualities he taught himself laboriously and painfully to acquire. To the writer objectivity and detachment were his writer's pride. Both subjected themselves to inconceivable restraints, endless disciplines to reach these ends. And both succeeded. Both writers and scholars freed themselves of the subjective passions, the emotional preconceptions which color conviction and judgment. Both writers and scholars freed themselves of the personal responsibility associated with personal choice. They emerged free, pure and single into the antiseptic air of objectivity. And by that sublimation of the mind they prepared the mind's disaster.

If it is a consolation to the philosophers of earlier civilizations to know that they lost the things they loved because of the purity of their devotion, then perhaps this consolation will be ours as well. I doubt if we will profit by it or receive much praise.

Further Resources

BOOKS

Donaldson, Scott, with R. H. Winnick. *Archibald MacLeish: An American Life.* Boston: Houghton Mifflin, 1992.

MacLeish, Archibald. *Archibald MacLeish: Reflections.* Bernard A. Drabeck and Helen E. Ellis, eds. Amherst: University of Massachusetts Press, 1986.

———. *Collected Poems.* Boston: Houghton Mifflin, 1962.

WEBSITES

"Archibald MacLeish." University of Illinois, Urbana-Champaign. Available online at http://www.english.uiuc.edu/maps/poets/m_r/macleish/macleish.htm; website home page: http://www.uiuc.edu (accessed February 24, 2003).

Speech on the Dedication of the National Gallery of Art
Speech

By: Franklin D. Roosevelt

Date: March 17, 1941

Source: Roosevelt, Franklin D. "Speech on the Dedication of the National Gallery." March 17, 1941. Reprinted online at http://www.nara.gov/ (accessed May 17, 2002).

About the Author: Franklin D. Roosevelt (1882–1945) was born in Hyde Park, New York. He attended Groton School, Harvard University, and Columbia University Law School. He served as the assistant secretary of the navy under Woodrow Wilson and was the 1920 Democratic vice presidential canidate. Crippled by polio in 1921, he perservered and was twice elected governor of New York State in the 1920s. In 1932, at the height of the Great Depression, he was elected president of the United States. He was reelected president in 1936, 1940, and 1944—the only president to ever win a third or fourth term—and died in office in April 1945. Roosevelt is considered one of America's greatest presidents for his efforts to fight the Depression with his "New Deal," and for leading the nation through World War II. ∎

Introduction

Andrew W. Mellon was one of the most successful financiers and industrialists of his time when he decided to heed the call of public office and serve the first of three Republican presidents as the secretary of the treasury during the 1920s. His policy of lowering personal and business taxes after World War I (1914–1918) led to business and job growth and higher tax revenues, which allowed the government to pay back its war debt. During this period, Mellon began to collect art as a private citizen. He accumulated one of the last great collections of European paintings, mainly due to the sound advice of Joseph Duveen, the advisor to the National Gallery in London.

On Christmas Day 1936, President Franklin D. Roosevelt received a letter from Mellon offering his art collection to the American people to establish a national gallery on the model of the National Gallery in London. The proposal included endowment funds and plans for a museum building. Some commentators called it the greatest gift ever made to any government by any individual.

One of the shrewdest businessmen in America, Mellon was equally savvy in his dealings with the other great

President Franklin Delano Roosevelt speaks at the dedication of the National Gallery of Art, 1941. © 2001 NATIONAL GALLERY OF ART, WASHINGTON D.C.

American collectors of art. Samuel Kress had the other major collection of Italian art, which had not been promised to any museum. Mellon knew that it must come to the National Gallery along with several other collections if the gallery was to take its place among the great national galleries of the world. Mellon requested that the institution not be named after him but instead be called the National Gallery of Art. This would entice the other great collectors to follow his example and add their treasures.

The act of Congress that created the gallery on March 24, 1937, provided that the American government would protect and care for the art and open the museum to the public free of charge. The building was completed in 1941, a few months after Mellon's death. In his speech, Roosevelt remembered Mellon as one of the most generous benefactors of the fine arts that the United States had ever known, which is how Mellon wanted to be regarded.

Significance

The United States was one of the last great nations in the world to establish a national gallery of art. It would have been impossible for the federal government to do this during the Great Depression. Thanks to Mellon, the United States was able to establish an art museum with a world-class collection of Italian Renaissance painting and sculpture, Dutch and Flemish old masters, and French

impressionist masterpieces that rivaled those in the capitals of Europe. Just as the Roosevelt presidency lifted the hearts of the American people, Mellon's gift (and those of the collectors who followed his example) symbolized a philanthropic generosity undreamed of in old regimes of Europe. Roosevelt makes this point in his speech, "The magnificence of the gift is matched by the humility of the giver. Not the Mellon Gallery but the National Gallery given to a grateful people and held in trust by them for their posterity. It belongs to all Americans."

The National Gallery of Art in Washington, D.C., immediately took its proud place among the great art galleries of the world, attracting millions of visitors each year. During World War II (1939–1945), a soldier passing through Washington on his way to the Pacific war wrote in the museum's guest book how important it was to visit such a place before he shipped out to serve his country.

Primary Source

Speech on the Dedication of the National Gallery of Art

SYNOPSIS: President Roosevelt's speech describes the enduring significance of institutions such as the National Gallery of Art and about the honorable men who created them.

[In this reproduced transcript, parentheses indicate words that Roosevelt omitted when reading the speech, italics indicate words that he added.]

Mr. Chief Justice, Ladies and Gentlemen:

It is with a very real sense of satisfaction that I accept for the people of the United States and on their behalf this National Gallery and the collections it contains. The giver of (the) *this* building has matched the richness of his gift with the modesty of his spirit, stipulating that the Gallery shall be known not by his name but by the nation's. And those other collectors of paintings and of sculpture who have already joined, or who propose to join, their works of art to Mr. Mellon's—Mr. Kress and Mr. Widemer— have felt the same desire to establish, not a memorial to themselves, but a monument to the art *that* they love and the country to which they belong. To these collections we now gratefully add the gift (from) of Miss Ellen Bullard and three anonymous donors, which marks the beginning of the Gallery's collection of prints; and also the loan collection of early American paintings from Mr. Chester Dale.

There have been, in the past, many gifts of great paintings and of famous works of art to the American people. Most of the wealthy men of the last century who bought, for their own satisfaction, the masterpieces of European collections, ended by presenting their purchases to their cities or *to* their towns. *And so* great works of art have a way of breaking out of private ownership into public use. They belong so obviously to all who love them—they are so clearly the property not of their single owners but of *all* men *everywhere*—that the private rooms and houses where they (are) *have lovingly* hung *in the past* become in time too narrow for their presence. The true collectors are the collectors who understand this—the collectors of great paintings who feel that they can never truly own, but only gather and preserve for all who love them, the treasures that they have found.

But though there have been many public gifts of art in the past, the gift of this National Gallery, dedicated to the entire nation, (and) containing a considerable part of the most important work brought to this country from the continent of Europe, has necessarily a new significance. *I think, I think* it signifies a relation—a new relation here made visible in paint and in stone—between the whole people of this country, and the old inherited tradition of the arts. And we shall remember that these halls of beauty, the (creation) *conception* of a great American architect, *John Russell Pope,* combine the classicism of the past with the convenience of today.

In accepting this building and the paintings *and other art that* it contains, the people of the United States accept a part in that inheritance for themselves. They accept it for themselves not because this Gallery is given to them—though they are thankful for the gift. They accept it for themselves because, in the past few years, they have come to understand that the inheritance is theirs and that, like other inheritors of other things of *great* value, they have a duty toward it.

There was a time when the people of this country would not have thought that the inheritance of art belonged to them or that they had responsibilities to guard it. A few generations ago, the people of this country were *often* taught by their writers and by their critics and by their teachers to believe that art was something foreign to America and to themselves—something imported from another continent, *something* (and) from an age which was not theirs—something they had no part in, save to go to see it in (a) *some* guarded room on holidays or Sundays.

But recently, within the last few years (,)—*yes, in our lifetime*— they have discovered that they *have* a part. They have seen in their own towns, in their own villages, in school houses, in post offices, in the back rooms of shops and stores, pictures painted by their sons, their neighbors—people they have known and lived beside and talked to. They have seen, across these last few years, rooms full of painting and *sculpture* by Americans, walls covered with the painting (of) *by* Americans—some of it good, some of it not so good, but all of it native, human, eager, and alive—all of it painted by their own kind in their own country, and painted about things *that* they know and look at often and have touched and loved.

The people of this country know now, whatever they were taught or thought *of, or thought* they knew before, that art is not something just to be owned (but) *or* something to be made: that it is the act of making and not the act of owning (which) *that* is art. And knowing this they know also that art is not a treasure in the past or an importation from another (country) *land,* but part of the present life of all the living and creating peoples—all who make and build; and, most of all, the young and vigorous peoples who have made and built our present wide country.

It is for this reason that the people of America accept the inheritance of these ancient arts. Whatever these paintings may have been to men who looked at them (a) generation*s* back—today they are not *only* works of art. Today they are the symbols of the human spirit, (and) *symbols* of the world the freedom of the human spirit *has* made—*and, incidentally,* a world against which armies now are raised and countries overrun and men imprisoned and their work destroyed.

To accept, today, the work of German painters such as Holbein and Durer, (and) of Italians like Botticelli and Raphael, (and) of painters of the Low Countries like Van Dyck and Rembrandt, and of famous Frenchmen, famous Spaniards—to accept this work today (on behalf of) *for* the people of this democratic nation is to assert the belief of the people of this *democratic* nation in a human spirit which now is everywhere endangered and which, in many countries where it first found form and meaning, has been rooted out and broken and destroyed.

To accept this work today is to assert the purpose of the people of America that the freedom of the human spirit and human mind which has produced the world's great art and all its science—shall not be utterly destroyed.

Seventy-eight years ago, in the third year of the War Between the States, men and women gathered here in *the Capital of a divided nation, here in* Washington, to see the dome above the Capitol completed and *to see* the bronze Goddess of Liberty set upon the top. It had been an expensive and laborious business, diverting money and labor from the prosecution of the war, and certain (citizens) *critics—for there were critics in 1863*—certain critics found much to criticize. There were new marble pillars in the Senate wing *of the Capitol;* (and) *there was* a bronze door for the central portal and other such expenditures and embellishments. But *the President of the United States, whose name was* Lincoln, when he heard (the) *those* criticisms, answered: "If people see the Capitol going on, it is a sign *that* we intend (the) *this* Union shall go on." (Applause)

We may borrow the words for our own. We too intend the Union shall go on. We intend it shall go on, carrying with it the great tradition of the human spirit which created it.

The dedication of this Gallery to a living past, and to a greater and more richly living future, is the measure of the earnestness of our intention that the freedom of a human spirit shall go on (,) *too.* (Applause)

Further Resources

BOOKS

Behrman, S. N. *Duveen.* New York: Random House, 1952.

Finley, David Edward. *A Standard of Excellence: Andrew W. Mellon Founds the National Gallery of Art.* Washington, D.C.: Smithsonian Institution Press, 1973.

Walker, John. *National Gallery of Art, D.C.* New York: Abrams, 1975.

WEBSITES

National Gallery of Art. Available online at www.nga.gov (accessed February 24, 2003).

"I Got It Bad (And That Ain't Good)"

Song

By: Duke Ellington and Paul Francis Webster

Date: 1941

Source: Ellington, Duke, and Paul Francis Webster. "I Got It Bad (And That Ain't Good)" song lyrics, 1941. Available online at http://www.thepeaches.com/music/composers/duke/IGotItBadandThatAintGood.txt; website home page: http://www.thepeaches.com (accessed April 1, 2003.)

About the Artists: Edward Kennedy "Duke" Ellington (1899–1974) was an American pianist and one of the nation's foremost jazz composers and bandleaders. Born in Washington, D.C., Ellington began to perform at age seventeen. As one of the fathers of big-band jazz, he composed or co-wrote thousands of scores. As an African American, he broke the race barrier in music.

Like Ellington, Paul Francis Webster (1907–1984) was an African American who helped break down color barriers in American music. Born in New York City he worked as a sailor, dance instructor, and eventually a Songwriter's Hall of Fame lyricist. He won Oscars for Best Original Song in 1953, 1955, and 1965, and worked with scores of artists from Ellington to Hoagy Carmichael, Peggy Lee, and Tony Bennett. ■

Introduction

Duke Ellington was a pioneer in big-band jazz, which combined a danceable appeal with blues-inspired lyrics about universal themes such as romantic love. His ascent into stardom was unusual, however. Born to a middle-class family that encouraged his interest in the fine arts, Ellington refused a scholarship to the prestigious Pratt Institute to follow the popular, raucous ragtime sound. Ragtime was born of an urban, African American tradition, and Ellington, as an African American musician, eventually translated that into a musical form that mainstream white America accepted. In the process, he created a place for sexuality, politics, and strong female voices—such as that of Ella Fitzgerald, who sang "I Got It Bad (And That Ain't Good).

Although his career spanned the 1920s to the 1970s, Ellington's greatest period was in the early 1940s, when

As one of the fathers of big-band jazz, Duke Ellington composed or cowrote thousands of scores. **THE GRANGER COLLECTION LTD.**

he composed several classic works such as "Concerto for Cootie," "Cotton Tail," "Ko-Ko," and "Harlem Air Shaft." His references to places such as Harlem were both autobiographical and political. Ellington performed for years (1927–1932, 1937–1938) at the famous Cotton Club in Harlem, one of the main stages for the African American cultural renaissance. By bringing Harlem into his music, he exposed mainstream America to the African American experience. He also wrote standards such as "Sophisticated Lady," "Satin Doll," "Don't Get Around Much Anymore," and "Prelude to a Kiss," which were sung by a wide variety of performers, from African American women such as Sarah Vaughan to Italian American men such as Frank Sinatra. Ellington captured the nation's attention when it most needed escape from the Depression during the 1930s and World War II (1939–1945) in the 1940s. By tapping into the youth and urban culture through dance music and jazz arrangements, he created a platform from which his music could speak to the nation. He became one of the first African American artists to gain a national, even international, following.

Significance

Duke Ellington had significant impact on American music, society, and politics. By fusing classical music technique and modern influences such as ragtime, he pioneered a new form of music that survived into the twenty-first century: big-band jazz. His music also paved the way for later developments such as rhythm and blues and rock and roll. By tapping into youth culture, providing dance music flavored with bold sexuality and honest lyrics, and basing his work on a foundation of exceptional musicianship, Ellington found a winning combination.

Moreover, Ellington had an important effect on American society because he was one of the first African American artists to gain mainstream national and international success. He performed at a time when many concert venues and audiences were segregated. Ellington, however, drew his inspiration from a variety of sources to create works with such widespread appeal that they could not be pigeonholed as "black music" for African American listeners, despite the efforts of some to do so. In the process, he exposed white listeners to musical trends that they had not previously encountered. His success translated into others' success, especially the African American women who sang so many of his compositions and interpreted his unapologetically sexy and strong lyrics. Perhaps most importantly, Ellington used his position of influence to educate his audience and celebrate his heritage. For example, his 1943 musical suite *Black, Brown and Beige* was a portrayal of African American history. Twenty years later, at the height of the civil rights movement, he composed the show *My People,* a celebration of African American culture. In short, Ellington created a new and welcome sound that influenced not only the musical world but the society and politics of the United States as well. His efforts opened the door for many generations and genres of music.

Primary Source

"I Got It Bad (And That Ain't Good)"

> **SYNOPSIS:** In this work, Duke Ellington and Paul Francis Webster create a blues-inspired jazz song that appeals to listeners regardless of race. The lighthearted emphasis on love, coupled with the adult themes of sex and alcohol, introduces a playful sensuality that was a welcome distraction from wartime concerns.

Never treats me sweet and gentle
The way he should
'Cause I got it bad, and that ain't good

My poor heart is sentimental
Not made of wood
I got it bad, and that ain't good

But when the weekend's over
And Monday rolls around
My man and me,

we pray some,
we gin some
and sin some

He don't love me
Like I love him
Nobody could
I got it bad, and that ain't good

Now folks with good intentions
Tell me to save my tears
I'm glad I'm mad about him
I can't live without him

Lord above me,
Make him love me
The way he should

Like a lonesome weeping willow
lost in the wood
The way I hug my pillow
No woman should
Because I got it bad, and that ain't good

Further Resources

BOOKS

Butcher, Geoffrey. *Next to a Letter from Home: Glenn Miller's Wartime Band.* Edinburgh, Scotland: Mainstream, 1986.

Dance, Stanley. *The World of Duke Ellington.* New York: Da Capo, 1981.

Ellington, Duke (Edward Kennedy). *Music Is My Mistress.* New York: Da Capo, 1973.

Fidelman, Geoffrey Mark. *First Lady of Song: Ella Fitzgerald for the Record.* Secaucus, N.J.: Carol, 1994.

Nicholson, Stuart. *Reminiscing in Tempo: A Portrait of Duke Ellington.* Boston: Northeastern University Press, 1999.

AUDIO AND VISUAL MEDIA

Ellington, Duke. *Beyond Category: The Musical Genius of Duke Ellington.* Washington, D.C.: Smithsonian Institution Press, 1994.

Let Us Now Praise Famous Men

Photographs

By: Walker Evans

Date: 1941

Source: Agee, James, and Walker Evans. *Let Us Now Praise Famous Men.* Boston: Houghton Mifflin, 1941.

About the Artist: Walker Evans (1903–1975) was a photographer, writer, and teacher. Born in St. Louis, Missouri, he graduated from Phillips Academy and spent a year at Williams College. His interest in documentary photography led him to record city streets, American nineteenth-century architecture of buildings and homes, and the people and places of the rural South, especially during the Great Depression. He worked for *Fortune* magazine for twenty years

and then taught graphic design at Yale University for ten years. ■

Introduction

Early on, Walker Evans wanted to be a writer and a painter. He spent a year in Paris auditing courses at the Sorbonne and reading Gustave Flaubert and Charles-Pierre Baudelaire. After his return to New York City, he took up the study of photography. In his early work photographing New York streets and inhabitants, he slowly developed an austere and honest style. One of his first projects was to illustrate *The Bridge* (1930), Hart Crane's epic poem about the Brooklyn Bridge. Later on, he saw the work of nineteenth-century photographer Eugene Atget, whose documentary style was to have a strong influence on his work. In 1938, he had his first major Museum of Modern Art exhibition, *American Photographs;* his catalogue of the same title became the touchstone by which every serious photography book since has been measured.

Two figures dominated American photography in Evans' youth: Alfred Stieglitz and Edward Steichen. Both men fought to establish photography as an art, but Evans rebelled against their views of what art is. To Evans, Stieglitz and Steichen believed art involved artiness and artifice. Evans favored the documentary approach he had learned from Atget. He hoped to attain in photography the cool objectivity of Flaubert's writings. Above all, he believed, like Baudelaire, that an artist's duty was to experience and document reality, no matter how bleak.

During the height of the Great Depression, Evans was a photographer for the Resettlement Administration, later known as the Farm Security Administration. Documenting the living and working conditions of poor agricultural workers in the South, he photographed deserted towns, shacks and shanties, and the people who lived in them.

Significance

In 1936, Evans took a leave of absence to collaborate with the writer James Agee on a *Fortune* magazine article about white sharecroppers hit hard by the Great Depression in Alabama. The two men spent three weeks living with the sharecroppers in Hale County, Alabama. *Fortune* declined to publish the article, saying it was too long and that its literary style, with its confrontational approach to the subject, was unsuitable for the magazine. Agee and Walker eventually published their material as a book, *Let Us Now Praise Famous Men,* in 1941.

The book focuses on the lives of three tenant cotton-farming families living in Hale County. It opens with fifty photographs. There are no quotations or captions to ac-

Primary Source

Walker Evans photograph from *Let Us Now Praise Famous Men* (1 OF 3)

SYNOPSIS: These pictures of a sharecropper, his wife, and little girl are among the most famous photographs ever taken by an American. Evans demonstrates his gift for selecting, capturing, and presenting the harsh beauty and hard-won dignity of the world of the rural southern farm worker. No quotations or captions accompanied the photographs as Evans and Agee believed that the images should stand alone. HULTON/ARCHIVE PHOTOS. REPRODUCED BY PERMISSION.

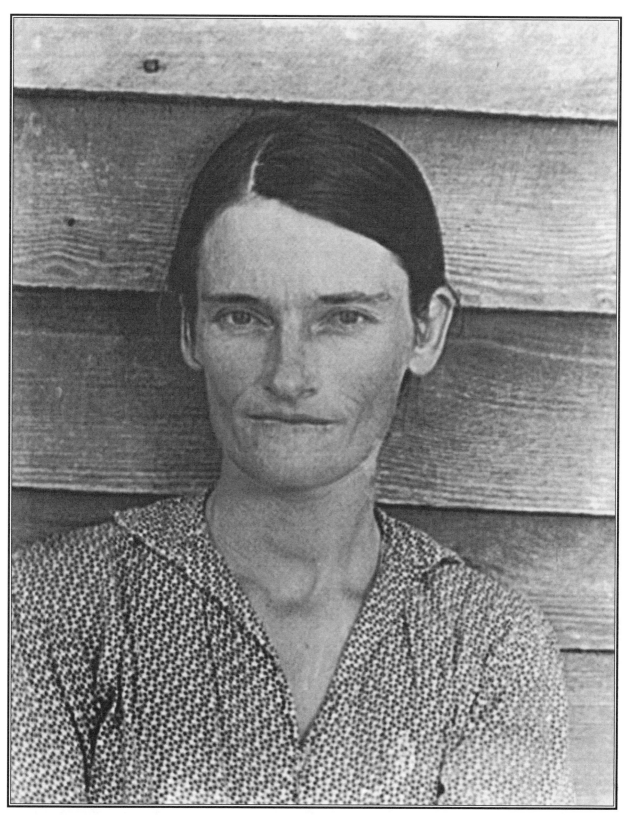

Primary Source

Walker Evans photograph from *Let Us Now Praise Famous Men* **(2 OF 3)** THE LIBRARY OF CONGRESS.

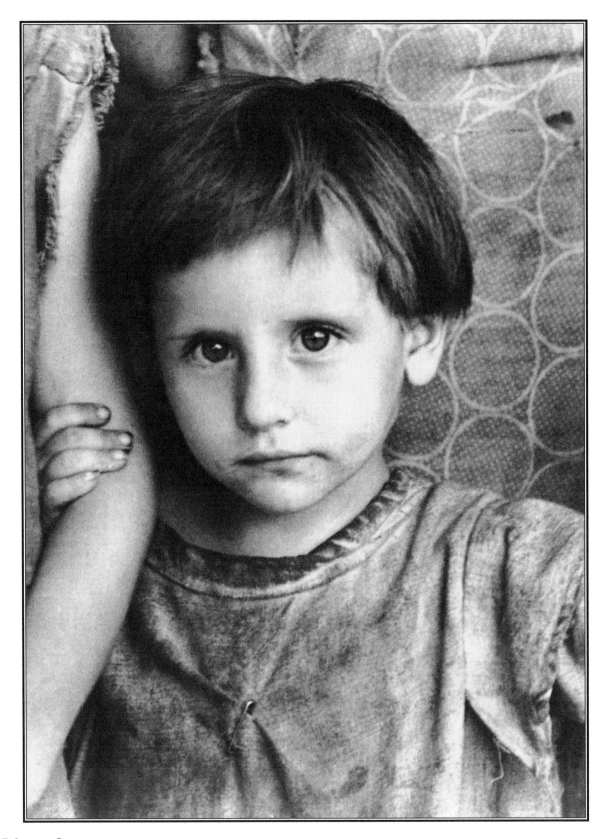

Primary Source

Walker Evans photograph from *Let Us Now Praise Famous Men* **(3 OF 3)** © BETTMANN/CORBIS. REPRODUCED BY PERMISSION.

company the images of the families, their homes, and their possessions. Evans and Agee believed that the images were self-explanatory and wanted the portraits of the families to confront the viewer with their strength, decency, and endurance in the face of poverty.

In *Let Us Now Praise Famous Men,* Evans pioneered the groundbreaking approach of using photography to document social issues. However, his method did not find an audience until 1960, when an expanded edition of the book was published. Its unsentimental but dignified account of rural life in the South inspired several generations of photographers and continues to open the eyes of readers to the artistic and cultural possibilities of documentary photography.

Evans had by then become the grand old man of photography and from his position at Yale University was to have a far-reaching effect on the way this art was taught and thought about in the United States. Throughout his career, his goal was to produce photographs that were evocative and mysterious, as well as an accurate record of the day. Evans initiated a tradition of American photographers interested in identifying and presenting the unique character of everyday American life.

Further Resources

BOOKS

Agee, James. *Let Us Now Praise Famous Men: Three Tenant Families, with an Introduction to the New Edition by John Hershey.* Boston: Houghton Mifflin, 1988.

Evans, Walker. *The Years of Bitterness and Pride: Farm Security Administration, Farm Security Administration Photographs, 1935–43.* New York: McGraw-Hill, 1975.

————. *Walker Evans: American Photographs, with an Essay by Lincoln Kirstein.* New York: Museum of Modern Art, 1991.

WEBSITES

"Walker Evans Before and After." Getty.edu. Available online at http://www.getty.edu/art/exhibitions/evans/; website home page: http://www.getty.edu (accessed February 24, 2003).

"Walker Evans Revolutionizes Documentary Photography." University of Virginia. Available online at http://xroads.virginia.edu/~UG97/fsa/welcome.html; website home page: http://www.virginia.edu (accessed February 24, 2003).

"Walker Evans." Masters-of-Photography.com. Available online at http://www.masters-of-photography.com/E/evans/evans.html; website home page: http://www.masters-of-photography.com (accessed February 24, 2003).

"Walker Evans." Artcyclopedia.com. Available online at http://www.artcyclopedia.com/artists/evans_walker.html; website home page: http://www.artcyclopedia.com (accessed February 24, 2003).

"The Life of John Brown" Series, No. 17
Painting

By: Jacob Lawrence

Date: 1941

Source: Lawrence, Jacob. "The Life of John Brown" Series, No. 17. 1941. Available online at http://www.jacoblawrence.org/art04.html; website home page: http://www.jacoblawrence.org (accessed February 24, 2003).

About the Artist: Jacob Lawrence (1917–2000) was born in Atlantic City, New Jersey. He began his career in painting as a young man. After the critical and financial breakthrough of the *Migration* series in 1941, he became widely known as the premier African American painter in the United States. He continued to paint series based on events in African American history, including notable works about World War II (1939–1945), the civil rights movement, and life in Africa. ■

Introduction

As a teenager, the lives of heroic, larger-than-life figures, especially revolutionaries, first captured Jacob Lawrence's imagination. In 1937, he began what was to be the first of his series of paintings on the life of Toussaint-Louverture. Next, he illustrated the stories of two former slaves who became major figures in American political life: Frederick Douglas and Harriet Tubman.

While working on the "Great Migration" series (depicting the period in which thousands of African Americans moved from the rural South to the urban North after World War I [1914–1918]), Lawrence began "The Life of John Brown" series. This series of twenty-two paintings was part of his continuing exploration of slavery in American history. Yet, here for the first time he turned from the heroic African American figures of his earlier work to tell the story of "a [white] man who had a fanatical belief that he was chosen by God to overthrow black slavery in America," as the caption from the first painting of the series reads. Each gouache (a water-based paint) is a vignette showing the relentless stages in the story of Brown's astonishing attack on Harpers Ferry that attempted to start a slave revolt in 1859. Each scene is accompanied by a concise statement of its theme.

Lawrence was not trying to spread false ideas. Considering the dramatic nature of the story—religious fanaticism and black guerilla warfare—his images are restrained and sobering. A good example is No. 17. As the title tells us, "John Brown remained a full winter in Canada drilling Negroes for his coming raid on Harpers Ferry." We see a somber group of twelve tall African

Primary Source

The Life of John Brown, no. 17. John Brown Remained a Full Winter in Canada, Drilling Negros for His Coming Raid on Harpers Ferry

SYNOPSIS: In this painting from "The Life of John Brown" series, Lawrence reveals his ability to "hit the nail on the head" in his storytelling: we see John Brown questioning a group of black followers for their planned raid on Harpers Ferry in Virginia.

© FRANCIS G. MAYER/CORBIS. REPRODUCED BY PERMISSION.

Americans disciples with heads bowed facing Brown, whose back is toward us. This gloomy man is clearly deformed by his religious fanaticism, and his black disciples seem to view their participation in this revolt as a necessary but unhappy obligation.

Significance

Previous series painting in the twentieth century had no narrative unity, meaning that the paintings did not tell a story about their subjects. Lawrence was clearly doing something new but at the same time, something old. His work told a thoroughly American story, but also hearkened to the beginnings of Western European painting: Giotto di Bondone's narrative cycles in the Arena Chapel. "The Life of John Brown," like "The Migration of the Negro" series of the same year, earned Lawrence the attention and admiration of the largely white "downtown audience" both for its talent and for its historical

ambitions. The "Migration" series was actually first exhibited at the Museum of Modern Art. Curators and audiences quickly saw that homegrown talents like Lawrence were soon going to challenge the dominance of Parisian artists. Within another decade, the art capital of the world would be New York City. Lawrence was not the first African American artist to have his work exhibited at the museum, but he was the first to have a one-man show.

For all these reasons, Lawrence's status as the leading African American painter was unrivaled during this period. His importance to the cause of historical truth and artistic achievement is still unrivaled. With the "John Brown" and "Migration" series, Lawrence confirmed his position as the major artistic historian of his people. Lawrence viewed art and history as forms of storytelling and never wavered in his belief that his role as an artist was to relate his people's story to the larger story of

Jacob Lawrence in Coast Guard uniform, standing before one of his paintings, 1945. CORBIS-BETTMANN. REPRODUCED BY PERMISSION.

America. Also, his artistry ensured that there would be a powerful imaginative recreation of the deeds and figures that made up the full story of the development of America.

Further Resources

BOOKS

Duggleby, John. *Story Painter: The Life of Jacob Lawrence.* San Francisco: Chronicle, 1998.

Nesbett, Peter T., and Michelle Dubois. *Complete Jacob Lawrence.* 2 vols. Seattle: University of Washington Press, 2000.

Wheat, Ellen. *Jacob Lawrence: American Painter* Seattle: University of Washington Press, 1986.

WEBSITES

"John Brown's Holy War." Public Broadcasting Service. Available online at http://www.pbs.org/wgbh/amex/brown/; website home page: http://www.pbs.org (accessed February 24, 2003).

What Is Modern Painting?
Pamphlet

By: Alfred H. Barr Jr.

Date: 1943

Source: Barr, Alfred H., Jr. *What Is Modern Painting?* New York: Museum of Modern Art, 1943. Revised 1974.

About the Author: Alfred H. Barr Jr. (1902–1981), an art historian, was born in Detroit, Michigan. He attended Princeton University, where he was influenced by Charles Rufus Morley and his course in medieval art. Barr received a graduate degree in art history and museum studies at Harvard University under Paul Sachs. In 1929, he became the first director of the Museum of Modern Art. During his years there, he was the curator for hundreds of exhibits and wrote definitive books on Pablo Picasso, Henri Matisse, and the cubists. He retired in 1968. ■

Introduction

Twentieth-century artists in their most well-known manifestations—expressionism, cubism, dadaism, futurism, surrealism, and abstract expressionism—seemed

Withdrawal from Dunkirk, by Richard Eurich. Oil on canvas, 30 x 40 inches. 1940. © **NATIONAL MARITIME MUSEUM, GREENWICH, LONDON. REPRODUCED BY PERMISSION.**

hostile to common sense if not common decency, made heavy demands on the viewer, and offered little of the pleasures of traditional art. Because of their adversarial stance toward the traditions of painting, modern artists became dependent on savvy dealers, rich patrons, art critics and curators, and, above all, the modern museum. The museum became a necessary intermediary between artist and the public, influencing both public taste and the life of art.

The Museum of Modern Art (MOMA), founded in New York in 1929, has been the single most important institution devoted to making twentieth-century art understandable and appreciated. More than any other institution of this kind, it was the creation of a single man, Alfred H. Barr Jr., whose ideas and judgments shaped the formation of MOMA in its early decades.

Barr's notion of art history, which was based on his historical training at Princeton and Harvard, focused on the sources, patterns, chronology, and spread of a style, and his approach was wide ranging. He went beyond painting, sculpture, and the graphic arts to architecture, industrial design, theater, movies, and literature. Barr was interested in promoting what we now call cultural literacy. He in-

sisted on artistic merit and historical significance as the two main criteria for inclusion in the museum.

Barr's conception of modernism, in his arrangement of MOMA's collections and in many of the museum's major exhibitions during his tenure, provided an account of both the master currents of modern art and its minor tributaries. He was also aware of the need to defend the artist's freedom to experiment, to express his or her deepest feelings, and even to fail in that attempt against those who would deny those freedoms.

Significance

Barr saw the need for a short pamphlet that was directed at people who were not informed about modern art. He invited such readers to make up their own minds by looking with their "own eyes and heart and head" only after they have given the new art of their time a chance. He pointed out that although people are bombarded with images all the time, they are rarely asked to look closely or read carefully.

In the introduction, Barr made readers aware of several considerations that go into the making and judging of modern painting. He appealed to the American love of invention, discovery, and challenge. He was sure that by doing so spectators would better understand that what is going on in the world of modern art is not that different from what is going on in other innovative sectors of national and international life. Above all, he considered the artist to be the "sensitive antennae" of the society who through his or her art makes us see the problems of our civilization. In his conclusion, he stated that the work of art is the visible symbol of the human spirit in its quest for perfection, truth, and freedom.

Barr's pamphlet enjoyed wide distribution and has been read for more than three decades. Many people owe their first impressions of modern art to the ideas presented in this work. Barr was responsible for hundreds of exhibits, which educated the New York audience and visitors about the new movements in modern art beginning with cubism. Barr was also one of the first to see that a visit to a museum should be thought of more like exploring an exciting territory on a vacation than as an educational undertaking or homework.

Primary Source

What Is Modern Painting? [excerpt]

> **SYNOPSIS:** In the following excerpt, Barr walks readers through some of the considerations they should keep in mind when first confronting modern painting.

What Is Modern Painting? It is not easy to answer this question in writing, for writing is done with words while paintings are made of shapes and colors. The best words can do is to give you some information, point out a few things you might overlook, and if, to begin with, you feel that you don't like modern painting anyway, words may help you to change your mind. But in the end you must look at these works of art with your own eyes and heart and head. This may not be easy, but most people who make the effort find their lives richer, more interesting, more worth living. . . .

. . . The variety of modern art reflects the complexity of modern life. Though this may give us mental and emotional indigestion, it does offer each of us a wide range to choose from.

But it is important not to choose too quickly. The art which makes a quick appeal or is easy to understand right away may wear thin like a catchy tune which you hear twice, whistle ten times and then can't stand any more.

It is just as important not to fool yourself. Don't pretend to like what you dislike or can't understand. Be honest with yourself. We don't all have to like the same things. Some people have no ear for music; a few have no eye for painting—or say they haven't because they are timid or don't want to make the effort.

Yet everybody who can see has an eye for pictures. Most of us see hundreds, maybe thousands, of pictures every week, a few of them very good ones too—photographs in newspapers and magazines, cartoons, illustrations and comics, advertising in buses and subways: Joe Palooka Happy Atom Scientists Buy Sweetie Pie Soap Buck Rogers Vote For McLevy Dallam Scores In Plane Crash Near Trenton Zowie The Pause That Refreshes—pictures which try to get you to buy this or that, tell you something you may forget tomorrow or give you a moment's lazy entertainment. (And do you remember the pictures on the walls of your home?) . . .

Some of them [modern paintings] may take a good deal of study, for although we have seen a million pictures in our lives we may never have learned to look at painting as an art. For the art of painting, though it has little to do with words, is like a language which you have to learn to read. Some pictures are easy, like a primer, and some are hard with long words and complex ideas; and some are prose, others are poetry, and others still are like algebra or geometry. But one thing is easy, there are no foreign languages in painting as there are in speech; there are only local dialects which can be understood internationally for painting is a kind of visual Esperanto. Therefore it has a special value in this riven world.

The greatest modern artists are pioneers just as are modern scientists, inventors and explorers. This makes modern art both more difficult and often more exciting than the art we are already used to. Galileo, Columbus, the Wright brothers suffered neglect, disbelief, even ridicule. Read the lives of the modern artists of eighty years ago, Whistler or van Gogh for instance, and you will keep an open mind about the art you may not like or understand today. Unless you can look at art with some spirit of adventure, the pioneer artists of our own day may suffer too. This might be your loss as well as theirs.

Perhaps you feel that these pictures have little to do with our everyday lives. This is partly true; some of them don't, and that is largely their value—by their poetry they have the power to lift us out of humdrum ruts. But others have a lot to do with ordinary life: vanity and devotion, joy and sadness, the beauty of landscape, animals and people, or even the appearance of our houses and our kitchen floors. And still others have to do with the crucial problems of our civilization: war, the character of democracy and tyranny, the effects of industrialization, the exploration of the subconscious mind, the survival of religion, the liberty and restraint of the individual.

The artist is a human being like the rest of us. He cannot solve these problems except as one of us; but through his art he can help us see and understand them, for artists are the sensitive antennae of society.

Beyond these comparatively practical matters art has another more important function: the work of art is a symbol, a visible symbol of the human spirit in its search for truth, for freedom, for perfection. . . .

Truth, freedom, perfection . . . words which might be proposed as the artist's equivalent of what liberty, equality, fraternity were to the French Revolution, or, in a somewhat different sense, what faith, hope and charity are to the Christian.

"War is hell!" This truth uttered by General Sherman, our nineteenth-century master of total war, has rung loud in recent years. A critic trying to make fun of Picasso's *Guernica* tells how a soldier standing before the canvas, remarked, "I wonder what Sherman would have said about Picasso." Out of occupied Paris came another story about the *Guernica*. The Germans, the legend tells, so valued the prestige of winning great foreign artists to their side that they sent their agent, Otto Abetz, to Picasso to persuade him to make a trip to Berlin as a friendly gesture toward the Nazis. Picasso refused curtly. On his way out of the studio the embarrassed German noticed a photograph of the *Guernica* and, forgetting the *Luftwaffe's* role in the picture said: "Ah, Monsieur Picasso, so it was you who did that." "No, Herr Abetz," replied Picasso, "you did."

Sherman in words, Picasso in paint were telling the same truth, each in his own language. Just as Picasso's forms are not to be found in nature, Sherman's "hell" is unknown to science. Indeed those who insist on facts will have to forgive the General his figure of speech, remembering that by his metaphor he won perhaps wider and more lasting fame than by his sword.

The truth which plumbs deeply, convinces the mind, brings joy to the heart or makes the blood run chill is not always factual; indeed it is rarely to be found in newsreels, statistics or communiqués. The soothsayer, that is, the truth-sayer, the oracle, the prophet, the poet, the artist, often speak in language which is not matter-of-fact or scientific. They prefer

the allegory, the riddle, the parable, the metaphor, the myth, the dream, for, to use Picasso's words, "Art is a lie that makes us realize the truth."

In order to tell this truth the artist must live and work in *freedom*. President Roosevelt, with the totalitarian countries in mind, put it clearly. "The arts cannot thrive except where men are free to be themselves and to be in charge of the discipline of their own energies and ardors. . . . What we call liberty in politics results in freedom in the arts. . . . Crush individuality in the arts and you crush art as well."

Sometimes in art galleries one hears a man who has just glanced at a cubist or expressionist picture turn away with the angry words, "It ought to be burned," or "There ought to be a law against it." That was just the way Hitler felt. When he became dictator he passed laws against modern art, called it degenerate, foreign, Jewish, international, Bolshevik; forced modern artists such as Klee, Kandinsky, Beckmann . . . out of art schools, drove them from the country and snatched their pictures from museum walls, to burn them or sell them abroad. . . .

Similarly the Soviet authorities, even earlier than the Nazis, began to suppress modern art, calling it leftist deviation, Western decadence, bourgeois, formalistic. About 1921 such painters as Chagall and Kandinsky left the U.S.S.R. in frustration. Even today paintings by these great expatriates are hidden away in museum storerooms (though "formalist" works by the foreigners Matisse and Picasso have gradually emerged from prison since the death of Stalin in 1953). The Soviet artists who remain are enjoined— and well paid—to paint pictures in a popular realistic style preferably with propaganda content. Other styles are forbidden and other subjects discouraged. In 1962 Khrushchev himself assaulted young artists with threats and scurrilous sarcasm because they deviated from Socialist Realism and dared exhibit their heresies in spite of official warning.

Why do totalitarian dictators hate modern art?

Because the artist, perhaps more than any other member of society, stands for individual freedom— freedom to think and paint without the approval of a Goebbels or a Central Committee of the Communist Party, to work in the style he wants, to tell the truth as he feels from inner necessity that he must tell it.

In this country there is little danger that the arts will suffer from the tyranny of a dictator but there are other less direct ways of crushing freedom in the arts. In a democracy the original, progressive artist often faces the indifference or intolerance of the public, the ignorance of officials, the malice of conservative artists, the laziness of the critics, the blindness or timidity of picture buyers and museums. Van Gogh was "free." He lived successively in two liberal democracies and painted as he wished. He also starved. In the end, desperate with disappointment, he shot himself, having sold only a couple of paintings in his lifetime for about $100 (they might be worth $300,000 now). Have we a van Gogh in America today? How has he been getting along? Has he found alert, courageous and generous admirers, and buyers, among private purchasers, business corporations, museums, city, state and Federal offices? Yes, more and more, but not enough.

Yet the American artist, since the war against Nazi tyranny abroad, has had to suffer occasional persecution here at home. Self-styled patriotic organizations and misguided congressmen, instigated by bitterly jealous academic artists, have accused modern artists and their supporters of communist sympathies. (It is true in the past that Communists once or twice did gain control over artists' groups, particularly during the depression and our military alliance with the U.S.S.R., but with very few exceptions, even the most gullible artists have lost their illusions about Communism—and those few exceptions have been for the most part "conservative" rather than "modern" in their art.)

At the 25th Anniversary of The Museum of Modern Art, President Eisenhower asserted "that freedom of the arts is a basic freedom, one of the pillars of liberty in our land. For our Republic to stay free, those among us with the rare gift of artistry must be able freely to use their talent. Likewise, our people must have unimpaired opportunity to see, to understand, to profit from our artists' work. As long as artists are at liberty to feel with high personal intensity, as long as our artists are free to create with sincerity and conviction, there will be healthy controversy and progress in art."

Freedom of expression, freedom from want and censorship and fear, these are desirable for the artist. But why should the artist's freedom particularly concern the rest of us? Because the artist gives us pleasure or tells us the truth? Yes, but more than this: his freedom as we find it expressed in his work of art is a symbol, an embodiment of the freedom which we all want but which we can never really find in everyday life with its schedules, obligations and compromises. Of course we can ourselves take up painting or some other art as amateurs and so increase our sense of personal freedom; but even in a nation of amateur artists there would still be a need for the artist who makes freedom of expression his profession. For art cannot be done well with the left hand: it is the hardest kind of work, consuming all a man's strength, partly for the very reason that it is done in greater freedom than other kinds of work.

For the arts thrive, to repeat President Roosevelt's phrase, where men are free "to be in charge of the discipline of their own energies and ardors." The greater the artist's freedom the greater must be his self-discipline. Only through the most severe self-discipline can he approach that excellence for which all good artists strive. And in approaching that goal he makes of his work of art a symbol not only of truth and freedom but also of perfection.

Perfection in a work of art is of course related to the perfection of a flawlessly typed letter, or an examination mark of 100, or a well-made shoe, but it differs in several important ways: it is usually far more complicated, combining many levels and varieties of human activity and thought; it cannot be judged by practical or material results, nor can it be measured scientifically or logically; it must satisfy not a teacher, a superior officer, or an employer but first and essentially the artist's own conscience; and, lastly, artistic perfection, unlike the perfection of the craftsman, the technician or the mathematician, can be, but should not be, "too" perfect.

The possibilities open to the painter as he faces his blank canvas, or to the composer before his untouched keyboard are so complex, so nearly infinite, that perfection in art may seem almost as unattainable as it is in life. Mondrian perhaps comes in sight of perfection by limiting his problem to the subtle adjustment of rectangles. . . . An "abstract" painter who passed beyond Mondrian into geometry would indeed find perfection, but he would leave art behind him just as, in another direction, the painters who go beyond Peto . . . in counterfeiting reality are expert craftsmen but scarcely artists. For complete perfection in art would probably be as boring as a perfect circle, a perfect Apollo, or the popular, harp-and-cloud idea of Heaven.

Yet the artist, free of outer compulsion and practical purposes, driven by his own inner passion for excellence and acting as his own judge, produces in his work of art a symbol of that striving for perfection which in ordinary life we cannot satisfy, just as we cannot enjoy complete freedom or tell the entire truth.

Truth, which in art we often arrive at through a "lie," *freedom,* which in art is a delusion unless controlled by self-discipline, and *perfection,* which if it were ever absolute would be the death of art—perhaps through pondering such ideas as these we can deepen our understanding of the nature and value of modern painting; but for most people the direct experience of art will always be more pleasurable and more important than trying to puzzle out its ultimate meaning. Listen to what Picasso has to say about attempting to answer such questions as "What is modern painting?" Let a painter have the last word:

> Everyone wants to understand art. Why not try to understand the song of a bird? Why does one love the night, flowers, everything around one, without trying to understand it? But in the case of a painting people have to understand. If only they would realize above all that an artist works because he must, that he himself is only a trifling bit of the world, and that no more importance should be attached to him than to plenty of other things in the world which please us, though we can't explain them. People who try to explain pictures are usually barking up the wrong tree.

Further Resources

BOOKS

Barr, Alfred H., Jr. *Defining Modern Art: Selected Writings of Alfred H. Barr, Jr.* Irving Sandler, ed. New York: Abrams, 1986.

———. *Matisse, His Art and His Public.* New York: Museum of Modern Art, 1974.

———. *Picasso: Fifty Years of His Art.* New York: Museum of Modern Art, 1974.

Kantor, Sybil Gordon. *Alfred H. Barr, Jr. and the Intellectual Origins of the Museum of Modern Art.* Cambridge: Massachusetts Institute of Technology Press, 2001.

WEBSITES

"Alfred Barr and Art Museums." Clemson University. Available online at http://people.clemson.edu/~methomp/museum/barr.html; website home page http://www.clemson.edu/ (accessed February 25, 2003).

Museum of Modern Art. Available online at http://www.moma.org (accessed February 25, 2003).

On the Town Caricature

Cartoon

By: Al Hirschfeld

Date: November 1944

Source: *On the Town.* Available online at http://www.leonardbernstein.com/studio/element.asp?FeatID=11&

Betty Comden and Adolph Green, Broadway writer/lyricist team, play with a filmstrip. The duo were also successful screenwriters. THE KOBAL COLLECTION. REPRODUCED BY PERMISSION.

AssetID=24; website home page: http://www.leonardbernstein.com (accessed February 25, 2003).

About the Artist: Al Hirschfeld (1903–2003), an American graphic artist, was born in St. Louis. He is famous for his caricatures of theater people and productions, thousands of which appeared in the Sunday Arts and Leisure section of *The New York Times* to signal the arrival of new shows. ∎

Introduction

After *Oklahoma!* opened in 1943, the Broadway musical changed. Richard Rodgers and Oscar Hammerstein showed everyone how the songs, music, dance, and plot could be integrated into a powerful and compelling whole. Now, a musical comedy needed to be written with the same unity of purpose as *Oklahoma!*, but this time it was to be funny.

The origins of *On the Town* lie in an idea for a ballet, which Jerome Robbins had in the fall of 1943. Robbins approached Leonard Bernstein, who was making his conducting debut with the New York Philharmonic. The ballet *Fancy Free* was the result.

Oliver Smith, who designed the sets for *Fancy Free*, suggested that it be turned into a full-length show. Bernstein was to write the score, and Robbins was to once again choreograph. Bernstein suggested his friends

Primary Source

On the Town Caricature

SYNOPSIS: Al Hirschfeld's cartoon was one of thousands of sketches he made of Broadway shows for the Arts and Leisure section of *The New York Times* Sunday Edition heralding the high points of the season. The following sketch shows a rehearsal for the original Broadway production of *On the Town,* with many of the principals giving a sense of the lightheartedness of the show and the team that created it. Composer Leonard Bernstein, conductor Max Goberman and director George Abbott are in the foreground. © AL HIRSCHFELD. DRAWING REPRODUCED BY SPECIAL ARRANGEMENT WITH HIRSCHFELD'S EXCLUSIVE REPRESENTATIVE, THE MARGO FEIDEN GALLERIES LTD., NEW YORK, NEW YORK. REPRODUCED BY PERMISSION.

Betty Comden and Adolph Green for the book and lyrics.

On the Town is set in New York City during World War II (1939–1945). Three sailors are on a twenty-four-hour shore leave. One of the sailors falls in love with a poster of Miss Subways, and his friends are determined to bring him together with the real woman for a date. *On the Town* contains three-dimensional characters, comic situations, and a wacky yet emotionally moving atmosphere derived from the dramatic demands of time against the background of war.

Significance

On the Town was an instant hit when it opened on Broadway in 1944. Wartime audiences were delighted with its tuneful score, which mixed romantic ballads with high-spirited and witty comic numbers. Its modern dances were set in various areas of New York City, and its cast included two of the show's creators, Comden and Green, and the young comedian Nancy Walker. Many great talents emerged from this show and went on to have successful careers.

During the next forty years, Bernstein, Robbins, and the team of Comden and Green were responsible for some of the most memorable shows during the greatest period of the Broadway musical. Although Bernstein was to become one of the leading symphony conductors of his day, he continued to write music for the concert hall and for Broadway throughout his career, including such legendary shows as *Candide, West Side Story,* and *Mass.* Bernstein worked with Comden and Green again on the New York–based musical *Wonderful Town,* as well as on *Peter Pan* for Mary Martin.

Robbins became one of the great Broadway choreographers with such shows as *The King and I, West Side Story,* and *Fiddler on the Roof,* as well as a major figure in the development of modern ballet. He was long associated with the New York City Ballet, for which he created more than sixty-six ballets.

Comden and Green became one of the most honored and successful teams of writers/lyricists in Broadway and Hollywood history. Their Broadway hits are notable for their wit and comic invention. Their shows, spanning four decades, include *Two on the Aisle, Bells Are Ringing, Say, Darling, Do Re Mi, Fade out Fade In, On the Twentieth Century,* and *The Will Rogers Follies.* They wrote the screenplay for *Singing in the Rain,* the classic movie musical about the early days of movies, as well as the screenplay for the cult classic *What a Way to Go!*

Further Resources

BOOKS

Mordden, Ethan M. *Beautiful Mornin': The Broadway Musical in the 1940s.* New York: Oxford University Press, 1999.

———. *Coming up Roses: The Broadway Musical in the 1950s.* New York: Oxford University Press, 1998.

WEBSITES

Al Hirschfeld.com. Available online at http://www.alhirschfeld .com/index2.html; website home page: http://www.alhirschfeld .com (accessed February 25, 2003).

Jerome Robbins Trust and Foundation. Available online at http://jeromerobbins.org/home0.htm; website home page: http://jeromerobbins.org (accessed February 25, 2003).

The Official Leonard Bernstein Website. Available online at http://www.leonardbernstein.com (accessed February 25, 2003).

AUDIO AND VISUAL MEDIA

Bernstein, Leonard, et al. *On the Town.* Nancy Walker, Chris Alexander, Betty Comden, and Adolph Green. Sony. CD, 1998.

On the Town. Directed by Gene Kelly and Stanley Donen. Warner Home Video. DVD, 2000.

"Richard Wright's Blues"

Book review

By: Ralph Ellison

Date: 1945

Source: Ellison, Ralph. "Richard Wright's Blues." In *Collected Essays of Ralph Ellison,* ed. John F. Callahan. New York: Modern Library, 1995, 128–133. Originally published in *The Antioch Review,* Summer 1945, 128–133.

About the Author: Ralph Ellison (1914–1994), a novelist and essay writer, was born in Oklahoma City, Oklahoma. He attended the Tuskegee Institute in Alabama on a music scholarship but soon turned to writing fiction. He moved to New York where as an editor for the *New Masses* he wrote influential essays, book reviews, and short stories. His novel *Invisible Man* (1952) established him as one of the foremost African American intellectuals in the years immediately following World War II (1939–1945). ∎

Introduction

Ralph Ellison's friend and fellow novelist Richard Wright is the subject of the review "Richard Wright's Blues," which Ellison wrote following the publication of Wright's autobiographical *Black Boy* (1945). In the review, Ellison demonstrated some of the qualities that made him the foremost African American intellectual of his generation. He spoke with a combination of intellectual erudition and hard-won experience.

In the opening, Ellison noted that Wright gave himself a twofold task as a writer: to portray the truth about the African American experience and to reveal the psychological and emotional obstacles that stand in the way of understanding between African Americans and whites. As "perhaps the most articulate Negro American," Wright was qualified to do so, projecting his own life in "lucid prose guided, say, by the insights of Freud and Marx." Ellison was just as qualified.

Ellison celebrated the intellectual and literary quality of Wright's autobiography, finding influences and debts to Jawaharlal Nehru, Fyodor Dostoyevsky, Jean-Jacques Rousseau, and James Joyce, but he insisted that these influences only came when Wright was in college. They were not what shaped Wright as a boy and a young man growing up in the South with only a "microscopic degree of cultural freedom." What then accounted for Wright's masterful prose? One factor was the presence of folk music among even the poorest blacks. The blues was a constant in the southern African American environment.

Thus, the folk culture of the African American South offered Wright a living art from which to learn how to talk and write about his experiences. After this, he was sensitive to what other writers could teach him about how to structure his own experience. In his books, Wright used two sources of inspiration: the lyric poetry of the southern African American folk experience and the intellectual heritage of twentieth-century Western man.

Significance

When we think about intellectual life in the United States in the 1940s, we think about a relatively small group of writers who lived in New York City and came together in the pages of little magazines such as *Partisan Review* and *The Nation.* These writers had many intellectual influences in common, above all, a commitment to Karl Marx and Sigmund Freud as the prophets of the twentieth century. Wright and Ellison were very much part of this group, contributing essays and fiction to these magazines. What set these two apart was the color of their skin and the sum of their experiences as children and young men in the "undemocratic South," as well as their similar experiences and treatment when they came to the urban North.

Ellison and Wright stand out in the history of twentieth-century American letters as the foremost African American writers of their time. Wright's *Native Son* (1940) and Ellison's *Invisible Man* had an impact unlike any other previous novels by African American authors. As widely read authors in the twentieth century, they conveyed the experiences of growing up African American during the Great Depression.

In his essays written during the seven years he was working on *Invisible Man,* Ellison diagnosed the African American condition in America by discussing the tension of educated African Americans in modern society. Ellison was very aware of the need human beings, African Americans as well as whites, have to find the

Richard Wright's writings concerning the African American experience were among the first to garner serious interest and criticism from white audiences. **ARCHIVE PHOTOS. REPRODUCED BY PERMISSION.**

strength to escape resentment, vengefulness, and self-justification.

Wright left the United States to live in Paris soon after the success of *Black Boy,* and never returned. He continued to produce fiction and essays. Ellison remained in the United States, wrote many essays and fiction and taught. He never published another novel after his masterpiece, *Invisible Man,* but after his death, his literary executor published *Juneteeth,* the manuscript of a novel that Ellison had been working on for thirty years.

Primary Source

"Richard Wright's Blues" [excerpt]

> **SYNOPSIS:** In this review, Ellison does more than simply recommend or summarize Wright's *Black Boy,* which had just been released. He provides an intelligent and insightful literary analysis of Wright's novel.

If anybody ask you
    who sing this song,
Say it was ole [Black Boy]
    done been here and gone.

As a writer, Richard Wright has outlined for himself a dual role: to discover and depict the meaning of Negro experience, and to reveal to both Negroes and whites those problems of a psychological and emotional nature which arise between them when they strive for mutual understanding.

Now, in *Black Boy,* he has used his own life to probe what qualities of will, imagination and intellect are required of a Southern Negro in order to possess the meaning of his life in the United States. Wright is perhaps the most articulate Negro American, and what he has to say is highly perceptive. Imagine Bigger Thomas projecting his own life in lucid prose guided, say, by the insights of Marx and Freud, and you have an idea of this autobiography.

Published at a time when any sharply critical approach to Negro life has been dropped as a wartime expendable, it should do much to redefine the problem of the Negro and American democracy. Its power can be observed in the shrill manner with which some professional "friends of the people" have attempted to strangle the work in a noose of newsprint.

What in the tradition of literary autobiography is it like, this work described as a "great American autobiography"? As a non-white intellectual's statement of his relationship to Western culture, *Black Boy* recalls the conflicting pattern of identification and rejection found in Nehru's *Toward Freedom.* In its use of fictional techniques, its concern with criminality (sin) and the artistic sensibility, and in its author's judgment and rejection of the narrow world of his origin, it recalls Joyce's rejection of Dublin in *A Portrait of the Artist.* And as a psychological document of life under oppressive conditions, it recalls *The House of the Dead,* Dostoevsky's profound study of the humanity of Russian criminals.

Such works were perhaps Wright's literary guides, aiding him to endow his life's incidents with communicable significance, providing him with ways of seeing, feeling and describing his environment. These influences, however, were encountered only after these first years of Wright's life were past, and were not part of the immediate folk culture into which he was born. In that culture the specific folk-art form which helped shape the writer's attitude toward his life and which embodied the impulse that contributes much to the quality and tone of his autobiography was the Negro blues.

This would bear a word of explanation. The blues is an impulse to keep the painful details and episodes of a brutal experience alive in one's aching consciousness, to finger its jagged grain, and to transcend it, not by the consolation of philosophy but by squeezing from it a near-tragic, near-comic lyricism.

As a form, the blues is an autobiographical chronicle of personal catastrophe expressed lyrically. And certainly Wright's early childhood was crammed with catastrophic incidents. In a few short years his father deserted his mother, he knew intense hunger, he became a drunkard begging drinks from black stevedores in Memphis saloons; he had to flee Arkansas, where an uncle was lynched; he was forced to live with a fanatically religious grandmother in an atmosphere of constant bickering; he was lodged in an orphan asylum; he observed the suffering of his mother, who became a permanent invalid, while fighting off the blows of the poverty-stricken relatives with whom he had to live; he was cheated, beaten and kicked off jobs by white employees who disliked his eagerness to learn a trade; and to these objective circumstances must be added the subjective fact that Wright, with his sensitivity, extreme shyness and intelligence, was a problem child who rejected his family and was by them rejected.

Thus, along with the themes, equivalent descriptions of milieu and the perspectives to be found in Joyce, Nehru, Dostoevsky, George Moore and Rousseau, *Black Boy* is filled with blues-tempered echoes of railroad trains, the names of Southern towns and cities, estrangements, fights and flights, deaths and disappointments, charged with physical and spiritual hungers and pain. And like a blues sung by such an artist as Bessie Smith, its lyrical prose evokes the paradoxical, almost surreal image of a black boy singing lustily as he probes his own grievous wound.

In *Black Boy* two worlds have fused, two cultures merged, two impulses of Western man become coalesced. By discussing some of its cultural sources I hope to answer those critics who would make of the book a miracle and of its author a mystery. And while making no attempt to probe the mystery of the artist (who Hemingway says is "forged in injustice as a sword is forged"), I do hold that basically the prerequisites to the writing of *Black Boy* were, on the one hand, the microscopic degree of cultural freedom which Wright found in the South's stony injustice, and, on the other, the existence of a personality agitated to a state of almost manic restlessness. There were, of course, other factors, chiefly ideological, but these came later.

Wright speaks of his journey north as

> . . . taking a part of the South to transplant in alien soil, to see if it could grow differently, if it could drink of new and cool rains, bend in strange winds, respond to the warmth of other

suns, and perhaps, to bloom. . . . And just as Wright, the man, represents the blooming of the delinquent child of the autobiography, just so does *Black Boy* represent the flowering—cross-fertilized by pollen blown by the winds of strange cultures—of the humble blues lyric. There is, as in all acts of creation, a world of mystery in this, but there is also enough that is comprehensible for Americans to create the social atmosphere in which other black boys might freely bloom.

For certainly in the historical sense Wright is no exception. Born on a Mississippi plantation, he was subjected to all those blasting pressures which in a scant eighty years have sent the Negro people hurtling, without clearly defined trajectory, from slavery to emancipation, from log cabin to city tenement, from the white folks' fields and kitchens to factory assembly lines, and which, between two wars, have shattered the wholeness of its folk consciousness into a thousand writhing pieces.

Black Boy describes this process in the personal terms of *one* Negro childhood. Nevertheless, several critics have complained that it does not "explain" Richard Wright. Which, aside from the notion of art involved, serves to remind us that the prevailing mood of American criticism has so thoroughly excluded the Negro that it fails to recognize some of the most basic tenets of Western democratic thought when encountering them in a black skin. They forget that human life possesses an innate dignity and mankind an innate sense of nobility; that all men possess the tendency to dream and the compulsion to make their dreams reality; that the need to be ever dissatisfied and the urge ever to seek satisfaction is implicit in the human organism; and that all men are the victims and the beneficiaries of the goading, tormenting, commanding and informing activity of that imperious process known as the Mind—the Mind, as Valéry describes it, "armed with its inexhaustible questions."

Perhaps all this (in which lies the very essence of the human, and which Wright takes for granted) has been forgotten because the critics recognize neither Negro humanity nor the full extent to which the Southern community renders the fulfillment of human destiny impossible. And while it is true that *Black Boy* presents an almost unrelieved picture of a personality corrupted by brutal environment, it also presents those fresh, human responses brought to its world by the sensitive child:

There was the *wonder* I felt when I first saw a brace of mountainlike, spotted, black-and-white horses clopping down a dusty road . . .

the *delight* I caught in seeing long straight rows of red and green vegetables stretching away in the sun . . . the faint, cool kiss of *sensuality* when dew came on to my cheeks . . . the vague *sense of the infinite* as I looked down upon the yellow, dreaming waters of the Mississippi . . . the echoes of *nostalgia* I heard in the crying strings of wild geese . . . the *love* I had for the mute regality of tall, moss-clad oaks . . . the hint of *cosmic cruelty* that I *felt* when I saw the curved timbers of a wooden shack that had been warped in the summer sun . . . and there was the *quiet terror* that suffused my senses when vast hazes of gold washed earthward from star-heavy skies on silent nights . . . [italics mine] And a bit later, his reactions to religion:

Many of the religious symbols appealed to my sensibilities and I responded to the dramatic vision of life held by the church, feeling that to live day by day with death as one's sole thought was to be so compassionately sensitive toward all life as to view all men as slowly dying, and the trembling sense of fate that welled up, sweet and melancholy, from the hymns blended with the sense of fate that I had already caught from life.

There was also the influence of his mother—so closely linked to his hysteria and sense of suffering—who (though he only implies it here) taught him, in the words of the dedication prefacing *Native Son*," to revere the fanciful and the imaginative." There were also those white men—the one who allowed Wright to use his library privileges and the other who advised him to leave the South, and still others whose offers of friendship he was too frightened to accept.

Wright assumed that the nucleus of plastic sensibility is a human heritage: the right and the opportunity to dilate, deepen and enrich sensibility—democracy. Thus the drama of *Black Boy* lies in its depiction of what occurs when Negro sensibility attempts to fulfill itself in the undemocratic South. Here it is not the individual that is the immediate focus, as in Joyce's *Stephen Hero*, but that upon which his sensibility was nourished.

Those critics who complain that Wright has omitted the development of his own sensibility hold that the work thus fails as art. Others, because it presents too little of what they consider attractive in Negro life, charge that it distorts reality. Both groups miss a very obvious point: that whatever else the environment contained, it had as little chance of prevailing against the overwhelming weight of the child's unpleasant experiences as Beethoven's quartets would have of destroying the stench of a Nazi prison.

We come, then, to the question of art. The function, the psychology, of artistic selectivity is to eliminate from an art form all those elements of experience which contain no compelling significance. Life is as the sea, art a ship in which man conquers life's crushing formlessness, reducing it to a course, a series of swells, tides and wind currents inscribed on a chart. Though drawn from the world, "the organized significance of art," writes Malraux, "is stronger than all the multiplicity of the world; . . . that significance alone enables man to conquer chaos and to master destiny."

Wright saw his destiny—that combination of forces before which man feels powerless—in terms of a quick and casual violence inflicted upon him by both family and community. His response was likewise violent, and it has been his need to give that violence significance which has shaped his writings.

Further Resources

BOOKS

Ellison, Ralph. *Invisible Man.* New York: Modern Library, 1992.

——. *Juneteeth: A Novel.* John Callahan, ed. New York: Random House, 1999.

——. *Shadow and Act.* New York: Random House, 1964.

Hersey, John. *Ralph Ellison: A Collection of Critical Essays.* Englewood Cliffs, N.J.: Prentice-Hall, 1974.

Macksey, Richard, and Frank E. Moorer, eds. *Richard Wright: A Collection of Critical Essays.* Englewood Cliffs, N.J.: Prentice-Hall, 1984.

Wright, Richard. *Twelve Million Black Voices: A Folk History of the Negro in the United States.* New York: Viking, 1941.

——. *Works.* New York: Library of America: Viking, 1991.

WEBSITES

"Ralph Ellison: An American Journey." Public Broadcasting Service. Available online at http://www.pbs.org/wnet/americanmasters/database/ellison_r_homepage.html; website home page: http://www.pbs.org (accessed February 25, 2003).

"Richard Wright: Black Boy." Public Broadcasting Service. Available online at http://www.pbs.org/rwbb/; website home page: http://www.pbs.org (accessed February 25, 2003).

The Iceman Cometh

"*Iceman Cometh* Has Its World Premiere at the Martin Beck"

Theatre review

By: Brooks Atkinson
Date: October 10, 1946

THE ICEMAN COMETH

THE PLAYBILL

REGISTERED IN U. S. PATENT OFFICE

FOR THE MARTIN BECK THEATRE

Playbill cover for Eugene O'Neill's *The Iceman Cometh* world premier at the Martin Beck Theatre in New York. © **PLAYBILL, INC. COURTESY OF PERFORMING ARTS BOOKS. REPRODUCED BY PERMISSION.**

Source: Atkinson, Brooks. "*Iceman Cometh* Has Its World Premiere at the Martin Beck." *The New York Times,* October 10, 1946. Reprinted online at http://www.eoneill.com/artifacts/reviews/ic1_times.htm; website home page: http://www.eoneill.com (accessed February 25, 2003).

About the Author: Brooks Atkinson (1894–1984), an American theater critic and journalist, was born in Melrose, Massachusetts. Atkinson was an editor of *The New York Times* before becoming its drama critic in 1925. His tenure as the drama critic lasted until 1960, making him the dean of New York newspaper critics. On his retirement, he became the first critic to have a theater named after him.

"*The Iceman Cometh* A Terrific Hit"

Theatre review

By: Robert Coleman
Date: October 11, 1946
Source: Coleman, Robert. "*The Iceman Cometh* A Terrific Hit." *New York Mirror,* October 11, 1946. Reprinted online at http://www.eoneill.com/artifacts/reviews/ic1_mirror.htm; website home page: http://www.eoneill.com (accessed February 25, 2003).

About the Author Robert Coleman was for many years the theater critic for the *New York Mirror*. ■

Introduction

Eugene O'Neill (1888–1953) wrote *The Iceman Cometh* in 1939. It is based on his youthful experiences when he was in his twenties in New York, living in flophouses as an alcoholic, often depressed and sometimes suicidal. When *Iceman* was first produced on Broadway in 1946, the critics welcomed it, though with reservations. Running for only 136 performances, it was not popular with postwar audiences. Everything about it seemed an insult to American's can-do sense of themselves in the years immediately after World War II (1939–1945).

One can get a very good sense of the state of the Broadway theater in October 1946 by reading Brooks Atkinson's and Robert Coleman's reviews that were published the day after the play opened. Atkinson, a much-respected reviewer for the influential *The New York Times,* called O'Neill "our first dramatist" and *Iceman* one of his best plays. Coleman, writing for the *New York Mirror,* said that the play was "theatre at its finest."

O'Neill's popular successes were all in the 1920s, and he had been absent from Broadway for thirteen years. Atkinson, writing for an elite college-educated audience, likened *Iceman* to the very best of O'Neill's previous work. Coleman's readers probably did not know O'Neill's work, so he referred to the contemporary Broadway theater "pernicious anemia," since his audience was likely to be familiar with that. He portrayed O'Neill as a "pep doctor" who gave Broadway theater, with this play, a "stimulating, revivifying shot in the arm." He praised the production and the play, insisting that the excessive length was part of the bargain. Neither reviewer sugarcoated the length and wordiness of *Iceman*. Nevertheless, Coleman insisted that the show would be a terrific hit; the show never became that.

Significance

The original production of *Iceman* ran only for 136 performances and closed without many people seeing it. It was forgotten, along with the man who wrote it, for almost ten years. How then did O'Neill's play become one of the classics of the postwar stage?

First, there was great interest in O'Neill in Sweden, where because of his debt to their greatest playwright, August Strindberg, his plays were never forgotten. There was also the fact that O'Neill had been writing several autobiographical plays he did not have produced while he lived. When *Long Days Journey into Night* was produced on Broadway in the mid-1950s, it electrified the New York audience and caused renewed interest in his work. *Iceman* also became a classic because of the cul-

tural changes that swept America and the world in the next decade. Many more people started going to college, where they were exposed to literature and no doubt to O'Neill's work.

Second, the revival of *Iceman* in the 1950s was produced off Broadway at a fraction of the cost of a Broadway production. Because of low ticket prices, it was possible for many interested theatergoers to see that production.

Third, the production was videotaped for television during the so-called golden age, when serious dramas became a staple of the television networks. A four-hour production of *Iceman* was shown to an audience that was the largest to ever see a serious play. There was even a movie version made in the 1970s.

Primary Source

"*Iceman Cometh* Has Its World Premiere at the Martin Beck"

> **SYNOPSIS:** This review of *The Iceman Cometh* is respectful, even reverent, toward the playwright, the play, and the larger issues the play raises. Wartime America was not receptive to this kind of play, and *Iceman* would not take its place as one of the greatest plays of the twentieth century until its revival in the 1950s.

Mr. O'Neill has written one of his best plays. Dipping back in his memory thirty-four years, reaching down to the tatter-demalions of a mouldy barroom, he has come up with a dark and somber play that compares with the best work of his earliest period. *The Iceman Cometh,* he calls it to no one's satisfaction but his own, and it was acted with rare insight and vitality at the Martin Beck last evening. Writing it for a performance that lasts more than four hours is a sin that rests between Mr. O'Neill and his Maker. Long plays have become nothing more than a bad label with our first dramatist.

But if that is the way Mr. O'Neill wants to afflict harmless play-goers, let us accept our fate with nothing more than a polite demurer. For the only thing that matters is that he has plunged again into the black quagmire of man's illusions and composed a rigadoon of death as strange and elemental as his first works. Taking his characters again out of the lower depths, as he did in the *S. S. Glencairn* series, he is looking them over with bleak and mature introspection. And like all his best work, this one is preeminently actable. The Theatre Guild performance, under Eddie Dowling's direction, is a masterpiece of tones, rhythms and illumination.

(Left to right) James Barton, Dudley Digges, Jeanne Cagney and Ruth Gilbert in the production of *The Iceman Cometh,* New York, 1946. **AP/WIDE WORLD PHOTOS. REPRODUCED BY PERMISSION.**

The whisky-ridden derelicts who drag their broken carcasses through Harry Hope's bar came out of O'Neill's youth when he, too, was drinking too much and dreaming of becoming a writer. They are men whose only lives are illusions—"pie dreams," O'Neill calls their memories which they foolishly translate into hopes for a future that will never exist. When the play opens they are happily living together in a spirit of human rancor, broken, tired and drunken but buoyed up by romantic illusions about themselves.

What shatters their stupor is the arrival of an old comrade who has reformed. He has found peace at last, he says. He does not need whisky any more, he says, because he has purged himself of illusions and knows the full truth of himself. Instead of mak-

ing them happy, however, his reform movement destroys their decaying contentment. Without illusions, they find themselves standing alone and terrified. They cannot face the hollowness of themselves without the opium of illusions. But they are released in the last act by the awful discovery that their teacher has freed himself from illusions by committing a crime that will sit him in the electric chair. He is free from illusions because he has resigned from life and is already dead in spirit. Whereupon, the derelicts drink up again and happily relapse into the stupor of the bottle.

That is the abstract story of *The Iceman Cometh.* But the concrete drama on the stage is infinitely more flavorsome. Among its battered wretches it includes a raffish lot of social outcasts in amazing variety—an I. W. W. émigré, a broken gambler, a cop who was thrown off the force, a British infantry officer who stole regimental funds, a Boer commando leader who showed the white feather, the well-educated son of an embezzler, some prostitutes and barkeeps. The Lord knows they talk too much, for Mr. O'Neill insists on grinding their bitterness into very small and precise pieces. But it is good talk—racy, angry, comic drumbeats on the lid of doom, and a strong undercurrent of elemental drama silently washes the gloomy charnel-house where they sit waiting.

Surely it is no accident that most of Mr. O'Neill's plays act well. Although he seems on the surface to be a literal writer, interminably fussing over minor details, his best plays move across the stage as methodically and resolutely as a heavy battle attack, and over-run strategic points with a kind of lumbering precision. The performance of *The Iceman Cometh* ranks among the theatre's finest works. To house these rags and tags of the human race, Robert Edmond Jones has created a mean and dingy last refuge that nevertheless glows with an articulate meaning, like a Daumier print, as one alert spectator observed.

To anyone who loves acting, Dudley Digges' performance as the tottering and irascible saloon proprietor is worth particular cherishing. Although the old man is half dead, Mr. Digges' command of the actor's art of expressing character and theme is brilliantly alive; it overflows with comic and philosophical expression. As the messenger of peace, James Barton is also superb—common, unctuous, cheerful and fanatical; and Mr. Barton reads one of the longest speeches on record without letting it drift off into sing-song or monotony.

As the barroom's master of cosmic thinking, Carl Benton Reid is vigorously incisive, and lends substance to the entire performance. Nicholas Joy is giving the best performance of his career as the unfrocked captain. As the garrulous night bartender, Tom Pedi with his querulous vitality streaks an amusing ribbon of color throughout the drama. There are also notable performances by John Marriott, as the discredited gambler; Paul Crabtree, as an I. W. W. traitor, and E. G. Marshall, as a fallen Harvard man.

If there were any justice in the world, all the actors would get a line of applause here. But this bulletin, like Mr. O'Neill's play, is already much too garrulous. Let us cut it short with one final salute to a notable drama by a man who writes with the heart and wonder of a poet.

Primary Source

"The Iceman Cometh A Terrific Hit"

SYNOPSIS: This review represents the state of critical opinion at the time *The Iceman Cometh* opened. Coleman insisted that the show would be a terrific hit; the show never became that.

With the theatre suffering from a case of pernicious anemia, Dr. Eugene O'Neill has after a 12-year absence, left retirement last evening to give it a stimulating, revivifying shot in the arm called *The Iceman Cometh.*

O'Neill's Iceman is a sort of Janus, one side being a peripatetic philanderer and the other death. He argues that most men live on illusion, on dreams of a brighter tomorrow, and when their illusions are shattered death arrives.

The Iceman Cometh is set in Harry's bar, circa 1912. Between Greenwich Village and the Hudson, it is a refuge for bums, tarts, radicals, adventurers and seamen. Harry, the host, does not press the guests when they get behind with the rent and he's fairly generous with his red-eye.

The annual event to which the regulars look forward is the coming of Hickey, a hardware salesman, for a toot. He always brings a big bankroll and the drinks are on him while the dough lasts. But Hickey's last visit proves disturbing.

He offers drinks to those who want 'em, but won't touch the stuff himself. He's found peace and doesn't need it any longer. And he tries to help his cronies find peace by shedding their illusions by facing tomorrow today. All because he has murdered his wife to destroy her illusions that he will turn out a decent husband if she waits long enough.

After nerve-wracking experiences with Hickey's panacea, most of the bums go back to their illusions and Harry's lousy booze, but the Iceman gets a couple who can't recapture the ability to dream.

The Theatre Guild has given the fascinating O'Neill script a fine production. The cast includes James Barton, Dudley Digges, Nicholas Joy, Car Benton Reid, Morton L. Stevens, Tom Pedi, Al McGranary, E. G. Marshall, John Marriott, Frank Twedell, Russell Collins, Paul Crabtree, Leo Chalzell, Joe Marr, Ruth Gilbert, Jeanne Cagney and Marcella Markham.

They are perfect types and give such perfect performances under Eddie Dowling's direction that it smacks of the ungracious to single out individuals for special salutes.

Robert Edmond Jones has contributed a setting so real that it fairly reeks of raw alcohol, perspiration, grime and cheap perfume.

The Iceman Cometh is a lengthy play. In four acts, it is given at matinee and evening performances. It is like seeing *The Deluge, The Wild Duck, The Time of Your Life* and reading Gautier's treatise on Bovaryism in two sittings. You really get your money's worth.

It's great to have O'Neill back with us. He loves theatre as much as he loves life. He is theatre at its finest. And though he is often garrulous—like life—and has an aversion for the editor's pencil, he is continuously absorbing.

Take our advice. Rush to the Martin Beck immediately. *The Iceman Cometh* will be a terrific hit, the "top ticket" at the brokers. Get your pasteboards now—or else.

Further Resources

BOOKS

Atkinson, Brooks. *Broadway.* New York: Limelight Editions, 1990.

———. *The Lively Years, 1920–1973.* New York: New York Association Press, 1973.

Bogard, Travis. *Contours in Time: The Plays of Eugene O'Neill.* New York: Oxford University Press, 1972.

O'Neill, Eugene. *Complete Plays.* New York: Library of America, 1988.

WEBSITES

"Eugene O'Neill: The Iceman Cometh." eOneill.com. Available online at http://www.eoneill.com/artifacts/Iceman_Cometh .htm; website home page: http://www.eoneill.com (accessed February 25, 2003).

"What Hollywood Can Do"

Movie review

By: James Agee

Date: December 7 and 14, 1946

Source: Agee, James. "What Hollywood Can Do," *Time,* December 7 and 14, 1946. Reprinted in Agee, James. *Agee on Film,* vol. 1. New York: Grosset & Dunlap, 1958, 229–233.

About the Author: James Agee (1909–1955) was a movie critic, screenwriter, poet, and novelist. Born in Knoxville, Tennessee, he attended Harvard University, worked for *Fortune* in the 1930s, and then reviewed movies for *Time* and *The Nation* throughout the 1940s. *A Death in the Family* (1957), his novel based on his experiences as a six-year-old boy when his father died, was published after his death and won the Pulitzer Prize. ∎

Introduction

At Harvard, James Agee discovered his poetic abilities under the mentorship of the influential critic and poet I. A. Richards. After graduating, Agee began writing poetry and went to work as a journalist for *Fortune.*

Although he did not agree with *Fortune*'s pro-capitalist agenda, Agee was a sensitive and productive writer who produced well-respected journalism on any subject that captured his attention. He thus became a favorite of the media giant Henry Luce, the discriminating founder and publisher of *Fortune. Fortune* commissioned Agee to research and write a study of rural poverty in the South during the Great Depression. Although the article was rejected, Agee copublished it with photographer Walker Evans as *Let Us Now Praise Famous Men* in 1941. In 1941, Agee left *Fortune* to become a movie critic for *The Nation* and *Time* (another Luce publication). His reviews appeared weekly throughout the 1940s.

In his review of *The Best Years of Our Lives,* Agee was writing about a contemporary film designed to appeal to adult postwar audiences. The film recounts the experiences of three American soldiers unsuccessfully attempting to return to the lives they led before World War II (1939–1945). Agee, in an unsentimental and uncompromising way, saw the film as an example of what can be expected from serious craftsmen working in the Hollywood "factory." In concluding his review, Agee stated "the limitations which will be inevitable in any Hollywood film, no matter how skillful and sincere. But it is also a great pleasure, and equally true, to say that it shows what can be done in the [Hollywood] factory by people of adequate talent when they get, or manage to make themselves, the chance." It is rare for a reviewer to devote so much space to showing both the limitation and the merits of a film.

Significance

Agee was one of the first writers to take popular movies seriously and to write about them weekly. He viewed Hollywood films as a compromise between the conflicting demands of capitalism and culture, which often produced work that was better than expected and worthy of serious people's consideration. These well-crafted, thoughtful weekly pieces about run-of-the-mill Hollywood films contrast with the occasional longer, more reflective pieces on the golden age of Hollywood. Agee's criticism earned him a small but influential readership.

Equally important, his writing caught the attention of film director John Huston, who asked Agee to write the screenplay for *The African Queen* (1951). Agee wrote a number of other screenplays, including one

Still from the movie *The Best Years of Our Lives,* with Dana Andrews, Frederic March, and Harold Russell, 1946. **THE KOBAL COLLECTION. REPRODUCED BY PERMISSION.**

about the life of French painter Paul Gauguin (unfilmed). He also wrote one for Charles Laughton's directorial debut, *The Night of the Hunter* (1955), which like so much of Agee's work was initially misunderstood and underrated and only later recognized as ahead of its time. Agee suffered a series of heart attacks and died in 1955.

The two-volume *Agee on Film* (1958–60), a collection of his reviews and screenplays, became an instant classic in the field of film criticism and an inspiration to aspiring screenwriters and critics. Dwight MacDonald, Stanley Kaufman, and especially Pauline Kael, whose reviews became essential reading for college education audiences beginning in the 1960s, were all in his debt. Equally important, Agee served as an example of the way a serious, sensitive, and honest writer could move from criticism of films to creating them. Filmmakers such as Peter Bogdanovich and Paul Schrader also began their careers as film critics.

Primary Source

"What Hollywood Can Do"

SYNOPSIS: Agee devoted two columns to analyzing the virtues and limitations of *The Best Years of Our Lives,* a film about the experiences of World War II veterans returning home.

The Best Years of Our Lives, a misfired title seems to have started as a gleam in Samuel Goldwyn's eye when he saw in a mid-war issue of *Time* a picture and article about returning veterans. At a later stage it was a verse novel by MacKinlay Kantor called *Glory for Me*—not a very good title either. Robert E. Sherwood turned this into a screen play; the director William Wyler and the cameraman Gregg Toland and a few hundred others turned the screen play into a movie. The movie has plenty of faults, and the worst of them are painfully exasperating; yet this is one of

Still from the movie *The Best Years of Our Lives,* with Myrna Loy, Fredric March, and Teresa Wright, 1946. **THE KOBAL COLLECTION. REPRODUCED BY PERMISSION.**

the very few American studio-made movies in years that seem to me profoundly pleasing, moving, and encouraging.

The story is of a sort that could have been, and often remains, just slick-paper fiction at its most sincere, and that could also have become, and occasionally suggests, a great and simple, limpid kind of fiction which few writers of serious talent seem able to attempt or even to respect, at present. An ex-bombardier (Dana Andrews), an ex-infantry sergeant (Fredric March), and an ex-sailor (Harold Russell) meet for the first time as they return to their home city, part to undertake the various pleasures and problems of their return, and meet again at various subsequent times as their lives and relationships shake down into new shape.

The bombardier, a highly intelligent proletarian, can find nothing better in the way of a job than his old place in a drugstore. He finds, too, that he and

the girl he married just before he went overseas no longer get along. The sergeant, who was once the kind of nervously well-married, vocationless, rather sensitive business man, too good for his job, who tries to sweep along his uneasiness in a momentum of alcohol, clowning, fairly sophisticated wit, and his real but seldom focused affections, finds that none of that has changed for the better. He is made vice-president of his bank, in charge of G.I. loans, and spends a good deal of his time drunk. The sailor, who has lost both hands and has learned to use a pair of hooks quite well, returns to the gentlest and most touching depths of the lower middle class. His chief problem is the girl he had always expected to marry; another is his extreme uneasiness about everybody's attempt to be good about his hooks; a hideous complication is that he is at once intuitively very perceptive and sensitive, and hopelessly inarticulate, and that most of the people he returns to are equally well-meaning and unsophisticated.

At its worst this story is very annoying in its patness, its timidity, its slithering attempts to pretend to face and by that pretense to dodge in the most shameful way possible its own fullest meanings and possibilities. Perhaps one shouldn't kick too hard at a "mere" device, but I feel very dubious about the invention of a nice bar in which the veterans keep meeting each other, perhaps because I suspect that one of the dodged truths is that, once they become civilians again, most men of such disparate classes or worlds would meet seldom, with greater embarrassment than friendliness, and that the picture is here presenting, instead of the unhappy likelihood, a hopeful and barely plausible lie. I feel a good deal of interest in the love affair that develops between Andrews and the banker's daughter, played by Teresa Wright, but again they have made it easy for themselves by showing Andrew's wife to be a bag, and they atone for this convenience only in part by making her as well-meaning and sympathetic and essentially innocent as, in terms invented for her, she could be. Thanks to much of the writing and all of the playing, this illicit affair is by implication remarkably real and mature; but in action, in the good old inevitable Sunday School way, the extra-marital activities are limited to a single Andrews-Wright kiss and a boy-friend, for Andrew's wife, lolling in his shirt-sleeves; and it is the wife who asks for a divorce.

Or again, they pretend to hit the banker's predicament between the eyes, and allow him to tell off his careful world which doesn't want to make loans to veterans without collateral in a speech which, on the movie scale of things, is reasonably bold. They even have the firmness to let March have the last word on that issue; he says that with nearly every loan without collateral he will have to put up the same fight all over again. Yet one is emotionally left with the impression that he has cleverly and lovably won his fight and will win it on every subsequent occasion, and the hints that his own bread and butter are and will be increasingly in jeopardy if he keeps his courage are so discreet as to be all but inaudible. As a footnote to this his boss, played by Ray Collins, is represented, not with the cool realism which could here have been so good and so nearly unprecedented in an American movie, but in the kind of skillful caricature which, like so much of Gilbert and Sullivan, makes every punch a kind of self-caress.

The only boss types represented cruelly are the manager and floor-walker of a chain drugstore—that is, men in a job predicament in which they are as much bullied as bullying; and it is not shown that they are bullied. The only business type who is represented with what seems like perfect justice is the father of the sailor's sweetheart, a specialized, fussy, feminine little man who nervously tries to badger the sailor about his plans for the future. Or for still another major fault—and here direction and playing are as much to blame as the script—the very interesting and, for movies, new character of the banker is only hinted at, not solidly presented. Only the psychologically sophisticated can gather from the film that his marriage is only nominally happy and is actually precarious, and that the people who made the movie may possibly be on to this; and March's benders, though extremely well done in their way, are staged with all but frantic gratitude as broad comic relief, as if professional entertainers who were also good artists were on these occasions very glad to betray their responsibilities as artists for the sake of getting a little bit of sure-fire—and commercially much-needed—fun into the show.

In fact, it would be possible, I don't doubt, to call the whole picture just one long pious piece of deceit and self-deceit, embarrassed by hot flashes of talent, conscience, truthfulness, and dignity. And it is anyhow more than possible, it is unhappily obligatory, to observe that a good deal which might have been very fine, even great, and which is handled mainly by people who could have done, and done perfectly, all the best that could have been developed out of the idea, is here either murdered in its cradle or reduced to manageable good citizenship in the early stages of grade school. Yet I feel a hundred times more liking and admiration for the film than distaste or disappointment.

It seems to me that the movie's basic weaknesses are in the script—or are more likely, in the writer's knowledge of all that he would have to go easy on as a part of the rather remarkable bargain by which he got away with all that he managed to. Yet this is a most unusually good screen play. Although the dialogue has a continuous sheen of entertainment slickness it is also notably well-differentiated, efficient, free of tricks of snap and punch and over-design, and modest in its feeling for how much weight it should carry on the screen; and most of the time there is an openness about the writing which I don't doubt every good screen writer tries for but which few achieve. By openness I mean simply that the scenes are so planned, and the lines so laid down, that every action and reaction, every motion and everything that is seen, is more centrally eloquent than the spoken lines. The movie thus has and takes its chance to be born in front of the camera, whereas the general run of screen plays force what takes place before the camera to be a mere redigestion of a predigestion.

With a director and camera man in charge so gifted as Messrs. Wyler and Toland it is impossible to guess which of them, or Mr. Sherwood, is most to be thanked for the great force, simplicity, and beauty of some of the scenes and countless of the camera set-ups; so it is purely my hunch, with apologies in advance, that the real heroes in this film are Wyler and Toland, with invaluable assists credited to the set designer and art director, who provide some of the best stages for the action that I have ever seen in a movie. I can't think of a single shot of Toland's that doesn't show the amount of will, creative energy, and taste, and doesn't add with perfect power and modesty its own special kind of expressiveness, which of course ought to be evident in every shot in every good movie, and which of course plenty of people try for without more than spasmodically achieving. I can't remember a more thoroughly satisfying job of photography, in an American movie, since *Greed*. Aesthetically and in its emotional feeling for people and their surroundings, Toland's work in this film makes me think of the photographs of Walker Evans. Toland either lacks or subsumes any equivalent intellect, irony, and delight in the varieties of texture, edge, meaning, mystery, and shape in clothing and in all inanimate things; but it is a question how much such powers of perception could be used in telling a story in motion.

William Wyler has always seemed to me an exceedingly sincere and good director; he now seems one of the few great ones. He has come back from the war with a style of great purity, directness, and warmth, about as cleanly devoid of mannerism, haste, superfluous motion, aesthetic or emotional over-reaching, as any I know; and I felt complete confidence, as I watched this work, that he could have handled any degree to which this material might have been matured as well as or even better than the job he was given to do. His direction of the nonprofessional, Harold Russell, is just an exciting proof, on the side, of the marvels a really good artist can perform in collaboration with a really good non-actor; much more of the time it was his job to get new and better things out of professionals than they had ever shown before. One conspicuous failure—good as it is in its regrettable way—is March in his drunk scenes; and Myrna Loy, as his wife, is surprisingly uneven. But March is far outside his normal habits, and very good indeed, in, for instance, his interview with Dana Andrews over the question of the March

daughter. And such a scene as that in which the sailor's father helps him get ready for bed seems to me so quietly perfect that I would set it in the world with the best fiction, or poetic drama, or movies that I know.

Almost without exception, down through such virtually noiseless bit roles as that of the mother of the sailor's fiancee, this film is so well cast and acted that there is no possible room to speak of all the people I wish I might. I cannot, however, resist speaking briefly, anyhow, of Teresa Wright. Like Frances Dee, she has always been one of the very few women in movies who really had a face. Like Miss Dee, she has also always used this translucent face with delicate and exciting talent as an actress, and with something of a novelist's perceptiveness behind the talent. And like Miss Dee, she has never been around nearly enough. This new performance of hers, entirely lacking in big scenes, tricks, or obstreperousness—one can hardly think of it as acting—seems to me one of the wisest and most beautiful pieces of work I have seen in years. If the picture had none of the hundreds of other things it has to recommend it, I could watch it a dozen times over for that personality and its mastery alone.

I can hardly expect that anyone who reads this will like the film as well as I do. It is easy, and true, to say that it suggests the limitations which will be inevitable in any Hollywood film, no matter how skillful and sincere. But it is also a great pleasure, and equally true, to say that it shows what can be done in the factory by people of adequate talent when they get, or manage to make themselves, the chance.

Further Resources

BOOKS

Agee, James. *Agee on Film*. 2 vols. New York: Grosset and Dunlap, 1958–60.

———. *The Collected Poems*. Robert Fitzgerald, ed. Boston: Houghton Mifflin, 1968.

———. *The Collected Short Prose*. Robert Fitzgerald, ed. Boston: Houghton Mifflin, 1968.

———. *Letters of James Agee to Father Flye*. Boston: Houghton Mifflin, 1971.

Barson, Alfred. *A Way of Seeing: A Critical Study of James Agee*. Amherst: University of Massachusetts Press, 1972.

Bergreen, Laurence. *James Agee: A Life*. New York: Dutton, 1984.

Böger, Astrid. *Documenting Lives: James Agee's and Walker Evans's "Let Us Now Praise Famous Men."* New York: Peter Lang, 1994.

WEBSITES
"James Agee." Public Broadcasting Service. Available online at http://www.pbs.org/wnet/ihas/poet/agee.html; website home page: http://www.pbs.org (accessed February 26, 2003).

"The Gangster As Tragic Hero"
Essay

By: Robert Warshow

Date: 1948

Source: Warshow, Robert. *The Immediate Experience: Movies, Comics, Theatre, and Other Aspects of Popular Culture.* Garden City, N.Y.: Doubleday, 1962, 85–88.

About the Author: Robert Warshow (1917–1955) was an influential writer on popular culture who was born in New York City. He graduated from the University of Michigan and served as a translator and research analyst for the U.S. Army during World War II. After the war, he returned to New York to work as an editor and writer for *Commentary* magazine. He wrote about popular culture, especially the movies, for *Commentary, The Nation,* and *Partisan Review.* He died of a heart attack at age thirty-seven. ∎

Introduction

Warshow wrote for the so-called little magazines, that is, small circulation journals that provided intelligent analysis and honest criticism of the arts, culture, and politics during the 1940s and 1950s, when such writing was in short supply. Unconventional ideas and serious writing appealed to a small pool of influential and elite readers. Despite their tiny readership, these journals had a great influence on culture. Popular mass-market magazines, such as *Life* and *Time,* were quick to hire their most talented writers, like James Agee.

In one of his articles, Warshow wrote, "a man watches a movie, and the critic must acknowledge that he is that man." Warshow was one of the first American intellectuals to see the moral and political significance of popular culture. He was interested in the motives that led him and others to read the work of scholars like T. S. Eliot and Henry James, on the one hand, and to view the popular culture movies of Humphrey Bogart, on the other hand. As he wrote in a grant application for a Guggenheim Fellowship, "That there is a connection between the two impulses I do not doubt, but the connection is not adequately summed up in the statement that the Bogart movie and the Eliot poem are both works of art. To define the connection seems to me to be one of the tasks of film criticism, and the definition must be a personal one."

Warshow wrote about certain genres of Hollywood movies, such as gangster and Western films, because he saw in them many subtle assumptions and convictions about our American way of life. They are unstated or unspoken because they are somehow beyond the realm of mature adult conversation and for that reason interesting and important to bring to light and analyze.

Significance

Warshow wrote about certain kinds of movies because of their "pervasive and disturbing power." Today, people may not realize how unusual it was for an intellectual to be engaged in thinking about popular culture. In the postwar period, few critics or academics were prepared to stake their reputations on anything so lowbrow as Hollywood movies. Fewer still wrote about them with Warshow's intelligence and sensitivity.

In his essay "The Gangster As Tragic Hero," Warshow wrote about the gangster film genre so as to illuminate a division in the American mind: between the pursuit of happiness and the rhetoric of "you can have it all" and the recognition that such a pursuit can never be satisfied. This contradiction underlies the popular appeal of the gangster film from 1932's *Scarface* to *The Godfather* (1972) and beyond. Warshow noted that the gangster appeals not only to feelings of impatience and alienation, but also more profoundly to that side of all of us "which refuses to believe in the normal possibilities of happiness and achievement." He observed, "The gangster is the 'no' to the great American 'yes' which is stamped so big over our official culture and yet has so little to do with the way we really feel about our lives." The gangster is popular in American culture because of our unspoken awareness that the moral and political limit set by democratic principles stands in the way of our full pursuit of happiness. The gangster is a tragic hero when even he cannot achieve happiness.

Warshow's insightful essay was widely read in the film schools of the 1960s, where it influenced the generation of filmmakers of the 1970s, such as George Lucas, Martin Scorsese, and Francis Ford Coppola. This is probably nowhere more clearly seen than in Coppola's *Godfather* trilogy and Lucas's *Star Wars* series.

Primary Source

"The Gangster As Tragic Hero" [excerpt]

> **SYNOPSIS:** In an excerpt from the following article, Warshow analyzes the cultural and social aspects of the character of the gangster and the genre of the gangster film, as well as what the gangster represented to American moviegoers in the 1940s.

Thus the importance of the gangster film, and the nature and intensity of its emotional and aesthetic

Paul Muni (second from left) stars in the 1932 film, *Scarface*, directed by Howard Hawks. Loosely based on the life of Al Capone, the film was the most violent and controversial of the gangster genre of that time. **COURTESY OF THE KOBAL COLLECTION. REPRODUCED BY PERMISSION.**

impact, cannot be measured in terms of the place of the gangster himself or the importance of the problem of crime in American life. Those European movie-goers who think there is a gangster on every corner in New York are certainly deceived, but defenders of the "positive" side of American culture are equally deceived if they think it relevant to point out that most Americans have never seen a gangster. What matters is that the experience of the gangster *as an experience of art* is universal to Americans. There is almost nothing we understand better or react to more readily or with quicker intelligence. The Western film, though it seems never to diminish in popularity, is for most of us no more than the folklore of the past, familiar and understandable only because it has been repeated so often. The gangster film comes much closer. In ways that we do not easily or willingly define, the gangster speaks for us, expressing that part of the American psyche which rejects the qualities and the demands of modern life, which rejects "Americanism" itself.

The gangster is the man of the city, with the city's language and knowledge, with its queer and dishonest skills and its terrible daring, carrying his life in his hands like a placard, like a club. For everyone else, there is at least the theoretical possibility of another world—in that happier American culture which the gangster denies, the city does not really exist; it is only a more crowded and more brightly lit country—but for the gangster there is only the city; he must inhabit it in order to personify it: not the real city, but that dangerous and sad city of the imagination which is so much more important, which is the modern world. And the gangster—though there are real gangsters—is also, and primarily, a creature of the imagination. The real city, one might say, produces only criminals; the imaginary city produces the gangster: he is what we want to be and what we are afraid we may become.

Thrown into the crowd without background or advantages, with only those ambiguous skills which the rest of us—the real people of the real city—can only pretend to have, the gangster is required to make his way, to make his life and impose it on others. Usually, when we come upon him, he has already made his choice or the choice has already been made for him, it doesn't matter which: we are not permitted to ask whether at some point he could have chosen to be something else than what he is.

The gangster's activity is actually a form of rational enterprise, involving fairly definite goals and various techniques for achieving them. But this rationality is usually no more than a vague background; we know, perhaps, that the gangster sells liquor or that he operates a numbers racket; often we are not given even that much information. So his activity becomes a kind of pure criminality: he hurts people. Certainly our response to the gangster film is most consistently and most universally a response to sadism; we gain the double satisfaction of participating vicariously in the gangster's sadism and then seeing it turned against the gangster himself.

But on another level the quality of irrational brutality and the quality of rational enterprise become one. Since we do not see the rational and routine aspects of the gangster's behavior, the practice of brutality—the quality of unmixed criminality—becomes the totality of his career. At the same time, we are always conscious that the whole meaning of this career is a drive for success: the typical gangster film presents a steady upward progress followed by a very precipitate fall. Thus brutality itself becomes at once the means to success and the content of success—a success that is defined in its most general terms, not as accomplishment or specific gain, but simply as the unlimited possibility of aggression. (In the same way, film presentations of businessmen tend to make it appear that they achieve their success by talking on the telephone and holding conferences and that success *is* talking on the telephone and holding conferences.)

From this point of view, the initial contact between the film and its audience is an agreed conception of human life: that man is a being with the possibilities of success or failure. This principle, too, belongs to the city; one must emerge from the crowd or else one is nothing. On that basis the necessity of the action is established, and it progresses by inalterable paths to the point where the gangster lies dead and the principle has been modified: there is really only one possibility—failure. The final meaning of the city is anonymity and death.

In the opening scene of *Scarface,* we are shown a successful man; we know he is successful because he has just given a party of opulent proportions and because he is called Big Louie. Through some monstrous lack of caution, he permits himself to be alone for a few moments. We understand from this immediately that he is about to be killed. No convention of the gangster film is more strongly established than this: it is dangerous to be alone. And yet the very conditions of success make it impossible not to be alone, for success is always the establishment of an *individual* pre-eminence that must be imposed on others, in whom it automatically arouses hatred; the successful man is an outlaw. The gangster's whole life is an effort to assert himself as an individual, to draw himself out of the crowd, and he always dies *because* he is an individual; the final bullet thrusts him back, makes him, after all, a failure. "Mother of God," says the dying Little Caesar, "is this the end of Rico?"—speaking of himself thus in the third person because what has been brought low is not the undifferentiated *man,* but the individual with a name, the gangster, the success; even to himself he is a creature of the imagination. (T. S. Eliot has pointed out that a number of Shakespeare's tragic heroes have this trick of looking at themselves dramatically; their true identity, the thing that is destroyed when they die, is something outside themselves—not a man, but a style of life, a kind of meaning.)

At bottom, the gangster is doomed because he is under the obligation to succeed, not because the means he employs are unlawful. In the deeper layers of the modern consciousness, *all* means are unlawful, every attempt to succeed is an act of aggression, leaving one alone and guilty and defenseless among enemies: one is *punished* for success. This is our intolerable dilemma. That failure is a kind of death and success is evil and dangerous, is—ultimately—impossible. The effect of the gangster film is to embody this dilemma in the person of the gangster and resolve it by his death. The dilemma is resolved because it is *his* death, not ours. We are safe; for the moment, we can acquiesce in our failure, we can choose to fail.

Further Resources
BOOKS
Warshow, Robert. *The Immediate Experience: Movies, Comics, Theatre, and Other Aspects of Popular Culture.* Garden City, N.Y.: Doubleday, 1962. Republished Cambridge, Mass.: Harvard University Press, 2002.

WEBSITES
"Crime and Gangster Films." The Greatest Films. Available online at · http://www.filmsite.org/crimefilms.html; website home page: http://www.filmsite.org (accessed February 26, 2003).

"The Public Enemy Website." Public Broadcasting Service. Available online at http://www.pbs.org/wgbh/amex/dillinger/index.html; website home page: http://www.pbs.org (accessed February 26, 2003).

The Ultimate Gangster and Crime Film Website. Available online at http://www.geocities.com/~mikemckiernan/ (accessed February 26, 2003).

"Jackson Pollock: Is He the Greatest Living Painter in the United States?"

Magazine article

By: *Life*

Date: August 8, 1949

Source: "Jackson Pollock: Is He the Greatest Living Painter in the United States?" *Life,* August 8, 1949, 42–45.

About the Artist: Jackson Pollock (1912–1956), born in Cody, Wyoming, was the leading painter of the abstract expressionism school. In 1930, he moved to Greenwich Village in New York City. Under the influence of surrealism and psychoanalytic therapy, he began to develop his own notions of artistic expression, which led to the drip technique. In 1945, he married Lee Krasner, another abstract expressionist painter. He was killed in an automobile accident in 1956. ■

Introduction

At the Art Students League in New York, Jackson Pollock studied under Thomas Hart Benton, one of the leading regionalists among American painters. Although a conservative painter, Benton was famous for twisting muscular forms and for his hard-living personality, both of which attracted Pollock. Benton was his friend and mentor for more than ten years. But Pollock was intellectually restless.

He soon found the work of the Mexican muralists Jose Clemente Orozco and Diego Rivera more exciting. In 1936, he joined the experimental workshop of David Alfaro Siqueiros. Toward the end of the decade, Pollock began Jungian psychoanalysis, partly to treat his alcoholism. This therapy led him to seek new ways to express art in the vast realms of the unconscious. Following the lead of the surrealists, many of whom were now living in New York, he began to experiment with accident and intuition.

By the mid-1940s, Pollock moved toward a completely abstract or nonrepresentational art in order to express feeling, rather than to illustrate it. In 1947–1948, he devised a radically new approach. By pouring and dripping paint onto a canvas on the floor, he created work that redefined the categories of painting and drawing. Pollock emphasized the expressive power of the artist's gestures, materials, and tools, often applying paint with sticks, trowels, and palette knives instead of with brushes. He challenged the concept of easel painting by working on large canvases placed either on the floor or fixed to a wall. With no apparent beginning or end, the resulting paintings extend beyond the edges of the canvas. The network of drips, splatters, and lines that animate his paintings was meant to unleash the artist's subconscious mood.

Engaged in psychoanalytic therapy, Jackson Pollock developed his own notions of artistic expression, which led to the drip technique used in many of his works. © 2002 THE POLLOCK-KRASNER FOUNDATION/ ARTISTS RIGHTS SOCIETY (ARS), NEW YORK. REPRODUCED BY PERMISSION OF ARTISTS RIGHTS SOCIETY, INC.

Significance

Although leading art critics such as Clement Greenberg supported him, Pollock nevertheless was subject to mockery. In 1956, just before his death, *Time* magazine dubbed him "Jack the Dripper." His unhappy personal life and his premature death in a car crash helped him become one of the legends of modern art; however, his work and its significance are still misunderstood.

Although Pollock's drip period lasted only from 1947 to 1951 (in the 1950s he went back to figurative work), his reputation and influence rest on these paintings. And even though these works now exemplify the extraordinary balance between accident and control that Pollock maintained, they were the subject of uncomprehending ridicule by people who only read the *Life*'s 1949 feature on him and looked at the poor-quality black-and-white reproductions.

The reaction of the general public to such an unorthodox approach to painting, along with the claims for its leading proponent in a popular magazine, led to a counterreaction. People mocked and sneered at Pollock. In the early 1950s, Pollock became a household name in America, but it was as a punch line to a bad joke. He was popularly considered to be a type of undisciplined bo-hemian or "beat" artist.

This was after all the period when Hollywood was grinding out movie versions of the lives of tortured mad foreign artists like Vincent van Gogh and Henri de Toulouse-Lautrec. The very terms that *Life* and other magazines used to describe his unorthodox creative process hardly suggested the diversity of Pollock's movements (flicking, splattering, and dribbling) or the lyrical, often spiritual, compositions they produced. Pol-lock was the victim as much as he was the beneficiary of the popular press's interest in him.

Primary Source

"Jackson Pollock: Is He the Greatest Living Painter in the United States?"

SYNOPSIS: Pollock's work was lauded by some of his contemporaries, and ridiculed by others. *Life*'s 1949 article on him reflects this. It describes Pol-lock's critical and commercial success, asking in the title: "Is He the Greatest Living Painter in the United States?" Yet the overall tone of the article borders on mockery. Pollock—a very serious man—was not amused.

Jackson Pollock paints onto a canvas on the floor, a technique that became his signature. © ESTATE OF RUDOLPH BURCKHARDT/LICENSED BY VAGA, NEW YORK, NY. BURCKHARDT RUDOLPH/ CORBIS SYGMA. REPRODUCED BY PERMISSION.

Recently a formidably high-brow New York critic hailed the brooding, puzzled-looking man [Pollock] . . . as a major artist of our time and a fine candi-date to become "the greatest American painter of the 20th Century." Others believe that Jackson Pol-lock produces nothing more than interesting, if in-explicable, decorations. Still others condemn his pictures as degenerate and find them as unpalat-able as yesterday's macaroni. Even so, Pollock, at the age of 37, has burst forth as the shining new phenomenon of American art.

Pollock was virtually unknown in 1944. Now his paintings hang in five U.S. museums and 40 private collections. Exhibiting in New York last winter, he sold 12 out of 18 pictures. Moreover his work has stirred up a fuss in Italy, and this autumn he is slated for a one-man show in *avantgarde* Paris, where he is fast becoming the most talked-of and controver-sial U.S. painter. He has also won a following among his own neighbors in the village of Springs, N.Y., who amuse themselves by trying to decide what his paint-ings are about. His grocer bought one which he iden-tifies for bewildered visiting salesmen as an aerial view of Siberia. . . .

Jackson Pollock was born in Cody, Wyo. He stud-ied in New York under Realist Thomas Benton but soon gave this up in utter frustration and turned to

his present style. When Pollock decides to start a painting, the first thing he does is to tack a large piece of canvas on the floor of his barn. "My paint-ing does not come from the easel," he explains, writ-ing in a small magazine called *Possibilities 1*." I need the resistance of a hard surface." Working on the floor gives him room to scramble around the can-vas, attacking it from the top, the bottom or the side (if his pictures can be said to have a top, a bottom or a side) as the mood suits him. In this way, "I can . . . literally be *in* the painting." He surrounds him-self with quart cans of aluminum paint and many hues of ordinary household enamel. Then, starting anywhere on the canvas, he goes to work. Some-times he dribbles the paint on with a brush. Some-times he scrawls it on with a stick, scoops it with a trowel or even pours it on straight out of the can. In with it all he deliberately mixes sand, broken glass, nails, screws or other foreign matter lying around. Cigaret ashes and an occasional dead bee some-times get in the picture inadvertently.

"When I am *in* my painting," says Pollock, "I'm not aware of what I'm doing." To find out what he has been doing he stops and contemplates the pic-ture during what he calls his "get acquainted" pe-riod. Once in a while a lifelike image appears in the painting by mistake. But Pollock cheerfully rubs it out because the picture must retain "a life of its own." Finally, after days of brooding and doodling, Pollock decides the painting is finished, a deduction few others are equipped to make.

Further Resources

BOOKS

Frank, Elizabeth. *Jackson Pollock.* New York: Abbeville, 1983.

Naifeh, Steven, and Gregory White Smith. *Jackson Pollock: An American Saga.* New York: HarperPerennial, 1991.

Solomon, Deborah. *Jackson Pollock: A Biography.* New York: Simon and Schuster, 1987.

Varnedoe, Kirk, and Pepe Karmel. *Jackson Pollock: New Approaches.* New York: Museum of Modern Art, 1999.

WEBSITES

"Jackson Pollock." National Gallery of Art. Available online at http://www.nga.gov/feature/pollock/pollockhome.html; website home page: http://www.nga.gov (accessed February 26, 2003).

"Jackson Pollock." Artcyclopedia.com. Available online at http://www.artcyclopedia.com/artists/pollock_jackson.html; website home page: http://www.artcyclopedia.com (accessed February 26, 2003).

AUDIO AND VIDUAL MEDIA

Jackson Pollock: Love and Death of Long Island. Directed by Teresa Griffiths. BBC Arts. Videocassette, 1999.

Pollock. Directed by Ed Harris. Sony Pictures Classics. 2000.

William Faulkner's Nobel Prize Acceptance Speech

Speech

By: William Faulkner

Date: December 10, 1950

Source: Faulkner, William. Nobel prize acceptance speech. December 10, 1950. Available online at http://www.nobel.se /literature/laureates/1949/; website home page: http://www .nobel.se (accessed February 26, 2003).

About the Author: William Faulkner (1897–1962) was born and lived most of his life Mississippi. In a series of novels and short stories he wrote a monumental history of Yoknapatawpha County, an imaginary place based on his home. *The Sound and the Fury* (1929) is the most famous of these works. He did not initially meet with success, but after World War II (1939–1945) critics took notice of his work and Faulkner is now regarded as one of the twentieth century's greatest novelists. He won the Nobel Prize for Literature in 1949. Faulkner also worked as a screenwriter on such films as *To Have and Have Not* (1944), *The Big Sleep* (1946), and *Land of the Pharaohs* (1955). ∎

Introduction

William Faulkner's early conviction that he was commercially unpublishable gave him the independence to write only for himself and a small group of readers. His determination to do it his way gave his work a depth, honesty, and complexity unmatched in the American literature of his time.

Although Faulkner did not finish high school and he spent only a year at the University of Mississippi, he was a serious reader of the nineteenth-century writers Honoré de Balzac and Charles Dickens, from whom he took his conception of the novelist as a historian of the human heart in a specific time and place. He also sympathized with the modernist experiments in the narrative technique of Joseph Conrad and James Joyce. It was no longer possible for Faulkner to tell a story the way the narrators in Balzac and Dickens did through an all-knowing character. Instead, he combined the historical ambitions of the nineteenth-century novelists with the methods of the twentieth-century modernists. For him to tell a story, it was necessary to create vivid but limited characters who could only tell their side of the story. By putting these characters' narratives together, he offered the best possibility of arriving at a better sense of the complex truth about "the human heart and its conflicts."

His choice of subject matter was dictated by a desire to penetrate to the intimate heart of the South and in particular of the little part of Mississippi where he and his ancestors had always lived. He sought the isolation of the small town of Oxford, where he lived most of his life and mined as the raw material for his imaginary history of Yoknapatawpha County.

Significance

French literary critics were among the first to recognize Faulkner's greatness. His books were studied and translated there, and he had a large and lasting influence on the French letters. Understanding and appreciation in the United States lagged far behind. This was in no small part due to Faulkner himself, who had no interest in marketing his work or even clarifying what he was doing. Malcolm Cowley, a friend and literary editor, had the idea of organizing the stories and novels chronologically for his edition of the *Portable Faulkner* in 1946. After this, Faulkner's achievements began to be more widely understood and appreciated in the United States. Cleanth Brooks, the dean of the New Critics, which was the most influential movement in English departments during this period, became his powerful champion. In *The Hidden God* (1963), he placed Faulkner with T. S. Eliot and Joyce as one of the greatest of modern writers.

By the time the Nobel committee picked him for the award in literature in 1949, Faulkner had become the

William Faulkner receives his 1949 Nobel Prize for literature by King Gustaf VI of Sweden at the Stockholm Concert Hall, on December 10, 1950. The 1949 prize was awarded in 1950 because judges could not decide on a winner. AP/WIDE WORLD PHOTOS. REPRODUCED BY PERMISSION.

highbrow American writer par excellence. Faulkner's speech, which seemed to have overcome whatever barrier there still was between him and the general reading public, was a great affirmation of the human spirit and the dignity of man to be made in the twentieth century; it was all the more inspiring to have come from a novelist whose work was devoted to an uncompromising and somewhat dispiriting analysis of the ultimate destruction of the aristocratic heritage of the old South after the Civil War (1861–1865).

Following his Nobel Prize Faulkner was lionized, with each of his new novels becoming best-sellers and many of his works adapted for the stage and screen. His influence can be seen in the work of such different writers as Norman Mailer, Truman Capote, and Toni Morrison.

Primary Source

William Faulkner's Nobel Prize Acceptance Speech

SYNOPSIS: Faulkner sums up his credo as a novelist and a man in his acceptance speech written in much the same poetic and almost Biblical style he used in his fiction. Faulkner delivered this speech in 1950 because a dispute among the Nobel judges delayed the delivery of his 1949 award until that year.

I feel that this award was not made to me as a man, but to my work—a life's work in the agony and sweat of the human spirit, not for glory and least of all for profit, but to create out of the materials of the human spirit something which did not exist before. So this award is only mine in trust. It will not be difficult to find a dedication for the money part of it commensurate with the purpose and significance of its origin. But I would like to do the same with the acclaim too, by using this moment as a pinnacle from which I might be listened to by the young men and women already dedicated to the same anguish and travail, among whom is already that one who will some day stand where I am standing.

Our tragedy today is a general and universal physical fear so long sustained by now that we can even bear it. There are no longer problems of the spirit. There is only one question: When will I be blown up? Because of this, the young man or woman writing today has forgotten the problems of the human heart in conflict with itself which alone can make good writing because only that is worth writing about, worth the agony and the sweat.

He must learn them again. He must teach himself that the basest of all things is to be afraid: and, teaching himself that, forget it forever, leaving no room in his workshop for anything but the old verities and truths of the heart, the universal truths lacking which any story is ephemeral and doomed—love and honor and pity and pride and compassion and sacrifice. Until he does so, he labors under a curse. He writes not of love but of lust, of defeats in which nobody loses anything of value, of victories without hope and, worst of all, without pity or compassion. His griefs grieve on no universal bones, leaving no scars. He writes not of the heart but of the glands.

Until he learns these things, he will write as though he stood among and watched the end of man. I decline to accept the end of man. It is easy enough to say that man is immortal simply because he will endure: that when the last ding-dong of doom has clanged and faded from the last worthless rock hanging tideless in the last red and dying evening, that even then there will still be one more sound: that of his puny inexhaustible voice, still talking. I refuse to accept this. I believe that man will not merely endure: he will prevail. He is immortal, not because he alone among creatures has an inexhaustible voice, but because he has a soul, a spirit capable of compassion and sacrifice and endurance. The poet's, the writer's, duty is to write about these things. It is his privilege to help man endure by lifting his heart, by reminding him of the courage and honor and hope and pride and compassion and pity and sacrifice which have been the glory of his past. The poet's voice need not merely be the record of man, it can be one of the props, the pillars to help him endure and prevail.

Further Resources

BOOKS

Brooks, Cleanth. *The Hidden God: Studies in Hemingway, Faulkner, Yeats, Eliot and Warren.* New Haven, Conn.: Yale University Press, 1963.

———. *William Faulkner: The Yoknapatawpha Country.* New Haven, Conn.: Yale University Press, 1966.

Faulkner, William. *As I Lay Dying.* New York: Random House, 1964.

———. *Novels.* New York: Library of America, 1985.

———. *The Portable Faulkner.* Malcolm Cowley, ed. New York: Penguin, 1977.

———. *The Sound and the Fury.* New York: Random House, 1984.

WEBSITES

"William Faulkner: Related Sites." Université Rennes 2, Haute Bretagne. Available online at http://www.uhb.fr/faulkner/WF/Related_Sites.htm; website home page: http://www.uhb.fr (accessed February 26, 2003).

"William Faulkner on the Web." University of Mississippi. Available online at http://www.mcsr.olemiss.edu/~egjbp/faulkner/faulkner.html; website home page: http://www.mcsr.olemiss.edu (accessed February 26, 2003).

"The American Theatre"

Magazine article

By: Arthur Miller

Date: 1954

Source: Miller, Arthur. "The American Theatre." *Holiday,* 1954. Reprinted in *The Passionate Playgoer.* George Oppenheimer, ed. New York: Viking, 1962, 29–32.

About the Author: Arthur Miller (1915–) is one of the foremost playwrights of the postwar American theater. Born and raised in New York City, he studied journalism at the University of Michigan. His works include *All My Sons* (1947), *Death of a Salesman* (1949), and *The Crucible* (1953). ∎

Introduction

Arthur Miller's first full-length play for Broadway, *The Man Who Had All the Luck* (1944), lasted less than a week. His first success was *All My Sons,* a play that centers on the corruption of a successful defense industry businessman and the consequences for his family. His next play, *Death of a Salesman,* won the Pulitzer Prize for drama and almost every other award for best play in 1949. It remains his greatest achievement. In the play, Willy Loman, a traveling salesman, suffers a nervous breakdown after being fired. This leads to the recognition of his failure as a businessman, father, and husband.

Miller was hailed as the great American playwright when *Salesman* opened. From the start, Miller wanted to write a different kind of play from other playwrights. Miller's plays were about the plight of ordinary men and women in postwar America struggling to attain the American dream and failing. Despite their failure and the fact that they were ordinary, he wanted to show the Broadway audience that "attention must finally be paid to such men." Miller's commitment to being natural on stage does not mean he was dead to the magic of the theater. His best plays are intensely theatrical with splendid monologues and searing debates.

In his article "The American Theatre," one sees that Miller is very much in love with the theater. He wrote this article a few years after his great successes on Broadway. It is a loving, discerning study of the trials and tribulations, triumphs and defeats of the actors who collaborate with the writer to create the characters. Miller provides a behind-the-scenes look at what makes the theater different from film or television: the mystery of the stage performance.

Critics have praised Arthur Miller's realistic dramas that explore the complex psychological and social issues that plagued humankind in the wake of World War II. THE LIBRARY OF CONGRESS.

Significance

Miller believed that it was possible to reinvent tragedy for contemporary audiences by replacing the protagonists of the traditional plays, kings, aristocrats, and the like, with middle-class men and women. By being scrupulously honest to the language of such people, he thought he could achieve his goal. Even today, professors of drama continue to debate the question of whether *Salesman* is a new kind of tragedy or a failed attempt to revive a dead form.

Regardless, the play's insistence on the importance of listening to "little" men who have been broken by society has had the greatest influence on both American and British playwrights. The careers of several key playwrights, most importantly David Mamet, owe everything to Miller's example. And *Salesman* has shown by its longevity around the world over for five decades that it is a dramatic masterpiece. The play speaks to a universal audience about the pressures of modern society on middle-class individuals who struggle to maintain their dignity, decency, and self-respect within the conditions that society imposes. Miller even directed a production of the play in Peking with a cast of Chinese actors.

Miller wrote timely plays after this, including *The Crucible,* which represents the communist witch-hunts

during the McCarthy era, and *A View From the Bridge* (1955), a modern Greek tragedy set in Brooklyn. But none of his other plays generated the acclaim of *Salesman.* Miller was an unfriendly witness before the House Un-American Activities Committee, which probably hurt his career in the 1950s. His marriage to Marilyn Monroe ended in divorce, and *After the Fall* (1964), his play about their relationship, was blasted by critics. He has continued to produce great work despite these personal and political setbacks.

Primary Source

"The American Theatre" [excerpt]

> **SYNOPSIS:** In the following excerpt, Miller describes what went on backstage during the auditions and rehearsals of *Death of a Salesman* on Broadway.

The production of a new play, I have often thought, is like another chance in life, a chance to emerge cleansed of one's imperfections. Here, as when one was very young, it seems possible again to attain even greatness, or happiness, or some otherwise unattainable joy. And when production never loses that air of hope through all its three-and-a-half-week rehearsal period, one feels alive as at no other imaginable occasion. At such a time, it seems to all concerned that the very heart of life's mystery is what must be penetrated. They watch the director and each other and they listen with the avid attention of deaf mutes who have suddenly learned to speak and hear. Above their heads there begins to form a tantalizing sort of cloud, a question, a challenge to penetrate the mystery of why men move and speak and act.

It is a kind of glamour that can never be reported in a newspaper column, and yet it is the center of all the lure theatre has. It is a kind of soul-testing that ordinary people rarely experience except in the greatest emergencies. The actor who has always regarded himself as a strong spirit discovers now that his vaunted power somehow sounds querulous, and he must look within himself to find his strength. The actress who has made her way on her charm discovers that she appears not charming so much as shallow now, and must evaluate herself all over again, and create anew what she always took for granted. And the great performers are merely those who have been able to face themselves without remorse.

In the production of a good play with a good cast and a knowing director a kind of banding together occurs; there is formed a fraternity whose members share a mutual sense of destiny. In these five blocks, where the rapping of the tap-dancer's feet and the bawling of the phonographs in the record-shop doorways mix with the roar of the Broadway traffic; where the lonely, the perverted, and the lost wander like the souls in Dante's hell and the life of the spirit seems impossible, there are still little circles of actors in the dead silence of empty theatres, with a director in their center, and a new creation of life taking place.

There are always certain moments in such rehearsals, moments of such wonder that the memory of them serves to further entrap all who witness them into this most insecure of all professions. Remembering such moments the resolution to leave and get a "real" job vanishes and they are hooked again.

I think of Lee Cobb, the greatest dramatic actor I ever saw, when he was creating the role of Willy Loman in *Death of a Salesman.* When I hear people scoffing at actors as mere exhibitionists, when I hear them ask why there must be a theatre if it cannot support itself as any business must, when I myself grow sick and weary of the endless waste and the many travesties of this most abused of all arts, I think then of Lee Cobb making that role and I know that the theatre can yet be one of the chief glories of mankind.

He sat for days on the stage like a great lump, a sick seal, a mourning walrus. When it came his time to speak lines, he whispered meaninglessly. Kazan, the director, pretended certainty, but from where I sat he looked like an ant trying to prod an elephant off his haunches. Ten days went by. The other actors were by now much further advanced: Milly Dunnock, playing Linda, was already creating a role; Arthur Kennedy as Biff had long since begun to reach for his high notes; Cameron Mitchell had many scenes already perfected; but Cobb stared at them, heavy-eyed, morose, even persecuted, it seemed.

And then, one afternoon, there on the stage of the New Amsterdam way up on top of a movie theatre on Forty-second Street (this roof theatre had once been Ziegfeld's private playhouse in the gilded times, and now was barely heated and misty with dust). Lee rose from his chair and looked at Milly Dunnock and there was a silence. And then he said, "I was driving along, you understand, and then all of a sudden I'm going off the road. . . ."

And the theatre vanished. The stage vanished. The chill of an age-old recognition shuddered my spine: a voice was sounding in the dimly lit air up front, a created spirit, an incarnation, a Godlike creation was taking place; a new human being was being formed before all our eyes, born for the first time on this earth, made real by an act of will, by an artist's summoning up of all his memories and his intelligence: a birth was taking place above the meaningless traffic below; a man was here transcending the limits of his body and his own history. Through the complete concentration of his mind he had even altered the stance of his body which now was strangely not the body of Lee Cobb (he was thirty-seven then) but of a sixty-year-old salesman; a mere glance of his eye created a window beside him, with the gentle touch of his hand on this empty stage a bed appeared, and when he glanced up at the emptiness above him a ceiling was there, and there was even a crack in it where his stare rested.

I knew then that something astounding was being made here. It would have been almost enough for me without even opening the play. The actors, like myself and Kazan and the producer, were happy, of course, that we might have a hit; but there was a good deal more. There was a new fact of life, there was an alteration of history for all of us that afternoon.

There is a certain immortality involved in theatre, not created by monuments and books, but through the knowledge the actor keeps to his dying day that on a certain afternoon, in an empty and dusty theatre, he cast a shadow of a being that was not himself but the distillation of all he had ever observed: all the unsingable heartsong the ordinary man may feel but never utter, he gave voice to. And by that he somehow joins the ages.

And that is the glamour that remains, but it will not be found in the gossip columns. And it is enough, once discovered, to make people stay with the theatre, and others to come seeking it.

I think also that people keep coming into these five blocks because the theatre is still so simple, so old-fashioned. And that is why, however often its obsequies are intoned, it somehow never really dies. Because underneath our shiny fronts of stone, our fascination with gadgets, and our new toys that can blow the earth into a million stars, we are still outside the doorway through which the great answers wait. Not all the cameras in Christendom nor all the tricky lights will move us one step closer to a better understanding of ourselves, but only, as it always was, the truly written word, the profoundly felt gesture, the naked and direct contemplation of man which is the enduring glamour of the stage.

Further Resources

BOOKS

Corrigan, Robert W. *Arthur Miller: A Collection of Critical Essays.* Englewood Cliffs, N.J.: Prentice-Hall, 1969.

Miller, Arthur. *Plays.* London: Methuen Drama, 1988.

Miller, Arthur, et al. *Arthur Miller Talks About His Work in the Company of Actors, Directors, Reviewers, and Writers.* Christopher Bigsby, ed. London: Methuen, 1990.

Oppenheimer, George, ed. *The Passionate Playgoer.* New York: Viking, 1962.

WEBSITES

The Arthur Miller Society Official Website. Available online at http://www.ibiblio.org/miller/ (accessed February 27, 2003).

AUDIO AND VISUAL MEDIA

Death of a Salesman. Directed by Alex Segal. Broadway Theatre Archive. DVD, 1965.

Death of a Salesman. Directed by Volker Schlondorff. Punch Productions Inc. Videocassette, 1985.

2
BUSINESS AND
THE ECONOMY

JONATHAN KOLKEY

Entries are arranged in chronological order by date of primary source. For entries with one primary source, the entry title is the same as the primary source title. Entries with more than one primary source have an overall entry title, followed by the titles of the primary sources.

der. The order is intended to prevent a march on Washington organized by A. Philip Randolph of the Brotherhood of Sleeping Car Porters.

• On July 24, the American Federation of Labor (AFL) and the Office of Production Management sign a no-strike pledge.

• On December 27, the OPA announces rubber rationing. Civilian consumption of rubber declines by 80 percent.

• On December 30, the first liberty ship is built and christened the *Patrick Henry*.

Important Events in Business and the Economy, 1940–1949

1940

• The U.S. Supreme Court rules that National Labor Relations Board (NLRB) decisions cannot be appealed and that only the NLRB, not labor unions, can enforce NLRB rulings.

• On October 24, the forty-hour workweek in industry begins as a result of the Fair Labor Standards Act, passed in 1938.

• On November 21, John L. Lewis of the United Mine Workers (UMW) resigns as head of the Congress of Industrial Organizations (CIO) in protest over President Franklin D. Roosevelt's election to a third term. Philip Murray succeeds him as president of the CIO.

1941

• On January 3, in anticipation of war the federal government calls for the construction of two hundred merchant vessels.

• On January 7, President Roosevelt creates the Office of Production Management to supervise defense production.

• On January 22, strikes at the Allied Chalmers plant initiate a series of defense-industry labor disputes.

• On January 24, Labor Secretary Frances Perkins reports the largest increase in employment in the past eleven years.

• On February 3, the U.S. Supreme Court rules that the Fair Labor Standards Act of 1938 is constitutional.

• On April 11, the Ford Motor Company signs its first union contract, settling a strike in which the CIO calls out 85,000 workers at the River Rouge plant.

• On April 11, Congress establishes the Office of Price Administration and Civilian Supply (OPA) to recommend price-control measures.

• On May 1, U.S. Defense Savings Bonds go on sale.

• On May 16, General Motors (GM) gives its workers a wage increase of ten cents per hour to prevent strikes. In return, the CIO drops its demand for a closed shop.

• On June 9, President Roosevelt orders troops to take over the Los Angeles plants of the North American Aviation Company to replace striking workers.

• On June 25, President Roosevelt issues Executive Order 8802, designed to end racial discrimination in government agencies, job-training programs, and industries with defense contracts. The order establishes the Committee on Fair Employment Practices to investigate racial violations of the or-

1942

• Industrialist Henry J. Kaiser perfects prefabrication and mass production techniques in shipbuilding. His Vancouver, Washington, shipworks constructs a 10,500-ton liberty ship in a record-setting seven and a half days.

• On January 1, the Office of Production Management bans the sale of new cars and trucks.

• On January 12, the National War Labor Board (NWLB) is created with the power to impose binding arbitration and to seize plants during labor disputes.

• On January 16, President Roosevelt establishes the War Production Board by executive order, replacing the Office of Production Management.

• On January 30, President Roosevelt signs the Price Control Bill into law, giving the OPA the power to establish prices for all products except farm goods.

• On March 17, William Green of the AFL and Philip Murray of the CIO announce a no-strike agreement.

• On April 18, the War Manpower Commission is established.

• On April 28, the OPA attempts to combat inflation with its General Maximum Price Regulation.

• On July 15, in what becomes known as the "Little Steel" formula, the War Labor Board allows a 15 percent wage increase to thousands of steelworkers in the smaller steel firms, pegging increases for most unionized workers to cost-of-living increases.

• In October, the Revenue Act of 1942 increases the number of people paying income taxes from 39 million to 42.6 million.

• On December 1, nationwide gasoline rationing begins.

• On December 4, President Roosevelt terminates the Works Projects Administration; the Civilian Conservation Corps had already been disbanded. With millions of men overseas and with women taking jobs in defense plants, unemployment is no longer a problem.

1943

• On February 9, to cope with labor shortages, President Roosevelt mandates a minimum workweek of forty-eight hours in war industries; overtime is paid for any work over forty hours.

• On March 25, Chester C. Davis is appointed U.S. food administrator and is given the task of alleviating food shortages.

- On March 29, rationing of meat, fat, and cheese begins.
- On April 17, the War Manpower Commission prohibits 27 million essential workers from leaving their jobs.
- On May 1, the national government seizes coal mines after 530,000 miners, under John L. Lewis's lead, walk out and refuse to obey a NWLB order to return to work. The miners will win wage concessions, but many Americans condemn Lewis and his followers as traitors.
- On May 27, the Office of War Mobilization is established to coordinate war efforts on the home front.
- On June 10, President Roosevelt signs the Current Tax Payment Act, requiring the withholding of federal income taxes from individual paychecks on a regular basis. This act revolutionizes the collecting of taxes and gives government more power to spend than before.
- On June 25, Congress overrides the president's veto to pass the Smith-Connally Labor Act that prohibits strikes in defense industries and mandates a 30-day cooling-off period in other industries.
- On December 27, the federal government, by presidential order, seizes the railroads in order to stop a nationwide rail strike. Owners regain control after the dispute is settled.

1944

- On April 26, federal troops seize the Montgomery Ward plant after company chairman Sewell Avery refuses to extend the company's contract with the CIO as ordered by the NWLB.
- On May 3, the OPA ends meat rationing, except for steak and choice cuts of beef.
- From July 1 to July 30, diplomats at the Bretton Woods Conference establish the World Bank, the International Monetary Fund, and the General Agreement on Tariffs and Trade.
- On August 14, the War Production Administration begins to allow manufacturers to resume the production of consumer goods.

1945

- From January 15 to May 8, a nationwide dim-out is ordered to conserve fuel.
- On May 25, military aircraft production is reduced by 30 percent.
- On June 28, Ford Motor Company completes the last of its war contracts. During the war Ford manufactured a total of 8,600 bombers, 278,000 jeeps, and 57,000 aircraft engines.
- On August 14, the War Manpower Commission lifts all controls on wages.
- On August 15, rationing of gasoline and fuel oil ends.
- On August 18, President Harry S. Truman orders the full restoration of civilian consumer production, collective bargaining, and the return of free markets. A wave of strikes by coal miners, steelworkers, longshoremen, autoworkers, and others follows.

- On December 20, tire rationing ends.
- On December 31, the NWLB is replaced by the National Wage Stabilization Board.

1946

- On February 21, President Truman creates the Office of Economic Stabilization to oversee reconversion to a peacetime economy.
- On April 29, the U.S. Department of Agriculture reports that farm prices, and hence the cost of food, are at record highs, underscoring the need for higher wages among workers.

1947

- On April 20, United States Steel and the steelworkers agree on a pay raise of 15 cents per hour, setting the standard for the industry.
- On May 9, the World Bank opens, loaning France $250 million for reconstruction.
- On June 5, U.S. Secretary of State George Marshall announces the Marshall Plan, intended to help Europe recover from the damage of the war.
- On June 23, over President Truman's veto, Congress passes the Taft-Hartley Act that limits the powers of labor unions by banning the closed shop, requiring an eighty-day cooling-off period before a strike, forbidding political contributions by unions, and requiring union leaders to swear they are not Communists.

1948

- On January 1, the General Agreement on Tariffs and Trades goes into effect, lowering international trade barriers.
- The U.S. Supreme Court nullifies the section of the Taft-Hartley Act that limits political spending by labor unions; in a later decision, it will uphold the provision of the act banning the closed shop.
- On May 25, the UAW and GM sign the first sliding-scale wage contract. Wages are adjusted based on the cost of living.
- On August 16, Congress passes the Anti-Inflation Act.

1949

- On January 14, in the first major antitrust suit brought by the government since before World War II, the Justice Department proposes to break up the American Telephone and Telegraph Company (AT&T) and separate its production subsidiary, Western Electric.
- On October 31, Walter Reuther, president of the Congress of Industrial Organizations (CIO), begins to purge the organization of Communists, who had long been allowed to operate within CIO unions.
- On November 18, Crucible Steel, the last holdout, signs a contract with the United Steelworkers.

Republican Criticism of New Deal Economics

Speech to the Union League Club of Chicago, Illinois

Speech

By: Robert A. Taft

Date: January 5, 1940

Source: Taft, Robert A. Speech to the Union League Club of Chicago, Illinois. January 5, 1940. Reprinted in Clarence E. Wunderlin, Jr., ed., *The Papers of Robert A. Taft, vol. 2, 1939–1944.* Kent, Ohio: The Kent State University Press, 2001, 104–05, 107–09.

Speech to the Lions Club of Wilmington, Delaware

Speech

By: Robert A. Taft

Date: March 1, 1940

Source: Taft, Robert A. Speech to the Lions Club of Wilmington, Delaware. March 1, 1940. Reprinted in Clarence E. Wunderlin, Jr., ed., *The Papers of Robert A. Taft, vol. 2, 1939–1944* Kent, Ohio: The Kent State University Press, 2001, 120–21.

About the Author: Robert A. Taft (1889–1953), son of Republican President William Howard Taft, was born in Cincinnati, Ohio. Taft graduated from Yale University and Harvard Law School. Taft was elected as a United States senator from Ohio in 1938. He quickly became the Republican Party's premier congressional leader and spokesman. Affectionately known as "Mr. Republican," Taft unsuccessfully sought the Republican Party's presidential nomination in 1940, 1944, 1948, and, most notably, in 1952. Always a bridesmaid in his quest to become president, a disheartened Taft died in 1953. ■

Introduction

By the end of the 1930s, Franklin D. Roosevelt's New Deal economic policies had proved extremely popular with the American people, producing large Democratic majorities. This popularity was understandable, in light of

Senator Robert A. Taft was an articulate critic of President Roosevelt's New Deal economic policies. THE LIBRARY OF CONGRESS.

the 1929 stock market crash and the terrible economic conditions inherited by Roosevelt. Despite its popularity, the New Deal failed to accomplish its major goal, restoring economic prosperity. The unemployment rate had been as high as 30.5 percent in 1933, Roosevelt's first year in office. It improved after that, but then surged back to 22.6 percent during a 1938 relapse. Even in 1940, seven years into Roosevelt's presidency, unemployment stood at 19.5 percent. While effective politically, the New Deal had not lived up to its promise to stimulate the economy.

At the dawn of the new decade, the American economy showed few signs of imminent recovery from the Great Depression. Also, Roosevelt and his advisers appeared to have exhausted policy initiatives to help the struggling economy. The New Deal policies were not working, and only American preparation for possible entry into World War II (1939–1945) kept the American economy from sinking even lower. Many Roosevelt critics saw the president's aggressive, interventionist policies aimed at Germany and Japan as an attempt to divert the public's attention from his administration's demonstrable economic failures.

Ohio Republican Senator Robert A. Taft, son of former President William Howard Taft, was the most knowledgeable and articulate critic of Roosevelt's economic and fiscal policies. Elected to the U.S. Senate from Ohio in 1938, Robert Taft quickly emerged as the New Deal's strongest political adversary. Prior to Taft's election, criticism of New Deal policies came primarily from discredited or fringe critics, including former President Herbert Hoover and Father Charles Coughlin, or from conservative members of the president's own Democratic Party. By 1940, Taft's role as chief opponent of the New Deal signaled a restoration of a more traditional, and effective, "loyal opposition" from the minority party so important to policy discussions. This corrected the temporary imbalance in American politics that had been created by the several sweeping Democratic Party election victories of the 1930s.

Significance

Although some members of the Roosevelt administration seemed sympathetic to communism, Taft's contention that the New Deal reflected the influence of dangerous foreign ideologies seems to be questionable in retrospect. On the other hand, Taft's conclusion that the New Deal fostered a government-centered, planned economy reflecting a philosophy of scarcity has proven quite perceptive. In theory, the New Deal imposed a series of controls on various aspects of the American economy to regulate business for the public interest. However, in practice, government regulation often supported certain favorite interests, at the expense of others, irrespective of the public good. This generally was accomplished by restricting market competition.

The "Deregulation Movement" began in the 1970s, peaked under President Ronald Reagan in the 1980s, and continues today. This legislative effort has repealed or modified many of the competitive restraints the New Deal placed on industries, including banking, the stock market, airlines, trucking, and communications. In this regard, Taft's critique of New Deal economics appears vindicated. The passage of time has dimmed much of the luster surrounding Roosevelt's New Deal. While correct on the failure of the New Deal to "fix" the economy, Taft was wrong in his conclusion that the New Deal would "inevitably lead to a totalitarian state." Eventually, the American political process proved able to remove or modify the onerous provisions of the New Deal, providing a solid foundation for the economic expansion of the 1980s and 1990s.

Primary Source

Speech to the Union League Club of Chicago, Illinois [excerpt]

SYNOPSIS: In 1940, Ohio Senator Robert A. Taft, a Republican, delivered this speech, strongly critical of Franklin D. Roosevelt's New Deal policies. Taft

decries the attempt to create a planned economy as "confused, illogical, and ineffective."

The underlying creed of every New Dealer is that the government can produce prosperity by regulation of everything, that it can run every man's business better than he can run it himself, and every farmer's farm better than the farmer. . . .

I have frequently denounced the theory of a planned economy which underlies these proposals. I believe that it leads inevitably to a totalitarian state in which individual enterprise is destroyed and all activity socialized and directed by an all-powerful government. I believe that such a state would destroy liberty without improving the condition of even the poorest families. I am convinced that no matter how well such a state is run, the American people would ultimately revolt against the attempt to direct all individual activity. One of the main reasons for the trend away from the New Deal today is the fact that more and more people are affected by the government's attempt to regulate their business or their livelihood.

But my experience in Washington has made me realize how ineffectively the present government regulation is worked out. The present government can hardly claim to be guided by anything that remotely resembles a plan. Those of us who believe in American liberty and the building up of a prosperity through private initiative should be thankful that the planned economy of the present administration is as far from planned as it is, for the people have been turned against it, not only by their belief that it is attempting a change in the whole American system which has made this country what it is, but because the administration of it is confused, illogical and ineffective. . . .

The administration promises to restore prosperity and find jobs for the unemployed, but it enacts a payroll tax which puts an absolute premium on every employer reducing the number of his employees. It enforces a wage-hour law which directly reduces the number of employees employed in many industries, including, for instance, porters at the union stations, and will drive many small businesses completely out of business, particularly in the small towns and rural sections, thus creating still more unemployment. . . .

Government regulation is bad enough, even if it were directed by a consistent policy. When every department moves without regard to the general policy of the government or the conflicting regulations of other departments, it is no wonder that the business man stops trying to figure what the government will do next, abandons all plans for expansion, and confines his activities to the simple business of keeping his business alive. Many people have pointed out that business lacks confidence. Perhaps the main reason why it lacks confidence is because it hasn't the faintest idea what the government is going to do next. Business men are quite willing to adjust themselves to new conditions. They can perhaps in time overcome the effect of some kinds of excessive government regulation, but they must know what the limits of government activity are. They must know what is going to happen to their business during the next twelve months.

Any new administration will have a man-sized job to reorganize the whole government as it must be reorganized. In doing so, however, it can eliminate many bureaus. It can reduce the field in which many bureaus operate. It can give some system to the administration of those activities which are concerned with eliminating abuses in the present system. In doing so, it can tremendously reduce expense of overlapping activities. The time has come to study every government activity, and reduce federal spending to a point where the current revenues will pay the bill. But after six and one-half years of experience, the people know it will never be done by the present administration. They look forward to the 1940 election as a time to clean house. The utter confusion of the present government is one of the main reasons why the people have decided that a complete change is needed in 1940.

Primary Source

Speech to the Lions Club of Wilmington, Delaware

> **SYNOPSIS:** In 1940, Taft delivered other speech strongly critical of Roosevelt. He criticizes the New Deal's economic philosophy. He claims that such interference with the market system inspired dangerous foreign ideologies—in particular Soviet Communism.

The New Deal has failed to produce the prosperity it promised, particularly to the underprivileged. There are still nine million unemployed, and national income is far below what it was in the twenties. The standard of living is lower, farm prices are substantially what they were before any of the elaborate New Deal control measures were initiated, and this failure has been brought about at an expense of more than $20,000,000,000, which you, your children and your grandchildren are going to have to pay.

Yet in spite of this failure, the administration is still dominated by the ideals of planned economy, and thinks that the government can run each man's business than he can run it himself. It hopes to bring prosperity to government spending, government regulation and government operation. There is still a large group in the government animated by the ideals of Socialism, if not Communism, men who desire to abolish the American system, which caused this country in one hundred and fifty years to become the greatest country in the world, and establish some kind of regimented state.

They still have that sympathy with the ideals of Communism which President Roosevelt had, as he admitted in his address before the American Youth Congress. He said: "In the early days of Communism I recognized that many leaders in Russia were bringing education and better health, and above all better opportunity to millions who had been kept in ignorance and serfdom under imperial regime . . . I hoped that Russia would work out its own problems and their government would eventually become a peace loving, popular government with free ballot."

While the President abhors the actions of Mr. Stalin, he does not seem to know that everything that Mr. Stalin is doing was done by Mr. Lenin and Mr. Trotsky. He does not seem to recognize that the ideals of Communism are, and always were, fundamentally at variance with the American system. In theory, though not in practice, a Communist government might some day have a free ballot, but even in theory it could not have had a free economy of the American style.

This sympathy for Communist ideals still dominates many bureaus in the government. It leads to more and more regulation of business and taxation of success. It discourages men from starting new enterprises. It drives little business out of business entirely. It checks the growth of small industry into big industry. It increases unemployment and prevents prosperity. Seven years after every previous depression, we have been on the crest of a new advance. In 1900, seven years after the depression of 1893; in 1928, seven years after the depression of 1921, we had a larger national income than we had ever had before, and we provided a job for every man who wanted a job. Our troubles today have resulted from the theory which dominates the New Deal, a planned economy in a regimented state.

Further Resources

BOOKS

Parker, James. *Mr. Republican: A Biography of Robert A. Taft.* Boston: Houghton Mifflin, 1972.

Rutland, Robert A. *The Republicans from Lincoln to Bush.* Columbia, Mo.: University of Missouri Press, 1996.

White, William Smith. *The Taft Story.* New York: Harper, 1954.

"Arsenal of Democracy"

Radio address

By: Franklin D. Roosevelt

Date: December 29, 1940

Source: Roosevelt, Franklin D. "Arsenal of Democracy" Fireside Chat on national security, December 29, 1940. Reprinted in *The Public Papers and Addresses of Franklin D. Roosevelt, 1940 Volume: War—and Aid to Democracies.* New York: The Macmillan Company, 1941, 633–36, 640–43.

About the Author: Franklin D. Roosevelt (1882–1945) was born at Hyde Park, New York. Educated at Harvard, Roosevelt was elected to the New York Senate in 1910, and served as assistant secretary of the navy from 1913 to 1920. After losing a bid for vice president in 1920, Roosevelt contracted polio, leaving his legs permanently paralyzed. Returning to politics, Roosevelt was elected governor of New York in 1928, and he defeated Herbert Hoover for the presidency in 1932. Roosevelt was reelected in 1936, 1940, and 1944. The only president to serve more than two terms, Roosevelt led the nation through the Great Depression and during World War II. ∎

Introduction

World War II began in Europe when Nazi Germany invaded Poland on September 1, 1939, bringing the Allies, most notably Great Britain and France, to Poland's aid. American popular opinion was against involvement in the war, and officially the United States was neutral in the conflict until after the Japanese bombed Pearl Harbor on December 7, 1941. Prior to Pearl Harbor, however, President Franklin D. Roosevelt had effectively aligned the nation with the Allied cause. Believing the Nazis and their allies, the Axis powers, to be a long-term threat to the United States, the Roosevelt administration actively sought to aid England and France against Hitler's Germany. After France fell to Germany in June 1940, Roosevelt made the decision to swap "destroyers for bases" with beleaguered England in September 1940.

American public opinion forced Roosevelt to stop well short of his private desire to bring about actual American participation in the war. This precise issue surfaced during his 1940 reelection campaign against Republican challenger, Wendell Willkie. FDR repeatedly reassured jittery voters that the United States did not entertain plans to send American soldiers into any "foreign wars." Most Americans undoubtedly desired a British victory over Nazi Germany, and they were eager to assist the British by providing materiel and financial backing. But Americans drew the line at committing American soldiers to combat. In the words of a popular slogan at the time, the United States should render to England, "All aid short of war."

Roosevelt was an excellent political communicator. He frequently spoke directly to nationwide radio audiences, something no president before him had done. These addresses, called "fireside chats" because of their feel of intimacy with Roosevelt, covered a wide array of topics, and were an important method of communicating policy initiatives during the Roosevelt administration. After winning reelection for a third term, Roosevelt used his fireside chat on December 29, 1940 to outline an ambitious new initiative for 1941. He explained in the radio address that the United States would significantly increase its defense outlays and set unprecedented industrial production targets. By accomplishing these goals, the United States would become the mighty "Arsenal of Democracy" that England and its allies needed to resist Nazi aggression. The following month, Roosevelt sent legislation to Congress greatly increasing military spending and establishing a program of material aid to the Allies that became known as the Lend-Lease program.

This strategy, as with other Roosevelt foreign policy initiatives during the early stages of World War II, was presented to a skeptical public as a means of avoiding active American military intervention in the war. This theory held that by providing the Allies with the supplies necessary to defeat Germany, America could avoid sending its troops into combat. Roosevelt, a veteran of President Woodrow Wilson's administration during World War I, surely recalled that a similar policy brought the United States into that conflict. Wilson stubbornly insisted that American merchant ships be permitted to supply Germany's enemy, England. The American public likely recognized that Roosevelt was not being entirely candid as to why the actions were being taken.

Significance

Whatever the true motivation for Roosevelt's proposal, the practical result of turning America into the "Arsenal of Democracy" was a significant increase in defense spending. The United States already had started the task of refurbishing its military, especially after the stunning Nazi victory over France in June 1940. The huge additional defense outlays in 1941 had enormous economic repercussions.

By injecting significantly more government money than envisioned, the accelerated rearmament of 1941 jump-started the long-dormant American economy. Within one year, unemployment in the United States dropped from 15 percent to only 5.2 percent—the fastest and most substantial employment turnaround in American history. The Gross National Product (GNP) for 1941 was the first since the beginning of the Great Depression to surpass the GNP of last pre-Depression year, 1929. The Great Depression in America was over.

Ostensibly a short-term expenditure, high levels of defense spending soon became a permanent policy. Defense spending was astronomical during World War II. Even after the war ended, a high level of defense remained a central feature of the Cold War. Only after the total collapse of the Soviet Union in the early 1990s did America finally revert to a genuine "peacetime" economy.

Primary Source

"Arsenal of Democracy" [excerpt]

SYNOPSIS: On December 29, 1940, President Franklin D. Roosevelt delivered perhaps his most celebrated "fireside chat" in a radio broadcast to the nation. In the address, Roosevelt outlines his intention during 1941 to increase defense outlays substantially and establish ambitious industrial production targets designed to make the United States the great "Arsenal of Democracy." Not only did this bold proposal fit perfectly with Roosevelt's avowed desire to assist England and its allies in resisting Nazi aggression, the enormous projected increase in defense-related spending would help the depressed American economy.

My friends:

This is not a fireside chat on war. It is a talk on national security; because the nub of the whole purpose of your President is to keep you now, and your children later, and your grandchildren much later, out of a last-ditch war for the preservation of American independence and all the things that American independence means to you and to me and to ours.

Tonight, in the presence of a world crisis, my mind goes back eight years to a night in the midst of a domestic crisis. It was a time when the wheels of American industry were grinding to a full stop, when the whole banking system of our country had ceased to function. . . .

We face this new crisis—this new threat to the security of our nation—with the same courage and realism.

Never before since Jamestown and Plymouth Rock has our American civilization been in such danger as now.

For, on September 27, 1940, by an agreement signed in Berlin, three powerful nations, two in Eu-

rope and one in Asia, joined themselves together in the threat that if the United States of America interfered with or blocked the expansion program of these three nations—a program aimed at world control—they would unite in ultimate action against the United States.

The Nazi masters of Germany have made it clear that they intend not only to dominate all life and thought in their own country, but also to enslave the whole of Europe, and then to use the resources of Europe to dominate the rest of the world. . . .

[If Great Britain falls] We should enter upon a new and terrible era in which the whole world, our hemisphere included, would be run by threats of brute force. To survive in such a world, we would have to convert ourselves permanently into a militaristic power on the basis of war economy. . . .

There is no demand for sending an American Expeditionary Force outside our own borders. There is no intention by any member of your Government to send such a force. You can, therefore, nail any talk about sending armies to Europe as deliberate untruth.

Our national policy is not directed toward war. Its sole purpose is to keep war away from our country and our people.

Democracy's fight against world conquest is being greatly aided, and must be more greatly aided, by the rearmament of the United States and by sending every ounce and every ton of munitions and supplies that we can possibly spare to help the defenders who are in the front lines. It is no more unneutral for us to do that than it is for Sweden, Russia and other nations near Germany, to send steel and ore and oil and other war materials into Germany every day in the week.

We are planning our own defense with the utmost urgency; and in its vast scale we must integrate the war needs of Britain and the other free nations which are resisting aggression.

This is not a matter of sentiment or of controversial personal opinion. It is a matter of realistic, practical military policy, based on the advice of our military experts who are in close touch with existing warfare. These military and naval experts and the members of the Congress and the Administration have a single-minded purpose—the defense of the United States.

This nation is making a great effort to produce everything that is necessary in this emergency—and with all possible speed. This great effort requires great sacrifice.

I would ask no one to defend a democracy which in turn would not defend everyone in the nation against want and privation. The strength of this nation shall not be diluted by the failure of the Government to protect the economic well-being of its citizens.

If our capacity to produce is limited by machines, it must ever be remembered that these machines are operated by the skill and the stamina of the workers. As the Government is determined to protect the rights of the workers, so the nation has a right to expect that the men who man the machines will discharge their full responsibilities to the urgent needs of defense.

The worker possesses the same human dignity and is entitled to the same security of position as the engineer or the manager or the owner. For the workers provide the human power that turns out the destroyers, the airplanes and the tanks.

The nation expects our defense industries to continue operation without interruption by strikes or lock-outs. It expects and insists that management and workers will reconcile their differences by voluntary or legal means, to continue to produce the supplies that are so sorely needed.

And on the economic side of our great defense program, we are, as you know, bending every effort to maintain stability of prices and with that the stability of the cost of living.

Nine days ago I announced the setting up of a more effective organization to direct our gigantic efforts to increase the production of munitions. The appropriation of vast sums of money and a well coordinated executive direction of our defense efforts are not in themselves enough. Guns, planes, ships and many other things have to be built in the factories and arsenals of America. They have to be produced by workers and managers and engineers with the aid of machines which in turn have to be built by hundreds of thousands of workers throughout the land.

In this great work there has been splendid cooperation between the Government and industry and labor; and I am very thankful.

American industrial genius, unmatched throughout the world in the solution of production problems, has been called upon to bring its resources and its talents into action. Manufacturers of watches, farm implements, linotypes, cash registers, automobiles, sewing machines, lawn mowers and locomotives are now making fuses, bomb packing crates, telescope mounts, shells, pistols and tanks.

But all our present efforts are not enough. We must have more ships, more guns, more planes—more of everything. This can only be accomplished if we discard the notion of "business as usual." This job cannot be done merely by superimposing on the existing productive facilities the added requirements of the nation for defense.

Our defense efforts must not be blocked by those who fear the future consequences of surplus plant capacity. The possible consequences of failure of our defense efforts now are much more to be feared.

After the present needs of our defenses are past, a proper handling of the country's peace-time needs will require all the new productive capacity—if not more.

No pessimistic policy about the future of America shall delay the immediate expansion of those industries essential to defense. We need them.

I want to make it clear that it is the purpose of the nation to build now with all possible speed every machine, every arsenal, every factory that we need to manufacture our defense material. We have the men—the skill—the wealth—and above all, the will.

I am confident that if and when production of consumer or luxury goods in certain industries requires the use of machines and raw materials that are essential for defense purposes, then such production must yield, and will gladly yield, to our primary and compelling purpose.

I appeal to the owners of plants—to the managers—to the workers—to our own Government employees—to put every ounce of effort into producing these munitions swiftly and without stint. With this appeal I give you the pledge that all of us who are officers of your Government will devote ourselves to the same whole-hearted extent to the great task that lies ahead.

As planes and ships and guns and shells are produced, your Government, with its defense experts, can then determine how best to use them to defend this hemisphere. The decision as to how much shall be sent abroad and how much shall remain at home must be made on the basis of our over-all military necessities.

We must be the great arsenal of democracy. For us this is an emergency as serious as war itself. We must apply ourselves to our task with the same resolution, the same sense of urgency, the same spirit of patriotism and sacrifice as we would show were we at war.

Further Resources

BOOKS

Dallek, Robert. *Franklin D. Roosevelt and American Foreign Policy.* New York: Oxford University Press, 1981.

Martel, Leon. *Lend-lease, Loans, and the Coming of the Cold War: A Study of the Implementation of Foreign Policy.* Boulder, Colo.: Westview Press, 1979.

Nelson, Donald M. *Arsenal of Democracy: The Story of American War Production.* New York: Harcourt, Brace and Company, 1946.

WEBSITES

"Arsenal of Democracy." Available at http://www.geocities .com/Pentagon/Quarters/5433/arsen.html (March 3, 2003).

Fireside Chat on the Cost of Living and the Progress of the War

Radio address

By: Franklin D. Roosevelt

Date: September 7, 1942

Source: Roosevelt, Franklin D. Fireside Chat on the Cost of Living and the Progress of the War. Radio address delivered on September 7, 1942. Reprinted in *The Public Papers and Addresses of Franklin D. Roosevelt, 1942 Volume: Humanity on the Defensive.* New York: Harper & Brothers Publishers, 1950, 368–72, 374, 376–77.

About the Author: Franklin D. Roosevelt (1882–1945) was born at Hyde Park, New York. Educated at Harvard, Roosevelt was elected to the New York Senate in 1910, and served as assistant secretary of the navy from 1913–1920. After losing a bid for vice president in 1920, Roosevelt contracted polio, leaving his legs permanently paralyzed. Returning to politics, Roosevelt was elected governor of New York in 1928, and he defeated Herbert Hoover for the presidency in 1932. Roosevelt was reelected in 1936, 1940, and 1944. The only president to serve more than two terms, Roosevelt led the nation through the Great Depression and during World War II. ■

Introduction

The Roosevelt administration's response to the early success of the Axis powers in World War II (1939–45) was to increase defense spending significantly and set aggressive production targets for American rearmament efforts in 1941. Even before the Japanese attack on Pearl Harbor on December 7, 1941, brought America into the war, unemployment was on the decline. After the attack, widespread unemployment ceased to be a major concern for the first time in more than a decade. The nation's factories now furiously produced unprecedented quantities of war materiel. Inflation (a general rise in prices mak-

ing the cost of living greater), an historic wartime scourge, surfaced quickly as the primary economic problem.

The high demand for labor in defense industries meant that workers received higher wages, production bonuses, and significant overtime pay. Businesses that had suffered for a decade during the Great Depression finally had customers with money to spend, and it was inevitable that they began to raise their prices. At the same time, the devotion of the economy to producing war goods meant fewer consumer items were available, driving up their prices as well. The result of all this was a steep jump in the cost of living, driving up food prices, rents, and an array of consumer items.

Several policy measures were instituted to reduce what was termed "excess consumer purchasing power." These included mandatory rationing of certain items, increasing taxes, and encouraging citizens to buy war bonds. However, the most controversial measure was the imposition of wage and price controls. As early as August 1941, Roosevelt responded to the onset of higher inflation by establishing an independent agency to address the crisis—The Office of Price Administration (OPA). The agency initially lacked statutory authority to control prices directly. Although the United States had experienced severe inflation during previous wars—most notably during the Revolutionary War, the Civil War, and World War I—the national government previously had never sought to impose strict price controls. A few weeks after Pearl Harbor, Congress passed the Emergency Price Control Act. This represented a step, however tentative, towards a comprehensive system of price controls. On September 7, 1942, Roosevelt asked Congress to enact the Stabilization Act. Later that evening in a fireside chat, Roosevelt explained to the American people the need for the legislation. Subsequently, Congress approved the legislation quickly, and the president signed the bill into law on October 2, 1942. The legislation granted the OPA unprecedented authority to stabilize both wages and prices.

Significance

Controls, especially on wages, appear to have "worked" during World War II, slowing the rate of inflation although they could not eliminate it completely. It was not that such action constituted sound economics, but, rather, that the American people recognized the gravity of the situation and patriotically agreed to work for less than they ordinarily might have commanded. The Truman administration's Korean War-era controls, imposed in January 1951, gave a similar illusion of "success." On the other hand, President Nixon's attempt to impose wartime price controls during the unpopular Vietnam War, the Wage and Price Freeze Act, was an economic disaster.

President Franklin D. Roosevelt delivers a "fireside chat" about inflation and his seven-point National Economic Policy. © BETTMANN/CORBIS. REPRODUCED BY PERMISSION.

Although Roosevelt's price and wage controls were successful, they were not without critics. Historically, wartime controls have placed a burden on citizens, and World War II was no exception. Willing to sacrifice some material comforts to help the war effort, the daily reality of the inconvenience caused by the controls tempted some to circumvent the measures. Predictably, a thriving black market emerged, as people sought to get around price controls and mandatory rationing.

Many observers objected to what they characterized as America's "partial economic controls" during World War II. Some wondered why wages and prices were controlled, but corporate profits were not. The slogan, "Draft soldiers, draft capital" highlighted the irony of asking soldiers to sacrifice their lives, while the wealthy avoided contributing their "fair share" of profits earned from business generated by the war. Proposals to limit corporate profits and to limit individual salaries to $25,000, touched on in Roosevelt's address, failed to garner sufficient support in Congress.

Primary Source

Fireside Chat on the Cost of Living and the Progress of the War [excerpt]

SYNOPSIS: On September 7, 1942, President Roosevelt requested that Congress pass the Stabilization Act, granting the OPA statutory authority to control wages and prices. The president then explained the proposed legislation in one of his famous "fireside chats," a national radio broadcast delivered that evening.

From left to right, union leaders David Dubinsky, George Meany, William Green, and George Harrison in New York, 1949. © HULTON-DEUTSCH COLLECTION/CORBIS. REPRODUCED BY PERMISSION.

Today I sent a message to the Congress, pointing out the over-whelming urgency of the serious domestic economic crisis with which we are threatened. Some call it "inflation," which is a vague sort of term, and others call it a "rise in the cost of living," which is much more easily understood by most families.

That phrase, "the cost of living," means essentially what a dollar can buy.

From January 1, 1941, to May of this year, nearly a year and a half, the cost of living went up about 15 percent. And at that point last May we undertook to freeze the cost of living. But we could not do a complete job of it, because the Congressional authority at the time exempted a large part of farm products used for food and for making clothing, although several weeks before, I had asked the Congress for legislation to stabilize all farm prices.

At that time I had told the Congress that there were seven elements in our national economy, all of which had to be controlled; and that if any one essential element remained exempt, the cost of living could not be held down.

On only two of these points—both of them vital, however—did I call for Congressional action. These two vital points were: first, taxation; and second, the stabilization of all farm prices at parity.

"Parity" is a standard for the maintenance of good farm prices. It was established as our national policy in 1933. It means that the farmer and the city worker are on the same relative ratio with each other in purchasing power as they were during a period some thirty years before—at a time when the farmer had a satisfactory purchasing power. One hundred percent of parity, therefore, has been accepted by farmers as the fair standard for the prices they receive.

Last January, however, the Congress passed a law forbidding ceilings on farm prices below 110 percent of parity on some commodities. And on other commodities the ceiling was even higher, so that the average possible ceiling is now about 116 percent of parity for agricultural products as a whole.

This act of favoritism for one particular group in the community increased the cost of food to everybody—not only to the workers in the city or in the munitions plants, and their families, but also to the families of the farmers themselves.

Since last May, ceilings have been set on nearly all commodities, rents, and services, except the exempted farm products. Installment buying, for example, has been effectively controlled.

Wages in certain key industries have been stabilized on the basis of the present cost of living.

But it is obvious to all of us that if the cost of food continues to go up, as it is doing at present, the wage earner, particularly in the lower brackets, will have a right to an increase in his wages. I think that would be essential justice and a practical necessity.

Our experience with the control of other prices during the past few months has brought out one important fact—the rising cost of living can be controlled, providing that all elements making up the cost of living are controlled at the same time. I think that also is an essential justice and a practical necessity. We know that parity prices for farm products not now controlled will not put up the cost of living more than a very small amount; but we also know that if we must go up to an average of 116 percent of parity for food and other farm products—which is necessary at present under the Emergency Price Control Act before we can control all farm prices—the cost of living will get well out of hand. We are face to face with this danger today. Let us meet it and remove it.

I realize that it may seem out of proportion to you to be over-stressing these economic problems at a time like this, when we are all deeply concerned about the news from far distant fields of battle. But I give you the solemn assurance that failure to solve this problem here at home—and to solve it now—will make more difficult the winning of this war.

If the vicious spiral of inflation ever gets under way, the whole economic system will stagger. Prices and wages will go up so rapidly that the entire production program will be endangered. The cost of the war, paid by taxpayers, will jump beyond all present calculations. It will mean an uncontrollable rise in prices and in wages, which can result in raising the over-all cost of living as high as another 20 percent soon. That would mean that the purchasing power of every dollar that you have in your pay envelope, or in the bank, or included in your insurance policy or your pension, would be reduced to about eighty cents' worth. I need not tell you that this would have a demoralizing effect on our people, soldiers and civilians alike.

Over-all stabilization of prices, salaries, wages, and profits is necessary to the continued increasing production of planes and tanks and ships and guns.

In my Message to Congress today, I have said that this must be done quickly. If we wait for two or three or four or six months it may well be too late.

I have told the Congress that the Administration cannot hold the actual cost of food and clothing down to the present level beyond October first.

Therefore, I have asked the Congress to pass legislation under which the President would be specifically authorized to stabilize the cost of living, including the price of all farm commodities. The purpose should be to hold farm prices at parity, or at levels of a recent date, whichever is higher. The purpose should also be to keep wages at a point stabilized with today's cost of living. Both must be regulated at the same time; and neither one of them can or should be regulated without the other.

At the same time that farm prices are stabilized, I will stabilize wages.

That is plain justice—and plain common sense.

And so I have asked the Congress to take this action by the first of October. We must now act with the dispatch which the stern necessities of war require.

I have told the Congress that inaction on their part by that date will leave me with an inescapable responsibility to the people of this country to see to it that the war effort is no longer imperiled by the threat of economic chaos.

As I said in my Message to the Congress:

In the event that the Congress should fail to act, and act adequately, I shall accept the responsibility, and I will act.

The President has the powers, under the Constitution and under Congressional Acts, to take measures necessary to avert a disaster which would interfere with the winning of the war. . . .

Today I have also advised the Congress of the importance of speeding up the passage of the tax bill. The Federal Treasury is losing millions of dollars each and every day because the bill has not yet been passed. Taxation is the only practical way of preventing the incomes and profits of individuals and corporations from getting too high.

I have told the Congress once more that all net individual incomes, after payment of all taxes, should be limited effectively by further taxation to a maximum net income of $25,000 a year. And it is equally important that corporate profits should not exceed a reasonable amount in any case.

The Nation must have more money to run the war. People must stop spending for luxuries. Our country needs a far greater share of our incomes. . . .

Battles are not won by soldiers or sailors who think first of their own personal safety. And wars are not won by people who are concerned primarily with their own comfort, their own convenience, their own pocketbooks. . . .

All of us here at home are being tested—for our fortitude, for our selfless devotion to our country and to our cause.

Further Resources

BOOKS

Graham, Otis I. Jr. *Toward a Planned Society: From Roosevelt to Nixon.* New York: Oxford University Press, 1976.

Vatter, Harold G. *The U.S. Economy in World War II.* New York: Columbia University Press, 1985.

Ware, Caroline Farrar. *The Consumer Goes to War: A Guide to Victory on the Home Front.* New York: Funk & Wagnalls, 1942.

The War Labor Board and What It Means to You
Pamphlet

By: Douglas Aircraft Company

Date: March 18, 1943

Source: *The War Labor Board Order and What It Means to You.* Santa Monica, Calif.: Douglas Aircraft Company, 1943.

About the Organization: A pioneering company in the aircraft manufacturing fields since 1920, Douglas Aircraft Company—builder of the legendary DC-3 and various military aircraft—was a prime defense contractor during World War II. Douglas Aircraft is headquartered in Santa Monica, California. ∎

Introduction

World War II (1939–1945) marked a major turning point in the history of the American workplace. For the first time, the national government sought to prohibit racial and gender discrimination in both hiring and promoting employees and to advance the then-novel concept of "equal-pay for equal-work." Franklin D. Roosevelt's landmark executive order in April 1941 established the Federal Fair Employment Practices Commission (FEPC). These provisions applied only to private firms awarded government contracts, and, therefore, had somewhat limited application. Once America entered World War II, the

reach of the FEPC expanded greatly. Although its edicts were frequently evaded, the FEPC set an important precedent for future efforts by the national government to combat workplace discrimination.

Meanwhile, other wartime government agencies also played a crucial role in this workplace revolution—chief among them the National War Labor Board (NWLB), an independent agency established by presidential order on January 12, 1942. The NWLB worked closely with the FEPC and the Department of Labor to handle much of the day-to-day enforcement of these new government antidiscriminatory regulations.

Founded in 1920 by legendary aircraft pioneer, Donald Douglas, the Santa Monica, California-based Douglas Aircraft Company was a prime example of a defense contractor that operated under the close scrutiny of the National War Labor Board. As such, Douglas Aircraft workers—whites and blacks, men and women—were impacted by the various administrative rulings of the National War Labor Board.

Significance

Unfortunately, it remains doubtful whether the majority of American corporations actually embraced the federal government's antidiscrimination ethos of the World War II era. The experience of the tumultuous 1960s demonstrated how long-standing cultural prejudices operated against minorities and women and hampered the economic progress of these groups. American corporations likely viewed these wartime workplace innovations as an inconvenient, but ultimately bearable, cost of doing business. The subsequent dissolution of the National War Labor Board after the war (along with the Congress' refusal to make the FEPC a permanent part of American policy) was no doubt appreciated by many of the leaders of corporate America.

Although substantially abated in the immediate postwar era, the government's various antidiscrimination efforts in 1941–45 did serve to establish both the legislative and cultural foundation for the Civil Rights movement's victories in the 1960s and 1970s.

Primary Source

The War Labor Board Order and What It Means to You [excerpt]

> **SYNOPSIS:** Among its various responsibilities, the National War Labor Board was charged with the task of promoting the smooth operation of the country's workplace—especially in private firms receiving government contracts. Defense contractor, Douglas Aircraft, of Santa Monica, California, issued the following booklet to its employees to clarify the often confusing edicts of the National War Labor Board.

Douglas Aircraft Company Employees work on planes in Long Beach, California. October 1942. THE LIBRARY OF CONGRESS.

Foreword

To Douglas Employees:

This booklet has been prepared to answer as many as possible of the questions you have asked about the Directive Order of the National War Labor Board issued March 3, 1943. The Order is printed in full, together with extracts from the majority opinion, statements of policies of this Company and other pertinent information. . . .

This company was the first, on May 2, 1942, to suggest to the National War Labor Board that consideration should be given to the increased cost of living and wage increases elsewhere before possible freezing of wages in all Southern California airplane plants. From the very beginning of the wage stabilization conferences last July we have followed the policy of presenting all facts to the government and carrying out its dictates in the light of national rather than individual, or group, interests. This we will continue to do so long as the government con-

siders it essential to the inflation control program and to our production effort.

I appreciate the patience, co-operation and loyalty with which you awaited the decision of the War Labor Board.

[Signature] Donald W. Douglas
Santa Monica, California
March 18, 1943.

The War Labor Board Order and What It Means To You

[Italicized text in the following excerpt was in bold in the original document.]

Equal pay for equal work, identical classifications for identical jobs, and individual up-grading on individual merit have been established for all aircraft workers, men and women alike, wherever they may be employed in Southern California aircraft factories. These conditions shall prevail for the duration of the unlimited National Emergency declared by the

President of the United States on May 27, 1941. Such is the intent of the Directive Order of the National War Labor Board of March 3, 1943, for Douglas workers, and for all other aircraft employees.

The ruling of the Board establishes minimum and maximum rates of pay for 291 classified occupations. All of these are grouped into ten labor grades with wages ranging from a minimum of 75 cents per hour up to a $1.45 maximum. While the order stabilizes and equalizes like jobs in all shops, it provides that no employee's present rate of pay shall be reduced. And all classified employees "shall immediately receive at least the minimum hourly wage rate attached to the labor grade in which his job is classified," according to the Order.

Job Evaluation

The advantages of the job classification plan are summarized in one paragraph from the opinion of the Board. It describes the method of evaluating each job and will clarify any questions about the differentials in minimum and maximum rates of pay from the bottom to the top of the ten labor grades. The Board says:

> The purpose of the new job classification plan is to remove those manifest inequities from the present haphazard wage structure. This is to be done by careful definition of individual jobs and a studied evaluation of wage rates for these jobs. The first step in the job evaluation plan was to decide upon a list of characteristics common to all jobs and a method of measuring the degree of value of each of these characteristics for each job. The chosen job characteristics are skill, mentality, responsibility for material and equipment, mental application, physical application, job conditions and unavoidable hazards. To give a true measure of the value of the work done by a competent workman on each of the classified jobs, each job is evaluated by carefully estimating the degree of each of these characteristics required to do the work of that job in a satisfactory way. When these evaluations have been completed for all the jobs or groups of jobs, they indicate the appropriate relationship between wage rates that should be paid for the several jobs, on the basis of skill, intelligence, responsibility, application, job conditions and hazards. *The plan as a whole is an equitable application, within the industry's internal wage structure, of the sound principle of equal pay for equal work.*

In this portion of the opinion of the Board it emphasizes that it is evaluating the JOB and not the MAN who performs it. Hence, only the wage rates for the JOB are frozen, and not the earning power of the MAN. The job, whatever its description, depends

for its execution upon the capacity of the man or woman who occupies that position—upon the effort of a human being.

Merit Reviews

The Labor Board's Directive Order assures every Douglas employee full opportunity for advancement. You will find in Part I, Section 1, Paragraph (f) the requirement that any classified employee who has been at the maximum rate for his grade for a period of sixteen (16) weeks may request a review of his qualifications to determine whether or not he should be upgraded to a better job if one is available. It has been and will continue to be our standard policy automatically to review the record of each employee every three months instead of the longer period of 16 weeks. In actual practice, a large number of records are reviewed more frequently, to accomplish, in the language of the Order, "more rapid advancement where that is in the interest of maximum production as determined by the employer."

Personnel and Payroll departments have completed the tremendous task of conversion of all classifications and have arranged the necessary pay adjustments to bring all factory employees at least to the minimum of their SCAI labor grade and rate range. In addition, work has already been started on reviews of all other employees' records to accomplish under the Douglas company's merit increase policy "necessary ingrade adjustments" or merit increases, according to their efficiency and work assignments. *All such wage adjustments will be effective as of the payroll period beginning March 18, 1943.*

Every Douglas employee covered by the Directive Order of the National War Labor Board of March 3, 1943, is entitled, individually and in his own right, to the full benefits of reclassification, pay adjustment, promotions, vacations with pay, and sick leave. Every measure necessary to the immediate and complete application of the spirit and the letter of the Order has been taken by the Company. Any employee, who desires to do so may at any time apply to his Supervisor or to his Employee Counselor for additional information or action.

Clerical Workers

Weekly and hourly paid clerical and technical employees, commonly known as the "white collar workers," gain equal benefits and advantages under Part II of the Order. All employees not included in Part I are to be reclassified. A schedule was submitted to the War Labor Board at the same time as the one for production workers. However, the Board directed that this schedule be submitted for the approval of the West Coast Aircraft Committee, on which management, labor and the public will have representation. Although their specific job classifications are not included in the Order, it is directed that their compensation shall be adjusted within 90 days and made retroactive to March 4, 1943, which was the Douglas payroll period nearest to the effective date of the Order. (See Appendix "A" Part V, Section 6, page 17). Administrative employees on the company's monthly payroll are not covered by the Board's Order.

Vacations with pay, and sick leave, for all Douglas employees have been authorized by the Board. Every worker will participate according to length of service with the Company. (See Appendix "A", Part III, Section 1.)

Wage Adjustments

Retroactive wage adjustments of three $25.00 war bonds and $10.00 in cash, or a cash payment of $64.75, and ranging downward to $1.85 per week, have been granted all aircraft employees.

The provisions of Section 2 of Part III dealing with the retroactive wage adjustment are clear insofar as they affect those employees who have remained on the payroll of the company from July 6, 1942, through Mar. 3, 1943. Many questions have arisen concerning the status of employees whose time and conditions of service are not specifically provided for under the Directive Order. It will be necessary to submit all doubtful cases to the West Coast Aircraft Committee for determination. Those who went from aircraft employment into the military services are given special consideration under Part III, Section 2, Paragraph (c). You may be assured that the company will adopt the most liberal interpretation permissable under the Order in compensating all other groups who are entitled to a partial retroactive wage adjustment. And payment will be made as quickly as possible.

Information contained in this booklet has been assembled from official copies of the National War Labor Board's Directive Order of March 3, 1943, and from the conversion table and other documents submitted by the Company to the Board. To the best of our knowledge and belief it is complete and accurate. Any inadvertant variations in this booklet from the official text of the Order or from the official interpretations of it will be modified to conform to the Order as promulgated by the Board or its representatives.

Further Resources

BOOKS

Baker Wise, Nancy, and Christy Wise. *A Mouthful of Rivets: Women at Work in World War II.* San Francisco: Jossey-Bass, 1994.

Hartmann, Susan. *The Home Front and Beyond: American Women in the 1940s.* Boston: Twayne Publishers, 1982.

National War Labor Board. *The Termination Report of the National War Labor Board: Industrial Disputes and Wage Stabilization in Wartime.* Washington, D.C.: National War Labor Board, 1949

"The Nine Hundred and Twenty-ninth Press Conference"
Press conference

By: Franklin D. Roosevelt

Date: December 28, 1943

Source: Roosevelt, Franklin D. "The Nine Hundred and Twenty-ninth Press Conference," December 28, 1943. Excerpts reprinted in *The Public Papers and Addresses of Franklin D. Roosevelt, 1943 Volume: The Tide Turns.* New York: Harper & Brothers, 1950, 569–75.

About the Author: Franklin D. Roosevelt (1882–1945) was born at Hyde Park, New York. Educated at Harvard, Roosevelt was elected to the New York Senate in 1910, and served as assistant secretary of the navy from 1913 to 1920. After losing a bid for vice president in 1920, Roosevelt contracted polio, leaving his legs permanently paralyzed. Returning to politics, Roosevelt was elected governor of New York in 1928, and he defeated Herbert Hoover for the presidency in 1932. Roosevelt was reelected in 1936, 1940, and 1944. The only president to serve more than two terms, Roosevelt led the nation through the Great Depression and during World War II. ∎

Introduction

Although the New Deal had enacted considerable legislation between 1933 and 1936 designed to restore the American middle class, widespread opposition hardened by 1937, as Franklin D. Roosevelt sought to enact programs targeted specifically to assist the nation's truly poor. Roosevelt's Second Inaugural Address of January 1939 called for bold action: "I see one-third of a nation ill-housed, ill-clad, ill-nourished." However a potent coalition of Republicans and conservative Democrats (mostly from the South) either successfully blocked most new initiatives or rendered ineffective those that did pass. The Bankhead-Jones Farm Tenancy Act of 1937—a well-intentioned measure that established the controversial Farm Security Administration, designed to enable long-suffering farmworkers to purchase their own lands—fell far short of its ambitious goals. In retrospect, the Fair Labor Standards Act of June 1938 can be considered the final New Deal bill.

Meanwhile, social critics lamented the lack of progress toward achieving true social and economic justice for the habitually downtrodden. Roosevelt repeatedly refused to concede publicly that further New Deal initiatives could not be passed. As a practical matter, the administration's primary battle was to protect and preserve the New Deal initiatives passed prior to 1939. Roosevelt's January 1939 State of the Union Address contained a tacit admission of this political reality, in which he called for the need "to invigorate the processes of recovery in order to preserve our reforms." The era of social and economic experimentation had ended.

Soon thereafter, the pressures of foreign affairs overshadowed domestic policy. The rearmament effort, followed by America's entry into World War II in December 1941, removed much of the pressure to adopt or extend new domestic reforms. The resulting prosperity even trickled down to the country's poorest citizens. The adage, a rising tide lifts all boats, proved true, if only in a modest fashion.

By December 1943, Americans were confident of victory in Europe and Asia. Americans began to think seriously about the shape of the postwar world, including domestic policy considerations. Not surprisingly, many voices—long stifled by the perceived need for wartime unity and distracted by wartime concerns—now demanded yet another round of ambitious social reform.

Significance

Roosevelt needed to garner support from the American business community for his ambitious interventionist foreign policy and to achieve his unprecedented industrial production goals and wartime mobilization efforts. In order to accomplish these goals, political realities forced Roosevelt—despite protests to the contrary—to abandon most of his unrealized hopes for extending the New Deal. The 1942 Congress, dominated by a conservative coalition of Republicans and southern Democrats, endeavored to eliminate or reduce the scope of many New Deal programs. In June 1943, Congress passed, over Roosevelt's veto, the Smith-Connally Act (the War Labor Disputes Act) favored by management, and opposed by unions.

After several years of heated denial, Roosevelt publicly acknowledged the political reality that the New Deal could not be expanded further on December 28, 1943. In a press conference, Roosevelt compared his two primary roles as president—"Dr. New Deal" and "Dr. Win-the-War."

Scholars continue to debate what Roosevelt intended these titles to signify, whether he would have resurrected the New Deal to tackle the pressing requirements of post-World War II America. Roosevelt won reelection in 1944, but died soon after his fourth inauguration. While he never again piloted a peacetime economy, Roosevelt's unfinished legacy served as an inspiration for several generations of progressive social reformers.

Vice President Harry S. Truman, who succeeded Roosevelt in April 1945, had strongly supported the New Deal. As president, Truman proposed several new reform programs, including a comprehensive system of national health care. Roosevelt's successor lacked the personal charisma, political skills, and—most importantly—the votes in Congress to institute these new social reforms. The impasse in American politics that prevented further expansion of New Deal initiatives began in 1937, and it lasted until 1964. In 1964, a new generation of liberal leaders—many of whom had themselves been enthusiastic young New Dealers, led by President Lyndon Johnson and Vice President Hubert Humphrey—helped enact major portions of Roosevelt's unfinished legacy, including civil rights legislation, Medicare, and increased federal aid to education.

Primary Source

"The Nine Hundred and Twenty-ninth Press Conference" [excerpt]

SYNOPSIS: President Franklin D. Roosevelt frequently used press conferences to communicate with the American people. During his press conference on December 28, 1943, Roosevelt acknowledged publicly, for the first time, a policy shift that had been a political reality for several years—the New Deal was over. While admitting this he nevertheless defended the New Deal programs and looked towards new programs "when the time comes."

Mr. President, after our last meeting with you, it appears that someone stayed behind and received word that you no longer like the term "New Deal." Would you care to express any opinion to the rest of us? . . .

How did the New Deal come into existence? It was because there was an awfully sick patient called the United States of America, and it was suffering from a grave internal disorder—awfully sick—all kinds of things had happened to this patient, all internal things. And they sent for the doctor. And it was a long, long process—took several years before those ills, in that particular illness of ten years ago, were remedied. But after a while they were remedied. And on all those ills of 1933, things had to be done to cure the patient internally. And it was done; it took a number of years.

And there were certain specific remedies that the old doctor gave the patient, and I jotted down a few of those remedies. The people who are peddling all this talk about "New Deal" today, they are not telling about why the patient had to have remedies. I am inclined to think that the country ought to have it brought back to their memories, and I think the country ought to be asked too, as to whether all these rather inexperienced critics shouldn't be asked directly just which of the remedies should be taken away from the patient, if you should come down with a similar illness in the future. It's all right now—it's all right internally now—if they just leave him alone.

But since then, two years ago, the patient had a very bad accident—not an internal trouble. Two years ago, on the seventh of December, he was in a pretty bad smashup—broke his hip, broke his leg in two or three places, broke a wrist and an arm, and some ribs; and they didn't think he would live, for a while. And then he began to "come to"; and he has been in charge of a partner of the old doctor. Old Dr. New Deal didn't know "nothing" about legs and arms. He knew a great deal about internal medicine, but nothing about surgery. So he got his partner, who was an orthopedic surgeon, Dr. Win-the-War, to take care of this fellow who had been in this bad accident. And the result is that the patient is back on his feet. He has given up his crutches. He isn't wholly well yet, and he won't be until he wins the war.

And I think that is almost as simple, that little allegory, as learning again how to spell "cat."

The remedies that the old Dr. New Deal used were for internal troubles. He saved the banks of the United States and set up a sound banking system. We don't need to change the law now, although obviously there are some people who don't like saving the banks who would like to change the whole system, so that banks would have the great privilege under American freedom of going "bust" any time they wanted to again.

Well, at the same time, one of the old remedies was Federal deposit insurance, to guarantee bank deposits; and yet I suppose there must be some people, because they make so much smoke, who would like to go back to the old system and let any bank, at will, go and lose all its depositors' money with no redress.

In those days, another remedy was saving homes from fore-closure, through the H.O.L.C.; saving farms from foreclosure by the Farm Credit Ad-

ministration. I suppose some people today would like to repeal all that and go back to the conditions of 1932, when the people out West mobbed a Federal Judge because he was trying to carry out the existing law of the land in foreclosing a farm; rescuing agriculture from disaster—which it was pretty close to—by the Triple A [Agricultural Adjustment Administration] and Soil Conservation; establishing truth in the sale of securities and protecting stock investors through the S.E.C. And yet I happen to know that there is an undercover drive going on in this country today to repeal the S.E.C., and "let's sell blue-sky securities to the widows and orphans and everybody else in this country." A lot of people would like to do that, take off all the rules and let old Mr. Skin skin the public again.

Well, we have got slum clearance—decent housing; and there hasn't been enough done on slum clearance. I don't think that people who go into slums in this country would advocate stopping that, or curtailing the program, although of course a small percentage of real-estate men would like to have slums back again, because they pay money.

Reduction of farm tenancy.

Well, your old doctor, in the old days, old Doctor New Deal, he put in old-age insurance, he put in unemployment insurance. I don't think the country would want to give up old-age insurance or unemployment insurance, although there are a lot of people in the country who would like to keep us from having it.

We are taking care of a great many crippled and blind people, giving a great deal of maternity help, through the Federal aid system. Well, some people want to abolish it all.

And the public works program, to provide work, to build thousands of permanent improvements—incidentally, giving work to the unemployed, both the P.W.A. and W.P.A.

Federal funds, through F.E.R.A., to starving people.

The principle of a minimum wage and maximum hours.

Civilian Conservation Corps.

Reforestation.

The N.Y.A., for thousands of literally underprivileged young people.

Abolishing child labor. It was not thought to be constitutional in the old days, but it turned out to be.

Reciprocal trade agreements, which of course do have a tremendous effect on internal diseases.

Stimulation of private home building through the F.H.A.

The protection of consumers from extortionate rates by utilities. The breaking up of utility monopolies, through Sam Rayburn's law.

The resettlement of farmers from marginal lands that ought not to be cultivated; regional physical developments, such as T.V.A.; getting electricity out to the farmers through the R.E.A.; flood control; and water conservation; drought control—remember the years we went through that!—and drought relief; crop insurance, and the ever normal granary; and assistance to farm cooperatives. Well, conservation of natural resources.

Well, my list just totaled up to thirty, and I probably left out half of them. But at the present time, obviously, the principal emphasis, the overwhelming first emphasis should be on winning the war. In other words, we are suffering from that bad accident, not from an internal disease. . . .

But it seems pretty clear that we must plan for, and help to bring about, an expanded economy which will result in more security, in more employment, in more recreation, in more education, in more health, in better housing for all of our citizens, so that the conditions of 1932 and the beginning of 1933 won't come back again. . . .

You have a program to meet the needs of the country. The 1933 program that started to go into effect that year took a great many years. If you remember what I said, it was a program to meet the problems of 1933. Now, in time, there will have to be a new program, whoever runs the Government. We are not talking in terms of 1933's program. We have done nearly all of that, but that doesn't avoid or make impossible or unneedful another program, when the time comes. When the time comes.

Further Resources

BOOKS

Brinkley, Alan. *The End of Reform: New Deal Liberalism in Recession and War.* New York: Alfred A. Knopf, 1985.

Burns, James MacGregor. *Roosevelt: The Soldier of Freedom.* New York: Harcourt Brace Jovanovich, 1970.

Porter, David L. *Congress and the Waning of the New Deal.* Port Washington, N.Y.: Kennikat Press, 1980.

"Seizure!"

Magazine article

By: *Time*

Date: May 8, 1944

Source: "Seizure!" *Time,* May 8, 1944, 11–13.

About the Publication: *Time* was the most influential, national magazine in the United States during the World War II era, and remains one of America's most widely read news magazines. ∎

Introduction

American industry realized high profits during the wartime economic boom. However, many business leaders considered the federal government heavy handed in allocating raw materials and imposing production quotas. Business leaders were also upset by what they viewed as government supervision of labor relations that highly favored unions. Despite this tension, public confrontation between business and the government rarely occurred.

One exception to this general rule of quiet tolerance, involving a showdown between the federal government and Montgomery Ward, captured national headlines. As Montgomery Ward did not recognize a particular union as the legitimate bargaining agent for its workers, the company steadfastly refused to negotiate with that union's representatives—virtually guaranteeing a walk-out. Rather than permitting the nation's second-leading retailer to shut down operations, the Roosevelt administration decided to take over day-to-day operations of the company. This was done to maintain a stable economic climate on the home front. Many Americans applauded the get-tough policy in this case, as the company had demonstrated a marked hostility to organized labor.

The government undoubtedly expected swift capitulation from Montgomery Ward management. It was hard to conceive that corporate executives would challenge the authority of a popular president and his administration. However, cantankerous Montgomery Ward chairman Sewell Avery (1874–1960) was spoiling for a fight. By April 1944, Avery already was embroiled in a running dispute with the National War Labor Board. Montgomery Ward had refused to accept contract proposals with its workforce, as Avery thought the provisions were too favorable to labor interests seeking to unionize his company. In response to government seizure of his corporation, Avery literally barricaded himself inside his Chicago headquarters, daring the Roosevelt administration to make the next move in this volatile atmosphere. Soldiers were dispatched to the scene instantly. Avery was carried unceremoniously out of the company's headquarters, while defiantly still seated in his expensive

Sewell L. Avery, chairman of Montgomery Ward & Co., is escorted by two military policemen for refusing to cooperate with President Roosevelt's directive. April 27, 1945. © BETTMANN/CORBIS. REPRODUCED BY PERMISSION.

leather-backed chair. This memorable moment splashed across the front pages of the nation's newspapers.

Significance

This bizarre incident provoked an immediate congressional inquiry into issues concerning the government's often coercive labor and management policies during World War II. Many Americans decried the government's heavy-handed actions against Montgomery Ward on general principles. Others wondered why a mere department store chain and mail-order house should be deemed an "essential" national industry. This was the classification necessary for government seizures under the Smith-Connally Act, also known as the War Labor Disputes Act. The Smith-Connally Act was passed to limit government seizures of businesses to essential national industries in order to avoid significant disruption of the nation's war efforts.

Sewell Avery electrified the nation, and especially the business community with his nonviolent, uncooperative tactics. The feisty Saginaw, Michigan, native and Michigan Law School graduate passively resisted government action, as did later leaders of heroic civil rights struggles in the 1960s. It is difficult to imagine today's

corporate leaders, more sensitive to public relations issues, would emulate Avery's defiant stance toward the government.

Primary Source

"Seizure!"

> **SYNOPSIS:** In this article, *Time* captures the drama of an intense (and bizarre) confrontation between the Roosevelt administration and one of the nation's most outspoken business leaders, Montgomery Ward chairman Sewell Avery. Avery was evicted from his office after the Roosevelt administration decided to assume the day-to-day operations of the firm because of an impending strike.

Serene and calm, Sewell Lee Avery sat down in the green leather chair in his paneled office, and waited. Day before, he had sent a telegram challenging the authority of the President of the U.S. to seize the Chicago plant of Montgomery Ward & Co., the $295,000,000 mail-order house of which Mr. Avery is the absolute, unchallenged boss. Mr. Avery had not long to wait.

The U.S. Government arrived, in the person of an old-family Chicagoan, Under Secretary of Commerce Wayne Chatfield Taylor—a rich man's son, product of St. Mark's and Yale, onetime investment banker, and by no means a wild-eyed New Dealer. Sewell Avery rose from his chair, his thin lips parting in an amiable smile, and courteously, gravely asked the U.S. Government to step in. The door closed.

With Wayne Taylor came short, balding Ugo Carusi, executive assistant to the U.S. Attorney General; with Sewell Avery were two top company executives. Out of his briefcase Wayne Taylor drew a certified copy of the Presidential order directing the Secretary of Commerce to take over operation of Montgomery Ward & Co. "for the successful prosecution of the war."

An hour later Wayne Taylor emerged, informed newsmen that Sewell Avery had bluntly refused to turn over his plant. Messrs. Taylor and Carusi seemed nonplussed. They telephoned Commerce Secretary Jesse Jones in Washington, huddled with U.S. District Attorney J. Albert Woll in Chicago's old Post Office. Presently they returned, accompanied by U.S. Deputy Marshal William H. McDonnell and eight gun-toting deputies. Facing the armed squadron, Sewell Avery politely told Marshal McDonnell that he would not surrender. Then a call went out to Camp Skokie Valley, just north of Chicago.

MONTGOMERY WARD PEOPLE:

FACTS ABOUT THE STRIKE AT WARDS

1. The contract which Wards signed at Chicago in December, 1942, under duress at the direction of the President, expired December 8, 1943.

2. On November 16, 1943, Wards told the union it would negotiate a new contract covering five of the seven bargaining units established at Chicago. Wards questioned whether the union represented a majority of employees in the mail order house and retail store because less than 20% in those two units were then having union dues checked off from wages.

3. Although five months have elapsed, the union has refused to show that it is the majority choice of the employees by either a card check or an election.

4. Under the law Wards is forbidden to bargain with a union which does not represent a majority.

5. The War Labor Board has illegally ordered Wards to extend the expired contract without requiring the union to prove its majority. Wards has brought suit to have this order set aside.

6. The union has called the strike to force Wards to accept this illegal order.

7. The company stands ready to recognize the union when proof of its representation has been presented.

MONTGOMERY WARD & CO.
SEWELL AVERY
Chairman

An ad taken out by Montgomery Ward explains its position on the employee strike. © TRIBUNE MEDIA SERVICES, INC. ALL RIGHTS RESERVED. REPRODUCED BY PERMISSION.

Time to Go Home

Shortly after 6 p.m., three olive-drab Army trucks rolled up to Montgomery Ward's main entrance. Out jumped a 44-man unit of battle-helmeted Military Police under command of Lieut. Ludwig Pincura.

Sewell Avery was not surprised to see them. He smiled. After a moment's embarrassed silence, Lieut. Pincura said: "Under authority vested in me by the President of the United States I am taking over this plant."

Asked Sewell Avery: "Does that mean I have to leave?"

"Yes," said the commander of the Army of Occupation.

"No," said Wayne Taylor, almost at the same time.

Sewell Avery, a tall, thin man with long thin hands, glanced calmly at his watch. "Well," he said, "time to go home anyway." He left by a rear door, ducking reporters, jumped into his waiting black Cadillac and drove to his Lake Shore Drive apartment. Lieut. Pincura's men posted the President's seizure order on company bulletin boards, began alternating on four-hour shifts in front of the eight-story brick office building. For the 16th time in World War II the U.S. Army had seized private property, at the direction of the President, as the result of a labor dispute. But this time there was a difference. That night on the radio, in the early editions of morning newspapers, in news offices and corner drugstores, the questions were asked: Is Ward's a war plant? Do the President's wartime powers cover seizure of a mail-order house?

"You New Dealer!"

Next morning 30 newsmen and photographers milled around Montgomery Ward's main entrance, their way barred by soldiers. A lieutenant came out, told the newsmen a press room had been set up on the seventh floor. Virtually imprisoned in this room for 20 minutes (a bayonet-wielding soldier barred the door), the newsmen were finally ushered into Sewell Avery's office.

Sewell Avery was not there. At his desk sat Wayne Taylor; at Wayne Taylor's right sat lank, bird-like Attorney General Francis Biddle, who had flown in from Washington at 4 a.m., rushed to Ward's after an hour's sleep at the Drake Hotel. His eyes were red-rimmed; his jaw set.

Said the Attorney General, in his best Philadelphia Main Line accent: "When Mr. Avery came in this morning I asked him if he would cooperate and turn over books to our bookkeepers. He refused to do this. . . . I asked him to call a staff meeting and explain what our purpose was. Mr. Avery said he would not cooperate in any way. We told Mr. Avery he would have to leave. Mr. Avery refused."

Francis Biddle looked nervously about the room, then quietly dropped his bombshell: "Mr. Taylor therefore directed Major Weber to conduct Mr. Avery out of the plant. Mr. Avery refused and had to be carried out."

Newsmen nearest the door scurried out of the room to telephones. Those who stayed badgered the Attorney General with questions:

"Did they actually carry him out?"

Replied Mr. Biddle: "He was actually picked up and carried out of this chair occupied by Mr. Taylor."

"How did he react?"

Francis Biddle seemed to welcome this question. He smiled: "Well, I'll tell you something. He got pretty mad when I said he had to go. Then the blood came to his face and he said to me, 'You New Dealer!'"

A newsman asked: Would Sewell Avery be barred from holding a stockholders' meeting in the building? Francis Biddle saw no reason why he should; then he blandly added: "We're not interfering with anybody. We were in charge here and were being interfered with." That afternoon, Chicago papers carried quarter-page Montgomery Ward advertisements stating that "because of the presence of trespassers," the stockholders' meeting would be held at the Blackstone Hotel.

Feet First

The actual ejection of the $100,000-a-year board chairman of Montgomery Ward was carried out by Sergeant Jacob L. Lepak of Milwaukee and Private Cecil A. Dies of Memphis. The two soldiers picked 170-lb. Sewell Avery up by his arms and thighs, carried him to the elevator. Mr. Avery refused to walk in; the soldiers picked him up again. In the elevator Sewell Avery said: "I'll be glad when this is over." On the main floor he again refused to budge. The soldiers hoisted him up, carried him past a handful of startled clerks in the lobby, and down the main steps. His grey hair unruffled, his blue suit coat buttoned, his hands folded benignly across his stomach, his eyes half-closed, Avery looked every inch an Oriental potentate being borne by slaves.

Photographers who had waited outside jammed plates into their cameras, snapped the most startling U.S. newspicture since a press agent set a midget on J. P. Morgan's lap in 1933. One Ward executive suggested putting the picture on the cover of Ward's next catalogue, with a caption "We take orders from everybody." Put down on the sidewalk, Sewell Avery bowed slightly to his carriers, walked across the Chicago, Milwaukee, St. Paul & Pacific Railroad tracks to a waiting limousine.

Told that newsmen had snapped the picture, Attorney General Biddle replied: "That's too bad. I felt sorry for the old boy."

"The Old Man"

The events of the two days had projected into the news and given at least a footnote in history to a man hardly known to the U.S. public. Son of a wealthy Michigan lumberman (six generations of Averys have been lumbermen), Sewell Avery was born in Saginaw in 1874. After graduation from Michigan University Law School (1894), he started at the bottom in a small gypsum plans owned by his father. At 22 he was manager. In 1901 the company was absorbed by the U.S. Gypsum Co.; four years later, Sewell Avery was president of U.S. Gypsum. A suave and brilliant supersalesman, he built the company into an $81,000,000 concern, made it one of the largest purveyors of building materials in the U.S. He is still the company's board chairman.

In deep-depression 1931, when Montgomery Ward was losing money, harried directors called in Salesman Avery as doctor. In twelve years he had changed a $5,700,000 loss (1932) into a $20,438,000 profit (1943). His formula, soon discovered by avid readers of Montgomery Ward catalogues: adding new luxury lines to Ward's stock in trade. Said he: "We no longer depend on hicks and yokels. We sell more than overalls and manure-proof shoes." Meanwhile the number of employes has jumped from 35,000 to 78,000.

Sewell Avery has run Ward's not only well but with an iron hand. In the late '30s, Ward's became famous in the business world for the number of top executives who left because of violent disagreement with "the Old Man." (Some of them: Walter Hoving, now president of Manhattan's swank Lord & Taylor; Brigadier General Albert J. Browning, now a top man in Lieut. General Somervell's A.S.F.; Raymond H. Fogler, now president of W. T. Grant Co.) By turns a kindly and domineering man, Sewell Avery once said: "If anybody ventures to differ with me, of course, I throw them out of the window."

In time, Sewell Avery also earned a quiet reputation as one of the nation's foremost Roosevelt-haters and labor-baiters. He has fought the New Deal since 1935 when Ward's lost its blue eagle for refusing to pay NRA assessments. No rough-&-tumble labor fighter, his union opponents say that he has learned the "a 300-page legal brief can be as deadly as a machine gun."

Union Security

The long battle which flared last week began in 1939 when C.I.O.'s United Mail Order, Warehouse & Retail Employes' Union laid siege in Ward's

Chicago plant. By February 1941 the union had won an NLRB election (by 3-to-1 majority), was duly certified as bargaining agent for the plant's 7,000 employes. But it did not get a contract with Ward's until Franklin Roosevelt had twice commanded Sewell Avery to sign. The bone of contention: a maintenance-of-membership clause, which WLB insisted on ramming down Sewell Avery's throat. To Mr. Avery, maintenance of membership was the wartime equivalent of the closed shop, to which he is bitterly, irreconcilably opposed.

The contract came up for renewal last December. This time Sewell Avery flatly informed the union that he would not sign come hell or high water. His reason: with a year's staggering 200% labor turnover, he doubted that the union still represented a majority of employes. WLB promptly asked NLRB to hold another election. The union screamed, while other Chicago employers rushed NLRB with requests for elections in their plants. But WLB also ordered Sewell Avery to renew the contract, pending the election.

When the union finally struck (*Time,* April 24), the contract had not been signed, nor the election called. To end the strike and to force Sewell Avery to terms, WLB turned the case over to the President. No one knew for sure whether the union had a majority. WLB and NLRB were playing the New Deal's favorite game of labor coddling; bureaucratic red tape delayed the election. Sewell Avery, at the very least, was guilty of intransigence in not continuing the old contract until the election should be held.

Presidential Power

But the overwhelming issue at stake was whether or not the President had authority to take over an industry that seemed to the U.S. public patently civilian. How far does Federal power extend? Attorney General Biddle tried manfully to class Montgomery Ward as a war industry, pointing out that one of its subsidiaries manufactures airplane parts. But he hastily sought refuge under the Constitution's broad mandate to the President "to take care that the laws be faithfully executed."

Swift public clamor almost drowned over the Attorney General's tortuous reacting. Cried Illinois' Republican Congressman Charles S. Dewey: "Gestapo methods!" Tart Senator Harry S. Byrd asked: "Does Francis Biddle cherish the ambition to be an American Himmler?" Echoing the fears of many a businessman, Mississippi's Senator James Eastland declared: "If the President has power to take over Montgomery Ward, he has the power to take over a grocery store or butcher shop in any hamlet in the U.S."

The House Rules Committee whipped through a resolution for a Congressional inquiry. But Nevada's maverick Senator Pat McCarran beat the House to the draw, dispatched an investigator to Chicago, and subpoenaed all WLB files in the case. Acting under a month-old resolution empowering the Judiciary Committee to investigate all executive orders, he promised a full-dress "nonpolitical" investigation.

The President seemed to be on shaky, if not altogether nonexistent, legal ground in seizing the plant. But he had a case: the office of President could not accept a preemptory rebuff from one citizen. (During all the pulling & hauling, Franklin Roosevelt was still at his Southland vacation spot.)

By week's end the case was headed firmly for the courts. In Chicago, Attorney General Biddle summoned U.S. District Judge William H. Holly, a longtime liberal. out of a meeting of the National Lawyer's Guild, asked for an injunction to bar Sewell Avery and other company officers from the plant. The judge granted a temporary injunction, ordered a further hearing for this week. Said Sewell Avery: "Fine. It shows the Government recognizes the Constitution. Now we can take our time." After four days of occupation, the Army withdrew.

This week, as Attorney General Biddle applied in Federal Court for a presidential injunction against Ward's the issues were underlined with startling clarity. Said Biddle: "No business or property is immune to a presidential order. Particularly in time of war the Court should not substitute its judgement for that of the Executive." Replied Ward's counsel, Harold A. Smith: "I have listened in vain for any reference . . . to the Bill of Rights or the rights of the people. . . . Spontaneous fear rose up in the country after this seizure. Why? Because never has anything like this happened since the days of King John. . . . Are we at Runnymead again?"

Further Resources

BOOKS

Atleson, James B. *Labor in the Wartime State: Labor Relations and Law During World War II.* Urbana, Ill.: University of Illinois Press, 1998.

Miller, Sally M., and Daniel A. Cornford, eds. *American Labor in the Era of World War II.* Westport, Conn.: Greenwood Press, 1995.

Sullivan, Lawrence. *Bureaucracy Runs Amuck.* Indianapolis: Bobbs-Merrill, 1944.

The Bretton Woods Proposals

Booklet

By: U. S. Treasury Department

Date: February 15, 1945

Source: *The Bretton Woods Proposals.* Washington, D.C.: U.S. Treasury Department, 1945.

About the Organization: The U. S. Treasury Department issued this booklet to enhance public support for the Bretton Woods Agreements. This was part of the Roosevelt administration's efforts to create a new global order that reflected American economic, military, and political leadership. ■

Introduction

The United States took a major step toward creating a truly global economy at the Bretton Woods Monetary Conference in July 1944. Held in rural New Hampshire, this conference helped establish a new world currency-exchange system. This system did not use a strict gold standard, but, rather, a more flexible combination of gold and the American dollar. Delegates also made plans to establish both the International Monetary Fund (IMF) and the International Bank for Reconstruction and Development (World Bank)—institutions destined to play important roles in international business in the postwar world and promoting American economic dominance.

The United States had emerged as the world's strongest economic power by 1890. Despite this, many Americans were reluctant for the nation to break its traditional policy of isolationism and assume a role of global leadership. In World War I (1914–18), the United States demonstrated a military might that complemented its economic power. However, after that war much of the country wanted the United States to turn away from what they saw as unnecessary entanglement in foreign affairs.

As World War II (1939–45) drew to a victorious conclusion, the strength of the United States was evident. Most Americans reluctantly accepted that the United States would continue in a role of world leadership. The Bretton Woods Agreements of June 1944, coupled with two 1944 conferences at Dumbarton Oaks in Washington, D.C. that laid the foundation for creating of the United Nations in 1945, signified that America would play the decisive role in world affairs. There would be no retreat into a period of isolationism as occurred after World War I.

Significance

Although unheralded at the time, the decisions at Bretton Woods and Dumbarton Oaks would have profound implications in the decades to come. The IMF and the World Bank soon became important sources of loans and other funds to the governments of the new nations that were created in the decades after World War II. They did not accomplish this without controversy, as their aid was generally conditional upon the recipients following certain economic policies.

The United States's decision to assume a leading financial role in the world committed the nation, possibly unwittingly, to a policy of free trade. This opened vast new markets for American products, as well as exposing American business to competition with foreign imports. The loss of many manufacturing jobs in the United States over the past half-century can be seen as an unintended consequence of adhering to an increasingly permissive trade policy.

The momentous decision to accept the burdensome role of world leadership embroiled America in the whirlpool of international politics to a larger degree than feared by even the staunchest opponents of globalization at the time. The decisions of 1944 also likely committed the United States in the long run to a new, more-expansive immigration policy, befitting one of the world's two reigning superpowers, that occurred after 1965.

Whatever the wisdom of adopting a long-term policy of globalization, American leaders of 1944 primarily embraced the policy due to their determination to avoid a repetition of World War II and the rise of German Nazism—which they saw as the result of national economic rivalries exacerbated by the Great Depression of the 1930s. American leaders embraced internationalism and free trade as antidotes to the unbroken cycle of international war, especially in Europe. The dismal record of continued worldwide violence since the end of World War II during this supposed new global era proved that the predictions of those favoring globalization were overly optimistic. The heralded arrival of a more peaceful and secure planet did not occur, at least not as envisioned by the 1944 conferences.

Primary Source

The Bretton Woods Proposals [excerpt]

SYNOPSIS: The following excerpt from a U.S. Treasury Department booklet extols the virtues of the recently-negotiated Bretton Woods Agreements, designed to promote a truly global system reflecting American economic, military, and political hegemony. The document provides a revealing glimpse of the internationalist mindset prevalent at that time.

The actual details of a financial and monetary agreement may seem mysterious to the general public. Yet at the heart of it lie the most elementary bread-and-butter realities of daily life. What we have

U.S. Secretary of the Treasury Henry Morgenthau Jr. speaks at the Bretton Woods Conference. July 2, 1944. © BETTMANN/CORBIS. REPRODUCED BY PERMISSION.

done here in Bretton Woods is to devise machinery by which men and women everywhere can exchange, on a fair and stable basis, the goods which they produce through their labor. And we have taken the initial step through which the nations of the world will be able to help one another in economic development to their mutual advantage and for the enrichment of all.

> *—From the address closing the Bretton Woods Conference. By Henry Morgenthau, Jr., Secretary of the Treasury, President of the Conference.*

Introduction

Bretton Woods is the symbol of a new kind of cooperation. It stands for proposals looking toward cooperation in the solution of international monetary and financial problems. Drafted by representatives of 44 nations in a conference called on the invitation of President Roosevelt at Bretton Woods, New Hampshire, in July 1944, the proposals are the outgrowth of three years of study by the technical staffs of the Treasury, State Department, Board of Governors of the Federal Reserve System, and other agencies of the United States government. For a period

of more than a year, informal discussions were held with representatives of other governments associated with us in winning the war.

As part of the economic foundation for a peaceful and prosperous world, the Bretton Woods proposals call for the establishment of two international institutions, the International Monetary Fund and the International Bank for Reconstruction and Development. Although related in purpose, these institutions will perform quite different functions. The Fund will be concerned with the maintenance of orderly currency practices as they relate to international trade, while the Bank will facilitate the making of long-term international investments for productive purposes.

Acceptance of the proposals by the United States will require Congressional action.

The International Monetary Fund
What the Fund Will Do

The fundamental purpose of the International Monetary Fund is to promote the balanced growth of international trade. It will do this in three ways. First, it will stabilize the value of all currencies in terms of each other. Second, it will progressively remove barriers against making payments across boundary lines. Third, it will provide a supplementary source of foreign exchange to which a member country may apply for the assistance necessary to enable it to maintain stable and unrestricted exchange relationships with other members. . . .

Cooperation vs. Isolation

The essence of the proposed International Monetary Fund is that it would substitute order and stability for the dog-eat-dog attitude that has in the past characterized international currency practices. Order and stability in exchange policies are objectives that can be attained not by a single country working alone but only by the united action of all of the 44 countries represented at Bretton Woods. Upon the attainment of these objectives hinges the realization of the ultimate goals of national policy—high levels of employment, rising standards of living, and economic development. In the shrunken world of tomorrow prosperity, like political security, lies not in isolation but in cooperation and mutual understanding.

The International Bank for Reconstruction and Development

What the Bank Will Do

The International Bank for Reconstruction and Development, like the International Monetary Fund, recognizes the need for worldwide cooperation in monetary and financial matters. Both aim at the balanced growth of trade as a means of achieving high levels of employment and rising standards of living. Each, however, will have its own separate function. The Fund will be concerned with orderly, stable exchange rates and freedom in exchange transactions; the Bank will be concerned with long-range productive international investment.

The Bank, therefore, will fill important needs in the postwar economies of all the 44 countries that assisted in preparing the Bretton Woods proposals.

Factories, dams, power plants, transportation systems, and public buildings in the countries ravaged by war have been shelled, bombed, and pillaged. Foreign capital will be needed to help replace this wealth. While it is fully recognized that the major portion of the reconstruction burden must be borne by the affected countries themselves, yet for many "seed corn" items of capital equipment they must look to their more fortunate neighbors. . . .

The Bank's Guarantee

The Bank is not intended to supplant but to supplement the private capital market. Loans will be made, as they have been in the past, by private lenders who see an opportunity to make an advantageous investment in a foreign country. The Bank will support and encourage these loans through the usual investment channels. . . .

Direct and guaranteed loans will for the most part be additional loans, over and above the private loans that would ordinarily be made, and will serve directly to increase the volume of international trade. . . .

Membership

Membership in the Bank, in the first instance, is to be limited to countries that participated in the Bretton Woods conference and become members of the International Monetary Fund. Other countries may become members after they have been admitted to the Fund. Membership has been tied in this way because both institutions are designed to solve closely related problems. A country's adherence to the Fund will mean greater currency stability and the progressive removal of exchange restrictions, which will in turn reduce the risks of long-term investment. Furthermore, it is believed that only those nations that have demonstrated their willingness to cooperate in the improvement of basic world trade conditions should be permitted to participate in the operations of the International Bank for Reconstruction and Development. . . .

What the Bank Means to the United States

. . . The plans are based on the conviction that stability and security in financial and commercial relationships will remove some of the important causes of war and at the same time help to open the way for increased trade and prosperity throughout the world.

The United States now, as never before, occupies a key position in world affairs. Whether we cooperate in maintaining the peace as we have in waging war will to a considerable extent shape the course of history for generations to come. Our acceptance and support of the Bretton Woods proposals, therefore, will be taken as a happy augury. It will mean to the rest of the world that instead of choosing economic isolation, which would inevitably lead to political isolation, we have determined to do our part toward the attainment of world peace and prosperity.

Further Resources

BOOKS

Schild, Georg. *Bretton Woods and Dumbarton Oaks: American Economic and Political Postwar Planning in the Summer of 1944.* New York: St. Martin's Press, 1995.

Van Dormael, Armand. *Bretton Woods: Birth of a Monetary System.* New York: Holmes & Meier Publishers, 1978.

WEBSITES

The International Monetary Fund Home Page. Available online at http://www.imf.org/ (accessed April 21, 2003).

The World Bank Group. Available online at http://www.worldbank.org/ (accessed April 21, 2003).

"It Must Not Happen Again"

Newspaper advertisement

By: West Virginia Coal Association

Date: October 21, 1945

Source: "It Must Not Happen Again." Advertisement published in the *Herald-Advertiser,* October 21, 1945, as cited in U.S. House Committee on Military Affairs. *Repeal of War Labor Disputes Act.* Hearings before the Committee on Military Affairs, House of Representatives, 79th Cong., 1st sess. Washington, D.C.: U.S. Government Printing Office, 1945, 45–46.

About the Organization: The West Virginia Coal Association spoke for the interests of the coal mine owners and operators engaged in long-standing, bitter labor disputes with the United Mine Workers Association (UMWA). The UMWA was led by its charismatic and combative president, John L. Lewis. ■

Introduction

The immediate pre–World War II era witnessed the most violent and widespread, yet effective, series of strikes in American history. Organized labor enjoyed, in retrospect, its "golden age." American businesses enjoyed a welcome respite from intense labor strife during the war. The Smith-Connally Act of June 1943 (the War Labor Disputes Act) effectively curtailed many potential strikes, and the National War Labor Board helped enforce a measure of industrial peace.

After the end of World War II (1939–45), the various government economic controls began to be repealed. Not surprisingly, business leaders from the coal industry voiced strong concern about a resurgence of union activism at the end of World War II. The coal industry had endured, perhaps, the most bitter labor strife of any single American industry during the twentieth century. John L. Lewis was the leader of the United Mine Workers of America, and he was legendary for making strong demands and striking if they were not met. Lewis even

Many Americans considered United Mine Workers' leader, John L. Lewis as an arrogant "labor baron." **THE LIBRARY OF CONGRESS.**

had sought to defy President Franklin D. Roosevelt, a one-time ally, who demanded a no-strike pledge from labor for the duration of the war. Lewis called for a nationwide coal strike in 1943, only to relent when Roosevelt threatened the federal government seizure of the mines. Lewis came to symbolize, for many Americans, an arrogant "labor baron" not unlike the businessmen he opposed.

Significance

As Congress debated the fate of the Smith-Connally Act, some businessmen called for the act to remain in effect. This was especially true of those in industries with the most contentious labor relations, like mining. These business leaders favored the retention of the strong wartime measure as a way to rein in union activities. Recalling the prewar situation, they feared that a return to normal peacetime conditions would allow union activists to unleash another round of labor strife. With the war over, labor leaders were indeed starting to push for better wages and conditions.

Despite the fears expressed by business leaders, the Smith-Connally Act (War Labor Disputes Act) was swiftly repealed, and the National War Labor Board was abolished. During 1945 and 1946, organized labor engaged in a wave of major strikes. While these achieved some short-term gains, this resurgence of labor militancy served primarily to provoke a firm reaction—the subsequent passage of the 1947 Taft-Hartley Act, viewed by many as "strongly anti-labor." In the end, the American business community won the ultimate victory over rival labor unions.

Primary Source

"It Must Not Happen Again"

SYNOPSIS: Typical of corporate rhetoric against labor immediately after World War II, this newspaper advertisement appeared in a West Virginia publication, *The Herald-Advertiser*. The October 21, 1945, message was paid for by the West Virginia Coal Association, and represents the interests of coal mine owners and operators who were experiencing the return of labor unrest now that the war was over. The article encourages an end to the National War Labor Board, perceived as pro-labor, but the continuation of the Smith-Connally Act, which was restrictive of organized labor.

A coal mine strike which began late in September, spreading rapidly throughout West Virginia as roving UMWA pickets forced a work stoppage at 90 percent of the State's mines, was ended abruptly by John L. Lewis when he instructed his handpicked local officers to put the miners back to work on Monday (tomorrow).

It was a stupid and senseless strike covertly called in violation of an existing wage agreement ratified by representatives of the miners and coal producers, intended to coerce mine foremen and other members of the supervisory mine forces into a Lewis union organized and controlled by the UMWA.

This stoppage of work in the mines also was a violation of the Federal Smith-Connally Act. In ending the strike John L. Lewis, at least by implication, admits his responsibility for the mine stoppage and revealed that while he had power to order the men to return to work on Monday, he could have exercised the same authority at each mine when the men ceased work. Six months before, Lewis had agreed to the following provisions in the labor contract:

> The mine workers intended no intrusion upon the rights of management as heretofore practiced and understood * * *. The term 'mine workers' in this agreement shall not include mine foremen, assistant mine foremen, fire bosses, or bosses in charge of any class of labor inside or outside the mine, or coal inspectors, weigh bosses, watchmen, clerks or members of the executive, supervisory, sales, and technical forces of the operators.

This contract had at least 6 months to run before it could be reopened by any party. Yet John L. Lewis, demanding immediate organization of these supervisory forces whom he had hitherto exempted, deliberately violated a contract of his own making by trying to force these exempt employees of management into his puppet union.

Miners Not Sympathetic

West Virginia miners were never sympathetic with the UMWA leaders in promoting the strike. They were forced from the mines by their own leaders—forced to strike—just as Lewis sought to force the management of the coal mines into his union. The miners, of course, will bear the heavy burden of the strike placed upon their shoulders through the avarice of their leaders.

The contract breakers, by this illegal strike, have cost West Virginia nearly a hundred million dollars. Miners have lost $15,000,000 in wages, are subject to fines aggregating $2,000,000, are denied unemployment compensation benefits, have cashed their war bonds and have impaired their savings. For a long time the miners must remember that "Lewis giveth and Lewis taketh away."

John L. Lewis did not end the illegal coal strike without an ominous threat that his effort to force the unionization of mine foremen would be resumed at "some more appropriate time."

This is a threat that Congress cannot ignore. It is a threat that Congress can stop at its source. It is an impending threat held over all industry to stop reconversion, to keep employers and employees embroiled in a stupid struggle, a constant menace to economic peace.

During this short and unlawful strike the public generally, and coal consumers particularly, have observed with intense indignation the economic ravages that result from a coal strike. The cruel and devastating power of one man to cripple or destroy the Nation, or freeze the people into submission, has been made evident. No individual should be entrusted with such power without accompanying responsibility. Such unregulated and uncontrolled power, vested in one man without responsibility for his acts, can be as devastating as an atomic bomb in the hands of a person running berserk.

Every Wrong Has Its Remedy

There is a remedy for this wanton disturbance of the economic peace. Leaders of labor, clothed with vast power, must be made responsible for the exercise of the privileges they are accorded by law. The employers cannot dodge responsibility. Those who represent labor and make contracts with the employer must be held to similar accountability.

Congress, which clothed labor leaders with these innumerable powers, also has authority to impose responsibility on these persons. Early action by Congress would avert similar outlaw strikes by malcontents who have no regard for the sanctity of a labor contract. Immediate legislation would lead to the restoration of economic peace and eliminate turbulence in the chaotic labor field.

The coal industry is not the only industry affected by the domineering attitude of arrogant labor leaders who seek to deprive employers of their managerial rights. It has been the unworthy objective sought in many other industries. If you are an employer of labor it is your privilege and duty to advise your Senators and Congressmen that they should act to impose responsibility with the same alacrity that marked their efforts in extending privileges to organized labor.

Management must never be divested of its right to manage its operation, else the entire economic and industrial structure topple into irreparable ruin. Supervisory employees, vested with managerial powers, cannot follow both management and the directives of union leadership. These supervisors can be responsible only to the management that clothes them with the managerial authority they exercise.

West Virginia Coal Association

Further Resources

BOOKS

Baratz, Morton S. *The Union and the Coal Industry.* New Haven, Conn.: Yale University Press, 1955.

Dubofsky, Melvyn. *John L. Lewis: A Biography.* New York: Quadrangle/New York Times Book Co., 1977.

Zieger, Robert H. *John L. Lewis: Labor Leader.* Boston: Twayne Publishers, 1988.

Statement before the Senate Committee on Banking and Currency

Statement

By: Robert F. Wagner

Date: June 30, 1945

Source: Wagner, Robert F. Statement before the Senate Committee on Banking and Currency, June 30, 1945. 79th Cong., 1st sess. Washington, D.C.: U.S. Government Printing Office, 1945, 1–2, 3–4, 5.

About the Author: Robert F. Wagner (1877–1953), a native of Germany, came to the United States with his parents in 1885. He attended the City College of New York and New York Law School. In 1926, Wagner was elected a United States senator from New York—an office he held until his retirement in 1949. Throughout his career, Wagner remained one of the most influential and effective leaders of American liberalism. ∎

Introduction

The United States suffered through five depressions during the nineteenth century. These periods of severe economic downturns—the panics of 1819, 1837, 1857, 1873, and 1893—featured a contraction of the economy, the failure of many banks and businesses, and a significant increase in unemployment. During these panics, the U.S. government took little or no corrective action, except perhaps acting to protect its own treasury.

However, the Great Depression of the 1930s saw the U.S. government, for the first time, pursue active policy initiatives to improve the economic situation. Both Presidents Herbert Hoover and Franklin D. Roosevelt instituted policies that enjoyed varying degrees of success. By 1945, the precedent had been established for government policy intervention to assist the economy. With the impending return of peacetime conditions, the American people expected that the federal government would stand poised to adopt any policy necessary to avoid or lessen the effects of future depressions. Americans, remembering all too well the decade-long economic slump of the 1930s, believed that only the advent of World War II had rescued the nation from its economic depression. They fully expected the Great Depression to return once the war and its related economic boom ended.

To address these various concerns, a subcommittee of the U.S. Senate Committee on Banking and Currency held hearings from July through September 1945 to examine the so-called "Full Employment Act of 1945." The legislation was officially enacted the following year as the Full Employment Act of 1946. This law made it the federal government's responsibility not only to control inflation and unemployment, but also to adopt economic and fiscal policies that promoted full employment and prosperity. The Full Employment Act of 1946 also created the Council of Economic Advisers—an advisory body within the executive branch charged with assisting the president in managing the nation's economy.

Significance

The Full Employment Act of 1946 represented the triumph in Washington of the economic and financial philosophy of "Keynesian economics." Named after the influential British economist, John Maynard Keynes (1883–1946), Keynesian economics signified a major departure from historic economic theory. Traditional emphasis on the importance of balanced government budgets and the maintenance of a strict gold standard were abandoned. These economic theories were replaced with a more flexible concept that held, as its central premise, that government should engage in countercyclical (also called pump-priming) spending. In other words, the government should combat future depressions by spending, borrowing heavily if necessary, to stimulate an otherwise weak economy.

The New Deal economy had unwillingly been forced into a version of such pump-priming tactics in preparing for and conducting World War II. Only the tremendous infusion of government money into the economy to wage World War II finally produced the jolt necessary to restore economic prosperity. Keynes's ideas were little known in the United States when the pre-war expansion was undertaken. Even the appearance of Keynes's classic book, *The General Theory of Employment, Interest and Money,* did not immediately influence American policy makers. However, the Full Employment Act of 1946 represented a full triumph of Keynesian thinking among government officials. Keynesian economics remained the preeminent American and world economic philosophy, largely unchallenged, until well into the 1970s.

Primary Source

Statement of Senator Robert F. Wagner before the Senate Committee on Banking and Currency [excerpt]

SYNOPSIS: New York Democratic Senator Robert Wagner, chair of the Subcommittee on Banking and Currency, presents his case for the proposed Full Employment Act of 1945—a measure that, for the first time in American history, assigned to the federal government the responsibility of managing the economy to achieve full employment during peacetime. The Full Employment Act was enacted in 1946.

Statement of Hon. Robert F. Wagner, Senior Senator from the State of New York

It is misleading to talk about the full employment bill as a Government commitment to provide jobs for all. This bill presents a program of, by, and for the people. This bill proposes a commitment on the part of the American people that we shall have continuing full employment after the war.

Let us not be distracted by those who quibble as to the meaning of the words "full employment." Certainly, we need facts. But let us not hold back

until all the statisticians agree whether full employment means 60,000,000 jobs or 57,000,000 jobs.

I can define full employment very simply, by quoting a statement which I made 15 years ago. Then I said:

> The right to work is synonymous with the inalienable right to live. The right to work has never been surrendered and cannot be forfeited. Society was organized to enlarge the scope of that right and to increase the fruits of its exercise.

I spoke these words here in the Senate, on December 30, 1930.

And today I say this: Whoever believes in this right to work, believes in it for every adult who is looking for an honest job at decent pay, must believe in full employment. Whoever believes that American society can benefit by enlarging the scope of this right and increasing the fruits of its exercise, must necessarily approve at least the objectives of the full employment bill.

Any person who accepts the proposition that the right to work is of all-prevailing practical importance; any person who recognizes that all other rights, the freedoms and liberties which we cherish, depend upon this all-important right to work; any such person is committed to the principle of full employment.

These few remarks sum up my argument for the full-employment bill—in human terms. I do not think that anything can be said to weaken the force of this argument—in human terms.

The people of America also have an economic right to continuous full employment, because that means the full enjoyment of the boundless resources and wealth with which providence has blessed us. With full employment we can have constantly higher standards of living, because our capacity to produce is constantly and magnificently on the increase. With full employment we can easily afford to sustain decent standards of health, education, housing, and nutrition for our 37,000,000 families. With full employment, we can assure an endless demand for the products of our factories and our farms. With full employment we can afford to enjoy the leisure that is necessary to the cultivation of the finer qualities of mankind.

Full employment in America is also a world-wide right, for it is the most vital single requirement for lasting peace among all the peoples of the earth.

Mass unemployment would drive us toward both economic isolationism and economic imperialism; economic isolationism in the vain hope of providing jobs in America by excluding the products of other nations; economic imperialism in the vain hope of creating markets abroad for American products at the threat of the sword.

World peace must rest on ever-increasing world prosperity. World prosperity without American prosperity is manifestly too preposterous to contemplate. The splendid edifice of the Charter which we are now building, if not accompanied by full employment in America would be like a factory building without a dynamo. . . .

To maintain full employment after the war, we shall need jobs for at least 7,000,000 more persons than had jobs in the last year before the war. This means at least 13,000,000 more persons than had jobs in the banner year 1929.

We shall need to absorb an almost unbelievable increase in our productive capacity, which already shows that in our more advanced industries, two men can now do the work that three did before the war.

We shall need to maintain an average postwar annual income for the Nation almost twice as high as in the so-called prosperity year 1929—a postwar annual income, on a per capita basis, at least 50 percent higher than it was before the war.

We shall have to do all these things and more, in the face of the release of 20,000,000 or more able-bodied adults from the armed forces and from immediate war production. We shall need to do these things in the face of a drop in the demand for war goods and services which runs up to $100,000,000,000 a year.

Even to contemplate failure in this task is unthinkable. Twenty million or even fifteen million or ten million unemployed in postwar America would spell disaster.

The size of the task before us, the great human issues involved, require complete candor in our examination of past experience. During the decade before the war, we in this country wrestled continuously with the problem of mass unemployment. Substantial gains were made toward reducing its volume. Even more substantial gains were made toward humanizing the methods of dealing with its victims. I do not need to catalogue here that record of progress—through improved banking and security exchange legislation, through social security, through reforms in private home financing, through slum clearance, public housing and public works. But no one can pretend that these measures alone, or even in combination, solved the problem to our satisfaction. The

bare truth is this: While unemployment was cut almost in half between 1933 and 1937, it was not reduced much below 7,000,000, and it rose considerably above the figure between 1937 and the beginning of the defense program. No thinking person can be smugly content with this record. No thinking person can fail to shrink from the results that would follow if we do not better this record in the future.

In 1940 we moved actively into defense activities. Then we were drawn into the war by the Japanese attack. We have achieved full employment, in fact, abnormal employment, during the war. But this did not happen automatically just because there was a war. It happened because under the pressure of war we marshalled all our resources and organized them systematically according to plan. We took the new instrumentalities forged by the people for their own use during the previous decade—we added these to what we had before, and we integrated them into a stable and efficient economic machinery. We demonstrated that there are literally no limits to the productive capacity of America.

No one would suggest that we should retain, in the postwar period the degree of centralization and controls that have been necessary during the war. But the war has taught us what the indispensable minimum requirements are for maintaining full production and full employment. These indispensable minimum requirements, and these alone, are incorporated in the full employment bill. . . .

The bill provides that the Government itself, through direct action, shall create useful and productive jobs, but only for those who have the right to work and who cannot otherwise freely exercise that right.

Thus the bill firmly rejects the proposition that public employment is the main avenue toward full employment. It rejects the proposition that full employment requires continued deficit spending. It embraces the idea that cooperation between enterprise and Government, guided by an annual inventory of the economic problems with which both must deal, will lead to increasingly high levels of employment in private enterprise. It is founded upon the undebatable fact that full employment and full production are the one sure escape from deficit financing.

But the bill does not blink the fact that any government worthy of the name has the bedrock responsibility to see that the right to work is fully realized, even where it means direct action. It recognizes also that public investment should be undertaken toward creating decent standards of living for all, in those areas where private enterprise does not operate; for example, with respect to health and education and the development of natural resources. . . .

Unity of action depends upon agreement about objectives. We have been unified during the war because our objective has been crystal clear; to defeat our enemies. We need an equally crystal-clear objective with regard to postwar enemy No. 1—mass unemployment. The full employment bill will provide a machinery for unity, in defining this enemy and accomplishing its total defeat. Unconditional defeat must be the only terms. . . .

The greatest problem of modern democracy is to reconcile our essential freedoms with reasonable efficiency in meeting our economic problems. There will be no such thing in the postwar world as the possibility of continuing freedom plus continuing mass unemployment. Either we must conquer unemployment, or unemployment will destroy our freedom.

The full-employment bill reflects an immense and entirely justified optimism in the future of America, a future based upon preserving our freedom and our liberties by making the free and democratic American system work.

Further Resources

BOOKS

Graham, Jr., Otis L. *Towards a Planned Society: From Roosevelt to Nixon.* New York: Oxford University Press, 1976.

Huthmacher, J. Joseph. *Robert F. Wagner and the Rise of Urban Liberalism.* New York: Atheneum, 1971.

Norton, Hugh Stanton. *The Employment Act: The Council of Economic Advisors, 1946–1976.* Columbia, S.C.: University of South Carolina Press, 1977.

WEBSITES

"Wagner, Robert Ferdinand, 1877–1953." Biographical Directory of the United States Congress. Available online at: http://bioguide.congress.gov/scripts/biodisplay.pl?index=W000021 (accessed April 21, 2003).

Investigation of Petroleum Resources

Congressional records

By: Special Committee Investigating Petroleum Resources
Date: 1945

Source: *Investigation of Petroleum Resources.* Hearings Before a Special Committee Investigating Petroleum Resources, United States Senate, Seventy-Ninth Congress, First Session. Washington: U.S. Government Printing Office, 1946, 1, 6, 7, 8, 33, 35–36, 66, 69, 94, 118–19, 161, 197, 275, 285, 319, 324, 502.

About the Author: This special committee of the U.S. Senate investigated the condition of U.S. petroleum reserves and the likely future petroleum needs of the United States in June 1945. A variety of experts representing petroleum corporations and experts from the American oil industry testified before the committee. ∎

Introduction

The world's first commercial oil well was drilled in Pennsylvania in 1859—an event that set in motion the nearly century-long American domination of the petroleum industry. Although the original Pennsylvania oil fields were eventually exhausted (today we recall a distant echo of the past with the names Pennzoil and Quaker State) by 1900, newly-discovered oil fields in Texas and California guaranteed continued American petroleum preeminence.

In July 1941, the United States, the world's leader in petroleum exports, slapped a crippling embargo on Japan. That country, totally dependent on imported oil, soon responded by bombing Pearl Harbor. By 1945, the United States was at a crossroads regarding its future energy policy. Soon the nation would no longer be capable of supplying its own rapidly increasing oil requirements. Even if it could, with the discovery and extraction of enormous petroleum reserves in the Middle East and other parts of the world, the era of American global oil domination would soon be over. In June 1945, a select committee of the United States Senate held hearings to investigate this potential problem.

Significance

The testimony offered at the June 1945 hearings raised vexing issues that still plague Americans to this day—the debate over offshore drilling, the production of synthetic fuels, the need for strict energy-conservation measures, and the role of private corporations in the search for new sources of oil. However, in hindsight it is clear that the policy makers and oil company executives present at the hearings did not appreciate the seriousness of these issues. Despite assurances during the testimony that America could always rely on its huge coal deposits, looming on the horizon was a predictable dependence on foreign sources of energy. Little was ultimately done to avoid this dependence, and it proved to be a dangerous policy. In the decades to come the United States would often be dragged into the turmoil of Middle East politics because of its need to protect oil supplies. Meanwhile, a new and serious environmental issue was also surfacing:

Two men stand by a Quaker State Motor Oil advertisement at a Gulf Gas Station. **THE LIBRARY OF CONGRESS.**

air pollution caused by the ever-increasing burning of fossil fuels. By 1947, *Time* magazine had coined the word "smog" to describe the brown haze that choked many American cities.

Primary Source

Investigation of Petroleum Resources [excerpt]

SYNOPSIS: In 1945, the U.S. Senate held hearings to investigate the current and future state of America's most important energy source, oil. A parade of expert witnesses from the oil industry painted a largely optimistic picture of the situation, failing to recognize the depth and seriousness of the possible problems they foresaw.

[In the excerpt below, speakers are identified by their last name or title. Their full names and positions are as follows: Senator Joseph C. Mahoney (committee chairman), Senators Brewster, Hatch, Moore, and Johnson, Henry S. Fraser (chief counsel to the Special Committee Investigating Petroleum Resources), Antonio M. Fernandez (Representative from New Mexico), Captain C.P. Franchot and Brigadier General H.L. Peckham (United States Naval Reserve), J. Edgar Pew (Vice President, Sun Oil, Chairman of committee on Petroleum Reserves for the American Petroleum Institute), Mr. J.C. Hunter (President, Mid-Continent Oil and Gas Association), Mr. Hallanan (President, Plymouth Oil), Mr. A.C. Matlei (President, Honolulu Oil of San Francisco, CA), Mr. E.L. DeGolyer (Consulting Engineer, DeGolyer and MacNaughton), Mr. Michael W. Straus, Mr. H.D. Miser (Government employee, in charge of section of geology of fuels, geological survey, Department of Interior).]

The Chairman: The committee will come to order.

This session of the Senate Special Committee Investigating Petroleum Resources has been called this morning to open the hearings to which the representatives of the oil industry have been invited to present evidence on all aspects of the petroleum industry.

Everybody attending this meeting is well aware of the fact that the United States has contributed extraordinary quantities of its petroleum resources to fight the war, not only for the operation of our own Army and Navy but for the military operations of our allies, and even for civilian purposes. We all also know that petroleum is one of the most essential, if not the most essential, commodity for industry, so that as we look forward to the coming peace for which we all earnestly pray, we want to be certain what our resources of oil will be.

The committee has invited representatives of the industry to come here today and tell their story. As a matter of fact we went further than that. We invited the industry to organize a committee on its own part to present this evidence. Out of the feeling that nobody knows better than the industry what the conditions in the industry are, we hope to be able to sit down here across the table, lay all the cards on the table, and find out what is best to be done in the future. . . .

Mr. Pew: . . . we find that within a few years after the discovery of the Drake well in 1859, periodic alarms have been raised that we could not satisfy for long the national need for petroleum. There has hardly been a 5-year period since that time in which someone—and most often someone in the Government—has not made dire predictions that our oil resources were nearing exhaustion. Yet, almost invariably immediately upon the heels of such alarms new discoveries have been made and new methods developed for the extraction of crude oil from the earth. The demand for petroleum products constantly has increased. Today, under the stress of war, it is 25 times greater than at the beginning of this century. Yet, the domestic industry, with negligible help from the outside world, has always met this demand in the long run. Price and demand have been the regulators of supply. So definite and firm is this pattern that it demonstrates beyond all doubt that the reason for any brief period of shortage is not any latent weakness in the resource but is to be found in other factors.

Strangely, pessimists and prophets of exhaustion constantly have dogged the heels of this industry. All the cries of alarm that we have heard in the last 2 or 3 years are but repetitions of similar dire predictions laid down through the years. All of the latter were proved false by time, and so shall the present pessimistic statements. A quick glance at these past prophecies, however, will enable us to view the present predictions in better perspective. . . .

Particularly during the period of the First World War and immediately thereafter, just as during the present war, there was a flood of pessimistic forecasts. In 1915 Dr. Ralph Arnold,

a noted geologist of that day, set off the alarm with a forecast that we had only 5,763,000,000 barrels of oil in the ground at the end of the previous year. . . .

The blackest forecast of all came in 1919 from David White, Chief Geologist of the United States Survey, placing oil remaining available in the ground on January 1, 1919, as 6,740,000,000 barrels. White contended that "the peak of the production of natural petroleum in this country will be reached by 1921." He foresaw the exhaustion of American resources within 17 years at the 1919 rate of production, namely, 380,000,000 barrels annually. . . .

The United States Geological Survey, in cooperation with the American Association of Petroleum Geologists, estimated that as of January 1, 1922, the reserves of oil recoverable by methods then in use totaled 9,150,000,000 barrels, of which, they stated, 5,000,000,000 barrels "may be classified as oil in sight." These reserves, the report added, were, "enough to justify the present requirements of the United States for only 20 years if the oil could be taken out of the ground as fast as it is wanted."

The Geological Survey asserted that the United States was, "already absolutely dependent on foreign countries to eke out her own production and, if the foreign oil can be produced, this dependence is sure to grow greater and greater as our own fields wane."

Very obviously all these predictions were wrong. I have cited them not to ridicule the prophets, for they had neither the facilities nor the information to make accurate prognostications such as we have today. I cite these now proved erroneous predictions solely to demonstrate the hazards inherent in speculating about the extent of our oil resources. In recent years there has been less speculation and greater reliance on known facts, scientifically developed and demonstrated. . . .

The result has been an abundant supply of petroleum that has made this Nation great, and that has been primarily responsible for its high standard of living in peace and its supremacy in the present highly mechanized war. Other nations possess similar or greater resources than we do, but have left them dormant and useless, either because the sole right of exploration and development has been lodged in the Government or other restrictions have hampered their peoples.

Even though the United States possesses a minor part of the area of the world where geologists believe oil can be found, there has been produced in this country 64 percent of the world's cumulative oil production; last year 65 percent of the world's production came from the United States, it was reported; and, we have in this country now approximately 39 percent of the estimated world-known crude oil reserves. Moreover, Americans have discovered and developed a large quantity of the oil found outside of our national borders, even after the areas involved had been tested and abandoned by foreigners.

American supremacy in the finding of oil does not come from any peculiar genius on the part of our people. Rather, it results from our system of enterprise and opportunity which provides incentives that spur the initiative and ingenuity of Americans to search for oil. By and large, Americans have been free to drill wells wherever they thought oil might be found; they have been free and have had incentives to develop and produce the oil they discovered. Destroy these freedoms and incentives and you kill the spirit that has been responsible for our achievements in this field.

. . .

Senator Brewster: You feel, then, that as far as the United States is concerned, there is no occasion for us to be particularly excited or interested in the oil reserves of foreign areas, that they are not things that will be of any tremendous consequence to us in the foreseeable future?

Mr. Pew: As far as I know the situation—and we do not have any foreign production—oil over there is, to an extent, controlled in this country. I do not mean the majority of it, but enough of it is controlled in this country to the end that we have such oil available for use here when and if we need it, if it can be brought in here under either war conditions or otherwise. It is just as available now as it ever was.

Senator Brewster: One of our very definite questions before we get through is going to be, first, the oil reserves of the Western Hemisphere, which I assume we will all agree

would be available, and the other question is the oil reserves of the Middle East.

As you know, this whole question was precipitated by the suggestion that the 50,000,000,000 barrels that were asserted to be in the Middle East was a matter that might be of very considerable concern to us hereafter, and it was on that basis that a considerable change in our whole foreign policy was proposed, that we ought to recognize that as one of the essential factors to our defense. I think before we get through it will be anticipated that we will want an opinion from the oil industry, at least, as to how far we ought to go in extending the interest of our foreign policy into the Middle East reserves. We are gratified as to the enterprise of American businessmen and geologists, as you pointed out, in discovering these reserves after others had failed, but we have to settle the question of whether those are vital to our defense.

Mr. Pew: Senator, I would say there has been a study of the foreign policy, and suggested foreign policy, by the oil committee of the PIWC, I believe it is, the details of which I am not in a position to discuss and would not know. Just speaking personally, I would say as long as we can get to that oil we have enough hold on it. If we were in trouble over there and could not get to it we would probably have just developed such oil for our enemies. . . .

Report of the Foreign Operations Committee of the Petroleum Administration for War

I. Factors that Create an International Oil Problem

. . . 2. Interest in oil is universal. All countries are consumers of petroleum, most countries are importers, many countries are exporters. Oil is used in every part of the world and is essential to all industrial activities. It is also the chief support of the newer forms of transportation, as exemplified in the motorcar, the truck, the diesel boat, and the airplane.

3. The known oil resources of the world are limited and concentrated. Five great regions contain an overwhelming proportion of the world's oil. These are: the United States, the Soviet Union, the Middle East, the Far East, and the Caribbean area. The Middle East and the Caribbean area together probably contain more known oil than the rest of the world.

4. Oil exploration and discovery present extraordinary difficulties, requiring rare and specialized

abilities. Undiscovered oil is a present asset to no one; if it is to serve an economic purpose, its discovery must be facilitated. Most of the oil so far discovered in the world has been found either by American enterprise or by techniques developed in the United States.

II. Special Interest of the United States in Oil

. . . 3. The economy of the United States probably faces partial dependence upon foreign oil resources. Long an oil exporter on balance, the United States may face a significant change in its status. Evidence points to the imminence of a shift from a condition in which this country has surplus oil for export to one in which the Nation will become a net importer of oil. This expected change will make the economy of the United States partly dependent upon foreign oil resources.

4. The national security of the United States is dependent upon adequate world oil developments. The security of the United States military power is enhanced by having adequate and strategically located sources of oil supplies throughout the world in the hands of American nationals.

III. Immediate Problems of Pressing Urgency

1. Changed conditions require changed policies. The war has brought about radical changes in the status of the United States in respect to the oil resources of the world.

(a) The United States is faced with the prospect of shifting from the status of a net exporter to that of a net importer of oil, thus bringing into view the possibility of partial dependence upon foreign sources of supply. . . .

2. A foreign oil policy must be established at once if the interests of the United States are not to be sacrificed.

Mr. Hunter: In World War I, straining to the ultimate, we produced only 90,000,000 more barrels in the last year than in the first year. In World War II, we produced 464,000,000 barrels more oil in 1944 than in the opening year, 1938. How did we do it? I can find no answer but, primarily, conservation—conservation developed through years of progress in State regulation; cooperative regulation with the oil industry during which restraint to non-wasteful producing rates has built up the potential capacity to produce. . . .

The truth of the matter is that we are nowhere near running out of oil, and, but for the inordi-

nate demands of war, we would today have a surplus of producing capacity that would have to be restricted in order to prevent physical waste and to conserve the supplies for the time when they would be needed. There are those who believe that this country should begin to hoard its oil, either in underground reservoirs or in storage tanks above ground. They question the ability of the country to meet its oil problems for the future and have a mistaken belief that we can protect the security of the Nation by freezing the situation we have today in terms of oil resources. This has never been the way to solve the problems of the petroleum or any other industry. We live in a dynamic and constantly changing world, and we only learn to deal with its problems by allowing them to develop in their normal and natural course. We are not in danger of running out of oil overnight. We are certain that we have supplies for many years to come, and that in the interval we will find more supplies, and, if given opportunity, we will develop new techniques that will provide additional supplies from other sources. . . .

Our country is particularly dependent upon oil for its way of life. We have by far the greatest proportion of the automobiles in the world, and we use 30 times as much oil per capita as the remainder of the world. This oil is a tremendous source of energy that carried us around the country in automobiles and railroads, and that drives thousands of machines in power plants and factories. It does work for us that could not be done if the rest of the world's population were our slaves, and it does that work very cheaply. The public has reason, therefore, to be tremendously interested in an abundant supply of petroleum as cheaply as possible and in the advantageous use of those supplies without waste. In this the industry and the public are in complete accord. Our task is to utilize petroleum efficiently to maintain and improve the standard of living with which it is so intimately related.

We have had an abundance of oil, not because this country was blessed with greater resources by nature than others but because of the inherent initiative of the people and the freedom to carry on their business as they chose. Foreign countries are known to have larger potential reserves of oil, but due to government restrictions and other handicaps they have not developed their resources to the same extent that we have. We were first to learn how to find oil efficiently and use it effectively, and Americans carried that knowledge to the far corners of the globe. As their resources are developed, they, too, may gain the benefits of this black gold that provides such tremendous amounts of energy at low cost. They will need the major part of their own resources, if they are to develop progressive economy and better standards of living.

In part, some of their reserves may be available to us, if needed, but we cannot depend on foreign reserves as a safeguard in time of war. Unless we can insure access to reserves by military control, ownership will be of no benefit whatever. If the United States Government, instead of American companies, had owned the oil resources in the Dutch East Indies and Saudi Arabia, those resources would not have been any more accessible today. . . .

National Policy Essential

Mr. Hallanan: A national oil policy resting upon the solid foundation of whole-hearted cooperation and mutual confidence between the oil industry on the one hand and the Government and people whom it serves on the other hand, is just as essential to the security and prosperity of the Nation as its policy of national defense. In this time—and for all the future we can visualize—oil is the most vital and integral part of any national defense program and it is likewise linked to the operation of our domestic economy with equal importance as an essential product. Indeed, oil is the one commodity which must be available in abundance if the Nation is to be secure, both from enemies without and from economic stagnation and disintegration within. We have learned in the recent years that for our own security we must be prepared to supply the requirements of other nations and peoples.

In 1919, Henri Berenger, French industrialist and oil commissioner of his country during the First World War, made a prophecy that has been borne out by the experience of the war in which we are presently engaged and which is just as true today as when it was uttered 26 years ago. He said: "He who owns the oil will own the world for he will rule the sea by means of the heavy oils, the air by means of

the ultra refined oils, and the land by means of petrol and illuminating oils. . . ."

Mr. Matlei: Our present proven oil reserves are only a part of the answer to our future oil supply. Much of our future production will come from fields not today discovered. This is historically the story of the development of oil. Today we are producing in excess of 400,000 barrels daily from fields not discovered in December 1941. New areas must be explored and much time, money, and effort expended by the oil industry in the search for new fields in the United States as well as in foreign lands. Individual initiative, private capital, and free competitive enterprise have enabled the petroleum industry to present the aspect of a "far-flung productive organism, capable, self-reliant, imbued with ideals of service, highly complex, yet integrated, practitioner of mass production, cost conscious, alive, growing, and dynamic"—an industry producing from less than 7 percent of the earth's surface 67 percent of the world total oil production. Its technology is world renowned. No foreign government, by direct engagement in, or regulation of, its oil industry, has had a success comparable to that of the privately owned and operated oil industry of the United States. Our national oil policy must recognize, protect, and hold harmless from unnecessary encroachment of bureaucracy that economic unit and preserve it intact. . . .

Mr. DeGolyer: I am not a pessimist with regard to the oil supply of the United States. We do not know how great the ultimate production of our country will be, how much oil remains to be found, but I presume that no one will dispute the conclusion that it is a finite amount—that we are dealing with a wasting asset.

The great problem is that of how much remains to be discovered, but the greater problem still is that of at what rate we will be able to find it—of its "findability," . . .

We do not know how much oil remains to be found in the United States. I believe that great quantities will be discovered. Mr. Wallace Pratt, whose book, Oil in the Earth, has been placed before your committee by Mr. Monroe Cheney, estimates the quantity still to be discovered at approximately 50,000,000,000 barrels. His implied assumption is that on acre-averages oil occurs in sedimentary rocks of proper type throughout the world in approximately equal amounts. This, I doubt. All other mineral deposits are notoriously of unequal distribution throughout the world, and this is particularly so for coal, the mineral nearest to petroleum in origin. . . .

General Peckham: American companies should continue and increase their ownership and production of foreign oil. Aside from the financial benefits to these companies, such ownership and production would give the United States a greater participation in world oil affairs. . . .

In determining the amount of foreign oil which should be imported into the United States, careful consideration must be given to the effect upon domestic production. Importation which would depress the domestic market price for crude oil to the extent that the capital and resources of domestic companies would be depleted with resulting injury to the domestic industry would be unwise for reasons hereafter stated. . . .

Mr. Straus: When it will become necessary to adopt synthetic fuels as the backbone of our gasoline operations in the United States, I do not know. That depends upon world economics, international developments, and world exploration beyond our control and probably beyond the control of any group represented here today. But we believe that the national interest requires a sure source of gasoline within the domestic confines of the United States, subject to the control of the United States and independent of any factors beyond our control. We will be ready with such a source of gasoline. A new great synthetic fuel industry in the United States is within our grasp when we need it. With this work on synthetic fuel development the unknowns are falling away one by one. . . .

And we also know where within the United States there are proven deposits of over 3,000,000,000,000 tons of coals and lignites which would be sufficient to supply all existing demands for these fuels, plus enough coal and lignite to give us all the gasoline at our present rate of consumption that we need for at least the next thousand years.

Mr. Fraser: What then?

Mr. Straus: That is to be handled by other people, I believe.

Mr. Fraser: There have been empires in the history of the world which have lasted for more than a thousand years, and I would hate to contemplate that within a thousand years the Republic of the United States will pass from the scene.

Mr. Straus: Of course, a thousand years isn't much when we are talking about petroleum and petroleum development. . . .

Mr. Miser: The United States has for many years produced about three-fifths of the world's petroleum. It is thus drawing on its supplies at a rapid rate. How much longer these supplies can meet fully our normal needs is not certain. It is certain, however, that the discovery rate of petroleum will some day decline to the point where our crude petroleum supplies will not meet fully our normal needs. Although our country may not face such a petroleum shortage for some years, adequate future supplies of petroleum products must at all times be assured for the security and welfare of the Nation. Sources of these products are not alone the crude petroleum in this and other countries but also substitute sources which include oil shale, coal, oil-saturated sands, and natural gas. The domestic deposits of these substitute sources are large and are capable of providing ample petroleum products for many centuries. The Nation must be equipped with adequate information concerning the extent, character, and reserves of these resources and concerning processes for large-scale recoveries of petroleum products from them. This is necessary so that they may be utilized promptly when the Nation is required to turn to them to augment domestic and imported supplies of crude petroleum.

Further Resources

BOOKS

O'Connor, Harvey. *The Empire of Oil.* New York: Monthly Review Press, 1955.

Randall, Stephen J. *United States Foreign Oil Policy, 1919–1948: For Profits and Security.* Montreal: McGill-Queen's University Press, 1985.

Yergin, Daniel. *The Prize: The Epic Quest for Oil, Money, and Power.* New York: Simon & Schuster, 1991.

"Housing and Full Employment"

Magazine article

By: Leon Keyserling

Date: June 1946

Source: Keyserling, Leon. "Housing and Full Employment," *American Federationist*, June 1946, 10–12.

About the Author: Leon H. Keyserling (1908–1987) a native of Charleston, South Carolina, attended Columbia University and Harvard Law School. Although later famed as an economist, Keyserling never finished his Ph.D. in economics at Columbia. After serving in various capacities for the Roosevelt administration, Keyserling was appointed by President S. Truman as the first vice chairman of the newly established Council of Economic Advisors in 1946. Keyserling became its chairman in 1950. After his departure from Washington in 1953, Keyserling worked as a consultant. ∎

Introduction

The end of World War II in 1945 unleashed a tremendous pent-up demand for housing. Young veterans were eager to marry and start families—something it had been difficult for them to do during the Depression and the war. The result was the postwar "baby boom" generation, which needed a place to live.

Little housing was available, however. There was little money available for new housing during the Great Depression, and during World War II (1939–45) most of America's industry and materials were devoted to supplying the war effort. With the supply of housing so short, prices for new and existing homes skyrocketed. In the immediate postwar period, no domestic problem was as pressing as the housing shortage.

Many liberal and some moderate politicians, including President Truman, wanted to deal with the housing crisis through government action. They did not believe that private industry could solve the problem alone, especially when it came to providing affordable housing for poor Americans. They wanted the federal government to fund public housing projects for the poor, and redevelop inner city slums. Such a program would also work toward their goals of using federal government power to ensure full employment and long-term prosperity for Americans.

In 1945, the proponents of federal public housing programs put forward the Wagner-Ellender-Taft bill (named for its Senate sponsors) to achieve these aims. Its provisions included: authorization for federal construction of hundreds of thousands of dwellings, federal assistance for the clearance and replacement of slums with better housing, a permanent federal agency concerned with housing, and enhancements to existing home loan and loan guarantee programs. The bill was met with fierce opposition from conservatives opposed to an expansion of government spending and bureaucracy, and by businessmen who saw government involvement in the housing industry as unnecessary and unfair interference with the free market.

The programs proposed in the Wagner-Ellender-Taft bill became the center of the controversy surrounding the government's role in the housing crisis. The bill was introduced, under various names, in one session of Congress after another throughout the late 1940s. There it would routinely pass in the Senate but be defeated in the House, leaving the matter unresolved. Its opponents denounced it as socialist, anti-capitalist, and possibly even Communist in nature. They insisted that the free market could solve the housing crisis, and laid blame for high housing prices on one of public housing's biggest supporters: organized labor. In the generally anti-labor and decidedly anti-Communist atmosphere of the late 1940s these were powerful criticisms.

Supporters of public housing like Leon Keyserling denounced their opponents as acting purely out of business self-interest, and blamed them for the inability of the government to act on the housing issue. In 1948, President Truman forced Congress to meet in special session and demanded that they pass the housing bill. The Republican-controlled body failed to do so, passing only the much weaker Housing Act of 1948. Truman was then able to lay the blame for the housing crisis on the Republicans, helping both himself and other Democrats to win elections that fall. This put the Democrats in control of Congress and paved the way for the passage of the Housing Act of 1949.

Significance

The Housing Act of 1949 embodied most of the reforms and programs that liberals had been pushing for in the Wagner-Ellender-Taft Act and similar acts. It became the basis for federal housing policy and spending for the next several decades. However it was plagued with problems from the moment it became law. Partly this was due to the continued opposition of conservatives and businessmen, who worked to reduce the scope and funding of public housing programs. The demands of the Korean War (1950-53) also led to reduced funding. It would take twenty years to build the 810,000 public housing units that were the 1949 Housing Act's six-year goal.

This is not to say that the general housing crisis continued. Private industry built tens of millions of homes during the late 1940s and 1950s, aided in part by federal home loan and loan guarantee programs. Most of these new homes were built surrounding cities at a distance, leading to the development of sprawling suburbs. These homes met the demand of most Americans, but, as predicted by liberals, were out of reach for low-income Americans.

The urban redevelopment and public housing aspects of the Housing Act of 1949 were supposed to meet the needs of these poorer Americans. Even those who supported the Act's ideals ultimately had to admit that it failed in practice. Some public housing and urban renewal projects were successful, but many others were conspicuous failures. Too often, urban renewal projects intended to improve low-income neighborhoods succeeded primarily by forcing the poor residents out, and into substandard housing elsewhere. Government housing projects intended to replace slums frequently became notorious slums themselves, lacking in community and social services and they were just as racially segregated as the housing they replaced. By the mid-1970s, the programs of the Housing Act of 1949 were being phased out. New and different policies were tried, but a shortage of low-income housing remained a problem into the twenty-first century.

Primary Source

"Housing and Full Employment"

> **SYNOPSIS:** The United States endured a severe housing shortage in the immediate post–World War II period. The Truman administration's response was a push for greater government involvement in housing, which led to a long political battle with conservatives and business interests. Writing for a supportive audience of union members, Leon Keyserling, one of Truman's advisors, explains here why federal action is necessary.

America has come through the war to face the greatest economic and social issue in its history. Or, more accurately, we now face an economic and social issue which has been with us for generations, but which now takes on unequaled magnitude.

This central issue is whether the productive capacity of America shall be given full scope for tremendous achievements or whether we shall, as in the past, produce at only a fractional part of our capacity. This issue is also whether the proceeds of this production shall be distributed generously and equitably, in a manner to assure the average citizen a fair reward for his toil and to bring a decent standard of living to every American family, or whether these proceeds of production shall be distributed in a selfish and inequitable manner which maintains poverty in a land of limitless plenty.

The way to determine this issue will decide the future of our system of private enterprise, individual freedom and political democracy. The words "private enterprise" should be underscored, because the true friends of private enterprise know that it cannot withstand the impact of another depression as much bigger than the last one as World War II was bigger than World War I. That is the kind of depression that we will have if we act now as we did in the 1920s.

And yet, while the future of private enterprise is clouded with doubt if the shortsighted policies of the past continue, never before was the future of private enterprise so bright if it adjusts itself, in moderation and good will, to the lessons of experience and the needs of our times.

For the production records hung up during the recent war have made it clear beyond question that we do not need socialism, and we certainly do not need a totalitarian form of government. The American economic system is strong enough and rich enough to provide decent standards of living for all without destroying the principle of different reward based upon different ability, without taking the means of production out of private ownership and management, and without confiscation or unusual levies.

But in order that our system of private enterprise may come through with flying colors, it must abandon the restrictive outlook which has characterized so much of its activity in the past and must accept instead the philosophy of full production and full employment.

Whenever anyone refers to a restrictive outlook, there are some misguided people who seize upon these words as a means of heaping criticism and calumnies upon the shoulders of working people in general and organized labor in particular. But in broad perspective, nothing is clearer in our history than that the organized labor movement has stood on the side of expanding our economy and multiplying its fruits. The organized opposition to this kind of progress has come from quite different sources.

The most recent illustration of this occurred when the Full Employment Bill was before Congress last year. The main purpose of this bill was to dedicate our people, our enterprise and our government to the proposition that the right to employment is a gift of nature which should not be withdrawn by man. The bill held that it was our obligation, as a people and as a nation, to make this right secure and to enjoy the benefits of prosperity, security and happiness which flow from the full exercise of this right.

On this great issue, putting aside matters of detail, the working people of America in all types of la-

"Don't Blame Labor" [excerpt]

[A prominent union leader responds to accusations that organized labor is behind the high cost of post-war housing.]

Are Home Prices Too High? They Are. But Building Unions Are Not at Fault.

Every worker knows that in the past six years the cost of living has steadily increased. Every family looking for a home today knows that nothing has increased as much as the cost of a place to live. The new $6000 dream home of 1940 is a not-so-new $10,000 house today. And the $500 lot you selected for your new home back then isn't any bigger today, but the price has gone up to $800 or more. Or if, last September, you found a $6000 house built during the war, but waited until February to buy it, the price had by then jumped to $7800—an average increase of $300 a month!

Everyone looking for a house wants to know why this dizzy rise in the price of homes. Where does that extra $4000, added on the prewar $6000 house, go? Who gets the money? Why should the price on this prewar house have increased 17 per cent in the first six months after V-J Day? Why should war housing have increased some 30 per cent in this same six months, although these war-built houses were often hastily and shoddily constructed?

Most of the rise in the cost of housing is a speculative increase created by the scarcity of housing. Whenever there is a shortage, the man with the long purse is able and willing to pay more, while the man with the short purse is forced to do without. Without price control, those who are richer bid up the price out of reach of those who are poorer. This is especially true of housing right now because there is no substitute for a house. Bread and butter, meat and cheese may be hard to buy, but at least you can eat something else. But only four walls and a roof can give shelter.

The profits from resale of this scarce housing go into the pockets of real estate speculators. And today the speculation in the housing market is almost as great as the speculation in the 1929 stock market. These speculative profits never go to the people who make the goods. They go only to those who sell and resell them.

Without price control on the sale of either, both the existing homes and new houses have commanded extremely high prices. However, there are those who allege that labor generally and the building workers specifically are responsible for the high cost of housing. Over and over again the charge is made that housing costs the consumer too much because the wages paid construction workers are too high. These attacks falsify facts and violate common sense.

The majority of wage-earners, both in and out of the building trades, have never been able to earn enough to afford decent, soundly built houses for themselves. Is there any truth then to the charge that building wages are too high and that labor costs must be cut? What are the wages of building workers? How much of the home buyer's dollar goes to the men who build his home? What is the best way of bringing well-built houses within the financial reach of every wage-earner and every wage-earner and every family in the country? . . .

The vast majority of American families, both on the farm and in the city, could afford the homes that private enterprise builds if the costs were reduced. . . .

Those who attack building labor by urging that the reduction in housing costs be taken out of the building workers' pocket know that they cannot make a case without falsifying the facts. Nor do they stop there in their attack and their false claims. They allege that it is the purpose of the building trades to restrict housing construction by a variety of means.

No charge could be more absurd. It was the Housing Committee of the American Federation of Labor, working in close cooperation with the A. F. of L. Building and Construction Trades Department, that as far back as 1940 began to formulate a comprehensive large-scale postwar housing program. It is this program, unanimously adopted by the 1944 A. F. of L. convention, which forms the basis of the Wagner-Ellender-Taft General Housing Bill. To launch a drive in Congress for the enactment of the largest permanent housing program ever is carrying restriction pretty far!

SOURCE: Shishkin, Boris. "Don't Blame Labor." *American Federationist,* July 1946, 7, 9, 10.

bor organizations have stood steadfastly in favor of full production and full employment.

The opposition to the Full Employment Bill came entirely from some spokesmen of narrow interests who were *afraid* of full employment. Some of these spokesmen were even frank enough to state that they preferred a certain amount of unemployment, even where involuntary. They said that a "pool" of unemployed was a necessary characteristic of a "free" or "healthy" economy.

It is not to be supposed that any of these spokesmen contemplated that this "free" or "healthy" state of affairs would require that *they* and *their families* might have to take their turn in sharing the desolation and deprivation of unwanted unemployment.

Those uninformed persons who in the press and on the radio rush to accuse labor of a restrictive outlook would do well to read through the hearings on the Full Employment Bill.

The whole subject of house production is closely connected with the goal of full production and full employment. It is also closely connected with the goal of a decent standard of living for every American family. And here again we have a close and dramatic illustration of those who seek to achieve these goals and also of those who stand deliberately against them in their desire to benefit by a restrictive economy.

The Wagner-Ellender-Taft bill (S. 1592), sometimes referred to as the General Housing Bill, has now passed the Senate and awaits action by the House of Representatives. The general purposes of this bill are simple. First, to stimulate an annual volume of house production sufficient for housing to play its full part in an economy of full part in an economy of full production and full employment. Second, to replace substandard housing, slums and shacks in urban and rural areas with decent housing at a sufficient rate of speed to make genuine progress toward the goal of a decent home for every American family. And third, to provide aid for local planning, so that a sound housing environment can be placed in the setting of a sound general community environment.

Before discussing any of the provisions of this bill in detail, it is important to note that the hearings on this bill have afforded another example of the lineup between those who favor a full economy and those who look yearningly backward to a restrictive economy.

Organized labor has expressed its unqualified and aggressive support of the Wagner-Ellender-Taft bill. Any criticism of the bill on the part of working people was only on the ground that it should be even more comprehensive and even more forward-looking.

On the other hand, the bill has been and is being fought tooth and nail by spokesmen of certain groups who wrongly think that their interests would be hurt by a program to achieve a decent home for every American family.

These spokesmen for restriction include some homebuilders, despite the fact that the bill would give the private homebuilding industry the greatest opportunity it has ever had to build more houses than it ever built before.

These spokesmen for restriction include some moneylenders, who claim that the bill would hurt them by reducing interest rates—although the true effect of the bill would be to create investment outlets in housing vastly greater than have ever existed before.

These spokesmen for restriction include some jerrybuilders, who opposed the warranty of sound construction which labor advocated—the very same jerrybuilders who for years through their propaganda have been trying to make the consumer believe that labor was responsible for poor housing standards.

These spokesmen for restriction include some private financing institutions, which object to the payment of the prevailing wage for labor working upon housing covered by government insurance—while at the same time some of these institutions are fearful that public housing may cut into the profits drawn from their ownership of the slums.

These spokesmen for restriction oppose the provisions of the Wagner-Ellender-Taft bill which would entrust the management of housing projects to cooperatives of working people—while at the same time they shed no tears for the veterans who, in the current shortage, are left to the tender mercies of certain unrepresentative types of real estate management.

Above all, these spokesmen for restriction are opposed to the public housing provisions of the Wagner-Ellender-Taft bill which, over a period of four years, would provide half a million units of low-rent public housing for urban wage-earners at costs within their means. It would also provide about 150,000 units of public housing for families of low income on farms and in other rural areas.

It is upon the public housing provisions of the Wagner-Ellender-Taft bill that the opposition is concentrated; and it is around these provisions of the bill that labor should rally as it rallies to the support of the whole measure.

The American Federation of Labor has a vital interest in public housing. It has this interest because the A. F. of L. participated vigorously in the establishment of the housing movement and also in the preparation and advocacy of the United States Housing Act of 1937, the parent statute of all public housing.

But beyond this interest which arises from close association, organized labor has a vital stake in public housing because there are millions of wage-earners and their families for whom public housing is the only means of providing decent housing. Even allowing for the present high level of national income, which we all hope to see maintained and bettered in the postwar years, only those whose lack of sympathy has made them blind to the problems of working people claim that private builders can meet in full the housing needs of workers and their families.

The country is now concentrating upon providing homes for veterans. Let the veterans themselves speak about what kind of homes they can afford. According to a survey at War Department separation centers, of those veterans who want to own their homes only 14 per cent believe that they can afford to pay more than $50 a month for shelter, 54 per cent believe that they can afford to pay between $30 and $50 a month, and 32 per cent state that they cannot afford to pay more than $30 a month. Of the veterans who desire rental housing, 11 per cent are in the more than $50 a month group, 55 per cent in the $30 to $50 a month group, and 34 per cent in the less than $30 a month group.

These are the figures for veterans but, after all, veterans are a good cross-section of the country at large.

Detailed statistics of past, present and prospective performance are not needed to prove that private enterprise does not and cannot provide any substantial quantity of decent housing in urban areas for families who cannot afford to pay more than $30 a month for their shelter. It follows from this that public housing for low-income families offers no competition to decent, privately owned housing. In short, public housing for low-income families is the only method of taking millions of families out of the slums into healthful homes.

If the public housing provisions of the Wagner-Ellender-Taft bill were to be defeated or delayed, it would mean a defeat for millions of typical wage-earners in their just aspiration to live in decent homes. It would mean the defeat of the desire of the workers who build homes to live in new houses which they themselves have built, rather than in sub-standard houses cast down to them from a previous generation. It would mean the defeat of the goal of full employment, because without a huge and steady house building program we cannot sustain full employment; and we cannot have a huge and steady house building program unless we build public housing for low-income families as well as housing for other elements in the population. It would mean the defeat of the simple, human goal of a decent home for every American family. Such a defeat is unthink-

able. But to avoid it, working people throughout the land should gather the facts about the existing public housing programs in their own communities, in order to be able to answer the misrepresentations that are raised against them.

They should know that, before the war, public housing really served families who could not get decent housing elsewhere. The rents which wage-earning families paid in new public housing projects were about the same as the rents which they had been paying previously in the slums from which they came.

They should know that during the war many of these public housing projects were temporarily converted for use by war workers with higher incomes. These war workers have generally been paying the full economic rent, and this explains why families of higher income are now living in some of the projects. As we return to a peacetime situation, the public housing projects are being returned to their original purpose.

The people should know that every public housing project represents not only sound standards of living but also sound labor standards applied to the construction of every house.

Armed with these facts, the people who believe in public housing because it is a just cause will be prepared to fight for it with all the force necessary to overcome an opposition which is well financed and determined.

Working people know perfectly well that many of them who are above the income levels prescribed for public housing are still unable to obtain decent housing through the methods of private financing which have prevailed in the past. They will therefore be deeply concerned about enactment of the other provisions of the Wagner-Ellender-Taft bill, designed for the purpose of bringing better financing terms to families of middle income who can afford to pay only between $30 and $50 a month for their shelter.

Labor, through its suggestions and its testimony at hearings, has played an important part in the development of the Wagner-Ellender-Taft bill. This bill is the most important single measure now before Congress on any subject relating to the general welfare and well-being of the average American citizen. It therefore relates to the general welfare and well-being of the people of America as a whole.

Consistently with their record over the years, working people will continue to be the central core of the fighting force against special privilege and greed, and for the welfare and well-being of the American people as a whole.

Further Resources

BOOKS

Davies, Richard. *Housing Reform During the Truman Administration.* Columbia, Mo.: University of Missouri Press, 1966.

Duany, Andres. *Suburban Nation: The Rise of Sprawl and the Decline of the American Dream.* New York: North Point Press, 2000.

Jackson, Kenneth T. *Crabgrass Frontier: The Suburbanization of the United States.* New York: Oxford University Press, 1985.

WEBSITES

von Hoffman, Alexander. "A Study in Contradictions: The Origins and Legacy of the Housing Act of 1949." Available online at http://www.mi.vt.edu/Research/PDFs/hoffman.pdf (accessed April 22, 2003).

"We Back America"

Magazine article

By: George Meany

Date: July 1946

Source: Meany, George. "We Back America." *American Federationist* 53, no. 7, July 1946, 3–6.

About the Author: George Meany (1894–1980) was born and raised in New York City, and entered the workforce as a journeyman plumber. He eventually climbed the ranks of the Plumbers International Union in New York State. A staunch advocate of social justice, Meany served in various capacities for his own union, and later for the nationwide American Federation of Labor (AFL) in Washington. He became the AFL president in 1952. After the celebrated reunification with the Congress of Industrial Organizations (CIO) in 1955, Meany served as the first president of the combined AFL-CIO until his retirement in 1979. ■

Introduction

After defeating its great rival, the Knights of Labor, for the allegiance of American workers, the American Federation of Labor (AFL) emerged after 1900 as the unchallenged leader of the American labor movement. Led by Samuel Gompers, a no-nonsense, hard-boiled trade unionist, the AFL sought to reassure the skeptical (and often hostile) American public that organized labor accepted capitalism and sought merely to ensure that workers received fair representation of their interests.

The AFL was a loose alliance, dominated by craft unions. Craft unions were unions of skilled tradesmen, like plumbers and electricians, who saw themselves as a cut above the typical factory worker, whose job required no special training or skills. Skilled tradesmen were distinguished from factory workers not only by having skills, but by the relatively high wages and good working conditions these skills guaranteed them.

There were some elements within the American labor movement that wanted to organize factory workers into European-style mass unions. The AFL was aware of this, and disapproved. One reason was that it saw little connection between the skilled trades it represented and factory workers. Another issue was that industrial unions in Europe were much more politically active and radical than American craft unions, having often plotted to overthrow governments and seize the factories in the name of socialism or Communism. The AFL did not want to be associated with such extremism, and Gompers and his successors sought to reassure the public of the AFL's loyalty to the nation and its essential moderation regarding economic affairs. Also, it actively tried to purge from its ranks various "troublemakers," who, it felt, gave all unions a bad name.

This tension came to a climax in 1935 when the most radical elements within the AFL ranks—those seeking to foster large, European-style industrial unions, led by United Mine Workers of America president John L. Lewis—formed the Congress of Industrial Organizations (CIO). In retaliation, the AFL expelled the CIO-dominated unions from its ranks the following year. The CIO went on to great success, however, helping its members to expand and encouraging the unionization of industries formerly neglected by the AFL.

Significance

The advent of the radical CIO in 1935 created serious problems for the more moderate AFL. The AFL had spent two generations trying mightily to convince the American public of organized labor's patriotism and complete acceptance of the free-enterprise system. The CIO, with its prominent Communist organizers and its heavy overtones of European-style class warfare, threatened to discredit all American unions, and the AFL worked hard to distance itself from them.

This was especially true after the end of World War II (1939–45) and the beginning of America's Cold War struggle against the Communist Soviet Union. The Communist issue, including the CIO's initial tepid response to the Cold War, became a prime weapon of the AFL in its efforts to distance itself from the CIO. In this the AFL reflected, and played upon, the anti-communism and fear that was prevalent in American society during the postwar "Red Scare." Ironically, the AFL and the CIO would soon drop their rivalry. In 1955 they merged and formed the AFL-CIO (with George Meany as the organization's first president) in order to better combat anti-unionism within business and government. The AFL's heated battle with the CIO is today largely forgotten—perhaps the inevitable result of their reconciliation.

Primary Source

"We Back America" [excerpt]

SYNOPSIS: In the following excerpt, future AFL-CIO President George Meany attacks the rival labor organization, the CIO. He takes direct aim at what he claims is a too-friendly attitude displayed by the CIO towards both the Soviet Union and various Communist organizations, including the Soviet-sponsored World Federation of Trade Unions. Meany charges that the CIO leadership, possibly unwittingly, has become a tool for those interests that seek to further the Soviet's subversive agenda.

Our country is first with us.
Can C.I.O. stay the same?

Every man and woman who prides himself or herself on his or her American citizenship must back to the limit our country's efforts to achieve a peace based on justice and decency.

In its relations with the other nations of the earth, our country must of necessity be a unit if it is to be effective. There cannot be one foreign policy for the American worker and another for the American businessman. We cannot have two foreign policies—one for the Republicans and another for the Democrats. We must succeed or fail as one indivisible unit.

We achieved military victory on this basis. There is no other basis on which we can win the peace. If we fail, we must and will face an ominous and uncertain future. . . .

Why We Fought

By force, or unilateral action, we find Soviet Russia exercising the prerogatives of a dictator in Poland, Eastern Germany, Iran, Czechoslovakia and the Balkan nations and, in addition, assuming a dominant antidemocratic position in Eastern Asia. While screaming loudly against an imaginary "western bloc," this same nation has set up a chain of dominated states from the North Sea to the Pacific Ocean. . . .

Free Men Can't Be Gagged

Certain individuals have been telling the American people that they should refrain from speaking out frankly against the evils in the recent actions of the Soviets, lest such criticism "impair" relations between the United States and Russia. No one need try to persuade the American Federation of Labor to accept this preposterous suggestion. We believe in freedom of speech and we regard silence in the face of manifest evil as contemptible. Moreover, all his-

tory plainly shows the utter futility of trying to correct wrong by refusing to expose it, and we are therefore going to keep speaking out—bluntly— concerning Russia's undemocratic actions. Let others try to ignore the tragic facts if they wish. We shall not emulate them.

It is crystal clear by now that Soviet policy calls for the complete elimination of every non-Soviet government. While we in America can discover no radical difference, either in methods or in purposes, between fascism and communism, the Russian line is to label all non-Soviet governments as fascist. In the final analysis, the Soviet idea for world peace seems to be complete acceptance on the part of all the world of Soviet domination and control. . . .

In Russia's program to control other nations an important role has been assigned to the Soviet-created and controlled organization which calls itself the World Federation of Trade Unions. This is a world-wide fifth-column organization formed by Russia for the purpose of inculcating world labor with the views of Soviet world policy. This is the so-called world labor organization which the American Federation of Labor has refused to join or even recognize as a trade union instrument.

The World Federation of Trade Unions came into being with a loud noise at the time the United Nations Conference on International Organization was held in San Francisco. It was formed by the so-called trade unions of Soviet Russia, which are not real unions at all, but merely instruments of oppression operated by the government for the purpose of enslaving the workers of Russia. Working in conjunction with the Soviet group was the dominant Communist group in the C.I.O. and the secretary of the British Trades Union Congress, who was lured into collaboration by the promise that he would be the dominant leader in this new setup.

The W.F.T.U. claims to represent 60,000,000 workers, of which the C.I.O. claims to represent 6,000,000. Needless to say, no proof of membership figures is offered. However, an analysis of the figures claimed—on which voting strength is, of course, determined—shows that Soviet Russia and the countries it controls have about 70 per cent of the votes. Russia alone has 27,000,000 members listed out of the 60,000,000 total claimed.

This organization has been loudly demanding a seat in the United Nations on a par with member states on the ground that it represents all world labor. It is very ardently following the party line with regard to world affairs. Among other things, it has been loudly insisting upon democratic rule for Spain and, until recently, Argentina. It has now had to pipe down insofar as the Argentine is concerned, for Russia and Argentina have kissed and made up. Dictator Perón will now, of course, be recognized as a staunch advocate of democracy and, of course, it is by no means impossible that Dictator Stalin may as suddenly discover that Dictator Franco isn't such a bad fellow after all.

This so-called World Federation of Trade Unions has a big assignment in soviet plans for the future. A program for world domination calls for worldwide power and influence over those who produce. The W.F.T.U. could well be a very effective instrument of world policy through the use of the fifth column methods which Hitler used so effectively.

As this article is being written, this called World Federation of Trade Unions is holding a meeting of its Executive Board in Moscow. Three officers of the C.I.O. are in Moscow, attending this meeting of Russia's world propaganda and pressure group. One may well wonder whether the C.I.O. boys approach their discussions with their Soviet friends with the same American ideals and principles as to world peace that are being advocated in Paris by our Secretary of State.

I am to some extent surprised that the C.I.O. allowed itself to be hooked into this outfit. But of course, there is no cause for astonishment in regard to people like Bridges and Curran, who have never by a single word or deed indicated any loyalty to America that overshadowed their allegiance to Moscow.

Entirely apart from the obvious purpose behind this organization, the American Federation of Labor would not under any circumstances join with the so-called Russian unions. The fundamental difference in ideals between the two groups would make cooperation utterly impossible.

We pride ourselves on having a free movement. We pride ourselves on the fact that we can strike, that we can quit and go where we will in search of better employment. We take pride in the fact that we can publicly disagree with our government. We like free speech. We dislike concentration camps. We abhor speedup systems. We are opposed to a secret police force which strikes terror in the hearts of all peoples in totalitarian countries. All of these matters represent fundamental and basic differences between our movement and Russia's labor front.

While we hope to see the day when the Russian worker is released from state slavery, we cannot give approval to his present status by joining with him in an organization which is as much a fraud as the Soviet unions themselves.

The American Federation of Labor is going to continue to follow its traditional American way. We are not going to put ourselves in a position similar to that in which the C.I.O. Communist group found itself back in June of 1941.

That was when the Communists in the C.I.O. had to turn quick somersaults in order to keep in step with Moscow.

The real trade unionists of our country have an obligation to see to it that American workers are not fooled by this so-called World Federation of Trade Unions. The greatest contribution we can make, outside of supporting a foreign policy based on justice and liberty, is to see to it that this organization is clearly identified in the minds of American workers in its true form—an instrument of Soviet power politics designed to undermine the allegiance of workers to their own nations. The American Federation of Labor is going to oppose to the limit this or any other effort which may be made to destroy the loyalty of American workers to the United States.

The record of achievement written by the American Federation of Labor during the past six and one-half decades is an American record. We have never faltered or deviated. Our only ism is Americanism. So it was in the past. So it will be in the future.

Further Resources
BOOKS
Robinson, Archie. *George Meany and His Times: A Biography.* New York: Simon & Schuster, 1981.

Rosswurm, Steve, ed. *The CIO's Left-Led Unions.* New Brunswick, N.J.: Rutgers University Press, 1992.

Zieger, Robert H. *The CIO, 1935–1955.* Chapel Hill, N.C.: University of North Carolina Press, 1995.

Truman Defends Taft-Hartley Act Veto
Radio address

By: Harry S. Truman
Date: June 20, 1947
Source: Truman, Harry S. Speech Defending the Taft-Hartley Act Veto. June 20, 1947. Reprinted in Koenig, Louis W, ed.

The Truman Administration: Its Principles and Practice.
Washington Square, NY: New York University Press, 1956,
241–45.

About the Author: Harry S. Truman (1884–1972) became
president of the United States in April 1945 upon the death
of Franklin D. Roosevelt. Elected to a second term, he served
until 1953. Truman actively supported liberal causes at home
in the form of his Fair Deal programs. His presidency saw
the beginning of the Cold War, and Truman's foreign policy
was both forceful and anti-Communist, helping to rebuild Europe and Japan while fighting the Korean War (1950–53).
Much maligned while in office, Truman's reputation in both
foreign and domestic affairs has grown over time. ∎

Introduction

The Wagner Labor Relations Act of 1935 shifted the
balance of power between business and labor toward organized labor for the first time in American history. The
Smith-Connelly Act of 1943 imposed some restrictions
on labor, but as a wartime measure it was repealed after
American victory in World War II (1939–45). Having
been held in check for several years, labor unions responded to the repeal with major strikes and other activities. Many began to feel that the labor unions were too
strong. Named after Ohio Republican senator Robert A.
Taft, and New Jersey Republican representative Frederick A. Hartley Jr., the Taft-Hartley Labor Relations Act
of 1947 (also known as the Labor Management Relations
Act) significantly reduced the power of unions, and was
generally perceived as correcting an imbalance in business and labor relations.

Although most Republicans and many Democrats in
Congress welcomed the passage of legislation intended
to strike a blow at the power of organized labor, both primary sponsors appear as somewhat unlikely candidates
for the assignment. Senator Taft's labor record prior to
1947 had been as a moderate. Taft's major complaint
against unions appears to have centered around his personal opposition to the labor tactic known as "secondary
boycotts"—where strikers would boycott companies that
did business with the real target of their strike. Representative Hartley, a congressman from New Jersey since
1928, abandoned his long-standing pro-labor stance in
sponsoring this bill.

The Taft-Hartley Act of 1947 reestablished the
availability of an injunction (a court order) as a significant deterrent to strikes. Specifically, it authorized the
federal government to obtain injunctions prohibiting
work stoppages during an "eighty-day cooling off period" if a strike threatened the safety and health of the
nation. Jurisdictional strikes—strikes called as part of a
dispute between unions over who would represent a
group of workers—were prohibited, as were secondary
boycotts. In addition, the Taft-Hartley Act outlawed the
practice of the closed shop, a workplace that required

union membership as a condition of employment. It also
permitted states the option of passing "right-to-work"
laws. These laws make it illegal for a union and businesses to agree that all jobs of a specific type would go
to union members (for example, that all engine assem-
blers at an auto plant must be United Auto Workers
members). The Taft-Hartley Act forbade members of the
Communist Party from serving as labor union officials—
a blow aimed directly at the Communist-infiltrated CIO
unions. It also banned direct political campaign contributions from unions, although this provision would
eventually be found unconstitutional.

Although a Democrat previously considered moderately friendly to the interests of organized labor, President Harry S. Truman privately sympathized with many
of the provisions of the Taft-Hartley Act. He too felt that
the Wagner Act of 1935 had given organized labor too
much clout, and Truman recognized the need to enact
some new corrective measure to remedy the balance between business and labor. Truman might have signed a
slightly less anti-labor measure had one emerged as the
final product of congressional deliberations. As it was,
there was considerable uncertainty until the last minute
as to whether Truman would sign or veto the bill.

Significance

In the end, political calculations, far beyond pure
economic concerns, guided Truman's actions. The president not only vetoed the measure, but surprised many
observers with his sharp public criticism of the legislation. With his action, Truman guaranteed that the Taft-
Hartley Act would become a major issue in his upcoming
1948 reelection campaign.

Despite Truman's strident opposition, the Republican-
dominated Congress easily overrode the presidential
veto, and the measure became law. A significant number
of conservative Democrats (mostly from the South) broke
ranks to join their Republican colleagues to enact the legislation. The passage of such a law, designed to reduce
drastically the power of a very potent special-interest
group and voting block—as organized labor was in the
postwar period—is rare in American history. Union conduct after World War II (1939–1945), in particular a series of disruptive strikes and flirtations with communism,
cost labor the support of the American public, once generally sympathetic toward the union movement. Organized labor became viewed as yet another power center
to be feared, along with big business and big government.

The American labor movement clearly overestimated
its strength in the immediate postwar period. Unwilling
to learn the lesson from the post–World War I era that
strikes during periods of inflation and shortages only
anger the public, the labor leaders after World War II re-

President Harry S. Truman defended his vetoing of the Taft-Hartley Act through a radio address in 1947. AP/WIDE WORLD PHOTOS. REPRODUCED BY PERMISSION.

peated the same mistake. During periods of rising consumer prices, the public is likely to blame the rising cost of living on increased wage hikes won by unions, even if these wages increases are themselves simply trying to keep up with the inflation.

Primary Source

Truman Defends Taft-Hartley Act Veto [excerpt]

> **SYNOPSIS:** President Harry S. Truman's veto of the Taft-Hartley Act was as much motivated by politics as by economics. Truman made a radio address to the nation on June 20, 1947, explaining in harsh terms why he was vetoing the bill. This excerpt might well have served as the blueprint for Truman's successful reelection campaign for the following year.

My fellow countrymen:

At noon today I sent to Congress a message vetoing the Taft-Hartley Labor Bill. I vetoed this bill because I am convinced it is a bad bill. It is bad for labor, bad for management, and bad for the country.

I had hoped that the Congress would send me a labor bill I could sign. . . .

But the Taft-Hartley bill is a shocking piece of legislation.

It is unfair to the working people of this country. It clearly abuses the right, which millions of our citizens now enjoy, to join together and bargain with their employers for fair wages and fair working conditions.

Under no circumstances could I have signed this bill!

The restrictions that this bill places on our workers go far beyond what our people have been led to believe. This is no innocent bill. . . .

We have all been told that the Taft-Hartley bill is favorable to the wage earners of this country. It has been claimed that workers need to be saved from their own folly and that this bill would provide the means of salvation. Some people have called this bill the "workers' bill of rights."

Let's see what this bill really would do to our working men.

The bill is deliberately designed to weaken labor unions. When the sponsors of the bill claim that by weakening unions they are giving rights back to the individual workingman, they ignore the basic reason why unions are important in our democracy. Unions exist so that laboring men can bargain with their employers on a basis of equality. Because of unions the living standards of our working people have increased steadily until they are today the highest in the world.

A bill which would weaken unions would undermine our national policy of collective bargaining. The Taft-Hartley bill would do just that. It would take us back in the direction of the old evils of individual bargaining. It would take bargaining power away from workers and give more power to management. This bill would even take away from our workingmen some bargaining rights which they enjoyed before the Wagner Act was passed twelve years ago. If we weaken our system of collective bargaining, we weaken the position of every workingman in the country.

This bill would again expose workers to the abuses of labor injunctions.

It would make unions liable for damage suits for actions which have long been considered lawful.

This bill would treat all unions alike. Unions which have fine records, with long years of peaceful relations with management, would be hurt by this bill just as much as the few troublemakers.

The country needs legislation which would get rid of abuses. We do not need, and we do not want, legislation which will take fundamental rights away from our working people. . . .

We have been told by the supporters of the Taft-Hartley bill that it would reduce industrial strife. On the contrary, I am convinced that it would increase industrial strife. The bill would soon upset security clauses in thousands of existing agreements between labor and management. These agreements were mutually arrived at and furnish a satisfactory basis for relations between worker and employer. They provide stability in industry. With their present types of agreements outlawed by this bill, the parties would have to find a new basis for agreement. The restrictions in this bill would make the process of reaching new agreements a long and bitter one. The bill would increase industrial strife because a number of its provisions deprive workers of legal protection of fundamental rights. They would then have no means of protecting these rights except by striking.

The bill would open up opportunities for endless lawsuits by employers against unions and by unions against employers. For example, it would make employers vulnerable to an immense number of lawsuits, since grievances, however minor, could be taken into court by dissatisfied workers.

In so far as employers are concerned, I predict that if this bill should become law they would regret the day that it was conceived. It is loaded with provisions that would plague and hamper management. It is filled with hidden legal traps that would take labor relations out of the plant, where they belong, and place them in the courts.

Another defect is that in trying to correct labor abuses the Taft-Hartley bill goes so far that it would threaten fundamental democratic freedoms.

One provision undertakes to prevent political contributions and expenditures by labor organizations and corporations. This provision would forbid a union newspaper from commenting on candidates in national elections. It might well prevent an incorporated radio network from spending any money in connection with the national convention of a political party. It might even prevent the League of Women Voters—which is incorporated—from using its funds to inform its members about the record of a political candidate. I regard this provision of the Taft-Hartley bill as a dangerous challenge to free speech and our free press.

One of the basic errors of this bill is that it ignores the fact that over the years we have been making real progress in labor-management relations. We have been achieving slow but steady improvement co-operation between employers and workers.

We must always remember that under our free economic system management and labor are associates. They work together for their own benefit and for the benefit of the public. The Taft-Hartley bill fails to recognize these fundamental facts. Many provisions of the bill would have the result of changing employers and workers from members of the same team to opponents on contending teams. I feel deep concern about what this would do to the steady progress we have made through the years.

I fear that this type of legislation would cause the people of our country to divide into opposing groups. If conflict is created, as this bill would create it—if seeds of discord are sown, as this bill would sow them—our unity will suffer and our strength will be impaired.

This bill does not resemble the labor legislation which I have recommended to the Congress. The whole purpose of this bill is contrary to the sound growth of our national labor policy.

Further Resources

BOOKS

McCullough, David. *Truman.* New York: Simon & Schuster, 1993.

Millis, Harry A. *From the Wagner Act to Taft-Hartley: A Study of National Labor Policy and Labor Relations.* Chicago: University of Chicago Press, 1950.

White, William Smith. *The Taft Story.* New York: Harper, 1954.

Photographs of Supermarkets in the 1940s

Photographs

Date: 1940s

Source: Photographs of Supermarkets in the 1940s. From *Progressive Grocer* magazine. Appearing in McAusland, Randolph. *Supermarkets: 50 Years of Progress.* Washington, D.C.: Food Marketing Institute, 1980, 38, 41, 42, 47, 49, 50, 51.

About the Publication: Founded in 1922, the publication *Progressive Grocer* is an important trade magazine for the grocery business. The magazine maintains a unique collection of photographs documenting the evolution of the American supermarket during the twentieth century. ■

Introduction

The American supermarket came of age during the 1940s, as it revolutionized the buying habits of the American public. Convenient "one-stop shopping" replaced separate trips to the corner grocer, butcher shop, bakery, the produce and flower stand, and the drug store.

The arrival of World War II (1939–1945) placed the supermarket at the forefront of the nation's efforts to help win the war on the home front. The supermarket helped administer the nation's food-rationing program, assisted in implementing consumer price controls, served as an important resource in the government's ambitious plans to sell war bonds, and provided opportunities for women and minorities to enter the workforce and obtain relatively well-paying jobs.

Following victory in the war, the supermarket's role expanded markedly as the headlong rush to suburbia continued the dramatic change in the American consumer's expectations. Supermarkets eclipsed the venerable neighborhood grocery store in both convenience and selection of merchandise. Also, the supermarket itself was part of wider retailing innovations that featured an increasing variety of frozen and prepared foods.

Significance

The supermarket stood as a perfect symbol of post-World War II American prosperity, especially when contrasted with the nations of war-ravaged Europe, whose citizens faced daily deprivations. This material abundance made America the envy of the world.

The image of the American supermarket also served as a potent weapon during the Cold War era. For Communists, while undoubtedly a substantial military threat to the global interests of the United States, had failed miserably in providing material comforts. The contrast between an American supermarket, stocked with fresh foods and goods from around the world, and the Soviet Union's long lines for basic goods such as toilet paper, could not be more marked.

Finally, the supermarket can be viewed as the first step in a larger retailing trend. The arrival of the supermarket usually meant the doom of the corner "mom-and-pop" store. As time elapsed, this trend became a noticeable feature of the entire American economy. Big chains of stores selling a wide variety of merchandise replaced small, independent merchants all across the land. By the century's end, giant superstores had driven out a large number local shopkeepers, impoverishing community after community as the traditional, hardy, self-sufficient merchants, once the middle-class backbone of their neighborhoods, found themselves replaced.

Further Resources

BOOKS

Mayo, James M. *The American Grocery Store: The Business Evolution of an Architectural Space.* Westport, Conn.: Greenwood Press, 1993.

Seth, Andrew, and Geoffrey Randall. *The Grocers: The Rise and Rise of the Supermarket Chain.* Dover, N.H.: Kogan Page, 2001.

Primary Source

Hinky Dinky Supermarket: Photographs of Supermarkets in the 1940s (1 OF 5)

SYNOPSIS: The following photo essay depicts the manner in which the supermarket became the center of retail business in the United States during the 1940s. With the demise already in sight for many independent local merchants, the supermarket emerged triumphant as a crucial center for both business and community interaction. This Hinky Dinky supermarket was built in the modernist style popular in 1941. It was also built before the United States's entrance into World War II, after which access to building materials and labor became restricted. PROGRESSIVE GROCER.

Primary Source

Frozen Food Section: Photographs of Supermarkets in the 1940s (2 OF 5)
Frozen foods were not introduced to American consumers until the late 1930s. PROGRESSIVE GROCER.

Primary Source

Meat Cuts with Ceiling Prices: Photographs of Supermarkets in the 1940s (3 OF 5)

An instructional photograph on meat rationing shows meat cuts with their ceiling prices and ration point values. PROGRESSIVE GROCER. THE LIBRARY OF CONGRESS.

Primary Source

"Point Free" Baked Beans: Photographs of Supermarkets in the 1940s (4 OF 5)

This supermarket aisle is stocked with "no point" items that were not rationed out, so families were able to stock up on them and save their ration points for high-point luxury items. PROGRESSIVE GROCER.

Primary Source

"Bring Your Own Shopping Bag": Photographs of Supermarkets in the 1940s (5 OF 5)

A supermarket worker points to a shopping bag rationing poster. Retailers were asked by the U.S. government to cut their use of paper bags in half. PROGRESSIVE GROCER.

3

EDUCATION

NADINE PINÈDE

Entries are arranged in chronological order by date of primary source. For entries with one primary source, the entry title is the same as the primary source title. Entries with more than one primary source have an overall entry title, followed by the titles of the primary sources.

Important Events in Education, 1940–1949

1940

- Students numbering 12,640,000 are enrolled in the federal lunch program at a cost of around twelve million dollars.

- The United States census lists nearly ten million adults as virtually illiterate. The median number of years of school attendance by persons over the age of 25 is 8.4.

- In June, the U.S. Supreme Court affirms a Pennsylvania law that allows any schoolchild who refuses to salute the American flag to be expelled. The Court reverses this ruling in 1943.

- On August 5, the National Education Association calls on educators to contribute to the nation's defense by fostering faith in American democracy.

- On October 3, the president of Columbia University calls for the resignation of faculty members who do not support the Allied cause.

1941

- On March 17, the New York Board of Higher Education votes to dismiss City College faculty members who belong to communist or fascist organizations.

- On July 1, deferment of military service for college students is eliminated.

- In July, Georgia governor Eugene Talmadge fires University of Georgia Dean of Education Walter Dewey Cocking, a proponent of racial equality, which leads to widespread resignations and the loss of accreditation for the university.

- On December 16, about five hundred liberal arts colleges decide to offer three-year degrees, with classes taken during the summer, allowing graduation before the draft age of twenty-one.

1942

- Correspondence courses sponsored by the U.S. Armed Forces Institute begin.

- In January, the College Entrance Examination Board decides to replace its traditional essay test with achievement tests measuring skills in reading and problem-solving as well as general knowledge.

- In July, U.S. education commissioner John W. Studebaker estimates a shortage of fifty thousand teachers across the United States.

- On December 1, the U.S. Office of Education announces that college enrollments had declined dramatically due to the military draft.

1943

- In January, second-, third-, and fourth-graders in Seattle are taught to prepare simple dishes such as oatmeal, scrambled eggs, and butterscotch pudding because many of their mothers are busy with wartime jobs.

- In April, Education Commissioner Studebaker vigorously promotes education at all levels for African Americans.

- On June 27, the National Education Association reports that 2 million children between the ages of 14 and 18 have left school for wage work.

- In October, the Thomas-Hill bill, providing federal supplements to state education, is defeated in the Senate due to a provision requiring that the funds be disbursed equally to all races.

- On November 26, the U.S. Office of Education announces that enrollment in institutions of higher education has declined by 8 percent since 1942.

1944

- The United Negro College Fund is established.

- More than 275 courses are offered to veterans by the United States Armed Forces Institute.

- On June 22, the Serviceman's Readjustment Act, popularly known as the "GI Bill of Rights," is signed into law by President Roosevelt. The bill funds veterans' education.

1945

- On February 20, the U.S. Office of Education urges the formation of schools specializing in foreign studies.

- In June, inspired by the military's success using movies to teach servicemen subjects such as machine guns, camouflage, and venereal disease, Virginia allocates $1,176,000 toward making educational movies for use in public schools.

- In July, Vannevar Bush publishes the results of a year-long study of federal science education, *Science: The Endless Frontier*. It urges increased federal expenditures for science education.

- In August, scientists meeting at the Conference on Science, Philosophy and Religion in New York urge the integration of ethics and humanities scholars into atomic weapons research.

- In September, the University of Maryland alters its curricular requirements, making courses in American history mandatory.

- From November 1 to November 16, the United Nations Educational, Scientific, and Cultural Organization (UNESCO) is founded following a conference of international scholars.

1946

- Fifty-three percent of all college students are veterans.

- In May, General Omar Bradley announces that 1.6 million veterans have applied for benefits under the GI Bill.

- In July, at the annual meeting of the National Education Association in Buffalo, it is revealed that 350,000 teachers have left the profession since 1941.

- On July 30, President Truman signs a bill authorizing American participation in UNESCO.

- In August, Senator James W. Fulbright introduces and Congress passes the Fulbright Act to fund scholarly exchanges between the United States and other countries.

- On August 18, a world conference of educators in Endicott, New York, advocates the adoption of universal history and geography textbooks; their goal is to "eliminate national bias."

1947

- UNESCO's educational efforts in developing countries are curtailed due to the growing Cold War.

- Allen Zoll's National Council for American Education produces the pamphlet *The Commies Are After Your Kids.*

- In February, the U.S. Supreme Court confirms the constitutionality of a statute allowing private-school students to be transported in publicly owned buses.

- On February 2, more than two thousand teachers in Buffalo, New York, go on a week-long strike for higher pay.

- In May, New York governor Thomas E. Dewey declares strikes by teachers and other public employees illegal. Similar laws are enacted in Ohio, Pennsylvania, and Texas.

- In May, Harvard University makes its coeducational arrangement with Radcliffe College permanent.

- On June 24, Gen. Dwight Eisenhower accepts the position of president of Columbia University.

- In July, the National Conference for the Improvement of Teachers issues a teachers' "Bill of Rights," calling for higher salaries, a forty-hour workweek, tenure, and retirement plans.

- In September, seventy-five thousand students nationwide receive no schooling due to teacher shortages.

- On October 21, southern governors meet in Asheville, N.C., to plan a regional system of racially segregated higher education.

- On December 15, the President's Commission on Higher Education releases the first volume of its report, *Higher Education for American Democracy*; among other goals, it calls for an end to racial segregation and quotas in college admissions.

1948

- New Jersey desegregates its public schools.

- In January, the Smith-Mundt Act, providing for foreign academic exchanges, becomes law.

- On January 12, in *Sipuel v. Oklahoma,* the U.S. Supreme Court orders Oklahoma to provide law education to Ada L. Sipuel. Rather than admit an African American student to the University of Oklahoma Law School, the state opens a one-pupil law school for her. She returns to court, but the Supreme Court rejects her appeal.

- On February 3, Silas Hunt becomes the first African American student accepted to University of Arkansas Law School.

- In March, Minneapolis teachers strike for twenty-seven days, demanding salary increases.

- On March 8, in *McCollum v. Board of Education,* the U.S. Supreme Court rules that there may be no religious instruction or activity in public-school facilities.

- On July 15, John W. Studebaker resigns as U.S. education commissioner. He had held the post since 1934.

- On September 22, the Census Bureau announces that illiteracy in America has reached a new low of 2.7 percent of the population.

- On October 6, bowing to a federal court ruling that African American students may not be rejected on racial grounds, the University of Oklahoma Law School accepts George McLaurin as a student, but only on a segregated basis.

1949

- The House Committee on Un-American Activities proposes that educators be required to submit for inspection lists of books used in courses.

- The first baby-boom children reach kindergarten age. Educators estimate a 39 percent increase in school attendance in the coming year.

- On June 30, Harvard and Brown universities announce their first African American faculty appointments.

- In July, the National Education Association votes 2,882-5 to bar Communists from the organization.

- In summer, spurred by controversy over public funds used for parochial school students, Francis Cardinal Spellman and Eleanor Roosevelt debate the issue of separation of church and state.

- On November 26, the National Intrafraternity Conference recommends that member groups eliminate racial and religious restrictions on membership.

"Whither the American Indian?"

Magazine article

By: Alden Stevens

Date: March 1, 1940

Source: Stevens, Alden. "Whither the American Indian?" *Survey Graphic* 29, no. 3, March 1, 1940, 168. Available online at http://newdeal.feri.org/survey/40b09.htm; website home page: http://newdeal.feri.org (accessed February 27, 2003).

About the Author: Alden Stevens (1907–1968) was born and raised in Chicago and later graduated from the University of Chicago. He was a well-traveled writer and museum exhibition designer whose assignments took him to numerous American Indian reservations. Stevens also wrote for several television shows, and in 1957, served as the field director of the *Mobil Travel Guide*. In 1941, he joined the American Association on Indian Affairs, an organization dedicated to promoting the welfare of American Indians. In 1964, he was elected president of the association, a position he held until his death. ■

As commissioner of the Bureau of Indian Affairs, John Collier was more sensitive to Indian traditions. **THE LIBRARY OF CONGRESS.**

Introduction

Ever since the establishment of mission schools by the Spaniards in the 1500s, continuous efforts had been made to convert American Indians to Christianity and to deprive them of their culture. Assimilation was the goal of American Indian education, especially at the hands of missionaries and in the American Indian boarding schools across the country. Students were forbidden to speak their native languages and were stripped of their customs. The regime at these boarding schools, such as the Carlisle Indian School in Pennsylvania, which was actually run by a former army officer, often resembled the military. Most graduates were left unprepared for returning to their home communities.

By 1933, the federal government's attitude toward the education of American Indians was beginning to change. President Franklin D. Roosevelt (served 1933–1945) appointed John Collier to reform the corrupt Bureau of Indian Affairs. Unlike past commissioners, Collier was sympathetic to American Indians' demands for political autonomy and sensitive to their traditions.

He also made certain that American Indians were hired in New Deal programs. That same year, Luther Standing Bear, an Oglala Lakota Sioux, published his autobiography *Land of the Spotted Eagle*, in which he called for a reform of American Indian education through greater self-determination. By 1934, Collier had convinced Congress to pass the Indian Reorganization Act, which provided American Indians self-rule and an end to the unfair land allotment system. The act was accepted by three-quarters of the American Indian nations.

Significance

As part of his new approach, Collier made sure that American Indian students received loans for vocational and higher education. He also closed down the sixteen federally operated boarding schools, replacing them with eighty-four reservation day schools. Most importantly, Collier rejected assimilation as the aim of education, and instead looked to anthropology as a tool for cross-cultural understanding.

Alden Stevens's article "Whither the American Indian" pointed out that in 1940 there were still debates about the merit of educating American Indian children on the reservation instead of in public schools. Despite record-high enrollments, at least ten thousand school-age

American Indian children were not enrolled in any school at all. However, Stevens concluded his overview by writing that "many Indian problems remain unsolved, but every one has been attacked."

Primary Source

"Whither the American Indian?" [excerpt]

SYNOPSIS: In this excerpt, Stevens provides a brief survey of the history of American Indian education from the colonial era through the 1930s. He shows how New Deal education policies were an about-face from earlier policies of assimilation.

The problem of education, so vital to the success of any government program, has been a sore spot for more than a century, and the present administration has characteristically applied to it a fresh viewpoint; at the same time building on the work done by the previous administration under Commissioner Rhoads, who was one of the first to recognize the hopeless inadequacy of traditional policies.

The original colonies showed little concern for Indian education, although several colleges, including Dartmouth and Harvard, made provision for tuition-free admission of Indians, and the Continental Congress in 1775 employed a schoolmaster for the Delaware and made motions toward doing something for other tribes. The Revolution interrupted, and until 1819 Indian education was left entirely to a few missionary societies. From that year to 1873, $10,000 was appropriated annually for the work, and most of this was turned over to the missions. From 1873 on, the appropriations increased fairly regularly, until 1932, when $11,224,000 was set aside. The next few years saw slight reductions; the budget for 1939–1940 allow[s] $10,523,745. (However, most post-1933 building was done with emerge[ncy] funds not included in the departmental budget.) Until 1929, Indian education was pretty much a hodgepodge. More Indians attended public schools than other kind—this is still true. Large numbers were in mission schools. Many attended boarding schools both on and off the reservation. These were established late in the last century when the accepted theory of Indian education called for removing the children from their parents and home life as much as possible so that they might be "civilized." Often the children were taken by force from their homes and subjected in the schools to a rigid discipline and a standardized, outmoded course of study. Half their time was devoted to schoolwork, the other half to doing routine institutional tasks

such as laundering, cleaning, wood-chopping and food preparation. Often this work was too hard and too many hours per day were devoted to it, so that it had a serious effect on health. Insufficient operating funds made the school and living standards dangerously low.

Forbidden to speak their own language in school, out of touch with family and tribal life, denied the normal experience and education needed to prepare them for life as Indians, the children would return home from school dissatisfied misfits, unable to readapt themselves to reservation life and equally unable to find a place in a white community. They had learned to read and write, but they were unfamiliar with the customs and language of [their] own people, and found their schooling of little use in making a living.

The problem was a hard one, and perhaps the earlier officials should not be too harshly criticized for their failure to solve it. Indians are very diverse; they represent hundreds of cultures vastly different one from another. More than two hundred mutually unintelligible languages are spoken in the United States. The school program must be carefully fitted to each group since the needs vary so much. And undoubtedly the success of the present program rests partly on a study of previous failures.

The "about-face" in Indian education is designed to mesh with the "about-face" in general policy. Recognizing attempts to drag children from their families and "civilize" them is a total failure, the aim now is to give a basic education in the three R's without detaching them from their families, to teach hygiene and such mechanical skills as will be useful to each group. This is accomplished to an increasing extent in day schools, which are being established on as many reservations as possible. The children live at home and walk or ride to school. Native tongues are not forbidden, and an increasing number of Indians are on the teaching staffs. In the past ten years the Indian day school population (in all-Indian schools distinct from public schools) has risen from 4,532 to 14,087. There are still over 10,000 in boarding schools on and off the reservations. . . .

The fact that facilities for education were so limited has made it impossible to abandon entirely the boarding schools, but the emphasis in these has been changed radically, and they are now used principally as vocational and trade schools. The boarding school at Flandreau, S.D., specializes in dairying; Haskell Institute (a high school) at Lawrence, Kan.,

Devil dancers in ceremonial costume prepare for a performance on the Mescalero Apache Reservation near Almagordo, N.M., on July 2, 1949. Sending Indian youth to schools where their native language and costume were banned was one way authorities tried to assimilate Indian Americans into white culture. **AP/WIDE WORLD PHOTOS. REPRODUCED BY PERMISSION.**

gives business and commercial courses and shop work; that at Santa Fe, N.M., is for [students] who wish to learn arts and crafts. Sherman Institute, at Riverside, Calif., teaches agriculture and industrial work. Thus it is possible for those who show aptitude and want training in trades to get it.

Some of these schools are accredited by higher institutions, and an educational loan fund of $250,000 enables young Indians to attend advanced trade and vocational schools as well as colleges. About 220 Indians are now receiving higher education, most of them in state universities.

Indian education is still much less complete than it should be. At least 10,000 children of school age are not enrolled in any school. But . . . never have there been as many school-age children in school as there are today. The importance of education [is] reflected in the fact that more than half the total staff [of] the Office of Indian Affairs is engaged in this work.

Of 86,747 Indians between six and eighteen, 33,645 attend public schools not operated by the Office of Indian Affairs. These are mostly in such states as California, Minnesota, and Oklahoma, where a certain amount of assimilation is actually taking place. The arrangement does not work badly; and some educators feel that Indian children who attend public schools are better adapted to meet their problems as adults for the contacts made there. Since Indian land is exempt from taxation, the government pays a small tuition to the school district for each Indian pupil.

For the first time adult Indians are taking a real interest in the education of their children and in the possibilities of the school as a community center. At the Rosebud reservation (Sioux, S.D.) a vegetable canning project by the women with some help from the school teacher was so successful that for the first time in many years a winter was passed without relief rations being sent into the area. There is an awakening of interest that has resulted in some rather astonishing initiative on the part of the Indians. In the Kallihoma district of Oklahoma some twenty-five children were without school facilities, but their parents got together, bought an abandoned hotel, remodeled it themselves, set up an Indian and his wife as teachers, and started a day school and community center which has been a most successful enterprise.

Further Resources

BOOKS

Coleman, Michael C. *American Indian Children at School, 1850–1930.* Jackson: University of Mississippi Press, 1993.

Katz, William Loren. *A History of Multicultural America: The New Freedom to the New Deal.* Austin, Tex.: Raintree Steck-Vaughn, 1993.

Szasz, Margaret Connell. *Education and the American Indian: The Road to Self-Determination since 1928.* Albuquerque: University of New Mexico Press, 1999.

PERIODICALS

Knott, Sarah Gertrude. "North of the Border." *Survey Graphic,* June 1, 1940, 339. Available online at http://newdeal.feri.org /survey/40c16.htm; website home page: http://newdeal.feri .org (accessed February 27, 2003).

WEBSITES

"Native American Education: Educ. 311 Colgate University Library Research Guide." Available online at http://exlibris .colgate.edu/Staff/EHutton/Nativeduc.html; website home page: http://www.colgate.edu (accessed February 27, 2003).

"Native American Authors Project." Internet Public Library. Available online at http://www.ipl.org/cgi/ref/native/browse .pl/A110; website home page: http://www.ipl.org (accessed February 27, 2003).

AUDIO AND VISUAL MEDIA

In the White Man's Image. American Experience. Produced by Christine Lesiak. PBS Home Video. Videocassette, 1992.

Mary McLeod Bethune's Letter to Eleanor Roosevelt

Letter

By: Mary McLeod Bethune

Date: April 22, 1941

Source: McCluskey, Audrey Thomas, and Elaine M. Smith, eds. *Mary McLeod Bethune: Building a Better World—Essays and Selected Documents.* Bloomington: Indiana University Press, 1999, 120–21.

About the Author: Mary McLeod Bethune (1895–1955) one of seventeen children whose parents were freed slaves, was born in Mayesville, South Carolina. She opened a school for girls in 1904, which later became Bethune-Cookman College,

Mary McLeod Bethune and singer Marian Anderson at the launch of the SS Booker T. Washington. California, September 29, 1942. THE LIBRARY OF CONGRESS.

where she served as president for many years. She was the director of the Division of Negro Affairs of the National Youth Administration (NYA) and the founder and first president of the National Council of Negro Women. In 1974, she was honored with a national monument in Washington, D.C. ∎

Introduction

The story of Mary McLeod Bethune's struggle to get an education and fund her own school was well known. In 1904, with "$1.50 and faith," she opened the Daytona Normal and Industrial Institute, patterned on the Scotia Seminary, a Presbyterian school for African American girls that she had attended. Three years later, she set up the Tomoka Mission as an extension to the school.

Bethune's school included a hospital and a farm. In 1923, Bethune merged her school of three hundred girls with the Cookman Institute in Jacksonville and in 1929 added Bethune-Cookman College, the postsecondary division. Even during the Great Depression, Bethune, a charismatic speaker, was a successful fund-raiser for her school and by 1943 had transformed it into one of the region's leading teacher training colleges for African Americans and a fully accredited four-year institution. Bethune served as president of Bethune-Cookman from 1923 to 1942 and again from 1946 to 1947.

Students at Bethune-Cookman College say goodbye to Dr. Bethune after her resignation, 1943. THE LIBRARY OF CONGRESS.

During the New Deal, Bethune, as the director of the Division of Negro Affairs of the NYA, was the first African American woman to head a federal agency. Other African American advisors had been appointed to federal agencies, but their power was minimal. Bethune, however, was able to gather these advisors and other prominent African Americans and to use her access to President Franklin D. Roosevelt (served 1933–1945) to put forward their agenda of racial equality and integration.

Bethune's group, the Federal Council on Negro Affairs, became known as the "Black Cabinet." As a member and leader of this group, Bethune served as an unofficial advisor to President Roosevelt. She praised his 1941 executive order that desegregated the defense in-

dustries and the government and promoted the war effort among African Americans.

Significance

In 1935, Bethune was appointed to the National Youth Administration, a New Deal agency responsible for helping young people stay in school or find work. She was instrumental in getting the agency to extend its benefits to African Americans and to hire many African Americans for government positions at both federal and state levels. By 1939, Bethune had become the director of Negro Affairs. Under her leadership, more than 150,000 African American teenagers went to high school, while 60,000 went on to college.

Bethune developed a close friendship with Eleanor Roosevelt in the 1930s and 1940s. Bethune was first introduced to Eleanor at a luncheon hosted by her mother-in-law, Sara Roosevelt, in the 1920s. The only African American present, Bethune had to face the horrified stares of several southern white ladies. Undaunted, Sara led her into the dining room, seated her as the guest of honor, and introduced her to Eleanor.

After Bethune resigned from the college presidency in 1944, she, like Eleanor, had a distinguished career that included honorary degrees and consulting with the United Nations. Although she had never attained her dream of being a missionary in Africa, Bethune traveled to Liberia in 1952 as a U.S. representative at the inauguration of its president and was given the highest honor of the government of Haiti in 1949.

Back home, Bethune remained faithful to the words that guided her for so many years, inscribed on the pedestal of her statue unveiled in 1974 in Washington, D.C., "I leave you love. I leave you hope. I leave you the challenge of developing confidence in one another. I leave you a thirst for education. I leave you respect for the use of power. I leave you faith. I leave you racial dignity."

Primary Source

Mary McLeod Bethune's Letter to Eleanor Roosevelt

SYNOPSIS: In this letter, Bethune personally thanks the First Lady for accepting a place as a trustee on the board of Bethune-Cookman College, articulates her vision of an institution for both vocational and academic training, and lists the physical needs of the school. The reference to Marian Anderson was probably not accidental; in 1939, Eleanor had publicly resigned from the Daughters of the American Revolution over its refusal to let Anderson, an African American, sing in Constitution Hall.

April 22, 1941

Mrs. Eleanor Roosevelt
The White House
Washington, D.C.

My dear Mrs. Roosevelt:

May I express to you my sincere gratitude for the opportunity you gave me to talk with you two weeks ago. It seemed that the way was so clear to say to you what I had in my mind and my heart to say. You were so receptive, so generous in your understanding of the things I tried to pour out to you.

First of all, I want to thank you for your acceptance of a place on our Board of Trustees of Bethune-Cookman College. Now you are able to think of our work in an official manner and through this affiliation you may feel free to bring our problems to the attention of friends who may be willing to give us their good-will.

I have such deep appreciation for the fine women who have stood so closely by Martha Berry and her work and who have helped her meet vital and pressing needs in her marvelous work. For thirty-six years I have been trying to unfold a vision similar to hers, in training Negro boys and girls of the deep South. We have tried to provide here opportunities for them for opportunities in this section are so few. We have tried to build here a little oasis where they might receive the type of rounded training that will make of them fine American citizens. The masses of our people are exposed to so little in the way of culture and skill. I am not concerned with the idea of "just another school" here. I am concerned about maintaining an Institution that will give unusual opportunity in the things that are needed most by young people in a day like this.

It is my heart's desire to have greater emphasis placed on the Crafts here. Vocational instruction in all of its phases is so very important. If we are to build strong bodies we must begin to put emphasis on physical training. I would like to see here a fine class in Commercial dietetics, for this [is] a field where fine men and women may be developed with splendid cultural background. I am deeply interested in the secretarial courses, particularly those that prepare young women for service in personal care as well as in stenography, typewriting and filing. We need here in Bethune-Cookman a large gymnasium that may be used for recreation and for large gatherings of a musical or literary nature. We would then be in position to have artists like Marian Anderson and be prepared to take care of occasions such as we had when you came to us. There is nothing in this section where we may find participation in the cultural things save what we can provide ourselves.

I am determined to have our vocational work go forward on a parallel with our academic work. We look forward to four years of college work, preparing our young people as strongly in the vocations as in their literary pursuits. You know, of course, our need for a Library building and for more books. Our Library—inadequate though it is—is the only one for Negroes in Volusia County. We want to help our young people in Music—not only in training them in vocal, instrumental and choral music, but in publicizing and preserving their natural talents along this line. This is such a great field for development in so many phases of endeavor.

This is a wonderful spot in the deep South for a fine woman like you to place her active interest and help. It would, through you, challenge the interest of many other fine women who might be willing to help perpetuate the vision of a Negro woman. We need you so much.

I have written you a rather long letter but I felt that I wanted to say these things to you at this time. Please take the time to read this letter calmly and be prayerful, with me, that our work may be preserved and strengthened, and that our service may be revised and expanded to meet the present-day needs of our young people. With you and the friends whom you may touch, with my own untiring effort, and with God as our Guide, I feel that we may go forward.

Always sincerely yours,
Mary McLeod Bethune

Further Resources

BOOKS

Carruth, Ella Kaiser. *She Wanted to Read: The Story of Mary McLeod Bethune.* New York: Abingdon, 1966.

Greenfield, Eloise. *Mary McLeod Bethune.* New York: Harper-Collins, 1977.

Holt, Rackham. *Mary McLeod Bethune: A Biography.* Garden City, N.Y.: Doubleday, 1964.

Smith, Elaine M. "Mary McLeod Bethune." In *Notable Black American Women.* Detroit: Gale Research, 1992.

PERIODICALS

Bennett, Lerone, Jr. "Chronicles of Black Courage: Mary McLeod Bethune Started College with '$1.50 and Faith.'" *Ebony,* February 2002, 156.

"First Lady Praises Mrs. Mary Bethune." *The New York Times,* May 3, 1943, 14.

Gault, Charlayne Hunter. "20,000 at Unveiling of Statue to Mary Bethune in Capital." *The New York Times,* July 11, 1974, 11.

WEBSITES

"Dr. Mary McLeod Bethune." Bethune-Cookman College. Available online at http://www.cookman.edu/Welcome/Founder/Default.html; website home page: http://www.bethune.cookman.edu (accessed February 28, 2003).

"Mary McLeod Bethune." Galenet.com. Available online at http://www.galenet.com/servlet/BioRC; website home page: http://www.galenet.com (accessed February 28, 2003).

AUDIO AND VISUAL MEDIA

"Mary McLeod Bethune Speaks of the Power of Education." New York Public Library. Available online at http://web.nypl.org/research/sc/scl/bethune.html; website home page: http://web.nypl.org (accessed February 28, 2003).

Brannon, Jean Marilyn, ed. *The Negro Woman.* Smithsonian Folkways Recordings. Audiocassette, 1966.

Black Americans of Achievement: Video Collection II. Directed by Amy A. Tiehel. Schlessinger Video Productions. Videocassette, 1994.

"Schools for New Citizens"
Magazine article

By: Viola Paradise

Date: September 1941

Source: Paradise, Viola. "Schools for New Citizens." *Survey Graphic* 30, no. 9, September 1941, 469. Available online at http://newdeal.feri.org/survey/sg41469.htm; website home page: http://newdeal.feri.org (accessed February 28, 2003).

About the Author: Viola Paradise (1887–1980) was born in Chicago, Illinois, and educated at the University of Chicago and the New York School of Social Work. She wrote several novels and contributed numerous articles to the leading publications of her time, including the *Pictorial Review, Harpers, Women's Home Companion, Scribner's,* and *The Dial.* She died in New York. ∎

Introduction

At the turn of the twentieth century, millions of immigrants entered America hoping to create a better life for themselves and their children. Many were from southern and eastern Europe: Italy, Russia, Austria-Hungary, and Greece. There was a wide diversity of languages, religions, and ethnic groups represented. By the 1930s, America's largest cities included ethnic enclaves like "Little Italy," "Greek town" and "Chinatown." Immigrants were taught that their ethnicity was somehow inferior and that "Americanization" was the process of getting rid of it as completely as possible.

In the early 1930s, a small but steady stream of refugees from Nazi Germany began arriving in the United States. The majority of these new arrivals were Jewish immigrants fleeing Nazi persecution, but they also included Catholics, Protestants, and antifascists. These new refugees comprised an estimated 110,000 of 527,000 immigrants who entered the United States between June 1931 and June 1940. They arrived in America ready to adjust to a new life and often used education as a means of adjustment.

Significance

Unlike some of the earlier non-English speaking immigrants, about half of these refugees had had some exposure to English in German high schools. As a group, the refugees were often highly educated, although they could rarely practice the same professions they had practiced at home. Through the Works Progress Administration, the public schools, the Adult Education Council, and other organizations, the refugees had many opportunities to take English and Americanization classes.

New York City offered a wide array of educational opportunities for the refugee. The Ethical Culture Society, among others, provided lectures on topics from "Life in the South" to "City Planning." Refugees were also invited to social events with Americans at the Walden School and the YWCA. As Viola Paradise indicated in her article, the refugees brought a diversity of experiences with them to the classroom, but they were generally more than willing to undergo the process of Americanization while also sharing their own cultures.

Primary Source

"Schools for New Citizens" [excerpt]

SYNOPSIS: In this excerpt, Paradise vividly brings to life the daily work of an Americanization classroom where German refugees and other immigrants learned English, among other things.

September . . . a new school term. Not only for America's millions of school children, but for some two and a half million adults, as well. Under the sponsorship of local school boards, WPA, settlements, unions, churches, they study subjects ranging from simple English to international relations, from Diesel-engine operators to dietetics. A class may be homogeneous—like one where thirty native Americans stand crowded in a Mississippi kitchen to learn to read and write their own language; or, in Arizona, where a group of Americans still speaking the language of their Spanish ancestors (who established missions in that territory in 1629) are now discovering their native tongue; or it may be a New York City school room, where students of a dozen different nationalities are also learning English.

But whatever the place and pace of learning, whatever the sponsorship, the classes have this in common: adults are eagerly acquiring knowledge in which they are absorbed or for which they will have immediate use.

Into this set-up comes the refugee.

He presents no new problems to the school systems of the country. Only some minor adjustments. For a while the public schools of New York and several other large cities did provide special refugee classes, both in day and evening schools. It was soon found, however, that nearly all the newcomers

Greek immigrant students study in an English class sponsored by the New York City Board of Education, 1940. © BETTMANN/CORBIS. REPRODUCED BY PERMISSION.

could fit into regular classes. And though some public schools and many private organizations still arrange special instruction for special groups, by and large public education takes the refugee in its stride.

The new refugee is in many ways easier to teach than the earlier immigrant. Schooling has been an important part of his life. Most of the adults have had the equivalent of our high school education. Many have had university training. Visit almost any evening English class and you will find a refugee engineer, chemist, scholar. But though many of the emigrés had acquired a little book-English in the course of their education and wanderings, most of them have still to learn to speak with ease, to think in English and, added one teacher, recalling many stories of horror and hardship, "even to forget in English."

The American school helps him forget. He has come expecting something rather forbidding. Instead he finds friendliness and individual attention. And a chance not only to pronounce words, but to contribute his own ideas.

Suppose you visit an advanced class in speech improvement.

A WPA poster promotes education, 1940. THE LIBRARY OF CONGRESS.

It is a little after seven. Twenty students have taken their seats. Others will be a little late, because of their working hours.

A new pupil presents his registration card. He clicks his heels and bows from the waist. His eyes are guarded. "In a few days," the teacher tells you, "he will come in with an easy American 'Good Evening.' Like these."

A Czechoslovak couple has just entered, the woman ahead of the man. "It is not only our language idioms they must learn," she continues, smiling, "but the idiom of our manners. Sometimes it is harder for a man to let his wife precede him into the room than to get words in the right order in a sentence."

The Czechoslovak couple—from the Sudetenland—appreciate the joke, and explain it to the new student in German. He thaws a little.

As the teacher writes a list of words on the board, you look at some of the other students. Afterwards you learn that the handsome white-pompadoured woman with earrings was a teacher in Italy; that the hollow-eyed German is an anthropologist who spent two years in a concentration camp; that the bowed bald man—once a Berlin factory owner—had almost starved on his then fantastic but now almost commonplace odyssey, via Poland, Lithuania, the whole width of Russia, Japan, and finally across the Pacific to the United States; that the distinguished looking man with the deeply lined face and long pliant fingers is a Hamburg surgeon, here only nine weeks, who must wait five years and become a citizen before he will be allowed to practice.

You see, too, many others, long in the United States: A Greek fruit store owner, spurred by the Alien Registration Act into a realization of the value of citizenship, is trying to learn the language he has been mispronouncing for two decades. And, with a start of surprise, you recognize a good sprinkling of American-born students.

A pronunciation drill begins the session. *This, those, thirty, thirsty, nothing. . . .* Will these tongue-biting words ever be conquered? And which will be hardest—for the Hamburg surgeon to change his *sirsty* to *thirsty,* for a Hungarian butcher to *think* instead of *tink,* for a sad-eyed Viennese anthropologist to transform *nossine* to *nothing;* or for an American machinist to wrench free of his life-time habit of saying *thoity* and *nutt'n?*

But before your very ears some amazing improvements are accomplished, and more are promised.

Next comes reading, with a current events magazine as text. The students read in turn, the others following silently with their lips, alert for the teacher's corrections, stopping for definition and comment. Then a lesson in dictation—a rather difficult poem. You feel sure it is beyond the ability of the class, but you are pleasantly surprised at the number who get it with only a few mistakes. The newest comers and the most backward students of course make a good many, and one or two have given up after a short try. The teacher looks at a number of papers, and chooses one student to copy his upon the board. The others compare and correct, and those who could not get the poem from dictation, copy it into their notebooks for home study.

Then the class moves on to its favorite stage—discussion.

Who will volunteer to give a two or three minute speech? A pause. Then a plump Italian gets up and makes an impassioned plea for all-out aid to Britain. The teacher interrupts only near the end, to call time, and to point out a few of the speaker's errors. An Irish-American woman—about fifty—is next. Twisting at her dress like an embarrassed little girl, she tells how she gets people to give bundles for Britain: she helps them clean out their closets. Next a shy girl, whose nationality you never learn, suggests that somebody speak on what to do about subversive propaganda. Now one of the Americans gets up. "I'm a subversive guy," he begins, and makes a speech maintaining that this is not our war. There is much head-shaking at this but no violent discussion, and most of the students write down the twelve books which the subversive guy recommends—books ranging from "In Place of Splendor" to "Red Star Over China." Next a White Russian, veteran refugee in many lands but only now come to America, answers in gentle but badly broken English. "You are mistakit. You are been foolished wit propaganda," he begins. Next the Greek makes a three sentence contribution. "Here in America is free speech. Here in this class everybody speak how he think. Nobody mad." Then the American machinist gives a brief and intelligent talk on unemployment insurance.

By now they all want to speak, but the bell rings. The hour-and-a-half is over. The teacher reminds them of an imminent expedition to the Museum of Natural History. They gather their notebooks and leave, some to go into other classes, some for home. They've learned a good bit, and they've had a good time.

Further Resources

BOOKS

Alinsky, Saul. *Reveille for Radicals.* New York: Random House, 1946.

Saenger, Gerhart. *Today's Refugees, Tomorrow's Citizens: A Story of Americanization.* New York: Harper and Brothers, 1941.

Stubblefield, Harold W., and Patrick Keane. *Adult Education in the American Experience: From the Colonial Period to the Present.* San Francisco: Jossey-Bass, 1994.

Weiss, Bernard J., ed. *American Education and the European Immigrant, 1840–1940.* Urbana: University of Illinois Press, 1982.

PERIODICALS

Saenger, Gerhart. "The Refugees Here." *Survey Graphic,* November 1, 1940, 576. Available online at http://newdeal.feri .org/survey/40c21.htm; website home page http://newdeal .feri.org (accessed February 28, 2003).

WEBSITES

"History of Adult, Vocational, Distance Education." Katholieke Universiteit Nijmegen. Available online at http://www.socsci .kun.nl/ped/whp/histeduc/links11b.html#adu; website home page: http://www.kun.nl (accessed May 16, 2002).

AUDIO AND VISUAL MEDIA

A Future Reborn, 1918–1945. American Stories: The American Dream. Discovery Channel Production. Videocassette, 1998.

"History DE-American History and Contemporary Civilization"

Exam, Chart

By: College Entrance Examination Board

Date: 1941

Source: College Entrance Examination Board. "History DE-American History and Contemporary Civilization." In *Questions Set at the Examinations of June, 1941.* Boston: Athenaeum, 1941, 88–90.

About the Organization: The College Entrance Examination Board, now known simply as the College Board, was established in 1900. A membership organization first composed of the Ivy League, Seven Sister, and other selective colleges, the College Board was interested in centralizing the admissions examination process to colleges and universities. It did so by developing standardized tests such as the Scholastic Assessment Test (SAT), with which students could apply to a number of institutions without having to sit for entrance examinations at each one. ∎

Introduction

At the turn of the twentieth century, standardized testing had been used sporadically in schools to measure students' mastery of a prescribed curriculum. Through the work of Alfred Binet, Lewis Terman, and others, another kind of standardized testing arose. The Stanford-Binet intelligence test measured people's intelligence quotient (IQ) by dividing a person's chronological age by his or her "mental age." First used on a mass scale during World War I (1914–1918) to measure the intelligence of army recruits, IQ tests were soon touted as a means of measuring a student's innate potential for achievement and "tracking" him or her into academic or vocational courses, a way of selecting and sorting the best and the brightest.

Significance

Since 1901, the College Entrance Examination Board had offered essay exams in subjects based on the traditional curriculum offered in the elite New England college preparatory schools. Students who had not attended those schools were at a disadvantage when taking the test.

A student pauses to think while taking an inductive reasoning test. June 7, 1942. © BETTMANN/CORBIS. REPRODUCED BY PERMISSION.

The standardized version of the SAT was developed in the 1930s, when Harvard University decided to offer scholarships to underprivileged students and asked the College Board to create a new test for selecting these scholarship recipients. Although the College Board continued to offer the essay tests for a decade, in 1942 the new exam became the standard requirement for college applicants.

As veterans returned from World War II (1939–1945) and began flocking to colleges under the G.I. Bill, the importance of the SAT grew along with enrollments. In 1941, ten thousand students took the test; seven years later, that number had doubled. The increase in demand for standardized testing brought about the birth of the Educational Testing Service (ETS).

In 1947, the College Board, the American Council on Education, and the Carnegie Foundation for the Advancement of Teaching turned over their testing programs, a portion of their assets, and some of their employees to form the ETS. The SAT became the preferred method of evaluating college applicants because the ETS, working with IBM, used machines to scan answer sheets quickly. Along with the ETS came the launching of the test-preparation industry, headed by Stanley Kaplan, who taught his first formal SAT prep class in 1946. Standardized testing has enjoyed considerable growth as an

industry, but it has also continually come under attack for what critics claim are its socioeconomic biases.

Primary Source

"History DE-American History and Contemporary Civilization"

SYNOPSIS: This is the complete examination (with accompanying chart, "Growth in City Population, 1790-1940") in American history and contemporary civilization offered in June 1941.

Friday, June 20

2 P.M. Three hours

Answer six questions.

Wherever the nature of the question permits, give dates, or otherwise indicate the time relation.

1. The chart ["Growth in City Population, 1790–1940"] shows the growth in population of Boston, Cincinnati, Los Angeles, and of the total population of all cities over 8,000 in the United States. For *each* of these three cities, answer the following questions (suggested time: 20 minutes):

a. In which decades did this city grow faster and in which decades did it grow less fast than the total population of all cities?

b. How do you explain the difference in rate of growth between this city and the total population of all cities?

2. The present scope and functions of the Federal Government under the Constitution are greater than those explicitly stated in that document. They have been partly determined by judicial decisions and by the development of administrative agencies. Illustrate this statement by reference to (a) at least one important judicial decision, and (b) the activities of at least one federal administrative agency (suggested time: 25 minutes).

3. Each one of the following statements was made by a president of the United States. For two of these statements, name the president who made it and tell how the ideas in the statement itself led you to recognize its author (suggested time: 25 minutes).

a. "We found our country hampered by special privilege, a vicious tariff, obsolete banking laws, and an inelastic currency. Our foreign affairs were dominated by commercial interests for their selfish ends."

b. "I have already intimated to you the danger of party in the State, with particular reference to

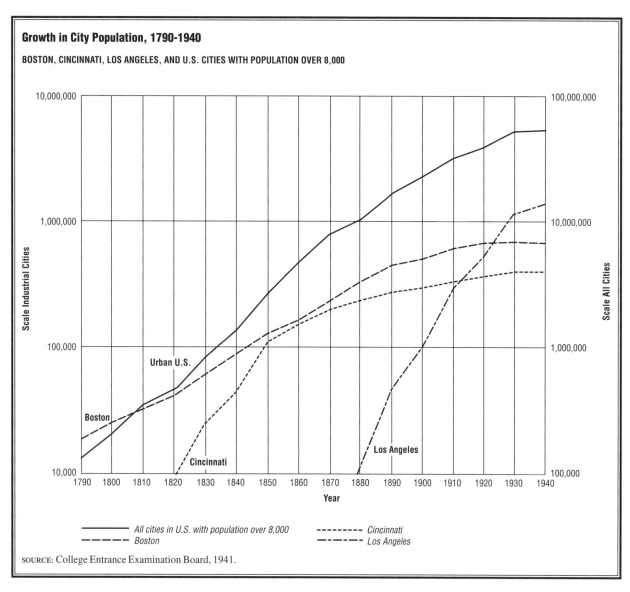

Growth in City Population, 1790-1940

BOSTON, CINCINNATI, LOS ANGELES, AND U.S. CITIES WITH POPULATION OVER 8,000

SOURCE: College Entrance Examination Board, 1941.

Primary Source

"History DE-American History and Contemporary Civilization": Chart

The chart, "Growth in City Population, 1790–1940," was included as part of question one of the exam on American history and contemporary civilization offered in June 1941.

the founding of them on geographical discriminations. Let me now take a more comprehensive view, and warn you, in the most solemn manner, against the baneful effects of the spirit of party generally. . . ."

c. "Yet our distress comes from no failure of substance. We are stricken by no plague of locusts. . . . [P]lenty is at our doorstep, but a generous use of it languishes in the very sight of the supply. Primarily, this is because the rules of the exchange of mankind's goods have failed through their own stubbornness

and their own incompetence. . . . Practices of the unscrupulous moneychangers stand indicted in the court of public opinion, rejected by the hearts and minds of men."

4. Criticize the following statement, supporting your criticism with concrete evidence (suggested time: 20 minutes):

The increased cooperation of the United States and Latin America since 1939 is a perfectly natural development. The United States has always had peaceful and harmonious relations with her sister republics to the South.

Number of Candidates Examined at the Quarterly Series, 1946–1947[1], Classified by Type of Candidate and Program Taken

Type of candi-date	Type of school	Sex	Candidates taking each combination of programs								Candidates taking each program				All candi-dates
			S.A.T. only	C.M.T. only	S.A.T. ACH.	S.A.T. VET.	C.M.T. ACH.	C.M.T. VET.	ACH. only	VET. only	S.A.T.	C.M.T.	ACH.	VET.	
All candi-dates	Public	Boys	6,949	329	7,496	19	1,530	25	515	517	14,464	1,884	9,541	561	17,380
		Girls	9,519	1	4,527	1	29		1,028	2	14,047	30	5,584	3	15,107
		Total	16,468	330	12,023	20	1,559	25	1,543	519	28,511	1,914	15,125	564	32,487
	Inde-pendent	Boys	4,990	137	6,271	34	1,072	12	481	557	11,295	1,221	7,824	603	13,554
		Girls	6,664	11	3,562		13		1,452	3	10,226	24	5,027	3	11,705
		Total	11,654	148	9.833	34	1,085	12	1,933	560	21,521	1,245	12,851	606	25,259
	Others	Boys	1,562	440	1,016	117	649	69	98	2,223	2,695	1,158	1,763	2,409	6,174
		Girls	865	1	339	2	3		55	54	1,206	4	397	56	1,319
		Total	2,427	441	1,355	119	652	69	153	2,277	3,901	1,162	2,160	2,465	7,493
	Total	Boys	13,501	906	14,783	170	3,251	106	1,094	3,297	28,454	4,263	19,128	3,573	37,108
		Girls	17,048	13	8,428	3	45		2,535	59	25,479	58	11,008	62	28,131
		Total	30,549	919	23,211	173	3,296	106	3,629	3,356	53,933	4,321	30,136	3,635	65,239

[1]Exclusive of veterans tested at the colleges or the semimonthly centers.

SOURCE: *Forty-Seventh Annual Report of the Director, 1947.* Princeton, NJ: College Entrance Examination Board, 1947, p. 113.

Number of Candidates Examined at the Quarterly Series, 1946–1947[a], Classified by Type of School, District of School, and District of Residence

Type of School	District of School[b]	District of residence[b]											Total
		East North Central	East South Central	Middle Atlantic	Moun-tain	New England	Pacific	South Atlantic	West North Central	West South Central	Foreign	Un-known	
Public	E. N. Central	2,146	1	4	...	2	...	1	2	...	1	1	2,158
	E. S. Central	1	181	...	...	...	...	3	...	...	...	...	185
	Mid Atlantic	1	1	19,781	...	21	3	4	...	1	...	3	19,815
	Mountain	...	...	...	310	2	...	...	...	1	1	...	314
	New England	...	...	29	2	6,931	...	3	...	...	1	1	6,967
	Pacific	1	...	1	...	2	513	...	1	1	...	...	519
	S. Atlantic	2	...	10	...	2	1	1,435	1	...	...	3	1,454
	W. N. Central	2	...	...	2	...	...	1	627	...	2	...	634
	W. S. Central	1	...	1	...	...	...	...	...	351	1	1	355
	Foreign	...	...	4	...	1	...	1	...	...	71	...	77
	Total	2,154	183	19,830	314	6,961	517	1,448	631	354	77	9	32,478
Inde-pendent	E. N. Central	1,511	9	56	5	10	8	26	33	7	12	...	1,677
	E. S. Central	12	238	12	1	...	2	31	3	10	4	...	313
	Mid. Atlantic	181	28	8,699	26	358	457	219	28	26	109	...	10,131
	Mountain	25	...	11	87	4	21	5	4	9	1	...	167
	New England	328	36	1,803	28	6,203	82	250	65	48	116	1	8,960
	Pacific	2	...	1	5	2	304	...	...	...	4	...	318
	S. Atlantic	96	59	389	2	88	15	1,657	17	20	20	...	2,363
	W. N. Central	35	1	10	7	5	17	11	599	19	3	...	707
	W. S. Central	2	1	...	4	...	...	2	2	163	1	...	175
	Foreign	...	...	20	...	8	3	3	...	...	423	...	457
	Total	2,192	372	11,001	165	6,678	909	2,204	751	302	693	1	25,268
Others	Unknown	505	64	4,316	98	1,379	270	428	175	97	159	2	7,493

[a]Exclusive of veterans tested at the colleges or the semimonthly centers.
[b]The states included in each geographical section are as follows: *E. N. Central:* Illinois, Indiana, Michigan, Ohio, Wisconsin. *E. S. Central:* Alabama, Kentucky, Mississippi, Tennessee. *Mid. Atlantic:* New Jersey, New York, Pennsylvania. *Mountain:* Arizona, Colorado, Idaho, Montana, Nevada, New Mexico, Utah, Wyoming. *New England:* Connecticut, Maine, Massachusetts, New Hampshire, Rhode Island, Vermont. *Pacific:* California, Oregon, Washington. *S. Atlantic:* Delaware, District of Columbia, Florida, Georgia, Maryland, North Carolina, South Carolina, Virginia, West Virginia. *W. N. Central:* Iowa, Kansas, Minnesota, Missouri, Nebraska, North Dakota, South Dakota. *W. S. Central:* Arkansas, Louisiana, Oklahoma, Texas.

SOURCE: *Forty-Seventh Annual Report of the Director, 1947.* Princeton, NJ: College Entrance Examination Board, 1947, p. 114.

Moreover, all the Americas are bound by a common spirit of democracy and common culture.

5. Answer *five* of the following questions briefly (suggested time: 30 minutes):

  a. With what one problem were these three men all concerned, and what part in the problem did each play? John D. Rockefeller, Sr., Theodore Roosevelt, Senator John Sherman.

  b. Why did New England oppose the War of 1812?

  c. From what sources did American railway builders obtain their funds?

  d. Why was immigration to the United States restricted during the twentieth century?

  e. What personal rights does the Constitution undertake to protect?

  f. Name three important American religious leaders and indicate why each was important.

6. One of the most urgent problems in the United States today is that of its Negro citizens. Analyze this problem, showing (a) its historical background, (b) the nature and extent of the problem today, (c) the efforts now being made to solve the problem, and (d) the practical steps which you believe to be most likely to lead toward a satisfactory solution (suggested time: 60 minutes).

Further Resources

BOOKS

Gould, Stephen Jay. *The Mismeasure of Man.* New York: Norton, 1996.

Lemann, Nicholas. *The Big Test: The Secret History of the American Meritocracy.* New York: Farrar Straus and Giroux, 1999.

PERIODICALS

"The Assessment Culture: An Introduction." *Education Week: The Century Series.* Available online at http://www.edweek.com/sreports/century6.htm; website home page: http://www.edweek.com (accessed February 28, 2003).

WEBSITES

"Americans Instrumental in Establishing Standardized Tests." Public Broadcasting Service. Available online at http://www.pbs.org/wgbh/pages/frontline/shows/sats/where/three.html; website home page: http://www.pbs.org (accessed February 28, 2003).

"Measuring Up: Tests, Curriculum, and Standards." Public Broadcasting Service. Available online at http://www.pbs.org/kcet/publicschool/roots_in_history/testing.html; website home page: http://www.pbs.org (accessed February 28, 2003).

"Where Did the Test Come From?" Public Broadcasting Service. Available online at http://www.pbs.org/wgbh/pages/frontline/shows/sats/where/; website home page: http://www.pbs.org (accessed February 28, 2003).

AUDIO AND VISUAL MEDIA

Frontline: Secrets of the SAT. PBS Home Video. Videocassette, 1999.

"The Eight-Year Study"

Speech

By: Wilford M. Aikin

Date: February 20, 1942

Source: Aiken, Wilford M. "High School and the Promise of the Future." *High School Journal* 25, Spring 1942, 149–55. Originally delivered as an address at the Southeastern Conference of the Progressive Education Association, Greenville, South Carolina, February 20, 1942. Reprinted in *American Education: An Introduction Through Readings.* Tyrus Hillway, ed. Boston: Houghton Mifflin, 1964, 217–20.

About the Author: Wilford M. Aikin (1882–1965) was born in Ohio. A leading progressive educator, he taught in various high schools before directing a private academy, the John Burroughs School, in St. Louis, Missouri. In 1930, Aikin became chairman of the Commission on the Relation of Schools and College of the Progressive Education Association (PEA), which sponsored the Eight-Year Study. He was made a professor of education at Ohio State University in 1935. ∎

Introduction

The PEA, founded in 1919, grew in the following decades to symbolize the experiments taking place in child-centered education, especially through its journal *Progressive Education.* The PEA encompassed many different approaches to progressive education. However, unlike the social reconstructionists associated with George Counts, the PEA never advocated using schools for social change. Instead, it focused on innovations in teaching and learning, emphasizing creativity and freedom for children. As was the case with John Dewey's laboratory school, many of these innovations took place not in public schools but in private institutions. The PEA provided a link between educational researchers at schools of education and these private laboratory schools, where innovative educational theory and technique could be tested.

In contrast, the public schools were being subjected to the frequent surveys of the "administrative" progressives, a group of educators who advocated testing and measurement for greater bureaucratic efficiency. The administrative progressives would conduct school surveys with their experts and make recommendations for change based on their findings. Although they seemed diametrically opposed to the child-centered progressives, both types of progressives focused on the internal workings of the school without engaging the social problems outside of the school, which the social reconstructionists insisted were important.

In 1928, Dewey, accepting the honorary presidency of the PEA, addressed the group and criticized its neglect of the school's social role in a democracy. This speech, like Counts's challenging speech "Dare Progressive Education Be Progressive?" in 1932, did little to change the PEA's orientation. Counts's speech, however, was provocative enough to stop the meeting for a discussion of his attack, which centered on how the PEA's child-centered progressivism was in fact upholding the status quo in the depth of the Great Depression. Nevertheless, the PEA continued to advocate curricular experimentation as the means to progress. The Eight-Year Study was the result of these efforts.

Significance

From 1932 to 1940, the PEA conducted its famous Eight-Year Study, a comparative analysis of students from thirty "progressive" high schools and their counterparts in more traditional institutions. The study was first conceived in response to problems of the secondary school curriculum and college admissions.

The study's goal was to compare the college performance of students from varying progressive high schools, some public, some private, and some laboratory schools, with that of students from traditional high schools. Each student from the progressive school was matched with one from a traditional school, and the pairs were followed through high school and college.

In general, the study concluded that graduates of the experimental schools earned slightly higher grade point averages and received slightly more academic honors, among other characteristics.

The study indicated that the students from the six most progressive schools did the best of any group in college. Since most of the leading progressive schools involved in the study were situated in affluent communities, however, it was difficult to assess the influence of socioeconomic background, which could have played a role in the results. Progressive educators had argued that their curriculum was more democratic because it eliminated such obscure subjects as Latin and Greek and instead emphasized critical thinking and problem solving. Thus, it could help students from less-privileged backgrounds to enter college and succeed there.

Progressive educators like Aikin felt that the Eight-Year Study vindicated their ideas. Regardless, as soon as the funding sources dried up many of the schools involved simply returned to more traditional practices. As for the PEA, waning interest and lack of funding contributed to it being disbanded in 1955. It could also be argued that the PEA was a victim of its own success: as the child-centered curriculum and problem-solving approach became part of the educational mainstream, the need for the organization diminished.

Primary Source

"The Eight-Year Study" [excerpt]

SYNOPSIS: In this excerpt, originally delivered as an address to the PEA and later published as "High Schools and the Promise of the Future," Aikin summarizes the results of the Eight-Year Study and argues for the benefits of a progressive curriculum in high school and its importance to a democratic society.

The Thirty Schools have demonstrated that secondary schools generally can be trusted with freedom from imposed requirements by the colleges. These are representative schools. They did not abuse their freedom; they did not engage in wild, irresponsible experimentation. In fact, their greater freedom brought with it a greater sense of responsibility. It led to profound study of the school's obligation to society and to each individual student. There is no reason to suppose that other schools would not accept their greater responsibility with equal seriousness and competence. As hundreds of teachers in the participating schools discovered in themselves unknown creative powers, so would thousands of others develop new vitality and strength in their attempts to perform new duties. Surely the freedom which produces such results will not long be denied.

We may confidently expect that schools and colleges throughout the country will develop relations which will make possible for all schools a considerable measure of the freedom which the Thirty Schools have had. Steps to that end are being taken by this Association, by the National Association of Secondary School Principals, and by other influential organizations. Many colleges are ready now; others are open-minded, willing to be persuaded and convinced. Some will resist every liberalizing influence. Full cooperation will come in time, for a democratic society can no longer permit the waste of material and human resources that now takes place because of our failure to unite the strength of schools and colleges for the greatest possible service to American youth.

But let us make no mistake at this point. Freedom does not of itself bring progress. High Schools generally now have more latitude for constructive effort than they use. Greater freedom will bring greater responsibility. By taking advantage of the opportunities that they now have to serve youth better, schools will demonstrate that a larger measure of freedom should be granted.

This takes us, then, to the heart of the matter. The democratic ideal of life and society demands a dynamic high school whose purposes and practices are consistent with that ideal. This we have not yet fully achieved, either among the Thirty Schools or elsewhere. Its achievement requires fundamental reconstruction of secondary education.

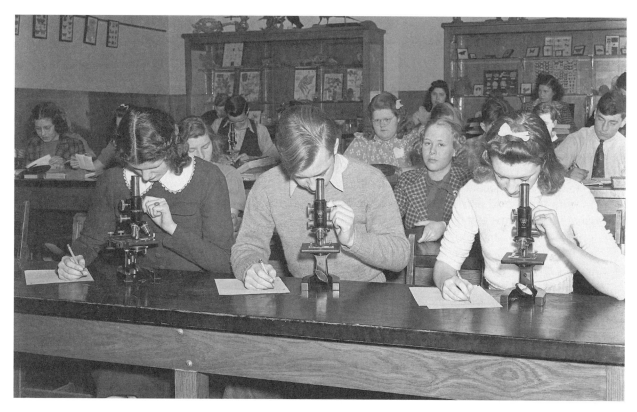

Students peer through microscopes at Teaneck High School in New Jersey. © BETTMANN/CORBIS. REPRODUCED BY PERMISSION.

The Thirty Schools have been engaged in this task. Other schools have been struggling with the same problem. Every school should join in this attempt. I now bring you some lessons which the schools of the Eight-Year Study have learned. Perhaps they will enable other schools to avoid mistakes and to find more quickly a sure sense of direction:

(1) Principals and teachers must be willing and able to reconsider and call in question everything they have been taking for granted. All of the present work of the school—its purposes, its practices, its organization, its curriculum—should be subjected to the most careful scrutiny. Vested interests should be laid aside, custom called in question, and tradition held up to the clear light of the present needs of youth in our society.

(2) Change should not be made hastily or piecemeal. Fundamental revision requires the most serious study of which teachers and administrators are capable. The democratic ideal of life cuts deep. To understand it clearly and fully, educators must bring all their powers of intellect and imagination to its study. The problems and concerns of youth are many and real. Earnest, careful, open-minded investigation is essential if a school faculty is to know what those concerns are and what should be done to meet them. The schools of the Study which plunged into change without sufficient deliberation found it necessary later to abandon some of their new work and to dig deeper for solid rock on which to build.

(3) Deliberation preparatory to reconstruction in any school should involve every teacher. No one should be left out. Even the teacher who opposes all change should have his say. Failure to include everyone resulted in some of the most serious difficulties encountered by the participating schools. Being left out of the discussions, many teachers felt hurt and were indifferent to the new work. Others were resentful, and some were so unprofessional as to obstruct and ridicule the efforts of those who were involved in the work of revision. Moreover, many teachers have unsuspected powers of creative thought and action. Many of the schools failed to draw upon these powers, to their distinct loss. Unanimity of thought and action is seldom achieved, but progress can be made without that if opportunity for full participation is provided.

(4) Participation by parents is essential. "Few of the Thirty Schools realized fully in the beginning that changes in the school cannot be satisfactorily made without both participation and understanding by parents.

"Most parents of the present high-school generation went to high school for at least a year. They think of it as they knew it when they were students. Anything different from their own school experience tends to disturb them. When their sons and daughters tell of 'integrated subjects,' 'core courses,' 'culture epochs,' excursions for community study, teacher-pupil planning, and the like, parents wonder what in the world is going on at school. They are inclined to have confidence in the teachers, but these strange things cause doubts to arise. Most parents want schools to be alive and to make progress, but they want to be sure that established curriculums and ways of teaching are not changed without good reason and that the new ways are sensible and sound. Of course, every school has a few patrons who object violently and noisily to any change from 'the good old days of the little red school-house on the hill.'

"If principal, teachers, and students have one concept of education and parents quite another, misunderstanding, conflict, and unhappiness are inevitable. The schools which did not draw patrons into the planning which preceded revision encountered parental misunderstanding. Unwarranted criticism and opposition were the results. In some instances worthy innovations had to be abandoned because of censure. This could have been avoided if these schools had taken pains to secure parental participation in the thinking which led to change in the curriculum. Moreover, these schools did not have the good counsel that many thoughtful laymen can give. Others of the member schools took parents into their confidence, consulted with them as plans were developed, and gained strength through their support in new undertakings. Out of these happy and unhappy experiences the Thirty Schools have learned that no school is fully prepared for reconstruction unless the cooperation of parents has been secured."

(5) Students, too, have important contributions to make to curriculum building. Seldom have teachers realized the capacity of young people to think constructively about their own education. Many teachers in the Thirty Schools have been surprised and delighted by the response of students when invited to think about what the school should be and do.

(6) "No school or teacher is fully ready for constructive change until plans for appraising results are carefully formulated. The school should find out whether changes in curriculum and methods of teaching achieve purposes more effectively. The Thirty Schools emphasize the necessity of taking time to secure all possible evidence of student progress and to study that evidence searchingly for clues to fur-

ther action. Equally important are adequate means for recording and reporting all significant aspects of pupil development. Evaluating, recording and reporting are inextricably interwoven in the whole fabric of education. Therefore, they cannot be ignored in any sound preparation for educational reconstruction."

(7) Let me now tell you that this Study reveals clearly that the school which undertakes thoroughgoing remaking of itself is in for the most difficult and, at the same time, the most thrilling and profitable experience in its history. When teachers cooperatively seek to help young people with their perplexing problems of growing up into a complex adult world, they give themselves without stint and to the point of exhaustion. Teaching ceases to be deadening routine and becomes the most exciting and challenging work in the world. In the Thirty Schools hundreds of teachers have discovered new and rich life for themselves as teachers and as persons. And they testify that all the cost of time and effort is repaid many fold in deep satisfaction and personal growth.

The ten million boys and girls now in our high schools cannot carry the nation's burden in this hour of world conflict. That burden is ours. We are determined that the earth they inherit shall not be in chains. Theirs will be the tasks that only free men can perform in a world of freedom. It will be an even greater task than ours. To prepare them for it is the supreme opportunity of the schools of our democracy.

Further Resources

BOOKS

Cremin, Lawrence A. *The Transformation of the School: Progressivism in American Education, 1876–1957.* New York: Knopf, 1961.

Graham, Patricia Albjerg. *Progressive Education: From Arcady to Academe.* New York: Teachers College Press, 1967.

Krug, Edward. *The Shaping of the American High School.* Vol. 2, *1920–1941.* Madison: University of Wisconsin Press, 1972.

Urban, Wayne, and Jennings Wagoner. *American Education: A History.* Boston: McGraw-Hill, 2000.

Zilversmit, Arthur. *Changing Schools: Progressive Education in Theory and Practice, 1930–1960.* Chicago: University of Chicago Press, 1993.

PERIODICALS

Manzo, Kathleen Kennedy. "The Legacy of an Influential Yet Often Forgotten Study." *Education Week,* May 19, 1999. Available online at http://www.edweek.com/ew/vol-18/36eight.h18; website home page: http://www.edweek.com (accessed February 28, 2003).

Olsen, Lynn. "Tugging at Tradition." *Education Week,* April 21, 1999. Available online at http://www.edweek.com/ew/vol-18/32debate.h18; website home page: http://www.edweek.com (accessed February 28, 2003).

WEBSITES

"School: The Story of American Public Education." Public Broadcasting Service. Available online at http://www.pbs .org/kcet/publicschool/index.html; website home page: http://www.pbs.org (accessed February 28, 2003).

AUDIO AND VISUAL MEDIA

As American As Public School, 1900–1950. School: The Story of American Public Education. Films for the Humanities and Sciences. Videocassette, 2001.

"Rupert, Idaho—Children Go to Swimming Classes in the School Bus"

Photograph

By: Russell Lee

Date: July 1942

Source: Lee, Russell. "Rupert, Idaho—Children Go to Swimming Classes in the School Bus." July 1942. Library of Congress. Card number fsa2000050772/PP. Available online at http://lcweb2.loc.gov/pp/mdbquery.html (accessed April 3, 2003).

About the Photographer: Russell Lee worked as a photographer for the Farm Security Administration during the Great Depression of the 1930s and into the 1940s, publicizing the conditions of America's rural poor to the public through his images. He continued to work at various posts as a photographer until his death in 1986. ■

Introduction

In 1937, Frank W. Cyr, a professor of rural education at Teachers College, Columbia University, conducted the first survey to investigate how students were getting to school. He found that most students who attended school shared the same mode of transportation: they walked. If they could hitch a ride, it was often in a farmer's horse-drawn cart or a covered wagon.

Urban schoolchildren might use public transportation, such as the streetcar, if they could afford the fare. For the wealthiest, getting to school was often not an issue. Children of the elite often attended boarding schools in the New England countryside, where they lived during the school term, and only left the pastoral campuses for holidays. Along with college students who had the means, boarding school students might have taken a Pullman railroad car to get home for the holidays.

Cyr discovered that among the children who didn't walk or hitch a ride, most rode a motorized school bus. These came in all shapes, sizes, and colors, including purple, red, white, and blue. First sold in the 1920s, these buses had no safety standards. Schools complained about

Advertisers Target Education

The subject of education and educators received increased attention from businesses during the 1940s as a way to appeal to potential consumers. Several advertisements are digitally reproduced and available online through Duke University's Digital Scriptorium project's Ad*Access database at the Rare Book, Manuscript, and Special Collections Library. The Scriptorium's website home page is http://scriptorium.lib.duke.edu/scriptorium/; to access the Ad*Access database, go to http://scriptorium .lib.duke.edu/adaccess/. The Scriptorium is a good online resource for accessing various U.S. historical documents, including advertisements, sheet music, and the women's liberation movement.

A 1947 Trans World Airlines advertisement targeted at teachers, "What Is It Like to Fly?" offers instructors university-sponsored tours to India, the Mediterranean, and Great Britain. Teachers have long been a symbol of stability in American culture and the combination of the high-flying teacher linked safety and responsibility with flying. To view the advertisement, search the Ad*Access database with "What Is It Like to Fly?" then select Transportation; Airlines: 1947.

The advertisement "Safe . . . and on Time to Modern Education" displays the yellow school bus and associates it with the Consolidated School as a sign of progress. Also included is a reference to the television show *Harvest of Stars,* sponsored by International Harvester. With its emphasis on safety, the ad was probably addressed to parents. Access this advertisement by searching the Ad*Access database with "Safe . . . and on Time to Modern Education," then select Transportation; Buses: 1947–1949.

A third advertisement, "We're Going Back to School at the Head of Our Class!" shows two college students heading back to school via a Pullman sleeping railcar. The 1948 ad shows the male student networking with an executive, while the female student arrives well groomed, thanks to the Pullman car's amenities. An African American porter is shown in the background. Known for the impeccable service provided by African American porters, Pullman cars were not an inexpensive way to travel. At one time, the Pullman Sleeping Car Company employed more African Americans than any other U.S. corporation, and its porters were organized in an influential union, the Brotherhood of Sleeping Car Porters. To view this add at Ad*Access, search on "We're Going Back to School at the Head of Our Class!" then select Transportation; Railroads: 1948.

Primary Source

"Rupert, Idaho—Children Go to Swimming Classes in the School Bus"

SYNOPSIS: This image depicts young, rural children in 1942 Idaho boarding a bus to take them to class. The bus was produced in the yellow color that was made standard for all school buses in 1939. THE LIBRARY OF CONGRESS.

the high cost of buying the buses, while the manufacturers complained that the lack of uniform standards made them expensive to produce on the assembly line.

In 1939, Cyr decided to convene a seven-day conference in New York City of state officials, school leaders, and bus engineers to establish school bus safety standards. The conference participants adopted forty-four new standards on bus size, engine specifications, and, most notably, color. The specific shade of yellow to be used, known as National School Bus Chrome, was chosen for its high visibility through fog and rain and from dusk until dawn. Many of the standards have been changed and others added, but the yellow color remains the same.

Significance

The problem of how to get to school worsened with the closing of rural schools, which began during the Great Depression in the 1930s and continued throughout the 1940s. Since schools were being consolidated to save

money, children now had to find a way of getting to a school that was often miles away.

In 1941, New Jersey enacted a law stating that if children lived far from any schoolhouse, the local board of education could provide for their transportation. This included children attending nonpublic schools, such as Catholic schools. Following World War II (1939–1945), the consolidated school and the ramifications of this and similar state laws would contribute to the greater use of yellow school buses. These buses eventually became a symbol of both American education and national culture.

Further Resources

BOOKS

Knight, Edgar W., and Clifton L. Hall. *Readings in American Educational History.* New York: Appleton-Century-Crofts, 1951.

Steinhilber, August W. *State Laws Relating to Transportation and Textbooks for Parochial School Students and Constitu-*

tional Protection of Religious Freedom. Washington, D.C.: U.S. Department of Health, Education, and Welfare, Office of Education, 1966.

PERIODICALS

White, Kerry A. "The Rise of the Big Yellow Bus." *Education Week,* January 27, 1999. Available online at http:// www .edweek.com/ew/vol-18/20bus.h18; website home page: http://www.edweek.com (accessed March 3, 2003).

WEBSITES

"Chasing the Sun: TWA." Public Broadcasting Service. Available online at http://www.pbs.org/kcet/chasingthesun /companies/twa.html; website home page: http://www.pbs .org (accessed March 3, 2003).

"History of American Education Project: Modern Period of American Education." University of Notre Dame. Available online at http://www.nd.edu/~rbarger/www7/m5.jpg; website home page: http://www.nd.edu (accessed March 3, 2003).

"Posters: International School Bus." International. Available online at http://www.internationaldelivers.com/school_bus /pictures.html; website home page: http://www.international delivers.com (accessed May 26, 2002).

"The Pullman Porter's Story." North by South. Available online at http://www.northbysouth.org/2000/Fraternal/pullman1 .htm; website home page: http://www.northbysouth.org (accessed March 3, 2003).

"School: The Story of American Public Education." Public Broadcasting Service. Available online at http://www.pbs .org/kcet/publicschool/index.html; website home page: http://www.pbs.org (accessed March 3, 2003).

AUDIO AND VISUAL MEDIA

As American As Public School, 1900–1950. School: The Story of American Public Education. Films for the Humanities and Sciences. Videocassette, 2001.

"America Was Schoolmasters"

Poem

By: Robert P. Tristram Coffin

Date: 1943

Source: Coffin, Robert P. Tristam. "America Was Schoolmasters." Reprinted in *Unseen Harvests: A Treasury of Teaching.* Claude M. Fuess and Emory B. Basford, eds. New York: Macmillan, 1947, 284–85.

About the Author: Robert P. Tristram Coffin (1892–1955) was born and grew up in Brunswick, Maine, on a saltwater farm. He attended Bowdoin College and Princeton University before going to Oxford University as a Rhodes scholar. He served two years in World War I (1914–1918). Coffin wrote more than forty books and was awarded many honors, including the 1936 Pulitzer Prize for poetry for his work *Strange Holiness.* He taught at Wells College from 1921 to 1934 and

eventually returned to Bowdoin, where he was Pierce Professor in English from 1934 until his death. ∎

Introduction

Coffin received his early education at a rural red-brick schoolhouse, where perhaps he had a schoolmaster not unlike the one he describes in his poem. In adulthood, he successfully combined the roles of artist and teacher, poet and prose writer. He wrote dozens of books of poems, novels, biographies, and essays. He was well known for his pastoral poetry of Maine that speaks of the human condition, a mood he evoked in the opening stanzas of his poem "America Was Schoolmasters."

Primer for America was published at the height of American involvement in World War II (1939–1945) and Coffin confessed that the war influenced his poetry. In his introduction, he wrote, "I was sitting in the exact center of the population of this country, in the Hoosier State. And I was also sitting in the middle of this War. Those two things sort of started me off, I guess."

A primer is an elementary text for teaching children to read. *The New England Primer* (c. 1683), one of the earliest and most famous of America's primers, began "In Adam's Fall / We Sinn'd All." The Puritans linked education and religion and early on instilled strong morals in their children. Coffin explicitly refers to the primer's broader purpose in his introduction, "The *New England Primer* was in the back of my mind and insisted on getting its title into mine from the start. For I meant these ballads to be first lessons in the first principles of being American, the primary stages of the American myth. So I used primary, heraldic colors, downright metaphors, and the straightforward lines of a song. Like the 'Now I lay me' of that first old first reader for New England children, I wanted these verses to appeal to everyone who reads."

Significance

"America Was Schoolmasters" was a ballad that celebrated certain American values, but it also urged the reader to remember the importance of those values in a time of war. The first stanza evoked the virginal natural beauty of America: its forests, grain, and rainbows. The second described the wildlife and only in the middle of the third did the mood shift from a pastoral one to introduce the schoolmaster.

The schoolmaster was introduced with a "but" in the third stanza, after "brown men / With eyes full of sun." Presumably, these were the American Indians that the first "schoolmasters" sought to "teach" through conversion. These Puritanical schoolmasters were described as "tall" and "lonely," working hard at piling on "loads of syntax / Till the small boys groaned."

The schoolmasters tried to "stiffen" the girls for life by teaching them spelling and manners, but they also took

A public school teacher teaches first-graders about American Indian culture, 1942. **THE LIBRARY OF CONGRESS.**

"wild" children and turned them into "reasoning / Sunny democrats." Through such education by the schoolmaster, a symbol of American hard work, Coffin implied that both nature and human "wildness" had to be tamed to create American civilization, which was worth fighting for. In the last stanza, Coffin concisely illustrated the schoolmasters' achievements by ending the poem with a final image of discipline that seems far removed from the poem's opening lines but is linked by its theme.

Primary Source

"America Was Schoolmasters"

> **SYNOPSIS:** Coffin's poem explores American values through the figure of the stern schoolmaster.

America was forests,
America was grain,
Wheat from dawn to sunset,
And rainbows trailing rain.

America was beavers,
Buffalo in seas,
Cornsilk and the johnnycake,
Song of scythes and bees.

America was brown men
With eyes full of the sun,
But America was schoolmasters,

Tall one by lonely one.

They hewed oak, carried water,
Their hands were knuckle-boned,
They piled on loads of syntax
Till the small boys groaned.

They taught the girls such manners
As stiffened them for life,
But made many a fine speller,
Good mother and good wife.

They took small wiry children,
Wild as panther-cats,
And turned them into reasoning
Sunny democrats.

They caught a nation eager,
They caught a nation young,
They taught the nation fairness,
Thrift, and the golden tongue.

They started at the bottom
And built up strong and sweet,
They shaped our minds and morals
With switches on the seat!

Further Resources

BOOKS

Coffin, Robert P. Tristram. *Lost Paradise: A Boyhood on a Maine Coast Farm.* St. Clair Shores, Mich.: Scholarly, 1971.

———. *Primer for America.* New York: Macmillan, 1943.

————. *Strange Holiness.* New York: Macmillan, 1935.

Nygard, Paul David. "Man of Maine: A Life of Robert P. Tristram Coffin." Ph.D. diss., Saint Louis University, 1997.

Serafin, Steven R., and Alfred Bendixen, eds. *Encyclopedia of American Literature.* New York: Continuum, 1999.

Swain, Raymond Charles. *A Breath of Maine: Portrait of Robert P. Tristram Coffin.* Boston: Branden, 1967.

WEBSITES

"Robert P. Tristram Coffin Papers, 1910–1955." University of New Hampshire. Available online at http://www.izaak.unh.edu/specoll/mancoll/coffin.htm; website home page: http://www.unh.edu (accessed March 1, 2003).

Soldiers and their dates dance and celebrate at Camp Patrick Henry on August 11, 1945, after the end of WWII. The soldiers just arrived home from Europe. © THE MARINERS' MUSEUM/ CORBIS. REPRODUCED BY PERMISSION.

Servicemen's Readjustment Act of 1944
Law

By: U.S. Congress

Date: June 22, 1944

Source: *Servicemen's Readjustment Act of 1944.* U.S. Public Law 346. 78th Cong. 2d sess., June 22, 1944. Available online at http://www.nara.gov:80/cgi-bin/starfinder/20769; website home page: http://www.nara.gov (accessed February 11, 2003). ∎

Introduction

While the war was still raging, American policy makers were trying to figure out what to do about the eventual prospect of sixteen million returning veterans. The possibility of another economic depression was alarming. As early as 1942, it was obvious that a plan would be needed to reintegrate the veterans into the civilian economy without causing massive unemployment. The National Resources Planning Board, a White House agency, studied postwar manpower needs and in June 1943 recommended a series of programs for education and training.

The *Servicemen's Readjustment Act of 1944,* more commonly known as the G.I. Bill of Rights, provided a solution to this problem and at the same time compensated the veterans for their service during the war. Not only would it provide tuition, fees, books, and a monthly subsistence payment for veterans in school, it would also provide them with the chance to set up their own businesses, buy their own homes, and receive other financial aid.

The American Legion designed the main features of the G.I. Bill and, after a nationwide campaign, it passed into law in a mere six months. The bill was signed by President Franklin D. Roosevelt (served 1933–1945) on June 22, 1944.

However, there were many educators who had serious misgivings about the legislation and worried about its effects on higher education. Some felt it was too expensive and would encourage laziness among the veterans, while others feared the veterans would lower standards at colleges and universities. Despite these fears, the G.I. Bill has achieved wide recognition as one of the most important acts of Congress.

Significance

The G.I. Bill provided one free year of higher education for each ninety days of service and one additional month of paid education for each month of service up to forty-eight months. In 1947, the program's peak year, veterans accounted for 49 percent of U.S. college enrollments. Slightly more than half of the eligible veterans participated, with an average length of time of support of nineteen months. Out of approximately 15.4 million veterans, 7.8 million were trained, including 2.2 million in college, 3.5 million in other schools, 1.4 million in on-the-job training, and 690,000 in farm training. The Veterans Administration paid the schools up to a maximum of $500 a year per student for tuition, books, fees, and other training costs. It also paid the single veteran a sub-

Number of Candidates Taking the Special Aptitude Test for Veterans at Each of the Semimonthly Centers, 1946–1947

Semimonthly Center	October	November	December	January	February	March	April	May	June	July	August	September	Total
Berkeley, Calif.	3	6	3	3	6	3	–	5	1	3	3	–	36
Buffalo, N. Y.	4	21	20	5	10	16	16	8	7	8	11	7	133
Cambridge, Mass.	14	39	49	40	41	98	139	235	201	134	83	15	1,088
Chicago, Ill.	10	6	9	6	7	6	5	5	7	9	16	–	86
Los Angeles, Calif.	1	4	–	3	2	2	4	2	3	–	2	–	23
New York, N. Y.	128	234	286	112	185	195	236	309	151	117	134	56	2,143
Philadelphia, Pa.	115	135	88	116	144	126	112	117	89	57	91	55	1,245
Pittsburgh, Pa.	6	12	8	4	14	8	7	7	18	13	18	2	117
Washington, D. C.	7	10	16	6	18	12	21	25	18	8	9	9	159
Total	288	467	479	295	427	466	540	713	495	349	367	144	5,030

SOURCE: *Forty-Seventh Annual Report of the Director, 1947.* Princeton, NJ: College Entrance Examination Board, 1947, p. 111.

sistence allowance of up to $50 a month, which was increased to $65 a month in 1946 and to $75 a month in 1948. Veterans with dependents could receive a higher allowance. The total cost of the World War II education program was $14.5 billion.

In the late 1930s, about 160,000 U.S. citizens graduated from college each year. By 1950, that number had increased to 500,000. The increased number of students brought in by the G.I. Bill greatly contributed to the post-war expansion of higher education in the United States, particularly in community colleges. Through its educational benefits, the G.I. Bill also created a significant opportunity for socioeconomic mobility for the working class. Those veterans who were better educated received better-paying jobs, and this resulted in more taxes for the government, whose initial investment could be considered more than repaid. Although the program ended on July 25, 1956, education benefits continue to be a part of the incentive to enter military service.

Primary Source

Servicemen's Readjustment Act of 1944 [excerpt]

SYNOPSIS: *Servicemen's Readjustment Act of 1944, or the G.I. Bill, providing free higher education for servicemen, increased the number of college students and contributed to the postwar expansion of higher education in the United States.*

Seventy-eighth Congress of
the United States of America

At the Second Session

An Act

To provide Federal Government aid for the readjustment in civilian life of returning World War II veterans.

Be it enacted by the Senate and House of Representatives of the United States of America in Congress assembled, That this Act may be cited as the "Servicemen's Readjustment Act of 1944."

Title I

Chapter I—Hospitalization, Claims, and Procedures

Sec. 100. The Veterans' Administration is hereby declared to be an essential agency and entitled, second only to the War and Navy Departments, to priorities in personnel, equipment, supplies, and material under any laws, Executive orders, and regulations pertaining to priorities, and in appointments of personnel from civil-service registers the Administrator of Veterans' Affairs is hereby granted the same authority and discretion as the War and Navy Departments and the United States Public Health Service: *Provided,* That the provisions of this section as to priorities for materials shall apply to any State institution to be built for the care or hospitalization of veterans.

Sec. 101. The Administrator of Veterans' Affairs and the Federal Board of Hospitalization are hereby authorized and directed to expedite and complete the construction of additional hospital facilities for war veterans, and to enter into agreements and contracts for the use by or transfer to the Veterans' Administration of suitable Army and Navy hospitals after termination of hostilities in the present war or after such institutions are no longer needed by the armed services; and the Administrator of Veterans' Affairs is hereby authorized and directed to establish necessary regional offices, sub-offices, branch offices, contact units, or other subordinate offices in centers of population where there is no Veterans' Administration facility, or where such a facility is not

Veteran William Oskay, Jr., attending Pennsylvania State College under the G.I. Bill, studies in the company of his wife and young daughter.
© BETTMANN/CORBIS. REPRODUCED BY PERMISSION.

readily available or accessible: *Provided,* That there is hereby authorized to be appropriated the sum of $500,000,000 for the construction of additional hospital facilities.

Sec. 302. (a) The Secretary of War, the Secretary of the Navy, and the Secretary of the Treasury are authorized and directed to establish, from time to time, boards of review composed of five commissioned officers, two of whom shall be selected from the Medical Corps of the Army or Navy, or from the Public Health Service, as the case may be. It shall be the duty of any such board to review, at the re-

quest of any officer retired or released to inactive service, without pay, for physical disability pursuant to the decision of a retiring board, the findings and decision of such retiring board. Such review shall be based upon all available service records relating to the officer requesting such review, and such other evidence as may be presented by such officer. Witnesses shall be permitted to present testimony either in person or by affidavit and the officer requesting review shall be allowed to appear before such board of review in person or by counsel. In carrying out its duties under this section such board of review shall have the same powers as exercised by, or vested in, the retiring board whose findings and decision are being reviewed. The proceedings and decision of each such board of review affirming or reversing the decision of the retiring board shall be transmitted to the Secretary of War, the Secretary of the Navy, or the Secretary of the Treasury, as the case may be, and shall be laid by him before the President for his approval or disapproval and orders in the case.

(b) No request for review under this section shall be valid unless filed within fifteen years after the date of retirement for disability or after the effective date of this Act, whichever is the later.

Title II

Chapter IV—Education of Veterans

Sec. 400. (a) Subsection (f) of section 1, title I, Public Law Numbered 2, Seventy-third Congress, added by the Act of March 24, 1943 (Public Law Numbered 16, Seventy-eighth Congress), is hereby amended to read as follows:

(f) Any person who served in the active military or naval forces on or after September 16, 1940, and prior to the termination of hostilities in the present war, shall be entitled to vocational rehabilitation.

The agency disbursing such adjusted compensation shall first pay the unpaid balance and accrued interest due on such loan to the holder of the evidence of such indebtedness to the extent that the amount of adjusted compensation which may be payable will permit.

Further Resources

BOOKS

Bound, John. *Going to War and Going to College: Did World War II and the G.I. Bill Increase Educational Attainment for Returning Veterans?* Cambridge, Mass.: National Bureau of Economic Research, 1999.

Goldberg, Vicki. *Margaret Bourke-White: A Biography.* New York: Harper and Row, 1986.

Greenberg, Milton. *The G.I. Bill: The Law That Changed America.* New York: Lickle, 1997.

Olson, Keith W. *The G.I. Bill, the Veterans, and the Colleges.* Lexington: University Press of Kentucky, 1974.

WEBSITES

"G.I. Bill Act of June 2, 1944." Higher Education Resource Hub. Available online at http://www.higher-ed.org/resources /GI_bill.htm; website home page: http://www.higher-ed.org (accessed March 3, 2003).

"The G.I. Bill of Rights (1944)." North Carolina State University. Available online at http://hcl.chass.ncsu.edu/garson /dye/docs/gibill.htm; website home page http://www.ncsu .edu (accessed March 3, 2003).

"Remembering the G.I. Bulge: An Exhibit Honoring the Students Who Attended S.U. Under the G.I. Bill." Syracuse University. Available online at http://archives.syr.edu/arch /gi/bulge.htm; website home page: http://www.syr.edu (accessed March 3, 2003).

AUDIO AND VISUAL MEDIA

The G.I. Bill: The Law That Changed America. PBS Home Video. Videocassette, 1997.

Constitution of the United Nations Educational, Scientific and Cultural Organisation (UNESCO)

Constitution

By: UNESCO

Date: November 16, 1945

Source: Constitution of the United Nations Educational, Scientific and Cultural Organisation (UNESCO). Reprinted in Knight, Edgar W., and Clifton L. Hall. *Readings in American Educational History.* New York: Appleton-Century-Crofts, 1951, 773–75.

About the Organization: In 1942, a Conference of Allied Ministers of Education representing eighteen governments met in London. Based on their proposals, the UN held a conference on the establishment of an educational and cultural organization in November 1945. Forty-four governments, including the United States, were represented. On November 16, 1945, the UN Educational, Scientific and Cultural Organisation (UNESCO) constitution was signed. ∎

Introduction

From the ashes of World War II (1939–1945) came the idea for an international cooperating body, the United Nations, and, within it, a specialized agency to handle education, science, and culture. The roots of UNESCO actually extend back to the 1920s. President Woodrow Wilson (served 1913–1921) helped to establish the League of Nations, only to suffer extreme disappointment at America's decision not to enter. Nevertheless, the idea of international cooperation had taken hold. Left to consider the devastation of World War I (1914–1918), Europe and America had hoped to avoid another such disaster by creating the League of Nations. Following World War II, the Allies established the United Nations, a stronger, more effective organization devoted to maintaining world peace.

Several agencies were precursors to UNESCO. The International Committee of Intellectual Cooperation in Geneva operated from 1922 to 1946 and its executing agency, the International Institute of Intellectual Cooperation, was based in Paris. The International Bureau of

Assembly of the second UNESCO Conference in Mexico City, November 6, 1947. **AP/WIDE WORLD PHOTOS. REPRODUCED BY PERMISSION.**

Education, also based in Geneva, existed from 1925 until 1969, when it became part of the UNESCO Secretariat in Paris under its own statutes.

The first session of the General Conference of UNESCO took place in Paris in 1946 with the participation of representatives from thirty governments entitled to vote. Among the founding member states were the Allied nations of World War II: the United States, France, and the United Kingdom. The defeated Axis powers, Japan and the Federal Republic of Germany, were not allowed to join until 1951.

Significance

In the difficult postwar years, Europe needed to be rebuilt. The United States headed the effort, both on its own and through international organizations like UNESCO, whose coupons overcame foreign exchange difficulties in buying books and other cultural materials. Beyond Europe, UNESCO began a translation program of representative works of world literature so that they could be preserved and distributed. Beginning in 1948, the organization also offered a fellowship program and undertook the education of Palestinian refugees displaced from their homes by the creation of the Israeli state.

Although UNESCO began in idealism, the agency suffered from the realities of the shifting geopolitical cli-

mate, with several member countries withdrawing and reentering. In 1984, citing "ineffectiveness and organizational abuses," the United States withdrew, but its reentry has been discussed. In 2000, UNESCO had 188 member states and operated its educational programs throughout the world with conferences, fellowships, publications, and multimedia.

The terminology may have changed, but most of the goals stated in the UNESCO constitution remain integral to its current work. UNESCO still states its strategic objectives for education as promoting education as a fundamental human right; improving the quality of education; and promoting experimentation, innovation, and the diffusion and sharing of information and best practices, as well as policy dialogue, in education. The effects of globalization and economic inequality, as well as ethnic and religious conflict, make reaching these objectives even more urgent. The broader goal remains the same, as the UNESCO constitution states, "Since wars begin in the minds of men, it is in the minds of men that the defences of peace must be constructed."

Primary Source

Constitution of the United Nations Educational, Scientific and Cultural Organisation (UNESCO) [excerpt]

SYNOPSIS: These extracts from the UNESCO constitution show how its founding member nations viewed education as a means of fostering international peace.

The governments of the States parties to this Constitution on behalf of their peoples declare:

that since wars begin in the minds of men, it is in the minds of men that the defences of peace must be constructed;

that ignorance of each other's ways and lives has been a common cause, throughout the history of mankind, of that suspicion and mistrust between the peoples of the world through which their differences have all too often broken into war;

that the great and terrible war which has now ended was a war made possible by the denial of the democratic principles of the dignity, equality and mutual respect of men, and by the propagation, in their place, through ignorance and prejudice, of the doctrine of the inequality of men and races;

that the wide diffusion of culture, and the education of humanity for justice and liberty and peace are indispensable to the dignity of man and constitute a sacred duty which all the nations must fulfill in a spirit of mutual assistance and concern;

that a peace based exclusively upon the political and economic arrangements of governments would not be a peace which could secure the unanimous, lasting and sincere support of the peoples of the world, and that the peace must therefore be founded, if it is not to fail, upon the intellectual and moral solidarity of mankind.

For These Reasons, the States parties to this Constitution, believing in full and equal opportunities for education for all, in the unrestricted pursuit of objective truth, and in the free exchange of ideas and knowledge, are agreed and determined to develop and to increase the means of communication between their peoples and to employ these means for the purposes of mutual understanding and a truer and more perfect knowledge of each other's lives;

In Consequence Whereof they do hereby create the United Nations Educational, Scientific and Cultural Organisation for the purpose of advancing, through the educational and scientific and cultural relations of the peoples of the world, the objectives of international peace and of the common welfare of mankind for which the United Nations Organisation was established and which its Charter proclaims.

Article I. Purposes and Functions

1. The purpose of the Organisation is to contribute to peace and security by promoting collaboration among the nations through education, science and culture in order to further universal respect for justice, for the rule of law and for the human rights and fundamental freedoms which are affirmed for the peoples of the world, without distinction of race, sex, language or religion, by the Charter of the United Nations.

2. To realise this purpose the Organisation will:

   a. collaborate in the work of advancing the mutual knowledge and understanding of peoples, through all means of mass communication and to that end recommend such international agreements as may be necessary to promote the free flow of ideas by word and image;

   b. give fresh impulse to popular education and to the spread of culture; by collaborating with Members, at their request, in the development of educational activities; by instituting collaboration among the nations to advance the ideal of equality of educational opportunity without regard to race, sex or any distinctions economic or social; by suggesting educational methods best suited to prepare the children of the world for the responsibilities of freedom;

   c. maintain, increase and diffuse knowledge; by assuring the conservation and protection of the world's inheritance of books, works of art and monuments of history and science, and recommending to the nations concerned the necessary international conventions; by encouraging cooperation among the nations in all branches of intellectual activity, including the international exchange of persons active in the fields of education, science and culture and the exchange of publications, objects of artistic and scientific interest and other materials of information; by initiating methods of international cooperation calculated to give the people of all countries access to the printed and published materials produced by any of them.

3. With a view to preserving the independence, integrity and fruitful diversity of the cultures and

educational systems of the States Members of this Organisation, the Organisation is prohibited from intervening in matters which are essentially within their domestic jurisdiction. . . .

Further Resources

BOOKS

Hoggart, Richard. *An Idea and its Servants: UNESCO From Within.* London: Chatto and Windus, 1978.

Preston, William. *Hope and Folly: The United States and UNESCO, 1945–1985.* Minneapolis: University of Minnesota Press, 1989.

UN Educational, Scientific and Cultural Organisation. *Conference for the Establishment of the United Nations Educational, Scientific and Cultural Organisation: Held at the Institute of Civil Engineers, London, from the 1st to the 16th November, 1945.* London: Preparatory Commission UNESCO, 1946.

———. *UNESCO, Twenty Years of Service to Peace, 1946–1966.* Paris: UN Educational, Scientific and Cultural Organisation, 1966.

———. *What Is UNESCO?* London: UN Educational, Scientific and Cultural Organisation, 1946.

WEBSITES

"Education." UN Educational, Scientific and Cultural Organisation. Available online at http://www.unesco.org/education/index.shtml; website home page: http://www.unesco.org (accessed March 4, 2003).

"Teaching and Learning for a Sustainable Future: A Multimedia Teacher Education Programme." UN Educational, Scientific and Cultural Organisation. Available online at http://www.unesco.org/education/tlsf/; website home page: http://www.unesco.org (accessed March 4, 2003).

UNESCO Institute for Statistics. Available online at http://www.uis.unesco.org (accessed March 4, 2003).

"United States and UNESCO: Together Again?" Woodrow Wilson International Center for Scholars. Available online at http://wwics.si.edu/NEWS/digest/unesco.htm; website home page: http://wwics.si.edu (accessed May 30, 2002).

"United States of America Education System." University of Southern California. Available online at http://www.usc.edu/dept/education/globaled/wwcu/background/United-States.htm; website home page: http://www.usc.edu (accessed March 4, 2003).

AUDIO AND VISUAL MEDIA

Achieving Education for All. UNESCO Publishing. Videocassette, 1996.

The Courage to Teach. UNESCO Publishing. Videocassette, 1997.

Science, the Endless Frontier
Report

By: Vannevar Bush

Date: 1945

Source: Bush, Vannevar. "Letter of Transmittal" and "Renewal of Our Scientific Talent." *Science, the Endless Frontier: A Report to the President.* Washington, D.C., 1945. Reprinted in *The Educating of Americans: A Documentary History.* Daniel Calhoun, ed. Boston: Houghton Mifflin, 1969.

About the Author: Vannevar Bush (1890–1974), born in Everett, Massachusetts, was an American electrical engineer and inventor who contributed to the development of computer hypertext. He was a professor and then dean of engineering at the Massachusetts Institute of Technology and then became president of the Carnegie Institution in Washington in 1939. During World War II (1939–1945), he headed the Office of Scientific Research and Development and after the war was instrumental in establishing the National Science Foundation. ■

Introduction

In June 1940, Adolf Hitler's troops were advancing in Europe. The previous year, German scientists had discovered nuclear fission and the Allies were alarmed at the prospect of further advances. Scientific research became a matter of national security.

In Washington, Vannevar Bush met with President Franklin D. Roosevelt (served 1933–1945) about unifying the efforts and resources of America's scientists. Consequently, the Office of Scientific Research and Development was created, with Bush as its director. Under his leadership, more than thirty thousand scientists upgraded America's defense system. Bush is personally credited with advancements in radar, the proximity fuse, fire control mechanisms, and amphibious vehicles. When the atom bomb was built in the early to mid-1940s, Bush discussed its use and effects with President Harry S. Truman (served 1945–1953) and defended scientist J. Robert Oppenheimer for his opposition to it.

After the Allied victory in 1945, Bush returned to his post as president of the Carnegie Institution, where he worked tirelessly to promote the importance of science in the national interest. In numerous speeches, articles, and books, he argued for a significant federal investment in scientific research and education.

Significance

Science, the Endless Frontier, written for President Roosevelt, was a report based on a year-long study of how the lessons of wartime mobilization could be used in peacetime. In it, Bush argued that "Scientific progress is one essential key to our security as a nation, to our better health, to more jobs, to a higher standard of living, and to our cultural progress."

Bush pointed to a "deficit" in scientists, only made worse by the wartime draft. Crucial to scientific progress is the cultivation of scientific talent that, Bush wrote, must be done through a merit-based system that removed barriers to higher education. It was a matter of national urgency that those who had not attended elite college preparatory schools should be given the opportunity to attend college if they had the ability.

When the United States dropped the atomic bomb on Japan in 1945, science's crucial role in national security became strikingly obvious. As a result of the increasing attention to scientific research, the federal government created the National Science Foundation in 1950. During the Cold War and the space race between the United States and the Soviet Union, the 1957 launching of *Sputnik*, a Soviet satellite, resulted in the passage of the massive National Defense Education Act in 1958. This act would greatly influence the teaching of math and science in America.

Primary Source

Science, the Endless Frontier [excerpt]

SYNOPSIS: In this excerpt, Bush discusses how to increase the number and quality of American scientists through changes in the education system. This excerpt includes a letter to President Roosevelt that introduces the report, and a section of chapter 4, "The Renewal of Our Scientific Talent." The section is entitled "A Program."

July 5, 1945

Office of Scientific Research and Development
1530 P Street, N.W.
Washington 25, D. C.

The President of the United States,
The White House,
Washington, D.C.

Dear Mr. President:

In a letter dated November 17, 1944, President Roosevelt requested my recommendations on the following points:

1. What can be done, consistent with military security, and with the prior approval of the military authorities, to make known to the world as soon as possible the contributions which have been made during our war effort to scientific knowledge?

2. With particular reference to the war of science against disease, what can be done now to organize a program for continuing in the future the work which has been done in medicine and related sciences?

3. What can the Government do now and in the future to aid research activities by public and private organizations?

4. Can an effective program be proposed for discovering and developing scientific talent in American youth so that the continuing future of scientific research in this country may be assured on a level comparable to what has been done during the war?

It is clear from President Roosevelt's letter that in speaking of science he had in mind the natural sciences, including biology and medicine, and I have so interpreted his questions. Progress in other fields, such as the social sciences and the humanities, is likewise important; but the program for science presented in my report warrants immediate attention.

In seeking answers to President Roosevelt's questions I have had the assistance of distinguished committees specially qualified to advise in respect to these subjects. The committees have given these matters the serious attention they deserve; indeed, they have regarded this as an opportunity to participate in shaping the policy of the country with reference to scientific research. They have had many meetings and have submitted formal reports. I have been in close touch with the work of the committees and with their members throughout. I have examined all of the data they assembled and the suggestions they submitted on the points raised in President Roosevelt's letter.

Although the report which I submit herewith is my own, the facts, conclusions, and recommendations are based on the findings of the committees which have studied these questions. Since my report is necessarily brief, I am including as appendices the full reports of the committees.

A single mechanism for implementing the recommendations of the several committees is essential. In proposing such a mechanism I have departed somewhat from the specific recommendations of the committees, but I have since been assured that the plan I am proposing is fully acceptable to the committee members.

The pioneer spirit is still vigorous within this nation. Science offers a largely unexplored hinterland

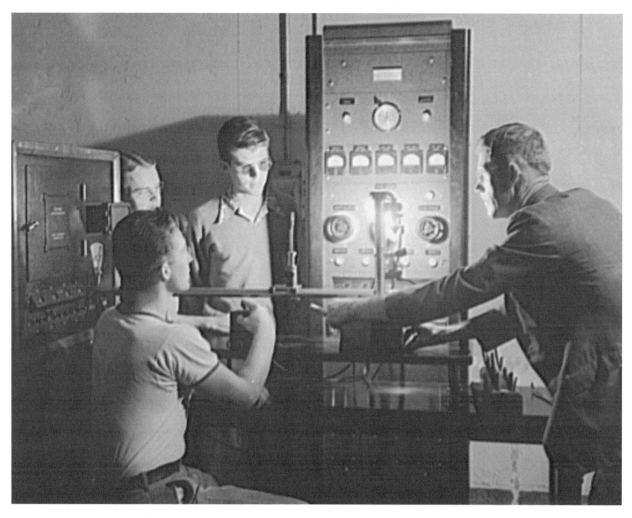

Students at the Colorado School of Mines use a spectograph to study minerals for use in defense industries. Students employ geophysical methods which will be applied to airplane detection and anti-submarine warfare. October 1942. **THE LIBRARY OF CONGRESS.**

for the pioneer who has the tools for his task. The rewards of such exploration both for the Nation and the individual are great. Scientific progress is one essential key to our security as a nation, to our better health, to more jobs, to a higher standard of living, and to our cultural progress.

Respectfully yours,
(s) V. Bush, Director

A Program

The country may be proud of the fact that 95 percent of boys and girls of fifth grade age are enrolled in school, but the drop in enrollment after the fifth grade is less satisfying. For every 1,000 students in the fifth grade, 600 are lost to education before the end of high school, and all but 72 have ceased formal education before completion of college. While we are concerned primarily with meth-

ods of selecting and educating high school graduates at the college and higher levels, we cannot be complacent about the loss of potential talent which is inherent in the present situation.

Students drop out of school, college, and graduate school, or do not get that far, for a variety of reasons: they cannot afford to go on; schools and colleges providing courses equal to their capacity are not available locally; business and industry recruit many of the most promising before they have finished the training of which they are capable. These reasons apply with particular force to science; the road is long and expensive; it extends at least 6 years beyond high school; the percentage of science students who can obtain first-rate training in institutions near home is small.

Improvement in the teaching of science is imperative; for students of latent scientific ability are particularly vulnerable to high school teaching which fails to awaken interest or to provide adequate instruction. To enlarge the group of specially qualified men and women it is necessary to increase the number who go to college. This involves improved high school instruction, provision for helping individual talented students to finish high school (primarily the responsibility of the local communities), and opportunities for more capable, promising high school students to go to college. Anything short of this means serious waste of higher education and neglect of human resources.

To encourage and enable a larger number of young men and women of ability to take up science as a career, and in order gradually to reduce the deficit of trained scientific personnel, it is recommended that provision be made for a reasonable number of (a) undergraduate scholarships and graduate fellowships and (b) fellowships for advanced training and fundamental research. The details should be worked out with reference to the interests of the several States and of the universities and colleges; and care should be taken not to impair the freedom of the institutions and individuals concerned.

The program proposed by the Moe Committee would provide 24,000 undergraduate scholarships and 900 graduate fellowships and would cost about $30,000,000 annually when in full operation. Each year under this program 6,000 undergraduate scholarships would be made available to high school graduates, and 300 graduate fellowships would be offered to college graduates. Approximately the scale of allowances provided for under the educational program for returning veterans has been used in estimating the cost of this program.

The plan is, further, that all those who receive such scholarships or fellowships in science should be enrolled in a National Science Reserve and be liable to call into the service of the Government, in connection with scientific or technical work in time of war or other national emergency declared by Congress or proclaimed by the President. Thus, in addition to the general benefits to the nation by reason of the addition to its trained ranks of such a corps of scientific workers, there would be a definite benefit to the nation in having these scientific workers on call in national emergencies. The Government would be well advised to invest the money involved in this plan even if the benefits to the nation were thought of solely—which they are not—in terms of national preparedness.

Further Resources

BOOKS

Barfield, Claude E., ed. *Science for the Twenty-first Century: The Bush Report Revisited.* Washington, D.C.: AEI Press, 1997.

Bush, Vannevar. *Modern Arms and Free Men: A Discussion of the Role of Science in Preserving Democracy.* New York: Simon and Schuster, 1949.

———. *Pieces of the Action.* New York: Morrow, 1970.

Kevles, Daniel J. *The Physicists: The History of a Scientific Community in Modern America.* New York: Knopf, 1978.

Mann, Alfred K. *For Better or for Worse: The Marriage of Science and Government in the United States.* New York: Columbia University Press, 2000.

Zachary, G. Pascal. *Endless Frontier: Vannevar Bush, Engineer of the American Century.* New York: The Free Press, 1997.

PERIODICALS

Bush, Vannevar. "As We May Think." *Atlantic Monthly,* July 1945. Available online at http://www.theatlantic.com/unbound/flashbks/computer/bushf.htm; website home page: http://www.theatlantic.com (accessed March 1, 2003).

WEBSITES

American Decades. Galenet.com. Available online at http://www.galenet.com/servlet/BioRC; website home page: http://www.galenet.com (accessed March 1, 2003).

"Events in the Life of Vannevar Bush." Brown University. Available online at http://www.cs.brown.edu/research/graphics/html/info/timeline.html; website home page: http://www.brown.edu (accessed March 1, 2003).

"History of the National Science Foundation." National Science Foundation. Available online at http://www.nsf.gov/od/lpa/nsf50/history.htm; website home page: http://www.nsf.gov (accessed March 1, 2003).

"Networking the Nerds." Public Broadcasting Service. Available online at http://www.pbs.org/opb/nerds2.0.1/networking_nerds/diana.html; website home page: http://www.pbs.org (accessed March 1, 2003).

"Slate, Slide Rules and Software: Teaching Math in America." Smithsonian Institution. Available online at http://www.americanhistory.si.edu/teachingmath/; website home page: http://www.si.edu (accessed March 1, 2003).

AUDIO AND VISUAL MEDIA

Inventing the Future: The K–16 Connection in Science. Films for the Humanities and Sciences. Videocassette, 2001.

Higher Education for American Democracy: Vol. I, Establishing the Goals

Report, Charts

By: President's Commission on Higher Education
Date: 1947

Source: President's Commission on Higher Education. *Higher Education for American Democracy: Vol. I, Establishing the Goals.* Washington, D.C.: Government Printing Office, 1947. Reprinted in *American Higher Education: A Documentary History.* Richard Hofstadter and Wilson Smith, eds. Chicago: University of Chicago Press, 1961, 984–86.

About the Organization: President Harry S. Truman (served 1945–1953) appointed his Commission on Higher Education in the summer of 1946. It was composed of twenty-eight educators and laymen and headed by George F. Zook, the president of the American Council on Education. The president asked the commission to "re-examine our system of higher education in terms of its objectives, methods, and facilities; and in the light of the social role it has to play." ∎

Introduction

With the prospect of several million returning veterans enrolling in colleges and universities through the G.I. Bill, American higher education faced an urgent challenge after World War II (1939–1945). Existing facilities were inadequate to meet the needs of these new students, and new faculty would have to be trained and hired for increased enrollment. Money for these expenditures was not available from diminishing endowments, a result of fewer gifts because of increased taxes. American higher education faced a potential crisis.

In response, President Truman appointed the Commission on Higher Education, which, by the end of 1947, had produced a six-volume report. The six volumes were: *Establishing the Goals, Equalizing and Expanding Individual Opportunity, Organizing Higher Education, Staffing Higher Education, Financing Higher Education,* and *Resource Data.*

As these titles indicate, the commission emphasized increasing educational opportunity. The commission recommended that federal aid be given in the form of scholarships for undergraduate students and fellowships for graduate students. Some opponents criticized federal aid to education on the grounds that it was not explicitly mentioned in the Constitution and therefore the responsibility of the states according to Article Ten. Others, especially in the South, simply did not want to give up local control of education to the federal government.

To deal with the postwar financial burden, some colleges raised money by turning themselves into businesses, and thus abusing their tax-exempt status. They openly violated a 1938 U.S. Supreme Court ruling that established taxes on any university's commercial ventures.

Significance

In defining greater educational opportunity as crucial to a democracy, the President's Commission on Higher Education may have also set the tone for further developments that would expand educational opportunity for African Americans and other excluded groups.

Students leave New York University's Main Building. © LUCIEN AIGNER/CORBIS. REPRODUCED BY PERMISSION.

The report paid close attention to segregation and educational inequality among the races and concluded that the talents of African Americans and other minorities could not afford to be wasted.

In 1948, a decade after the *Missouri ex rel. Gaines v. Canada* decision of 1938, the Supreme Court again ruled in the favor of an African Americans who had been denied access to higher education in the student's home state. In *Sipuel v. Board of Regents of University of Oklahoma* (1948), the Court ruled that Ada Lois Sipuel Fisher was entitled to attend the state law school (there was no "separate but equal" law school for African Americans), and that the state must provide her with a legal education since she was qualified, in conformity with the equal protection clause of the Fourteenth Amendment. Future Supreme Court Justice Thurgood Marshall of the National Association for the Advancement of Colored People represented the petitioner; it would only be six more years until his victory in *Brown v. Board of Education* (1954), the landmark antisegregation case.

Fisher graduated from the University of Oklahoma's law school in 1951; forty years later she was asked to serve on the university's Board of Regents. Her story was featured in the 1948 New York *Herald Tribune* report *Our Imperiled Resources,* and her experience was dramatized in the play *Halls of Ivory.*

Direct Cost of Higher Education and Its Relationship to the Gross National Product, 1932-1947

Fiscal year	Amount (in millions)[1]	Proportion of gross national product (percent)[2]
1932	$ 421	0.63
1940	522	.55
1947	1,005	.46

[1]Source: General and educational expenditures, not including capital expansion, as reported by U.S. Office of Education.
[2]Source of gross national product: U.S. Bureau of Foreign and Domestic Commerce.

SOURCE: *American Higher Education; A Documentary History.* Edited by Richard Hofstadter and Wilson Smith. Chicago: University of Chicago Press, 1961, p. 977.

Primary Source

Higher Education for American Democracy: Vol. I, Establishing the Goals: Chart (1 OF 3)

SYNOPSIS: This primary source comprises three charts as well as the excerpt "Toward Equalizing Opportunity," from *Higher Education for American Democracy: Vol. I, Establishing the Goals.*

The postwar years inaugurated a new era in American higher education. After having fought a war against fascism and Nazism in the name of democratic ideals, many Americans, among them African American veterans, were ready to apply those ideals at home.

Primary Source

Higher Education for American Democracy: Vol. I, Establishing the Goals [excerpt]

SYNOPSIS: This excerpt, "Toward Equalizing Opportunity," highlights the commission's comments on why broadening access to higher education is a crucial part of American democracy. Three charts are included in this primary source.

The American people should set as their ultimate goal an educational system in which at no level—high school, college, graduate school, or professional school—will a qualified individual in any part of the country encounter an insuperable economic barrier to the attainment of the kind of education suited to his aptitudes and interests.

This means that we shall aim at making higher education equally available to all young people, as we now do education in the elementary and high schools, to the extent that their capacity warrants a further social investment in their training.

Obviously this desirable realization of our ideal of equal educational opportunity cannot be attained immediately. But if we move toward it as fast as our economic resources permit, it should not lie too far in the future. Technological advances, that are already resulting in phenomenal increases in productivity per worker, promise us a degree of economic well-being that would have seemed wholly Utopian to our fathers. With wise management of our economy, we shall almost certainly be able to support education at all levels far more adequately in the future than we could in the past.

The Commission recommends that steps be taken to reach the following objectives without delay:

1. High school education must be improved and should be provided for all normal youth.

This is a minimum essential. We cannot safely permit any of our citizens for any reason other than incapacity, to stop short of a high school education or its equivalent. To achieve the purpose of such education, however, it must be improved in facilities and in the diversity of its curriculum. Better high school education is essential, both to raise the caliber of students entering college and to provide the best training possible for those who end their formal education with the twelfth grade.

2. The time has come to make education through the fourteenth grade available in the same way that high school education is now available.

Enrollment of Institutions of Higher Education and Index of Change[1]

	Enrollments in Institutions Accepting			
	Negroes only		All other	
Year	Number	Index of change (1932 = 100)	Number	Index of change (1932 = 100)
1932	21,880	100	1,132,237	100
1936	32,628	149	1,175,599	104
1940	41,839	191	1,452,364	128
1947[2]	63,500	290	2,290,500	202

[1]Source is resident enrollment as reported by U.S. Office of Education.
[2]Estimated.

SOURCE: *American Higher Education; A Documentary History.* Edited by Richard Hofstadter and Wilson Smith. Chicago: University of Chicago Press, 1961, p. 981.

Primary Source

Higher Education for American Democracy: Vol. I, Establishing the Goals: Chart (2 OF 3)

This means that tuition-free education should be available in public institutions to all youth for the traditional freshman and sophomore years or for the traditional 2-year junior college course.

To achieve this, it will be necessary to develop much more extensively than at present such opportunities as are now provided in local communities by the 2-year junior college, community institute, community college, or institute of arts and sciences. The name used does not matter, though community college seems to describe these schools best; the important thing is that the services they perform be recognized and vastly extended.

Such institutions make post-high-school education available to a much larger percentage of young people than otherwise could afford it. Indeed, as discussed in the volume of this Commission's report, "Organizing Higher Education," such community colleges probably will have to carry a large part of the responsibility for expanding opportunities in higher education.

3. The time has come to provide financial assistance to competent students in the tenth through fourteenth grades who would not be able to continue without such assistance.

Tuition costs are not the major economic barrier to education, especially in college. Costs of supplies, board, and room, and other living needs are great. Even many high-school students are unable to continue in school because of these costs.

Arrangements must be made, therefore, to provide additional financial assistance for worthy students who need it if they are to remain in school. Only in this way can we counteract the effect of family incomes so low that even tuition-free schooling is a financial impossibility for their children. Only in this way can we make sure that all who are to participate in democracy are adequately prepared to do so.

4. The time has come to reverse the present tendency of increasing tuition and other student fees in the senior college beyond the fourteenth year, and in both graduate and professional schools, by lowering tuition costs in publicly controlled colleges and by aiding deserving students through inaugurating a program of scholarships and fellowships.

Only in this way can we be sure that economic and social barriers will not prevent the realization of the promise that lies in our most gifted youth. Only in this way can we be certain of developing for the common good all the potential leadership our soci-

Proportion of Young Persons Attending School by Age and Color, April 1947

Age	Attending School	
	White	Nonwhites (about 95 percent Negro)
	Percent	Percent
6 years of age	67.8	63.4
7 to 9 years of age	97.1	89.2
10 to 13 years of age	98.2	93.7
14 to 17 years of age	82.5	71.9
18 to 19 years of age	28.2	24.2
20 to 24 years of age	11.3	6.7

SOURCE: *American Higher Education; A Documentary History.* Edited by Richard Hofstadter and Wilson Smith. Chicago: University of Chicago Press, 1961, p. 980.

Primary Source

Higher Education for American Democracy: Vol. I, Establishing the Goals: Chart (3 OF 3)

ety produces, no matter in what social or economic stratum it appears.

5. The time has come to expand considerably our program of adult education, and to make more of it the responsibility of our colleges and universities.

The crisis of the time and the rapidly changing conditions under which we live make it especially necessary that we provide a continuing and effective educational program for adults as well as youth. We can in this way, perhaps, make up some of the educational deficiencies of the past, and also in a measure counteract the pressures and distractions of adult life that all too often make the end of formal schooling the end of education too.

6. The time has come to make public education at all levels equally accessible to all, without regard to race, creed, sex or national origin.

If education is to make the attainment of a more perfect democracy one of its major goals, it is imperative that it extend its benefits to all on equal terms. It must renounce the practices of discrimination and segregation in educational institutions as contrary to the spirit of democracy. Educational leaders and institutions should take positive steps to overcome the conditions which at present obstruct free and equal access to educational opportunities. Educational programs everywhere should be aimed at undermining and eventually eliminating the attitudes that are responsible for discrimination and segregation—at creating instead attitudes that will make education freely available to all.

Further Resources

BOOKS

Brint, Steven, and Jerome Karabel. *The Diverted Dream: Community Colleges and the Promise of Educational Opportunity in America, 1900–1985.* New York: Oxford University Press, 1989.

Fisher, Ada Lois Sipuel, with Danney Goble. *A Matter of Black and White: The Autobiography of Ada Lois Sipuel Fisher.* Norman: University of Oklahoma Press, 1996.

Forest, James J. F., and Kevin Kinser, eds. *Higher Education in the United States: An Encyclopedia.* 2 vols. Santa Barbara, Calif.: ABC-CLIO, 2002.

Goodchild, Lester, and Harold S. Wechsler, eds. *The History of Higher Education.* Needham Heights, Mass.: Simon and Schuster, 1997.

Kennedy, Gail, ed. *Education for Democracy: The Debate Over the Report of the President's Commission on Higher Education.* Boston: Heath, 1952.

New York *Herald Tribune* Forum (1948). *Our Imperiled Resources.* New York: New York *Herald Tribune,* 1948.

Olevnik, Peter P. *American Higher Education: A Guide to Reference Sources.* Westport, Conn.: Greenwood, 1993.

Rudolph, Frederick. *The American College and University: A History.* Athens: University of Georgia Press, 1990.

Russell, James Earl. *Federal Activities in Higher Education After the Second World War: An Analysis of the Nature, Scope, and Impact of Federal Activities in Higher Education in the Fiscal Year 1947.* New York: King's Crown Press, Columbia University, 1951.

Solomon, Barbara Miller. *In the Company of Educated Women: A History of Women and Higher Education in America.* New Haven, Conn: Yale University Press, 1985.

WEBSITES

"History and Archival Resources in Higher Education." Higher Education Resource Hub. Available online at http://www .higher-ed.org/history.htm; website home page: http://www .higher-ed.org (accessed March 3, 2003).

AUDIO AND VISUAL MEDIA

Beyond the Dream III: A Celebration of Black History. Cox, Matthews and Associates. Videocassette, 1991.

A Community School in a Spanish-Speaking Village

Memoir

By: Loyd S. Tireman and Mary Watson

Date: 1948

Source: Tireman, Loyd S., and Mary Watson. *A Community School in a Spanish-Speaking Village.* Albuquerque: University of New Mexico Press, 1948, 74–78.

About the Authors: Loyd S. Tireman (1896–1959), a pioneer in bilingual education, was born into a farming community in Orchard, Iowa. He graduated from Upper Iowa State University in 1917, in time to enlist for service in World War I (1914–1918). After the war, he returned to Iowa, married, and assumed a position as a school superintendent in Hanlontown, the first of several such positions he held. He did graduate work in education at the University of Iowa, Iowa City, receiving his master's in 1924 and his doctorate in 1927. That same year, he joined the faculty of the University of New Mexico, Albuquerque, and remained in New Mexico until his death.

Mary Watson, a former rural teacher, was the principal of the Nambé School in New Mexico. When the school closed, she rejoined the state department of education in New Mexico and later became the state superintendent of education. ∎

Introduction

During the 1930s, Loyd S. Tireman conducted some of the first bilingual education experiments in the United States at the San José Demonstration and Experimental School in Bernalillo County, New Mexico. School surveys had shown that English- and Spanish-speaking children performed equally well on reading exams in the first three grades but that the disparity in scores increased as the children grew older. Unlike the native English speakers, the Hispanic children could not receive the same reading reinforcement at home. Tireman's school sought to use innovative methods that would help the rural Hispanic children with their reading.

Following progressive education theory and practice, he designed a curriculum based on the children's own experiences and linked the classroom with the community to increase student and parent interest in his program. He hired a school nurse and taught health and hygiene classes, began a preschool reading program, and made Spanish an elective for the higher grades, one of the first bilingual education efforts in the country. The San José school quickly became a model for others in New Mexico despite the prejudice that existed against Hispanics. By 1938, however, Tireman's funding had run out and he moved on to a new experimental school in Nambé, an agricultural village in northern New Mexico.

Significance

Like other towns, Nambé had suffered during the Great Depression of the 1930s. However, it had a benefactor in the form of Cyrus McCormick, Jr., who was the heir to the International Harvester fortune. In the early 1930s, McCormick had moved nearby and had decided to fund a school based on the San José school, with Tireman as its head.

Tireman set to work redesigning the curriculum to reflect the experience of the Nambé children. Just as the progressive philosopher of education, John Dewey, had

A Spanish American girl sings folk songs to her little brothers and sisters. **THE LIBRARY OF CONGRESS.**

advocated, Tireman sought to reinforce the relation between the school and society by creating a curriculum based on solving the community's problems. The Nambé Community School's teachers and students would walk through town and use its problems as the basis for their lessons. At the same time, several New Deal agencies taught Nambé's adults such skills as scientific farming techniques.

Just as at San José, however, Tireman encountered opposition to his innovations. On the one hand, white educators often assumed a bilingual community-based curriculum was undemanding, and on the other hand, Hispanics were often suspicious of the education offered to their children by white, urban teachers. With the outbreak of World War II (1939–1945) and the demise of many New Deal agencies, the Nambé school closed in 1942.

Tireman continued to publish his research on bilingual and bicultural education throughout the 1940s and also authored the Mesaland series of children's readers. After the war, he was sent to Bolivia to help organize its

schools. Suffering from heart disease and leukemia, he died in 1959.

Primary Source

A Community School in a Spanish-Speaking Village [excerpt]

> **SYNOPSIS:** These excerpts, taken from a teacher's diary, highlight some of the innovative methods used at Nambé to create a bilingual and bicultural community-based curriculum.

A Day in the Upper Grades Room

As I left the house this morning, Roberto and Mike were going by and I walked along with them. It was 8:15 when we got to school. Several children were already there, and as I opened the door of the room they rushed in to get balls and bats. Some of the children listened to the newscast, to be able to contribute something during our discussion of current events. The children are vitally interested in the developments of the war, for during the first part of the year they learned much about the present war. This interest has been kept up by reading newspapers, magazines, as well as through discussions and listening to the radio. Another group of children took the Chinese checkers and gathered around one of the small tables to play a game; several went to their desks to practice multiplication tables with which they had been having trouble; some went to work on some summaries of a current study on conservation; some had carving to do; some played blackboard games; some gathered in small groups to talk; others had brought their guitars and were strumming them and practicing new strokes, for it was the day for the WPA music teacher to come. Reuben and Betty were discussing a copy of a mural by Diego Rivera, which was posted on the bulletin board in the hall. Antonia and Manuel started a basketball game. Irene helped me put up some conservation pictures and captions, which the children had written, stimulated by some pictures which they had secured on loan by writing to the regional office of the Soil Conservation Service. . . .

Our room is arranged so that there are four rows of movable desks placed close together, leaving space for a circle of chairs, in which groups can come together for planning, discussion, or reading without disturbing people who are working at their seats. We also have three small tables which we use for display of work or other needs. In one corner we have a supply cupboard. There are also three bookcases in the room, one reserved for reference materials—encyclopedias and dictionaries; the other two for readers, arithmetics, library books, and social science materials. We have three large outline maps made by the children: one of New Mexico, another of the United States, and another of Europe. The boys and girls had felt the lack of a map on which to show the German conquests in Europe and mark the changes taking place, so they made the outline map of Europe, and when it proved a success, the other two were suggested. Many of the geographical concepts and historical movements have been traced on these maps; and as these maps are washable, it is easy to keep them clean. In addition we had a set of commercial maps.

When the bell rang, at nine, the children came in. . . .

When all were settled, I asked if there were any news to bring up. Pedro told us about a death with which we were all concerned. A young man from the community had died in an accident in Arizona and his body had been brought home. Pedro said the accident was caused because the driver had been going too fast and was drunk. We discussed the matter of excess speed and intoxication while driving.

Antonio volunteered that he had read in the Santa Fe *New Mexican* that the Croats and Serbs had united in Yugoslavia to fight against possible German aggression. We located Yugoslavia on our outline map. A discussion followed on the possibility of conquest of the Balkan Peninsula. Basilia said she didn't know it was called the Balkan Peninsula. The present war has given us many opportunities to learn about countries of the world. A common misconception we have encountered is: the children thought Europe and Africa were countries or sometimes continents, using these interchangeably. The use of maps has corrected this.

Ted, our only Anglo, remarked that the newspapers were full of news about strikes at the Ford plant. We got into a discussion of labor rights, unions, agitators, and workers. Adela thought the laborers were right, because she could see why they should have a share of the profits during the war boom. Soilo thought labor was taking advantage of the situation. Ernestine thought the President ought to call out the army and make the strikers work. We all agreed the country needs armaments to help Britain. I suggested that a weakness of democracy was that when individuals were given responsibilities and didn't meet them adequately, everyone suffered. Reuben said, "Yes, like Librado yesterday, when he took advantage of the freedom in the room." During our first study on the present war, the children had learned much about other forms of government in the world. They had been much concerned with the preservation of democracy and had made a list of the ways in which they, in their daily lives, could live more democratically. They had read several books on democracy and were still very much interested.

Further Resources

BOOKS

Bachelor, David L. *Educational Reform in New Mexico: Tireman, San Jose, and Nambé.* Albuquerque: University of New Mexico Press, 1991.

Forest, Suzanne. *The Preservation of the Village: New Mexico's Hispanics and the New Deal.* Albuquerque: University of New Mexico Press, 1989.

Sánchez, George. *Forgotten People: A Study of New Mexicans.* Albuquerque: University of New Mexico Press, 1940.

Tireman, Loyd S. *Teaching Spanish-Speaking Children.* Albuquerque: University of New Mexico Press, 1948.

PERIODICALS

Tireman, Loyd S. "Bilingual Children." *Review of Educational Research,* June 14, 1944, 273–278.

———. "Elementary Curriculum As a Tool for Improving the Community." *Progressive Education,* February 17, 1940, 130–133.

Vogel, Albert W., and Martin L. Berman. "The School at Nambé." *New Mexico School Review* 53, 1977, 12–15.

WEBSITES

Gonzales, Carolyn. "Looking Back: The Work of Some of UNM's Most Prominent Early Researchers Recalls a Proud Tradition." University of New Mexico. Available online at http://www.unm.edu/~quantum/quantum_fall_1999/looking_back.html; website home page: http://www.unm.edu (accessed March 4, 2003).

"The L. S. Tireman Papers, 1923–1957." University of New Mexico. Available online at http://elibrary.unm.edu/oanm/NmU/nmu1%23mss573bc/; website home page: http://www.unm.edu (accessed March 4, 2003).

AUDIO AND VISUAL MEDIA

Victim of Two Cultures: Richard Rodriguez. Films for the Humanities and Sciences, 1990.

Education in a Japanese American Internment Camp

Farewell to Manzanar

Memoir

By: Jeanne Wakatsuki Houston

Date: 1973

Source: Houston, Jeanne Wakatsuki, and James D. Houston. *Farewell to Manzanar.* Boston: Houghton Mifflin, 1973, 89–90, 93.

About the Author: Jeanne Wakatsuki Houston (1934–) was born in Inglewood, California. Her Japanese American family was among the first to be interned at the Manzanar War Relocation Center during World War II (1939–1945). Houston studied sociology and journalism at San Jose State College, where she and her husband, a novelist, first met. They were married in 1957 and live in California. Houston was awarded both the Humanities Prize in 1976 and the Christopher Award for the screenplay of *Farewell to Manzanar.*

"A Teacher at Topaz"

Memoir

By: Eleanor Gerard Sekerak

Date: 2000

Source: Sekerak, Eleanor Gerard. "A Teacher at Topaz." In *Only What We Could Carry: The Japanese American Internment Experience.* Lawson Fusao Inada, ed. Berkeley, Calif.: Heyday, 2000, 132–33.

About the Author: Eleanor Gerard Sekerak was born in California. She graduated from the University of California, Berkeley, before taking up an assignment to teach at Topaz Relocation Center in Utah during World War II. After the war, Sekerak returned to California and was a social studies teacher and counselor for thirty years before retiring. ■

Introduction

Since the turn of the twentieth century, the Japanese had immigrated into the United States, primarily settling on the West Coast as farmers. They encountered discrimination in immigration and naturalization, housing, and employment. During World War I (1914–1918), they formed an American Loyalty League in San Francisco to serve in the army. After the war, however, the Japanese were no longer allowed to immigrate to the United States and were denied citizenship.

In California, the Alien Land Law forbid the *Issei,* or first-generation immigrants, from buying land, even in the name of their *Nisei,* or American-born, children. Japanese Americans made up only 2 percent of California's population but produced 13 percent of the state's crops, with less land than their white neighbors. When whites boycotted their products, Japanese Americans started their own farmers' markets. They also challenged their exclusion from citizenship and immigration through the Japanese American Citizens League. During the 1930s, some progress was made, as Japanese Americans were elected to office in Hawaii, including a federal judgeship. However, the progress of the New Deal era would be catastrophically reversed with Japan's attack on Pearl Harbor on December 7, 1941.

Significance

Americans reacted to the attack on Pearl Harbor with racial hostility toward Japanese Americans, although most of them had never even lived in Japan and had become U.S. citizens. The Federal Bureau of Investigation searched hundreds of Japanese American homes, froze bank accounts, and arrested 1,370 people. Fearing another attack on the West Coast, leaders in California, Oregon, and Washington called for the detention of all Japanese Americans, whether *Issei* or *Nisei.*

In February 1942, President Franklin D. Roosevelt (served 1933–1945) signed Executive Order 9066 to counter espionage and sabotage. As a result, the government established "relocation camps" for about 120,000 people of Japanese ancestry. Families were given from forty-eight hours to two weeks to pack and were forced to sell their homes, businesses, and farms to whites at whatever price was offered. More than two-thirds of those interned under the executive order were citizens of the United States and more than half were children.

Relocation began the following month. The War Relocation Authority (WRA) was created to administer the

Interned students, Kiyo Yoshida, Lillian Watkatsuki and Yoshiko Yamasaki attend high school at the Manzanar Relocation Center, 1943. THE LIBRARY OF CONGRESS.

internment camps, which were scattered in isolated desert areas of Arizona, California, Utah, Idaho, Colorado, and Wyoming; a camp in New Jersey imprisoned those from the East Coast.

Schools were built in the camps, in some cases by internees, but had very little equipment. Students tried not to fall behind in their studies despite the circumstances. Many children kept diaries, wrote haiku poetry, and sketched pictures of their experiences at the camps.

When Japanese radio propaganda mentioned the camps as an example of America's "racial war" against Asians, President Roosevelt began to change his policies: the army was opened to internees and a Japanese American unit was created, eventually becoming among the most decorated of the war. Internees were also allowed to leave the camps if they could find work in another part of the country. Finally, a government employee, Mitsuye Endo, sued for her freedom and in 1944 the Supreme Court agreed with her. President Roosevelt rescinded Executive Order 9066 in 1944 and the last of the camps closed in March 1946. After their release, eight thousand of the former detainees decided to leave for Japan. In 1991, Congress offered each person who had been interned a reparations payment of $20,000.

Primary Source

Farewell to Manzanar [excerpt]

SYNOPSIS: In this excerpt, Jeanne Wakatsuki Houston describes growing up in the Manzanar Relocation Center, including her school days and extracurricular activities and her attempts to be "unmistakably American."

Once we settled into Block 28 that ache I'd felt since soon after we arrived at Manzanar subsided. It didn't entirely disappear, but it gradually submerged, as semblances of order returned and our pattern of life assumed its new design.

For one thing, Kiyo and I and all the other children finally had *a school.* During the first year, teachers had been volunteers; equipment had been makeshift; classes were scattered all over camp, in mess halls, recreation rooms, wherever we could be squeezed in. Now a teaching staff had been hired. Two blocks were turned into Manzanar High, and a third block of fifteen barracks was set up to house the elementary grades. We had blackboards, new desks, reference books, lab supplies. That second, stable school year was one of the things *Our World* commemorated when it came out in June of 1944.

My days spent in classrooms are largely a blur now, as one merges into another. What I see clearly is the face of my fourth-grade teacher—a pleasant face, but completely invulnerable, it seemed to me at the time, with sharp, commanding eyes. She came from Kentucky. She wore wedgies, loose slacks, and sweaters that were too short in the sleeves. A tall, heavyset spinster, about forty years old, she always wore a scarf on her head, tied beneath the chin, even during class, and she spoke with a slow, careful Appalachian accent. She was probably the best teacher I've ever had—strict, fair-minded, dedicated to her job. Because of her, when we finally returned to the outside world I was, academically at least, more than prepared to keep up with my peers.

I see her face. But what I hear, still ringing in my mind's ear, is the Glee Club I belonged to, made up of girls from the fourth, fifth, and sixth grades. We rehearsed every day during the last period. In concert we wore white cotton blouses and dark skirts. Forty voices strong we would line up at assemblies or at talent shows in the firebreak and sing out in unison all the favorites school kids used to learn: *Beautiful Dreamer, Down By the Old Mill Stream, Shine on Harvest Moon, Battle Hymn of the Republic. . . .*

In addition to the regular school sessions and the recreation program, classes of every kind were being offered all over camp: singing, acting, trumpet playing, tap-dancing, plus traditional Japanese arts like needlework, judo, and kendo. The first class I attended was in baton twirling, taught by a chubby girl about fourteen named Nancy. In the beginning I used a sawed-off broomstick with an old tennis ball stuck on one end. When it looked like I was going to keep at this, Mama ordered me one like Nancy's from the Sears, Roebuck catalogue. Nancy was a very good twirler and taught us younger kids all her tricks. For months I practiced, joined the baton club at school, and even entered contests. Since then I have often wondered what drew me to it at that age. I wonder, because of all the activities I tried out in camp, this was the one I stayed with, in fact returned to almost obsessively when I entered high school in southern California a few years later. By that time I was desperate to be "accepted," and baton twirling was one trick I could perform that was thoroughly, unmistakably American—putting on the boots and a dress crisscrossed with braid, spinning the silver stick and tossing it high to the tune of a John Philip Sousa march.

Primary Source

"A Teacher at Topaz" [excerpt]

SYNOPSIS: In this excerpt, Eleanor Gerard Sekerak describes her experience as a teacher trying to choose the appropriate civics curriculum for the school at Topaz Relocation Center.

In the beginning, faculty meetings were an exercise in how to tolerate frustration, as we wrestled with the "how to" of a core curriculum in a community school with few supplies and practically no library. Then we ran into opposition from the community itself—the parents did not want an experimental curriculum. They wanted their children to be prepared for college and to lose no academic ground because of the evacuation. So, with apologies to Stanford's Professor Paul Hanna, we modified the curriculum procedures by combining social studies and English as the "core" for the 1942–43 school year.

The first semester we covered federal, state, county, and city government and administration. An update on the creation and administration of wartime agencies was included. Then an intensive study of the WRA calling our project a "federally created municipality" followed. Staff members came to class to discuss the various phases of the administration of Topaz, and students took field trips and participated in an actual week of work experience in one phase of the community.

In May 1942 our community participation took a very active form when all seniors and their teachers went into the fields to plant onions and celery in areas of tillable ground scattered beyond the alkali deposits. Thereafter, whenever crooked celery stalks appeared on mess hall tables, much merriment ensued concerning whose responsibility it was to have produced such a deformity.

The second semester each student decided on the town in which he wished to resettle, and we set up a community survey of this locality and state. Using a Russell Sage publication, *Your Community* by Joanna Colcord, they sent for materials (writing model letters), did primary and secondary research, and wrote a term paper in college manuscript form summing up their results. At a recent reunion, there was amusement as alumni recounted that they had arrived at their chosen resettlement destinations knowing more than the natives.

Underlying all this was my personal determination that standards of behavior and of learning and performance were in no way to be lessened. As I faced my first day I wondered how I could teach American government and democratic principles while we sat in classrooms behind barbed wire! I never ceased to have a lump in my throat when classes recited the Pledge of Allegiance, especially the phrase, "liberty and justice for all."

Further Resources

BOOKS

Daniels, Roger, Sandra C. Taylor, and Harry H. L. Kitano. *Japanese Americans: From Relocation to Redress.* Seattle: University of Washington Press, 1991.

Kaneshiro, Takeo, comp. *Internees: War Relocation Center Memoirs and Diaries.* New York: Vantage, 1976.

Katz, William Loren. *A History of Multicultural America: World War II to the New Frontier.* Austin, Tex.: Raintree Steck-Vaughn, 1993.

Okihiro, Gary Y. *Storied Lives: Japanese American Students and World War II.* Seattle: University of Washington Press, 1999.

Tajiri, Vincent, ed. *Through Innocent Eyes: Writings and Art from the Japanese American Internment by Poston I Schoolchildren.* Los Angeles: Keiro Services Press and the Generations Fund, 1990. Reprint of *Out of the Desert,* Ray Bianchi and Paul Takeda, comp., 1943.

Takaki, Ronald. *Strangers from a Different Shore.* New York: Penguin, 1991.

Tunnell, Michael O., and George W. Chilcoat. *The Children of Topaz: The Story of a Japanese-American Internment Camp Based on a Classroom Diary.* New York: Holiday House, 1996.

PERIODICALS

Manzanar Free Press. Manzanar Internment Camp, Inyo County, California, 1942–1945.

Topaz Times. Topaz Internment Camp, Topaz, Utah, 1942–1945.

WEBSITES

"AHC Primary Sources in the Classroom: Heart Mountain Relocation Center." American Heritage Center, University of Wyoming. Available online at http://uwadmnweb.uwyo.edu /AHC/classroom/hm/index.htm; website home page: http:// uwadmnweb.uwyo.edu (accessed March 4, 2003).

"Children of the Camps: Resources and Links." Children of the Camps: The Documentary. Available online at http://www .children-of-the-camps.org/resources/index.html; website home page: http://www.children-of-the-camps.org (accessed March 4, 2003).

"Images from Topaz." University of Utah. Available online at http://www.lib.utah.edu/spc/photo/9066/topaz.htm; website home page: http://www.utah.edu (accessed March 4, 2003).

"Only What We Could Carry: The Japanese American Internment Experience." Heyday Books. Available online at http:// www.heydaybooks.com/books/owc.html; website home page: http://www.heydaybooks.com (accessed March 4, 2003).

AUDIO AND VISUAL MEDIA

Children of the Camps. National Asian American Telecommunications Association. Videocassette, 1999.

Farewell to Manzanar. Universal Studios. Videocassette, 1976.

From a Different Shore: The Japanese-American Experience. Films for the Humanities and Sciences. Videocassette, 1994.

Chronicles of Faith: The Autobiography of Frederick D. Patterson

Autobiography

By: Frederick Douglass Patterson

Date: 1991

Source: Patterson, Frederick Douglass. *Chronicles of Faith: The Autobiography of Frederick D. Patterson.* Martia Graham Goodson, ed. Tuscaloosa: University of Alabama Press, 1991, 121–23.

About the Author: Frederick Douglass Patterson (1901–1988), born in Washington, D.C., was named after Frederick Douglass, the famous nineteenth-century abolitionist. Orphaned at the age of two, he was raised by an aunt in Texas. Patterson went on to earn a master of science, a doctor of veterinary medicine degree, and a doctorate in philosophy. He became the president of Tuskegee Institute in Alabama in 1935 and founded the United Negro College Fund in 1944. ■

Introduction

For most of this country's history, African Americans who wanted a higher education faced the barriers of outright discrimination and Jim Crow segregation. A lucky few, like the sociologist W.E.B. DuBois, who was also the first African American Harvard doctoral recipient, could attend schools in the North or go to Europe but most could not. The private African American colleges created after the Civil War (1861–1865) sought to fill this gap, but they often faced problems with funding.

Some private colleges received financial support from northern white philanthropists like the Rockefellers or from organizations like the Rosenwald Fund or the General Education Board. During the Great Depression of the 1930s, however, even these sources diminished or dried up completely. A new way of raising money had to be found.

Frederick Douglass Patterson had spent four years at Prairie View State College in Texas before entering Iowa State, where he earned his degree in veterinary science. He had picked cotton and waited tables to finance his education. In 1928, he was hired by Tuskegee Institute to direct its veterinary science department and teach bacteriology. Booker T. Washington had founded Tuskegee in 1881 and had emphasized the importance of a more practical vocational education over a liberal education, which was favored by DuBois. At Tuskegee, Patterson was quickly promoted to director of the School of Agriculture and then, in 1935, to president.

Significance

Even though there was slow but steady progress in the National Association for the Advancement of Colored People's legal battles against segregation in higher education, such as the Supreme Court decision of *Missouri ex. rel. Gaines* (1938), most African Americans who wanted a higher education at this time turned to African American colleges, which were very affordable and accessible. Inspired by the success of the March of Dimes, Patterson thought of employing the same fund-raising technique of a combined appeal on behalf of historically African American colleges and universities (HBCU). The United Negro College Fund (UNCF) was incorporated on April 25, 1944, with twenty-seven member colleges, twelve thousand students, and an income of $765,000.

When Patterson died in 1988, the UNCF had grown to forty-two member colleges, forty-five thousand students, and an income of $42 million. It has provided staff salaries, student scholarships, laboratories, and libraries for HBCUs, which are open to students of all races. The UNCF motto, "A mind is a terrible thing to waste," is well known.

The UNCF is the largest independent source of money for America's private HBCUs. Some famous graduates of HBCUs include civil rights leaders such as Martin Luther King, Jr., and Andrew Young. In 1999, the UNCF had thirty-nine members and was named the administrator of the $1 billion Bill and Melinda Gates Millennium Scholars Program. The success of the UNCF also led to the creation of the American Indian College Fund. For his efforts in education and philanthropy, Patterson received the Presidential Medal of Freedom, the nation's highest civilian honor, in 1987.

Primary Source

Chronicles of Faith: The Autobiography of Frederick D. Patterson [excerpt]

SYNOPSIS: As the president of Tuskegee Institute, Patterson had often been asked for help by other African American colleges. In this excerpt from his memoir, he discusses what led him to create the UNCF.

In 1943 we had the first meeting to consider the feasibility of a combined appeal program, which became the United Negro College Fund. Our first national campaign was in 1944. Until then, practically all of the money for the black colleges had been raised largely by the president himself. I came to the

At the Tuskegee Institute in Alabama, a statue shows Booker T. Washington, the school's founder, lifting the veil off a slave. © BETTMANN/CORBIS. REPRODUCED BY PERMISSION.

presidency of Tuskegee at a time when the methods that Dr. Moton had used successfully to raise money were becoming passé.

In most small private colleges, the president based one of his primary appeals on the fact that the college had a deficit caused by enrolling so many financially poor students who wanted an education. The school just couldn't turn them down. The tuition at Tuskegee then was about fifty dollars a year. As a result, we had to raise just about all the money needed to run the institution from sources other than tuition. So we would go out and make the appeal to erase the deficit.

Tuskegee was fortunate, as was Hampton [University], in having some endowment, but ours was approximately $10 million, which produced only about $500,000 a year, at 5 percent, to operate the institution. Our budget was about $3 million. We had to find the difference between that and the modest tuition paid by the students and the yearly grant of five thousand dollars from the state of Alabama.

Tuskegee's fifty thousand dollar deficit became very important for two reasons. First, it meant unpaid bills. And if it was fifty thousand this year and noth-

United Negro College Fund founder and Tuskegee president Frederick D. Patterson with botanist George Washington Carver, 1940. ©
BETTMANN/CORBIS. REPRODUCED BY PERMISSION.

ing improved, it was going to be another fifty thousand the next year or perhaps even seventy-five thousand. Second, a college which is coping with deficit financing is not a college that can do new things to keep up with the times. Therefore, it stagnates. The stagnation can be worse than the deficit itself.

Either we had to reduce substantially the number of courses we were offering or we had to find new sources of funds. My analysis was that the things we were doing were sufficiently important and that we should be doing even more. Under the cir-

cumstances, I opted to see how Tuskegee could raise more money. I decided that since all private black colleges faced similar, if not identical, financial hardships, and since Tuskegee Institute, as a single institution, was having relatively little success, why not suggest to other private black colleges that we pool our resources—tell a better story and appeal to a broad base of donors as a financial constituency?

I wrote a letter to a number of private colleges. The immediate impetus for writing the letter was that

I had to prepare a little paper for presentation to a group known as the Atheneum Club on the campus of Tuskegee Institute. The club was composed of faculty members and doctors at the Veterans Hospital next door to the campus. Each member was expected to present a paper which reflected something of the speaker's interests, particularly his professional interests. At the time, I had no intention of doing anything more than talking about an interest which was very close to my heart, namely the fact that Tuskegee needed money, as did, perhaps, a lot of other private black colleges.

At the time I wrote the letter, it was purely an inquiry, so I could report to the club on the general condition of the colleges, of which the members were probably unaware. I received a prompt response from most of the college presidents. They said, "We are having an even worse time than Tuskegee Institute in raising funds, and we are in serious financial trouble."

When I received such quick replies, I wondered whether the respondents thought that perhaps I had some money to give out. When Booker Washington headed Tuskegee, certain wealthy philanthropists, and the Rosenwald Fund in particular, gave him money to help Tuskegee and to distribute among other schools. This arrangement became well known, and people remembered it long after such funds had ceased to be available. I had to write an additional letter to the private black colleges explaining that I was merely trying to find out whether they were as poor as Tuskegee was. This, I am sure, was disappointing news.

My initial survey revealed that Tuskegee was better off than most of the black private schools to which I had written. Tuskegee had a comparatively long history of reasonably well organized fund raising. We had a specific office dedicated to this purpose, and two field agents who lived in the North and who, on a regular schedule, presented Tuskegee's case to people who they knew to be interested. We were raising about forty thousand dollars a year at that time, but it cost more than twenty thousand to raise it.

In my earlier efforts to find money for Tuskegee, I had already been made aware that two or three changes were taking place in the philanthropic marketplace. As I've said before, many of the wealthy people who had given to Tuskegee had lost their wealth in the depression. Others had died, and their children did not necessarily inherit the philanthropic interests of their parents. Furthermore, the Roo-

sevelt administration was blamed, as I have said, for the changing tax situation. Despite the fact that most blacks were denied the vote, many potential contributors believed that blacks were responsible for Roosevelt's election and said they would not give for that reason.

Still another part of the picture which the record should show is that as little as we presidents—going out individually—were raising, we were competing with each other for the same philanthropic dollar, because not many people were interested in this group of institutions.

I can recall bumping into some of the presidents of other black colleges in the offices of the General Education Board. Our meeting wasn't intentional; it was just happenstance. They were going for their interests, and I was going for mine. There was no secret about who was donating what: reports were usually available indicating the gifts a particular foundation had made to various colleges.

The GEB and the Julius Rosenwald Fund of Chicago had strong minority interests in their philanthropy. While they gave to whites, they frequently gave to blacks. We, as presidents of black colleges, felt that the extent of their interest and the level of giving left much to be desired. For although the two foundations were among the major contributors to black colleges, they made greater gifts to white colleges, whose needs were comparatively less staggering than ours. As Benjamin Mays, former president of Morehouse College, has said, they always seemed to assume that blacks don't *need* as much money as whites. The Rosenwald Fund initially concentrated on helping primary and secondary schools, whereas the GEB seemed to be more interested in helping the black colleges. Very few other foundations at that time were equally interested in black higher education.

All of these factors combined to create a bleak financial future if our survival depended on traditional sources. Such at least was my conclusion in a paper that I presented to the Atheneum Club. And that was the end of my probe, or so I thought at the time.

Further Resources
BOOKS

A Salute to Historic Black Educators. Chicago: Empak, 1990.

Sammons, Vivian O. *Blacks in Science and Education.* Washington, D.C.: Hemisphere, 1989.

"United Negro College Fund." In *United Negro College Fund Archives: A Guide and Index.* Ann Arbor, Mich.: University Microfilms International, 1985.

PERIODICALS

Obituary. *Washington Post,* April 28, 1988, D4.

Patterson, Frederick Douglass. *Presidential Medal of Freedom Remarks at the Presentation Ceremony.* Public Papers of the Presidents, June 23, 1987. 23 Weekly Comp. Pres. doc. 730.

WEBSITES

"Frederick Douglass Patterson: Veterinarian." Princeton University. Available online at http://www.princeton.edu/~mcbrown/display/patterson.html; website home page: http://www.princeton.edu (accessed March 4, 2003).

United Negro College Fund. Available online at http://www.uncf.org (accessed March 4, 2003).

4

FASHION AND DESIGN

JOSEPH R. PHELAN

Entries are arranged in chronological order by date of primary source. For entries with one primary source, the entry title is the same as the primary source title. Entries with more than one primary source have an overall entry title, followed by the titles of the primary sources.

Important Events in Fashion and Design, 1940–1949

1940

- Architect Frank Lloyd Wright completes the People's Church in Kansas City, bringing modernism to church architecture.

- Colorfast textiles are improved, allowing prints to be more durable through many washings.

- Japanese silk supplies to the United States continue to dwindle under the trade embargo between the two countries.

- In fall, with the fall of Paris to the Nazis, the United States experiences its first fashion season without French designers.

- New automobiles and trucks numbering 4,476,000 are produced in the United States, a 25 percent increase over 1939. Americans own 69 percent of the world's cars.

1941

- College women and debutantes go hatless, a trend that alarms the millinery industry.

- New York mayor Fiorello H. La Guardia, acting as national director of civil defense, appoints a committee of stylists to submit designs for women's uniforms.

- Ludwig Mies van der Rohe's master plan for the Illinois Institute of Technology applies his distinctive design to low buildings.

- Charles Eames and Eero Saarinen win first prize in the Museum of Modern Art competition for functional furniture.

- Architects Walter Gropius and Marcel Breuer are commissioned by the U.S. government to design a 250-unit defense housing project called Aluminum City in New Kensington, Pennsylvania.

- In August, rationing of silk stockings begins.

- In September, under pressure from the U.S. government to conserve fabric, clothing designers begin the debate over hemlines.

- On November 24, *Life* magazine publishes an article on movie star Veronica Lake's "peek-a-boo" hairdo, claiming that it is "comparable in value, fame and world influence to Deanna Durbin's voice, Fred Astaire's feet or Marlene Dietrich's legs."

1942

- Claire McCardell's "popover" dress wins a *Harper's Bazaar* competition for the most attractive and practical housedress.

- With restrictions on metal, U.S. designers start producing dresses that fasten without any of the traditional devices such as hooks, snaps, buttons, or zippers.

- A range of household goods is produced for the first time in glass and plastic rather than in metal, including the glass kettle, ceramic ware, and a plastic juicer.

- Mid-nineteenth-century ironwork decorating buildings throughout the country is claimed for the war effort and melted down for munitions, resulting in the disappearance of cast-iron lacework and metallic horse troughs as urban architectural embellishments.

- The nave of the great Cathedral of Saint John the Divine in New York, begun in 1892, is completed.

- Henry-Russell Hitchcock publishes his monograph on Frank Lloyd Wright, *In the Nature of Materials,* and identifies what he calls a uniquely American kind of architecture.

- Prefabricated buildings are put into military service.

- In February, the War Production Board commandeers all of DuPont's supply of nylon for parachutes, tires, netting, and tents.

- On February 22, the manufacture of motor vehicles for the civilian market ceases as the auto industry aids in the war effort by building planes, anti-aircraft guns, ambulances, and tanks for the military.

- In April, in response to government restrictions on fabric, clothing manufacturers introduce cuffless pants for men.

- In April, Order L-41 is issued, prohibiting all but essential war construction.

- In June, the American Institute of Architects, with the Producers' Council, issues a bulletin, *The Conservation of Critical Materials in Construction,* to serve as a guideline for building construction during the war.

- In July, the War Production Board limits the manufacture of beauty supplies because of the need to conserve the metal used in cosmetic packaging. The ban lasts only four months, as women across the country protest.

1943

- Designer Norman Norell wins the first Coty American Fashion Critics' Award.

- Designers introduce glitter into their evening wear, with sequins, beads, and embroidery appearing on wools, crepes, sheer fabrics, and sweaters.

- A rumored shortage of black fabric triggers a run on women's black dresses.

- The U.S. government averts a wool shortage by releasing millions of pounds of wool and ending restrictions on its use.

- Frank Lloyd Wright begins designing the circular, spiral-ramp interior for the Guggenheim Museum in New York; his innovative, ambitious design takes a decade to complete.

- In response to shortages in housing, manufacturers develop a fold-up "suitcase" house to ship to Europe to house military personnel and the growing numbers of refugees.
- On January 25, the world's largest office building, the thirty-four-acre Pentagon, is completed in Arlington, Virginia.
- On February 7, shoe rationing begins, limiting civilians to three pairs per year.
- On May 17, *Life* magazine declares the "safe and stylish" wardrobe designed for Boeing's new female workforce a new fashion fad on the West Coast.

1944

- Eero Saarinen shares first prize with Oliver Lundquist in a contest to design small, affordable postwar houses; the design helps to introduce prefabricated houses as a solution to the problem of postwar housing.
- Air conditioning is introduced in motor vehicles.
- On June 22, President Roosevelt signs the Servicemen's Readjustment Act, better known as the GI Bill of Rights, which includes provisions for low-interest housing loans for World War II veterans.
- On August 25, Paris is liberated by Allied troops, allowing French clothing designers to return to the fashion stage.

1945

- As the war ends, U.S. cities report a growing housing crisis: 98 percent of cities report shortages of houses, and more than 90 percent report shortages of apartments.
- On July 16, movie star Rita Hayworth wins the title of "Number One Back Home Glamour Girl" in an overseas poll of U.S. enlisted men.
- In September, Paris designers hold their first fashion show since the outbreak of World War II.
- On October 1, the U.S. government lifts the ban on housing construction to permit the building of thirty-two thousand units for citizens not involved in the war effort.
- On October 29, War Production Board chairman J. A. Krug revokes Ration Order 2-B, which limited the sale of automobiles to civilians with special government-issued certificates.

1946

- *Life* magazine reports a frenzy of consumer buying by a public weary of rationing and shortages.
- Walter Gropius publishes *Rebuilding Our Communities,* in which he gives details of his city-planning and urban-decentralization projects.
- Marcel Breuer completes the Robinson House in Williamstown, Massachusetts; it becomes the model for the popular split-level house.
- Charles Eames exhibits his designs in the first one-man furniture show by the Museum of Modern Art.
- Advances in car design include the Nash 600, made with a single unit of welded steel; the Studebaker Champion, with

aircraft-style "no-glare" dials on the instrument panel; and the Chrysler Town and Country, a luxury station wagon.
- In January, the Franklin D. Roosevelt dime goes into circulation.
- On July 1, the U.S. military drops an atomic bomb with a photo of Rita Hayworth on the Bikini Atoll. Days later, Louis Reard christens his skimpy, two-piece bathing suit "the bikini."

1947

- Designer Christian Dior single-handedly restores the supremacy of French couture with his controversial New Look; small waistlines, padded hips, longer hems, and full skirts revive the feminine silhouette and set the dominant look for the postwar United States.
- A comprehensive exhibit of Ludwig Mies van der Rohe's work is held at the Museum of Modern Art in New York.
- The 1947 Studebaker Starlight surprises and delights consumers and car experts; its great sweep of glass in the wraparound rear window inspires countless jokes about whether the car is coming or going.
- *Vogue* magazine compares the new Oldsmobile, the "dynamic design of the Future," to the architecture of Frank Lloyd Wright.

1948

- American architects post record employment levels, as the nation's construction volume for the first half of the year runs 25 percent above 1947 levels.
- Architect Eleanor Raymond completes the Sun House, the last of three houses in which she explores the new potentials of plywood, paneling, and prefabrication.
- Architect Alvar Aalto challenges the dominance of the International Style with the completion of the Baker House dormitory at the Massachusetts Institute of Technology, foreshadowing the postmodern experimentation of the 1970s.
- Ludwig Mies van der Rohe's first executed tall buildings, the Promontory Apartments, are completed in Chicago.
- Independent automakers Hudson and Studebaker capture a record-breaking 18 percent of the domestic automobile market.
- General Motors produces a new high-compression engine, the V-8.
- On March 1, Eero Saarinen wins first prize in the competition for a Saint Louis memorial to Thomas Jefferson and the western expansion of the frontier. The *New York Herald Tribune* declares that his design will "rank among the nation's great monuments."
- In September, designer Adrian opens the Adrian Room in New York's Gunthers.
- On September 28, New York house builders Levitt and Sons build a sample Levittown on Long Island and sell fifty-three houses for a total of $1.1 million, breaking the world record for house selling. By the end of the week forty-seven more have been sold, and hundreds of customers have been put on a waiting list.

• In the fall, Christian Dior announces the opening of the U.S. branch of his design house, consolidating his influence on U.S. fashion. He starts mass-producing a line of about ninety dresses for wholesale in the United States at $59.75 and up. His first American collection debuts in November, making him the first French designer to be successful in designing and producing in the United States.

1949

• The Gunnison Homes division of U.S. Steel Corporation announces a twenty-four by twenty-eight foot, two-bedroom, steel and plywood house to sell for six thousand dollars. The firm's factories produce a house every twenty minutes.

• In Pacific Palisades, California, Charles Eames designs one of the first stylish and expensive prefabricated houses; that year he is also given the first annual award of the American Institute of Decorators.

• Architect Philip Johnson incorporates the design principles of Ludwig Mies van der Rohe in his New Canaan, Connecticut residence, the Glass House.

• The rubber industry unveils its tubeless tire, which does away with the inner tube. The tubeless tire is resistant to blowouts and is expected to make motorists' travels safer and more trouble free.

• Fashion designer Adele Simpson opens her medium-priced line of clothing in New York.

• In July, after prolonged debate Congress passes President Truman's public housing bill, the largest public housing program in U.S. history. The act calls for the construction of 810,000 units of low-rent housing.

Rita Hayworth on the Cover of *Life*

Magazine cover

By: Robert Landry

Date: August 11, 1941

Source: Landry, Robert. "Rita Hayworth." Photograph, August 11, 1941. *Life* Cover Collection Website. Available online at http://www.life.com/Life/search/covers/1941/cv081141.html; website home page: http://www.life.com/Life/search/covers (accessed March 8, 2003).

About the Artist: Rita Hayworth (1918–1987) was born in Brooklyn, New York. She achieved stardom in a series of movie musicals, including *You'll Never Get Rich* (1941) and *You Were Never Lovelier* (1942), both with Fred Astaire, and *Cover Girl* (1944). She also appeared in some of the classic film noirs (movies featuring corrupt characters, bleak urban settings, and lots of shadows), most notably *Gilda* (1945). In 1948, she starred in *The Lady From Shanghai,* which was directed by her second husband, Orson Welles, who was also her costar. In 1949, the divorced Hayworth married the playboy prince Aly Khan. The marriage was a controversial union for both parties. ∎

Introduction

Rita Hayworth was born Margarita Carmen Cansino. Her mother was a Ziegfeld Follies chorus girl and her father was a Spanish-born dancer. She began dancing in her father's nightclub at age twelve.

Hayworth appeared in small roles in Hollywood films beginning in 1935. An agent for Twentieth Century Fox discovered Rita dancing. The movie studio cast the sixteen-year-old in *Dante's Inferno* (1935) starring Spencer Tracy. Rita was soon typecast as an ethnic dancer in a series of B-movies. In 1937, she married Edward C. Judson, a businessman and a salesman, who advised her to dye her hair auburn and to have her hairline and eyebrows altered through electrolysis (application of electric current to remove hair). Rita also changed her professional name, taking her mother's maiden name, Haworth, and adding a "y" to ensure proper pronunciation.

A series of magazine and newspaper photos of the new Rita Hayworth caught the attention of Harry Cohn,

Rita Hayworth starred as the title character in *Gilda,* released in 1946.
THE KOBAL COLLECTION. REPRODUCED BY PERMISSION.

the head of Columbia Pictures, who signed her to a seven-year contract. Hayworth's first leading role was opposite Cary Grant in *Only Angels Have Wings* (1939), followed by *Strawberry Blonde* (1941) with James Cagney. Hayworth achieved star status when she danced with Astaire in *You'll Never Get Rich* and *You Were Never Lovelier* (1942). She appeared on the cover of *Time* and was called the "Great American Love Goddess" by *Life* magazine.

By the early 1940s, Hayworth was Columbia Pictures' leading actress. After Hayworth starred in the musical *Cover Girl* (1944), this time with Gene Kelly, *Life* published a seductive photograph of Hayworth wearing black lace. This photograph became one of the most popular pinups among American servicemen. Hayworth's popularity continued with *Gilda,* widely held to be her

Primary Source

Rita Hayworth on the Cover of *Life*

SYNOPSIS: One of the most popular covers that *Life* ever published of a Hollywood beauty was this one of Rita Hayworth in a bathing suit at the beach. PHOTOGRAPH BY ROBERT LANDY/TIMEPIX. REPRODUCED BY PERMISSION.

best film in which she sang "Put the Blame on Mame" while stripping off her long black gloves.

Significance

Hollywood movie stars of the World War II period (1939–1945) held a special place in the hearts of the American public. The most popular Hollywood actors—Grant, Astaire, and James Cagney—Rita Hayworth's costars, were sometimes referred to as America's royalty. Wartime audiences invested these stars with a special quality, which seemed at first glance out of place in a democracy. Yet, democracy, especially one that was digging itself out of the Depression and asking its young men to risk their life in war, needed models of perfection, beauty, and grace under pressure. To Americans, Hollywood royalty provided these qualities.

However, America perhaps needed something more. The description of Hayworth as the "Great American Love Goddess" suggested a deeper need in the American spirit to lift it out of the misery and uncertainty of war. Audiences were looking for a characteristic that transcended beauty. Hayworth's appeal went beyond celebrity status. The public saw her as a love goddess. Her radiant beauty, self-possession, and sex appeal, whether on a magazine cover or the silver screen, promised a level of pleasure, well-being, excitement, and satisfaction, which most of us seek but never attain.

Hayworth's phenomenal appeal to American servicemen reached its greatest height in their decision to paste her pinup on the most powerful weapon of mass destruction in the history of the world. In 1946, the United States tested one of its atomic bombs at Bikini Atoll in the Pacific Ocean. The bomb was called *Gilda,* after Hayworth's famous movie.

Further Resources

BOOKS

Higham, Charles. *Hollywood in the Forties.* New York: Barnes, 1968.

Leaming, Barbara. *If This Was Happiness.* New York: Viking, 1989.

WEBSITES

"Rita Hayworth." The Internet Movie Database. Available online at http://us.imdb.com/Name?Hayworth,+Rita; website home page: http://us.imdb.com (accessed March 8, 2003).

Wilkins, Peggy L. "Rita Hayworth." Glamournet.com. Available online at http://glamournet.com/legends/Rita; website home page: http://glamournet.com (accessed March 8, 2003).

AUDIO AND VISUAL MEDIA

Gilda. Original release, 1946. Directed by Charles Vidor. Columbia Pictures/Columbia Classics. VHS, DVD.

The Lady From Shanghai. Original release, 1948. Directed by Orson Welles. Columbia Pictures/Columbia Classics. VHS, DVD.

Cover Girl. Original release, 1944. Directed by Charles Vidor. Columbia Pictures/Columbia Home Video. VHS.

You'll Never Get Rich. Original release, 1941. Directed by Sidney Lanfield. Columbia Pictures/Columbia Home Video. VHS.

You Were Never Lovelier. Original release, 1942. Directed by William A. Seitter. Columbia Pictures/Columbia Home Video. VHS.

"Veronica Lake's Hair: It Is a Cinema Property of World Influence"

Magazine article

By: *Life*

Date: November 24, 1941

Source: "Veronica Lake's Hair: It Is a Cinema Property of World Influence." *Life* 11, November 24, 1941, 58–61.

About the Artist: Veronica Lake (1919–1973) was chosen by director Preston Sturges as the leading lady in his semi-autobiographical film *Sullivan's Travels* (1941), which Lake herself considered her best performance. In 1942, she was teamed with Alan Ladd in *This Gun for Hire,* the first of several films they made together. *Life* named Lake the top box-office star of 1943. Her other film roles included *The Blue Dahlia* (1946) and *The Glass Key* (1942), both examples of classic Hollywood film noir (a genre of movie featuring corrupt characters, bleak urban settings, and lots of shadows). ∎

Introduction

It was in a minor role in an Eddie Cantor film that an actress called Constance Keane (born Constance Frances Marie Ockleman) introduced what many consider the hairstyle of the twentieth century. When her hair fell over one eye while she was playing a bit part in *Forty Little Mothers* (1940), director Busby Berkeley, a connoisseur of over-the-top style, recognized a new one. He advised the makeup man, "Let it fall. It distinguishes her from the others." The hair didn't make Keane a star, however, until producer Arthur Hornblow Jr., who rechristened her Veronica Lake, cast her as the femme fatale in *I Wanted Wings* (1940). It was in this role that her long, blonde hair, falling over her right eye, caused a sensation. The media dubbed Lake the "girl with the peek-a-boo bang," and the tag stuck for years afterward.

Paramount executives were the first to recognize Lake's potential impact on audiences. A shoulder glamor shot of her and her peek-a-boo hairstyle dominated ads for *I Wanted Wings.* Lake's peek-a-boo hair was the ultimate nonutilitarian (impractical) hairstyle for women. For that very reason, it became a kind of ideal for both men and

Veronica Lake was once dubbed the "girl with the peek-a-boo bang." AP/WIDE WORLD PHOTOS. REPRODUCED BY PERMISSION.

women during World War II (1939–1945), when utilitarian considerations governed most people's lives. Lake held a special place in the hearts of moviegoers for her marvelous sultriness and glamor. The image she projected effortlessly transcended the realities of most people's lives. It is no wonder that she was chosen to star in the leading role in Rene Clair's delightful comedy *I Married a Witch* (1942), one of her best roles. It is also no surprise that she became of one of the ultimate "bad girls" of film noir.

Significance

When the dashing young Clark Gable took off his shirt to reveal his undershirt in *It Happened One Night* (1934), millions of men were said to start wearing undershirts. Millions more T-shirts were certainly sold. Thus began America's love affair with the way Hollywood stars dress and look.

Americans spend billions of dollars on their appearance each year. In the 1940s, Hollywood played a key role in defining both men's images of female desirability and women's self-image. Whether by design or accident, Lake's long, sensual hair became a symbol of both.

Although Lake's hairstyle was copied by many women during the war years, it was certainly far from an ideal style, especially given the time period. In the early 1940s, more and more women were entering the workforce, taking over the jobs of men who had gone off to war, and a hairstyle that got in the way was not really suitable for work. In addition, taking care of such a hairstyle required a lot of effort and was very time consuming. A November 24, 1941, *Life* article noted that Lake had to get up extra early to prepare her hair and had to spend her evenings combing and treating it. At some point, Hollywood regretfully told Lake to cut her hair. But the style has persisted.

Hollywood continues to influence hairstyles. In the 1950s, Yul Brynner's masculine sex appeal even made bald heads seem desirable. Crew cuts were popular with American men for most of the 1950s and early 1960s, thanks to Rock Hudson, Tab Hunter, and other Hollywood heartthrobs. But the greatest revolution in men's hairstyles was not due to Hollywood, but to the Beatles, who came to America in the mid-1960s, consigning the crew cut to oblivion for almost thirty years.

Primary Source

"Veronica Lake's Hair: It Is a Cinema Property of World Influence"

SYNOPSIS: *Life* magazine was famous for its photojournalism, offering a higher ratio of photographs to text than American readers had been used to. In this article, we see the way photographs carry the weight of the story, while the text becomes almost an afterthought.

The 19th minute of the movie *I Wanted Wings* is already marked as one of the historic moments of the cinema. It was the moment when an unknown young actress named Veronica Lake walked into camera range and waggled a head of long blonde hair at a suddenly enchanted public. Not since the late Jean Harlow launched the platinum-blonde fad in 1930 had the movies produced such a trichological sensation. Veronica Lake's hair has been acclaimed by men, copied by girls, cursed by their mothers and viewed with alarm by moralists. It is called the "strip-tease style," the "sheep-dog style" and the "bad-girl style" (though few except nice girls wear it), but to most moviegoers it is simply "the Veronica Lake style."

Miss Lake thus finds herself, seven months later, the owner and custodian of a personal property comparable in value, fame and world influence to Deanna Durbin's voice, Fred Astaire's feet or Marlene Dietrich's legs.

Facts and Figures

In a cold, scientific light, Miss Lake has some 150,000 hairs on her head, each measuring about .0024 inches in cross-section. The hair varies in length from 17 inches in front to 24 inches in back and falls about 8 inches below shoulders. For several inches it falls straight from the scalp and then begins to wave gently.

All her life Miss Lake has worn her hair long, except for one brief period in grade school when she had it cut in a windblown bob. Before that, as a little girl, she let it fall in curls almost down to her waist and since the bob era she has always had it more than shoulder length. "If I had my way," she says now, "I'd let it grow until I tripped over it." Since she stands only 5 ft. 1 ½ in. tall and her hair grows an inch a month, that would, as a matter of fact, take only a little more than three years.

Care and Training

Miss Lake's head of hair is, in most respects, a delight to its possessor. It waves naturally. It practically never snarls. It has just enough natural oil to keep it bright without ointments. And it does not need to be done up in curlers at night.

It takes a lot of time, though. Because of her hair, Miss Lake must get up even earlier than other movie actresses. On a worki 6 A.M., and gets to the studio about 6:30. To wash, set and dry her hair takes an hour and 45 minutes. It is washed twice in Nulava shampoo, once in Maro oil and then, because of Hollywood's hard water, rinsed in vinegar. She uses no lotions, brilliantines or setting ointments. The only fixing the hairdresser does is to put one wave, just above the point where the natural waves begin. This is done by flipping the hair once around a finger and then inserting a bobby pin to hold it.

In the evening Miss Lake gives her hair a good brushing at home and either braids it or puts it in a net. She never uses curlers, partly because she considers them bad for the hair and partly because she feels sorry for any man whose wife does her hair up at night.

Perils and Problems

The owner of such a head of hair inevitably faces certain problems. One is the problem on boys on street corners who hoot rudely at it. For this reason Miss Lake finds it convenient to ride in a closed car when her hair is down and to have it up when she is walking.

Much more serious is its natural tendency to get caught in things. By dint of constant watchfulness, Miss Lake manages to keep it from being caught in car doors, elevators and electric fans, but it has a bad habit of snagging on men's buttons. If Miss Lake were in fact the kind of girl she portrays on the screen, this might lead to all kinds of fascinating complications, but as it is, the button interludes are merely a bother. It also catches frequently on bracelets and necklaces and once got so badly snarled on her wrist watch that it broke the winding stem.

When she goes anywhere except to the studio Miss Lake always wears a net or a turban or braids her hair. This prevents it from falling into her food at dinner and keeps her from having to fuss with it constantly. If she does have to fix it while dining in a restaurant, she retires to the ladies' room. "I get very disgusted," she says, "when I see other women combing their hair into their soup."

The only major accident that has ever befallen Miss Lake's hair occurred some years ago when she bent down too close to an oven she was lighting and the flames leaped up, singeing off her eyebrows and forelock. Nowadays she keeps away from stoves but her hair catches fire fairly often when she is smoking. This, though a constant concern, is not a serious peril. When it happens the hair of the screen's most inflammable blonde merely sizzles a little and goes out.

Further Resources

BOOKS

Higham, Charles. *Hollywood in the Forties.* New York: Barnes, 1968.

Spoto, Donald. *Madcap: The Life of Preston Sturges.* Boston: Little, Brown, 1990.

WEBSITES

Dirks, Tim. "Sullivan's Travels." The Greatest Films. Available online at http://www.filmsite.org/sull.html; website home page: http://www.filmsite.org (accessed March 8, 2003).

AUDIO AND VISUAL MEDIA

Sullivan's Travels. Original release, 1942. Directed by Preston Sturges. Paramount Pictures. DVD, VHS.

This Gun for Hire. Original release, 1942. Directed by Frank Tuttle. Columbia Pictures. VHS.

"United States Auto Plants Are Cleared for War"

Magazine article

By: *Life,*

Date: February 16, 1942

Source: "United States Auto Plants Are Cleared for War." *Life,* February 16, 1942.

About the Publication: *Life* was founded in 1936 as a pictorial news magazine by publisher Henry R. Luce (1898–1967), who also founded *Time* (1923), *Fortune* (1930), and *Sports Illustrated* (1954). It was published weekly until 1972, and beginning in 1978 it shifted to publishing monthly issues. After its first few issues, *Life* quickly became noted for its photojournalism, especially for offering more pages of photos than its competitors provided. ∎

Introduction

With their involvement in World War II (1939–1945), Americans had gone from the pursuit of pleasure to the waging of war. The automobile companies stopped the production of automobiles for civilians so that they could manufacture tanks, trucks, and airplanes, as well as bombs, shells, and artillery. The contracts for war-related production that the government gave the automakers more than doubled.

America's transition from civilian to wartime production reveals the flexibility of the American system of government. The Founding Fathers intended a limited government, one that is restricted to providing a framework for social freedom. Church is to be separated from state and the economy from government. The persons and property of American citizens are supposed to be free from government interference without clear and compelling reasons. World War II was a compelling reason.

When the United States entered the war, the whole American economy rose to the challenge. The system of American production changed, from civilian to wartime effort. Such an overnight transformation was not possible through the ordinary operating laws of the market place and free enterprise. This was because by and large these laws assumed that conditions of normalcy and stability prevailed. In order for America to respond to war, it was imperative that the mighty auto industry, which like all other enterprises in the business sector had been dedicated to private profit, conform to government directive.

Significance

History has proven again and again that war always engenders unforeseen social change at a tremendous rate. World War II was no exception. The emergency reforms necessary during wartime resulted in new industrial, scientific, technological, and administrative possibilities. These innovations became the norm when peace returned. The blending of the car industry's brilliant mass production and the aviation industry's advanced technology meant better transportation for people all over the world at the end of the war. In addition, these innovations transformed the daily lives of individuals through the development of new industries, products, technologies, means of communication, and job opportunities.

The roots of the computer revolution, which has transformed the economy, and with it our lives, in the

The last fenders are produced by a Detroit auto factory before its conversion to production of military airplane parts. February 1942. THE LIBRARY OF CONGRESS.

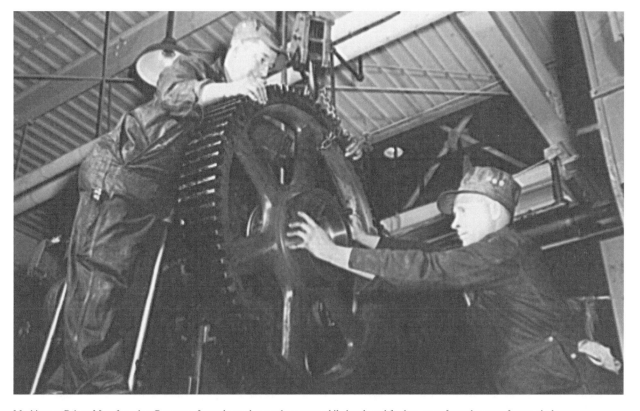

Machines at Briggs Manufacturing Company, formerly used to produce automobile hoods and fenders, are reformed to manufacture airplane parts. Detroit, February 1942. THE LIBRARY OF CONGRESS.

last decade or so, go back to World War II research. Soon after the war, the National Aeronautics and Space Administration (NASA) launched the program that would, in a remarkably short period, put a man on the Moon.

Primary Source

"United States Auto Plants Are Cleared for War"

SYNOPSIS: This *Life* magazine article announces and illustrates dramatically the transformation, by government directive, of the automobile manufacturing plants in America into factories for the production of war matériel.

Last week an era in U.S. history came to an end in a factory in Pontiac, Mich., 25 miles north of Detroit. At exactly 1:31 P.M. on Feb. 2, the last pleasure car that will be made until the war is won rolled off the assembly line in Pontiac's Plant A. Other famous makers—Ford, Plymouth Studebaker and the rest—had already ended production. Now the $4,000,000,000-a-year auto industry had only one customer and only one boss—the U.S. Government-at-war.

In Detroit and its 100-mile belt of auto-making cities, men no longer talked of what the auto industry could do. They went ahead and did it. The hush that fell on the assembly lines was soon shattered. Crews of workmen ripped down mile after mile of overhead conveyers. Huge machines were torn loose from their concrete moorings and rushed out into storage yards. Workmen with drills cut gaping holes in the floors to set foundations for even heavier machinery, needed in tank and plane production. Some plants were closed up just as they stood, because new ones could be built more cheaply and more quickly than the machinery could be dismantled. But every automobile company could show two, three, four, sometimes a dozen big factories humming with war work.

Word came from Washington that all existing war plants were to be enlarged, even the newest and biggest. All auto factories that could be converted were to be converted. Many new factories were to be built. War contracts awarded to the auto industry topped ten billions (compared with four billions before Pearl Harbor), but this was just a beginning. By the time the auto plants finish that much stuff they will be tooled up to produce several times ten billions more.

Up to last week 250,000 men lost their jobs as the auto lines halted. That was serious for them (Michigan law allows $16-a-week compensation for 18 weeks), but it was temporary. Ernest Kanzler, the auto "czar" appointed by Donald Nelson, estimated

the auto plants will need at least 700,000 men and women for their war work, which is 275,000 more than they ever employed before.

These figures were a revolution in themselves. Last week another revolution, which Americans will not feel for a long time, was taking shape in and around Detroit. The auto industry's genius for mass production was being merged—forcibly, some said—with the advanced engineering and design ideas of the younger aviation industry. This meant that when peace comes 130,000,000 Americans and their neighbors around the world will be able to enjoy speed, convenience and luxuries in transportation that are now undreamed of.

Further Resources

BOOKS

Nelson, Donald Marr. *Arsenal of Democracy: The Story of American War Production.* New York: Harcourt, Brace, 1946.

WEBSITES

"The Arsenal of Democracy." History, Arts and Libraries. Available online at http://www.sos.state.mi.us/history /museum/explore/museums/hismus/1900-75/arsenal; website home page: http://www.michigan.gov/hal (accessed March 8, 2003).

Ford Heritage. Available online at http://www.fordheritage.com (accessed March 8, 2003).

Nolan, Jenny. "Willow Run and the Arsenal of Democracy." *Detroit News.* Available online at http://detnews.com/history /arsenal/arsenal.htm; website home page: http://detnews .com (accessed July 23, 2002).

American Men in Three Wartime Posters

"Man the Guns—Join the Navy"; "Keep 'Em Fighting"; "Get Hot—Keep Moving"

Posters

By: McClelland Barclay; National Safety Council; Unknown
Date: 1942
Source: McClelland, Barclay; National Safety Council; Unknown. "Man the Guns—Join the Navy"; "Keep 'Em Fighting"; "Get Hot—Keep Moving." 1942. National Archives and Records Administration, Still Picture Branch, Washington, D.C. Available online at http://www.archives.gov/exhibit _hall/powers_of_persuasion/man_the_guns/man_the_guns .html; website home page: http://archives.gov (accessed March 28, 2003).

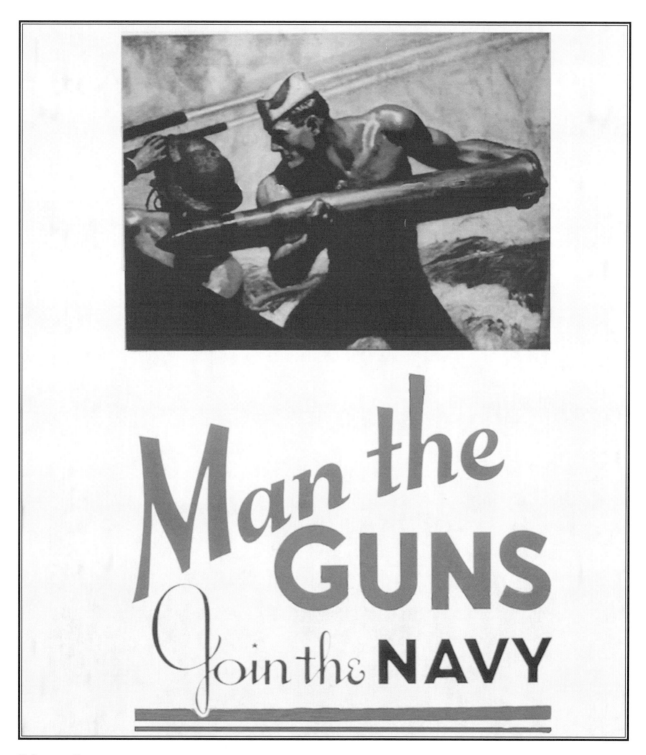

Primary Source

American Men in Three Wartime Posters (1 OF 3)

SYNOPSIS: These three posters were produced during World War II to encourage ordinary citizens to serve their country. They convey images of America's strength and commitment through its brave and strong men. These men were serving the cause of democracy on the high seas with the navy and in the nation's factories through dedicated labor. This recruitment poster uses men with guns to depict American strength. POSTER BY MCCLELLAND BARCLAY, 1942. PRODUCED FOR THE NAVY RECRUITING BUREAU. COURTESY OF NATIONAL ARCHIVES (NWDNS-44-PA-24).

Primary Source

American Men in Three Wartime Posters (2 OF 3)

This poster, produced in 1942 by McClelland Barclay, promotes more and safer gun production. PRINTED FOR THE NATIONAL SAFETY COUNCIL, INC. COURTESY OF NATIONAL ARCHIVES (NWDNS-44-PA-1171B).

Primary Source

American Men in Three Wartime Posters (3 OF 3)
This poster symbolizes the American tradition of hard work. COURTESY OF NATIONAL ARCHIVES (NWDNS-179-WP-1256).

About the Artist: McClelland Barclay (1891–1943) was a lieutenant commander in the U.S. Navy Reserve until he was pronounced missing in action in the Pacific theater. Before World War II (1939–1945), he did illustrations of beautiful women for the *Saturday Evening Post* and the *Pictorial Review*. He drew many posters for the U.S. Navy, including those for recruitment purposes. He also drew officer portraits. ■

Introduction

America had an isolationist policy (nonalliance with other countries) in the period before World War II. A majority of the electorate supported the struggle of the European nations to remain free but was convinced that it was Europe's struggle and not that of the United States. Franklin D. Roosevelt (served 1933–1945) had in fact run for reelection with a promise not to send American soldiers to Europe. However, after the Japanese attacked Pearl Harbor on December 7, 1941, Americans, realizing their national interests were at stake, had a change of heart.

The government reminded Americans it was inevitable that they had to get involved in the war. The wartime posters' invitation to potential navy volunteers that they would "Man the Guns" appealed to the American soul.

The posters were an appeal for manpower. The armed services needed men, and posters were an ideal tactic to communicate this need to potential volunteers. The government also wanted to encourage industrial productivity. Under war conditions, the normal incentives to productivity, such as pay raises and promotions, could not be called on to drive workers to perform better. The government sought to boost workers' morale and ensure their job commitment. Thus, the images of servicemen loading shells were designed to foster the connection in the worker's mind between his effort at the plant and the serviceman's effort at the war front.

The posters portrayed Americans doing "heavy lifting" rather than enjoying themselves as normal advertising tends to do. At the height of the war, Winston Churchill told the British people that he had only "blood, toil, tears and sweat" to give them. These posters by Barclay and others conveyed essentially the same message to the American public.

Significance

We notice in these posters one common theme: the men are shirtless. On the one hand, Barclay and the other artists wanted to portray the manliness and physical attributes of men who joined the war movement. The artists wished to show the natural power and strength underneath the servicemen's uniforms. Posters such as "Man the Guns—Join the Navy" and "Keep 'Em Fighting" presented images of the American male in action. Broad-shouldered, superbly fit men were shown holding huge shells, which would be fed into the guns of a battleship facing the enemy on the high seas. Even the poster "Get Hot—Keep

Moving" shows a male figure working in a foundry (place for molding metal), holding a steel pole as would a pikeman (foot soldier) during the Middle Ages, holding his weapon recently tempered in a glowing furnace.

On the other hand, the shirtless men were symbols of America's strength and power as it waged war against the enemy, both in the battlefield and on the home front. The posters appealed to the American tradition of rising to the challenge posed by an enemy who would put an end the American democratic way of life.

One cannot but suspect that these posters influenced young males in the direction of bodybuilding, a pursuit that became tremendously popular after the war, making Charles Atlas, a famous weight lifter, a household name. Also, the posters conveyed the images of men dressed for hard work. To the extent these posters exercised an influence on clothing trends, it would be in the direction of tough, durable work wear. The rise of denim to a dominant position in American fashion could be said to be prefigured by the men in these wartime posters.

Further Resources

BOOKS

Laurie, Clayton D. *The Propaganda Warriors: America's Crusade against Nazi Germany.* Lawrence: University Press of Kansas, 1996.

Rubenstein, Harry, and William L. Bird. *Design for Victory: World War II Posters on the American Home Front.* New York: Princeton Architectural Press, 1998.

WEBSITES

"Powers of Persuasion: Poster Art From World War II." U.S. National Archives and Records Administration. Available online at http://www.archives.gov/exhibit_hall/powers_of _persuasion/powers_of_persuasion_home.html; website home page: http://www.archives.gov (accessed March 8, 2003). *This site contains additional poster art from World War II.*

American Women in Three Wartime Posters

"Victory Waits on Your Fingers"; "Longing Won't Get Him Back Sooner . . . Get a War Job!"; "We Can Do It!"

Posters

By: Royal Typewriter Company; Lawrence Wilbur; J. Howard Miller

Date: ca. 1942

Source: Royal Typewriter Company; Lawrence Wilbur; J. Howard Miller. "Victory Waits on Your Fingers"; "Longing

Primary Source

American Women in Three Wartime Posters (1 OF 3)

SYNOPSIS: These three vivid and colorful posters are among the most beloved of all the propaganda posters produced by the U.S. government during the war. This poster illustrates that women are encouraged to do what they can to win the war.

PRODUCED BY THE ROYAL TYPEWRITER COMPANY FOR THE U.S. CIVIL SERVICE COMMISSION. COURTESY OF NATIONAL ARCHIVES (NWDNS-44-PA-2272).

Primary Source

American Women in Three Wartime Posters (2 OF 3)

This World War II poster by Lawrence Wilbur encourages women to contribute to the end of the war by working. POSTER BY LAWRENCE WILBUR, 1944. PRODUCED BY THE GOVERNMENT PRINTING OFFICE FOR THE WAR MANPOWER COMMISSION. COURTESY OF NATIONAL ARCHIVES (NWDNS-44-PA-389).

Primary Source

American Women in Three Wartime Posters (3 OF 3)
The character of Rosie the Riveter has greater resonance than any other character created by artists to symbolize strong, dedicated female factory workers who retained their femininity even while doing what was then considered men's work. NATIONAL ARCHIVES AND RECORDS ADMINISTRATION.

Won't Get Him Back Sooner . . . Get a War Job!"; "We Can Do It!" ca. 1942. National Archives and Records Administration, Still Picture Branch, Washington, D.C. Available online at http://archives.gov/exhibit_hall/powers_of_persuasion /its_a_womans_war_too/its_a_womans_war_too.html; website home page: http://www.archives.gov (accessed March 28, 2003). ■

Introduction

In her influential treatise *A Vindication of the Rights of Women* (Peter Edes for Thomas and Andrews, Boston, 1792), English author Mary Wollstonecraft argued that if women are to have civil and political rights equal to those of men, they should not be put on a pedestal. They should instead take their places beside men in the life of the community. The wartime poster announcing "Longing Won't Bring Him Back Sooner—Get a War Job!" symbolizes this deromanticizing sought by Wollstonecraft. If the woman in the poster feels lost without her man who is at war, she should make herself useful by joining the war effort.

The posters of World War II (1939–1945) represent the contributions of American women, who took part in winning the war as did the soldiers in the field. The posters also point to a future time when women would enter the workforce in large numbers, dominating many key sectors of economic activity and occupying some of the most powerful positions in the country. It was during the war that American women redefined their role in the workforce. Such posters as "Keep 'Em Flying, Miss U.S.A." symbolize a social change, in which women were no longer just the caretakers of children and the home.

These posters were also the government's efforts to influence public opinion through the artistic representation of the domestic war effort. The federal program gave talented illustrators the opportunity to gain a public presence that would have been impossible in peacetime. By far the most famous of these posters is "Rosie the Riveter," originally known as "We Can Do It!" Created by J. Howard Miller, it was produced by Westinghouse.

Significance

The change in the life of American women from the prewar domestic sphere to the wartime workforce had a tremendous impact on fashion and style. At home one is free to dress as one pleases. But in the factory or office, one dresses for work. However, at the same time, a woman is not necessarily dressing for others when she goes to the factory or office. Instead, she dresses for the type of work she has been hired to do.

"Rosie the Riveter" was not the kind of woman who gave a moment's thought to messy hair, chipped nails, or even some grease on her brow. She was strong, confident, dedicated, and represented the kind of woman en-

visaged by Wollstonecraft. In the poster, Rosie flexes her biceps while wearing a scarf over her hair, much like that worn by the stereotypical housewife when she scrubs the kitchen floor at home. Rosie also wears a pair of overalls similar to those worn by the mechanic at the local garage. While combining the domestic and the "industrial" look, she looks surprisingly attractive and feminine.

It is not hard to see what the long-term impact of the Rosie "look" would be on subsequent female styles. Today, it is taken for granted that women will wear clothes similar, if not identical, to those worn by men, depending on job location, occasion, and activity. These days, when shopping for clothes, American women are not always looking for that perfect feminine look. They consider a variety of styles, depending on where they will wear the clothing—at work, for sports, or for leisure.

What Rosie represents then is a reinvention of the ideal American woman, confident in her hair style and clothing, as well as in the work environment. She is the symbol of later generations of women who would retain their femininity while performing jobs traditionally assumed by men.

Further Resources
BOOKS
Honey, Maureen. *Creating Rosie the Riveter: Class, Gender, and Propaganda During World War II*. Amherst: University of Massachusetts Press, 1984.

Wise, Christy, and Nancy Baker Wise. *A Mouthful of Rivets: Women at Work in World War II*. San Francisco: Jossey-Bass, 1994.

WEBSITES
"Powers of Persuasion: Poster Art From World War II." U.S. National Archives and Records Administration. Available online at http://www.archives.gov/exhibit_hall/powers_of _persuasion/powers_of_persuasion_home.html; website home page: http://www.archives.gov (accessed March 8, 2003). *This site contains additional poster art from World War II.*

Address at the Dedication of the Thomas Jefferson Memorial
Speech

By: Franklin D. Roosevelt

Date: April 13, 1943

Source: Roosevelt, Franklin D. Address at the Dedication of the Thomas Jefferson Memorial, Washington, D.C. April 13, 1943. *The Public Papers and Addresses of Franklin D. Roosevelt*. Vol. 12. New York: Random House, 1943.

Dedicated on the third president's bi-centennial anniversary, April 12, 1943, the Jefferson Memorial is constructed of marble from Vermont, Missouri, Georgia, and Tennessee. **THE LIBRARY OF CONGRESS.**

About the Author: Franklin D. Roosevelt (1882–1945), the thirty-second president of the United States, was born in Hyde Park, New York. In 1910, he was elected state senator of New York. From 1913 to 1920, he served as the assistant secretary of the navy. He was twice elected governor of New York State. At the height of the Great Depression, Roosevelt became president of the United States in 1932. He was re-elected president four times, dying in office in April 1945 during the first few months of his last term. ∎

Introduction

President Franklin D. Roosevelt dedicated the Jefferson Memorial monument on the two hundredth birthday of the nation's third president, Thomas Jefferson (served 1801–1809). Roosevelt's speech was intended to awaken Americans' appreciation of democracy in the face of the country's involvement in World War II (1939–1945). The speech was marked by a sense of the continuing significance of the leadership and achievements of Jefferson to the American experiment in self-government.

Roosevelt argued that his generation of Americans, although burdened with war, could be grateful for the opportunity to rededicate themselves to the principles of the Declaration of Independence. He observed that Ameri-

cans, who were living through World War II, could relate to Jefferson's life and work of which previous generations may have lost sight. Just as Jefferson realized that the colonial Americans might not attain their independence from Great Britain if they were not willing to fight for their freedom, Americans during World War II had come to the same realization, eventually declaring war against the Axis powers (Japan, Germany, and Italy) after Japan attacked Pearl Harbor on December 7, 1941.

Americans in the early 1940s could relate to Jefferson. Jefferson lived at a time when the principles of freedom were threatened by others who disagreed. During Roosevelt's presidency, Americans lived in a world threatened by powerful tyrants like Adolf Hitler. And just as Jefferson, who cherished both peace and freedom, had to sacrifice peace on more than one occasion to protect freedom, Americans gave up their peaceful existence to fight enemies worldwide. Therefore, although 150 years separated Jefferson and his countrymen living in the 1940s, they shared a common goal of protecting their liberties and the common determination to commit the ultimate sacrifice if necessary.

Significance

The Jefferson Memorial was designed in the 1930s by John Russell Pope in the neoclassical style of architecture that Jefferson had been known to favor. A bronze statue of Jefferson, designed by Rudolph Evans, stands facing the White House. While the building was viewed by some in the architectural community as anachronistic (out of date), it has endured and become one of the most beloved of U.S. historic monuments. The architecture, once regarded as a throwback to a bygone era, is now viewed with renewed respect. It is regarded as a brilliant example of the classical style adapted to American conditions.

Jefferson, like the memorial built in his honor, has enjoyed a revival of interest. He is considered one of the most fertile thinkers that our democracy has ever produced. Not a decade goes by without a new interpretation of the man and his vision. This is testimony as much to the brilliance of his mind as to the continuing relevance of his ideas. Jefferson was among other things an architect. He designed Monticello, his home in central Virginia. In the 1980s, the American Association of Architects voted his architectural plans for the University of Virginia as the most significant architectural achievement in American history.

It is fitting that Roosevelt, who dedicated the Jefferson Memorial during wartime, was honored with a monument of his own in 1997. The Roosevelt Memorial is symbolic. Roosevelt's leadership during the greatest crisis the United States faced in the twentieth century restored the nation's confidence in the noble experiment in self-government and made it once again a model for the world.

Primary Source

Address at the Dedication of the Thomas Jefferson Memorial, Washington, D.C.

SYNOPSIS: In this speech, President Roosevelt dedicates a neoclassical temple to his great predecessor, Thomas Jefferson, with whom he shares a commitment to champion the cause of democracy.

Today, in the midst of a great war for freedom, we dedicate a shrine to freedom.

To Thomas Jefferson, Apostle of Freedom, we are paying a debt long overdue.

Yet, there are reasons for gratitude that this occasion falls within our time; for our generation of Americans can understand much in Jefferson's life which intervening generations could not see as well as we.

He faced the fact that men who will not fight for liberty can lose it. We, too, have faced that fact.

He lived in a world in which freedom of conscience and freedom of mind were battles still to be fought through—not principles already accepted of all men. We, too, have lived in such a world.

He loved peace and loved liberty—yet on more than one occasion he was forced to choose between them. We, too, have been compelled to make that choice.

Generations which understand each other across the distances of history are the generations united by a common experience and a common cause. Jefferson, across a hundred and fifty years of time, is closer by much to living men than many of our leaders of the years between. His cause was a cause to which we also are committed, not by our words alone but by our sacrifice.

For faith and ideals imply renunciations. Spiritual advancement throughout all our history has called for temporal sacrifices.

The Declaration of Independence and the very purposes of the American Revolution itself, while seeking freedoms, called for the abandonment of privileges.

Jefferson was no dreamer—for half a century he led his State and his Nation in fact and in deed. I like to think that this was so because he thought in terms of the morrow as well as the day—and this was why he was hated or feared by those who thought in terms of the day and the yesterday.

We judge him by the application of his philosophy to the circumstances of his life. But in such applying we come to understand that his life was given for those deeper values that persist throughout all time.

Leader in the philosophy of government, in education, in the arts, in efforts to lighten the toil of mankind—exponent of planning for the future, he led the steps of America into the path of the permanent integrity of the Republic.

Thomas Jefferson believed, as we believe, in Man. He believed, as we believe, that men are capable of their own government, and that no king, no tyrant, no dictator can govern for them as well as they can govern for themselves.

He believed, as we believe, in certain inalienable rights. He, as we, saw those principles and freedoms challenged. He fought for them, as we fight for them.

He proved that the seeming eclipse of liberty can well become the dawn of more liberty. Those who fight the tyranny of our own time will come to learn that old lesson. Among all the peoples of the earth, the cruelties and the oppressions of its would-be masters have taught this generation what its liberties can mean. This lesson, so bitterly learned, will never be forgotten while this generation is still alive.

The words which we have chosen for this Memorial speak Jefferson's noblest and most urgent meaning; and we are proud indeed to understand it and share it:

"I have sworn upon the altar of God, eternal hostility against every form of tyranny over the mind of man."

Further Resources

BOOKS

Rosenman, Samuel Irving. *Working with Roosevelt.* New York: Harper, 1952.

Rosenman, Samuel Irving, and Dorothy Rosenman. *Presidential Style: Some Giants and a Pygmy in the White House.* New York: Harper and Row, 1976.

WEBSITES:

Franklin D. Roosevelt Presidential Library and Museum. Available online at http://www.fdrlibrary.marist.edu (accessed March 8, 2003).

"National Mall." National Park Service. Available online at http://www.nps.gov/nama/monuments/monument.htm; website home page: http://www.nps.gov (accessed March 8, 2003).

"Samuel Rosenman." Museum of Tolerance Online: Multimedia Learning Center. Available online at http://motlc.wiesenthal.com/pages/t066/t06621.html; website home page: http://motlc.wiesenthal.com (accessed March 8, 2003).

"Thomas Jefferson Digital Archive." University of Virginia Library. Available online at http://etext.lib.virginia.edu/jefferson; website home page: http://etext.lib.virginia.edu (accessed March 8, 2003).

Eames Chairs

Furniture designs

By: Charles and Ray Eames

Date: 1945, 1948

Source: Eames, Charles, and Ray Eames. Eames chairs. Lounge chair prototype, 1945; "La Chaise," 1948. Available online at http://www.loc.gov/exhibits/eames/images/vc9671.jpg; http://www.loc.gov/exhibits/eames/images/vcf23a.jpg; website home page http://www.loc.gov (accessed March 24, 2003).

About the Designers: Charles Eames (1907–1978) and Ray Eames (1912–1988) were a husband-and-wife team of interior designers and curators. Ray was also a painter, while

Charles and Ray Eames designed mass-produced furniture that was also modern and elegant. **ASSOCIATED PRESS/THE LIBRARY OF CONGRESS. REPRODUCED BY PERMISSION.**

Charles was an architect. Charles collaborated with Eero Saarinen, an architect and designer, on various design projects, most notably the formfitting shell chair. The Eameses are best known for designing mass-produced but comfortable and elegant furniture. An example is the famous Eames chair (1946), constructed of two pieces of molded plywood and joined by stainless steel tubing. They also designed houses and produced films. ■

Introduction

During World War II (1939–1945), Charles and Ray Eames worked with plywood to make aircraft parts and stretchers. After the war, they saw the need for furniture that the average consumer could afford. They understood at the same time that such furniture had to meet a high standard of quality. In particular, the Eameses realized how important the simple chair was in the daily life of modern society. Looking to make a functional piece of furniture, they departed from the traditional upholstered chair.

Their first experiment was the molded plywood chair, which could be mass-produced. These chairs were simple, functional, and inexpensive. They could be stacked by the dozen for storage and easily moved around because of their comparatively light weight. These chairs were shaped in the seat area and the back to give comfort. As inspiration

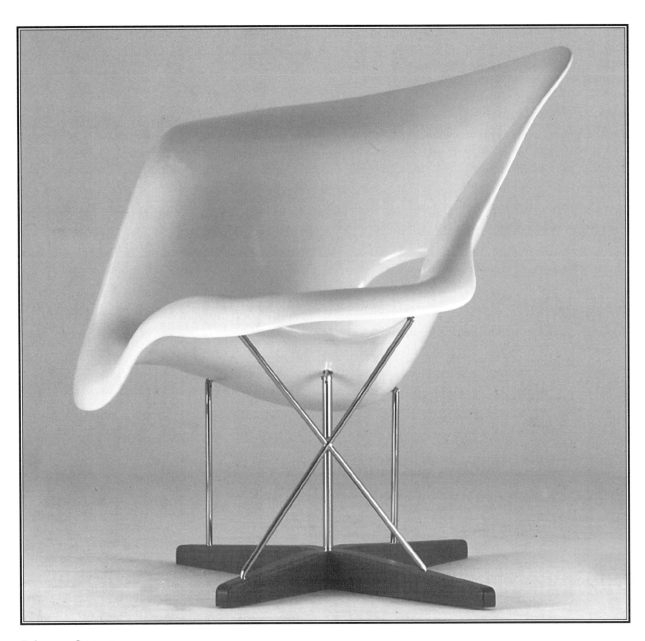

Primary Source

"La Chaise": Eames Chairs (1 OF 3)

SYNOPSIS: These photographs exhibit the creative energies of the Eameses by showing a representative variety of their contributions to the field of interior and industrial design. Especially important are the images of the various chairs, which had a huge impact on the nature of institutional furniture in America. This piece, called "La Chaise," was designed in 1948.
COURTESY OF VITRA DESIGN MUSEUM, WEIL AM RHEIN. REPRODUCED BY PERMISSION.

for the form of the chairs, the Eameses looked to such objects as animal traps, trays, baskets, and dress forms. For this new kind of furniture, they developed special production methods, including new welding techniques and special mold formations. The Eameses also made chairs out of plastic, wire mesh, and aluminum. In the medium of aluminum, the Eameses developed a multiple-seating system well suited for institutions. This involved hanging the

seating along the rails of an aluminum frame. In 1950, they switched to plastic material, creating the first one-piece fiberglass-reinforced plastic chairs.

Significance

The significance of the Eameses' contribution to American life is illustrated by the fact that versions of their plywood-and-wire chairs are still in production half

Primary Source

Eames Adjustable Jig for Chair: Eames Chairs (2 OF 3)
An adjustable jig, designed by Charles and Ray Eames, was used to determine the best shape for their molded plywood
chairs. Circa 1945. COURTESY OF VITRA DESIGN MUSEUM, WEIL AM RHEIN. REPRODUCED BY PERMISSION.

a century after their introduction. The Eameses' innovative designs were a perfect match for the post-World War
II economy and society. In the years since the war, our
economy has been transformed from the industrial blue-
collar kind, to the postindustrial, high-technology, white-
collar system. Millions of people make their living in
offices these days. Such offices need furniture, which has
to be functional, durable, and inexpensive. Also, students
attend schools, colleges, and universities in numbers not
seen before the war. They, too, need to sit in comfort-

able, inexpensive chairs in a myriad of classrooms, libraries, and cafeterias.

What the Eameses were confronting was a mass society, the needs of which had to be met on a massive
scale in terms of goods and services. This could be accomplished only through industrial production and marketing. The question then was whether mass-produced
items could be functional, as well as aesthetically pleasing to the eye. The Eameses believed that just because a
home or office had to be utilitarian did not mean it could

Primary Source

Lounge Chair Prototype: Eames Chairs (3 OF 3)
Designed by Charles and Ray Eames, this is a prototype of a lounge chair to be constructed of molded plywood, rubber, and "slunk-skin" upholstery, which was made from the skin of an unborn calf. COURTESY OF VITRA DESIGN MUSEUM, WEIL AM RHEIN. REPRODUCED BY PERMISSION.

not be attractive. The chairs they designed were not only colorful, but were also elegant, thereby positively affecting the moods and frames of mind of their users, and thus their quality of life.

Further Resources

BOOKS

Eames, Charles. *The World of Franklin and Jefferson: The American Revolution Bicentennial Exhibit.* Los Angeles: Rice, 1976.

Kirkham, Pat. *Charles and Ray Eames: Designers of the Twentieth Century.* Cambridge: MIT Press, 1995.

WEBSITES

"Charles and Ray Eames: A Legacy of Inventions." Library of Congress. Available online at http://www.loc.gov/exhibits /eames; website home page: http://www.loc.gov (accessed March 8, 2003).

"Building a Democracy"
Essay

By: Frank Lloyd Wright

Date: October 1946

Source: Wright, Frank Lloyd. "Building a Democracy." *Taliesin Square-Paper Number 10,* October 1946. Reprinted in Pfeiffer, Bruce Brooks, ed. *Frank Lloyd Wright: Collected Writings.* New York: Rizzoli, 1992.

About the Author: Frank Lloyd Wright (1867–1959) is considered the foremost twentieth-century American architect. For six decades Wright was responsible for the most innovative and beautiful designs for private homes and public buildings of any American architect. ■

Introduction

Frank Lloyd Wright opened his practice in 1893. From architect Louis Sullivan's doctrine that form should follow function in architecture, meaning that the style and materials of a building should embody its purpose, Wright developed his own belief that in a good building form and function are the same. He called his architecture "organic," or natural. He believed that a building should be an extension of the natural surroundings. The rooms should not be enclosed spaces but should flow into one another through shared spaces. Wright also developed a new vision of midwestern domestic architecture, the "Prairie Style," with its trademark long horizontals, overhanging eaves, and open interior spaces that echo the surrounding landscape.

Wright's design of the Imperial Hotel in Tokyo (1916–1922) was a resounding success, even more so when the building survived the 1923 earthquake. To complement his building projects, he began a regime of teaching and mentoring young architects, which continued throughout his career. At the beginning of the 1940s, Wright was considered the grand old man of American architecture. Many would have expected him to retire at the age of seventy-three, but Wright had a good many working years ahead of him. In the 1950s, he took fewer commissions, marshalling his forces for the fresh vision, which he was to bring to the Guggenheim commission (1957–1959). His idea for a circular museum building with a ramp taking the place of floors was as novel then as it is now.

In "Building a Democracy," a 1946 article, Wright discussed the similarities between organic architecture and organic democracy. He believed that just as organic architecture stems from nature and is intended for the life lived in that house or building, organic democracy comes from humanity's nature, or the essence of humanity, which is its independence and freedom to be itself.

Significance

Wright encapsulated the spirit of his career in his 1946 article. He stood for the development of a thor-

Architect Frank Lloyd Wright's unique style remained influential years after his death. **CORBIS-BETTMANN. REPRODUCED BY PERMISSION.**

oughly American approach to architecture. The neoclassical, Georgian, and Gothic revival styles that dominated America in the nineteenth and early twentieth centuries were unacceptable to Wright and the progressive architects of his generation because they had no real relationship to the experience of Americans in the twentieth century.

Wright's whole career was based on developing a uniquely American style of building, one that respected and enhanced the sovereignty of the individual. Some would argue that the events in Europe at this time called attention to the deficiencies in humanity's nature and to its inability to govern itself well. But Wright held that only the self-respecting citizen had any respect for others and humanity. Without this "sound human foundation," governments are founded on servility and secret hate. Democracy is founded on humanity's self-respect. It unleashes humanity's enterprise and demands its sacrifice and vigilance if democracy is to be preserved as a form of government. Democracy and a democratic architecture will prevail if the faith in the self-governing capacity of the individual prevails and is respected by architects.

In his emphasis on the need for builders to think of the human scale of projects, he was prophetic. Beginning in

"The American Quality" [excerpt]

No matter by what evidence the truth may be confronted, mankind in these United States is more individualized from day to day. Men *are* getting more and more concerned for their individuality. They *do* take increasing pride in the personal element. . . .

And now, we the people of these United States should stop this vain bluffing the enemy with out-moded murder-machines and prepare to defend ourselves permanently by building up defense from the beginning on a solid foundation. Build defense as straightforward as possible. Build up our own peculiar strength as single-mindedly from within as it is possible for us to build it. And build as unconcerned for everything remote or external as we can. The more we do this *as individuals* the purer and stronger we will become as a united people championing human Freedom.

The less we ally ourselves with alien forces; the less we rely upon these forces; the more we take of ourselves upon our own shoulders—the more nature will smile upon us in our effort to build an impregnable free nation. Our true defense is not military now, nor will it be ever if we know the truth about ourselves. Let this truth come through. If it is allowed to work, Democracy is far stronger than Fascism or Communism or any other ism. The idea of the absolute autonomy of a free man has created a power in this world mightier than anything that can be opposed to it!

We of this American Democracy are the natural bearers of this power. Let us stop wasting it and now make it felt. Military leaders equipped with all the planes, tanks, and guns in the world couldn't make it take effect.

■ ■ ■

Our national weakness lies in the fact that with us Faith and Being are yet to become one. . . .

Being and belief coincide, or nothing happens. The one great significance that will lead to this noble self-realization on our part is that the developed individual believes in himself, believes implicitly that innate good is in him. The more we, the people of these United States, discover of the hidden forces of nature, the more we will realize that self-realization, a noble selfhood, alone matters. Being and belief must coincide—be one power. Our country then is forever a great power, and only so is it a free country. God does become mightier in that process of self-realization, and it is irrelevant whether there are gods or not. In other words, whether Fascism or Communism, or all isms whatsoever, win or lose. . . .

For Democracy is of such sense and courage: the highest form of Aristocracy the world has ever known because it is integral in the nature of materials. Who would want to fight a nation built that way?

Certainly not Hitler.

SOURCE: Wright, Frank Lloyd. "The American Quality." *Scribner's Commentator,* October 1941, 35, 36, 46

---

the late 1970s, several urban planners of housing developments began to embrace Wright's ideas in the notion of human scale and defensible space. The "small is beautiful" movement owes everything to Wright's insistence on human scale. And if his notion of a "relaxed" building seems counterintuitive, one has only to look at some of the most recent triumphs of Frank Gehry, America's most celebrated living architect, to understand how Wright's vision is still the most farsighted in the American architectural tradition.

Primary Source

"Building a Democracy"

> **SYNOPSIS:** Wright's article is one of his many efforts to link democracy and architecture in the minds of Americans. He aims to make them more attentive and receptive to the work of progressive architects at a time of great change and confusion about the aims of these men.

Democracy and architecture, if both are organic, cannot be two separate things. Neither can democ- racy nor architecture be enforced, in any sense. Both must come from within, spontaneously. In architecture, as in democracy, this organic or natural way is new to us only because the interior nature of man is still new to mankind, and democracy is still a search for organic form.

Democracy is not so much a form—even were we to find it—or a policy—even were we to make it—as it is abiding faith in man's indivisible right to himself as himself. That faith is the natural essence of manhood and is therefore the only safe foundation for creative building. In so far as the State is concerned, it is the same. It is only the man with self respect who has any respect for others, and so is capable of faith in mankind, and thus of constructing a government. Lacking this sound human foundation, no government can rise above servility and secret hate. Collective security without this foundation *first* is merely illusion. Internationalism without this foundation *first* is coercion.

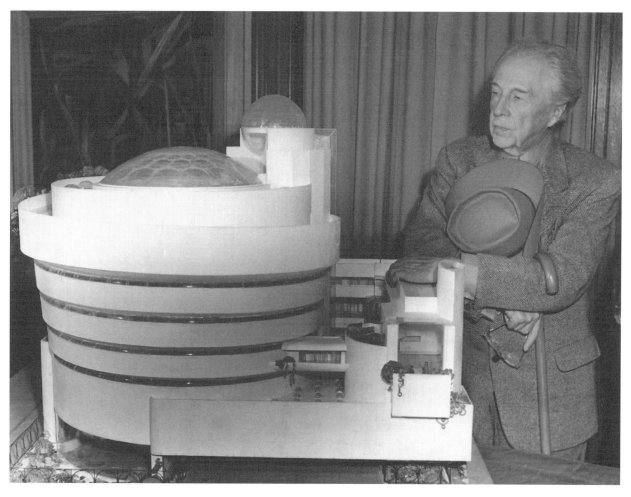

Frank Lloyd Wright displays a model of the New York City Guggenheim Museum, which he designed. Completed in 1959, it houses modern and contemporary art. **AP/WIDE WORLD PHOTOS. REPRODUCED BY PERMISSION.**

Man-made codes come in to obstruct, expropriate or punish only when we lose sight of the way to live naturally, as we build, and build naturally as we live.

Unfortunately for us, and the nature of democracy at this moment as well, the way of our literate official architecture is, owing to academic education, utterly inorganic. It is by code, and our way of life therefore is no longer free nor inspired by principle. How can a man's life keep its course if he will not let it flow from within? The democratic code must be designed to *complete,* not to *prevent* the man.

The mass to which we belong calls itself Democracy while betraying the courageous idea that the soulful source of all inspiring life flows from the individual. The other mass is obsessed by the cowardly idea of taking cover under a State supreme with no individual responsibility whatever.

To overcome false ideas, bad work or violent men, democracy has only to mind its own business,

stand its own ground, build its own way, the natural or organic way.

Were we genuinely a Democracy this violent division would be resolved, and there would be no adversary.

The structure Democracy must know is the living kind, and that kind of structure is of life at its best for the best of life itself. In itself, organic character is sound social foundation: integral or organic structure grown up from the ground into the light by way of the nature of man's life on earth, the method of building to show man to himself as nobly himself. The true architecture of democracy will be the externalizing of this inner seeing of the man as Jesus saw him, from within—not an animal or a robot, but a living soul. Organic life cannot grow from anything less than the independence of the individual as such—the independence of the individual: his freedom to be true to himself! And

"Falling Water House," designed by Frank Lloyd Wright. Wright captured the imagination of the American public by building this and other homes that embraced the natural landscape. **PHOTOGRAPH BY BILL HEDRICH/HEDRICH-BLESSING. CHICAGO HISTORICAL SOCIETY. REPRODUCED BY PERMISSION.**

since that cannot be enforced it cannot even be standardized.

Force is futile. It can organize nothing. Nor can science help us now. Science has put miraculous tools in our toolbox, but no science can ever show us how to use these tools for humanity. It is only natural or organic architecture, interior philosophy, and a living religion—not the institutionalized kind (I am talking now about the heart and the deep-seated instincts of man)—it is these three alone, organic

architecture, interior philosophy, and a living religion, that can make life again creative, make men as safe as is good for them, or ever make government tolerable. These three need each other at this crucial moment as never before. In the light of these three organic inspirations, revived and alive, we could build an organic democracy.

Here in America, if we will only discover what our vast good ground is good for, and use it to build with and build upon, a native culture would come to us from loving our own ground and allowing our ground to love us. A great integrity! The integrity! The integrity we lack!

We have no good reason here in America to give an imitation of a great industrial nation confined to a small island like England, whose only way out is manufacturing. Our entire nation from border to border and coast to coast is still just a neglected back yard while we have this cinder strip here in the East. A marvelous range of individual expression awaits us as a people when we do discover our own ground. Why are houses alike all over America? Why do we think they have to be so? Why are we as a people inhibited so early? Because we build by code. Sometimes I think we were born, live, and die by code. Give us freedom!

Let inspiration come to us the natural way. Why plant more Oxford-gothic on the plains of Oklahoma? Let us mimic no more. If we build in the desert let the house know the desert and the desert be proud of the house by making the house an extension of the desert. So that when you're in the house, the desert seems the house's own extension. The same thought, in the same feeling, goes for whatever we build wherever we build it. Organic buildings are always of the land and for the life lived in the building. They are not merely on a site, they are of it. Native materials for native life where such exist are better than plastics which have to be brought it. According to circumstances, both may be equally desirable.

And this idea that seems to have invaded our country from somewhere that architecture is one thing, landscape architecture another, and interior decoration a third is absurd. In organic architecture all three of these are one.

Whether a structure be life, a building, or a state, why buy more monstrosity?

Look at Washington. Is there a single-minded democratic, that is to say, organic, building there, one sincerely devoted to the nature of its purpose? Bureaucrats are there to work. How can they work in these miles of stone quarries erected to satisfy a grandomania as insatiable as it is insignificant?

Not satisfied, look at Moscow. The case is much the same. A new civilization, unable to find a way of building that is its own, slavishly reproduces the buildings of the culture it overthrew. It overthrew the great high ceilings, high chandeliers, pornographic statues playing on grand terraces. Only now they want the ceilings higher, five chandeliers. where

there was one before, and they want it all everywhere, even in the subway!

Not liking Moscow, see London! The greatest habituation on earth sunk in its own traditions, unable to see daylight anywhere—part of its charm, of course.

If you see within at all, you will see the same degradation in all. You will find them poisoned for democracy, one and all militaristic, their columns marshaled like soldiers menacing the human spirit, their opposing major and minor center lines of classic architecture—the true crucifixion.

A democratic building is at ease, it stands relaxed. A democratic building, again, is for and belongs to the people. It is of human scale, for men and women to live in and feel at home.

No wonder we were bound as things were and must struggle to be unbound as things are.

Were we to build a building for the United Nations we could not build for an incongruous idea anything but incongruity. The attempt of the nations now to get together is a hopeful sign. All this struggle is good. I have a feeling—it is only a hunch—that we have to make mistakes; we can't come upon the ideal thing right side up all at once.

I do know that when the home for the United Nations is built it must be a modern high-spirited place of great repose, an unpretentious building, abandoning all specious symbolism, having the integrity of organic character in itself, an example of great faith in humanity. Let the Assembly room be a place of light as wide open to the sky as possible (that influence is auspicious). Make it no screen to hide ignoble fears or cherish native hypocrisy cultured anywhere by any tradition. Like the human being it would prophesy—its basis the earth, its goal the universal.

If the United Nations is to be a success, it is all up to each of us right where we now are, in the citadels of democracy, our own homes. We love to call them our own. We wish to live there the life of brotherly love and creative sensitivity with full individual responsibility. But we want to live as potent individuals craving immortality, believing in ourselves, and therefore in each other, as with worldwide hospitality we strive for the things that seem more fair to live with and to live for.

When the organic architecture of Democracy is allowed to build for democratic life the organic or natural way, we the American people will recover nobility. Our creative sensitivity will then learn from right-minded architecture to see a man noble as MAN, a brick that is a BRICK, see wood beautiful as WOOD (not falsified by some demented painter). We will wish to have a board live as a BOARD and use steel as STEEL—the spider spinning—and we want glass to be the miracle life itself is. We will see, by means of it, interior space come alive as the reality of every building. We will learn that our greatest lack as a civilization is the beauty of organic integrity and that Beauty itself is the highest and finest kind of morality. When Democracy builds it will build the organic way and every man's building—his chosen government no less—will be benign.

If we love Democracy, the way to *do* is to *be.* I can see no fight for freedoms. In a democracy there is only FREEDOM.

Further Resources

BOOKS

Brooks, H. Allen. *Frank Lloyd Wright and The Prairie School.* New York: George Braziller, 1984.

Fitch, James Marston. "Architects of Democracy: Jefferson and Wright." In *Architecture and the Esthetics of Plenty.* New York: Columbia University Press, 1961.

Gill, Brendan. *Many Masks: A Life of Frank Lloyd Wright.* New York: Putnam, 1987.

Kaufmann, Edgar, Jr. *Fallingwater: A Frank Lloyd Wright Country House.* New York: Abbeville Press, 1986.

Pfeiffer, Bruce Brooks, ed. *Frank Lloyd Wright: Collected Writings, 1939–1949.* Vol. 4. New York: Rizzoli, 1995.

Sergeant, John. *Usonian Houses: Designs for Moderate Cost One-Family Homes.* New York: Whitney Library of Design, 1976.

Wright, Frank Lloyd. *Autobiography.* New York: Duell, Sloan and Pearce, 1943.

Periodicals

Secrest, Meryle. "An Architect with Love for Nature and Lots of Fight." *Smithsonian,* February 11, 1994.

WEBSITES

All-Wright Site: An Internet Guide to Frank Lloyd Wright. Available online at http://www.geocities.com/SoHo/1469/flw.html (accessed March 8, 2003).

"Frank Lloyd Wright: Designs for an American Landscape, 1922–1932." Library of Congress. Available online at http://www.loc.gov/exhibits/flw/flw.html; website home page: http://www.loc.gov (accessed March 8, 2003).

"Frank Lloyd Wright: Life and Work." Public Broadcasting Service. Available online at http://www.pbs.org/flw; website home page: http://www.pbs.org (accessed March 8, 2003).

AUDIO AND VISUAL MEDIA

Frank Lloyd Wright. Directed by Ken Burns and Lynn Novick. PBS Home Video, 1998, VHS.

The Farnsworth House

Architectural design

By: Ludwig Mies van der Rohe

Date: 1946–1951

Source: Mies van der Rohe, Ludwig. The Farnsworth House. 1946–1951. Friends of the Farnsworth House. Available online at http://www.farnsworthhousefriends.org/house.html (accessed March 8, 2003).

About the Architect: Ludwig Mies van der Rohe (1886–1969) was one of the major innovators of twentieth-century architecture. He was also an influential designer. His revolutionary architectural work is summed up in his famous phrase, "Less is more." ∎

Introduction

Ludwig Mies van der Rohe first achieved prominence with his designs for all-glass skyscrapers, which were never built but captured the imagination of generations of young architects. He would later realize part of these designs in the twin-tower apartment block of Chicago's Lake Shore Drive (1951) and the Seagram Building (1958) in New York.

Mies van der Rohe designed the German Pavilion for the 1929 Barcelona International Exposition, which

German-born architect Ludwig Mies van der Rohe moved to the United States in 1937. AP/WIDE WORLD PHOTOS. REPRODUCED BY PERMISSION.

Primary Source

The Farnsworth House (1 OF 3)

SYNOPSIS: The Farnsworth House is pictured in these photos as completed, showing both its modernistic beauty and its impractical aspects. An exterior view is pictured above. © 1997, 2001 PETER G. PALUMBO. REPRODUCED BY PERMISSION OF LORD PETER G. PALUMBO.

Primary Source

The Farnsworth House (2 OF 3)

An exterior, front view of the Farnsworth House. © 1997, 2001 PETER G. PALUMBO. REPRODUCED BY PERMISSION OF LORD PETER G. PALUMBO.

Primary Source

The Farnsworth House (3 OF 3)

An interior view of the Farnsworth House. © 1997, 2001 PETER G. PALUMBO. REPRODUCED BY PERMISSION OF LORD PETER G. PALUMBO.

attracted international acclaim for its classical poise and elegance, refinement of detail, and high degree of craftsmanship. In 1937, he moved to the United States to head the department of architecture at the Armour Institute of Chicago (now the Illinois Institute of Technology) until his retirement in 1958. He helped develop a comprehensive plan for the campus and designed nearly twenty individual buildings, which comprise the largest and most important collection of his work anywhere.

Mies van der Rohe's buildings transformed the downtown cores of major metropolitan cities in Europe and the United States. The clean lines and elegant profiles of his creations were an expression of the ambition felt by the cities' populations following World War II (1939–1945). In addition, he designed houses, which were as revolutionary as his commercial building designs.

In 1945, Edith Farnsworth commissioned him to design a weekend place on her ten-acre property located near Chicago. She instructed him to design an inexpensive home, giving him freedom to bring together his idea of universal space and the reality of steel structure. He arrived at a novel plan for the house: a transparent box, framed by eight exterior steel columns. Its interior was a simple room, subdivided by partitions and completely enclosed by glass. The exterior was an open, flexible space, and the floor hovered five feet above the ground, in part because the house was located on a floodplain. The house was constructed between 1949 and 1951.

Significance

The Farnsworth House is an example of post-World War II American home architecture. It is also Mies van der Rohe's summary statement of the spatial and architectural principles he first realized in the Barcelona Pavilion.

As the house neared completion, Farnsworth challenged Mies van der Rohe over the expenses and the lack of privacy. His philosophical ideas about the house interacting with nature made it expensive to build and maintain, as well as impractical to live in. For example, the glass walls, which were intended to dissolve the distinction between indoors and outdoors, made it stiflingly hot in the summer and afforded no privacy. In addition, the open porch gave no protection from mosquitoes. In the winter, the house was very expensive to heat and the glass walls fogged up. These problems created a rift between Farnsworth and Mies van der Rohe, leading to a lawsuit that the latter eventually won.

Then, in the April 1953 issue of *House Beautiful* magazine, the editor claimed that a sinister group of International Style architects supported by the Museum of Modern Art in New York City was trying to force Americans to accept a certain architectural design. The magazine indicated that the architecture was barren, impoverished, impractical, and destructive of individual possessions and of individuals themselves. It was hinted that communists were behind the undertaking. A list of International Style architects, including Mies van der Rohe's name, was published to warn readers.

For all her public complaints, Farnsworth continued to live in the house for almost twenty years. The house was acquired in the early 1970s by Lord Peter Palumbo, a wealthy British businessman. The Farnsworth House is now preserved as a state historical site.

Further Resources

BOOKS

Lambert, Phyllis. *Mies in America.* New York: Abrams, 2001.

Riley, Terrance, and Barry Bergdoll. *Mies in Berlin.* New York: Museum of Modern Art, 2001.

WEBSITES

"The Farnsworth House: Mies van der Rohe, 1946–1951." Graduate School of Architecture, Planning and Preservation, Columbia University. Available online at http://www.cc .columbia.edu/cu/gsapp/BT/GATEWAY/FARNSWTH /farnswth.html; website home page: http://www.arch .columbia.edu (accessed March 8, 2003).

"New Look and Revolt Against New Look"

Magazine article

By: *Time*

Date: September 15, 1947

Source: "New Look and Revolt Against New Look." *Time* 50, September 15, 1947, 49–50.

About the Publication: The first issue of *Time* appeared in 1923. Since that time, it has become one of the world's most widely read news magazines. The international publication is perhaps best known for its "Person of the Year" issue. This edition is published at the close of each year, and profiles the individual who, in the magazine's view, has had the most impact on world history in the previous twelve months. ∎

Introduction

The end of World War II (1939–1945) meant a return to normalcy, one aspect of which was women's fashion. American fashion designers could make the clothing they wanted without government restrictions. Although the clothing industry came out with various designs, none excited the public's interest; the result was that sales went down rather than up. A new style was needed and as American designers were creating new fashions, so were their Parisian counterparts.

Christian Dior (1905–1957) established his fashion house in Paris in 1946 and became famous for the New Look in 1947, which consisted of narrow shoulders, constricted waist, and long, full skirts. His designs were popular because of their classic elegance and feminine look. Dior was in some sense continuing the tradition of the royal court with its exaggerated features in dress and hair. Thus, he would accent the natural features of the female body almost to the point of absurdity, as had his predecessors in the royal court.

Sophie Gimbel's (1898–1981) "new look" was the counter-revolution to Dior's design. She avoided the extremes of his design. She realized that her more simple and unaffected rendition of what was causing a stir on the Paris runways could be achieved without pain to either the body or to the pocket book.

Significance

The idea that the public often benefits from the private ambition of private individuals is very well illustrated in the world of fashion. In the case of Dior, his novel idea of selling "licenses" for accessories, cosmetics, and hosiery bearing his name resulted in the global distribution of his creations toward the end of the 1940s.

In the case of Gimbel, we see a fashion designer in tune with the time. Instead of copying Dior's New Look, she made clothing that had the ease and comfort of male styles while retaining the elegance and charm desirable in women's clothing. For this, she is sometimes said to have contributed to the emancipation of women. The drive for success of these innovative designers has fueled the fashion revolutions of the twentieth century and, in the process, helped sustain a major industry and a key part of the consumer economy.

Primary Source

"New Look and Revolt Against New Look" [excerpt]

SYNOPSIS: In this excerpt on the fashion counter-revolution, we see the emergence of three things: the announcement of a new center of fashion in New York, the emergence of Sophie Gimbel, a new fashion leader, and finally, *Time* magazine's role in informing and shaping American opinion.

Not since Irene Castle bobbed her hair in 1914 had there been such turmoil, twitting and posturing among American women. What was going on? The

Women don bustle gowns in the style of those worn in the 1890s on an Atlantic City boardwalk. © BETTMANN/CORBIS. REPRODUCED BY PERMISSION.

search for the "New Look." What was the New Look? No one knew precisely.

Some fashion designers proposed hobble skirts, hoop skirts and skirts that flapped about the ankles. Some went in for padded shoulders; others padded hips. Some placed their trust in the back bustle, side bustle and the wasp-waist corset whose constrictions in the last century had been a mainstay of jokesmiths and had made its wearers subject to fainting fits and worse.

In short, fashion was up to its old trick—peddling, as Oscar Wilde observed, "that by which the fantastic becomes for a moment universal."

All this dithering convinced many a woman that the New Look was merely locked. In Georgia, a group of outraged men formed the League of Broke Husbands, hoped to get "30,000 American husbands to hold that hemline." In Louisville 1,265 Little Below the Knee Club members signed a manifesto against any change in the old knee-high style. And in . . . California, Mrs. Louise Horn gave a timely demonstration of the dangers lurking in the New Look. As she alighted from a bus, her new long, full skirt caught in the door. The bus started up and she had to run a block before the bus stopped and she was freed.

Revolution

Despite such minor setbacks, the style revolution rolled on. It had been too carefully planned to be stopped by such molehills as unorganized scoffers or individual critics. When war-time clothing restrictions were abandoned a year ago, designers had cautiously lowered hems a bit. This excited so little interest that the $4 billion women's clothing industry, one of the biggest in the U.S., fell into a frightening slump this spring. Orders in many lines fell off as much as 60% (some of this was due to manufacturers' waiting for fabric price cuts that never came). Obviously, what was needed was a sweeping change—a revolution in style that would make all the present styles unwearable.

As U.S. designers fell to this job with a will, they were ably abetted by Paris. There the brasshats of fashion, indifferent as always to the wishes or even the shapes of their subjects, panted to regain the attention, if not the prestige, which they had lost during the war. Almost before anyone could say *haute couture,* such Parisian newcomers as Christian Dior were making a great to-do about squeezing waists into wasp lines and padding out hips—and the revolution was on.

Counter-Revolution

As with most revolutions, this one bred its own counter-revolution. Last week, in the perfumed air of a pale blue room on the third floor of Manhattan's Saks Fifth Avenue, one act of that counter-revolution was being staged. There Designer Sophie Gimbel was displaying her fall collection of 125 models. In the world of high fashion, it was a notable event.

The collection constituted Sophie Gimbel's conception of the New Look. As head of Saks's famed Salon Moderne, its custom dress shop, Sophie is one of the top U.S. designers. Moreover, as the U.S. dress industry is well aware, she has a razor-keen sense, as sharp as any other designer's, of what U.S. women will finally choose to wear out of the hodge-podge of new styles. As far as the great mass-producing dress shops of Manhattan's Seventh Avenue are concerned, that makes Sophie a fashion chart. What she displays one week—at $255 a dress and up—is often what the Seventh Avenue lofts will be busily making into a reasonable facsimile a year later, for $49.50.

As Sophie's slim-waisted models swept about her salon last week, the carefully curried audience of women (and one sad husband looking like a Displaced Person) cooed with pleasant surprise. Nowhere was there a sign of fantastic extremes that had given the New Look its painful expression. Sophie had simply gone her own, independent way and created a New Look that was an easily recognizable alteration of the Old. Shoulders were padded slightly less than before and waists were narrower, but few were corseted, and daytime hemlines, only slightly lower, were still a long way from the ankles. ("Everyone," said Sophie, "knows that dresses were too short.")

In a word, Sophie was reassuring: she was telling the world that the New Look could be acquired with comparatively little pain to either torsos or pocketbooks. "After all," said she, "our girls have beautiful figures. Do you think they'll want to spoil them with padded hips? Even if they do like this tight waistline, how many are willing to go through the agony to get it? I put on one of those new corsets and after 15 minutes I had to take it off. I've never been so uncomfortable in my life."

Conservative Manifesto

Sophie has always been content to let more flashy designers go their own gait, and doesn't worry

about trying to set a trend. She believes in the maxim that the best-dressed women follow the fashions at a discreet distance. Her style is to be simple and unaffected. Says she: "I try to make a woman look as sexy as possible and yet look like a perfect lady." Many women want to look like that. Consequently, Sophie probably sells more clothes than any other designer, with the possible exception of her archrival, Hattie Carnegie.

At 49, her tall (5 ft. 8½ in.), slim figure is still a fashionable model's size (35 in. bust, 26 waist, 36 hips). She keeps it that way by calisthenics, by often walking to work from her Manhattan house, by dieting and by plenty of golf, which she plays in the high 80s. (She wears a girdle, as thin as possible, only because she doesn't think it's "nice" to go ungirdled.) Her working dress is usually one of her own simple black $300 daytime dresses.

She puts in a concentrated working day. Usually she is in her salon by 10 and works straight through, often without lunch, until 6. Her corner office is tiny (12 ft. by 15 ft.). Her desk has a bargain-basement clutter of sketches, snapshots and a teacup or two. For her big-spending customers, such as Mrs. E. F. Hutton, Mrs. Pierre du Pont and Mrs. James Van Alen, Sophie usually pops out of her office and plays salesgirl herself. She is quite a salesgirl, and can usually manage to charm the customers into wearing what she thinks they should. Before an adamantine customer who knows exactly what she wants, regardless, Sophie gracefully gives in. "I used to tell everyone when something wasn't becoming to them," she says. "Then they went right out to other shops and bought something like it anyway. Now I only tell it to those who'll take my advice."

Nor does Sophie worry about that bugaboo of smart shops—selling the same $500 dress to two women and having them both wear it to the same party. She tells her regular customers what their friends have bought. But occasional customers have to take their chances.

For designing, selling and overseeing the 300 fitters, seamstresses, etc. in her workshop, Sophie is paid $34,000 a year by her boss, who is also her husband—Adam Gimbel, president of Saks and cousin of Bernard Gimbel, president of the parent company, Gimbel Brothers, Inc.

Model at Work

Sophie and Adam live with her son, Jay Rossbach (by Sophie's first marriage), in a modernized four-story house on Manhattan's East 64th Street. (Their twin beds have "Sophie" and "Adam" cosily embroidered on the pillowslips.) Sophie's hobbies are collecting china dogs and raising tulips and rhododendrons in the small garden in the rear. They also lease a small, seven-room country house near Red Bank, N.J.

As boss of Saks, and as a genial extrovert who likes to air his opinions, Adam is not above telling Sophie how she ought to run her fashion business. Sophie usually ends such discussions: "Now, Adam dear, we've been all over that before. You know how familiar I am with the subject so let's not discuss it again."

Although Sophie works hard, she has enough time for an active social life and usually is not in bed before 1 A.M. Even at parties she is really working at modeling her own clothes. She seldom comes home from a party without a handful of orders for whatever she had on.

Further Resources

BOOKS

Burns, Leslie Davis, and Nancy C. Bryant. *The Business of Fashion.* New York: Fairchild, 1997.

De Rethy, Esmeralda. *Christian Dior: The Early Years, 1947–57.* London: Thames and Hudson, 2001.

Mulvagh, Jane. *Vogue: History of Twentieth Century Fashion.* London: Viking, 1988.

Olian, JoAnne, ed. *Everyday Fashions of the Forties.* New York: Dover, 1992.

PERIODICALS

Arnaud, Jean-Louis. "When Paris Sets the Tone." *Label France,* March 1996. Available online at http://www.france.diplomatie .fr/label_france/ENGLISH/DOSSIER/MODE/par.html; website home page: http://www.france.diplomatie.fr/label_france (accessed March 8, 2003).

WEBSITES

Fashion in the Forties. Available online at http://www.geocities .com/bloomergirl01970/wood.htm (accessed March 8, 2003).

"Vogue Archive." Cntraveller.com. Available online at http:// www.cntraveller.co.uk/content/ie4/159/1315-0-1-1.html; website home page: http://www.cntraveller.co.uk (accessed July 23, 2002).

"The Glass House, New Canaan, Connecticut"

Architectural designs

By: Philip Johnson

Date: 1949

Source: Johnson, Philip. "The Glass House, New Canaan, Connecticut." 1949. Reprinted in *Writings.* New York: Oxford University Press, 1979.

About the Architect: Philip Johnson (1906–) is a leading American architect and critic. He was already one of the most influential writers and curators on modern architecture, when he went back to school to become an architect. His notable collaboration with Ludwig Mies van der Rohe led to the construction of the Seagram Building skyscraper in New York (1958). In his later architectural work, he is credited with the invention of postmodernism, which consisted of an eclectic mix of modernism and other styles from the whole history of architecture. ■

Introduction

Philip Johnson made every effort to publicize the fact that his Glass House at New Canaan, Connecticut, was derivative in nature and could not have been created if it were not for the works of earlier figures in the field. He explained that "we are [the] descendants" of the "intellectual revolutionaries" from the baroque period because like them we are attached to the cube, the sphere, and other mathematical shapes. Johnson's taking the cube as the "absolute" form for his glass house (actually comprised of several structures) comes from a French legacy. He explained that the layout of the buildings is "pure neo-Classic Romantic" and reflects the Greek site planning as explained by Auguste de Choisy. His acknowledgment of his indebtedness to a wide range of architectural ideas was groundbreaking for an adherent of the International Style.

Johnson's house was a "modestly sized domestic grouping" and yet managed to concentrate a tremendously broad range of historical influences. His repeated borrowings from the historical past and avowed submissiveness to various classical and baroque influences, along with various modern trends, shows us that Plato's statement that "there is nothing new under the sun" has much to recommend it.

Johnson acknowledged that the idea for a glass house came from Mies van der Rohe, his mentor. Mies van der Rohe had suggested how easy it would be to construct a house out of large sheets of glass. He himself had designed a glass house called the "Farnsworth House" (1949–1951). The use of eighteen-foot panels of plate glass to construct a house was obviously going to have novel effects. The reflections generated by the glass sheets affect the view from the house—reflection, rather than light and shadow, plays the key role in what one sees.

Significance

Johnson's Glass House symbolizes the creative use of building materials, in this case, glass and steel beams. Johnson admitted that he drew on a wide variety of classical and contemporary styles. Obviously, the house was highly experimental and did not lead to a wave of urban subdivisions shimmering in the sun because of the glass material. But the modernistic style of the structure was part of the modern movement that had influenced housing

Primary Source

"The Glass House, New Canaan, Connecticut" (1 of 2)

SYNOPSIS: Built in 1949, Philip Johnson's Glass House is essentially a box with walls made entirely of glass with only a small cylindrical brick enclosure to house a bathroom and a fireplace. It has become a famous example of the possibilities of an open plan carried to its logical, extreme conclusion. JOHNSON GLASS HOUSE, DESIGNED BY PHILIP JOHNSON, NEW CANAAN, CONNECTICUT, 1986, PHOTOGRAPH BY RICHARD PAYNE. REPRODUCED BY PERMISSION.

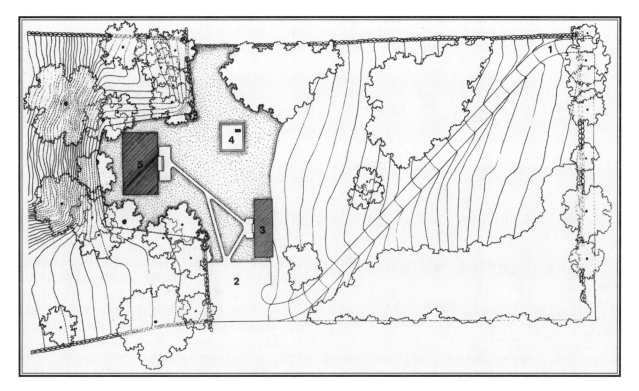

Primary Source

"The Glass House, New Canaan, Connecticut" (2 of 2)

Site plan for Glass House. Key to site plan: 1. Entrance. 2. Car park. 3. Guest house. 4. Sculpture. 5. Glass house. JOHNSON GLASS HOUSE, DESIGNED BY PHILIP JOHNSON, NEW CANAAN, CONNECTICUT, 1986, ILLUSTRATION FROM ARCHITECTURAL REVIEW, CVII, SEPTEMBER, 1950. REPRODUCED BY PERMISSION OF ARCHITECTURAL REVIEW.

design in the years following World War II (1939–1945). The date of the house's construction—1949—is significant in itself. It indicates that the structure was built in the early phase of the great postwar economic expansion, when both the cities and the suburbs were developing rapidly and in new ways.

Johnson's house reflects Americans' twin desires to enjoy the great outdoors and to have the creature comforts of home. His house makes the traditional brick and windows seem claustrophobic by comparison. When owners of the older-style houses came to renovate and modernize their more Victorian-style dwellings, they would do so under the influence of the ideas embodied in Johnson's Glass House.

Further Resources

BOOKS

Johnson, Philip. *Architecture, 1949–1965.* New York: Holt, Rinehart and Winton, 1966.

Johnson, Philip, and Henry-Russell Hitchcock. *International Style: Architecture Since 1922.* New York: Norton, 1966.

Johnson, Philip, Hilary Lewis, and John T. O'Connor, eds. *Philip Johnson: The Architect in His Own Words.* New York: Rizzoli International, 1994.

WEBSITES

"Philip Johnson." Fine Arts Department, Boston College. Available online at http://www.bc.edu/bc_org/avp/cas/fnart /fa267/pjohnson.html; website home page: http://www .bc.edu/bc_org/avp/cas/fnart/default.html (accessed March 8, 2003).

"Philip Johnson." The Great Buildings Collection. Available online at http://www.greatbuildings.com/architects/Philip _Johnson.html; website home page: http://www.greatbuildings .com (accessed March 8, 2003).

"Portrait of an Artist." Public Broadcasting Service. Available online at http://www.pbs.org/newshour/bb/environment /johnson_7-9a.html; website home address: http://www.pbs .org (accessed March 8, 2003).

"The Curse of Conformity"

Magazine article

By: Walter Gropius

Date: 1958

Source: Gropius, Walter. "The Curse of Conformity." *Saturday Evening Post,* 1958. Reprinted as "Unity in Diversity." In *Apollo in the Democracy: The Cultural Obligations of the Architect.* New York: McGraw-Hill, 1968, 21–32.

About the Architect: Walter Gropius (1883–1969) was a German American architect and educator. He was the founder of the Bauhaus (literally "house of building") school. His leadership led to a new unified and integrated approach to design education, which supplanted older schools and has

dominated the study of design in the twentieth century. After leaving Germany, he became chair of the school of architecture at Harvard University. ■

Introduction

It is impossible to imagine daily life in urban American without the glass-and-steel lines of its modern buildings. The movement that brought about the American modernist architectural revolution can very much be traced to two men: Walter Gropius and Ludwig Mies van der Rohe. Neither of these master builders of modern America was American-born, however. Born in Germany at the end of the 1800s, they came to America as the Nazis rose to power in Germany to direct architects and designers on a wholly new path—one as the chair of the architecture department at Harvard, the other as the designer and director of the Armour Institute of Chicago (now the Illinois Institute of Technology).

Gropius's article "Unity in Diversity" is based on his many years as the head of two of the most significant departments of architecture in Germany and the United States, as well as his practical architectural experience in both countries. He reflected on what he saw as the characteristic shortcomings of the "American mind" in this period: its emphasis on specialization, its worship of mass production, and the consequent stifling of individual diversity and independence of thought.

According to him, the artist and the artisan do not work together in America. He found the Puritan heritage, with its emphasis on the ethical over the aesthetic, to be the leading cause of this split. The Puritans, suspicious of art and emotions, placed emphasis on book learning, morality, and good works. This heritage has made the American education system stress book learning and specialization, rather than the importance of craft and the interrelationship of arts and technology.

Significance

Gropius called for a reform of precollege education along the lines of his reform of education in Germany at the Bauhaus and in the United States at Harvard. He advocated that scientific and technological education be integrated with practical and aesthetic activities by training students in the language of form, materials, and techniques, and allowing active participation by the students in planning and improving their environment.

Gropius and his followers were so successful in advocating their education reform that many of the problems he addressed in his article no longer exist in the United States. Students are taught at an early age to become comfortable with technological tools and with the principles of design so that they will be masters, rather than slaves, of their environment.

However, Gropius mentioned one problem that is still pervasive in American society as a whole: the worship of technological innovation for its own sake. One could say that this love affair with technology drives the economy. Yet, the growth of technology is so rapid and complex that we still feel uncomfortable programming most of the electronic appliances that we cannot live without. So we buy a new gadget to program the old ones. We have become two societies as a result: one of technicians, the other, their clients.

Primary Source

"The Curse of Conformity"

SYNOPSIS: In this article, Gropius brings a lifetime of experience as an architect and teacher to bear on the limitations of design education in the United States and sketches some principles that would improve such education.

Though American technique is the envy of the world, the "American way of life" does not command unqualified respect abroad. We have proved to all the peoples of the earth that it is possible for an energetic nation to raise its material and civic standards to undreamed of heights. The example has been zealously studied. Other nations are eager to adopt our magic formula. Yet they are reluctant to accept the idea that the American brand of technology provides the ultimate blueprint for the good life. Indeed, we ourselves are beginning to suspect that economic abundance and civic freedom may not be enough.

Wherein have we failed? In this attempt to analyze some of our shortcomings and to suggest remedies, I draw from my experience as an educator and practicing architect both in this country and abroad. I have also had considerable opportunities to observe the impact of American culture on older countries, especially those which have recently emerged from a feudal or colonial past . . . of a modern industrial society. Everywhere the introduction of mechanization has produced such confusion that the problems of the conversion have been more evident than the benefits.

I have become more and more convinced that we have failed to give leadership in the right direction. We have not exported, along with our technical and scientific skills, principles of wise application—mainly because we have not formulated such principles at home. For example, our biggest man-made objects, our cities, have steadily grown more chaotic

Walter Gropius was the founder of the Bauhaus architecture school, whose aesthetic was influenced by notions of industry and technology. THE BETTMANN ARCHIVE/CORBIS-BETTMANN. REPRODUCED BY PERMISSION.

and ugly, despite brilliant individual contributions to planning and design. For all the heroic efforts of conservationists, a good deal of our loveliest countryside is being bulldozed out of existence, a sacrifice to commercial exploitation. In our smaller towns people try hard to preserve a certain regional character and community spirit—a losing struggle against conformity imposed by mass production. Increasingly, patterns of taste dictated by purely commercial considerations win acceptance, and the natural feeling for quality and appropriateness is dissipated in the giddy tumble from novelty to novelty. The individual is so dazed by the profusion of goods which merchandising propagandists press upon him that he no longer retains much personal initiative or sales resistance.

What should be the goal of our stupendous economic progress? What do we really want to accomplish with our splendid new techniques for faster transportation and wider communication? So far they have merely accelerated our pace without bringing us near enough to our original democratic goal. Instead, the tools of civilization have outgrown us, and their multiplicity has exerted a dominance of its own, a dominance which impairs the individual's capability to seek and understand deeper potentialities. Our subservience to our own brain child, the machine, tends to stifle individual diversity and independence of thought and action—two factors which used to be strong components of the American image. We know, after all, that diversity in unity, not conformity, constitutes the fabric of democracy. Unless we can reconcile diversity with unity, we may end up as robots.

To this world we have transmitted our enthusiasm for new scientific and technical invention, but we worship the machine to such a degree that we have been accused of forsaking the human standards of value in its service. Our apologia is that the rapid progress of technology and science has confounded our concepts of beauty and the good life; as a result, we are left with loose ends and a sense of helplessness in the midst of plenty.

We can overcome this defeatism only by understanding that the inertia or alertness of our brain and heart, not the machine, decides our destiny. It is not the tool, it is the mind that is at fault when things get out of hand.

Extreme specialization has dulled our faculty to bring unity to our complicated existence, and this has led to a dissolution of cultural relationships. Consequently, life has become immeasurably impoverished. The spiritual life is being throttled by the all-engulfing rationalism of the "organization man." Man is in danger of losing his entity.

There is only meager evidence that we Americans recognize the urgent task confronting us—to shift the emphasis from "bigger" to "better," from the quantitative to the qualitative, and to give significant form and beauty to our environment. An evolution of this kind would add moral authority to material abundance and would open up frontiers that we have been slow to explore.

Why have we been so hesitant to implement the ideals implicit in the development of our particular way of life? Why does a nation committed to the promise of free universal education take so long to provide enough schools and teachers for its children? Why have we shown so little interest in good housing? And why have we not seen to it that our cities and towns are models of sound organic planning and architectural harmony?

One probable explanation for this last shortcoming is that America's Puritan colonizers, in their preoccupation with the development of an ethical code, paid little attention to the development of an aesthetic code. We are therefore to this day largely dominated by the tenets of a bygone world. The Puritans ignored the fact that aesthetic principles may release ethical powers, and that the codes should have been developed interdependently. The consequent absence in our society of a cultivated sense of beauty has left natural talent underdeveloped and has relegated the artist to an ivory tower.

Where aesthetic standards do prevail in this country, they stem mainly from a preindustrial era—vide our fondness for collecting antiques. But there can be no true relation between the artistic inspiration of that era and the present requirements of a mass audience.

These requirements have not been satisfied by the material production of the eight-hour working day. We are beginning to realize that two important ingredients—beauty and inner resourcefulness—are missing in our brave new world. Cultural problems cannot be solved by intellectual processes only. We must go down to the roots to reawaken in every individual the ability to understand and create form.

How can such a renascence be achieved in a society almost exclusively devoted to commercial exploits and the accumulation of factual data? This may seem a strange question to ask in a country that fosters so many institutions designed to preserve art treasures and to encourage artistic activities. It is true that these institutions—the museums, art associations, and foundations—perform a valuable service, but they can do no more than impart "art appreciation" to those who feel they can afford what they consider a luxury. They exert little influence on schools, where art is of secondary importance to the study of English, history, and mathematics.

At one time, standards of taste were imposed through power or example by the leading feudal caste. Later on the business tycoons, for better or worse, influenced others to follow their personal preferences or whims. Our generation takes its cultural guidance from groups of their fellow citizens—school boards, city councils, women's clubs—chosen by popular consent to make important cultural decisions. This is as it should be, for democratic principles not only permit but demand that each individual bring his personal conviction and insight to bear upon his surroundings.

But how have these citizens trained themselves to deserve confidence in their judgment? How have they learned to distinguish between diversity and anarchy, between organic planning and mere accumulation? We assume too much if we expect them to function properly in this role without having had a chance to develop powers of discrimination. They must first be made aware of the possibilities of promoting a stimulating environment for themselves and their community rather than resorting to clichés or pinchpenny expediency. As it is, their education rarely leads to a grasp of organic development and visual beauty. The pseudoartistic examples of design that reach them through aggressive sales techniques, with their competitive assault of chaotic shapes and colors, is apt to reduce them to a state of sensorial apathy.

We need to revitalize our natural creative capacities which for so long have been allowed to atrophy. It will not, of course, be easy to recapture a birthright almost completely forsaken. The effort must begin in school, during the child's formative years.

To accomplish this, our educational system, with its overemphasis on fact-finding, must cultivate altitudes which will integrate emotional experience with scientific and technical knowledge. The strong puritan bias in our national origin, mistrustful of emotional responses, has so influenced education that natural impulses have been inhibited and the artistic imagination cannot take wing. We must overcome such prejudices and broaden our educational approach to include the recognition of emotional impulses, controlling rather than suppressing them, an atmosphere in which the artist could flourish not as an isolated phenomenon, ignored or rejected by the crowd, but as an integral part of our public life.

We already let our children in kindergarten recreate their surroundings in imaginative play. This interest, in one form or another, should be intensified and perpetuated all the way through school and college. Practical design problems in form, color, and space relations should be studied and actual materials used for their representation. In such an educational concept I do not view book learning as an end in itself, but rather as a means to illuminate practical experience. It should become second nature for the student to adopt a constructive attitude toward the appearance of his own habitat so that in later life he may creatively participate in its development.

Nothing promotes an understanding of environmental planning better than active participation in it. If such a general spirit penetrates society at all levels, the artistically gifted will then respond naturally and exuberantly, giving expression to the common desire. The artist's work and message will be understood by all people, not just by one group or clique.

The modern artist is frequently accused of moving in an exclusive world of his own, a stranger to his fellow men. But a true artist is always a candid interpreter of his society. If his society has few clear aims and standards, his work will reflect that lack. Instead of condemning him if he does not produce soothing entertainment, we should heed and try to understand his message. The interpretation of beauty constantly changes with the development of philosophy and science, and as the artist is sensitive to the spiritual and scientific concepts of his time, he intuitively expresses them. If we cannot always follow him, the fault may lie in our complacency toward the very forces that shape our times. There is no cause to berate the artist for deliberate mystification or frivolity when we, his audience, have lost interest in his search for a symbolic expression of contemporary phenomena. Our society desperately needs his stabilizing influence to moderate the furious tempo of science and industry.

What kind of educational climate must we provide to fire the imagination of a potential artist and equip him with an infallible technique? Out of a passionate concern with this problem, realizing that the lone "visionary" had little chance to change the general education or industrial system, I took it upon myself almost forty years ago to found a pilot institute. This was the Bauhaus School of Design in Weimar and later Dessau, Germany. The faculty, whom I recruited from the ranks of the most advanced painters, sculptors, and architects of the day, and I shared the belief that it was essential to select talented young people before they had either surrendered to the conformity of the industrial community or withdrawn into ivory towers. We proposed to train them to bridge the gap between the rigid mentality of the businessman and technologist and the imagination of the creative artist. We wanted our students to come to terms with the machine without sacrificing their initiative, so that they might bring to mass production, to architecture, and to community planning a sense of order and beauty.

To that end we combined our efforts to evolve a teachable, supra-individual language of form based on psychological and biological factors. This language was to furnish the student with an objective knowledge of visual facts. Beyond that, it was to establish a common background for spontaneous artistic creation, saving the work of the artist from arbitrariness or isolation and making it part of the development of a genuine *Zeitgeist,* away from the I-cult. Our object was not to supply a new set of recipes, but to inculcate a new set of values reflecting the thought and feeling of our time. That goal could be approached only by an unfettered search for the laws governing materials and techniques as well as those governing human psychology. Our students were first taught the psychological effects of form, color, texture, contrasts, rhythm, light, and shade. They were familiarized with the rules of proportion and human scale. They were encouraged to explore the fascinating world of optical illusions, indispensable to the creation of form. The student was led through many stages of creative experience with various materials and tools to make him aware of their potentialities as well as his own talents and limitations.

After this basic course the students were trained in a specialized craft of their own choice. The instruction in craftsmanship given in the Bauhaus workshops was not an end in itself, but a means of education. The aim was to turn out designers able, by their intimate knowledge of materials and working processes, to produce models for industrial mass production, which were not only designed but made at the Bauhaus. These designers had to be fully acquainted with the methods of production on an industrial scale and so, during their training, they were assigned temporarily to practical work in factories. Conversely, skilled factory workmen came to the Bauhaus to discuss the needs of industry with the staff and the students.

The Bauhaus was not concerned with producing designs of ephemeral commercial gadgets. It was rather a laboratory for basic research into design problems of all types. Staff and students succeeded in giving their work a homogeneity based not on external, stylistic features, but on a fundamental approach to design which resulted in standard products rather than novelties.

In short, the purpose of the Bauhaus was not to propagate any style, system, or dogma, but to exert a revitalizing influence on design. We sought an approach to education which would promote a creative state of mind and thus help to reestablish contemporary architecture and design as a social art.

The influence of the Bauhaus on American design and design curricula has been widespread. Its lesson is particularly applicable in this country because nowhere else is the assembly-line method so firmly entrenched and, consequently, nowhere does a greater need exist for a guide to standards of excellence in mass production. A firm resolve to mass-produce goods of both technical quality and cultural

significance would have far-reaching effect because the world has learned to watch the United States for signposts to where the journey into the machine age is heading. So far, the rest of the world has been thrilled by some of the achievements of United States designers and manufacturers, but more often it has been merely snowed under by an avalanche of poorly designed gadgets, the modish fluctuations of an industry bent on attracting customers by entertainment value rather than by quality. Respect for a sound standard product, combining function with aesthetic value, is at a low ebb. Merchandising catch-words attempting to glorify every trilling industrial product have beclouded the issue. There is no sustained effort to determine which features of our vast industrial civilization represent the best and lasting values and should therefore be cultivated to form the nucleus of a new cultural tradition for the machine age. Instead of recognizing that cultural achievement stems from the selection of the essential and typical, we exalt quantity.

Selectivity is a criterion of a balanced culture. Indiscrimination leads to cultural anarchy. To achieve true standards, we must first cultivate a voluntary discipline, acknowledging that there is greater excitement and promise of beauty in purposeful limitation than in mere accumulation. Variety for variety's sake as a continuous national program will eventually surfeit even the most voracious consumers and alienate our warmest admirers abroad.

The idea of limitation has never greatly appealed to Americans. Early in their history they embarked on the ambitious plan of proving that material blessings could be shared by all. But having largely accomplished this we must now open new doors. One of the brightest prospects will be the creation of visual order out of our chaotic modern scene by cooperative efforts and coordinated planning.

Obviously, the ideas which finally crystallize into an aesthetic principle must be rooted in society as a whole, not in individual genius alone. *But it is a common background of distinct altitudes that the artist needs to relate his own contribution successfully to an established social order.* In all great cultural periods unity of form has been given to the man-made environment. This, in retrospect, we call "style." To reach this goal, we must restore the influence of the artist. We must establish him in our industrial framework as a full-fledged member of the production team along with the engineer, the scientist, and the businessman. Only together can they combine low cost, good technique, and beautiful form in our products. Initiative in business must be balanced by initiative in cultural fields. *To become fully mature a democracy must bestow the highest prestige upon the artist.*

The American sophisticate roams the world today nostalgically searching for products that do not bear the stamp of mass production and sales organization. This is a sentimental journey to recover what he has lost at home. He seeks standard products whose usefulness and beauty have been patiently developed by the skill and unwavering good sense of generations of craftsmen, and which, ironically, have now become curios for connoisseurs. The thrill of acquisition grows rarer as economic pressures force other countries to remake themselves in the American image of mechanical mass production. Meanwhile, whoever turns his back on his own civilization forfeits the chance to perform a service which his heritage, his basic philosophy, and present need urgently demand of him—namely, to turn the calamities of the machine age into assets by inculcating the desire for quality and beauty in the producer as well as in the consumer.

As long as our "cultured" elite insist that undiscriminating popular taste is beyond repair, that salvation lies only in imposing upon an uncomprehending public an authoritative aesthetic formula, they will sidestep the particular obligation of a democratic society—to work from the ground up instead of from the top down. The dicta of the illuminati derive from an epoch when cultural matters were the concern of an elite who could enforce standards of taste, as well as of production. This cannot suffice in our present democratic system. *A social organization that has conferred equal privileges on everybody must fi-*

nally acknowledge its duty to prevent such privileges from being wasted through ignorance and unresponsiveness. This can be accomplished only by gradually raising the general level of perceptiveness and discrimination, not by handing down formulas from above. Aesthetic creativeness cannot survive either as the privilege and occupation of an esoteric few or as an embellishing cloak thrown over the unlovely features of the contemporary scene. It should be a primary function of all, with a solid foundation in popular custom. *Unity in diversity*—the symbol of culture and its sublime manifestation.

The next generation may witness such a unification of society. The role of the artist will then be to find the humanized image for society's aspirations and ideals. By virtue of his ability to give visible symbols to significant order, he may once again become society's seer and mentor and as a custodian of its conscience solve the American paradox.

Further Resources

BOOKS

Gropius, Walter. *The New Architecture and the Bauhaus.* London: Faber and Faber, 1935.

WEBSITES

Lilleystone, Angela. "Walter Gropius." University of Massachusetts, Boston. Available online at http://www.cs.umb.edu/~alilley/baugropius.html; website home page: http://www.cs.umb.edu (accessed March 8, 2003).

"Walter Gropius." The Great Buildings Collection. Available online at http://www.greatbuildings.com/architects/Walter_Gropius.html; website home page: http://www.greatbuildings.com (accessed March 8, 2003).

"Walter Gropius." Vitruvio.ch. Available online at http://www.vitruvio.ch/arc/masters/gropius.htm; website home page: vitruvio.ch (accessed March 8, 2003).

5

GOVERNMENT AND POLITICS

AMY H. STURGIS

Entries are arranged in chronological order by date of primary source. For entries with one primary source, the entry title is the same as the primary source title. Entries with more than one primary source have an overall entry title, followed by the titles of the primary sources.

Important Events in Government and Politics, 1940–1949

1940

- On January 3, in his State of the Union Address, President Franklin D. Roosevelt asks Congress for $1.8 billion for defense, an unprecedented sum that alarms isolationists.

- On January 26, the 1911 U.S.-Japan Treaty of Commerce expires, and Secretary of State Cordell Hull informs the Japanese government that trade will continue only on a day-to-day basis.

- On June 3, the War Department agrees to sell Britain millions of dollars' worth of outdated munitions and aircraft.

- On June 10, President Roosevelt declares that U.S. policy is changing from "neutrality" to "non-belligerency." Isolationists predict that this shift will lead to America's entrance into the war.

- From June 11 to June 13, Congress passes both the Naval Supply Act and the Military Supply Act, authorizing $3.3 billion for defense projects.

- On June 28, Republicans nominate Wendell L. Willkie as their presidential candidate; Charles McNary is nominated as his running mate two days later.

- On June 28, Congress passes the Alien Registration Act (Smith Act), which requires registration and fingerprinting of all foreigners in the United States and makes it illegal to advocate the overthrow of the U.S. government.

- From July 15 to July 19, the Democratic National Convention nominates Roosevelt for an unprecedented third term. Henry A. Wallace is chosen as his running mate.

- On September 3, the United States agrees to give fifty destroyers to Great Britain in exchange for rights to construct naval and air bases on British territories in the Western Hemisphere.

- On September 16, President Roosevelt signs the Selective Service Act, requiring men ages twenty-one to thirty-five to register for military training.

- On September 26, President Roosevelt announces an embargo on exporting scrap iron and steel except to Britain and the Western Hemisphere, cutting off Japan from vital raw materials.

- On September 27, the Tripartite Pact, a ten-year military and economic alliance between Germany, Italy, and Japan, is formalized. The three Axis powers pledge mutual assis-

tance to one another in case of attack by any nation not already at war with another member.

- On November 5, President Roosevelt is reelected.

- On December 29, President Roosevelt delivers his "arsenal of democracy" speech, pledging to become the chief munitions supplier of the Allies.

1941

- On January 6, in his State of the Union Address President Roosevelt asks Congress to support the Lend-Lease program. He also outlines the "four essential freedoms" for which the Allies are fighting: freedom of speech, freedom of worship, freedom from want, and freedom from fear.

- On March 11, Congress passes the Lend-Lease Act, extending credit or arms to Britain in exchange for items or services of equal value. The initial appropriation is $7.8 billion.

- On June 22, Germany declares war on the Soviet Union, betraying the Hitler-Stalin Pact. President Roosevelt promises Joseph Stalin Lend-Lease assistance to aid the Soviets.

- On June 25, to avert a march on Washington by civil rights advocates, the president establishes the Fair Employment Practices Committee to prevent racial discrimination in defense plants.

- On July 25, in response to the Japanese invasion of Indochina on June 24 the United States freezes all Japanese assets.

- On August 14, President Roosevelt and British prime minister Winston Churchill meet to discuss the Atlantic Charter, which becomes the blueprint for the United Nations.

- On September 11, after the September 4 German attack on the U.S.S. *Greer,* President Roosevelt orders a "shoot on sight" policy against all Axis ships within the U.S. sea frontier, beginning an undeclared naval war in the North Atlantic.

- On November 17, in Washington, D.C., Japanese ambassador Nomura Kichisaburo and special envoy Kurusu Saburo suggest that war could result if the United States does not remove its economic embargo and refrain from interfering with Japanese activities in China and the Pacific.

- On December 7, Japan attacks Pearl Harbor, Hawaii, as well as U.S. bases in the Philippines, Guam, Midway, and Wake Island.

- On December 8, calling the Japanese attack "a date which will live in infamy," President Roosevelt asks Congress for a declaration of war against Japan. Only one member fails to vote for the declaration: Rep. Jeannette Rankin of Montana, a committed pacifist who also voted against American involvement in World War I.

- On December 11, Germany declares war on the United States, with Italy following suit.

- On December 22, President Roosevelt signs a new draft act requiring all males ages eighteen to sixty-five to register for military service and all males twenty to forty-four to be prepared to enter active duty.

1942

- On January 1, with twenty-five other nations, the United States signs the Declaration of United Nations. All of the countries affirm their alliance against the Axis and pledge not to make a separate peace with Germany.

- On January 12, the National War Labor Board is established to settle labor disputes.

- On January 30, the Emergency Price Control Act takes effect, placing ceilings on prices and rents.

- On February 19, President Roosevelt issues Executive Order 9066, authorizing the removal of Japanese Americans on the West Coast from their homes and their internment in concentration camps.

- From May 4 to May 9, in the Battle of the Coral Sea, the first sea battle in which ships do not confront each other but dispatch aircraft to attack the other's fleet, the United States wins its first significant victory and thwarts Japan's advance southward to Australia.

- On May 6, all U.S. forces in the Philippines surrender after the fall of Corregidor.

- From June 4 to June 6, in the turning point of the Pacific naval war the Japanese lose the Battle of Midway, which stops their advance across the Pacific. After this crucial battle the Japanese will fight a defensive war.

- On June 25, Major General Dwight D. Eisenhower is appointed commander of U.S. forces in Europe.

- On November 3, in midterm elections the Republicans gain significantly. Though Congress is still run by Democrats, a loose coalition of conservatives from both parties dominates.

- On November 8, Operation Torch begins with four hundred thousand Allied troops landing in Algeria and Morocco in northern Africa. Under the command of General Eisenhower, the invasion is intended to secure the Suez Canal and oil reserves of the Levant, to aid in the assault on Italy, to relieve pressure on the Red Army, and to support the British offensive in Egypt.

- On November 13, the Selective Service Act is amended to draft males as young as eighteen.

1943

- On January 14, the Casablanca Conference begins. By January 24, President Roosevelt and Prime Minister Churchill decide to demand unconditional surrender from the Axis.

- From May 7 to May 9, Axis troops surrender in North Africa.

- On May 27, President Roosevelt creates the Office of War Mobilization to coordinate the nation's total war effort. He also issues an executive order requiring anti-discrimination clauses in all government/industry war contracts.

- On July 10, the Allied invasion of Sicily begins.

- On August 17, Axis troops surrender in Sicily.

- On September 3, the Allies launch an invasion of Italy.

- On November 26, at the conclusion of the Cairo Conference, Roosevelt, Churchill, and Chiang Kai-shek of China

agree that all Chinese territories seized by Japan will be returned and that Korea will be granted independence.

- From November 28 to December 1, in the first meeting with all three Allied leaders present, Roosevelt, Churchill, and Stalin meet at Tehran to plan the Allied invasion of Europe.

- On December 17, Congress repeals all Chinese Exclusion Acts enacted throughout the century.

- On December 24, General Eisenhower is named commander of all Allied forces in Europe.

1944

- On June 6, the long-planned "Operation Overlord," the invasion of Nazi-occupied France, begins on D-Day on the beaches of Normandy in northern France.

- On June 22, President Roosevelt signs the Serviceman's Readjustment Act, better known as the GI Bill of Rights. Providing low-interest loans for postwar housing and funds for education, the act will change the demographic map of the United States by fostering suburbanization and will open up higher education to many working-class Americans for the first time.

- On June 28, meeting in Chicago, the Republican Party nominates Governor Thomas E. Dewey of New York for president and Governor John Bricker of Ohio for vice president.

- On July 21, the Democratic Party nominates Roosevelt for an unprecedented fourth term as president. Senator Harry S. Truman of Missouri is nominated to replace Henry Wallace as vice president.

- On July 22, the Bretton Woods Conference in New Hampshire, begun July 1, ends. Representatives of forty-four nations, not including the Soviet Union, establish the International Monetary Fund (IMF) and the International Bank for Reconstruction and Development (the World Bank). The United States provides 25 percent of the capital for the IMF and 35 percent for the World Bank, giving it effective leadership of the postwar economy.

- On August 25, Paris is liberated by Allied forces.

- On September 11, American forces enter Germany.

- On September 16, at the second Quebec Conference, Roosevelt and Churchill agree on the division of Germany into occupied zones.

- On October 7, the Dumbarton Oaks Conference in Washington, D.C., ends, with the United States, Britain, the Soviet Union, and China agreeing on the basis for the United Nations Charter and the structure of the organization.

- On October 20, U.S. forces invade Leyte Island in the Philippines under the leadership of General Douglas MacArthur.

- On November 7, President Roosevelt wins an unprecedented fourth term.

- On December 16, German forces launch a surprise counteroffensive, seeking to thwart the Allied invasion. Succeeding at first in throwing back Allied troops, the Germans push deep into the Ardennes Forest of Belgium, creating a bulge in the Allied lines. Within a month the Germans have lost the Battle of the Bulge.

1945

- On February 11, the Yalta Conference ends with Roosevelt, Churchill, and Stalin agreeing on the postwar division of Europe and Asia, on the treatment of war criminals, and on holding the first meeting of the United Nations to discuss further issues.

- On April 12, President Roosevelt dies. Truman is sworn in as president.

- On April 25, American and Russian troops meet at the Elbe River in a great show of camaraderie and fraternity.

- On May 8, Germany surrenders, ending the European war. Victory in Europe (V-E) Day is declared in the United States as massive celebrations erupt.

- On June 5, the United States, Britain, France, and the Soviet Union agree to the division and occupation of Germany and to a similar division of Berlin. Future failure to agree on terms for the reunification of Germany will lead to tensions between the West and the Soviets.

- On June 21, Japanese troops surrender at Okinawa.

- On July 16, the first atomic bomb is detonated at Alamogordo, New Mexico.

- On July 17, President Truman attends the first session of the final wartime conference between the Allies at Potsdam, Germany, and issues an ultimatum to Japan.

- On July 28, the Senate ratifies the United Nations Charter by a vote of 89-2.

- On August 6, the United States drops an atomic bomb on Hiroshima, Japan. The resulting devastation amazes even the scientists who created it. More than fifty thousand people perish in seconds, and four square miles of the city are reduced to rubble.

- On August 8, in keeping with previous agreements, the Soviet Union enters the war in the Far East.

- On August 9, a second atomic bomb is dropped on Nagasaki in southern Japan, killing forty thousand Japanese civilians immediately. Tokyo announces its intention to surrender.

- On August 27, the Allies begin to divide Korea, with the Soviets occupying territory north of the thirty-eighth parallel, the Americans the southern half of the peninsula.

- On September 2, Japan signs a formal surrender onboard the U.S.S. *Missouri* in Tokyo Bay.

- On September 6, President Truman presents his economic recovery plan to Congress. Later known as the "Fair Deal," the program promises full employment, a substantial raise in the minimum wage, the extension of Social Security, national health insurance, federal aid to education, and government-sponsored housing for the poor.

- On October 2, the London Conference ends with the failure of Soviets and Western Allies to reach agreement about peace treaties to be signed with Germany and her allies.

- On November 19, President Truman asks Congress to establish a compulsory universal health-insurance program.

1946

- On January 10, the first General Assembly of the United Nations meets in London.

- On February 21, President Truman establishes the Office of Economic Stabilization to guide conversion to a peacetime economy.

- On February 22, at the U.S. embassy in Moscow, George F. Kennan dictates his influential "Long Telegram" assessing Soviet foreign policy; it is an early articulation of his theory that the U.S. government must contain Soviet expansion.

- On March 5, former prime minister Churchill delivers his "Iron Curtain" speech at Westminster College in Fulton, Missouri, with President Truman in attendance.

- On July 4, the United States grants political independence to the Philippines, though maintaining the right to station ships and planes on Philippine territory at Subic Bay and Clark Air Base.

- On July 25, reacting to the concerns of consumers and labor, President Truman signs a bill extending wartime price controls for one more year.

- On September 20, U.S. secretary of commerce Henry A. Wallace is forced to resign after publicly criticizing President Truman's conduct of U.S.-Soviet relations. Wallace proclaims that American actions are promoting a dangerous arms race, advocating instead "friendly, peaceful competition" with the Soviets.

- On November 5, Republicans gain control of both the House of Representatives and the Senate.

- On November 9, responding to pressures from business and conservatives, President Truman lifts price controls on most consumer goods even though recently enacted legislation is supposed to safeguard against this for six more months.

- On December 5, despite conservative opposition, especially in the South, President Truman issues Executive Order 9809, creating the Committee on Civil Rights to investigate the treatment of African Americans in the United States.

1947

- On March 12, announcing his "containment policy," President Truman declares that the United States will provide four hundred million dollars to Greece and Turkey to fight communism. The "Truman Doctrine" will commit the United States to becoming a global anticommunist policeman.

- On March 21, reflecting concern about the growing power of the presidency, Congress approves the Twenty-second Amendment to the U.S. Constitution, which would limit the president to two four-year terms or to ten years in office.

- On March 22, both reflecting the rising tide of anticommunism and spurring it on, President Truman announces a program to investigate the loyalty of government employees.

- On June 5, at Harvard University commencement exercises, Secretary of State Marshall announces the European Recovery Plan that will bear his name. Ultimately the nations of western Europe will receive more than twelve billion dollars in aid for reconstruction.

• On June 23, over President Truman's veto, Congress passes the Taft-Hartley Act (Labor Management Relations Act), which bans the closed shop by which only union members may be hired and which permits employers to sue unions for damages incurred in strikes. The act also allows the government to enforce an eighty-day cooling-off period, forbids political contributions by unions, and requires union leaders to swear they are not Communists.

• On July 26, the National Security Act abolishes the old Department of War, replacing it with a new Defense Department. The act also creates the National Security Council and the Central Intelligence Agency.

• On September 2, President Truman signs the Inter-American Treaty of Reciprocal Assistance (Rio Pact), in which nineteen American nations commit themselves to "collective defense against aggression."

• On October 29, President Truman endorses the report of his Committee on Civil Rights calling for an end to segregation in every aspect of American life, urging that steps be taken to implement social, political, and economic equality.

• On December 29, Henry A. Wallace announces that he will run for president as a third-party candidate.

1948

• On April 30, the International Conference of American States, with twenty-one members in attendance at Bogotá, Colombia, establishes the Organization of American States (OAS).

• On May 1, the Democratic People's Republic of Korea (North Korea) is established. The Republic of South Korea is established later in the year.

• On May 14, Israel declares its independence from Britain as a sovereign state. The United States becomes the first nation to recognize the new country.

• On June 7, the United States and its western European allies formulate a plan to create West Germany.

• On June 24, President Truman signs a new Selective Service Act requiring all males eighteen to twenty-five to register for military service.

• On June 24, Republicans nominate Thomas E. Dewey as their presidential candidate. Earl Warren is named as his running mate.

• On June 26, in response to the Soviet shutdown of all traffic from the West into Berlin on June 24, the United States initiates the Berlin airlift. For the next year nearly 275,000 flights will provide Berliners with 2.3 million tons of food and fuel.

• On July 15, the Democratic National Convention nominates Truman for reelection, with Senator Alben Barkley of Kentucky as his running mate.

• On July 17, having walked out of the Democratic convention, Southern Democrats form the States Rights Party ("Dixiecrats") and nominate Governor Strom Thurmond of South Carolina for president. Their platform stresses states' rights and racial segregation.

• On July 22, in Philadelphia other dissident Democrats form a fourth party, the Progressive Party, and nominate Henry A. Wallace for president.

• On July 26, President Truman issues executive orders intended to end racial discrimination in the armed forces and federal civil service.

• On August 3, former Communist Whittaker Chambers accuses Alger Hiss, a high-ranking State Department diplomat, of membership in the Communist Party, lending credence to right-wing charges that subversives have infiltrated the government.

• On November 2, defying the polls and the political pundits, President Truman is reelected.

1949

• On April 4, the North Atlantic Treaty Organization (NATO) is founded as a mutual defense pact among the Western Allies.

• On May 12, the Soviet Union lifts the Berlin blockade.

• On May 23, the Federal Republic of Germany (West Germany) is formally established.

• On July 21, the Senate ratifies the NATO treaty.

• On September 23, President Truman announces that the Soviets have detonated their first atomic bomb.

• On October 1, Mao Tse-tung announces the creation of the People's Republic of China. The United States does not recognize the new government.

"The Four Freedoms"

Speech

By: Franklin D. Roosevelt

Date: January 6, 1941

Source: Roosevelt, Franklin D. "The Four Freedoms." State of the Union speech, January 6, 1941. Available at the Institute for the Study of Civic Values online at http://www.libertynet.org/~edcivic/fdr.html; website home page: http://www.libertynet.org (accessed August 28, 2002).

About the Author: Franklin Delano Roosevelt (1882–1945), born in Hyde Park, New York, served as the thirty-second president of the United States, from 1933 to 1945. He became the only person in the nation's history to be elected to the presidency four times. Roosevelt is best remembered for leading the nation through two of its greatest challenges, the Great Depression and World War II (1939–1945). He died in office in April 1945. ■

Introduction

When President Roosevelt made his State of the Union address to Congress on January 6, 1941, he did not know that within the year Japan would attack Pearl Harbor and the United States would be drawn into World War II. He considered the nation in a state of emergency nonetheless. He spoke of national defense and the support of U.S. allies but focused mainly on a broader picture. Roosevelt believed that democracy was in danger not only from military power but also from social revolution, namely the spread of dictators and philosophies that threatened individual freedom. He outlined national policy in his speech, urging citizens to place unnecessary domestic concerns behind the larger cause of democracy and warning them that sacrifices were necessary to maintain the American way of life.

The most significant part of the address, which became known as the "Four Freedoms Speech," was not Roosevelt's outline of U.S. policy, however. Roosevelt also presented four goals he hoped the United States would support and foster across the globe. He identified four freedoms to which he believed all people were entitled: the freedom of speech and expression, the freedom of religion, the freedom from want, and the freedom from fear. He admitted that not all American citizens enjoyed these freedoms and explained ways in which the U.S. government could provide and protect them. The president also expanded notions of American duty. According to Roosevelt, the country had the obligation to export these freedoms elsewhere as well as to defend them at home. His ambitions for freedom did not stop at the U.S. borders.

Significance

Roosevelt's "Four Freedoms Speech" was important in four main ways. First, it prepared the American public for the possibility of war. Although the United States had been committed to noninterference, Roosevelt's speech planted a seed in the public's mind. It helped to increase U.S. military activity and pave the way for the declaration of war against Japan that followed the bombing of Pearl Harbor. Second, Roosevelt's emphasis on the plight of democracy set the stage for the Cold War. After World War II, dictators such as Germany's Adolph Hitler no longer threatened democracy, but communist regimes such as that in the Soviet Union remained. Roosevelt's warning about international challenges to freedom helped to justify the United States' part in the Cold War, the clash of superpowers that defined world politics through the 1980s.

Third, the goals Roosevelt described served as a foundation for the post-World War II creation of the United Nations, in which the United States played a key role. Roosevelt's four freedoms informed the purpose and policy of this international organization. Fourth, and perhaps most importantly, the president's speech expanded traditional notions of U.S. responsibility. According to Roosevelt, the United States had a duty to the entire world as its primary example of democracy and freedom. Although the idea that the United States was exceptional had existed for some time, the concept of the nation as the world's leader and model was significant. Later perceptions of the United States as "the world's police" owe much to Roosevelt's belief in America as the defender of democracy across the world. The "Four Freedoms Speech" was more than a simple summary of domestic and international policy. The speech redefined Roosevelt's, and ultimately the nation's, understanding of U.S. identity.

Primary Source

"The Four Freedoms" [excerpt]

> **SYNOPSIS:** In this State of the Union address, President Roosevelt outlines his social and political goals not only for the United States, but also for the world. His objectives were a major factor in the U.S. entry into World War II and, even more importantly, strongly influenced post-war foreign policy. Roosevelt's idealism, however, contrasted sharply in some cases with World War II and Cold War realities.

World War II poster inspired by President Roosevelt's "Four Freedoms" speech. **COURTESY NATIONAL ARCHIVES (NWDNS-44-PA-2066).**

Mr. Speaker, members of the 77th Congress:

I address you, the members of this new Congress, at a moment unprecedented in the history of the union. I use the word "unprecedented" because at no previous time has American security been as seriously threatened from without as it is today. . . .

As long as the aggressor nations maintain the offensive they, not we, will choose the time and the place and the method of their attack. And that is why the future of all the American Republics is today in serious danger. That is why this annual message to the Congress is unique in our history. That is why every member of the executive branch of the government and every member of the Congress face great responsibility—great accountability.

The need of the moment is that our actions and our policy should be devoted primarily—almost exclusively—to meeting this foreign peril. For all our domestic problems are now a part of the great emergency. Just as our national policy in internal affairs

has been based upon a decent respect for the rights and the dignity of all of our fellow men within our gates, so our national policy in foreign affairs has been based on a decent respect for the rights and the dignity of all nations, large and small. And the justice of morality must and will win in the end.

Our national policy is this:

First, by an impressive expression of the public will and without regard to partisanship, we are committed to all-inclusive national defense.

Second, by an impressive expression of the public will and without regard to partisanship, we are committed to full support of all those resolute people everywhere who are resisting aggression and are thereby keeping war away from our hemisphere. By this support we express our determination that the democratic cause shall prevail, and we strengthen the defense and the security of our own nation.

Third, by an impressive expression of the public will and without regard to partisanship, we are committed to the proposition that principle of morality and considerations for our own security will never permit us to acquiesce in a peace dictated by aggressors and sponsored by appeasers. We know that enduring peace cannot be bought at the cost of other people's freedom. In the recent national election there was no substantial difference between the two great parties in respect to that national policy. No issue was fought out on the line before the American electorate. And today it is abundantly evident that American citizens everywhere are demanding and supporting speedy and complete action in recognition of obvious danger. . . .

In fulfillment of this purpose we will not be intimidated by the threats of dictators that they will regard as a breach of international law or as an act of war our aid to the democracies which dare to resist their aggression. Such aid is not an act of war, even if a dictator should unilaterally proclaim it so to be. And when the dictators—if the dictators—are ready to make war upon us, they will not wait for an act of war on our part.

They did not wait for Norway or Belgium or the Netherlands to commit an act of war. Their only interest is in a new one-way international law which lacks mutuality in its observance and therefore becomes an instrument of oppression. The happiness of future generations of Americans may well depend on how effective and how immediate we can make our aid felt. No one can tell the exact character of the emergency situations that we may be called upon to meet. The nation's hands must not be tied when the nation's life is in danger.

Yes, and we must prepare, all of us prepare, to make the sacrifices that the emergency—almost as serious as war itself—demands. Whatever stands in the way of speed and efficiency in defense, in defense preparations at any time, must give way to the national need. A free nation has the right to expect full cooperation from all groups. A free nation has the right to look to the leaders of business, of labor and of agriculture to take the lead in stimulating effort, not among other groups but within their own groups.

The best way of dealing with the few slackers or trouble-makers in our midst is, first, to shame them by patriotic example, and if that fails, to use the sovereignty of government to save government. As men do not live by bread alone, they do not fight by armaments alone. Those who man our defenses and those behind them who build our defenses must have the stamina and the courage which come from unshakeable belief in the manner of life which they are defending. The mighty action that we are calling for cannot be based on a disregard of all the things worth fighting for.

The nation takes great satisfaction and much strength from the things which have been done to make its people conscious of their individual stake in the preservation of democratic life in America. Those things have toughened the fiber of our people, have renewed their faith and strengthened their devotion to the institutions we make ready to protect. Certainly this is no time for any of us to stop thinking about the social and economic problems which are the root cause of the social revolution which is today a supreme factor in the world. For there is nothing mysterious about the foundations of a healthy and strong democracy.

The basic things expected by our people of their political and economic systems are simple. They are:

Equality of opportunity for youth and for others.

Jobs for those who can work.

Security for those who need it.

The ending of special privilege for the few.

The preservation of civil liberties for all.

The enjoyment of the fruits of scientific progress in a wider and constantly rising standard of living.

These are the simple, the basic things that must never be lost sight of in the turmoil and unbelievable complexity of our modern world. The inner and abiding strength of our economic and political systems is dependent upon the degree to which they fulfill these expectations.

Many subjects connected with our social economy call for immediate improvement. As examples:

We should bring more citizens under the coverage of old-age pensions and unemployment insurance.

We should widen the opportunities for adequate medical care.

We should plan a better system by which persons deserving or needing gainful employment may obtain it.

I have called for personal sacrifice, and I am assured of the willingness of almost all Americans to respond to that call. A part of the sacrifice means the payment of more money in taxes. In my budget message I will recommend that a greater portion of this great defense program be paid for from taxation than we are paying for today. No person should try, or be allowed to get rich out of the program, and the principle of tax payments in accordance with ability to pay should be constantly before our eyes to guide our legislation.

If the Congress maintains these principles the voters, putting patriotism ahead of pocketbooks, will give you their applause. In the future days which we seek to make secure, we look forward to a world founded upon four essential human freedoms.

The first is freedom of speech and expression—everywhere in the world.

The second is freedom of every person to worship God in his own way—everywhere in the world.

The third is freedom from want, which, translated into world terms, means economic understandings which will secure to every nation a healthy peacetime life for its inhabitants—everywhere in the world.

The fourth is freedom from fear, which, translated into world terms, means a world-wide reduction of armaments to such a point and in such a thorough fashion that no nation will be in a position to commit an act of physical aggression against any neighbor—anywhere in the world. That is no vision of a distant millennium. It is a definite basis for a kind of world attainable in our own time and generation. That kind of world is the very antithesis of the so-called "new order" of tyranny which the dictators seek to create with the crash of a bomb.

To that new order we oppose the greater conception—the moral order. A good society is able to face schemes of world domination and foreign revolutions alike without fear. Since the beginning of our American history we have been engaged in change, in a perpetual, peaceful revolution, a revolution which goes on steadily, quietly, adjusting itself to changing conditions without the concentration camp or the quicklime in the ditch. The world order which we seek is the cooperation of free countries, working together in a friendly, civilized society.

This nation has placed its destiny in the hands, heads and hearts of its millions of free men and women, and its faith in freedom under the guidance of God. Freedom means the supremacy of human rights everywhere. Our support goes to those who struggle to gain those rights and keep them. Our strength is our unity of purpose.

To that high concept there can be no end save victory.

Further Resources

BOOKS

Davis, Kenneth Sydney. *FDR—The War President, 1940–1943: A History.* New York: Random House, 2000.

Freidel, Frank. *Franklin D. Roosevelt: A Rendezvous with Destiny.* New York: Little, Brown & Company, 1991.

Goodwin, Doris Kearns. *No Ordinary Time: Franklin and Eleanor Roosevelt: The Home Front in World War II.* New York: Touchstone Books, 1995.

WEBSITES

Franklin D. Roosevelt Library and Digital Archives. Available online at http://www.fdrlibrary.marist.edu/ (accessed May 9, 2002).

"Powers of Persuasion: Poster Art from World War II." National Archives and Records Administration. Available online at http://www.archives.gov/exhibit_hall/powers_of_persuasion /four_freedoms/four_freedoms.html; website home page http:// www.archives.gov/ (accessed March 14, 2003).

"Franklin D. Roosevelt's Pearl Harbor Speech"

Speech

By: Franklin D. Roosevelt

Date: December 8, 1941

Source: Roosevelt, Franklin D. "Franklin D. Roosevelt's Pearl Harbor Speech." December 8, 1941. Available at the Boulder Community Network Government/Political Center online at http://bcn.boulder.co.us/government/national /speeches/spch2.html; website home page http://bcn.boulder .co.us (accessed March 14, 2003).

About the Author: Franklin Delano Roosevelt (1882–1945), born in Hyde Park, New York, served as the thirty-second president of the United States, from 1933 to 1945. The only person in the nation's history to be elected to the presidency four times, he is best remembered for leading the nation through two of its greatest challenges: the Great Depression and World War II (1939–1945). He died in office in April 1945. ∎

Introduction

Even as World War II flared overseas, the United States government adopted a policy of nonintervention and chose to stay out of the conflict as long as possible. For the most part, this policy corresponded to the mainstream public desire to avoid the casualties and hardships of another conflict like World War I (1914–1918). By 1941, however, President Roosevelt moved the nation closer to involvement in two main ways. First, the United States began supplying military and other aid to Great Britain and its allies, going so far as to accept noncash payment for such materials under the Lend-Lease Act. Second, Roosevelt instructed the U.S. Navy to shoot at German submarines on sight. Despite these actions, the United States was not officially at war.

Then, on December 7, 1941, Japanese forces bombed Pearl Harbor, Hawaii. The attack destroyed nearly all of the U.S. Pacific fleet and hundreds of airplanes and killed approximately 2,500 U.S. military personnel and civilians. The next day Roosevelt addressed Congress and requested that the United States declare war on Japan. The president's speech was not only a formal step toward an official declaration but also an attempt to rally public support for the war. Japan was one of the Axis powers, along with Germany and Italy, so a declaration of war would engage the United States in a preexisting world conflict alongside the Allies (Great Britain, France, and the Soviet Union). American popular opinion strongly supported the president, and Congress immediately complied with Roosevelt's request to declare war.

Significance

Three days after the United States declared war on Japan, Germany and Italy declared war on the United States. The United States found itself joining Great Britain, France, the Soviet Union, and, to a lesser extent, China against the Axis powers in a conflict that continued until 1945. Like the other nations in the war, the United States suffered many casualties. The war had a unique impact on the United States, however, in five major ways. First, the nation's economy, which had failed to return to its pre-Great Depression health, experienced a great rebound due to wartime spending and production. The country emerged from the war, in fact, with a

The *U.S.S. Shaw* explodes after being hit by three bombs during the Japanese raid on Pearl Harbor, December 7, 1941. **NATIONAL ARCHIVES AND RECORDS ADMINISTRATION.**

thriving economy. Second, the United States experienced great scientific developments because of advances in military technology. The most notable of these was the development of the atomic bomb, which ultimately played a significant role in ending World War II. Third, the nation emerged from the war as a political and economic world leader. This led to U.S. commitments to help rebuild war-torn Europe. In addition, it placed the United States in opposition to the other global superpower, the Soviet Union, in what would become a decades-long Cold War.

U.S. entry into World War II also changed everyday life in the United States. A fourth impact of the war was the great influx of women into the domestic workforce as they filled positions previously occupied by men. Fifth, the returning war veterans received unprecedented benefits from the government, including the opportunity to attend college through the G.I. Bill. This helped to create a new, young, college-educated middle class in the United States. The declaration of war achieved by President Roosevelt's Pearl Harbor speech was the first step in a war effort that forever changed the face of the nation.

Primary Source

"Franklin D. Roosevelt's Pearl Harbor Speech"

SYNOPSIS: In this speech, President Roosevelt responds to the Japanese attack on Pearl Harbor by explaining the international situation to Congress and then requesting a declaration of war against Japan. Congress quickly granted the president's request and declared war. This effectively brought the United States into World War II.

To the Congress of the United States:

Yesterday, Dec. 7, 1941—a date which will live in infamy—the United States of America was suddenly and deliberately attacked by naval and air forces of the Empire of Japan.

The United States was at peace with that nation and, at the solicitation of Japan, was still in conversation with the government and its emperor looking toward the maintenance of peace in the Pacific.

Indeed, one hour after Japanese air squadrons had commenced bombing in Oahu, the Japanese ambassador to the United States and his colleagues delivered to the Secretary of State a formal reply to a recent American message. While this reply stated that it seemed useless to continue the existing diplomatic negotiations, it contained no threat or hint of war or armed attack.

It will be recorded that the distance of Hawaii from Japan makes it obvious that the attack was deliberately planned many days or even weeks ago. During the intervening time, the Japanese government has deliberately sought to deceive the United States by false statements and expressions of hope for continued peace.

The attack yesterday on the Hawaiian islands has caused severe damage to American naval and military forces. Very many American lives have been lost. In addition, American ships have been reported torpedoed on the high seas between San Francisco and Honolulu.

Yesterday, the Japanese government also launched an attack against Malaya.

Last night, Japanese forces attacked Hong Kong.

Last night, Japanese forces attacked Guam.

Last night, Japanese forces attacked the Philippine Islands.

Last night, the Japanese attacked Wake Island.

This morning, the Japanese attacked Midway Island.

Japan has, therefore, undertaken a surprise offensive extending throughout the Pacific area. The facts of yesterday speak for themselves. The people of the United States have already formed their opinions and well understand the implications to the very life and safety of our nation.

As commander in chief of the Army and Navy, I have directed that all measures be taken for our defense.

Always will we remember the character of the onslaught against us.

No matter how long it may take us to overcome this premeditated invasion, the American people in their righteous might will win through to absolute victory.

I believe I interpret the will of the Congress and of the people when I assert that we will not only defend ourselves to the uttermost, but will make very certain that this form of treachery shall never endanger us again.

Hostilities exist. There is no blinking at the fact that our people, our territory and our interests are in grave danger.

With confidence in our armed forces—with the unbounding determination of our people—we will gain the inevitable triumph—so help us God.

I ask that the Congress declare that since the unprovoked and dastardly attack by Japan on Sunday, Dec. 7, a state of war has existed between the United States and the Japanese empire.

Further Resources

BOOKS
Davis, Kenneth Sydney. *FDR—The War President, 1940–1943: A History.* New York: Random House, 2000.

Lord, Walter. *Day of Infamy: The Classic Account of the Bombing of Pearl Harbor.* 60th Anniversary Edition. New York: Henry Holt & Company, 2001.

Prange, Gordon W., et al. *December 7, 1941: The Day the Japanese Attacked Pearl Harbor.* Reissue edition. New York: Warner Books, 1991.

WEBSITES
"Pearl Harbor." National Archives. Available online at http://www.archives.gov/exhibit_hall/treasures_of_congress/Images/page_21/67b.html; website home page http://www.archives.gov/ (accessed March 14, 2003).

"The Pearl Harbor Attack." U.S. Navy Historical Center. Available online at http://www.history.navy.mil/faqs/faq66-1.htm; website home page http://www.history.navy.mil/index.html (accessed March 14, 2003).

"Remembering Pearl Harbor." National Geographic. Available online at http://www.nationalgeographic.com/pearlharbor; website home page http://www.nationalgeographic.com (accessed March 14, 2003).

Letter from James Y. Sakamoto to President Franklin D. Roosevelt

Letter

By: James Y. Sakamoto

Date: March 23, 1942

Source: Sakamoto, James Y. "Letter from James Y. Sakamoto of the Emergency Defense Council Seattle Chapter of the Japanese American Citizens League dated March 23, 1942. Emergency Defense Council of the Seattle Chapter, Japanese American Citizens League. March 23, 1942. Camp Harmony Exhibit. University of Washington. Available online at http://www.lib.washington.edu/exhibits/harmony/Documents/fdr.html; website home page http://www.lib.washington.edu (accessed March 19, 2003).

About the Author: James Y. Sakamoto (1903–1955) was an American by birth and a leader in the Seattle and national Japanese American community. He founded the first

English-language newspaper for Japanese Americans, the *Japanese American Courier,* in 1928. He also founded the Japanese American Citizen's League and served as its second national president. At the time he wrote to President Roosevelt, Sakamoto was a member of the Emergency Defense Council of the Seattle Chapter of the Japanese American Citizens League. He was one of many Japanese American leaders who urged the U.S. government to rethink its violations of Japanese Americans' civil rights. ■

Introduction

Japanese Americans formed a small minority, barely one-tenth of one percent of the U.S. population, in 1941 when the United States entered World War II (1939–1945). Their numbers were concentrated on the West Coast, where they already had faced discrimination and racism from the area's mainstream population. After the Japanese bombed Pearl Harbor on December 7, 1941, anti-Japanese sentiment intensified, even against those who were U.S. citizens. Panic spread as journalists and politicians suggested that Americans of Japanese descent might be undercover agents for the Japanese government planning to attack the United States from within. Even reputable newspapers and magazines such as *Time* and *Life* ran stories catering to the paranoia of the U.S. public.

This popular fear led President Roosevelt to agree to a drastic plan that clearly violated the rights of Japanese American citizens and noncitizens alike. On February 19, 1942, he signed Executive Order 9066, which authorized the secretary of war to create the War Relocation Authority (WRA). The WRA forcibly removed 110,000 people of Japanese descent to ten internment camps situated in remote parts of the United States. These people were not under investigation for acts of treason against the U.S. government; they were targeted and removed from their homes simply because of their ethnic heritage. The internment camps were similar to prisoner-of-war camps, complete with wooden barracks, armed guards, and barbed-wire fences. Because the relocation process was speedy, many Japanese Americans could not secure their belongings adequately and thus lost homes, businesses, and other property. The camps existed until 1945, when all captives were allowed to leave and try to rebuild their lives.

Significance

In a decade in which women, African Americans, and other groups enjoyed new opportunities, if not equal treatment with others, the internment of Japanese Americans starkly illustrated the injustices minorities suffered when mainstream Americans united against them. The internment policy contrasted sharply with the patriotism of Japanese Americans who fought for the United States against Japan. More than 17,000 Japanese Americans

fought on behalf of the United States and approximately 1,200 of those volunteered for service from U.S. internment camps. The internment experience altered many Japanese American lives forever. Not only did these people face the indignity of relocation, but many lost their savings, livelihoods, and homes. Years later, the example of Japanese American internment served as a warning to the government of what not to do when a minority group—for example, Arab Americans during the Gulf War of the 1990s or after the terrorist attacks of September 11, 2001—faces mass fear from a nation in a state of emergency.

The internments spawned a number of legal cases, most notably the 1944 Supreme Court case *Korematsu v. United States.* Although the majority of justices found in favor of the U.S. government, saying "the military urgency of the situation demanded that all citizens of Japanese ancestry be segregated," the case is best remembered for the dissenting opinion that stated Executive Order 9066 was a case of "obvious racial discrimination." In 1988 Congress and President Ronald Reagan acknowledged publicly that Japanese Americans' rights had been violated and offered each surviving internee a tax-free reparation payment of $20,000. Although this gesture came too late to repair the damage done in the 1940s, it did prove that the United States had learned a lesson from the experience and intended not to repeat its mistake.

Primary Source

Letter from James Y. Sakamoto to President Franklin D. Roosevelt

SYNOPSIS: In this letter, James Y. Sakamoto urges President Roosevelt to respect the rights of loyal Japanese American citizens. His concern extended both to civilians who faced relocation to U.S. government internment camps, and to Japanese American soldiers who served in the U.S. armed forces and yet remained under suspicion because of their heritage.

March 23, 1942

The Honorable Franklin D. Roosevelt
President of the United States of America
The White House
Washington, D.C.

Mr. President:

We, the American Citizens of Japanese parentage in these United States, have taken seriously your various statements on the Four Freedoms. Our parent generation too has taken comfort from those assertions. They have not enjoyed the rights of citizenship in this country. For that reason they are at this time particularly open to accusation and suspicion.

We were reassured when war broke out and heard your directions as to the treatment to be accorded aliens of enemy countries. We felt those were commands upon all American citizens to pull together for a common objective. Even when the clamor against us raised by a national organization whose patriotic motives are undoubted seemed about to threaten our very lives, we trusted in your protection.

The picture has changed since then. Evacuation has now become a certainty for all of us, non-citizen and citizen alike. We citizens have been singled out for treatment that has hitherto not been meted out to any American. Though the medicine was bitter, we have attempted to obey without criticism, and to swallow it.

We were prepared to go where we might be sent, to be uprooted permanently from the homes we have known since childhood. Our parents before us had in many instances built up the only homes we knew. They had given us an American education and in some thousands of instances sent us gladly into the service of our country. They, too, were to accompany us. We thought it would simply be a matter of transfer to another locality in which we might carry on, under a cloud indeed, but demonstrating our loyalty none the less, by obeying a humiliating and distasteful command.

We are still so minded. We shall obey willingly. We shall continue to trust you and to give our allegiance to the ideals you enunciate.

In the working out of the details of evacuation, we have noticed an insistence upon the necessity for speed in going to places not designated by anyone. We are willing to go, glad to escape from even the possibility of ever being accused of even being present in the area where sabotage might conceivably take place.

Under the circumstances prevailing, we have been so completely discredited by the American people at large that it is impossible for us to appear anywhere without giving rise to some hysterically false assumption that we are engaged in some nefarious design against a country that is as much ours as it is that of our fellow citizens. So marked is this that had we any intention such as we are popularly credited with, the easiest manner in which it might be accomplished would be for us to simply pick up and spread our unwanted presence over the Ameri-

A military police officer posts an order that requires Japanese living on Bainbridge Island, near Seattle, Washington, to evacuate the area, 1942. © BETTMANN/CORBIS. REPRODUCED BY PERMISSION.

can map and so precipitate, under Army decree, that complete disruption of the war effort.

Our people have not been unconscious of the extent to which our country has been dependent upon them for the production of certain articles of food in areas now filled with Army installations and all lines of war work. Certainly, had they any mind to sabotage they could have done so no more completely than by ceasing to produce the food upon which so much of the war effort depended.

Mr. President, we have protested our loyalty in the past. We have not been believed. We are willing to assume the burden of continuing to demonstrate it under all but impossible conditions. We would be deeply grateful if you would point it out to our fellow citizens that we are not traitors to our country as the above facts, in our opinion amply demonstrate.

Restore our good name to us that our soldiers of Japanese ancestry need no longer hang their heads in shame as their hearts secretly bleed in anxiety over the whereabouts of their parents and loved ones possibly stranded penniless in some desert of the Southwest, or begging their bread in the streets of some strange place.

Give to us some refuge in the heart of the country far removed from even the suspicion or possibility to do harm. We have helped to feed the nation in the past. Let us continue to do so now that it is needed the more. Only let us do so freely and not under that compulsion made notorious in an enemy country. We do not have to be driven to work for a country in which we believe for ideals more precious than our life-blood.

We know there have been dissident elements among us, often unknown to ourselves. We know that some of the customs brought from abroad do lay some members of our parents open to suspicion even yet. We, like our fellow citizens, have complete confidence in the all-seeing eye of the Federal Bureau of Investigation. We have seconded their efforts when told what it was they were searching for and we shall continue to do so.

We hope to find in the hearts of those like ours some understanding of our problems and some surcease from the burdens that oppress us. We have confidence that you yourself may present our case to them as a demonstration here of sincerity toward the promises you have made to the world.

Trusting that you will give us your sympathetic assistance and with the greatest hope for your continued good health, I am, my dear Mr. President,

Faithfully yours,
James Y. Sakamoto

Further Resources

BOOKS

Daniels, Roger, et al. *Japanese Americans, From Relocation to Redress.* Seattle: University of Washington Press, 1991.

Harth, Erica. *Last Witnesses: Reflections on the Wartime Internment of Japanese Americans.* New York: Palgrave, 2001.

Ng, Wendy L. *Japanese American Internment During World War II: A History and Reference Guide.* Westport, Conn.: Greenwood Press, 2002.

Yamamoto, Eric K. *Race, Rights, and Reparation: Law and the Japanese American Internment.* Gaithersburg, N.Y.: Aspen Law & Business, 2001.

WEBSITES

"Behind Barbed Wire at Amanche." University of Denver Museum of Anthropology. Available online at http://www.du .edu/~anballar/BehindBarbedWire.html; website home page http://www.du.edu (accessed May 14, 2002).

"Camp Harmony Exhibit." University of Washington. Available online at http://www.lib.washington.edu/exhibits/harmony /exhibit/; website home page http://www.lib.washington.edu (accessed May 14, 2002).

"Suffering Under A Great Injustice: Ansel Adams's Photographs of Japanese American Internment at Manzanar." American Memory: Historical Collections for the National Digital Library. Library of Congress. Available online at http://memory.loc.gov/ (accessed March 14, 2003).

The Discovery of Freedom: Man's Struggle Against Authority

Nonfiction work

By: Rose Wilder Lane

Date: 1943

Source: Lane, Rose Wilder. *The Discovery of Freedom: Man's Struggle Against Authority.* Fiftieth Anniversary Edition. San Francisco: Fox & Wilkes, 1993.

About the Author: Rose Wilder Lane (1886–1968) was the first child of Almanzo and Laura Ingalls Wilder. Her family later became famous thanks to the *Little House* children's book series written by her mother, which Lane herself edited and heavily modified. As a columnist and author in her own right, Lane explored ideas about individual rights and international affairs and was one of a handful of highly visible U.S. women political commentators in the first half of the twentieth century. ∎

Introduction

The Discovery of Freedom: Man's Struggle Against Authority served as Rose Wilder Lane's personal manifesto, an explanation of a political philosophy built over a lifetime of travel and publication. Years of writing for popular newspapers and magazines established Lane as a respected journalist. Novels such as *Diverging Roads* and nonfiction books such as *The Making of Herbert Hoover* added to her reputation. Her time as a reporter for the American Red Cross brought her face-to-face with the aftermath of World War I (1914–1918) and the issue of human rights. After visiting war-torn countries, Lane wrote about the conditions she witnessed. *The Peaks of Shala* and *Travels with Zenobia,* for example, chronicle her experiences as an American and a woman confronting the devastation of war in Albania. Such reports focused on the need to limit government, protect individual liberties, and value freedom, not only for the United States but for all citizens of the world.

In *The Discovery of Freedom,* Lane sketches a historical and geographic overview of the cause of liberty from "Old World" times through what she calls the "Third Attempt" at freedom, namely the American experiment after the War of Independence. She ends her passionate volume on a positive note, saying, "Americans are fighting a World War now because the Revolution is a World Revolution. Freedom creates this new world, that cannot exist half slave and half free. It will be free." By linking the efforts of the United States and the Allies in World War II (1939–1945) to the ongoing evolution of liberty, Lane not only showed her support for the war effort but helped place the war in a historical context for her readers. Rather than being a mystifying and terrifying event, World War II through Lane's eyes became another link in a long struggle for freedom, one built on the experience of World War I and destined for a happy ending for those who championed individual rights.

Significance

The Discovery of Freedom was important for four main reasons. First, it marked a new era for woman political commentators. Its publication in 1943 not only garnered attention in its own right but also coincided with the publication of other highly visible political works by women authors, such as Ayn Rand's *The Fountainhead* and Isabel Paterson's *The God of the Machine.* Second, Lane's highly personal style made her message accessible to those who did not read political theory, economic texts, or even fiction such as Rand's. Since she wrote from her own experiences and observations, and without the jargon of scholars, her insights seemed more relevant and clear than similar ones by authors who wrote for more specialized audiences. In short, Lane brought philosophy to the mainstream. Third, Lane's work served as a uniquely powerful endorsement of U.S. involvement in World War II, because she herself had often opposed U.S. policy, especially those actions that she believed unnecessarily expanded the power of the national government to the detriment of individual freedom. (Her vocal opposition to the Social Security program and the rise of the welfare state, for example, is legendary.) Lane's support of U.S. involvement in World War II reflected the strong public consensus about joining the war effort.

Most importantly, *The Discovery of Freedom* presented a view of history that was both libertarian (supporting free will) and nationalist (championing one nation over others). Lane's book tells the story of the evolution of freedom, with the United States as its focal point. Like many of her generation, Lane viewed the early American republic as the world's best experiment in liberty and its greatest achievement until the twentieth century, when the United States' entry into World War II cemented its role as the world's political leader. Significantly, only a few years earlier, most Americans had shared the president's desire to remain neutral. The Japanese bombing of Pearl Harbor and the increasing threat of Hitler's Nazi Germany, however, caused a reversal in this position. By

Rose Wilder Lane, in her *The Discovery of Freedom* related that U.S. involvment in WWII was part of the struggle for worldwide freedom. **AP/WIDE WORLD PHOTOS. REPRODUCED BY PERMISSION.**

1943, the mainstream American public, like Lane, embraced the U.S. war effort as yet another example of the United States' exceptional nature, its position as a role model to other nations, and its duty to spread an American "revolution" across the world.

Primary Source

The Discovery of Freedom: Man's Struggle Against Authority [excerpt]

> **SYNOPSIS:** In this excerpt, journalist and author Rose Wilder Lane describes World War II as the American Revolution expanded to a global scale, a fight for individual liberty in which the United States plays a leading role. Lane's work reflects a U.S. consensus about America's growing position in the world and the importance of its involvement in the war effort.

The World Revolution

Fewer than three million men and women began the Revolution, not two centuries ago. On a very small area of this earth, a small percentage of its population have been able to use their natural freedom;—to the greatest extent in these States, to a lesser extent in the British Commonwealth, and a little on the western rim of continental Europe.

A converted food machinery plant, formerly used for production of cube-steak machines, now helps produce anti-tank guns. **THE LIBRARY OF CONGRESS.**

For little more than a century, human energy has been effectively attacking the enemies of human life—most effectively in these States, a little less effectively in the British Commonwealth, and somewhat on the western rim of Europe.

Americans have been most vigorously creating the industrial revolution: steamships, railroads, telegraph, trans-oceanic cables, telephones, farm machinery, elevators, skyscrapers, subways, bridges, dams, hydroelectric plants, radios, airplanes—the New World.

Americans created the machine age; mass production, and mass distribution of the produced wealth. (For wealth produced *must* be consumed.) Americans created modern medicine, modern hygiene, modern sanitation, modern dietetics.

Americans are now creating the power age; they are gathering the power of gravitation that keeps the stars in their places, and transforming it into streams of power flowing through the machines and driving the stream-lined trains and the hyro-compasses and the radio beams, and lighting the cities and the farmers' barns and toasting the bread for breakfast.

Americans are creating the chemical age; new chemicals, new metals, new fabrics, synthetics, plastics, innumerable ways of subduing to human uses the infinitesimal tininess within the invisible electron, that is totally imperceptible to any human sense or any instrument—a root of power that only human imagination can grasp.

Three generations—grandfather to grandson—have created wonders surpassing the utmost imaginings of all previous time.

Never before in their long history have Europeans lived ninety-five years without a famine. In the Americas, in the British Commonwealth, and in western Europe (but nowhere else) no mass-population has starved utterly to death (until this war) since the year 1848.

The free use of human energy in these States has completely transformed living for every American. Twenty years ago, American energy began transforming the whole human world for everyone living on this planet.

Since 1920, American energy, American techniques, Americans in person, have been building the New World around the earth. Americans industrialized Russia (a man from Connecticut built Dnieperstroy dam, that the retreating Russians have just destroyed). Americans rationalized German industries. Americans modernized China, Japan, Persia, Arabia, Africa.

All Europeans and Asiatics have one word for this creation of the New World in their countries. It is, "Americanization." (Their intellectuals hate it; it attacks the very basis of their Old World thinking.)

Only once before in known history has there been anything resembling this New World in character. That was the Saracens' world, that stretched across three continents, from the Atlantic to China and the Ganges, and lasted for eight hundred years.

This New World embraces the whole planet. It reaches the most remote islands, it includes the Eskimos beyond the Arctic circle and the naked savages in equatorial jungles. And it is not yet fifty years old. . . .

The Revolution has been causing upheavals in almost every country on earth, for a hundred years. Now the counter-revolutionists come out of Germany, determined to end it.

New tyrants, defending the ancient tyranny, intend to destroy utterly this new idea that men are free. They do not believe it. As firmly as Lycurgus or Nebuchadnezzar, they believe that all men are naturally subject to Authority (all but themselves.) Government, they believe, is Authority; they are Government. They accept that responsibility. They believe that they should, and that they do, control the inferior masses. And by the use of the real power, force (permitted by the false beliefs of their wretched subjects) they intend to make their imaginary static world orderly, as it was before the Revolution began.

Mussolini will bring back the grandeur that was ancient Rome. Hitler will resurrect the Holy Roman Empire of the 16th century and establish it with pagan gods older than Rome, to endure for a thousand years. The Japanese will have all Asia for the Asiatics, as it was before Mohammed was born.

Fanatic reactionaries, counter-revolutionists, defenders of a tyranny older than history, they imagine that they can go back to the past before America was discovered. And they dare to claim that *they* are creating a new world!

And now they are armed. The Revolution has armed them as tyrants never were armed before.

The caterpillar tractor that Americans invented to plow the peaceful fields and multiply the farmer's productive energy as if by magic, now armored and armed it charges in battalions of tanks over the bodies of men. The submarine, that an American invented to rescue a broken man from imprisonment on St. Helena, now it lurks hidden under all the seas to kill men. The machine that two brothers invented in their bicycle shop, to give all men wings, now it makes the moonlit sky a terror that drives men underground. This is what Authority does with the tools of the Revolution.

Blind, ignorant, bestially unable to understand this New World, these counter-revolutionists use free men's discoveries, their inventions, their techniques and their tools, to tear this earth-encircling network of dynamic, productive energies to pieces and to destroy the freedom that creates it. Idiots who would kill the living thing they want, by clutching it.

This is war around the whole earth *because* human energy, working under its natural individual control and therefore working naturally and effectively to satisfy human needs, has created this New World encircling the whole earth.

This is war in the air and war under all the seas, because for the first time in all known history, individuals have used their energy freely to explore the depths of the sea and to rise to the farthest heights of air.

Americans are fighting a World War now because the Revolution is World Revolution. Freedom creates this new world, that cannot exist half slave and half free. It will be free.

> Ignorance is of a peculiar nature; once dispelled, it is impossible to re-establish it. It is not originally a thing of itself, but is only the absence of knowledge; and though man may be *kept* ignorant, he cannot be *made* ignorant.
>
> There does not exist in the compass of language an arrangement of words to express so much as the means of effecting a counter-revolution. The means must be an obliteration of knowledge; and it has never yet been discovered how to make a man *unknow* his knowledge.
>
> Thomas Paine, "The Rights of Man"

Americans know that all men are free. All over this world there are men who know it now. The pigmy Republic has become a colossus. And too late and too little, the Old World tyrants attack this Revolution with its own tools.

Win this war? Of course Americans will win this war. This is only a war; there is more than that. Five generations of Americans have led the Revolution, and the time is coming when Americans will set this whole world free.

Further Resources

BOOKS

Holtz, William V. *The Ghost in the Little House: A Life of Rose Wilder Lane*. Columbia, Mo.: University of Missouri Press, 1995.

Lane, Rose Wilder. *Free Land*. Reprint. Lincoln, Neb.: University of Nebraska Press, 1984.

MacBride, Roger Lea, ed. *The Lady and the Tycoon: The Best of Letters Between Rose Wilder Lane and Jasper Crane*. Caldwell, Idaho: Caxton Publishers, 1973.

WEBSITES

Prairie Homestead. Available online at http://www.geocities.com/prairiehomestead (accessed March 14, 2003).

"Letters from Los Alamos"

Letters

By: Phyllis Fisher

Date: November 1944, August 1945

Source: Fisher, Phyllis. "Letters from Los Alamos." November 1944, August 1945. Reprinted in *America Firsthand*, edited by Robert D. Marcus and David Burner, vol. 2, *Readings from Reconstruction to the Present*, 4th ed. Boston: Bedford Books, 1997.

About the Author: Phyllis Fisher and her son moved to Los Alamos, New Mexico, in 1944. Her husband, physicist Leon Fisher, was sent to Los Alamos to work on developing the first nuclear bomb for the United States government through the so-called Manhattan Project. The entire project was classified, so the Fishers could not tell family or friends where they were going or why. After August 6, 1945, when the United States dropped an atomic bomb on Hiroshima, Japan, the entire world learned what had been done in Los Alamos. Phyllis Fisher then could write to her loved ones and discuss life on a secret military base and her reaction to the product of her husband's work. ■

Introduction

In 1939, the U.S. government organized a project with scientists—many them refugees from enemy nations—to explore how it could use the newly discovered fission process for military purposes. These scientists, working with the armed forces, sought to build the first atomic bomb. The famous physicist Albert Einstein himself persuaded President Franklin D. Roosevelt (served 1933–1945) to set aside funds to begin research. In 1943, physicist J. Robert Oppenheimer created an isolated, secret laboratory base in Los Alamos, New Mexico, to house what had been named the Manhattan Project. The U.S. government gathered a number of outstanding scientific and military minds, along with their families and support personnel, and created a self-contained, secret world in which to work on the classified research. The researchers seemed to disappear, because they could not tell family and friends where they were or what they were doing. The Los Alamos site was cut off from American consciousness as the mainstream public focused on the events of World War II (1939–1945).

By 1945, the Manhattan Project's $6,000 budget had grown to $2,000,000,000 and the first atomic bomb had been created. On July 16, 1945, a controlled explosion was staged on the Alamogordo air base in New Mexico. The resulting explosion created a 40,000-foot mushroom cloud and fused the desert surface to glass over an 800-yard radius. The bomb's explosion equaled a blast of 15,000 to 20,000 tons of TNT. The scientists and the military were satisfied by the result. One month after the successful test, the United States dropped one atomic bomb each on Hiroshima and Nagasaki, Japan. With the two bombings, the American public learned about the Manhattan Project and those who had worked in secret for years at Los Alamos.

Significance

The Manhattan Project proved a turning point in U.S. and world history. It created the only two atomic bombs ever used in warfare. On August 6, 1945, the bombing of Hiroshima killed 66,000, injured 69,000, and damaged almost seventy percent of the city's structures. On August 9, the bombing of Nagasaki killed 39,000, injured 25,000, and damaged approximately forty percent of the city's structures. The detonations brought World War II to an abrupt close. A day after the bombing of Nagasaki, the Japanese government initiated surrender negotiations, effectively ending World War II with a victory for the Allies and a particular success for the United States. The unveiling, use, and destructive power of the bombs awed the entire world, including most Americans, who had been unaware of the weapons' development. The bombs inflicted drastic and devastating long-term effects on the Japanese, especially in terms of human life and the environment.

The bombings immediately altered the United States' international status. The fact that the country: 1) possessed nuclear weapons, 2) had proven willing to use them, and 3) in doing so had ended World War II, put the nation in a unique world leadership position. The United States already possessed increased international status and authority because it had a thriving economy despite the war and had experienced little battle on its own soil compared to its allies. Being the only nuclear power on the planet, however, put the country in a league of its own.

The development and use of the bombs ushered in the atomic age for all nations. The Soviet Union developed its own nuclear capabilities, leading to an arms race between it and the United States. Other nations developed similar weapons, and the breakup of the Soviet Union beginning in 1989 dispersed existing bombs into even more hands. Once the atomic bomb was developed, the world could not return to its pre-nuclear life. Weapons of mass destruction have remained a reality since 1945.

Primary Source

"Letters from Los Alamos" [excerpt]

SYNOPSIS: In these excerpted letters, Phyllis Fisher reacts with surprise to the media attention paid to the formerly secret Los Alamos and to the reality of the U.S. bombing of Japan. Although she had known about the development of the nuclear bomb through her husband's work, she was unprepared for the emotions she felt when she heard reporters discussing Japanese death tolls. As she said in one letter, "hey, those are people!"

November, 1944

Now, listen to this very carefully and try to understand. I can't. We have a gate here that isn't a gate at all. It consists of a guardhouse and an unfriendly signpost surrounded by sentries. Regulations governing passage of said "gate" top any screwy regulation of any Army post anywhere. It seems that you can drive past it in an automobile without showing a pass, but you can't walk past it. Pedestrians must show passes. No exceptions.

I drove past the gate (to the vet's) with Fawn and, naturally, wasn't stopped. The veterinary hospital is only about 100 yards beyond and is visible from the gate. After our visit to the vet, I rushed out with my shivering dog, climbed into the car to start back, and—you guessed it—the car wouldn't start. By this time, it was snowing. I began to run as best I could, with Fawn held securely inside my coat. Of course, I was promptly stopped at the gate. I had no pass! In my rush to get Fawn to the vet's and back, I had neglected to take it. I explained to the sentries that my car wouldn't start. I had to get back. My hus-

Major General Leslie Groves and Dr. Oppenheimer at the site where the first atomic bomb was tested near Alamogrado, September 11, 1945. ARCHIVE PHOTOS, INC. REPRODUCED BY PERMISSION.

band had to get to work. My baby would be alone! My dog was dying! None of which made any difference. Only one word seemed to have meaning, the word "regulations." There were, it seemed, no provisions for someone who drove out the gate and had to walk back through it. Too bad. By then the snow was slanting and spinning angrily, and I wasn't getting any warmer. Fawn wasn't getting any lighter. They could see my car standing there, but that didn't make any difference. One MP suggested that I phone someone who could come out and identify me. Fine help! No one I knew had a phone. Lee couldn't be reached by phone until he left Bobby and went to work. And he wouldn't do that (I certainly hope he wouldn't do that) until I was safely home. What to do?

Monday, August 6, 1945

Please note——LOS ALAMOS, NEW MEXICO

Well, today's news makes everything else seem pretty unimportant! You can't possibly imagine how strange it is to turn on the radio and hear the outside world talking about us today! After all the extreme secrecy, it seems positively unreal to hear stories about the bomb, the site, and everything.

A mushroom cloud rises from an atomic bomb test on Bikini Atoll in 1946. © CORBIS. REPRODUCED BY PERMISSION.

The "gadget" worked better (!) than anyone dare to expect, and Hiroshima a city we have never heard of, and its population of 350,000 has been wiped out. The radio announcers could hardly control their voices. They told the whole story. How had they gotten the information so quickly? They named names! Who had told them? They described our hill, our hill. They located us on a barren plateau in the mountains north and west of Santa Fe.

They identified us as LOS ALAMOS!

We couldn't believe what we heard! "Over one hundred thousand Japs killed by one bomb," the announcers bragged. They ticked off the figures as though they were reporting scores at a sporting event. But, hey, those are people! A radius of one mile vaporized, they cheered as I shuddered. They are talking about a populated target, a city. And part of me keeps saying, "This can't be real." It's also actually unreal to hear names connected with the project, names like Oppenheimer, Segre, Fermi, Bohr, and others. After months of caution and secrecy, it's too much.

Kaltenborn [a news commentator] somehow seemed more detached and more objective than the others. He took time, in spite of the hysteria, to consider the bomb's potential for good or evil. Then he described the first test atomic explosion in the southern "arid part of the state" in New Mexico and named the date, the place, and even the code name, "Trinity."

After "Trinity," days went by while we waited to hear how and when the gadget (maybe I'd better get used to writing the word "bomb") would be used. Which brings us up to today. By comparison the excitement on the hill today has put that of July 16th far down the scale of insane rejoicing. You can't imagine it. I can't describe it. I'm certain that it will take time for the emotional bits in all of us that were triggered by "Trinity" and that blew up with the bomb to settle down into place.

August 10, 1945

Now I am upset! Yesterday's bombing of Nagasaki was shocking! I cannot understand the necessity of a second bomb. The Japanese were known to be suing for peace and trying to negotiate terms that they could accept. Why destroy another city and its inhabitants? Why couldn't both bombs have been dropped over some unimportant unpopulated island as a demonstration of what could happen to Japan?

Further Resources

BOOKS

Bailey, Janet. *The Good Servant: Making Peace With the Bomb at Los Alamos.* New York: Simon & Schuster, 1995.

Fermi, Rachel, and Esther Samra. *Picturing the Bomb: Photographs from the Secret World of the Manhattan Project.* New York: H.N. Adams, 1995.

Howes, Ruth. *Their Day in the Sun: Women of the Manhattan Project.* Philadelphia: Temple University Press, 1999.

Lee, Wen Ho, *My Country Versus Me: The First-hand Account by the Los Alamos Scientist Who Was Falsely Accused of Being A Spy.* New York: Hyperion, 2001.

Szasz, Ferenc Morton. *The Day the Sun Rose Twice: The Story of the Trinity Site Nuclear Explosion, July 16, 1945.* Albuquerque: University of New Mexico Press, 1984.

WEBSITES

"Atomic Spaces: Living on the Manhattan Project." University of Illinois. Available online at http://tigger.uic.edu/~pbhales /atomicspaces/; website home page http://tigger.uic.edu/index .html/ (accessed March 17, 2003).

"Fifty Years from Trinity." *The Seattle Times.* Available online at http://seattletimes.nwsource.com/trinity/; website home page http://seattletimes.nwsource.com/ (accessed March 17, 2003).

Friedrich A. Von Hayek, an Austrian economist, argued against Roosevelt's New Deal and Truman's Fair Deal government programs. THE LIBRARY OF CONGRESS.

The Road to Serfdom

Nonfiction work

By: Friedrich A. Hayek

Date: 1944

Source: Hayek, Friedrich A. *The Road to Serfdom: A Classic Warning Against the Dangers to Freedom Inherent in Social Planning.* Reprint edition. Chicago: University of Chicago Press, 1976.

About the Author: Friedrich A. Hayek (1899–1992), an Austrian economist, served as the Took Professor of Economic Science and Statistics at the University of London from 1931 to 1950. In 1950, he became Professor of Social and Moral Science at the University of Chicago. He taught at the University of Freiburg, Germany, from 1962 to 1967. Hayek received the Nobel Prize in Economics in 1974. ■

Introduction

As the 1940s began, Keynesian economic theory was the primary guide of U.S. public policy. This theory took its name from its founder, English economist, journalist, and financier John Maynard Keynes. In his influential work *The General Theory of Employment, Interest and Money* (1935–1936), Keynes suggested that a government-sponsored policy of full employment would solve the problems of economic recession. This kind of centralized economic planning formed the basis of President Franklin D. Roosevelt's New Deal and President Harry S. Truman's Fair Deal programs. Roosevelt (served 1933–1945) and Truman (served 1945–1953) both agreed with Keynes that the government could coordinate and plan the economy for the betterment of the United States. They implemented strategies based on Keynesian economics to help the nation recover from the Great Depression and meet the challenge of World War II (1939–1945).

A voice of opposition surfaced in 1944, however, when Austrian economist Friedrich Hayek published *The Road to Serfdom.* An admittedly political work, the book argued that economic planning by a centralized government was, in fact, a form of socialism. Socialism, Hayek continued, inevitably led to totalitarianism—a form of government that subordinates all aspects of an individual's life to the authority of the government. In other words Hayek argued that expanded government control of the economy was incompatible with democracy. If the United States and other nations continued to drift toward such socialism, he warned, individual freedom would be threatened. Even as the United States and its allies fought the totalitarian powers of Germany, Italy, and Japan, Hayek boldly predicted that the Allies themselves might become totalitarian powers unless they limited government control of their economies and supported ureglated, free market economies instead.

Significance

The Road to Serfdom made Hayek a well-known author. Reviewers either loved his work or hated it. On September 24, 1944, *The New York Times* economist Henry Hazlitt wrote that "Friedrich Hayek has written one of the most important books of our generation." *Reader's Digest* ran a twenty-page excerpt of the book and the Book-of-the-Month Club distributed some 600,000 copies of it in a condensed version. Such popular attention to a work of political economics was unusual, to say the least. Hayek intended to address fellow specialists, to be sure, but his work reached the average reader as well.

Furthermore, the book inspired great controversy by challenging the Keynesian view held by most political leaders. As others debated his ideas, Hayek began a decades-long written and verbal rivalry with Keynes. Hayek did not overthrow Keynes to become the favored economist of U.S. policymakers in the 1940s, but his ideas eventually prevailed. A significant portion of the academic community later discredited the fundamental ideas of Keynesian economics. History proved that government intervention in economies creates misleading signals that result in misallocation of resources. Free, unregulated markets proved to be far more efficient. The experience and ultimate failure of planned economies such as the Soviet Union's offered vivid illustrations to economists and politicians alike. Roosevelt's and Truman's welfare-state policies lost favor as Hayek's plea for limited government and individual freedom gained popularity. By the 1980s, leaders such as U.S. President Ronald Reagan (served 1981–1989) and British Prime Minister Margaret Thatcher (served 1979–1990) not only followed free market policies but named Hayek specifically as one of the fathers of modern economic thought.

Primary Source

The Road to Serfdom [excerpt]

SYNOPSIS: In his controversial work *The Road to Serfdom* (1944), Friedrich Hayek argues that "the unforeseen but inevitable consequences of socialist planning create a state of affairs in which, if the policy is to be pursued, totalitarian forces will get the upper hand." In other words, he suggests that government planning, though conducted with good intentions, is incompatible with democracy and liberty.

Nothing distinguishes more clearly conditions in a free country from those in a country under arbitrary government than the observance in the former of the great principles known as the Rule of Law. Stripped of all technicalities, this means that government in all its actions is bound by rules fixed and announced beforehand—rules which make it possible to foresee with fair certainty how the authority will use its coercive powers in given circumstances and to plan one's individual affairs on the basis of

this knowledge. Though this ideal can never be perfectly achieved, since legislators as well as those to whom the administration of the law is intrusted are fallible men, the essential point, that the discretion left to the executive organs wielding coercive power should be reduced as much as possible, is clear enough. While every law restricts individual freedom to some extent by altering the means which people may use in the pursuit of their aims, under the Rule of Law the government is prevented from stultifying individual efforts by *ad hoc* action. Within the known rules of the game the individual is free to pursue his personal ends and desires, certain that the powers of government will not be used deliberately to frustrate his efforts.

The distinction we have drawn before between the creation of a permanent framework of laws within which the productive activity is guided by individual decisions and the direction of economic activity by a central authority is thus really a particular case of the more general distinction between the Rule of Law and arbitrary government. Under the first the government confines itself to fixing rules determining the conditions under which the available resources may be used, leaving to the individuals the decision for what ends they are to be used. Under the second the government directs the use of the means of production to particular ends. The first type of rules can be made in advance, in the shape of *formal rules* which do not aim at the wants and needs of particular people. They are intended to be merely instrumental in the pursuit of people's various individual ends. And they are, or ought to be, intended for such long periods that it is impossible to know whether they will assist particular people more than others. They could almost be described as a kind of instrument of production, helping people to predict the behavior of those with whom they must collaborate, rather than as efforts toward the satisfaction of particular needs.

Economic planning of the collectivist kind necessarily involves the very opposite of this. The planning authority cannot confine itself to providing opportunities for unknown people to make whatever use of them they like. It cannot tie itself down in advance to general and formal rules which prevent arbitrariness. It must provide for the actual needs of people as they arise and then choose deliberately between them. It must constantly decide questions which cannot be answered by formal principles only, and, in making these decisions, it must set up distinctions of merit between the needs of different people. When the government has to decide how many pigs are to be raised or how many busses are to be run, which coal mines are to operate, or at what prices shoes are to be sold, these decisions cannot be deduced from formal principles or settled for long periods in advance. They depend inevitably on the circumstances of the moment, and, in making such decisions, it will always be necessary to balance one against the other the interests of various persons and groups. In the end somebody's views will have to decide whose interests are more important; and these views must become part of the law of the land, a new distinction of rank which the coercive apparatus of government imposes upon the people. . . .

Where the precise effects of government policy on particular people are known, where the government aims directly at such particular effects, it cannot help knowing these effects, and therefore it cannot be impartial. It must, of necessity, take sides, impose its valuations upon people and, instead of assisting them in the advancement of their own ends, choose the ends for them. As soon as the particular effects are foreseen at the time a law is made, it ceases to be a mere instrument to be used by the people and becomes instead an instrument used by the lawgiver upon the people and for his ends. The state ceases to be a piece of utilitarian machinery intended to help individuals in the fullest development of their individual personality and becomes a "moral" institution—where "moral" is not used in contrast to immoral but describes an institution which imposes on its members its views on all moral questions, whether these views be moral or highly immoral. In this sense the Nazi or any other collectivist state is "moral," while the liberal state is not.

Perhaps it will be said that all this raises no serious problem because in the kind of questions which the economic planner would have to decide he need not and should not be guided by his individual prejudices but could rely on the general conviction of what is fair and reasonable. This contention usually receives support from those who have experience of planning in a particular industry and who find that there is no insuperable difficulty about arriving at a decision which all those immediately interested will accept as fair. The reason why this experience proves nothing is, of course, the selection of the "interests" concerned when planning is confined to a particular industry. Those most immediately interested in a particular issue are not necessarily the best judges of the interests of society as a whole. To take only the most

characteristic case: when capital and labor in an industry agree on some policy of restriction and thus exploit the consumers, there is usually no difficulty about the division of the spoils in proportion to former earnings or on some similar principle. The loss which is divided between thousands or millions is usually either simply disregarded or quite inadequately considered. If we want to test the usefulness of the principle of "fairness" in deciding the kind of issues which arise in economic planning, we must apply it to some question where the gains and the losses are seen equally clearly. In such instances it is readily recognized that no general principle such as fairness can provide an answer. When we have to choose between higher wages for nurses or doctors and more extensive services for the sick, more milk for children and better wages for agricultural workers, or between employment for the unemployed or better wages for those already employed, nothing short of a complete system of values in which every want of every person or group has a definite place is necessary to provide an answer.

In fact, as planning becomes more and more extensive, it becomes regularly necessary to qualify legal provisions increasingly by reference to what is "fair" or "reasonable"; this means that it becomes necessary to leave the decision of the concrete case more and more to the discretion of the judge or authority in question. One could write a history of the decline of the Rule of Law, the disappearance of the *Rechtsstaat,* in terms of the progressive introduction of these vague formulas into legislation and jurisdiction, and of the increasing arbitrariness and uncertainty of, and the consequent disrespect for, the law and the judicature, which in these circumstances could not but become an instrument of policy. It is important to point out once more in this connection that this process of the decline of the Rule of Law had been going on steadily in Germany for some time before Hitler came into power and that a policy well advanced toward totalitarian planning had already done a great deal of the work which Hitler completed.

There can be no doubt that planning necessarily involves deliberate discrimination between particular needs of different people, and allowing one man to do what another must be prevented from doing. It must lay down by a legal rule how well off particular people shall be and what different people are to be allowed to have and do. It means in effect a return to the rule of status, a reversal of the "movement of progressive societies" which, in the famous phrase of Sir Henry Maine, "has hitherto been a movement from status to contract." Indeed, the Rule of Law, more than the rule of contract, should probably be regarded as the true opposite of the rule of status. It is the Rule of Law, in the sense of the rule of formal law, the absence of legal privileges of particular people designated by authority, which safeguards that equality before the law which is the opposite of arbitrary government.

Further Resources

BOOKS

Ebenstein, Alan O. *Friedrich Hayek: A Biography.* New York: Palgrave, 2001.

Gray, John. *Hayek on Liberty.* Third edition. New York: Routledge, 1998.

Steele, G.R. *Keynes and Hayek: The Money Economy.* New York: Routledge, 2001.

PERIODICALS

Sturgis, Amy H. "The Rise, Decline, and Reemergence of Classical Liberalism." *The LockeSmith Review,* vol. 1, *Great Thinkers in Classical Liberalism.* Nashville: The LockeSmith Institute, 1994, 20–63.

Taylor, Robert S. "The Social Theory of Friedrich A. Hayek." *The LockeSmith Review,* vol. 1, *Great Thinkers in Classical Liberalism.* Nashville: The LockeSmith Institute, 1994, 152–174.

WEBSITES

"Commanding Heights: The Battle for the World Economy." Public Broadcasting Service. Available online at http://www .pbs.org/wgbh/commandingheights/index.html; website home page http://www.pbs.org (accessed May 16, 2002).

Hayek Center for Multidisciplinary Research. Available online at http://www.hayekcenter.org/ (accessed May 16, 2002).

AUDIO AND VISUAL MEDIA

Commanding Heights: The Battle for the World Economy. Heights Productions, Inc. Videocassette, 2002.

"Serve your country in the WAVES"

Poster

By: U.S. Navy

Date: 1944

Source: "Serve your country in the WAVES." 1944. Navy Historical Center. Department of the Navy. Available online at http://www.history.navy.mil/ac/posters /wwiiwomen/wavep1.htm; website home page http://www .history.navy.mil/index.html (accessed March 17, 2003).

About the Organization: Throughout World War II (1939–1945), the U.S. government recruited men into national service, urged citizens to ration scarce resources such as food and gasoline, warned Americans against sharing confidential military information, and encouraged people to buy war bonds. It also conducted campaigns to draw women into the military. The U.S. Navy, for example, advertised on behalf of its female corps, the WAVES. Such advertisements reinforced the notion of U.S. servicewomen as patriots and as inspirational role models for the next generation of Americans. ■

Introduction

The U.S. Navy formed the WAVES, or Women Accepted for Volunteer Emergency Service, as a military unit on July 30, 1942. The WAVES immediately became a popular choice, drawing approximately 100,000 women during World War II. These servicewomen filled a number of different roles within the United States, from clerical workers to instructors for male pilots during flight training. The Navy actively recruited professional women in the fields of mathematics, engineering, and the physical sciences. These WAVES members undertook delicate tasks such as designing operations and calculating bomb trajectories. Many WAVES recruits filled positions previously reserved for men. At least one-third of the WAVES, for example, were assigned to naval aviation duties.

The WAVES treated its recruits in an unusually progressive way compared to its counterparts in other branches of the U.S. armed forces. The army's female unit, the Women's Auxiliary Corps (WACS), was subsidiary to male units. Women in the WAVES, however, could attain the same status as men who served in the reserves. The WAVES drew many influential civilians. The first WAVES commander, for example, was Mildred McAfee, the president of Wellesley College. Its ranks also included Grace Hopper, a pioneering mathematician who developed advanced computer technology such as UNIVAC I, the first commercial electronic computer. Hopper eventually became a rear admiral in the U.S. Navy.

Significance

The women of the WAVES played vital roles in the war effort, from training troops to planning precise military operations. Their efforts brought new attention to women in positions of authority and leadership and thus made military careers an option for American women. Women in uniform competed with working women such as Rosie the Riveter and Jenny on the Job, and pinup girls such as Betty Grable as symbols of American femininity, power, and wartime patriotic spirit. Ironically, the WAVES' refusal to accept African

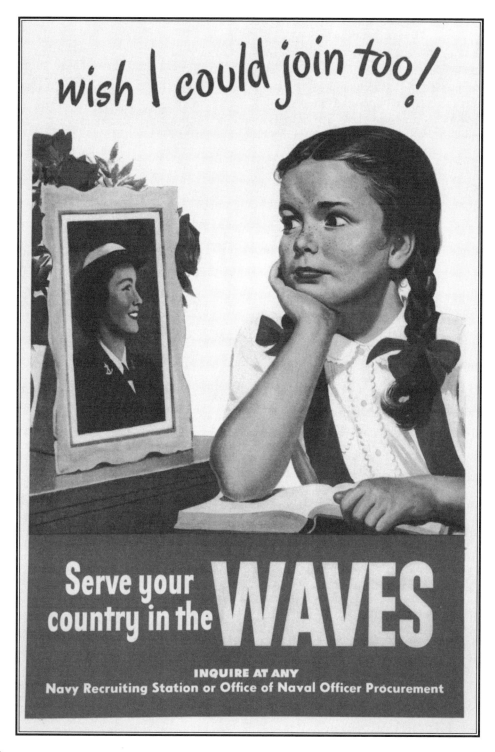

Primary Source

"Serve your country in the WAVES"

SYNOPSIS: This recruitment poster shows how a young girl might look up to women in the WAVES and dream of someday serving her country in a similar way. The poster demonstrates how U.S. military recruitment campaigns encouraged and capitalized on the image of WAVES members as patriotic role models for young Americans. COURTESY OF THE NAVAL HISTORICAL FOUNDATION.

Americans helped integrate the armed services. The WAVES' discriminatory policy drew vocal complaints and placed pressure on Washington to integrate all branches of the American military. After President Harry S. Truman (served 1945–1953) ordered racial integration of the armed services through Executive Order 9981, the WAVES accepted their first African-American members.

The WAVES' significance is underscored by its continuation after World War II. In 1948, the Women's Armed Services Integration Act made the WAVES a permanent part of the U.S. Navy. Eventually some women served in the WAVES overseas; several thousand members, for instance, took part in the Korean War. The WAVES existed until 1978, when separate women's units of the armed forces were integrated with their formerly all-male counterparts. The WAVES began a tradition of women's involvement in the U.S. Navy that remained unbroken into the twenty-first century.

Further Resources

BOOKS

Gruhitz-Hoyt, Olga. *They Also Served: American Women in World War II.* Secaucus, N.J.: Carol Publishing Group, 1995.

Larson, C. Kay. *'Til I Come Marching Home: A Brief History of American Women in World War II.* Pasadena, M.D.: Minerva Center, 1995.

Litoff, Judy Barett, and David C. Smith. *American Women in a World at War: Contemporary Accounts From World War II.* Wilmington, Del.: Scholarly Resources, 1997.

WEBSITES

Naval Historical Center. Available online at http://www.history .navy.mil/index.html (accessed March 17, 2003).

"Postcard Collection: WAVES—World War II." Smith College Archives. Available online at http://clio.fivecolleges.edu/smith /postcards/wave.htm; website home page http://clio.fivecolleges.edu/smith (accessed March 17, 2003).

"Charter of the United Nations Preamble"

Charter

By: Representatives of the Governments of the United Nations

Date: June 26, 1945

Source: "Charter of the United Nations Preamble." June 26, 1945. Available at the University of Minnesota Human Rights Library online at http://www1.umn.edu/humanrts/instree /preamble.html; website home page http://www1.umn.edu /humanrts/index.html (accessed March 19, 2003).

Inscription taken from the Bible (Isaiah 2:4) on a staircase leading through the United Nations buildings in New York City. GETTY IMAGES. REPRODUCED BY PERMISSION.

About the Organization: Although the United Nations Charter had no one single author, the so-called "Big Three" nations—the United States, the United Kingdom, and the Soviet Union—took the lead in establishing the organization. The charter itself resulted primarily from international wartime conferences held in Dumbarton Oaks, Washington, D.C.; Yalta, Crimea; and San Francisco, California. ∎

Introduction

The name "United Nations" (UN) originally referred to those nations allied against Germany, Italy, and Japan in World War II (1939–1945). These nations, also known as the Allies, agreed that a new global organization would be needed after the war to help manage international affairs and prevent another world war. A year after World War I (1914–1918), the Treaty of Versailles had established the first such body, known as the League of Nations. As World War II made painfully obvious, the League of Nations proved unable to ensure global peace and security. Its many weaknesses, however, provided the starting point for dialogue about a new international body. Eventually the United States, the United Kingdom, and the Soviet Union took the lead in devising a new plan. Chief concerns among the three were how the UN would recognize membership, colonies, and voting formulas. Through the Dumbarton

Secretary of State James Byrnes looks on as Truman signs the document that ratifies the United Nations Charter, August 1945. © HULTON-DEUTSCH COLLECTION/CORBIS. REPRODUCED BY PERMISSION.

Oaks, Yalta, and San Francisco wartime conferences, representatives of the nations eventually reached agreement on these issues and created a charter to give the organization shape.

The UN Charter was unanimously adopted on June 26, 1945, by representatives of fifty countries: nine from continental Europe, 21 from American republics, seven from Middle East states, five from Commonwealth nations, two from Soviet republics and one from the Soviet Union itself, two from East Asian nations, and three from African states. The charter took effect on October 24, 1945. The UN located its headquarters in New York City and established offices in Geneva and Vienna, with field stations around the world.

Significance

The UN inherited the purpose, structure, and functions of the League of Nations, which disbanded in 1946. While the two organizations shared some striking similarities, the UN proved more aggressive and dedicated to maintaining international peace and security. The UN's effectiveness stemmed in part from changes in the decision-making process, as outlined in the charter. The shift in international relations wrought by the war also increased the UN's clout. Member nations, well aware that the League of Nations had not been able to prevent

World War II, intended to make the UN capable of preventing World War III.

Nevertheless, the UN faced considerable obstacles in its first decades. Tension between the United States and the Soviet Union during the Cold War strained the organization's ability to function. The dismantling of European colonies in the Middle East, Asia, and Africa after World War II also presented stiff challenges. The UN, however, survived its difficult birth. Its location in New York City, coupled with the ongoing leadership of the United States, helped to secure the U.S. role in world affairs after 1945. The Preamble to the UN Charter, in particular, reflects the philosophy and influence of U.S. presidents, including Woodrow Wilson (served 1913–1921), who was instrumental in establishing the League of Nations, and Franklin D. Roosevelt (served 1933–1945), whose Four Freedoms speech outlined social and political goals that anticipated the spirit of the United Nations.

Primary Source

"Charter of the United Nations Preamble"

> **SYNOPSIS:** In the Preamble to the Charter of the United Nations, the representatives of member governments set forth the guiding principles on which

the organization was founded. The main purpose of the United Nations remains the preservation of international peace and security.

We the peoples of the United Nations determined

- to save succeeding generations from the scourge of war, which twice in our lifetime has brought untold sorrow to mankind, and

- to reaffirm faith in fundamental human rights, in the dignity and worth of the human person, in the equal rights of men and women and of nations large and small, and

- to establish conditions under which justice and respect for the obligations arising from treaties and other sources of international law can be maintained, and

- to promote social progress and better standards of life in larger freedom,

and for these ends

- to practice tolerance and live together in peace with one another as good neighbors, and

- to unite our strength to maintain international peace and security, and

- to ensure by the acceptance of principles and the institution of methods, that armed force shall not be used, save in the common interest, and

- to employ international machinery for the promotion of the economic and social advancement of all peoples,

have resolved to combine our efforts to accomplish these aims.

Accordingly, our respective Governments, through representatives assembled in the city of San Francisco, who have exhibited their full powers found to be in good and due form, have agreed to the present Charter of the United Nations and do hereby establish an international organization to be known as the United Nations.

Further Resources

BOOKS

Basic Facts about the United Nations. New York: United Nations, 1998.

Meisler, Stanley. *The United Nations: The First Fifty Years.* New York: Atlantic Monthly Press, 1997.

Simma, Bruno, and Hermann Mosler, eds. *The Charter of the United Nations: A Commentary.* New York: Oxford University Press, 1995.

WEBSITES

United Nations. Available online at http://www.un.org (accessed May 9, 2002).

"United Nations Milestones." Truman Presidential Museum and Library. Available online at http://www.trumanlibrary .org/whistlestop/teacher_lessons/un_milestones.htm; website home page http://www.trumanlibrary.org (accessed May 9, 2002).

"President Harry S. Truman's Address Before a Joint Session of Congress, March 12, 1947"

Speech

By: Harry S. Truman

Date: March 12, 1947

Source: Truman, Harry S. "President Harry S. Truman's Address Before a Joint Session of Congress, March 12, 1947." The Avalon Project at the Yale Law School. Available online at http://www.yale.edu/lawweb/avalon/trudoc.htm; website home page http://www.yale.edu (accessed March 18, 2003).

About the Author: Harry S. Truman (1884–1972) was president of the United States from 1945 to 1953. Born in Missouri, he held a seat in the U.S. Senate before becoming vice president during the last term of President Franklin D. Roosevelt (served 1933–1945). When Roosevelt died suddenly in 1945, Truman became the thirty-third president of the United States. He remained in the White House until 1953. Truman is best remembered for his decision to use the atomic bomb against the Japanese in World War II (1939–1945), his opposition to Soviet expansionism across the globe, and his precedent-setting Truman Doctrine. ∎

Introduction

On March 12, 1947, President Harry S. Truman addressed a joint session of Congress to request immediate economic and military aid for the governments of Greece and Turkey. At the time the Greek government was threatened by communist rebellion, and Turkey was endangered by Soviet expansion in the Mediterranean area. Great Britain faced severe financial challenges caused by heavy human and materiel losses in World War II and could not continue providing assistance to Mediterranean countries that struggled to withstand internal instability and external pressure from the Soviet Union. Other nations of the West agreed with Great Britain's assessment that these nations were in danger of falling to the communists, but they were likewise unable to assist. Truman stated that the duty of providing aid therefore fell to the United States.

President Harry S. Truman addresses a joint session of Congress to request aid for Greece and Turkey, March 12, 1947. AP/WIDE WORLD PHOTOS. REPRODUCED BY PERMISSION.

Truman deliberately referred to the recent world war in his appeal to Congress. He noted how the United States fought Germany and Japan, governments that tried to coerce other nations against the will of their people. Then he explained how the United States could once again fight coercion by helping Greece and Turkey to remain free and self-ruling. Truman's speech was ironic because the Soviet Union had been a U.S. ally during the war, and it was the Soviet Union and its practice of communism that now presented the perceived threat to Greece and Turkey. Irony aside, however, Truman's speech convinced Congress to intervene in the Mediterranean and provide approximately four million dollars in assistance to Greece and Turkey.

Significance

Truman's speech had lasting impact in four primary ways. First and most obviously, the speech had its desired effect; Congress appropriated funds to aid Greece and Turkey. Second, in the bigger picture, the specific request for this assistance set a precedent known as the Truman Doctrine. This doctrine held that it was the duty of the United States, based on both philosophical principle and political self-interest, to support free peoples across the world who resisted communist domination. For Truman's purposes, "free peoples" did not necessarily

mean democracies or republics, but rather any state with Western, anticommunist sympathies. The U.S. government later used this doctrine to justify U.S. intervention in Korea (1950–1953) and Vietnam (1964–1975), among other places.

The third impact of the Truman Doctrine was the establishment of a pattern of U.S. financial aid to other countries. Before the war, the United States was one actor among many on the world stage. Afterward it emerged as a leading nation, largely because its economy had survived and even thrived on the war effort. The precedent of extending financial assistance to other nations opened the door for other policies such as the Marshall Plan, which provided economic help for European nations rebuilding after the war.

Truman's position had a fourth impact as well: The United States took over the job of helping struggling countries, a task previously shouldered by Great Britain and other Western nations. The Truman Doctrine also set up the United States as the chief opponent of the Soviet Union politically, economically, and militarily in the postwar world. This opposition between the democratic United States and the communist Soviet Union defined the Cold War era, which was characterized by proxy wars across the world, the competition to reach and conquer space, and the nuclear arms race until its conclusion in the late 1980s.

Primary Source

"President Harry S. Truman's Address Before a Joint Session of Congress, March 12, 1947" [excerpt]

SYNOPSIS: In this excerpt from Truman's speech, he explains the situation in the Mediterranean and calls for U.S. aid to Greece and Turkey. Truman argues that the United States has a duty to assist free peoples resisting coercion from other nations, thus setting the policy precedent known as the Truman Doctrine.

Mr. President, Mr. Speaker, Members of the Congress of the United States:

The gravity of the situation which confronts the world today necessitates my appearance before a joint session of the Congress. The foreign policy and the national security of this country are involved.

One aspect of the present situation, which I wish to present to you at this time for your consideration and decision, concerns Greece and Turkey.

The United States has received from the Greek Government an urgent appeal for financial and economic assistance. Preliminary reports from the American Economic Mission now in Greece and reports from the American Ambassador in Greece corroborate the statement of the Greek Government that assistance is imperative if Greece is to survive as a free nation.

I do not believe that the American people and the Congress wish to turn a deaf ear to the appeal of the Greek Government. . . .

As in the case of Greece, if Turkey is to have the assistance it needs, the United States must supply it. We are the only country able to provide that help.

I am fully aware of the broad implications involved if the United States extends assistance to Greece and Turkey, and I shall discuss these implications with you at this time.

One of the primary objectives of the foreign policy of the United States is the creation of conditions in which we and other nations will be able to work out a way of life free from coercion. This was a fundamental issue in the war with Germany and Japan. Our victory was won over countries which sought to impose their will, and their way of life, upon other nations.

To ensure the peaceful development of nations, free from coercion, the United States has taken a leading part in establishing the United Nations. The United Nations is designed to make possible lasting freedom and independence for all its members. We shall not realize our objectives, however, unless we are willing to help free peoples to maintain their free institutions and their national integrity against aggressive movements that seek to impose upon them totalitarian regimes. This is no more than a frank recognition that totalitarian regimes imposed on free peoples, by direct or indirect aggression, undermine the foundations of international peace and hence the security of the United States.

The peoples of a number of countries of the world have recently had totalitarian regimes forced upon them against their will. The Government of the United States has made frequent protests against coercion and intimidation, in violation of the Yalta agreement, in Poland, Rumania, and Bulgaria. I must also state that in a number of other countries there have been similar developments.

At the present moment in world history nearly every nation must choose between alternative ways of life. The choice is too often not a free one.

One way of life is based upon the will of the majority, and is distinguished by free institutions, representative government, free elections, guarantees of individual liberty, freedom of speech and religion, and freedom from political oppression.

The second way of life is based upon the will of a minority forcibly imposed upon the majority. It relies upon terror and oppression, a controlled press and radio; fixed elections, and the suppression of personal freedoms.

I believe that it must be the policy of the United States to support free peoples who are resisting attempted subjugation by armed minorities or by outside pressures.

I believe that we must assist free peoples to work out their own destinies in their own way.

I believe that our help should be primarily through economic and financial aid which is essential to economic stability and orderly political processes.

The world is not static, and the status quo is not sacred. But we cannot allow changes in the status quo in violation of the Charter of the United Nations by such methods as coercion, or by such subterfuges as political infiltration. In helping free and independent nations to maintain their freedom, the United States will be giving effect to the principles of the Charter of the United Nations.

It is necessary only to glance at a map to realize that the survival and integrity of the Greek nation are of grave importance in a much wider situation. If Greece should fall under the control of an armed minority, the effect upon its neighbor, Turkey, would be immediate and serious. Confusion and disorder might well spread throughout the entire Middle East.

Moreover, the disappearance of Greece as an independent state would have a profound effect upon those countries in Europe whose peoples are struggling against great difficulties to maintain their freedoms and their independence while they repair the damages of war.

It would be an unspeakable tragedy if these countries, which have struggled so long against overwhelming odds, should lose that victory for which they sacrificed so much. Collapse of free institutions and loss of independence would be disastrous not only for them but for the world. Discouragement and possibly failure would quickly be the lot of neighboring peoples striving to maintain their freedom and independence.

Should we fail to aid Greece and Turkey in this fateful hour, the effect will be far reaching to the West as well as to the East.

We must take immediate and resolute action.

I therefore ask the Congress to provide authority for assistance to Greece and Turkey in the amount of $400,000,000 for the period ending June 30, 1948. In requesting these funds, I have taken into consideration the maximum amount of relief assistance which would be furnished to Greece out of the $350,000,000 which I recently requested that the Congress authorize for the prevention of starvation and suffering in countries devastated by the war.

In addition to funds, I ask the Congress to authorize the detail of American civilian and military personnel to Greece and Turkey, at the request of those countries, to assist in the tasks of reconstruction, and for the purpose of supervising the use of such financial and material assistance as may be furnished. I recommend that authority also be provided for the instruction and training of selected Greek and Turkish personnel.

Finally, I ask that the Congress provide authority which will permit the speediest and most effective use, in terms of needed commodities, supplies, and equipment, of such funds as may be authorized.

If further funds, or further authority, should be needed for purposes indicated in this message, I shall not hesitate to bring the situation before the Congress. On this subject the Executive and Legislative branches of the Government must work together.

This is a serious course upon which we embark.

I would not recommend it except that the alternative is much more serious. The United States contributed $341,000,000,000 toward winning World War II. This is an investment in world freedom and world peace.

The assistance that I am recommending for Greece and Turkey amounts to little more than 1 tenth of 1 per cent of this investment. It is only common sense that we should safeguard this investment and make sure that it was not in vain.

The seeds of totalitarian regimes are nurtured by misery and want. They spread and grow in the evil soil of poverty and strife. They reach their full growth when the hope of a people for a better life has died. We must keep that hope alive.

The free peoples of the world look to us for support in maintaining their freedoms.

If we falter in our leadership, we may endanger the peace of the world—and we shall surely endanger the welfare of our own nation.

Great responsibilities have been placed upon us by the swift movement of events.

I am confident that the Congress will face these responsibilities squarely.

Further Resources

BOOKS

Jones, Howard. *"A New Kind of War": America's Global Strategy and the Truman Doctrine in Greece.* New York: Oxford University Press, 1989.

McGhee, George Crews. *The U.S.-Turkish-NATO Middle East Connection: How the Truman Doctrine Contained the Soviets in the Middle East.* New York: St. Martin's Press, 1990.

Rossides, Eugene T., ed. *Truman Doctrine of Aid to Greece: A Fifty-Year Retrospective.* Washington, D.C.: American Hellenic Institute Foundation, 1998.

PERIODICALS

Ivie, Robert L. "Fire, Flood, and Red Fever: Motivating Metaphors of Global Emergency in the Truman Doctrine Speech." *Presidential Studies Quarterly,* September 1999, 570–591.

Shogan, Robert. "Truman Doctrine Holds Lessons, Cautions for Today's Leaders." *Los Angeles Times,* March 11, 1997, A5.

WEBSITES

Harry S. Truman Library and Museum. Available online at http://www.trumanlibrary.org/ (accessed May 1, 2002).

The Testimony of J. Edgar Hoover Before the House Un-American Activities Committee

Testimony

By: J. Edgar Hoover

Date: March 26, 1947

Source: "The Testimony of J. Edgar Hoover Before the House Un-American Activities Committee." March 26, 1947. Reprinted in *Cold War*. Cable News Network. Available at CNN online at http://www.cnn.com/SPECIALS/cold.war /episodes/06/documents/hoover/; website home page http:// www.cnn.com (accessed March 17, 2003).

About the Author: J[ohn] Edgar Hoover (1895–1977) served as the director of the Federal Bureau of Investigation from 1924 until his death. The size and scope of the FBI expanded greatly under his controversial leadership. He is best known for his aggressive investigation of communists both inside and outside of the U.S. government, his surveillance of so-called "political radicals" from Ku Klux Klan members to Martin Luther King, Jr., and his toleration of Mafia activity in the United States. ∎

Introduction

After the World War II alliance between the United States and the Soviet Union ended, American anticommunist sentiment exceeded its pre-war level because the chief communist power, the Soviet Union, was the sole superpower competing with the United States. Its political system of centralized planning and government ownership was in opposition to the U.S. political system of democratic elections and capitalism. The Soviet Union was also blatantly hostile to U.S. interests. Moreover, communist influence was expanding because of military efforts by the Soviet Union and later China and because the theory of communism proved attractive to many across the globe. Some in the United States feared not only attack by external communist powers but also infiltration by American communists. Subversive communist ideas and propaganda, they argued, were as dangerous to the U.S. government as bombs and soldiers. Fear turned to hysteria and spawned what became known as the "Red Scare."

U.S. leaders played into the hands of Red Scare proponents. President Harry S. Truman (served 1945–1953) established the Federal Employee Loyalty Program in order to detect alleged communists in state service. The Dies Committee and the State of California Joint Fact-Finding Committee on Un-American Activities paved the way for the House Un-American Activities Committee (HUAC), which was created to investigate and expose communists nationally. The committee scrutinized many private industries as well as governmental bodies. Between 1947 and 1954, HUAC paid particular attention to the film business. Hollywood screenwriters, producers, directors, and actors suspected of having communist sympathies were "blacklisted," effectively shunned and ignored by their colleagues. This was not the first time. In 1938, the Dies Committee even called ten-year-old screen star Shirley Temple to testify about her knowledge of communists in Hollywood. HUAC took the investigation further, however, jailing those who took the Fifth Amendment and refused to testify about their alleged political beliefs and affiliations. Testimony such as J. Edgar Hoover's helped to maintain the momentum behind HUAC and the fear behind the Red Scare.

Significance

Fear of communism and the Soviet system propelled U.S. policy for decades and thus had lasting repercussions. Notably it led to U.S. intervention in Korea (1950–1953) and Vietnam (1964–1975). The Truman Doctrine, which initiated U.S. support of democracies all over the world, was integral to this policy. The U.S.-Soviet rivalry was enhanced by competition in space exploration, which became intense when the Soviet Union launched the first satellite. Both nations also competed militarily by stockpiling nuclear weapons.

Domestically, the United States faced a difficult challenge in preserving the rights of free speech, expression, and assembly in light of the Red Scare. HUAC's activities, for example, ended many careers in Hollywood and greatly increased the government's ability to censor artists and their work. Individuals were penalized for claiming their constitutional rights and denied due process of the law in the name of national security. Some later movements reacted against the precedent set by the most fervent anticommunists. The antiwar, student, and free speech movements of the 1960s, for example, criticized the panic of the 1940s and 1950s. The pendulum of public opinion eventually reached the other side; communism even became fashionable in certain settings, particularly Marxism on university campuses. With the end of the Cold War and the fall of the Soviet Union by the 1990s, the subject of communism became less timely. The debate about how to ensure national defense without violating individual rights, however, has remained.

Primary Source

The Testimony of J. Edgar Hoover Before the House Un-American Activities Committee [excerpt]

SYNOPSIS: The following excerpts come from J. Edgar Hoover's testimony to the House Un-American Activities Committee. Hoover argues that communists in the United States are dangerous and destructive

FBI Director J. Edgar Hoover gives his speech regarding communism to the House Un-American Activities Committee (HUAC) on March 26, 1947. ©
BETTMANN/CORBIS. REPRODUCED BY PERMISSION.

and calls for a "vigorous, intelligent, old-fashioned Americanism" to defend against them. This speech and others like it attempted to combat communism by describing the situation as a national emergency.

My feelings concerning the Communist Party of the United States are well known. I have not hesitated over the years to express my concern and apprehension. As a consequence its professional smear brigades have conducted a relentless assault against the FBI. You who have been members of this committee also know the fury with which the party, its sympathizers and fellow travelers can launch an assault. I do not mind such attacks. What has been disillusioning is the manner in which they have been able to enlist support often from apparently well-meaning but thoroughly duped persons. . . .

The communist movement in the United States began to manifest itself in 1919. Since then it has changed its name and its party line whenever expedient and tactical. But always it comes back to fundamentals and bills itself as the party of Marxism-Leninism. As such, it stands for the destruction of our American form of government; it stands for the destruction of American democracy; it stands for the destruction of free enterprise; and

it stands for the creation of a "Soviet of the United States" and ultimate world revolution. . . .

The communist, once he is fully trained and indoctrinated, realizes that he can create his order in the United States only by "bloody revolution." Their chief textbook, *The History of the Communist Party of the Soviet Union,* is used as a basis for planning their revolution. Their tactics require that to be successful they must have:

1. The will and sympathy of the people.

2. Military aid and assistance.

3. Plenty of guns and ammunition.

4. A program for extermination of the police as they are the most important enemy and are termed "trained fascists."

5. Seizure of all communications, buses, railroads, radio stations, and other forms of communications and transportation. . . .

One thing is certain. The American progress which all good citizens seek, such as old-age security, houses for veterans, child assistance, and a host of others, is being adopted as window dressing by the communists to conceal their true aims and entrap gullible followers. . . .

The mad march of Red fascism is a cause for concern in America. But the deceit, the trickery, and the lies of the American communists are catching up with them. Whenever the spotlight of truth is focused upon them they cry, "Red-baiting." Now that their aims and objectives are being exposed, they are creating a Committee for the Constitutional Rights of Communists, and are feverishly working to build up what they term a quarter-million-dollar defense fund to place ads in papers, to publish pamphlets, to buy radio time. They know that their backs will soon be to the wall. . . .

I feel that this committee could render a great service to the nation through its power of exposure in quickly spotlighting existing front organizations and those which will be created in the future. There are easy tests to establish the real character of such organizations:

1. Does the group espouse the cause of Americanism or the cause of Soviet Russia?

2. Does the organization feature as speakers at its meeting known communists, sympathizers, or fellow travelers?

3. Does the organization shift when the party line shifts?

4. Does the organization sponsor causes, campaigns, literature, petitions, or other activities sponsored by the party or other front organizations?

5. Is the organization used as a sounding board by or is it endorsed by communist-controlled labor unions?

6. Does its literature follow the communist line or is it printed by the communist press?

7. Does the organization receive consistent favorable mention in the communist publications?

8. Does the organization present itself to be nonpartisan yet engage in political activities and consistently advocate causes favored by the communists?

9. Does the organization denounce American and British foreign policy while always lauding Soviet policy?

10. Does the organization utilize communist "double-talk" by referring to Soviet dominated countries as democracies, complaining that the United States is imperialistic and constantly denouncing monopoly-capital?

11. Have outstanding leaders in public life openly renounced affiliation with the organization?

12. Does the organization, if espousing liberal progressive causes, attract well-known honest patriotic liberals or does it denounce well-known liberals?

13. Does the organization have a consistent record of supporting the American viewpoint over the years?

14. Does the organization consider matters now directly related to its avowed purposes and objectives?

The Communist Party of the United States is a fifth column if there ever was one. It is far better organized than were the Nazis in occupied countries prior to their capitulation. They are seeking to weaken America just as they did in their era of obstruction when they were aligned with the Nazis. Their goal is the overthrow of our government. There is no doubt as to where a real communist's loyalty rests. Their allegiance is to Russia, not the United States. . . .

What can we do? And what should be our course of action? The best antidote to communism is vigorous, intelligent, old-fashioned Americanism, with eternal vigilance. I do not favor any course of action which would give the communists cause to portray and pity themselves as martyrs. I do favor unrelenting prosecution wherever they are found to be violating our country's laws.

As Americans, our most effective defense is a workable democracy that guarantees and preserves our cherished freedoms.

I would have no fears if more Americans possessed the zeal, the fervor, the persistence and the industry to learn about this menace of Red fascism. I do fear for the liberal and progressive who has been hoodwinked and duped into joining hands with the communists. I confess to a real apprehension so long as communists are able to secure ministers of the gospel to promote their evil work and espouse a cause that is alien to the religion of Christ and Judaism. I do fear so long as school boards and parents tolerate conditions whereby communists and fellow travelers, under the guise of academic freedom, can teach our youth a way of life that eventually will destroy the sanctity of the home, that undermines faith in God, that causes them to scorn respect for constituted authority and sabotage our revered Constitution.

I do fear so long as American labor groups are infiltrated, dominated or saturated with the virus of communism. I do fear the palliation and weasel-worded gestures against communism indulged in by some of our labor leaders who should know better, but who have become pawns in the hands of sinister but astute manipulations for the communist cause.

I fear for ignorance on the part of all our people who may take the poisonous pills of communist propaganda.

Further Resources

BOOKS

Barson, Michael, and Steven Heller. *Red Scared!: The Commie Menace in Propaganda and Popular Culture.* San Francisco: Chronicle Books, 2001.

Hoover, J. Edgar. *Masters of Deceit: The Story of Communism in America and How to Fight It.* Reprint edition. New York: Buccaneer Books, 1994.

O'Reilly, Kenneth. *Hoover and the Unamericans: The FBI, HUAC, and the Red Menace.* Philadelphia: Temple University Press, 1983.

WEBSITES

"Excerpts from HUAC Hearings." *Cold War.* Cable News Network. Available online at http://www.cnn.com/SPECIALS /cold.war/episodes/06/documents/huac/; website home page http://www.cnn.com (accessed March 17, 2003).

"HUAC and Censorship Changes." Available online at http:// www.moderntimes.com/palace/huac.htm; website home page http://www.moderntimes.com/palace/index.html (accessed March 17, 2003).

"HUAC, McCarthy, and the Reds." Available online at http:// huac.tripod.com/ (accessed March 17, 2003).

"Address by General George C. Marshall Secretary of State of the United States at Harvard University, June 5, 1947"

Speech

By: George C. Marshall

Date: June 5, 1947

Source: "Address by General George C. Marshall Secretary of State of the United States at Harvard University." June 5, 1947. Available at the Organisation for Economic Co-operation and Development online at http://www.oecd.org/EN/document/0,,EN-document-0 -nodirectorate-no-16-9362-0,,00.html; website home page http://www.oecd.org (accessed March 17, 2003).

About the Author: General George C. Marshall (1880–1959) served as U.S. Army chief of staff during World War II (1939–1945) and later as secretary of state (1947–1949) and secretary of defense (1950–1951). He is best remembered for the European Recovery Program he proposed in 1947, which became known as the Marshall Plan. In 1953 he received the Nobel Prize for Peace. ∎

Introduction

World War II dealt a harsh blow to the economies of many European nations. It also left the democratic United States vying with the communist Soviet Union for influence across the globe. In an address at Harvard University in 1947, U.S. Secretary of State George Marshall suggested the idea of a European self-help program, financed by the United States, to deal with Europe's economic problems. Marshall explained that helping these nations rebuild and stabilize their economies would ensure that democratic institutions survived in Europe. Allowing the economies to struggle, he argued, would be an invitation for communist expansion in Europe. He believed that disheartened and suffering European citizens might vote for communist parties within their nations if solutions to their hardships did not arrive soon. A European Recovery Program therefore would not only help European nations but would also further U.S. interests in preserving democracies and fighting communism during the Cold War.

The European Recovery Program described by Marshall went into effect in 1948 and became known as the Marshall Plan. A committee of 16 countries met to discuss how to solve the poverty, unemployment, and dislocation created in Europe by the war; the resulting reconstruction plan became the basis for U.S. policy. From 1948 to 1951, Austria, Belgium, Denmark, France, Greece, Iceland, Ireland, Italy, Luxembourg, The Netherlands, Norway, Portugal, Sweden, Switzerland, Turkey, the United Kingdom, and West Germany all participated in the plan. Although the United States assisted Eastern European nations, the Soviet Union withdrew its participation in aiding nations under its military control.

Significance

The Marshall Plan brought about several important changes, not only reconstructing Europe after World War II but also changing the United States and its place in the world. First, the program succeeded in helping Europe back to its feet. Some Western European nations experienced increases of 15 to 25 percent in their gross national products; European chemical, engineering, and steel industries in particular experienced rapid recovery. Second, the Marshall Plan succeeded in political terms. The communist expansion in Europe that Marshall and others feared did not happen. Furthermore, the plan's success cemented a leadership position for the United States on

A poster that promotes the European Recovery (or Marshall) Plan. THE LIBRARY OF CONGRESS.

the world stage. The U.S. program distributed $13 billion in economic aid to help restore industry, agriculture, and trade in Europe. As the architect of European reconstruction, the United States gained a power unimaginable only a few years earlier, when the nation had been only one of many global forces and certainly not a superpower.

Third, the program established the Economic Cooperation Administration (ECA) to divide and distribute the relief funds. The temporary ECA was replaced later by the permanent Organisation for European Economic Cooperation (OEEC), which admitted West Germany to its ranks. Fourth, the Marshall Plan set a precedent for how the United States offered economic aid to other nations. President Harry S. Truman (served 1945–1953), for example, used the plan as a model for assistance to less developed countries in his Point Four Program of 1949.

Primary Source

"Address by General George C. Marshall Secretary of State of the United States at Harvard University, June 5, 1947" [excerpt]

SYNOPSIS: In this excerpt, Secretary of State Marshall introduces the idea of giving U.S. aid to European nations in order to rebuild economies shattered by World War II. Not only would this assist the nations in question, he argues, but it would help U.S. interests by supporting fellow democracies and discouraging the spread of communism.

But to speak more seriously, I need not tell you, gentlemen, that the world situation is very serious. That must be apparent to all intelligent people. I think one difficulty is that the problem is one of such enormous complexity that the very mass of facts presented to the public by press and radio make it exceedingly difficult for the man in the street to reach a clear appraisement of the situation. Furthermore, the people of this country are distant from the troubled areas of the earth and it is hard for them to comprehend the plight and consequent reactions of the long-suffering peoples, and the effect of those reactions on their governments in connection with our efforts to promote peace in the world.

In considering the requirements for the rehabilitation of Europe, the physical loss of life, the visible destruction of cities, factories, mines and railroads was correctly estimated but it has become obvious during recent months that this visible destruction was probably less serious than the dislocation of the entire fabric of European economy. For the past 10 years conditions have been highly abnormal. The feverish preparation for war and the more feverish maintenance of the war effort engulfed all aspects of national economies. Machinery has fallen into disrepair or is entirely obsolete. Under the arbitrary and destructive Nazi rule, virtually every possible enterprise was geared into the German war machine. Long-standing commercial ties, private institutions, banks, insurance companies, and shipping companies disappeared, through loss of capital, absorption through nationalization, or by simple destruction. In many countries, confidence in the local currency has been severely shaken. The breakdown of the business structure of Europe during the war was complete. Recovery has been seriously retarded by the fact that two years after the close of hostilities a peace settlement with Germany and Austria has not been agreed upon. But even given a more prompt solution of these difficult problems the rehabilitation of the economic structure of Europe quite evidently will require a much longer time and greater effort than had been foreseen.

There is a phase of this matter which is both interesting and serious. The farmer has always produced the foodstuffs to exchange with the city dweller for the other necessities of life. This division of labor is the basis of modern civilization. At the present time it is threatened with breakdown. The town and city industries are not producing adequate goods to exchange with the food-producing farmer. Raw materials and fuel are in short supply. Machinery is lacking or worn out. The farmer or the peasant cannot find the goods for sale which he desires to purchase. So the sale of his farm produce for money which he cannot use seems to him an unprofitable transaction. He, therefore, has withdrawn many fields from crop cultivation and is using them for grazing. He feeds more grain to stock and finds for himself and his family an ample supply of food, however short he may be on clothing and the other ordinary gadgets of civilization. Meanwhile people in the cities are short of food and fuel. So the governments are forced to use their foreign money and credits to procure these necessities abroad. This process exhausts funds which are urgently needed for reconstruction. Thus a very serious situation is rapidly developing which bodes no good for the world. The modern system of the division of labor upon which the exchange of products is based is in danger of breaking down.

The truth of the matter is that Europe's requirements for the next three or four years of foreign food and other essential products—principally from America—are so much greater than her present ability to pay that she must have substantial additional help or face economic, social, and political deterioration of a very grave character.

The remedy lies in breaking the vicious circle and restoring the confidence of the European people in the economic future of their own countries and of Europe as a whole. The manufacturer and the farmer throughout wide areas must be able and willing to exchange their products for currencies the continuing value of which is not open to question. . . .

An essential part of any successful action on the part of the United States is an understanding on the part of the people of America of the character of the problem and the remedies to be applied. Political passion and prejudice should have no part. With foresight, and a willingness on the part of our people to face up to the vast responsibility which history has clearly placed upon our country, the difficulties I have outlined can and will be overcome.

I am sorry that on each occasion I have said something publicly in regard to our international situation, I've been forced by the necessities of

Highly regarded by the top goverment leaders, George C. Marshall was called out of retirement to serve as U.S. Secretary of State. **PUBLIC DOMAIN.**

the case to enter into rather technical discussions. But to my mind, it is of vast importance that our people reach some general understanding of what the complications really are, rather than react from a passion or a prejudice or an emotion of the moment. As I said more formally a moment ago, we are remote from the scene of these troubles. It is virtually impossible at this distance merely by reading, or listening, or even seeing photographs or motion pictures, to grasp at all the real significance of the situation. And yet the whole world of the future hangs on a proper judgment. It hangs, I think, to a large extent on the realization of the American people, of just what are the various dominant factors. What are the reactions of the people? What are the justifications of those reactions? What are the sufferings? What is needed? What can best be done? What must be done? Thank you very much.

Further Resources
BOOKS
Hogan, Michael J. *The Marshall Plan: America, Britain, and the Reconstruction of Western Europe, 1947–1952.* Cambridge: Cambridge University Press, 1989.

Montgomery, John Dickey, and Dennis A. Rondinelli, eds. *Great Policies.* New York: Praeger, 1995.

Schain, Martin, ed. *The Marshall Plan: Fifty Years After.* New York: Palgrave, 2001.

WEBSITES

"Featured Documents: The Marshall Plan." National Archives and Records Administration. Available online at http://www .archives.gov/exhibit_hall/featured_documents/marshall_plan /index.html; website home page http://www.archives.gov/ (accessed March 17, 2003).

"For European Recovery: The Fiftieth Anniversary of the Marshall Plan." Library of Congress. Available online at http:// lcweb.loc.gov/exhibits/marshall/; website home page http:// www.loc.gov/ (accessed March 17, 2003).

"The Marshall Plan." United States Agency for International Development. Available online at http://www.usaid.gov /multimedia/video/marshall/; website home page http:// www.usaid.gov/ (accessed March 17, 2003).

"Dewey Defeats Truman"

Photograph

By: Frank Cancellare

Date: November 4, 1948

Source: "Dewey Defeats Truman." Photograph. November 4, 1948. United Press International.

About the Publication: The editors of the *Chicago Daily Tribune* were not alone in assuming that President Harry S. Truman (served 1945–1953) could not win the 1948 U.S. presidential election. Most polls and political analysts predicted a victory by his Republican opponent, Thomas E. Dewey. Truman did win the race, however, thanks to aggressive personal campaigning across the country and his strategy of attacking the Republican Congress instead of the Republican presidential candidate. Papers with partisan Republican leanings, such as the *Chicago Daily Tribune,* pictured below, were anxious to report the defeat of the Democrat Truman. The *Chicago Daily Tribune*'s error is best remembered because of the famous photograph of President Truman posing with its mistaken headline that Dewey, not Truman, won the election of 1948. ∎

Introduction

Vice President Harry S. Truman, a former senator from Missouri, became president of the United States on April 12, 1945, after Franklin D. Roosevelt (served 1933–1945) died in office. He agreed with Roosevelt's New Deal policy, which was based on the idea that the government needed to take an active role in providing economic justice and equality to U.S. citizens. As president Truman extended this policy through what he called the Fair Deal. Unlike Roosevelt, however, Truman appeared to the public as disorganized and restless, sug-

gesting new policies in each speech and failing to prioritize his most important initiatives. In other words, he seemed more of a confused bureaucrat than a visionary leader. In response the Congress, controlled by Republicans, opposed Truman's Democratic proposals and tried to limit, not increase, the size of government. This political opposition ensured that the Fair Deal would not have the success of Roosevelt's New Deal.

It seemed certain to most U.S. political and media insiders that Truman did not stand a chance of election when he decided to run for the presidency in 1948. The southern section of the Democratic Party split from the main party and formed the States' Rights, or "Dixiecrat," Party and nominated South Carolina governor Strom Thurmond to run for the presidency. The left wing of the Democratic Party supported Roosevelt's third vice president, Henry Wallace, as a candidate. This disharmony within the Democratic Party, combined with Truman's lackluster record, led most insiders to favor Republican nominee Thomas E. Dewey to win the race. Truman organized an aggressive campaign, however, traveling the nation by train and speaking directly to the people. Rather than attacking the opposition's candidate, he attacked what he called the "do-nothing Congress" in a series of fiery and eloquent speeches. His hard work paid off in the form of a surprise victory.

Significance

The election of 1948 was important for three reasons. First, it proved how much impact an effective campaign strategy could have. Truman turned the tide of public opinion toward him thanks to passionate speeches and personal appearances. His train trip across the nation was the difference between victory and defeat. Second, the campaign helped to set the precedent of presidents blaming Congress for the failure of policies and the obstruction of plans. Competing against Congress rather than the opposing presidential candidate became a pattern seen many times when presidents sought reelection in the twentieth century.

Third, the election had lasting importance because it gave Truman four more years as president. Although he ran on a Fair Deal platform, the program continued to disappoint both Truman and the American people. By the end of his term in 1952, Truman knew he could not win reelection. Popular opinion turned to the Republican Party with the election of Dwight Eisenhower (served 1953–1961). President Eisenhower's approach was quite different from Truman's. He wanted to cut spending, reduce taxes, limit the power of the presidency, and give more authority to the legislature and judiciary. The welfare-state era of the New Deal and Fair Deal ended with Truman's administration. Although Truman's election

Primary Source

"Dewey Defeats Truman"

SYNOPSIS: The editors of the *Chicago Daily Tribune* believed, like many others in the media, that Republican presidential candidate Thomas E. Dewey would win the election of 1948. They printed an edition of the newspaper that claimed "Dewey Defeats Truman" before the votes were even counted. In this photograph, President Harry S. Truman, having won the election, happily poses for a picture with the mistaken headline. UPI/CORBIS-BETTMANN. REPRODUCED BY PERMISSION.

seemed like a victory at the time, it did not guarantee success for the economic and political policies he supported.

Further Resources

BOOKS

Byrnes, Mark S. *The Truman Years, 1945–1953.* New York: Longman, 2000.

Donaldson, Gary. *Truman Defeats Dewey.* Lexington: University Press of Kentucky, 1999.

Karabell, Zachary. *The Last Campaign: How Harry Truman Won the 1948 Election.* New York: Knopf, 2000.

WEBSITES

Harry S. Truman Library and Museum. Available online at http://www.trumanlibrary.org/ (accessed May 16, 2002).

"Harry S. Truman." The White House. Available online at http://www.whitehouse.gov/history/presidents/ht33.html; website home page http://www.whitehouse.gov (accessed March 17, 2003).

"Communists Should Not Teach in American Colleges"

Journal article

By: Raymond B. Allen

Date: May 1949

Source: Allen, Raymond B. "Communists Should Not Teach in American Colleges." *Educational Forum,* vol. 13, no. 4, May 1949. Available online at http://www.english.upenn.edu/~afilreis/50s/raymond-allen.html (accessed March 17, 2003).

About the Author: Raymond B. Allen (1902–1986) was a physician who worked as a professor and administrator in several medical schools before rising to the presidency of the University of Washington at Seattle in 1946. Two years later, he was responsible for the controversial dismissal of three professors who allegedly held communist sympathies. In 1949, he published an article, "Communists Should Not Teach in American Colleges," in the journal *Educational Forum.* Allen left the university in 1951 and served as chancellor of the University of California at Los Angeles from 1952 to 1959. ∎

Introduction

Like many other U.S. groups, the academic world fell prey to the so-called "Red Scare" in the early years of the Cold War. Anticommunism in the United States was as old as communism itself; panic about the communist threat against democracy had surfaced as early as the opening decades of the twentieth century. The rise of Joseph Stalin (in power 1927–1953) as leader of the Soviet Union, however, brought new urgency to Americans' fear. After World War II (1939–1945) the Soviet Union seemed a powerful political and military threat to the United States. The standoff between American democracy and Soviet communism was heightened by the fact that the two nations emerged from the war as global superpowers. China's shift to communism and the Soviet Union's successful test of an atomic bomb helped to tip the scales from concern to hysteria.

The Red Scare affected not only the U.S. government but also institutions such as colleges and universities. Ironically, in the place where the "dialogue of ideas" was most praised, some were shut out of the conversation due to the nature of their ideas. Academic leaders such as President Raymond B. Allen of the University of Washington at Seattle argued that communists should not be allowed to teach at institutions of higher learning. Allen asserted that the rigid beliefs of communist political philosophy would not allow those who followed it to engage in the scholarly search for truth. In other words, Allen believed communists were too closed-minded to be effective in the classroom. Certainly fear influenced

Allen's position as well. If professors who did not believe in the capitalism and rugged individualism of mainstream U.S. political philosophy taught the country's young people, then those professors might foster a new generation of communists who would topple the United States from the inside.

Significance

The immediate impact of the Red Scare was that many people in government, the film industry, universities, and elsewhere lost their jobs because they were suspected of sympathizing with communism. Some were members of the Communist Party. Others were the victims of political or personal attacks for other, less obvious, reasons. Still others simply had the misfortune of being associated with people who were held in suspicion. Anticommunists couched their efforts in terms of loyalty and treason, while those who defended themselves couched their efforts in terms of freedom and conscience. Open debate about the nature of communism suffered as fear made the political theory a taboo subject of discussion.

Articles such as Raymond B. Allen's are significant because they proved that anticommunism, and Red Scare hysteria in particular, had transferred from governmental politics—congressional hearings, special subcommittees, and targeted programs—to popular politics. The private sector was mimicking the public sector; therefore organizations such as institutions of higher education conducted their own hunts for those who held communist beliefs. Communists serving in the U.S. government were no longer the only concern: communists anywhere in the country were seen as a problem. The spread of this crusade from state to private leaders proved the power of and general consensus about anticommunism at the time. Popular fear was strongest regarding enterprises that held sway over the nation's youth such as universities, which influenced the worldview of their students, and movies, which conveyed messages to their audiences. Just as many Americans feared physical attack from communist powers outside the country, they feared subtle, even invisible attack on the American way of life from ideas within the nation.

Primary Source

"Communists Should Not Teach in American Colleges" [excerpt]

> **SYNOPSIS:** In this excerpt from the *Educational Forum* article "Communists Should Not Teach in American Colleges," Raymond B. Allen claims that the communist worldview does not allow teachers to participate in the open search for truth. Teachers restrained by dogma, he asserts, are not really teachers at all. Communists therefore could not fulfill the obligations of college teaching.

A witness gives testimony at the state legislature's anti-Communist Canwell Committee, in Seattle, Washington, May 4, 1949. © SEATTLE POST INTELLIGENCER COLLECTION; MUSEUM OF HISTORY & INDUSTRY/CORBIS. REPRODUCED BY PERMISSION.

The question of whether a member of the Communist Party should be allowed to teach in an American college is by no means a simple one. Despite the fact that many persons in educational circles appear to find easy answers to this question, those of us who have examined the question most carefully perhaps find the answers more difficult.

The general outlines of the examination of this problem in the recent cases at the University of Washington are probably well enough known that they need not be reviewed in detail here. Suffice it to say that the question was surveyed from every angle and with every facility available to the administration and faculty of the University of Washington. The decision, while it may not be fully satisfactory to everyone concerned, is in my opinion the most thoroughly considered and best documented study of the relationship between Communism and higher education yet attempted in America.

Out of this long and painstaking examination I have come reluctantly to the conclusion that members of the Communist Party should not be allowed to teach in American colleges. I am now convinced that a member of the Communist Party is not a free man. Freedom, I believe is the most essential in-

gredient of American civilization and democracy. In the American scheme educational institutions are the foundation stones upon which real freedom rests. Educational institutions can prosper only as they maintain free teaching and research. To maintain free teaching and research the personnel of higher education must accept grave responsibilities and duties as well as the rights and privileges of the academic profession. A teacher must, therefore, be a free seeker after the truth. If, as Jefferson taught, the real purpose of education is to seek out and teach the truth wherever it may lead, then the first obligation and duty of the teacher is to be a free man. Any restraint on the teacher's freedom is an obstacle to the accomplishment of the most important purposes of education.

This kind of freedom, without restraint from any quarter, is the keystone of the unparalleled progress with which America and the American way of life have faced the world. The justification for this kind of freedom, especially as it relates to teaching and research, may be seen in the great accomplishments of our classrooms and laboratories. In my own lifetime, for instance, I have seen the free minds of scholarly men solve most of the mysteries of travel in the air. I have also seen free research evolve a whole new science of electronics that has revolutionized men's ability to communicate with one another. As a medical man I have seen free research wipe out some of the most hideous diseases that have afflicted mankind down through the centuries. Even my young children have seen free and scholarly men unlock and control the vast and frightening power of the atom. In the past decade, all of us have seen the virility of a free people win out in a death struggle with the slave-states of Germany, Italy and Japan, only now to be faced again by another and perhaps more vicious adversary. These accomplishments I submit are some of the material fruits of freedom in scholarship and teaching.

The freedom that America prizes so much, then, is a positive and constructive concept. It starts, of course, by maintaining a freedom from restraint. Its greatest glory, however, derives from freedom considered in a more positive sense; that is, a freedom "for," a freedom to accomplish. In this best sense, freedom is not only a right and a privilege, but a responsibility which must rest heavily upon the institutions of freedom upon which we depend for the progress and virility of our way of existence.

This kind of freedom, I submit, is not allowed the membership the Communist Party. I have come to this conclusion painfully and reluctantly through a long series of hearings and deliberations. In my opinion these careful studies by faculty and administrative agencies of the University of Washington have proved beyond any shadow of a doubt that a member of the Communist Party is not a free man, that he is instead a slave to immutable dogma and to a clandestine organization masquerading as a political party. They have shown that a number of the Communist Party has abdicated control over his intellectual life.

Further Resources

BOOKS

Foster, Stuart J. *Red Alert: Educators Confront the Red Scare in American Public Schools, 1947–1954.* New York: Peter Lang, 2000.

Haynes, John Earl. *Red Scare or Red Menace?: American Communism and Anti-communism in the Cold War Era.* Chicago: Ivan R. Dee, 1990.

Isaacs, Jeremy, et al., *Cold War: An Illustrated History, 1945–1991.* New York: Little Brown & Company, 1998.

Stein, R. Conrad. *The Great Red Scare.* New Jersey: Silver Burdett Press, 1998.

WEBSITES

"Allen, Raymond B." *UCLA Past Leaders.* Available online at http://www.ucla.edu/chancellor/pastleaders/allen.html; web-site home page http://www.ucla.edu (accessed July 10, 2002).

"The Effect of McCarthyism on American Universities." Barnard Electronic Archive and Teaching Laboratory. Available online at http://beatl.barnard.columbia.edu/students/his3464y/grinberg+perry/mccarthyism.html; website home page http://beatl.barnard.columbia.edu/ (accessed March 17, 2003).

"Wipe Out Discrimination"

Poster

By: Committee for Industrial Organization (CIO)

Date: 1949

Source: "Wipe Out Discrimination." Poster. 1949. Reprinted in Boyer, Paul S., et al. *The Enduring Vision.* Second edition. Lexington, Mass.: D.C. Heath and Company, 1993.

About the Organization: Public-service announcements on posters and in other media not only reflected social trends and movements by expressing popular sentiments but also allowed organizations to advertise themselves by linking their names with successful ideas. In this case, the Committee for Industrial Organization (CIO), a labor union, sought to link its agenda with the growing emphasis on civil rights. Despite this and other efforts to revitalize itself, the CIO did not thrive. In 1955, it joined the American Federation of Labor (AFL) to form the AFL-CIO. The AFL-CIO had internal problems as well, however, and its membership decreased over time. ■

Introduction

Civil rights became a more visible issue during the Truman administration for several reasons. First, increased racial violence in the South made the problem difficult to ignore. Second, leaders of the Soviet Union focused much of their anti-U.S. rhetoric on the U.S. mistreatment of blacks. In part this was a response to U.S. criticisms of Soviet human rights abuses and painted Americans as hypocrites. Such rhetoric also undercut U.S. attempts to make overtures to African and Asian nations that U.S. leaders feared might be attracted to communism. President Harry S. Truman (1945–1953) established the first President's Committee on Civil Rights to explore the subject. On October 29, 1947, the committee issued a pathbreaking report, titled *To Secure These Rights,* which immediately captured the public's attention and interest. The president followed it up with a special message to Congress requesting that legislators enact most of the proposals in the report, which he called "an American charter of human freedom." By 1949, clearly, the question of discrimination was a part of the mainstream U.S. consciousness. The CIO tried to capitalize on this by publicizing its embrace of civil rights.

Primary Source

"Wipe Out Discrimination" Poster

SYNOPSIS: The Committee for Industrial Organization, a labor union, created this poster to show the group's position on the growing issue of civil rights. The poster calls for an end to discrimination "against races" and "religions," "on the job," "in restaurants," and "in housing." THE LIBRARY OF CONGRESS.

Nineteen forty-nine was not the best year, however, for labor unions such as the CIO. Unions had grown in membership and power during the 1940s, and a number of large-scale strikes had followed. This created an antiunion backlash in popular opinion. In addition, the "Red Scare," a pervasive fear of communism in the United States, led to widespread concern about communist infiltration of labor unions. One result of this was the Labor-Management Relations Act of 1947, also known as the Taft-Hartley Act. This act amended prior pro-union legislation, guaranteeing employees the right not to join unions, requiring unions to give sixty-day advance notification of a strike, and narrowing the definition of unfair labor practices, among other things. Weakened by law and suffering from a public-relations dilemma, unions such as the CIO sponsored public-service announcements linking the ailing labor movement with the rising cause of civil rights.

Significance

Public-relations campaigns such as the CIO's "Wipe Out Discrimination" effort could not revive the vitality of labor unions. In fact, the CIO did not survive long as an independent organization. In 1955, it merged with the American Federation of Labor (AFL). The AFL-CIO experienced many internal and publicity problems, such as when they expelled the Teamsters Union in 1957 due to that union's problems with corruption and racketeering. Membership in the AFL-CIO and similar organizations declined steadily thereafter.

The Committee on Civil Rights' report, *To Secure These Rights,* spawned some immediate changes, including Executive Order 9981 (1948), which desegregated the U.S. armed forces. Not all Americans were committed to civil rights, however. Southern segregationists criticized Truman's attention to the issue and left the Democratic Party during the 1948 election to form the States' Rights, or "Dixiecrat," Party. The Dixiecrats nominated South Carolina governor Strom Thurmond to run against Truman for the presidency. The political party was short-lived but the opposition to civil rights legislation continued for some time.

The goals endorsed by the "Wipe Out Discrimination" poster were not addressed directly or comprehensively until the Civil Rights Act of 1964, legislation created to end discrimination based on race, color, religion, and national origin. The act also created the Equal Employment Opportunity Commission to enforce its provisions. Therefore, although public-service announcements like those sponsored by the CIO did not have an immediate effect, they did bring the issue to national awareness, encouraged members of the civil rights movement, and prepared the way for later changes in laws and lifestyles. Ironically, Title VII of the Civil Rights Act

banned discrimination by trade unions; clearly, the CIO's philosophy had not been put into practice in all labor unions.

Further Resources

BOOKS

Gardner, Michael R. *Harry Truman and Civil Rights: Moral Courage and Political Risks.* Carbondale, Ill.: Southern Illinois University Press, 2002.

To Secure These Rights: The Report of the President's Committee on Civil Rights. Washington, D.C.: U.S. Government Printing Office, 1947.

Zieger, Robert H. *The CIO, 1935–1955.* Chapel Hill, N.C.: University of North Carolina Press, 1995.

WEBSITES

AFL-CIO. Available online at http://www.afl-cio.org/home/htm (accessed March 17, 2003).

"Milestones: The Early Years." U.S. Equal Employment Opportunity Commission. Available online at http://www.eeoc.gov/35th/milestones/early.html; website home page http://www.eeoc.gov/ (accessed March 17, 2003).

"Indian Self-Government"

Essay

By: Felix S. Cohen

Date: 1949

Source: Cohen, Felix S. "Indian Self-Government." *American Indian,* 1949. Reprinted In *Red Power: The American Indians' Fight for Freedom,* second edition. Edited by Josephy, Alvin M., Jr., et al. Lincoln, Neb.: University of Nebraska Press, 1999, 69–72.

About the Author: Felix S. Cohen (1907–1953) was a distinguished legal theorist and an activist for Native American rights. From 1933 to 1948 he served as an assistant solicitor with the U.S. Department of the Interior, where he worked on American Indian issues. He later entered private practice and taught law at the City College of New York and Yale Law School. As an attorney and author he worked with the Association on American Indian Affairs until his death in 1953. He is best known for his influential book *Handbook of Federal Indian Law* (1942). ∎

Introduction

As early as President Thomas Jefferson's so-called "Indian Civilization Campaign" in the early nineteenth century, political thinkers and legal theorists—not to mention Native American leaders—have called for more opportunities for American Indians to enjoy self-rule, or sovereignty. The U.S. government's forced removal of native nations in the mid- to late nineteenth century, and the reorganization and reallocation of "Indian territories" in the late nineteenth and early twentieth centuries kept the native nations in a constant state of political, economic, and legal flux. As the United States constantly redefined and altered its authority over Native American peoples, native nations and their advocates continued to call for greater freedom and self-determination.

Felix S. Cohen used his position as a noted and respected U.S. legal scholar to revisit the issue of American Indian self-rule. His 1949 article "Indian Self-Government" brought the issue to national attention. Another article published in 1953 in the *Yale Law Journal* went even further in criticizing the U.S. government for blocking the path of Native American political, legal, and economic progress. He even compared the U.S. Bureau of Indian Affairs to an extortion racket and explained how agency officials threatened Native American communities with losing their hospitals, schools, and oil and natural gas rights if they did not support the agency and its agenda. Cohen's writings not only exposed injustices done by the United States against Native America but also called for the reconsideration and reform of the government's relation to American Indian nations. Cohen's credibility as a theorist, professor, scholar, and activist brought new urgency to the issue of Native American rights.

Significance

Cohen's many efforts on behalf of Native American issues in the 1930s, 1940s, and early 1950s helped to force the U.S. government into exploring ways of reforming U.S.-Native American relations. The first visible result of Cohen's and others' activism came in 1948. That year the Hoover Commission evaluated the organization of the executive branch of the U.S. government and issued its report. The commission suggested—along the lines of Cohen's proposals—that the Bureau of Indian Affairs be dismantled in favor of a state-based system that allowed native nations more opportunities and legal freedom. Other, later, calls for similar action followed. When more than 450 Native American leaders met at the 1961 Voice of the American Indian Conference, they issued the "Declaration of Indian Purpose" that called for American Indian self-rule. The *Presidential Task Force Report on the American Indian* (1966) and national Josephy Study (1969) both called for a fundamental overhaul of the Bureau of Indian Affairs as well. For decades after Cohen raised the issue of the U.S. government's control over and mismanagement of native nations, both U.S. government and Native American studies confirmed his findings and echoed his suggestions.

The work of Cohen and those who followed him helped to pave the path for the 1975 Indian Self-Determination Act, which granted all tribes the right to manage programs and services formerly administered by the Bureau of Indian Affairs. Although this did not end

President Truman signs a bill that creates a commission to handle Indian Claims, August 1946. © BETTMANN/CORBIS. REPRODUCED BY PERMISSION.

U.S. control over native nations—the Bureau of Indian Affairs remained under investigation for alleged misdoings into the twenty-first century—the act was a first step in addressing the problems Cohen and others identified. The many years that it took to develop this act does not lessen the achievement of activists such as Cohen who championed the cause of Native Americans.

Primary Source

"Indian Self-Government" [excerpt]

SYNOPSIS: This commentary by Felix S. Cohen, titled "Indian Self-Government," explores the promise and possibilities of Native American self-government and how they relate to the U.S. government's connection with native nations. As with all of Cohen's work, this excerpt reflects sympathy and concern for the legal plight of Native Americans. This work was first published in the 1949 book *The American Indian*.

Not all who speak of self-government mean the same thing by the term. Therefore let me say at the outset that by self-government I mean that form of government in which decisions are made not by the people who are wisest, or ablest, or closest to some throne in Washington or in Heaven, but, rather by the people who are most directly affected by the decisions. I think that if we conceive of self-government in these matter-of-fact terms, we may avoid some confusion.

Let us admit that self-government includes graft, corruption, and the making of decisions by inexpert minds. Certainly these are features of self-government in white cities and counties, and so we ought not to be scared out of our wits if somebody jumps up in the middle of a discussion of Indian self-government and shouts "graft" or "corruption."

Self-government is not a new or radical idea. Rather, it is one of the oldest staple ingredients of the American way of life. Many Indians in this country enjoyed self-government long before European immigrants who came to these shores did. It took the white colonists north of the Rio Grande about 170 years to rid themselves of the traditional European pattern of the divine right of kings or, what we call today, the long arm of bureaucracy, and to substitute the less efficient but more satisfying Indian pattern of self-government. South of the Rio Grande the process took more than three centuries, and there are some who are still skeptical as to the completeness of the shift.

This is not the time and place to discuss the ways in which the Indian pattern of self-government undermined the patterns which the colonists first brought to this country, patterns of feudalism, land-lordism and serfdom, economic monopoly and special privilege, patterns of religious intolerance and nationalism and the divine right of kings. It was not only Franklin and Jefferson who went to school with Indian teachers, like the Iroquois statesman Canasatego, to learn the ways of federal union and democracy. It was no less the great political thinkers of Europe, in the years following the discovery of the New World, who undermined ancient dogmas when they saw spread before them on the panorama of the Western Hemisphere new societies in which liberty, equality, and fraternity were more perfectly realized than they were realized in contemporary Europe, societies in which government drew its just powers from the consent of the governed. To Vitoria, Grotius, Locke, Montaigne, Montesquieu, Voltaire, and Rousseau, Indian liberty and self-government provided a new polestar in political thinking. But, for the present, I want merely to emphasize that Indian self-government is not a new or radical policy but an ancient fact. It is not something friends of the Indi-

ans can confer upon the Indians. Nobody can grant self-government to anybody else. We all recall that when Alexander was ruler of most of the known civilized world, he once visited the philosopher Diogenes, who was making his home in an old bathtub. Diogenes was a rich man because he did not want anything that he did not have. He was a mighty man because he could master himself. Alexander admired Diogenes for these qualities, and standing before him said, "Oh, Diogenes, if there is anything that I can grant you, tell me and I will grant it." To which Diogenes replied, "You are standing in my sunlight. Get out of the way." The Federal Government which is, today, the dominant power of the civilized world cannot give self-government to an Indian community. All it can really do for self-government is to get out of the way. . . .

I recall very vividly in 1934 working on a study for the Indian Office of legal rights of Indian tribes which was to serve as a guide in the drafting of tribal constitutions under the Wheeler-Howard Act. I found that the laws and court decisions clearly recognized that Indian tribes have all the governmental rights of any state or municipality except insofar as those rights have been curtailed or qualified by Act of Congress or by treaty, and such qualifications are relatively minor, in fact. When, at last, my job was done and the Solicitor's opinion had been reviewed and approved by the proper authorities of the Interior Department and properly mimeographed, I learned to my dismay that all copies of the opinion in the Indian Office had been carefully hidden away in a cabinet and that when an Indian was found reading this opinion, the copy was forthwith taken from his hands and placed under lock and key. Incidentally, the Indian whose reading was thus interrupted had spent more years in school and college than the men who controlled the lock and key. The Indian Office was sure that the opinion, if released to the public, would be more disturbing. I suppose they were right. The opinion was disturbing to the Indian Office. Its suppression was equally disturbing to me. My despondency was somewhat relieved when I found that Chief Justice Marshall and Pope Paul III and Bartholomew de las Casas had all received the same treatment. It was of John Marshall's decision upholding the rights of self-government of the Cherokee Tribe that an old Indian fighter in the White House, President Jackson, said, "John Marshall has made his decision. Now let him enforce it." The sovereign State of Georgia paid no attention to the decision of the United States Supreme Court and the good missionary whom the Supreme Court had freed continued to languish in a Georgia prison. And what happened to John Marshall in 1832 was not novel. The same thing happened to Bartholomew de las Casas 300 years earlier when, as Archbishop of Chiapas, he endeavored to read to his flock of Spanish landowners the guarantees of Indian freedom signed by the Pope and by the King of Spain. He was not allowed to read these documents by the outraged landowners of his archdiocese. In fact, he was driven from his church. History has a strange way of repeating itself. I was relieved to find myself in such good company, and so, instead of resigning, I distributed copies of the opinion where I thought they would do the most good.

How can we explain the fact that despite all the respect and reverence shown to the principle of Indian self-government across four centuries, there is so little left today of the fact of Indian self-government? How can we explain this discrepancy between word and deed?

Further Resources

BOOKS

Anderson, Terry L. *Sovereign Nations or Reservations? An Economic History of American Indians.* San Francisco: Pacific Research Institute for Public Policy, 1995.

Lyons, Oren, et al. *Exiled in the Land of the Free: Democracy, Indian Nations, and the U.S. Constitution.* Santa Fe: Clear Light Publishers, 1992.

Wilkins, David E. *American Indian Sovereignty and the U.S. Supreme Court.* Austin, Tx.: University of Texas Press, 1997.

PERIODICALS

Sturgis, Amy H. "Tale of Tears." *Reason,* March 1999, 46–52.

WEBSITES

"American Indian Sovereignty." Alaska Justice Statistical Analysis Center. University of Alaska Anchorage. Available online at http://www.uaa.alaska.edu/just/rlinks/natives/sovereignty.html; website home page http://www.uaa.alaska.edu/just/index.html (accessed March 17, 2003).

"Resources for Indigenous Cultures Around the World." NativeWeb. Available online at http://www.nativeweb.org (accessed March 17, 2003).

6

LAW AND JUSTICE

SCOTT A. MERRIMAN

Entries are arranged in chronological order by date of primary source. For entries with one primary source, the entry title is the same as the primary source title. Entries with more than one primary source have an overall entry title, followed by the titles of the primary sources.

Important Events in Law and Justice, 1940–1949

1940

• On January 15, the Senate approves Frank Murphy's appointment to the Supreme Court.

• On June 28, the Alien Registration Act (Smith Act) is passed. This law makes it unlawful for any individual to call for the overthrow of any government in the United States by force. It also makes it unlawful to join or found any group which teaches such a doctrine.

1941

• On January 31, Justice James Clark McReynolds retires from the Supreme Court after serving for twenty-six years.

• On June 12, Senator James F. Byrnes is nominated and confirmed on the same day to an appointment as an associate justice of the Supreme Court.

• On June 27, Justice Harlan Fiske Stone is confirmed by the Senate to replace Charles Evans Hughes as chief justice upon Hughes's retirement.

• On July 1, Chief Justice Hughes retires after serving as chief justice for eleven years.

• On July 11, Robert H. Jackson is sworn in as an associate justice of the Supreme Court.

1942

• On January 7, Attorney General Francis Biddle announces the arrest of 3,234 Axis nationals in the United States.

• On January 12, the Supreme Court declares Georgia's contract labor law unconstitutional.

• On February 19, per executive order of the president, the secretary of war is authorized to prescribe areas on the West Coast from which persons might be excluded.

• By March 29, more than 110,000 Japanese Americans from California, Arizona, Oregon, and Washington have been moved to relocation camps.

• On October 3, after serving only sixteen months, Supreme Court Justice James Byrnes resigns to accept appointment as the director of the Office of Economic Stabilization.

• On October 19, Attorney General Biddle announces that Italians residing in the United States will no longer be treated as enemy aliens.

1943

• On January 11, U.S. Court of Appeals Judge Wiley B. Rutledge is nominated as an associate justice of the Supreme Court.

• On May 10, the U.S. Supreme Court rules that the Federal Communications Commission (FCC) has the legitimate authority to regulate the major broadcasting chains on behalf of the public.

• On May 17, the Supreme Court refuses to review a lower court decision that held that Japanese who are born in this country are American citizens and are therefore entitled to vote. A challenger, John T. Regan, had argued unsuccessfully that "dishonesty, deceit and hypocrisy are racial characteristics of the Japanese," thus making them unfit for American citizenship.

• On November 13, after a protest by about 1,000 Japanese American internees, martial law is imposed at the Tule Lake Detention Center.

1944

• On April 3, in its decision in *Smith v. Allwright*, the Supreme Court outlaws the white primary, ruling that African American voters cannot be excluded from Texas primary elections.

• On July 3, President Roosevelt signs a law withdrawing the citizenship of Japanese Americans who refuse to pledge allegiance to the United States.

• From August 21 to October 7, the Dumbarton Oaks Conference is held near Washington, D.C. The initial proposals to which the participants (the United States, the Soviet Union, Great Britain, and China) agree serve as the guidelines for the charter of the United Nations.

• On December 17, the U.S. Army announces that effective January 2, 1945, it will end the mass exclusion of Japanese Americans from the West Coast.

• On December 18, in its decision on *Korematsu v. U.S.*, the Supreme Court affirms the government's power to intern Japanese American citizens.

1945

• From April 25 to June 26, the United Nations Conference on International Organization is held in San Francisco. Over the course of two months a charter is worked out; it is unanimously approved on June 25.

• On July 28, the U.S. Senate ratifies the United Nations Charter by a vote of 89-2. President Harry S. Truman signs the charter on August 8.

• On July 31, Justice Owen J. Roberts, who supervised an inquiry into the attack on Pearl Harbor and who headed a commission that traced art objects stolen by the Germans during World War II, resigns from the Supreme Court after serving since 1930.

• On October 1, Senator Harold H. Burton takes the oath of office as an associate justice of the Supreme Court.

• On November 20, war-crime trials of Nazis begin in Nuremburg, Germany.

• On December 13, Josef Kramer, "The Beast of Belsen," two of his female guards, and eight other Nazis are hanged in Hameln (Hamelin), Germany, after a British military court convicted them for atrocities.

1946

• On January 10, the first session of the United Nations General Assembly is held in London.

• On January 19, the International Military Tribunal for the Far East is established to try Japanese leaders on war-crime charges.

• On June 3, the Supreme Court rules that racial segregation on interstate buses is unconstitutional.

• On June 24, Fred M. Vinson, former secretary of the treasury, takes the oath of office as the new chief justice of the Supreme Court.

• On July 3, the American Bar Association establishes a committee to evaluate the qualifications of candidates for the federal bench.

• On July 28, African Americans vote for the first time in the Texas Democratic primary.

1947

• On March 21, President Truman issues Executive Order 9835, which requires the investigation of all government employees or applicants for government positions.

• On March 24, the Twenty-second Amendment to the U.S. Constitution is proposed. This amendment prohibits any person from holding more than two full terms as president of the United States or two full terms and more than two years in addition as acting president (for a theoretical total of ten years). This amendment is subsequently ratified on February 26, 1951.

• On July 18, President Truman signs the Presidential Succession Act, rewriting the law passed in 1886 regarding presidential succession. The new law makes the Speaker of the House next, after the vice president, followed by the president pro tempore of the Senate, the secretary of state, and the cabinet members according to rank.

• On October 29, President Truman's Committee on Civil Rights recommends the abolition of poll taxes and the creation of new laws to protect African American rights to equal access to education, housing, and public services.

• On December 8, the Supreme Court overturns the conviction of an African American man for murder on the grounds of the exclusion of African American jurors.

1948

• On January 12, in *Sipuel v. Oklahoma,* the U.S. Supreme Court orders Oklahoma to provide law education to Ada L. Sipuel. Rather than admit an African American student to the University of Oklahoma Law School, the state opens a one-pupil law school for her. She returns to court, but the Supreme Court rejects her appeal.

• On March 8, the U.S. Supreme Court rules in *McCollum v. Board of Education* that religious training in public schools is unconstitutional.

• On April 26, William T. Coleman becomes the first African American Supreme Court law clerk.

• On April 29, a San Francisco federal court restores the U.S. citizenship of Japanese Americans who renounced it while interned.

• On May 3, the Supreme Court rules that covenants barring African Americans from purchasing or inhabiting property are unenforceable.

• On July 26, President Truman issues executive order 9981 establishing equal treatment and opportunity in the military. It is a first step toward the goal of ending racial segregation in the U.S. armed forces.

• On August 3, the House Committee on Un-American Activities hears testimony from admitted Communist courier Whittaker Chambers that a State Department official, Alger Hiss, had been a member of a Communist organization prior to World War II. Hiss is later indicted for perjury and, after a first trial ending in a hung jury, is found guilty and sentenced to five years in prison.

1949

• On March 28, the Supreme Court invalidates a provision in Alabama's constitution designed to exclude African American voters.

• On June 17, Governor James E. Folsom of Alabama, following raids by hooded men who whipped several people, signs a bill forbidding the wearing of masks.

• On August 2, Attorney General Tom C. Clark is nominated as an associate justice of the Supreme Court by President Truman.

• On September 15, U.S. Court of Appeals Judge Sherman Minton is nominated as an associate justice to the Supreme Court.

• On October 14, eleven leaders of the U.S. Communist Party are convicted of violation of the Smith Act of 1940. Their convictions are subsequently affirmed by the U.S. Supreme Court in 1951.

Gobitas Perspectives

"Here Comes Jehovah!"

Memoir

By: Lillian Gobitas

Date: 1986

Source: Irons, Peter. *The Courage of Their Convictions: Sixteen Americans Who Fought Their Way to the Supreme Court.* New York: Penguin Books, 1988, 26–27, 29, 30–33.

About the Author: Lillian Gobitas's family lived above the small store they owned in Pennsylvania. They converted to the Watchtower Society of Jehovah's Witnesses when Gobitas's maternal grandparents moved in with them. In adulthood Gobitas's religion took her to Europe and Canada before she returned to the United States with her husband. A clerical error changed the family's name from Gobitas to Gobitis during the Supreme Court case.

"Billy Gobitas to school directors, Minersville, Pennsylvania, November 5, 1935"

Letter

By: William Gobitas

Date: November 5, 1935

Source: Gobitas, William. Letter to school directors, Minersville, Pennsylvania. November 5, 1935. Library of Congress American Memory Collection, search "William Gobitas." Available online at http://memory.loc.gov/ammem /mdbquery.html (accessed April 30, 2003).

About the Author: William "Billy" Gobitas, a Jehovah's Witness, refused to stand and recite the pledge of allegiance in school. Together, he and his sister Lillian were part of a Supreme Court case that challenged the requirement that all students recite the pledge in class. ∎

Introduction

Jehovah's Witnesses doctrine opposes killing anyone, leading many to become conscientious objectors, or people who refused to go to war on religious or moral grounds, during World War I (1914–1918) and World War II (1939–1945). Nevertheless Jehovah's Witnesses were often not recognized as conscientious objectors.

During World War I many of them, then called the Russellites, were convicted under the Espionage and Sedition Acts for refusing to fight. One original leader of the Jehovah's Witnesses, Charles Rutherford, and several of his followers were sentenced to 20-year jail terms. They did not have to serve these sentences, as they were released in 1919 when their convictions were overturned.

Jehovah's Witnesses and other religious minorities, such as the Amish and Mennonites, who also chose not to support World War I, often wound up in prison for draft evasion or refusal to follow orders. In jail they were given the choice of supporting the war in noncombatant positions, such as farming or working in a hospital, or staying in prison. Many chose the former; those who chose the latter suffered greatly in military prisons as the guards frequently beat them in an attempt to convince them to change their minds and support the war.

During the period leading up to World War II there was a superpatriotic feeling in the United States. This led to strong hatred against those did not salute the flag. In 1940 the Supreme Court ruled against the Gobitas children for refusing to salute the flag in school. Justice Frankfurter's language in the *Gobitis* decision echoed the argument that everyone must support the country in times of crisis. He argued that "national unity" is "the basis of national security." He also attempted to avoid limiting governmental power, writing that he did not want to deny the legislature the right to select "appropriate means" for the "attainment" of national unity.

Significance

The public reacted very negatively to Jehovah's Witnesses after the *Gobitis* decision. Mobs, public officials, and some vigilantes carried out violent assaults. Lillian Gobitas recalled how she was "witnessing house to house" when a mob formed and "the police called me into the car and took me past the mob into the fire house. I remember one girl punched me and the mob was trying to break down the doors of the fire house."

In her personal account of these events Lillian Gobitas conveyed her belief that the Witnesses's cause would eventually triumph, even after the Supreme Court ruled against her family. In 1943 another flag salute case, *West Virginia State Board of Education v. Barnette,* was heard by the Supreme Court. In this second case the Supreme Court overturned *Gobitis,* holding that Jehovah's Witnesses did not have to salute the flag. In another case, heard between these two decisions, justices Douglas, Black, and Murphy stated that the Gobitas decision was wrong. Public opinion seemed to shift somewhat in favor of allowing Witnesses not to salute the flag as the issue became tied up with allowing freedom, the whole "purpose" (in some people's minds) of fighting World War II.

Walter Gobitas poses with his two children, William and Lillian. February 16, 1938. UPI/CORBIS-BETTMANN. REPRODUCED BY PERMISSION.

While Jehovah's Witnesses have won support from the courts in flag salute cases other issues remain controversial. For example some legislatures and city councils have tried to ban door-to-door solicitation to protect people's privacy. These laws are aimed primarily at door-to-door sales and Jehovah's Witnesses. In these cases governing officials must decide whether such laws prevent the Jehovah's Witnesses from enjoying freedom of religion, as door-to-door solicitation is one of the primary methods of promoting their religion.

Primary Source

"Here Comes Jehovah!" [excerpt]

SYNOPSIS: In this personal account Lillian Gobitas discusses the reasons underlying her decision to stop saluting the flag. She also describes the severe prejudice she faced both during the trials and after the Supreme Court's decision. This account includes her family's optimism about the potential for their case's success at the Supreme Court level, their disappointment at its eventual defeat, and their elation at the *Barnette* decision. The letter Lillian's brother Billy wrote to the school director is also reproduced.

In the summer of 1935, Judge Rutherford, the president of the Watchtower Society of Jehovah's

Witnesses, gave this talk on the radio about what the Scriptures say on emblems. He said that he himself wouldn't give a salute to the flag, not because he didn't respect the flag as a symbol of the country but because of what the Scripture says about worshipping an image of the State.

We were all at different schools, but we liked them very much. I loved school, and I was with a nice group. I was actually kind of popular. I was class president in the seventh grade, and I had good grades. And I felt that, Oh, if I stop saluting the flag, I will blow all this! And I did. It sure worked out that way. I really was so fearful that, when the teacher would look my way, I would quick put out my hand and move my lips. We knew that Carleton Nicholls up in Lynn, Massachusetts, took a stand against the salute in school. He was expelled from school, and the story was in the newspapers.

My brother William was in the fifth grade at that time, the fall of 1935. The next day Bill came home and said, I stopped saluting the flag. So I knew this was the moment! This wasn't something my parents forced on us. They were very firm about that, that what you do is your decision, and you should understand what you're doing. I did a lot of reading and checking in the Bible and I really took my own stand.

I went first to my teacher, Miss Anna Shofstal, so I couldn't chicken out of it. She listened to my explanation and surprisingly, she just hugged me and said she thought it was very nice, to have courage like that. But the students were awful. I really should have explained to the whole class but I was fearful. I didn't know whether it was right to stand up or sit down. These days, we realize that the salute itself is the motions and the words. So I sat down and the whole room was aghast. After that, when I'd come to school, they would throw a hail of pebbles and yell things like, Here comes Jehovah! They were just jeering at me. Some of my girl friends would come and ask what it was about. That was nice. One-on-one is a lot easier.

They watched us for two weeks, my brother and I and Edmund Wasliewski, who was another Witness who wouldn't salute. With my brother, the teacher tried to force his arm up and he just held onto his pocket. After two weeks, they had the school-board meeting and Dad and Mom both went. They had grown up with these men on the school board and gone to school with them. The superintendent, Dr. Roudabush, was a very firm type of person, and Dr. McGurl, the board president, was also very firm. The others kind of followed suit.

Dad told the school board why we couldn't take part in the flag salute. Dad told us he was very nervous at the meeting. The board made its decision right then, without much discussion. The idea was that we were insubordinate, and there would be immediate expulsion. They said at the meeting, Don't even come to school tomorrow! . . .

One time when we did street work with our literature in Minersville, two girls passed by. They were my close friends in school, and I overheard them saying, Just think, we used to be friends with *her!* I remember knocking at a door and the girl inside said to her family, There's that Lillian Gobitis. But because we went to the Kingdom School we were kind of out of sight, out of mind. One girl in my school, who was really the smartest in the whole class, became a Witness and nine days ago I met her in Florida at one of our conventions. She told me that she asked her mother, Where are the Gobitises? Where's Lillian? They must have moved away! What happened to us really wasn't publicized until it got into the courts.

After we had been expelled, one of the Catholic churches in Minersville announced a boycott of our store, and it meant a great deal to us. More children had been born, and it was our living, so it was very important. Business fell off quite a lot. Sometimes my Dad sent my brother to my aunt's house next door for a loan, because it was kind of critical. After a while, though, time went by and the people felt that this was kind of ridiculous, that the priest would tell them where to buy their groceries. Dad was really well known and he made a go of it by making farmer sausage and kielbasi. People came from everywhere for these things and this is how we survived the boycott. So they came back. . . .

We wouldn't have done anything about our expulsion, but since the school board was so firm in our case, the Watchtower Society said they would like to use ours as a test case. Some schools were very kind and took the children back, but there were thousands that had hard, hard treatment, who were knocked against the wall and beaten and went home crying and almost hysterical.

I remember the trial in our case very vividly. It was in Philadelphia, at the federal court. Judge Maris was a quiet-looking person, a calm-looking person. He was a very agreeable person, not formidable at all. Bill and I had to go on the stand and testify. He explained that the Ten Commandments in Exodus 20 was our reason for not saluting the flag. When it was my turn I explained First John 5:21, "little children, keep yourselves from idols." I remember the school-board lawyer saying, I object! We have had one scripture and that's enough, he said. But he was overruled. Dr. Roudabush was very feisty on the stand, very angry and hostile. But we never felt any animosity on our part toward him. Like the Scriptures show, you hope that some day they'll change, and many do.

We felt completely optimistic about the case. Judge Maris had given such a marvelous opinion, and the three judges on the appellate court gave a favorable opinion. So when it went to Washington, my family went down to hear the argument in the Supreme Court. First there was a corporation case, and there was a lot of shuffling and noise and questions. Then they started our case with Mr. Gardner from the Civil Liberties Union. The justices still were not completely attentive to him. After that, Judge Rutherford argued our case. He did it a lot from a Biblical standpoint, like with Shadrach, Meshach, and Abednego, when they took a stand and wouldn't bow down to the image of Nebuchadnezzar. And of course he discussed legal things too. It was extremely arresting. You could really hear a pin drop! The justices listened so attentively.

With all this rapt attention, we felt very optimistic. And then, months later, we were in the kitchen with

> Minersville, Pa.
> Nov. 5, 1935
>
> Our School Directors
> Dear Sirs
>
> I do not salute the flag be
> cause I have promised to do
> the will of God. That means
> that I must not worship anything
> out of harmony with God's law.
> In the twentieth chapter of
> Exodus it is stated, "Thou shalt
> not make unto thee any graven
> image, nor bow down to them nor
> serve them for I the Lord thy God
> am a jealous God visiting the in-
> iquity of the fathers upon the children
>
> unto the third and fourth generation
> of them that hate me. I am a true
> follower of Christ. I do not salute the
> flag because I do not love my country
> but I love my country and I love God
> more and I must obey His comm-
> andments.
>
> Your Pupil,
> Billy Gobitas

Primary Source

"Billy Gobitas to school directors, Minersville, Pennsylvania, November 5, 1935"

SYNOPSIS: The William Gobitas Papers contain the letter in which Billy Gobitas tells the Minersville, Pennsylvania, school directors why he, a Jehovah's Witness, refused to salute the American flag. The letter states that Gobitas loves God more than his country and that saluting the flag would be out of harmony with God's law. THE LIBRARY OF CONGRESS.

Dissent Between Justices

Although the Supreme Court majority opinion has the force of law and appears to speak with one voice, in reality the Court is made up of individuals, whose often divergent perspectives represent a variety of viewpoints (even in unanimous decisions). These become apparent when readers note the different approaches in the concurring and dissenting opinions the Justices issue alongside the majority opinion. In his introduction to Gobitas' account, Peter Irons relates the following anecdote. When Justice Frankfurter learned that Justice Black had changed his mind and now felt that the *Gobitis* decision should be overturned, he "scornfully asked if Black had been reading the Constitution. 'No, but he has read the papers,' [Justice] Douglas replied (23)." Frankfurter's remark refers to his belief that the Constitution's meaning had not changed in the few years since the *Gobitis* decision and implies that Black has only just bothered to read the Constitution. Contrarily, Justice Black felt that the *Gobitis* decision had resulted in such extreme violence against Jehovah's Witnesses that the relationship between flag salute laws and people's Constitutional Rights should be reevaluated.

the radio on and it was time for the news, and they said, In Washington today, the Supreme Court decided the flag case. It was against us, eight to one. Talk about a cold feeling! We absolutely did not expect that. That just set off a *wave* of persecution. It was like open season on Jehovah's Witnesses. That's when the mobs escalated. The Kingdom Hall in Litchfield, Illinois was totally destroyed by a mob, and there were more than three thousand Witnesses arrested every year for the next three years.

Sometimes a bunch of us teenagers would go out, calling on the homes in a town, and pretty soon a group starts to form, throwing tin cans and rocks at us. We would keep a car nearby and just go to another part of the territory. I remember on Wednesday nights we all did free family home Bible studies with people who wanted to learn more, and we would drop each other off along the road and the last one would pick us up. In this one place, I was driving to pick up Daddy, and a group came and started to let the air out of the tires and surround the car. I stepped on the gas and my father said, Don't you *ever* do that again! You could have hurt someone. . . .

After our case was decided, my brother Bill was called to the world headquarters of the Jehovah's Witnesses in Brooklyn. First he was doing what we call Pioneering, full-time service. We were in a bad situation at home, because the store always needed him, and he really was not able to make his quotas in home visits. So he had an opportunity to move to New York and live with a couple in the Bronx for a very nominal rent. Then he said, Lillian, why don't *you* come too. By that time, the husband was in prison in Danbury, Connecticut, because of the military. Hundreds of Witnesses went to prison during the war because they were turned down for exemption as ministers. We consider all Witnesses to be ministers, and draft boards refused to recognize that. . . .

After a few months, I was called to the world headquarters in Brooklyn. This was a tremendous privilege, because there were people from all over the country and around the world who were giants of faith. They all had been in full-time service before they went there, and they were from all walks of life. There weren't many girls called to work there; it was mostly heavy work and we did mostly cleaning.

But we also had a radio station that served New York and Connecticut, and I was given a little part on the show after school every day. It was called Rachel and Uncle John. I was Rachel and Uncle John was played by an elderly gentleman, Mr. Macmillan, who would tell me Bible stories. Working with Brother Macmillan was no ordinary privilege. He had been one of the eight Watchtower officials who were incarcerated in Atlanta Penitentiary in 1919, and during the war years of the 'forties he visited a circuit of twenty-one prisons to encourage the men who were there for their Christian neutrality. Mr. Knorr, who became president of the Watchtower Society after Judge Rutherford died, said that the reason he chose me for the show was because of the flag salute case! So that opened doors.

After we lost our case, we thought that this is it and we'll just have to endure. Problems in the world were escalating, and we would get reports from Germany about hideous things. There were ten thousand Witnesses in the concentration camps and two thousand were finally killed. We just thought things would escalate until what the Scriptures call Armageddon and it would be the end of this system of things. We just need to endure, that was the feeling.

In 1943, we went back to Washington for the Supreme Court hearing in the Barnette case from West Virginia. This was a case that was almost the same as our flag-salute case. The people in that case were all cousins; the Stulls and McClures were cousins of the Barnettes. They were in the courtroom too, but no one thought to introduce us. A few years ago, we had a traveling minister down here in Atlanta named Dave McClure, and we went to a meeting where my husband told his experiences from the German concentration camps. And Erwin said, Dave, why don't you tell us your experiences from your case. And that was really an occasion, because it's like, you know this story but you really don't know how it ended. So he told about how on the school bus the kids were always picking fights with him. He was kind of a tough one and he'd battle his way out of the fights, and this was a daily thing. When their case went before the courts, the opposition lawyer didn't prepare because he thought it was an open-and-shut case. We'll just go by the Gobitis precedent and that's all!

In the Barnette case, we felt more optimistic this time, like there's a light at the end of the tunnel. We *never* thought it would come to court again. Already, there were rumors that Justices Murphy and Douglas and Black were changing their minds. We also knew that Justice Murphy was having his portrait done for the capitol in Michigan, where he had been governor, and the artist was one of Jehovah's Witnesses. He had long conversations with Justice Murphy while he was sitting for his portrait, and Murphy was expressing that he surely had second thoughts. And the newspapers, and Eleanor Roosevelt in her column, My Day, and Attorney General Biddle, all began to express sympathy for us. This was ridiculous, they said, treating us like Communists. These are little children, following their convictions. So the atmosphere changed, and the Court was won over on Flag Day—June 14, 1943. We really never thought that day would come.

Further Resources

BOOKS

Eastland, Terry. *Religious Liberty in the Supreme Court: The Cases That Define the Debate Over Church and State.* Grand Rapids, Mich: W. B. Eerdmans Pub. Co., 1993.

Mathisen, Robert R. *The Role of Religion in American Life: An Interpretive Historical Anthology.* Washington, DC: University Press of America, 1982.

Barth, Alan. *Prophets With Honor; Great Dissents and Great Dissenters in the Supreme Court.* New York: Knopf, 1974.

PERIODICALS

Russo, Charles J. and Joseph R. McKinney. "Resolved: As a Matter of Basic Principle, Regardless of Particular Court Interpretation." *Curriculum Review* 33(1) September 93: 3–8.

Danzig, Richard R. "Justice Frankfurter's Opinions in the Flag Salute Cases: Blending Logic and Psychologic in Constitutional Decisionmaking." *Stanford Law Review* 36(3) February 1984: 675–723.

U.S. v. Darby

Supreme Court decision

By: Harlan F. Stone

Date: February 3, 1941

Source: *U.S. v. Darby,* 312 U.S. 100 (1941). Reprinted in Kutler, Stanley, ed. *The Supreme Court and the Constitution: Readings in American Constitutional History,* 3rd ed. New York: W.W. Norton, 1984, 402–406.

About the Author: Harlan F. Stone (1872–1946) was a professor and dean at Columbia Law School in the late 1910s and early 1920s. Calvin Coolidge (served 1923–1929) appointed Stone to the Supreme Court in 1925 after he served as attorney general. President Franklin D. Roosevelt (served 1933–1945) named him chief justice in 1941. Illness struck him suddenly in 1946, in the middle of delivering an opinion in *Girouard v. United States,* and he died of a cerebral hemorrhage later that night. ∎

Introduction

Before the 1930s federal power to regulate commerce was extremely limited, particularly by the commerce clause of the U.S. Constitution. This clause states that Congress may "regulate Commerce with foreign nations, and among the several states, and with the Indian tribes." In one of the earliest commerce cases after the Civil War (1861–1865), *U.S. v. E.C. Knight* (1895), even manufacturing was held to be outside the U.S. government's control, as "commerce succeeds to manufacturing, and is not a part of it." The court eventually slightly expanded this view but government powers remained extremely limited, especially in terms of local commerce, wages, and hours.

Child labor was a particular evil that Congress attempted to outlaw with legislation. However, this was struck down by the Supreme Court as an interference with the police power of the states. Congress then decided to tax the products of child labor and the Court struck down this legislation as well. These issues moved off the national radar screen in the 1920s as conditions seemed to improve and the desire of the public for commercial regulation seemed to abate. With the onset of the Great Depression in the early 1930s, however, the need for federal regulations on commerce became increasingly clear. Attempts to regulate hours and wages with the National Recovery Act and other acts were struck down by the Supreme Court as unconstitutional, as the issue of wages and hours did not directly relate to interstate commerce.

Roosevelt's "court-packing" plan, a presidential attempt to appoint new justices who would agree with New Deal legislation, failed. Nevertheless such legislation did begin to receive support from the Court. The Fair Labor Standards Act of 1938 was the first national legislation to regulate hours and wages for those businesses in interstate commerce and to prohibit the interstate shipment of goods produced at factories that used child labor. The act was tested in the Supreme Court in *U.S. v. Darby.*

Significance

The Supreme Court's unanimous opinion upholding the Fair Labor Standards Act was a clear victory for the New Deal and an enlargement of the commerce clause. The earlier precedent of *Hammer v. Dagenhart,* which had struck down a congressional attempt to ban child labor, was overruled. With Supreme Court support of the Fair Labor Standards Act, Congress could regulate worker wages and hours, as well as child labor, as long as the goods being affected went into interstate commerce. Later decisions built upon this, labeling nearly all commerce "interstate." This was a clear victory for those who wanted wage and hour laws and a ban on child labor. The decision's significance has carried into the twenty-first century because it greatly expanded federal power, improved wages and working conditions, and saved children from being worked to death. This also allowed future Congresses to go after what they perceived as dangers, as long as those issues were remotely connected to interstate commerce.

This broader view of the commerce clause gave Congress a great deal more power to deal with the problems and issues that arose in the later twentieth century. For instance, the 1964 Civil Rights Act prohibits discrimination but does not use the Fourteenth Amendment's due process or equal protection clause to equalize public accommodations. It uses instead the commerce clause, which would have been impossible without *Darby.* Congress has also used, with varying treatment by the courts, a broader view of the commerce clause to ban drug sales near schools and to regulate handgun purchases.

Primary Source

U.S. v. Darby [excerpt]

SYNOPSIS: Justice Stone explains that shipping goods between states, rather than manufacturing itself, is interstate commerce, and that Congress can control such shipment. He then explains that the Fair Labor Standards Act allows Congress to prevent one manufacturer from outselling another manufacturer in another state because the first manufacturer underpays and overworks its employees. Because the Court believes Congress is not infringing on states' rights to make such legislation, it overrules the precedent of *Dagenhart* and upholds the Fair Labor Standards Act. The case was decided on February 3, 1941.

Justice Stone delivered the opinion of the Court.

The two principal questions raised by the record in this case are, *first,* whether Congress has constitutional power to prohibit the shipment in interstate commerce of lumber manufactured by employees whose wages are less than a prescribed minimum or whose weekly hours of labor at that wage are greater than a prescribed maximum, and, *second,* whether it has power to prohibit the employment of workmen in the production of goods "for interstate commerce" at other than prescribed wages and hours. A subsidiary question is whether in connection with such prohibitions Congress can require the employer subject to them to keep records showing the hours worked each day and week by each of his employees including those engaged "in the production and manufacture of goods to wit, lumber, for 'interstate commerce.'" . . .

The prohibition of shipment of the proscribed goods in interstate commerce. . . .

While manufacture is not of itself interstate commerce, the shipment of manufactured goods interstate is such commerce and the prohibition of such shipment by Congress is indubitably a regulation of the commerce. The power to regulate commerce is the power "to prescribe the rule by which commerce is governed." It extends not only to those regulations which aid, foster and protect the commerce, but embraces those which prohibit it. . . . It is conceded that the power of Congress to prohibit transportation in interstate commerce includes noxious articles, . . . stolen articles, . . . kidnapped persons, . . . and articles such as intoxicating liquor or convict-made goods, traffic in which is forbidden or restricted by the laws of the state of destination. . . .

But it is said that the present prohibition falls within the scope of none of these categories; that while the prohibition is nominally a regulation of the commerce its motive or purpose is regulation of wages and hours of persons engaged in manufacture, the control of which has been reserved to the states and upon which Georgia and some of the states of destination have placed no restriction; that the effect of the present statute is, . . . under the guise of a regulation of interstate commerce, . . . to regulate wages and hours within the state contrary to the policy of the state which has elected to leave them unregulated.

The power of Congress over interstate commerce "is complete in itself, may be exercised to its utmost extent, and acknowledges no limitations other than are prescribed in the Constitution." That power can neither be enlarged nor diminished by the exercise or non-exercise of state power. . . . Congress, following its own conception of public policy concerning the restrictions which may appropriately be imposed on interstate commerce, is free to exclude from the commerce articles whose use in the states for which they are destined it may conceive to be injurious to the public health, morals or welfare, even though the state has not sought to regulate their use. . . .

Such regulation is not a forbidden invasion of state power merely because either its motive or its consequence is to restrict the use of articles of commerce within the states of destination; and is not prohibited unless by other Constitutional provisions. It is no objection to the assertion of the power to regulate interstate commerce that its exercise is attended by the same incidents which attend the exercise of the police power of the states. . . .

The motive and purpose of the present regulation are plainly to make effective the Congressional conception of public policy that interstate commerce should not be made the instrument of competition in the distribution of goods produced under substandard labor conditions, which competition is injurious to the commerce and to the states from and to which the commerce flows. The motive and purpose of a regulation of interstate commerce are matters for the legislative judgment upon the exercise of which the Constitution places no restriction and over which the courts are given no control. . . . Whatever their motive and purpose, regulations of commerce which do not infringe some constitutional prohibition are within the plenary power conferred on Congress by the Commerce Clause. Subject only to that limitation, presently to be considered, we conclude that the prohibition of the shipment interstate of goods produced under the forbidden substandard labor conditions is within the constitutional authority of Congress.

In the more than a century which has elapsed since the decision of *Gibbons v. Ogden,* these principles of constitutional interpretation have been so long and repeatedly recognized by this Court as applicable to the Commerce Clause, that there would be little occasion for repeating them now were it not for the decision of this Court twenty-two years ago in *Hammer v. Dagenhart.* In that case it was held by a bare majority of the Court over the powerful and now classic dissent of Mr. Justice Holmes setting forth the fundamental issues involved, that Congress

Harlan Fiske Stone, Chief Justice of the Supreme Court, 1941–1946. COLLECTION OF THE SUPREME COURT OF THE UNITED STATES.

was without power to exclude the products of child labor from interstate commerce. The reasoning and conclusion of the Court's opinion there cannot be reconciled with the conclusion which we have reached, that the power of Congress under the Commerce Clause is plenary to exclude any article from interstate commerce subject only to the specific prohibitions of the Constitution.

Hammer v. Dagenhart has not been followed. The distinction on which the decision was rested that Congressional power to prohibit interstate commerce is limited to articles which in themselves have some harmful or deleterious property—a distinction which was novel when made and unsupported by any provision of the Constitution—has long since been abandoned. . . . The thesis of the opinion that the motive of the prohibition or its effect to control in some measure the use or production within the states of the article thus excluded from the commerce can operate to deprive the regulation of its constitutional authority has long since ceased to have force. . . . And finally we have declared "The authority of the federal government over interstate commerce does not differ in extent or character from that retained by the states over intrastate commerce." . . .

The conclusion is inescapable that *Hammer v. Dagenhart* was a departure from the principles which have prevailed in the interpretation of the Commerce Clause both before and since the decision and that such vitality, as a precedent, as it then had has long since been exhausted. It should be and now is overruled.

Validity of the wage and hour requirements

Section 15 (a) (2) and §§ 6 and 7 require employers to conform to the wage and hour provisions with respect to all employees engaged in the production of goods for interstate commerce. . . .

There remains the question whether such restriction on the production of goods for commerce is a permissible exercise of the commerce power. The power of Congress over interstate commerce is not confined to the regulation of commerce among the states. It extends to those activities intrastate which so affect interstate commerce or the exercise of the power of Congress over it as to make regulation of them appropriate means to the attainment of a legitimate end, the exercise of the granted power of Congress to regulate interstate commerce. . . .

Congress, having by the present Act adopted the policy of excluding from interstate commerce all goods produced for the commerce which do not conform to the specified labor standards, it may choose the means reasonably adapted to the attainment of the permitted end, even though they involved control of intrastate activities. . . .

The Sherman Act and the National Labor Relations Act are familiar examples of the exertion of the commerce power to prohibit or control activities wholly intrastate because of their effect on interstate commerce. . . .

The means adopted for the protection of interstate commerce by the suppression of the production of the condemned goods for interstate commerce is so related to the commerce and so affects it as to be within the reach of the commerce power. . . . Congress, to attain its objective in the suppression of nationwide competition in interstate commerce by goods produced under substandard labor conditions, has made no distinction as to the volume or amount of shipments in the commerce or of production for commerce by any particular shipper or producer. It recognized that in present day industry, competition by a small part may affect the whole and that the total effect of the competition of many small producers may be great. . . .

So far as *Carter v. Carter Coal Co.* is inconsistent with this conclusion, its doctrine is limited in principle by the decisions under the Sherman Act and the National Labor Relations Act, which we have cited and which we follow. . . .

Our conclusion is unaffected by the Tenth Amendment. . . . The amendment states but a truism that all is retained which has not been surrendered. There is nothing in the history of its adoption to suggest that it was more than declaratory of the relationship between the national and state governments as it had been established by the Constitution before the amendment or that its purpose was other than to allay fears that the new national government might seek to exercise powers not granted, and that the states might not be able to exercise fully their reserved powers. . . .

From the beginning and for many years the amendment has been construed as not depriving the national government of authority to resort to all means for the exercise of a granted power which are appropriate and plainly adapted to the permitted end. . . .

Validity of the wage and hour provisions under the Fifth Amendment

Both provisions are minimum wage requirements compelling the payment of a minimum standard wage with a prescribed increased wage for overtime of "not less than one and one-half times the regular rate" at which the worker is employed. Since our decision in *West Coast Hotel Co. v. Parrish* it is no longer open to question that the fixing of a minimum wage is within the legislative power and that the bare fact of its exercise is not a denial of due process under the Fifth more than under the Fourteenth Amendment. Nor is it any longer open to question that it is within the legislative power to fix maximum hours. . . .

The Act is sufficiently definite to meet constitutional demands. One who employs persons, without conforming to the prescribed wage and hour conditions, to work on goods which he ships or expects to ship across state lines, is warned that he may be subject to the criminal penalties of the Act. No more is required.

Further Resources
BOOKS
Cushman, Barry. *Rethinking the New Deal Court: The Structure of a Cultural Revolution.* New York: Oxford University Press, 1998.

Mason, Alpheus Thomas. *Harlan Fiske Stone: Pillar of the Law.* New York: Viking Press, 1956.

Renstrom, Peter G. *The Stone Court: Justices, Rulings, and Legacy.* Santa Barbara, Calif.: ABC-CLIO, 2001.

Urofsky, Melvin I. *Division and Discord: The Supreme Court under Stone and Vinson, 1941–1953.* Columbia, S.C.: University of South Carloina Press, 1997.

WEBSITES

Craddock, Ashley. "In Court, Arguing for Net Speech as Commerce." *Wired News,* April 23, 1997. Available online at http://www.wired.com/news/politics/0,1283,3361,00.html; website home page: http://www.wired.com (accessed April 20, 2003).

Reynolds, Glenn Harlan. "Kids, Guns, and the Commerce Clause: Is the Court Ready for Constitutional Government?" *Policy Analysis* 216, October 10, 1994. Available online at http://www.cato.org/pubs/pas/pa-216.html; website home page: http://www.cato.org (accessed April 20, 2003).

United States v. Lopez. 514 U.S. 549 (1995). Available online at http://caselaw.lp.findlaw.com/scripts/getcase.pl?court=us&vol;=514&invol;=549; website homepage: http://findlaw.com (accessed April 20, 2003).

U.S. Constitution, Article I. Available online at http://www.law.cornell.edu/constitution/constitution.articlei.html; website home page: http://www.law.cornell.edu (accessed April 20, 2003).

Executive Order 8802

Executive order

By: Franklin D. Roosevelt

Date: June 25, 1941

Source: President. Executive Order 8802. "Reaffirming Policy Of Full Participation In The Defense Program By All Persons, Regardless Of Race, Creed, Color, Or National Origin, And Directing Certain Action In Furtherance Of Said Policy." *Federal Register* 6, 3109, June 25, 1941. Available online at http://www.eeoc.gov/35th/thelaw/eo-8802.html; website home page: http://www.eeoc.gov (accessed April 24, 2003).

About the Author: Franklin D. Roosevelt (1882–1945) was born in Hyde Park, New York. He survived an adulthood bout with polio and rarely revealed his dependence upon a wheelchair. He and his wife Eleanor had six children, one of whom died in infancy. First elected in 1932, Roosevelt went on to win three more bids for the presidency, causing a Constitutional Amendment limiting presidents to two terms. He died while in office in April 1945, shortly before the end of World War II. ∎

Introduction

African Americans have long suffered workplace discrimination. Well into the twentieth century they were denied the best jobs and were the last hired and first fired. Although America fought for democracy abroad in World War I (1914–1918), such democracy was not universally present at home. During the war some African Americans, including educator and writer W.E.B. DuBois, suggested unified support of the war. After the war many African-American soldiers returned with a fresh outlook, in part because soldiers fighting with the French had been treated fairly. Equality was not forthcoming, though. Prejudice persisted throughout the 1920s and discriminatory groups like the Ku Klux Klan enjoyed a revival. Roosevelt's New Deal programs during the Great Depression of the 1930s segregated, and often excluded, African Americans. For instance the first Agricultural Adjustment Act paid benefits mostly to white farmers who owned large amounts of land. In the South this led to sharecroppers, many of whom were African American, being thrown off the land.

A marked instance of racism occurred when nine young African-American men in Alabama were falsely accused of rape and quickly convicted in the 1930s. Eight of them were sentenced to death. Although the Supreme Court overturned their convictions, Alabama tried them again and the trials dragged on throughout the 1930s. The last "Scottsboro Boy" did not leave prison until 1950. All of the publicity in this case, and the prejudice it demonstrated, drew attention to the plight of African Americans in the South.

For this reason, among others, African Americans determined to fight both civilian and military racism as U.S. involvement in World War II (1939–1945) grew more likely. A. Philip Randolph, head of the Brotherhood of Sleeping Car Porters, an important African-American union, called for integration of defense contractors. When his demand met with little response he threatened a march on Washington. Roosevelt responded with Executive Order 8802 and the promise of a Fair Employment Practices Commission (FEPC) to oversee the order.

Significance

The FEPC was underfunded and not wholly successful. Through Order 8802 antidiscrimination clauses were written into war contracts but were not always enforced. Facilities in the South were still segregated, even for Army troops. The Army itself was still segregated, with many African Americans under the command of Southern officers on the theory that Southern whites knew "how to deal with" African Americans. Outside of the military, racial tensions flared several times during World War II, including race riots in Detroit and New York, largely between African Americans and whites who lived in overly close conditions. African Americans were fighting for victory both abroad against U.S. enemies and at home against racism; the FEPC assisted with this "Double V," or double victory, campaign.

A group of employees read a poster printed by the Labor Division of the Office of Production Management and the President's Committee on Fair Employment Practice, that states there will be no discrimination in defense employment. © BETTMANN/CORBIS. REPRODUCED BY PERMISSION.

Executive Order 8802 and the FEPC also led, in some ways, to the Equal Employment Opportunity Commission (EEOC) that exists today. However the EEOC was not launched until the 1960s, under the Civil Rights Act of 1964, because southern conservatives opposed any agency promoting equality throughout the 1940s. Although Executive Order 8802 publicized racism, validated the struggles of African Americans, and lent some amount of support to cries for increased equality in the 1940s, most of the impetus for the Civil Rights movement of the 1950s and 1960s came from individuals, rather than the government.

Primary Source

Executive Order 8802

SYNOPSIS: After setting out his reasons for issuing the executive order, Roosevelt says the defense program needs the support of all citizens of all races to survive and explains that workers have been barred from employment in the defense industry on the basis of their race.

WHEREAS it is the policy of the United States to encourage full participation in the national defense program by all citizens of the United States, regardless of race, creed, color, or national origin, in the firm belief that the democratic way of life within the Nation can be defended successfully only with the help and support of all groups within its borders; and

WHEREAS there is evidence that available and needed workers have been barred from employment in industries engaged in defense production solely because of considerations of race, creed, color, or national origin, to the detriment of workers' morale and of national unity.

NOW, THEREFORE, by virtue of the authority vested in me by the Constitution and the statutes, and as a prerequisite to the successful conduct of our national defense production effort, I do hereby reaffirm the policy of the United States that there shall be no discrimination in the employment of workers in defense industries or government because of race, creed, color, or national origin, and I do hereby declare that it is the duty of employers and of labor organizations, in furtherance of said policy and of this order, to provide for the full and equitable participation of all workers in defense industries, without discrimination because of race, creed, color, or national origin;

And it is hereby ordered as follows:

1. All departments and agencies of the Government of the United States concerned with vocational and training programs for defense production shall take special measures appropriate to assure that such programs are administered without discrimination because of race, creed, color, or national origin;

2. All contracting agencies of the Government of the United States shall include in all defense contracts hereafter negotiated by them a provision obligating the contractor not to discriminate against any worker because of race, creed, color, or national origin;

3. There is established in the Office of Production Management a Committee on Fair Employment Practice, which shall consist of a chairman and four other members to be appointed by the President. The Chairman and members of the Committee shall serve as such without compensation but shall be entitled to actual and necessary transportation, subsistence and other expenses incidental to performance of their duties. The Committee shall receive and investigate complaints of discrimination in violation of the provisions of this order and shall take appropriate steps to redress grievances which it finds to be valid. The Committee shall also recommend to the several de-

partments and agencies of the Government of the United States and to the President all measures which may be deemed by it necessary or proper to effectuate the provisions of this order.

Franklin D. Roosevelt
The White House
June 25, 1941

Further Resources

BOOKS

Jones, Jacqueline. *Four Centuries of Black and White Labor.* New York: Norton, 1998.

Feagin, Joe R., and Melvin P. Sikes. *Living with Racism: The Black Middle Class Experience.* Boston: Beacon Press, 1994.

PERIODICALS

Day, John Cocci. "Retelling the Story of Affirmative Action: Reflections on a Decade of Federal Jurisprudence in the Public Workplace." *California Law Review* 89, no. 1, January 2001, 59–128.

WEB SITES

"Milestones: The Early Years." Equal Employment Opportunity Commission. Available online at http://www.eeoc.gov/35th/milestones/early.html; website home page: http://www.eeoc.gov (accessed April 20, 2003).

"Executive Order 8802." *The First Measured Century.* The Corporation for Public Broadcasting. Available online at http://www.pbs.org/fmc/timeline/eexec8802.htm; website home page: http://www.pbs.org (accessed June 8, 2002).

Japanese Internment and the Law

Executive Order 9066

Executive order

By: Franklin D. Roosevelt
Date: February 19, 1942
Source: President. Executive Order 9066. "Authorizing the Secretary of War to Prescribe Military Areas." *Federal Register* 7, no. 38, 1407, February 19, 1942. Available online at http://www.library.arizona.edu/images/jpamer/execordr.html; website home page: http://www.library.arizona.edu (accessed April 24, 2003).
About the Author: Franklin D. Roosevelt (1882–1945) was born in Hyde Park, New York. He survived an adulthood bout with polio and rarely revealed his dependence upon a wheelchair. He and his wife Eleanor had six children, one of whom died in infancy. First elected in 1932, Roosevelt went on to win three more bids for the presidency, causing a Constitutional Amendment limiting presidents to two terms. He died while in office in April 1945, just before the end of World War II.

Hirabayashi v. U.S.

Supreme Court decision

By: Harlan F. Stone (majority), Frank Murphy (concurrence)
Date: June 21, 1943
Source: *Hirabayashi v. United States* 320 U.S. 81 (1943). Reprinted in Hall, Kermit L., William M. Wiecek, and Paul Finkelman, eds. *American Legal History: Cases and Materials,* 2d ed. New York: Oxford University Press, 1996, 429–430.
About the Authors: Harlan F. Stone (1872–1946) came to the Supreme Court in 1925 after a stint as attorney general. He was named chief justice in 1941. One of his primary concerns while on the bench was judicial restraint.

Like Stone, Frank Murphy (1890–1949) came to the Supreme Court after serving as attorney general. Appointed in 1939, Murphy consistently supported civil liberties. He was also known for his tendency to judge cases based on his conscience.

Korematsu v. U.S.

Supreme Court decision

By: Hugo L. Black (majority), Frank Murphy (dissent)
Date: December 18, 1944
Source: *Korematsu v. United States* 323 U.S. 214 (1944). Reprinted in Kutler, Stanley, ed. *The Supreme Court and the Constitution: Readings in American Constitutional History,* 3rd ed. New York: W.W. Norton, 1984, 708–712.
About the Author: Hugo Lafayette Black (1886–1971) represented Alabama in the U.S. Senate for two terms. He was appointed to the Supreme Court in 1937. His term was generally distinguished by his support of civil rights. ∎

Introduction

There has long been anti-Asian prejudice in the United States. One early sign of this was the Chinese Exclusion Act of 1882, which banned Chinese immigration for ten years and prevented Chinese already in America from becoming citizens. People who had left the country on visits back to China before the act's passage were not allowed to return. The act was made permanent in 1902. The National Origins Act of 1924 went even further, banning immigration from anywhere in East Asia. Neither act was revoked until the latter half of the twentieth century.

After the Japanese bombed Pearl Harbor on December 7, 1941, many began agitating for the removal of Japanese Americans from the West Coast. Vote-hungry politicians responded to baseless racial fears to support these demands. Businesses that competed with Japanese Americans saw the opportunity to eliminate their rivals and supported the demands as well. In response President Roosevelt issued Executive Order 9066, which Congress later ratified with legislation. Approximately

two-thirds of the Japanese Americans removed and detained under the order were U.S. citizens. Those born outside the United States, the *Issei,* were unable to become citizens, regardless of how long they had lived in the country. Only second-generation Japanese Americans (born in the United States), the *Nisei,* were citizens.

This order was more damaging than anything done in the xenophobia, or fear of people of foreign origin, of World War I (1914–1918). In that conflict only those German immigrants who violated exclusion orders were forced into detention camps. During World War II (1939–1945) German Americans and Italian Americans who were not citizens were generally not relocated but only kept under curfew for a short time. In contrast, about 110,000 of the 127,000 Japanese Americans who lived on the mainland were relocated, mostly from the West Coast. Those in Hawaii were generally left alone, probably because they made up such a large percentage of the population that their removal would have disrupted the local economy.

Gordon Hirabayashi, an American citizen of Japanese ancestry, sued to challenge a curfew order issued in accordance with Executive Order 9066. He argued that Congress had illegally delegated power and that the curfew order was racial discrimination that violated the Fifth Amendment due process clause. Hirabayashi also tried to challenge the relocation order but due to his attorney's errors in preparing the record, and due to the fact that both his two jail sentences ran concurrently, the Supreme Court considered only the curfew order and not the relocation order. However, the Supreme Court did make itself clear in *Hirabayashi* that the president and Congress have the power to do whatever is needed in wartime.

Another Japanese American, Fred Korematsu, sued to challenge the relocation of Japanese Americans surrounding the San Leandro, California, area. He had volunteered for the army but was refused and had begun working for a defense plant before his arrest for violating the order. Korematsu initially claimed that he was a Mexican American to prevent being excluded and relocated. Then he insisted on his loyalty to America and protested the unconstitutionality of the government's relocation of people for racial reasons. Unlike the Hirabayashi case, the Supreme Court considered the relocation order itself in *Korematsu.*

Significance

Japanese Americans fought well in World War II in spite of, or perhaps because of, the intense racial prejudice they faced. The 442nd Regimental Combat Team in Europe, made up entirely of Japanese Americans, had the highest rate of commendations and won over 18,000 medals. Japanese Americans were not allowed to fight in the Pacific, though. *Hirabayahsi* and *Korematsu* set a dangerous precedent as they allowed the government to do anything which it saw fit in wartime.

Only in the *Ex Parte Endo* case, decided December 18, 1944 (the same day as *Korematsu*) did the Court rule somewhat in favor of Japanese Americans, determining that only those whose loyalty was questionable could be held. In *Endo* the Court ordered the release of Mitsuye Endo, whose loyalty was unquestioned. The Court did not rule directly on the detention issue, however, only ruling that the War Relocation Authority could not hold those whose loyalty was never doubted. Hirabayashi's case is one of the two most frequently studied Japanese-American internment cases, along with *Korematsu*.

It was not until 1976 that Executive Order 9066 was repealed. Moreover, the *Korematsu* and *Hirabayashi* decisions have never been formally overturned. Hirabayashi only had his conviction vacated, or pronounced invalid, in the 1980s and even then the government still defended Executive Order 9066 in the courts. Roughly ten years passed before Japanese Americans received a formal apology and it was not until the late 1980s that internees received some small compensation for their economic losses. The relocation ruined the lives of numerous Japanese Americans and cost them businesses, homes, and property. At a very basic level it demonstrated an ugly side of the United States and showed the depths to which the country might sink during war.

Primary Source

Executive Order 9066

SYNOPSIS: The president orders the secretary of war to designate areas from which civilians may be excluded and further instructs him to provide food and shelter for those excluded citizens. Roosevelt also says this executive order does not affect another order instructing the FBI to regulate alien enemies. Effectively this allows for the creation of relocation camps. Although the order nowhere mentions Japanese Americans they were understood to be the intended target of Roosevelt's instructions.

WHEREAS the successful prosecution of the war requires every possible protection against espionage and against sabotage to national-defense material, national-defense premises, and national-defense utilities as defined in section 4, Act of April 20, 1918, 40 Stat. 533, as amended by the act of November 30, 1940, 54 Stat. 1220, and the Act of August 21, 1941, 55 Stat. 655 (U. S. C., Title 50, Sec. 104):

NOW, THEREFORE, by virtue of the authority vested in me as President of the United States, and

Commander in Chief of the Army and Navy, I hereby authorize and direct the Secretary of War, and the Military Commanders whom he may from time to time designate, whenever he or any designated Commander deems such actions necessary or desirable, to prescribe military areas in such places and of such extent as he or the appropriate Military Commanders may determine, from which any or all persons may be excluded, and with such respect to which, the right of any person to enter, remain in, or leave shall be subject to whatever restrictions the Secretary of War or the appropriate Military Commander may impose in his discretion. The Secretary of War is hereby authorized to provide for residents of any such area who are excluded therefrom, such transportation, food, shelter, and other accommodations as may be necessary, in the judgment of the Secretary of War or the said Military Commander, and until other arrangements are made, to accomplish the purpose of this order. The designation of military areas in any region or locality shall supersede designations of prohibited and restricted areas by the Attorney General under the Proclamations of December 7 and 8, 1941, and shall supersede the responsibility and authority of the Attorney General under the said Proclamations in respect of such prohibited and restricted areas.

I hereby further authorize and direct the Secretary of War and the said Military Commanders to take such other steps as he or the appropriate Military Commander may deem advisable to enforce compliance with the restrictions applicable to each Military area here in above authorized to be designated, including the use of Federal troops and other Federal Agencies, with authority to accept assistance of state and local agencies.

I hereby further authorize and direct all Executive Departments, independent establishments and other Federal Agencies, to assist the Secretary of War or the said Military Commanders in carrying out this Executive Order, including the furnishing of medical aid, hospitalization, food, clothing, transportation, use of land, shelter, and other supplies, equipment, utilities, facilities and services.

This order shall not be construed as modifying or limiting in any way the authority heretofore granted under Executive Order No. 8972, dated December 12, 1941, nor shall it be construed as limiting or modifying the duty and responsibility of the Federal Bureau of Investigation, with respect to the investigation of alleged acts of sabotage or the duty and responsibility of the Attorney General and the

Department of Justice under the Proclamations of December 7 and 8, 1941, prescribing regulations for the conduct and control of alien enemies, except as such duty and responsibility is superseded by the designation of military areas there under.

Franklin D. Roosevelt
February 19, 1942

Primary Source

Hirabayashi v. U.S. [excerpt]

SYNOPSIS: Justice Stone states that war can make racial distinctions necessary, even though such would normally be forbidden, in order to protect the majority of the population. However Justice Murphy's concurrence demonstrates the tenuous nature of the Court's unanimous decision to uphold the curfew. He says American law is based on a tradition requiring legal equality. Noting the unique nature of the racial restrictions imposed upon Japanese Americans he calls the curfew barely constitutional. The case was decided on June 21, 1943.

Mr. Chief Justice Stone delivered the opinion of the Court.

. . . The challenged orders were defense measures for the avowed purpose of safeguarding the military area in question, at a time of threatened air raids and invasion by the Japanese forces, from the danger of sabotage and espionage. As the curfew was made applicable to citizens residing in the area only if they were of Japanese ancestry, our inquiry must be whether in the light of all the facts and circumstances there was any substantial basis for the conclusion . . . that the curfew as applied was a protective measure necessary to meet the threat of sabotage and espionage which would substantially affect the war effort and which might reasonably be expected to aid a threatened enemy invasion. The alternative which appellant insists must be accepted is for the military authorities to impose the curfew on all citizens within the military area, or on none. In a case of threatened danger requiring prompt action, it is a choice between inflicting obviously needless hardship on the many, or sitting passive and unresisting in the presence of the threat. We think that constitutional government, in time of war, is not so powerless and does not compel so hard a choice if those charged with the responsibility of our national defense have reasonable ground for believing that the threat is real. . . .

But appellant insists that the exercise of the power is inappropriate and unconstitutional because it discriminates against citizens of Japanese ancestry. . . .

Distinctions between citizens solely because of their ancestry are by their very nature odious to a free people whose institutions are founded upon the doctrine of equality. For that reason, legislative classification or discrimination based on race alone has often been held to be a denial of equal protection. . . .

We may assume that these considerations would be controlling here were it not for the fact that the danger of espionage and sabotage, in time of war and of threatened invasion, calls upon the military authorities to scrutinize every relevant fact bearing on the loyalty of populations in the danger areas. Because racial discriminations are in most circumstances irrelevant and therefore prohibited, it by no means follows that, in dealing with the perils of war, Congress and the Executive are wholly precluded from taking into account those facts and circumstances which are relevant to measures for our national defense and for the successful prosecution of the war, and which may in fact place citizens of one ancestry in a different category from others. . . . The adoption by Government, in the crisis of war and of threatened invasion, of measures for the public safety, based upon the recognition of facts and circumstances which indicate that a group of one national extraction may menace that safety more than others, is not wholly beyond the limits of the Constitution and is not to be condemned merely because in other and in most circumstances racial distinctions are irrelevant. . . .

Mr. Justice Murphy, concurring:

Distinctions based on color and ancestry are utterly inconsistent with our traditions and ideals. They are at variance with the principles for which we are now waging war. We cannot close our eyes to the fact that for centuries the Old World has been torn by racial and religious conflicts and has suffered the worst kind of anguish because of inequality of treatment for different groups. There was one law for one and a different law for another. Nothing is written more firmly into our law than the compact of the Plymouth voyagers to have just and equal laws. To say that any group cannot be assimilated is to admit that the great American experiment has failed, that our way of life has failed when confronted with the normal attachment of certain groups to the lands of their forefathers. As a nation we embrace many groups, some of them among the oldest settlements in our midst, which have isolated themselves for religious and cultural reasons.

A Japanese family gathers in their living room at the Manzanar Relocation Camp in 1943. **THE LIBRARY OF CONGRESS.**

Today is the first time, so far as I am aware, that we have sustained a substantial restriction of the personal liberty of citizens of the United States based upon the accident of race or ancestry. Under the curfew order here challenged no less than 70,000 American citizens have been placed under a special ban and deprived of their liberty because of their particular racial inheritance. In this sense it bears a melancholy resemblance to the treatment accorded to members of the Jewish race in Germany and in other parts of Europe. The result is the creation in this country of two classes of citizens for purposes of a critical and perilous hour—to sanction discrimination between groups of United States citizens on the basis of ancestry. In my opinion this goes to the very brink of constitutional power.

Primary Source

Korematsu v. U.S. [excerpt]

> **SYNOPSIS:** In this case the U.S. Supreme Court justifies Executive Order 9066, which led to the relocation of Japanese Americans to internment camps. Justice Black claims evidence of Japanese-American

disloyalty existed and argues the camps were necessary because it is impossible to separate the loyal from the disloyal. Justice Murphy's dissent challenges the blanket relocation of all Pacific Coast Japanese Americans, arguing that such exclusion is racist and that the relocated citizens posed no immediate public danger. The case was decided on December 18, 1944.

Justice Black delivered the opinion of the Court.

The petitioner, an American citizen of Japanese descent, was convicted in a federal district court for remaining in San Leandro, California, a "Military Area," contrary to Civilian Exclusion Order No. 34 of the Commanding General of the Western Command, U.S. Army, which directed that after May 9, 1942, all persons of Japanese ancestry should be excluded from that area. No question was raised as to petitioner's loyalty to the United States. . . .

It should be noted, to begin with, that all legal restrictions which curtail the civil rights of a single racial group are immediately suspect. That is not to say that all such restrictions are unconstitutional. It is to say that courts must subject them to the most rigid scrutiny. Pressing public necessity may sometimes justify the existence of such restrictions; racial antagonism never can. . . .

[E]xclusion of those of Japanese origin was deemed necessary because of the presence of an unascertained number of disloyal members of the group, most of whom we have no doubt were loyal to this country. It was because we could not reject the finding of the military authorities that it was impossible to bring about an immediate segregation of the disloyal from the loyal that we sustained the validity of the curfew order as applying to the whole group. In the instant case, temporary exclusion of the entire group was rested by the military on the same ground. The judgment that exclusion of the whole group was for the same reason a military imperative answers the contention that the exclusion was in the nature of group punishment based on antagonism to those of Japanese origin. That there were members of the group who retained loyalties in Japan has been confirmed by investigations made subsequent to the exclusion. Approximately five thousand American citizens of Japanese ancestry refused to swear unqualified allegiance to the United States and to renounce allegiance to the Japanese Emperor, and several thousand evacuees requested repatriation to Japan.

We uphold the exclusion order as of the time it was made and when the petitioner violated it. . . . In doing so, we are not unmindful of the hardships imposed by it upon a large group of American citizens. . . . But hardships are part of war, and war is an aggregation of hardships. All citizens alike, both in and out of uniform, feel the impact of war in greater or lesser measure. Citizenship has its responsibilities as well as its privileges, and in time of war the burden is always heavier. Compulsory exclusion of large groups of citizens from their homes, except under circumstances of direst emergency and peril, is inconsistent with our basic governmental institutions. But when under conditions of modern warfare our shores are threatened by hostile forces, the power to protect must be commensurate with the threatened danger. . . .

It is said that we are dealing here with the case of imprisonment of a citizen in a concentration camp solely because of his ancestry, without evidence or inquiry concerning his loyalty and good disposition towards the United States. Our task would be simple, our duty clear, were this a case involving the imprisonment of a loyal citizen in a concentration camp because of racial prejudice. Regardless of the true nature of the assembly and relocation centers—and we deem it unjustifiable to call them concentration camps with all the ugly connotations that term implies—we are dealing specifically with nothing but an exclusion order. To cast this case into outlines of racial prejudice, without reference to the real military dangers which were presented, merely confuses the issue. Korematsu was not excluded from the Military Area because of hostility to him or his race. He *was* excluded because we are at war with the Japanese Empire, because the properly constituted military authorities feared an invasion of our West Coast and felt constrained to take proper security measures, because they decided that the military urgency of the situation demanded that all citizens of Japanese ancestry be segregated from the West Coast temporarily, and finally, because Congress, reposing its confidence in this time of war in our military leaders—as inevitably it must—determined that they should have the power to do just this. There was evidence of disloyalty on the part of some, the military authorities considered that the need for action was great, and time was short. We cannot—by availing ourselves of the calm perspective of hindsight—now say that at that time these actions were unjustified.

Justice Murphy, dissenting.

This exclusion of "all persons of Japanese ancestry, both alien and non-alien," from the Pacific Coast area on a plea of military necessity in the absence of martial law ought not to be approved. Such exclusion goes over "the very brink of constitutional power" and falls into the ugly abyss of racism.

In dealing with matters relating to the prosecution and progress of a war, we must accord great respect and consideration to the judgments of the military authorities who are on the scene and who have full knowledge of the military facts. The scope of their discretion must, as a matter of necessity and common sense, be wide. And their judgments ought not to be overruled lightly by those whose training and duties ill-equip them to deal intelligently with matters so vital to the physical security of the nation.

At the same time, however, it is essential that there be definite limits to military discretion, especially where martial law has not been declared. Individuals must not be left impoverished of their constitutional rights on a plea of military necessity that has neither substance nor support. . . .

The judicial test of whether the Government, on a plea of military necessity, can validly deprive an individual of any of his constitutional rights is whether the deprivation is reasonably related to a public danger that is so "immediate, imminent, and impending" as not to admit of delay and not to permit the intervention of ordinary constitutional processes to alleviate the danger. . . . Civilian Exclusion Order No. 34, banishing from a prescribed area of the Pacific Coast "all persons of Japanese ancestry, both alien and non-alien," clearly does not meet that test. Being an obvious racial discrimination, the order deprives all those within its scope of the equal protection of the laws as guaranteed by the Fifth Amendment. It further deprives these individuals of their constitutional rights to live and work where they will, to establish a home where they choose and to move about freely. In excommunicating them without benefit of hearings, this order also deprives them of all their constitutional rights to procedural due process. Yet no reasonable relation to an "immediate, imminent, and impending" public danger is evident to support this racial restriction which is one of the most sweeping and complete deprivations of constitutional rights in the history of this nation in the absence of martial law.

It must be conceded that the military and naval situation in the spring of 1942 was such as to generate a very real fear of invasion of the Pacific Coast, accompanied by fears of sabotage and espionage in that area. The military command was therefore justified in adopting all reasonable means necessary to combat these dangers. In adjudging the military action taken in light of the then apparent dangers, we must not erect too high or too meticulous standards; it is necessary only that the action have some reasonable relation to the removal of the dangers of invasion, sabotage and espionage. But the exclusion, either temporarily or permanently, of all persons with Japanese blood in their veins has no such reasonable relation. And that relation is lacking because the exclusion order necessarily must rely for its reasonableness upon the assumption that *all* persons of Japanese ancestry may have a dangerous tendency to commit sabotage and espionage and to aid our Japanese enemy in other ways. It is difficult to believe that reason, logic or experience could be marshalled in support of such an assumption.

That this forced exclusion was the result in good measure of this erroneous assumption of racial guilt rather than bona fide military necessity is evidenced by the Commanding General's Final Report on the evacuation from the Pacific Coast area. In it he refers to all individuals of Japanese descent as "subversive," as belonging to "an enemy race" whose "racial strains are undiluted," and as constituting "over

A recess period at the Manzanar Relocation Center, California, 1943.
THE LIBRARY OF CONGRESS.

112,000 potential enemies . . . at large today" along the Pacific Coast. In support of this blanket condemnation of all persons of Japanese descent, however, no reliable evidence is cited to show that such individuals were generally disloyal, or had generally so conducted themselves in this area as to constitute a special menace to defense installations or war industries, or had otherwise by their behavior furnished reasonable ground for their exclusion as a group.

Justification for the exclusion is sought, instead, mainly upon questionable racial and sociological grounds not ordinarily within the realm of expert military judgment, supplemented by certain semi-military conclusions drawn from an unwarranted use of circumstantial evidence. . . .

No one denies, of course, that there were some disloyal persons of Japanese descent on the Pacific Coast who did all in their power to aid their ancestral land. Similar disloyal activities have been engaged in by many persons of German, Italian and even more pioneer stock in our country. But to infer that examples of individual disloyalty prove group disloyalty and justify discriminatory action against the entire group is to deny that under our system of law individual guilt is the sole basis for deprivation of rights. . . . To give constitutional sanction to that inference in this case, however well-intentioned may have been the military command on the Pacific Coast is to adopt one of the cruelest of the rationales used by our enemies to destroy the dignity of the individual and to encourage and open the door to discriminatory actions against other minority groups in the passions of tomorrow.

No adequate reason is given for the failure to treat these Japanese Americans on an individual basis by holding investigations and hearings to separate the loyal from the disloyal, as was done in the case of persons of German and Italian ancestry. . . . It is asserted merely that the loyalties of this group "were unknown and time was of the essence." Yet nearly four months elapsed after Pearl Harbor before the first exclusion order was issued. . . .

Moreover, there was no adequate proof that the Federal Bureau of Investigation and the military and naval intelligence services did not have the espionage and sabotage situation well in hand during this long period. Nor is there any denial of the fact that not one person of Japanese ancestry was accused or convicted of espionage or sabotage after Pearl Harbor while they were still free. . . .

I dissent, therefore, from this legalization of racism. Racial discrimination in any form and in any degree has no justifiable part whatever in our democratic way of life. It is unattractive in any setting but it is utterly revolting among a free people who have embraced the principles set forth in the Constitution of the United States. All residents of this nation are kin in some way by blood or culture to a foreign land. Yet they are primarily and necessarily a part of the new and distinct civilization of the United States. They must accordingly be treated at all times as the heirs of the American experiment and as entitled to all the rights and freedoms guaranteed by the Constitution.

Further Resources

BOOKS

Arrington, Leonard J. *The Price of Prejudice: The Japanese-American Relocation Center in Utah during World War II.* Logan, Utah: Faculty Assn., 1962.

Daniels, Roger, and Eric Foner. *Prisoners Without Trial: Japanese Americans in World War II.* New York: Hill and Wang, 1993.

Dudley, William. *Japanese American Internment Camps.* San Diego, Calif.: Greenhaven Press, 2002.

Hath, Erica. *Last Witnesses: Reflections on the Wartime Internment of Japanese Americans.* New York: Palgrave, 2001.

Hosokawa, Bill. *Nisei, The Quiet Americans: The Story of a People.* Boulder: University Press of Colorado, 2002.

Houston, Jeanne Wakatsuki, and James D. Houston. *Farewell to Manzanar: A True Story of the Japanese American Experience During and After the World War II Internment.* New York: Bantam Books, 1995.

Inada, Lawson Fusau. *Only What We Could Carry: The Japanese-American Internment Experience.* Berkeley: Heyday, 2000.

Irons, Peter H. *Justice At War: The Story of the Japanese American Internment Cases.* New York: Oxford University Press, 1983.

James, Thomas. *Exile Within: The Schooling of Japanese Americans, 1942–1945.* Cambridge, Mass.: Harvard University Press, 1987.

Uchida, Yoshiko. *Desert Exile: The Uprooting of a Japanese-American Family.* Seattle: University of Washington Press, 1982.

Weglyn, Michi. *Years of Infamy: The Untold Story of America's Concentration Camps.* New York: Morrow, 1976.

PERIODICALS

Brooks, Charlotte. "In the Twilight Zone Between Black and White: Japanese American Resettlement and Community in Chicago, 1942–1945." *Journal of American History* 86, no. 4, 1655–1688.

Maga, Timothy P. "Ronald Reagan and Redress for Japanese-American Internment 1983–1988." *Presidential Studies Quarterly,* Summer 1998, 606.

Mizono, Takeya. "Newspapers, Content and Construct—The Creation of 'Free Press' in Japanese-American Camps: The War Relocation Authority's Planning and Making of the Camp Newspaper Policy." *Journalism and Mass Communication Quarterly,* 78, no. 3, 503–519.

Okamura, Johnathan Y. "Race Relations in Hawai'i During World War II: The Non-Internment of Japanese Americans." *Amerasia Journal* 26, no. 2, 117–142.

Regalado, Samuel O. "Incarcerated Sport: Nisei Women's Softball and Athletics During Japanese American Internment." *Journal of Sport History* 27, no. 3, 431–445.

WEB SITES

Beckwith, Jane. "Topaz Camp." Available online at http://www.millardcounty.com/topazcamp.html; website home page: http://www.millardcounty.com (accessed April 9, 2002).

"Evacuation and Internment of San Francisco's Japanese 1942." Museum of the City of San Francisco. Available online at http://www.sfmuseum.org/war/evactxt.html; website home page: http://www.sfmuseum.org (accessed April 20, 2003).

The Japanese American Internment. Available online at http://www.geocities.com/Athens/8420/main.html (accessed March 28, 2002).

Mudrock, Theresa. "Camp Harmony Exhibit." *Japanese American Exhibit and Access Project.* University of Washington. Available online at http://www.lib.washington.edu/exhibits/harmony/Exhibit/default.htm; website home page: http://www.lib.washington.edu (accessed April 20, 2003).

Myers, Roger. "War Relocation Authority Camps in Arizona, 1942–1946." *Images of the Southwest.* Available online at http://dizzy.library.arizona.edu/images/jpamer/wraintro.html; website home page: http://www.library.arizona.edu (accessed April 20, 2003).

"Japanese-Americans Internment Camps During World War II." Special Collections Department, J. Willard Marriott Library, Photograph Archives, University of Utah. Available online at http://www.lib.utah.edu/spc/photo/9066/9066.htm; website home page: http://www.lib.utah.edu (accessed April 20, 2003).

Wickard v. Filburn

Supreme Court decision

By: Robert Jackson

Date: November 9, 1942

Source: *Wickard v. Filburn*, 317 U.S. 111 (1942). Reprinted in Kutler, Stanley, ed. *The Supreme Court and the Constitution: Readings in American Constitutional History*, 3d ed. New York: W.W. Norton, 1984, 406–412.

About the Author: Robert Jackson (1892–1954) was appointed to the Supreme Court in 1941. Like several Supreme Court justices in the twentieth century, Jackson came to the bench after being attorney general. He was a strong supporter of First Amendment rights and his term was distinguished by a long-standing feud with fellow justice Hugo Black. While Black often wanted the Court to take a stronger role in curbing government infringement on civil liberties, Jackson resisted this in favor of judicial restraint. ∎

Introduction

Wickard v. Filburn affected two very different aspects of American congressional power. First, it defined what the commerce clause of the U.S. Constitution meant when it stated that Congress had the power "to regulate [c]ommerce with foreign Nations, and among the several States, and with the Indian Tribes." Second, it redefined interstate commerce. The interstate portion of this clause had served as the basis for much federal power but questions remained about how far this power reached into the states. Questions also remained about the extent to which the commerce clause could regulate all aspects of production, even those far removed from commerce.

In addition, questions remained about Congress's power to regulate agriculture. While Congress had not been granted specific control over agriculture, many in the nineteenth century, especially those from farming states, agreed that the general welfare clause ("We the people . . . in order to . . . promote the General Welfare . . . do ordain and establish this Constitution . . .") allowed Congress to regulate agriculture. Others disagreed and the Supreme Court, in *United States v. Butler* (1936), stated the general welfare clause did not allow agriculture regulation. The first Agricultural Adjustment Act (1933) was struck down in *Butler* but the New Deal passed a Second Agricultural Adjustment Act in 1938. The Supreme Court upheld this second act, but mostly as it affected interstate commerce. The *Wickard* case tested the act as it affected grains used purely on the farm as food for livestock, household food, and seed, all areas far removed from any direct effect on interstate commerce. Upholding the act in this area would completely redefine interstate commerce as well as greatly expand the power of Congress in the area of both the commerce clause and the general welfare clause.

Significance

The Supreme Court determined that Wickard's use of his own production above the quota for his household did affect interstate commerce. The Court stated that if he had *not* used his own grain he would have bought grain that might have been from another state. This meant that even if his grain did not appear on an interstate market his production above the quota still affected interstate commerce. The Supreme Court here destroyed the nearly fifty-year-old distinction between production and commerce, which meant that Congress could regulate both of these activities. The only requirement now was that the item regulated must have "a substantial economic effect on interstate commerce." The decision also recalled and put into law Chief Justice John Marshall's early nineteenth-century comment that "restraints on its [the commerce clause's] exercise must proceed from political rather than judicial processes." With this expansion of the commerce clause few areas were immune from potential regulation. This expansion greatly increased the government's ability to control the economy.

Congress went on to use the commerce clause to accomplish its goals in other areas. For instance many civil rights regulations are based on the commerce clause. Discrimination in certain areas may be prohibited if the activity has an effect upon interstate commerce. In addition, by expanding the idea of the general welfare clause to include agriculture, the Wickard decision greatly expanded the government's power and gave a judicial stamp of approval to the system of price supports, quotas, and production controls that continues to exist. Thus *Wickard v. Filburn* helped set the stage for powers that the government has held into the twenty-first century, both in agriculture and in the larger world. In addition *Wickard* symbolized the completion of the constitutional revolution of the 1930s, as it directly repudiated the idea of limited government symbolized by *United States v. Butler*.

Primary Source

Wickard v. Filburn [excerpt]

SYNOPSIS: Justice Jackson rules that the power of Congress to control agricultural commerce is to be decided by the effect of a product on the economy. He notes that wheat production generally exceeds consumption in the states. Therefore private consumption, in which a farmer uses his own excess grain for use on his farm rather than buying it from another farmer, does affect market demand for the product. Thus the court rules the regulations legal, allowing farmers to be penalized for selling or using grain they produce above the quota. The case was decided on November 9, 1942.

Justice Jackson delivered the opinion of the Court.

It is urged that under the Commerce Clause of the Constitution, Article I, § 8, clause 3, Congress does not possess the power it has in this instance sought to exercise. The question would merit little consideration since our decision in *United States v. Darby* . . . sustaining the federal power to regulate production of goods for commerce, except for the fact that this Act extends federal regulation to production not intended in any part for commerce but wholly for consumption on the farm. The Act includes a definition of "market" and its derivatives, so that as related to wheat, in addition to its conventional meaning, it also means to dispose of "by feeding (in any form) to poultry or livestock which, or the products of which, are sold, bartered, or exchanged, or to be so disposed of." Hence, marketing quotas not only embrace all that may be sold without penalty but also what may be consumed on the premises. Wheat produced on excess acreage is designated as "available for marketing" as so defined, and the penalty is imposed thereon. Penalties do not depend upon whether any part of the wheat, either within or without the quota, is sold or intended to be sold. The sum of this is that the Federal Government fixes a quota including all that the farmer may harvest for sale or for his own farm needs, and declares that wheat produced on excess acreage may neither be disposed of nor used except upon payment of the penalty, or except it is stored as required by the Act or delivered to the Secretary of Agriculture.

Appellee says that this is a regulation of production and consumption of wheat. Such activities are, he urges, beyond the reach of Congressional power under the Commerce Clause, since they are local in character, and their effects upon interstate commerce are at most "indirect." In answer the Government argues that the statute regulates neither production nor consumption, but only marketing; and, in the alternative, that if the Act does go beyond the regulation of marketing it is sustainable as a "necessary and proper" implementation of the power of Congress over interstate commerce.

The Government's concern lest the Act be held to be a regulation of production or consumption, rather than of marketing, is attributable to a few dicta and decisions of this Court which might be understood to lay it down that activities such as "production," "manufacturing," and "mining" are strictly "local" and, except in special circumstances which are not present here, cannot be regulated under the commerce power because their effects upon interstate commerce are, as matter of law, only "indirect." Even today, when this power has been held to have great latitude, there is no decision of this Court that such activities may be regulated where no part of the product is intended for interstate commerce or intermingled with the subjects thereof. We believe that a review of the course of decision under the Commerce Clause will make plain, however, that questions of the power of Congress are not to be decided by reference to any formula which would give controlling force to nomenclature such as "production" and "indirect" and foreclose consideration of the actual effects of the activity in question upon interstate commerce.

At the beginning Chief Justice Marshall described the federal commerce power with a breadth never yet exceeded. . . . He made emphatic the embracing and penetrating nature of this power by warning that effective restraints on its exercise must proceed from political rather than from judicial processes. . . .

For nearly a century, however, decisions of this Court under the Commerce Clause dealt rarely with questions of what Congress might do in the exercise of its granted power under the Clause, and almost entirely with the permissibility of state activity which it was claimed discriminated against or burdened interstate commerce. During this period there was perhaps little occasion for the affirmative exercise of the commerce power, and the influence of the Clause on American life and law was a negative one, resulting almost wholly from its operation as a restraint upon the powers of the states. In discussion and decision the point of reference, instead of being what was "necessary and proper" to the exercise by Congress of its granted power, was often some concept of sovereignty thought to be implicit in the status of statehood. Certain activities such as "production," "manufacturing," and "mining" were occasionally said to be within the province of state governments and beyond the power of Congress under the Commerce Clause.

It was not until 1887, with the enactment of the Interstate Commerce Act, that the interstate commerce power began to exert positive influence in American law and life. This first important federal resort to the commerce power was followed in 1890 by the Sherman Anti-Trust Act and, thereafter, mainly after 1903, by many others. These statutes ushered in new phases of adjudication, which required the Court to approach the interpretation of the Commerce Clause in the light of an actual exercise by Congress of its power thereunder.

When it first dealt with this new legislation, the Court adhered to its earlier pronouncements, and allowed but little scope to the power of Congress. These earlier pronouncements also played an important part in several of the five cases in which this Court later held that Acts of Congress under the Commerce Clause were in excess of its power.

Even while important opinions in this line of restrictive authority were being written, however, other cases called forth broader interpretations of the Commerce Clause destined to supersede the earlier ones, and to bring about a return to the principles first enunciated by Chief Justice Marshall. . . .

Not long after the decision of *United States v. Knight Co.,* . . . Mr. Justice Holmes, in sustaining the exercise of national power over intrastate activity, stated for the Court that "commerce among the States is not a technical legal conception, but a practical one, drawn from the course of business." It was soon demonstrated that the effects of many kinds of intrastate activity upon interstate commerce were such as to make them a proper subject of federal regulation. In some cases sustaining the exercise of federal power over intrastate matters the term "direct" was used for the purpose of stating, rather than of reaching, a result; in others it was treated as synonymous with "substantial" or "material"; and in others it was not used at all. Of late its use has been abandoned in cases dealing with questions of federal power under the Commerce Clause.

In the *Shreveport Rate Cases,* . . . the Court held that railroad rates of an admittedly intrastate character and fixed by authority of the state might, nevertheless, be revised by the Federal Government because of the economic effects which they had upon interstate commerce. The opinion of Mr. Justice Hughes found federal intervention constitutionally authorized because of "matters having such a close and substantial relation to interstate traffic that the control is essential or appropriate to the security of that traffic, to the efficiency of the interstate service, and to the maintenance of conditions under which interstate commerce may be conducted upon fair terms and without molestation or hindrance." . . .

The Court's recognition of the relevance of the economic effects in the application of the Commerce Clause, exemplified by this statement, has made the mechanical application of legal formulas no longer feasible. Once an economic measure of the reach of the power granted to Congress in the Commerce Clause is accepted, questions of federal power can-

Supreme Court Justice Robert H. Jackson, 1941. © BETTMANN/CORBIS. REPRODUCED BY PERMISSION.

not be decided simply by finding the activity in question to be "production," nor can consideration of its economic effects be foreclosed by calling them "indirect." The present Chief Justice [Stone] has said in summary of the present state of the law:

> The commerce power is not confined in its exercise to the regulation of commerce among the states. It extends to those activities intrastate which so affect interstate commerce, or the exertion of the power of Congress over it, as to make regulation of them appropriate means to the attainment of a legitimate end, the effective execution of the granted power to regulate interstate commerce. . . . The power of Congress over interstate commerce is plenary and complete in itself, may be exercised to its utmost extent, and acknowledges no limitations other than are prescribed in the Constitution. . . . It follows that no form of state activity can constitutionally thwart the regulatory power granted by the commerce clause to Congress. Hence the reach of that power extends to those intrastate activities which in a substantial way interfere with or obstruct the exercise of the granted power. . . .

Whether the subject of the regulation in question was "production," "consumption," or "marketing" is, therefore, not material for purposes of deciding the question of federal power before us. That an activity is of local character may help in a doubtful case to determine whether Congress intended to reach it. The same consideration might help in determining whether in the absence of Congressional action it would be permissible for the state to exert its power on the subject matter, even though in so doing it to some degree affected interstate commerce. But even if appellee's activity be local and though it may not be regarded as commerce, it may still, whatever its nature, be reached by Congress if it exerts a substantial economic effect on interstate commerce, and this irrespective of whether such effect is what might at some earlier time have been defined as "direct" or "indirect."

The parties have stipulated a summary of the economics of the wheat industry. Commerce among the states in wheat is large and important. Although wheat is raised in every state but one, production in most states is not equal to consumption. Sixteen states on average have had a surplus of wheat above their own requirements for feed, seed, and food. Thirty-two states and the District of Columbia, where production has been below consumption, have looked to these surplus-producing states for their supply as well as for wheat for export and carry-over.

The wheat industry has been a problem industry for some years. Largely as a result of increased foreign production and import restrictions, annual exports of wheat and flour from the United States during the ten-year period ending in 1940 averaged less than 10 per cent of total production, while during the 1920's they averaged more than 25 per cent. The decline in the export trade has left a large surplus in production which, in connection with an abnormally large supply of wheat and other grains in recent years, caused congestion in a number of markets; tied up rail-road cars; and caused elevators in some instances to turn away grains, and railroads to institute embargoes to prevent further congestion.

Many countries, both importing and exporting, have sought to modify the impact of the world market conditions on their own economy. Importing countries have taken measures to stimulate production and self-sufficiency. The four large exporting countries of Argentina, Australia, Canada, and the United States have all undertaken various programs for the relief of growers. Such measures have been designed, in part at least, to protect the domestic price received by producers. Such plans have generally evolved towards control by the central government.

In the absence of regulation, the price of wheat in the United States would be much affected by world conditions. During 1941, producers who coöperated with the Agricultural Adjustment program received an average price on the farm of about $1.16 a bushel, as compared with the world market price of 40 cents a bushel.

Differences in farming conditions, however, make these benefits mean different things to different wheat growers. There are several large areas of specialization in wheat, and the concentration on this crop reaches 27 per cent of the crop land, and the average harvest runs as high as 155 acres. Except for some use of wheat as stock feed and for seed, the practice is to sell the crop for cash. Wheat from such areas constitutes the bulk of the interstate commerce therein.

On the other hand, in some New England states less than one per cent of the crop land is devoted to wheat, and the average harvest is less than five acres per farm. In 1940 the average percentage of the total wheat production that was sold in each state, as measured by value, ranged from 29 per cent thereof in Wisconsin to 90 per cent in Washington. Except in regions of large-scale production, wheat is usually grown in rotation with other crops; for a nurse crop for grass seeding; and as a cover crop to prevent soil erosion and leaching. Some is sold, some kept for seed, and a percentage of the total production much larger than in areas of specialization is consumed on the farm and grown for such purpose. Such farmers, while growing some wheat, may even find the balance of their interest on the consumer's side.

The effect of consumption of home-grown wheat on interstate commerce is due to the fact that it constitutes the most variable factor in the disappearance of the wheat crop. Consumption on the farm where grown appears to vary in an amount greater than 20 per cent of average production. The total amount of wheat consumed as food varies but relatively little, and use as seed is relatively constant.

The maintenance by government regulation of a price for wheat undoubtedly can be accomplished as effectively by sustaining or increasing the demand as by limiting the supply. The effect of the statute before us is to restrict the amount which may be produced for market and the extent as well to which one may forestall resort to the market by producing to meet his own needs. That appellee's own contribution to the demand for wheat may be trivial by itself is not enough to remove him from the scope of federal regulation where, as here, his contribution, taken together with that of many others similarly situated, is far from trivial. . . .

It is well established by decisions of this Court that the power to regulate commerce includes the power to regulate the prices at which commodities in that commerce are dealt in and practices affecting such prices. One of the primary purposes of the Act in question was to increase the market price of wheat, and to that end to limit the volume thereof that could affect the market. It can hardly be denied that a factor of such volume and variability as home-consumed wheat would have a substantial influence on price and market conditions. This may arise because being in marketable condition such wheat overhangs the market and, if induced by rising prices, tends to flow into the market and check price increases. But if we assume that it is never marketed, it supplies a need of the man who grew it which would otherwise be reflected by purchases in the open market. Home-grown wheat in this sense competes with wheat in commerce. The stimulation of commerce is a use of the regulatory function quite as definitely as prohibitions or restrictions thereon. This record leaves us in no doubt that Congress may properly have considered that wheat consumed on the farm where grown, if wholly outside the scheme of regulation, would have a substantial effect in defeating and obstructing its purpose to stimulate trade therein at increased prices.

It is said, however, that this Act, forcing some farmers into the market to buy what they could provide for themselves, is an unfair promotion of the markets and prices of specializing wheat growers. It is of the essence of regulation that it lays a restraining hand on the self-interest of the regulated and that advantages from the regulation commonly fall to others. The conflicts of economic interest between the regulated and those who advantage by it are wisely left under our system to resolution by the Congress under its more flexible and responsible legislative process. Such conflicts rarely lend themselves to judicial determination. And with the wisdom, workability, or fairness, of the plan of regulation we have nothing to do.

Further Resources

BOOKS

Cushman, Barry. *Rethinking the New Deal Court: The Structure of a Constitutional Revolution.* New York: Oxford University Press, 1998.

Desmond, Charles S. *Mr. Justice Jackson: Four Lectures in His Honor.* New York: Columbia University Press, 1969.

Gerhart, Eugene C. *Supreme Court Justice Jackson, Lawyer's Judge.* Albany, N.Y.: Q Corporation, 1961.

Hockett, Jeffrey D. *New Deal Justice: The Constitutional Jurisprudence of Hugo L. Black, Felix Frankfurter, and Robert H. Jackson.* Lanham, Md.: Rowman & Littlefield Publishers, 1996.

WEBSITES

Craddock, Ashley. "In Court, Arguing for Net Speech as Commerce." *Wired News,* April 23, 1997. Available online at http://www.wired.com/news/politics/0,1283,3361,00.html; website home page: http://www.wired.com (accessed June 8, 2002).

Reynolds, Glenn Harlan. "Kids, Guns, and the Commerce Clause: Is the Court Ready for Constitutional Government?" *Policy Analysis* 216, October 10, 1994. Available online at http://www.cato.org/pubs/pas/pa-216.html; website home page: http://www.cato.org (accessed June 8, 2002).

United States v. Lopez. 514 U.S. 549 (1995). Available online at http://caselaw.lp.findlaw.com/scripts/getcase.pl?court=us&vol;=514&invol;=549; website homepage: http://findlaw.com (accessed April 20, 2003).

U.S. Constitution, Article I. Available online at http://www.law.cornell.edu/constitution/constitution.articlei.html; website home page: http://www.law.cornell.edu (accessed April 20, 2003).

West Virginia State Board of Education v. Barnette

Supreme Court decision

By: Robert Jackson (majority), Felix Frankfurter (dissent)
Date: June 14, 1943
Source: *West Virginia Board of Education v. Barnette,* 319 U.S. 624 (1943). Reprinted in Kutler, Stanley, ed. *The Supreme Court and the Constitution: Readings in American Constitutional History,* 3d ed. New York: W.W. Norton, 1984, 511–519.
About the Authors: Robert Jackson (1892–1954) was appointed to the Supreme Court in 1941. Like several Supreme Court justices in the twentieth century, Jackson came to the bench after being attorney general. He was a strong supporter of First Amendment rights.

Before his Supreme Court Appointment in 1939 Felix Frankfurter (1882–1965) was a Harvard Law professor who advised President Roosevelt (served 1933–1945). His strong nationalism appears in many of the opinions he wrote while on the bench. ■

Introduction

Jehovah's Witnesses were often disliked and felt intense pressure to conform prior to and during World War II (1939–1945). Jehovah's Witnesses were not well treated during wars in general. One of the religious group's original leaders, Charles Rutherford, and several of his followers were sentenced to 20-year jail terms for their pacifist positions during World War I (1914–1918). They did not have to serve the full sentences as their convictions were overturned in 1919.

The *Minersville School District v. Gobitis* (1940) decision, which held that Jehovah's Witnesses could be forced to salute the flag, resulted in widespread violence against Jehovah's Witnesses. Vigilantes, mobs, and even public officials attacked Jehovah's Witnesses for their beliefs. The *Gobitis* decision clashed with most Supreme Court decisions of the period, which had moved toward greater protection of minorities. Thus it was not surprising that the court decided to hear another flag salute case only three years after *Gobitis.* The West Virginia law in question in *Barnette* considered failure to salute the flag "insubordination" and allowed expulsion of children and imprisonment of parents for up to 30 days, as well as a fine of up to $50. Parents who removed their children from schools in response to the law disobeyed state compulsory education laws.

Significance

The Court's ruling that the Barnette children could not constitutionally be forced to salute the flag may seem surprising, given that it had ruled against Jehovah's Witnesses only three years earlier in *Gobitis.Gobitis* was decided on a vote of 8-1 and only three years later the Court switched completely, voting 8-1 to overturn its previous flag salute rulings. In the years between these two decisions Justices Douglas, Black, and Murphy stated in another opinion that *Gobitis* had been wrong, demonstrating that the violence following the case likely affected the Court's opinion. This caused a debate within the court. While Douglas, Black, and Murphy were moved, in part, by the violence against Jehovah's Witnesses to vote in favor of the Barnette family, Frankfurter felt the Court ought to defer to the local legislature in this case. Although Jackson and Frankfurter found themselves on opposite sides of the flag salute issue, the division of the court typifies its division between the Frankfurter-Jackson wing, which gave more deference to the government, and the Black-Douglas wing, which held that the government was prohibited from making "any law" that interfered with the freedom of speech, press, or religion.

The *Barnette* ruling foreshadowed the Court's expansion of constitutional freedoms in the 1950s and 1960s. The perspective represented by the Black-Douglas wing appeared again in *Taylor v. Mississippi* (1943). This decision held that states could not convict Jehovah's Witnesses under sedition statutes, laws that prohibited resistance to governmental authority, without direct evidence of a clear and present danger. Throughout the

1950s and 1960s freedom of religion was slowly expanded. The Warren Court in *Engle v. Vitale* (1962) held that students did not have to recite a state-generated prayer at the start of each school day. The Court said this use of state facilities, supported by public taxes, was a violation of the separation between church and state. The Supreme Court, in *School District of Abington Township v. Schempp* (1963), also overturned a law requiring daily Bible reading, stating that the First Amendment both prohibited favoring one religion over another and aiding religion in general. State aid to religious schools was, however, allowed by the Warren Court (1953–1969) in order to help pay for textbooks.

In other areas the Supreme Court allowed public officials to drop references to God in the oaths they swore. The Court also expanded conscientious objector status, granted to individuals who refused to go to war on religious or moral grounds, so that it applied to all religions, even ones that did not involve belief in a god. These decisions generally increased protections to religions outside the mainstream. Often such decisions went against public opinion, leading to campaigns and billboards suggesting "Impeach Earl Warren." Some claimed the Supreme Court had taken God out of schools (referring to *Engle*) while allowing the criminals to go unpunished (referring to other decisions of the Warren Court increasing defendants' rights such as *Miranda v. Arizona,* which guaranteed that police would read people their rights when arresting them).

Primary Source

West Virginia State Board of Education v. Barnette
[excerpt]

> **SYNOPSIS:** Justice Jackson, delivering the opinion of the Court, argues the state cannot impose patriotism on its subjects. He explains that the Fourteenth Amendment prohibits the government from denying individuals liberty, including the First Amendment's freedom of religion, without due process of law. He reasons that West Virginia's flag salute law violates due process and therefore goes against the Fourteenth Amendment. Justice Frankfurter, in a dissenting opinion, maintains that the Fourteenth Amendment does not forbid a state from passing a flag salute law. The case was decided on June 14, 1943.

Mr. Justice Jackson delivered the opinion of the Court

. . . As the present Chief Justice [Stone] said in dissent in the *Gobitis* case, the State may "require teaching by instruction and study of all in our history and in the structure and organization of our government, including the guaranties of civil liberty, which tend to inspire patriotism and love of country." Here, however, we are dealing with a compulsion of students to declare a belief. They are not merely made acquainted with the flag salute so that they may be informed as to what it is or even what it means. The issue here is whether this slow and easily neglected route to aroused loyalties constitutionally may be short-cut by substituting compulsory salute and slogan. This issue is not prejudiced by the Court's previous holding that where a State, without compelling attendance, extends college facilities to pupils who voluntarily enroll, it may prescribe military training as part of the course without offense to the Constitution. It was held that those who take advantage of its opportunities may not on ground of conscience refuse compliance with such conditions. In the present case attendance is not optional. . . .

There is no doubt that the flag salute is a form of utterance. Symbolism is a primitive but effective way of communicating ideas. The use of an emblem or flag to symbolize some system, idea, institution, or personality, is a short cut from mind to mind. Causes and nations, political parties, lodges and ecclesiastical groups seek to knit the loyalty of their followings to a flag or banner, a color or design. The State announces rank, function, and authority through crowns and maces, uniforms and black robes; the church speaks through the Cross, the Crucifix, the altar and shrine, and clerical raiment. Symbols of State often convey political ideas just as religious symbols come to convey theological ones. Associated with many to these symbols are appropriate gestures of acceptance or respect: a salute, a bowed or bared head, a bended knee. A person gets from a symbol the meaning he puts into it, and what is one man's comfort and inspiration is another's jest and scorn.

Over a decade ago Chief Justice Hughes led this Court in holding that the display of a red flag as a symbol of opposition by peaceful and legal means to organized government was protected by the free speech guaranties of the Constitution. Here it is the State that employs a flag as a symbol of adherence to government as presently organized. It requires the individual to communicate by word and sign his acceptance of the political ideas it thus bespeaks. Objection to this form of communication when coerced is an old one, well known to the framers of the Bill of Rights.

It is also to be noted that the compulsory flag salute and pledge requires affirmation of a belief and an attitude of mind. . . . It is now a commonplace that censorship or suppression of expression of opin-

Supreme Court Justice Felix Frankfurter. © BETTMANN/CORBIS. REPRODUCED BY PERMISSION.

ion is tolerated by our Constitution only when the expression presents a clear and present danger of action of a kind the State is empowered to prevent and punish. It would seem that involuntary affirmation could be commanded only on even more immediate and urgent grounds than silence. But here the power of compulsion is invoked without any allegation that remaining passive during a flag salute ritual creates a clear and present danger that would justify an effort even to muffle expression. To sustain the compulsory flag salute we are required to say that a Bill of Rights guards the individual's right to speak his own mind, left it open to public authorities to compel him to utter what is not in his mind. . . .

The *Gobitis* decision, however, *assumed* . . . that power exists in the State to impose the flag salute discipline upon school children in general. The Court only examined and rejected a claim based on religious beliefs of immunity from an unquestioned general rule. The question which underlies the flag salute controversy is whether such a ceremony so touching matters of opinion and political attitude may be imposed upon the individual by official authority under powers committed to any political organization under our Constitution. We examine rather than assume

Saluting the Flag

When the *Barnette* case came before the Supreme Court, a flag salute did not resemble the modern fingers to the forehead or hand over the heart gesture. Instead, it involved raising the right arm straight ahead of the body, palm down, much like the "Heil Hitler" salute. Justice Jackson notes that many states, including West Virginia, had modified their salute to be palm up in response to complaints about its resemblance to the Nazi gesture.

existence of this power and . . . re-examine specific grounds assigned for the *Gobitis* decision.

1. It was said [in Frankfurter's *Gobitis* opinion] that the flag-salute controversy confronted the Court with "the problem which Lincoln cast in memorable dilemma: 'Must a government of necessity be too *strong* for the liberties of its people, or too *weak* to maintain its own existence?' and that the answer must be in favor of strength."

We think issues may be examined free of pressure or restraint growing out of such considerations.

It may be doubted whether Mr. Lincoln would have thought that the strength of government to maintain itself would be impressively vindicated by our confirming power of the State to expel a handful of children from school. Such oversimplification, so handy in political debate, often lacks the precision necessary to postulates of judicial reasoning. If validly applied to this problem, the utterance cited would resolve every issue of power in favor of those in authority and would require us to override every liberty thought to weaken or delay execution of their policies.

Government of limited power need not be anemic government. Assurance that rights are secure tends to diminish fear and jealousy of strong government, and by making us feel safe to live under it makes for its better support. Without promise of a limiting Bill of Rights it is doubtful if our Constitution could have mustered enough strength to enable its ratification. To enforce those rights today is not to choose weak government over strong government. It is only to adhere as a means of strength to individual freedom of mind in preference to officially disciplined uniformity for which history indicates a disappointing and disastrous end.

2. It was also considered in the *Gobitis* case that functions of educational officers in States, coun-

ties and school districts were such that to interfere with their authority "would in effect make us the school board for the country." . . .

Such Boards are numerous and their territorial jurisdiction often small. But small and local authority may feel less sense of responsibility to the Constitution, and agencies of publicity may be less vigilant in calling it to account. The action of Congress in making flag observance voluntary and respecting the conscience of the objector in a matter so vital as raising the Army contrasts sharply with these local regulations in matters relatively trivial to the welfare of the nation. There are village tyrants as well as village Hampdens, but none who acts under color of law is beyond reach of the Constitution.

3. The *Gobitis* opinion reasoned that this is a field "where courts possess no marked . . . competence," that it is committed to the legislatures as well as the courts to guard cherished liberties and that it is constitutionally appropriate to "fight out the wise use of legislative authority in the forum of public opinion and before legislative assemblies rather than to transfer such a contest to the judicial arena. . . ."

The very purpose of a Bill of Rights was to withdraw certain subjects from the vicissitudes of political controversy, to place them beyond the reach of majorities and officials and to establish them as legal principles to be applied by the courts. One's right to life, liberty, and property, to free speech, a free press, freedom of worship and assembly, and other fundamental rights may not be submitted to vote; they depend on the outcome of no elections.

4. Lastly, and this is the very heart of the *Gobitis* opinion, it reasons that "National unity is the basis of national security," that the authorities have "the right to select appropriate means for its attainment," and hence reaches the conclusion that such compulsory measures toward "national unity" are constitutional. Upon the verity of this assumption depends our answer in this case. . . .

Struggles to coerce uniformity of sentiment in support of some end thought essential to their time and country have been waged by many good as well as by evil men. Nationalism is a relatively recent phenomenon but at other times and places the ends have been racial or territorial security, support of a dynasty or regime, and particular plans for saving souls. As . . . moderate methods to attain unity have failed, those bent on its accomplishment must resort to an ever-increasing severity. . . . Ultimate futility of such attempts to compel coherence is the lesson of every such effort from the Roman drive to stamp out Christianity as a disturber of its pagan unity, the Inquisition, as a means to religious and dynastic unity, the Siberian exiles as a means to Russian unity, down to the fast failing efforts of our present totalitarian enemies. Those who begin coercive elimination of dissent soon find themselves exterminating dissenters. Compulsory unification of opinion achieves only the unanimity of the graveyard.

It seems trite but necessary to say that the First Amendment to our Constitution was designed to avoid these ends by avoiding these beginnings. There is no mysticism in the American concept of the State or of the nature or origin of its authority. We set up government by consent of the governed, and the Bill of Rights denies those in power any legal opportunity to coerce that consent. Authority here is to be controlled by public opinion, not public opinion by authority.

The case is made difficult not because the principles of its decision are obscure but because the flag involved is our own. Nevertheless, we apply the limitations of the Constitution with no fear that freedom to be intellectually and spiritually diverse or even contrary will disintegrate the social organization. To believe that patriotism will not flourish if patriotic ceremonies are voluntary and spontaneous instead of a compulsory routine is to make an unflattering estimate of the appeal of our institutions to free minds. We can have intellectual individualism and the rich cultural diversities that we owe to exceptional minds only at the price of occasional eccentricity and abnormal attitudes. When they are so harmless to others or to the State as those we deal with here, the price is not too great. But freedom to differ is not limited to things that do not matter much. That would be a mere shadow of freedom. The test of its substance is the right to differ as to things that touch the heart of the existing order.

If there is any fixed star in our constitutional constellation, it is that no official, high or petty, can prescribe what shall be orthodox in politics, nationalism, religion, or other matters of opinion or force citizens to confess by word or act their faith therein. If there are any circumstances which permit an exception, they do not now occur to us.

We think the action of the local authorities in compelling the flag salute and pledge transcends constitutional limitations on their power and invades the sphere of intellect and spirit which it is the purpose of the First Amendment to our Constitution to reserve from all official control.

The decision of this Court in *Minersville School District v. Gobitis* . . . [is] overruled, and the judgment enjoining enforcement of the West Virginia Regulation is Affirmed.

Mr. Justice Frankfurter, dissenting:

One who belongs to the most vilified and persecuted minority in history is not likely to be insensible to the freedoms guaranteed by our Constitution. Were my purely personal attitude relevant I should wholeheartedly associate myself with the general libertarian views in the Court's opinion, representing as they do the thought and action of a lifetime. But as judges we are neither Jew nor Gentile, neither Catholic nor agnostic. We owe equal attachment to the Constitution and are equally bound by our judicial obligations whether we derive our citizenship from the earliest or the latest immigrants to these shores. As a member of this Court I am not justified in writing my private notions of policy into the Constitution, no matter how deeply I may cherish them or how mischievous I may deem their disregard. The duty of a judge who must decide which of two claims before the Court shall prevail, that of a State to enact and enforce laws within its general competence or that of an individual to refuse obedience because of the demands of his conscience, is not that of the ordinary person. It can never be emphasized too much that one's own opinion about the wisdom or evil of a law should be excluded altogether when one is doing one's duty on the bench. The only opinion of our own even looking in that direction that is material is our opinion whether legislators could in reason have enacted such a law. In the light of all the circumstances, including the history of this question in this Court, it would require more daring than I possess to deny that reasonable legislators could have taken the action which is before us for review. Most unwillingly, therefore, I must differ from my brethren with regard to legislation like this. I cannot bring my mind to believe that the "liberty" secured by the Due Process Clause gives this Court authority to deny to the State of West Virginia the attainment of that which we all recognize as a legitimate legislative end, namely, the promotion of good citizenship, by employment of the means here chosen. . . .

That claims are pressed on behalf of sincere religious convictions does not of itself establish their constitutional validity. Nor does waving the banner of religious freedom relieve us from examining into the power we are asked to deny the states. Otherwise the doctrine of separation of church and state, so cardinal in the history of this nation and for the

School children in Southington, Connecticut, pledge allegiance to the American flag, May 1942. **THE LIBRARY OF CONGRESS.**

liberty of our people, would mean not the disestablishment of a state church but the establishment of all churches and of all religious groups.

The subjection of dissidents to the general requirement of saluting the flag, as a measure conducive to the training of children in good citizenship, is very far from . . . exacting obedience to general laws that have offended deep religious scruples. Compulsory vaccination . . . food inspection regulations . . . the obligation to bear arms . . . testimonial duties . . . compulsory medical treatment . . . these are but illustrations of conduct that has often been compelled in the enforcement of legislation of general applicability even though the religious consciences of particular individuals rebelled at the exaction.

Law is concerned with external behavior and not with the inner life of man. It rests in large measure upon compulsion. Socrates lives in history partly because he gave his life for the conviction that duty of obedience to secular law does not presuppose consent to its enactment or belief in its virtue. The consent upon which free government rests is the consent that comes from sharing in the process of making and unmaking laws. . . . The individual conscience may profess what faith it chooses. . . . [B]ut it cannot thereby restrict community action through political organs in matters of community concern, so long as the action is not asserted in a discriminatory way either openly or by stealth. One may have

the right to practice one's religion and at the same time owe the duty of formal obedience to laws that run counter to one's beliefs. . . .

The flag salute exercise has no kinship whatever to the oath tests so odious in history. For the oath test was one of the instruments for suppressing heretical beliefs. Saluting the flag suppresses no belief nor curbs it. Children and their parents may believe what they please, avow their belief and practice it. It is not even remotely suggested that the requirement for saluting the flag involves the slightest restriction against the fullest opportunity on the part both of the children and of their parents to disavow as publicly as they choose to do so the meaning that others attach to the gesture of salute. All channels of affirmative free expression are open to both children and parents. Had we before us any act of the state putting the slightest curbs upon such free expression, I should not lag behind any member of this Court in striking down such an invasion of the right to freedom of thought and freedom of speech protected by the Constitution. . . .

One's conception of the Constitution cannot be severed from one's conception of a judge's function in applying it. . . . Our system is built on the faith that men set apart for this special function, freed from the influences of immediacy and from the deflections of worldly ambition, will become able to take a view of longer range than the period of responsibility entrusted to Congress and legislatures. We are dealing with matters as to which legislators and voters have conflicting views. Are we as judges to impose our strong convictions on where wisdom lies? That which three years ago had seemed . . . to lie within permissible areas of legislation is now outlawed by the deciding shift of opinion of two Justices. What reason is there to believe that they or their successors may not have another view a few years hence? Is that which was deemed to be of so fundamental a nature as to be written into the Constitution to endure for all times to be the sport of shifting winds of doctrine? Of course, judicial opinions, even as to questions of constitutionality, are not immutable. As has been true in the past, the Court will from time to time reverse its position. But I believe that never before these Jehovah's Witnesses cases . . . has this Court overruled decisions so as to restrict the powers of democratic government. Always heretofore, it has withdrawn narrow views of legislative authority so as to authorize what formerly it had denied. . . .

Of course patriotism can not be enforced by the flag salute. But neither can the liberal spirit be enforced by judicial invalidation of illiberal legislation. Our constant preoccupation with the constitutionality of legislation rather than with its wisdom tends to preoccupation of the American mind with a false value. The tendency of focusing attention on constitutionality is to make constitutionality synonymous with wisdom, to regard a law as all right if it is constitutional. Such an attitude is a great enemy of liberalism. Particularly in legislation affecting freedom of thought and freedom of speech much which should offend a free-spirited society is constitutional. Reliance for the most precious interests of civilization, therefore, must be found outside of their vindication in courts of law. Only a persistent positive translation of the faith of a free society into the convictions and habits and actions of a community is the ultimate reliance against unabated temptations to fetter the human spirit.

Further Resources

BOOKS

Eastland, Terry. *Religious Liberty in the Supreme Court: The Cases That Define the Debate Over Church and State.* Grand Rapids, Mich.: W.B. Eerdmans, 1993.

Gaustad, Edwin S. *Religious Issues in American History.* New York: Harper & Row, 1968.

Mauro, Tony. *Illustrated Great Decisions of the Supreme Court.* Washington, D.C.: Congressional Quarterly Press, 2000.

Newton, Merlin O. *Armed With the Constitution: Jehovah's Witnesses in Alabama and the U.S. Supreme Court.* Tuscaloosa: University of Alabama Press, 1994.

PERIODICALS

Danzig, Richard. "Justice Frankfurter's Opinions in the Flag Salute Cases: Blending Logic and Psychologic in Constitutional Decisionmaking." *Stanford Law Review* 36, no. 3, February 1984, 675–723.

"Judge Backs Berkeley in Dispute over Salute." *The New York Times,* May 10, 1984, B21.

AUDIO AND VISUAL MEDIA

"Congress Shall Make No Law: Six Cases that Helped Define the First Amendment." Terre Haute, Ind.: The Library, 1988.

Smith v. Allwright

Supreme Court decision

By: Stanley F. Reed

Date: April 3, 1944

Source: *Smith v. Allwright,* 321 U.S. 649 (1944). Reprinted in Kutler, Stanley, ed. *The Supreme Court and the Constitution: Readings in American Constitutional History,* 3d ed. New York: W.W. Norton, 1984, 589–592.

About the Author: Justice Stanley F. Reed (1884–1980) acted as the general prosecutor for the Federal Farm Board

and was solicitor general under President Franklin D. Roosevelt (served 1933–1945) before his 1938 appointment to the Supreme Court. In 1949 he testified on behalf of Alger Hiss, who was accused of perjury in connection with charges of spying for the Soviet Union. Reed retired from the Court in 1957. When he died in 1980 he was the longest lived member of the Supreme Court. ■

Introduction

Many southern states denied African Americans the right to vote well into the twentieth century. They did so using a variety of tactics including poll taxes, grandfather clauses, and literacy tests. Even after all of these methods of preventing African Americans from registering to vote had failed, southern states still upheld voter restrictions with the "white primary" rule, which stated only whites could vote in the Democratic primary in the South. As most registered voters in the South were Democrats, a victory in the Democratic primary meant a near certain victory in the regular election.

This Democratic stranglehold persisted because Republicans were still identified as the party of the North which had defeated the South in the Civil War (1861–65) and, in the eyes of many Southerners, tried to destroy their traditions and way of life. All participation in the southern Democratic party was limited to whites until the practice was outlawed in *Nixon v. Herndon* (1927) and *Nixon v. Condon* (1932). The Texas Democratic party, supposedly independent of the state apparatus, then called a convention that limited voting in the Democratic primary to those who were white. The Supreme Court ruled this legal in *Grovey v. Townsend* (1935), as it allegedly involved no state action. However, changes in court personnel, along with a decision upholding the conviction of Louisiana officials who did not count African American votes, *United States v. Classic* (1941), encouraged the National Association for the Advancement of Colored People (NAACP) to challenge this law. Texas officials were so sure the white primary would be upheld that they did not even send counsel to argue on its behalf. However, on April 3, 1944, the Supreme Court voted down the white primary in Texas in *Smith v. Allwright,* effectively ending its practice throughout the South.

Significance

Smith v. Allright was a firm step toward establishing voting equality. It held that states could not allow discrimination in party elections and, by application, held that the federal government was going to rule in favor of African Americans' voting rights. *Smith v. Allwright* signaled the beginning of the end of many discriminatory practices and led to a string of other decisions outlawing such practices. In addition it gave African Americans hope that the Supreme Court, at the very least, was on their side, even though the level of support for civil rights from the president and Congress varied greatly between 1944 and 1968.

Although the Supreme Court effectively settled the white primary issue the poll tax had to be outlawed through a constitutional amendment and no court decision could change the views of those southern registrars who were firmly opposed to any African Americans voting. These individuals were willing to put any number of obstacles between African Americans voters and the ballot box, including literacy and education tests. It finally took federal legislation, the Voting Rights Act of 1965, to truly end discriminatory practices and give most African Americans in the South a chance to vote. When African Americans were finally allowed to vote throughout the South, southern politics underwent a drastic change. The southern Democratic party became much more liberal and in response many conservative whites fled the Democratic party for the Republican party or at least voted for Republicans in some federal elections. In the elections of 1980 and 1984, for example, southern Democrats helped to elect Ronald Reagan (served 1981–1989) to the presidency and provided him with much of his congressional support.

Primary Source

Smith v. Allwright [excerpt]

> **SYNOPSIS:** Justice Reed explains the Texas Democratic party's argument that it is not subject to constitutional constraints, like the Fourteenth Amendment, because it is a voluntary organization and because primaries are not responsible for the election of candidates. However Reed notes that since primaries play such an integral role in the election process, the action of a political party can, in some cases, become fused with the action of the state. Thus the court overrules its earlier decision in *Grovey* and requires Texas to allow African Americans to vote in the Democratic primary. The case was decided on April 3, 1944.

Justice Reed delivered the opinion of the Court.

This writ of certiorari brings here for review a claim for damages in the sum of $5,000 on the part of the petitioner, a Negro citizen of the 48th precinct of Harris County, Texas, for the refusal of respondents, election and associate election judges respectively of that precinct, to give petitioner a ballot or to permit him to cast a ballot in the primary election of July 27, 1940, for the nomination of Democratic candidates for the United States Senate and House of Representatives, and Governor and other state officers. The refusal is alleged to have been solely because of the race and color of the proposed voter. . . .

Texas is free to conduct her elections and limit her electorate as she may deem wise, save only as her action may be affected by the prohibitions of the United States Constitution or in conflict with powers delegated to and exercised by the National Government. The Fourteenth Amendment forbids a state from making or enforcing any law which abridges the privileges or immunities of citizens of the United States and the Fifteenth Amendment specifically interdicts any denial or abridgement by a state of the right of citizens to vote on account of color. Respondents appeared in the District Court and the Circuit Court of Appeals and defended on the ground that the Democratic party of Texas is a voluntary organization with members banded together for the purpose of selecting individuals of the group representing the common political beliefs as candidates in the general election. As such a voluntary organization, it was claimed, the Democratic party is free to select its own membership and limit to whites participation in the party primary. Such action, the answer asserted, does not violate the Fourteenth, Fifteenth or Seventeenth Amendment as officers of government cannot be chosen at primaries and the Amendments are applicable only to general elections where governmental officers are actually elected. Primaries, it is said, are political party affairs, handled by party, not governmental, officers. No appearance for respondents is made in this Court. Arguments presented here by the Attorney General of Texas and the Chairman of the State Democratic Executive Committee of Texas, as amici curiae, urged substantially the same grounds as those advanced by the respondents. . . .

In *Grovey v. Townsend* [1935] . . . this Court had before it another suit for damages for the refusal in a primary of a county clerk, a Texas officer with only public functions to perform, to furnish petitioner, a Negro, an absentee ballot. The refusal was solely on the ground of race. . . . This Court went on to announce that to deny a vote in a primary was a mere refusal of party membership with which "the state need have no concern," . . . while for a state to deny a vote in a general election on the ground of race or color violated the Constitution. Consequently, there was found no ground for holding that the county clerk's refusal of a ballot because of racial ineligibility for party membership denied the petitioner any right under the Fourteenth or Fifteenth Amendments.

Since *Grovey v. Townsend* and prior to the present suit, no case from Texas involving primary elections has been before this Court. We did decide, however, *United States v. Classic* [1941]. . . . We there held that § 4 of Article I of the Constitution authorized Congress to regulate primary as well as general elections, . . ."where the primary is by law made an integral part of the election machinery." . . . The fusing by the *Classic* case of the primary and general elections into a single instrumentality for choice of officers has a definite bearing on the permissibility under the Constitution of excluding Negroes from primaries. This is not to say that the *Classic* case cuts directly into the rationale of *Grovey v. Townsend*. This latter case was not mentioned in the opinion. *Classic* bears upon *Grovey v. Townsend* not because exclusion of Negroes from primaries is any more or less state action by reason of the unitary character of the electoral process but because the recognition of the place of the primary in the electoral scheme makes clear that state delegation to a party of the power to fix the qualifications of primary elections is delegation of a state function that may make the party's action the action of the state. When *Grovey v. Townsend* was written, the Court looked upon the denial of a vote in a primary as a mere refusal by a party of party membership. . . . As the Louisiana statutes for holding primaries are similar to those of Texas, our ruling in *Classic* as to the unitary character of the electoral process calls for a re-examination as to whether or not the exclusion of Negroes from a Texas party primary was state action. . . .

It may now be taken as a postulate that the right to vote in such a primary for the nomination of candidates without discrimination by the State, like the right to vote in a general election, is a right secured by the Constitution. . . . By the terms of the Fifteenth Amendment that right may not be abridged by any state on account of race. Under our Constitution the great privilege of the ballot may not be denied a man by the State because of his color. . . .

Primary elections are conducted by the party under state statutory authority. The county executive committee selects precinct election officials and the county, district or state executive committees, respectively, canvass the returns. These party committees or the state convention certify the party's candidates to the appropriate officers for inclusion on the official ballot for the general election. No name which has not been so certified may appear upon the ballot for the general election as a candidate of a political party. No other name may be printed on the ballot which has not been placed in nomination by qualified voters who must take oath that they did not participate in a primary for the se-

Stanley Reed, U.S. Supreme Court associate justice, 1938–1957.
© CORBIS. REPRODUCED BY PERMISSION.

lection of a candidate for the office for which the nomination is made.

The state courts are given exclusive original jurisdiction of contested elections and of mandamus proceedings to compel party officers to perform their statutory duties. . . .

The United States is a constitutional democracy. Its organic law grants to all citizens a right to participate in the choice of elected officials without restriction by any state because of race. This grant to the people of the opportunity for choice is not to be nullified by a state through casting its electoral process in a form which permits a private organization to practice racial discrimination in the election. Constitutional rights would be of little value if they could be thus indirectly denied. . . .

The privilege of membership in a party may be, as this Court said in *Grovey v. Townsend,* . . . no concern of a state. But when, as here, that privilege is also the essential qualification for voting in a primary to select nominees for a general election, the state makes the action of the party the action of the state. In reaching this conclusion we are not unmindful of the desirability of continuity of decision in constitutional questions. However, when convinced of former error, this Court has never felt constrained to follow precedent. In constitutional questions, where correction depends upon amendment and not upon legislative action, this Court throughout its history has freely exercised its power to re-examine the basis of its constitutional decisions. This has long been accepted practice, and this practice has continued to this day. This is particularly true when the decision believed erroneous is the application of a constitutional principle rather than in interpretation of the Constitution to extract the principle itself. Here we are applying, contrary to the recent decision in *Grovey v. Townsend,* the well established principle of the Fifteenth Amendment, forbidding the abridgement by a state of a citizen's right to vote. *Grovey v. Townsend* is overruled.

Further Resources

BOOKS

Patterson, James T. *Brown v. Board of Education: A Civil Rights Milestone and Its Troubled Legacy.* New York: Oxford University Press, 2001.

Lawson, Steven F. *In Pursuit of Power: Southern Blacks and Electoral Politics 1965–1982.* New York: Columbia University Press, 1985.

Lusane, Clarence. *No Easy Victories: Black Americans and the Vote.* New York: Franklin Watts, 1996.

WEBSITES

Greenberg, Sanford N. "White Primaries." *The Handbook of Texas Online.* Available online at http://www.tsha.utexas .edu/handbook/online/articles/view/WW/wdw1.html (Accessed June 8, 2002).

Executive Order 9835

Executive order

By: Harry S. Truman

Date: March 21, 1947

Source: President. Executive Order 9835. "Prescribing Procedures for the Administration of an Employees Loyalty Program in the Executive Branch of the Government." *Federal Register* 12, 1935, March 21, 1947. Available online at http:// coursesa.matrix.msu.edu/~hst203/documents/loyal.html; website home page: http://www.msu.edu (accessed April 1, 2003).

About the Author: Harry S. Truman (1884–1972) grew up on a farm in Missouri. He served his home state as a U.S. senator from 1935–1944. Elected vice president in 1944, he became president when Franklin D. Roosevelt died in office in April 1945. He was elected to a second term in 1948. President Truman's "Fair Deal" tried, mostly unsuccessfully, to expand Roosevelt's liberal domestic policies. His Truman Doctrine of vigorous opposition to Communist expansion abroad became

the basis for America's Cold War foreign policy, and led America into the Korean War (1950–53). He returned to Missouri upon his retirement and died there in 1972. ∎

Introduction

The end of World War II left the United States fearful of the Soviet Union and communism. Americans had long distrusted and feared the Soviet Union. Its establishment in 1917 led to the first "Red Scare," when many American communists and other dissidents were arrested or deported out of fear that they would try to overthrow the government. The United States was allied with the Soviets during the war, and an effort was made to forget past differences, but these differences resurfaced rapidly in 1945, even before the defeat of the German and Japanese armies. Moreover the United States perceived World War II as a battle for peace and freedom and the Soviet Union seemed to be challenging these goals with its aggressive moves in Eastern Europe following the war. The Soviet Union was involved in massive spying against the United States and stole a fair amount of information used in building the atomic bomb. The Soviets probably would have succeeded in building the bomb anyway, as they had many brilliant atomic scientists, but the information stolen hastened the process. The development of the atomic bomb, which most scientists and politicians publicly proclaimed would take the Soviet Union a decade but which only took four years, also greatly increased the fear of the American public. Republican politicians began to use this issue against the Democrats, describing them as "soft" on communism. In response to political issues and public fears, both legitimate and paranoid, Truman developed a loyalty program that investigated many government employees.

Significance

The loyalty program contributed to the second Red Scare, during which the United States became fanatically obsessed with eliminating communism. This program did not find many communists. Loyalty programs and loyalty oaths did result in the firing of some Quakers, who refused to swear oaths, and others who did not believe in forced displays of loyalty. There were some communists and genuine threats but the threats did not match the level of hysteria. Julius and Ethel Rosenberg were convicted of spying on the United States for the Soviet Union and consequently executed, even though recent evidence suggests that the U.S. government may have known of Ethel's innocence at the time.

One of the prime promoters of the Red Scare was Senator Joseph McCarthy, who made a crusade out of accusing, with little or no proof, government agencies of hiding communists. McCarthy and "McCarthyism," the specter that he founded, ran Washington for four years until he began investigating the Army and was exposed for the bully he was. A blacklist existed in Hollywood where people who refused to "name names" and reveal current and former Communist party members were systematically refused employment. Campuses were also affected by the Red Scare. Professors could be fired if they were found to have communist ties, had ever been members of the Communist party, or were left-leaning politically. Professors would also be fired if they refused to identify those who they knew to have been members of the Communist party. All of this served to stifle intellectual freedom in the United States. Dwight Eisenhower (served 1953–1961) used the communist hysteria to boost his political hopes and his presidential run. He did not come to the defense of George Marshall, chief of staff of the U.S. army during World War II and Eisenhower's former superior, when Marshall was falsely accused of being a communist. Not many people were imprisoned during the second Red Scare, unlike the Red Scare that followed World War I, and few were deported, but many lives were ruined by the communist paranoia.

Primary Source

Executive Order 9835

SYNOPSIS: Truman states that government employees are each somewhat responsible for the democratic processes of the United States. Therefore this order allows extensive background investigations of those applying for federal jobs, as well as current employees. It empowers the Civil Services Commission to oversee such investigations and creates a Loyalty Review Board to conduct them.

WHEREAS each employee of the Government of the United States is endowed with a measure of trusteeship over the democratic processes which are the heart and sinew of the United States; and

WHEREAS it is of vital importance that persons employed in the Federal service be of complete and unswerving loyalty to the United States; and

WHEREAS, although the loyalty of by far the overwhelming majority of all Government employees is beyond question, the presence within the Government service of any disloyal or subversive person constitutes a threat to our democratic processes; and

WHEREAS maximum protection must be afforded the United States against infiltration of disloyal persons into the ranks of its employees, and equal protection from unfounded accusations of disloyalty must be afforded the loyal employees of the Government:

NOW, THEREFORE, by virtue of the authority vested in me by the Constitution and statutes of the United States, including the Civil Service Act of 1883 (22 Stat. 403), as amended, and section 9A of the act approved August 2, 1939 (18 U.S.C. 61i), and as President and Chief Executive of the United States, it is hereby, in the interest of the internal management of the Government, ordered as follows:

Part I—Investigation of Applicants

1. There shall be a loyalty investigation of every person entering the civilian employment of any department or agency of the executive branch of the Federal Government.

2. Investigations of persons entering the competitive service shall be conducted by the Civil Service Commission, except in such cases as are covered by a special agreement between the Commission and any given department or agency.

3. Investigations of persons other than those entering the competitive service shall be conducted by the employing department or agency. Departments and agencies without investigative organizations shall utilize the investigative facilities of the Civil Service Commission.

4. The investigations of persons entering the employ of the executive branch may be conducted after any such person enters upon actual employment therein, but in any such case the appointment of such person shall be conditioned upon a favorable determination with respect to his loyalty.

5. Investigations of persons entering the competitive service shall be conducted as expeditiously as possible; provided, however, that if any such investigation is not completed within 18 months from the date on which a person enters actual employment, the condition that his employment is subject to investigation shall expire, except in a case in which the Civil Service Commission has made an initial adjudication of disloyalty and the case continues to be active by reason of an appeal, and it shall then be the responsibility of the employing department or agency to conclude such investigation and make a final determination concerning the loyalty of such person.

President Harry S. Truman meets with advisors. **CORBIS-BETTMANN. REPRODUCED BY PERMISSION.**

6. An investigation shall be made of all applicants at all available pertinent sources of information and shall include reference to:

7. Federal Bureau of Investigation files.

8. Civil Service Commission files.

9. Military and naval intelligence files.

10. The files of any other appropriate government investigative or intelligence agency.

11. House Committee on un-American Activities files.

12. Local law-enforcement files at the place of residence and employment of the applicant, including municipal, county, and State law-enforcement files.

13. Schools and colleges attended by applicant.

14. Former employers of applicant.

15. References given by applicant.

16. Any other appropriate source.

17. Whenever derogatory information with respect to loyalty of an applicant is revealed a full investigation shall be conducted. A full field investigation shall also be conducted of those applicants, or of applicants for particular positions, as may be designated by the head of the employing department or agency, such designations to be based on the determination by any such head of the best interests of national security.

Part II—Investigation of Employees

1. The head of each department and agency in the executive branch of the Government shall be personally responsible for an effective program to assure that disloyal civilian officers or employees are not retained in employment in his department or agency.

2. He shall be responsible for prescribing and supervising the loyalty determination procedures of his department or agency, in accordance with the provisions of this order, which shall be considered as providing minimum requirements.

3. The head of a department or agency which does not have an investigative organization shall utilize the investigative facilities of the Civil Service Commission.

4. The head of each department and agency shall appoint one or more loyalty boards, each composed of not less than three representatives of the department or agency concerned, for the purpose of hearing loyalty cases arising within such department or agency and making recommendations with respect to the removal of any officer or employee of such department or agency on grounds relating to loyalty, and he shall prescribe regulations for the conduct of the proceedings before such boards.

5. An officer or employee who is charged with being disloyal shall have a right to an administrative hearing before a loyalty board in the employing department or agency. He may appear before such board personally, accompanied by counsel or representative of his own choosing, and present evidence on his own behalf, through witnesses or by affidavit.

6. The officer or employee shall be served with a written notice of such hearing in sufficient time, and shall be informed therein of the nature of the charges against him in sufficient detail, so that he will be enabled to prepare his defense. The charges shall be stated as specifically and completely as, in the discretion of the employing department or agency, security considerations permit, and the officer or employee shall be informed in the notice (1) of his right to reply to such charges in writing within a specified reasonable period of time, (2) of his right to an administrative hearing on such charges before a loyalty board, and (3) of his right to appear before such board personally, to be accompanied by counsel or representative of his own choosing, and to present evidence on his behalf, through witness or by affidavit.

7. A recommendation of removal by a loyalty board shall be subject to appeal by the officer or employee affected, prior to his removal, to the head of the employing department or agency or to such person or persons as may be designated by such head, under such regulations as may be prescribed by him, and the decision of the department or agency concerned shall be subject to appeal to the Civil Service Commission's Loyalty Review Board, hereinafter provided for, for an advisory recommendation.

8. The rights of hearing, notice thereof, and appeal therefrom shall be accorded to every officer or employee prior to his removal on grounds of disloyalty, irrespective of tenure, or of manner, method, or nature of appointment, but the head of the employing department or agency may suspend any officer or employee at any time pending a determination with respect to loyalty.

9. The loyalty boards of the various departments and agencies shall furnish to the Loyalty Review Board, hereinafter provided for, such reports as may be requested concerning the operation of the loyalty program in any such department or agency.

Part III—Responsibilities of Civil Service Commission

1. There shall be established in the Civil Service Commission a Loyalty Review Board of not less than three impartial persons, the members of which shall be officers or employees of the Commission.

2. The Board shall have authority to review cases involving persons recommended for dismissal on grounds relating to loyalty by the loyalty board of any department or agency and to make advisory recommendations thereon to the head of the employing department or agency. Such cases may be referred to the Board either by the

employing department or agency, or by the officer or employee concerned.

3. The Board shall make rules and regulations, not inconsistent with the provisions of this order, deemed necessary to implement statutes and Executive orders relating to employee loyalty.

4. The Loyalty Review Board shall also:

(1) Advise all departments and agencies on all problems relating to employee loyalty.

(2) Disseminate information pertinent to employee loyalty programs.

(3) Coordinate the employee loyalty policies and procedures of the several departments and agencies.

(4) Make reports and submit recommendations to the Civil Service Commission for transmission to the President from time to time as may be necessary to the maintenance of the employee loyalty program.

2. There shall also be established and maintained in the Civil Service Commission a central master index covering all persons on whom loyalty investigations have been made by any department or agency since September 1, 1939. Such master index shall contain the name of each person investigated, adequate identifying information concerning each such person, and a reference to each department and agency which has conducted a loyalty investigation concerning the person involved.

1. All executive departments and agencies are directed to furnish to the Civil Service Commission all information appropriate for the establishment and maintenance of the central master index.

2. The reports and other investigative material and information developed by the investigating department or agency shall be retained by such department or agency in each case.

3. The Loyalty Review Board shall currently be furnished by the Department of Justice the name of each foreign or domestic organization, association, movement, group or combination of persons which the Attorney General, after appropriate

investigation and determination, designates as totalitarian, fascist, communist or subversive, or as having adopted a policy of advocating or approving the commission of acts of force or violence to deny others their rights under the Constitution of the United States, or as seeking to alter the form of government of the United States by unconstitutional means.

4. The Loyalty Review Board shall disseminate such information to all departments and agencies.

Part IV—Security Measures in Investigations

1. At the request of the head of any department or agency of the executive branch an investigative agency shall make available to such head, personally, all investigative material and information collected by the investigative agency concerning any employee or prospective employee of the requesting department or agency, or shall make such material and information available to any officer or officers designated by such head and approved by the investigative agency.

2. Notwithstanding the foregoing requirement, however, the investigative agency may refuse to disclose the names of confidential informants, provided it furnishes sufficient information about such informants on the basis of which the requesting department or agency can make an adequate evaluation of the information furnished by them, and provided it advises the requesting department or agency in writing that it is essential to the protection of the informants or to the investigation of other cases that the identity of the informants not be revealed. Investigative agencies shall not use this discretion to decline to reveal sources of information where such action is not essential.

3. Each department and agency of the executive branch should develop and maintain, for the collection and analysis of information relating to the loyalty of its employees and prospective employees, a staff specially trained in security techniques, and an effective security control system for

protecting such information generally and for protecting confidential sources of such information particularly.

Part V—Standards

1. The standard for the refusal of employment or the removal from employment in an executive department or agency on grounds relating to loyalty shall be that, on all the evidence, reasonable grounds exist for belief that the person involved is disloyal to the Government of the United States.

2. Activities and associations of an applicant or employee which may be considered in connection with the determination of disloyalty may include one or more of the following:

3. Sabotage, espionage, or attempts or preparations therefore[e], or knowingly associating with spies or saboteurs;

4. Treason or sedition or advocacy thereof;

5. Advocacy of revolution or force or violence to alter the constitutional form of government of the United States;

6. Intentional, unauthorized disclosure to any person, under circumstances which may indicate disloyalty to the United States, of documents or information of a confidential or non-public character obtained by the person making the disclosure as a result of his employment by the Government of the United States;

7. Performing or attempting to perform his duties, or otherwise acting, so as to serve the interests of another government in preference to the interests of the United States.

8. Membership in, affiliation with or sympathetic association with any foreign or domestic organization, association, movement, group or combination of persons, designated by the Attorney General as totalitarian, fascist, communist, or subversive, or as having adopted a policy of advocating or approving the commission of acts of force or violence to deny other persons their rights under the Constitution of the United States, or as seeking to alter the form of government of the United States by unconstitutional means.

Part VI—Miscellaneous

1. Each department and agency of the executive branch, to the extent that it has not already done so, shall submit, to the Federal Bureau of Investigation of the Department of Justice, either directly or through the Civil Service Commission, the names (and such other necessary identifying material as the Federal Bureau of Investigation may require) of all of its incumbent employees.

2. The Federal Bureau of Investigation shall check such names against its records of persons concerning whom there is substantial evidence of being within the purview of paragraph 2 of Part V hereof, and shall notify each department and agency of such information.

3. Upon receipt of the above-mentioned information from the Federal Bureau of Investigation, each department and agency shall make, or cause to be made by the Civil Service Commission, such investigation of those employees as the head of the department or agency shall deem advisable.

4. The Security Advisory Board of the State-War-Navy Coordinating Committee shall draft rules applicable to the handling and transmission of confidential documents and other documents and information which should not be publicly disclosed, and upon approval by the President such rules shall constitute the minimum standards for the handling and transmission of such documents and information, and shall be applicable to all departments and agencies of the executive branch.

5. The provisions of this order shall not be applicable to persons summarily removed under the provisions of section 3 of the act of December 17, 1942, 56 Stat. 1053, of the act of July 5, 1946, 60 Stat. 453, or of any other statute conferring the power of summary removal.

6. The Secretary of War and the Secretary of the Navy, and the Secretary of the Treasury with respect to the Coast Guard, are hereby directed to continue to enforce and maintain the highest standards of loyalty within the armed services, pursuant to the applicable statutes, the Articles of War, and the Articles for the Government of the Navy.

7. This order shall be effective immediately, but compliance with such of its provisions as require the expenditure of funds shall be deferred pending the appropriation of such funds.

8. Executive Order No. 9300 of February 5, 1943, is hereby revoked.

Further Resources

BOOKS

Herman, Arthur. *Joseph McCarthy: Reexamining the Life and Legacy of America's Most Hated Senator.* New York: Free Press, 2000

Powers, Richard. *Not Without Honor: A History of American Anticommunism.* New York: Free Press, 1995.

Schrecker, Ellen. *Many Are the Crimes: McCarthyism in America.* Princeton, NJ: Princeton University Press, 1999.

————. *The Age of McCarthyism: A Brief History With Documents.* Boston: Bedford/St. Martin's, 2002.

PERIODICALS

Gibson, J.L. "Pluralism, Federalism, and the Protection of Civil Liberties." *Western Political Quarterly* 43:3 (Sept.1990): 511–36.

Fred M. Vinson, Chief Justice of the Supreme Court, 1946–1953. COLLECTION OF THE SUPREME COURT OF THE UNITED STATES.

Shelley v. Kraemer

Supreme Court decision

By: Fred M. Vinson

Date: May 3, 1948

Source: *Shelley v. Kraemer,* 334 U.S. 1 (1948). Reprinted in Leeson, Susan M. and James C. Foster, eds. *Constitutional Law: Cases in Context.* New York: St. Martin's Press, 1992, 384–385.

About the Author: Fred M. Vinson (1890–1953), the son of a Kentucky jailer, became the thirteenth chief justice of the Supreme Court. As a congressional representative from Kentucky in the 1930s he generally supported President Franklin D. Roosevelt's (served 1933–1945) New Deal legislation. Afterward he acted as an advisor to President Harry S. Truman (served 1945–1953), who appointed him chief justice in 1946. His most sensational decision, also his last, was to overturn a stay of execution for Julius and Ethel Rosenberg, allowing their executions to proceed in 1953. Vinson died later that year. ∎

Introduction

Restrictive covenants inserted into home deeds forbade the sale of the land to anyone failing to meet certain criteria, such as being white, Anglo-Saxon, and Protestant. These clauses obviously aimed to keep an area all white. Originally this goal had been accomplished through municipal ordinances that ordered segregation of neighborhoods, but these were outlawed in *Buchanan v. Warley* (1917). Because this decision only directly applied to laws passed by a city or municipal body, those opposed to desegregation quickly included restrictive covenants in private contracts. In 1926 the Court limited *Buchanan's* effect, upholding the legality of restrictive covenants. Even though restrictive covenants had to be enforced in the state courts the Court held they were not state actions. The Court also refused to apply *Buchanan* to the District of Columbia, even though the Fifth Amendment forbids federal denial of due process. These two decisions rendered *Buchanan* ineffective. Until the Shelley case, states and municipalities could not prohibit African Americans from moving into areas but private individuals could.

When the Shelley family moved into a home with a restrictive covenant designed to exclude African-American families from the neighborhood, a neighbor attempted to enforce the covenant. The family received lukewarm support from the National Association for the Advancement of Colored People (NAACP), which greatly feared losing a restrictive covenant case and wanted to wait for a stronger case to take before the Supreme Court. However a St. Louis attorney intended to pursue the issue to the Supreme Court with or without NAACP sanction, so the group eventually agreed to back the case. The Truman Administration then stepped in on behalf of the NAACP, an important gesture of federal support. On May 3, 1948, the Supreme Court ruled in favor of the Shelley family, outlawing restrictive covenants.

Significance

The Court heard the case of *Hurd v. Hodge,* intended to forbid judicial enforcement of restrictive covenants in the District of Columbia, at the same time as *Shelley,* rendering this decision effective nationwide. This was a sizable victory for the NAACP as it allowed people to move wherever they wanted and forbade enforcement of covenants designed to prevent integration. However two federal agencies, the Federal Housing Authority and the Veterans Administration, still discriminated. In the 1950s these two agencies would not give loans to African Americans to move into white areas; nor would they give loans so that African Americans could move to the new suburbs. Thus African Americans were largely excluded from the great suburbanization movement of the 1950s, making it difficult for the African-American community to build on the victory of *Shelley.* The government did not force the Federal Housing Authority and Veterans Administration to stop engaging in discrimination until the 1960s when Title VIII of the Civil Rights Act of 1968 (Fair Housing Act) forbade racial discrimination in bank loans for home rental and sale and empowered the federal government to act to remedy discrimination. Racial housing discrimination still exists, however. For instance some landlords will list an apartment as vacant but claim the apartment has been filled when an African American or person of another minority comes to look at it. African Americans are also more often denied loans than whites with similar credit situations. However *Shelley's* primary impact has not been diminished, as it made it impossible to write discrimination into a lease and have it be enforced.

Primary Source

Shelley v. Kraemer

SYNOPSIS: Justice Vinson first affirms that the right to own and enjoy property is a guaranteed civil right. He says that though the Fourteenth Amendment guarantees no protection against private discrimination, state enforcement of restrictive covenants takes such covenants beyond the bounds of private action. Thus he decrees that restrictive covenants, by denying rights based on race or color, are illegal. The case was decided on May 3, 1948.

Mr. Justice Vinson delivered the opinion of the Court.

. . . It cannot be doubted that among the civil rights intended to be protected from discriminatory

state action by the Fourteenth Amendment are the rights to acquire, enjoy, own and dispose of property. Equality in the enjoyment of property rights was regarded by the framers of that Amendment as an essential precondition to the realization of other basic civil rights and liberties which the Amendment was intended to guarantee. . . .

Since the decision of this Court in the *Civil Rights Cases* [of 1883], the principle has become firmly embedded in our constitutional law that the action inhibited by the first section of the Fourteenth Amendment is only such action as may fairly be said to be that of the States. That Amendment erects no shield against merely private conduct, however discriminatory or wrongful.

We conclude, therefore, that the restrictive agreements standing alone cannot be regarded as violative of any rights guaranteed to petitioners by the Fourteenth Amendment. So long as the purposes of those agreements are effectuated by voluntary adherence to their terms, it would appear clear that there has been no action by the State and the provisions of the Amendment have not been violated.

But here there was more. These are cases in which the purposes of the agreements were secured only by judicial enforcement by state courts of the restrictive terms of the agreements. . . .

[F]rom the time of the adoption of the Fourteenth Amendment until the present, it has been the consistent ruling of this Court that the action of the States to which the Amendment has reference includes action of state courts and state judicial officials. Although, in construing the terms of the Fourteenth Amendment, differences have from time to time been expressed as to whether particular types of state action may be said to offend the Amendment's prohibitory provisions, it has never been suggested that state court action is immunized from the operation of those provisions simply because the act is that of the judicial branch of the state government. . . .

We have no doubt that there has been state action in these cases in the full and complete sense of the phrase. The undisputed facts disclose that petitioners were willing purchasers of properties upon which they desired to establish homes. The owners of the properties were willing sellers; and contracts of sale were accordingly consummated. It is clear that but for the active intervention of the state courts, supported by the full panoply of state power, petitioners would have been free to occupy the properties in question without restraint. . . .

We hold that in granting judicial enforcement of the restrictive agreements in these cases, the States have denied petitioners the equal protection of the laws and that, therefore, the action of the state courts cannot stand. We have noted that freedom from discrimination by the States in the enjoyment of property rights was among the basic objectives sought to be effectuated by the framers of the Fourteenth Amendment. That such discrimination has occurred in these cases is clear. Because of the race or color of these petitioners they have been denied rights of ownership or occupancy enjoyed as a matter of course by other citizens of different race or color. . . .

Reversed.

Further Resources

BOOKS

Irons, Peter. *The Courage of Their Convictions: Sixteen Americans Who Fought Their Way to the Supreme Court.* New York: Penguin, 1990.

Maruo, Tony. *Illustrated Great Decisions of the Supreme Court.* Washington, DC: Congressional Quarterly Press, 2000.

PERIODICALS

Darden, Joe T. "Black Residential Segregation Since the 1948: *Shelley v. Kraemer* Decision." *Journal of Black Studies* 25:6 (July 1995): 680–692.

Cashin, Sheryll D. "Middle-class Black Suburbs and the State of Integration: a Post-Integrationist Vision for Metropolitan America." *Cornell Law Review.* 86:4 (May 2001): 729–777.

WEBSITES

"Shelley House." *We Shall Overcome: Historic Places of the Civil Rights Movement.* National Park Service. Available online at http://www.ca1.bluestreak.com/ (Accessed June 8, 2002).

"Local Cases With National Impacts." *The Struggle for Fair Housing in St. Louis.* Metropolitan St. Louis Equal Housing Opportunity Council. Available online at http://www.stlouis.missouri.org/501c/ehoc/cases.html (Accessed June 8, 2002).

Executive Order 9981

Executive Order

By: Harry S. Truman

Date: July 26, 1948

Source: President. Executive Order 9981. "Establishing the President's Committee on Equality of Treatment and Opportunity in the Armed Services." *Federal Register* 13, 4313, July 26, 1948. Available online at http://www.yale.edu/lawweb/avalon/presiden/execord/eo9981.htm; website home page: http://www.yale.edu (accessed April 21, 2003).

About the Author: Harry S. Truman (1884–1972) grew up on a farm in Missouri. He served as a U.S. senator from Missouri from 1935–1941 and again from 1941–1944. In 1944 he ran and won as Franklin D. Roosevelt's (served 1933–1945) vice president and became president when Roosevelt died in office in 1945. To win reelection in 1948 Truman rode a train around the country in a "whistlestop" campaign. He returned to Missouri upon his retirement and died there in 1972. ∎

Introduction

African Americans have fought on behalf of the United States in all of its conflicts. Crispus Attucks died in the Boston Massacre five years before the start of the American Revolution (1775–1783). After the Emancipation Proclamation of 1863 the United States organized the U.S. Colored Troops to fight in the Civil War (1861– 1865). African Americans also served in the army during the campaigns against the Native Americans, who nicknamed them "Buffalo Soldiers." Fully one-quarter of the troops fighting in Cuba during the Spanish-American War (1898) were African American; the Cubans, who called them "smoked yankees," treated them with much more respect than fellow U.S. troops did. African Americans served bravely in both World War I (1914–1918) and World War II (1939–1945), despite receiving poor social and military treatment. Not until 51 years after the war ended was the first African American awarded the Medal of Honor for World War II actions.

During World War II African Americans espoused the "Double V" campaign—victory at home over racism and victory abroad over U.S. enemies. However several returning soldiers were viciously lynched in the South. Harry S. Truman reacted to these atrocities by establishing the President's Committee on Civil Rights. Upon its recommendation Truman issued Executive Order 9981, which ended segregation in the armed forces and placed the U.S. Justice Department on the side of the National Association for the Advancement of Colored People (NAACP) in some court fights, including *Shelley v. Kraemer*.

Significance

Truman suffered politically for his forward stance on Civil Rights. In 1948 the southern (Dixiecrat) wing of the Democrat party bolted from the Democratic Convention and nominated J. Strom Thurmond, governor of South Carolina, for president. Thurmond won much of the Deep South and 39 electoral votes. Because of this defection and the opposition of Progressive candidate Henry Wallace, most thought Truman would lose the election. Although Truman did win reelection by a small margin he did not accomplish much legislatively during the remainder of his presidency, largely due to opposition from those who disagreed with his stance on race.

Six Tuskegee Airmen pose together. The Tuskegee Airmen were an all black squadron of fighter pilots who fought in World War II. UPI/CORBIS-BETTMANN. REPRODUCED BY PERMISSION.

Despite the order, the race issue in the military reared its head again during the Korean War (1950–1953). Many segregated units still existed. Military commanders delayed integrating the fighting forces and the military technically called divisions integrated even if they still had some all-black platoons or squads. In addition a higher percentage of African Americans than whites were court-martialed in this period and generally received more serious punishments than whites. The NAACP was forced to investigate the issue and publicize it before many of these sentences were reduced.

Racism was still an issue during the Vietnam War (1964–1975). A higher percentage of African Americans than whites died because more African Americans were sent into combat and fewer were able to get into technical, non-combat positions. Also more African Americans were drafted than their percentages suggest, as few were able to get college deferments. Many people have suggested that Colin Powell, chairman of the Joint Chiefs of Staff from 1989–1993, finally forced the Army to rec-

ognize the African-American contribution to the Vietnam conflict. In spite of the difficulties enacting Executive Order 9981 and the long road to equality that still lay ahead, this order demonstrates some of the first signs of government commitment to equality in the military.

Primary Source

Executive Order 9981—Establishing the President's Committee on Equality of Treatment and Opportunity in the Armed Services

SYNOPSIS: After defining the importance of democracy in the armed forces, Truman orders equality in the armed forces without regard to race, color, religion, or national origin. He allows a delay in implementation of the policy, which military commanders used to postpone integration of fighting troops during the Korean War. He then creates the President's Committee on Equality of Treatment and Opportunity in the Armed Services to oversee the order's implementation.

Lieutenant Colonel Benjamin Davis talks to Lieutenant Charles Dryden in his cockpit before he takes off in a P-40 Warhawk at the training base for the Tuskegee Airmen, 1945. © BETTMANN/CORBIS. REPRODUCED BY PERMISSION.

WHEREAS it is essential that there be maintained in the armed services of the United States the highest standards of democracy, with equality of treatment and opportunity for all those who serve in our country's defense:

NOW, THEREFORE, by virtue of the authority vested in me as President of the United States, by the Constitution and the statutes of the United States, and as Commander in Chief of the armed services, it is hereby ordered as follows:

1. It is hereby declared to be the policy of the President that there shall be equality of treatment and opportunity for all persons in the armed services without regard to race, color, religion or national origin. This policy shall be put into effect as rapidly as possible, having due regard to the time required to effectuate any necessary changes without impairing efficiency or morale.

2. There shall be created in the National Military Establishment an advisory committee to be known as the President's Committee on Equality of Treatment and Opportunity in the Armed Services, which shall be composed of seven members to be designated by the President.

3. The Committee is authorized on behalf of the President to examine into the rules, proc[ed]ures and practices of the armed services in order to determine in what respect such rules, procedures and practices may be altered or improved with a view to carrying out the policy of this order. The Committee shall confer and advise with the Secretary of Defense, the Secretary of the Army, the Secretary of the Navy, and the Secretary of the Air Force, and shall make such recommendations to the President and to said Secretaries as in the judgment of the Committee will effectuate the policy hereof.

4. All executive departments and agencies of the Federal Government are authorized and directed to cooperate with the Committee in its work, and to furnish the Committee such information or the services of such persons as the Committee may require in the performance of its duties.

5. When requested by the Committee to do so, persons in the armed services or in any of the executive departments and agencies of the Federal Government shall testify before the Committee and shall make available for the use of the Committee such documents and other information as the Committee may require.

6. The Committee shall continue to exist until such time as the President shall terminate its existence by Executive order.

Further Resources

BOOKS

Powell, Colin L., and Harry S. Truman. *President Truman and the Desegregation of the Armed Forces: A 50th Anniversary Review of Executive Order 9981.* Washington D.C.: National Legal Center for the Public Interest, 1998.

Dornfield, Margaret. *The Turning Tide: From the Desegregation of the Armed Forces to the Montgomery Bus Boycott.* New York: Chelsea House, 1995.

WEBSITES

Geselbracht, Raymond H. "The Truman Administration and the Desegregation of the Armed Forces." Available online at http://www.trumanlibrary.org/deseg1.htm; website home page: http://www.trumanlibrary.org (accessed June 7, 2002).

"LBJ School Record Military Symposium." *The Record: The Online Newsletter of the LBJ School of Public Affairs,* Spring 1998. Available online at http://www.utexas.edu/lbj /pubs/record/spring98/events/military.html; website home page: http://www.utexas.edu/lbj (accessed June 8, 2002).

Simpson, Diana. "African-Americans in Military History." Available online at http://www.au.af.mil/au/aul/bibs/afhist /aftoc.htm; website home page: http://www.au.af.mil (accessed June 8, 2002).

"Hiss and Chambers: Strange Story of Two Men"

Newspaper article

By: Robert G. Whalen

Date: December 12, 1948

Source: Whalen, Robert G. "Hiss and Chambers, Strange Story of Two Men." *The New York Times,* December 12, 1948, sec. 4, p. 6.

About the Author: Robert G. Whalen (1913–1969) was an editor for *The New York Times.* He often wrote anonymously and was little known outside the paper, though he had published articles in *Reader's Digest* and *Scholastic Magazine* before coming to the *Times.* He edited the *Times's* "Week in Review" column and acted as assistant to the Sunday editor. At the time of his death from cancer in 1969 he was known among colleagues for his fairness and pioneering use of "perspective" journalism. ■

Introduction

Alger Hiss was seen by many as the embodiment of the liberal establishment. He clerked for Supreme Court justice Oliver Wendell Holmes Jr.; worked for the State Department during the presidency of Franklin D. Roosevelt (served 1933–1945); and was considered a lead-

ing young diplomat. Hiss was accused first of being a communist and later of passing secret documents to the Soviet Union by Whittaker Chambers, an ex-communist who "saw the light," quit the Communist party, became a "man of the right," and testified before the House Un-American Activities Committee (HUAC). HUAC originated in the late 1930s as a place for conservatives to sound off against the "excesses" and "communism" of the New Deal. However with the extensive fear of communism in the late 1940s, HUAC rose in importance. The era following World War II (1939–1945) was marked by widespread American concern about the dangers of communism. Soviet expansion brought on the Cold War, as many in the United States feared the worldwide spread of communism. Many were also disillusioned about the Soviet Union, which had been a U.S. ally during World War II but now was racing toward creating an atomic bomb of its own. Many people, with the help of the Republicans, saw the national Democratic party as being too soft on communism; the Hiss case confirmed their fears.

Significance

The Alger Hiss trial in front of HUAC is important for several reasons. Notably this trial gave Richard Nixon his political start. The young California congressman's persecution of Hiss catapulted him into a Senate run, where he labeled his opponent Helen Gahagan Douglas "the pink lady." The HUAC investigations also led many people to believe in the need to "root" communists out of Washington, D.C., and elsewhere. This belief rose to the level of fervor. One person commented "I don't know what communism is, but there better not be any of it in Washington." From 1950 to 1954 anti-communism remained center stage in large part due to Joseph McCarthy, junior senator from Wisconsin, who dominated the news.

When McCarthy needed an issue to campaign on in 1950 he selected anticommunism. Even though he seldom had any reasonable documentation for any of his charges and often altered evidence to create "proof," his attacks ruined many people's lives. His reckless attacks spawned the term "McCarthyism." While McCarthy had no evidence for his attacks and ran roughshod over any semblance of justice, some of the concern might have been justified. There were, in fact, Soviet attempts to steal atomic secrets. In 1950 Ethel and Julius Rosenberg were convicted of espionage on grounds that they had assisted the Soviet Union in stealing atomic secrets. Although the FBI at the time believed Ethel to be innocent (which Russian documents later contradicted, revealing her as a sympathetic accessory to her husband's activities, though not herself a spy) and only indicted her to put pressure on Julius to name his co-conspirators, both were executed.

The Red Scare created a blacklist in the movie industry that prevented some writers and directors from working for mainstream studios for many years. Many professors were fired from universities for past communist ties or for refusing to name others as communists. While few were actually imprisoned many people's lives were ruined.

Convicted of perjury Hess spent five years in prison. He died in the 1990s still proclaiming his innocence, even though the latest evidence confirms that he did spy for the Soviet Union in the 1930s.

Primary Source

"Hiss and Chambers: Strange Story of
Two Men"

> **SYNOPSIS:** Whalen's article came after HUAC had decided to prosecute Hiss for perjury. HUAC could not prosecute him for handing secrets to the Soviets as the statute of limitations had expired before Chambers accused him of passing documents. The article is easy to read, being designed to give *The New York Times* readers a neutral account of events up to the point of the trials. Whalen concentrates on the relationship between Hiss and Chambers, giving the piece more of a human interest, rather than legal, focus.

This is the story of the two men who have been involved in one of the strangest headline dramas of recent years. It is the story of Alger Hiss and Whittaker Chambers and of their relationship. It is far from complete because [the] finish is not yet written and more than that, because so much of it is shrouded in mystery and contradiction.

What follows is an attempt to reconstruct, out of the testimony and known facts, what seems definite in the story and to clarify the mysteries so far as possible.

■ ■ ■

The principal characters in the drama are these two men:

Whittaker Chambers, 47, short and plump. Native of Philadelphia, studied at Columbia. A Quaker, joined the Communist party in 1924, worked as operating editor of *The Daily Worker* and writer for *The New Masses*. Quit the Communist party in 1938, joined the staff of *Time* magazine in 1939. Was a senior editor of *Time* until his resignation last week. Did most of his writing on his farm at Westminster, Md. His associates at *Time* describe him as an "intellectual" and they add: "None of us knows him very well."

Alger Hiss, 44, tall and slender. Native of Baltimore, Phi Beta Kappa from Johns Hopkins, graduate of Harvard Law School, protégé of Felix Frankfurter, former secretary to Supreme Court Justice Oliver Wendell Holmes. An Episcopalian. Entered Government in minor post in 1933. Served as a counsel to Senate Munitions Investigating Committee, joined the State Department in 1936, rose rapidly to become adviser at Yalta, executive secretary of Dumbarton Oaks conference, secretary general of United Nations Charter Conference in San Francisco. In 1946 succeeded the late Dr. Nicholas Murray Butler as president of Carnegie Endowment for International Peace.

The drama falls into two parts: an early period, beginning around 1934 and running to the middle of this year, the events of which are obscure; and the subsequent period when the drama broke into the open. The first period might be called The Prologue, and the second can be divided into these six chapters: (1) The Accusation; (2) The Denial; (3) The Chambers Rebuttal; (4) The Hiss Rebuttal; (5) The Confrontation; (6) The New Chapter.

The Prologue

The two men met in Washington about 1934. The atmosphere of the city was one of change and experiment. The capital abounded with "bright young men," eager to take part in building the New Deal. Ideas were freely exchanged. Communists were regarded with a certain tolerance. The Soviet Union, recently recognized by the Roosevelt Administration, was looked upon as a friendly nation.

The relationship of the two men in this setting is a matter of dispute. According to Mr. Chambers, he was at this time a paid "courier" of the Communist "underground" and Mr. Hiss, a Government official, was associated with him in espionage on behalf of the Soviet Union.

According to Mr. Hiss, they met while he was with the Senate committee; Mr. Chambers—under another name—posed as a free-lance writer and sought material on the investigation; they parted after a brief acquaintance when Mr. Hiss decided Mr. Chambers was a "sponger."

At any rate, it is certain that the two men knew each other in Washington, and eventually broke off their relationship, however close or casual it may have been.

Approach to Berle

In 1939, when the Nazi-Soviet pact was signed, Mr. Chambers—no longer a Communist—decided

Nine of ten Hollywood writers, directors, and producers are held in contempt of Congress for refusing to state whether they were communists or not, December 12, 1947. © BETTMANN/CORBIS. REPRODUCED BY PERMISSION.

that the story of the Communist "underground" should be told. He sought an interview at the White House and was referred to Adolf A. Berle Jr., an outspoken anti-Communist, then Assistant Secretary of State. He gave Mr. Berle the impression that Mr. Hiss belonged to a pro-Soviet group, but he refused to make open charges. Mr. Berle made some inquiries but found no grounds for action.

Eight years passed. The atmosphere in the nation was markedly different from that of the Nineteen Thirties. The Soviet Union was regarded as a potential enemy. Communists were widely suspected of being Russian agents.

The Thomas Committee

In April of last year, J. Parnell Thomas, chairman of the House Un-American Activities Committee, demanded that the Department of Justice prosecute Communist leaders. He said that committee hearings on legislation to outlaw the Communist party had proved that there was a "fifth column in our midst." In June, Attorney General Tom Clark ordered an investigation by a Federal grand jury in New York. The hearings were secret, but it is now known that Mr. Hiss and Mr. Chambers both testified before that grand jury. Last July, the jury indicted twelve Communist party leaders on charges of conspiracy to overthrow the Government. There were reports that the jury had also taken considerable testimony on espionage. The Thomas committee called open hearings to make the espionage and other charges public.

1—The Accusation

The Hiss-Chambers case came before the Un-American Activities Committee on Aug. 3. The scene was a hearing room in the New House Office Building in Washington. Mr. Chambers was in the witness chair. He told how he had quit the Communist party in 1938 and went on:

> For a year I lived in hiding, sleeping by day and watching through the night with a gun or revolver within easy reach. . . . I had sound reason for supposing that the Communists might try to kill me. For a number of years I had myself served in the underground, chiefly in Washington, D.C. . . . I knew it at its top level, a group of seven or so men. . . . A member of this group . . . was Alger Hiss.

Several times Mr. Chambers emphasized that the aim of the group was "infiltration" of the Government rather than espionage. He said: "I should perhaps make the point that these people were specifically not wanted to act as sources of information." Mr. Chambers said that the chief effort was to place Communists in positions of influence, that espionage was an "ultimate objective."

2—The Denial

On Aug. 4, in a telegram to the subcommittee, Mr. Hiss asked an opportunity to testify "formally and under oath." The next day, in the Washington hearing room, he read a statement declaring:

> I am not and have never been a member of the Communist party. I do not and have not adhered to the tenets of the Communist party. . . . I have never followed the Communist party line. . . . To the best of my knowledge I never heard of Whittaker Chambers until 1947, when two representatives of the Federal Bureau of Investigation asked me if I knew him. . . . So far as I know I have never laid eyes on him, and I should like to have the opportunity to do so.

There were these exchanges:

Robert Stripling, chief committee investigator: "I have here a picture which was made last Monday. . . . I understand from people who knew Mr. Chambers during 1934 and 1935 that he is much heavier . . . But I show you this picture, Mr. Hiss. . . ."

Hiss: "I would much rather see the individual. . . . If this is a picture of Mr. Chambers he is not particularly unusual looking."

In view of the flat Chambers accusation and the flat Hiss denial, it was apparent that one of the two had committed perjury. The subcommittee now set about requestioning the two men, seeking circumstantial detail that might tend to corroborate the story of either Mr. Chambers or Mr. Hiss.

3—The Chambers Rebuttal

On Aug. 7, in the Federal Court House in New York, Mr. Chambers was questioned at an executive (non-public) subcommittee session.

An investigator asked: "By what name did he [Mr. Hiss] know you?"

Chambers: "He knew me by the party name of Carl. . . . To have questioned me [about my last name] would have been a breach of party discipline."

Mr. Chambers' circumstantial statements included these: He and Mr. Hiss had been "close friends." Mr. Chambers collected Mr. Hiss' Communist party dues for two or three years. He stayed overnight at the Hiss home in Georgetown several times in the mid-Thirties. Mrs. Hiss had a son, "Timmy," by a previous marriage. She called her husband "Hilly" and he called her "Dilly" and "Pross." They had a cocker spaniel. They vacationed on the Eastern Shore of Maryland, were amateur ornithologists, went out mornings to watch birds along the Potomac and "once they saw, to their great excitement, a prothonotary warbler." In 1936 Mr. Hiss gave a car—a "dilapidated" Ford roadster—to the Communist party.

Mr. Chambers agreed to submit to a lie-detector test.

4—The Hiss Rebuttal

On Aug. 16, in Washington, Mr. Hiss was questioned, also at an executive session. He said he knew no such Carl as Mr. Chambers claimed to have been. But he declared he had been trying to think who might have been as familiar with his household as the Chambers testimony indicated. Mr. Hiss said: "I have written a name on the pad in front of me of a person whom I knew in 1933 and 1934 who not only spent some time in my house but sublet my apartment. . . . The name . . . is . . . George Crosley."

Mr. Hiss said he knew Crosley as a free-lance writer, "obviously not successful," and with markedly discolored teeth. He said he sublet his apartment to Crosley, threw in an old Ford roadster as part of the deal, lent him money, and got nothing in return but a rug. He came to the conclusion that "I had been a sucker and he was sort of a deadbeat."

Among circumstantial statements made by Mr. Hiss were these: His stepson was called "Timmy." Mr. Hiss called his wife "Prossy," she called him "Hill" or "Hilly." They had a cocker spaniel. They vacationed on the Eastern Shore of Maryland and were amateur ornithologists. He had seen a prothonotary warbler along the Potomac.

Mr. Hiss refused to submit to a lie-detector test, on the ground that lie detectors had not been proven reliable.

The big question now was that of "George Crosley." The subcommittee moved to bring Mr. Hiss and Mr. Chambers face to face.

5—The Confrontation

On the evening of Aug. 17, in Room 1400 of the Commodore Hotel in New York City, Representatives Richard M. Nixon and John McDowell held an executive session. Mr. Hiss appeared first. When Mr. Chambers entered the room, Mr. Hiss was asked whether he had "ever known that man before."

Hiss: "May I ask him to speak?" . . .

Chambers: "My name is Whittaker Chambers."

Mr. Hiss walked over to Mr. Chambers and said: "Would you mind opening your mouth wider?"

Chambers: "I am senior editor of *Time* magazine."

Hiss: "I think this is George Crosley, but I would like to hear him talk a little longer."

Mr. Chambers said his teeth had been in "very bad shape" in the Thirties but had been treated, whereupon Mr. Hiss positively identified him as George Crosley. After a few moments Mr. Hiss again strode toward Mr. Chambers.

Hiss: "May I say for the record at this point that I would like to invite Mr. Whittaker Chambers to make those same statements out of the presence of this committee without their being privileged for suit for libel? I challenge you to do it, and I hope you will do it damned quickly. (Addressing investigator) I am not going to touch him. You are touching me."

Investigator: "Please sit down, Mr. Hiss. . . . I want no disturbance."

Hiss: "I don't—."

McDowell: "Sit down, please."

Hiss: "You know who started this." After further sessions in Washington, the hearings recessed.

Summarizing the hearings, the committee declared that Mr. Chambers had been a "forthright and emphatic" witness, while Mr. Hiss had been "evasive." In discussing the events of a dozen years ago,

for example, Mr. Hiss prefaced 198 statements with the phrase: "To the best of my knowledge." The records were turned over to the Department of Justice, to determine which of the two might be prosecuted for perjury. Lacking further evidence, there was little likelihood that either could be indicted.

6—The New Chapter

Then, on Aug. 30, on a radio broadcast, Mr. Chambers repeated his charge that Mr. Hiss was a Communist. This statement was not protected by Congressional immunity. Mr. Hiss filed a slander suit in Baltimore, demanding $75,000 damages. The slander suit led to developments which put the mystery in a new and more sinister light.

Three weeks ago in Baltimore, Mr. Chambers was questioned by Mr. Hiss' attorney as a preliminary to the trial of the slander suit. Asked whether he could corroborate his charges against Mr. Hiss, Mr. Chambers produced a sheaf of documents which he said had been stolen from State Department and other Government files for transmission to Russia.

Bykov Story

Mr. Chambers said that in 1937 he introduced Mr. Hiss to a Russian agent named Colonel Bykov, and that thereafter Mr. Hiss "began a fairly consistent flow of such material as we have before us here." He declared that the routine was for Mr. Hiss to bring the documents home, have Mrs. Hiss type copies, and then return the papers to the files. Where it was difficult to remove papers, Mr. Chambers charged, Mr. Hiss supplied notations in his own handwriting.

There followed the dramatic events of the past nine days—the appearance of Un-American Activities Company investigators at Mr. Chambers' farm in Maryland, with a subpoena for further evidence; his "surrender" of microfilms secreted in a pumpkin; the reopening of committee hearings and of the investigation by the Federal grand jury in New York.

Further Resources
BOOKS
Tanenhaus, Sam. *Whittaker Chambers: A Biography.* New York: Random House, 1997.

Fariello, Griffin. *Red Scare: Memories of the American Inquisition. An Oral History.* New York: Norton, 1995.

PERIODICALS
Tannenhaus, Sam. "Open Secrets." *New Republic,* November 8, 1999, p.60.

Weiser, Benjamin. "Nixon Lobbied Grand Jury to Indict Hiss in Espionage Case, Transcripts Reveal." *The New York Times,* October 12, 1999, pA25.

WEBSITES
Kisseloff, Jeff, ed. The Alger Hiss Story. Available online at http://homepages.nyu.edu/~th15/ (Accessed June 7, 2002).

"The Good War": An Oral History of World War II

Eyewitness account

By: Studs Terkel

Date: 1984

Source: Terkel, Studs, ed. *"The Good War": An Oral History of World War II.* New York: Pantheon Books, 1984, 146–49.

About the Author: Studs Terkel (1912–) was born in the Bronx, New York. He built his early career as a radio commentator. His concern for the common man led him to begin taping oral interviews with average citizens and transcribing them into books. His most famous work is the Pulitzer Prize-winning *"The Good War,"* which presents the perspectives of average citizens on World War II (1939–1945). Terkel lives in the Chicago area, where he hosts a program on WFMT radio. ■

Introduction

In the nineteenth century prejudice against Hispanics led to tension between Mexican sheep farmers and Western cattle ranchers. Mexican Americans were by far the largest group of Hispanics in the United States throughout this period. Often easy to identify by accented speech, though not always skin coloration, Hispanic Americans made easy targets for prejudice. The Great Depression of the 1930s encouraged hostility against Hispanics, many of whom had been working at jobs that no whites would consider until the stock market collapsed in the late 1920s. When whites suddenly wanted these jobs in the depressed economy, the perception that "those Mexicans" were stealing "American" jobs gained popularity. It has been estimated that 500,000 Hispanics left the United States in the Great Depression; some were forcibly taken across the border to Mexico (even though not all were Mexican), while others left more willingly.

White racist attitudes persisted into the 1940s, when the Zoot Suit Riots took place. This oral interview displays the focus of a bystander rather than a victim. Although the interview represents only one person's account of what occurred, that view touches on some of the key concerns during the riots, including police violence and prejudice against Hispanics.

The shortage of laborers during World War II allowed many Mexican Americans and other Hispanics to get factory jobs for the first time, bringing them to West-

ern cities in large numbers and prompting white resentment. The Zoot Suit Riots sprung from a number of sources, including a belief on the part of whites that Mexican Americans were not "doing their part" to help the United States win World War II. These same whites believed Hispanics wearing tailored "zoot suits" were flaunting American values.

The riots were triggered by an alleged attack on a serviceman by a Mexican American. This provoked sailors stationed in San Francisco to attack all Hispanics wearing zoot suits. Hispanic Americans retaliated and the riots continued for four days in June 1943, with police arresting Hispanics far more often than whites. Sometimes the Hispanics would be arrested for defending themselves and sometimes for their own protection. After the riots, laws were passed outlawing the "zoot suit."

Significance

The Zoot Suit Riots are a measure of anti-Hispanic prejudice in the United States in the 1940s. Although conditions have improved dramatically since then, prejudiced minds still often believe Hispanics holding jobs of any sort in the United States are stealing "American" jobs. Especially along the Mexican border such prejudice encourages the racist assumption that all Hispanic workers are illegal aliens. Issues important to Hispanics did not gain wide social recognition until the 1960s with activists such as Cesar Chavez. Problems like inequality in education still trouble the Hispanic community. Many school districts are funded largely with property taxes, meaning rich districts generally have much more money to spend on their schools. This system discriminates against low-income students. Since a high percentage of Hispanic and African-American children come from low-income families, this represents an area of racial as well as economic prejudice. California has tried to ban bilingual education in an effort aimed against schools that teach Spanish-speaking Hispanic students in their native tongue. Attempts to make English the official U.S. language have been aimed largely against Hispanics. Anti-Hispanic prejudice in the United States receives far more unofficial support than prejudice against African Americans. However activists publicizing the presence of prejudice against Hispanics and promoting cultural pride within Hispanic communities have begun to change views across the nation.

Primary Source

"The Good War": An Oral History of World War II
[excerpt]

> **SYNOPSIS:** In this account, Don McFadden, a retired deputy sheriff from Los Angeles County, describes his experiences as a young man during the Zoot Suit

Riots, including his brush with police brutality. Arrested for violation of curfew, he and his brother wound up in jail with zoot suiters arrested for their own protection. McFadden describes these victims' condition and that of other Hispanics attacked by servicemen during the riots.

In the summer of '43, they had these zoot-suit riots. Zoot suit was a style of dress, mostly Mexican American kids went into it at that time. It actually started in East L.A., and they would spread out to Hollywood and down around the beach. Once in a while they'd have a ruckus, okay? They were called rat packs.

There were some sailors down at the beach. Apparently, they got into some kind of confrontation with these zoot-suits. A sailor had been stabbed, that was the word. When the word got back to San Diego, where all the servicemen were—well, you know the navy and the marines. (Laughs.) This was in June of '43. Thousands of servicemen came up en masse. They started out in East L.A. They started grabbing anybody that had a zoot suit on. Anybody wearing that was fair game. They just really did a number on 'em—ripped their clothes up, beat 'em up. Then it spread downtown, and the police really had a problem.

I heard about it on the radio and was reading about it. This had been going on maybe a week. One night myself, my brother, and two friends decided to go down and see what was going on, right? We figured: Hey, we're big men. We're gonna get involved in this. We really just wanted to see firsthand what was happening.

They had the streets blocked off for about six blocks. No traffic at all on Main Street. Pretty soon, we see these servicemen confronting the zoot-suiters. Sometimes they didn't even have zoot suits on. If they happened to be Mexican, that was enough.

We walked into a little restaurant on Main Street, just standing there, nothing going on. All of a sudden, I see a guy in civilian clothes, he's really giving my brother a hard time. I'm wondering what's goin' on, we weren't doing anything. He just grabs him and hauls him outside. My brother was fourteen at the time. One of my buddies went out to talk to him, and he starts doing the same thing to him—grabbed 'im and shakin' him.

It turned out he was a detective. He is in plain clothes and didn't identify himself. So I went out and said, "What's going on?" He kinda came on strong, so I took a swing at him. (Laughs.) That was my mis-

A zoot suit outfit that was popular among Mexican American youths in the 1940s. UPI/CORBIS-BETTMANN. REPRODUCED BY PERMISSION.

take. I was seventeen and in good shape. I don't know what ever made me do it. Down the street, there were a couple of six-foot-six motorcycle cops. They had their clubs out. They ran down and really started takin' care of me. They did a number on my head with their clubs. I covered up and it was all over. I did get cut up, but at that time I had a little more hair than I got now, so it gave me some padding.

We were all under curfew age, so they took us to jail for violation. We ended up in about half a dozen jails. We went to the old Plaza jail that was really old. It was still made out of adobe. (Laughs.) They took us to the Georgia Street jail. They put three of us in one cell. We were the only non-zoot-suiters there, the only non-Mexicans.

The rest of the jail was packed with all these zoot-suiters. They'd been picking 'em up all over town, not because they'd done anything wrong, but because they were victims and they were tryin' to keep 'em from gettin' hurt. Most of 'em had their clothes in shreds. Their tailor-made suits were just hangin' on 'em. They'd been really worked over.

All these taunts were going back and forth between the three of us and all these zoot-suiters. You no-good zoot-suiters and this and that. (Laughs.) We were tryin' to rile 'em. How's it feel to be in jail? Of course, they didn't put us in with them or we'da probably been beaten up. We really didn't have anything against 'em. We were just out for a lark. Anyway, we ended up bein' transferred to another jail. We spent the night there. My parents couldn't find out what happened to us. They hadn't been notified. The next afternoon, they came and got me out.

A lotta people got hurt, a lot of innocent people, a lot of these young Mexican kids. I saw a group of servicemen stop a streetcar. They spotted one zoot-suiter on it. They got on, he couldn't get off. They carried him off unconscious. Here's a guy riding a streetcar and he gets beat up 'cause he happens to be a Mexican. I actually saw that happen.

Servicemen would go into theaters in downtown L.A. They'd go up and make the projectionist shut off the movie, right? Turn the lights on. They'd go down both aisles. Any zoot-suiters they saw (laughs), they'd drag him right out by his seat and—(clap hands)—beat him, tear his clothes up, what have

you. They were mostly sailors and marines. They came from San Diego.

I went in the service, the navy, in August of '43. I got out in April of '46. I think the war pulled us out of isolation and pulled us out of the Depression. And L.A. became a big metropolis—too big, actually. (Laughs.)

It was just an interesting time to be alive, and history was being made. There was a feeling of optimism. It will be a better world—afterwards, you know. I'm not really too optimistic about what's happening today.

The war made me grow up a lot faster. It was good for me because of the discipline I received. It probably kept me out of serious trouble. I was a wild kid and had friends that did some crazy things. (Laughs.) By the grace of God, we survived without endin' up in jail.

Further Resources

BOOKS

Mazon, Mauricio. *The Zoot Suit Riots: The Psychology of Symbolic Annihilation.* Austin: University of Texas Press, 1984

Mirande, Alfredo. *Gringo Justice.* Notre Dame, IN: University of Notre Dame Press, 1987.

PERIODICALS

del Castillo, Richard Griswold. "The Los Angeles 'Zoot Suit Riots' Revisited: Mexican and Latin American Perspectives." *Mexican Studies* 16:2 (Summer 2000): 367–92.

WEBSITES

"American Experience: Zoot Suit Riots." Corporation for Public Broadcasting. Available online at http://www.pbs.org /wgbh/amex/zoot/ (Accessed June 8, 2002).

AUDIO AND VISUAL MEDIA

Cherry Poppin' Daddies. "Zoot Suit Riot." *Zoot Suit Riot: The Swingin' Hits of The Cherry Poppin' Daddies.* Mojo Records, 1997.

7

LIFESTYLES AND SOCIAL TRENDS

AMY H. STURGIS

Entries are arranged in chronological order by date of primary source. For entries with one primary source, the entry title is the same as the primary source title. Entries with more than one primary source have an overall entry title, followed by the titles of the primary sources.

Important Events in Lifestyles and Social Trends, 1940–1949

1940

TRENDS AND FADS: Fifty-one percent of women between the ages of twenty and twenty-four are married. The average size of American families has shrunk to 3.8 members. Annual attendance at baseball games is estimated at ten million. Weekly movie attendance is estimated at eighty million. Nickel jukeboxes appear in restaurants, taverns, tearooms, variety stores, and gas stations; sixteen records play for fifty cents.

• The National Association for the Advancement of Colored People (NAACP) denounces the military's policy of racial segregation.

• The House Committee on Un-American Activities (HUAC) denounces the Communist Party and the German-American Bund as un-American.

1941

TRENDS AND FADS: The median age at first marriage is twenty-four for men and 21.5 for women. With the improvement of the economy, car sales soar. Alcohol consumption also rises.

• "Rosie the Riveter," named for Rosina Bonavita, becomes the emblem of the American woman working in the defense industries.

• A national committee is formed to work for abolition of the poll tax, which prevents many African Americans from voting in southern states.

• On January 15, A. Philip Randolph and other civil rights leaders call for a march on Washington on July 1 to demand an end to discrimination in defense-industry employment. President Franklin D. Roosevelt issues Executive Order 8802, banning racial discrimination in the defense industries and creating the Fair Employment Practices Committee in order to prevent this march.

• On May 17, the Justice Department begins its round-up of illegal immigrants.

• On December 15, because of the war, Harvard, Yale, Princeton, and other American universities announce that they are cutting the undergraduate program from four to three years by offering year-round sessions. Seventy-six medical schools also cut their programs from four years to three.

• On December 27, rationing of automobile tires begins.

1942

TRENDS AND FADS: A victory garden fad sweeps the nation; forty percent of the vegetables consumed in the United States are grown in victory gardens.

• The Congress of Racial Equality (CORE) is founded by James Farmer, Bayard Rustin, and A.J. Muste, Christian pacifists who plan to use the nonviolent-resistance tactics of Mohandas Gandhi to fight racial discrimination and segregation.

• Single men ages eighteen to thirty-five and married men ages eighteen to twenty-six are eligible for the draft.

• Willow Run, near Detroit, becomes the fastest-growing city in the United States, as thousands move there to work in the B-24 bomber plant.

• On January 2, the Office of Civilian Supply announces that all civilian car and truck production will cease for the duration of the war.

• On January 18, workers walk out at Hudson Naval Ordnance Arsenal in Detroit when African American workers take over machines formerly operated by whites.

• On February 19, President Roosevelt issues Executive Order 9066, ordering the removal of all Japanese Americans on the West Coast to internment camps for the duration of the war.

• On April 27, the Office of Price Administration (OPA) halts sugar sales for about a week while consumers register for sugar-rationing coupon books.

• On December 1, nationwide gasoline and fuel-oil rationing begins.

1943

TRENDS AND FADS: The 1943 birth rate is the highest yet in U.S. history. Teenage fads include slumber parties, pep rallies, beach parties, and Saturday nights at soda shops with jukeboxes and meeting dates at hamburger "joints." Boys wear army boots while girls favor baggy, rolled-up blue jeans and sloppy shirttails.

• Cabs are required to take as many passengers as they can carry.

• A scarcity of goods combined with increased individual income create long lines at grocery stores, movies, bars, and restaurants.

• The government orders a minimum forty-eight-hour work-week in key defense plants. Labor shortages result in new practices that "pamper" employees. Awards, fringe benefits, piped-in music, coffee breaks, and suggestion boxes are all introduced in the workplace.

• On January 1, meat is rationed to twenty-eight ounces per person per week, butter is rationed at four ounces per week, the sale of sliced bread is banned, and flour and canned goods are also rationed. Shoes are rationed to three pairs a year; new sneakers are not available because of a rubber shortage.

• On January 7, opera singer Marian Anderson is the first African American to perform in Constitution Hall, Washington, D.C. The Daughters of the American Revolution

(DAR), who own the hall, gained considerable notoriety when they refused Anderson's request to rent the hall in 1939.

- On June 22, following dozens of deaths and the deployment of federal troops, the nation's worst race riot ends in Detroit.

- In June, in Los Angeles, a weeklong riot breaks out when white servicemen attack Mexican American civilians, many of them employed in local shipyards. Afterwards, the city council outlaws the "zoot suits" worn by many of the Chicanos involved in the incident.

- On August 1, five African Americans are killed and five hundred are injured during race riots in Harlem, New York. Damages are estimated at five million dollars.

- On August 2, the federal government begins the Emergency Maternity and Infant Care Program (EMIC), under which the government pays the entire cost of medical care for wives and infant children of enlisted men in the four lowest pay grades.

1944

TRENDS AND FADS: Census statistics show a population increase of four million in the southern and western United States between 1940 and 1944. Fifty-eight percent of women between the ages of twenty and twenty-four are married. Thirty percent of the nineteen million working-women in the United States are employed in factory jobs; 3.27 million women are employed in defense industries. The U.S. Census Bureau estimates that 2.75 million employed women have 4.5 million children under the age of fourteen. Slacks become popular with workingwomen. Sales of baking powder fall because workingwomen are baking less often.

- The United Negro College Fund is established.

- Swedish economist Gunnar Myrdal publishes his analysis of American race relations, *An American Dilemma: The Negro Problem and Modern Democracy.*

- In January, *The Races of Mankind,* a forty-six-cent YMCA pamphlet attacking Nazi racial doctrines, is deemed controversial by many people because it opposes racism; the YMCA is ordered to stop distributing it at USO clubs, even though fifty thousand copies have been sold.

- On April 3, in its decision in *Smith v. Allwright,* the U.S. Supreme Court rules that African Americans cannot be barred from voting in political party primaries.

- In June, ballpoint pens are introduced into the U.S. consumer market.

- On August 14, the War Production Board allows the production of various domestic appliances, such as electric ranges and vacuum cleaners, to resume.

1945

TRENDS AND FADS: The birthrate stands at 2.4 births per thousand women. One abortion occurs for every 150 live births. There are 18,610,000 employed outside their homes; the Women's Bureau reports that 80 percent of them want to continue working after the war. Children buy Defense Stamps weekly; schools have air-raid drills. Toys are scarce; stores have no bicycles, skates, sleds, or electric trains.

- Laid off because their jobs have been given to returning veterans, women autoworkers stage a protest march with posters reading "Stop Discrimination Because of Sex."

- On May 21, the U.S. Supreme Court affirms the right of states to recognize or reject Nevada divorce decrees.

- In February, the U.S. government imposes a midnight curfew on entertainment nationwide. The curfew is lifted in May.

- In August, gasoline rationing ends.

- In November, all previously rationed items except sugar are available.

- In December, many families take their first vacations since the bombing of Pearl Harbor.

- In December, cabaret shows open in many cities. They are by-products of the army's USO shows for the troops.

- On December 24, the National Community Christmas Tree is lit by President Harry Truman for the first time since 1941.

1946

TRENDS AND FADS: The Baby Boom begins; the birthrate is up 20 percent over 1945. Seventy-four percent of couples have their first child during their first year of marriage.

- Dr. Benjamin Spock's *The Commonsense Book of Baby and Child Care* is published.

- The cost of living has increased 33 percent since 1941, creating dissatisfaction among consumers.

- On July 2, for the first time since Reconstruction African Americans vote in the Mississippi Democratic primary.

- On September 15, the Federal Security Agency reports a rise in the proportion of divorces to marriages, but this upsurge in divorce is short-lived and soon overshadowed by a much larger and longer-lasting increase in marriage.

- In September, speaking before the American Legion, FBI director J. Edgar Hoover warns of 100,000 communist operatives who have infiltrated U.S. organizations.

- On December 5, President Harry Truman's Executive Order 9809 establishes the President's Committee on Civil Rights.

1947

TRENDS AND FADS: The birthrate reaches 2.8 births per thousand women. Housing shortages cause six million families to double up with friends or relatives. College enrollments rise to an all-time high of 6.1 million students as four million returning veterans use the opportunities for education, housing, and business provided by the GI Bill of Rights. All but 3 percent of male veteran heads of households are employed.

- Sugar rationing ends, sparking an enormous increase in ice-cream consumption.

- Women lose one million factory jobs, half a million clerical positions, three hundred thousand jobs in commercial services, and one hundred thousand jobs in sales as companies hire returning veterans.

- The Georgia Supreme Court revokes the charter of the Ku Klux Klan.

- Bernard Baruch coins the expression "Cold War." Journalist Walter Lippmann popularizes the phrase.

- On April 10, Jackie Robinson signs with the Brooklyn Dodgers, becoming the first African American in major league baseball.

- On December 3, the U.S. Motion Picture Association votes to regulate against glorification of crime on the screen. The Screen Directors Guild bars members of the Communist Party from holding office. A Hollywood blacklist compiled by studio executives includes three hundred writers, directors, and actors who are alleged to be Communist sympathizers.

1948

- In North Carolina a government-supported program provides children with a well-balanced lunch of black-eyed peas, eggs, cheese, potatoes, a biscuit, milk, and a tangerine—all for five cents.

- The Baskin-Robbins chain of ice-cream shops opens.

- Alfred Kinsey's report on the sexual behavior of the human male is published.

- The bikini bathing suit, named for the 1946 Bikini Atoll nuclear test site, arrives on American beaches.

- On February 2, President Truman asks Congress to pass strong civil rights legislation. Passage is blocked by powerful Southern Democrats.

- On July 9, a Nevada court declares prostitution legal in Reno.

- On July 26, President Truman issues executive orders intended as first steps toward integrating the armed forces and the federal civil service.

- On September 13, Margaret Chase Smith of Maine becomes the first woman to be elected to the U.S. Senate.

1949

TRENDS AND FADS: The Baby Boom levels off at 3.58 million live births. Ninety percent of boys and 74 percent of girls questioned in a national poll of high-school-age young people think it is "all right for young people to pet or 'neck' when they are out on dates."

- Abraham Levitt and his sons William and Alfred convert a Long Island potato field into a prefabricated, "carbon copy" suburban community called "Levittown." For $7,990 (sixty dollars per month and no down payment) the consumer can purchase a four-room house with attic, outdoor barbecue, washing machine, and 12 1/2-inch built-in television set.

- General Mills and Pillsbury introduce prepared cake mixes, one in a growing list of new convenience foods.

- In January, for the first time African Americans are invited to events surrounding a presidential inauguration and stay in the same Washington, D.C., hotels as whites.

- On March 17, South Carolina becomes the last state in the U.S. to legalize divorce.

- In July, Jackie Robinson testifies before HUAC on black loyalty to the United States.

- On September 25, Charlie Lupica of Cleveland, Ohio, sets a flagpole-sitting record of 177 days, two hours, and twenty-five minutes.

"I'd Rather Not Be on Relief"

Song

Date: 1938

Source: Anonymous. "I'd Rather Not Be on Relief." As performed by Lester Hunter. *Voices from the Dust Bowl: The Charles L. Todd and Robert Sonkin Migrant Worker Collection.* American Memory digital primary source collection, Library of Congress. Available online at http://memory .loc.gov/cgi-bin/query/r?ammem/todd:@field(DOCID+st045); website home page: http://memory.loc.gov (accessed April 20, 2003). ■

Introduction

Songs such as "I'd Rather Not Be on Relief" evolved as a means of self-expression in communities of people who all faced the same economic obstacles. This song emerged from the Shafter Farm Security Organization migrant labor camp, but it was typical of songs that were sung across the nation by migrant workers and others who found themselves hurt by the Great Depression. The themes of such songs were clear: the workers did not want charity. They wanted to work. They believed that stopgap governmental measures were short-term solutions to long-term problems. Many such songs appealed to other institutions such as churches, families, and labor unions to provide hope in what seemed an almost hopeless situation.

Although the 1940s are remembered mostly for international affairs, specifically World War II (1939–1945) and the beginning of the Cold War, the decade began under the shadow of the Great Depression. President Franklin D. Roosevelt (served 1933–1945) intended his New Deal policies to increase employment and relieve poverty, but the U.S. economy did not rebound from the Depression until wartime production began in full force. World War II, in effect, brought the Great Depression to an end. In 1940, many Americans were struggling for the barest necessities. Many of these were migrant laborers who had originally been farmers themselves or employees in other businesses. When they found themselves without a way to make a living during the Depression, they traveled looking for employment. Thus, migrant workers found themselves facing two challenges. First, the Depression hit the agriculture industry hard, and farmers who were barely surviving themselves could not afford to pay workers well. Second, because so many unemployed people tried to find work as migrant laborers, there were too many workers available for too few jobs.

One New Deal program was intended specifically to help migrant workers. The Farm Security Administration, or FSA, built camps to house migrant workers across the country. This was a short-term success; it created jobs for those who built the housing and provided shelter for those who otherwise would not have had it. It failed, however, to solve the larger problems of failing farms and the overabundance of migrant workers. Another program, the Works Progress Administration, or WPA, employed people to work on special government projects. This policy, too, only solved short-term problems. Once projects were completed, the original problems of poverty and unemployment returned. Some looked to labor unions such as the Committee for Industrial Organization, or CIO, to offer solutions. The era of labor union growth had passed, however. Concerns about ethics, business practices, and communist influence began a decline in labor union prestige and membership that continued from the 1940s onward.

Significance

Songs such as "I'd Rather Not Be on Relief" captured the experience of those who were hit hardest by the Great Depression. These kinds of records remain invaluable because there are now few sources that document the political and economic struggles of migrant workers. The era the songs described was important chiefly because it brought into being the modern welfare state. Through President Roosevelt's New Deal policies, the size, scope, and expense of the national government greatly increased; after the need for the New Deal had lessened, the bureaucracy that had been created never shrank to its pre-Depression size. Many of the projects undertaken by New Deal programs preserved important historical data such as songs and pictures of U.S. migrant workers.

The nation's economic wounds did not begin to heal until the nation entered World War II at the end of 1941. Wartime production solved what the New Deal could not. In fact, the war left the United States in better shape economically than it had been before the war. This was a direct contrast to all other nations involved in World War II, whose economies suffered because of the conflict.

Primary Source

"I'd Rather Not Be on Relief"

SYNOPSIS: This song reflects the frustration of unemployed and impoverished laborers who lived in the Shafter Farm Security Organization migrant labor camp in the early 1940s. The song explains that the laborers did not want to work for special government projects. Instead, they simply wanted a thriving economy that allowed farmers to be successful and, in turn, pay their workers fairly. The author of this song believed that labor unions offered the solution to the problems he faced.

We go around all dressed in rags
While the rest of the world goes neat,
And we have to be satisfied
With half enough to eat.
We have to live in lean-tos,
Or else we live in a tent,
For when we buy our bread and beans
There's nothing left for rent.
I'd rather not be on the rolls of relief,
Or work on the W. P. A.,
We'd rather work for the farmer
If the farmer could raise the pay;
Then the farmer could plant more cotton
And he'd get more money for spuds,
Instead of wearing patches,
We'd dress up in new duds.
From the east and west and north and south
Like a swarm of bees we come;
The migratory workers
Are worse off than a bum.
We go to Mr. Farmer
And ask him what he'll pay;
He says, "You gypsy workers
Can live on a buck a day."
I'd rather not be on the rolls of relief,
Or work on the W. P. A.,
We'd rather work for the farmer
If the farmer could raise the pay;
Then the farmer could plant more cotton
And he'd get more money for spuds,
Instead of wearing patches,
We'd dress up in new duds.
We don't ask for luxuries
Or even a feather bed.
But we're bound to raise the dickens
While our families are underfed.
Now the winter is on us
And the cotton picking is done,
What are we going to live on
While we're waiting for spuds to come?
Now if you will excuse me
I'll bring my song to an end.
I've got to go and chuck a crack
Where the howling wind comes in.
The times are going to better
And I guess you'd like to know
I'll tell you all about it,
I've joined the C. I. O.

Further Resources

BOOKS

Curtis, James. *Mind's Eye, Mind's Truth: FSA Photography Reconsidered.* Philadelphia: Temple University Press, 1989.

Edsforth, Ronald. *The New Deal: America's Response to the Great Depression.* Malden, Mass.: Blackwell, 2000.

Lichtenstein, Nelson. *Labor's War at Home: The CIO in World War II.* Cambridge, N.J.: Cambridge University Press, 1982.

Sternsher, Bernard. *Hope Restored: How the New Deal Worked in Town and Country.* Chicago: Ivan R. Dee, 1999.

Zieger, Robert H. *The CIO, 1935–1955.* Chapel Hill, N.C.: University of North Carolina Press, 1995.

WEBSITES

American Social History Project/Center for Media and Learning, and Center for History and New Media. "Every Picture Tells a Story: Documentary Photography and the Great Depression." History Matters. Available online at http://chnm.gmu.edu/fsa; website home page: http://historymatters.gmu.edu (accessed April 20, 2003).

Shahn, Ben et. al. *Documenting America. America from the Great Depression to World War II: Black-and-White Photographs from the FSA-OWI, 1935–1945.* American Memory digital primary source collection, Library of Congress. Available online at http://lcweb2.loc.gov/ammem/fsahtml/fadocamer.html; website home page: http://memory.loc.gov (accessed April 20, 2003).

Letter to Jesse O. Thomas

Letter

By: Snow F. Grigsby

Date: January 23, 1940

Source: Grigsby, Snow F. Letter to Jesse O. Thomas, January 23, 1940. Reproduced in "Cavalcade of the American Negro" in the Library of Congress exhibit *African-American Mosaic.* Available online at http://www.loc.gov/exhibits/african/images/nulbooth.jpg; website home page: http://www.loc.gov (accessed April 20, 2003).

About the Author: Snow F. Grigsby was extensively involved in civil rights activism in Detroit, Michigan. His primary concern was achieving equality in employment and housing. In 1933, he established the Detroit Civic Rights Committee to complement the activities of the Detroit office of the National Association for the Advancement of Colored People (NAACP). ∎

Introduction

In 1940, Americans observed the seventy-fifth anniversary of the end of the Civil War (1861–1865). African Americans, in particular, felt they had much to celebrate: since the Civil War and the abolition of slavery, African American culture had thrived. The art and literature of the Harlem Renaissance had spawned a new era of artistic recognition, and both jazz and blues music were enjoying mainstream success. In politics, a national network of organizations had emerged to promote African American economic and political opportunity. The 1940 anniversary provided an opportunity to showcase these achievements and, in the process, encourage even more.

African American leaders organized two key events that year: the Seventy-Five Years of Negro Progress Exposition held in Detroit in May, and the Diamond Jubilee Exposition held in Chicago. They invited different groups to contribute educational exhibits to the expositions. One was the National Urban League. By 1940, the league was an established presence on a national scale. It began in 1911 when three organizations—the Committee for Improving the Industrial Conditions Among Negroes in New York, the League for the Protection of Colored Women, and the Committee on Urban Conditions Among Negroes—merged to create the National League on Urban Conditions Among Negroes. This group helped African Americans, particularly those from the rural South, relocate to New York City and find housing, training, and jobs. The organization soon became national when affiliate groups sprang up in other major cities. In 1919, the association shortened its name to the National Urban League. Organizations such as the National Urban League took part in the 1940 expositions to foster pride in and awareness of African American achievements and inspire more in the following decades.

Significance

The expositions of 1940 served as successful community-building events that educated blacks and nonblacks alike about the history and achievements of African Americans. Both provided a centralized location for individuals and organizations from across the country to meet, share information, and make future plans. The expositions also helped to refocus mainstream national attention on domestic issues. In 1940, most Americans were preoccupied by World War II (1939–1945), which raged overseas, and worried about potential U.S. involvement in the hostilities. The expositions not only offered the chance for celebration and pride but also reminded people that unresolved problems of inequality, segregation, and discrimination plagued the nation from within.

Most importantly the expositions helped build momentum for African American social and political activism in the 1940s and afterward. The impressive attendance at the events proved that the community, when united, was a significant force. The networking opportunities the ex-

positions provided allowed leaders to find areas of similar concern and form alliances for future cooperation. For example, after the two expositions, African American leaders were able to convince President Harry S. Truman (served 1945–1953) to appoint the first President's Committee on Civil Rights. In 1947, this committee produced the landmark report *To Secure These Rights,* which launched significant civil rights legislation. Civil rights leaders also coordinated protests about military practices, which led in 1948 to Executive Order 9981, desegregating the U.S. armed forces. The civil rights movement of the 1950s and 1960s also was built on the collaboration of groups that were brought together by cultural events such as the expositions in Detroit and Chicago.

Primary Source

Letter to Jesse O. Thomas

SYNOPSIS: When he wrote this letter, Grigsby was the coordinator of Exhibits and Organizations for the Seventy-Five Years of Negro Progress Exposition held in Detroit in May 1940. In it, he invites National Urban League Secretary Jesse O. Thomas to contribute an exhibit about the National Urban League to the exposition. Grigsby hoped such an exhibit would raise awareness about the league's efforts on behalf of African Americans.

January 23, 1940

Mr. Jesse O. Thomas, Secretary
National Urban League
1133 Broadway
New York City

Dear Sir:

No doubt you are aware of the fact that there will be held in the City of Detroit in May, 1940 a Seventy-Five Years of Negro Progress Exposition at which time we shall try to show through exhibits the progress that the Negro has made in the past seventy-five years since freedom was declared. This Exposition will be held in Convention Hall which is the largest convention hall in Michigan and is located in the heart of downtown Detroit. Incidentally, the Quadrennial Session of the General Conference of the African Methodist Episcopal Church will meet here at the same time.

The Urban League has done some fine work. We would be very much pleased to have an exhibit from the National Urban League office depicting its service to Negroes throughout the country. Booths 10′ × 10′, 10′ × 15′, and 15′ × 15′ are available. Space for your exhibit will be given gratis. Kindly inform us how much space to reserve.

We are enclosing folders which will give you an idea of the broad scope of this Exposition.

Respectfully yours,
Seventy-Five Years of Negro Progress Exposition Committee
Snow F. Grigsby, Co-ordinator of Exhibits and Organizations

Further Resources

BOOKS

Meriwether, James Hunter. *Proudly We Can Be Africans: Black Americans and Africa, 1935–1961.* Chapel Hill, N.C.: University of North Carolina Press, 2002.

Moore, Jesse Thomas. *A Search for Equality: The National Urban League, 1910–1961.* University Park, Pa.: Pennsylvania State University Press, 1981.

Parris, Guichard. *Blacks in the City: A History of the National Urban League.* Boston: Little, Brown, 1971.

Trotter, Joe William. *African Americans in the Industrial Age: A Documentary History, 1915–1945.* Boston: Northeastern University Press, 1996.

Writers' Program of the Work Projects Administration in the State of Illinois. *Cavalcade of the American Negro.* Chicago: Diamond Jubilee Exposition Authority, 1940.

"Yellow Men of Mars"

Illustrations

By: J. Allen St. John

Date: August 1941

Source: St. John, J. Allen. "Yellow Men of Mars" illustrations. In *Amazing Stories* 15, no. 8, August 1941, front cover and page 6. Reproduced in "Life on Mars." Digital Library and Archives, University Libraries, Virginia Technological University. Available online at http://spec.lib.vt.edu/lifemars/lmarsdir1.htm; website home page: http://spec.lib.vt.edu (accessed April 20, 2003).

About the Artist: James Allen St. John (1872–1957) developed his artistic talents under the influence of his mother, Susan Hely St. John. He provided drawings for books, including *The Works of Mark Twain* (1899), but it was St. John's artwork for the adventure stories of Edgar Rice Burroughs that gained him the most attention. Over two decades, St. John provided cover and interior art for thirty of the author's novels. After 1940, St. John mainly drew for pulp magazines devoted to science fiction, inlcuding *Weird Tales, AMZ, Fantastic Adventures, Amazing Stories,* and *Other Worlds.* ∎

Introduction

As the United States moved from the Great Depression to World War II (1939–1945), society demanded escapist entertainment to give people a break from fear and uncertainty. Pulp magazines, one form of that entertainment, got their name from the poor quality of paper on which they were printed. The premise behind inexpensive printing was twofold. First, the content of the magazines was assumed to be disposable; the publications were not intended to be kept and reread as masterpieces. Second, by using inexpensive materials, publishers kept the purchase price of the magazines low, so more people could afford them. One such pulp magazine, which published science fiction, was *Amazing Stories.*

Hugo Gernsback (1884–1967), first published *Amazing Stories* as a companion to the publication *Science and Invention* in 1926. Gernsback hoped the new magazine would foster interest in the sciences. He named the fiction he wished to publish "scientification," which later became known as "science fiction." The publication's editor in 1941, Ray Palmer, expanded the magazine by reprinting works by traditional action-oriented authors, such as Edgar Rice Burroughs. *Amazing Stories* also targeted a younger reading audience with formulaic, mass-produced stories, also known as "fiction factory" works. Balancing these lighter pieces were contributions from such notable authors as Edmond Hamilton and Walter M. Miller.

As *Amazing Stories* gained success, competitors soon entered the market. Stories about evil subterranean powers controlling the earth and its people abounded, as did tales of threatening Martians and their plans for conquest. Imaginative art, such as that by J. Allen St. John, became as important to the magazines as the stories themselves. As escapes went, pulp magazines were inexpensive, accessible, and dependable at a time when the unknown horrors of distant worlds were a comforting distraction from the frightening realities of the daily news.

Significance

Throughout its history *Amazing Stories* preserved classic works such as those by Edgar Rice Burroughs and launched the careers of new talents such as Roger Zelazny, Ursula K. LeGuin, and Ben Bova. The annual science fiction achievement awards are now called the "Hugos" in his honor; he received a special Hugo in 1960 for his contribution to science fiction.

Magazines such as *Amazing Stories* were important for three main reasons. First, stories of future technologies and extraterrestrial adventures helped set the stage for the atomic age, which brought new attention to science and technology and their relevance to Americans' daily lives. Pulp magazines like *Amazing Stories* helped maintain public focus on science and technology. They also tapped into U.S. fear and uncertainty about what technology could mean. When the Cold War with the Soviet Union began in the 1940s, the two nations competed in scientific research in general and the space race in particular. These struggles were mirrored and reinforced in science fiction stories of the time. Second, as pulp magazines looked to attract younger readers, they helped to develop a youth

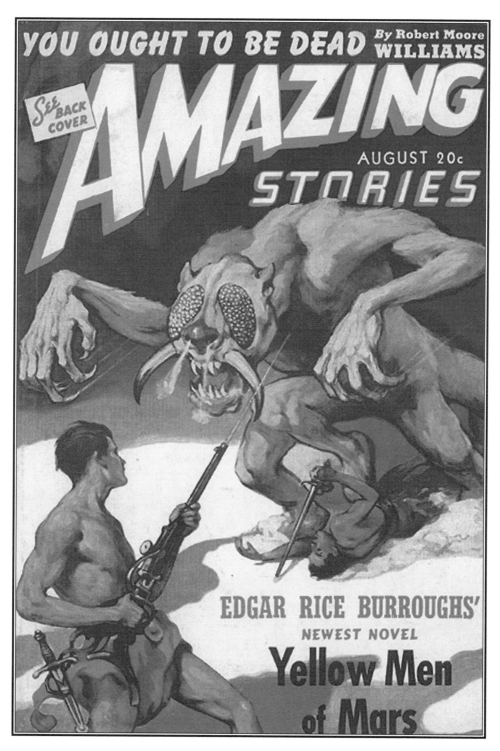

Primary Source

"Yellow Men of Mars" (1 OF 2)

SYNOPSIS: This artwork from *Amazing Stories* illustrates stories about Mars by Edgar Rice Burroughs, who wrote such classics as the *Tarzan* series and *At the Earth's Core*. The vivid, action-oriented art of pulp science fiction magazines became as important to the publications as the stories themselves.This illustration by J. Allen St. John illustrates a scene from "Yellow Men of Mars" featured in the August 1941 issue of *Amazing Stories*. © 1941 EDGAR RICE BURROUGHS. ALL RIGHTS RESERVED. REPRODUCED BY PERMISSION.

culture that blossomed as baby boomers, children born following World War II, reached school age. The inexpensive, brightly colored magazines were accessible to young readers, and they grew in popularity along with related publications such as comic books. As the postwar economy boomed and consumer spending rose, pulp magazines flourished in tandem with the youth culture.

Perhaps most importantly, *Amazing Stories* and publications like it helped to create the Golden Age of Science Fiction, often dated from 1940 to 1965. While earlier science fiction had appealed to the specialized taste of an educated few, its audience expanded among both youth and adults. As television and films gained popularity, serials such as *Flash Gordon* built on the foundation laid by the pulp magazines. British and French authors paved the way for science fiction, but the Golden Age made the genre a specifically American product. Science fiction in the twenty-first century owes a debt to the early pulp magazines that boosted interest in stories of other worlds and possible futures.

Further Resources

BOOKS

Aldiss, Brian W. *Trillion Year Spree: The History of Science Fiction.* New York: Avon, 1973.

Asimov, Isaac, and Martin H. Greenberg, eds. *Amazing Stories: Sixty Years of the Best Science Fiction.* New York: Random House, 1985.

Bleiler, Everett F. *Science-Fiction: The Gernsback Years.* Kent, Ohio: Kent State University Press, 2000.

Clareson, Thomas D. *Understanding Contemporary Science Fiction: The Formative Period (1926–1970).* Columbia, S.C.: University of South Carolina Press, 1992.

Landon, Brooks. *Science Fiction After 1900: From the Steam Man to the Stars.* New York: Twayne, 1997.

Seed, David. *American Science Fiction and the Cold War: Literature and Film.* Edinburgh, Scotland: Edinburgh University Press, 1999.

PERIODICALS

Orlando, Maria. "Hugo Gernsback: The Inventor, the Prophet, and the Father of Science Fiction." *Poptronics,* February 2002, 23–26.

WEBSITES

"The Lynx's Pulp Magazine Cover Gallery." Available online at http://pulpcovers.itgo.com (accessed April 20, 2003).

"Jenny on the Job—Steps ahead with Low Heels"

Poster

By: U.S. Public Health Service
Date: c. 1941–1945

Source: Office for Emergency Management, Office of War Information, Domestic Operations Branch, Bureau of Special Services. "Jenny on the Job—Steps ahead with Low Heels." c. 1941–1945. National Archives, College Park, Md. Records of the Office of Government Reports. Record Group 44. Available online at http://arcweb.archives.gov/arc/arch_results_detail.jsp?&pg=3&si=0&nh=8&st=b; website home page: http://www.archives.gov (accessed April 18, 2003).

About the Organization: The U.S. government actively encouraged the entry of women into the workforce during World War II. A series of posters published by the Federal Security Agency and U.S. Public Health Service, among other agencies, gave women hints about how to make the transition to the workplace. "Jenny on the Job," like her counterpart "Rose the Riveter," became a national symbol of working women in the 1940s. ∎

Introduction

Women had appeared in the U.S. workforce before the 1940s, but most left employment to become homemakers when they married or gave birth to their first child. Moreover, they held positions in customarily female professions such as teaching, nursing, and secretarial work. During World War II (1939–1945), married women, even mothers, took part- and full-time employment not only in typical women's positions but also in factories and other traditionally male settings, substituting for soldiers who had gone to war. Perhaps the most famous image of the era was "Rosie the Riveter," a patriotic woman whose factory work helped produce materials necessary for the war effort.

Although women served in the armed forces during World War II, women also were necessary in the private workforce in order to maintain production in U.S. industries, provide materials necessary for the war, and stabilize the American economy. To encourage women to take the place of servicemen in the workforce and to educate them about how to do so, the government created the "Jenny on the Job" poster series. In the posters, Jenny encountered a number of on-the-job situations and served as a role model to women in the workplace. For example, women's fashions in the early 1940s, including shoes with high, slender heels, were designed for appearance and sex appeal rather than work. In the poster shown below, Jenny recognized that she could not move crates while wearing such shoes. Her solution was to wear low-heeled, commonsense shoes on the job. Other aspects of her dress—her hair netted back rather than worn down and styled, her slacks instead of a traditional skirt—further illustrated job-friendly habits to women.

Significance

Public-service campaigns such as the "Jenny on the Job" poster series helped to bring women into the workforce in record numbers and keep them there throughout

Primary Source

"Jenny on the Job—Steps ahead with Low Heels"

SYNOPSIS: In this poster, one of a series about "Jenny on the Job," Jenny practices good work skills by wearing low-heeled shoes while working. Women's fashions traditionally were impractical for physical work; as a public service, therefore, the government reminded American women not to wear high heels as they moved into the workplace. NATIONAL ARCHIVES. REPRODUCED BY PERMISSION.

World War II. Although many women chose to return to the home after servicemen returned, others remained at work and carved a lasting place for women in the U.S. economy. The entertainment industry reflected this change by portraying women as professional, career-oriented people, just like men. Perhaps the most famous example was Katharine Hepburn, who played a number of outspoken, competitive heroines who held positions previously considered to be for men.

Images of working women such as "Jenny on the Job" and "Rosie the Riveter" also offered a contrast to the other dominant view of women during World War II: the pinup girl. While the pinup girl was a scantily clad, seductive version of the "girl next door," waiting for her man to come home to her, Rosie and Jenny were capable, no-nonsense, self-motivated women who were not waiting for men but instead were busy with their own important tasks. They maintained their femininity, tying back their long hair in scarves or nets rather than wearing so-called boy cuts, but they were in a male space, doing men's work, performing physical labor. The pampered pinup depended on men. The independent working woman not only depended on herself but also supported men by helping to fuel the war effort. Both the pinup girl and the working woman were necessary parts of the war effort, one for morale and one for the economy. Perhaps the working woman, however, had the greater impact, because the experience of women in the workplace planted a seed in the American consciousness. That seed germinated during the women's movement of later decades and changed the roles and options of women in the United States forever.

Further Resources

BOOKS

Baxandall, Rosalyn, and Linda Gordon, eds. *America's Working Women: A Documentary History, 1600 to the Present.* New York: Norton, 1995.

Blackwelder, Julia Kirk. *Now Hiring: The Feminization of Work in the United States, 1900–1995.* College Station, Tex.: Texas A & M University Press, 1997.

Gluck, Sherna Berger. *Rosie the Riveter Revisited: Women, the War, and Social Change.* Boston: G.K. Hall, 1987.

Honey, Maureen. *Creating Rosie the Riveter: Class, Gender, and Propaganda During World War II.* Amherst, Mass.: University of Massachusetts Press, 1984.

Laughlin, Kathleen A. *Women's Work and Public Policy: A History of the Women's Bureau, U.S. Department of Labor, 1945–1970.* Boston: Northeastern University Press, 2000.

WEBSITES

Rosie the Riveter Trust. Available online at http://www .rosietheriveter.org (accessed April 18, 2003).

"Lead Kindly Light"

Advertisement

By: Ray-O-Vac

Date: c. 1941

Source: Ray-O-Vac. "Lead Kindly Light." Ray-O-Vac batteries advertisement, c. 1941. Reproduced in Cayton, Andrew, Elizabeth Israels Perry, and Allan M. Winkler. *America: Pathways to the Present.* Englewood Cliffs, N.J.: Prentice-Hall, 1995, 699.

About the Organization: The Ray-O-Vac company manufactured a major brand of batteries during and after the 1940s. The company, like many others, understood the demand of a growing consumer culture and created advertisements to increase sales. ∎

Introduction

One of the basic principles of advertising is that the seller must show the consumer why he or she needs a given product. Telling consumers that an item is necessary for some unusual event or practice does not inspire demand; however, showing them that an item is necessary for some everyday, commonplace event or practice is good advertising. In its advertisements, Ray-O-Vac sought to prove that its batteries met the daily needs of consumers and could be not only useful but even invaluable. It is telling, then, that between 1941 and 1945 Ray-O-Vac chose the image of a school bomb drill to sell its flashlight batteries. The advertisers assumed that schools, air raid shelters, and bomb drills were part of everyday American experience. They were correct.

To prepare for the possibility that the United States could be bombed during World War II (1939–1945), air raid shelters, also bomb shelters, became the norm in public buildings, schools, and even some private homes. These shelters were underground structures much like small basements that were reinforced to survive the impact of bombs. Often they held food, water, and other supplies in case people had to remain in the shelters for extended periods during an attack. After the invention of the atomic bomb, many of these shelters were upgraded so that people could live in them for a long while until the effects of nuclear fallout diminished and it was safe to return to the surface. Schools conducted bomb drills—much like they did earthquake, tornado, and other disaster drills—to practice evacuating students to air raid shelters safely and quickly.

Significance

The prevalence of advertisements such as Ray-O-Vac's proved that the wartime experience had become second nature to the U.S. public. Alarming, frightening things such as the need for air raid shelters became usual, even normal parts of life. The American people had for some time resisted being drawn into World War II, so this

Primary Source

"Lead Kindly Light"

SYNOPSIS: In this advertisement for Ray-O-Vac flashlight batteries, the batteries are depicted in use by a teacher as she leads her students to an air raid shelter during a bomb drill. This not only shows the commercialization of the war—using the war to sell products—but it also shows how deeply ingrained the war experience was for the average consumer. REPRODUCED BY PERMISSION.

change of attitude was significant. It showed that once Americans supported the war effort, they did so whole-heartedly. Even the purchase of batteries could seem like a patriotic act. Furthermore, the advertisements not only reflected a certain view of the war but encouraged it. When a schoolchild's knowledge that an enemy might attack his or her school became the subject of battery advertisements, it lost its mystique and became just another part of life. Ray-O-Vac did not suggest that war would end the next day; if anything, the company suggested that the war would continue for some time, and therefore the need for batteries in the future would remain. Taking warfare and its associated danger as "a given" helped to reinforce calm and acceptance among the American people.

Advertisements' use of war images also helped set the cultural stage for the transition from World War II—where the enemy was the Axis powers of Germany, Japan, and Italy—to the Cold War where the new enemy was the Soviet Union. The wartime vigilance of World War II accustomed Americans to an ongoing threat of violence, even when traditional warfare ended. The air raid shelter, for example, became such a symbol of American life that it was easily converted in U.S. minds into a nuclear bomb shelter during the Cold War. The American comfort level with the threat of violence—a comfort level heightened by advertisements such as Ray-O-Vac's—eased the shift from one kind of warfare to another.

Further Resources

BOOKS

Brown, Bruce W. *Images of Family Life in Magazine Advertising, 1920–1978*. New York: Praeger, 1981.

Henriksen, Margot A. *Dr. Strangelove's America: Society and Culture in the Atomic Age*. Berkeley and Los Angeles: University of California Press, 1997.

May, Elaine Tyler. *Homeward Bound: American Families in the Cold War Era*. New York: Basic Books, 1988.

Rose, Kenneth D. *One Nation Underground: The Fallout Shelter in American Culture*. New York: New York University Press, 2001.

Whitfield, Steven J. *The Culture of the Cold War*, 2d ed. Baltimore, Md.: Johns Hopkins University Press, 1996.

Betty Grable Bathing Suit Pinup

Photograph

Date: c. 1942

Source: "Betty Grable Bathing Suit Pinup, ca. 1942." Corbis. Image no. BE001136. Available online at http://pro.corbis.com (accessed February 17, 2003). ∎

Introduction

Pinup pictures were a phenomenon of World War II (1939–1945). Meant to encourage and motivate U.S. troops, pinups of beautiful, often scantily clad women appeared in magazines and on posters, calendars, and postcards. Soon they became the mascots for servicemen. Actress and model Betty Grable was perhaps the most popular of the pinup girls.

Entertainers and musicians traveled to perform for U.S. troops stationed abroad during World War II, but few morale boosters were as successful as the pinup girl. An industry built up around producing images of women: some famous actresses and models, some unknown hopefuls, and even some fictional women. These pictures were intended to be "pinned up" wherever the troops were stationed and then taken down and carried to the next post. Soldiers adopted these images as mascots and decorated their surroundings, including the sides of aircraft, with portrayals of pinup girls. Betty Grable, for example, adorned the sides of a number of U.S. bomber planes.

The pinup walked a fine line between two images. On the one hand, the picture was meant to capture the likeness of a wholesome "girl next door," the sweetheart who might be waiting at home for every soldier as soon as the war ended. On the other hand, the pinup girl was also meant to be an unattainable ideal, the perfect woman, the ultimate sex symbol. The women were often dressed in bathing suits, lingerie, or revealing shorts and midriff-baring tops while striking sexy, flirtatious poses. Most images, however, stopped short of pornography. The women were seen as sensual and desirable, but in a teasing way: they were "good girls," chaste enough to be a serviceman's girlfriend or even wife. This blend of the sexy and the sweet was, in a sense, a metaphor for home, for all that U.S. forces were fighting for overseas. Some of the most gifted artists and photographers of the 1940s contributed to the lucrative and lasting art of the pinup girl.

Significance

The pinup girl was important for three main reasons. First, pinup images helped make careers. Although Betty Grable was an actress before she posed for this picture, its phenomenal popularity among U.S. forces brought her superstardom. American servicemen voted Grable their favorite pinup girl; it is no coincidence that, in the same year this pinup appeared, Grable was the year's number one box-office star. She went on to become one of the top ten box-office draws in Hollywood for ten consecutive years. Her visibility as a pinup girl translated to success on the silver screen. Second, pinup girls fulfilled their goal: they helped to raise the morale of U.S. forces. Servicemen's letters, diaries, and memorabilia—not to

Primary Source

Betty Grable Bathing Suit Pinup

SYNOPSIS: Perhaps the most famous pinup image of Betty Grable, this photograph cheered U.S. servicemen across the globe during World War II. In the picture, Grable balanced her "girl-next-door" reputation from film with a more provocative "sex symbol" image meant to inspire American troops. © BETTMANN/CORBIS. REPRODUCED BY PERMISSION.

mention the impressive sales of pinup images—proved the importance of the pinup to the everyday life of the American soldier.

Third, and perhaps most importantly, the pinup girl image reinforced certain stereotypes about the ideal woman and her role. Brainy actress Katharine Hepburn, dressed for one of her roles as an ace reporter or talented attorney, was not considered "pinup material." Pinup girls—and they were called girls, not women—were valued not for their intelligence but for being curvaceous, long-legged, slender, and beautiful. Their attire and poses emphasized their roles as sex objects meant to satisfy men. This image was in direct contrast to the "Rosie the Riveter" image of women as capable, independent actors in the workforce who could substitute for men and even carve their own places in labor and the professions. The contrast between the pinup girl and the emerging working woman of the 1940s led to a national rethinking of society's expectations for women.

Further Resources

BOOKS

Collins, Max Allan. *For the Boys: The Racy Pin-Ups of WWII.* Portland, Ore.: Collectors Press, 2000.

Higonnet, Margaret Randolph. *Behind the Lines: Gender and the Two World Wars.* New Haven, Conn.: Yale University Press, 1987.

McGee, Tom. *Betty Grable: The Girl with the Million Dollar Legs.* New York: Vestal Press, 1997.

Weatherford, Doris. *American Women and World War II.* New York: Facts on File, 1990.

PERIODICALS

Christian, Shirley. "A Trove of Pinups at the University of Kansas Is Admired by All Sorts, Including Feminists." *The New York Times,* November 25, 1998, E1.

World War II Ration Stamp Books

World War II Ration Stamps, Book No. 2

Booklet

By: U.S. Office of Price Administration
Date: c. 1942
Source: U.S. Office of Price Administration. World War II Ration Stamps, Book No. 2. c. 1942. Farm Security Administration-Office of War Information Photograph Collection. Library of Congress Prints & Photographs Division, Wash-

ington, D.C. 20540. Available online at http://lcweb2.loc.gov /pp/pphome.html; website home page: http://lcweb2.loc.gov (accessed April 20, 2003).

"War Ration Book No. 3"

Booklet

By: U.S. Office of Price Administration
Date: c. 1942
Source: "War Ration Book no. 3." Photograph. 1940–1946. Library of Congress. Call number LC-USE6–D-010120. Available online at http://lcweb2.loc.gov/pp/fsaquery .html#Number; website home page: http://lcweb2.loc.gov (accessed April 29, 2003). ∎

Introduction

With the entry of the United States into World War II (1939–1945), the domestic economy was retooled for wartime production. This meant that materials once purchased by consumers were now used in producing military supplies. Factories that had made automobiles and household appliances began to make weapons and ammunition. Shoe producers sidelined fashionable footwear and began to make boots for U.S. soldiers. The silk and nylon that had been used to make women's hosiery was used instead to make parachutes for the armed forces. Supplies of other resources were limited, as well. The supply routes in the Pacific Ocean that had transported metals and rubber to the United States came under enemy control, and those items, like sugar, grew scarce as well. Philippine imports were cut off, ships that had carried sugar from Puerto Rico and Cuba were used for national defense, and much of the sugar that was available went into making explosives. Moreover, perishables such as meats and dairy products, when they were produced, were sent first to the armed services. Suddenly, the Great Depression question "Can I afford this item?" was replaced with the World War II question "Where is this item?"

What could have been a divisive problem on the home front instead became a unifying experience that most Americans met with acceptance and even teamwork. The experience made lasting changes, some of which endured into the twenty-first century. When bananas grew scarce, Hostess Twinkies substituted vanilla-flavored cream for the banana filling. The change became a consumer favorite and was never reversed. The meat product SPAM became a best-seller during the war and has remained on grocery shelves. Ironically enough, the forced change from red meats and fatty dairy products to fresh produce and low-fat meat alternatives created a healthier citizenry during World War II than existed before or after the conflict. The end of the war brought an end to rationing, and shortages eventually disappeared as supply once again met demand.

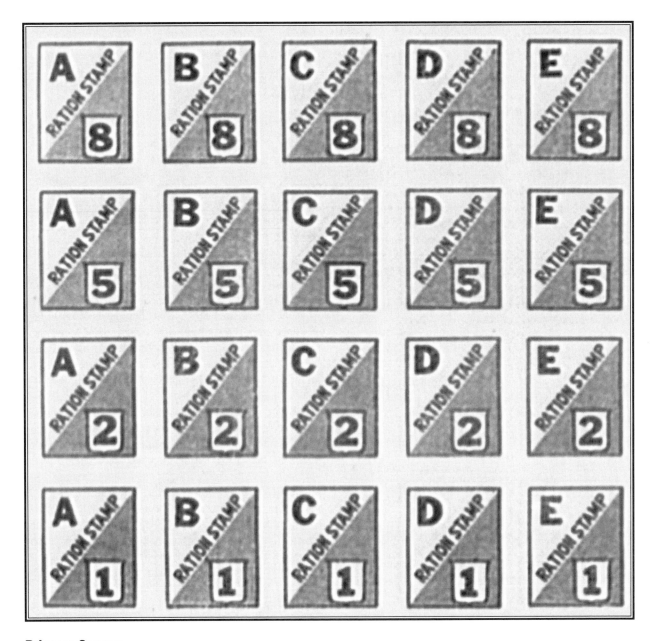

Primary Source

"War Ration Book No. 3"

SYNOPSIS: Stamps from a World War II Ration book. Consumers were required to submit these stamps when purchasing certain goods. THE LIBRARY OF CONGRESS.

Significance

War rationing was important for three main reasons. First, it united the nation in the war effort. Everyone, in effect, was in the same boat. That unity translated to a sense of teamwork unrivaled in recent U.S. war experiences. Second, rationing affected the way people lived their lives on a day-to-day basis. Tires were patched and repatched. Fashions changed. Most importantly, family meals took careful, advance planning. Cookbooks immediately hit the press with recommendations for how to substitute molasses, honey, or sorghum for sugar or stretch meat with oatmeal, nuts, or soybean flours. Consumers mixed light cream, custard, and unflavored gelatin with butter to make it last. To prepare meals for celebrations and special events, cooks had to save coupons and plan shopping strategies. The simple act of eating became a complicated proposition. Each lifestyle change reminded consumers that the nation was at war.

The most significant impact of shortages was the evolution of the patriotism of rationing. Advertisers hailed potted meat products that used cheaper cuts of meat as the patriotic choice for shoppers. Posters reminded consumers that each bite of steak they ate took a dinner from a soldier; conversely, passing on steak at the market was an act of heroism. Empty lots, school fields, and private yards were tilled to plant so-called victory gardens to supplement American tables. The rhetoric of the time elevated acts of simple self-interest to valor in an international struggle; a schoolchild planting squash in her backyard was striking a blow against Hitler. This turned a potentially nightmarish situation—too few goods for too many people—into a morale-building experience. The public-relations aspects of rationing proved as important as the rationing itself.

Primary Source

World War II Ration Stamps, Book No. 2 [excerpt]

SYNOPSIS: This ration booklet represented the government's efforts to help consumers deal with shortages brought by World War II. Its coupon point system allowed every American limited purchasing power for certain products, many of which were food. The three years of the "use it all, wear it out, make it do, or go without" message of rationing not only helped the war effort but also built morale.

Instructions

1. This book is valuable. Do not lose it.

2. Each stamp authorizes you to purchase rationed goods in the quantities and at the times designated by the Office of Price Administration. Without the stamps you will be unable to purchase those goods.

3. Detailed instructions concerning the use of the book and the stamps will be issued from time to time. Watch for those instructions so that you will know how to use your book and stamps.

4. Do not tear out stamps except at the time of purchase and in the presence of the storekeeper, his employee, or a person authorized to make delivery.

5. Do not throw this book away when all of the stamps have been used, or when the time for their use has expired. You may be required to present this book when you apply for subsequent books.

■ ■ ■

Rationing is a vital part of your country's war effort. This book is your Government's guarantee of your fair share of goods made scarce by war, to which the stamps contained herein will be assigned as the need arises.

Any attempt to violate the rules is an effort to deny someone his share and will create hardship and discontent.

Such action, like treason, helps the enemy.

Give your whole support to rationing and thereby conserve our vital goods. Be guided by the rule:

If you don't need it, DON'T BUY IT.

Further Resources

BOOKS

Bentley, Amy. *Eating for Victory: Food Rationing and the Politics of Domesticity.* Urbana, Ill.: University of Illinois Press, 1998.

Litoff, Judy Barrett. *Since You Went Away: World War II Letters From American Women on the Home Front.* Oxford, England: Oxford University Press, 1991.

Thomas, Mary Martha. *Riveting and Rationing in Dixie: Alabama Women and the Second World War.* Tuscaloosa, Ala.: University of Alabama Press, 1987.

U. S. Office of Price Administration. "Rationing in World War II." Washington, D.C.: U.S. Government Printing Office, 1946.

Ward, Barbara McLean. *Produce and Conserve, Share and Play Fair: The Grocer and the Consumer on the Home-Front Battlefield During World War II.* Portsmouth, N.H.: Strawberry Banke Museum: Distributed by University Press of New England, 1994.

Spencer Tracy and Katharine Hepburn in *Woman of the Year*

Movie still

By: MGM Studios
Date: 1942
Source: Spencer Tracy and Katharine Hepburn in *Woman of the Year.* Movie still. 1942. The Kobal Collection/MGM/Clarence Sinclair Bull. Image number WOM003CD. ■

Introduction

The film industry enjoyed great success in the 1940s as Americans looked to escape the memory of the Great Depression of the previous decade and the threat and later reality of World War II (1939–1945). Light fare such as comedies, musicals, and romances were particular favorites. Katharine Hepburn and Spencer Tracy rose to prominence as gifted actors and as a winning box-office

Primary Source

Spencer Tracy and Katharine Hepburn in *Woman of the Year*

SYNOPSIS: This image shows Spencer Tracy and Katharine Hepburn starring together in the first of their many romantic comedies, *Woman of the Year*. The film began a series of similar movies starring the two actors and providing audiences with witty, escapist fun. The film also challenged stereotypes about women's roles at home and in the workplace. THE KOBAL COLLECTION/ MGM/ BULL, CLARENCE SINCLAIR. REPRODUCED BY PERMISSION.

combination. As the Cold War political and military situation grew more complex, the appeal of escapist entertainment grew.

The film *Woman of the Year* is a romantic comedy about the marriage of a laid-back sportswriter, played by Spencer Tracy, and a clever international reporter, played by Katharine Hepburn. In many ways, the movie reflects the tastes of the moviegoing audiences of its time. First,

it is escapist. While the main characters face conflicts, these conflicts are within the characters' control and can be solved, unlike economic depression or a world war. Second, it is funny; the characters' humor is punctuated with fast-paced, witty dialogue as they fight, trade insults, and eventually reconcile. Third, romantic comedies of this type have happy endings. Audiences valued uplifting stories during the war era, when the news was full of uncertain and frightening events beyond most Americans' control.

Romantic comedies such as *Woman of the Year* hinge on the familiar theme of competition between the sexes. Hepburn's heroines operated in professional settings as journalists, attorneys, and other respected positions formerly held by men, and they were good at what they did. They held their own in competition with men, even if one of those men was a boyfriend or husband. This often led to romantic tension as the hero, played by Spencer Tracy in *Woman of the Year,* tried and failed to assert dominance at work as well as in the relationship. Such films mirrored the public's struggle with—and eventual understanding and acceptance of—women's changing roles in the workplace as well as the home. The fact that *Woman of the Year* led to a series of films with the same stars and basic formula proved its widespread appeal.

Significance

Woman of the Year was important for two key reasons. First, it began the legendary collaboration of Spencer Tracy and Katharine Hepburn, who continued to make films together until Tracy's death in 1967. Among their most memorable later films were *Adam's Rib* (1949), *Pat and Mike* (1952), *The Desk Set* (1957), and the groundbreaking *Guess Who's Coming to Dinner?* (1967). The term "Tracy-Hepburn film" became synonymous with witty, fast-paced, dry-humored romantic comedies that often featured a feisty professional woman both in love with and in competition against an equally feisty professional man. Both actors also gained great respect in solo ventures. Tracy became the first actor to win two consecutive Academy Awards for Best Actor. Hepburn won four Academy Awards across several decades and in 1999 was named the top female screen legend of all time by the American Film Institute.

The second impact of *Woman of the Year* and films like it lay in the portrayal of women as tough, gutsy, and ambitious. Katharine Hepburn's roles rarely placed her in the traditional setting of the home with an idealized view of domestic life and motherhood. On the contrary, her heroines were outspoken participants in what had been considered "the man's world" of business, sports, and politics. These films mirrored what was happening in the United States as women joined the workforce in record numbers and encouraged them to stay there even after the war was over. Hepburn served as a role model to American women as society's view of "a woman's place" began to change. Her women were not merely "Rosie the Riveter" characters, filling in for men in the factories; they were educated, professional women creating a place for themselves in all walks of life.

Further Resources

BOOKS

Basinger, Jeanine. *A Woman's View: How Hollywood Spoke to Women, 1930–1960.* Hanover, N.H.: Wesleyan University Press, 1995.

Britton, Andrew. *Katharine Hepburn: Star as Feminist.* London: Studio Vista, 1995.

Edwards, Anne. *A Remarkable Woman: A Biography of Katharine Hepburn.* New York: Morrow, 1985.

Hepburn, Katharine. *Me: Stories of My Life.* New York: Knopf, 1991.

Karlyn, Kathleen Rowe. *The Unruly Woman: Gender and the Genres of Laughter.* Austin, Tex.: University of Texas Press, 1995.

Leaming, Barbara. *Katharine Hepburn.* New York: Crown, 1995.

WEBSITES

"Tracy & Hepburn." Available online at http://www.themave .com/Tracy/ST_Hep.htm; website home page: http://www .themave.com (accessed February 17, 2003).

AUDIO AND VISUAL MEDIA

Adam's Rib. MGM. Directed by George Cukor. 1949.

The Desk Set. Twentieth Century Fox. Directed by Walter Lang. 1957.

Guess Who's Coming to Dinner? Columbia Pictures. Directed by Stanley Kramer. 1967.

Pat and Mike. MGM. Directed by George Cukor. 1952.

Woman of the Year. Original release, 1942, MGM. Directed by George Stevens. DVD/VHS, 2000, Warner Home Video.

A Guide for All-American Girls
Guidebook

By: All-American Girls Professional Baseball League
Date: 1943
Source: All-American Girls Professional Baseball League. *A Guide for All-American Girls.* 1943. National Baseball Hall of Fame Library. Reproduced online at http://www .baseballhalloffame.org/education/primary%5Fsources /women/document_01_small.htm; website home page: http://www.baseballhalloffame.org (accessed March 24, 2003).
About the Organization: In 1943, Philip K. Wrigley, owner of the Chicago Cubs, founded the All-American Girls Baseball League (AAGBL). Originally a softball league, the AAGBL evolved into the first women's professional baseball circuit. The league had franchises in fifteen cities, all in the Midwest. Two hundred sixty-one players from twenty-four states, Canada, and Cuba played in the AAGBL. The first several seasons were successful, but eventually poor management, financial troubles, aging players, and a decline in fan interest led the AAGBL to fold after twelve years of existence. ■

Jean Marlowe of the Chicago Colleens winds up for a pitch.
© BETTMANN/CORBIS. REPRODUCED BY PERMISSION.

Introduction

Opportunities for women to make money playing professional sports at the beginning of World War II were exceptionally rare. But the war provided an opportunity, if only temporarily. The idea of a women's professional baseball—or at first, softball—league was the brainchild of Philip K. Wrigley, the chewing gum magnate and owner the Chicago Cubs. Wrigley's main reason for starting a women's league was to provide a baseball alternative in the event that major league men's baseball was shut down during World War II.

The AAGBL began with softball rules, with a few modifications including greater distance between bases

(to encourage stolen bases) and greater distance between the pitcher's mound and home plate. A larger ball, the size of a softball, was used. Over the AAGBL's history, the ball size shrunk to that of a regulation baseball. The league had four teams in its inaugural season; Rockford (Illinois) Peaches, South Bend (Indiana) Blue Sox, Racine (Wisconsin) Belles, and Kenosha (Wisconsin) Comets. The players initially received $45 to $85 per week, a better wage than the average worker earned during the war ($10-$20 per week).

Over the course of the league's twelve-year history, a number of outstanding players performed. One star was Dorothy "Dottie" Schroeder from Illinois, who signed with the AAGBL as a fifteen-year-old high school student in 1943. Although she batted only .188 in her first season, Schroeder became a great hitting and fielding shortstop for several teams. Schroeder was so good that she was nicknamed "Honey Wagner"—a reference to Honus Wagner, Hall of Fame shortstop of the Pittsburgh Pirates. Connie Mack, the long-time Philadelphia Athletics owner and manager, reportedly said of Schroeder, "If she were a man, I'd give $50,000 for her." Tall at 5' 8" and known for her signature pigtails, Schroeder was the only woman to play all twelve seasons in the AAGBL (1943–1954).

Philip Wrigley's vision of women ballplayers was a combination of skill in the field like men, but "femininity" off it. The AAGBL players were required to attend "charm school," where they were given lessons in how to walk, sit, apply makeup, and conduct themselves in social situations. League officials brought in Helena Rubenstein, whose chain of beauty salons made her name synonymous with the image of femininity, to assist in the effort. As Dottie Schroeder remembered, "We learned how to walk and how to talk. They were deadly earnest about it. . . . They're going to teach me how to be graceful. I learned how to be graceful by playing out in the pasture, side-steppin' all the cow pies." Each team had a chaperone that accompanied players wherever they went, dealt with personal matters, and acted as a buffer between the players and their male managers. Along with charm school, the AAGBL distributed to every player a ten-page "Guide for All-American Girls." While the charm schools were discontinued after several years, beauty kits were given annually to the players. Even as late as 1950, there were rules requiring feminine attire, when not in uniform, and long hair, not "boyish bobs." There was a ban on smoking, drinking in public, and using obscene language at anytime. During the league's last several years, enforcement of the rules became lax. Players frequently got into trouble for drinking and speeding.

Significance

The All-American Girls Baseball League went through many changes in its twelve-year history. The game evolved from softball to baseball. The league's administration changed over the years. Wrigley ran the league in 1943 and 1944. He lost interest when it appeared the war would end soon, and that major league baseball would return to normal. After 1950, the teams operated as independent entities with no centralized administration. Even the name of the league changed several times, from All-American Girls Softball League to All-American Girls Professional Baseball League to All-American Girls Baseball League.

After 1948, the league began to decline. Teams were stocked with aging players. With fewer young prospects, most teams lost money and cut expenses by eliminating spring training and paying lower salaries. Fan interest waned. By 1954, the AAGBL had run its course, and the league disbanded after the season. Although a few players—Dottie Schroeder for one—played on touring teams for several more years, women's baseball ceased after 1957, The AAGBL was forgotten to history, with reunions among the former league players a chief reminder of their trailblazing accomplishments.

In 1987, a Public Broadcasting Service documentary on the league, co-produced by the son of a AAGBL player, received positive notice and attracted the attention of Hollywood. In 1992, Director Penny Marshall released *A League of Their Own,* a fictionalized account of women's lives in the AAGBL, starring Tom Hanks, Geena Davis (as a character based on Dottie Schroeder), and Madonna. In 1943, Philip Wrigley predicted that photos of star women players some day would be framed next to the male major leaguers in baseball's Hall of Fame in Cooperstown, New York. This happened in 1988, after lobbying from AAGBL alumni. Baseball's Hall of Fame recognized women's baseball by unveiling an exhibit of their accomplishments—a long overdue honor for these women pioneers.

Primary Source

A Guide for All-American Girls [excerpt]

SYNOPSIS: This guide was given to players in the All-American Girls Professional League as a part of the "charm school" training the women were required to attend. It highlights the concern of the era that women athletes retain their femininity. Along with the suggested beauty routine below, the guide also gave instruction in physical exercises, etiquette, and appropriate attire for wear outside the playing field.

When you become a player in the All-American Girls Baseball League you have reached the highest position that a girl can attain in this sport. The All-American Girls Baseball League is getting great public attention because it is pioneering a new sport for women.

You have certain responsibilities because you too are in the limelight. Your actions and appearance both on and off the field reflect on the whole profession. It is not only your duty to do your best to hold up the standard of this profession but to do your level best to keep others in line.

The girls in our League are rapidly becoming the heroines of youngsters as well as grownups all over the world. People want to be able to respect their heroines at all times. The All-American Girls Baseball League is attempting to establish a high standard that will make you proud that you are a player in years to come.

We hand you this manual to help guide you in your personal appearance. We ask you to follow the rules of behavior for your own good as well as that of the future success of girls' baseball.

In these few pages you will find many of the simple and brief suggestions which should prove useful to you during the busy baseball season. If you plan your days to establish an easy and simple routine, so that your meals are regular and well balanced, so that you have time for outside play and relaxation, so that you sleep at least eight hours each night and so that your normal functions are regular, you will be on the alert, do your job well and gain the greatest joy from living. Always remember that your mind and your body are interrelated and you cannot neglect one without causing the other to suffer. A healthy mind and a healthy body are the true attributes of the All-American girl.

Suggested Beauty Routine

After the Game

Remember, the All-American girl is subjected to greater exposure through her activities on the diamond, through exertion in greater body warmth and perspiration, through exposure to dirt, grime and dust and through vigorous play to scratches, cuts, abrasions and sprains. This means extra precaution to assure all the niceties of toilette and personality. Especially "after the game," the All-American girl should take time to observe the necessary beauty ritual, to protect both her health and appearance. Here are a few simple rules that should prove helpful and healthful "after the game."

1. Shower well and soap the skin.

2. Dry thoroughly to avoid chapping or chafing.

3. Apply cleansing cream to face—remove with tissue.

4. Wash face with soap and water.

5. Apply skin astringent.

6. Apply rouge moderately but carefully.

7. Apply lipstick with moderate taste.

8. Apply eye make-up if considered desirable.

9. Apply powder.

10. Check all cuts, abrasions or minor injuries.

If you suffer any skin abrasion or injury, or if you discern any aches or pains that do not appear to be normal, report them at once to your coach-chaperon or the person responsible for treatment and first aid. Don't laugh off slight ailments as trivialities because they can often develop into serious infection or troublesome conditions that can handicap your play and cause personal inconvenience. See that your injuries, however slight, receive immediate attention. Guard your health and welfare.

Additional Beauty Routine

Morning and Night

In the morning, when you have more time to attend to your beauty needs, you will undoubtedly be enabled to perform a more thorough job. Use your cleansing cream around your neck as well as over the face. Remove it completely and apply a second time to be sure that you remove all dust, grease and grime. Wipe off thoroughly with cleansing tissue. Apply hand lotion to keep your hands as lovely as possible. Use your manicure set to preserve your nails in a presentable condition and in keeping with the practical needs of your hands in playing ball.

Teeth

Not a great deal need be said about the teeth, because every All-American girl instinctively recognizes their importance to her health, her appearance and her personality. There are many good tooth cleansing preparations on the market and they should be used regularly to keep the teeth and gums clean and healthy. A regular visit to a reliable dentist is recommended and certainly no tooth ailment should be neglected for a moment.

Body

Unwanted or superfluous hair is often quite common and it is no problem to cope with in these days when so many beauty preparations are available. If you have such hair on arms or legs, there are a number of methods by which it can be easily removed. There is an odorless liquid cream which can be applied in a few moments, permitted to dry and then showered off.

Deodorants

There are a number of very fine deodorants on the market which can be used freely all over the body. The most important feature of some of these products is the fact that the fragrance stays perspiration-proof all day long. These deodorants can be used especially where excess perspiration occurs and can be used safely and effectively without retarding natural perspiration. The All-American girl is naturally susceptible because of her vigorous activities and it certainly pays dividends to be on the safe side. Deodorant keeps you fresh and gives you assurance and confidence in your social contacts.

Eyes: The Eyes are the Windows of the Soul

The eyes indicate your physical fitness and therefore need your thoughtful attention and care. They bespeak your innermost thoughts—they reflect your own joy of living—or they can sometimes falsely bespeak the listlessness of mind and body. Perhaps no other feature of your face has more to do with the impression of beauty, sparkle and personality which you portray.

A simple little exercise for the eyes and one which does not take much time can do much to strengthen your eyes and add to their sparkle and allure. Turn your eyes to the corner of the room for a short space of time, then change to the other corner. Then gaze at the ceiling and at the floor alternately. Rotating or rolling your eyes constitutes an exercise and your eyes will repay you for the attention that you give to them. There are also vitamins prescribed for the care of the eyes. Drink plenty of water and eat plenty of vegetables. We all know well that the armed forces found carrots a definite dietary aid to eyesight. Use a good eyewash frequently and for complete relaxation at opportune moments, lie down and apply an eye pad to your eyes for several minutes.

Hair: Women's Crowning Glory

One of the most noticeable attributes of a girl is her hair, woman's crowning glory. No matter the features, the clothes, the inner charm or personality—they can all suffer beneath a sloppy or stringy coiffure. Neither is it necessary to feature a fancy or extravagant hair-do, because a daily program for the hair will help to keep it in healthful and attractive condition.

Neatness is the first and greatest requirement. Arrange your hair neatly in a manner that will best retain its natural style despite vigorous play. Off the diamond, you can readily arrange it in a softer and more feminine style, if you wish. But above all, keep your hair as neat as possible, on or off the field.

Brushing the hair will help a great deal more than is realized. It helps to stimulate the scalp which is the source of healthful hair growth. It develops the natural beauty and lustre of the hair, And it will not spoil the hair-do. When brushing, bend over and let your head hang down. Then brush your hair downward until the scalp tingles. Just a few minutes of this treatment each day will tend to keep your scalp in fine condition and enhance the beauty of your "crowning glory."

Mouth

Every woman wants to have an attractive and pleasing mouth. As you speak, people watch your mouth and you can do much, with a few of the very simplest tools, to make your mouth invitingly bespeak your personality. Your beauty aids should, of course, include an appropriate type of lipstick and a brush. They should be selected with consideration and care.

With your lipstick, apply two curves to your upper lip. Press your lips together. Then, run your brush over the lipstick and apply it to your lips, outlining them smoothly. This is the artistic part of the treatment in creating a lovely mouth. Patient practice and care make perfect. Open your mouth and outline your own natural curves. If your lips are too thin to please you, shape them into fuller curves. Now, use a tissue between your lips and press lightly to take off excess lipstick. If you wish to have a "firmer foundation," use the lipstick a second time and use the tissue "press" again.

Caution: Now that you have completed the job, be sure that the lipstick has not smeared your teeth. Your mirror will tell the tale—and it is those little final touches that really count.

Further Resources

BOOKS

Berlage, Gai Ingham. *Women in Baseball: The Forgotten History.* Westport, Conn.: Praeger, 1994.

Browne, Lois. *Girls of Summer: In Their Own League.* Toronto: Harper-Collins, 1992.

Gregorich, Barbara. *Women at Play: The Story of Women in Baseball.* New York: Harcourt, Brace, and Company, 1993.

Johnson, Susan E. *When Women Played Hardball.* Seattle: Seal Press, 1994.

Madden, W.C. *The Women of the All-American Girls Professional Baseball League: A Biographical Dictionary.* Jefferson, N.C.: McFarland and Company, 1997.

WEBSITES

All-American Girls Professional Baseball League, 1943–1954. Available at http://www.aagpbl.org (Accessed March 1, 2003).

"Rosie the Outfielder." The National Baseball Hall of Fame and Museum. Available at http://www.baseballhalloffame.org /exhibits/online_exhibits/baseball_enlists/rosie.htm; website home page: http://www.baseballhalloffame.org (Accessed March 1, 2003).

AUDIO AND VISUAL MEDIA

A League of Their Own. Original release 1992, Columbia Pictures/Parkway. Directed by Penny Marshall. DVD, 1997, Columbia TriStar Home Video.

A League of Their Own. Documentary. Filmmakers Library, 1987, VHS.

The Case of the Black-Eyed Blonde
Novel

By: Erle Stanley Gardner

Date: 1943

Source: Gardner, Erle Stanley. *The Case of the Black-Eyed Blonde.* New York: William Morrow, 1944. Reprint, New York: Pocket Books, 1968, 227–228, 230–231.

About the Author: Erle Stanley Gardner (1889–1970) was a lawyer, but as an author he wrote almost one hundred mystery and detective novels that sold more than a million copies each, making him the best-selling American author of his era. Under the pen name A.A. Fair, he wrote a series based on the adventures of detective Bertha Cool and legalist Donald Lam. He is best known for his character Perry Mason. Gardner adapted his Mason stories for radio programs, television shows, and motion pictures beginning in the 1930s. ■

Introduction

Beginning with his 1933 novels *The Case of the Velvet Claws* and *The Case of the Sulky Girl*, Erle Stanley Gardner had a hit with Perry Mason. Mason was an intelligent, courageous, determined attorney who accepted the tough murder cases, uncovered their hidden mysteries, and almost always pulled out astounding victories in court despite the odds. Perry Mason novels, like the later radio, television, and movie series, adhered to a certain formula. Clients most often sought out Mason because of his superior reputation. These clients were

Eric Stanley Gardner, lawyer and prolific writer of detective novels, created the famous Perry Mason character. AP/WIDE WORLD PHOTOS. REPRODUCED BY PERMISSION.

falsely accused of murder, but circumstantial evidence pointed to their guilt. With the help of private investigator Paul Drake and secretary Della Street—both of whom, like Mason himself, often bent the rules while searching for the truth—Mason not only cleared the name of the innocent but discovered the guilty and brought them to justice.

Many of the characters appearing in the Perry Mason cases were exotic and romantic: beautiful models, mysterious millionaires, secret lovers. The settings could be equally interesting. Gardner described in detail the era's elegant, sophisticated cultural tastes for fur coats, dry martinis, and cigarettes. Mason usually raced against law enforcement officers to track down the evidence necessary to clear his client, often finding himself in life-threatening peril, or at least significant danger, in the process. His exploits captivated readers and made them return for more.

Significance

Novels such as Gardner's played three important roles in the United States. First, they provided much-needed escapist entertainment for the American public in the 1940s. Absent from Perry Mason novels were depressions, wars, and communists. Although the action might be frightening and at times violent, the reader could be certain that Mason, Street, and Drake would be safe and successful at the end of each adventure. Even the most desperate plot moments were punctuated by witty dialogue and fast-paced action. Mason was ever cool, Della always poised under threat. Such novels allowed audiences to forget the uncertainty of the times and find interest and enjoyment. Second, the books represented a kind of mass-produced culture. The plots and purposes of the novels at some level all looked the same, much like the preassembled, manufactured homes of the new 1940s suburbs. Many could be marketed in a short time, creating a rapid-fire, disposable product; no one expected to reread a Perry Mason novel as one might savor a classic piece of literature. The goals of inexpensive book series such as Gardner's were to provide temporary pleasure, not timeless classics. Chances were that a reader who enjoyed one Perry Mason case would enjoy the next one as well, since the formula for one applied to all.

Perhaps most importantly, the Perry Mason series both challenged and reinforced typical gender stereotypes. On the one hand, Della Street was a single working woman rather than a traditional married homemaker and mother. She took part in fieldwork and sensitive investigations, and her acute observations and instincts often helped unravel mysteries. She could be tough when she needed to be and held her own with her male employer and acquaintances. On the other hand, Street was not an equal to Mason or Drake. She was a subordinate, a secretary, a step below the career men in terms of education and prestige. The flirtatious behavior and sexual banter she shared with both Mason and Drake blurred the lines of the professional and personal, as did comments about her appearance and charm made by clients and colleagues. In other words, Street's work life was defined not by her abilities but by her gender. In this sense, the Perry Mason novels reflected the tension American society felt between traditional notions of femininity and emerging ideas about feminism.

Primary Source

The Case of the Black-Eyed Blonde [excerpt]

SYNOPSIS: The 1943 Gardner novel *The Case of the Black-Eyed Blonde* is a typical Perry Mason story, covering one case from its beginning to the courtroom conclusion. Each Perry Mason mystery also included masculine banter with detective Paul Drake and not-so-subtle flirting with secretary Della Street.

"Oh, tracing the family resemblance. He pointed out to me how the boy had his mother's forehead and his son's mouth, and his eyes were the exact image of Bartsler's mother's, and . . ."

"Good heavens!" Della Street interrupted. "And *that* from a skeptic who prides himself on being hard to convince."

"Exactly," Mason said. "It simply goes to show how credulous a man can be despite his efforts to be cynical and hard-boiled when it comes to something he wants to believe. How many men look at themselves in the mirror and see themselves as they actually are? They see the mental image they have created of themselves, ten to twenty years younger than they actually are."

Della Street laughed. "You're talking about women now," she said.

"No," Mason said, "a woman is more honest with herself, a little more critical in her appraisal. Women don't kid themselves the way men do. They're more romantic and more realistic."

Mason swung the car around the corner into a side street. "Remember this little isolated place, Della?" he said with enthusiasm. "It's where they serve you that heavy bread-like pastry with cheese and spices melted over it."

"Oh yes!" Della exclaimed, "And they have some perfectly marvelous wine! It's been a long time since we've eaten here, Chief." . . .

"Some one coming," Della Street said in a low voice.

Mason looked up toward the man who had left a woman companion at the table and was coming toward him.

"Shucks, Della," Mason said, "we seem to have no privacy at all."

"Oh, I'll leave if you're going to be surly about it," Drake grinned. "I thought perhaps Della would give me a dance before. . . ."

The man stood in the entrance of the booth and cleared his throat. "You'll pardon me for interrupting," he said, "but you're Perry Mason. I've seen you in court, and I have been trying to get you all evening. When you walked in here, I thought it was fate that had brought you here. I simply *must* consult you about something that bothers me, something rather mysterious, and something very important."

Mason smiled and shook his head. "Not until after I've had another cocktail, some hors d'oeuvres, some steaks, and. . . ."

"I'll wait," the man said anxiously, "if you'll only talk with me."

"And we'll be eating garlic," Mason warned. "What is it all about?"

"It's about a fish."

"Are you, by any chance, trying to kid me?"

"No, no," the man said, "a goldfish."

"And it's important?"

"Of course, it's important. It's driving me crazy! But don't let me detain you now, Mr. Mason. I'll be waiting over there with my companion, and if you'll join us for an after-dinner brandy, I'll give you the high lights."

Further Resources

BOOKS

Hughes, Dorothy B. *Erle Stanley Gardner: The Case of the Real Perry Mason.* New York: William Morrow, 1978.

Mundell, E.H. *Erle Stanley Gardner: A Checklist.* Kent, Ohio: Kent State University Press, 1968.

Van Dover, J. Kenneth. *Murder in the Millions: Erle Stanley Gardner, Mickey Spillane, Ian Fleming.* New York: F. Ungar, 1984.

WEBSITES

Miller, John Anthony. The Official Erle Stanley Gardner Website. Available online at http://www.erlestanleygardner.com (accessed April 18, 2003).

Wartime Conservation Posters

Posters

"Save Waste Fats for Explosives"; "When You Ride Alone You Ride with Hitler!"; "Waste Helps the Enemy"

By: Henry Koerner; Weimer Pursell; Vanderlaan

Date: c. 1943

Source: Koerner, Henry; Weimer Pursell; Vanderlaan. "Save Waste Fats for Explosives"; "When You Ride Alone You Ride with Hitler!"; "Waste Helps the Enemy." 1943. National Archives, College Park, Md. Still Picture Branch. Available online at http://www.archives.gov/exhibit_hall/powers_of _persuasion/use_it_up/use_it_up.html; website home page: http://www.archives.gov (accessed March 8, 2003).

About the Artists: The artists who created these posters were commissioned by the U.S. government during World War II (1939–1945) to use their talents to motivate Americans to participate in the war effort. By putting these artists on the public payroll, the government allowed them to invest their energies in creating propaganda posters, which also enabled wide exposure of their work. ■

Primary Source

"Save Waste Fats for Explosives" (1 OF 3)

SYNOPSIS: The U.S. government published these three posters to encourage domestic austerity during World War II. They were designed to remind Americans that they were all in the war effort together and that frugality in the home and workplace could play a major part in achieving victory abroad. This 1943 poster by Henry Koerner encouraged Americans to save food fats for use as explosives in the war effort. POSTER BY HENRY KOERNER, 1943. PRINTED BY THE GOVERNMENT PRINTING OFFICE OF WAR INFORMATION. COURTESY OF NATIONAL ARCHIVES (NWDNS-44-PA-380).

Primary Source

"When You Ride Alone You Ride With Hitler!" (2 OF 3)

This 1943 poster by Weimer Pursell encouraged American motorists to carpool by playing on their sense of national loyalty.

POSTER BY WEIMER PURSELL, 1943. PRINTED BY THE GOVERNMENT PRINTING OFFICE FOR THE OFFICE OF PRICE ADMINISTRATION. COURTESY OF NATIONAL ARCHIVES (NWDNS-44-PA-2415).

Primary Source

"Waste Helps the Enemy" (3 OF 3)
This poster by Vanderlaan portrayed U.S. conservation as a means of defeating Hitler and Nazi Germany. POSTER BY VANDER-LAAN. PRODUCED BY THE DOUGLAS AIRCRAFT COMPANY. COURTESY OF NATIONAL ARCHIVES (NWDNS-79-WP-103).

Introduction

American society has often been characterized as one of consumerism and consumption. But this is a somewhat misleading image. Deep in the American soul is a tradition of frugality and saving, not to say miserliness and penny-pinching. The Puritans who first settled America brought with them an austere and spartan view of life, which no doubt served them well in the trackless wildernesses of the New World.

Even as the nation grew and expanded, the tradition of austerity and saving never disappeared, surfacing when the Great Depression occurred in 1929 and put the American economy into a tailspin. World War II followed, requiring Americans to ration essentials so that troops in the field had all they needed to fight the war. In the early 1940s, the government, using poster art, called on the American people to practice caution, frugality, and resourcefulness.

To Americans, messages from Uncle Sam in the form of poster art were not new. They were all too familiar with the World War I (1914–1918) recruiting poster by illustrator James Montgomery Flagg, depicting a pointing Uncle Sam saying, "I Want You for the U.S. Army." This time, the government again used poster art to promote restraint in the public's consumption of gasoline, rubber, sugar, butter, and meat.

These wartime posters encouraged Americans to tighten their belts. They sought to make civilians feel like foot soldiers, even as they performed such mundane tasks as using both sides of writing paper, sharing car rides, and saving the fat from meal preparations for the manufacture of explosives. These seemingly small tasks, when collectively done by millions of Americans, would help turn the tide against the enemy. In addition, these posters made every American feel that he or she would have a part in the ultimate victory.

Significance

The American people did indeed practice frugality and resourcefulness during World War II, a resourcefulness reflected by the Victory Garden Campaign of 1942, during which people cultivated backyard vegetable lots. The wartime posters recommending "doing more with less" had struck a chord with the American people, who wanted to do their part in the war effort by living economically.

The conservationism fostered by these wartime posters is significant not only in the historical role it played in bringing the war effort to a successful conclusion, but also for anticipating contemporary "reuse and recycle" campaigns. Just as wartime conservationism harkened back to the early Americans' resourcefulness and frugality, so too today's conservationist movements learn from the World War II practice of finding new ways to get by while consuming less.

Like the wartime campaign, today's conservationism seeks the public's large-scale involvement to consume natural resources more prudently for the long-term interests of the country. During the war, the restraint exercised by the civilian population was seen in the light of the freedoms of generations to come. Similarly, today's campaign to reduce waste and consume in an environmentally friendly way are justified in terms of the interests of future generations.

Further Resources

BOOKS

Laurie, Clayton D. *The Propaganda Warriors: America's Crusade against Nazi Germany.* Lawrence: University Press of Kansas, 1996.

Rubenstein, Harry, and William L. Bird. *Design for Victory: World War II Posters on the American Home Front.* New York: Princeton Architectural Press, 1998.

WEBSITES

"Powers of Persuasion: Poster Art From World War II." U.S. National Archives and Records Administration. Available online at http://www.archives.gov/exhibit_hall/powers_of_persuasion/powers_of_persuasion_home.html; website home page: http://www.archives.gov (accessed March 8, 2003). *This site contains additional poster art from World War II.*

The Fountainhead
Novel

By: Ayn Rand

Date: 1943

Source: Rand, Ayn. *The Fountainhead.* Philadelphia: Blakiston, 1943, 694, 695, 736, 737, 743.

About the Author: Ayn Rand (1905–1982) was born in St. Petersburg, Russia, and emigrated to the United States after the Russian Revolution. She worked as a screenwriter in Hollywood and became a naturalized U.S. citizen in 1931. Her first novel, *We, The Living,* was published in 1936. Her 1943 work, *The Fountainhead,* became her first best-seller. She followed this with a second literary hit, *Atlas Shrugged,* in 1957. She is best remembered for promoting her individualist philosophy of objectivism in her novels, nonfiction books, and journals. ∎

Introduction

The turn to communism by her native Russia influenced Ayn Rand deeply; all of her work, both fiction and nonfiction, was an indictment of any regime or system of thought that placed the individual's well-being beneath that of the group. Her books and articles expressed what she termed the philosophy of objectivism: 1) no person should live for another, 2) each person's highest moral end was his or her own happiness, and 3) any notion of "the group"

Ayn Rand gives testimony before the House Un-American Activities Committee on October 20, 1947. © BETTMANN/CORBIS. REPRODUCED BY PERMISSION.

instead of "the individual" was ultimately a threat that endangered every person. The heroes of her works were creators, inventors, entrepreneurs, and artists who worked to fulfill their own visions rather than please or serve anyone else. Perhaps the most stunning articulation of Rand's objectivist philosophy came in *The Fountainhead,* which was a best-selling novel in 1944 and turned into a popular film in 1949 starring Gary Cooper and Patricia Neal.

The Fountainhead tells the story a brilliant young architect named Howard Roark, who battles with conventional standards of beauty and utility because his vision is far ahead of his time. Rather than copying old patterns of architecture, Roark is an artist who creates new structures unlike anything ever seen. In the midst of his creative struggles, Roark stands alone, expelled from school, mocked at parties and in the media, and attacked by those close to him, including his lover. During his struggle, he witnesses the amazing success of a fellow architect, the conniving Peter Keating, who is the most popular architect of the time even though he really knows nothing about designing buildings. Ultimately, Roark discovers and rejects the seductive power of money and reputation. In the end, he chooses to be true to his own genius despite the great unhappiness that such a decision could mean. His individualism marks him as a true Randian hero.

Significance

The Fountainhead had lasting importance for American culture and politics. The first of Rand's novels to gain popular attention, it has become a classic text studied in schools and reprinted often. This opened the way for Rand's later work, including fiction such as *Atlas Shrugged* (1957), and nonfiction such as *For the New Intellectual* (1961), *The Virtue of Selfishness* (1961), *Capitalism: The Unknown Ideal* (1966), *Introduction to Objectivist Epistemology* (1967), and *Philosophy: Who Needs It?* (1982). In 1991, nine years after Rand's death, a Gallup survey concerning influential authors in the United States named Ayn Rand second in importance, surpassed only by *The Bible.* Rand's success reflected the growing U.S. interest in popular philosophy beginning in the 1940s. As more Americans attended college, thanks in no small part to the effects of the GI Bill that financed veterans' education, more people became interested in questions of philosophy. Rand, among others, addressed the issue in a way that was accessible to an educated but nonspecialist audience. Her use of fiction as well as nonfiction to convey her message made her work all the more appealing to the public. The success of Rand's periodicals, such as *The Objectivist* (1962–1971) and *The Ayn Rand Newsletter* (1971–1976), gave longer life to the interest in popular philosophy.

Finally, Rand's achievements put a more cultural and less political face on the American preoccupation with communism. In a sense, all of Rand's work was a reaction to and an attack on the rise of communism in the Soviet Union and around the world. Her writings reinforced U.S. concerns about the nature of the communist threat to individualism and thus to the American way of life.

Primary Source

The Fountainhead [excerpt]

> **SYNOPSIS:** Ayn Rand's heroes are known for passionate speeches that explain their ideas and motivations. In *The Fountainhead,* architect Howard Roark is the mouthpiece of Rand's philosophy as he denies the demands of others and remains true to his creative vision.

"Look around you. Pick up any newspaper and read the headlines. Isn't it coming? Isn't it here? Every single thing I told you? Isn't Europe swallowed already and we're stumbling on to follow? Everything I said is contained in a single word—collectivism. And isn't that the god of our century? To act together. To think—together. To feel—together. To unite, to agree, to obey. To obey, to serve, to sacrifice. Divide and conquer—first. But then—unite and rule. We've discovered that one at last. Remember the Roman Emperor who said he wished humanity had a single neck so he could cut it? People have laughed at him for centuries. But we'll have the last laugh. We've accomplished what he couldn't accomplish. We've taught men to unite. This makes one neck ready for one leash. We've found the magic word. Collectivism. Look at Europe, you fool. Can't you see past the guff and recognize the essence? One country is dedicated to the proposition that man has no rights, that the collective is all. The individual held as evil, the mass—as God. No motive and no virtue permitted—except that of service to the proletariat. That's one version. Here's another. A country dedicated to the proposition that man has no rights, that the State is all. The individual held as evil, the race—as God. No motive and no virtue permitted—except that of service to the race. Am I raving or is this the cold reality of two continents already? Watch the pincer movement. If you're sick of one version, we push you into the other. We get you coming and going. We've closed the doors. We've fixed the coin. Heads—collectivism, and tails—collectivism. Fight the doctrine which slaughters the individual with a doctrine which slaughters the individual. Give up your soul to a council—or give it up to a leader. But give it up, give it up, give it up. My technique, Peter. Offer poison as food and poison as antidote. Go fancy on the trimmings, but hang on to the main objective. Give the fools a choice, let them have their fun—but don't forget the only purpose you have to accomplish. Kill the individual. Kill man's soul. The rest will follow automatically. . . ."

"Thousands of years ago, the first man discovered how to make fire. He was probably burned at the stake he had taught his brothers to light. He was considered an evildoer who had dealt with a demon mankind dreaded. But thereafter men had fire to keep them warm, to cook their food, to light their caves. He had left them a gift they had not conceived and he had lifted darkness off the earth. Centuries later, the first man invented the wheel. He was probably torn on the rack he had taught his brothers to build. He was considered a transgressor who ventured into forbidden territory. But thereafter, men could travel past any horizon. He had left them a gift they had not conceived and he had opened the roads of the world.

"That man, the unsubmissive and first, stands in the opening chapter of every legend mankind has recorded about its beginning. Prometheus was chained to a rock and torn by vultures—because he had stolen the fire of the gods. Adam was condemned to suffer—because he had eaten the fruit of the tree of knowledge. Whatever the legend, somewhere in the shadows of its memory mankind knew that its glory began with one and that that one paid for his courage.

"Throughout the centuries there were men who took first steps down new roads armed with nothing but their own vision. Their goals differed, but they all had this in common: that the step was first, the road new, the vision unborrowed, and the response they received—hatred. The great creators—the thinkers, the artists, the scientists, the inventors—stood alone against the men of their time. Every great new thought was opposed. Every great new invention was denounced. The first motor was considered foolish. The airplane was considered impossible. The power loom was considered vicious. Anesthesia was considered sinful. But the men of unborrowed vision went ahead. They fought, they suffered and they paid. But they won.

"No creator was prompted by a desire to serve his brothers, for his brothers rejected the gift he offered and that gift destroyed the slothful routine of their lives. His truth was his only motive. His own truth, and his own work to achieve it in his own way. A symphony, a book, an engine, a philosophy, an airplane or a building—that was his goal and his life. Not those who heard, read, operated, believed, flew or inhabited the thing he had created. The creation, not its users. The creation, not the benefits others derived from it. The creation which gave form to his truth. He held his truth above all things and against all men.

"His vision, his strength, his courage came from his own spirit. A man's spirit, however, is his self. That entity which is his consciousness. To think, to feel, to judge, to act are functions of the ego.

"The creators were not selfless. It is the whole secret of their power—that it was self-sufficient, self-motivated, self-generated. A first cause, a fount of energy, a life force, a Prime Mover. The creator served nothing and no one. He had lived for himself.

"And only by living for himself was he able to achieve the things which are the glory of mankind. Such is the nature of achievement. . . ."

"I came here to say that I do not recognize anyone's right to one minute of my life. Nor to any part of my energy. Nor to any achievement of mine. No matter who makes the claim, how large their number or how great their need.

"I wished to come here and say that I am a man who does not exist for others.

"It had to be said. The world is perishing from an orgy of self-sacrificing.

"I wished to come here and say that the integrity of a man's creative work is of greater importance than any charitable endeavor. Those of you who do not understand this are the men who're destroying the world.

"I wished to come here and state my terms. I do not care to exist on any others."

Further Resources

BOOKS

Den Uyl, Douglas J. *The Fountainhead: An American Novel.* New York: Twayne, 1999.

Gladstein, Mimi Reisel. *The New Ayn Rand Companion.* Westport, Conn.: Greenwood, 1999.

Machan, Tibor. *Ayn Rand.* New York: Peter Lang, 1999.

Peikoff, Leonard. *Objectivism: The Philosophy of Ayn Rand.* New York: Dutton, 1991.

Rand, Ayn. *For the New Intellectual: the Philosophy of Ayn Rand.* New York: Penguin, 1961.

———. *The Ayn Rand Reader.* Gary Hull and Leonard Peikoff, eds. New York: Plume, 1999.

PERIODICALS

Sturgis, Amy H. "The Rise, Decline, and Reemergence of Classical Liberalism." *The LockeSmith Review: Vol. I, Great Thinkers in Classical Liberalism.* Nashville, Tenn.: The LockeSmith Institute, 1994, 20–63.

WEBSITES

The Journal of Ayn Rand Studies. Available online at http://www.aynrandstudies.com (accessed April 20, 2003).

Servicemen's Readjustment Act of 1944

Law

By: U.S. Congress

Date: 1944

Source: *Serviceman's Readjustment Act.* Public Law 346. 78th Congress, 2d sess., June 22, 1944. Reproduced in *American Passages: A History of the United States.* Available online at http://azimuth.harcourtcollege.com/history/ayers/chapter27/27.1.gibill.html; website home page: http://azimuth.harcourtcollege.com (accessed April 18, 2003). ∎

Introduction

After the end of World War II (1939–1945), the nation faced the challenge of demobilizing the military. The number of persons serving in the U.S. armed forces dropped dramatically in a relatively short period of time. The Army, for example, dropped to six hundred thousand individuals in 1947 from a wartime peak of eight million. National lawmakers recognized that they owed a debt of gratitude to the armed forces personnel returning from World War II; on a more pragmatic level, they also realized that the the nation faced an economic and political challenge in reabsorbing the GIs into society. To assist discharged veterans returning home to build a new life, the U.S. Congress with the support of President Franklin D. Roosevelt's administration passed the *Servicemen's Readjustment Act of 1944.*

This legislation, also known as the GI Bill of Rights, or simply "GI Bill," provided $13 million in assistance to returning military veterans. Some of the funds went to programs such as low-interest mortgages so veterans could afford to buy houses. Perhaps the most important provision of the act was the providing of a free college education to more that fifteen million veterans. The college experience changed as the swarm of veterans entered universities across the country. The "Vic the Vet" cartoon series—created by Gabe Josephson, an artist attending Syracuse University thanks to the GI Bill—and similar works of popular culture explained and parodied the experience of the older students who went from battlefields back to the books. Before the GI Bill, a college education was an expensive and often exclusive proposition. The GI Bill brought a new generation and demographic into higher education.

Significance

The GI Bill was important for three main reasons. First, it altered the landscape of U.S. higher education. Existing colleges and universities could not handle the influx of students, so new institutions, especially state universities, sprang into being to meet the demand. Many other schools expanded their physical campus, and number of classroom and dormitory buildings to accommodate more students. This rapid expansion in turn created a need for more professors, so graduate schools around the nation likewise grew. Second, the GI Bill produced the largest number of college graduates the United States had known to that point, many of them first-generation students. This meant the professional workforce grew much larger, and more middle-class individuals expected the nine-to-five, suburban, house-and-car lifestyle that came to be synonymous with the American dream. Moreover, this expanded number of college graduates included more women, both veterans and wives of veterans who returned to school with or after their husbands.

The GI Bill also garnered support for Roosevelt's administration, due in no small part to the fact that the GIs it benefited were active voters as well as veterans.

More importantly, though, the GI Bill created a lasting effect because its impact did not stop with the World War II generation. Many of those who attended school through the GI Bill became college-educated parents who expected their children to study at a university. The ongoing demand for higher education caused permanent growth in old schools even as it created new ones. Later versions of the bill offered similar opportunities to veterans of military service as well. Although the *Serviceman's Readjustment Act of 1944* expired in 1956, it changed the culture of the United States into the twenty-first century.

Primary Source

Servicemen's Readjustment Act of 1944 [excerpt]

SYNOPSIS: This excerpt from the *Servicemen's Readjustment Act of 1944* provided the opportunity for World War II veterans to obtain a college education. The so-called GI Bill of Rights also provided assistance such as unemployment benefits and low-interest loans for homes and other investments.

Title II

Chapter IV—Education of Veterans

Part VIII

1. Any person who served in the active military or naval service on or after September 16, 1940, and prior to the termination of the present war, and who shall have been discharged or released therefrom under conditions other than dishonorable, and whose education or training was impeded, delayed, interrupted, or interfered with by reason of his entrance into the service, or who desires a refresher or retraining course, . . . shall be eligible for and entitled to receive education or training under this part. . . .

3. Such person shall be eligible for and entitled to such course of education or training as he may elect, and at any approved educational or training institution at which he chooses to enroll, whether or not located in the State in which he resides, which will accept or retain him as a student or trainee in any field or branch of knowledge which such institution finds him qualified to undertake or pursue. . . .

5. The Administrator shall pay to the educational or training institution, for each person enrolled in full time or part time course of education or training, the customary cost of tuition, and such laboratory, library, health, infirmary, and other similar fees as are customarily charged, and may pay for books, sup-

plies, equipment, and other necessary expenses, exclusive of board, lodging, other living expenses, and travel, as are generally required for the successful pursuit and completion of the course by other students in the institution: *Provided,* That in no event shall such payments, with respect to any person, exceed $500 for an ordinary school year. . . .

6. While enrolled in and pursuing a course under this part, such person, upon application to the Administrator, shall be paid a subsistence allowance of $50 per month, if without a dependent or dependents, or $75 per month, if he has a dependent or dependents.

Further Resources

BOOKS

Bennett, Michael J. *When Dreams Came True: The G.I. Bill and the Making of Modern America.* Washington, D.C.: Brassey's, 1996.

Hyman, Harold Melvin. *American Singularity: The 1787 Northwest Ordinance, the 1862 Homestead–Morrill Acts, and the 1944 G.I. Bill.* Athens, Ga.: University of Georgia Press, 1987.

Kaledin, Eugenia. *Daily Life in the United States, 1940–1959: Shifting Worlds.* Westport, Conn.: Greenwood, 2000.

Olson, Keith W. *The G.I. Bill, the Veterans, and the Colleges.* Lexington, Ky.: University Press of Kentucky, 1974.

WEBSITES

Department of Veteran Affairs. Available online at http://www.va.gov (accessed April 20, 2003).

"The GI Bill of Rights (1944)." Available online at http://hcl.chass.ncsu.edu/garson/dye/docs/gibill.htm; website home page: http://www.ncsu.edu (accessed April 20, 2003).

"Servicemen's Readjustment Act (1944)." Our Documents. Available online at http://ourdocuments.gov/content.php?page=document&doc=76; website home page: http://ourdocuments.gov (accessed April 20, 2003).

"Vic the Vet." Syracuse University Archives and Records Management. Available online at http://archives.syr.edu/accessions/vicvet.htm; website home page: http://archives.syr.edu (accessed April 14, 2003).

"RAAF Captures Flying Saucer on Ranch in Roswell Region"

Newspaper article

By: *Roswell Daily Record*
Date: July 8, 1947
Source: "RAAF Captures Flying Saucer on Ranch in Roswell Region." *Roswell Daily Record,* July 8, 1947. Avail-

Army Airforce officers Brigadier General Roger M. Ramey and Colonel Thomas J. Dubose, identify metallic fragments found near Roswell to be pieces of a weather balloon, July 8, 1947. © BETTMANN/CORBIS. REPRODUCED BY PERMISSION.

able online at http://www.roswell-record.com/july8.html; website home page: http://www.roswell-record.com (accessed April 20, 2003). ■

Introduction

In 1947, the staff of the *Roswell Daily Record* found the eyes of the nation trained on their New Mexico town. After strange events took place on a ranch near Roswell, locals and government officials both suggested that a flying saucer had crashed there. Officials later denied this, but the idea had already caught the attention of the U.S. public and laid the foundation for a legend. Although unidentified flying objects (UFOs) had been reported before—including so-called foo fighters seen by pilots in World War II (1939–1945)—no single UFO event before or since has drawn so much national interest.

Something mysterious happened in Roswell, New Mexico, in the summer of 1947, and within days, multiple theories had developed about what exactly it was. According to local residents, the intelligence office of the 509th Bombardment Group at Roswell Army Air Field (RAAF), and the *Roswell Daily Record,* a flying saucer crashed in a field near Roswell and was recovered by U.S. officials. Within days, however, the gov-

ernment amended the original report and explained that the recovered craft was really parts of a downed weather balloon. By the time this information came to light, the idea of an alien craft perhaps from outer space had taken hold of the nation's imagination. Apparent discrepancies in governmental press statements did little to help matters. Weeks, years, and even decades later, additional official statements offered new explanations. At various times, the incident was linked to a downed weather balloon, a military experiment gone wrong, and a test flight of classified aircraft. As the government revised its story, alleged witnesses emerged with tales of flying saucers, secret cover-ups, and even autopsies of alien beings. Because military operations in and near Roswell were classified, full disclosure of the event was and is doubtful. Only two things are certain: something happened near Roswell and the government was involved. Perhaps even more intriguing than the facts, however, was the reaction of the U.S. public. The Roswell mystery became a standard American myth, spawning television series, films, books, and even songs. The town of Roswell became a symbol of the unknown and a tourist destination for science fiction enthusiasts. The significant timing of the event at the beginning of the atomic age and cold war and the intense interest of the American people made the Roswell mystery an important reflection of 1940s consciousness.

Significance

Popular fascination with the Roswell mystery showed the uncertainty, even fear, that plagued the American public after World War II. If an alien craft had crashed in Roswell, some thought, it might be an extraterrestrial version of the attack on Pearl Harbor. Once again, an unexpected, possibly hostile force had touched U.S. soil. The unleashing of the atomic bomb also had created deep concern. Unfamiliar, deadly technology had changed the way people viewed the world. Once the power of the atom had been harnessed for such destruction, the world could not return to its former state. The idea that even more sophisticated, potentially threatening technology existed beyond Americans' understanding terrified many. A wave of "alien attack" films and stories became popular. "Technology gone wrong" novels and movies—many dealing with anxieties about radiation and mutation—also followed in the late 1940s and 1950s. The Roswell incident tapped into fears about the postwar world and its dangers.

Equally important, the government's changing and contradictory stories about what happened at Roswell fed into a growing postwar distrust of the government. The climate of patriotism and support during the war gave way to doubts. Some were shaken because something as powerful as the atomic bomb had been created in secret and used so boldly. Many more were concerned that communists had infiltrated the U.S. State Department and other engines of government to overthrow the nation from the inside. As the Red Scare grew and U.S. leaders traded allegations of disloyalty and un-Americanism, many citizens were unsure whom, if anyone, to believe. Conspiracy theories about the Roswell incident and an alleged government cover-up multiplied as other factors brought the trustworthiness of the government into question. In later decades, interest in the Roswell mystery resurfaced, especially in times when dissatisfaction and disillusionment with the government were highest.

Primary Source

"RAAF Captures Flying Saucer on Ranch in Roswell Region"

> **SYNOPSIS:** This article from the *Roswell Daily Record* offers reports from Roswell locals Mr. and Mrs. Dan Wilmot and from the intelligence office of the 509th Bombardment Group at Roswell Army Air Field. These reports were the first reactions to the mysterious events in Roswell. Although both reports suggest that a flying saucer had crashed, the U.S. government later denied that this was the case.

The intelligence office of the 509th Bombardment group at Roswell Army Air Field announced at noon today, that the field has come into possession of a flying saucer.

According to information released by the department, over authority of Maj. J. A. Marcel, intelligence officer, the disk was recovered on a ranch in the Roswell vicinity, after an unidentified rancher had notified Sheriff Geo. Wilcox, here, that he had found the instrument on his premises.

Major Marcel and a detail from his department went to the ranch and recovered the disk, it was stated.

After the intelligence officer here had inspected the instrument it was flown to higher headquarters.

The intelligence office stated that no details of the saucer's construction or its appearance had been revealed.

Mr. and Mrs. Dan Wilmot apparently were the only persons in Roswell who saw what they thought was a flying disk.

They were sitting on their porch at 105 South Penn. last Wednesday night at about ten o'clock when a large glowing object zoomed out of the sky from the southeast, going in a northwesterly direction at a high rate of speed.

Wilmot called Mrs. Wilmot's attention to it and both ran down into the yard to watch. It was in sight less then a minute, perhaps 40 or 50 seconds, Wilmot estimated.

Wilmot said that it appeared to him to be about 1,500 feet high and going fast. He estimated between 400 and 500 miles per hour.

In appearance it looked oval in shape like two inverted saucers, faced mouth to mouth, or like two old type washbowls placed together in the same fashion. The entire body glowed as though light were showing through from inside, though not like it would inside, though not like it would be if a light were merely underneath.

From where he stood Wilmot said that the object looked to be about 5 feet in size, and making allowance for the distance it was from town he figured that it must have been 15 to 20 feet in diameter, though this was just a guess.

Wilmot said that he heard no sound but that Mrs. Wilmot said she heard a swishing sound for a very short time.

The object came into view from the southeast and disappeared over the treetops in the general vicinity of six mile hill.

Wilmot, who is one of the most respected and reliable citizens in town, kept the story to himself hoping that someone else would come out and tell about having seen one, but finally today decided that he would go ahead and tell about it. The announcement that the RAAF was in possession of one came only a few minutes after he decided to release the details of what he had seen.

Further Resources
BOOKS

Booker, M. Keith. *Monsters, Mushroom Clouds, and the Cold War: American Science Fiction and the Roots of Postmodernism, 1946–1964.* Westport, Conn.: Greenwood, 2001.

Clark, Jerome. *The Emergence of a Phenomenon—UFOs from the Beginning Through 1959.* Detroit: Omnigraphics, 1992.

McAndrew, James. *The Roswell Report: Case Closed: Executive Summary.* Washington, D.C.: U.S. Air Force, 1997.

Peebles, Curtis. *Watch the Skies!: A Chronicle of the Flying Saucer Myth.* Washington, D.C.: Smithsonian Institution Press, 1994.

The Roswell Report: Fact Versus Fiction in the New Mexico Desert. Washington, D.C.: U.S. Air Force, 1995.

Levittown, New York

Photographs

By: William J. Levitt

Date: April 13, 1949; May 14, 1954

Source: Green, Arthur. "Levittown, New York Seen from Above." April 13, 1949. Corbis. Image no. U901794ACME; Bettmann/Corbis. "Houses In Levittown, Long Island." May 14, 1954. Corbis. Image no. BE041725. Available online at http://pro.corbis.com (accessed March 27, 2003).

About the Architect: William J. Levitt (1907–1994) attended New York University for three years before joining his father's construction company. He eventually came to manage the organization, finances, advertising, sales, and land transactions of the company. Levitt's first housing development was begun during the early years of the Great Depression. His initial attempts to enter the field of low-cost housing were unsuccessful, but by 1947 his first mass-

Primary Source

Levittown, New York (1 OF 2)

SYNOPSIS: The following photographs present different views of Levittown's legendary tract housing. Founded in 1947, Levittown, with its affordable housing and proximity to New York City, set the standard by which future suburbs would be judged. This photo features an aerial view of Levittown. UPI/CORBIS-BETTMANN. REPRODUCED BY PERMISSION.

Primary Source

Levittown, New York (2 OF 2)
There were only two models for houses in the Long Island Levittown, but many homeowners chose different colors for brick or roofing, and made other modifications to distinguish their home from their neighbor's. © BETTMAN/CORBIS. REPRODUCED BY PERMISSION.

produced housing development, Levittown, opened on Long Island, New York. ■

Introduction

The United States has been called the "First New Nation" because it left behind the long-standing historical legacies of the older nations of Europe and had an opportunity to begin everything afresh in a spirit of innovation and experimentation. This great historical saga

was in some sense repeated in microcosm in the story of Levittown. It was a replay of the story of the *Mayflower* on a more mundane but nonetheless humanly significant scale. Just as the Puritans had been looking to establish a "shining city upon a hill," the servicemen returning from World War II (1939–1945) were also hoping for a future life of peace and prosperity. Now was the time to achieve the "American dream." And the character of this dream has been shaped by U.S. history itself.

It has been a long tradition in the United States to be suspicious of the "big city." Thomas Jefferson's experience in Paris had taught him that large urban centers become the home of vice, corruption, violence, and despotism. But by the turn of the twentieth century, the United States had become one of the world's leading industrial powers and Jefferson's dream of an agrarian republic had attained the status of an American myth.

William Levitt's contribution was to imagine a compromise between this historical American agrarianism and the demands of postwar industrial society. His answer was the modern suburb.

Levitt's mass-produced suburban houses brought the landed estate of the gentry to the ordinary working man and his family. No longer would such families be packed into the crowded tenement houses of the big city. Rather, they would live comfortably in a dwelling to which they had title and which they were free to adapt to their own purposes within the limits of location and space.

Significance

The homogeneity and interchangeability of such living accommodations has been a subject of criticism from the outset. American folk singer Pete Seeger expressed his contempt for bourgeois, suburban life in the 1960s when he sang, "Little boxes, little boxes, little boxes all the same . . . And they all get put in boxes, little boxes all the same . . . and they're all made out of ticky-tacky and they all look just the same." This has been the persistent complaint of the bohemian-intellectual class about suburban life and its alleged lack of culture, character, and sophistication. But this criticism is at the same time a hearkening back to the Jeffersonian ideal of freedom and independence, which is in part the inspiration for the very Levittown of which they are so critical. But Seeger had perhaps forgotten that which Levitt in fact confronted: a workable solution to the housing problem is the best way to deal with the question of self-sufficient, "individualized" living for Americans.

With thousands of servicemen returning from the war to begin their lives anew, the pressing practical question was how to find large numbers of people decent accommodation under modern conditions of space and transportation. Levitt's suburb was a practical and pragmatic answer. The Levittown phenomenon changed the American city by giving rise to the suburban lifestyle. Workers commuted to city jobs during the week and returned to spend evenings and weekends in residential areas. As the decades progressed, suburbs of suburbs developed until so-called urban sprawl resulted. As a result, ever-larger cities spread across expanding miles and no longer had central downtown areas, distinctive personalities, or a unifying sense of community. Those who could afford to abandoned the traditional city for neighborhoods with people of similar social, ethnic, economic, and religious backgrounds.

The rise of the Levittown-inspired suburbs also significantly altered many consumer trends. Commuting into the city for work, for example, required a car. The automobile industry thrived in concert with the rise of suburbia. High-tech, electrical household appliances also became fashionable. Where once the theater, cinemas, and other city events provided entertainment, now radios and televisions became necessary to bring music, drama, and even advertising to the American home. U.S. consumer spending in effect reordered itself around the reality of suburban life.

The innovations of Levittown, therefore, made a quality of life available to ordinary people which had been unthinkable to earlier generations. Levitt's vision of a new way of living for a new era was a model of American practical intelligence responding to difficult circumstances and novel needs. The innovation represented by Levittown in due course led to the baby boom, which had such a huge demographic impact on American society. In one of those historical paradoxes that sometimes distinguish American life, today's baby boomers who are heading for retirement may be destined for a seniors' Levittown in the Sunbelt or for an "empty-nester" condominium in the heart of the city from which their parents moved years before.

Further Resources

BOOKS
Duncan, Susan Kirsch. *Levittown: The Way We Were.* Huntington, N.Y.: Maple Hill Press, 1999.

Gans, Herbert. *The Levittowners: Ways of Life and Politics in a New Suburban Community.* New York: Pantheon, 1967. Reprinted New York: Columbia Univeristy Press, 1982.

Jackson, Kenneth T. *Crabgrass Frontier: The Suburbanization of the United States.* Oxford, England: Oxford University Press, 1987.

Martinson, Tom. *American Dreamscape: The Pursuit of Happiness in Postwar Suburbia.* New York: Carrol & Graf, 2000.

Navarra, Tova, et al. *Levittown: The First Fifty Years.* Gloucestershire, England: Arcadia Tempus, 1997.

PERIODICALS
Harvey, Dennis. "Chronicle of an American Suburb." *Variety,* April 8–14, 2002, 32.

Holohan, Dan. "The Treasure That Is Levittown." *PM Engineer,* February 2002, 26–28.

WEBSITES
"Levittown: Documents of an Ideal American Suburb." University of Illinois, Chicago. Available online at http://tigger.uic.edu/~pbhales/Levittown.html; website home page: http://tigger.uic.edu (accessed March 8, 2003).

"Levittown at Fifty." Long Island: Our Story. Available online at http://www.lihistory.com/specsec/levmain.htm; website home page: http://www.lihistory.com (accessed March 8, 2003).

AUDIO AND VISUAL MEDIA
Reynolds, Malvina. "Little Boxes." As performed by Pete Seeger on the album *Pete Seeger at Carnegie Hall.* Smithsonian/Folkways, 1963.

8

THE MEDIA

DAN PROSTERMAN

Entries are arranged in chronological order by date of primary source. For entries with one primary source, the entry title is the same as the primary source title. Entries with more than one primary source have an overall entry title, followed by the titles of the primary sources.

Important Events in the Media, 1940–1949

1940

- On January 5, Edwin H. Armstrong demonstrates high-fidelity radio, broadcast in frequency modulation (FM), over station WIMOJ in Worcester, Massachusetts.

- In February, *Whiz Comics,* introducing C.C. Beck's Captain Marvel, is published.

- On February 12, the radio show *Superman* begins, providing the source for such lines as "Up, up, and away!" and "This looks like a job for Superman!"

- In spring, the first issue of *Batman* is published.

- On March 20, Radio Corporation of America (RCA) begins a publicity campaign for broadcasts of the visual technology, television, which it hopes to begin September 1, 1940.

- On April 8, the Federal Communications Commission (FCC) begins hearings to determine whether RCA has a monopoly on television technology and manufacturing. On May 28, it condemns RCA's monopolistic practices.

- On May 20, the FCC authorizes commercial FM radio stations to begin broadcasting January 1, 1941.

- In June, Will Eisner's *The Spirit* debuts as a weekly comic book distributed in newspapers.

- On September 4, the Columbia Broadcasting System (CBS) demonstrates color television transmission over its New York station, W2XAB.

- On November 5, election returns are telecast for the first time.

1941

- On January 16, in an important licensing decision, the FCC forbids partisan political activities by broadcasters, asserting that "the broadcaster cannot be an advocate."

- On February 26, the Justice Department drops its antitrust suit against the American Society of Composers, Authors and Publishers (ASCAP) following the signing of a consent decree that opens the field of royalty collections to a new company, Broadcast Music Incorporated (BMI).

- In March, Captain America is created by Joe Simon and Jack Kirby for *Timely Comics.*

- From March to April, Blondie and Dagwood Bumstead become parents for a second time in Chic Young's *Blondie.* The baby girl is named Cookie by one of the 431,275 readers who submit names in a contest.

- Parents Magazine Institute, concerned about the amount of fantasy in comic books, offers the first issue of *True Comics,* with stories about historic events and real-life heroes. It is the first educational comic book.

- On May 2, the FCC issues a study, *Report on Chain Broadcasting,* calling for sweeping changes to combat monopolies in the ownership of radio stations and networks.

- On May 3, the FCC establishes industrywide standards for television manufacturing and broadcasting.

- On June 25, RCA introduces the Orthicon Television Camera, a vast improvement over previous television cameras.

- In fall, Archie makes his comic-book debut.

- In fall, *Ellery Queen's Mystery* magazine appears on the newsstands.

- In October, Gilberton Comics introduces comic-book adaptations of literary works in *Classic Comics*; the name is later changed to *Classics Illustrated.*

- On November 13, National Broadcasting Corporation (NBC) and Mutual Broadcasting Service cancel broadcasts by Berlin correspondents due to Nazi censorship; the following day, the German government bans broadcasts by NBC, Mutual, and CBS reporters.

- On November 20, *Reader's Digest* announces that its circulation has reached a record 5 million.

- In December, Walt Kelly's Pogo is introduced in *Animal Comics.*

- In December, Charles Moulton's Wonder Woman debuts.

- On December 8, after the Japanese attack on Pearl Harbor, amateur radio stations are shut down for the duration of World War II.

- On December 19, the Office of Censorship is established to supervise voluntary self-censorship by newspapers, magazines, films, and radio broadcasts.

1942

- *Business Week* estimates that the comic-book industry is enjoying sales of $15 million a year.

- On January 15, the National Association of Broadcasters (NAB) issues its "Code of Wartime Practices for American Broadcasters," guidelines for stations regarding the reporting of war news and information.

- On February 23, the FCC announces that no new radio or television station permits will be issued for the duration of the war in order to channel construction and electronic equipment toward military purposes.

- In spring, Crockett Johnson's comic strip *Barnaby* debuts.

- On April 17, *Stars and Stripes* begins publishing from England.

- On June 13, President Roosevelt establishes the Office of War Information to control official news and propaganda. Elmer Davis, a newspaper writer and radio commentator, is placed in charge.

- In November, *Negro Digest* debuts.

- In December, the A.C. Nielsen company introduces a mechanical box attached to radios to determine which programs have the most listeners. The device becomes the basis of the radio and television ratings system.

1943

- On January 1, *Time* magazine selects Joseph Stalin as its Man of the Year for 1942.

- On May 10, in *NBC v. the United States,* the U.S. Supreme Court upholds the right of the FCC to regulate broadcasting.

- On December 10, revised censorship codes give the U.S. government greater control over the dissemination of information.

- On December 30, charging the magazine with obscenity, the postmaster general announces that *Esquire's* second-class postage privileges will be revoked. On January 21, 1944, *Esquire* sues to prevent the postmaster from doing so.

1944

- *Seventeen* magazine debuts.

- On September 28, the Radio Technical Planning Board (RTPB) of the FCC begins hearings with the leaders of the electronic, broadcast, and defense industries to determine postwar allocation of the electromagnetic spectrum and to determine how to introduce new broadcast technologies to the public.

- On October 8, *Ozzie and Harriet* debuts on CBS radio.

1945

- On April 12, the death of Franklin D. Roosevelt, who used radio effectively in his "fireside chats," is the first death to receive extensive broadcast coverage.

- On May 18, after V-E Day, the Office of Censorship lifts many of its restrictions on news from Europe.

- On June 4, the U.S. Court of Appeals in Washington, D.C., voids the postmaster general's revocation of *Esquire's* second-class postage privileges.

- On June 27, the RTPB issues its final report on the division of the electromagnetic spectrum, assigning television spectrum bandwidths in the very high and ultrahigh frequency ranges, from 44 to 216 MHz.

- On August 22, after the Japanese defeat, the FCC allows amateur radio stations to resume operations.

- In November, *Ebony* magazine is founded by John H. Johnson.

1946

- RCA markets its 630TS television to consumers; the ten-inch set sells for $374.

- On March 7, the FCC issues its report, *Public Service Responsibility of Broadcast Licensees,* defining the parameters of public conduct for broadcasters, including limits to advertising, local obligations, and political fairness.

- On April 16, President Harry S. Truman signs the Lea Act, limiting the legal power of labor unions in the broadcasting industry.

- On August 31, *The New Yorker* devotes an entire issue to John Hersey's *Hiroshima.*

1947

- In January, Milton Caniff begins a new comic strip, *Steve Canyon,* two weeks after ending work on *Terry and the Pirates.*

- In May, American Business Consultants, a for-profit anti-Communist group, begins publication of its *Counterattack* newsletter, which will aid in widespread blacklisting of suspected communist-sympathizers.

- On October 2, the International Telecommunications Union meets in Atlantic City to discuss issues of international channel allocation and interference.

- On October 5, the president uses the new medium of television to speak to the American public for the first time.

1948

- Peter Goldmark develops the first long-playing record.

- The communist weekly, *New Masses,* suspends publication.

- On January 7, *United States News* announces a merger with *World Report.*

- In summer, both the Democratic and Republican Party conventions are televised.

- On June 29, the Audience Research branch of the Gallup Poll reports that 354,000 television sets are in use in the United States.

- In July, in response to criticism over the growing number of crime comics and over scantily clad women in comics, a handful of comic-book publishers form the Association of Comics Magazine Publishers and establish a code of standards in order to encourage self-regulation in the face of possible censorship. The effort is ignored by most comic-book publishers.

- On September 29, due to increased television interference, the FCC suspends licensing of new television stations. The "temporary" freeze on television lasts nearly four years.

- On October 4, Walt Kelly's *Pogo* first appears in the *New York Star.*

1949

- On January 20, President Truman's inauguration is telecast.

- On June 1, the FCC issues guidelines regarding the presentation of news and editorializing to broadcasters, asserting that editorializing should occur only after broadcasters have presented "all reasonable viewpoints" to the public.

- In fall, the *Magazine of Fantasy and Science Fiction* appears for the first time.

"London Blitz: September 1940"

Radio broadcast

By: Edward R. Murrow

Date: September 18, 21, and 22, 1940

Source: Murrow, Edward R. "London Blitz: September 1940." Radio transcript. Reprinted in Hynes, Samuel et al., eds. *Reporting World War II: Part One, American Journalism, 1938–1944.* New York: Library of America, 1995.

About the Author: Born Egbert Roscoe Murrow (1908–1965) in rural North Carolina, Edward R. Murrow became a true pioneer in broadcast journalism. He worked first in radio, gaining worldwide acclaim for his dramatic broadcasts during the London Blitz, then moved to the emerging medium of television after World War II (1939–1945). Murrow died of lung cancer on April 27, 1965, at the age of 57. Numerous awards are now named for the famed journalist, who remains the most revered broadcaster in the history of news reporting. ■

CBS correspondent Edward R. Murrow at his typewriter during World War II. Murrow's broadcasts from London during the Blitz brought the war home to Americans. © BETTMANN/CORBIS. REPRODUCED BY PERMISSION.

Introduction

By the fall of 1940 Germany had successfully invaded Poland and France, leaving Great Britain and Russia as the only opposition to a Hitler-led Europe. On the evening of September 7, 1940, the German Air Force *(Luftwaffe)* began a nightly bombing campaign against London, England, designed to destroy the British fighting spirit and weaken defenses against a German military takeover. These raids continued for 57 consecutive nights and did not stop altogether until May 10, 1941. The air raids killed more than 13,000 Londoners, destroyed more than 200,000 homes, and nearly resulted in the fall of Great Britain to Germany.

During Hitler's takeover of Austria in 1937, CBS cultural broadcast coordinator Edward R. Murrow offered his first of 5,000 broadcasts to the American public. Following the start of World War II in Europe in 1939 American journalists struggled to maintain a safe distance from German-occupied territory while getting close enough to report the terrible struggle. Murrow moved to London to cover the war with an elite troop of journalists. The "Murrow Boys," as they came to be known, in-

cluded some of the foremost figures in broadcast journalism history—Eric Sevareid, William L. Shirer, Charles C. Collingwood, and Howard K. Smith. This band of reporters would provide the American public with some of the most consistently vital and vivid reporting of World War II.

Significance

For Americans World War II in 1940 was still a "European conflict." Pearl Harbor was more than one year away and isolationist sentiment governed policymaking. The *Luftwaffe*'s attacks against London began to change how Americans perceived the war. President Franklin D. Roosevelt (served 1933–1945) first provided Britain with armaments in response to the Blitz.

Murrow's reports from bomb-riddled London offered Americans terrifying, first-hand descriptions of the German air raids. The journalist spoke to his audience from rooftops overlooking the devastated city, from air-raid shelters crammed with civilians whose homes had been destroyed, with bomb after bomb exploding in the background—"Now you'll hear two bursts a little nearer in a moment. There they are! That hard, stony sound."

Murrow's reporting style foreshadowed later coverage of the Vietnam and Gulf wars, as he brought the war into American's homes night after night after night. Using emotional but concise, steady language and a serious tone, Murrow forged an inescapable connection between the war raging in Europe and his audience in the United States.

Murrow's coverage brought him stature on both sides of the Atlantic that endured long after the war. Recruited by both the BBC in London and CBS in New York, he developed television programs based on lengthy interviews with popular figures as well as in-depth investigations of important issues in the postwar world. These programs for CBS News served as the precursors to modern television newsmagazine programs. Murrow was awarded the Presidential Medal of Freedom in 1964 and an honorary knighthood by Great Britain in the year of his death, 1965.

Primary Source

"London Blitz: September 1940" [excerpt]

SYNOPSIS: The following three reports, transcribed exactly as they were delivered, provide succinct examples of how Murrow reported the Blitz. Broadcast just as the air raids began in September 1940, these reports convey the immediate context in which Murrow, and millions of Londoners, lived and worked. In two of the scripts the journalists are standing on a rooftop, peering over the London skyline moments after German bombers have descended upon the city in waves. The stark newscasts provided haunting depictions for Americans just beginning to comprehend the global reach of the so-called "European war."

September 18, 1940

I'd like to say one or two things about the reporting of this air war against London. No one person can see it all. The communiqués are sparing of information because details of damage would assist the Germans. No one can check by personal observation the damage done during a single night or a single week. It would take a lifetime to traverse the streets of this city, but there's a greater problem involved; it's one of language. There are no words to describe the thing that is happening. Today I talked with eight American correspondents in London. Six of them had been forced to move—all had stories of bombs and all agreed that they were unable to convey through print or the spoken word an accurate impression of what's happening in London these days and nights. I may tell you that Bond Street has been bombed; that a shop selling handkerchiefs at $40 the dozen has been wrecked; that these words

were written on a table of good English oak which sheltered me three times as bombs tore down in the vicinity, but you can have little understanding of the life in London these days—the courage of the people; the flash and roar of the guns rolling down streets where much of the history of the English-speaking world has been made; the stench of air-raid shelters in the poor districts. These things must be experienced to be understood.

A woman inspecting a sweater, taking it to the bright sunlight shining through a smashed skylight for close inspection. A row of automobiles, with stretchers racked on the roofs like skis, standing outside of bombed buildings. A man pinned under wreckage where a broken gas main sears his arm and face. These things must be seen if the whole impact of this war is to be felt.

If we talk at times of the little flashes of humor that appear in this twilight of suffering, you must understand that there is humor in these people, even when disaster and hell come down from heaven. We can only tell you what we see and hear.

The individual's reaction to the sound of falling bombs cannot be described. The moan of stark terror and suspense cannot be encompassed by words, no more can the sense of relief when you realize that you weren't where that one fell. It's pleasant to pick yourself up out of the gutter without the aid of a searcher party. Between bombing one catches glimpses of the London one knew in the distant days of peace. The big red busses roll through the streets. The tolling of Big Ben can be heard in the intervals of the gunfire. The little French and Italian restaurants in Soho bring out their whitest linens and polish their glass and silver for the two or three guests who brave the blackout, the bombs, and the barrage. There are advertisements in the papers extolling the virtues of little rubber ear plugs which prevent one from hearing the bombs and guns. In many buildings tonight people are sleeping on mattresses on the floor. I've seen dozens of them looking like dolls thrown aside by a tired child. In three or four hours they must get up and go to work just as though they had had a full night's rest, free from the rumble of guns and the wonder that comes when they wake and listen in the dead hours of the night.

September 21, 1940

I'm standing on a rooftop looking out over London. At the moment everything is quiet. For reasons of national as well as personal security, I'm unable to tell you the exact location from which I'm speaking. Off to my left, far away in the distance, I can see just that faint-red, angry snap of antiaircraft bursts against the steel-blue sky, but the guns are so far away that it's impossible to hear them from this location. About five minutes ago the guns in the immediate vicinity were working. I can look across just at a building not far away and see something that looks like a flash of white paint down the side, and I know from daylight observation that about a quarter of that building has disappeared—hit by a bomb the other night. Streets fan out in all directions from here, and down on one street I can see a single red light and just faintly the outline of a sign standing in the middle of the street. And again I know what that sign says, because I saw it this afternoon. It says DANGER—UNEXPLODED BOMB. Off to my left still I can see just that red snap of the antiaircraft fire.

I was up here earlier this afternoon and looking out over these housetops, looking all the way to the dome of St. Paul's. I saw many flags flying from staffs. No one ordered these people to put out the flag. They simply feel like flying the Union Jack above their roof. No one told them to do it, and no flag up there was white. I can see one or two of them just stirring very faintly in the breeze now. You may be able to hear the sound of guns off in the distance very faintly, like someone kicking a tub. Now they're silent. Four searchlights reach up, disappear in the light of a three-quarter moon. I should say at the moment there are probably three aircraft in the general vicinity of London, as one can tell by the movement of the lights and the flash of the antiaircraft guns. But at the moment in the central area everything is quiet. More searchlights spring up over on my right. I think probably in a minute we shall have the sound of guns in the immediate vicinity. The lights are swinging over in this general direction now. You'll hear two explosions. There they are! That was the explosion overhead, not the guns themselves. I should think in a few minutes there may be a bit of shrapnel around here. Coming in—moving a little closer all the while. The plane's still very high. Earlier this evening we could hear occasional . . . again those were explosions overhead. Earlier this evening we heard a number of bombs go sliding and slithering across to fall several blocks away. Just overhead now the burst of the antiaircraft fire. Still the near-by guns are not working. The searchlights now are feeling almost directly overhead. Now you'll hear two bursts a little nearer in a moment. There they are! That hard, stony sound.

September 22, 1940

I'm standing again tonight on a rooftop looking out over London, feeling rather large and lonesome. In the course of the last fifteen or twenty minutes there's been considerable action up there, but at the moment there's an ominous silence hanging over London. But at the same time a silence that has a great deal of dignity. Just straightaway in front of me the searchlights are working. I can see one or two bursts of antiaircraft fire far in the distance. Just on the roof across the way I can see a man standing wearing a tin hat, with a pair of powerful night glasses to his eyes, scanning the sky. Again looking in the opposite direction there is a building with two windows gone. Out of one window there waves something that looks like a white bed sheet, a window curtain swinging free in this night breeze. It looks as though it were being shaken by a ghost. There are a great many ghosts around these buildings in London. The searchlights straightaway, miles in front of me, are still searching that sky. There's a three-quarter moon riding high. There was one burst of shell-fire almost straight in the Little Dipper. The guns are too far away to be heard.

Down below in the streets I can see just that red and green wink of the traffic lights; one lone taxicab moving slowly down the street. Not a sound to be heard. As I look out across the miles and miles of rooftops and chimney pots, some of those dirty-gray fronts of the buildings look almost snow white in this moonlight here tonight. And the rooftop spotter across the way swings around, looks over in the direction of the searchlights, drops his glasses, and just stands there. There are hundreds and hundreds of men like that standing on rooftops in London tonight watching for fire bombs, waiting to see what comes out of this steel-blue sky. The searchlights now reach up very, very faintly on three sides of me. There is a flash of a gun in the distance, but too far away to be heard.

Further Resources
BOOKS
Cloud, Stanley. *The Murrow Boys: Pioneers on the Front Lines of Broadcast Journalism.* Boston: Houghton Mifflin, 1996.

Hynes, Samuel et al., eds. *Reporting World War II: Part One, American Journalism, 1938–1944.* New York: Library of America, 1995.

———. *Reporting World War II: Part Two, American Journalism, 1944–1945.* New York: Library of America, 1995.

Persico, Joseph E. *Edward R. Murrow: An American Original.* New York: McGraw-Hill, 1988.

Sperber, A.M. *Murrow: His Life and Times.* New York: Freundlich Books, 1986.

WEBSITES

American National Biography. Available online at http://www .anb.org (accessed July 30, 2002).

"Murrow, Edward R." *The Museum of Broadcast Communications.* Available online at http://www.museum.tv/archives /etv/M/htmlM/murrowedwar/murrowedwar.htm (accessed July 30, 2002).

AUDIO AND VISUAL MEDIA

"Edward (Egburt) Roscoe Murrow." Old Time Radio (OTR). Available online at http://www.otr.com/murrow.html (accessed July 30, 2002).

"WWII News and Speeches: 1938–Dec. 1941." The Authentic History Center. Available online at http://www .authentichistory.com/audio/ww2/ww2_1938-1941_04 .html (accessed July 30, 2002).

Captain America, No. 1
Comic book

By: Joe Simon and Jack Kirby

Date: March 1941

Source: Simon, Joe, and Jack Kirby. *Captain America,* No. 1, March 1941. Reprinted in Spillane, Mickey, et al. *Golden Age of Marvel, Vol. 2.* New York: Marvel Comics, 1999.

About the Authors: Joe Simon wrote and Jack Kirby (1918–1994) illustrated some of the most vibrant comic books of the 1940s, the "Golden Age" of comics. The pair created Captain America, the embodiment of American ideals and patriotism, and continued working for Marvel Comics until the comic book industry failed after the end of World War II (1939–1945). Kirby and Simon resurrected their careers as the comic business boomed again in the 1960s, the beginning of the "Silver Age" of comic books . Along with Marvel icon Stan Lee, Kirby developed several characters whose popularity continues to the present, including the Incredible Hulk, the Fantastic Four, and the X-Men. Kirby died at the age of 76 on February 6, 1994. Simon has continued in comics for more than 50 years, sketching comic art at his residence in New York City. He lost his legal battle with Marvel Comics over the copyright for Captain America in March 2002. Sold for a dime in 1941, a near pristine copy of *Captain America,* No. 1, sold for $265,000 in 2000. ∎

Introduction

Coming on the heels of the comic book boom created by Jerry Siegel and Joe Schuster in the late 1930s, Joe Simon and Jack Kirby encountered an audience eager for new comics. By 1941 DC Comics' Superman and Batman titles each sold more than one million copies per issue. Timely Comics, later to become Marvel Comics, offered Americans superheroes designed precisely to protect them against the Axis powers (Germany, Italy, and Japan).

By March 1941 Germany had overtaken France and much of Eastern Europe and Japan increasingly threat-

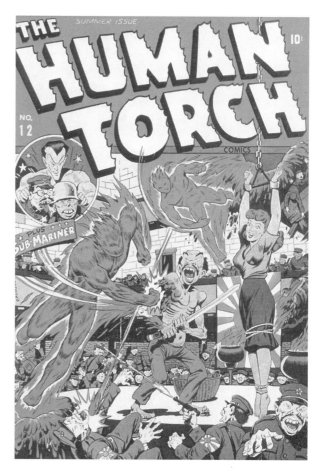

The cover of *Human Torch,* No. 12, vividly depicts the hero burning the flesh from the arm of a Japanese swordsman. The hero and his companion rain fire onto their enemies in a macabre foreshadowing of the firebombings of Tokyo and the atomic attacks on Hiroshima and Nagasaki in 1945. **COVER OF *HUMAN TORCH,* NO. 12, SUMMER, 1943, PHOTOGRAPH. TM & © 2002 MARVEL CHARACTERS, INC. REPRODUCED BY PERMISSION.**

ened American installations in the Pacific. The public continued to debate whether they should enter the war. Simon and Kirby's Captain America would not play the waiting game. Instead, this character gave Americans a forceful hero who never wavered in his struggle for democracy and freedom.

Significance

In stark opposition to the isolationist argument that the United States probably would lose a war with Germany, *Captain America,* No. 1, depicted "Cap" socking Hitler in the jaw. Drawn by Kirby in a dynamic artistic style, Captain America virtually leapt from the pages in full color and constant action. The power he conveyed was no accident. According to Joe Simon, a Jew, this superhero presented him with a way to express his hatred of the Nazis. Published months prior to Pearl Harbor, *Captain America,* No. 1, and other comics articulated the

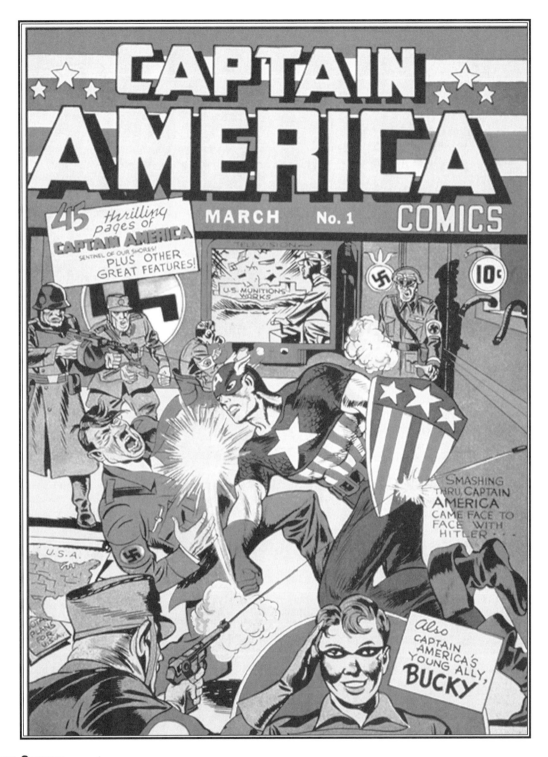

Primary Source

Captain America, No. 1 [excerpt] (1 OF 4)

SYNOPSIS: As with other propaganda pieces of the early 1940s, the following comic book excerpt provides modern readers with a sense of how Americans distinguished between their German and Japanese foes. Captain America battles cunning, technologically advanced Germans; here, Captain America punches Hitler in the jaw on the cover of *Captain America*, No. 1, March 1941. COVER OF *CAPTAIN AMERICA*, NO. 1, MARCH 1941, PHOTOGRAPH. TM & © 2002 MARVEL CHARACTERS, INC. REPRODUCED BY PERMISSION.

Primary Source

Captain America, No. 1 [excerpt] (2 OF 4)
The first page from *Captain America*, No. 1, March 1941. CAPTAIN AMERICA, NO. 1, MARCH 1941, PHOTOGRAPH. TM & © 2002 MARVEL CHARACTERS, INC. REPRODUCED BY PERMISSION.

Primary Source

Captain America, No. 1 [excerpt] (3 of 4)

Page 8 of *Captain America,* March 1941. Young sidekicks in the comics, like Bucky, were meant to give the boys who bought comics a character they could relate to directly. CAPTAIN AMERICA, "MEMBER SENTINELS OF LIBERTY," NO. 1, MARCH 1941, PHOTOGRAPH. TM & © 2002 MARVEL CHARACTERS, INC. REPRODUCED BY PERMISSION.

Primary Source

Captain America, No. 1 [excerpt] (4 OF 4)
A panel from the first issue of *Captain America.* From the beginning, Captain America's mission was to protect the United States against attempts to undermine its way of life, both overt and covert. CAPTAIN AMERICA, "CAPTAIN AMERICA CAPTURES SPY RING!" NO. 1, MARCH 1941, PHOTOGRAPH. TM & © 2002 MARVEL CHARACTERS, INC. REPRODUCED BY PERMISSION.

realization held by many that joining World War II would be inevitable. According to Simon and other interventionists, avoiding the war only served to strengthen the opposition and would make the battle that much harder when it eventually came.

In fact, the plot of Captain America's first issue may be regarded as a rallying cry for the American public to support the war effort. The story focused directly on the belief that the Axis powers sought to destroy America. Faced with "the danger of foreign attack," Americans also needed to defend against "the threat of invasion from within . . . the dreaded fifth column." As a result, Kirby and Simon declared, Americans must "heed the call to arm for defense." The final page of this comic book even provided young readers with a means of supporting this cause by joining "Captain America's Sentinel of Liberty" and helping Cap "in his war against the spies and enemies in our midst who threaten our very independence." In an atmosphere rife with debates over the United States's role in global affairs, *Captain America,* No. 1, provided a clear argument for brave, patriotic support of bold intervention.

Further Resources

BOOKS

Goulart, Ron. *Comic Book Culture: An Illustrated History.* Portland, Ore.: Collectors Press, 2000.

Lee, Stan. *Origins of Marvel Comics.* New York: Simon & Schuster, 1976.

Simon, Joe, and Jim Simon, *The Comic Book Makers.* Stoneham, Mass.: Vanguard Productions, 2002.

Spillane, Mickey et al. *Golden Age of Marvel, Vol. 2.* New York: Marvel Comics, 1999.

PERIODICALS

"Jack Kirby, 76; Created Comic-Book Superheroes." *The New York Times,* February 8, 1994.

Sacks, Ethan. "Comic Books Imitate Life; WTC Attack Changes the Myth." *New York Daily News,* October 31, 2001.

WEB SITES

American National Biography Online. Available online at http://www.anb.org (accessed July 30, 2002).

Goldenagecomix.com. Available online at http://www .goldenagecomix.com (accessed July 30, 2002).

"The Jack Kirby Collector." *Twomorrows Publishing.* Available online at http://www.twomorrows.com/kirby/jack.html (accessed July 30, 2002).

Simon Entertainment Properties. Available online at http:// www.simoncomics.com (accessed July 30, 2002).

Isolationist Speeches by Charles Lindbergh

Speeches

By: Charles Lindbergh
Date: April 23, 1941; September 11, 1941
Source: Lindbergh, Charles. America First Speeches Advocating Isolationism. New York, New York, April 23, 1941; Des Moines, Iowa, September 11, 1941. Reprinted online

at Ranfranz, Patrick, ed. Charles Lindbergh: An American Aviator. http://www.charleslindbergh.com (accessed March 26, 2003).

About the Author: The son of a Minnesota congressman, Charles A. Lindbergh (1902–1974) emerged as one of the most popular figures in the United States in 1927, when he became the first pilot to fly solo, nonstop, across the Atlantic Ocean. The life of an American idol, though, proved to be far from safe and secure. In March 1932 Lindbergh's baby was kidnapped, and the ensuing media maelstrom forced Charles and his wife to flee the country. Lindbergh returned to the United States following the outbreak of World War II (1939–1945) in Europe and became a prominent spokesman for isolationism. After serving in the Pacific he won a Pulitzer Prize for his account of his transatlantic flight. Late in life Lindbergh became an ardent conservationist, touring the globe to argue that aviation and air travel actually harmed the environment. A pioneer in world aviation, Lindbergh died at the age of 72 on August 26, 1974. The *Spirit of St. Louis,* the plane he flew across the Atlantic in 1927, hangs in the Smithsonian Institution Air and Space Museum in Washington, D.C. ∎

Introduction

Seeking privacy from the spectacle surrounding the manhunt, trial, and execution of his baby's kidnapper, Lindbergh toured the military installations of several European nations in the 1930s. Germany's Nazi regime invited Lindbergh to inspect its air force and awarded the American with the Service Cross of the German Eagle in 1938. During his several inspections, Lindbergh became convinced that the German military, particularly its air force, was unstoppable. These opinions, along with his amiable relations with the Nazis, fueled his isolationist belief that the United States should avoid allying with Britain against Germany in World War II (1939–1945). Charles and his wife returned to the United States in April 1939, eager to avoid the oncoming European war—Germany had already taken over Austria and Czechoslovakia and would invade Poland only four months later. The Lindberghs returned to a tense nation, rife with debate over whether to enter the global conflict.

Significance

Founded in September 1940, the America First Committee quickly grew to become the leading isolationist group in the United States, possessing nearly one million official members at the height of its popularity. Lindbergh joined the organization in April 1941 and offered the following, nationally broadcast address in support of isolationism. The speech immediately positioned Lindbergh as the America First Committee's most prominent member—and interventionists' most ardent foe. In the speech, Lindbergh bluntly asserted that the "we should not enter a war unless we have a reasonable chance of winning" and "that the United States is not prepared to wage war in Europe successfully at this time."

Lindbergh's conclusion that the war was unwinnable caused another media frenzy for the flier, as interventionists attacked him as unpatriotic and pro-German. The United States' most famous aviator resigned his military commission following criticism by President Franklin D. Roosevelt (served 1933–1945) and then struggled to reenlist following the attack on Pearl Harbor in December 1941. The America First Committee dissolved less than one week after the attack and isolationist sentiment ended. Finally able to rejoin the military as an adviser in the Pacific, Lindbergh eagerly volunteered for more than fifty combat missions.

Primary Source

Isolationist Speeches by Charles Lindbergh

SYNOPSIS: Having recently joined the America First Committee in April 1941, Charles Lindbergh addresses an audience in New York City to offer his argument for U.S. non-intervention in World War II. Listened to live by millions of Americans, the speech would deepen the divide between isolationists and interventionists. Lindbergh concludes the address by admonishing listeners to avoid succumbing to the mass media's calls for war. With the likes of Lindbergh, Edward R. Murrow, Captain America, and Dr. Seuss influencing the American public, it would take the Japanese attack on Pearl Harbor in December 1941 to finally close the issue and bring the nation fully behind a massive war effort. Delivered on September 11, 1941, Lindbergh's controversial speech in Des Moines, Iowa, backfired, greatly harming the America First Committee and the broader isolationist movement. Critics of America First had long argued that anti-Semitism and pro-German ideology drove isolationism. Lindbergh's characterization of Jews in this speech stoked these criticisms and even caused many of Lindbergh's sympathizers to distance themselves from the aviator and his cause.

New York City Speech

There are many viewpoints from which the issues of this war can be argued. Some are primarily idealistic. Some are primarily practical. One should, I believe, strive for a balance of both. But, since the subjects that can be covered in a single address are limited, tonight I shall discuss the war from a viewpoint which is primarily practical. It is not that I believe ideals are unimportant, even among the realities of war; but if a nation is to survive in a hostile world, its ideals must be backed by the hard logic of military practicability. If the outcome of war depended upon ideals alone, this would be a different world than it is today.

I know I will be severely criticized by the interventionists in America when I say we should not en-

Charles Lindbergh delivers his speech at the America First Rally in Manhattan Center, April 25, 1941. AP/WIDE WORLD PHOTOS. REPRODUCED BY PERMISSION.

ter a war unless we have a reasonable chance of winning. That, they will claim, is far too materialistic a viewpoint. They will advance again the same arguments that were used to persuade France to declare war against Germany in 1939. But I do not believe that our American ideals, and our way of life, will gain through an unsuccessful war. And I know that the United States is not prepared to wage war in Europe successfully at this time. We are no better prepared today than France was when the interventionists in Europe persuaded her to attack the Siegfried Line.

I have said before, and I will say again, that I believe it will be a tragedy to the entire world if the British Empire collapses. That is one of the main reasons why I opposed this war before it was declared, and why I have constantly advocated a negotiated peace. I did not feel that England and France

had a reasonable chance of winning. France has now been defeated; and, despite the propaganda and confusion of recent months, it is now obvious that England is losing the war. I believe this is realized even by the British government. But they have one last desperate plan remaining. They hope that they may be able to persuade us to send another American Expeditionary Force to Europe, and to share with England militarily, as well as financially, the fiasco of this war.

I do not blame England for this hope, or for asking for our assistance. But we now know that she declared a war under circumstances led to the defeat of every nation that sided with her from Poland to Greece. We know that in the desperation of war England promised to all these nations armed assistance that she could not send. We know that she misinformed them, as she has misinformed us, concerning her state of preparation, her military strength, and the progress of the war.

In time of war, truth is always replaced by propaganda. I do not believe we should be too quick to criticize the actions of a belligerent nation. There is always the question whether we, ourselves, would do better under similar circumstances. But we in this country have a right to think of the welfare of America first, just as the people in England thought first of their own country when they encouraged the smaller nations of Europe to fight against hopeless odds. When England asks us to enter this war, she is considering her own future, and that of her Empire. In making our reply, I believe we should consider the future of the United States and that of the Western Hemisphere.

It is not only our right, but it is our obligation as American citizens to look at this war objectively, and to weigh our chances for success if we should enter it. I have attempted to do this, especially from the standpoint of aviation; and I have been forced to the conclusion that we cannot win this war for England, regardless of how much assistance we extend.

I ask you to look at the map of Europe today and see if you can suggest any way in which we could win this war if we entered it. Suppose we had a large army in America, trained and equipped. Where would we send it to fight? The campaigns of the war show only too clearly how difficult it is to force a landing, or to maintain an army, on a hostile coast. Suppose we took our navy from the Pacific, and used it to convoy British shipping. That would not win the war for England. It would, at best, permit her to exist under the constant bombing of the German air fleet. Suppose we had an air force that we could send to Europe. Where could it operate? Some of our squadrons might be based in the British Isles; but it is physically impossible to base enough aircraft in the British Isles alone to equal in strength the aircraft that can be based on the continent of Europe.

I have asked these questions on the supposition that we had in existence an army and an air force large enough and well enough equipped to send to Europe; and that we would dare to remove our navy from the Pacific. Even on this basis, I do not see how we could invade the continent of Europe successfully as long as all of that continent and most of Asia is under Axis domination. But the fact is that none of these suppositions are correct. We have only a one-ocean navy. Our army is still untrained and inadequately equipped for foreign war.

Our air force is deplorably lacking in modern fighting planes.

When these facts are cited, the interventionists shout that we are defeatists, that we are undermining the principles of Democracy, and that we are giving comfort to Germany by talking about our military weakness. But everything I mention here has been published in our newspapers, and in the reports of congressional hearings in Washington. Our military position is well known to the governments of Europe and Asia. Why, then, should it not be brought to the attention of our own people?

I say it is the interventionist in America, as it was in England and in France, who gives comfort to the enemy. I say it is they who are undermining the principles of Democracy when they demand that we take a course to which more than eighty percent of our citizens are opposed. I charge them with being the real defeatists, for their policy has led to the defeat of every country that followed their advice since this war began. There is no better way to give comfort to an enemy than to divide the people of a nation over the issue of foreign war. There is no shorter road to defeat than by entering a war with inadequate preparation. Every nation that has adopted the interventionist policy of depending on some one else for its own defense has met with nothing but defeat and failure.

When history is written, the responsibility for the downfall of the democracies of Europe will rest squarely upon the shoulders of the interventionists who led their nations into war uninformed and unprepared. With their shouts of defeatism, and their disdain of reality, they have already sent countless thousands of young men to death in Europe. From the campaign of Poland to that of Greece, their prophecies have been false and their policies have failed. Yet these are the people who are calling us defeatists in America today. And they have led this country, too, to the verge of war.

There are many such interventionists in America, but there are more people among us of a different type. That is why you and I are assembled here tonight. There is a policy open to this nation that will lead to success—a policy that leaves us free to follow our own way of life, and to develop our own civilization. It is not a new and untried idea. It was advocated by Washington. It was incorporated in the Monroe Doctrine. Under its guidance, the United States became the greatest nation in the world. It is based upon the belief that the security of a nation lies in the strength and character of its own people. It recommends the maintenance of armed forces sufficient to defend this hemisphere from attack by any combination of foreign powers. It demands faith in an independent American destiny. This is the policy of the America First Committee today. It is a policy not of isolation, but of independence; not of defeat, but of courage. It is a policy that led this nation to success during the most trying years of our history, and it is a policy that will lead us to success again.

We have weakened ourselves for many months, and still worse, we have divided our own people by this dabbling in Europe's wars. While we should have been concentrating on American defense, we have been forced to argue over foreign quarrels. We must turn our eyes and our faith back to our own country before it is too late. And when we do this, a different vista opens before us. Practically every difficulty we would face in invading Europe becomes an asset to us in defending America. Our enemy, and not we, would then have the problem of transporting millions of troops across the ocean and landing them on a hostile shore. They, and not we, would have to furnish the convoys to transport guns and trucks and munitions and fuel across three thousand miles of water. Our battleships and submarines would then be fighting close to their home bases. We would then do the bombing from the air, and the torpedoing at sea. And if any part of an enemy convoy should ever pass our navy and our air force, they would still be faced with the guns of our coast artillery, and behind them, the divisions of our army.

The United States is better situated from a military standpoint than any other nation in the world. Even in our present condition of unpreparedness, no foreign power is in a position to invade us today. If we concentrate on our own and build the strength that this nation should maintain, no foreign army will ever attempt to land on American shores.

War is not inevitable for this country. Such a claim is defeatism in the true sense. No one can make us fight abroad unless we ourselves are willing to do so. No one will attempt to fight us here if we arm ourselves as a great nation should be armed. Over a hundred million people in this nation are opposed to entering the war. If the principles of Democracy mean anything at all, that is reason enough for us to stay out. If we are forced into a war against the wishes of an overwhelming majority of our people, we will have proved Democracy such a failure at home that there will be little use fighting for it abroad.

The time has come when those of us who believe in an independent American destiny must band together, and organize for strength. We have been led toward war by a minority of our people. This minority has power. It has influence. It has a loud voice. But it does not represent the American people. During the last several years, I have travelled over this country, from one end to the other. I have talked to many hundreds of men and women, and I have had letters from tens of thousands more, who feel the same way as you and I. Most of these people have no influence or power. Most of them have no means of expressing their convictions, except by their vote which has always been against this war. They are the citizens who have had to work too hard at their daily jobs to organize political meetings. Hitherto, they have relied upon their vote to express their feelings; but now they find that it is hardly remembered except in the oratory of a political campaign. These people—the majority of hard-working American citizens are with us. They are the true strength of our country. And they are beginning to realize, as you and I, that there are times when we must sacrifice our normal interests in life in order to insure the safety and the welfare of our nation.

Such a time has come. Such a crisis is here. That is why the America First Committee has been formed—to give voice to the people who have no newspaper, or news reel, or radio station at their command; to the people who must do the paying, and the fighting, and the dying, if this country enters the war.

Whether or not we do enter the war, rests upon the shoulders of you in this audience, upon us here on this platform, upon meetings of this kind that are being held by Americans in every section of the United States today. It depends upon the action we take, and the courage we show at this time. If you believe in an independent destiny for America, if you believe that this country should not enter the war in Europe, we ask you to join the America First Committee in its stand. We ask you to share our faith in the ability of this nation to defend itself, to develop its own civilization, and to contribute to the progress of mankind in a more constructive and intelligent way than has yet been found by the warring nations of Europe. We need your support, and we need it now. The time to act is here.

Des Moines Speech [excerpt]

. . . The second major group I mentioned is the Jewish.

It is not difficult to understand why Jewish people desire the overthrow of Nazi Germany. The persecution they suffered in Germany would be sufficient to make bitter enemies of any race.

No person with a sense of the dignity of mankind can condone the persecution of the Jewish race in Germany. But no person of honesty and vision can look on their pro-war policy here today without seeing the dangers involved in such a policy both for us and for them. Instead of agitating for war, the Jewish groups in this country should be opposing it in every possible way for they will be among the first to feel its consequences.

Tolerance is a virtue that depends upon peace and strength. History shows that it cannot survive war and devastations. A few far-sighted Jewish people realize this and stand opposed to intervention. But the majority still do not.

Their greatest danger to this country lies in their large ownership and influence in our motion pictures, our press, our radio, and our government.

I am not attacking either the Jewish or the British people. Both races, I admire. But I am saying that the leaders of both the British and the Jewish races, for reasons which are as understandable from their viewpoint as they are inadvisable from ours, for reasons which are not American, wish to involve us in the war.

We cannot blame them for looking out for what they believe to be their own interests, but we also must look out for ours. We cannot allow the natural passions and prejudices of other peoples to lead our country to destruction.

Further Resources

BOOKS

Bak, Richard. *Lindbergh: Triumph and Tragedy.* Dallas: Taylor Publishing, 2000.

Berg, A. Scott. *Lindbergh.* New York: Berkley Publishing Group, 1999.

Cole, Wayne S. *Charles A. Lindbergh and the Battle Against American Intervention in World War II.* New York: Harcourt, Brace, Jovanovich, 1974.

Lindbergh, Charles A. *The Wartime Journals of Charles A. Lindbergh.* New York: Harcourt, Brace, Jovanovich, 1970.

PERIODICALS

Whitman, Alden. "Lindbergh Dies of Cancer in Hawaii at the Age of 72." *The New York Times,* August 27, 1974.

WEBSITES

American Experience: Lindbergh. Available online at http://www.pbs.org/wgbh/amex/lindbergh/ (accessed July 30, 2002).

American National Biography Online. Available online at http://www.anb.org (accessed July 30, 2002).

AUDIO AND VISUAL MEDIA

"Lindbergh." *The American Experience.* PBS.

Editorial Cartoons of Dr. Seuss
Political cartoons

By: Theodor Seuss Geisel

Date: May 22, 1941; December 9, 1941

Source: Geisel, Theodore Seuss. Political cartoons. *PM.* May 22, 1941; December 9, 1941. Reprinted online at http://orpheus.ucsd.edu/speccoll/dspolitic/pm/10522cs.jpg and http://orpheus.ucsd.edu/speccoll/dspolitic/pm/11209cs.jpg; website home page: http://orpheus.ucsd.edu/speccoll/dspolitic/index.htm (accessed March 14, 2003).

About the Author: Theodor Seuss Geisel (1904–1991) is best known as "Dr. Seuss," the famous author of nearly fifty children's books featuring such original characters as the Lorax, the Grinch, and Yertle the Turtle. Prior to writing his most famous works—*The Cat in the Hat* (1957), *How the Grinch Stole Christmas* (1957), and *Green Eggs and Ham* (1960), among others—Geisel drew vibrant, politically charged cartoons for the liberal New York City newspaper *PM.* ∎

Introduction

In 1940 Geisel came to *PM* after illustrating for various magazines and creating advertisements for the Standard Oil Corporation. As the publication's chief editorial cartoonist from 1941 to 1943, Geisel drew cartoons concerning issues of vital importance, primarily the Great Depression and World War II (1939–1945). By the time Geisel joined *PM* the war in Europe and Asia was well underway. Germany had invaded France and Poland, and Japan had overtaken portions of China and was preparing an assault on U.S. bases throughout the Pacific. The dominant question on the minds of Americans was whether they should join in the struggle against Germany and Japan. Isolationists argued that the United States would gain nothing by entering the fray and quite possibly would be defeated alongside allies Britain, France, and China. Interventionists contended that the country must join the global war before Japan and Germany gained too much strength and eventually threatened the United States directly.

Significance

Geisel's drawings for *PM* conveyed his staunch advocacy of U.S. military intervention in World War II. He chastised the isolationists, most prominently Charles A.

Primary Source

Editorial Cartoons of Dr. Seuss (1 OF 2)

SYNOPSIS: These two political cartoons provide a sense of how Geisel approached the war before and immediately after Pearl Harbor. The May 22, 1941, drawing shows a smiling Uncle Sam, representing the United States, completely unaware of the threat he will soon face from Germany after it has destroyed England. PUBLIC DOMAIN. GRADUATE LIBRARY, UNIVERSITY OF MICHIGAN.

Primary Source

Editorial Cartoons of Dr. Seuss (2 OF 2)
The December 9, 1941 editorial cartoon shows the Japanese attacks on Pearl Harbor literally waking up and reviving the sleeping giant. Like many American artists, Geisel portrayed the Japanese in unflattering caricature, with buck teeth and glasses. PUBLIC DOMAIN. GRADUATE LIBRARY, UNIVERSITY OF MICHIGAN.

Lindbergh (see Lindbergh entry in this chapter), for their argument that the United States could, and *should,* avoid entering the conflict. Before the Japanese attacked Pearl Harbor in December 1941, Geisel depicted a fatigued, worried, and often oblivious Uncle Sam, unable to see how powerful he is or how immediate the Axis threat really is. The isolationists, according to Geisel, actually aided the Axis powers by asserting that the United States could not win the war even if it tried. Following U.S. entry into the war, the artist shifted tone and provided readers with several cartoons urging them to support President Franklin D. Roosevelt (served 1933–1945) and the war effort. Geisel's war bonds cartoons even included a popular motto from his Standard Oil ads, "Quick, Henry, the Flit!" In the 1930s the insecticide Flit was sold to prevent mosquito infestations; in World War II, Geisel suggested, U.S. aid for the war effort would inoculate the world against fascism.

Geisel's support for exterminating the enemy, as well as his drawings of the enemy, express the vicious nature of wartime propaganda. Hitler represented Germany, but a series of increasingly grotesque, inhuman figures came to represent Japan. The Japanese, according to Geisel's drawings, possessed extremely large teeth, squinty eyes, and large noses. Moreover, these cartoons depicted the Japanese as ignorant dupes of Hitler. A cartoon two days before Pearl Harbor showed a small, monkey-like figure labeled "Japan," asking Hitler, his "Master," about how to provoke a smiling, benign Uncle Sam to fight. Geisel, of course, was certainly not the only writer to utilize racist depictions of the enemy to support the U.S. war effort.

Further Resources

BOOKS

MacDonald, Ruth K. *Dr. Seuss.* Boston: Twayne Publishers, 1988.

Minear, Richard H., ed. *Dr. Seuss Goes to War: The World War II Editorial Cartoons of Theodor Seuss Geisel.* New York: New Press, 1999.

Morgan, Judith, and Neil Morgan, *Dr. Seuss and Mr. Geisel: A Biography.* New York: Random House, 1995.

PERIODICALS

Pace, Eric. "Dr. Seuss, Modern Mother Goose, Dies at 87." *The New York Times,* September 26, 1991.

WEBSITES

American National Biography Online. Available online at http://www.anb.org (accessed July 30, 2002).

"Dr. Seuss Went to War: A Catalogue of Political Cartoons by Dr. Seuss." Mandeville Special Collections Library. Available online at http://orpheus.ucsd.edu/speccoll/dspolitic/index .htm (accessed August 30, 2002).

Seussville. Available online at http://www.seussville.com (accessed July 30, 2002).

AUDIO AND VISUAL MEDIA

"How the Grinch Stole Christmas!" (1966)

"The Lorax" (1972)

"Concentration Camp: U.S. Style"
Editorial

By: Ted Nakashima

Date: June 15, 1942

Source: Nakashima, Ted. "Concentration Camp: U.S. Style." *The New Republic* 106, no. 24, June 15, 1942, 822–823.

About the Author: Ted Nakashima's life mirrored that of many of the nearly 120,000 people of Japanese descent interned during World War II (1939–1945). While not much is known about Nakashima's life after his internment, his opinion piece for *The New Republic* in 1942 provided a clear portrait of his family's history. As a U.S. citizen born and raised in Seattle, Washington, Nakashima worked as an architectural draftsman prior to the war. The U.S. military relocated his family to "Camp Harmony," a temporary assembly center in Puyallup, Washington. Following a four-month stay in this temporary center, Nakashima and the other 7,200 residents of the camp were moved to a relocation center in Minidoka, Idaho. ∎

Introduction

President Franklin D. Roosevelt (served 1933–1945) signed Executive Order 9066 on February 19, 1942. The order declared that the West Coast was a "military zone from which 'any or all persons may be excluded'," but did not specify that Japanese Americans should or would be excluded from the region. Over the course of the next several months, however, more than 110,000 people of Japanese ancestry, the majority of whom were American citizens, were forcibly removed from the Pacific Coast states. The military first moved internees to assembly centers throughout California, Oregon, and Washington.

Following a stay of about four months, the internees were then relocated to ten larger camps further inland, primarily in the Western Mountain states and Arkansas. The internees remained in these camps until the Roosevelt administration and the military gradually phased them out between 1944 and 1946.

Significance

As is shown by *The New Republic* article, Americans vehemently debated the internment policy. The main argument for internment held that Japanese Americans were more loyal to Japan than to the United States and therefore posed distinct threats to national security after the United States declared war on Japan in December 1941. Another argument, which gained supporters as internment continued during the war, justified internment as a means of protecting Japanese Americans against racist attacks. Of course, as this editorial shows, proponents of this argument still suspected that people of Japanese descent would attempt an act of "sabotage" if allowed to remain on their property. The idea that the U.S. government would protect Japanese Americans' property proved to be a fallacy— virtually none of the property held by Japanese Americans before the war was returned to them after the conflict.

African American journalists also debated the internment policy, as many writers concluded that the racist aspects of imprisoning Japanese Americans because of their ancestry could easily threaten African Americans after the war. While *The Crisis,* the journal of the National Association for the Advancement of Colored People (NAACP), sharply rebuked the government's policy, African American newspapers on the West Coast lauded the internment policy and urged their readers to show their loyalty for the U.S. war effort. The Double-V Campaign, first urged in the *Pittsburgh Courier* in 1942, focused on the opportunities offered by the war, maintaining that victory abroad against fascism could bring victory at home in the struggle for equal rights.

In *The New Republic*'s "Concentration Camp: U.S. Style" and *The Crisis*'s "Americans in Concentration Camps," critics of the internment emphasized the similarities between the imprisonment of Japanese Americans and the widespread murder of Jews in concentration camps in Europe.

After acknowledging that not a single act of espionage was committed by any person of Japanese descent during the war, the U.S. military ordered the first internment camp closings in December 1944. That year the armed forces had actually begun drafting internees to serve in the military. Comprised of Japanese Americans, the 442nd Regimental Combat Team became one of the

"Their Best Way to Show Loyalty"

Japanese leaders in California who are counseling their people, both aliens and native-born, to co-operate with the Army in carrying out the evacuation plans are, in effect, offering the best possible way for all Japanese to demonstrate their loyalty to the United States.

Many aliens and practically all the native-born have been protesting their allegiance to this Government. Although their removal to inland districts outside the military zones may inconvenience them somewhat, even work serious hardships upon some, they must certainly recognize the necessity of clearing the coastal combat areas of all possible fifth columnists and saboteurs. Inasmuch as the presence of enemy agents cannot be detected readily when these areas are thronged by Japanese the only course left is to remove all persons of that race for the duration of the war.

That is a clear-cut policy easily understood. Its execution should be supported by all citizens of whatever racial background, but especially it presents an opportunity to the people of an enemy race to prove their spirit of co-operation and keep their relations with the rest of the population of this country on the firm ground of friendship.

Every indication has been given that the transfer will be made with the least possible hardship. General DeWitt's order was issued in such a way as to give those who can make private moving arrangements plenty of time to do so. All others will not be moved until arrangements can be made for places for them to go. They may have to be housed in temporary quarters until permanent ones can be provided for them, but during the summer months that does not mean they will be unduly uncomfortable.

Their property will be carefully protected by the Federal Government, their food and shelter will be provided to the extent they are not able to provide it for themselves, and they will be furnished plenty of entertainment and recreation. That is not according to the pattern of the European concentration camp by any means.

Real danger would exist for all Japanese if they remained in the combat area. The least act of sabotage might provoke angry reprisals that easily could balloon into bloody race riots.

We must avoid any chance of that sort of thing. The most sensible, the most humane way to insure against it is to move the Japanese out of harm's way and make it as easy as possible for them to go and to remain away until the war is over.

SOURCE: "Their Best Way to Show Loyalty." *San Francisco News,* March 6, 1942.

---

most decorated units in the war. Decades later President Ronald Reagan (served 1981–1989) formally apologized for the internment and Congress passed a bill providing for $20,000 in compensation to be paid to all living victims of the relocation.

Primary Source

"Concentration Camp: U.S. Style"

SYNOPSIS: In June 1942 the U.S. War Relocation Authority had begun its plans to move more than 110,000 Japanese-American detainees from assembly centers to isolated relocation centers. Written prior to this lengthy transfer to even harsher conditions in rural Idaho, Ted Nakashima's article focuses on the contradiction presented by the United States's fight for democracy abroad and denial of constitutional liberties at home. Several times the author professes his loyalty as an American citizen and rails against the government's duplicitous rhetoric. Nakashima concludes his argument by actually using the racist slur "Japs" when arguing that patriotic Japanese Americans should be allowed to fight the Japanese enemy, or "Japs."

Unfortunately in this land of liberty, I was born of Japanese parents; born in Seattle of a mother and father who have been in this country since 1901. Fine parents, who brought up their children in the best American way of life. My mother served with the Volunteer Red Cross Service in the last war— my father, an editor, has spoken and written Americanism for forty years.

Our family is almost typical of the other unfortunates here at the camp. The oldest son, a licensed architect, was educated at the University of Washington, has a master's degree from the Massachusetts Institute of Technology and is a scholarship graduate of the American School of Fine Arts in Fontainebleau, France. He is now in camp in Oregon with his wife and three-months-old child. He had just completed designing a much needed defense housing project at Vancouver, Washington.

The second son is an M.D. He served his internship in a New York hospital, is married and has two fine sons. The folks banked on him, because he was the smartest of us three boys. The army took him a

The Manzanar Relocation Camp, California, 1942. Over 10,000 Japanese Americans and Japanese immigrants to the United States were imprisoned here during World War II. NATIONAL ARCHIVES AND RECORDS ADMINISTRATION.

month after he opened his office. He is now a lieutenant in the Medical Corps, somewhere in the South.

I am the third son, the dumbest of the lot, but still smart enough to hold down a job as an architectural draftsman. I have just finished building a new home and had lived in it three weeks. My desk was just cleared of work done for the Army Engineers, another stack of 391 defense houses was waiting (a rush job), when the order came to pack up and leave for this resettlement center called "Camp Harmony."

Mary, the only girl in the family, and her year-old son, "Butch," are with our parents—interned in the stables of the Livestock Exposition Buildings in Portland.

Now that you can picture our thoroughly American background, let me describe our new home.

The resettlement center is actually a penitentiary—armed guards in towers with spotlights and deadly tommy guns, fifteen feet of barbed-wire fences, everyone confined to quarters at nine, lights out at ten o'clock. The guards are ordered to shoot anyone who approaches within twenty feet of the fences. No one is allowed to take the two-block-long hike to the latrines after nine, under any circumstances.

The apartments, as the army calls them, are two-block-long stables, with windows on one side. Floors are shiplaps on two-by-fours laid directly on the mud, which is everywhere. The stalls are about eighteen by twenty-one feet; some contain families of six or seven persons. Partitions are seven feet high, leaving a four-foot opening above. The rooms aren't too bad, almost fit to live in for a short while.

The food and sanitation problems are the worst. We have had absolutely no fresh meat, vegetables or butter since we came here. Mealtime queues extend for blocks; standing in a rainswept line, feet in the mud, waiting for the scant portions of canned wieners and boiled potatoes, hash for breakfast or canned wieners and beans for dinner. Milk only for the kids. Coffee or tea dosed with saltpeter and stale bread are the adults' staples. Dirty, unwiped dishes, greasy silver, a starchy diet, no butter, no milk, bawling kids, mud, wet mud that stinks when it dries, no vegetables—a sad thing for the people who raised them in such abundance. Memories of a crisp head of lettuce with our special olive oil, vinegar, garlic and cheese dressing.

Today one of the surface sewage-disposal pipes broke and the sewage flowed down the streets. Kids

Japanese American internees peel potatoes and onions in the Santa Anita Internment Camp, California, 1942. AP/WIDE WORLD PHOTOS. REPRODUCED BY PERMISSION.

play in the water. Shower baths without hot water. Stinking mud and slops everywhere.

Can this be the same America we left a few weeks ago?

As I write, I can remember our little bathroom—light coral walls. My wife painting them, and the spilled paint in her hair. The open towel shelving and the pretty shower curtains which we put up the day before we left. How sanitary and clean we left it for the airlines pilot and his young wife who are now enjoying the fruits of our labor.

It all seems so futile, struggling, trying to live our old lives under this useless, regimented life. The senselessness of all the inactive manpower. Electricians, plumbers, draftsmen, mechanics, carpenters, painters, farmers—every trade—men who are able and willing to do all they can to lick the Axis. Thousands of men and women in these camps, en-

ergetic, quick, alert, eager for hard, constructive work, waiting for the army to do something for us, an army that won't give us butter.

I can't take it! I have 391 defense houses to be drawn. I left a fine American home which we built with our own hands. I left a life, highballs with our American friends on week-ends, a carpenter, laundry-truck driver, architect, airlines pilot—good friends, friends who would swear by us. I don't have enough of that Japanese heritage *"ga-man"*—a code of silent suffering and ability to stand pain.

Oddly enough I still have a bit of faith in army promises of good treatment and Mrs. Roosevelt's pledge of a future worthy of good American citizens. I'm banking another $67 of income tax on the future. Sometimes I want to spend the money I have set aside for income tax on a bit of butter or ice cream or something good that I might have smuggled through the gates, but I can't do it when I think that every dollar I can put into "the fight to lick the Japs," the sooner I will be home again. I must forget my stomach.

What really hurts most is the constant reference to us evacuees as "Japs." "Japs" are the guys we are fighting. We're on this side and we want to help.

Further Resources

BOOKS
Adams, Ansel. *Manzanar*. New York: Times Books, 1988.

Daniels, Roger. *Prisoners Without Trial: Japanese Americans in World War II*. New York: Hill and Wang: 1993.

Hynes, Samuel et al., eds. *Reporting World War II: Part One, American Journalism, 1938–1944*. New York: Library of America, 1995.

Uchida, Yoshiko. *Desert Exile: The Uprooting of a Japanese American Family*. Seattle: University of Washington Press, 1982.

PERIODICALS
"Americans in Concentration Camps." *The Crisis,* September 1942.

Daniels, Roger. "Incarcerating Japanese Americans." *Magazine of History* 16 (Spring 2002): 19–23.

WEBSITES
"Internment of San Francisco Japanese." *Museum of the City of San Francisco.* Available online at http://www.sfmuseum .org/war/evactxt.html (accessed July 30, 2002).

Mudrock, Theresa. "Camp Harmony Exhibit." Available online at http://www.lib.washington.edu/exhibits/harmony/exhibit/ (accessed July 30, 2002).

"Suffering Under a Great Injustice: Ansel Adams' Photographs of Japanese-American Internment at Manzanar." *American Memory*. Available online at http://memory.loc.gov/ammem /aamhtml/ (accessed July 30, 2002).

AUDIO AND VISUAL MEDIA
Come See the Paradise, 1990, 20th Century Fox. VHS, 1992.

"This One Is Captain Waskow"
Newspaper article

By: Ernie Pyle
Date: January 10, 1944
Source: Pyle, Ernie. "This One Is Captain Waskow." Scripps-Howard wire service, January 10, 1944. Reprinted in Hynes, Samuel et al., eds. *Reporting World War II: Part One, American Journalism, 1938–1944*. New York: Library of America, 1995.

About the Author: Born in rural Indiana, Ernie Pyle (1900–1945) threw himself into newspaper reporting with

such verve that he was writing for the Washington (D.C.) *Daily News* by the age of 23. By 1935 he wrote for a paper owned by the Scripps-Howard newspaper chain and found himself reporting for a nationwide audience. Once World War II (1939–1945) had erupted in Europe, Pyle was once again ready to thrust all of his energies into journalism. He provided some of the most memorable copy of the conflict and gained wide acclaim for his stories of common individuals forced into spectacular circumstances. He won the Pulitzer Prize in 1944 for his portrayals of combat the previous year. Pyle was killed by a Japanese sniper on April 18, 1945. Not yet 45 years old when he died, Pyle's work became legendary and he is still revered as the quintessential war reporter. ∎

Introduction

After declaring war on December 8, 1941, the United States slowly built its military forces to compete with the Axis powers (Germany, Japan, and Italy). The United States-led invasion at Normandy, France, would not occur until June 1944. In the meantime, Josef Stalin, the leader of the Soviet Union, complained several times to President Franklin D. Roosevelt (served 1933–1945) that the United States should attack Germany immediately. Instead the president decided first to encounter German forces in North Africa (1942–1943) before moving into Italy (1943–1944). Ernie Pyle wrote "This One Is Captain Waskow" during the Italian campaign in winter 1943–1944.

Significance

Pyle had rushed to Europe to cover the Blitz in 1940. Since then, he had written several pieces for *Stars and Stripes,* a newspaper for U.S. military personnel. By the Italian campaign, Pyle's reporting had achieved widespread appeal with Americans at home and in the military. He sought to provide readers with a "worm's-eye view" of war. He focused on the experience of infantrymen rather than high officers and abhorred propaganda about the joys of fighting in war. Like political cartoonists Bill Mauldin and Howard Brodie, Pyle attempted to provide a realistic sense of the war that encapsulated the horrors, boredom, comradery, and humor he encountered at the front lines. John Steinbeck, the Nobel Prize-winning author and a friend of Pyle, described Pyle's reporting perspective:

> There are really two wars and they haven't much to do with each other. There is the war of maps and logistics, of campaigns, of ballistics, armies, divisions and regiments—and that is General [George] Marshall's war. Then there is the war of the homesick, weary, funny, violent, common men, who wash their socks in their helmets, complain about the food, whistle at Arab girls, or any girls for that matter, and lug themselves through as dirty a business as the world has ever seen and do it with humor and dignity and courage—and that is Ernie

War correspondant Ernie Pyle in Normandy, France during the Allied invasion, 1944. AP/WIDE WORLD PHOTOS. REPRODUCED BY PERMISSION.

Pyle's war. He knows it as well as anyone and writes about it better than anyone.

Following Italy, Pyle landed at Normandy Beach one day after D-Day, marched through Paris during its liberation, and then traveled to the Pacific to cover the invasions of Okinawa and Iwo Jima. Following Pyle's death on a nearby island, a soldier found a piece of paper on the slain journalist's body. The paper contained the column Pyle planned to submit following the end of the war. As with the reporter's previous stories, this piece would provide a ferociously realistic depiction of war and its aftermath:

But there are many of the living who have had burned into their brains forever the unnatural sight of cold dead men scattered over the hillsides and in the ditches along the high rows of hedge throughout the world. Dead men by mass production—in one country after another—month after month and year after year. Dead men in winter and dead men in summer. Dead men in such familiar promiscuity that they become monotonous. Dead men in such monstrous infinity that you come almost to hate them. These are the things that you at home need not even try to understand. To you at home they are columns of figures, or he is a near

one who went away and just didn't come back. You didn't see him lying so grotesque and pasty beside the gravel road in France. We saw him, saw him by the multiple thousands. That's the difference. . . .

Primary Source

"This One Is Captain Waskow"

SYNOPSIS: By the time he wrote "This One Is Captain Waskow," Pyle had endured more than three years of warfare. He battled his own depression and coped with his wife's suicide attempts but continued to cover the war. In the vein of broadcaster Edward R. Murrow, Pyle avoided emotional language. He chose, instead, to honor his subjects by presenting detailed portraits of their lives. This article provided readers with a harsh portrait of World War II—but, nevertheless, an utterly realistic one.

At the front lines in Italy, Jan. 10—(by wireless)— In this war I have known a lot of officers who were loved and respected by the soldiers under them. But never have I crossed the trail of any man as beloved as Capt. Henry T. Waskow, of Belton, Tex.

Captain Waskow was a company commander in the 36th Division. He had been in this company since long before he left the States. He was very young, only in his middle 20s, but he carried in him a sincerity and gentleness that made people want to be guided by him.

"After my own father, he comes next," a sergeant told me.

"He always looked after us," a soldier said. "He'd go to bat for us every time."

"I've never known him to do anything unkind," another one said.

■ ■ ■

I was at the foot of the mule trail the night they brought Captain Waskow down. The moon was nearly full, and you could see far up the trail, and even part way across the valley. Soldiers made shadows as they walked.

Dead men had been coming down the mountain all evening, lashed onto the backs of mules. They came lying belly down across the wooden packsaddle, their heads hanging down on the left side of the mule, their stiffened legs sticking awkwardly from the other side, bobbing up and down as the mule walked.

The Italian mule skinners were afraid to walk beside dead men, so Americans had to lead the mules down that night. Even the Americans were reluctant to unlash and lift off the bodies, when they got to the bottom, so an officer had to do it himself and ask others to help.

The first one came early in the morning. They slid him down from the mule, and stood him on his feet for a moment. In the half light he might have been merely a sick man standing there leaning on the other. Then they laid him on the ground in the shadow of the stone wall alongside the road.

I don't know who that first one was. You feel small in the presence of dead men, and you don't ask silly questions.

We left him there beside the road, that first one, and we all went back into the cowshed and sat on watercans or lay on the straw, waiting for the next batch of mules.

Somebody said the dead soldier had been dead for four days, and then nobody said anything more about him. We talked for an hour or more; the dead man lay all alone, outside in the shadow of the wall.

■ ■ ■

Then a soldier came into the cowshed and said there were some more bodies outside. We went out into the road. Four mules stood there in the moonlight, in the road where the trail came down off the mountain. The soldiers who led them stood there waiting.

"This one is Captain Waskow," one of them said quickly.

Two men unlashed his body from the mule and lifted it off and laid it in the shadow beside the stone wall. Other men took the other bodies off. Finally, there were five lying end to end in a long row. You don't cover up dead men in the combat zones. They just lie there in the shadows until somebody else comes after them.

The uncertain mules moved off to their olive groves. The men in the road seemed reluctant to leave. They stood around, and gradually I could sense them moving, one by one, close to Captain Waskow's body. Not so much to look, I think, as to say something in finality to him and to themselves. I stood close by and I could hear.

One soldier came and looked down, and he said out loud:

"God damn it!"

That's all he said, and then he walked away.

Another one came, and he said, "God damn it to hell anyway!" He looked down for a few last moments and then turned and left.

Another man came. I think he was an officer. It was hard to tell officers from men in the dim light, for everybody was grimy and dirty. The man looked down into the dead captain's face and then spoke directly to him, as though he were alive:

"I'm sorry, old man."

Then a soldier came and stood beside the officer and bent over, and he too spoke to his dead captain, not in a whisper but awfully tenderly, and he said:

"I sure am sorry, sir."

Then the first man squatted down, and he reached down and took the captain's hand, and he sat there for a full five minutes holding the dead hand in his own and looking intently into the dead face. And he never uttered a sound all the time he sat there.

Finally he put the hand down. He reached up and gently straightened the points of the captain's shirt collar, and then he sort of rearranged the tattered edges of his uniform around the wound, and then he got up and walked away down the road in the moonlight, all alone.

The rest of us went back into the cowshed, leaving the five dead men lying in a line end to end in the shadow of the low stone wall. We lay down on the straw in the cowshed, and pretty soon we were all asleep.

Further Resources

BOOKS

Hynes, Samuel et al., eds. *Reporting World War II: Part One, American Journalism, 1938–1944.* New York: Library of America, 1995.

———. *Reporting World War II: Part Two, American Journalism, 1944–1945.* New York: Library of America, 1995.

Miller, Lee Graham. *The Story of Ernie Pyle.* New York: Viking Press, 1950.

Pyle, Ernie. *Ernie's War: The Best of Ernie Pyle's World War II Dispatches.* New York: Random House, 1986.

Tobin, James. *Ernie Pyle's War: America's Eyewitness to World War II.* New York: The Free Press, 1997.

Voss, Frederick S. *Reporting the War: The Journalistic Coverage of World War II.* Washington, D.C.: Smithsonian Institution Press for the National Portrait Gallery, 1994.

PERIODICALS

"Ernie Pyle Is Killed on Ie Island; Foe Fired When All Seemed Safe." *The New York Times*, April 19, 1945.

Lancaster, Paul. "Ernie Pyle: Chronicler of 'The Men Who Do the Dying.'" *American Heritage* 32 (Feb.–Mar. 1981): 30–41.

WEBSITES

American National Biography Online. Available online at http://www.anb.org (accessed July 30, 2002).

"On This Day." *The New York Times on the Web.* Available online at http://www.nytimes.com/learning/general/onthisday /bday/0803.html (accessed July 30, 2002).

Sweeny, Michael S. "Appointment at Hill 1205: Ernie Pyle and Captain Henry T. Waskow." *Texas Military Forces Museum.* Available online at http://www.kwanah.com/txmilmus /36division/sweeney.htm (accessed July 30, 2002).

AUDIO AND VISUAL MEDIA

"The Story of G. I. Joe." (1945)

"For the Jews—Life or Death?"

Editorial

By: I.F. Stone

Date: June 10, 1944

Source: Stone, I.F. "For the Jews—Life or Death?" *The Nation* 158, no. 24, June 10, 1944, 670–671.

About the Author: Born in Philadelphia, Isidor Feinstein (1907–1989) did not wait long before making a name for himself in journalism. By the age of 14, Feinstein had published his first newspaper, a left-leaning journal titled *The Progress.* The young writer attacked racism and human rights abuses—topics he would continue to cover passionately for the next 65 years. In response to growing anti-Semitism in Europe and the possibility that it would spread across the Atlantic, he changed his name to I.F. Stone in 1937. Stone wrote for liberal publications such as *The Nation* and *PM* during the 1930s and 1940s but remained a fiercely independent journalist. His most famous works came after World War II (1939–1945). He published his own weekly newsletter, *I. F. Stone's Weekly,* for nearly twenty years until health problems forced him to stop in 1971. By the time Stone died, more than a dozen compilations of his editorials had been published on topics ranging from World War II and the creation of Israel to the Cold War struggles in Korea (1950–1953) and Vietnam (1964–1975). ∎

Introduction

The American people had the opportunity to learn of Nazi discrimination against and later mass killings of Jews long before I.F. Stone wrote his dramatic editorial for *The Nation* in June 1944. In May and June 1939, reporters covered the S.S. *St. Louis* as it made a harrowing, futile journey across the Atlantic, carrying more than 900 Jewish refugees from Germany who attempted to gain asylum first in Cuba and then in the United States. Refused entry, the ship traveled along the Florida coast for several

"A Vast Slaughterhouse: 1,000,000 Jews Slain By Nazis, Report Says"

London, June 29 (U.P.)—The Germans have massacred more than 1,000,000 Jews since the war began in carrying out Adolf Hitler's proclaimed policy of exterminating the people, spokesmen for the World Jewish Congress charged today.

They said the Nazis had established a "vast slaughterhouse for Jews" in Eastern Europe and that reliable reports showed that 700,000 Jews already had been murdered in Lithuania and Poland, 125,000 in Rumania, 200,000 in Nazi-occupied parts of Russia and 100,000 in the rest of Europe. Thus about one-sixth of the pre-war Jewish population in Europe, estimated at 6,000,000 to 7,000,000 persons, had been wiped out in less than three years.

A report to the congress said that Jews, deported en masse to Central Poland from Germany, Austria, Czechoslovakia and the Netherlands, were being shot by firing squads at the rate of 1,000 daily.

Information received by the Polish Government in London confirmed that the Nazis had executed "several hundred thousand" Jews in Poland and that almost another million were imprisoned in ghettos.

A spokesman said 10,232 persons died in the Warsaw ghetto from hunger, disease, and other causes between April and June last year and that 4,000 children between the ages of 12 and 15 recently were removed from there by the Gestapo to work on slave-labor farms.

The pre-Nazi Jewish population of Germany, totaling about 600,000 persons, was said to have been reduced to a little more than 100,000.

SOURCE: "A Vast Slaughterhouse: 1,000,000 Jews Slain by Nazis, Report Says." *The New York Times,* June 30, 1942.

days as advocates tried to convince President Franklin D. Roosevelt (served 1933–1945) to allow it safe harbor. The U.S. government refused to permit the ship entry, sending its passengers back across the Atlantic to what most believed would be certain death. By 1939 Germany had eliminated all Jewish civil rights and had ordered the removal of all Jews under Nazi authority. In the winter of 1941–1942 German Chancellor Adolf Hitler ordered the "Final Solution"—the use of concentration camps for the express purpose of exterminating all European Jews.

Significance

This horrifying policy of mass executions was not a secret. *The New York Times* first reported the killings as the creation of the War Refugee Board in January 1944 and the Board eventually safeguarded more than 200,000 Jews by the end of the conflict. Nevertheless, Stone argued, the United States needed to take more immediate action to protect the Jews. As Washington, D.C., editor for *The Nation* during the war, Stone urged not only politicians but also fellow "newspapermen" to "shake loose from customary ways and bureaucratic habit, to risk inexpedience and defy prejudice, to be whole-hearted" in the fight for "justice and humanity." In 1944 and 1945, even as Germany began to lose the war, the killings increased to their highest levels. More than six million Jews and millions of others died in what came to be known as the Holocaust.

Primary Source

"For the Jews—Life or Death?"

SYNOPSIS: The editorial insert preceding Stone's article notes the immediacy of the topic under discussion. The day after the story's completion, President Roosevelt "indicated that he was considering" the creation of "'free ports' for refugees." As the introduction warned, however, the president seemed "indefinite." Also evoking the rapidly changing nature of news during the war, a monumental event occurred between the writing of this piece on June 1 and its publication on June 10—D-Day. The Allied invasion of German-occupied France on June 6, 1944, began the downfall of Nazi power and the ultimate end of the Holocaust in April 1945.

At his press conference on June 2, after this article was written; the President indicated that he was considering the conversion of an army camp in this country into a "free port" for refugees. Unfortunately, as the New York Post has pointed out, "his statement was conditional, indefinite. The check is still on paper and we don't even know what the amount is." In these circumstances Mr. Stone's analysis of the urgency of the situation and his plea for public pressure to secure action from the Administration are no less valid than they were before Mr. Roosevelt spoke.

Washington, June 1

This letter, addressed specifically to fellow-newspapermen and to editors the country over, is an appeal for help. The establishment of temporary internment camps for refugees in the United States, vividly named "free ports" by Samuel Grafton of the New York *Post,* is in danger of bogging down. Every similar proposal here has bogged down until it was too late to save any lives. I have been over a mass

The body of a Holocaust victim, burned to death by S.S. troops, 1945, Gardelegen, Germany. **PHOTOGRAPH BY SGT. E.R. ALLEN. NATIONAL ARCHIVES AND RECORDS ADMINISTRATION.**

early as June 1942. This relatively brief, six-paragraph article did not appear in bold headlines, and the coverage seemed to almost understate the deaths of "more than 1,000,000 Jews since the war began." Nevertheless, the sheer numbers listed in the report conveyed the atrocities underway as "about one sixth of the pre-war Jewish population in Europe, estimated at 6,000,000 to 7,000,000 persons, had been wiped out in less than three years."

Stone's piece reflected the evolving debate over whether the United States should take greater steps to save European Jewry. President Roosevelt had ordered of material, some of it confidential, dealing with the plight of the fast-disappearing Jews of Europe and with the fate of suggestions for aiding them, and it is a dreadful story.

Anything newspapermen can write about this in their own papers will help. It will help to save lives, the lives of people like ourselves. I wish I were eloquent, I wish I could put down on paper the picture that comes to me from the restrained and diplomatic language of the documents. As I write, the morning papers carry a dispatch from Lisbon reporting that the "deadline"—the idiom was never more literal—has passed for the Jews of Hungary. It is approaching for the Jews of Bulgaria, where the Nazis yesterday set up a puppet regime.

I need not dwell upon the authenticated horrors of the Nazi internment camps and death chambers for Jews. That is not tragic but a kind of insane horror. It is our part in this which is tragic. The essence of tragedy is not the doing of evil by evil men but the doing of evil by good men, out of weakness, indecision, sloth, inability to act in accordance with what they know to be right. The tragic element in the fate of the Jews of Europe lies in the failure of their friends in the West to shake loose from customary ways and bureaucratic habit, to risk inexpediency and defy prejudice, to be whole-hearted, to care as deeply and fight as hard for the big words we use, for justice and for humanity, as the fanatic Nazi does for his master race or the fanatic Jap for his Emperor. A reporter in Washington cannot help seeing this weakness all about him. We are half-hearted about what little we could do to help the Jews of Europe as we are half-hearted about our economic warfare, about blacklisting those who help our enemies, about almost everything in the war except the actual fighting.

There is much we could have done to save the Jews of Europe before the war. There is much we could have done since the war began. There are still things we could do today which would give new lives to a few and hope to many. The hope that all is not black in the world for his children can be strong sustenance for a man starving in a camp or entering a gas chamber. But to feel that your friends and allies are wishy-washy folk who mean what they say but haven't got the gumption to live up to it must brew a poisonous despair. When Mr. Roosevelt established the War Refugee Board in January, he said it was "the policy of this government to take all measures within its power . . . consistent with the suc-

cessful prosecution of the war . . . to rescue the victims of enemy oppression."

The facts are simple. Thanks to the International Red Cross and those good folk the Quakers, thanks to courageous non-Jewish friends in the occupied countries themselves and to intrepid Jews who run a kind of underground railway under Nazi noses, something can still be done to alleviate the suffering of the Jews in Europe and some Jews can still be got out. Even under the White Paper there are still 22,000 immigration visas available for entry into Palestine. The main problem is to get Jews over the Turkish border without a passport for transit to Palestine. "Free ports" in Turkey are needed, but the Turks, irritated by other pressures from England and the United States, are unwilling to do for Jewish refugees what we ourselves are still unwilling to do, that is, give them a temporary haven. Only an executive order by the President establishing "free ports" in this country can prove to the Turks that we are dealing with them in good faith; under present circumstances they cannot but feel contemptuous of our pleas. And the longer we delay the fewer Jews there will be left to rescue, the slimmer the chances to get them out. Between 4,000,000 and 5,000,000 European Jews have been killed since August, 1942, when the Nazi extermination campaign began.

There are people here who say the President cannot risk a move of this kind before election. I believe that an insult to the American people. I do not believe any but a few unworthy bigots would object to giving a few thousand refugees a temporary breathing spell in their flight from oppression. It is a question of Mr. Roosevelt's courage and good faith. All he is called upon to do, after all, is what Franco did months ago, yes, *Franco.* Franco established "free ports," internment camps, months ago for refugees who fled across his border, refugees, let us remember, from his own ally and patron, Hitler. Knowing the Fuhrer's maniacal hatred for Jews, that kindness on Franco's part took considerably more courage than Mr. Roosevelt needs to face a few sneering editorials, perhaps, from the Chicago *Tribune.* I say "perhaps" because I do not know that even Colonel McCormick would in fact be hostile.

Official Washington's capacity for finding excuses for inaction is endless, and many people in the State and War departments who play a part in this matter can spend months sucking their legalistic thumbs over any problem. So many things that might have been done were attempted too late. A little more than a year ago Sweden offered to take

20,000 Jewish children from occupied Europe if Britain and the United States guaranteed their feeding and after the war their repatriation. The British were fairly rapid in this case, but it took three or four months to get these assurances from the American government, and by that time the situation had worsened to a point that seems to have blocked the whole project. In another case the Bulgarian government offered visas for 1,000 Jews if arrangements could be made within a certain time for their departure. A ship was obtained at once, but it took seven weeks for British officials to get clearance for the project from London, and by that time the time limit had been passed. The records, when they can be published, will show many similar incidents.

The news that the United States had established "free ports" would bring hope to people who have now no hope. It would encourage neutrals to let in more refugees because we could take out some of those they have already admitted. Most important, it would provide the argument of example and the evidence of sincerity in the negotiations for "free ports" in Turkey, last hope of the Balkan Jews. I ask fellow-newspapermen to show the President by their expressions of opinion in their own papers that if he hesitates for fear of an unpleasant political reaction he badly misconstrues the real feelings of the American people.

Further Resources

BOOKS

Cottrell, Robert C. *Izzy: A Biography of I.F. Stone.* New Brunswick, N.J.: Rutgers University Press, 1992.

Patner, Andrew. *I.F. Stone: A Portrait.* New York: Pantheon Books, 1988.

Stone, I.F. *The War Years, 1939–1945.* Boston: Little, Brown, 1988.

Wyman, David S. *The Abandonment of the Jews: America and the Holocaust.* New York: Pantheon Books, 1984.

PERIODICALS

Flint, Peter B. "I.F. Stone, Iconoclast of Journalism, Is Dead at 81." *The New York Times,* June 19, 1989.

WEBSITES

"America and the Holocaust." *Public Broadcasting Service Online.* Available online at http://www.pbs.org/wgbh/amex /holocaust/index.html (accessed July 30, 2002).

American National Biography. Available online at http://www .anb.org (accessed July 30, 2002).

The New York Review of Books. Available online at http:// www.nybooks.com/authors/4880 (accessed July 30, 2002).

United States Holocaust Memorial Museum. Available online at http://www.ushmm.org/ (accessed July 30, 2002).

World War II Cartoons

"Willie and Joe"

Cartoons

By: Bill Mauldin

Date: 1945

Source: Mauldin, Bill. *Up Front.* New York: W.W. Norton, 1945.

About the Artist: Born in New Mexico, Bill Mauldin (1921–2003) realized a passion for drawing early in life and later attended the Academy of Fine Arts in Chicago. Rather than stunting his artistic drive, World War II (1939–1945) provided Mauldin with the setting for his greatest, most influential work. In 1945 he produced *Up Front,* a compilation of his war cartoons originally published in the U.S. Army newspaper *Stars and Stripes.* After the war Mauldin continued to publish sharp critiques of U.S. society for United Features Syndicate, attacking the likes of the Ku Klux Klan and Senator Joseph McCarthy. After winning another Pulitzer in 1959

"Let 'im in. I wanna see a critter I kin feel sorry fer."

Primary Source

"Willie and Joe" (1 OF 3)

SYNOPSIS: While U.S. fighting with Japanese troops in the Pacific began in December 1941, U.S. troops did not enter the war in Europe until the fall of 1943, when they began an assault on the weakest Axis power, Italy. Mauldin drew the following cartoons during the Allied invasion of Italy during the winter of 1943–1944. REPRODUCED BY PERMISSION OF BILL MAULDIN AND THE WATKINS/LOOMIS AGENCY.

"Wisht I could stand up an' git some sleep."

Primary Source

"Willie and Joe" (2 OF 3)
Cartoon and caption by Bill Mauldin from his book *Up Front*.
REPRODUCED BY PERMISSION OF BILL MAULDIN AND THE
WATKINS/LOOMIS AGENCY.

he drew his most famous piece following the assassination of
President John F. Kennedy in 1963. The drawing depicted
Abraham Lincoln, seated at the Lincoln Memorial, mourning
the young president's death with his head in his hands.

Cartoons for *Yank* Magazine

Cartoons

By: Howard Brodie
Date: March–April 1945
Source: Brodie, Howard. *Yank,* March–April 1945.
About the Artist: Howard Brodie (1915–), like Mauldin,
drew cartoons for a U.S. Army magazine, *Yank,* during
World War II. He joined troops on the front lines in many
dangerous settings and received the Bronze Star for risking
his life to convey to readers the agony of war. Following the
war Brodie continued to cover both domestic and foreign
conflicts for the next several decades, including the Korean
(1950–1953) and Vietnam (1964–1975) wars and Watergate.
He continued to draw for CBS News until 1989. ∎

Introduction

Joining the U.S. Army at the age of 19, Bill Mauldin
advanced to become a full-time cartoonist for *Stars and*

Stripes by 1944. *Stars and Stripes* provided news to U.S.
servicemen stationed throughout the world. Howard
Brodie performed similar work for the Army magazine
Yank. The pair's attention to the travails of life in the military quickly made them quite popular with readers.
United Feature Syndicate distributed Mauldin's cartoons
to an even wider audience. Mauldin, still not yet 25 years
old, became the youngest winner of the Pulitzer Prize in
1945 for his sympathetic, somewhat subversive depictions of life for common infantrymen fighting in Europe.
Both artists accompanied their drawings with textual accounts of military life during World War II. The combination of visuals and terse, powerful writing offered
readers vivid depictions of war.

Significance

Howard Brodie accompanied his drawings with dramatic descriptions of soldiers fighting in fierce combat.
For "Compassion," a drawing of one soldier comforting
another in the midst of battle, Brodie wrote:

> I remember the young soldier well, he screamed,
> he was just out of control, and he screamed, and

"Maybe Joe needs a rest. He's talkin' in his sleep."

Primary Source

"Willie and Joe" (3 OF 3)
Cartoon and caption by Bill Mauldin from his book *Up Front*.
REPRODUCED BY PERMISSION OF BILL MAULDIN AND THE WATKINS/
LOOMIS AGENCY.

"We passed a still doughboy on the side of the road with no
hands, his misshapen, ooze-filled mittens a few feet from him."

Primary Source

Cartoons for *Yank* Magazine (1 OF 3)

SYNOPSIS: By April 13, 1945, the publication date for Brodie's cartoons, the war in Europe had neared its end. In the months leading up to Germany's surrender on May 7, 1945, though, American troops encountered staunch opposition from retreating German troops. Brodie's drawings convey how approaching victory did not make the fighting any less intense.

DRAWING BY HOWARD BRODIE, FROM THE MAGAZINE "YANK," FROM APRIL 13, 1945.

there was another soldier next to him who consoled him, and embraced him. That was a moving moment for me, to see that compassion in combat. And these are the things a person feels when he's in proximity to death—his buddy, that next human being, that person in the foxhole is the most important person in your life.

Brodie's compelling work conveyed the agony and despair of war—decades later these images remain indelibly linked not only to World War II, but to the devastation wrought by war in general. The artist's influence centered on his ability to portray the humanity of individuals faced with death and destruction all around them. Brodie's drawings did not differentiate between ally and enemy but instead provided an immediate sense of the horrors people encountered in a conflict that cost the world fifty million lives.

Although more humorous in tone and lighter in style, Bill Mauldin's characters nonetheless provided their own biting critique of the war. He focused specifically on the problems caused by military hierarchy and the treatment endured by millions of ordinary troops. Mauldin's mockery of officials resulted in his great popularity with soldiers but sharp rebuke from high commanders. Hoping to quash "Mauldin's scurrilous attempts to undermine military discipline," General George S. Patton actually petitioned *Stars and Stripes* to stop publishing the cartoons. The publication refused. Mauldin later explained his reasoning behind such depictions: "I drew pictures for and about the soldiers because I knew what their life was like and understood their gripes. I wanted to make something out of the humorous situations which come up even when you don't think life could be any more miserable." ("Bill Mauldin."

"I saw a GI in his hole, slumped in his last living position."

Primary Source

Cartoons for *Yank* Magazine (2 OF 3)
Cartoon and caption by Howard Brodie from *Yank,* April 13, 1945. DRAWING BY HOWARD BRODIE, FROM THE MAGAZINE "YANK," FROM APRIL 13, 1945.

Available online at http://www.spartacus.schoolnet.co .uk/ARTmauldin.htm; website home page: http://www .spartacus.schoolnet.co.uk)

In *Up Front*, Mauldin balanced his comical drawings with serious commentary on soldiers' daily travails. He contextualized his amusing depiction of a soldier sleep-marching by explaining the very unfunny subtext that forced the soldier to sleep while he marched:

> One thing is pretty certain if you are in the infantry—you aren't going to be very warm and dry while you sleep. . . . You do most of your sleeping while you march. It's not a very healthy sleep; you might call it a sort of coma. You can't hear anybody telling you to move faster but you can hear a whispering whoosh when the enemy up ahead stops long enough to throw a shell at you.

Further Resources

BOOKS
Brodie, Howard. *Drawing Fire: A Combat Artist at War.* Los Altos, Calif.: Portola Press, 1996.

Hynes, Samuel et al., eds. *Reporting World War II: Part Two, American Journalism, 1944–1945.* New York: Library of America, 1995.

"Two doughs had their arms around each other; one was sobbing."

Primary Source

Cartoons for *Yank* Magazine (3 OF 3)
Cartoon and caption by Howard Brodie from *Yank,* April 13, 1945. DRAWING BY HOWARD BRODIE, FROM THE MAGAZINE "YANK," FROM APRIL 13, 1945.

Mauldin, Bill. *Bill Mauldin's Army: Bill Mauldin's Greatest World War II Cartoons.* Novato, Calif.: Presidio Press, 1983.

———. *The Brass Ring.* New York: W.W. Norton, 1971.

———. *Up Front: Text and Pictures.* New York: Henry Holt, 1945. Reprint, W.W. Norton, 2000.

Voss, Frederick S. *Reporting the War: The Journalistic Coverage of World War II.* Washington, D.C.: Smithsonian Institution Press for the National Portrait Gallery, 1994.

WEBSITES

Spartacus Educational. Available online at http://www .spartacus.schoolnet.co.uk/ARTmauldin.htm (accessed July 30, 2002).

"They Drew Fire: Combat Artists of WWII." *Public Broadcasting Service Online.* Available online at http://www.pbs .org/theydrewfire/artists/brodie.html (accessed July 30, 2002).

Reporting the Holocaust

"33,000 Dachau Captives Freed by 7th Army"

Newspaper article

By: Marguerite Higgins

Date: May 1, 1945

Source: Higgins, Marguerite. "33,000 Dachau Captives Freed by 7th Army." *New York Herald Tribune,* May 1, 1945. Reprinted in Hynes, Samuel et al., eds. *Reporting World War II: Part Two, American Journalism, 1944–1945.* New York: Library of America, 1995.

About the Author: Marguerite Higgins (1921–1966) joined the staff of the New York *Herald Tribune* at the age of 21 and became one of the first female war reporters. She wrote the following piece on the Dachau concentration camp at 24. Higgins devoted her life to covering world conflict, travelling throughout the world to provide readers with dramatic reporting from the battlefronts of Europe, Korea, and Vietnam. She became the first woman to receive a Pulitzer Prize for foreign reporting for her coverage of the Korean War (1950–1953). While covering the conflict in Vietnam (1964–1975) in 1966, she contracted a tropical disease and died at the age of 45.

"Dachau"

Magazine article

By: Martha Gellhorn

Date: June 23, 1945

Source: Gellhorn, Martha. "Dachau." *Collier's,* June 23, 1945. Reprinted in Hynes, Samuel et al., eds. *Reporting World War II: Part Two, American Journalism, 1944–1945.* New York: Library of America, 1995.

About the Author: Martha Gellhorn (1908–1998) began her journalistic career after dropping out of Bryn Mawr college to become a writer. Over the next decade she worked first in Paris, and then for the Federal Emergency Relief Administration documenting the Depression. In 1937 she was hired by *Collier's Weekly* to cover the Spanish Civil War. It was here that she met Ernest Hemingway, whom she would marry in 1940, and divorce in 1945. Gellhorn was in Germany to cover the rise of Hitler and in Czechoslovakia when the Nazis seized that country. She continued to work for *Collier's* throughout World War II, traveling to every theatre of the war. Gellhorn continued to cover foreign conflicts long after the end of World War II (1939–1945). She journeyed to danger zones in Southeast Asia, Central America, and the Middle East throughout the second half of the twentieth century. By the time of her death in 1998 at the age of 89, this forceful female pioneer in international reporting had also written five novels and more than a dozen novellas. ∎

Introduction

Like many of the Nazi concentration camps, the installation in Dachau, Germany, began as a prison for political dissidents. Dachau began operations in 1933, shortly after Adolf Hitler became Chancellor of Germany, and acquired nearly 5,000 inmates by the end of the year. By the end of World War II the camp had held more than 200,000 prisoners, with about one-third of the population being Jewish. Although military and journalist reports from the liberation of Dachau described gas chambers and crematoria being used for mass extermination, it is generally acknowledged today that the tens of thousands of deaths at the camp resulted from disease, shootings, starvation, and torturous "medical experiments."

Significance

By the time Marguerite Higgins and Martha Gellhorn visited the concentration camp at Dachau in the spring of 1945, the Nazis' policy of mass executions had taken the lives of more than six million Jews and millions of other civilians. The Allied armies that marched through former German-occupied Europe liberated hundreds of thousands of prisoners sure to die under Nazi rule. As Higgins noted, the Germans actually increased the killings as their defeat approached.

The American journalists who visited the concentration camps each remarked about the "stench of death and sickness" that engulfed them as they entered. In Dachau, Auschwitz, Buchenwald, and other prisons, reporters struggled to express the horror the victims had experienced. Famed broadcaster Edward R. Murrow simply stated, "For much of it, I have no words." Writing for *Collier's,* Gellhorn utilized the extra space afforded by the magazine to question why and how such unimaginable actions could be committed:

> You are ashamed for mankind . . . We are not entirely guiltless, we the Allies, because it took us twelve years to open the gates of Dachau. We were blind and unbelieving and slow, and that we can

never be again. We must know now that there can never be peace if there is cruelty like this in the world. And if ever again we tolerate such cruelty we have no right to peace.

Primary Source

"33,000 Dachau Captives Freed by 7th Army" [excerpt]

SYNOPSIS: Marguerite Higgins accompanied Allied troops into Dachau as they liberated the concentration camp on April 29, 1945. She confirmed the unthinkable—thousands of bodies piled upon one another and horrifying evidence of countless more executions. As was the case in other camps, scores of prisoners died as they ran into electrically charged barbed wire to greet their saviors.

Dachau, Germany, April 29 (Delayed)—Troops of the United States 7th Army liberated 33,000 prisoners this afternoon at this first and largest of the Nazi concentration camps. Some of the prisoners had endured for eleven years the horrors of notorious Dachau. The liberation was a frenzied scene. Inmates of the camp hugged and embraced the American troops, kissed the ground before them and carried them shoulder high around the place. . . .

The Dachau camp, in which at least a thousand prisoners were killed last night before the S.S. (Elite Guard) men in charge fled, is a grimmer and larger edition of the similarly notorious Buchenwald camp near Weimar.

This correspondent and Peter Furst, of the army newspaper "Stars and Stripes," were the first two Americans to enter the inclosure at Dachau, where persons possessing some of the best brains in Europe were held during what might have been the most fruitful years of their lives.

While a United States 45th Infantry Division patrol was still fighting a way down through S.S. barracks to the north, our jeep and two others from the 42d Infantry drove into the camp inclosure through the southern entrance. As men of the patrol with us busied themselves accepting an S.S. man's surrender, we impressed a soldier into service and drove with him to the prisoners' barracks. There he opened the gate after pushing the body of a prisoner shot last night while attempting to get out to meet the Americans.

There was not a soul in the yard when the gate was opened. As we learned later, the prisoners themselves had taken over control of their inclosure

Marguerite Higgins gets into a jeep during World War II. One of the first female war correspondents, Higgins won fame and praise for her coverage of World War II and the Korean War. AP/WIDE WORLD PHOTOS. REPRODUCED BY PERMISSION.

the night before, refusing to obey any further orders from the German guards, who had retreated to the outside. The prisoners maintained strict discipline among themselves, remaining close to their barracks so as not to give the S.S. men an excuse for mass murder. But the minute the two of us entered a jangled barrage of "Are you Americans?" in about sixteen languages came from the barracks 200 yards from the gate. An affirmative nod caused pandemonium.

Tattered, emaciated men, weeping, yelling and shouting "Long live America!" swept toward the gate in a mob. Those who could not walk limped or crawled. In the confusion, they were so hysterically happy that they took the S.S. man for an American. During a wild five minutes he was patted on the back, paraded on shoulders and embraced enthusiastically by prisoners. The arrival of the American soldier soon straightened out the situation.

I happened to be the first through the gate, and the first person to rush up to me turned out to be a Polish Catholic priest, a deputy of August Cardinal

Hlond, Primate of Poland, who was not a little startled to discover that the helmeted, uniformed, be-goggled individual he had so heartily embraced was not a man.

In the excitement, which was not the least dampened by the German artillery and the sounds of battle in the northern part of the camp, some of the prisoners died trying to pass through electrically charged barbed wire. Some who got out after the wires were decharged joined in the battle, when some ill-advised S.S. men holding out in a tower fired upon them.

The prisoners charged the tower and threw all six S.S. men out the window. . . .

The barracks at Dachau, like those at Buchenwald, had the stench of death and sickness. But at Dachau there were six barracks like the infamous No. 61 at Buchenwald, where the starving and dying lay virtually on top of each other in quarters where 1,200 men occupied a space intended for 200. The dead—300 died of sickness yesterday—lay on concrete walks outside the quarters and others were being carried out as the reporters went through.

The mark of starvation was on all the emaciated corpses. Many of the living were so frail it seemed impossible they could still be holding on to life.

The crematorium and torture chambers lay outside the prisoner inclosures. Situated in a wood close by, a new building had been built by prisoners under Nazi guards. Inside, in the two rooms used as torture chambers, an estimated 1,200 bodies were piled.

In the crematorium itself were hooks on which the S.S. men hung their victims when they wished to flog them or to use any of the other torture instruments. Symbolic of the S.S. was a mural the S.S. men themselves had painted on the wall. It showed a headless man in uniform with the S.S. insigne on the collar. The man was astride a huge inflated pig, into which he was digging his spurs.

The prisoners also showed reporters the grounds where men knelt and were shot in the back of the neck. On this very spot a week ago a French general, a resistance leader under General Charles de Gaulle, had been killed.

Just beyond the crematorium was a ditch containing some 2,000 more bodies, which had been hastily tossed there in the last few days by the S.S. men, who were so busy preparing their escape they did not have time to burn the bodies.

Below the camp were cattle cars in which prisoners from Buchenwald had been transported to Dachau. Hundreds of dead were still in the cars due to the fact that prisoners in the camp had rejected S.S. orders to remove them. It was mainly the men from these cattle cars that the S.S. leaders had shot before making their escape. Among those who had been left for dead in the cattle cars was one man still alive who managed to lift himself from the heap of corpses on which he lay.

Primary Source

"Dachau" [excerpt]

SYNOPSIS: Gellhorn visited Dachau shortly after its liberation by U.S. troops. She began her article by describing conversations she had with American G.I.s after leaving the camp. "'No one will believe us,' a soldier said. . . . One of the men said suddenly, 'We got to talk about it, see? We got to talk about it if anyone believes us or not." Gellhorn described not only what she saw, but conveyed some of the horrors that prisoners had experienced during their imprisonment.

The doctor spoke with great detachment about the things he had watched in this hospital. He had watched them, and there was nothing he could do to stop them. All the prisoners talked in the same way—quietly, with a strange little smile as if they apologized for talking of such loathsome things to someone who lived in a real world and could hardly be expected to understand Dachau.

"The Germans made here some unusual experiments," he said. "They wished to see how long an aviator could go without oxygen; how high in the sky he could go. So they had a closed car from which they pumped the oxygen. It is a quick death," he said. "It does not take more than fifteen minutes. But it is a hard death. They killed not so many people, only eight hundred, in that experiment. It was found that no one can live above 36,000 feet altitude without oxygen."

"Whom did they choose for this experiment?" I asked.

"Any prisoner," he said, "so long as he was healthy. They picked the strongest. The mortality was one hundred per cent, of course."

"It is very interesting, is it not?" said another doctor. We did not look at one another. I do not know how to explain it, but aside from the terrible anger you feel, you are ashamed. You are ashamed for mankind.

"There was also the experiment of the water," said the first doctor. "This was to see how long pilots could survive when they were shot down over water like the Channel, let us say. For that, the German doctors put the prisoners in great vats of sea water, and they stood in water up to their necks. It was found that the human body can resist for two hours and a half in water eight degrees below zero. They killed six hundred people on this experiment. Though sometimes a man had to suffer three times, for he fainted early in the experiment and then he was revived, and a few days later the experiment was again undertaken."

"Didn't they scream? Didn't they cry out?" I said.

He smiled at that question. "There was no use in this place for a man to scream or cry out. It was no use for any man ever."

A colleague of the doctor's came in. He was the one who knew about the malaria experiment. The German doctor who was chief of the army tropical medicine research used Dachau as an experimental station. He was attempting to find a way to immunize German soldiers against malaria. To that end, he inoculated 11,000 Dachau prisoners with tertiary malaria. The death rate from the malaria was not too heavy; it simply meant that these prisoners weakened by fever died more quickly afterward from hunger. However, in one day three men died of overdoses of pyramidon with which, for some unknown reason, the Germans were then experimenting. No immunization for malaria was ever found.

Down the hall in the surgery, the Polish surgeon got out the record book to look up some data on operations performed by the SS doctors. These were castration and sterilization operations. The prisoner was forced to sign a paper beforehand saying that he willingly undertook this self-destruction. Jews and gypsies were castrated; any foreigner who had had relations with a German woman was sterilized. The woman was sent to a concentration camp.

The surgeon mentioned another experiment, really a very bad one, he said, and obviously quite useless. The guinea pigs were Polish priests. (Over two thousand Catholic priests passed through Dachau, but only one thousand are alive.) The German doctors injected streptococcus germs in the upper leg of the prisoners between the muscle and the bone. An extensive abscess formed, accompanied by fever and extreme pain.

The Polish doctor knew of more than a hundred cases who had been treated this way; there may

Martha Gellhorn in 1940. Gellhorn covered World War II for *Collier's* magazine, traveling all over the world, and occasionally masquerading as a man, to do so. © **BETTMANN/CORBIS. REPRODUCED BY PERMISSION.**

have been more. He had a record of thirty-one deaths, but it took usually from two to three months of ceaseless pain before the patient died, and all of them died after several operations performed during the last few days of their lives. The operations were a further experiment to see if a dying man could be saved, but the answer was that he could not. Some prisoners recovered entirely because they were treated with the already known and proved antidote, but there were others who were now moving around the camp as best they could, crippled for life.

And then because very simply I could listen to no more, my guide who had been in Dachau for ten and a half years took me across the compound to the jail. In Dachau if you want to rest from one horror you go and see another. . . .

I have not talked about how it was the day the American Army arrived, though the prisoners told me. In their joy to be free and longing to see the friends who had come at last, the prisoners rushed to the fence and died—electrocuted. There were those who died cheering, because that effort of happiness was more than their bodies could endure. There were those who died because at last they had food and they ate before they could be stopped and

A photograph taken by Margaret Bourke-White the day after liberation at the Nazi concentration camp in Buchenwald, Germany, April, 1945. This and many of the other photos taken by Bourke-White at Buchenwald were published in the May 7, 1945 issue of *Life* magazine. © ESTATE OF MARGARET BOURKE-WHITE. REPRODUCED BY PERMISSION.

it killed them. I do not know words fine enough to talk of the men who have lived in this horror for years—three years, five years, ten years—and whose minds are as clear and unafraid as the day they entered.

I was in Dachau when the German armies surrendered unconditionally to the Allies. It was a suitable place to be. For surely this war was made to abolish Dachau and all the other places like Dachau and everything that Dachau stands for. To abolish it forever. That these cemetery prisons existed is the crime and shame of the German people.

We are not entirely guiltless, we the Allies, because it took us twelve years to open the gates of Dachau. We were blind and unbelieving and slow, and that we can never be again. We must know now that there can never be peace if there is cruelty like this in the world.

And if ever again we tolerate such cruelty we have no right to peace.

Further Resources

BOOKS

Edwards, Julia. *Women of the World: The Great Foreign Correspondents.* Boston: Houghton Mifflin, 1988.

Gellhorn, Martha. *The Face of War.* New York: Simon & Schuster, 1959.

———. *The View From the Ground.* New York: Atlantic Monthly Press, 1988.

Marzolf, Marion. *Up From the Footnote: A History of Women Journalists.* New York: Hastings House, 1977.

May, Antoinette. *Witness to War: A Biography of Marguerite Higgins.* New York: Beaufort Books, 1983.

Mills, Kay. *A Place in the News: From the Women's Pages to the Front Page.* New York: Dodd, Mead, 1988.

Rollyson, Carl E. *Nothing Ever Happens to the Brave.* New York: St. Martin's, 1990. (Also published as *Beautiful Exile: The Life of Martha Gellhorn.* London: Aurum Press, 2001.)

Wyman, David S. *The Abandonment of the Jews: America and the Holocaust.* New York: Pantheon Books, 1984.

PERIODICALS

Gellhorn, Martha. "Dachau: Experimental Murder." *Collier's,* June 23, 1945.

Lyman, Rick. "Martha Gellhorn, Daring Writer, Dies at 89." *The New York Times,* February 17, 1998.

Obituary for Marguerite Higgins. *The New York Times,* January 4, 1966.

WEBSITES

"America and the Holocaust." *Public Broadcasting Service Online.* Available online at http://www.pbs.org/wgbh/amex/holocaust/index.html (accessed July 30, 2002).

American National Biography. Available online at http://www.anb.org (accessed July 30, 2002).

Mazal, Harry W. "The Dachau Gas Chambers." *The Holocaust History Project.* Available online at http://www.holocaust-history.org/dachau-gas-chambers (accessed July 30, 2002).

United States Holocaust Memorial Museum. Available online at http://www.ushmm.org/ (accessed July 30, 2002).

"Hiroshima"

Magazine article

By: John Hersey

Date: August 31, 1946

Source: Hersey, John. "Hiroshima." *The New Yorker,* August 31, 1946.

About the Author: Born to missionary parents in China, John Richard Hersey (1905–1993) spent nearly the first two decades of life living in eastern Asia. The family did not return to the United States until 1924, after which Hersey began studies for a lengthy journalism career that saw his return to the region of his birth for his most influential work, *Hiroshima.* Despite his other Pulitzer Prize-winning war reporting and a later novel about the destruction of the Warsaw ghetto (*The Wall,* 1950), Hersey is still best remembered for his 1946 story about six survivors of the atomic blast. He died in 1993 at the age of 88. ■

Introduction

Hersey provided readers with some of the most incisive reporting of the evolution of the Pacific War from Asia, China, Japan, Russia, and the South Pacific during World War II (1939–1945). He wrote for *Time* magazine from 1937 to 1944, and *Life* from 1944 through the end of the conflict. Shortly after winning the Pulitzer Prize for his 1944 novel about Italians and the U.S. Army, *A Bell for Adano, Life* magazine and the *The New Yorker* co-sponsored Hersey's return to Japan for a year in which the author would research the aftermath of the atomic bombing of Hiroshima.

One year after the blasts in Hiroshima and Nagasaki, the United States had entered a new conflict of international importance—the Cold War with the Soviet Union. Throughout the Cold War, Americans faced the possibility of nuclear attacks much like those that devastated the

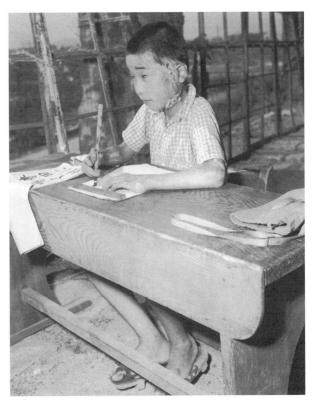

A child with scars on her face from the Hiroshima bomb. **CORBIS-BETTMANN. REPRODUCED BY PERMISSION.**

Japanese during World War II. Hersey's harrowing account of the Hiroshima bombing would provide a startling tale of the horrors wrought by atomic warfare. The story would cast the threat of the Cold War in a new light, as well as dramatically alter readers' opinions concerning this nation's use of atomic bombs to end World War II.

Significance

After a year of interviews, Hersey decided to narrow his story to the lives of six individuals who directly experienced the atomic bombing of Hiroshima: Miss Toshiko Sasaki, a clerk; Dr. Masakazu Fujii, a physician; Mrs. Hatsuyo Nakamura, a tailor's widow with three small children; Father Wilhelm Kleinsorge, a German missionary priest; Dr. Terufumi Sasaki, a young surgeon; and Reverend Mr. Kiyoshi Tanimoto, a Methodist pastor. Hersey's decision to focus on common civilians, two doctors, two clergymen, and two working women, added to the overall humanity of the piece and increased its dramatic effect for his American audience.

Despite the viciousness with which both sides fought in the Pacific and the racist propaganda that dominated mass media during the war, Hersey's realistic portrait of ordinary people encountering extraordinary hardship resonated with the public. He intentionally avoided emotional language and instead focused on providing detailed

Victims of the first atomic bomb, Hiroshima, Japan, 1945. GETTY IMAGES/GAMMA LIAISON, INC. REPRODUCED BY PERMISSION.

accounts of a few individuals who barely escaped death in August 1945. Hersey later explained his reasoning in a letter to historian Paul Boyer, "The flat style was deliberate, and I still think I was right to adopt it. A high literary manner, or a show of passion, would have brought me into the story as a mediator; I wanted to avoid such mediation, so the reader's experience would be as direct as possible." (Boyer, Paul S. *By the Bomb's Early Light*. New York: Pantheon, 1985, 206.)

Rather than offer portions of Hersey's report over several issues, *The New Yorker* made an unprecedented decision to devote an entire issue to this single article. The magazine's predominantly upscale readership received their August 31, 1946, edition to find a cover design depicting a pleasant afternoon at the park—people enjoying themselves by dancing, swimming, and playing during a leisurely summer day. Readers did not open the cover to see their expected commentaries about theater, literature, and politics, however. Instead, they saw the headline "A Reporter at Large: Hiroshima, I—A Noiseless Flash." The editors justified this content with a brief explanation on the opening page, calling for readers to "take time to consider the terrible implications of [the atomic bomb's] use."

The piece would have an immediate impact. The Book-of-the-Month Club sent a free copy of the article to every subscriber. On September 9, 1946, ABC Radio broadcasted a reading of the entire text during its most popular evening hours. Alfred A. Knopf published the article in book form that same year. For the 1989 edition, the author returned to Japan for interviews with the six survivors and added a chapter describing their lives since the bombing. When *The New York Times* published a century's end list of the "Best 100" works of journalism of the twentieth century, John Hersey's "Hiroshima" topped the list.

Primary Source

"Hiroshima" [excerpt]

> **SYNOPSIS:** The following excerpts include the initial reactions of the Reverend Kyoshi Tanimoto and Dr. Masakazu Fujii when the atomic bomb exploded over the center of Hiroshima, Japan. Tanimoto had graduated from Emory College in Atlanta, Georgia, five years earlier and spoke near-fluent English. Fortunately Tanimoto had awakened at 5 a.m. the morning of August 8, 1945, and traveled two miles from the city center to move furniture from his parish to

a friend's house. Dr. Fujii had awakened earlier than usual as well that day to see a guest off at the train station. At 8:15 a.m. the fifty-year-old doctor sat in his private hospital, reading the daily newspaper on the porch.

Then a tremendous flash of light cut across the sky. Mr. Tanimoto has a distinct recollection that it travelled from east to west, from the city toward the hills. It seemed a sheet of sun. Both he and Mr. Matsuo reacted in terror—and both had time to react (for they were 3,500 yards, or two miles, from the center of the explosion). Mr. Matsuo dashed up the front steps into the house and dived among the bedrolls and buried himself there. Mr. Tanimoto took four or five steps and threw himself between two big rocks in the garden. He bellied up very hard against one of them. As his face was against the stone, he did not see what happened. He felt a sudden pressure, and then splinters and pieces of board and fragments of tile fell on him. He heard no roar. (Almost no one in Hiroshima recalls hearing any noise of the bomb. But a fisherman in his sampan on the Inland Sea near Tsuzu, the man with whom Mr. Tanimoto's mother-in-law and sister-in-law were living, saw the flash and heard a tremendous explosion; he was nearly twenty miles from Hiroshima, but the thunder was greater than when the B-29 hit Iwakuni, only five miles away.)

When he dared, Mr. Tanimoto raised his head and saw that the rayon man's house had collapsed. He thought a bomb had fallen directly on it. Such clouds of dust had risen that there was a sort of twilight around. In panic, not thinking for the moment of Mr. Matsuo under the ruins, he dashed out into the street. He noticed as he ran that the concrete wall of the estate had fallen over—toward the house rather than away from it. In the street, the first thing he saw was a squad of soldiers who had been burrowing into the hillside opposite, making one of the thousands of dugouts in which the Japanese apparently intended to resist invasion, hill by hill, life for life; the soldiers were coming out of the hole, where they should have been safe, and blood was running from their heads, chests, and backs. They were silent and dazed.

Under what seemed to be a local dust cloud, the day grew darker and darker. . . .

Dr. Fujii sat down cross-legged in his underwear on the spotless matting of the porch, put on his glasses, and started reading the Osaka *Asahi*. He liked to read the Osaka news because his wife was there. He saw the flash. To him—faced away from

Journalist John Hersey during World War II. Hersey's article on Hiroshima was among the first to bring home to Americans the terrible destruction they had caused by dropping the atomic bomb. © **BETTMANN/CORBIS. REPRODUCED BY PERMISSION.**

the center and looking at his paper—it seemed a brilliant yellow. Startled, he began to rise to his feet. In that moment (he was 1,550 yards from the center), the hospital leaned behind his rising and, with a terrible ripping noise, toppled into the river. The Doctor, still in the act of getting to his feet, was thrown forward and around and over; he was buffeted and gripped; he lost track of everything, because things were so speeded up; he felt the water.

Dr. Fujii hardly had time to think that he was dying before he realized that he was alive, squeezed tightly by two long timbers in a V across his chest, like a morsel suspended between two huge chopsticks—held upright, so that he could not move, with his head miraculously above water and his torso and legs in it. The remains of his hospital were all around him in a mad assortment of splintered lumber and materials for the relief of pain. His left shoulder hurt terribly. His glasses were gone. . . .

Dr. Masakazu Fujii's hospital was no longer on the bank of the Kyo River; it was in the river. After the overturn, Dr. Fujii was so stupefied and so tightly squeezed by the beams gripping his chest that he

Cover of the *New Yorker*. August 31, 1946. This issue of the magazine was devoted entirely to John Hersey's story: "Hiroshima." © 1946 BY THE NEW YORKER MAGAZINE, INC. ALL RIGHTS RESERVED. REPRODUCED BY PERMISSION.

was unable to move at first, and he hung there about twenty minutes in the darkened morning. Then a thought which came to him—that soon the tide would be running in through the estuaries and his head would be submerged—inspired him to fearful activity; he wriggled and turned and exerted what strength he could (though his left arm, because of the pain in his shoulder, was useless), and before long he had freed himself from the vise. After a few moments' rest, he climbed onto the pile of timbers and, finding a long one that slanted up to the river-bank, he painfully shinnied up it.

Dr. Fujii, who was in his underwear, was now soaking and dirty. His under-shirt was torn, and blood ran down it from bad cuts on his chin and back. In this disarray, he walked out onto Kyo Bridge, beside which his hospital had stood. The bridge had not collapsed. He could see only fuzzily without his glasses, but he could see enough to be amazed at the num-

ber of houses that were down all around. On the bridge, he encountered a friend, a doctor named Machii, and asked in bewilderment, "What do you think it was?"

Dr. Machii said, "It must have been a *Molotoffano hanakago*"—a Molotov flower basket, the delicate Japanese name for the "bread basket," or self-scattering cluster of bombs.

At first, Dr. Fujii could see only two fires, one across the river from his hospital site and one quite far to the south. But at the same time, he and his friend observed something that puzzled them, and which, as doctors, they discussed: although there were as yet very few fires, wounded people were hurrying across the bridge in an endless parade of misery, and many of them exhibited terrible burns on their faces and arms. "Why do you suppose it is?" Dr. Fujii asked. Even a theory was comforting that day and Dr. Machii stuck to his. "Perhaps because it was a Molotov flower basket," he said.

There had been no breeze earlier in the morning when Dr. Fujii had walked to the railway station to see a friend off, but now brisk winds were blowing every which way; here on the bridge the wind was easterly. New fires were leaping up, and they spread quickly, and in a very short time terrible blasts of hot air and showers of cinders made it impossible to stand on the bridge any more. Dr. Machii ran to the far side of the river and along a still unkindled street. Dr. Fujii went down into the water under the bridge, where a score of people had already taken refuge, among them his servants, who had extricated themselves from the wreckage. From there, Dr. Fujii saw a nurse hanging in the timbers of his hospital by her legs, and then another painfully pinned across the breast. He enlisted the help of some of the others under the bridge and freed both of them. He thought he heard the voice of his niece for a moment, but he could not find her; he never saw her again. Four of his nurses and the two patients in the hospital died, too. Dr. Fujii went back into the water of the river and waited for the fire to subside.

Further Resources

BOOKS

Boyer, Paul S. *By the Bomb's Early Light*. New York: Pantheon, 1985.

Hersey, John. *Hiroshima*. New York: Random House, 1989.

Hynes, Samuel et al., eds. *Reporting World War II: Part One, American Journalism, 1938–1944*. New York: Library of America, 1995.

———. *Reporting World War II: Part Two, American Journalism, 1944–1945*. New York: Library of America, 1995.

PERIODICALS

Hersey, John. "The Novel of Comtemporary History." *Atlantic History,* November 1949.

Obituary of John Hersey. *The New York Times,* March 25, 1993.

WEBSITES

American National Biography. Available online at http://www .anb.org (accessed July 30, 2002).

"Hiroshima and Nagasaki." *Trinity Atomic Web Site.* Available online at http://nuketesting.enviroweb.org/hiroshim/index .html (accessed July 30, 2002).

Rothman, Steve. "The Publication of 'Hiroshima' in *The New Yorker.* Available online at http://www.geocities.com /Heartland/Hills/6556/hiro.html (accessed July 30, 2002).

"Superman vs. The Atom Man"

Radio script

By: Ben Peter Freeman

Date: November 6, 1946

Source: Freeman, Ben Peter. "The Atom Man—Episode L851." Reprinted in DC Comics, ed., comp. *The Superman Radio Scripts. Volume I: Superman vs. the Atom Man.* New York: Watson-Guptill, 2001, 78–79.

About the Author: Ben Peter Freeman (1901–1992) wrote for the *Saturday Evening Post* and *The New York Times* prior to creating television and radio scripts for the wildly popular Superman series of the 1940s and 1950s. After leaving the program in 1953, he served as a sales manager for a Chicago Construction Company until his retirement. Freeman died on December 11, 1992, at the age of 91. ∎

Introduction

Action Comics #1, which featured the debut of Superman, ushered in a new era of comic book superheroes that quickly spawned series in other media formats, such as novels, cartoons, newspaper comics, radio, film, and, later, television. Only eight years elapsed between the first appearance of Superman and his monumental battles with The Atom Man broadcast in the fall of 1946, but in that time the cultural terrain had changed immensely. The end of World War II (1939–1945) brought the temporary demise of comic books, as Americans opted instead for radio programs. Broadcast entertainment thrived in the 1940s, with the first Superman radio series beginning only two years after *Action Comics #1* appeared in June 1938. "The Adventures of Superman" hit the airwaves in 1940 and continued to thrill listeners until 1951. As radio gave way to television, the Superman TV series ran for 104 episodes during the 1950s and continues to be syndicated.

As media formats changed during the 1940s, so too did the political context in which they were produced. The end of World War II brought the downfall of the Axis powers (Germany, Japan, and Italy) but the fear of war remained. The Cold War between the Soviet Union and the United States started as the atomic bombs fell over Hiroshima and Nagasaki in August 1945. These nuclear attacks spawned an unprecedented arms race and an inescapable fear of atomic destruction.

Significance

In the latter months of World War II, the U.S. War Department censored DC Comics and prevented it from running storylines concerning atomic testing and nuclear technology until after the war. The increasing fascination with nuclear weaponry and the destructive capacity of atomic warfare greatly influenced the plotlines of radio programs such as "The Adventures of Superman." In the fall of 1946, just over one year after the atomic bombings of Japan, Superman began a titanic, nearly 50-part battle with his newest arch-enemy—The Atom Man.

Still in the shadow of war with Germany, the series began with the villain Der Teufel (meaning The Devil in German) stealing a batch of kryptonite, which the audience knew rendered Superman powerless. Seeking to engulf the world in Nazi tyranny, Der Teufel used the radioactive powers of kryptonite to create The Atom Man, whose radioactive energy could feasibly destroy Superman and the United States with him.

This plot joined Americans' lingering fear of Nazism and new-found anxiety over atomic weaponry. The Atom Man, who "threatened to destroy the entire city unless the Nazi swastika was raised over City Hall," represented the troubles both known and unknown posed by "atomic energy." At almost the same moment that the public first encountered The Atom Man, they witnessed the destructive capacity of atomic weapons in John Hersey's article "Hiroshima." Most likely, a listener would immediately understand the horrible ramifications of this exchange between the naïve young journalist Jimmy Olsen and his editor, Perry White: "[L]ook, Mayor—it's one thing to *say* you're going to destroy Metropolis, and another thing to be able to do it. This is the biggest city in the world. Olsen: . . . . [L]ook what just one atomic bomb did to Hiroshima!"

Primary Source

"Superman vs. The Atom Man"

SYNOPSIS: The following episode, transcribed in its entirety, marked the conclusion of the 47-part "Atom Man" story that ran during the fall of 1946. As with nearly all radio entertainment programs of this period, this broadcast began with an opening and closing promotion for the show's sponsor, the Kellogg's cereal company. The final scene noted that danger had not completely left Metropolis, providing eager listeners with further reason to return to their radio sets the next evening for more adventures of Superman. This story proved so popular that it was reproduced as a 15-part film serial, "Atom Man vs. Superman," in 1950.

Cast

Announcer

Henry Miller

Superman

Inspector Henderson

General Niles

Theme

Announcer: Superman!

Wind effect . . . and down. End of track one.

Announcer: Boasting that he would destroy every man, woman and child in Metropolis as his first step in avenging the defeat of Germany, Henry Miller, the fanatical young Nazi, in whose veins flows the deadly kryptonite which enables him to generate atomic power, prepared to explode the dam guarding the great billion-gallon reservoir in the hills above the city. While the police and army guarded the river and canal, and Superman searched for him from the night skies, Miller, hidden in a dark patch of woods in the hills, attacked the reservoir! The first sparks of jagged green lightning which leaped from his weirdly gloved hands landed just short of the dam, plowing an enormous crater in the earth. From aloft, Superman heard the explosion, and launched himself down through space at his deadly foe.

As we continue now, a titanic battle is raging in the pale moonlight. Miller, the Atom Man, pointing his metal-gloved hands aloft, sends fierce shafts of green lightning hissing and crackling at Superman, who wheels and spins and darts from them like some great bird—seeking an opportunity to flash in and rip the electronic converter from Miller's throat. Screaming like a maniac, Miller hurls bolt after bolt at the Man of Steel—watches him falter in midair like a wounded bird—and then barely swoop out of range.

Sneak in atomics and swooping wind above.

Miller: (*screaming just off mike*) Come closer, I dare you! You're afraid of me! (*mad laugh*) Superman is afraid of me!

Feature atomics at full, then down for Announcer—no wind.

Announcer: (*on cue*) Gasping for breath, his mighty muscles weakened by the bombardment of atomic power, Superman clings to the top of a tall tree, regaining his lost strength. But the Atom Man, whirling about, sees him and advances, his strange meshed hands outstretched, forked green lightning hurtling from them to pierce and shrivel the trees in his path—to rend and uproot them, and send them crashing to earth with a roar like Jovian thunder!

The works on the trees for about five seconds—bending, exploding, crashing.

Miller: (*on cue*) (*screaming*) Now for you, Superman!

Announcer: (*low and tense*) His eyes gleaming like a madman's, the Nazi monster points his hands at the tree to which Superman clings—laughing triumphantly as the green atomic lightning strikes the giant trunk, coils around it like fierce, twining snakes, uproots and hurls it, blackened and scorched, to the earth! And as Superman falls to the ground in the crashing branches, the Atom Man rushes toward him.

Miller: Now, I've got you! This time, you're through!

Superman: No! Keep away!

Announcer: His atomic power raking and exploding the earth and branches about his fallen foe, the Atom Man races forward—

Explosions.

Announcer: (*on cue*) But suddenly—when he is only a few paces away, there is a violent burst of wind—(*burst wind*)—a blur of red and blue, and Superman bounds high from the ground—flashing up into the heavens like a comet!

Enraged, the Atom Man points his hands aloft and hurls deadly green lightning after him!

Feature atomics for about three seconds.

Announcer: (*on cue*) One bolt—another—strikes the Man of Steel, and his swift ascent is halted. He struggles in midair—threshes his powerful arms and legs like a desperate swimmer—and then as a third bolt strikes him, he shudders—and begins to fall!

Wind of fall over atomics.

Announcer: Faster and faster he falls—the pale moon lighting his billowing red cape and shimmering on the silvery waters of the vast reservoir below. There is a mighty splash.

Mighty splash and fade out all sound.

Announcer: And Superman disappears beneath the surface of the lake.—For a long minute—*two* minutes—there is nothing to be seen but an ever-widening circle of ripples on the smooth bosom of the water. And at the edge of the blackened, ravaged woods, the Atom Man, who has turned the switch on the converter at his throat and stilled his deadly power, laughs long and loud.

Miller: (*keep Atom Man voice*) (*great laugh*) I said I'd finish you, and I did! You're dead now—drowned!—and when I explode the dam and send a billion gallons of water pouring down on Metropolis, your useless body will be carried with it. (*wild laugh*)

Click, hum of kryptonite, atomics and build.

Announcer: Once again, the Atom Man touches the switch on the converter strapped to his throat, flashing the electronic impulse to the deadly kryptonite atoms in his blood and surging toward his gloved hands, from which they emerge in the jagged green sparks of atomic energy.

And now, triumphantly, he lifts his hands again—points them at the high concrete dam protecting the great reservoir. The green lightning leaps—ever lengthening—and is almost at the dam, when (*burst wind and sustain*) Superman flashes upward from the deep waters of the reservoir, his costume and cape dripping—and rockets like a bullet at the Atom Man!

Superman: (*fading in above*) (*project*) No, you don't, Miller!

Miller: (*wild with rage*) *You,* again! What does it take to kill you?

Superman: More than *you've* got, my friend!

Miller: You're crazy, you fool! I'll finish you now! Now!

Superman: It's *you* who'll be finished tonight, Miller!

Miller: We'll see!—Stop this if you can!

Feature atomics for couple seconds and swirl wind through—then down just enough to let Announcer over.

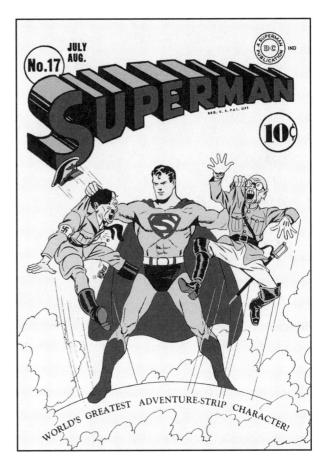

Superman dangles a terrified Hitler and Tojo high above the Earth on this comic book cover from July-August, 1942. DC COMICS, INC.

Announcer: Once more, the strange and terrible battle rages. Mouthing wild curses, the Atom Man hurls his green power again and again at his flying foe, who darts and twists from it—circles and turns in the air like a giant falcon.

Superman: You'll exhaust your power, Miller! What'll you do then?

Miller: It won't be exhausted before I finish you—and Metropolis too!—(*wild triumph*) There! Now, I've go you!—*There!*

Superman: (*off, fading*) (*cry out in pain*). No! No!

Feature atomics briefly, then jump to landing off.

Announcer: (*on cue*) Suddenly caught by a dozen bolts of atomic lightning, Superman cries out—stricken—tries to zoom away—falters—and thuds to earth twenty yards from where Miller stands.—He lies there—groaning—trying desperately to rise—as the Atom Man rushes toward him, his wild, gloating laugh ringing through the woods.

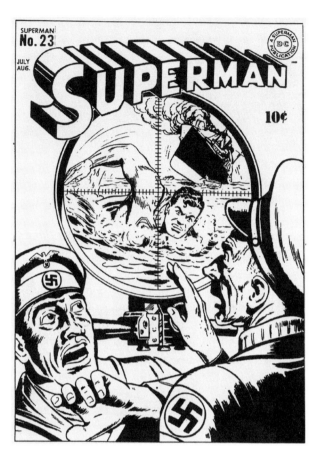

Nazi submariners are terrified by the approach of Superman on this comic book cover from July-August, 1943. DC COMICS, INC.

Miller: (*laugh*) The mighty Superman! This is the end!

Superman: (*off, fade in groaning*) No—I can't—I can't—

Announcer: As the Atom Man is almost upon him, Superman makes one final, frenzied effort—rolls and clutches at a fallen tree—manages to throw it into the path of his murderous foe. Unable to check his wild rush in time, the Atom Man trips over the tree trunk, and falls!

Studio: *Miller falls, then series of muffled explosions.*

Miller: (*cry out as falls*).

Announcer: His hands thrown out, the Atom Man lies stunned for a brief moment, as the ghastly lightning pours from his fingers and shatters the earth around him. And in that brief moment, Superman rises to his feet—his eyes bulging and red-rimmed—his costume stained and torn.

Superman: Now's my chance! Now!

Announcer: Like a staggering giant, Superman reaches the Atom Man, and swoops him into his arms.

Superman: (*ring out triumphantly*) Up!—Up! And Awaay!

Super wind in burst and lower under with atomics.

Announcer: High into the pale moonlight leaps the Man of Steel, the fiercely struggling Atom Man in his arms. Five thousand feet! Ten thousand feet!

Miller: (*screaming*) I'll kill you! I'll kill you!

Superman: (*effort*) I want that converter on your throat!

Miller: No!—(*fighting*) No!

Superman: (*effort*) I'll get it if I have to—(*weakening*) take your hands off my shoulders!

Wind down and atomics up.

Miller: I'll kill you! I'll kill you!

Superman: (*gasping*) Take your hands off, I said!—The atomic power—it's—it's weakening me!

Miller: I warned you, you fool! I said I'd finish you! Now, I will! (*wild laugh*)

Feature atomics briefly, and down to let Announcer over.

Announcer: (*on cue*) Fastening his metal gloved hands on Superman's shoulders, the Atom Man's wild laugh rings insanely through the heavens as he witnesses his powerful foe shudder—feels him weaken and grow limp.

Miller: (*screaming*) Die, Superman, die!

Superman: Stop it!—Stop it! My strength—is almost gone—I—I'll drop you! (*groan and pass out*) Aagh—

Miller: Die!—Die!—(*scream of terror*)

Announcer: As the terrible atomic power smashes again and again at his weakened body, Superman loses consciousness. His head falls on his chest—his eyes close, and his strong arms relax their grip on his opponent.

Miller: (*scream and fade fast*) I'm falling! I'm falling! (*screaming*)

Rush of Miller's and Superman's fall over atomics and lose atomics. Build wind.

Announcer: Screaming in terror, the Atom Man feels himself falling—shrieks in panic as he sees the ground miles below rushing up to meet him. A few feet away, his red cape bil-

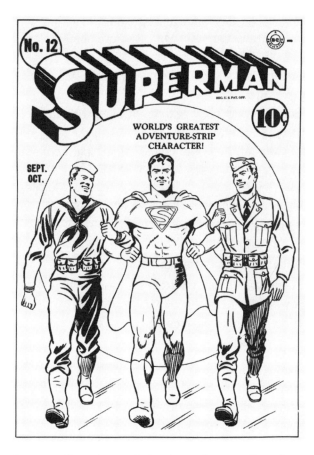

Superman walks arm in arm with American servicemen on this comic book cover from September-October, 1941. DC COMICS, INC.

lowing about his limp body, Superman falls, too. Faster and faster the two deadly enemies—both of them helpless now—plummet down toward the bank of the city's north canal—where police officers and soldiers, attracted by the amazing green lightning miles above, stare upwards in open mouthed wonder. And then—

Studio: *Wind up to full for second and two great thuds, one right after the other, and then all sound out.*

Announcer: (*on cue*) There are two smashing, sickening thuds, as first the Atom Man, and then the Man of Steel, strike the earth and lie still.

A few minutes later, Superman opens his eyes to see the anxious faces of Police Inspector Henderson and General Niles of the army, looking down at him.

Sneak in harbor, B.G.

Superman: (*fading in dazedly*) Oh, hello—hello, Inspector.

Henderson: Are you all right, Superman?

Superman: (*halting*) Yes, I think so.

Studio: *Scrambling to feet.*

Henderson: Don't try to get up yet.

Superman: I'm all right.—Miller—the Atom Man. What about him?

Henderson: He's finished.

Superman: Are you sure?

Henderson: No doubt about it. What's left of him is under that canvas over there. You saved Metropolis tonight, Superman.

General: You certainly did, and I want to extend my thanks and the thanks of the army. I'm General Niles, by the way.

Superman: Thank you, sir. I didn't mean to let Miller die. But I carried him into the air to prevent him from exploding the dam—and then he tried to finish me. I lost consciousness.

General: You did a wonderful job. Simply wonderful. We've had a report of what happened at the reservoir. If not for you—(*shiver*) every man, woman, and child in Metropolis would be dead by now.

Henderson: We owe you more than we can ever repay.

Superman: You don't owe me anything. I'm fighting for the same things you are—the end of tyranny and intolerance—all the things that Miller and the Nazis stood for.

Henderson: Then I'll only say thank heaven that the worst threat America ever faced is over.

General: I'll second that.

Superman: I'm sorry, gentlemen, but the threat is *far* from over.

Henderson & General: (*startled*) It isn't? What do you mean?

Superman: I mean that a terrible threat still remains—to *me*—to you, and to the entire world.

Fade out harbor.

Announcer: Amazed, Inspector Henderson and General Niles stare at Superman. Henry Miller, the deadly Atom Man, is no more, so what can his conqueror mean? You, who have followed this story closely, may be able to guess what Superman means, and know why, at this very moment of his greatest triumph, his own life, and the lives of all humanity, are still in mortal danger! In tomorrow's episode, the Man of Steel explains, and begins a new and thrilling adventure which is even more exciting than the one from which he has just emerged. So don't fail to be with us tomorrow, same time, same station, for the beginning of one of the most exciting stories in all THE ADVENTURES OF SUPERMAN!

Announcer: Faster than a speeding bullet!

Studio: *Rifle bullet ricochet.*

Announcer: More powerful than a locomotive!

Studio: *Locomotive effect.*

Announcer: Able to leap tall buildings at a single bound!

Studio: *Burst of wind, level and fluctuate behind Announcer and Voices.*

Announcer: Look! Up in the sky!

Voice 1: It's a bird!

Voice 2: It's a plane!

Voice 3: (*big*) It's Superman!

Announcer: Follow The Adventures of Superman, brought to you every day, Monday through Friday, same time, same station, by the great old Kellogg Company of Battle Creek. And—for other thrilling adventures of Superman, see your local newspaper. Superman is also a copyrighted feature appearing in *Superman* D.C. Publications.

Further Resources

BOOKS

Daniels, Les. *Superman, The Complete History: The Life and Times of the Man of Steel.* San Francisco: Chronicle Books, 1998.

PERIODICALS

"Ben Peter Freeman, Superman Serialist." *Chicago Sun-Times,* December 30, 1992.

WEBSITES

The Antique Radio Collector. Available online at http://www.oldtimeradioprograms.com (accessed July 30, 2002).

"Superman Radio." *DC Comics.* Available online at http://www.dccomics.com/radio/index.html (accessed July 30, 2002).

Younis, Steven. *Superman Homepage.* Available online at http://www.supermanhomepage.com (accessed July 30, 2002).

AUDIO AND VISUAL MEDIA

Superman vs. Atom Man on Radio: Smithsonian Historical Performances. Smithsonian Institution and Radio Spirits, 1999.

Superman on Radio: Smithsonian Historical Performances (Historical Radio Plays). Smithsonian Institution, 1998.

Superman with Batman & Robin on Radio: Smithsonian Historical Performances (Historical Radio Plays). Smithsonian Institution, 1998.

Superman: The Movie. (1978)

"1948 Is Television's Big Boom Year"
Magazine article, Photographs

By: Joanne Melniker
Date: July 20, 1948
Source: Melniker, Joanne. "1948 Is Television's Big Boom Year." *Look* 12, no. 15, July 20, 1948, 28–33.
About the Author: In the publication's table of contents for its July 20, 1948, edition, *Look* magazine introduced its readers to a staff writer who was both "pretty" and "hard-working"—24-year-old Joanne Melniker. Despite the numerous reporters who provided crucial reports during World War II (1939–1945), female journalists remained a distinct minority in the profession at the close of the decade. Thus, the publication relied upon several gendered references to increase the impact of Melniker's story, particularly how her fourteen consecutive nights of television viewing "made New York night life pretty dull for several men about town." Besides referring to her movie-watching habits and predilection for ballet music, the introduction noted that its youngest writer graduated from Smith College at the age of 19 and quickly advanced to become *Look*'s "Eastern head of the Entertainment Department." ∎

Introduction

Americans experienced television sporadically prior to the end of World War II. Commerce Secretary, and later President, Herbert Hoover (served 1929–1933) starred in the first public demonstration when he gave a speech in Washington, D.C., that American Telephone and Telegraph transmitted to viewers in New York City. In 1939 millions of visitors to the World's Fair in New York saw a massive exhibit declaring television the wave of the future. Right after the Federal Communications Commission (FCC) decided to permit commercial television in 1941, the United States became embroiled in World War II (1939–1945). The conflict halted virtually all television broadcasting, hindering public use throughout the early 1940s. All research and development efforts centered on war production, eventually leading to major technological innovations in broadcasting. Between the war's end in August 1945 and the end of the decade, television grew to become a major force in American mass media.

Significance

As *Look* magazine noted, 1948 proved to be "Television's Big Boom Year." Only nine television broadcast

Number of Television Stations in the United States in 1948

Number of Stations Now in Operation

Baltimore, Md.	2	Newark, N.J.	1
Boston, Mass.	1	New Haven, Conn.	1
Buffalo, N.Y.	1	New York, N.Y.	4
Chicago, Ill.	2	Philadelphia, Pa.	3
Cincinnati, Ohio	1	Richmond, Va.	1
Cleveland, Ohio	1	St. Louis, Mo.	1
Detroit, Mich.	1	St. Paul, Minn.	1
Los Angeles, Calif.	1	Schenectady, N.Y.	1
Milwaukee, Wis.	1	Washington, D.C.	3

Number of Additional Stations to Begin Operating Within Year

Albuquerque, N.M.	1	Memphis, Tenn.	1
Ames, Iowa	1	Miami, Fla.	1
Atlanta, Ga.	3	Minneapolis, Minn.	2
Baltimore, Md.	1	New Orleans, La.	3
Binghamton, N.Y.	1	New York, N.Y.	2
Birmingham, Ala.	2	Oklahoma City, Okla.	1
Bloomington, Ind.	1	Omaha, Nebr.	2
Boston, Mass.	1	Phoenix, Ariz.	1
Charlotte, N.C.	1	Pittsburgh, Pa.	1
Chicago, Ill.	2	Portland, Ore.	1
Cincinnati, Ohio	2	Providence, R.I.	1
Cleveland, Ohio	2	Riverside, Calif.	1
Columbus, Ohio	3	Rochester, N.Y.	1
Dallas, Tex.	2	Rome, N.Y.	1
Davenport, Iowa	1	St. Petersburg, Fla.	1
Dayton, Ohio	2	Salt Lake City, Utah	1
Detroit, Mich.	2	San Antonio, Tex.	2
Erie, Pa.	1	San Diego, Calif.	1
Ft. Worth, Tex.	1	San Francisco, Calif.	3
Greenboro, N.C.	1	Seattle, Wash.	1
Houston, Tex.	1	Stockton, Calif.	1
Indianapolis, Ind.	2	Toledo, Ohio	1
Jacksonville, Fla.	1	Tulsa, Okla	1
Johnstown, Pa.	1	Utica, N.Y.	1
Kansas City, Mo.	1	Waltham, Mass.	1
Lancaster, Pa.	1	Washington, D.C.	1
Los Angeles, Calif.	6	Wilmington, Del.	1
Louisville, Ky.	2		

SOURCE: "1948 Is Television's Big Boom Year." *Look Magazine*, March 4, 1947, p. 28

rest of the century. The writer noted that only about one in ten Americans had even seen television by July 1948. Besides the limited number of stations in operation at the time, the price of television sets made widespread TV ownership virtually impossible. The 10-inch G.E. model was priced at $449.95, or more than $3,300 in 2002 dollar values. The gigantic 20-inch DuMont priced at $2,495 in 1948—more than $18,000 in 2002 U.S. dollars.

Writing many years before 24-hour television programming and hundreds of channel choices, Melniker declared that "an adult finds little to keep him in his chair" in 1948. Yet the shows described in her piece present many similarities to modern television schedules, with sports, comedy, music, fashion, drama, and children's programs providing the most popular viewing options.

This article also foreshadowed the "sweeping" changes that television brought to American media and culture in the coming years. Unfortunately for the workers at *Look* magazine, one of mass media's sacrifices to TV would be the once popular, large-format, picture-based magazine. Started in 1937, one year after its main competitor, *Life, Look* lost more and more advertising revenue to television and ceased publication in 1971. One year later, *Life* suspended operations until 1978.

Primary Source

"1948 Is Television's Big Boom Year": Magazine article

SYNOPSIS: Just two years prior to the publication of Melniker's article, the FCC officially described the public service responsibilities held by radio and television broadcasters as controlling "not merely a means of entertainment, but also an unequaled medium for the dissemination of news, information, and opinion, and for the discussion of public issues." As Joanne Melniker conveys in her opening paragraphs, viewers were only just beginning to see the radical changes television would bring to U.S. society. Some of the photographs that accompanied the original article are reproduced here as well.

Television is no longer just around the corner. It's here. Never has an industry grown up so fast. Reports about it one day are out of date the next. It is still too early to say exactly how television will alter America's cultural pattern, but even its detractors admit that the changes will be sweeping. Not only the home, but also the schoolroom and the factory will feel its effect.

Lots will be happening to television in 1948. Here are some of the predictions. There will be more

stations operated in the entire United States in 1946, with only a single station operating west of the Mississippi River. More than half of these stations resided in the nation's two largest cities—Chicago and New York City. By 1947 the total number of stations had doubled. In October of that year President Harry Truman (served 1945–1953) delivered the first presidential telecast, in which he explained the importance of food conservation. Thirty additional stations began operations in 1948 and 49 starts occurred in 1949.

Joanne Melniker's task for *Look* was to examine the state of the television industry in 1948. To undertake such a project, she researched television programming, viewer demographics, and the massive changes then underway that would reshape global media for the

Public Service Responsibility of Broadcast Licensees: Report By Federal Communications Commission, March 7, 1946 [excerpt]

C. Discussion of Public Issues

The use of broadcasting as an instrument for the dissemination of news, ideas, and opinions raises a multitude of problems of a complex and sometimes delicate nature, which do not arise in connection with purely entertainment programs. A few such problems may be briefly noted, without any attempt to present an exhaustive list:

1. Shall time for the presentation of one point of view on a public issue be sold, or shall all such presentations of points of view be on sustaining time only?

2. If presentations of points of view are to be limited only to sustaining time, what measures can be taken to insure that adequate sustaining time during good listening hours is made available for such presentations, and that such time is equitably distributed?

3. If time is also on occasion to be sold for presentation of a point of view, what precautions are necessary to insure that the most time shall not gravitate to the side prepared to spend the most money?

4. Are forums, town meetings, and round-table type broadcasts, in which two or more points of view are aired together, intrinsically superior to the separate presentation of points of view at various times?

5. Should such programs be sponsored?

6. What measures will insure that such programs be indeed fair and well-balanced among opposing points of view?

7. Should locally originated discussion programs, in which residents of a community can themselves discuss issues of local, national, or international importance be encouraged, and if so, how?

8. How can an unbiased presentation of the news be achieved?

9. Should news be sponsored, and if so, to what extent should the advertiser influence or control the presentation of the news?

10. How and by whom should commentators be selected?

11. Should commentators be forbidden, permitted, or encouraged to express their own personal opinions?

12. Is a denial of free speech involved when a commentator is discharged or his program discontinued because something which he has said has offended (a) the advertiser, (b) the station, (c) a minority of his listeners, or (d) a majority of his listeners?

13. What provisions, over and above Section 315 of the Communications Act of 1934, are necessary or desirable in connection with the operation of broadcast stations during a political campaign?

14. Does a station operate in the public interest which charges a higher rate for political broadcasts than for commercial programs?

15. The Federal Communications Commission is forbidden by law to censor broadcasts. Should station licensees have the absolute right of censorship, or should their review of broadcasts be limited to protection against libel, dissemination of criminal matter, etc.?

16. Should broadcasters be relieved of responsibility for libel with respect to broadcasts over which they exercise no control?

17. Should the "right to reply" to broadcasts be afforded; and if so, to whom should the right be afforded, and under what circumstances?

18. When a station refuses time on the air requested for the discussion of public issues, should it be required to state in writing its reasons for refusal? Should it be required to maintain a record of all such requests for time, and of the disposal made of them?

19. What measures can be taken to open broadcasting to types of informational programs which contravene the interests of large advertisers—for example, news of the reports and decisions of the Federal Trade Commission concerning unfair advertising; reports of the American Medical Association concerning the effects of cigarette-smoking; temperance broadcasts; etc?

These are only a few of the many questions which are raised in complaints to the Commission from day to day. The future of American broadcasting as an instrument of democracy depends in no small part upon the establishment of sound solutions to such problems, and on the fair and impartial application of general solutions to particular cases. . . .

The carrying of any particular public discussion, of course, is a problem for the individual broadcaster. But the public interest clearly requires that an adequate amount of time be made available for the discussion of public issues; and the Commission, in determining whether a station has served the public interest, will take into consideration the amount of time which has been or will be devoted to the discussion of public issues.

SOURCE: Federal Communications Commission. *Public Service Responsibility of Broadcast Licensees.* Washington, D.C.: GPO, March 7, 1946, 39–40.

than 750,000 sets in use by the end of the year. Instead of 27 stations, there will be over 100. By the end of two years, there will be an audience of 65,000,000 and 100,000 persons will be employed in the industry. Within five years, it will be established as one of ten largest industries of the nation.

How and Where You Can See Television

At this point, only one American in every ten has seen television. But now that broadcasters in 63 major U. S. cities have their feet in the television door, this will soon be remedied—see list on facing page.

It takes more than a will, however, to put over a television station. The average capital investment for a station is $375,000. In the larger cities, the investment will be approximately $1,000,000 per station and the operating loss is estimated at $500,000 per year in each of the first two years thereafter. In general, to estimate the cost of a television operation, you multiply radio costs by ten.

Not only broadcasters have rushed into the act, but advertisers too. In the past year the number of sponsors has increased 800 per cent. Gillette paid $100,000 for the right to televise the Louis-Walcott return match. It's said that the television rights for baseball games in New York City cost $700,000. The reason for the broadcasters' hurry is based on the limited number of stations allotted industry by the Federal Communications Commission. Each city is given a certain number of channel's according to its population, selling possibilities and lack of interference between stations. There are 12 available channels. And FCC hearings are being held in cities where there are more applicants than facilities to determine who shall receive licenses.

At the moment, the longest TV network is from Boston to Richmond, and the first coast-to-coast network will not be in operation until 1951. But national advertisers are planning to spend $10,000.000 this year on television. Compared to the $447,000.000 which went into radio advertising last year, this may seem insignificant. But the trend is there, and it will keep building up each year.

Television Sets

The sixteen sets shown on this page give a good idea of what's on the market today—prices quoted are subject to change. They range from the cheapest, Tele-Tone's, to the most expensive, DuMont's. To the prices must be added installation costs ranging from $50 to $300. Not pictured is Pilot's new

15 lb. model with a 3″ image, priced at less than $100.

Most television receivers are direct-view models—the image is seen on the tube itself. Projection models, like the RCA machine, left, have a small tube but they use an arrangement of lenses to throw a larger image on the screen. To increase the size of the image on the small, direct-view model, a magnifying lens can be fitted over the screen.

At present there are about 350,000 television receivers in operation in the U. S. Three-fourths of them are in the Eastern network cities and at least half around New York City. This still represents a mere drop in the bucket compared to the 66,000,000 radios in 37,000,000 homes.

Here's What You Can See On Television

The program end of television is still in the try-and-hope-it-works stage. It has far to go to catch up to the technical marvels that gave it birth. With some exceptions, an adult finds little to keep him in his chair. But more money and removal of barriers like the ban on live music make the future brighter.

The programs pictured here are typical of what is available to a viewer in the New York area. Sports "telecasts" (TV word for broadcast), usually excellent, are the mainstay. Despite grumbles to the contrary, most experts agree that this will stimulate, not kill, interest in live sporting events. Although presently most stations are on an average of only four hours a day, plans are going ahead for more daytime shows. Question still being raised, still unanswered: Will the housewife take time from her chores to watch?

General Foods, which sponsored 217 television programs last year, recently released a report on the average television family in New York City. This family owns a set bought within the last year, with a seven-inch or ten-inch screen. It pays more than $75 a month for rent, has a phone. There are 3.3 persons in the family. They invite friends in for a telecast about three times a week. The head of the family is an executive, professional man or owns his own business. An average of 3.47 persons watch the set every night. Of the 42 hours available at the time of the survey, the average televiewer's set was turned on for 17 of them. Further checks showed that more than 68 per cent of the viewers remembered the names of the programs' sponsors. Sports, dramatic shows and movies were preferred, in that order.

How and Where You Can See Television

At this point, only one American in every ten has seen television. But now that broadcasters in 63 major U. S. cities have their feet in the television door, this will soon be remedied—see list on facing page.

It takes more than a will, however, to put over a television station. The average capital investment for a station is $375,000. In the larger cities, the investment will be approximately $1,000,000 per station and the operating loss is estimated at $500,000 per year in each of the first two years thereafter. In general, to estimate the cost of a television operation, you multiply radio costs by ten.

Not only broadcasters have rushed into the act, but advertisers too. In the past year the number of sponsors has increased 800 per cent. Gillette paid $100,000 for the right to televise the Louis-Walcott return match. It's said that the television rights for baseball games in New York City cost $700,000. The reason for the broadcasters' hurry is based on the limited number of stations allotted industry by the Federal Communications Commission. Each city is given a certain number of channels according to its population, selling possibilities and lack of interference between stations. There are 12 available channels. And FCC hearings are being held in cities where there are more applicants than facilities to determine who shall receive licenses.

At the moment, the longest TV network is from Boston to Richmond, and the first coast-to-coast network will not be in operation until 1951. But national advertisers are planning to spend $10,000,000 this year on television. Compared to the $447,000,000 which went into radio advertising last year, this may seem insignificant. But the trend is there, and it will keep building up each year.

Transmitters are changing city skylines.

TELE-TONE
$149.95
7" Image

HALLICRAFTERS
$169.50
7" Image

MOTOROLA
$179.95
7" Image

EMERSON
$269.50
10" Image

PHILCO
$339.50
10" Image

U. S. TELEVISION
$375
10" Image

FARNSWORTH
$375*
10" Image

ADMIRAL
$309.95
10" Image

GENERAL ELECTRIC
$449.95
10" Image

WESTINGHOUSE
$685
10" Image

STEWART-WARNER
$682
10" Image

ANDREA
$685
12" Image

CROSLEY
$795
10" Image

STROMBERG-CARLSON
$1,195*
12" Image

*Includes installation

RCA
$1,195
15" x 20" (projection)

DUMONT
$2,495
20" Image

TELEVISION SETS

The sixteen sets shown on this page give a good idea of what's on the market today—prices quoted are subject to change. They range from the cheapest, Tele-Tone's, to the most expensive, DuMont's. To the prices must be added installation costs ranging from $50 to $300. Not pictured is Pilot's new 15 lb. model with a 3" image, priced at less than $100.

Most television receivers are direct-view models—the image is seen on the tube itself. Projection models, like the RCA machine, left, have a small tube but they use an arrangement of lenses to throw a larger image on the screen. To increase the size of the image on the small, direct-view model, a magnifying lens can be fitted over the screen.

At present there are about 350,000 television receivers in operation in the U. S. Three-fourths of them are in the Eastern network cities and at least half around New York City. This still represents a mere drop in the bucket compared to the 66,000,000 radios in 37,000,000 homes.

(Continued on next page)

Primary Source

"1948 Is Television's Big Boom Year": Photographs (1 OF 2)

SYNOPSIS: Accompanying the article on "1948 Is Television's Big Boom Year: How and Where You Can See Television," *Look* magazine, July 20, 1948, was this image of sixteen television sets. LOOK MAGAZINE, JULY 20, 1948, VOL. 12, #15, P. 29.

Primary Source

"1948 Is Television's Big Boom Year": Photographs (2 OF 2)

The article "1948 Is Television's Big Boom Year" included photos from popular TV programs to illustrate what was available to watch, *Look* magazine, July 20, 1948. LOOK MAGAZINE, JULY 20, 1948, VOL. 12, #15, P.30.

These are the BASIC INGREDIENTS

- Sports
- Quiz
- Children's
- Educational
- Service
- Discussion
- Amateur
- News
- Musical
- Movies
- Fashion
- Crime
- Participation
- Drama
- Comedy
- "How To"

Since January, Television Milestones Have Come Thick and Fast

The television events on these pages have occurred since the first of the year. Although they are just an inkling of what is to come, they represent a great miracle of our civilization. This miracle started in 1873 when scientists discovered the conductivity of a metal called selenium. It provided a means of converting light waves into electrical impulses. The photoelectric cell was the next step. But still only the total amount of light reflected by an image was caught, not the image itself. In 1883, Paul Nipkow invented a whirling disk which broke the image into small parts, transmitted them one after another. This became the basis for today's television receiver. The wireless and motion picture added sound and movement.

Then men began to look for a way to do this electronically. In 1932, Dr. Vladimir Zworykin patented the iconoscope. This recorded the image with a cathode-ray tube instead of a disk and photoelectric cell.

Once electronic scanning was initiated, the course of television was set. In 1931, Dr. Allen B. DuMont came up with a workable receiver.

Although television had been on view at the New York World's Fair, it wasn't until 1941 that the FCC gave the go-ahead on commercial televising. Then the war got in the way. When television came into the news again there was a new gimmick—color, developed by CBS. RCA, king of black-and-white, bristled. Color needed costlier equipment, different channels, was still impractical commercially.

In March, 1947, the FCC banished color television to the laboratory for further work, and the rush for black-and-white was on. People bought sets, not afraid that they would be obsolete the next day. Bars put in television, and New York City's Hotel Roosevelt led the way with sets in its rooms.

Today the potentialities of television are tremendous. Like anything else, it can work for both good and evil. This will be largely determined by the men who control it. But in the long run it is up to the public.

Further Resources

BOOKS

Barnouw, Erik. *Tube of Plenty: The Evolution of American Television.* New York: Oxford University Press, 1975.

Lichty, Lawrence W. *American Broadcasting: A Source Book on the History of Radio and Television.* New York: Hastings House, 1975.

Sterling, Christopher H. *Stay Tuned: A Concise History of American Broadcasting.* Belmont, Calif.: Wadsworth Publishing Company, 1978, 2002.

WEBSITES

Miller, Jeff. *History of American Broadcasting.* Available online at http://members.aol.com/jeff560/jeff.html (accessed July 30, 2002).

Television History—The First 75 Years. Available online at http://www.tvhistory.tv/ (accessed July 30, 2002).

The Hollywood Blacklist

Testimony of Ronald Reagan Before the House Un-American Activities Committee, October 23, 1947

Testimony

By: Ronald Reagan
Date: October 23, 1947

Source: Reagan, Ronald. Testimony before the House Un-American Activities Committee, October 23, 1947. Reprinted in Bentley, Eric, ed. *Thirty Years of Treason: Excerpts From Hearings Before the House Committee on Un-American Activities, 1938–1968.* New York: Viking, 1971, 146–147.

About the Author: Ronald Reagan (1911–) worked in several Hollywood films in the 1940s and 1950s before forgoing movies altogether to pursue a career in politics in the 1960s. Winning the California governorship in 1966, Reagan quickly rose to become the popular leader of a new conservative movement in the United States. In the 1980s he resurrected the Republican Party by winning the presidency in 1980 and gaining reelection in 1984 by the largest electoral vote margin in history. The "Reagan Right," as it came to be known, has proved a powerful, lasting influence in public policy into the twenty-first century.

Testimony of Edward Dmytryk Before the House Un-American Activities Committee, October 29, 1947

Testimony

By: Edward Dmytryk
Date: October 29, 1947

Source: Dmytryk, Edward. Testimony before the House Un-American Activities Committee, October 29, 1947. Reprinted in Bentley, Eric. *Thirty Years of Treason: Excerpts From Hearings Before the House Committee on Un-American Activities, 1938–1968.* New York: Viking, 1971, 167–168.

About the Author: Edward Dmytryk (1909–1999) directed films in Hollywood in the 1930s and 1940s. In 1944 he joined the Communist Party while continuing his career in filmmaking. Called to testify before the House Un-American Activities Committee in 1947, Dmytryk was punished for his previous associations with left-wing groups and sentenced to a year in jail for his refusal to cooperate with the Committee. He later moved to Europe before resurrecting his Hollywood career in the 1950s. He directed more than 25 films in his long career before dying at the age of 90 in 1999. ∎

Introduction

Congress created the House Un-American Activities Committee (HUAC) in 1937 to investigate radical organizations on the left, such as the Communist Party, and the right, such as the Ku Klux Klan, as a means of protecting internal security. From its inception until its demise in 1968, however, the Committee focused virtually all of its attention squarely on left-leaning groups. It spent much of its energies in the 1930s and 1940s criticizing the New Deal policies of President Franklin D. Roosevelt (served 1933–1945) for posing a communist threat to the United States. After the end of World War II (1939–1945), as tensions increased with the Soviet Union, the Committee continued to investigate domestic communists both real and imagined.

The HUAC pointed its conservative crosshairs at the Hollywood movie industry in 1947. Although liberals, socialists, and communists had worked in films for years, the Committee now declared that "Red" filmmakers threatened to control American culture in order to foster a communist takeover. Republican Chairman J. Parnell Thomas of New Jersey called ten Hollywood executives, all suspected communist sympathizers, to testify in October 1947. The group, known as the Hollywood Ten, refused to cooperate with the Committee and argued that the First and Fifth Amendments to the Constitution justified their actions. The Committee disagreed and sentenced each to six to twelve months in federal prison.

Significance

In testimony from October 30, 1947, Chairman Thomas questioned Ring Lardner Jr., an Academy Award-winning screenwriter who refused to testify about his political background. Thomas's tone, refusal to let Lardner complete sentences, and abrupt eviction of Lardner from the hearings all convey how the Committee often operated. Lardner later won a second Academy Award for his screenplay for *M*A*S*H* (1970). Interestingly Chairman Thomas was later convicted of corruption and served a prison sentence alongside two of the Hollywood Ten he helped convict.

"Red Scares" flared in the United States following both World War I (1914–1918) and World War II (1939–1945). After each conflict, the United States government investigated leftist media outlets that officials believed criticized the government in any way. At both times the government saw the media as possessing great power in American culture and politics. Many moviemakers and journalists scrambled to depict themselves as loyal and patriotic. Hollywood produced films such as *The Red Menace* and *I Married a Communist*. The editors of *Look* magazine produced several articles outlining the supposed communist threat to the United States. The articles even enlisted citizens in the fight against domestic subversion and foreign invasion. One article, "How to Spot a Communist" (March 4, 1947), included the list "How to Identify an American Communist."

Primary Source

Testimony of Ronald Reagan Before the House Un-American Activities Committee, October 23, 1947 [excerpt]

SYNOPSIS: As president of the Screen Actors Guild in 1947, Ronald Reagan staunchly opposed left-wing influence in the motion picture industry. Called to testify as a "friendly" witness for the Committee, he eagerly took the opportunity to voice his opposition to communists and "their propaganda," and to defend his loyalty to the ideals of American democracy.

Mr. Stripling: Mr. Reagan, what is your feeling about what steps should be taken to rid the motion-picture industry of any Communist influences?

Mr. Reagan: Well, sir, ninety-nine per cent of us are pretty well aware of what is going on, and I think, within the bounds of our democratic rights and never once stepping over the rights given us by democracy, we have done a pretty good job in our business of keeping those people's activities curtailed. After all, we must recognize them at present as a political party. On that basis we have exposed their lies when we came across them, we have opposed their propaganda, and I can certainly testify that in the case of the Screen Actors Guild we have been eminently successful in preventing them from, with their usual tactics, trying to run a majority of an organization with a well-organized minority. In opposing those people, the best thing to do is make democracy work. In the Screen Actors Guild we make it work by insuring everyone a vote and by keeping everyone informed. I believe that, as Thomas Jefferson put it, if all the American people know all of the facts they will never make a mistake. Whether the Party should be outlawed, that is a matter for the Government to decide. As a citizen, I would hesitate to see any political party outlawed on the basis of its political ideology. We have spent a hundred and seventy years in this country on the basis that democracy is strong enough to stand up and fight against the inroads of any ideology. However, if it is proven that an organization is an agent of a foreign power, or in any way not a legitimate political party—and I think the Government is capable of proving that—then that is another matter. I happen to be very proud of the industry in which I work; I happen to be very proud of the way in which we conducted the fight. I do not believe the Communists have ever at any time been able to use the motion picture screen as a sounding board for their philosophy or ideology.

Mr. Chairman: There is one thing that you said that interested me very much. That was the quotation from Jefferson. That is just why this Committee was created by the House of Rep-

How to Identify an American Communist

There is no simple definition of an American Communist. However, certain general classifications can be set up. And if either a person or an organization falls within most of these classifications, that person or organization can be said to be following the Communists' lead.

1. The belief that the war waged by Great Britain and her allies during the period from August, 1939, to June, 1941 (the period of the war before Russia was invaded), was an "imperialistic" war and a game of power politics.

2. The support of a foreign policy which agrees always with that followed by Soviet Russia, and which changes as the USSR policy changes.

3. The argument that any foreign or domestic policy which does not fit the Communist plan is advanced for ulterior motives and is not in the best interests of either the people or of world peace.

4. The practice of criticizing only American, British and Chinese policies, and never criticizing Soviet policies.

5. Continually receiving favorable publicity in such Communist publications as the *Daily Worker* and the *New Masses*.

6. Continually appearing as sponsor or co-worker of such known Communist-front groups as the Committee to Win the Peace, the Civil Rights Congress, the National Negro Congress and other groups which can be described as Communist inspired because they fall within the classifications set forth here.

7. Continually charging critics with being "Fascists," no matter whether the criticism comes from liberals, conservatives, reactionaries or those who really are Fascists.

8. Arguing for a class society by pitting one group against another; and putting special privileges ahead of community needs as, for example, claiming that labor has privileges but has no responsibilities in dealing with management.

9. Declaring that capitalism and democracy are "decadent" because some injustices exist under those systems.

Of course, actual membership in the Communist Party is 100 per cent proof, but this kind of proof is difficult to obtain.

SOURCE: Cherne, Leo. "How to Spot a Communist." *Look*, March 4, 1947, 23.

---

resentatives: to acquaint the American people with the facts. Once the American people are acquainted with the facts there is no question but what the American people will do the kind of a job that they want done: that is, to make America just as pure as we can possibly make it. We want to thank you very much for coming here today.

Mr. Reagan: Sir, I detest, I abhor their philosophy, but I detest more than that their tactics, which are those of the fifth column, and are dishonest, but at the same time I never as a citizen want to see our country become urged, by either fear or resentment of this group, that we ever compromise with any of our democratic principles through that fear or resentment. I still think that democracy can do it.

Primary Source

Testimony of Edward Dmytryk Before the House Un-American Activities Committee, October 29, 1947 [excerpt]

SYNOPSIS: Edward Dmytryk faced a fate similar to Ring Lardner's when he testified on October 29, 1947. Committee members bristled when Dmytryk refused to answer whether he was or had ever been a member of the Communist Party. Following his prison sentence and a sojourn in Europe, Dmytryk returned to testify again in 1951. He instantly resurrected his filmmaking career by "naming names," providing the Committee with the names of 26 individuals in Hollywood who he claimed were members of left-wing groups. Aided by Dmytryk's testimony and others, the Committee and sympathetic executives blacklisted more than 300 individuals, preventing them from working in Hollywood for several years if not for the rest of their lives.

Mr. Stripling: Are you now or have you ever been a member of the Communist Party, Mr. Dmytryk?

Mr. Dmytryk: Well, Mr. Stripling, I think that there is a question of constitutional rights involved here. I don't believe that you have—

The Chairman: When did you learn about the Constitution? Tell me when you learned about the Constitution?

Actors Thomas Gomez, "Vanning," and Janis Carter, "Christine." They are the Communist villains of "I Married a Communist." **COURTESY OF THE KOBAL COLLECTION. REPRODUCED BY PERMISSION.**

Mr. Dmytryk: I will be glad to answer that question, Mr. Chairman. I first learned about the Constitution in high school and again—

Mr. McDowell: Let's have the answer to the other question.

Mr. Dmytryk: I was asked when I learned about the Constitution.

Mr. Stripling: I believe the first question, Mr. Dmytryk, was: Are you now, or have you ever been, a member of the Communist Party?

Mr. Dmytryk: All right, gentlemen, if you will keep your questions simple, and one at a time, I will be glad to answer.

Mr. Stripling: That is very simple.

Mr. Dmytryk: The Chairman asked me another question.

The Chairman: Never mind my question. I will withdraw the question.

Mr. Dmytryk: I have been advised that there is a question of constitutional rights involved. The Constitution does not ask that such a question be answered in the way that Mr. Stripling wants it answered. I think that what organizations I belong to, what I think, and what I say cannot be questioned by this Committee.

Mr. Stripling: Then you refuse to answer the question?

Mr. Dmytryk: I do not refuse to answer it. I answered it in my own way.

Mr. Stripling: You haven't answered whether or not you are a member of the Communist Party.

Mr. Dmytryk: I answered by saying I do not think you have the right to ask—

Mr. Stripling: Mr. Chairman, it is apparent that the witness is pursuing the same line as the other witnesses.

The Chairman: The witness is excused.

Further Resources

BOOKS

Barson, Michael. *Red Scared! The Commie Menace in Propaganda and Popular Culture.* San Francisco: Chronicle, 2001.

Bentley, Eric, ed. *Thirty Years of Treason: Excerpts From Hearings Before the House Committee on Un-American Activities, 1938–1968.* New York: Viking, 1971.

Ceplair, Larry. *The Inquisition in Hollywood: Politics in the Film Community, 1930–1960.* Garden City, N.Y.: Doubleday, 1980.

Dmytryk, Edward. *Odd Man Out: A Memoir of the Hollywood Ten.* Carbondale, Ill.: Southern Illinois University Press, 1996.

Goodman, Walter. *The Committee: The Extraordinary Career of the House Committee on Un-American Activities.* New York: Farrar, Straus, and Giroux, 1968.

McMilligan, Patrick, and Paul Buhle. *Tender Comrades: A Backstory of the Hollywood Blacklist.* New York: St. Martin's, 1997.

Reagan, Ronald. *An American Life.* New York: Simon & Schuster, 1990.

PERIODICALS

Cherne, Leo. "How to Spot a Communist." *Look* 11, March 4, 1947, 21–25.

"Is There A 'Witch Hunt'?" *Life,* January 12, 1948, 26.

WEBSITES

American National Biography. Available online at http://www.anb.org (accessed July 30, 2002).

"'Are You Now or Have You Ever Been . . .' Testimony From HUAC Hollywood Hearings." *A CNN Perspective Series: Cold War.* Available online at http://www.cnn.com/SPECIALS/cold.war/episodes/06/documents/huac (accessed July 30, 2002).

"Reagan." *Public Broadcasting Service.* Available online at http://www.pbs.org/wgbh/amex/reagan (accessed July 30, 2002).

"Un-American Activities Committee." *Spartacus Educational.* Available online at http://www.spartacus.schoolnet.co.uk/USAhuac.htm (accessed July 30, 2002).

AUDIO AND VISUAL MEDIA

Reagan. Part of the PBS series *American Experience.* WGBH, 1998, DVD.

"Could the Reds Seize Detroit?"

Magazine article, Magazine cover

By: James Metcalfe

Date: August 3, 1948

Source: Metcalfe, James. "Could the Reds Seize Detroit?" *Look* 12, no. 16, August 3, 1948, 21–27.

About the Publication: First published in 1937, *Look* magazine drew readers with colorful pictures and lively articles concerning all facets of American society. Fashion, sports, arts, politics, science, and health provided its core sections, as "America's Family Magazine" competed primarily with *Life,* started in 1936, for subscribers. As opposed to weekly newsmagazines such as *Time* and *Newsweek, Look* and *Life* lured readers primarily with large, vibrant photography that provided the backbone for their editorial content. ■

Introduction

The end of World War II (1939–1945) brought only temporary solace for war-weary Americans. Within only a matter of months the United States found itself involved in an entirely new struggle against tyranny and oppression. Communist Russians rather than fascist Germans, Italians, and Japanese provided the primary enemies during the Cold War with the Soviet Union. As with the massive propaganda campaigns of World War II, the Cold War shaped popular culture in fundamental ways. Media writers in film, newspapers, magazines, radio, and television depicted communists plotting to destroy democracy abroad and at home. Communists, so the storylines often went, manipulated ordinary citizens into becoming threats to domestic security. These Americans could turn "Red" and hatch treacherous schemes to take control of the United States from within. This domestic "menace" allegedly provided the Soviet Union with means of destabilizing the United States enough to permit a full-scale invasion or nuclear attack by the Soviet Union.

Articles such as "The Reds Have a Standard Plan for Taking Over a New Country" (*Life,* June 7, 1948) and "We Can Lose the Next War in Seven Days," (*Look,* July 8, 1947) bombarded Americans with tales of Soviet re-

pression, U.S. military weakness, and lack of civilian preparation for an attack.

The actions of world leaders supported these terrifying assertions. Following the Soviet takeover of several formerly Nazi-occupied countries in Eastern Europe, the Truman administration declared that the United States must halt the spread of communism before it gained control of Europe. The Truman Doctrine (March 12, 1948) and the Marshall Plan (June 5, 1948) called for billions of dollars to be given to European nations to prevent the spread of communism. On June 24, 1948, the Soviet Union began a blockade of Berlin, the capital of Germany, further heightening tensions between the superpowers.

Significance

In this tumultuous context, the editors of *Look* decided to investigate the possibility of a Soviet takeover of a major U.S. city. Due to its proximity to Canada, high union population, racial demographics, and a host of other factors, the magazine's reporters concluded that Detroit, Michigan, faced imminent invasion. With the cooperation of city officials, the publication staged several dramatic photographs of costumed "communists" gaining control of the metropolis.

Although greeted with a sultry picture of a blond model lounging seductively on the magazine's cover, readers opened their August 3, 1948, edition to find communists killing police officers and telephone operators in a mad struggle to seize Detroit and thereby control the heart of American industry. Writer James Metcalfe sensationally described how small disturbances could lead to Soviet conquest: "Now, caught in the madness of the moment, emboldened by the darkness, intoxicated by an unbridled license to kill, loot, and destroy, mobs would swarm in the streets." This lengthy portrayal of an imagined successful communist attack concluded with a brief assurance that Detroit's police commanders would probably win the battle. After all, "Detroit's defense against Communist disorders rests in capable hands."

As in "Is This Tomorrow?", a widely distributed comic book, "Could the Reds Seize Detroit?" posed the outcome of a war between communism (Soviet Union) and democracy (United States) as an open-ended question. The reader then possessed the ability to decide the matter. Only through intense civilian preparation and the funding of massive military projects, such pieces warned, could national security be preserved against the "Red menace." No evidence of a Soviet plot to overthrow the U.S., or Detroit, government existed. Nevertheless American mass media fanned the fears of Americans in order to defend liberty and sell more magazines.

Primary Source

"Could the Reds Seize Detroit?"

SYNOPSIS: *Look* magazine composed the following piece as an exposé that would reveal how communists threatened to conquer a large American city. Because of its high union population and other factors Detroit became the publication's choice for a likely Soviet target. Several municipal officials, including the mayor and police commissioner, helped stage the scenes for photographs. The text and pictures complement one another and provide modern readers with a sense of how anticommunist propaganda appeared in the late 1940s.

Detroit, home of mass production, city of assembly lines, maker of weapons in time of war, creator of tools for progress in time of peace, is the industrial heart of America. Today, a sickle is being sharpened to plunge into that heart.

There are Communists in Detroit. Estimates of their strength vary from 3,000 to twice that number. Protected by the Constitution of the government that they are seeking to destroy, the Reds are going boldly about their sinister business. A major depression with its attendant unemployment and unrest or war with Russia—will show how effectively they have spent their time.

Many factors make Detroit a focal point of Communist activity. Not the least of these is its geographical location. Only a narrow river separates the city from Canada, a foreign country. Ignoring the formalities of legal entrance, Red agents can shuttle back and forth as rum-runners did during Prohibition days.

That same river gives Detroit's position strategic value, controlling as it does an essential link in a vital inland waterway.

But factories alone would make Detroit a magnet for Communists. Their endless flow of planes, tanks, weapons and vehicles made them arsenals during the last war. They would become so again in another conflict.

With all of the theatrical props at hand for their favorite drama—*Chaos*—the Communists need only to recruit a cast of characters and school them in their parts. Having done this, they can start the show with a bang at curtain time—iron curtain time. Stooges, either willing tools or Red dupes, are available in Detroit.

Oaths are Meaningless to Communists

Like most industrial cities, Detroit is highly unionized. Labor organizations long have been tempting pastures for Communist infiltration. But reputable unions are making strenuous efforts to purge their ranks of Reds.

A union-member may be asked to swear that he is not a member of the Communist Party, but the sanctity of an oath is meaningless to a Red. Only a searching investigation could prove his good faith. In such an inquiry, every effort must be used to avoid injury to innocent people. Fellow travelers are quick to protest that their civil rights are being invaded whenever they are called upon to account for their subversive activities.

There are many minority groups in Detroit. They fall within the four broad categories of nationality, race, low income and a polyglot collection of all the foregoing. In the main, their status as good citizens of this country cannot be challenged. They are assets to the city in which they live.

Agents Stir Up Discord

As in all minorities, however, there are those who chafe at fancied social and economic discrimination. Quick to seize upon any source of discontent—regardless of its origin—the Communists are not overlooking these opportunities to exploit ignorance and prejudice to serve their own purposes.

Detroit is within District 7 of the Communist Party of Michigan. The district is divided into twelve sections. Each of the sections contains a large number of clubs. The clubs, identified as either community or industrial units, are the smallest offshoots of the parent body.

They are the nerve-ends of a complex system whose lines make a serpentine course through intermediate headquarters of the Communist Party of America to terminate finally in Moscow.

The number in each club is not fixed, but the practice is to keep within general limits of from five to twenty. It is easier to hold frequent meetings with small numbers, and all can convene within the privacy of a member's home. Small groups are cohesive, can be tightly controlled and permit more thorough indoctrination.

The Front Organizations

It can be assumed that every meeting of every club is not a nefarious conspiracy. But the clubs are creatures of the Kremlin and ultimately, it will be the Politburo that will determine the purpose they are to serve.

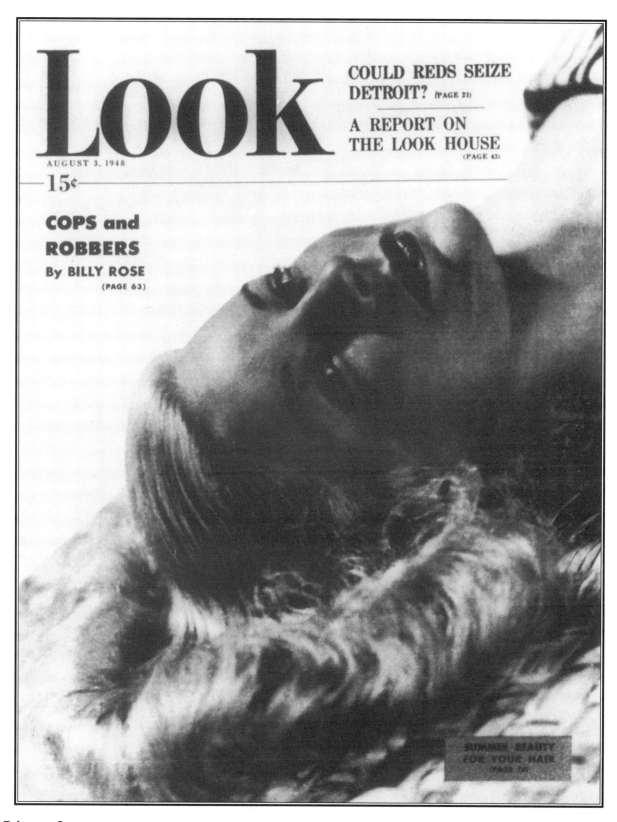

COULD REDS SEIZE
DETROIT? (PAGE 21)

A REPORT ON
THE LOOK HOUSE
(PAGE 43)

COPS and
ROBBERS
By BILLY ROSE
(PAGE 63)

AUGUST 3, 1948

15¢

Primary Source

"Could the Reds Seize Detroit?": *Look* magazine cover

SYNOPSIS: The August 3, 1948, cover of *Look* that contained the article "Could the Reds Seize Detroit?" COVER OF LOOK MAG-
AZINE, AUGUST 3, 1948.

Fully aware that a self-confessed Communist organization as such offends a hostile public, the Reds are adroit at using misnomers or *fronts* to cloak the origin of agencies they themselves have created. These Communist fronts are innocent sounding, and their objectives are often, on the surface, worthy ones. The House Committee on Un-American Activities has exposed many of them.

Playing the field, the Reds not only launch their own front organizations but they climb aboard any other cause or crusade that will further their designs. These are usually movements that, in a city like Detroit, receive ready support. Known Communists have been identified there in such controversies as strikes, attacks on the Taft-Hartley Law, and opposition to conscription.

Hitch-Hikers on Popular Issues

The fact that sincere people, themselves bitter opponents of Communism, are fighting for or against a cause, doesn't discourage Reds from joining the issue.

Non-Communist groups organized to fight Jim Crowism, anti-Semitism, immigration restrictions and similar prejudices or practices, are often surprised and embarrassed to discover that Reds have sneaked into their ranks. Actually, it is an old and familiar Red stratagem. Agent provocateurs wait until a movement gathers momentum, then climb aboard and attempt to influence its policies and objectives. While doing so, they plant more seeds of hatred and discord.

When a front organization has been exposed and denounced, the Reds don't disband it. They merely change its name. To a Communist, the title of an organization has no more enduring qualities than that of a sworn oath or an agent's alias.

This artful dodging in matters of identity is effective. When the pressure is on, the Red units go into evasive action, disappear from the public ken and emerge a short time later under another tag.

The Detroit police admit the difficulty of proving actual Communist affiliation or membership in the Party. A Red is instructed to deny any connection with communism if it will ease his plight upon arrest or while undergoing questioning. Since membership in the Communist Party is not illegal, the police can't do much more than keep an eye on certain key people. When taken into custody for violation of existing statutes, however, the Communists are given an opportunity to tell the police about their left-wing activities. They never do.

Skeptics who doubt the existence of a Red menace, parlor pinks enjoying a coy flirtation with their Communist cousins, and the complacent who ignore the subject, would do well to view some of the Red documents in the Detroit Police Department files. One of the more interesting papers is a *Questionnaire on the Life and Activities of Leading Party Functionaries.*

Record of Violence Is an Asset

A Leading Party Functionary is an important figure in the Red chain of command—one whose standing is enhanced by a life record of violence and trouble-making.

The questionnaire requires the functionary to give his *real name.* He is then asked such questions as: *When did you enter the revolutionary movement? . . . To what trade unions have you belonged? . . . Have you taken part in strikes and demonstrations? . . . What prison sentences have you served? . . .*

Do a mere three- to six-thousand Reds constitute a threat to a metropolitan area of nearly two and a half million inhabitants? The answer is a qualified one—*Yes, if the time and conditions are right.* There are tragic cities in Europe today that prove how well the Communists can create the right conditions and how skillfully they time their blows. The same pattern that marked the fall of Prague, and of other cities that went to bed in freedom and woke up behind the iron curtain, would lend itself to a Communist coup in Detroit. It was mentioned earlier that either war with Russia or a severe depression would set the stage and provide the time for a Red uprising.

Assume that Russia declared war upon the United States; not in the obsolete fashion of serving formal notice, but in a sneak offensive an all-out initial blow in the best *blitzkrieg* style.

Red Uprising Geared to Russian Attack

Synchronizing their revolt with the start of the Russian attack, Communists in this country would lash out in every major city, striking swiftly while a nation reeled from shock.

The first few minutes would be busy ones for the Communist flying squads. On split-second schedule, groups would be liquidating certain civic and political leaders. Other units would take previously selected hostages into custody. At the same time, equally ruthless storm units would capture all broadcasting stations, the police and sheriff's office, radio transmitters.

Meanwhile, demolition crews would have sealed off the city from immediate assistance by blasting highway bridges and rail lines, and by placing obstacles on landing fields and seizing airport control towers.

Rabble-rousers, using sound trucks, would roll into those sections of the city where years of preparation had conditioned the people to Communist leadership. Now, caught in the madness of the moment, emboldened by the darkness, intoxicated by an unbridled license to kill, loot and destroy, mobs would swarm in the streets.

Prisoners, many of them hoodlums with long police records, would be freed from the Wayne County Jail and provided with arms. So for at least one night, Detroit could know the chaos and horror that Bogota, Colombia, knew this spring when a Red-inspired revolt, timed to embarrass the Pan-American Conference, unleashed a reign of terror and destruction.

Now, using the straw-man technique of creating a crisis, then solving it, the Reds would utilize captured press and radio facilities to urge a restoration of calm and order. City officials, either at gun-point or to avoid further bloodshed, would caution the populace against resistance, advise them to bow to Red leadership. Quislings would take their appointed posts, top-flight agents would arrive to master-mind future developments, and Detroit could conceivably become another Prague.

The foregoing events represent both an extreme and a hypothetical situation. Suppose, however, that the Reds were merely concentrating on hampering an American war effort by fomenting strikes and carrying out sabotage. The years they have spent in consolidating their position would not have been wasted.

Reds Would Like a Depression

Or visualize conditions during a great depression when factories are idle, when hundreds of thousands of men—all normally employed by Detroit's automobile plants—are out of work, bitter, discontented and susceptible to influence by subversive agents who offer them an antidote for despair.

Much of America may be apathetic to the dangers of communism. But certain exceptions must be made to that indictment. *Detroit is not napping.* The F.B.I. keeps its own secrets, but there can be no doubt about the efforts of the Detroit Police Department. It is a force of some 4,000 men that never relaxes its vigilance.

Police Commissioner Harry Toy, like Mayor Eugene I. Van Antwerp, is a strong, fearless personality who attacks problems effectively. His name is a hated one among Communists. Recently, when he revived the war-time Red Squad—a special police detail whose sole job is to keep an eye on subversive activities—Communist headquarters in Detroit published a flood of handbills demanding Toy's removal from office.

Under direct supervision of Superintendent Edwin Morgan, the police carry on their activities, keep up extensive training, rehearse their "M"-Day plan for emergency action, and keep a sharp eye on the left-wingers in the area.

Edward Behrendt, sheriff of Detroit's surrounding Wayne County, is an experienced officer. He keeps his own force of 300 deputies and a uniformed road patrol on the alert.

Men familiar with Communist activities in Detroit are not minimizing the dangers lurking in their plotting.

With the Communists and their cohorts aligned against the local law-enforcement agencies, could the Reds seize Detroit? Previously, it was suggested that they could—if the time and conditions were right. But as long as the Detroit Police Department maintains its present standards of alertness and efficiency, the Communists won't find it easy to seize control.

Have Reds infiltrated into the ranks of the Police Department? No. Detroit screens its police thoroughly. On guard against such tactics, officials have effectively maintained the integrity of their personnel. The force is made up of high-caliber men.

Does the vigilance of the Police Department eliminate the possibility of the Communists causing trouble? No. Like fire wardens, policemen can only anticipate trouble and minimize it when it occurs. With men like Toy and Morgan, and with senior inspectors like Furlong, Throop and Wysocki heading the three major divisions of the force, Detroit's defense against Communist disorders rests in capable hands.

Members of the Police Department and the Sheriff's office co-operated in enacting the scenes depicted in this story. They felt that they should do everything possible to enlighten all people to the danger of Communism.

Further Resources

BOOKS
Barson, Michael. *Red Scared!: The Commie Menace in Propaganda and Popular Culture.* San Francisco: Chronicle Books, 2001.

Fried, Richard M. *The Russians Are Coming! The Russians Are Coming!: Pageantry and Patriotism in Cold-War America.* New York: Oxford University Press, 1998.

Schrecker, Ellen. *Many Are the Crimes: McCarthyism in America.* Boston: Little, Brown, 1998.

PERIODICALS

Cherne, Leo. "How to Spot a Communist." *Look* 11 (March 4, 1947): 21–25.

Finney, Nat S. "We Can Lose the Next War in Seven Days." *Look* 11 (July 8, 1947): 21–27.

"The Reds Have a Standard Plan for Taking Over a New Country." *Life* (June 7, 1948): 36–37.

WEBSITES

"'Are You Now or Have You Ever Been . . .' Testimony from HUAC Hollywood hearings." *A CNN Perspective Series: Cold War.* Available online at http://www.cnn.com/SPECIALS/cold.war/episodes/06/documents/huac (accessed July 30, 2002).

Spartacus Educational. Available online at http://www.spartacus.schoolnet.co.uk/USAred.htm (accessed July 30, 2002).

9

MEDICINE AND HEALTH

SUSAN P. WALTON

Entries are arranged in chronological order by date of primary source. For entries with one primary source, the entry title is the same as the primary source title. Entries with more than one primary source have an overall entry title, followed by the titles of the primary sources.

Important Events in Medicine and Health, 1940–1949

1940

- A team of researchers at the Rockefeller Institute discovers the Rh factor in blood.

- Rebecca Lancefield identifies streptococcus group A as the cause of rheumatic fever.

- The Rockefeller Foundation announces it will make a recently developed vaccine available to Britain to fight influenza in the war zone.

- On May 22, the Council of Foods of the American Medical Association (AMA) gives its first seal of approval to the Bird's Eye Corporation for its quick-frozen foods.

- In August, there are deadly outbreaks of polio in West Virginia and Indiana during the summer.

- On October 10, the medical faculty at Stockholm University announces it will not award the Nobel Prize for medicine in 1940 because of the ongoing war.

- On October 21, the Clinical College of the American College of Surgeons recommends a detailed plan for having doctors serve in the military without causing hardships at home.

- On October 31, sulfaguanidine is announced as a cure for bacterial dysentery, a common disease among troops in the tropics.

- In December, influenza reaches epidemic proportions in California, Oregon, Washington, New Mexico, Arizona, and Idaho.

1941

- Clinical use of oral anticoagulants is initiated.

- Penicillin enters clinical use.

- Doctors at New York's Bellevue Hospital advance the diagnosis of heart disease by experimenting with cardiac catheterization.

- On March 25, the U.S. Public Health Service reports the most serious measles outbreak in seven years along the Eastern Seaboard and spreading westward.

- On March 27, Group Health Association, Inc., a nonprofit organization chartered by New York State, offers preventive medical care as well as treatment to state residents for twenty-four dollars or less a year.

- On May 22, the American Social Hygiene Association reports that 0.3 percent of U.S. adults have syphilis.

- On April 4, a federal jury convicts the AMA of violating the Sherman Antitrust Act. A federal appeals court upholds the conviction in 1942.

- On June 5, Dr. Louis Dublin announces that infant mortality has declined by 45 percent over the previous 20 years.

- On December 4, the National Foundation for Infantile Paralysis announces its approval of the polio treatment developed by Elizabeth Kenny: heat, massage, and exercise. Other medical professionals debate the value of this treatment.

1942

- The American Red Cross begins collecting blood for treating battle casualties.

- Canadian physicians introduce the use of curare as a relaxant during surgical procedures.

- Radioactive iodine is used to treat hyperthyroidism.

- On October 16, in response to a venereal disease epidemic, Georgia health officials order the quarantine of all venereal disease cases and the detention and treatment of all victims of venereal diseases not receiving medical care.

- On October 26, six New York hospitals announce they will teach the Kenny treatment for infantile paralysis.

- On November 7, the AMA council on foods and nutrition recommends that consumption of sugar in candy and soft drinks, which are low in nutritional value, be limited.

- On November 28, the *Journal of the American Medical Association* (*JAMA*) reports that albumin in human blood can be injected or transfused in a highly concentrated form to relieve shock.

1943

- Selman Waksman isolates and discovers streptomycin, the first antibiotic to prove effective against tuberculosis.

- Hepatitis A and B are found to be two distinct diseases.

- John Friend Mahoney and colleagues at the U.S. Public Health Service pioneer the use of penicillin to treat syphilis.

- The U.S. Supreme Court upholds a lower court decision against the AMA, ruling that the organization violated antitrust laws by impeding the activities of cooperative health groups.

- In the summer, an infantile paralysis epidemic spreads through Texas, California, Washington, Kansas, and New York.

1944

- Helene Deutsch publishes *The Psychology of Women, A Psychoanalytic Interpretation.*

- H.T.J. Berk designs the first therapeutically effective artificial kidney.

- Benjamin Duggar discovers the first tetracycline antibiotic, aureomycin.

- Early ambulation after surgery and childbirth is introduced.

- On March 3, the magazine *Air Force* reports that the drug benzedrene has been used to help pilots fight off sleepiness and fatigue on return trips of combat missions.

- On April 10, the annual report of the National Foundation for Infantile Paralysis expresses regret at the publicity given the Kenny method for treating the disease. A month later, an AMA committee will publicly criticize Kenny's method.

- On June 29, the American Red Cross announces development of a serum to prevent measles.

- On July 13, Mayo Clinic physicians report that cigarettes may harm wounded men by constricting blood vessels.

- On August 7, the U.S. Public Health Service announces gonorrhea can be cured in 7½ hours with penicillin.

- On August 17, an infantile paralysis outbreak reaches epidemic proportions in New York, North Carolina, Kentucky, Pennsylvania, and Virginia.

- On August 26, the New York State Hospital Commission reports that insulin shock treatment has enabled 55 percent of those treated for dementia praecox to become useful members of society.

- On September 9, Harvard Medical School announces the development of a synthetic skin from blood plasma to heal burns.

- On November 3, the U.S. Army announces a 25 percent reduction in the incidence of malaria since the beginning of the war.

- On November 23, the *Journal of the American Medical Association* claims Americans with a normal diet do not benefit from vitamins.

1945

- Helen Taussig and Alfred Blalock pioneer an operation to increase oxygenation of the blood of blue-babies whose malformed hearts cannot pump enough blood to their lungs.

- The American Cancer Society is incorporated.

- In February, oral penicillin is introduced.

- On March 23, the Census Bureau reports that the death rate from cancer in the United States has more than doubled since 1900.

- On November 14, the *Journal of the American Medical Association* reports successful treatment of scarlet fever by injecting penicillin into the muscles every three hours for seven days.

- On November 19, President Harry Truman asks Congress for a comprehensive national health program.

- On November 24, the U.S. Navy reports a cure for cholera.

- In December, an influenza epidemic grips the nation.

1946

- Benadryl becomes the first oral antihistamine sold over the counter.

- Psychiatrist Benjamin Spock publishes the first edition of his *Common Sense Book of Baby and Child Care.*

- The Communicable Disease Center is established in Atlanta.

- On March 31, the American Geographic Society announces plans for an atlas of diseases to aid in the study of the relationship between environment and health.

- On April 6, Oklahoma City public-health officials are the first to use penicillin to treat venereal disease among civilians.

- On April 17, the American Cancer Society reveals a proposed three million dollar cancer research program using radioactive isotopes produced in atom-bomb research.

- On August 2, the U.S. nuclear plant at Oak Ridge, Tennessee, makes the first sale of a radioactive isotope to a private institution when it sells one millicurie of carbon 14 to the Barnard Free Skin and Cancer Hospital in Saint Louis for use in cancer research.

- On August 9, the U.S. Public Health Service reports the worst infantile paralysis epidemic since 1916.

- On October 2, the Association for the Advancement of Research on Multiple Sclerosis is formed in New York.

- On October 27, the American Social Hygiene Association announces that reported cases of syphilis increased 42 percent in the twelve months ending June 30.

1947

- Claude Beck successfully uses James Rand's defibrillator to treat ventricular fibrillation by direct application of electric shock.

- The electrokymograph for recording heart motion is introduced.

- Work on the artificial kidney begins at Peter Bent Brigham Hospital in Boston.

- On January 7, Spring Grove Street Hospital in Maryland announces the release of several "incurable" psychiatric patients who had undergone prefrontal lobotomies, separating the emotional and action centers of the brain.

- On February 10, the Planned Parenthood Federation of America announces that a recent poll of U.S. doctors shows 97.8 percent in favor of birth control.

- On March 18, the Atomic Bomb Casualty Commission reports abnormalities among children recently born to atomic-bomb victims in Hiroshima and Nagasaki.

- On June 21, the War Department announces plans to build the world's largest medical research center at Forest Glen, Maryland.

- On November 24, the Southern Medical Association, meeting in Baltimore, drops its ban on attendance of African-American physicians at its scientific sessions.

1948

- The World Health Organization is established by the United Nations.

- Cortisone is first used to treat rheumatoid arthritis.

- On March 6, the U.S. Atomic Energy Commission announces free distribution of certain radioactive isotopes for use in cancer treatment.

- On April 21, investigators at Ohio State University report the successful use of irradiated cobalt to treat cancer.

- On May 18, the Medical Society of the State of New York adopts a resolution urging elimination of racial discrimination in admission to the AMA.

- On June 27, Army researchers report that chloromycetin, a new drug, can cure typhoid fever within three days.

- On August 4, the Public Health Service reports new polio outbreaks in North Carolina, Texas, and California.

- On October 15, the U.S. Public Health Service announces that a five-minute test to detect diabetes will be used in a nationwide effort to find an estimated one million hidden diabetes cases.

- On October 18, New York City begins a fluoridation program by coating the teeth of fifty thousand children with sodium fluoride to prevent decay.

- On December 3, the AMA ends a four-day meeting in Saint Louis after making plans to raise $3.5 million to fight President Truman's national health insurance program.

- On December 6, the American Dental Association announces its opposition to Truman's proposed national health insurance.

- On December 20, researchers at nuclear laboratories in the United States report that five scientists are going blind as a result of their work with cyclotrons.

1949

- Antibiotics and immunization bring infant deaths down to 31.3 per thousand, from 47 per thousand in 1940.

- Maternal mortality plunges from 37.6 per ten thousand live births in 1940 to 8.3 per ten thousand in 1949.

- Linus Pauling and his colleagues report that sickle-cell anemia is caused by molecular abnormality.

- In work that will pave the way for Jonas Salk's vaccine, David Bodian and his colleagues demonstrate that polio is caused by not just one but three distinct types of viruses.

- G.D. Searle & Company introduces dramamine as a motion-sickness remedy.

- The National Institute of Mental Health is established.

- Lithium is first used in the treatment of psychiatric disease.

- On February 2, the AMA presents an alternative to Truman's compulsory medical insurance plan, stressing expansion of voluntary medical plans and greater state aid to the indigent.

- On February 27, the American Cancer Society and National Cancer Institute meeting hears a report linking increased cigarette smoking to the rapid rise in incidence of lung cancer during the previous twenty-five years.

- On February 28, the New York County Medical Society, the largest member of the AMA, refuses to support the AMA's fight against Truman's compulsory medical insurance proposal.

- On May 16, Johns Hopkins University doctors report that the motion-sickness drug dramamine relieves morning sickness in many pregnant women.

- On August 12, the African-American-dominated National Medical Association refuses to take a position on the issue of national health insurance at its Detroit convention, despite a request from the AMA to oppose the plan.

- On August 16, the U.S. Public Health Service reports that the average life span of an American is 66.8 years, up from the prewar average of 65.

- On August 29, a 22-million-volt betatron is used to treat two cancer patients at the University of Illinois at Chicago hospital, the first application of a nuclear device in cancer therapy.

- On September 23, the Senate approves a five-year, $280 million program for the construction of medical schools and other health-professional training facilities.

- On December 8, the House of Delegates of the AMA unanimously approves a twenty-five dollar levy on all AMA members to fight Truman's proposed national health insurance plan.

"The Lessons of the Selective Service"

Magazine article

By: Lewis B. Hershey

Date: July 1941

Source: Hershey, Lewis B. "The Lessons of the Selective Service." *Survey Graphic,* July 1941, p. 383. Available at the New Deal Network online at http://newdeal.feri.org/survey /sg41383.htm; website home page at http://newdeal.feri.org (accessed March 18, 2003).

About the Author: General Lewis B. Hershey (1893–1977) worked as deputy director of the Selective Service, the government agency in charge of drafting men for military service, before serving as its director from 1941 to 1970. ∎

Introduction

Seeking Men to Fight

When the Japanese bombed Pearl Harbor on December 7, 1941, triggering U.S. involvement in World War II (1939–1945), the American military had to mobilize quickly. The Selective Service had already begun examining men of draft age and had found that many did not meet the physical standards the armed forces required of soldiers.

The "lesson" was not new. A study of World War I (1914–1918) draftees had found that out of each 1,000 men examined, 468 had at least one defect that rendered them unfit for full military service. Some were defects that could be easily remedied. The most common defects were mechanical, with "weak feet" topping the list. Tuberculosis and venereal disease together accounted for 11 percent. Others suffered from nutrition-related problems. Five percent were underweight, while others had goiter or were under the required height.

When General Hershey proposed to fight these problems by introducing physical fitness education in the schools, many states already had such programs in place. By 1925, 30 states had enacted legislation that mandated some form of physical education in the schools. While the general implied that some potential recruits had ruined their health and strength through studying too hard,

widespread malnutrition during the 1930s seems a more likely cause. According to an article by Federal Security Administrator Paul McNutt, a 1938 report from a Texas county found that "20 percent of the deaths in this county were hastened by a lack of sufficient amount and balanced diets."

Significance

The Goal of Fitness

General Hershey's was one of many voices contributing to the discussion on how the nation could improve the health of its population in the expectation of war. Although others did not discount the need for better physical training, most people, including President Franklin D. Roosevelt (served 1933–1945), placed more emphasis on better nutrition. "If people are undernourished, they cannot be efficient in producing what we need in our unified drive for dynamic strength," Roosevelt wrote in a 1941 letter to McNutt.

Only after World War II did the goal of physical fitness become more of a priority. This came about not because of a military initiative but because in 1953 a physical fitness evaluation called the Kraus-Weber test revealed that American children were less fit than their European counterparts. Two years later President Dwight D. Eisenhower (served 1953–1961) founded the President's Council on Physical Fitness, which continues to conduct annual tests on schoolchildren. These tests have generally shown that American children are still less fit than their European counterparts.

The efforts to create a more physically fit America have, by and large, failed within the general population. Although many individuals are keenly aware of the need to stay fit and exercise regularly, most do not. An increasing percentage of the population was considered obese by the end of the twentieth century. This included, alarmingly, an increasingly large percentage of children; obese children are more likely to become obese adults. Many children now spend long hours in front of computer terminals and television screens instead of exercising and playing actively. In 1941, however, General Hershey could not know that television and computers would further reduce children's chances of leaving school in fighting trim.

Primary Source

"The Lessons of the Selective Service"

> **SYNOPSIS:** In this article Brigadier General Hershey puts forth his proposal for achieving greater fitness among American youth.

Out of a million men examined by Selective Service and about 560,000 excepted by the army, a

Army officers perform the draft lottery for WWII. The Selective Service found that many draftees had to be rejected due to lack of physical fitness, leading to efforts to solve this national problem. **AP/WIDE WORLD PHOTOS. REPRODUCED BY PERMISSION.**

total of 380,000 have been found unfit for general military service. It has been estimated that perhaps one third of the rejections were due either directly or indirectly to nutritional deficiencies. In terms of men, the army today has been deprived of 150,000 who should be able to do duty as soldiers. This is 15 percent of the total number physically examined by the Selective Service System.

It is perhaps of little use to speculate on what should have been done by our schools, by parents, by health bodies, or by the government. Probably the depression years left their marks. Undoubtedly the automobile and the cash it required for monthly payments and for gas, oil, and tires, has cost us as a people in physical fitness. Whether we are worse off physically than we were in 1917–18 is undoubtedly controversial. That our physical standards are higher now, let us admit. The fact remains that while we may be no worse now than twenty-four years ago we seem certainly to be no better. Better or worse or the same, we are physically in a condition of which we nationally should be thoroughly ashamed. It is a condition we should recognize as dangerous and which we should take immediate, positive and vigorous measures to correct.

Prevention is always better than cure. Far-reaching results will follow basic programs to develop our people physically. This is a long range task in which parents, schools, and government must each bear a part. I believe the most fundamental step must be a basic change in our conception of the nature of our educational system. We must place a decided emphasis on physical training and physical education. This recognition must be on a plane above the recreational level. Today we pay our tribute to outstanding athletes, but only as they entertain us. Our educational system must place the youth who has developed a perfect healthy body on a plane above the scholarship giant who in reaching this goal has ruined his eyes, his digestion, and his health in general.

America cannot be strong when half of her sons are substandard physically. America needs whole men, not half men. She must develop vigorous and healthy youths; she must prehabilitate those whose defects are slight; she must rehabilitate those examined and found deficient. The task before us, like all tasks in a democracy, is the duty and responsibility of each and every citizen. The Selective Service System by its very nature will play a vital part in the solution of this all important problem. It dedicates itself to a participation in the movement for a healthier citizenry.

Further Resources

WEBSITES

McNutt, Paul. "The First Step Toward Fitness." *Survey Graphic,* July 1941. Available online at http://newdeal.feri.org/texts /461.htm; website home page: http://newdeal.feri.org (accessed August 22, 2002).

"The Job Ahead"

Magazine article

By: Thomas Parran

Date: July 1941

Source: Parran, Thomas. "The Job Ahead." *Survey Graphic,* July 1941. Available at the New Deal Network online at http://newdeal.feri.org/survey/sg41396.htm; website home page at http://newdeal.feri.org (accessed April 18, 2003).

About the Author: Thomas Parran (1892–1968) was surgeon general during most of President Franklin Roosevelt's administration (1933–1945). Known for his active promotion of many public health initiatives, Parran was behind campaigns against venereal disease, malnutrition, and other conditions. ∎

Introduction

In the wake of the Great Depression of the 1930s, public health officials were well aware that many Americans suffered the lingering effects of malnutrition (not eating a balanced diet) and undernutrition (not eating enough of any sort of food). They were equally aware that this was in large part because people could not afford to buy nutritious foods. Fresh food was more healthful but also more expensive. Lean meat was better than white "fat" meat such as salt pork but cost a lot more. Paul McNutt, the Federal Security Administrator, wrote:

> Thousands of families live on sow belly and corn. Other thousands live on beans and tortillas. Most of these should grow kitchen gardens, some say. . . . [But] it must not be forgotten that there are other thousands—without a square foot of real estate within five miles of their homes in which they could put a spade—who cannot buy meal-balancing foods at the prices they would have to pay.

McNutt and other officials noted that many Americans had opposed government spending on improved nutrition during the years of the New Deal. Although many people had relied on government assistance to survive during the Depression, they did not like the idea of the government telling anyone—including them—what to eat. They spoke scornfully of the young social workers who handed out nutrition advice and viewed these advisers, correctly in many cases, as college-educated, well-off young women who had never suffered a day's want in their lives. One Works Progress Administration writer, for example, described a social worker visiting her struggling clients in her full riding gear, on her way to the stables.

Significance

Well before the United States entered World War II (1939–1945) in December 1941, government officials began addressing Americans' health. The threat of war succeeded in putting good nutrition at the top of the national agenda in a way that the Depression never had. People could rally around the idea that American soldiers and civilians alike needed all their strength to fight the enemy.

One early result of this was the National Nutrition Conference convened in Washington, D.C., by President Roosevelt in 1941 to "secure recommendations for a national program of policy and action." The conference marked the first truly national effort to improve nutrition. It was attended by some 900 delegates representing all fields of medicine and service organizations.

Russell Wilder, M.D., the chairman of the National Research Council's (NRC) Committee on Food and Nutrition, fired the opening shot at the conference by pointing out that the so-called surplus of food did not mean that Americans were well nourished. Citing 1936 government surveys, he noted that only one-fourth of all families had food that would provide a "good" diet, while one-third bought food that could provide, at best, a "poor" diet.

Another result of the wartime "mobilization" for good nutrition was a surge in nutrition research, an often neglected area of medicine. Chemists' study of vitamins and the amounts that people required for optimum health gave physicians a concrete tool in the fight against malnutrition. At the same time food producers began to fortify certain foods, notably flour and bread, to make them more nutritious. By this time physicians could also rely on the work of the NRC's Committee on Food and Nutrition, which had the previous year published the first recommended daily amounts of some nutrients.

The government was equally concerned about giving soldiers a good diet. A program of careful meal planning was put into effect under the direction of the president of the American Dietetic Association. The diet may not have offered gourmet fare, but officials at the time pointed out that it was probably a lot better than what the early recruits had been eating as civilians.

The long-term consequences of the wartime campaign for good nutrition have lasted into the twenty-first

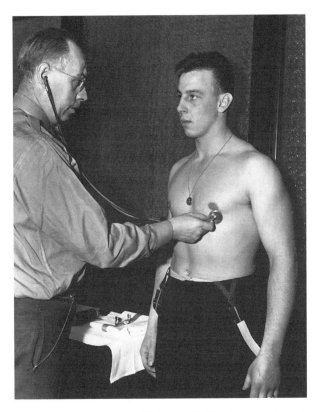

A Navy doctor listens to a recruit's heart, 1942. Though malnutrition and undernutrition were problematic results of the Depression, national emphasis was not placed on good nutrition until WWII required that Americans have all their strength to fight the enemy. **UPI/CORBIS-BETTMANN. REPRODUCED BY PERMISSION.**

century. The NRC continues to issue revised dietary guidelines periodically. The U.S. Department of Agriculture provides extensive nutrition information. Physicians devote more of their education to the study of nutrition, although critics still contend that their knowledge is frequently insufficient. Shoppers now read labels that tell them how much of each nutrient foods provide. Hunger and malnutrition still exist in the United States but to a much lesser degree.

Primary Source

"The Job Ahead" [excerpt]

SYNOPSIS: In "The Job Ahead," Surgeon General Thomas Parran issues a nutritional call to arms to create a strong and well-nourished nation in preparation for the United States's involvement in World War II.

All of us today are conscious of the grave task lying before us. The President has declared a state of unlimited national emergency. In the weeks and months to come, we shall need not only planes and munitions, a growing army and navy, but also rugged health and courage. All these defenses are within our reach. Given the national will to do it, we have the power to build here in America a nation of people more fit, more vigorous, more competent; a nation with better morale, a more united purpose, more toughness of body, and greater strength of mind than the world has ever seen. . . .

In the past half-century we in this country have added twenty years to the average span of human life, largely by saving the lives of babies and of young people. But life expectancy for those beyond the age of forty has not increased since Pasteur's time. On the contrary, many diseases have increased because more people grow old enough to acquire them. Deaths have increased from cancer, heart conditions, kidney diseases, mental illness—in fact, from all of the so-called degenerative causes. It is easy to say that this is due to the strain of modern life. Yet every disease, every malfunction of an organ, results from a derangement in the functioning of the individual body cell. The individual cell functions properly if it is properly fed; and if it is not killed by the invasion of bacterial, virus, or chemical poisons, or by endogenous toxins. The food available to each of the body cells probably determines to a large degree the health of that cell, its proper functioning, its reciprocal relations with other cells, which make up bodily organs and systems. . . .

While the full extent of the Nation's nutritional problem is undetermined, we know that, as President Roosevelt stated to the Washington conference, "every survey of nutrition, by whatever method conducted, in whatever part of the country, shows malnutrition to be widespread and serious." Studies of family diets by the Department of Agriculture in all income groups of nation show that one third of the people are getting food inadequate to maintain good health. Less than one fourth are getting a "good diet," even when measured by the old standards which are lower than the "gold standard." Some people cannot afford to buy food they need; others spend their food budget unwisely; still others have fixed and faulty food habits. Americans want good health to be the heritage of all, on as dramatic a basis as the suffrage itself. We want no property qualifications for health.

In practical terms, we need every drop of milk, every egg, every legume, every pound of meat and of fish we can produce for Anglo-American nutrition, plus substantial quantities of animal and vegetable fats, fish liver oils, and certain vitamins. I believe that the program of the Department of Agriculture which will convert most of our ever-normal granary of feed into concentrated human protein foods represents a long step forward. We may have to go even further during this emergency. . . .

Beyond today's emergency, food offers a foundation stone in an after-war world economy. Food for defense involving, as it should, intimate cooperation between the United Kingdom, the British Commonwealth, the United States, and the other American Republics lay the basis for a world policy to meet effectively this elemental human need. Toward the realization of that hope for the future, immediate domestic responsibilities for food nutrition will point the way. . . .

After this war, when cities and civilizations lie in ruins and the impulse toward human brotherhood is smothered with hate, all the strength and courage that America can muster will be needed for the rebuilding of a shattered world. As a people, we must be conscious of our destiny, for America is the last great hope on earth.

Further Resources

BOOKS

Cummings, Richard Osborne. *The American and His Food,* Rev. ed. New York: Arno Press, 1970.

WEBSITES

Sherman, Henry. "A Longer, Stronger Life." *Survey Graphic,* July 1941. Available online at http://www.newdeal.feri/org /survey (accessed April 18, 2003).

"The Diagnostic Value of Vaginal Smears in Carcinoma of the Uterus"

Journal article

By: George N. Papanicolaou and Herbert F. Traut

Date: August 1941

Source: Papanicolaou, George N., and Herbert F. Traut. "The Diagnostic Value of Vaginal Smears in Carcinoma of the Uterus." *The American Journal of Obstetrics and Gynecology* 42, no. 2 (August 1941): 193–206.

About the Primary Author: George Papanicolaou (1883–1962), who gave his name in shortened form to the Pap smear, was born in Greece, but he and his wife moved to the United States in 1913. His work in the estrous cycle in mice led to the first isolation of estrogen. This interest led to the work with cancer that eventually made him famous. He

was a member of the Cornell University faculty for several years, and after his work gained widespread acceptance, he won numerous awards, including the Honor Award of the American Cancer Society. ■

Introduction

Cervical cancer and other cancers of the female reproductive organs were not widely discussed in the nineteenth and early twentieth centuries, in part because of prevailing Victorian notions of modesty. While cancer was the eighth leading cause of death in 1900, for women, cancer of the reproductive organs was the leading cause of cancer deaths. In the early twentieth century, cervical cancer generally went untreated because there was no way to detect it. Doctors thus needed an early diagnostic technique that could be widely used, and Papanicolaou's test provides just that. It took a long time for this test to be developed, though. Papanicolaou began his work on this method and made significant breakthroughs in the 1920s, even determining his method of testing, but it was not until 1941 that he and Traut published this article.

Significance

Papanicolaou's goal was to develop a test for both uterine and cervical cancer. But while the Pap test is not very effective in detecting uterine cancer, it effectively detects cervical cancer, so that even in the 1940s the cure rate for cervical cancer was fairly high if it was found early. Since 1941 annual Pap smears have been recommended for every woman over the age of eighteen. One problem with Pap smears is that they may be uncomfortable and, like most medical care, can be expensive if not covered by insurance. Another difficulty is that they are somewhat inaccurate, sometimes reporting false negatives when in fact cancerous cells are present. A third complication is that the Pap smear is more reliable if it is done at a certain time in the menstrual cycle. If the cancer is detected early, or if it is detected at a precancerous stage, the prognosis is extremely good. If it becomes more established, however, it can invade other organs, lowering the patient's chances of being cured. Pap smears, although not foolproof, are still the best diagnostic tool widely available. Doctors are constantly doing research to improve the use of Pap smears and have just determined that combining a Pap smear with an HPV (human papillomavirus) test improves the chances of accurately screening for cervical cancer.

While progress has been made, cancer has remained the second leading cause of death (after heart disease) for the last half-century in the United States, and cancer of the reproductive organs is still one of the leading causes of cancer deaths for women.

Primary Source

"The Diagnostic Value of Vaginal Smears in Carcinoma of the Uterus"

SYNOPSIS: Papanicolaou and Traut note that an early diagnosis of female cervical cancer is needed to allow treatment. They discuss the difficulties of doing this in 1941 and how the use of the vaginal smear overcomes those difficulties. They go on to discuss how cancer cells from vaginal smears can be recognized with the proper training.

The death rate from carcinoma of the female genital tract is approximately 32,000 per year in the United States and of this figure, four-fifths, or 26,000 deaths per year, may be said to be due to cancer of the uterus. This rate has remained practically constant during the past twenty-five years.

One of the factors probably responsible for this rather discouraging situation is the fact that, despite the progress in methods of treatment, no significant improvement has been achieved in the diagnosis of malignant growths of the female genital tract, more particularly in their early stages. Indeed, it seems very likely that until enough is known about the etiology of cancer to make it possible to place efficient prophylactic weapons in physicians' hands, no radical change in the picture can be expected unless the introduction of new methods makes possible an early diagnosis of the disease.

Early diagnosis and treatment yield a high percentage of cures in both carcinoma of the fundus and of the cervix. The present difficulty in accomplishing an early diagnosis lies in the fact that we must depend largely upon the subjective symptoms of the disease to bring the patient to the physician, and by the time the patient becomes sufficiently aware of discomforts to seek help, the disease is far advanced. Even when the patient is seen early, the technique for making a positive diagnosis is not simple, as it involves a biopsy followed by the procedures necessary for microscopic examination, all of which are time consuming and relatively expensive. If by any chance a simple, inexpensive method of diagnosis could be evolved which could be applied to large numbers of women in the cancer-bearing period of life, we would be in a position to discover the disease in its incipiency much more frequently than is now possible. It is our purpose to present in this preliminary report the results of experimentation with such a method of diagnosis which appears to have great possibilities and which has been in use at the New York Hospital for the past eighteen months.

One of us (Papanicolaou) has studied the normal and abnormal variations in the vaginal smear in women and in animals for many years. Through these studies, which have been conducted since 1923 at the Woman's Hospital, at the New York Hospital, and at the Memorial Hospital, he has become aware of the fact that carcinoma of the fundus and carcinoma of the cervix are to some extent exfoliative lesions, in the sense that cells at the free surface of the growth tend to be dislodged and subsequently find their way into the vagina. Furthermore, a technique for collecting the cellular debris, smearing it upon glass slides, and staining it has been perfected, so that the various components may be studied. The method is so simple and inexpensive that it may be applied to large numbers of women. . . .

Discussion

It will be seen from the foregoing descriptions that the interpretation of the smear depends upon an intimate knowledge of the cytologic characteristics of the vaginal fluid. It may also be inferred that this is a somewhat more difficult matter than the problem presented by the diagnosis of carcinomatous tissues. However, it is safe to say that the requirements are not above the powers of any trained cytologist or pathologist after these have had adequate training and sufficient experience. From our experience it should be said that in general gynecologic diagnosis, the vaginal smear technique presents greater difficulties than those presented by some of the conditions in which it has been widely used, such as the evaluation of estrogenic effect upon the vaginal epithelium.

During the past two years we have collected and studied many hundreds of vaginal smears from normal women and those suffering from gynecologic disease, and we feel that cells pathognomonic of cervical and fundal carcinoma can be definitely recognized. We are not yet in a position to offer a statistical proof of the reliability of this method of diagnosis, but we can say that in our experience it yields a high percentage of correct diagnoses when checked by tissue biopsies. There is evidence that a positive diagnosis may also be obtained in some cases of early disease. The simplicity of the method, the lack of inconvenience to the patient during its application and the possibility of obtaining daily information over a long period of time makes it very useful in following the progress of the disease after operative procedures or x-ray treatments.

In presenting this method of diagnosis at this time, we hope that it may prove to be a dependable means whereby the principal malignant diseases of the uterus can be recognized; and further that because of its simplicity, it may eventually be applied widely so that the incipient phases of the disease may come more promptly within the range of our modern modes of treatment which have been proved highly effective in early carcinoma. In conclusion, it may be well to reiterate that whereas the method makes the material for examination easily and frequently obtainable at low cost, the interpretation of the smear requires the services of a careful and discriminating cytologist who has had experience in this field. Few persons can be depended upon for this work at the present time; however, if the method proves to be worthy of further development, as we expect it to be, then it will be possible in a relatively short time to provide the necessary facilities for instruction.

Further Resources

BOOKS

Alison, Malcolm, ed. *The Cancer Handbook.* London: Nature Publishing Group, 2002.

Carmichael, D. Erskine. *The Pap Smear: Life of George N. Papanicolaou.* Springfield, Ill.: Thomas, 1973.

Cervical Cancer Screening: The Pap Smear. Bethesda, Md.: National Institutes of Health, 1981.

National Institutes of Health. *Pap Tests: A Healthy Habit for Life.* Bethesda, Md.: National Institutes of Health, 1998.

National Institutes of Health. *Pap Tests for Older Women: A Healthy Habit for Life.* Baltimore, Md.: U.S. Department of Health and Human Services, Public Health Service, National Institutes of Health, National Cancer Institute, Health Care Financing Administration, 2001.

New Devices Aim at Improving Pap Test Accuracy. Rockville, Md.: U.S. Department of Health and Human Services, Public Health Service, Food and Drug Administration, 1997.

WEBSITES

"George Papanicolaou, MD." American Society for Clinical Pathology. Available online at http://www.ascp.org/general/about/pioneers/papanicolaou.asp; website home page http://www.ascp.org (accessed May 15, 2003).

Penicillin

"The Mold Penicillium"

Journal article

By: Charles Hill

Date: November 1941

Source: Hill, Charles. "The Mold Penicillium." *Science* Supplement 94 (2447): November 21, 1941.

Alexander Fleming works in his laboratory. His accidental discovery of the first antibiotic—penicillin—in 1929 is one of the best-known stories of scientific advancement. **CORBIS-BETTMANN. REPRODUCED BY PERMISSION.**

About the Publication: *Science* was and remains one of the most prestigious scientific journals in the world. Published by the American Association for the Advancement of Science, the journal has reported the results of hundreds of studies that have marked vital advances in science and medicine. Publishing an account of penicillin very shortly after it had been produced in purified form suggests that the scientists who edited the journal immediately recognized the revolutionary nature of the drug.

"Penicillin Shown to Cure Syphilis"

Newspaper article

By: *The New York Times*

Date: December 16, 1949

Source: "Penicillin Shown to Cure Syphilis." *The New York Times,* December 16, 1949. ■

Introduction

The British microbiologist Alexander Fleming discovered penicillin in 1929. The story of this accidental find is one of the best known in the history of medicine. Fleming stopped by his lab during his summer holiday and happened to notice a petri dish in which he was growing the bacteria staphylococcus. A spore of mold had

Magnification of the penicillium mold, the source of penicillin.
© BETTMANN/CORBIS. REPRODUCED BY PERMISSION.

fallen into the dish, and the bacteria near the mold had been broken down. Fleming recognized the significance of his discovery but was not successful in purifying the mold into a form that could be used to treat infection. The mold was purified by Howard Florey and his colleagues at Oxford University in 1941 and produced in a more concentrated form by a group of American scientists that same year. Penicillin was the first of a class of drugs called antibiotics. They are effective against bacteria but not viruses, and not all antibiotics are effective against all bacteria.

Until the 1930s physicians had no effective way to cure bacterial infections, although they certainly tried. In the eighteenth and nineteenth centuries common practices included bleeding (excess blood was thought to fuel infection) and purging the body of "toxins" using emetics and laxatives. Infections such as syphilis were treated with various toxic substances that reduced some symptoms but did not cure the disease. In what microbiologist and historian of penicillin Milton Wainwright terms a "bizarre interlude in the story of antibiotics," doctors used "maggot therapy." This involved placing live maggots in an infected wound and letting them feed on the infected, dying tissue. The treatment was effective, although unpleasant, and researchers subsequently discovered that it was not only the removal of the dead flesh that made it so. Maggots secrete several antibacterial substances that aid in fighting infection. Maggot therapy was used as recently as the 1970s on a patient whose infection had become resistant to all antibiotics.

Sulfa drugs, developed in Germany in 1932, offered some hope but were useful for only a limited number of bacterial infections. Many people experienced side effects from them, some minor like rashes, but some life-threatening, such as kidney failure. Subsequently refined and improved, sulfa drugs are still used today.

Significance

The discovery of penicillin ended centuries of failure to cure infections. Like electricity, the telephone, and the internal combustion engine, its importance is difficult to overstate. The discovery of penicillin not only revolutionized medicine but changed the world.

Penicillin's immediate impact was to lessen wartime deaths, at least for the United States and its allies. During World War II (1939–1945), the Allies had penicillin in their arsenal of weapons, but Germany and its allies did not. When the United States entered World War II in December 1941, pharmaceutical companies went into high gear to try to produce enough to treat wounded soldiers. Techniques for the mass production of penicillin were developed at a U.S. Department of Agriculture laboratory in Peoria, Illinois, and commercial production was taken over by Pfizer, a drug manufacturer. The drug saved the lives of countless soldiers who would have died of infectious diseases or infected wounds. Some historians argue that the availability of penicillin was a direct factor in the Allied victory.

After the war, penicillin became available to civilians. Its effects on common ailments were as dramatic as they had been on war-related infections. Physicians and nurses reported cases in which patients had been on death's door when an infusion of penicillin brought them back. Women who would have died from infections that they developed after childbirth lived to raise their children. Bacterial pneumonia, long a major killer, became a treatable disease. Syphilis, deemed "the great plague," became a much more treatable disease due to the miracle of penicillin.

Penicillin itself had an enormous effect on public health. Beyond that, however, its discovery also turned the minds of scientists toward molds as a source of antibacterial drugs. Researchers went on to discover more such drugs and developed methods to create penicillin synthetically, without the use of the actual molds. Penicillin was the first and perhaps most important weapon in the campaign against infections diseases. Scientists may no longer be seeking molds, but the discovery of penicillin opened a door in the scientific imagination.

Primary Source

"The Mold Penicillium"

> **SYNOPSIS:** This account of penicillin very shortly after it had been produced in purified form suggests the immediate recognition of the revolutionary nature of the drug.

"500 Cases Prove Penicillin's Value"

[This news account describes a systematic study of the treatment of infections with the drug penicillin. The original study was published in the *Journal of the American Medical Association.*]

Scientists Find It 'Remarkably Potent Anti-Bacterial Agent' in Survey

Medical scientists, writing in the *Journal of the American Medical Association* today, described penicillin, the new drug developed at the Peoria Experimental Laboratories of the Department of Agriculture, as "a remarkably potent antibacterial agent." It can be given to patients by injection into a vein or a muscle or by local application, the article states, but warned that it is ineffective when given by mouth.

The report was submitted by the Committee on Chemotherapeutic and Other Agents of the division of medical sciences, National Research Council, in which the committee's findings from a study of 500 cases of infection treated with the substance are outlined.

On the committee are Dr. Chester S. Keefer of Boston, chairman; Dr. Francis G. Blake of New Haven,

Conn.; Dr. E. Kennerly Marshall Jr. of Baltimore; Dr. John S. Lockwood of Philadelphia; and Dr. W. Barry Wood Jr. of Baltimore.

Other conclusions from the study reported by the committee are that following intravenous or intramuscular injection, penicillin is excreted rapidly, "so that in order to obtain an adequate amount in the circulating blood and tissues it is necessary to inject penicillin continuously or at frequent intervals."

"Penicillin has been found to be most effective in the treatment of staphylococcic, gonococcic, pneumococcic and hemolytic (blood-destroying) streptococcus infections," the report added. It has been disappointing in the treatment of bacterial endocarditis (inflammation of the membrane lining of the heart). Its effect is particularly striking in sulfonamide resistance gonococcic infections."

The report of the committee is based on the studies conducted by twenty-two groups of investigators accredited to the committee. As has been stressed in recent announcements, the amount of penicillin that can be produced is not sufficient to meet the needs of the armed forces. As a result, little, if any, is likely to be available for civilian use for some time.

SOURCE: "500 Cases Prove Penicillin's Value." *The New York Times,* August 25, 1943.

For most human beings the age of cannibalism is over. But not so with microbes. One eats another with the careless abandon of a vegetarian tucking into his beans. This cannibalism amongst microbes has led to a discovery by British investigators of profound importance to doctors and patients the world over. The story is found in recent issues of two British medical journals. It opened some years ago in the department of bacteriology of one of London's largest teaching hospitals, St. Mary's.

Professor A. Fleming was engaged in his daily routine work in his bacteriology laboratory. He was growing colonies of different germs on specially prepared plates. One of his plates he noticed was contaminated by a mold, not unlike the molds that grow on stale bread or cheese or sausages. This too is a common occurrence in a laboratory, for one of the most difficult tasks is to grow germs pure and uncontaminated.

Most of us would have removed the mold and started again, but Professor Fleming went one better. He allowed the mold and germ to remain on the plate, only to find that while the mold was there the germ would not grow. In fact the mold killed the germ. This was the first, indeed the fundamental,

discovery—if the microbe did not eat its fellow microbe it certainly killed it.

The professor pursued the matter further. He discovered that it was only some germs which found it impossible to live side by side with the mold. So whenever he wanted to get rid of one of the germs he knew the mold could not live with, he added some mold to his plates. He exploited their known unneighborliness.

So far the discovery was interesting, but not of great importance. Then came the suggestion that this mold, *Penicillium,* might be used to kill germs which were actually in the human body. Could not the germ-killing substance which *Penicillium* contains be used as an antiseptic to kill germs inside the human body?

Professor Florey, of the University of Oxford, headed a team of workers to tackle this problem. After many experiments they succeeded in extracting from the mold the substance in it which possesses the antiseptic quality. From the mold *Penicillium* they extracted the germ-killing substance penicillin. This done, further experiments soon showed that penicillin was the most powerful germ-killer both inside and outside the body, superior even

A poster espouses the benefits of the antibiotic penicillin, especially for soldiers during World War II. THE ADVERTISING ARCHIVE, LTD. REPRODUCED BY PERMISSION.

to the latest drugs. That is saying a great deal, for in recent years medical science has made enormous strides in antiseptic drugs.

Prontosil, sulfanilamide, M & B 693, sulfathiazol—already these new drugs all in the same big family have saved thousands of lives. In pneumonia, meningitis and in severe infections of many kinds they have been found to be immensely useful. But penicillin goes one better—it is both the strongest and the safest germ-killer yet discovered. It does its work even when diluted to the astonishing extent of one in a million. It can be given by mouth or injected directly into a vein. Most important of all, it kills the germ inside the body without harming the body itself. Its work of germ-killing done, it passes through the body into the urine, from which it can be extracted by the chemist and used again.

There is one snag. Although there are plenty of molds in this world, there is not enough *Penicillium* mold of the right kind to give us large quan-

tities of penicillin. That difficulty may not prove insuperable. Research is now being undertaken to discover other sources of penicillin. Its chemical composition is being investigated in the hope that chemists may be able to manufacture it artificially in the laboratory.

We do well to remember that the value of lemon juice in preventing scurvy was known before vitamins were ever heard of. But when it was found that lemon juice prevented scurvy because it contained vitamin C, the chemists got busy and made the vitamin artificially in their laboratories. Let us hope that the story of penicillin is the story of vitamin C. Hopes are very high. *The British Medical Journal,* known for its cautious attitude, has gone so far as to say that penicillin is to other antiseptics what radium is to other metals. In view of that praise it is not too much to say that St. Mary's Hospital, London, and the University of Oxford have made a most important contribution to human knowledge.

Primary Source

"Penicillin Shown to Cure Syphilis"

> **SYNOPSIS:** Syphilis, deemed "the great plague," was widely and successfully treated after the discovery of penicillin.

The first four patients treated with penicillin for syphilis were recently re-examined, after a lapse of six years, and found still to be entirely free of symptoms of the disease.

This was reported yesterday by Dr. John F. Mahoney, a medical director of the United States Public Health Service, who six years ago thought penicillin should be effective against syphilis and promptly put his theory to the test with four patients. He re-examined the patients last October after tracing them around the world.

Dr. Mahoney will retire today, after thirty years in the service, to become director of the city Bureau of Laboratories. He has been director of the venereal disease laboratory at the United States Marine Hospital on Staten Island.

The initial disclosure that penicillin might be the long-sought-after, non-toxic compound for use against syphilis was made Oct. 14, 1943. A cautiously worded report written by Dr. Mahoney and his associates, Dr. R.C. Arnold and Dr. Ad Harris, held promise that the search for an anti-syphilitic drug might be at an end.

But the disease is one that naturally tends to reoccur after periods during which no symptoms are evident, and for this reason it was difficult to prove that penicillin "cures" syphilis.

The original four patients were seamen. They received a total of forty-eight injections at four-hour intervals. The period of treatment used at first was eight days. After this course of medication the investigators were able only to affirm that all the symptoms of the disease had disappeared.

After seventy-two months, Dr. Mahoney reported in the December issue of the Journal of Venereal Disease Information, the symptoms were still missing and this proved that the antibiotic had been effective for at least six years.

With improvements in the technique for using penicillin, the standard treatment for syphilis has been reduced in many cases to a single injection that does not incapacitate the patient.

Wide-spread use of the injections has caused the rate of new cases of the disease to decrease recently and Dr. Mahoney said "we believe that we are getting the disease well under control."

Dr. Mahoney urged that new drugs that are known to be non-toxic be used to treat human patients before they are completely assayed in tests with laboratory animals.

Further Resources

BOOKS

Horvitz, Leslie Ann. *Eureka!* New York: John Wiley & Sons, 2002.

Sheenan, J. C. *The Enchanted Ring: The Untold Story of Penicillin.* Boston: MIT Press, 1982.

Wainright, Milton. *Miracle Cure: The Story of Penicillin and the Golden Age of Antibiotics.* London: Blackwell, 1990.

PERIODICALS

Dowell, S. F. et al. "Mortality from Pneumonia in Children in the United States, 1939 through 1996." *New England Journal of Medicine,* May 11, 2000.

Elder, Albert L. "Penicillin." *The Scientific Monthly,* June 1944.

Meyer, Karl, et al. "On Penicillin." *Science,* July 3, 1942.

WEBSITES

"Medicine Through Time: Howard Florey and Ernst Chain." Available online at http://www.bbc.co.uk/education/medicine/nonint/modern/dt/modtbi3.shtml; website home page: http://www.bbc.co.uk/ (accessed August 22, 2002).

"The Pharmaceutical Century: Antibiotics and Isotopes." American Chemical Society. Available online at http://pubs.acs.org/journals/pharmcent; website home page: http://pubs.acs.org/ (accessed August 22, 2002).

"Cut Excess Weight, Women Are Urged"

Newspaper article

By: *The New York Times*

Date: November 9, 1942

Source: "Cut Excess Weight, Women Are Urged." *The New York Times,* November 9, 1942.

About the Organization: Since the publication of this table in 1942, the Metropolitan Life Insurance Company has continued to set standards for height/weight ratios that are widely followed by the public and health-care providers. ∎

Introduction

Nutrition was a major public health concern before and during World War II (1939–1945). Public health officials initially worried that people's diets were inadequate both in terms of containing enough calories and enough key nutrients. During the 1930s the Depression had left many people underweight as they struggled to find enough food of any sort.

By the second year of the U.S. involvement in the war, however, the situation had changed. Unemployment was low as more people joined the wartime workforce or the military. They worked hard and long and made enough money to buy the food they needed. Although the country had an ample supply of most food items, it also had to feed the troops at home and overseas and attempt to help its allies who were suffering food shortages.

Perhaps as both a psychological and physical response to the deprivation of the Depression years, some people began to overeat. According to surveys by the Metropolitan Life Insurance Company, this was particularly a problem among women. The company suggested that by overeating, women were consuming more than their fair share of food during a period when supplies had to be watched carefully. The company also pointed out that weighing too much was also bad for health (a commonplace statement at the beginning of the twenty-first century). At the time the idea that weight gain was not an automatic part of growing older was novel.

Particularly novel was the Metropolitan Life's statement that existing weight and height tables did not take into account the decreasing activity that accompanied age. Although no hard evidence exists to support this, this omission may well be because most women, in earlier decades, did *not* decrease their activity much with increasing age. They continued to work to support their families and did not have the advantages of buying prepared food or manufactured clothes. As a result they engaged in a lot of physical activity.

Metropolitan Life Insurance Company Table of Ideal Weights, 1942

Applies to women over 25 years of age

Height (with shoes)	Weight in pounds (as ordinarily dressed)		
	Small frame	Medium frame	Large frame
5 ft. 0	105–113	112–120	119–129
1	107–115	114–122	121–131
2	110–118	117–125	124–135
3	113–121	120–128	127–138
4	116–125	124–132	131–142
5	119–128	127–135	133–145
6	123–132	130–140	138–150
7	126–136	134–144	142–154
8	129–139	137–147	145–158
9	133–143	141–151	149–162
10	136–147	145–155	152–166
11	139–150	148–158	155–169
6 ft. 0	141–153	151–163	160–174

SOURCE: Metropolitan Life Insurance Company Statistical Bulletin, 1942; published in *The New York Times*, November 9, 1942.

Interestingly, the company points out that the "severe limitations in war-torn areas" had reduced rates of chronic ailments such as diabetes and heart disease. Although the company was not advocating starvation as a means of avoiding chronic health problems, it foretold what has since become universally accepted in the nutrition community.

Significance

The Metropolitan Insurance Company's height/weight chart has had a profound influence on what women (and later men, when they developed another chart) came to think of as being overweight. In the 1920s young women, in particular, put great stock in having slim and boyish figures. The deprivations of the 1930s altered Americans' perceptions of what represented a good weight, and most came to believe that being underweight was definitely bad.

The insurance company's statistical report changed that. Again, slimmer was better. Not only did it help ensure a longer and healthier life, it also prevented anyone from eating more than her or his "fair share." Over the years Metropolitan has revised its tables. Most recently the company decided that the weights it assigned to the height ranges were too narrow and that a higher weight could also be acceptable.

Metropolitan also broke ground by introducing the notion that women come in various basic sizes that are not influenced by height or weight. A short woman might still have a large frame, and thus her healthy weight range would be higher. A tall woman could have a slim build, placing her ideal weight at the lower end of the range.

Although the Metropolitan tables were an important factor in encouraging women to curb overeating and try to maintain a healthful weight, the notion of a "correct" weight may also have encouraged the fixation with weight that now affects many women and men.

Since 1942, when Metropolitan first introduced its table, other groups have come up with similar guidelines for height and weight. Metropolitan, however, is a significant debt for raising the issue of the negative health effects of being overweight and the positive effects of maintaining a good weight for one's height.

Primary Source

"Cut Excess Weight, Women Are Urged"

SYNOPSIS: The Metropolitan Life Insurance Company report, summarized in this news story, challenged existing ideas about the ideal weight for a woman. It presented new ideal weights based on body type, and urged women to meet those healthier and more obtainable goals.

Many Who Are Too Heavy Use Up Food Unnecessarily, Insurance Report Says

The average overweight woman is digging unnecessarily into the country's food supplies and constitutes a national health problem "of the first order," health authorities of the Metropolitan Life Insurance Company assert in their current Statistical Bulletin.

Wartime rationing of foods can help instead of hinder sensible reduction programs, the company points out, heartily recommending such programs for a substantial increase in the health and longevity of adults. Believing that commonly used weight tables show unneeded and undesirable increases in weight with advancing age, it proposes a new "ideal" table, which takes into account three separate groups of women, those with slight, medium and heavy builds.

Current tables, it is said, reflect a tendency to consume the same amount of food at a time when physical activity is decreasing. Between the ages of 30 and 50 years the weight of short women increases 13 to 14 pounds, or more than 10 per cent, while tall women gain as much as 15 pounds. A large-scale survey by the company showed that a moderate degree of overweight was beneficial to the "young adult," but that after 35 the advantage lay with women of average weight. Women who are under weight at middle age or older have the best longevity records.

"Frank obesity was bad at every age," the company found.

Discussing overweight as a national health problem, the company lists a dozen ailments that afflict heavy women. Severe food limitations in many war-torn areas have caused death rates from diabetes and other chronic diseases associated with overweight to decline, it is pointed out.

For health and longevity, the company has prepared the following table of "ideal" weights, which considers the variations in the body structure and can be applied to any woman past 25.

Further Resources

BOOKS

Bentley, Amy. *Eating for Victory: Food Rationing and the Politics of Domesticity.* Urbana, Ill.: University of Illinois Press, 1998, 238.

McIntosh, Elaine N. *American Food Habits in Historical Perspective.* Westport, Conn.: Praeger, 1995, 251.

Schwartz, Hillel. *Never Satisfied: A Cultural History of Diets, Fantasies, and Fat.* New York: Free Press, 1986, 468.

WEBSITES

The History of Diets and Dieting. Available online at http://www.karlloren.com/diet/p119.htm; website home page: http://www.karlloren.com (accessed April 4, 2003).

"America Is Learning What to Eat"

Newspaper article, Illustration

By: Clive M. McCoy

Date: March 28, 1943

Source: "America Is Learning What to Eat." *The New York Times,* March 28, 1943.

About the Author: Clive M. McCoy was a professor of nutrition at Cornell University in Ithaca, New York, a school well known for its research in agriculture and human nutrition. ∎

Introduction

The traditional American diet in the early twentieth century wasn't fancy. The Great Depression of the 1930s left many households short of money, forcing housewives to stretch their food dollars further. While they did have to worry about affording food, they did not have to wonder whether they could find the foods they wanted to buy. A standard cookbook published in 1931 lists dinner menus that include meat, potatoes, several vegetables, bread or rolls, and dessert—sometimes all preceded by an appetizer of soup or salad. A recipe for beef stroganoff required 1.5 pounds of beef filet for four servings, or six ounces per serving. That was one meal; breakfast and the midday meal often also included meat. Cakes, cookies, and other sweets were standard fare. The result was that Americans could, and did, eat more than they needed.

Americans experienced many changes after the United States entered World War II (1939–1945) in 1941. Eating habits, for example, changed when feeding the troops and shipping food to the nation's allies in Europe became top priorities. In 1942 President Franklin Roosevelt (served 1933–1945) included in a speech a suggestion that Americans have "Meatless Days" to conserve supplies. That same year Americans registered for ration books that contained stamps that they used when shopping. The stamps carried "points," and shoppers could not use more than their allotted points for a particular item. Since meat and sugar were two of the major foods rationed, Americans were no longer able to take their meaty and sweet diets for granted. Civilians were allotted five ounces of meat daily, and whipping cream was no longer available. Those with the space to do so grew victory gardens to produce their own fruits and vegetables, which they could also can for later consumption.

Significance

Rationing achieved significant results in several ways, although some lasted no longer than the duration of the war. First, it forced Americans to think about the nutritional quality of their diets. As some standards became less available, people could no longer assume they would get what they needed. This new awareness coincided with a growing body of knowledge about vitamins and minerals and the effects of their underconsumption and marked the beginning of a concern about nutrition that continues. Henry C. Sherman, chief of the U.S. Department of Agriculture's Bureau of Home Nutrition and Home Economics, noted "We have lately been learning not only that even our everyday foods have properties previously unknown but also that one's choice of food can actually change that internal environment of the body which science for three generations past had regarded as something fixed by nature."

Information about nutrition is now virtually inescapable; it is the topic of books, magazine and newspaper articles, and television offerings. Although many people still consume diets that are far from ideal (too many calories, too much fat, and too few fruits and vegetables, for example), they are constantly being urged to change their ways. Schoolchildren are taught about nutrition, and food producers use nutritional value as a selling point in their advertising.

THIS IS THE FOOD NEEDED BY THE AVERAGE AMERICAN
(150 LBS.—MODERATELY ACTIVE)

Primary Source

"America Is Learning What to Eat": Illustration

SYNOPSIS: Illustration from "America Is Learning What To Eat," *The New York Times*, March 28, 1943, an article that suggests ways in which Americans can achieve a balanced diet. *THE NEW YORK TIMES*. GRADUATE LIBRARY, UNIVERSITY OF MICHIGAN. REPRODUCED BY PERMISSION.

Rationing also helped people to become aware of different kinds of food. One major example of this was soybeans. Wartime cookbooks, such as the 1943 edition of Irma S. Rombauer's *The Joy of Cooking,* quickly added supplements that included such dishes as soybean loaf and soybean soufflé. Their nutritional value was their primary virtue because, as Rombauer notes, "They really need an uplift, being rather on the dull side." Although the end of meat rationing doubtless saw many cooks gratefully abandon soybean soufflé in favor of steak or hamburger, soy meat substitutes have in recent years made a comeback. Soy "burgers" and hot dogs are now found in most grocery stores and are favored by those who want to reduce their meat consumption.

Third, although no national statistics are available on the topic, it seems likely that the victory gardens grown by every patriotic household with enough space sparked the now-common habit of planting a summer vegetable garden. While surveys show that many Americans still do not eat the recommended amounts of fresh produce, the backyard garden certainly helps them to do so for part of the year.

Primary Source

"America Is Learning What to Eat" [excerpt]: Newspaper article

> **SYNOPSIS:** In this report, the author describes the positive health effects of wartime rationing of food and offers suggestions on how Americans can achieve a balanced diet.

In the pre-ration era we did not bother much about nutrition. Now we face its challenge. An expert gives the basis of a wholesome diet.

The problem facing every American housewife today is how to keep her family well nourished with the limited supplies of standard foodstuffs available under present and imminent rationing programs. Fortunately it is a question for which there is a ready answer, but it is one that requires of her a greater knowledge of the foods her family eats and a revision of her cookery in order to get the full value from the food she buys.

The experience of Great Britain in three and a half years of war has proved that good health can be maintained without many of the standard foods that both Americans and Britons relied on in prewar times. Indeed, although the average Briton eats less and works harder today than he did before 1939, his health is generally better and his nutritive standards are vastly improved. This is true in the face of a food shortage far more severe—chiefly because of the lack of shipping space and the loss of European sources of supply—than anything the United States is likely to experience.

What the British Food Ministry has achieved for the British people bears out what American nutritionists have known for many years past. Briefly stated, this is that—

1. Men can live in excellent health for their entire lives upon very simple diets.
2. Natural foods that are available in abundance in America can be fitted into combinations that are entirely adequate for good health.
3. Thousands of Americans have gone to premature graves from overeating and keeping their bodies too fat.
4. Natural foods with good cooking can be made to provide more complete diets than can processed foods supplemented with vitamin concentrates.

The problem of the housewife, then, simmers down to two questions: What are the essentials of a wholesome diet? How can I provide these essentials from the rationed and non-rationed foods available in the markets?

According to the National Research Council, a man weighing 150 pounds and living a moderately active life needs daily: 3,000 calories, 70 grams of protein, .8 grams of calcium, 12 milligrams of iron, 5,000 international units of vitamin A, 1.8 milligrams of thiamin (vitamin B1), 2.7 milligrams of riboflavin (vitamin B2), 18 milligrams of niacin (vitamin P-P), 75 milligrams of ascorbic acid (vitamin C) and an unknown amount of vitamin D and other assorted vitamins.

In the pre-ration era very few house-wives concerned themselves with this scientific jargon. Nutrition was a hit-or-miss matter, and because of the abundance of foods in the markets and the tendency of Americans to eat more than they required, the housewife often succeeded willy-nilly in providing her family with the essential nutrients. A pound of American beefsteak alone provided 880 calories, a generous ham sandwich 500, an ordinary serving of butter 100. And the average meat serving also went a long way toward meeting the body's requirements of protein and was an important source of minerals as well.

However, under the rationing program, the allotment per day is a little over five ounces of meat a person—the equivalent of about 275 calories in beef, slightly more in ham, 300 to 400 in pork and 150 to 200 in veal.

Providing the 3,000 calories for the 150-pound average man poses the least of the difficulties the housewife faces. A good part will be made up by better use of the fats from what meats are available under rationing. Bread will provide more of our caloric requirements, sugar less. Poultry, fish, soybeans, nuts, dried beans, lentils, peas and whole grains are high in caloric content. Butter is a rich source and most butter substitutes have similar qualities. In fact, many of the familiar foods of the American table besides meat are important contributors of calories.

The chronic shortage of various cuts of meat that preceded the introduction of rationing helped to prepare the housewife for the change in her food buying. She had been using more eggs and poultry and had been preparing non-meat dishes composed of dairy products and soybeans and other vegetables. Whether she realized it or not, she was introducing substitutes to maintain the high protein requirement of the daily diet.

As the war progresses and food-buying is further adjusted, she will begin to find soybeans an increasingly more important source of protein in her foods. Besides being a protein food, the soya is also valuable as a source of calories and supplies large quantities of some of the vitamins that are essential to health. It is not unlikely that soybean flour will become a component of all bread in the not too distant future, an objective that has the endorsement of many of the country's nutritionists.

A movement is on foot in New York State, backed by one of the leading women's organizations, to have all bread made by an open formula, containing dry skim milk and 5 per cent soybean flour in addition to enrichment in vitamins and iron. As this development proceeds to include whole wheat bread, one of the greatest nutritional advances of all time will have been made. And it will have relieved the housewife of one of her major concerns.

The third essential in the balanced diet—calcium—may prove one of the more difficult to get as time passes. The ice cream supply has been reduced by one-third and in many cases milk has become more expensive and more difficult to buy. A large percentage of dry skim milk, of which more than 1 per cent is calcium, is being shipped abroad.

However, the body's daily requirement can be provided by the foods that are still at the disposal of the housewife. Cheese, broccoli, cauliflower and various greens are important sources of the mineral. But . . . they should [be] used to set up a store of vitamins for the Winter months.

In further pursuit of vitamin sufficiency the housewife will use many of the parts of food that she had previously thrown away. Citrus parings, which may be as much as five times as rich in vitamin C as the juice, will be served in jellies, candies and other forms. As canned juices become rarer salads will be an increasingly important staple in the daily fare.

The chart that accompanies this article shows a few of the foods that are high in vitamin content. Many more could be added. But even in this abbreviated list there are many vegetables that are unfamiliar to the American table. The common dandelion weed that grows freely in every meadow and persistently in the most carefully tended lawn is among the richest of the greens in vitamin content. One small serving of it contains double the daily requirement of Vitamin A and more than enough Vitamin C as well.

Spinach, beet grains, brussels sprouts, strawberries, citrus fruits, tomatoes, endive, swiss chard and collards in various combinations should appear frequently on the menu. A judicious choice among them will account for the vitamin A and C requirements.

Wise use of ration coupons will help the housewife to get the daily requirements of thiamin, riboflavin and niacin. Kidneys, liver and hearts of beef, lamb and pork are rich in both thiamin and riboflavin. Bread, some greens and oysters are also sources. Three slices of liver will meet the niacin requirement; two slices of chicken.

Once the housewife has familiarized herself with the nutrients and explored the culinary possibilities, she will find that she will not have to surrender tastiness to obtain nutrition. Her meals will be appetizing and attractive. They may have a lower caloric content than in the prewar era, but for many adults that will be an advantage rather than a handicap. Adults eating well-planned diets will not gather unnecessary weight. They will be healthier, stronger, and they may escape some of the diseases that result from overeating.

Rationing will influence the eating habits of rich and poor alike. It will result in a fairer distribution of the food that is available and it will inevitably improve the nutritional health of the population, as more and more housewives discover the fascinating relationships between food and the health of their families.

Rationing also will make the housewife better acquainted with her grocer to the mutual advantage of both. She should not hesitate to tell him what she wants in the quality of food she buys. The grocer is sorely burdened with new troubles, but he is still attentive to his customers' needs.

The buyer should scrutinize more closely the nutritive value of the bread and pastries she is buying, and her grocer will help.

Further Resources

BOOKS
Hoopes, Roy. *Americans Remember: The Home Front.* New York: Hawthorn, 1977.

Rombauer, Irma S. *The Joy of Cooking.* New York: Bobbs-Merrill, 1943 edition.

PERIODICALS
Sherman, Henry C. "Budgeting the Basic 7." *The New York Times* October 3, 1943.

WEBSITES
"Global World War II Rationed Items List and Timeline." Voices: The Kansas Collection Online Magazine. Available online at http://www.ku.edu/carrie/kancoll/voices/1997/0597ratn.htm; website home page: http://www.ku.edu (accessed August 22, 2002).

"Demerol, Newly Marketed as a Synthetic Substitute For Morphine, Ranks With Sulfa Drugs and Penicillin"

Newspaper article

By: *The Wall Street Journal*
Date: August 31, 1943
Source: "Demerol, Newly Marketed as a Synthetic Substitute

For Morphine, Ranks With Sulfa Drugs and Penicillin." *The Wall Street Journal,* August 31, 1943. ∎

Introduction

Pain has existed as long as creatures have had nervous systems. Humans have sought ways to reduce or eliminate pain for millennia. Painkillers fall into two categories: anti-inflammatory drugs, which reduce pain caused by inflammation, and opiates, such as opium, which affect the central nervous system. Many of the opiates that reduce pain are addictive and have effects on the central nervous system that reduce their safety.

Alcoholic spirits, although not strictly a painkiller, were given to those who had to undergo painful, sometimes excruciating, procedures or who suffered from painful injuries. Alcohol's primary effect was to cause the victim who ingested enough to pass out. While this did indeed spare the person pain, alcohol's depressant effect on the central nervous system created a potentially dangerous situation.

Perhaps the earliest safe, though mild, painkillers were the aspirin-like substances that the ancient Greeks and Romans extracted from the bark of the willow tree. Willow contains salicin, which was later synthesized into acetylsalicylic acid, or aspirin. In 1897 a German chemist, Felix Hoffman, who worked for Friedrich Bayer and Company, began to research acetylsalicylic acid. As a result, he developed a product in powder form. By 1899, Bayer sold aspirin to physicians to give to their patients. In 1915 the medicine became available from pharmacies without a doctor's prescription.

During the same centuries that people were using salicin and related substances to reduce inflammation, they were also using opium and its by-products to kill pain. Initially they used it in crude, unrefined forms. People also smoked opium to induce a state of euphoria that was addictive. By the end of the nineteenth century, physicians regarded opium, in the words of one of England's most prominent surgeons, Sir William Osler, as "God's Own Medicine." Its painkilling properties prevented untold suffering from injury, disease, and surgery. If physicians of the time were aware of opiates' negative side effects, undoubtedly they viewed them as minor compared with its advantages. Nevertheless opiates such as morphine did pose some danger. They cause slow breathing, which can be particularly serious in someone already compromised by disease or physical injury.

Significance

In the early 1940s an alternative painkiller, Demerol (whose chemical name is meperidine), was developed by the Winthrop Chemical Company. Demerol marked the first of many synthetic, or man-made, opiates that are now widely used in pain control. Winthrop announced its production of Demerol in 1943, when casualties from World War II (1939–1945) were at their peak. The *Physician's Desk Reference* (PDR), a reference book on pharmaceuticals, now warns that Demerol "may be habit forming" and should be prescribed with the same caution for possible addiction as morphine. The 2001 issue of the PDR also notes that when used during childbirth, Demerol does cross the placental barrier and can slow breathing and other functions in the newborn. Subsequent experience with the drug has also shown, according to the PDR, that it should be given with "extreme caution" to patients with asthma or other respiratory ailments.

Primary Source

"Demerol, Newly Marketed as a Synthetic Substitute For Morphine, Ranks With Sulfa Drugs and Penicillin"

SYNOPSIS: Demerol marked the first of many synthetic, or man-made, opiates that are now widely used in pain control.

Demerol, the first satisfactory synthetic substitute for morphine, the essential pain relieving drug, is being put on the market by the Winthrop Chemical Co. Demerol has been in production for some time, but was not released for general use until a stock-pile had been built up sufficient to meet expected demands, Dr. Theodore G. Klumph, president of Winthrop, states.

The new drug takes rank along with the sulfa drugs, penicillin, and blood plasma as a major contribution to medical science. It possesses most of the advantages of morphine, derived from opium poppies, and has very few of the disadvantages.

Used in childbirth, it not only greatly relieves pain but also noticeably shortens labor. It has already been successfully used in thousands of test cases. Demerol is not habit forming in the physical sense that morphine is, and when used in childbirth has no effect on the infant.

Like most new drugs, a large part of the supply will go to wounded men in the armed forces. One of its notable advantages is that, unlike morphine, it does not slow down breathing. Morphine is now carried by fighting men for use in relieving the pain of severe wounds. Morphine, however, cuts down the normal essential oxygen supply of the body and so increases the handicaps of the patient and lowers resistance. Because Demerol has no effect on respiration it may be used on asthma patients who cannot be given morphine safely.

Russia is understood to be greatly interested in the new American production of this drug because of the large numbers of serious casualties, and may want to take a good part of the current production.

Further Resources

BOOKS

Booth, Martin. *Opium: A History.* New York: St. Martin's Press, 1996.

Physician's Desk Reference 2001. Montvale, N.J.: Medical Economics Company, 2001.

Vertosick, Frank T., Jr. *Why We Hurt: The Natural History of Pain.* New York: Harcourt, 2000.

WEBSITES

Bayer Aspirin. Available online at http://www.bayeraspirin.com (accessed August 22, 2002).

"Tell 37-Year Rise in Better Eating"

Newspaper article

By: *The New York Times*
Date: July 19, 1946
Source: "Tell 37-Year Rise in Better Eating." *The New York Times,* July 19, 1946. ■

Introduction

The first four decades of the twentieth century were an era of rapid ups and downs in the nation's economic state. These fluctuations were mirrored in Americans' well-being, including their diets. The prosperous 1920s brought no national food shortages, but scientific research on nutrition was still in its infancy. The 1930s were a decade of want for many, and even people who ate sufficient calories may not have been eating enough nutritious foods. The 1940s and World War II (1939–1945) created a new situation for nutrition. Although food supplies were adequate, America faced the extra task of feeding troops and helping its allies.

Studies of particular populations, particularly draft-age men, had found that many suffered from nutritional deficiencies. The early years of the war saw many women becoming overweight from eating too much and, perhaps, not being active enough. Thus, the USDA's long-range, large-scale look at American's eating habits was a useful look at the bigger picture.

The USDA report was issued three years after another branch of the Agriculture Department issued a re-

port that applied the seven basic food groups to improved nutrition and the war effort. "Budgeting our 7 Basic Foods: How we Can Keep Well-Nourished Ourselves While Sharing With Allies in Order To Win the War" emphasized the need for flexibility. One week might find the grocery shelves empty of potatoes; another nutritious carbohydrate food will do just as well. Henry C. Sherman, the USDA official who wrote the article, urged Americans to use this as a chance to introduce variety into their diets.

The victory gardens that Americans planted during World War II were also a source of nutrition. They provided fresh vegetables during summer and home-canned produce for the winter months. They also accustomed people to the notion of eating fresh vegetables; many previously had relied on canned goods.

Significance

By 1946 the science of nutrition had come of age. Because the report covered only national trends, not regions or particular income groups, it may have overlooked malnutrition among particular groups or in certain parts of the country. The general trend, however, was extremely positive. That the survey was conducted points out, too, that government officials had developed a system for monitoring the nutritional habits of Americans. This enabled them to design education programs that could help improve eating habits.

The report also is evidence that nutrition research had been translated into effective nutrition education. In some cases Americans might have been making a virtue of necessity, as in the example of drinking more milk because it was more widely available than other kinds of foods. Decreased consumption of potatoes and grain products suggests that these foods had been replaced with more fresh foods. Americans certainly did not stop eating bread or other bakery products, but the introduction of enriched flours meant that they could consume fewer calories and get the same or more vitamins. Their willingness to follow nutrition advice—although their patriotic duty—suggests that they no longer resented the advice of professional nutritionists, a trend noted during the Depression among people who were accepting government food aid.

The USDA survey also suggested that Americans had developed more of a taste for more nutritious foods. Victory gardens were suggested as both a practical and a patriotic gesture, but Americans were certainly under no obligation to plant them since most people were employed during wartime and earned enough money to buy food rather than grow it.

In the decades since World War II, gardening has become an increasingly popular practice among Americans. Even apartment dwellers plant tomatoes on their terraces, and those with a little patch of land, however small, put in a little garden that provides them with fresh produce during the summer. Americans may no longer garden in the interest of military victory, but perhaps they garden as a way to return to a simpler time and enjoy the "victory" of growing their own produce.

Primary Source

"Tell 37-Year Rise in Better Eating"

SYNOPSIS: This article reported findings of the Bureau of Human Nutrition and Home Economics, a branch of the U.S. Department of Agriculture (USDA). The bureau monitored what foods Americans consumed.

U. S. Economists Report Wide Advances in Civilians' Nutrition During War

Important advances in civilian nutrition in this country during the war years were reported today by the Bureau of Human Nutrition and Home Economics on the basis of a thirty-seven-year study of the per capita food supply, 1909 to 1945.

American gains in consuming during the war years more of the vitamins and minerals which scientists have prescribed for protecting health and promoting growth, calcium, iron, B vitamins and vitamins A and C, than in any other equal span in the thirty-seven-year period was ascribed to changing food habits which resulted in increased eating of milk, eggs, meat, poultry, vegetables and fruit.

The enrichment of white bread and flour was also given great credit for general better eating in this country. Said the report:

> Because of the enrichment program, grain products now furnish a much greater share of the total available supply of iron, and B vitamins, thiamine and niacin, than before World War II.

The rise of calcium and riboflavin in the diet was ascribed largely to greater consumption of milk. This rise was from a per capita of 169 quarts in 1909 to 212 quarts in 1939, a 205-quart average for the thirty years; followed by a quick jump from 215 quarts in 1940 to 257 in 1944. The early gradual increase in milk consumption was ascribed to increased use of manufactured dairy products other than butter. During World War II, the report said, fluid milk consumption reached new highs because of substitution for other foods, greater consumer purchasing power, and emphasis on the nutritive value of milk.

The rise in consumption of vitamins A and C was said to be due to increased use of fruits and vegetables. Citrus fruit and tomatoes jumped from a 44-pound per person average annual consumption in 1909 to 119 pounds in 1945; leafy green and yellow vegetables from 77 pounds in 1909 to 134 in 1945. The consumption in citrus fruit alone was a 400 per cent increase in the thirty-seven years.

Changing eating habits were also shown in the fact that there was a 30 per cent decrease in the consumption of potatoes and grain products.

The thirty-five-page report represents the longest-range study of the nutritional value of this country's diet ever made, and is probably the one such study for any nation. All figures given are national averages, and do not give regional variations or diet differences by income levels.

Further Resources

BOOKS

Burdett, James H. *Victory Garden Manual.* Chicago: Ziff Davis, 1943, 128.

McIntosh, Elaine N. *American Food Habits in Historical Perspective.* Westport, Conn.: Praeger, 1995, 251.

WEBSITES

Northwestern University Library World War II Poster Collection. Available online at http://www.library.northwestern.edu /govpub/collections/wwii-posters/; website home page: http:// www.library.northwestern.edu/ (accessed April 3, 2003).

Smithsonian Victory Garden Exhibition. Available online at http:// americanhistory.si.edu/house/yourvisit/victorygarden.asp; website home page: http://americanhistory.si.edu/ (accessed April 3, 2003).

Hill-Burton Act

Law

By: U.S. Congress

Date: August 13, 1946

Source: Hill-Burton Act, August 13, 1946. Available at the Schiller Institute online at http://www.schillerinstitute.org /health/hill_burton.html; website home page at http://www .schilerinstitute.org (accessed March 18, 2003). ∎

Introduction

In 1800, the United States had two hospitals: New York Hospital in New York City and Pennsylvania Hospital in Philadelphia. Before the days of antiseptic, or anti-infection, procedures, contagion in hospitals could pose a danger greater than disease or injury. Patients were looked after at home by families and physicians who spent a good deal of their time making house calls. By the beginning of the twentieth century, however, more people began to turn to hospital care for a number of reasons. By the 1920s, hospitals were booming. In 1922, Americans spent approximately 53 million days in the hospital, which represented one day for every two people. Hospital construction also flourished, with a total of $890 million spent between 1925 and 1929, an 80 percent increase over the previous five years.

The rise of scientific medicine made possible by increased knowledge and new pharmaceuticals gave hospitals more to offer. Diseases once treated at home now could be treated more successfully in the hospital. Improvements in surgical techniques and understanding made previously inoperable conditions treatable. Hospitals also had an increasing array of diagnostic tools in the form of X-rays and laboratories. Between 1935 and 1946, admissions to general hospitals rose by 32 percent. During World War II (1939–1945), however, hospitals lost ground. There were shortages of medical staffs as doctors and nurses joined the military. As the country poured most of its resources into the war effort, existing hospitals received little attention. By 1944, Surgeon General Thomas Parran estimated that at least 25 percent of existing hospitals were obsolete or would be so shortly.

At the same time, hospital construction was a very controversial issue politically. Politicians and physicians debated whether hospitals should be large regional research centers or community, or voluntary, hospitals. The debate over hospital construction had also become entangled with the debate over federal health insurance. The medical establishment, in the form of the American Medical Association, was strenuously opposed to this proposal. Thus, to craft legislation for funding hospital construction required congressmen to confront myriad special interest groups and negotiate political minefields.

Significance

The American Hospital Association (AHA), together with the associations for Catholic and Protestant hospitals, crafted a bill that maintained the idea of the "voluntary," not-for-profit community hospital. These groups worked with members of Congress who wanted to create legislation that combined people's need for hospitals with a larger vision of the future of health care in America. The AHA's executive director tapped Senator Harold Burton of Ohio, who recruited Senator Robert Taft, then running for president. They in turn secured the support of Senator Lister Hill of Alabama.

The resulting legislation, known as Hill-Burton, was the first major health facility construction program in the United States. Officially called P.L. 79–725, the Hospi-

tal Survey and Construction Act, it established a partnership between the existing voluntary hospital system and the federal and state governments. States that wanted to take part in Hill-Burton had to conduct comprehensive surveys of their available facilities and study their future needs. The legislation included the plan that hospitals serve as scientific research facilities and created the Federal Hospital Council, which included both government and non-government representatives. In return for the grants, hospitals had to agree to provide some free or reduced-price care for poor patients for a fixed period of time. That provision appealed to supporters of President Harry S. Truman's (served 1945–1953) national health plan, which was bitterly opposed by the medical establishment for fear that it would reduce its power and authority. One provision of the bill, dropped before its passage, would have provided for primary-care and preventive-medicine clinics.

The Hill-Burton Act changed the landscape of American medicine in ways that went beyond the construction of physical facilities. Since 1946, the program has distributed more than $4.6 billion in grants and $1.5 billion in loans to almost 7,000 health-care facilities in more than 4,000 communities. Hill-Burton has since been augmented by Title XVI of the Public Health Service Act, which requires facilities funded under the amendment to provide free services "in perpetuity."

Primary Source

Hill-Burton Act [excerpt]

> **SYNOPSIS:** The legislation, known as Hill-Burton, was the first major health facility construction program in the United States.

Declaration of Purpose

The purpose of this title is (a) to assist the several States in the carrying out of their programs for the construction and modernization of such public or other nonprofit community hospitals and other medical facilities as may be necessary, in conjunction with existing facilities, to furnish adequate hospital, clinic, or similar services to all their people; (b) to stimulate the development of new or improved types of physical facilities for medical, diagnostic, preventive, treatment, or rehabilitative services; and (c) to promote research, experiments, and demonstrations relating to the effective development and utilization of hospital, clinic, or similar services, facilities, and resources, and to promote the coordination of such research, experiments, and demonstrations and the useful application of their results.

Further Resources

BOOKS

Rosenberg, Charles E. *The Care of Strangers: The Rise of America's Hospital System.* New York: Basic Books, 1987.

Stevens, Rosemary. *In Sickness and in Wealth: American Hospitals in the Twentieth Century.* Rev. ed. Baltimore, Md.: The Johns Hopkins University Press, 1999.

The Common Sense Book of Baby and Child Care

Guidebook

By: Benjamin Spock, M.D.

Date: 1946

Source: Spock, Benjamin. *The Common Sense Book of Baby and Child Care.* New York: Duell, Sloan and Pearce, 1946.

About the Author: Benjamin Spock (1903–1998) was the oldest of six children. He graduated from Columbia University's College of Physicians and Surgeons in 1929. After training as a pediatrician, he sought further education in psychology and psychoanalysis in an effort to understand the emotional needs of babies and children. First published in 1946, *The Common Sense Book of Baby and Child Care* has produced multiple editions, sold millions, and remains a popular and trusted source of information for parents. ∎

Benjamin Spock. Dr. Spock's parenting guide, *The Common Sense Book of Baby and Child Care* (1946), was enormously influential and remains popular even today. **THE LIBRARY OF CONGRESS.**

Introduction

With the end of World War II (1939–1945), Americans wanted a quick return to normal life. Millions of couples settled down in the suburbs that were growing around the cities and produced what became known as the baby boom generation. As the birthrate soared so did the number of questions that mothers and fathers had about the best way to raise children.

Like all new parents these mothers and fathers wanted to do what was right for their children, and plenty of experts were ready to advise them. The experts of the time, notably Dr. Luther Emmett Holt and the psychologist John B. Watson, were firm proponents of what was termed "scientific parenthood." In the debate over whether "nature" (genetics) or "nurture" (environment) was more important, Watson came down firmly on the side of nurture—babies began with unformed minds and were shaped by their environments. In essence, they became what their parents made them.

What their parents should make them into, according to these experts, was little adults. Holt, Watson, and others firmly advised a detached, no-nonsense style of parenting so that babies would learn to toe the line at a very early age. This included toilet-training infants when they were several months old (even if they weren't strong

enough to sit alone on a potty); allowing babies to cry to teach them that crying would not get them what they wanted; and not showing children too much affection, as that would make them spoiled and demanding. Experts told parents to put babies on strict schedules for eating and sleeping lest they turn into little tyrants, whining for mothers to always be at their beck and call. Physical punishment was considered a good way to teach children what behavior wasn't acceptable.

Spock, himself raised under these principles, started to see conflicts between the experts' advice and what he heard from parents in his pediatric practice. He began writing *The Common Sense Book of Baby and Child Care* after working out a set of beliefs that combined his practical experience with some of the principles of psychoanalysis. In an era when experts charted out a strict route that parents should follow, Spock traveled without a map. He advised that parents pay equal attention to the child's emotional and physical needs and broke new ground when he wrote with the assumption that each baby was a distinctive individual.

Spock became the champion of the middle ground: don't go overboard in either direction. In a conversational and relaxed style, he told parents not to believe these experts, but to trust their own instincts instead. This alone was revolutionary; the advice itself, to followers of Holt and Watson, was pediatric heresy. Without using either the name of Sigmund Freud, the founder of modern psychoanalysis, or the still-controversial terms he used, Spock nevertheless outlined child development as a process in which the child's emerging sense of self included sexual feelings. At the same time, he politely suggested that many of the current practices were wrong. They were wrong in large part because children differ in their rate of development, in their readiness to start new behavior, and in their maturity. They begin speaking at different ages, which does not mean that the child who starts talking early is any smarter than the child who waits a bit longer.

Significance

The publication of *The Common Sense Book of Baby and Child Care* was significant because it brought about a major shift in thinking about child rearing. Spock's book marked the end of the era when parents clung to the advice of the "scientific" experts regardless of whether their children fit into the mold. Treat children with a mixture of love and firmness, Spock counseled, and they would feel secure. Avoid extremes of both control and permissiveness. Stay in the middle of the road. Spock's advice had a particularly strong impact in three areas: paying attention to babies' cries; toilet training; and discipline.

Ignore a crying baby, the experts said, advice with which Spock disagreed. He believed that a crying baby was sending a message—I'm hungry, I'm lonely, I'm uncomfortable—and that parents should respond to the message. Particularly revolutionary was the idea that parents should respond to a baby who was lonely and wanted to be comforted. Physical contact was vital, he argued—the main way that infants bond with parents.

Toilet training was another area about which parents obsessed. The childcare experts of the day told them that their infants could be toilet trained when they were only a few months old. Spock countered—to the relief of many parents—that babies of this age could not control these functions and so it was futile to try to force them. Rather, he suggested, wait until the child shows that she is ready, after which the process will proceed much more quickly and with less stress for everyone.

Discipline was another concern for parents. "Spare the rod and spoil the child" remained the standard rule—a child who was not punished physically would end up spoiled. Not so, Spock argued. Although he recognized that parents, being human, would occasionally lose their tempers and slap a child's hand, he believed that the regular use of spanking would not solve discipline problems. What it would do was produce angry, resentful children.

In the 1960s, when young people in particular began to protest the Vietnam War (1964–1975), critics of the antiwar movement blamed Spock. His advice, they claimed, had produced a generation that did not respect authority, a group of people whose parents, following Spock's advice, had raised children who rejected the "Establishment." Spock himself became an outspoken antiwar activist.

Primary Source

The Common Sense Book of Baby and Child Care [excerpt]

> **SYNOPSIS:** In this excerpt from the chapter "Preparing for the Baby: Trust Yourself," Spock expounds his fundamental premise: parents are the experts. His sympathetic and chatty style was a major departure from other child care books of the time.

You know more than you think you do. Soon you're going to have a baby. Maybe you have him already. You're happy and excited, but, if you haven't had much experience, you wonder whether you are going to know how to do a good job. Lately you have been listening more carefully to your friends and relatives when they talked about bringing up a child. You've begun to read articles by experts in the magazines and newspapers. After the baby is born, the doctor and nurses will begin to give you instructions, too. Sometimes it sounds like a very complicated business. You find out all the vitamins a baby needs and all the inoculations. One mother tells you you must use the black kind of nipples, another says the yellow. You hear that a baby must be handled as little as possible, and that a baby must be cuddled plenty; that spinach is the most valuable vegetable, that spinach is a worthless vegetable; that fairy tales make children nervous, and that fairy tales are a wholesome outlet.

Don't take too seriously all that the neighbors say. Don't be overawed by what the experts say. Don't be afraid to trust your own common sense. Bringing up your child won't be a complicated job if you take it easy, trust your own instincts, and follow the directions that your doctor gives you. We know for a fact that the natural loving care that kindly parents give to their children is a hundred times more valuable than their knowing how to pin a diaper on just right, or making a formula expertly. Every time you pick your baby up, even if you do it a little awkwardly at first, every time you change him, bathe him, feed him, smile at him, he's getting a feeling that he belongs to you and that you belong to him.

Nobody else in the world, no matter how skillful, can give that to him.

It may surprise you to hear that the more people have studied different methods of bringing up children the more they have come to the conclusion that what good mothers and fathers instinctively feel like doing for their babies is usually best after all. Furthermore, all parents do their best job when they have a natural, easy confidence in themselves. Better to make a few mistakes from being natural than to do everything letter-perfect out of a feeling of worry. . . .

You can be both firm and friendly. It's probably a good idea, after I have been emphasizing how you handle a young child by distraction and consideration, to point out that there are limits. Some gentle, unselfish parents devote so much effort to being tactful and generous to a child, that they give him the feeling that he's the crown prince, or rather the king. They speak to him sweetly no matter how disagreeable he is or how unreasonable his demands. This isn't good for him or for them. He needs to feel that his mother and father, however agreeable, still have their own rights, know how to be firm, won't let him be unreasonable or rude. He likes them better that way. It trains him from the beginning to get along reasonably with other people. The spoiled child is not a happy creature even in his own home. Then, when he gets out into the world, whether it's at 2 or 4 or 6, he is in for a rude shock. He finds that nobody is willing to kowtow to him; in fact, everybody dislikes him for his selfishness. Either he must go through life being unpopular, or learn the hard way how to be agreeable.

Conscientious parents often let a child take advantage of them for awhile—until their patience is exhausted—and then turn on him crossly. But neither of these stages is really necessary. If parents have a healthy self-respect, they can stand up for themselves while they are still feeling friendly. For instance, if your child is insisting that you continue to play a game after you are exhausted, don't be afraid to say cheerfully but definitely, "I'm all tired out. I'm going to read a book now and you can read *your* book, too."

If he is being very balky about getting out of the express wagon of another child who has to take it home now, though you have tried to interest him in something else, don't feel that you must go on being sweetly reasonable forever. Lift him out, even if he yells for a minute.

Punishment. Is punishment necessary? Most parents decide it is, at one time or another. But that doesn't prove that children themselves *need* a certain amount of punishment, the way they need milk and cod-liver oil, to grow up right.

What makes a child learn table manners? Not scolding—that would take a hundred years—but the fact that he wants to handle a fork and knife the way he sees others doing it. What makes him stop grabbing toys from other children as he grows older? Not the slaps that he might get from the other child or his parent. (I've seen boys and girls who were slapped regularly for years, and still grabbed.) The thing that changes him is learning to love his regular playmates and discovering the fun of playing *with* them. What makes him considerate and polite with his parents? Not the fear that they will punish him if he's rude, but the loving and respecting feeling he has for them. What keeps him from lying and stealing? Not the fear of the consequences. There are a few children, and adults, too, who go right on lying and stealing in spite of repeated and severe punishment. The thing that keeps us all from doing "bad" things to each other is the feelings we have of liking people and wanting them to like us.

In other words, if a child is handled in a friendly way, he wants to do the right thing, the grown-up thing, most of the time. When he occasionally goes wrong in his early years, he is best straightened out by such methods as distracting, guiding, or even removing him bodily. As he grows older, his parents at times have to explain firmly why he must do this, not do that. If they are sure in their own minds how they expect him to behave, and tell him reasonably, not too irritably, they will have all the control over him that they need. It's not that he'll *always* obey perfectly, but that's not necessary.

Then where does punishment fit in? People who have specialized in child care feel that it is seldom required. A first-rate nursery school teacher can guide eight small children through a day's session without punishing. A good camp councilor can do the same thing with a group of older boys, and most parents realize that when they themselves are most happy and reasonable they need to use punishment least.

But no parent (or non-parent, either) is always happy and reasonable. We all have our troubles, great or small, and we all take them out on our children to some degree. Come to think of it, it wouldn't be good training for a child to be brought up by perfect parents, because it would unsuit him for this world.

But even if we admit that we don't always do a good job of leading our children, and that we turn to punishment instead, that doesn't mean that punishment can be highly recommended. I don't think an agreeable parent should feel ashamed or a failure because he gets cross and uses punishment occasionally. But I disagree with the grim or irritable parent who seriously believes that punishment is a good regular method of controlling a child. The best I can do is explain why one punishment seems less desirable than another.

The best test of a punishment is whether it accomplishes what you are after, without having other serious effects. If it makes a child furious, defiant, and worse behaved than before, then it certainly is missing fire and doing more harm than good. If a punishment seems to break a child's heart or have a tendency to break his spirit, then it's probably too strong for him.

There are times when a child breaks a plate or rips his clothes through accident or carelessness. If he gets along well with his parents, he will feel just as unhappy as they do, and no punishment is needed. (In fact, you sometimes have to comfort him.) Jumping on a child who feels sorry already sometimes banishes his remorse, and makes him argue.

If you're dealing with an older child who is always fooling with the dishes and breaking them, it may be fair to make him buy replacements from his allowance. A child beyond the age of 6 is developing a sense of justice and sees the fairness of reasonable penalties. However, I'd go light on the legalistic, "take-the-consequences" kind of punishment before 6, and I wouldn't try to use it at all before the age of 3. You don't want a small child to develop a heavy sense of guilt. The job of a parent is to keep him from getting into trouble, rather than act as a severe judge after it's happened.

In the olden days children were spanked plenty, and nobody thought much about it. Then a reaction set in, and parents were taught that it was shameful. But that didn't settle everything. If an angry parent keeps himself from spanking, he may show his irritation in other ways, for instance, by nagging the child for half the day, or trying to make him feel deeply guilty. I'm not advocating spanking, but I think it is less poisonous than lengthy disapproval, because it clears the air, for parent and child. You sometimes hear it recommended that you never spank a child in anger but wait until you have cooled off. That seems unnatural. It takes a pretty grim parent to whip a child when the anger is gone.

I wouldn't advise putting a child in his room for punishment—that makes it seem like a prison. You want him to love his room for play or sleeping.

Avoid threats as much as possible. They tend to weaken discipline. It may sound reasonable to say, "If you don't keep out of the street with your bicycle, I'll take it away." But in a sense a threat is a dare—it admits that the child may disobey. It should impress him more to be firmly told he must keep out of the street, if he knows from experience that his mother means what she says. On the other hand, if you see that you may have to impose a drastic penalty like taking away a beloved bike for a few days, it's better to give fair warning. It certainly is silly, and quickly destroys all a parent's authority, to make threats that aren't ever carried out or that can't be carried out. Scary threats, such as bogiemen and cops, are 100 percent wrong in all cases.

If you seem to be needing to punish your child frequently, something is definitely wrong in his life or you are using the wrong methods. You need a wise outsider to help you—a children's psychiatrist, or, if that's not possible, perhaps a very understanding and successful teacher.

In general, remember that what makes your child behave well is not threats or punishment but loving you for your agreeableness and respecting you for knowing your rights and his. Stay in control as a friendly leader rather than battle with him at his level.

Further Resources

BOOKS

Colon, A. R., with P. A. Colon. *A History of Children: A Socio-Cultural Survey Across Millennia.* Westport, Conn.: Greenwood, 2001.

Grant, Julia. *Raising Baby by the Book: The Education of American Mothers.* New Haven, Conn.: Yale University Press, 1998.

Maier, Thomas. *Dr. Spock: An American Life.* New York: Harcourt Brace, 1998.

WEBSITES

The Dr. Spock Company: Expert Parenting and Children's Health Advice and Information. Available online at http://www.drspock.com (accessed August 22, 2002).

"Text of Truman Plea for Public Health Program"

Speech

By: Harry S. Truman
Date: May 19, 1947

Source: Truman, Harry S. "Text of Truman Plea for Public Health Program." Reprint of Truman's speech in *The New York Times,* May 19, 1945.
About the Author: President Harry S. Truman (1884–1972) was born in Missouri. After serving as a U.S. senator and later as vice president during Franklin D. Roosevelt's final term, Truman became president in April 1945, and served in that office until 1953. He had backed Roosevelt in his New Deal policies during the 1930s and proposed his own "Fair Deal" legislation in the 1940s and early 1950s. ∎

Introduction

The first crusade for some sort of national health insurance began around the beginning of the twentieth century. It was the product of the Progressive movement, a political reform effort whose backers sought to reduce, if not eliminate, social inequities caused by poverty and failures of justice.

The American reformers were following in the steps of their European counterparts, with one important exception. In other countries, the movements succeeded, at least to a degree. In 1883 Germany became the first nation to protect workers who could not work because of disease or injury. Other countries quickly followed suit. By 1911, according to Monte E. Poen, writing in *Harry S. Truman Versus the Medical Lobby,* "nearly every major European nation, including England, had legislated some kind of tax-supported health insurance program."

The Progressives made major efforts to educate the public and convince them of the practicality of such measures. Philanthropic foundations supported them by providing money for studies of the effectiveness of the European plans. At the same time, while plans for national health insurance became enmeshed in politics, the movement and others did succeed in getting some states to pass workers' compensation insurance for workers those injured on the job. By the time Woodrow Wilson (1913–1921) was elected president, ten states had passed such laws and, in cases where there were legal challenges, the courts were ruling that the laws were constitutional.

Success, however, did not come. Notes Poen, "In great measure, then, the history of the American social-insurance movement for health protection, both in the formative period and later . . . must be viewed as an evolving struggle between the conflicting branches of government and the competing lobbies, the former constructed to forestall action and the latter to promote or defeat the program."

In 1943 three congressmen introduced a bill that, among other social programs, included national medical care. The Wagner-Murry-Dingell bill never got off the ground. President Roosevelt (1933–1945) supported the idea of health care as a national right, but he never got beyond the social protection measures that had been part of the New Deal.

When Truman took office in 1945, following the death of President Roosevelt, he did so as a supporter of national health insurance. On November 19, 1945, Truman became the first president to propose such a plan to Congress. The plan had five components: hospital construction, public health, medical education and research, payments to the disabled, and compulsory pre-paid medical care. The same day that Truman presented his plan, Congressmen Wagner, Murry, and Dingell introduced a bill translating its provisions into legislation.

Significance

Truman's proposal, even before it was tested in the political cauldron, was significant for its very existence. It set in motion a debate in the United States that continues today. Truman did not succeed in convincing Congress to pass the national health insurance act. In having the political courage to try, however, he ensured the survival of the issue.

The story of Truman's defeat is the story of the power of special interests, in this case the American Medical Association (AMA). The president had the backing of some powerful leaders. Shortly after Truman delivered his speech, the *The New York Times* reported, a group of 191 leaders from all fields and professions issued a strong endorsement of the plan. New York City Mayor Fiorello La Guardia and other politicians were joined by judges, academics, medical professionals, and others. They described the plan as "a thoroughly American plan, consistent with our tradition of using Government to aid the people in doing things themselves."

Truman's nemesis was the AMA, whose money and influence were very substantial. A few months after Truman's message to Congress, the AMA issued a statement that denounced the plan as a "scourge." To physicians, the medical group argued that the bill would spell the end of professional freedom and independence. To the general population, the AMA claimed that the health-care plan would ruin the quality of medical care in the United States. According to the group, "The inevitable deterioration in the quality of care which would result from Government-herding of patients and doctors in assembly-line medical care would lower the standards of healthy America to those of sick, regimented Europe." The argument relied on emotion rather than facts; America was by no means "healthy," and large numbers of Americans lacked access to good medical care or the means to pay for it.

Truman did not retreat, but included his plan in his 1949 inaugural address. His plan lost. In 1951, however, Truman began to campaign for coverage for a highly vulnerable segment of the population, the elderly. He did not get the legislation through Congress, but fourteen

President Harry S. Truman speaks at a press conference, 1945. Truman was the first president to propose a national health care plan to Congress, though his plan was met with strong opposition by the American Medical Association. **AP/WIDE WORLD PHOTOS. REPRODUCED BY PERMISSION.**

years later, President Lyndon B. Johnson (1963–1969) achieved what Truman had started. He traveled to Independence, Missouri, where Truman lived in retirement, to sign the bill. It had, Johnson said, "all started with the man from Independence."

Primary Source

"Text of Truman Plea for Public Health Program"

SYNOPSIS: Harry Truman was a supporter of national health insurance. On November 19, 1945, he became the first president to propose such a plan to Congress. The plan had five components: hospital construction, public health, medical education and research, payments to the disabled, and compulsory pre-paid medical care.

To the Congress of the United States:

Healthy citizens constitute our greatest national resource. In time of peace, as in time of war, our ultimate strength stems from the vigor of our people. The welfare and security of our nation demand that the opportunity for good health be made available to all, regardless of residence, race or economic status.

At no time can we afford to lose the productive energies and capacities of millions of our citizens. Nor can we permit our children to grow up without a fair chance of survival and a fair chance for a healthy life. We must not permit our rural families to suffer for lack of physicians, dentists, nurses and hospitals. We must not reserve a chance for good health and a long productive life to the well-to-do alone. A great and free nation should bring good health care within the reach of all its people.

In my message to the Congress on Nov. 19, 1945, I said that every American should have the right to adequate medical care and to adequate protection from the economic threat of sickness. To provide this care and protection is a challenging task, requiring action on a wide front.

Long-Range Program

I have previously outlined the long-range health program which I consider necessary to the national welfare and security. I say again that such a program must include:

1. Adequate public health services, including an expanded maternal and child health program.

2. Additional medical research and medical education.

3. More hospitals and more doctors—in all areas of the country where they are needed.

4. Insurance against the costs of medical care.

5. Protection against loss of earnings during illness.

I am pleased to observe that important advances were made by the last Congress toward realization of some of the goals which I set forth in my earlier message. But we must not rest until we have achieved all our objectives. I urge this Congress to enact additional legislation to authorize the program I have outlined, even though the fulfillment of some aspects of it may take time.

Our public health services—Federal, State and local—provide our greatest and most successful defense against preventable diseases. But in many States, cities and counties in America, limited funds reduce the work of our public health services to a dangerously inadequate level. Public services related to maternal and child health were expanded by the Seventy-ninth Congress, through amendments to the Social Security Act. This action was gratifying, but the long-range need for additional health services for children and expectant mothers, and for care of crippled or otherwise physically handicapped children, should be carefully studied by the Congress.

Wants Research Expanded

The nation's medical research programs must in the future be expanded so that we can learn more about the prevention and cure of disease. The Congress has already recognized this by providing for research into the causes of cancer and mental diseases and abnormalities. Further dividends will accrue to our nation—and to our people—if research can point the way toward combatting and overcoming such major illnesses as arthritis and rheumatic fever and diseases of the heart, kidney and arteries.

We still face a shortage of hospitals, physicians, dentists and nurses. Those we have are unfairly distributed. The shortage of doctors, dentists and nurses can be met only through expanded educational opportunities. The shortage of hospitals will be met in part through the action of the last Congress, which provided Federal aid for the construction of hospitals.

In the last analysis the patient's ability to pay for the services of physicians or dentists for hospital care determines the distribution of doctors and the location of hospitals. Few doctors can be expected to practice today in sparsely settled areas or where prospective patients are unable to pay for their services. Doctors tend to concentrate in communities where hospitals and other facilities are best and where their incomes are most secure. The unequal distribution of doctors and hospitals will plague this nation until means are found to finance modern medical care for all of our people.

Need for Health Insurance

National health insurance is the most effective single way to meet the nation's health needs. Because adequate treatment of many illnesses is expensive and its cost cannot be anticipated by the individual, many persons are forced to go without needed medical attention. Children do not receive adequate medical and dental care. Symptoms which should come early to the attention of a physician are often ignored until too late. The poor are not the only ones who cannot afford adequate medical care. The truth is that all except the rich may at some time be struck by illness which requires care and services they cannot afford. Countless families who are entirely self-supporting in every other respect cannot meet the expense of serious illness.

Although the individual or even small groups of individuals cannot successfully or economically plan to meet the cost of illness, large groups of people can do so. If the financial risk of illness is spread among all our people, no one person is overburdened. More important, if the cost is spread in this manner more persons can see their doctors, and will see them earlier. This goal can be reached only through a medical insurance program, under which all people who are covered by an insurance fund are entitled to necessary medical, hospital and related services.

A national health insurance program is a logical extension of the present social-security system which is so firmly entrenched in our American democracy.

Of the four basic risks to the security of working people and their families—unemployment, old age, death and sickness—we have provided some insurance protection against three. Protection against the fourth—sickness—is the major missing element in our national social insurance program.

An insurance plan is the American way of accomplishing our objective. It is consistent with our democratic principles. It is the only plan broad enough to meet the needs of all our people. It is—in the long run—far less costly and far more effective than public charity or a medical dole.

Patients Would Choose Doctors

Under the program which I have proposed patients can and will be as free to select their own doctors as they are today. Doctors and hospitals can and will be free to participate or to reject participation. And a national health insurance plan can and should provide for administration through state and local agencies, subject only to reasonable national standards.

Finally, I should like to repeat to the Congress my earlier recommendation that the people of America be protected against loss of earnings due to illness or disability not connected with their work. Protection against temporary disability is already provided by two states and is being considered in others. Comprehensive disability insurance should exist throughout the nation. It can and should be a part of our social insurance system.

The total health program which I have proposed is crucial to our national welfare. The heart of that program is national health insurance. Until it is a part of our national fabric we shall be wasting our most precious national resource and shall be perpetuating unnecessary misery and human suffering.

I urge the Congress to give immediate attention to the development and enactment of national health and disability insurance programs.

Further Resources

BOOKS

Maioni, Antonia. *Parting at the Crossroads: The Emergence of Health Insurance in the United States and Canada.* Princeton, N.J.: Princeton University Press, 1998.

Poen, Monte M. *Harry S. Truman Versus the Medical Lobby: The Genesis of Medicare.* Columbia, Mo: University of Missouri Press, 1979.

PERIODICALS

"191 Leaders Back Health Program." *The New York Times,* November 24, 1945.

"AMA Assails Health Plan of Truman as a 'Scourge.'" *The New York Times,* April 24, 1946.

"Drug Aiding Fight on Tuberculosis"

Newspaper article

By: *The New York Times*

Date: December 4, 1947

Source: "Drug Aiding Fight on Tuberculosis." *The New York Times,* December 4, 1947.

About the Scientists: This article reported on the research of Selman A. Waksman (1888–1973) and Hubert A. Lechevalier. They worked at Rutgers University in New Jersey and were among the foremost bacteriologists of the era. Five years earlier they had announced the development of streptomycin, the first pharmaceutical agent that effectively treated tuberculosis. ∎

Introduction

The first drug used to treat tuberculosis was streptomycin, a relative of penicillin that was derived from antibiotic substances found in the soil. The drug, introduced in 1945, was effective for a while but, as has been happening continuously since the development of antibiotics, the bacteria began to develop strains that resisted the effects of the drugs, rendering them powerless. At the same time, it produced toxic effects to the nervous system. Other drugs were added to the treatment regime, but they, too, were followed by the development of resistant bacteria.

Meanwhile, the number of cases of tuberculosis continued to grow. In 1949 the National Tuberculosis Association estimated that the disease cost the nation more than $350,000,000. The money went to both care and prevention attempts. In New York City, for example, officials reported that the number of patients admitted for treatment rose 20 percent between 1945 and 1947 and rose another 18 percent between 1947 and 1949. The city's 20 tuberculosis hospitals were operating at 101 percent capacity in 1948.

During this time physicians were also treating tuberculosis with surgery, by removing diseased portions of the lungs. This was effective in some cases but, as with attempts to remove any diseased part of the body by surgery, doctors could never be sure that they'd taken out all the affected parts.

Efforts to develop a vaccine had long been underway in Europe. Albert Calmette, a French researcher, began working with a weakened strain of the bacillus in the second decade of the twentieth century. The outbreak of World War I (1914–1918) halted their testing efforts, but not have helped. In 1949 another group found "striking similarity in personality patterns" of schizophrenia patients and tuberculosis patients, based on their response to a psychological test. Further investigation by other researchers failed to find this link.

Significance

The discovery of neomycin was significant for several reasons. One was the method that researchers used to find it. Beginning in 1939, Waksman and Lechevalier reported, they had tested thousands of microorganisms for antibiotic action, most of them harvested from different soils, composts, and the like. Casting such a wide net, they found that many of these microorganisms did have antibiotic action, but were not suitable candidates for transformation into a drug. They narrowed their search and next focused on microorganisms that were active against streptomycin-resistant TB. One such agent, neomycin, showed promise for use in humans. Although more and more drug research is focusing on *designing* drugs, researchers still use the approach that led to neomycin. They test hundreds of chemical compounds in the hope of finding one that will be effective against a given condition.

Neomycin's major significance, however, was that it showed that more than one agent was effective against tuberculosis. It was quickly followed by other drugs, the most significant being a compound known as PAS. Developed by Jorgen Lehmann, a Danish researcher, PAS did not directly kill the bacilli. Rather, it stopped the production of two acids that he had discovered stimulated their growth.

Primary Source

"Drug Aiding Fight on Tuberculosis"

SYNOPSIS: This newspaper article describes the work that the microbiologists Waksman and Lechevalier published in the leading scientific journal *Science*.

Streptomycin Is Hailed as Ally by Dr. Hinshaw at Meeting of Chemical Engineers

Streptomycin can challenge penicillin as the No. 1 antibiotic because the former has proved beneficial in treatment of tuberculosis and other devastating human diseases that previously had not been touched by any direct drug action, Dr. H. Corwin Hinshaw of the Mayo Clinic, Rochester, Minn., told 1,000 chemical engineers last night in the Waldorf-Astoria Hotel. The common diseases now treated with penicillin already had been conquered essentially by the preceding sulfa drugs, he said.

Works Progress Administration poster from Cook County Public Health Unit, 1940. In the late 1940s, tuberculosis was an increasing epidemic in the United States. The discovery of neomycin was the first in a line of improvements in the disease's treatment. THE LIBRARY OF CONGRESS.

they continued after the war. The vaccine, called BCG for the initials of the researchers involved, was tested on 249 babies in Germany in 1930, with tragic results; the vials of the vaccine were intermingled with vials of live TB sent for research purposes, and at least 90 of the babies died. Scandinavian researchers continued to work on the vaccine, however, and produced a safe vaccine that did not give absolute immunity but boosted natural immunity significantly. The vaccine was widely used in Europe after World War II (1939–1945). It was never widely used in the United States.

Meanwhile research into TB continued. One group of researchers concluded that the disease was triggered by an allergic reaction to the bacilli and reported success in treating it with a combination of antihistamines and streptomycin. Because streptomycin alone was generally effective, the addition of the antihistamine may or may

While tuberculosis has been declining steadily in the United States it is still the most infectious disease of mankind, according to Dr. Hinshaw. In Europe and the Orient, he said, tuberculosis is many times more frequent than in this country, with the situation getting steadily worse.

Dr. Hinshaw spoke at a dinner marking the presentation of the Chemical Achievement Award to Merck & Co., Inc., Rahway, N. J., largest manufacturers of streptomycin. The biennial award is sponsored by Chemical Engineering, a McGraw-Hill publication.

Streptomycin has "very great value in some of the most fulminating types of lung tuberculosis." Dr. Hinshaw said, and is specially helpful in combination with some of the more radical forms of surgical treatment. Because of its production now by the ton instead of by the gram as two years ago, streptomycin is sometimes the most economical treatment for tuberculosis, according to the speaker.

Streptomycin has been helpful also in the treatment of certain wounds and intractable infections of the urinary tract, Dr. Hinshaw said. He added that it was a remarkable specific for the hitherto unconquered disease of tularemia, or rabbit fever, and was of value in treating plague.

The speaker said other forms of tuberculosis that yielded to streptomycin were miliary tuberculosis, which spreads through the blood stream; tuberculosis meningitis, attacking the spine and brain, which has been 100 per cent fatal; tuberculosis of the larynx and vocal cords, which produces ulcers of the windpipe and larger bronchial tubes, and types of tuberculosis of the intestines.

Dr. Vannevar Bush, chairman of the Research and Development Board of the Department of Defense, declared that to face the future without fear we must vote attention to science and technology, military strength and the industrial health of the country.

Dr. Alfred H. White, Professor Emeritus of Chemical Engineering, University of Michigan, presented the award to George W. Merck president of Merck & Co. Dr. White said chemical engineers, although working now for competing firms, still were willing to pool their resources in cases of urgent need, as in wartime.

Further Resources

BOOKS

Horvitz, Leslie Alan. *Eureka! Scientific Breakthroughs that Changed the World.* New York: John Wiley & Sons, 2002.

Rothman, Sheila M. *Living in the Shadow of Death: Tuberculosis and the Social Experience of Illness in American History.* New York: Basic Books, 1994.

Wainright, Milton. *Miracle Cure: The Story of Penicillin and the Golden Age of Antibiotics.* Cambridge, Mass.: Basil Blackwell, 1990.

State Mental Hospitals

The Shame of the States

Nonfiction work

By: Albert Deutsch

Date: 1948

Source: Deutsch, Albert. *The Shame of the States.* New York: Harcourt Brace, 1948.

About the Author: Albert Deutsch (1905–1961) was a well-known investigative journalist in the 1930s and author of multiple books.

The Snake Pit

Novel

By: Mary Jane Ward

Date: 1948

Source: Ward, Mary Jane. *The Snake Pit.* New York: Random House, 1946.

About the Author: Mary Jane Ward (1905–1981) was a novelist who suffered a mental breakdown and wrote an autobiographical novel of her experience in a state hospital. ■

Introduction

Several schools of psychology and psychiatry gained prominence in the 1930s and 1940s. One was the mental hygiene movement, pioneered by Clifford Beers and championed by many physicians and other health-care workers. A second was talk therapy, or psychoanalysis, pioneered by the Austrian physician Sigmund Freud in the early twentieth century. A third consisted of the so-called "somatic" therapies, which held that physical treatment could cure mental disorders. Insulin and convulsive shock therapies were examples of these, as was the highly controversial prefrontal lobotomy.

Although proponents of any of the three schools might claim otherwise, none really helped people with chronic major psychiatric disorders such as schizophrenia. Overwhelmed families often could not look after a seriously disturbed member, who was often sent to a state-owned and -operated mental hospital or asylum. Depending on the hospital, the person might be cared for well and receive some therapy or might receive only custodial care (a practice that came to be known as warehousing).

At the time state mental hospitals did not house only those with clear-cut psychiatric disorders. The poor, alcoholics, epileptics, and the mentally handicapped no longer had poorhouses to live in after 1890 legislation unintentionally led to their demise. Thus, although the state hospitals had many flaws, they also bore an enormous burden in caring for a diverse population, most of whom were likely to be there for life.

As an investigator of mental hospitals, Deutsch was preceded by John Maurice Grimes, a physician who undertook his survey of 600 mental hospitals against the wishes of the powerful American Medical Association (AMA). His report was taken over by the AMA, which was in turn heavily influenced by the American Psychiatric Association (APA). He published the report himself, noting that only about 20 percent of beds in mental hospitals were filled by psychiatric patients and that the patients were either confined to save work for the staff or made to work for the hospital themselves. Grimes proposed deinstitutionalization, recommending that patients who did not need assistance at the level of hospital care be discharged and cared for in the community. This course would become a reality in the 1960s.

World War II (1939–1945) also heightened awareness of the squalid conditions of many state hospitals. Conscientious objectors, people who refused to serve military duty on religious or moral grounds, assigned to work in state hospitals as alternative service, were horrified by conditions and formed the National Mental Health Foundation. Conscientious objectors' efforts and internal strife within the APA led to government action. In 1946, Congress enacted legislation that created the National Institute of Mental Health, one of the National Institutes of Health, to coordinate policy and research on mental health.

Significance

Grimes and the men who formed the National Mental Health Foundation successfully awoke the interest of government officials. Albert Deutsch and Mary Jane Ward, however, made the world inhabited by state hospital residents real to the average person through their writing. In *The Shame of the States,* Deutsch recommended building clean, well-run, therapeutic state institutions. His book did not inspire policy makers to work toward that aim. The ultimate effect of the exposes of the state hospitals was the dissolution of most of them. They were replaced by deinstitutionalization in the 1960s. Like Deutsch's book, *The Snake Pit* brought home the plight of ordinary people who found themselves in mental hospitals. The issue gained even greater prominence when the book was made into a film starring Olivia de Haviland.

Primary Source

The Shame of the States [excerpt]

SYNOPSIS: Albert Deutsch made the world inhabited by state hospital residents real to the average person. The ultimate effect of this expose was the dissolution of most of state institutions.

New York's Isle of Despair

Nonetheless, as you walk through the wards of the institution exposed by Nellie Bly—taken over by the State of New York a half-century ago and now known as Manhattan State Hospital—you see many cases that don't properly belong there. More than half of the 4,000 patients on Ward's Island are "seniles"—elderly folk whose mental processes have deteriorated because of arteriosclerosis (hardening of the arteries) or other conditions due to old age. Many of these have developed the harmless eccentricities often seen in old people—querulousness, memory gaps, childish traits, etc. Their families, finding them troublesome burdens, dump them in state hospitals in lieu of sending them to the poorhouse. They are shipped to mental hospitals mainly because there is a terrible lack of decent homes for the aged at rates the average family can afford to pay. Then, too, it is far more difficult to keep a feeble old father or mother in a cramped city apartment than on a farm where there's plenty of room.

"We've got to take them," Dr. Frederick Mac-Curdy, State Mental Hygiene Commissioner, told me. "But it would seem that more suitable institutional provision should be made for this group—perhaps in hospitals for the chronically ill." The piling up of these "crotchety" old people in our mental institutions, people who can't be helped by psychiatric treatment, is one of the gravest problems of our state hospital system. They tie up psychiatric personnel and facilities that are desperately needed to treat actively the acute and hopeful cases of mental disorder.

They jam the wards of the Manhattan State Hospital, where they are sent in large numbers because of the institution's proximity to the center of the metropolis. About 60 per cent of Manhattan's patients are over sixty years of age; some are past ninety. That's why Manhattan State has such a terrific mortality rate; about one out of six patients dies in the course of a year.

The institution itself is aged and decaying. Some of its buildings date back to the Civil War period. In 1923 its tinder-box buildings were swept by a horrible fire in which 21 patients and employees lost their lives. As a result of this holocaust, the state floated a $50,000,000 bond issue to finance a statewide hospital construction and fireproofing program.

But by 1933 the institution had become so hopelessly unfit that it was officially condemned. Its total abandonment no later than 1943 was ordered by legislative enactment. The pressure of chronic overcrowding on other state hospitals, added to the war crisis, caused a postponement in the abandonment plan till 1948. Now the state plans gradually to rebuild the hospital instead of giving it up entirely. A 3,000–bed institution is proposed, to occupy fifty acres on Ward's Island in place of the one hundred and fifty acres now covered. The rest of the Island will be turned back to New York City to be used as a park and recreational center.

The present institution is in an appalling state of deterioration and disrepair as a result of the years of neglect in expectation of abandonment. It is grossly over-crowded and undermanned, like most state hospitals. Some of its wards are crowded double beyond capacity.

A survey of Manhattan State Hospital was made in 1942 by Dr. Samuel W. Hamilton, leading mental hospital expert and past president of the American Psychiatric Association, with the assistance of Miss Mary E. Corcoran, R.N. They noted, in their confidential report to the mental hygiene authorities, a deterioration of staff morale at the hospital in addition to physical deterioration.

"An unhappy frame of mind has prevailed in the organization during the last several years," they reported, "while disintegration of the hospital had been agreed on and appeared inevitable. Conservatism, always a strong force in an old institution, was strengthened so that it has been sometimes difficult to persuade the whole organization of the need or even the propriety of steps in advance. What has 'always been done' seemed the only right standard. It is not easy to restore an active aggressive spirit to an organization that for several years has been permeated with a genteel gloom."

This low level of staff morale was evident in several Manhattan State Hospital doctors I talked to. The hospital has some fine psychiatrists on its staff—men who were attracted to it because of its convenient location. It has had a long tradition of active medical treatment, going back to the time when Dr. Adolf Meyer, the great American psychiatrist, made his headquarters there.

Manhattan State is still an active treatment center, in comparison with other state hospitals. Its tradition is maintained largely by the frequent contacts with men from the various medical schools and hospital centers of New York who use it as a research and teaching institution. But staff doctors can't practice good psychiatry when they have to handle hundreds of patients a piece. One had a load of more than 800 patients, spread over three different buildings, including many on suicidal and homicidal wards.

The average doctor at Manhattan State Hospital, I was told, spends about half his time in paper work—checking patients in and out, making up requisition orders in triplicate and quadruplicate, counting clothes, bed sheets, towels, writing up case reports, accident reports, death certificates, etc. On Sundays only one physician was left in charge of a total of 2,500 patients spread over 32 wards. Besides the impossible task of making rounds on all these wards, the Sunday physician had to see visitors and attend to necessary paper work.

"It means that the doctor is exhausted, the patient is neglected, and the family is discouraged," one physician observed.

Each Manhattan State Hospital doctor had to work a 32-hour uninterrupted, sleepless stretch every fifth day as officer of the day. He went on duty at 8:30 A.M. and worked continuously until 4:30 P.M. the next day. He received no additional compensation for this extra duty.

The official state regulations require that each hospital patient has to be interviewed at least twice a year. Yet Manhattan State doctors told me of many cases that had not been interviewed for as long as five years.

It was generally conceded that Dr. John W. Travis—short, chubby, bald-domed superintendent of Manhattan State—was an efficient business executive, but several doctors complained that he did little to stimulate scientific interest in his subordinates. Yet the institution's shock therapy units—both electric shock and insulin shock—compared favorably with those of other institutions I've seen.

Manhattan State Hospital receives mainly two types of mental patients—the very feeble and the very disturbed—both of whom can be transported long distances only with great difficulty or danger.

Both the physically feeble and the mentally disturbed patients are in need of special attention, which makes the problem of undermanning more serious at Manhattan than at other institutions. Nearly one fourth the regular ward jobs were unfilled at the time of my official visit, and 106 of the 432 ward attendants and nurses on the payroll were away on passes, vacations, or sick leave. I was much impressed, however, by the good caliber of a number of hard-working, sympathetic ward nurses and attendants.

Shortage of trained personnel was one reason for the relatively high accident rate among patients of Manhattan State. An official monthly report listed at least 12 serious accidents among patients during April, 1946, four of which terminated in death. Here are some samples:

Fracture neck of right femur. Caused by fall—pushed by another patient. Resulted in death.

Fracture of nose. Caused by altercation with another patient.

Fracture of left hip. Accidental fall here. Patient died.

Fracture right hip. Accidental fall here.

At Manhattan, as at most state mental hospitals, there is a form of labor exploitation that needs long-overdue correction. A considerable number of able-bodied patients are put at institutional labor on a full eight-hours-a-day basis—in the coal yards, laundry, repair shops, etc. But they get no pay for their full-time work. They get only extra rations of tobacco. Time was, at Manhattan, when patient-workers were paid ten dollars a month as recompense. This payment, niggardly enough, was canceled some years ago. It is a good policy to give patient-workers some monetary returns for their labor. It gives them a sense of independence, of being able to earn something. It helps build up self-confidence so strikingly lacking in many mental patients. It's a pity that the old policy was scrapped.

I have seen patients even more miserably exploited in other state hospitals. I've seen them, in some places, reduced to slaves and serfs, worked for 12 and 14 hours a day, seven days a week, with no return but candy and tobacco handouts. Sometimes this exploitation operates under the guise of "industrial therapy," when the real motive is not to speed the patient's recovery but to squeeze all possible labor out of him.

Shortly before the day of my official, announced visit to Manhattan State Hospital, I made a preliminary, unannounced inspection of some of the wards. I found several in indescribable stages of filth and general neglect, especially on the women's side.

But when I was officially shown around by Superintendent Travis, these same wards were meticulously scrubbed and tidied up. Wards teeming with untended patients had almost miraculously been emptied, and one which had on my earlier visit presented a bedlamic scene was now transformed into one of patient-less quiet and order.

It was quite evident that Dr. Travis possessed a noble consideration for the sensitivity of visitors to his institution and was bent on avoiding as much unpleasantness as possible. As one institutional employee later told me: "Gee, you must be something special. We sure did some tall cleaning up for you."

It must be said, in fairness, that Dr. Travis and his staff are doing everything possible to keep the decaying, doomed institution as clean as circumstances permit. It's mighty hard, with plaster falling constantly in some wards, paint peeling off the walls in huge blobs, and floors rotting steadily. The location of the hospital in the middle of the East River makes the job of warding off river rats a most difficult one.

An old-timer told me: "We're actually better off than we were a while ago in the way of keeping down rats and vermin, in spite of present appearances. You should have been here a few years ago, when one poor family came to claim a dead relative in the morgue. When the light was turned on, there was a big rat right on the chest of the corpse."

Primary Source

The Snake Pit [excerpt]

SYNOPSIS: Mary Jane Ward suffered a mental breakdown and wrote of her experience in a state hospital.

The smell of Ward Three, after you had been out in the open, was overpowering. When they stepped into the dayroom Virginia identified the smell. Paraldehyde. One romantic book she read while doing research into mental ailments stated that the stench of paraldehyde has vanished from our mental institutions. I remember I wondered what paraldehyde was and I looked it up and it said hypnotic, a hypnotic.

So it is paraldehyde and not formaldehyde. Grace knew a lot, but she did not know that. I have worked it out for myself from the sound and from the stench and also from the memory. I am therefore not so sick as Grace was when she left us. I am therefore ready to be transferred, more than that, I am ready to go home. What is the matter with that doctor who is one of the best? Months since I saw the man.

"Miss Hart," she said, after she had given her store order, that is, after she had said yes, she would like some more cigarettes, "when am I going to see my doctor again?"

"Wouldn't you like to order some candy too? You have a five-dollar credit at the store," said the nurse. "Have you heard the news? There's going to be a movie tomorrow night and you're on the list."

"I never will be missed."

"What?"

"Oh, I was just thinking about that Gilbert and Sullivan thing about having him on the list and so on."

"Say, I'd forgotten that show," said Miss Hart.

"Hitchy-Koo. My goodness, I was just a child then, of course."

"Of course," said Virginia. "You think it won't be long before I get to see my doctor again?"

"Aren't you feeling well? It's probably just from Petey."

"There are some things I want to ask him."

"Can't they wait until next week? You saw him just the day before yesterday, you know."

Another patient pushed up to Miss Hart to give a store order. Virginia went off to a corner and sat down. She tried to think, but the gray chiffon wound closer.

Further Resources

BOOKS

Grob, Gerald N. *Mental Illness and American Society, 1875–1940*. Princeton, N.J.: Princeton University Press, 1983.

Johnson, Ann Braden. *Out of Bedlam: The Truth about Deinstitutionalization*. New York: Basic Books, 1990.

Whitaker, Robert. *Mad in America: Bad Science, Bad Medicine, and the Enduring Mistreatment of the Mentally Ill*. New York: Perseus, 2002.

WEBSITES

"The Snake Pit." *Raintree County*. Available online at http://www.raintreecounty.com/SnakePit.html (accessed August 22, 2002).

AUDIO AND VISUAL MEDIA

The Snake Pit. 1948/1982. Directed by Anatole Litvak. 108 min. 20th Century Fox/Fox Studio Classic Series, 1982. VHS.

Sexual Behavior in the Human Male

Study

By: Alfred C. Kinsey

Date: 1948

Source: Kinsey, Alfred C., Wardell B. Pomeroy, and Clyde E. Martin. *Sexual Behavior in the Human Male*. Philadelphia: W. B. Saunders Company, 1948.

About the Author: Alfred C. Kinsey (1894–1956) was born in Hoboken, New Jersey. The son of an engineering instructor and a homemaker, he worked his way through college and then was employed as an instructor in biology and zoology at Harvard University while working for his doctorate degree. After becoming one of the world's experts on the gall wasp, Kinsey abruptly changed directions and began studying humans. His first study, the controversial and pioneering *Sexual Behavior in the Human Male,* was published in 1948. ∎

Introduction

Sexual drive is a basic human instinct, like eating and sleeping. In the mid-twentieth century, however, few people talked about sex openly, and scholarly books on the subject relied largely on generalizations, not on interviews with people. The most prominent sex researcher before Kinsey was Havelock Ellis, a physician. Ellis's massive two-volume work, *Studies in the Psychology of Sex,* was first published in Germany in 1897. When Ellis had it published in English, however, the result was a tangled and unsuccessful legal case in England. That being resolved, Ellis went next to the United States, where the first part of the book was published in 1901. The publisher marketed the book to medical professionals, not the general public, which probably saved it from further controversy and legal action. The book sold so well that it was still being published in 1942, six years after Ellis's death.

When American physicians wrote about sex, they generally did so to warn the public about its dangers. Masturbation would cause mental disorder. Sexual intercourse was the province of married couples for the purpose of procreation. Other sexual activity was "perversion." One exception was the work of Katharine Bement Davis, who surveyed graduates of the top women's colleges of the time in 1910. Davis's work won the support of John D. Rockefeller, who then involved the federally funded National Research Council. The result was that research into sexual practices became the province of universities, and the council wanted to sponsor further investigation.

What the Research Council sought, however, was a scientist of perfect credentials to carry out these studies. Alfred C. Kinsey, a zoologist, was the right person. With his Harvard degree and his many publications, he was someone who could apply the scientific method to the study of sex. At the University of Indiana, where he taught biology, Kinsey was involved in forming new courses on marriage and the family. At the same time, he was a taxonomist, a scientist whose specialty was the classification of species.

Significance

Kinsey and his team broke new ground in several areas. The group of about 6,000 men that he and his team interviewed was not a random sample (the kind of sample you might get by choosing every tenth name in the telephone book). Nevertheless, that the people were interviewed at all was a change that definitively separated Kinsey from those who came before. He believed that people generally tend to lie about their sex lives and that personal interviews with well-trained interviewers might better elicit the truth. Kinsey's interviewers were taught how to make their subjects feel more comfortable about answering highly personal questions.

Kinsey also pioneered research among "normal" males on forms of behavior that were definitely considered abnormal. Kinsey's findings were as surprising as his methods were innovative. His material on homosexuality was particularly startling. Unlike the medical establishment at the time, he did not view it as an illness. He also acknowledged that someone could have a homosexual experience, but not be exclusively homosexual. The number of men who had homosexual experiences, though, surprised even the researchers. Equally surprising were Kinsey's statistics on sexual activity with farm animals.

Although the book was written in a dry, scholarly style, the findings it contained struck a chord in a reading public eager for information. In 1949, Kinsey's book was high on *The New York Times* best-seller list and had 185,000 copies in print, despite a price of $6.50. By 1952, a summary of "Published Reactions to the Kinsey Report" in the journal *Social Forces* reported that Kinsey's work had generated 58 magazine articles, 19 newspaper articles, four books, and four conferences to discuss the findings.

Some conservatives and religious denominations used phrases such as "an insult to the American people" and "an assault on the family" to describe the report. Most Americans, though, believed that Kinsey's data contained information that should come out. A Gallup poll found that five out of six Americans thought that the Kinsey report was a "good thing." One of the most common reactions was that the report suggested the need to liberalize laws and examine attitudes toward sex. Those who favored changes in the law cited Kinsey's finding that 97

Alfred Charles Kinsey. Kinsey's "Sexual Behavior in the Human Male" was a pioneering study in human sexual behavior—a subject never before studied academically or scientifically. © HULTON GETTY/LIASON AGENCY. REPRODUCED BY PERMISSION.

percent of those surveyed had participated in some sexual practice that was illegal. The door that Kinsey opened never closed. The Kinsey Institute in Indiana is one of many academic institutions that study human biology and behavior as they relate to sex.

Primary Source

Sexual Behavior in the Human Male [excerpt]

SYNOPSIS: In the following excerpts from the introduction and several chapters of the report, Kinsey outlines his general beliefs about the study of sex and presents some of his more surprising findings.

Historical Introduction

For some time now there has been an increasing awareness among many people of the desirability of obtaining data about sex which would represent an accumulation of scientific fact completely divorced from questions of moral value and social custom. Practicing physicians find thousands of their patients in need of such objective data. Psychiatrists and analysts find that a majority of their patients need help in resolving sexual conflicts that have arisen in their

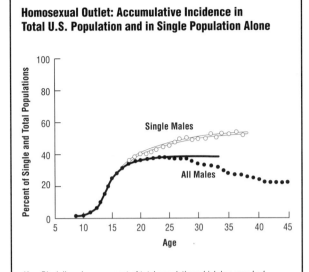

Homosexual Outlet: Accumulative Incidence in Total U.S. Population and in Single Population Alone

Key: Black line shows percent of total population which has ever had homosexual experience by each of the indicated ages. Hollow line shows percent of the population of single males which has ever had experience. All data corrected for U.S. Census distribution.

SOURCE: Alfred Kinsey, W. Pomeroy, and Clyde Martin. *Social Behavior in the Human Male*. Philadelphia: W.B. Saunders Co., 1948, p. 625.

lives. An increasing number of persons would like to bring an educated intelligence into the consideration of such matters as sexual adjustments in marriage, the sexual guidance of children, the pre-marital sexual adjustments of youth, sex education, sexual activities which are in conflict with the mores, and problems confronting persons who are interested in the social control of behavior through religion, custom, and the forces of the law. Before it is possible to think scientifically on any of these matters, more needs to be known about the actual behavior of people, and about the inter-relationships of that behavior with the biologic and social aspects of their histories.

Hitherto, there have not been sufficient answers to these questions, for human sexual behavior represents one of the least explored segments of biology, psychology, and sociology. Scientifically more has been known about the sexual behavior of some of the farm and laboratory animals. In our Western European-American culture, sexual responses, more than any other physiologic activities, have been subject to religious evaluation, taboo, and formal legislation. It is obvious that the failure to learn about human sexual activity is the outcome of the influence which the custom and the law have had upon scientists as individuals, and of t he not unmaterial restrictions which have been imposed upon scientific investigations in this field.

The statistics given throughout this volume on the incidence of homosexual activity, and the statistics to be given in the present section of this chapter, are based on those persons who have had physical contacts with other males, and who were brought to orgasm as a result of such contacts. By any strict definition such contacts are homosexual, irrespective of the extent of the psychic stimulation involved, of the techniques employed, or of the relative importance of the homosexual and the heterosexual in the history of such an individual. These are not data on the number of persons who are "homosexual," but on the number of persons who have had at least some homosexual experience—even though sometimes not more than one experience—up to the ages shown in the tables and curves. The incidences of persons who have had various amounts of homosexual experience are presented in a later section of this chapter. An individual who engages in a sexual relation with another male without, however, coming to climax, or an individual who is erotically aroused by a homosexual stimulus without ever having overt relations, has certainly had a homosexual experience. Such relations and reactions are, however, not included in the incidence data given here nor in most other places in this volume, because the volume as a whole has been concerned with the number and sources of male orgasms. On the other hand, the data on the heterosexual-homosexual ratings which are presented later in the present chapter, do take into account these homosexual contacts in which the subject fails to reach climax. Accumulative incidence curves based upon heterosexual-homosexual ratings may, therefore, be somewhat higher than the accumulative incidence curves based upon overt contacts carried through to the point of actual orgasm.

Data on the homosexual activity of the preadolescent boy have been presented in another chapter (Chapter 5) and no male is included in any of the calculations shown in the present chapter unless he has had homosexual experience beyond the onset of adolescence.

In these terms (of physical contact to the point of orgasm), the data in the present study indicate that at least 37 per cent of the male population has some homosexual experience between the beginning of adolescence and old. This is more than one male in three of the persons that one may meet as he passes along a city street. Among the males who remain unmarried until the age of 35, almost exactly

50 per cent have homosexual experience between the beginning of adolescence and that age. Some of these persons have but a single experience, and some of them have much more or even a lifetime of experience; but all of them have at least some experience to the point of orgasm. . . .

We ourselves were totally unprepared to find such incidence data when this research was originally undertaken. Over a period of several years we were repeatedly assailed with doubts as to whether we were getting a fair cross section of the total population or whether a selection of cases was biasing the results. It has been our experience, however, that each new group into which we have gone has provided substantially the same data.

Whether the histories were taken in one large city or another, whether they were taken in large cities, in small towns, or in rural areas, whether they came from one college or from another, a church school or a state university or some private institution, whether they came from one part of the country or from another, the incidence data on the homosexual have been more or less the same. . . .

Animal Contacts

No biologist exactly understands why males of a species are attracted primarily, even if not exclusively, to females of the same species. What is there to prevent insects of one species from mating with insects of many other species? What is there to prevent a frog from mating with frogs of other species? Why should mammals mate only with mammals of their own kind? In the animal kingdom as a whole, is it to be believed that the sources of sexual attraction are of such a nature that they provide stimuli only for other individuals of the same species? For the scientist it does not suffice to be told that nature allows nothing else but interspecific mating because she considers reproduction to be the objective of all sexual activities, and because the production of offspring is supposed to be impossible as a product of an interspecific cross. It does not suffice to think of inner forces which draw individuals together in their sexual relations. . . .

Such concepts concern intangibles with which science can have no dealing and, in the last analysis, the biologist and psychologist must look for material stimuli which, originating in one individual, may so affect other individuals that mating is the inevitable consequence. . . .

In any event, it is certain that human contacts with animals of other species have been known since

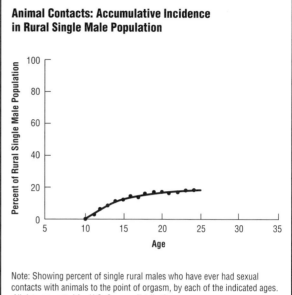

Animal Contacts: Accumulative Incidence in Rural Single Male Population

Note: Showing percent of single rural males who have ever had sexual contacts with animals to the point of orgasm, by each of the indicated ages. *All data corrected for U.S. Census distribution.*

SOURCE: Alfred Kinsey, W. Pomeroy, and Clyde Martin. *Social Behavior in the Human Male.* Philadelphia: W.B. Saunders, 1948, 670.

the dawn of history, they are known among all races of people today, and they are not uncommon in our own culture, as the data in the present chapter will show. Far from being a matter for surprise, the record simply substantiates our present understanding that the forces which bring individuals of the same species together in sexual relations, may sometimes serve to bring individuals of different species together in the same types of sexual relations. . . .

. . . [Among both] single and married males, only a fraction of 1 per cent of the total number of orgasms is derived from animal intercourse. In the period when such contacts are most frequent, namely between adolescence and 20 years of age, a little less than 1 per cent of the total outlet is so derived; but the figure drops rapidly in successive age groups, and it amounts to only 0.04 per cent among those males who remain single after the age of 25.

In the total population, only one male in twelve or fourteen (estimated at about 8%) ever has sexual experiences with animals. In this total population, it is not more than 6 per cent which is involved in the most active period (between adolescence and 20). The percentage drops in successive age groups to a little more than 1 per cent in the early twenties, and to a still lower figure at older ages.

Frequencies of animal contacts are similarly low in the population taken as a whole. For most individuals, they do not occur more than once or twice, or a few times in a lifetime.

On the other hand, the significance of such interspecific relationships becomes more apparent if we confirm the calculations simply to that segment of the population which has access to animals, namely to the males who are raised on farms. For that group, the incidences and frequencies of animal contacts are more nearly comparable to the incidences and frequencies of contacts with prostitutes, or of homosexual contacts, in the population. There are a number of city-bred boys (4% between adolescence and age 15 alone) who have animal contacts in their histories, and the fact that most of their experiences occur when they visit on farms suggests that the entire human male population might have animal contacts as frequently as farm boys do if animals were available to all of them.

Among boys raised on farms, about 17 per cent experience orgasm as the product of animal contacts which occur sometime after the onset of adolescence. As many more have contacts which do not result in orgasm, and there are still others who have pre-adolescent experience which is not included in the above calculations. It is, in consequence, something between 40 and 50 per cent of all farm boys who have some sort of animal contact, either with or without orgasm, in their pre-adolescent, adolescent, and/or later histories. These must be minimum data, for there has undoubtedly been some cover-up in the reports of these activities. The data given in the remainder of this chapter are confined to those contacts which have resulted in orgasm for the human subject; but all of these figures may be doubled if one wishes to determine the total number of persons involved in any sort of relation, whether with or without orgasm. Such data begin to show what the significance of animal intercourse might be if conditions were more favorable for such activity.

In fact, in certain Western areas of the United States, where animals are most readily available and social restraints on this matter are less stringent, we have secured incidence figures of as high as 63 per cent in some communities, and there are indications of still higher incidences in some other areas. The cases, however, are still too few to warrant a specific statement on these regional differences.

Ultimately, 14 to 16 per cent of the rural males of the grade school level, 20 per cent of the rural males of the high school level, and 26 to 28 per cent of the rural males of the college level have some animal experience to the point of orgasm. In this upper educational level, nearly one rural male in three has such contacts to the point of orgasm, and well over half of these upper level males have some kind of sexual contact with animals.

Further Resources

BOOKS

Bullough, Vern L. *Science in the Bedroom: A History of Sex Research.* New York: Basic Books, 1994.

Geddes, Donald Porter, ed. *An Analysis of the Kinsey Reports.* New York: New American Library, 1954.

PERIODICALS

Bullough, Vern L. "Alfred Kinsey and the Kinsey Report: Historical Overview and Lasting Contributions." *The Journal of Sex Research* 35 (May 1998): 127–31.

Palmore, Erdman. "Published Reactions to the Kinsey Report." *Social Forces* 31, no. 2 (1952): 165–72.

WEBSITES

Kinsey Institute home page. Available online at http://www.kinseyinstitute.org (accessed September 9, 2002).

McLemee, Scott. "The Man Who Took Sex Out of the Closet." Salon.com. Available online at http://www.salon.com/books/feature/1997/11/cov_05kinsey.html (accessed September 9, 2002).

"27,658 Polio Cases Listed Last Year"

Newspaper article

By: *The New York Times*
Date: 1949
Source: "27,658 Polio Cases Listed Last Year." *The New York Times,* 1949.
About the Organization: This newspaper article summarizes the findings of the National Foundation for Infantile Paralysis. The foundation's creation was announced in 1937 by President Franklin D. Roosevelt (served 1933–45). By its tenth year, the foundation was the major supporter of polio research and treatment in the United States. ∎

Introduction

In the years after the founding of the National Foundation for Infantile Paralysis, the number of polio cases continued to grow. The years after World War II (1939–1945) were particularly bad. The increase in cases reflected the rapid growth in the most susceptible segment of the population, children. The postwar baby boom, unfortunately, fueled a parallel explosion of polio cases.

Treatment methods were essentially a matter of trying to keep people alive and to minimize the disease's

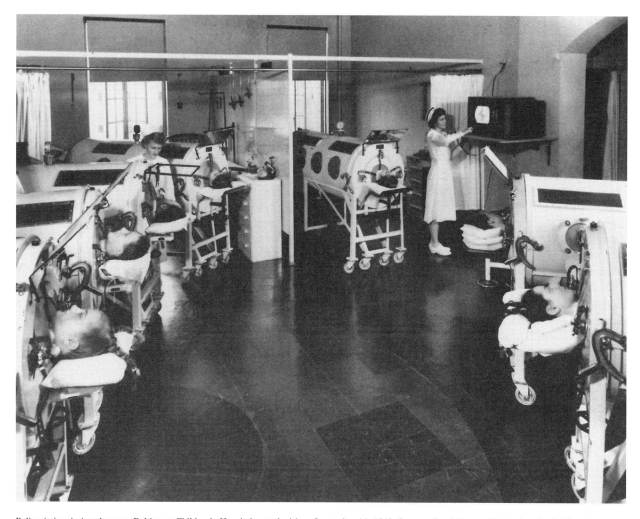

Polio victims in iron lungs at Baltimore Children's Hospital get television, September 14, 1948. Some polio victims could only breathe inside an iron lung. These devices encased the body, and within them air pressure was regulated to force air in and out of the patient's lungs. UPI/CORBIS-BETTMANN. REPRODUCED BY PERMISSION.

permanent effects whenever possible. Iron lungs were the only option to try to maintain respiration when a person could not breathe independently. Jane Smith, in *Patenting the Sun,* a history of polio, writes of a woman who gave birth in an iron lung. If they were lucky, polio victims were confined to the devices only for a short while, but even so, Smith describes the difficulty of "weaning" them. Having stayed alive only because of the machine, patients feared leaving its security, anxious that their fragile strength would fail them and that they would not be able to breathe on their own.

The most revolutionary change in treating polio's effects came from the Australian nurse, Sister Elizabeth Kenny. (The term "sister" in British English is the equivalent of "nurse" in American English.) Controversial in her own country and in England, Sister Kenny came to the United States in 1940, where she gained the support of the national foundation, although many physicians did not agree with her methods. The theory at the time was that to keep limbs of polio victims straight, they should be put in splints or casts. Only some muscles in an arm or leg might be paralyzed, and physicians believed that the strong muscles contracted the weak ones. The result would be a deformed limb.

Sister Kenny believed that polio was a disease of the muscles, not the central nervous system. This was wrong, but her methods were effective even if she did not understand the nature of the disease. She believed that all the muscles should be kept moving, not immobilized. To allow this, they needed to be relaxed. She developed her system by watching the Aboriginal peoples in Australia, who treated polio's paralysis by wrapping limbs in hot cloths. Sister Kenny did likewise and also used massage and physical therapy. This "retraining" of muscles succeeded in many victims, and the medical establishment came to respect her.

Significance

The number of polio cases reported by the March of Dimes in 1948 was significant not because it marked a peak, but because it never dropped any lower until the development of the first effective polio vaccine by Jonas Salk, which went into mass use in 1959. The epidemic hit 58,000 people in 1952 and 35,000 in 1953, according to March of Dimes statistics.

The number of cases also had an impact in that it made the quest for a vaccine even more urgent. Researchers had been trying for a successful vaccine for years. In 1935 trials were held for two vaccines, but one resulted in cases of polio and a few deaths and the other did not generate immunity.

As significant as the number of cases is the amount of money that the foundation raised and the kind of help it provided to communities, which would increase in the coming years. Smith describes the foundation as second only to the Red Cross in the amount of money it raised. The provision of equipment, through a network of "polio depots," helped communities that lacked sophisticated health care facilities. The professionals dispatched to epidemic areas gave essential help to overwhelmed local doctors and nurses. The physical therapists (trained in the Kenny method) were simply not available in most communities. Because of the foundation, polio became one of the few—perhaps the only—disease for which anyone could get help.

During these peak years of polio, the foundation used whatever tactics worked to generate money. Critics of these tactics found them too sensational, playing a bit too hard on the heartstrings of the would-be contributors. Smith describes one such effort, a movie called *The Crippler*, in which a sinister presence, the cloud of polio, spreads over playgrounds and schools. It is driven off by a brave young foundation volunteer played by Nancy Davis, a starlet who later became better known as Mrs. Ronald Reagan. The fund-raising was also among the first of such campaigns to heavily involve members of women's clubs, transforming them from purely social entities into important community fund-raising groups.

Primary Source

"27,658 Polio Cases Listed Last Year"

SYNOPSIS: The newspaper report summarizes the number of cases, their geographic distribution, and the details of the National Foundation for Infantile Paralysis's work in fighting polio nationwide.

$17,000,000 March of Dimes Funds Spent in Second-Worst Epidemic of the Disease

There were 27,658 reported cases of infantile paralysis in 1948, the second highest figure in the history of the disease in the United States, a statistical study by the National Foundation for Infantile Paralysis showed yesterday. In fighting the disease, the organization spent an estimated $17,000,000 from the March of Dimes.

The total of cases was exceeded only in 1916 when, the foundation estimated, the figure reached 50,000.

The study showed that California, North Carolina, and Texas accounted for more than 35 per cent of the 1948 figure. California had the largest number of cases, 5,560. South Dakota, with 940 cases, showed the extremely high incidence rate of 151 cases in 100,000 population.

As polio incidence mounted in epidemic areas in fifteen states, the foundation was called on to furnish medical personnel and extensive material aid. Two hundred and fifty physical therapists, 2,046 nurses and other personnel were sent into the field, as well as 141 respirators and other special equipment.

Commenting on the nation-wide drain on funds of the foundation and its chapters, Basil O'Connor, president, said the organization was "in the most difficult financial position in its eleven years."

"The National Foundation is on trial for its life," he declared. "Our hope for continued efficient work in the fight against polio lies in the coming March of Dimes, Jan. 14 to Jan. 31. This annual drive is the sole source of income for the foundation and its more than 2,800 chapters. This year we must realize a goal of not less than $30,000,000 to meet the continuing cost of caring for polio patients, of continued educational and research programs."

Mr. O'Connor said foundation grants for research in the last eleven years had provided for 691 projects in 114 institutions at a cost of $17,630,000. An additional $6,000,000 has been authorized for further scientific work, he said.

Further Resources

BOOKS

Seavey, Nina Gilden, Jane S. Smith, and Paul Wagner. *A Paralyzing Fear: The Triumph Over Polio in America.* New York: TV Books, 1998.

Smith, Jane S. *Patenting the Sun.* New York: William Morrow, 1990.

WEBSITES

Lincolnshire Post-Polio Library. The Lincolnshire Post-Polio Network. Available online at http://www.ott.zynet.co.uk/polio/lincolnshire/library.html (accessed August 22, 2002).

10

RELIGION

PETER J. CAPRIOGLIO

Entries are arranged in chronological order by date of primary source. For entries with one primary source, the entry title is the same as the primary source title. Entries with more than one primary source have an overall entry title, followed by the titles of the primary sources.

Important Events in Religion, 1940–1949

1940

INFLUENTIAL PUBLICATIONS: E. Stanley Jones, *Is the Kingdom of God Realism?*; Roland H. Bainton, *Here I Stand*; William E. Hocking, *Living Religions and a World Faith.*

- The United Jewish Appeal is founded.

- In February, the United States establishes a diplomatic counsel at the Vatican for the first time since 1868.

- On March 21, Rabbi Abraham J. Heschel arrives in the United States insisting humanity must make a distinction between good and evil.

1941

- Catholic leaders reform and reissue the Baltimore Catechism, the basis of Catholic educational instruction.

- On January 19, the Institute for Propaganda Analysis estimates there are 450,000 Christian pacifists in the United States.

- On September 6, the Presbyterian Church in the United States reports a membership decrease of 8,654 to a new total of 2,013,247.

- On November 30, more than sixteen thousand attend the opening of the entire interior length of the Cathedral of Saint John the Divine in New York, the longest Gothic cathedral in the world (601 feet).

1942

- On April 14, the *Saturday Evening Post* disclaims any anti-Semitic bias in an article by Milton Mayer titled "The Case Against the Jew."

- On April 30, the official Catholic Directory reports there are 22,556,242 Catholics in the United States.

- In June, an interracial group dedicated to nonviolent action forms the Congress of Racial Equality.

- In June, Presbyterian and Episcopalian church officials conclude discussions of a proposed merger.

- On August 14, the National Lutheran Council announces combined membership of 5,052,000 in 1941.

- In October, the Evangelican Reformed denomination and the Congregational Christian Church agree to a merger.

1943

INFLUENTIAL PUBLICATIONS: Trude Weiss-Rosmarin, *Judaism and Christianity: The Differences.*

- On January 6, the Selective Service System reports that of the more than 5 million men called in the draft, only 6,277 (0.1 percent) are conscientious objectors.

- On March 26, the National Jewish Welfare Board reports that Rabbi Alexander Goode is the first Jewish chaplain killed in the war.

- On April 26, U.S. Jews begin a six-week period of "mourning and intercession" on behalf of European Jews "exterminated by Hitler."

- On June 7, membership in the Methodist Church is reported at 6,640,424.

- On June 29, Pope Pius XII issues an encyclical called *Mystici Corporis Christi* that equates the Roman Catholic Church with the "mystical body of Christ."

- On July 19, the American Bible Society announces plans to distribute 1.8 million Bibles during the year.

- On August 29, the American Jewish Congress holds a memorial service for victims of Nazi persecution.

- On October 7, the Episcopal Church, while meeting in Cleveland, retains its ban on divorce.

1944

- A Gallup poll reveals that 58 percent of adult Americans had attended religious services at least once in the four weeks before the poll.

- In January, Evangelist Billy Graham takes over the Chicago religious radio program *Songs in the Night.*

- On January 2, the Federal Council of Churches announces that 256 religious bodies in the United States report a membership of 68,501,186 in 1942.

- On May 3, the General Conference of Methodism rejects a resolution to admit women to full rights as ministers.

- On May 18, the official Catholic Directory reports the U.S. Catholic population at 23,419,701—an increase of 474,564 over 1943.

- On August 6, the Theological Institute of the Russian Orthodox Church opens for the first time since 1917.

- On September 22, the Presbyterian Church in the United States reports membership at 2,098,091—an increase of 46,222 from the previous year.

1945

- The National Opinion Research Center reports that only 6 percent of those identifying themselves as Catholics said they seldom or never attended worship, in comparison with 19 percent of Protestants and 32 percent of Jews.

- On February 4, Alexei, metropolitan of Leningrad, is crowned patriarch of the Russian Orthodox Church in Moscow.

- In June, the Union of Orthodox Rabbis of the United States and Canada excommunicates Mordecai M. Kaplan for his modification of traditional doctrine in his *Sabbath Prayer Book.*

• On December 23, Pope Pius XII names thirty-two cardinals, including Francis J. Spellman of New York.

1946

INFLUENTIAL PUBLICATIONS: Rabbi Morris Silverman edits the first authoritative prayer book in the Conservative movement.

• On January 1, the Japanese emperor, Hirohito, announces that he is no longer divine.

• On February 11, a new translation of the New Testament, the Revised Standard Version, is published by the International Council of Religious Education.

• On February 20, representatives from one hundred Protestant and Orthodox churches from thirty-two countries meet in Geneva to plan a 1948 general assembly in the Netherlands to establish the World Council of Churches on a permanent basis.

• On March 5, the Federal Council of Churches of Christ in America, representing 27 million church members, condemns the atomic bombing of Japan.

• On April 28, the Alliance for the Preservation of American Reform Judaism is founded.

• On July 7, Mother Frances Xavier Cabrini, the second American to achieve sainthood, is canonized by the Pope.

• On August 25, the National Stewardship Institute reports that contributions to U.S. churches dropped $1,055,345,483 in the thirteen-year period from 1933 through 1945.

• On November 12, African American and white Baptists meet together for the first time at a joint session of the General Missionary Baptist Convention.

• On November 21, the North Carolina Baptist Convention rejects a resolution banning racial segregation in churches.

1947

• Two Bedouin boys discover the first of the Dead Sea Scrolls in a cave at Qumran, in British-occupied Palestine.

• On July 17, Archbishop Gregory arrives in the United States with the goal of uniting the U.S. Russian Orthodox Church with the Church in Russia.

• On July 23, a Southern Methodist women's conference condemns race discrimination and the recent Greenville, South Carolina, lynching acquittals.

• On October 23, the National Catholic Education Association reports that a record three million students attend Catholic schools.

• On December 1, the American Jewish Congress is reorganized as a permanent agency.

1948

• On January 10, a Gallup poll shows that 94 percent of Americans believe in God and 68 percent believe in life after death.

• On January 11, the Reverend Dr. G. Bromley Oxnam, Methodist bishop of Washington, D.C., helps found Protestants and Others Organized for the Separation of Church

and State, an organization designed to limit Roman Catholic influence in American politics.

• On February 25, Martin Luther King, Jr., is ordained and appointed assistant pastor at Ebenezer Baptist Church in Atlanta.

• On May 1, the Southern Baptist handbook reports a membership of 27,804,047.

• In July, the World Jewish Congress calls for support for Israel and an end to anti-Semitism.

• On August 1, the *Christian Herald* reports that a record 77,386,188 Americans are church members—a gain of 3,713,000 over 1946.

• On August 19, at its founding meeting, the International Council of Christian Churches, a fundamentalist organization of forty-five Protestant churches from eighteen countries, assails the World Council of Churches as antibiblical.

• On August 22, the first assembly of the World Council of Churches opens in Amsterdam, with 450 delegates and one thousand other officials of 150 Protestant and Orthodox churches from 42 nations present. The Vatican forbids Catholics to attend even as observers.

• On December 3, delegates to the national convention of the Federated Council of Churches pass a resolution calling on members to end racial segregation.

1949

• On January 22, Athenagoras, Greek Orthodox archbishop of North and South America, is enthroned patriarch of Constantinople. President Truman provides his own plane to assist the patriarch's move to Turkey.

• On April 21, a new U.S. Catholic catechism is issued, the first revision in sixty years; it maintains that "outside the Church there is no salvation."

• On April 21, the United Church of Christ is founded.

• In May, the Rabbinical Council of America votes to recognize the Chief Rabbinate of Israel as the central authority for all Jews.

• On May 9, Methodist Church membership has grown from 7,856,060 in 1939 to 8,651,062.

• On June 9, Vatican Radio announces there are 338,250,000 Catholics in the world.

• On June 25, the Vatican announces that ten years of excavation at the Basilica of Saint Peter in Rome confirms the tradition that Saint Peter is buried there.

• In summer, spurred by controversy over public funds used for parochial school students, Francis Cardinal Spellman and Eleanor Roosevelt debate the issue of separation of church and state.

• On September 9, a U.S. expedition abandons its search for Noah's Ark after twelve days of futile hunting on Mount Ararat in Turkey.

• On September 25, thirty-one-year-old evangelical minister Billy Graham begins a revival in Los Angeles, attended by more than 350,000 people.

Cantwell v. Connecticut

Supreme Court decision

By: Owen J. Roberts

Date: May 20, 1940

Source: *Cantwell v. Connecticut.* 310 U.S. 296 (1940). Available online at http://laws.findlaw.com/us/310 /296.html; website home page: http://www.findlaw.com (accessed April 21, 2003).

About the Author: Justice Owen J. Roberts (1875–1955), became well known to the American public when President Calvin Coolidge (served 1923–1929) appointed him to prosecute the Teapot Dome oil scandal, a case involving the misuse of public lands, in 1924. President Herbert Hoover (served 1929–1933) named Roberts to the United States Supreme Court in 1930. Roberts retired from the court in 1945 and became dean of the University of Pennsylvania Law School three years later. ■

Introduction

In *Cantwell v. Connecticut* Newton Cantwell sued the state of Connecticut for violating his First Amendment right of freedom of religion by requiring him to get prior official approval before soliciting door-to-door. Cantwell and his sons, Jesse and Russell, all Jehovah's Witnesses, were arrested while individually soliciting residents in a heavily Catholic neighborhood of New Haven, Connecticut.

The Cantwells asked residents if they would like to accept a pamphlet or hear a record, both of which contained statements attacking Roman Catholicism. If the residents refused to buy a book, the Cantwells would then ask for a donation that would go toward publication of more pamphlets.

At the time Connecticut law required individuals to obtain permission from the secretary of public welfare before engaging in solicitation. Since the Cantwells had not sought permission, the police arrested them. After being convicted in trial court they appealed to the state supreme court, which upheld their convictions. The Cantwells then appealed to the United States Supreme Court.

The Court, in an opinion written by Justice Roberts, rejects the state's argument that the First Amendment

A young Jehovah's witness gains the attention of an elderly passer-by. In 1940 Newton Cantwell, a Jehovah's Witness, was arrested for soliciting door-to-door to spread the word of God. Cantwell sued and took his case all the way to the Supreme Court. © HULTON-DEUTSCH COLLECTION/CORBIS. REPRODUCED BY PERMISSION.

does not apply to Connecticut statutes. Clearly, the Court said, the Due Process Clause of the Fourteenth Amendment—which says that no state shall "deprive any person of life, liberty, or property without due process of law"—makes the First Amendment applicable at the state level. The Court specifically stated for the first time that the Free Exercise of Religion Clause of the First Amendment applies to states as well as to the federal government: "The First Amendment declares that Congress shall make no law respecting an establishment of religion or prohibiting the free exercise thereof. The Fourteenth Amendment has rendered the legislatures of the states as incompetent as Congress to enact such laws."

The Court pointed out that there are two aspects to freedom of religion: freedom of conscience and freedom of acts of religious adherence. The first cannot be restricted by law since the freedom to believe is absolute, but some restraints can be placed on the second because the freedom to act must be balanced with the protection of society as a whole. The Court noted that no one would argue that a state may enact a law that prohibits the right to preach or to disseminate religious views. Plainly such a restraint would interfere with the free exercise of religion. However a state may enact general and nondiscriminatory laws to regulate the time, place, and manner of soliciting or holding meetings on the streets.

Significance

Federal courts would hear many more cases concerning "time, place, and manner" restrictions, not all of them centering on freedom of religion. In each case the courts tried to determine whether the regulation at issue was truly neutral or nondiscriminatory. If so the courts then had to balance the interests of those who wished to practice their religion publicly against the interests of the larger society.

The "time, place, and manner" rule established by the Supreme Court means that federal and state governments are all bound by the First Amendment's guarantees for religious freedom. The rights of citizens to follow whatever religious beliefs they wish is protected and absolute, but the right of citizens for free exercise of their religion is not absolute. A citizen's free-exercise right must be weighed against the public interest, and a state can regulate to ensure that it is practiced in a reasonable time, place, and manner.

The Court would base future decisions on the "reasonableness" factor. If the state restricted the practice of religion in reference to time, place, and manner, it had to demonstrate the reasonableness of such an action. If the state could not do so to the satisfaction of the court, then the question of a violation of the freedom of religion would have had to be raised.

Primary Source

Cantwell v. Connecticut [excerpt]

SYNOPSIS: Newton Cantwell claimed that a Connecticut state law requiring prior official approval before soliciting door-to-door violated the First Amendment guarantee of freedom of religion. The Supreme Court, while asserting that a state has the

right to issue appropriate time, place, or manner restrictions on solicitation, unanimously struck down the Connecticut statute as a violation of the First Amendment. Thus the Court upheld the freedom to spread religious ideas. The case was decided on May 20, 1940.

Mr. Justice Roberts delivered the opinion of the Court.

Newton Cantwell and his two sons, Jesse and Russell, members of a group known as Jehovah's witnesses [sic], and claiming to be ordained ministers, were arrested in New Haven, Connecticut, and each was charged by information in five counts, with statutory and common law offenses. After trial in the Court of Common Pleas of New Haven County each of them was convicted on the third count, which charged a violation of 6294 of the General Statutes of Connecticut, and on the fifth count, which charged commission of the common law offense of inciting a breach of the peace. On appeal to the Supreme Court the conviction of all three on the third count was affirmed. The conviction of Jesse Cantwell, on the fifth count, was also affirmed, but the conviction of Newton and Russell on that count was reversed and a new trial ordered as to them.

By demurrers to the information, by requests for rulings of law at the trial, and by their assignments of error in the State Supreme Court, the appellants pressed the contention that the statute under which the third count was drawn was offensive to the due process clause of the Fourteenth Amendment because, on its face and as construed and applied, it denied them freedom of speech and prohibited their free exercise of religion. In like manner they made the point that they could not be found guilty on the fifth count, without violation of the Amendment.

We have jurisdiction on appeal from the judgments on the third count, as there was drawn in question the validity of a state statute under the federal Constitution, and the decision was in favor of validity. Since the conviction on the fifth count was not based upon a statute, but presents a substantial question under the federal Constitution, we granted the writ of certiorari in respect of it.

The facts adduced to sustain the convictions on the third count follow. On the day of their arrest the appellants were engaged in going singly from house to house on Cassius Street in New Haven. They were individually equipped with a bag containing books and pamphlets on religious subjects, a portable phonograph and a set of records, each of which, when played, introduced, and was a description of, one of the books. Each appellant asked the person who responded to his call for permission to play one of the records. If permission was granted he asked the person to buy the book described and, upon refusal, he solicited such contribution towards the publication of the pamphlets as the listener was willing to make. If a contribution was received a pamphlet was delivered upon condition that it would be read.

Cassius Street is in a thickly populated neighborhood, where about ninety per cent of the residents are Roman Catholics. A phonograph record, describing a book entitled "Enemies," included an attack on the Catholic religion. None of the persons interviewed were members of Jehovah's witnesses.

The statute under which the appellants were charged provides:

> No person shall solicit money, services, subscriptions or any valuable thing for any alleged religious, charitable or philanthropic cause, from other than a member of the organization for whose benefit such person is soliciting or within the county in which such person or organization is located unless such cause shall have been approved by the secretary of the public welfare council. Upon application of any person in behalf of such cause, the secretary shall determine whether such cause is a religious one or is a bona fide object of charity or philanthropy and conforms to reasonable standards of efficiency and integrity, and, if he shall so find, shall approve the same and issue to the authority in charge a certificate to that effect. Such certificate may be revoked at any time. Any person violating any provision of this section shall be fined not more than one hundred dollars or imprisoned not more than thirty days or both.

The appellants claimed that their activities were not within the statute but consisted only of distribution of books, pamphlets, and periodicals. The State Supreme Court construed the finding of the trial court to be that "in addition to the sale of the books and the distribution of the pamphlets the defendants were also soliciting contributions or donations of money for an alleged religious cause, and thereby came within the purview of the statute." It overruled the contention that the Act, as applied to the appellants, offends the due process clause of the Fourteenth Amendment, because it abridges or denies religious freedom and liberty of speech and press. The court stated that it was the solicitation that brought the appellants within the sweep of the Act and not their other activities in the dissemination of literature. It declared the legislation consti-

tutional as an effort by the State to protect the public against fraud and imposition in the solicitation of funds for what purported to be religious, charitable, or philanthropic causes.

The facts which were held to support the conviction of Jesse Cantwell on the fifth count were that he stopped two men in the street, asked, and received, permission to play a phonograph record, and played the record "Enemies," which attacked the religion and church of the two men, who were Catholics. Both were incensed by the contents of the record and were tempted to strike Cantwell unless he went away. On being told to be on his way he left their presence. There was no evidence that he was personally offensive or entered into any argument with those he interviewed.

The court held that the charge was not assault or breach of the peace or threats on Cantwell's part, but invoking or inciting others to breach of the peace, and that the facts supported the conviction of that offense.

First. We hold that the statute, as construed and applied to the appellants, deprives them of their liberty without due process of law in contravention of the Fourteenth Amendment. The fundamental concept of liberty embodied in that Amendment embraces the liberties guaranteed by the First Amendment. The First Amendment declares that Congress shall make no law respecting an establishment of religion or prohibiting the free exercise thereof. The Fourteenth Amendment has rendered the legislatures of the states as incompetent as Congress to enact such laws. The constitutional inhibition of legislation on the subject of religion has a double aspect. On the one hand, it forestalls compulsion by law of the acceptance of any creed or the practice of any form of worship. Freedom of conscience and freedom to adhere to such religious organization or form of worship as the individual may choose cannot be restricted by law. On the other hand, it safeguards the free exercise of the chosen form of religion. Thus the Amendment embraces two concepts,—freedom to believe and freedom to act. The first is absolute but, in the nature of things, the second cannot be. Conduct remains subject to regulation for the protection of society. . . .

Second. We hold that, in the circumstances disclosed, the conviction of Jesse Cantwell on the fifth count must be set aside. . . .

We find in the instant case no assault or threatening of bodily harm, no truculent bearing, no intentional discourtesy, no personal abuse. On the contrary, we find only an effort to persuade a willing listener to buy a book or to contribute money in the interest of what Cantwell, however misguided others may think him, conceived to be true religion.

In the realm of religious faith, and in that of political belief, sharp differences arise. In both fields the tenets of one man may seem the rankest error to his neighbor. To persuade others to his own point of view, the pleader, as we know, at times, resorts to exaggeration, to vilification of men who have been, or are, prominent in church or state, and even to false statement. But the people of this nation have ordained in the light of history, that, in spite of the probability of excesses and abuses, these liberties are, in the long view, essential to enlightened opinion and right conduct on the part of the citizens of a democracy.

The essential characteristic of these liberties is, that under their shield many types of life, character, opinion and belief can develop unmolested and unobstructed. Nowhere is this shield more necessary than in our own country for a people composed of many races and of many creeds. There are limits to the exercise of these liberties. The danger in these times from the coercive activities of those who in the delusion of racial or religious conceit would incite violence and breaches of the peace in order to deprive others of their equal right to the exercise of their liberties, is emphasized by events familiar to all. These and other transgressions of those limits the states appropriately may punish. Although the contents of the record not unnaturally aroused animosity, we think that, in the absence of a statute narrowly drawn to define and punish specific conduct as constituting a clear and present danger to a substantial interest of the State, the petitioner's communication, considered in the light of the constitutional guarantees, raised no such clear and present menace to public peace and order as to render him liable to conviction of the common law offense in question.

The judgment affirming the convictions on the third and fifth counts is reversed and the cause is remanded for further proceedings not inconsistent with this opinion. So ordered.

Reversed and remanded.

Further Resources

BOOKS

Flowers, Ronald B. *That Godless Court?: Supreme Court Decisions on Church-State Relationships* Louisville, Ky.: Westminster John Knox Press, 1994.

Harrell, Mary Ann. *Equal Justice under Law: The Supreme Court in American Life.* Washington, D.C.: Supreme Court Historical Society, 1982.

Lee, Francis Graham. *Church-State Relations.* Westport, Conn.: Greenwood Press, 2002.

PERIODICALS

"High Court Shifts Church-State Stance." *U.S. News & World Report,* March 19, 1984, 10.

McGreevy, John T. "Paying the Words Extra: Religious Discourse in the Supreme Court of the United States." *Commonweal,* June 16, 1995.

"New Legislation on Religious Liberty." *The Christian Century,* August 2, 2000, 786.

WEBSITES

"Separation of Church and State FAQ: Jehovah's Witnesses & Religious Liberty." Available online at http://atheism.about.com/library/FAQs/cs/blcs_jw_index.htm (accessed April 23, 2003).

"Christian Faith and the World Crisis"

Journal article

By: Reinhold Niebuhr

Date: February 10, 1941

Source: Niebuhr, Reinhold. "Christian Faith and the World Crisis." *Journal of Christianity and Crisis,* February 10, 1941. Available online at http://www.religion-online.org/cgi-bin/relsearchd.dll/showarticle?item_id=381; website home page: http://www.religion-online.org (accessed February 12, 2002).

About the Author: Reinhold Niebuhr (1892–1971), born in Wright City, Missouri, became a major figure in Christian theology. He served as an evangelical pastor in Detroit from 1915 to 1928 and worked as a professor of Christian ethics at the Union Theological Seminary in New York City from 1928 to 1960. A political activist and influential theological author, he was renowned for his theology of Christian Realism. ■

Introduction

Theologian Reinhold Niebuhr's article "Christian Faith and the World Crisis" was published in the *Journal of Christianity and Crisis* on February 10, 1941, almost ten months before the Japanese bombed Pearl Harbor on December 7, 1941. The United States was still at peace but the possibility of entering World War II (1939–1945) was on the minds of many Americans. Some Christians argued that the United States had no moral right to enter the war and that if all Christians and others of good will would refuse to go to war, then all wars could be eliminated. Other Christians, while seeing war

As the nation struggled with whether or not to enter World War II, Reinhold Niebuhr published "Christian Faith and the World Crisis," an article which examined the arguments in terms of Christian morality. THE LIBRARY OF CONGRESS.

as the last resort against injustice, thought the atrocities being committed by the Nazis gave the United States not only the moral right but the moral obligation to declare war against them.

Understanding this conflict in American Christianity, Niebuhr examined both views to determine which made the most moral sense. After considering both sides he concluded that Christians had a moral right to fight the evil of Nazism. Those who believed that war was always immoral, he argued, tried to apply an unrealistic perfectionism and utopianism, or belief in an ideal world, to the crisis in Europe and Asia. Proposing that war could be eliminated if Christians would just refuse to fight was simplistic and dangerous to the cause of justice. Perfectionist and pacifist interpretations of Christianity did not apply to the international situation America faced in 1941.

Niebuhr's theology can be labeled "Christian Realism," a realization that humans, institutions, and societies are and always will be imperfect. Christian Realists contended that only Christ's love was perfect, so much so that he gave his life to save humanity. In "Christian Faith and the World Crisis," Niebuhr maintained that Christians must bear this in mind when dealing with

powerful political, economic, and social forces. Idealistic thinking will not bring about peace and social justice in the real world.

Before adopting this stance of Christian Realism, Niebuhr belonged to a movement in liberal Christianity that believed the inherent goodness of humanity would overcome evil in society. As he matured in his theological thinking, he decided that this approach could not effectively solve critical human problems.

Significance

An influential theologian, Niebuhr affected the thinking of many Christians who were uncertain about the morality of going to war. Still haunted by the tremendous loss of life in World War I (1914–1918) just a generation before, Americans feared involvement in another major military conflict. Niebuhr's theological support of fighting Nazism, along with that of other noted Christians, gave a much-needed moral boost to the nation as it witnessed the devastation in Europe. His justification helped to provide the moral guidance necessary for a people to go to war.

The lasting importance of Niebuhr's Christian Realism theology is attested to by the continued renown of his Serenity Prayer: "God, give us the serenity to accept what cannot be changed; give us the courage to change what should be changed; give us the wisdom to distinguish one from the other."

Primary Source

"Christian Faith and the World Crisis" [excerpt]

SYNOPSIS: Niebuhr discusses how Christians should morally interpret the problems facing the United States and the world during the 1940s. He examines the moral conflict between Christians who hold anti-war or pacifist positions and those who believe that war, under certain conditions, is not only morally justifiable but a moral obligation.

At the present moment a basic difference of conviction with regard to what Christianity is and what it demands runs through the whole of American Protestantism and cuts across all the traditional denominational distinctions. There is, on the one hand, a school of Christian thought that believes war could be eliminated if only Christians and other men of good will refused resolutely enough to have anything to do with conflict. Another school of thought, while conceding that war is one of the most vivid revelations of sin in human history, does not find the disavowal of war so simple a matter. The proponents of the latter position believe that there are historic situations in which refusal to defend the inheritance of a civilization, however imperfect, against tyranny and aggression may result in consequences even worse than war.

This journal intends to express and, if possible, to clarify this second viewpoint. We do not believe that the Christian faith as expressed in the New Testament and as interpreted in historic Christianity, both Catholic and Protestant, implies the confidence that evil and injustice in history can be overcome by such simple methods as are currently equated with Christianity. We believe that modern Christian perfectionism is tinctured with utopianism derived from a secular culture. In our opinion this utopianism contributed to the tardiness of the democracies in defending themselves against the perils of a new barbarism, and (in America at least) it is easily compounded with an irresponsible and selfish nationalism.

We intend this journal to be both polemic and irenic, as far as human frailty will permit the combination of these two qualities. It will be polemic in the sense that we shall combat what seem to us false interpretations of our faith, and consequent false analyses of our world and of our duties in it. It will be irenic in the sense that we shall seek to appreciate the extent to which perfectionist and pacifist interpretations of Christianity are derived from genuine and important elements in our common faith.

Perfectionists are right in their conviction that our civilization stands under the judgment of God; no one can have an easy conscience about the social and political anarchy out of which the horrible tyranny that now threatens us arose. But they are wrong in assuming that we have no right or duty to defend a civilization, despite its imperfections, against worse alternatives. They are right in insisting that love is the ultimate law of life. But they have failed to realize to what degree the sinfulness of all men, even the best, makes justice between competing interests and conflicting wills a perennial necessity of history.

The perfectionists rightly recognize that it may be very noble for an individual to sacrifice his life or interests rather than participate in the claims and counterclaims of the struggle for justice (of which war may always be the *ultima ratio*). They are wrong in making no distinction between an individual act of self-abnegation and a political policy of submission to injustice, whereby lives and interests other than our own are defrauded or destroyed. They seek erroneously to build a political platform upon individual perfection. Medieval perfectionism, whatever

its limitations, wisely avoided these errors. It excluded even the family from the possible consequences of an individual's absolute ethic, and it was profoundly aware of the impossibility of making its rigorous standards universal.

We believe that there are many Christians whose moral inclinations might persuade them to take the same view of current problems as our own, except for the fact that they are inhibited by religious presuppositions that they regard as more "purely" Christian than those represented by the consensus of the Church through all the ages. Therefore we will begin with an analysis of these religious presuppositions.

Christians are agreed that the God who is revealed in Christ is source and end of our existence and that therefore his character and will are the norm and standard of our conduct. It is only in recent decades, however, that it has been believed that the "gentleness" of Jesus was a sufficient and final revelation of the character of God, that this character was one of pure love and mercy, and that this revelation stood in contradiction to an alleged portrayal of a God of wrath in the Old Testament. . . .

The biblical answer to the problem of evil in human history is a radical answer, precisely because human evil is recognized as a much more stubborn fact than is realized in some modern versions of the Christian faith. These versions do not take the problem of justice in history seriously, because they have obscured what the Bible has to say about the relation of justice to mercy in the very heart of God. Every sensitive Christian must feel a sense of unworthiness when he is compelled by historic destiny to act as an instrument of God's justice. Recognition of the common guilt that makes him and his enemy kin must persuade him to imitate the mercy of God, even while he seeks to fulfill the demands of justice. But he will seek to elude such responsibilities only if he believes, as many modern Christians do, that he might, if he tried a little harder, achieve an individual or collective vantage point of guiltlessness from which to proceed against evil doers. There is no such vantage point. . . .

The measures now being taken for the support of the democracies are a logical expression of the unique conditions of America's relation to the world. They do justice on the one hand to our responsibilities for a common civilization that transcends the hemispheres, and on the other hand to the fact that we are not as immediately imperiled as other nations. Whether our freedom from immediate peril will enable us to persevere in the reservations that we still maintain cannot be decided in the abstract. The exigencies of the future must determine the issue.

We cannot, of course, be certain that defeat of the Nazis will usher in a new order of international justice in Europe and the world. We do know what a Nazi victory would mean, and our first task must therefore be to prevent it. Yet it cannot be our only task, for the problem of organizing the technical civilization of the western world upon a new basis of economic and international justice, so that the anarchy and decay that have characterized our life in the past three decades will be arrested and our technical capacities will be made fruitful rather than suicidal, is one which must engage our best resources. We must give some thought and attention to this great issue even while we are forced to ward off a horrible alternative.

We believe that the Christian faith can and must make its own contribution to this issue. The task of building a new world, as well as the tragic duty of saving the present world from tyranny, will require resources of understanding and resolution which are inherent in the Christian faith. The profoundest insights of the Christian faith cannot be expressed by the simple counsel that men ought to be more loving, and that if they became so the problems of war and of international organization would solve themselves.

Yet there are times when hopes for the future, as well as contrition over past misdeeds, must be subordinated to the urgent, immediate task. In this instance, the immediate task is the defeat of Nazi tyranny. If this task does not engage us, both our repentance and our hope become luxuries in which we indulge while other men save us from an intolerable fate, or while our inaction betrays into disaster a cause to which we owe allegiance.

Further Resources

BOOKS

Bingham, June. *Courage to Change: An Introduction to the Life and Thought of Reinhold Niebuhr.* New York: Scribners, 1961.

Landon, Harold R. *Reinhold Niebuhr: A Prophetic Voice in Our Time; Essays in Tribute.* Greenwich, Conn.: Seabury Press, 1962.

Niebuhr, Reinhold. *The Essential Reinhold Niebuhr: Selected Essays and Addresses.* New Haven, Conn.: Yale University Press, 1986.

PERIODICALS

Ostling, Richard N. "The Definitive Reinhold Niebuhr: An Admirable New Biography of the Apostle of Christian Realism." *Time*, Jan 20, 1986.

WEBSITES

Freeman, Paul. "The Neo-Orthodox Theology of Reinhold Niebuhr." International School of Theology. Available online at http://www.leaderu.com/isot/docs/niehbr3.html (accessed July 2, 2002).

Hodges, Miles. "In Depth Biographies: Niebuhr." Available online at http://www.newgenevacenter.org/biography/nieb (accessed July 2, 2002).

Niebuhr, Reinhold. "Original Serenity Prayer." Available online at http://www.soulfoodministry.org/docs/TheOriginalSerenityPrayeraswrittenbyReinholdNiebuhr.htm (accessed February 21, 2003).

"On Anti-Semitism"
Journal article

By: Jacques Maritain

Date: October 6, 1941

Source: Maritain, Jacques. "On Anti-Semitism." *Journal of Christianity and Crisis,* October 6, 1941. Available online at http://www.religion-online.org/cgi-bin/relsearchd.dll/showarticle?item_id=383; website home page: http://www.religion-online.org (accessed February 9, 2002).

About the Author: Jacques Maritain (1882–1973), one of the most important Catholic theologians and authors of the twentieth century, was born in Paris, France. From 1914 to 1940 he was a professor at the Institut Catholique in Paris. During World War II (1939–1945) he lived in the United States, which he considered his second home, and taught at Princeton and Columbia universities and the University of Chicago. Maritain is noted especially for his work on the moral philosophy of the medieval theologian St. Thomas Aquinas. ∎

Introduction

In the late 1930s and early 1940s Maritain became extremely concerned about the growth of anti-Semitism, especially in his native France. In June 1940, just months after the start of World War II, the German army defeated France and occupied two-thirds of the country. In the remaining one-third, France set up an authoritarian government, led by Marshal Pétain and Pierre Laval. This government, known as "Vichy" for its capital city, was openly anti-Semitic and cooperated fully in the Nazi plan to exterminate the Jews.

In "On Anti-Semitism," written shortly after the German occupation, Maritain establishes an extraordinary philosophical and theological position: anyone who holds anti-Jewish beliefs also speaks against Jesus Christ. Maritain argues that anti-Semitic words and behavior are anti-Christ on two levels: first because Christ himself was born a Jew of Jewish parents and second because Christ commanded his followers to love all people, regardless of their religious identity.

The earliest followers of Jesus, many of whom were Jewish, still followed the Judaic traditions of their families and ancestors while also following the new directions and law given to them by Jesus. A Christian religion distinct from the practice of Judaism did not develop until later, when large numbers of non-Jews became followers of Christ. Christianity still honors its Jewish heritage, holding the Old Testament, the Jewish Bible, as sacred as the New Testament, the gospels of Jesus. Many Christian worship services include readings from both the Old and the New Testament.

In one of his other writings Maritain comments on a statement by Pope Pius XI (served 1922–1939) that it was not possible for Christians to have any part in anti-Semitism. The pope asserted that because it attacked the people of Christ's roots, anti-Semitism was automatically anti-Christian. He also pointed out that all Christians were converts to the God of Israel who is the true God.

Significance

Maritain's influence on Christian and Jewish relations affected the advancement of the Catholic Church's thinking about Judaism and Jews. He helped change the Catholic view of the role of Jews in the world. For example, the church now teaches that prejudice and discrimination against Jews, as well as any other group, whether religious or nonreligious, is a serious offense against God. Maritain's theological perspective had a significant influence at the Second Vatican Council, a Catholic assembly that met four times between 1962 and 1965 under the leadership of Pope John XXIII. One of the council's most important documents, the "Declaration on the Relation of the Church to Non-Christian Religions" *(Nostra Aetate),* noted the special importance of the spiritual relationships between Jews and Christians. It condemned all types of anti-Semitism and laid the foundation for better relations and respect between these two faiths.

Maritain's influence also extended to the international community. His moral and political philosophy on human rights in general, and anti-Semitism in particular, is reflected in three other major post-World War II documents: the preamble to the Constitution of the Fourth French Republic (1946), the United Nations's Universal Declaration of Human Rights (1948), and the Canadian Charter of Rights and Freedoms (1982).

Primary Source

"On Anti-Semitism" [excerpt]

SYNOPSIS: Jacques Maritain, a Roman Catholic theologian, expresses deep concern about the spread of anti-Semitism around the world. He argues that the persecution of Jews in Europe in the 1940s

Jacques Maritain argues in "On Anti-Semitism" that in persecuting Jews one also persecutes Christ. Maritain helped influence Christian and Jewish relations, particularly the Catholic Church's position on the treatment of those from other religions. **AP/WIDE WORLD PHOTOS. REPRODUCED BY PERMISSION.**

echoes the persecution that Jesus Christ withstood almost two thousand years before. Those who express hatred toward Jews, he states, directly and indirectly demonstrate hatred toward Christ.

I have already spoken of anti-Semitism many times. I never would have thought that I would have to do so in connection with anti-Semitic laws promulgated by a French government—which are a denial of the traditions and the spirit of my country. I am well aware that these decrees have been adopted under German pressure and through the machinations of Laval. I also know that the French people by and large are astounded at and disgusted with these laws. The fact remains, however, that the Vichy leaders have enforced anti-Semitic laws in a more and more strict and iniquitous fashion, depriving French Jews of every governmental and cultural position, imposing upon them all kinds of restrictions with regard to liberal and commercial professions, mercilessly striking many of them who were wounded for their country during the present war, and hypocritically trying to hide a bad conscience under a pseudonational pathos in which religious and racial considerations are shamefully mixed.

A small part of the bourgeoisie and the country gentry, poisoned by filthy newspapers, is letting itself be permeated by racist baseness. Anti-Semitic German films are shown in movie-theaters even in the unoccupied part of France, and we have been told that a Catholic periodical was suspended for one month for having boldly protested against such an action. Despite innumerable private testimonies of help and solidarity given—often at great risk—to persecuted Jews, despite innumerable touching signs of friendship and fidelity that dismissed Jewish professors received from their students, no public protest has been made by any educational body; and some new corporative institutions, among the liberal professions, are willingly admitting a kind of numerus clausus.

The psychic poisons are more active than the physical ones; it is unfortunately inevitable that, little by little, many souls should bow down. If the anti-Semitic regulations and propaganda are to endure for some years, we may imagine that many weak people will resign themselves to the worst. They will think that, after all, the concentration camps are more comfortable for their neighbors than the Jews say, and finally they will find themselves perfectly able to look at or contribute to the destruction of their friends, with the smile of a clear conscience (life must go on!).

I have firm confidence in the natural virtues and the moral resistance of the common people of France. I know we must trust them; yet it is not only in thinking of the Jews, but in thinking of my country that I feel horrified by the anti-Semitic corruption of souls that is being furthered in France by a leadership that still dares speak of honor.

It is also for Christianity that I fear. Perhaps the danger is greater in countries that have not—not as yet—experienced Nazi terrorism. We have been told that in some countries of South America anti-Semitism is spreading among some sections of Catholic youth and Catholic intellectuals, despite the teachings of the Pope and the efforts of their own bishops. It is impossible to compromise with anti-Semitism; it carries in itself, as in a living germ, all the spiritual evil of Nazism. Anti-Semitism is the moral Fifth Column in the Christian conscience.

"Spiritually we are Semites," Pius XI said. "Anti-Semitism is unacceptable." I should like to emphasize in this paper the spiritual aspect of this question.

May I point out that the most impressive Christian formulas concerning the spiritual essence of anti-Semitism may be found in a book recently published by a Jewish writer who seems himself strangely unaware of their profoundly Christian meaning. I do not know whether Maurice Samuel shares even in Jewish piety; perhaps he is a God-seeking soul deprived of any definite dogmas, believing himself to be "freed" from any trust in divine revelation, of either the Old or the New Covenant. The testimony that he brings appears all the more significant because prophetic intuitions are all the more striking when they pass through slumbering or stubborn prophets who perceive only in an obscure way what they convey to us.

"We shall never understand," Mr. Samuel says, "the maniacal, world-wide seizure of anti-Semitism unless we transpose the terms. It is of Christ that the Nazi-Fascists are afraid; it is in his omnipotence that they believe; it is he that they are determined madly to obliterate. But the names of Christ and Christianity are too overwhelming, and the habit of submission to them is too deeply ingrained after centuries and centuries of teaching. Therefore they must, I repeat, make their assault on those who were responsible for the birth and spread of Christianity. They must spit on the Jews as the 'Christ-killers' because they long to spit on the Jews as the Christ-givers." (Maurice Samuel, *The Great Hatred.* New York, 1940)

The simple fact of feeling no sympathy for the Jews or being more sensitive to their faults than to their virtues is not anti-Semitism. Anti-Semitism is fear, scorn and hatred of the Jewish race or people, and a desire to subject them to discriminative measures. There are many forms and degrees of anti-Semitism. Not to speak of the demented forms we are facing at present, it can take the form of a supercilious nationalist and aristocratic bias of pride and prejudice; or a plain desire to rid oneself of competitors; or a routine of vanity fair; or even an innocent verbal mania. In reality no one is innocent. In each one the seed is hidden, more or less inert or active, of that spiritual disease which today throughout the world is bursting out into a homicidal, myth-making phobia, and the secret soul of which is resentment against the Gospel: "Christophobia."

Leon Bloy said that the "veil" to which Saint Paul refers and which covers the eyes of Israel is now passing "from the Jews to the Christians." This statement, which is harsh on the Gentiles and on the Christian distorters of Christianity, helps us understand something of the extensive and violent persecution of which the Jews today are victims, and of the spiritual upheaval that has been going on for years among many of them, denoting deep inward changes, particularly in respect to the person of Christ.

The growing solicitude in Israel's heart for the Just Man crucified through the error of the high priests is a symptom of unquestionable importance. Today in America representative Jewish writers like Sholem Asch and Waldo Frank are trying to reintegrate the Gospel into the brotherhood of Israel. While not yet recognizing Jesus as the Messiah, they do recognize him as the most pure Jewish figure in human history. They themselves would be disturbed to be considered as leaning toward Christianity. Yet while remaining closer than ever to Judaism, they believe that the Gospel transcends the Old Testament and consider it a divine flower issuing from the stem of the Patriarchs and the Prophets.

Never forgetful of the conflicts of history and of the harsh treatment received by their people, the authors of *Salvation* and of *The New Discovery of America* have long known and loved mediæval Christianity and Catholic spiritual life. They agree with Maurice Samuel that "Christophobia" is the spiritual essence of the demoniacal racism of our pagan world. Many other signs give evidence that Israel is beginning to open its eyes, whereas the eyes of many self-styled Christians are blinded, darkened by the exhalations of the old pagan blood suddenly, ferociously welling up once more among Gentiles.

"Jesus Christ is in agony until the end of the world," said Pascal. Christ suffers in every innocent man who is persecuted. His agony is heard in the cries of so many human beings humiliated and tortured, in the suffering of all those images and likenesses of God treated worse than beasts. He has taken all these things upon himself, he has suffered every wound. "Fear not, my child, I have already travelled that road. On each step of the abominable way I have left for you a drop of my blood and the print of my mercy."

Further Resources

BOOKS

Abel, Ernest L. *The Roots of Anti-Semitism.* Rutherford, N.J.: Fairleigh Dickinson University Press, 1975.

Belth, Nathan C. *A Promise to Keep: A Narrative of the American Encounter with Anti-Semitism.* New York: Times Books, 1979.

Selzer, Michael. *"Kike!" A Documentary History of Anti-Semitism in America.* New York: World Publishers, 1972.

WEBSITES

"Jacques Maritain." Acton Institute. Available online at http://www.acton.org/research/libtrad/maritain.html (accessed July 2, 2002).

"Jacques Maritain." Biography Online Database. Available online at http://search.biography.com/print_record.pl?id=9767 (accessed July 2, 2002).

Spring Hill College. Theology Library Resources for the Study of Antisemitism. Available online at http://www.shc.edu/theolibrary/antisem.htm (accessed July 2, 2002).

Constitution of the American Council of Christian Churches
Constitution

By: American Council of Christian Churches
Date: 1941
Source: Constitution of the American Council of Christian Churches. Available online at http://www.amcouncilcc.org/constitu.htm (accessed February 13, 2002).
About the Organization: The American Council of Christian Churches, headquartered in Bethlehem, Pennsylvania, is composed of representatives from a number of fundamentalist churches belonging to various denominations and fellowships. Established in 1941, the council has always considered itself multidenominational in that each member church maintains its own identity and has complete autonomy over its own affairs. ∎

Introduction

The American Council of Christian Churches (ACCC) consists of pastors, churches, and church members who adhere to biblical fundamentalism, the belief that everything in the Bible is literally true. The ACCC supports the goals of seeking the truth as presented in the Bible and preserving traditional Christian heritage.

In its efforts to affirm and promote biblical fundamentalism, the ACCC has tried to distance itself from liberal theological thought and practice. Council members, in defense of the Bible, view liberal theology as leading to ecumenical apostasy, or the abandonment of the Christian faith. They see liberal Christians as more concerned about social and political causes than the basics of their religion.

The fundamentalist Christian tradition traces its roots to the organized evangelical movement in the 1920s. The evangelical movement consisted of Protestant churches that centered their teachings on the Christian gospel as presented in the Bible. Fundamentalism was a collective response of Christians who disagreed with liberalism and secularism. Liberalism, a Protestant movement that originated in the nineteenth century, stresses the humanitarian and ethical dimensions of Christianity and deemphasizes traditional dogmatic, or authoritative, theology. Secularism is a philosophy that emphasizes human rather than religious values.

The ACCC deliberately organized itself as multidenominational but not interdenominational. The Council did not intend to form a new Christian group or denomination. Rather it wanted to preserve the individual identities and characteristics of existing groups and retain the historic diversity of the Christian faith. Primarily the ACCC strived to involve "Bible-believing" churches in their mission, to provide a meeting ground for common theological discussion, and to deal with issues that affected Christian fundamentalists.

The theological common ground of ACCC members is evident in its list of fundamental doctrines of the Christian faith: "the inspiration and inerrancy of Scripture; the deity of Jesus Christ, His virgin birth, substitutionary blood atonement [Jesus died so human beings could have eternal salvation], His literal bodily resurrection and His Second Coming 'in power and great glory.'"

Significance

The ACCC grew to about two million members in 2000. Member churches that year included Bible Presbyterian Church, Evangelical Methodist Church, Fellowship of Fundamental Bible Churches, Free Presbyterian Church of North America, Fundamental Methodist Church, General Association of Regular Baptist Churches, Independent Baptist Fellowship of North America, and Independent Churches Affiliated. In addition hundreds of independent local churches belonged.

The ACCC, a conservative assembly of churches, should not be confused with the National Council of Churches of Christ in the United States of America (NCC), a more liberal assembly established in 1950. About 52 million American Christians belong to churches that hold membership in the NCC. Although smaller than the NCC and the even larger World Council of Churches (WCC), the ACCC has not avoided taking unpopular and controversial positions and has often found itself at the opposite end of the theological spectrum from the NCC and WCC.

Primary Source

Constitution of the American Council of Christian Churches [excerpt]

SYNOPSIS: The preamble or introduction to the ACCC's constitution presents the theological reasons for the Council's formation. The first three articles of the constitution follow. Article I identifies

the religious group, Article II contains its basic beliefs, and Article III lists the rules for membership. The remaining articles of the constitution, which are not included below, deal with voting power, meetings, authority, officers, expenses, bylaws and amendments.

> Contending for the faith which was once delivered unto the saints (Jude 3).

Preamble

WHEREAS, It is the duty of all true churches of the Lord Jesus Christ to make a clear testimony to their faith in Him, especially in these darkening days of apostasy in many professing churches, by which apostasy whole denominations in their official capacity, as well as individual churches, have been swept into a paganizing stream of modernism under various names and in varying degree; and

WHEREAS, There has been a notable growth of autocratic domination especially on the part of modernistic leaders by whom the rightful powers of true churches are often usurped and are now being usurped; and

WHEREAS, The commands of God to His people to be separate from all unbelief and corruption are clear and positive; and

WHEREAS, We believe the times demand the formation of an agency, for fellowship and cooperation on the part of Bible-believing churches for the maintenance of a testimony pure and steadfast to the great fundamental truths of the Word of God as held by the historic Christian Church through the centuries, for the accomplishment of tasks which can better be done in cooperation than separately, and to facilitate the discharge of the obligations which inhere in the Commission of Christ to His Church.

THEREFORE, the constituent denominations forming this Council, do now establish it as an agency, without compromise or evasion, unreservedly dedicated as a witness to "the faith once delivered unto the saints."

Article I: Name

The name of this organization shall be The American Council of Christian Churches.

Article II: Doctrinal Statement

Among other equally biblical truths, we believe and maintain the following:

The plenary divine inspiration of the Scriptures in the original languages, their consequent inerrancy and infallibility, and, as the Word of God, the supreme and final authority in faith and life;

The Triune God: Father, Son and Holy Spirit;

The essential, absolute, eternal deity, and the real and proper, but sinless, humanity of our Lord Jesus Christ;

His birth of the Virgin Mary;

His substitutionary, expiatory death, in that He gave His life "a ransom for many";

His resurrection from among the dead in the same body in which He was crucified, and the second coming of this same Jesus in power and great glory;

The total depravity of man through the Fall;

Salvation, the effect of regeneration by the Spirit and the Word, not by works, but by grace through faith;

The everlasting bliss of the saved, and the everlasting suffering of the lost;

The real spiritual unity in Christ of all re-deemed by His precious blood;

The necessity of maintaining, according to the Word of God, the purity of the Church in doc-trine and life.

Article III: Membership

Section 1. Relationship to this Council shall be of two kinds: CONSTITUENT MEMBERS and INDI-VIDUAL MEMBERS.

Section 2. CONSTITUENT MEMBERS shall be of two classes; General Constituent Members shall be such autonomous national churches or associations of Christians as shall be in full agreement with the purposes of this Council as expressed in its Pre-amble and Doctrinal Statement, and may be admit-ted by a three-fourths vote of the delegates of the Council present and voting at a duly called meeting.

Local Constituent Members shall be of such lo-cal or regional congregations, churches or associa-tions of Christians as shall be in full agreement with the purposes of the Council as expressed by its Pre-amble and Doctrinal Statement, and may be admit-ted by a three-fourths vote of the delegates of the Council present and voting at a duly called meeting.

Section 3. INDIVIDUAL MEMBERS shall be such individual Christians as shall be in full agreement with the purposes of the Council as expressed by its Preamble and Doctrinal Statement, and who may be admitted by majority vote of the delegates of the Council present and voting at a duly called meeting.

Section 4. LIMITATIONS TO MEMBERSHIP: No denomination, association of churches, Bible-believ-ing society, individual or church affiliated with, or rep-resented in any manner by, the World Council of Churches (WCC) or any of its affiliates, such as the National Council of Churches of Christ in the U.S.A. (NCC), the World Evangelical Fellowship (WEF) or any of its affiliates, such as the National Association of Evangelicals (NAE), the modern Charismatic Move-ment, or the Ecumenical Movement shall be con-sidered for membership in the Council.

Section 5. EXPULSION FROM MEMBERSHIP: Ex-pulsion from membership may occur when a Con-stituent Body, local church or individual member does not maintain a separatist position in harmony with the ACCC doctrine and practice. Expulsion will require prior notification of the proposed action fol-lowed by a three-fourths vote of the Executive Com-mittee and majority approval of the Council Members at an Annual Meeting.

Further Resources

BOOKS

Falwell, Jerry, ed. *The Fundamentalist Phenomenon: The Resurgence of Conservative Christianity.* Garden City, N.Y.: Doubleday & Co., 1981.

Hunter, James Davison. "The Evangelical Worldview Since 1890." In *Piety and Politics: Evangelicals and Fundamen-talists Confront the World.* Richard John Neuhaus and Michael Cromartie, eds. Washington, D.C.: Ethics and Pub-lic Policy Center, 1987.

———. *Evangelicalism: The Coming Generation.* Chicago: University of Chicago Press, 1987.

WEBSITES

"Group Watch: American Council of Christian Churches." Pub-lic Eye. Available online at http://www.publiceye.org /research/Group_Watch/Entries-02.htm (accessed July 2, 2002).

"Introducing ACCC." American Council of Christian Churches. http://www.amcouncilcc.org/introduc.htm (accessed July 2, 2002).

"Why Do the Members of Christ Tear One Another?"

Newspaper article

By: Dorothy Day
Date: February 1942
Source: Day, Dorothy. "Why Do the Members of Christ Tear One Another?" *The Catholic Worker,* February 1942. Available online at http://www.catholicworker.org/dorothyday/daytext.cfm

?TextID=390; website home page: http://www.catholicworker .org (accessed April 22, 2003).

About the Author: Dorothy Day (1897–1980), born in Brooklyn, New York, was a committed Marxist until her conversion to Roman Catholicism in 1927. As a result, she developed into a famous social reformer and activist. In 1933 she co-founded the Catholic Worker Movement and guided its work in peace advocacy, civil rights, and labor union justice. Even during World War II (1939–1945), when most Americans supported the war effort, she remained a staunch anti-war activist. ■

Introduction

Despite the unpopularity of Dorothy Day's anti-war stance prior to and during World War II, she maintained her strongly held beliefs and denounced all wars. Her condemnation of war, based on her interpretations of Catholicism and Christianity, led her to accept pacifism as a strategy for social change and as a goal in itself.

During the 1930s Day was deemed newsworthy not so much for her pacifism but for her "hospitality houses" and other charitable work with the unemployed, the poor, and the oppressed during the Great Depression. Day's work during this time was part of the Catholic Worker Movement that she helped establish in 1933. She and her co-founder Peter Maurin applied Christian values to the solution of social problems. They traveled around the country visiting Catholic Worker communities and speaking about the movement to whatever groups would listen.

Day's anti-war position became very controversial in the early 1940s. By then it seemed inevitable that the United States would be drawn into the conflict in Europe. When the United States finally entered the war in December 1941 in retaliation for Japan's attack on Pearl Harbor, Day stayed true to her belief that war is never justifiable and that it is always morally wrong to kill another human being, whether civilian or soldier. To her, pacifism meant that one would not fight back even if physically attacked.

Some American Catholics and other Christians agreed with Day's position, but most did not. Official Roman Catholic theology stated that war was morally acceptable if it were just, that is, defended a right or corrected a wrong. Completely disagreeing with the Church's official position, Day said that war can never be justified under any conditions.

Significance

Once the United States entered the war, the large audiences that listened to Day's speeches grew sparser. Americans no longer wanted to hear anti-war, pacifist talks. Most supported the war effort and viewed such talks as unpatriotic. Even with the pro-war mood of the country working against her, Day continued her campaign, stat-ing that Christians had a moral obligation to disobey laws that they considered unjust. When the military draft was required by law in 1940, she encouraged Christians not to fight and told those who would listen that they should pray, fast, and give to the poor instead.

After World War II Day and the Catholic Worker movement persisted in their anti-war activism, protesting the Korean War (1950–1953) and the Vietnam War (1964–1975). They also participated in the civil rights movement during the 1960s.

Day's influence continues into the twenty-first century. Her moral justifications against war and her philosophy of pacifism are very much alive. Anti-war groups still use them in explaining their positions. She is so well respected and admired for her work that there is a movement among American Roman Catholics to have her canonized as a saint.

Primary Source

"Why Do the Members of Christ Tear One Another?"

SYNOPSIS: Dorothy Day defends her opposition to war in the February 1942 issue of *The Catholic Worker* newspaper. She defends the pacifist position of the Catholic Worker Movement by saying that its members do not avoid war because they are afraid of suffering, as proven by their regular battles with poverty, disease, filth, and cold in the slums of America's cities.

Fr. Stratman writes: "We think with Cardinal Faulhaber that Catholic moral theology must in fact begin to speak a new language, and that what the last two Popes have already pronounced in the way of general sentences of condemnation on modern war should be translated into the systematic terminology of the schools. The simple preacher and pastor can, however, already begin by making his own, words of the reigning Holy Father (Pius XI), 'murder,' 'suicide,' 'monstrous crime.'"

"But we are at war," people say. "This is no time to talk of peace. It is demoralizing to the armed forces to protest, not to cheer them on in their fight for Christianity, for democracy, for civilization. Now that it is under way, it is too late to do anything about it." One reader writes to protest against our "frail" voices "blatantly" crying out against war. (The word blatant comes from bleat, and we are indeed poor sheep crying out to the Good Shepherd to save us from these horrors.) Another Catholic newspaper says it sympathizes with our sentimentality. This is a charge always leveled against pacifists. We are supposed to be afraid of the suffering, of the hardships of war.

But let those who talk of softness, of sentimentality, come to live with us in cold, unheated houses in the slums. Let them come to live with the criminal, the unbalanced, the drunken, the degraded, the pervert. (It is not decent poor, it is not the decent sinner who was the recipient of Christ's love.) Let them live with rats, with vermin, bedbugs, roaches, lice (I could describe the several kinds of body lice).

Let their flesh be mortified by cold, by dirt, by vermin; let their eyes be mortified by the sight of bodily excretions, diseased limbs, eyes, noses, mouths.

Let their noses be mortified by the smells of sewage, decay and rotten flesh. Yes, and the smell of the sweat, blood and tears spoken of so blithely by Mr. Churchill, and so widely and bravely quoted by comfortable people.

Let their ears be mortified by harsh and screaming voices, by the constant coming and going of people living herded together with no privacy. (There is no privacy in tenements just as there is none in concentration camps.)

Let their taste be mortified by the constant eating of insufficient food cooked in huge quantities for hundreds of people, the coarser foods, the cheaper foods, so that there will be enough to go around; and the smell of such cooking is often foul.

Then when they have lived with these comrades, with these sights and sounds, let our critics talk of sentimentality.

"Love in practice is a harsh and dreadful thing compared to love in dreams."

Our Catholic Worker groups are perhaps too hardened to the sufferings in the class war, living as they do in refugee camps, the refugees being as they are victims of the class war we live in always. We live in the midst of this war now these many years. It is a war not recognized by the majority of our comfortable people. They are pacifists themselves when it comes to the class war. They even pretend it is not there.

Many friends have counseled us to treat this world war in the same way. "Don't write about it. Don't mention it. Don't jeopardize the great work you are doing among the poor, among the workers. Just write about constructive things like Houses of Hospitality and Farming Communes. "Keep silence with

a bleeding heart," one reader, a man, pro-war and therefore not a sentimentalist, writes us.

But we cannot keep silent. We have not kept silence in the face of the monstrous injustice of the class war, or the race war that goes on side by side with this world war (which the Communist used to call the imperialist war.)

Read the letters in this issue of the paper, the letter from the machine shop worker as to the deadening, degrading hours of labor. Read the quotation from the missioner's letter from China. Remember the unarmed steel strikers, the coal miners, shot down on picket lines. Read the letter from our correspondent in Seattle who told of the treatment accorded agricultural workers in the North West. Are these workers supposed to revolt? These are Pearl Harbor incidents! Are they supposed to turn to arms in the class conflict to defend their lives, their homes, their wives and children?

Another Pearl Harbor

Last month a Negro in Missouri was shot and dragged by a mob through the streets behind a car. His wounded body was then soaked in kerosene. The mob of white Americans then set fire to it, and when the poor anguished victim had died, the body was left lying in the street until a city garbage cart trucked it away. Are the Negroes supposed to "Remember Pearl Harbor" and take to arms to avenge this cruel wrong? No, the Negroes, the workers in general, are expected to be "pacifist" in the face of this aggression.

Love Is the Measure

Perhaps we are called sentimental because we speak of love. We say we love our president, our country. We say that we love our enemies, too. "Hell," Bernanos said, "is not to love any more."

"Greater love hath no man than this," Christ said, "that he should lay down his life for his friend."

"Love is the measure by which we shall be judged," St. John of the Cross said.

"Love is the fulfilling of the law," St. John, the beloved disciple said.

Read the last discourse of Jesus to his disciples. Read the letters of St. John in the New Testament. And how can we express this love—by bombers, by blockades?

Here is a clipping from the *Herald Tribune,* a statement of a soldier describing the use of the bayonet against the Japanese: "He (his father) should have been with us and seen how good it was. We got into them good and proper, and I can't say I remember much about it, except that it made me feel pretty good. I reckon that was the way with the rest of the company, by the way my pals were yelling all the time."

Is this a Christian speaking?

"Love is an exchange of gifts," St. Ignatius said.

Love is a breaking of bread.

Remember the story of Christ meeting His disciples at Emmaus? All along the road He had discoursed to them, had expounded the scriptures. And then they went into the inn at Emmaus, and sat down to the table together. And He took bread and blessed it and broke it and handed it to them, and they knew Him in the breaking of bread! (St. Luke, 24, 13-35.)

Love is not the starving of whole populations. Love is not the bombardment of open cities. Love is not killing, it is the laying down of one's life for one's friend.

Worse Than Others

Hear Fr. Zossima, in the brothers Karamazev [sic]: "Love one another, Fathers," he said, speaking to his monks.

> Love God's people. Because we have come here and shut ourselves within these walls, we are no holier than those that are outside, but on the contrary, from the very fact of coming here, each of us has confessed to himself that he is worse than others, than all men on earth . . . And the longer the monk lives in his seclusion, the more keenly he must recognize that. Else he would have no reason to come here.

Responsible for All Sins

> When he realizes that he is not only worse than others, but that he is responsible to all men for all and everything, for all human sins, national and individual, only then the aim of our seclusion is attained. For know, dear ones, that every one of us is undoubtedly responsible for all men and everything on earth, not merely through the general sinfulness of creation, but each one personally for all mankind and every individual man. For monks are not a special sort of man, but only what all men ought to be. Only through that knowledge, our heart grows soft with infinite, universal, inexhaustible love. Then every one of you will have the power to win over the whole world by love and to wash away the sins of the world with your tears . . . Each of you keep watch over your heart and confess your sins to yourself

unceasingly . . . Hate not the atheists, the teachers of evil, the materialists, and I mean not only the good ones—for there are many good ones among them, especially in our day—hate not even the wickedness. Remember them in your prayers thus: Save, O Lord, all those who have none to pray for them, save too all those who will not pray. And add, it is not in pride that I make this prayer, O Lord, for I am lower than all men . . .

"Holier Than Thou"

I quote this because that accusation "holier than thou" is also made against us. And we must all admit our guilt, our participation in the social order which has resulted in this monstrous crime of war.

We used to have a poor demented friend who came into the office to see us very often, beating his breast, quoting the penitential psalms in Hebrew, and saying that everything was his fault. Through all he had done and left undone, he had brought about the war, the revolution.

That should be our cry, with every mouthful we eat, "We are starving Europe!" When we look to our comfort in a warm bed, a warm home, we must cry, "My brother, my mother, my child is dying of cold."

"I am lower than all men, because I do not love enough. O God take away my heart of stone and give me a heart of flesh."

Further Resources

BOOKS

Miller, William D. *Dorothy Day: A Biography.* San Francisco: Harper & Row, 1982.

O'Connor, June. *The Moral Vision of Dorothy Day: A Feminist Perspective.* New York: Crossroad, 1991.

O'Grady, Jim. *Dorothy Day: With Love for the Poor.* Staten Island, N.Y.: Ward Hill Press, 1993.

PERIODICALS

Anderson, George M., "Dorothy Day Centenary." *America,* November 29, 1997.

Krupa, Stephen J., "Celebrating Dorothy Day: Dorothy Day Continues to Represent the Radical Conscience of American Catholicism." *America,* August 27, 2001.

WEBSITES

"Dorothy Day." Resources for Catholic Educators. Available online at http://www.silk.net/RelEd/day.htm (accessed August 28, 2002).

Riegle, Rosalie G. "Mystery and Myth: Dorothy Day, the Catholic Worker, and the Peace Movement." *Fellowship Magazine,* Nov–Dec. 1997. Available online at http://www.forusa.org/fellowship/Archives/fel1197-11.htm (accessed April 22, 2003).

Peace of Mind

Theological work

By: Joshua Loth Liebman

Date: 1946

Source: Liebman, Joshua Loth. *Peace of Mind.* New York: Simon and Schuster, 1946. Excerpts available online at http://akoven.tripod.com/jewishhealingtherapies/id2.html; website home page: http://akoven.tripod.com (accessed February 9, 2002).

About the Author: Joshua Loth Liebman (1907–1948), born in Hamilton, Ohio, was a well-known Jewish Reform rabbi, author, and radio preacher. He entered college when he was only 13 years old and graduated from the University of Cincinnati at 19. In 1930, at the age of 23, he was ordained at the Hebrew Union College in Cincinnati, Ohio. Nine years later, he became a rabbi at Temple Israel in Boston, where he served until his death. ■

Introduction

In his best-selling book, *Peace of Mind: Insights on Human Nature that Can Change Your Life,* Rabbi Liebman argued that religion and psychology can find common ground in helping people achieve inner security and strength. His book provided Americans with much-needed reassurance following World War II (1939–1945). During the war 405,000 Americans died and 671,000 were wounded. Surviving soldiers were finally coming home, but many of them had lasting physical and mental wounds from the horrors they had experienced.

To help war-weary Americans find inner peace, Liebman combined religion with a psychological framework that interpreted the functioning of the human mind. Psychology by itself would not be enough to achieve the peace of mind people wanted, Liebman maintained. Religion would provide the missing ingredients: a proper interpretation of life, a proper commitment, and a proper perspective. In other words, psychology would help people to realize what is and religion would reveal what ought to be.

By "proper interpretation of life" Liebman meant the realization that life is difficult and not always filled with goodness. Experiencing life sometimes included personal defeats and tragedies. Trying to achieve complete success in what one attempts is frustrating because perfection is an illusion.

"Proper commitment," in conjunction with a proper interpretation of life, leads to personal growth and the attainment of moral and emotional maturity. This commitment involves giving to the world and others in one's life as much as one demands from them. Meeting the needs of others is as important as meeting one's own needs. By avoiding selfishness and self-centeredness, people can achieve their desired maturity.

An elderly Rabbi studies the Talmud with a student in 1944 New York. After the traumas of World War II, hundreds of thousands of Jews, as well as people from other religious traditions, received guidance from Rabbi Joshua Liebman's *Peace of Mind.* © LUCIEN AIGNER/CORBIS. REPRODUCED BY PERMISSION.

Once a person has attained proper interpretation and commitment, he or she must develop "proper perspective." This requires the realization that occasional bouts of depression or attacks of the blues are normal for all human beings, regardless of how well life is going or how bad things become at times. Human beings are complex creations with a mixture of passing feelings and emotions. Everyone feels sad at times, but the sadness should pass away. Feeling relatively happy and contented should replace these down episodes.

Liebman assured his readers that God would help them in their time of need. With the help of God and through prayer everyone can develop peace of mind. The formula must include the proper interpretation of life, proper commitment, and proper perspective. To Liebman God was the Power who would provide for righteousness, personal salvation, and social salvation. It was up to human beings to embrace God's goodness and actively work toward their own inner peace and happiness.

Significance

Peace of Mind helped heal the psychological scars of a generation that had undergone considerable pain and suffering. The book was ranked either first or second on the national nonfiction best-seller lists for much of 1946, and for a time sold more than 5,000 copies a week. It has had more than forty printings and been translated into several languages. The need for healing was already present and Rabbi Liebman offered one way to help answer that dire need.

Hundreds of thousands of Jews, as well as people from other religious traditions, received guidance from *Peace of Mind* after the traumas of World War II. Liebman's work is still relevant as new generations seek to attain the goal of inner peace in the twenty-first century.

Primary Source

Peace of Mind [excerpt]

> **SYNOPSIS:** The following excerpts from Rabbi Joshua Liebman's best-selling spiritual self-help book contain samples of practical insights on human nature. Liebman explains peace of mind and how to attain it. Many of the ideas in *Peace of Mind* were also presented in his sermons at Temple Israel in Boston.

"This is the gift [peace of mind] that God reserves for His special protégés," he [Liebman's spiritual mentor] said. "Talent and beauty He gives to many. Wealth is commonplace, fame not rare. But peace of mind—that is . . . the fondest sign of His love. . . . Most men are never blessed with it; others wait all their lives—yes, far into advanced age—for this gift to descend upon them." . . .

I have come to understand that peace of mind is the characteristic mark of God Himself, and that it has always been the true goal of the considered life. . . . Slowly, painfully, I have learned that peace of mind may transform a cottage into a spacious manor hall; the want of it can make a regal park an imprisoning nutshell.

The quest for this unwearied inner peace is constant and universal. Probe deeply into the teachings of Buddha, Maimonides, or à Kempis, and you will discover that they base their diverse doctrines on the foundations of a large spiritual serenity. Analyze the prayers of troubled, overborne mankind of all creeds in every age—and their petitions come down to the irreducible common denominators of daily bread and inward peace. . . .

Especially today, when the prayers of men ascend, mourning and wailing to the Bestower of Gifts, they plead for an inward tranquility that is both a fortress and a sanctuary. And with reason. Modern man is treading a narrow defile that skirts an Inferno of such destruction as Dante could not envision nor Doré depict. Stricken by psychic anxieties, cloven by emotional conflicts, beset by economic insecurities, assailed by political doubts and cynicisms, the plucked rooster, man, is a peculiarly vulnerable fowl as he struts along the path of civilization. He has crowed a good deal in his time, rather bravely in spots. But now he begins to suspect that the ax of destiny is being sharpened for his neck. He trembles, pales, calls for madder music, stronger wine to drown the approaching specter of his fate. For the fact emerges that contemporary man, like T. S. Eliot's fatigued and pitiful Prufrock, is afraid!

In his fear he casts about for devices and techniques of salvation—something that will carry him through new dangers and give him sorely needed courage to face the old ones. What he needs (what we all need) is not a set of reassuring answers—for no such formula of reassurance exists—but rather an inner equilibrium, a spiritual stability that is proof against confusion and disaster. Peace of mind must not be identified with ivory-tower escapism from the hurly-burly of life, nor is it, as Whitehead points out, "a negative conception of anesthesia." Rather, it enables us to accept the pummelings of fate and fortune with a kind of equanimity—even with a kind of eagerness sprung of the sure knowledge that such buffetings cannot divert us from our creative life course.

Serious-minded social reformers ask in all sincerity: "Have men the *right* to peace of mind today? Is anyone morally justified even in contemplating this state when the world is in such a tumult of reconstruction?" We reply: "No reconstructed society can be built on unreconstructed individuals. Personal unbalance *never* leads to social stability. And Peace of mind is the indispensable prerequisite of individual and social balance."

Further Resources

BOOKS

Liebman, Joshua Loth. *Hope for Man: An Optimistic Philosophy and Guide to Self-fulfillment.* New York: Simon and Schuster, 1966.

———. *Meaning of Life.* Cincinnati, Ohio: Hebrew Union College, Jewish Institute of Religion, 1950.

———. *Morality and Immorality: the Problem of Conscience.* Cincinnati, Ohio: Hebrew Union College, Jewish Institute of Religion, 1950.

WEBSITES

The Judaism Site. Available online at http://www.torah.org (accessed April 22, 2003).

"Spirituality: Judaism." Seattle Community Network. Available online at http://www.scn.org/spiritual/judaism (accessed April 22, 2003).

Everson v. Board of Education of Ewing

Supreme Court decision

By: Hugo LaFayette Black

Date: February 10, 1947

Source: *Everson v. Board of Education of Ewing TP.* 330 U.S. 1 (1947). Available online at http://laws.findlaw.com/us/330/1.html; website home page: http://www.findlaw.com (accessed February 5, 2003).

About the Author: Justice Hugo LaFayette Black (1886–1971), born in Harlan, Alabama, was a Democratic senator from 1927 to 1937. President Franklin D. Roosevelt (served 1933–1945) appointed him to the United States Supreme Court in 1937, a position he held until 1971. Controversial and contradictory as a justice, Black was noted especially for his strong defense of the rights of citizens as guaranteed by the First Amendment of the Constitution. ■

Introduction

Arch R. Everson, a resident and taxpayer in Ewing, New Jersey, challenged a state law allowing local boards of education to reimburse parents for the expense of sending their children to either public or private schools on public transportation buses. Specifically Everson argued that the state should not reimburse parents who sent their children to Catholic schools because this violated the principle of separation of church and state.

The Everson case went to a New Jersey trial court which ruled that the state law was unconstitutional. The New Jersey Supreme Court reversed that decision and upheld the state law. Everson then appealed this ruling to the U. S. Supreme Court, the highest court in the nation.

The Supreme Court also upheld the state statute, ruling that it was constitutionally permissible to reimburse parents of parochial school students for transportation expenses. The majority opinion of the Court, signed by five out of nine justices, ruled that the law benefited the parents and not the church-affiliated schools; therefore it did not violate the separation of church and state principle.

The separation of church and state principle, also called the Establishment Clause, grew out of the Supreme Court's interpretation of the First Amendment of the U.S. Constitution. The First Amendment states: "Congress shall make no law respecting an establishment of religion or prohibiting the free exercise thereof." The Court has

determined that the Establishment Clause applies to individual states as well as the federal government.

Justice Black, in writing the decision for the court, observed that while the Constitution required a separation of church and state, the state should not be hostile to religion. The state must remain neutral in its actions toward religion. On the one hand it cannot legally promote any specific religion; on the other hand it cannot act to suppress a religion or place unnecessary and unreasonable obstacles in its way.

Significance

Those who opposed the use of public funding for any religious activity under any conditions were extremely disappointed by this Supreme Court decision. They viewed the use of state money to reimburse parents' expenses in sending their children to Catholic schools as direct government aid to religious institutions and thus as a clear violation of the Constitution.

Those in favor of this type of public funding argued that it helped parents who paid taxes to support public schools even though their children did not attend them. The proponents believed that it was only fair for those parents to get some kind of relief since the state did not have to provide public school education for their children.

The *Everson v. Board of Education* decision remained a valid legal precedent, affecting at least five other related decisions: *McGowan v. Maryland* (1961), *Engel v. Vitale* (1962), *Lemon v. Kurtzman* (1971), *Abington School District v. Schempp* (1973), and *The Committee for Public Education and Religious Liberty v. Nyquist* (1973).

Primary Source

Everson v. Board of Education of Ewing [excerpt]

SYNOPSIS: In this decision the U.S. Supreme Court rules it is constitutional for the government to reimburse parents for bus transportation costs whether they send their children to a religious or public school. The court finds that the First Amendment provision for separation between church and state was not being violated in this case. The case was decided on February 10, 1947.

Mr. Justice Black delivered the opinion of the Court.

A New Jersey statute authorizes its local school districts to make rules and contracts for the transportation of children to and from schools. The appellee, a township board of education, acting pursuant to this statute authorized reimbursement to parents of money expended by them for the bus

A school bus waits outside of Holy Child School in Suffern, New York, 1942. In *Everson v. Board of Education* (1947), the Supreme Court ruled that parents could receive reimbursement from the state for bus transportation costs whether their children attend public *or* parochial schools. **THE LIBRARY OF CONGRESS.**

transportation of their children on regular busses operated by the public transportation system. Part of this money was for the payment of transportation of some children in the community to Catholic parochial schools. These church schools give their students, in addition to secular education, regular religious instruction conforming to the religious tenets and modes of worship of the Catholic Faith. The superintendent of these schools is a Catholic priest.

The appellant, in his capacity as a district taxpayer, filed suit in a State court challenging the right of the Board to reimburse parents of parochial school students. He contended that the statute and the resolution passed pursuant to it violated both the State and the Federal Constitutions. That court held that the legislature was without power to authorize such payment under the State constitution. The New Jersey Court of Errors and Appeals reversed, holding that neither the statute nor the resolution passed pursuant to it was in conflict with the State constitution or the provisions of the Federal Constitution in issue. . . .

. . . [W]e cannot say that the First Amendment prohibits New Jersey from spending tax-raised funds

to pay the bus fares of parochial school pupils as a part of a general program under which it pays the fares of pupils attending public and other schools. It is undoubtedly true that children are helped to get to church schools. There is even a possibility that some of the children might not be sent to the church schools if the parents were compelled to pay their children's bus fares out of their own pockets when transportation to a public school would have been paid for by the State. The same possibility exists where the state requires a local transit company to provide reduced fares to school children including those attending parochial schools, or where a municipally owned transportation system undertakes to carry all school children free of charge. Moreover, state-paid policemen, detailed to protect children going to and from church schools from the very real hazards of traffic, would serve much the same purpose and accomplish much the same result as state provisions intended to guarantee free transportation of a kind which the state deems to be best for the school children's welfare. And parents might refuse to risk their children to the serious danger of traffic accidents going to and from parochial schools, the approaches to which were not protected by policemen. Similarly, parents might be reluctant to permit their children to attend schools which the state had cut off from such general government services as ordinary police and fire protection, connections for sewage disposal, public highways and sidewalks. Of course, cutting off church schools from these services, so separate and so indisputably marked off from the religious function, would make it far more difficult for the schools to operate. But such is obviously not the purpose of the First Amendment. That Amendment requires the state to be a neutral in its relations with groups of religious believers and non-believers; it does not require the state to be their adversary. State power is no more to be used so as to handicap religions, than it is to favor them.

This Court has said that parents may, in the discharge of their duty under state compulsory education laws, send their children to a religious rather than a public school if the school meets the secular educational requirements which the state has power to impose. It appears that these parochial schools meet New Jersey's requirements. The State contributes no money to the schools. It does not support them. Its legislation, as applied, does no more than provide a general program to help parents get their children, regardless of their religion, safely and expeditiously to and from accredited schools.

The First Amendment has erected a wall between church and state. That wall must be kept high and impregnable. We could not approve the slightest breach. New Jersey has not breached it here.

Affirmed.

Further Resources

BOOKS

Eastland, Terry, ed. *Religious Liberty in the Supreme Court: The Cases that Define the Debate Over Church and State.* Washington, D.C.: Ethics and Public Policy Institute, 1993.

Howe, Mark De Wolfe. *The Garden and the Wilderness: Religion and Government in American Constitutional History.* Chicago: University of Chicago Press, 1965.

Levy, Leonard Williams. *The Establishment Clause: Religion and the First Amendment,* 2d ed. Chapel Hill: University of North Carolina Press, 1994.

WEBSITES

Batte, Susan. "Important Establishment Clause Cases Dealing with Religion and Education: 1899 to 1970." Constitutional Principle: Separation of Church and State. Availabe online at http://members.tripod.com/~candst/table1.htm (accessed April 22, 2003).

Optatissima Pax
Papal encyclical

By: Pius XII

Date: December 18, 1947

Source: Pope Pius XII. *Optatissima Pax.* Rome, December 18, 1947. Available online at http://www.vatican.va/holy_father/pius_xii/encyclicals/documents/hf_p-xii_enc_18121947_optatissima-pax_en.html; website home page: http://www.vatican.va (accessed February 5, 2003).

About the Author: Pope Pius XII (1876–1958), born Eugenio Maria Guiseppe Giovanni Pacelli, was ordained a priest in 1899. After becoming a papal diplomat, he was elevated to cardinal in 1929. In 1930 he served as Vatican secretary of state until his election as pope in 1939, a post he held until his death. ∎

Introduction

By the end of World War II (1939–1945), Americans, along with the rest of the world, felt weary and dispirited. Years of bloodshed, destruction, and ruin had left people physically, mentally, and spiritually exhausted. Nevertheless, most believed that the post-war era would introduce a new age and that they must prepare themselves to rebuild and to maintain the shaky peace threatened by the pending "Cold War" between communist and democratic nations.

As Christmas 1947 approached, people yearned for hope and the restoration of peaceful normality. In response, Pope Pius XII wrote an encyclical, or letter to the leadership of the Catholic Church, shortly before Christmas, a season of hope and joy for Christians. On December 18 he issued *Optatissima Pax* to Catholics and all others in the world, calling for public prayers for social and world peace.

The pope believed that public prayers would focus group consciousness on achieving peace. Private prayers said by individual Christians would not be enough. People needed to pray together openly and publicly if they hoped to achieve the peace they desired.

In America tens of thousands of wounded soldiers with debilitating handicaps were home from the war zones in Europe and Asia, trying to rebuild their lives. Families of dead soldiers had to cope somehow without their missing loved ones and years of public anger against the enemy had to be transformed into caring and concern for its future. Pius told his followers that God must have an important part in meeting these challenges and that public prayers would help heal these wounds.

Trusting in and relying on the power of prayer, Pope Pius XII believed that petitions to God by millions of people would improve the spiritual life of both the individual and of the society. Group prayers had been em-

Pope Pius XII. The pope's encyclical *Optatissima Pax* called for public prayers for social and world peace. PUBLIC DOMAIN.

ployed by soldiers in battle as they faced enemy fire and many of them reported that praying helped them to find the strength and courage to carry on the fight. If prayers seemed to be answered in wartime by a merciful God, then they certainly should be powerful in seeking peace, brotherhood, and social justice in the postwar era.

Significance

The encyclical was very well received by Catholics and people of other faiths in the United States. The call for public prayers was addressed in Sunday church sermons, newspaper articles, and radio programs. American Catholics and non-Catholics realized that what the pope advocated made good spiritual sense. Public prayer would help in the healing process that the nation needed.

Pope Pius XII also stated that prayers for peace alone would not be sufficient for the good Christian. Practical measures for achieving world peace must be actively sought. Bringing relief to the needy, feeding the hungry, and helping to reduce hatred among people were some of the measures the pope hoped Catholics would actively work toward accomplishing.

In the United States a number of Catholic organizations have been established to deal with these problems. Catholic Charities, Catholic Social Services, the Knights of Columbus, and the Catholic Worker move-

ment are examples of organized efforts to bring about internal peace within the country by providing for those in need. American Catholic international relief organizations have also worked toward helping the needy around the world and have labored in promoting peaceful cooperation among nations.

Primary Source

Optatissima Pax

> **SYNOPSIS:** Following World War II Pope Pius XII saw a need to encourage Catholics and others to pray publicly for social and world peace and to work actively toward its accomplishment. He chose to release his encyclical *Optatissima Pax* one week before Christmas, the celebration of the birth of Christ, to demonstrate Christ's concern and commitment during his life on earth for the attainment of peace.

To the Patriarchs, Primates, Archbishops, Bishops and other Ordinaries in Peace and Communion with the Apostolic See.

Venerable Brethren, Greeting and Apostolic Blessing.

Peace, longed for so hopefully, which should signify the tranquillity of order and serene liberty, even after the cruel experience of a long war, still hangs in uncertain balance, as everyone must note with sadness and alarm. Moreover, people's hearts and minds are kept in a state of anxious suspense, while in not a few nations—already laid waste by the world-conflict and its sorry aftermath of ruin and distress—the social classes are being incited to mutual hatred as their continuous rioting and agitation plainly threaten to subvert the very foundations of civil society.

2. With this scene of disaster and misery before Us, Our heart is heavy with the weight of bitter sorrow and We cannot but feel compelled, by reason of the charge of universal fatherhood which God has laid upon Us, not only to entreat the nations one and all to have done with rancor and make peace once more as friends, but also to urge all Our children in Christ to storm heaven with more fervent prayers, never forgetting that all efforts are inadequate and unavailing if God's good pleasure is not first obtained, according to the inspired words of the Psalmist: "unless the Lord build the house, they labor in vain that build it."

3. The crisis is most serious indeed. Remedies must be found, and found without further delay. On the one hand the economic system of many nations, as a result of fabulous military expenditures and enormous destruction wrought by the war, has been dislocated and weakened to such an extent as to

be powerless to meet the problems with which it is faced, and to provide the materials for appropriate constructive enterprise, where work might be available for the unemployed who now must live their lives in forced and fruitless idleness. On the other hand there is no lack of those who, sad to say, embitter and exploit the working man in his distress, following a secret and astute plan, and thus obstruct the heroic efforts which the forces of justice and order are making to rebuild scattered fortunes.

4. But everyone must come to realize that lost wealth will not be recovered, or present wealth secured, by discord, public tumult, fratricide. This result can be achieved only by working together in harmony, by cooperation, by peaceful labor.

5. Those who deliberately and rashly plan to incite the masses to tumult, sedition, or infringement of the liberty of others are certainly not helping to relieve the poverty of the people but are rather increasing it by fomenting mutual hatred and disturbing the established order; this can even lead to complete chaos. Factional strife "has been and will be to many nations a greater calamity than war itself, than famine or disease."

6. At the same time it is the duty of all to realize that the world crisis is so serious today and so menacing for the future that it is imperative for all, especially the rich, to place the common welfare above their private advantage and profits.

7. But it must be clearly and constantly borne in mind that the first and most urgent need is to reconcile the hearts of men, to bring them to fraternal agreement and cooperation, so that they may set to work upon plans and projects in keeping with the demands of Christian teaching and needs of the present situation.

8. Let all remember that the flood of evil and disaster that has over-taken the world in past years was due chiefly to the fact that the divine religion of Jesus Christ, that provider of mutual charity among citizens, peoples and nations, did not govern, as it should, private, domestic and public life. If things have gone wrong on account of the desertion from Christ, public and private life must return to Him as soon as possible: if error has clouded the minds of men, they must return to that truth which, revealed from on high, indicates the right way to heaven: if hatred has brought them fatal results, they must return to Christian love which alone can heal their many wounds, and carry them over the crisis so filled with danger.

9. At the approach of the consoling feast of Christmas, which recalls the Child Jesus in the cra-

dle and the choir of Angels singing peace to men, We think it opportune to exhort all Christians, especially those in the flower of youth, to crowd around the holy crib and there to pray the Divine Infant to be pleased to ward off the threats of impending struggles and to quench the torches of revolt. May He illumine with light from above minds which are less often moved by stubborn malice than deceived by errors under the semblance of truth; may He repress and soothe rancor in men's minds, compose discords and give new life and vigor to Christian charity. May He teach those who are wealthy, generosity to the poor, and may He console by His example and aid from on high those who are in need and distress and lead them to desire above all those heavenly gifts which are more precious and lasting.

10. During the present difficulties, We place much trust in the prayers of innocent children for whom the Divine Redeemer cherishes a special love. Particularly during Christmas time, let them raise to Him their limpid voices and tiny hands, tokens of interior innocence, in united prayer, imploring peace, harmony and mutual charity. To their fervent prayers, We desire them to add the works of Christian piety and those gifts of Christian generosity which may placate the Divine Justice offended by so many crimes, and, as their means allow, bring relief to the needy.

11. We are confident, Venerable Brethren, that your prompt and zealous action will insure a hearty response to Our paternal exhortation, and that all, especially the young, will answer with enthusiasm this appeal which you will make your own.

12. Relying on this hope, to each and all of you, Venerable Brethren, as well as the flocks confided to your care, We impart with overflowing heart the Apostolic Benediction, a testimony of Our fatherly affection and a pledge of heavenly graces.

Further Resources

BOOKS

Blet, Pierre. *Pius XII and the Second World War: According to the Archives of the Vatican.* New York: Paulist Press, 1999.

Holmes, J. Derek. *The Papacy in the Modern World, 1914-1978.* New York: Crossroad, 1981.

Sanchez, Jose M. *Pius XII and the Holocaust: Understanding the Controversy* Washington, D.C.: Catholic University of America Press, 2002.

WEBSITES

"Papacy." Resources for Catholic Educators. Available online at http://www.silk.net/RelEd/papacy.htm (accessed August 28, 2002).

Hardon, John, S.J. "Papacy Unites the Catholic Church." Available online at http://www.catholic.net/rcc/Periodicals/Faith (accessed August 28, 2002).

McCollum v. Board of Education

Supreme Court decision

By: Hugo Black

Date: March 8, 1948

Source: *McCollum v Board of Education.* 333 U.S. 203 (1948). Available online at http://laws.findlaw.com/us/333 /203.html; website home page: http://www.findlaw.com (accessed February 11, 2002).

About the Author: Hugo LaFayette Black (1886–1971), born in Harlan, Alabama, was a Democratic senator from 1927 to 1937. President Franklin D. Roosevelt (served 1933–1945) appointed him to the United States Supreme Court in 1937, a position he held until 1971. Controversial and contradictory as a justice, he is noted especially for his strong defense of the rights of citizens, as guaranteed by the First Amendment of the U.S. Constitution. ∎

Introduction

In the early 1940s a group of Champaign, Illinois, citizens formed the Champaign Council on Religious Education. This organization, consisting of representatives from local Roman Catholic, Jewish, and Protestant groups, devised a proposal to offer voluntary classes in religion to public school students right in their own schools.

The local board of education agreed to this proposal and cleared the way for weekly religious instruction in public school buildings. The board agreed that all three major faiths in the community—Protestantism, Catholicism, and Judaism—would supply teachers and would have equal access to the school. A time would be set aside during the regular school day for these religious classes. With their parents' permission, students who wished to take these classes would be given release time and sent to certain classrooms. They could choose to attend a class conducted by a Protestant minister, a Roman Catholic priest, or a Jewish rabbi. Students who chose not to take these classes would be assigned to other classrooms or activities in the school. They would not receive instruction in their regular subjects so that students attending the religion classes would not be penalized by missing any academic material.

A resident and taxpayer of the school district, Vashti McCollum, who had a child in the Champaign school system, charged that the religious program violated the constitutional principle of separation of church and state and should not be permitted.

The courts hearing the case had to decide if the use of the public school system for religious classes, even voluntary ones, violated the Establishment Clause. This clause refers to the First Amendment of the Constitution

While her son Terry was a student, Vashti McCollum sued the Champaign (Illinois) school district for providing voluntary religion classes during the school day. **AP/WIDE WORLD PHOTOS. REPRODUCED BY PERMISSION.**

which states: "Congress shall make no law respecting an establishment of religion, or prohibiting the free exercise thereof." The Supreme Court had previously determined that the state cannot favor one religion over another, but had to determine if that condition applied in this case. The board of education believed that it did not because all three major Western religions were given access to the school facilities.

Significance

The majority opinion of the Supreme Court, delivered by Justice Black, stated that allowing religious classes to be taught in public schools was unconstitutional. By giving permission to religious groups to teach these students right in the public schools, the government allowed these groups to spread their faith. This clearly violated the separation of church and state and, therefore, the Establishment Clause.

The Supreme Court ruled that in the future no governmental agencies, including public schools, could help any religious group in the dissemination of its doctrine. Allowing a religious group to use space in a public building to teach its faith amounted to helping that group spread its message, which was unconstitutional. It did not matter if the program were voluntary for the students; it would still be a clear-cut case of the government, through its schools, helping to disseminate religious information.

Since then the practice of allowing religious education to take place in public schools during the regular school day has been prohibited. The justices stated that the decision should not be construed as hostility to religion but rather an enforcement of the Establishment Clause. These principles established by the court would be used in future cases involving questions of separation of church and state.

Primary Source

McCollum v. Board of Education [excerpt]

SYNOPSIS: This landmark Supreme Court decision disallowed the practice of providing space for religious education in public school classrooms during the school day. Allowing this practice would violate the doctrine of separation of church and state stated in the Establishment Clause of the First Amendment to the U. S. Constitution. The case was decided on March 8, 1948.

Mr. Justice Black delivered the opinion of the Court.

This case relates to the power of a state to utilize its tax-supported public school system in aid of religious instruction insofar as that power may be restricted by the First and Fourteenth Amendments to the Federal Constitution.

The appellant, Vashti McCollum, began this action for mandamus [a writ issued by a superior court commanding the performance of a specified official act or duty] against the Champaign Board of Education in the Circuit Court of Champaign County, Illinois. Her asserted interest was that of a resident and taxpayer of Champaign and of a parent whose child was then enrolled in the Champaign public schools. Illinois has a compulsory education law which, with exceptions, requires parents to send their children, aged seven to sixteen, to its tax-supported public schools where the children are to remain in attendance during the hours when the schools are regularly in session. Parents who violate this law commit a misdemeanor punishable by fine unless the children attend private or parochial schools which meet educational standards fixed by the State. District board of education are given general supervisory powers over the use of the public school buildings within the school districts. . . .

Appellant's petition for mandamus alleged that religious teachers, employed by private religious

groups, were permitted to come weekly into the school buildings during the regular hours set apart for secular teaching, and then and there for a period of thirty minutes substitute their religious teaching for the secular education provided under the compulsory education law. The petitioner charged that this joint public-school religious-group program violated the First and Fourteenth Amendments to the United States Constitution. . . .

The board first moved to dismiss the petition on the ground that under Illinois law appellant had no standing to maintain the action. This motion was denied. An answer was then filed, which admitted that regular weekly religious instruction was given during school hours to those pupils whose parents consented and that those pupils were released temporarily from their regular secular classes for the limited purpose of attending the religious classes. The answer denied that this coordinated program of religious instructions violated the State or Federal Constitution. Much evidence was heard, findings of fact were made, after which the petition for mandamus was denied on the ground that the school's religious instruction program violated neither the federal nor state constitutional provisions invoked by the appellant. On appeal the State Supreme Court affirmed. Appellant appealed to this Court . . . and we noted probable jurisdiction.

The appellee presses a motion to dismiss the appeal on several grounds, the first of which is that the judgment of the State Supreme Court does not draw in question the "validity of a statute of any State." . . . This contention rests on the admitted fact that the challenged program of religious instruction was not expressly authorized by statute. But the State Supreme Court has sustained the validity of the program on the ground that the Illinois statutes granted the board authority to establish such a program. . . .

Although there are disputes between the parties as to various inferences that may or may not properly be drawn from the evidence concerning the religious program, the following facts are shown by the record without dispute. In 1940 interested members of the Jewish, Roman Catholic, and a few of the Protestant faiths formed a voluntary association called the Champaign Council on Religious Education. They obtained permission from the Board of Education to offer classes in religious instruction to public school pupils in grades four to nine inclusive. Classes were made up of pupils whose parents signed printed cards requesting that their children

Practice and Usage in Aid to Sectarian Schools and Sectarianism in Public Schools, 1949

States	Rental of church-owned buildings for public-school purposes	Free textbooks furnished parochial-school pupils	Transportation of parochial-school pupils at public expense	Bible-reading in public schools	Excusing pupils for attendance at "week-day church" schools	Religious instruction by church teachers inside public schools during school hours	Use of public schools by religious groups after school hours	Employment of public-school teachers wearing religious garb
1	2	3	4	5	6	7	8	9
Alabama	Yes	No	No	Required	Yes	Yes	Yes	Yes
Alaska	Yes	No	No	No answer	Yes	No	No	No
Arizona	Yes	No	No	No	No	No	Yes	No
Arkansas	Yes	No	No	Required	Yes	No	Yes	Yes
California	Yes	No	Yes	No	Yes	No	No	No
Colorado	Yes	No	Yes	Permitted	Yes	No	Yes	Yes
Connecticut	Yes	No	Yes	Permitted	Yes	No[a]	Yes	No
Delaware	b	No	No	Required	No	No	No[e]	b
District of Columbia	No	No	No	Required	No	No	No	No
Florida	No	No	No	Required	Yes	No	Yes	No
Georgia	b	No	No	Required	Yes	No	Yes	No
Hawaii	Yes	No	Yes	Permitted	Yes	Yes	Yes	Yes
Idaho	Yes	No	No	Required	Yes	No	Yes	No
Illinois	b	No	Yes	No	Yes	No	Yes	Yes
Indiana	No	No	Yes[d]	Permitted	Yes	No	Yes	No
Iowa	No	No	No	Permitted	No	No	Yes	No
Kansas	Yes	No	No	Permitted	Yes	No	Yes	Yes
Kentucky	Yes	No	Yes	Required	Yes	No	Yes	b
Louisiana	Yes	Yes	Yes	No	Yes	Yes	Yes	No
Maine	b	No	No	Required	Yes	No	No	Yes
Maryland	b	No	Yes	Permitted	No	No	No[a]	No
Massachusetts	b	No	Yes	Required	Yes	No	Yes	b
Michigan	Yes	No	Yes	Permitted	Yes	f	Yes	Yes
Minnesota	Yes	No	No	b	Yes	No	Yes	No
Mississippi	b	Yes	No	Permitted	Yes	No	Yes	No
Missouri	Yes	–	No	Permitted	Yes	No	Yes	Yes
Montana	–	No	–	–	–	–	–	–
Nebraska	Yes	No	No	Permitted	No	No	No	No
Nevada	–	–	–	–	–	–	–	–
New Hampshire	b	No	Yes	Premitted	No	No	Yes	b
New Jersey	b	No	Yes	Required	Yes	No	Yes	b
New Mexico	Yes	Yes	Yes	Yes	No	No	Yes	Yes
New York	No	No	Yes	No	Yes	No	No	No
North Carolina	g	No	No	Premitted	No	Yes	No	No
North Dakota	Yes	No	No	Permitted	No	No	Yes	Yes
Ohio	Yes	No	Yes	Permitted	Yes	Yes	Yes	Yes
Oklahoma	Yes	No	No	Permitted	Yes	Yes	Yes	Yes
Oregon	Yes	Yes	Yes	Permitted	Yes	Yes	Yes	No
Pennsylvania	Yes	No	No	Required	Yes	No	No	No
Rhode Island	b	No	Yes	Premitted	Yes	No	Yes	b
South Carolina	Yes	No	No	Permitted	Yes	No	Yes	No
South Dakota	Yes	No	No	No	Yes	No	No	Yes
Tennessee	Yes	No	No	Required	No	No	b	Yes
Texas	b	No	No	Permitted	No	Yes	No[c]	Yes
Utah	Yes	No	No	Permitted	Yes	No	Yes	b
Vermont	b	No	No	Permitted	Yes	Yes	b	b
Virginia	Yes	No	No	Permitted	Yes	Yes	Yes	b
Washington	Yes	No	No	No	No	No	Yes	No
West Virginia	Yes	Yes	No	Permitted	Yes	No	Yes	No
Wisconsin	f	No	No	No	Yes	No	No	b
Wyoming	Yes	No	Yes	Permitted	No	No	Yes	b

[a] Was tried out and found unsuccessful and so discontinued.
[b] Law silent; state superintendent did not comment on practice.
[c] Except when church burned.
[d] If no extra expense is entailed.
[e] Except for church festivals.
[f] No answer.
[g] "No parochial schools in state," reported state superintendent.

SOURCE: "The Status of Religious Education in the Public Schools." Washington, DC: Research Division, National Education Association, 1949, p. 23.

be permitted to attend; They were held weekly, thirty minutes for the lower grades, forty-five minutes for the higher. The council employed the religious teachers at no expense to the school authorities, but the instructors were subject to the approval and supervision of the superintendent of schools. The classes were taught in three separate religious groups by Protestant teachers, Catholic priests, and a Jewish rabbi, although for the past several years there have apparently been no classes instructed in the Jewish religion. Classes were conducted in the regular classrooms of the school building. Students who did not choose to take the religious instruction were not released from public school duties; they were required to leave their classrooms and go to some other place in the school building for pursuit of their secular studies. On the other hand, students who were released from secular study for the religious instructions were required to be present at the religious classes. Reports of their presence or absence were to be made to their secular teachers.

The foregoing facts, without reference to others that appear in the record, show the use of tax-supported property for religious instruction and the close cooperation between the school authorities and the religious council in promoting religious education. The operation of the state's compulsory education system thus assists and is integrated with the program of religious instruction carried on by separate religious sects. Pupils compelled by law to go to school for secular education are released in part from their legal duty upon the condition that they attend the religious classes. This is beyond all question a utilization of the tax-established and tax-supported public school system to aid religious groups to spread their faith. And it falls squarely under the ban of the First Amendment (made applicable to the States by the Fourteenth) as we interpreted it in *Everson v. Board of Education.* There we said: "Neither a state nor the Federal Government can set up a church. Neither can pass laws which aid one religion, aid all religions, or prefer one religion over another. . . . Neither can force or influence a person to go to or to remain away from church against his will or force him to profess a belief or disbelief in any religion. No person can be punished for entertaining or professing religious beliefs or disbeliefs, for church attendance or nonattendance. No tax in any amount, large or small, can be levied to support any religious activities or institutions, whatever they may be called, or whatever form they may adopt to teach or practice religion. Neither a state nor the Federal Government can, openly or secretly,

participate in the affairs of any religious organizations or groups, and vice versa. . . .

To hold that a state cannot consistently with the First and Fourteenth Amendments utilize its public school system to aid any or all religious faiths or sects in the dissemination of their doctrines and ideals does not, as counsel urge, manifest a governmental hostility to religion or religious teachings. . . .

Here not only are the state's tax-supported public school buildings used for the dissemination of religious doctrines. The State also affords sectarian groups an invaluable aid in that it helps to provide pupils for their religious classes through use of the state's compulsory public school machinery. This is not separation of Church and State.

The cause is reversed and remanded to the State Supreme Court for proceedings not inconsistent with this opinion.

Reversed and remanded.

Further Resources

BOOKS

Eastland, Terry, ed. *Religious Liberty in the Supreme Court: The Cases That Define the Debate Over Church and State.* Washington, D.C.: Ethics and Public Policy Institute, 1993.

Howe, Mark De Wolfe. *The Garden and the Wilderness: Religion and Government in American Constitutional History.* Chicago: University of Chicago Press, 1965.

Levy, Leonard Williams. *The Establishment Clause: Religion and the First Amendment.* 2d ed.. Chapel Hill: University of North Carolina Press, 1994.

WEBSITES

"Court Decisions." Religious Freedom Page. Available online at http://religiousfreedom.lib.virginia.edu/court/mcco_v_boar .html (accessed April 23, 200).

"Religion, The Establishment Clause And Public Schools." ACLU Issues. Available online at http://www.aclu.org/issues /religion/pr3.html (accessed April 23, 200).

"Vashti Cromwell McCollum." Available online at http://www .clss.com/mccollum/vashti.htm. (accessed April 23, 2003).

Universal Declaration of Human Rights
Declaration

By: United Nations
Date: December 10, 1948
Source: United Nations. Universal Declaration of Human Rights. General Assembly Resolution 217 A (III). December

Eleanor Roosevelt reads the Universal Declaration of Human Rights on May 3, 1949, which was adopted the previous year by the United Nations. This document asserts that certain human freedoms and rights are possessed by every individual of every country in the world. © BETTMANN/CORBIS. REPRODUCED BY PERMISSION.

10, 1948. Available online at http://www.un.org/Overview /rights.html; website home page: http://www.un.org (accessed February 6, 2003).

About the Organization: President Franklin D. Roosevelt (served 1933–1945) coined the name "United Nations" during World War II (1939–1945) when referring to 26 nations that had pledged to continue fighting together against Germany, Italy, and Japan. In 1945 representatives of 50 countries met in San Francisco at the United Nations Conference on International Organization to draw up the United Nations Charter. The United Nations (UN) officially came into existence on October 24, 1945. ■

Introduction

At the end of World War II member countries of the UN wished to establish a *Universal Declaration of Human Rights* to guarantee the rights of individuals in all nations. This document would help assure that the Nazi atrocities against Jews and others, committed before and during the war, would never be allowed to occur again.

The UN's Commission on Human Rights, a permanent commission of the Economic and Social Council, was charged with the task of drafting a declaration. Five prominent people participated in the development of this historic document. Eleanor Roosevelt, the widow of President Franklin Roosevelt, was the American delegate and chairperson of the commission.

Two other members of the commission also took part in developing the document: P. C. Chang, the Chinese representative and vice chairperson of the commission, and Charles Malik, the Lebanese representative and Commission rapporteur, or reporter. John Humphrey, the director of the Division of Human Rights, and René Cassin, the French delegate to the Commission, were the two main writers of the declaration. The General Assembly of the UN adopted the declaration on December 10, 1948.

The preamble to the declaration states: "The recognition of the inherent dignity and of the equal and inalienable rights of all members of the human family is the foundation of freedom, justice and peace in the world." The preamble further declares, "Disregard and contempt for human rights have resulted in barbarous acts which have outraged the conscience of mankind. The advent of a world in which human beings shall enjoy freedom of speech and belief and freedom from fear and want has been proclaimed as the highest aspiration of the common people." Simply put, human rights must be protected by the rule of international law.

Significance

The declaration's effectiveness has received mixed reviews from the religious community in the United States. Proponents of the document have argued that, at the very least, it makes an international statement concerning people's rights to freedom of religion, including the freedom to change their religion or belief, and the freedom to teach, practice, worship and observe the religion of their choice. An international statement was better than no statement at all.

Others in the religious community have criticized the declaration for lacking any way to enforce its principles. They have pointed out a number of cases in which the violation of religious freedom has met with no effective response from the UN. Although the UN ratified a binding treaty and created the International Human Rights Covenants to establish international monitoring procedures and an international legal force, violations still take place. Many violations have occurred in communist countries. The former Union of Soviet Socialist Republics and China have been especially notorious for their suppression of religion and its practitioners.

Primary Source

Universal Declaration of Human Rights [excerpt]

SYNOPSIS: The Universal Declaration of Human Rights was adopted in 1948 by the United Nations in a General Assembly meeting in New York City. It contains 30 articles, of which five (1, 2, 16, 18, and 19) directly address religious freedoms. The remaining 25 articles concern other human freedoms.

Article 1

All human beings are born free and equal in dignity and rights. They are endowed with reason and conscience and should act towards one another in a spirit of brotherhood.

Article 2

Everyone is entitled to all the rights and freedoms set forth in this Declaration, without distinction of any kind, such as race, color, sex, language, religion, political or other opinion, national or social origin, property, birth or other status.

Furthermore, no distinction shall be made on the basis of the political, jurisdictional or international status of the country or territory to which a person belongs, whether it be independent, trust, non-self-governing or under any other limitation of sovereignty.

Article 16

(1) Men and women of full age, without any limitation due to race, nationality or religion, have the right to marry and to found a family. They are entitled to equal rights as a marriage, during marriage and at its dissolution.

(2) Marriage shall be entered into only with the free and full consent of the intending spouses.

(3) The family is the natural and fundamental group unit of society and is entitled to protection by society and the State.

Article 18

Everyone has the right to freedom of thought, conscience and religion; this right includes freedom to change his religion or belief, and freedom, either alone or in community with others and in public or private, to manifest his religion or belief in teaching, practice, worship and observance.

Article 19

Everyone has the right to freedom of opinion and expression; this right includes freedom to hold opinions without interference and to seek, receive and impart information and ideas through any media and regardless of frontiers.

Further Resources

BOOKS

And Justice for All: "The Universal Declaration of Human Rights" at 50. New York: Foreign Policy Association, 1998.

Glendon, Mary Ann. *A World Made New: Eleanor Roosevelt and the "Universal Declaration of Human Rights."* New York: Random House, 2001.

Johnson, M. Glen. *"The Universal Declaration of Human Rights": A History of Its Creation and Implementation, 1948-1998.* Paris: UNESCO Publications, 1998.

WEBSITES

"History of the Declaration." *Universal Declaration of Human Rights.* Available online at http://www.udhr50.org/history (accessed April 23, 2003).

History of the United Nations http://www.un.org/aboutun/history.htm (accessed April 23, 2003).

The First Assembly of the World Council of Churches Official Report
Report

By: World Council of Churches

Date: 1948

Source: World Council of Churches. The First Assembly of the World Council of Churches. Official Report. New York: Harper & Bros, 1949, 160–64. Available online at http://www.jcrelations.net/en/displayItem.php?id=1489; website home page: http://www.jcrelations.net (accessed February 5, 2003).

About the Organization: The World Council of Churches, established in 1948 in Amsterdam, the Netherlands, is a worldwide association consisting of approximately 350 Protestant, Orthodox, Anglican, and Old Catholic churches. The Roman Catholic Church, although not a member of the council, cooperates in joint efforts with the World Council of Churches. The council, which is headquartered in Geneva, Switzerland, was established primarily to encourage cooperation among all branches of Christianity worldwide. ∎

Introduction

After World War II (1939–1945) the process of reconstruction included not only rebuilding cities but also a rethinking of Christian attitudes and behavior toward Jewish people. The World Council of Churches (WCC) made a reexamination of the Christian approach to Jews and Judaism one of its foremost goals.

This first WCC assembly established committees to deal with the multiple concerns of member churches. One committee was directed to study the relationship between Christians and Jews over almost two thousand years and to draw up a statement indicating what changes should

The World Council of Churches assembles for the first time in August 1948, Amsterdam, the Netherlands. One of its initial committees was charged with examining Christian-Jewish relations in the post-World War II era. AP/WIDE WORLD PHOTOS. REPRODUCED BY PERMISSION.

occur in the future. A document titled "The Christian Approach to the Jews" resulted from the committee's work.

The WCC came to the realization that for centuries the Jews had been mistreated directly and indirectly by Christians and Christian-controlled societies. Too often Christians and their churches looked down upon the Jews and subjected them to prejudice, discrimination, and segregation because they would not accept Jesus Christ as the Messiah.

Jews had been persecuted not only by the Nazis who killed approximately six million Jews before and after World War II, but also by Christian-dominated nations and their citizenry in previous times. The history of the treatment of Jews was a tragic one and the WCC was determined to prevent its repetition. Christians had to extend the hand of reconciliation and help heal the wounds they had inflicted on Jews. The council prayed that a new era of friendship, love, and understanding between Christians and Jews would mark the second half of the twentieth century.

The WCC called upon all churches to reject and condemn anti-Semitism, regardless of whether it originated from religious, social, economic or political causes. Anti-

Semitism was declared to be a sin against God and human beings. A person could not call himself or herself a true Christian if he or she engaged in any practices that denied Jews justice or their rightful place in society.

The change occurring in the perception of the Jewish people and Judaism as a religion was not an easy one. The problem of conversion of the Jews to Christianity, a major point of contention between the two faiths, had to be addressed. The missionary stance of Christian churches toward all non-Christians including Jews would continue, but the council advised Christians to "scrupulously avoid all unworthy pressures or inducements" in mission work among the Jews.

Significance

American Jews greeted "The Christian Approach to the Jews" with mixed emotions. On one hand it suggested a positive change of attitude in a world body representing many Protestant churches. At the very least this change was a sign of hope for better Jewish and Christian relations. On the other hand the thorny question of missionary actions taken to convert Jews to the Christian faith still remained.

American Christians of goodwill toward the Jews welcomed the council's document, but with concern about how to apply it to the realities of everyday life. Sympathy toward the plight of the Jewish people, especially since the revelations of the mass killings in the Nazi concentration camps, motivated Christians to examine their own feelings toward Jews. They had heard firsthand anti-Semitic comments expressed by other Christians and knew it would be difficult to change the biases that had been part of American culture for so long. This Jewish-Christian dialogue, begun at the end of the 1940s, continues into the twenty-first century.

Primary Source

The First Assembly of the World Council of Churches Official Report [excerpt]

SYNOPSIS: The First Assembly of the World Council of Churches, which met in 1948, charged one of its special committees with developing a document that would examine how Christians should relate to Jews in the post-World War II era. The Assembly, held at Amsterdam from August 22 to September 4, 1948, received a report, part of which pertained to "The Christian Approach to the Jews." This document, excerpted below, has helped establish a new dialogue between Christians and Jews in the United States and Europe.

The Christian Approach to the Jews

A concern for the Christian approach to the Jewish people confronts us inescapably, as we meet together to look with open and penitent eyes on man's disorder and to rediscover together God's eternal purpose for His Church. This concern is ours because it is first a concern of God made known to us in Christ. No people in His one world have suffered more bitterly from the disorder of man than the Jewish people.

We cannot forget that we meet in a land from which 110,000 Jews were taken to be murdered. Nor can we forget that we meet only five years after the extermination of 6 million Jews. To the Jews our God has bound us in a special solidarity linking our destinies together in His design. We call upon all our churches to make this concern their own as we share with them the results of our too brief wrestling with it.

1. The Church's commission to preach the Gospel to all men

All of our churches stand under the commission of our common Lord, "Go ye into all the world and preach the Gospel to every creature." The fulfillment of this commission requires that we include the Jewish people in our evangelistic task.

2. The special meaning of the Jewish people for Christian faith

In the design of God, Israel has a unique position. It was Israel with whom God made His covenant by the call of Abraham. It was Israel to whom God revealed His name and gave His law. It was to Israel that He sent His Prophets with their message of judgment and of grace. It was Israel to whom He promised the coming of His Messiah. By the history of Israel God prepared the manger in which in the fullness of time He put the Redeemer of all mankind, Jesus Christ.

The Church has received this spiritual heritage from Israel and is therefore in honour bound to render it back in the light of the Cross. We have, therefore, in humble conviction to proclaim to the Jews, "The Messiah for Whom you wait has come." The promise has been fulfilled by the coming of Jesus Christ. For many the continued existence of a Jewish people which does not acknowledge Christ is a divine mystery which finds its only sufficient explanation in the purpose of God's unchanging faithfulness and mercy.

3. Barriers to be overcome

Before our churches can hope to fulfill the commission laid upon us by our Lord there are high bar-

riers to be overcome. We speak here particularly of the barriers which we have too often helped to build and which we alone can remove. We must acknowledge in all humility that too often we have failed to manifest Christian love towards our Jewish neighbours, or even a resolute will for common social justice. We have failed to fight with all our strength the age-old disorder of man which anti-semitism represents.

The churches in the past have helped to foster an image of the Jews as the sole enemies of Christ, which has contributed to anti-semitism in the secular world. In many lands virulent anti-semitism still threatens and in other lands the Jews are subjected to many indignities. We call upon all the churches we represent to denounce anti-semitism, no matter what its origin, as absolutely irreconcilable with the profession and practice of the Christian faith. Anti-semitism is sin against God and man. Only as we give convincing evidence to our Jewish neighbours that we seek for them the common rights and dignities which God wills for His children, can we come to such a meeting with them as would make it possible to share with them the best which God has given us in Christ.

4. The Christian witness to the Jewish people

In spite of the universality of our Lord's commission and of the fact that the first mission of the Church was to the Jewish people, our churches have with rare exceptions failed to maintain that mission. This responsibility should not be left largely to independent agencies. The carrying on of this mission by special agencies has often meant the singling out of the Jews for special missionary attention, even in situations where they might well have been included in the normal ministry of the church. It has also meant in many cases that the converts are forced into segregated spiritual fellowship rather than being included and welcomed in the regular membership of the church.

Owing to this failure our churches must consider the responsibility for missions to the Jews as a normal part of parish work, especially in those countries where Jews are members of the general community. Where there is no indigenous church or where the indigenous church is insufficient for this task it may be necessary to arrange for a special missionary ministry from abroad. Because of the unique inheritance of the Jewish people, the churches should make provision for the education of ministers specially fitted for this task. Provision should also be made for Christian literature to interpret the gospel to Jewish people. . . .

In reconstruction and relief activities the churches must not lose sight of the plight of Christians of Jewish origin, in view of their special suffering. Such provision must be made for their aid as will help them to know that they are not forgotten in the Christian fellowship.

5. The emergence of Israel as a state

The establishment of the state "Israel" adds a political dimension to the Christian approach to the Jews and threatens to complicate anti-semitism with political fears and enmities.

On the political aspects of the Palestine problem and the complex conflict of "rights" involved we do not undertake to express a judgment. Nevertheless, we appeal to the nations to deal with the problem not as one of expediency—political, strategic or economic—but as a moral and spiritual question that touches a nerve centre of the world's religious life.

Whatever position may be taken towards the establishment of a Jewish state and towards the "rights" and "wrongs" of Jews and Arabs, of Hebrew Christians and Arab Christians involved, the churches are in duty bound to pray and work for an order in Palestine as just as may be in the midst of our human disorder; to provide within their power for the relief of the victims of this warfare without discrimination; and to seek to influence the nations to provide a refuge for "Displaced Persons" far more generously than has yet been done.

Recommendations

We conclude this report with the recommendations which arise out of our first exploratory consideration of this "concern" of the churches.

1. To the member churches of the World Council we recommend:

- that they seek to recover the universality of our Lord's commission by including the Jewish people in their evangelistic work;

- that they encourage their people to seek for brotherly contact with and understanding of their Jewish neighbours, and cooperation in agencies combating misunderstanding and prejudice;

- that in mission work among the Jews they scrupulously avoid all unworthy pressures or inducements;

- that they give thought to the preparation of ministers well fitted to interpret the Gospel to Jewish people and to the provision of literature which will aid in such a ministry.

2. To the World Council of Churches we recommend:

- that it should give careful thought as to how it can best stimulate and assist the member churches in the carrying out of this aspect of their mission;

- that it give careful consideration to the suggestion made by the International Missionary Council that the World Council of Churches share with it a joint responsibility for the Christian approach to the Jews;

- that it be resolved:

that, in receiving the report of this Committee, the Assembly recognize the need for more detailed study by the World Council of Churches of the many complex problems which exist in the field of relations between Christians and Jews and in particular of the following:

(a) the historical and present factors which have contributed to the growth and persistence of anti-semitism, and the most effective means of combating this evil;

(b) the need and opportunity in this present historical situation for the development of cooperation between Christians and Jews in civic and social affairs;

(c) the many and varied problems created by establishment of a State of Israel in Palestine. The Assembly therefore asks that these and related questions be referred to the Central Committee for further examination.

Further Resources

BOOKS

Caroll, James. Constantine's Sword: *The Church and the Jews: A History.* N.Y.: Houghton Mifflin Co., 2001.

Falk, Randall, and Harrelson, Jacob. *Jews and Christians in Pursuit of Social Justice.* Nashville, Tenn.: Abingdon Press, 1996.

WEBSITES

"Archbishop of Canterbury Addresses Jewish-Christian Relations." Episcopal Church. Available online at http://www.episcopalchurch.org/ens/2001-123.html (accessed July 2, 2002).

Brockway, Allan R. "Assemblies of the World Council of Churches." Available online at http://www.abrock.com/Assemblies.html (accessed July 2, 2002).

"Jewish-Christian Relations. A Statement about Christianity."
    Available online at http://www.religioustolerance.org/jud
    _chrr.htm (accessed July 3, 2002).

A Guide to Confident Living
Guidebook

By: Norman Vincent Peale

Date: 1948

Source: Peale, Norman Vincent. *A Guide to Confident Living.* Englewood Cliffs, N.J.: Prentice Hall, Inc., 1948, 1–22.

About the Author: Norman Vincent Peale (1898–1993), born in Bowersville, Ohio, became a minister notable for his application of psychology to religion. He spread his message through church sermons, radio and television programs, and popular books and other writings. Ordained to the Methodist ministry in 1922, Peale changed his denomination to Dutch Reformed in 1932 when he accepted a position at the 300-year-old Marble Collegiate Church in New York City. Peale remained there for the next 50 years. ■

Introduction

Dr. Norman Vincent Peale broke new ground in the American ministry by using the principles of psychology in counseling members of his congregation. He saw the value of applying scientific information on human behavior directly to his ministry. *A Guide to Confident Living* contains his basic theories about the interplay of psychology and religion, stories from men and women he has counseled, and practical advice on taking charge of one's life by living confidently with the grace of God.

Before Peale developed this approach most pastors and religious leaders believed there was a dividing line between religion and psychology. Many viewed psychology as the enemy of religion and feared it would take over religion's traditional role of helping people with their problems. Few of them saw psychology's potential as an aid to the ministry. Peale challenged this perspective with *A Guide to Confident Living.*

Peale's book demonstrates how people achieve a more meaningful, happy, and successful existence by changing their thinking patterns through religious activity and spiritual growth. In a step-by-step approach he presents a guide to discovering inner strengths and gaining the confidence to live a healthy life. Peale tells readers that God is always at the center of these changes, helping people achieve their best by giving them the strength to fulfill their potential. Psychology and religion proved to be a powerful combination for those who chose to follow what Peale preached.

Norman Vincent Peale, author of *Guide to Confident Living,* challenged religious leaders' notion that religion and psychology are mutually exclusive. **THE LIBRARY OF CONGRESS.**

Significance

A Guide to Confident Living met a genuine need in the United States following World War II (1939–1945). Just as people regained hope for peace and prosperity a new conflict, the Cold War between the United States and the Union of Soviet Socialist Republics began to emerge. People feared that a war between these two superpowers would involve devastating nuclear weapons. While individuals could do little to solve such immense problems, they could do much to relieve their own personal difficulties, according to Peale. His book presented ways of overcoming consuming worries, tension, fear, and frustration through his spiritual techniques.

The application of psychology to religion proved very useful for many Americans. *A Guide to Confident Living* was well received by the reading public and became a huge success. Peale's second work *The Power of Positive Thinking* proved even more popular. A prolific writer, Peale eventually produced forty-six books and became one of the foremost motivational speakers of the twentieth century.

For more than 50 years he preached encouraging sermons at the Marble Collegiate Church in New York City. In addition to that ministry, he spoke to an average of

100 groups a year until the age of 93. His work so impressed Ronald Reagan (served 1981–1989) that the president awarded him the Presidential Medal of Freedom. Although Peale died in 1993, his message that faith works powerfully in ordinary lives is still widely read.

Primary Source

A Guide to Confident Living [excerpt]

> **SYNOPSIS:** In his very popular self-help book *A Guide to Confident Living,* Peale establishes his anecdotal style for conveying inspirational messages. In the following excerpts from chapter one, "A New-Old Way to Free Your Powers," Peale explains that most problems people face are personal in nature and can be reduced by applying religion and psychology to everyday life.

May I outline my own practice? Theories began to develop in my mind some years ago as the number of persons with whom I was privately counseling increased. I came to the ministry of a Fifth Avenue church at the low point of the depression, back in 1932. New York City, as the financial center of the nation, was profoundly affected by the depression and I soon became aware of the fear, anxiety, insecurity, disappointment, frustration, and failure everywhere at hand. I began to preach on these themes and stressed how faith in God could give courage and wisdom together with new insights for the solution of problems. Advertising such topics in the press brought large congregations to hear these discussions. Soon my schedule of personal interviews was more than I could possibly handle and long waiting lists developed. Recognizing my lack of specialized knowledge, I turned to a highly competent psychiatrist, Dr. Smiley Blanton, for help and thus began the counseling clinic in the church. . . .

We shall proceed to outline a simple but workable technique for successful living. As stated in the Introduction, nothing is offered here on a theoretical basis. Every principle in this book has been worked out in verifiable laboratory tests. These principles will work when they are worked. Confidence in these teachings is based on the fact that they have been developed out of the lives of real people, not once but many times. They have the effect of law because they have been proven by repeated demonstration. Let me drive home this fact: If you will utilize the principles of faith stated in this book, you, too, can solve the difficult problems of your personality. You, too, can really learn to live. It is not important what church you attend—Protestant, Catholic, or Jewish—nor does it make any difference how much you have failed in the past or how unhappy your present state of mind. Regardless of how apparently hopeless your condition may be, if you will believe in the principles outlined in this book and seriously start to work with them, you will get positive results.

I urge you to consider carefully the amazing things that often happen in church and suggest that you submit yourself not only to the private therapy of faith but to the astounding effect that group therapy may have upon you. But to attend church successfully, skill is required. Worship is not a hit or miss affair. There is an art to it. Those who by study and practice become expert in church going master one of the greatest of all skills, that of spiritual power. That you may learn to go to church efficiently, I suggest the following ten rules to guide you in mastering the art of church going.

Consistently put these rules into practice and one of these days the great thing may happen to you.

1. Think of church going as an art, with definite rules to follow, an art you can acquire.

2. Go regularly to church. A prescription designed by a physician to be taken at regular intervals is not effective if taken once a year.

3. Spend a quiet Saturday evening and get a good sleep. Get in condition for Sunday.

4. Go in a relaxed state of body and mind. Don't rush to church. Go in a leisurely manner. The absence of tension is a requisite to successful worship.

5. Go in a spirit of enjoyment. Church is not a place of gloom. Christianity is a radiant and happy thing. Religion should be enjoyed.

6. Sit relaxed in the pew, feet on floor, hands loosely in lap or at the side. Allow the body to yield to the contour of the pew. Don't sit rigid. God's power cannot get through to your personality through a tied-up body and mind.

7. Don't bring a "problem" to church. Think hard during the week, but let the problem "simmer" in the mind over Sunday. God's peace brings creative energy to help the intellectual process. You will receive insight to solve your problem.

8. Do not bring ill will to church. A grudge blocks the flow of spiritual power. To cast out ill will, pray in church for those you do not like or who dislike you.

9. Practice the art of spiritual contemplation. In church do not think about yourself. Think about God. Think of some beautiful and peaceful thing, perhaps even of the stream where you fished last summer. The idea is to get mentally away from the world, into an atmosphere of peace and refreshment.

10. Go to church expecting some great thing to happen to you. Believe that a church service is the creation of an atmosphere in which a spiritual miracle can take place. Men's lives have been changed in church through faith in Christ. Believe it can happen to you.

Further Resources

BOOKS

George, Carol V. R. *God's Salesman: Norman Vincent Peale & the Power of Positive Thinking.* New York: Oxford University Press, 1993.

Westphal, Clarence. *Norman Vincent Peale, Christian Crusader: A Biography.* Minneapolis, Tenn.: Denison, 1964.

WEBSITES

"Daily Guideposts." *Guideposts.* Available online at http://www.guideposts.org/aboutus/ (accessed April 23, 2003).

"Norman Vincent Peale." Horatio Alger Association of Distinguished Americans. Available online at http://www.horatioalger.com/member/pea52.htm (accessed April 23, 2003).

"Norman Vincent Peale: Turning America On To Positive Thinking." U.S. Dreams. Available online at http://www.usdreams.com/Peale28.html (accessed April 23, 2003).

"Beyond Religious Socialism"

Magazine article

By: Paul Tillich

Date: June 15, 1949

Source: Tillich, Paul. "Beyond Religious Socialism." *Christian Century,* June 15, 1949. Available online at http://www.religion-online.org/cgi-bin/relsearchd.dll/showarticle?item_id=475; website home page: http://www.religion-online.org (accessed April 23, 2003).

About the Author: Paul Tillich (1886–1965), born in Starzeddel, Prussia, taught theology and philosophy at several German universities before coming to the United States in 1933. He was appointed Professor of Philosophical Theology at Union Theological Seminary in New York City, where he remained until 1955. He then completed his career as University Professor at Harvard University. Tillich has been called the most prominent Protestant theologian of the twentieth century. ∎

Introduction

In "Beyond Religious Socialism," Paul Tillich presents a brief history of his experiences in theology and philosophy after coming to America from Germany in 1933. He notes particularly the important role of social ethics in American theology. The practice of social ethics involves the study of right and wrong, good and bad, moral judgments, and the rules or standards governing the conduct or behavior of people toward one another.

In Germany Tillich taught theology and philosophy at various universities and so was a "seasoned veteran" in religious studies when he came to the United States to resume his teaching career. He brought three distinct ideas with him from Germany: the theology of crisis, religious socialism, and the philosophy of existence.

The theology of crisis links theological concerns with the examination of crises. Theology is the systematic study of religious truth, the nature of God, and other religious questions. A crisis is a critical or decisive turning point usually involving impending change. Theology was meant to help people resolve problems, especially in times of crisis.

Religious socialism is the interrelationship of religion and politics as religious bodies work with a government trying to bring about economic and political changes. As Tillich noted in "Beyond Religious Socialism," before World War II (1939–1945) some hoped that the religious-socialist spirit would lessen tension developing between East and West. That did not occur.

Tillich's philosophy of existence evolved into what has become known as existentialism. This philosophical movement embraces different doctrines but focuses largely on the meaning of individual existence in an incomprehensible universe. Existentialists emphasize human freedom and abilities to make choices, but maintain there is no way to determine with certainty what may be good or bad, right or wrong. This condition places people in a dilemma because they must take responsibility for their actions without knowing if they are morally right or morally wrong.

Significance

Tillich has been characterized by experts as one of the twentieth century's most prominent and important religious thinkers. His theology and philosophy are still significant, but this does not mean that religious thinkers necessarily agree with his controversial and debatable views. His religious concepts still elicit both positive and negative commentary in many schools of theology in the United States as well as Europe.

Tillich answered a basic human question: where is God in all of this? He asserted that God is a dimension of man's existence. God is one's participation in the depth

Paul Tillich was a prominent figure in the examination of theological questions after the two world wars. His essay "Beyond Religious Socialism" offers an immigrant's perspective on the significance of social ethics in American theological thought. HARVARD UNIVERSITY NEWS OFFICE.

of one's own being. God exists, Tillich said, when one experiences the depth of one's being when responding to reality with ultimate concern. He stated, "Religion is man's response to ultimate concerns in terms of the ultimate." The objective of theology, according to Tillich, is to explain the individual's ultimate concern that determines his or her being or non-being.

Some Christians have been satisfied with Tillich's answer and found comfort and truth in it; others have not. For the latter, the question still remains to be answered: where is God in relation to what is happening in the world today?

Primary Source

"Beyond Religious Socialism" [excerpt]

SYNOPSIS: One of the most outstanding theologians and philosophers of the twentieth century, Tillich presents his thoughts about the state of theology in this article. In addition to his references to religious socialism, he discusses the theology of crisis and his views on existentialism. He also points out the significance of social ethics in American theological thought.

It was not a dramatic change of mind that I experienced during the past decade—such a change is hardly to be expected in the sixth decade of one's life—but a slow, often unconscious, always effective transformation in various respects. One of these changes arose from the fact that the past ten years belong to the fifteen that I have lived in this country and that they were consequently years of continuing adaptation to the ways and thoughts of America.

The summer of 1948, when I returned to Germany for the first time since 1933, gave me a clear test of the amount of adaptation I have undergone. The change has been first of all a change in my mode of expression. The English language has worked on me what my German friends and former students considered a miracle: it has made me understandable. No Anglicisms occurred in the innumerable speeches I delivered, but the spirit of the English language dominated every sentence—the spirit of clarity, soberness and concreteness. This forced itself upon me, often against my natural inclinations. It taught me to avoid the accumulation of substantives to which German is prone and to use verbs instead. It forbade the ambiguities in which, because of its origin in medieval mystical literature, German philosophical language so often indulges. It prohibited the use of logically unsharp or incomplete propositions. It pricked my conscience when I dwelt too long in abstractions. All this was very well received by my German audiences and was felt as my most impressive change of mind.

Reporting in Germany on the state of theology in the U.S.A. I said that America, while still following Europe's lead in historical and systematic theology, is far ahead of it in ethics. I could say this because I had become increasingly aware that ethics is an integral element of systematic theology, and that I had much to learn in social as well as individual ethics from American thought and reality. In social ethics I was partly prepared by my work as a "religious socialist" in Germany. But only slowly did I realize the central importance social ethics has in American theology and come to appreciate the abundant and advanced treatment it has received.

While in my first years in the United States I was surprised and worried by the tremendous emphasis put on the question of pacifism—a question that seemed to me of minor importance and often the result of confused thinking—I presently discovered that all theological problems were implicit in this problem. When therefore, in the years before, during and after the Second World War, the pacifist ideology was shattered in large numbers of people, I understood that this was an indication of a new attitude toward the doctrine of man and toward the whole of Christianity. And this change in the mind of others made it easier for me to feel at home in the theological work of this country.

When I first came to America, in 1933, I was labeled a "neo-orthodox" or a "neo-supernaturalist." This was certainly incorrect, but I must admit that some of my early utterances before American audiences could have created such an impression. My task in the thirties was to give my students and other listeners an account of my theological, philosophical and political ideas as they had developed during the critical years from 1914 to 1933. I brought with me from Germany the "theology of crisis," the "philosophy of existence" and "religious socialism," and I tried to interpret these to my classes and readers. In all three of these fields—the theological, the philosophical and the political—my thinking has undergone changes, partly because of personal experiences and insights, partly because of the social and cultural transformations these years have witnessed.

Most obvious of the changes on the world stage is the political one—from the uncertainties of the thirties to the establishment in the forties of a world-splitting dualism, in reality as well as in ideology. While before the Second World War there was some ground for hope that the religious-socialist spirit penetrating into East and West alike, though in different forms, would mitigate the contrast and prevent the conflict between them, no such hope has a foundation today. The expectation we had cherished after the First World War that a *kairos,* a "fulfillment of time," was at hand, has been twice shaken, first by the victory of fascism and then by the situation after its military defeat.

I do not doubt that the basic conceptions of religious socialism are valid, that they point to the political and cultural way of life by which alone Europe can be built up. But I am not sure that the adoption of religious-socialist principles is a possibility in any foreseeable future. Instead of a creative *kairos,* I see a vacuum which can be made creative only if it is accepted and endured and, rejecting all kinds of premature solutions, is transformed into a deepening "sacred void" of waiting. This view naturally implies a decrease of my participation in political activities. My change of mind in this connection was also influenced by the complete breakdown of a se-

rious political attempt I made during the war to bridge the gap between East and West with respect to the organization of postwar Germany.

It has been said that the repudiation of civil liberties and the rights of man in the Communist-dominated countries means the disillusionment of liberals all over the world. This is certainly true of those who had more illusions than my religious-socialist understanding of man ever allowed me to entertain. But it cannot be denied that this widespread repudiation of human rights had a depressing effect also on those who, like myself, without being utopian, saw the dawn of a new creative era in a moment which actually presaged a deeper darkness.

To turn now to philosophy: "Existentialism" was familiar to me long before the name came into general use. The reading of Kierkegaard in my student years, the thorough study of Schelling's later works, the passionate devotion to Nietzsche during the First World War, the encounter with Marx (especially with his early philosophical writings), and finally my own religious-socialist attempts at an existential interpretation of history—all had prepared me for more recent existential philosophy as developed by Heidegger, Jaspers and Sartre. In spite of the fact that existentialism has become fashionable and has been dangerously popularized, I have been confirmed in my conviction of its basic truth and its adequacy to our present condition. The basic truth of this philosophy, as I see it, is its perception of the "finite freedom" of man, and consequently of his situation as always perilous, ambiguous and tragic. Existentialism gains its special significance for our time from its insight into the immense increase in anxiety, danger and conflict produced in personal and social life by the present "destructive structure" of human affairs.

On this point existential philosophy has allied itself with therapeutic or depth psychology. Only through the late war and its aftermath has it become manifest that psychic illness—the inability to use one's finite freedom creatively—is more widespread in this country than any other disease. At the same time depth psychology has removed what remnants of the nineteenth-century mechanistic world view still remained, and has come to understand the sociological, ontological and even theological implications of phenomena like anxiety, guilt and compulsion neurosis. Out of this new co-operation of ontology and psychology (including social psychology) a doctrine of man has developed which has already exercised considerable influence in all cultural realms, especially in theology. . . .

In this way, it seems to me, it is possible to avoid two contradictory errors in theology, the supernaturalistic and the naturalistic. The first makes revelation a rock falling into history from above, to be accepted obediently without preparation or adequacy to human nature. The second replaces revelation by a structure of rational thought derived from and judged by human nature. The method of correlation, by overcoming the conflict of supernaturalism and naturalism, shows a way out of the blind alley in which the discussion between fundamentalism or neo-orthodoxy on the one hand, and theological humanism or liberalism on the other, is caught.

In the course of this mediating attempt it became increasingly clear to me that one achievement of so-called liberal theology has to be defended with great religious, ethical and scientific passion; namely, the right and duty of philological-historical criticism of the biblical literature without any condition except integrity of research and scientific honesty. Any dogmatic interference with this work would drive us into new or old superstitions—myths and symbols not understood as myths and symbols—and, since this cannot be done without the unconscious suppression of sounder knowledge, to fanaticism. The power of this neo-biblicism is obvious in continental Europe, but it can already be felt in this country also, and even among old-fashioned liberals.

Looking at the past decade of my life I see no dramatic changes of mind but a slow development of my convictions in the direction of greater clarity and certainty. Above all I have come to realize that a few great and lasting things are decisive for the human mind, and that to cling to them is more important than to look for dramatic changes.

Further Resources

BOOKS

Heywood, Thomas. *Paul Tillich.* Richmond, Va.: John Knox Press, 1966.

Newport, John P. *Paul Tillich.* Waco, Tex.: Word Books, 1984.

Pauck, Wilhelm. *Paul Tillich, His Life & Thought.* New York: Harper & Row, 1976.

WEBSITES

"Paul Tillich." Evansville University. Available online at http://www2.evansville.edu/ck6/bstud/tillich.html (accessed April 23, 2003).

"Paul Tillich Online Sites." Irish Theological Association. Available online at http://www.theology.ie/theologians/tillich.htm (accessed April 23, 2003).

"Greater L.A.'s Greatest Revival Continues!"

Newspaper advertisement

Date: October 26, 1949

Source: *Daily News* (Los Angeles), October 26, 1949. Reproduced in the Billy Graham Center Archives. Wheaton College. Available online at http://www.wheaton.edu/bgc/archives/images/laad1.jpg; website home page: http://www.wheaton.edu (accessed April 23, 2003). ■

Introduction

Billy Graham (1918–), born in Charlotte, North Carolina, preached his first sermon in 1937. He was ordained a Southern Baptist minister in 1939. After a period as minister of the First Baptist Church in Western Springs, Illinois, he became a traveling "tent evangelist," holding his first mass religious rally at Chicagoland Youth for Christ in 1944. The following year he became the field representative of a growing evangelistic movement known as Youth for Christ and served as its first vice president from 1945 to 1948. In this role he toured the United States and much of Great Britain and Europe, teaching local church leaders how to organize youth rallies.

Graham organized his first major crusade in Los Angeles in 1949 in obedience to Christ's command to go into the world and preach the Gospel to all. Historians consider Graham's eight-week crusade for Christ in Los Angeles the launching point for his career as the leading religious revivalist in the United States. Graham gained attention through nationally publicized crusades first in Los Angeles and then in Boston, Washington, and other major cities from 1949 to 1952. His message, that "through Christ sins are forgiven and people can live in peace," was also spread through his Hour of Decision radio program that began in 1950.

Graham's ministry consciously avoided association with any particular Christian group or doctrine. He wanted to appeal to Christians from all backgrounds and traditions as well as non-Christians, who were searching for God. His sermons dealt with the fundamentals of Christianity, like the literal truth of the Bible and the bodily resurrection of Jesus, but he didn't sound like a typical fundamentalist.

Significance

The crusade in Los Angeles brought Graham into the national spotlight. Two contemporary reports provide insight into the crusade. Richard Reynolds wrote in the *Daily News* (Los Angeles) on September 30, 1949 that old time religion has gone as modern as an atomic bomb in

Primary Source

"Greater L.A.'s Greatest Revival Continues!"

SYNOPSIS: Rev. Billy Graham, one of America's most famous preachers, achieved national recognition with his Christ for Greater Los Angeles crusade that ran from September 25 to November 20, 1949, and was attended by about 350,000 people. This newspaper advertisement for Graham's revival in Los Angeles ran in the *Los Angeles Daily News* on October 26, 1949. ARCHIVES OF THE BILLY GRAHAM CENTER, WHEATON, ILLINOIS. REPRODUCED BY PERMISSION.

the thunderous revival meetings that Rev. Billy Graham conducts nightly in a giant tent at Washington Boulevard and Hill Street. But its modernity is in externals. Nothing detracts from the traditional fury and power of an old-fashioned gospel gathering. That's what his listeners, many of whom remember with pleasure the late Billy Sunday, want. And that's what they get.

An Associated Press news release from November 1949 gives the following account. "Old-time religion is sweeping Los Angeles. In six weeks, 200-thousand people have filed into a circus tent on the outskirts. And they're still pouring in at the rate of 10-thousand every night. . . . Thousands have hit the sawdust trail [and] announced their return to Christ."

Since the 1949 Los Angeles crusade, Graham has became a noted charismatic preacher not only in the United States but worldwide, leading hundreds of thousands of people to make personal decisions to live for Christ. Advocating the public testimony of faith, an important part of his revival meetings, he has become America's leading evangelical Christian. His approach to Christianity is distinctively American because it differs from the European kind of Protestantism with which most Christians in America are familiar. During his ministry over 210 million people in more than 185 countries and territories have been exposed to his revivals. Hundreds of millions more have been reached through television, radio, video, film, and webcasts.

Further Resources

BOOKS

Graham, Billy. *The Faith of Billy Graham.* Anderson, S.C.: Droke House, 1968.

High, Stanley. *Billy Graham: the Personal Story of the Man, His Message, and His Mission.* New York: McGraw-Hill, 1956.

Pollock, John C. *Billy Graham: The Authorized Biography.* New York: McGraw-Hill, 1966.

PERIODICALS

Aikman, David. "Preachers, Politics and Temptation," *Time,* May 28, 1990.

Gibbs, Nancy, and Richard N. Ostling. "God's Billy Pulpit." *Time,* Nov 15, 1993.

Martin, William. "Billy Graham." *Christian History,* Feb 1, 2000.

WEBSITES

"About Billy Graham." http://www.billygraham.org/aboutUs /biographies.asp?b=1 (accessed April 23, 2003).

Billy Graham Center Archives. Wheaton College. Available online at http://www.wheaton.edu/bgc/archives/archhp1.html (accessed April 23, 2003).

Interviews With Holocaust Survivors
Eyewitness accounts

By: Rudy Herz, Ben Stern, and Pincus Kolender
Date: 1991
Source: Herz, Rudy; Ben Stern; and Pincus Kolender. Interviews by South Carolina Educational Television Studios. September 19, 1991 [Herz]; August 8, 1991 [Stern]; September 26, 1991 [Kolender]. Directed by Linda J. DuRant. VHS. Available through SCETV at http://www.scetv.org/Holocaust-Forum/INDEX.html; website home page: http://www.scetv.org (accessed February 5, 2003). Transcribed excerpts reproduced in The Holocaust: A Tragic Legacy. Available online at http://library.thinkquest.org/12663/?tqskip1=1&tqtime=0206; website home page: http://library.thinkquest.org (accessed February 10, 2002).

About the Authors: Rudy Herz, Ben Stern, and Pincus Kolender are three of the millions of Jews imprisoned at Nazi concentration camps during World War II. Before being sent to the camps, they and thousands of others were confined to ghettos, or separate Jewish sections, in European cities. Rudy spent almost two years in the Theresienstadt ghetto in Czechoslovakia; Ben lived in Kilce, a Polish ghetto, for six months; and Pincus spent an undetermined amount of time in the Bochnia ghetto, also in Poland. All three were later sent to Auschwitz, the notorious Nazi death camp. ∎

Introduction

These eyewitness accounts are only a few of the horrific testimonies by concentration camp survivors the United States and its allies liberated from these camps at end of World War II. Many survivors migrated to the United States after their release and became American citizens.

Before and during World War II (1939–1945), most Americans had either no knowledge or inaccurate information about the systematic killing of Jewish civilians. The Nazis deliberately killed about six million Jewish men, women, and children just because of their faith and ethnic background; many of these deaths occurred in gas chambers at concentration camps. Why weren't more Americans aware of the atrocities being committed against Jews? Where was the American response to this Holocaust?

Americans were ill-informed about the massacre of Jews because not many in the United States talked about it openly, if at all. President Franklin Roosevelt (served 1933–1945), though very much aware of the situation, said nothing about it publicly until the later years of the war. The Christian clergy, for the most part, either did not know about the calamity or chose to ignore it. Major newspapers published infrequent reports and popular

After years of ignoring the horrors Jews faced under the Nazis, President Roosevelt in 1944 created the War Refugee Board to assist in the rescue of victims of enemy oppression. MAIN COMMISSION FOR THE INVESTIGATION OF NAZI WAR CRIMES/USHMM PHOTO ARCHIVES.

magazines relating little or nothing about the killings. Hitler conducted his attacks against European Jews for more than three years before *The New York Times* carried the first authenticated account of Germany's policy to "exterminate" the Jewish race. On November 25, 1942, the newspaper reported that the U.S. State Department had confirmed that the Nazis had killed over two million Jews. Usually a story of this magnitude would appear on page one; the *Times* ran it on page 10.

Anti-Semitism, or anti-Jewish prejudice and discrimination, led even informed Americans to ignore the plight of the Jews. In 1942 a public opinion poll asked Americans which groups menaced the country the most. Respondents listed the Germans and the Japanese as numbers one and two, respectively. That could be expected, as those countries were the United State's primary enemies in the war. The poll indicated that Americans found Jews the third most menacing group, clearly a result of anti-Jewish bias.

Significance

Finally, in 1944, the United States government took an active measure to help European Jews. Some American Christian and Jewish groups pressured President Roosevelt into signing Executive Order 9417, which created the War Refugee Board. The board was given the responsibility to do all that it could to rescue victims of enemy oppression in imminent danger of death. This measure saved the lives of about 200,000 Jews by offering assistance to those trying to flee the Nazi terror. If the War

Refuge Board had been created just a year earlier, perhaps hundreds of thousands more could have been saved.

Eyewitness accounts of camp survivors, documents written by Nazi officers, stories of the allied soldiers who liberated the death camps, and the Nuremberg Trials of Nazi war criminals fully exposed the nature of the Holocaust. Most Americans became much more aware of what had happened to the Jewish people during World War II, but a minority of extremists still deny that the Holocaust ever happened.

Primary Source

Interviews with Holocaust Survivors [excerpt]

> **SYNOPSIS:** Three Jewish survivors who later moved to the United States tell about their experiences in a concentration camp in Auschwitz, Poland. At Auschwitz, the largest concentration camp during World War II, the Nazis systematically murdered hundreds of thousands of Jews.

Rudy at Auschwitz

In March or April, 1944, we got the dreaded notice that we had been selected for resettlement farther east. The train cars they took us in were actually cattle cars. We entered the cars and sat on our baggage. There was not very much room between us and the roof of the cattle car. Our car had from 80 to 100 people in it so it was quite crowded. We were sitting tight on tight. We had some water and some food but no comfort whatsoever. The cars

A sign on the entrance to the main concentration camp at Auschwitz reads, "Arbeit Macht Frei," which translates as "work brings freedom." Even after many eyewitness accounts have been published, to this day some still deny that the horrors of the Holocaust actually happened. **MAIN COMMISSION FOR THE INVESTIGATION OF NAZI WAR CRIMES/USHMM PHOTO ARCHIVES.**

were sealed. We could not open them from the inside. The windows were small, open rectangles. Perhaps we could have jumped off the train and run into the countryside, but we did not know if anyone on the outside would help us. We thought most civilians would probably turn us in. We could not speak the Czech language. It seemed better to go along with the SS and do what they wanted. By that time the war had been going on four or five years. We thought the end might be in sight and we would be liberated.

Our train left the ghetto at six o'clock in the evening. At night as we traveled, we heard gun shots. We did not know why these shots were fired. After the war, I learned the SS troops were on the roofs of the cattle cars shooting past the windows to discourage people from sticking their heads out. The train was moving at a fairly great speed. We did not know what country we were going through. There was no stopping.

At four o'clock the next afternoon, we arrived in Auschwitz in Poland. When the train stopped, we again thought of trying to escape. But we knew that in Germany most Germans would turn us over to the local authorities for a reward of money or food. We had no way of knowing if the Poles would be any different. Someone would have to hide us or bring us food. We had no money to pay for our keep. So in the end, to keep our family together, we dropped any plans of attempting to escape.

The doors of the cattle car were yanked opened. The first thing we heard was shouts of, "Out, as soon as you can, out. Your belongings you leave there." Despite this we grabbed what we could and assembled outside. Before us stood an immense rectangle of land surrounded by electrically-charged barbed wire. This was the Auschwitz death camp.

We were assembled in long rows and marched between the troops of the SS special death-head division into the camp. We were marched up and down a broad avenue for four or five hours between posts of barbed wire with a huge sign, EXTREME DANGER, HIGH VOLTAGE ELECTRICAL WIRES. We saw guard towers high above us. We saw men with machine guns inside them, but even then we did not know that we were in a death camp. Back and forth and back and forth, they just kept us in motion. As it got closer to one o'clock in the morning, we were more and more desperate. You could hear more and more cries for food.

Finally they set out large boxes. Everybody had to put in their valuables. Women and men were forced to strip off their wedding rings and hand over their prized possessions like lockets of relatives no longer there. Whatever we had, we lost. Those who did not give up their possessions willingly or quickly were beaten. Then we were separated into male and female groups and walked to what they called the B camp of Auschwitz. The women's camp was separated from the men's camp by a wide road. There were about 24 barracks for men and the same number for women. . . .

Ben at Auschwitz

I'd heard rumors that Jews were going to Auschwitz. But I didn't know what Auschwitz meant. I didn't know what "extermination camp" meant. People told me, but I couldn't imagine or understand it. We were rounded up and packed into cattle cars like sardines. We could not move our arms or legs. We traveled for two days—day and night. The heat was unbearable. Then one morning at dawn, we looked through the cracks in the cattle car. I saw the name Auschwitz or *Oswiecim* in Polish. I was paralyzed. I got numb. I didn't feel anything. When daylight came, they slid the car door open. All we heard was, *"Raus, raus,* get out of here, get out of here!"* I had to crawl over people who had died from the heat and from lack of food and water.

When they opened the doors to the cattle car, we jumped off as quickly as we could because we were under orders. SS men with the skulls on their hats and collars stood in front of us stretched out at intervals about every ten feet. The SS officer in charge stood with his German shepherd. The officer had one foot propped up on a little stool. We lined up and filed by him. Right there the selection took place. As each person passed by him, he pointed left or right. The thumb left and right was your destiny. The people sent to the left went to the gas chambers, and we went to the right.

They told us we were going to be given some new clothing, but before that, we were sent into the showers. Luckily, when we turned the faucets we saw water instead of gas. We started washing ourselves. We got out and stood there. We were deloused because we had lice. One guard stood there putting some kind of a chemical on our heads. Another put it under our arms. A third one shaved our heads. Then we were given some prisoner's uniforms, very similar to the uniforms a prison chain gang used to wear here. We got wooden shoes. We didn't get the sizes we normally wore. We had to make do with what we got. Then we were lined up again in single file and tattooed on the forearm. My number was B-3348.

We were marched to a barracks in Birkenau. Birkenau was a part of Auschwitz. Above the entrance was an arch with an inscription which said in German, Work Makes Men Free, pretending that this was a work camp. There were two rows of barracks with a wide street between them. In front of us was a crematorium and gas chambers. We smelled the flesh of human bodies burning. We couldn't mistake that smell for anything else. . . .

Pincus at Auschwitz

When we left the ghetto, they put us on cattle trains. They packed 100 to 120 people into a sealed car. There was no food on the train. Fortunately it took us only about two days to get to the concentration camp. Trains from places farther east or south, like Greece, sometimes took ten days. Many of the people on these trains did not survive the trip. . . .

The capos woke us at five o'clock each morning. The capos were prisoners who were in charge of the barracks and the work groups. They were mostly Germans, Poles, and some Jews. The Nazis assigned them to guard us. In the morning they gave us one piece of bread mixed with sawdust to eat. We also got a piece of margarine and a cup of coffee. It was not real coffee. We had to work until the evening. In the evening we got soup. If we were fortunate, we might sometimes find a few potatoes and a piece of meat in the liquid. Most of the time it was just hot water and a few potatoes. For that we had to work 9 or 10 hours a day. When we first came there, we worked unloading gravel and coal from trains. If you didn't finish your assigned task, you got a beating. We were clothed in an undershirt and a thin, striped coat. We worked outside when it was often 10 to 15 below zero. People just froze to death.

The hunger was also terrible. We used to search for a potato peel and fight over it. We were constantly, 24 hours a day, always hungry. We would think about food and dream about it.

To survive in Auschwitz you had to get a break. My break came when I met a friend of mine from my hometown. He gave me the name of a man who had been in Auschwitz for a long time and was a good friend of my family. At Auschwitz, he supervised other inmates. I went to see him and asked if he could give my brother and me different jobs. Lucky for me, he gave us work making metal cabinets. Our job was to carry things. We were not cabinet makers, but we did the lifting. It was indoors. I don't think I could have survived the winter doing more outdoor work. I think he saved my life.

Every few months we had what they called a selection. They came into the barracks and picked out the people who looked very skinny and couldn't work anymore. They looked you over, and if they didn't see much fat on you, they put down your number. The next morning they came with trucks, picked up these people and put them right in the crematorium. It was heartbreaking.

Further Resources

BOOKS

Contemporary Portrayals of Auschwitz: Philosophical Challenges. Amherst, N.Y.: Humanity Books, 2000.

Greenspan, Henry. *On Listening to Holocaust Survivors: Recounting and Life History.* Westport, Conn.: Praeger, 1998.

Lagerwey, Mary D. *Reading Auschwitz.* Walnut Creek, Calif.: Alta Mira Press, 1998.

Langer, Lawrence L. *Holocaust Testimonies: The Ruins of Memory.* New Haven, Conn.: Yale University Press, 1991.

WEBSITES

Jaher, Frederic Cople. "America Views the Holocaust." *Historian,* Summer 2000. Available online at http://www.findarticles.com/cf_dls/m2082/4_62/64910252/print.jhtml (accessed April 22, 2003).

"Nuremberg Indictments." Court TV Casefiles. Available online at http://www.courttv.com/casefiles/nuremberg/indictments.html (accessed April 22, 2003).

Simon Wiesenthal Center. Multimedia Learning Center Online. Available online at http://motlc.wiesenthal.com/pages/ (accessed April 22, 2003).

11

SCIENCE AND TECHNOLOGY

JACQUELINE LESHKEVICH

Entries are arranged in chronological order by date of primary source. For entries with one primary source, the entry title is the same as the primary source title. Entries with more than one primary source have an overall entry title, followed by the titles of the primary sources.

Important Events in Science and Technology, 1940–1949

1940

- On May 15, the Vought-Sikorsky corporation conducts the first completely successful helicopter flight.
- On June 15, President Franklin D. Roosevelt establishes the National Defense Research Committee (NDRC), a new federal agency headed by Vannevar Bush to mobilize science for military purposes.
- In July, Physicist James Hillier of RCA completes construction of the first high-resolution electron microscope.
- In October, the Radiation Laboratory, a microwave-radiation lab nicknamed "Rad Lab," is established at the Massachusetts Institute of Technology to develop an airborne radar-intercept system.

1941

- John Vincent Atanasoff and Clifford Berry complete the Atanasoff Berry Computer (ABC), an unworkable prototype of the programmable digital computer.
- The Grand Coulee Dam begins operations in Washington state.
- Plutonium is isolated by Edwin M. McMillan and Glenn Theodore Seaborg.
- On June 28, an executive order by President Roosevelt establishes the Office of Scientific Research and Development (OSRD) to oversee and coordinate all wartime research and development. The OSRD will coordinate the development of radar, sonar, and the first stages of the atomic bomb.
- In August, the Rad Lab ASV (air-to-surface-vessel radar) detects ships twenty to thirty miles away and surfaced submarines two to five miles away.

1942

- Biologist Konrad E. Bloch and colleagues describe the biosynthesis of cholesterol.
- Napalm is developed by Harvard scientist Louis F. Fieser for use in U.S. Army flamethrowers.
- In January, physicists working on nuclear fission unite to form the Metallurgical Laboratory at the University of Chicago.
- In June, President Roosevelt gives Vannevar Bush approval for the Manhattan Project, a secret, large-scale effort to build an atomic bomb.

- On October 1, the Bell Aircraft Corporation tests the first American jet aircraft, the XP-59.
- In December, President Roosevelt approves $400 million for the Manhattan Project.
- On December 2, physicist Enrico Fermi achieves the first controlled release of nuclear energy in a chain reaction.

1943

- Biologists Salvador Luria and Max Delbruck demonstrate spontaneous mutation in bacteria.
- Physicist Luis Alvarez guides a distant plane to a landing using radar.
- In December, Howard Aiken completes the Harvard-IBM Mark I Automatic Sequence-Controlled Calculator (ASCC).

1944

- Biologist Oswald Avery and his colleagues at the Rockefeller Institute extract DNA from bacteria; the published results of their research lead to more intensive studies of the mechanisms of inheritance.
- The U.S. military uses the insecticide DDT to eradicate body lice among troops and civilians.
- Ralph Wyckoff and Robley Williams develop the metal-shadowing technique, permitting three-dimensional photographs with the electron microscope.
- On March 1, the Manhattan Project laboratory at Oak Ridge, Tennessee, produces the first milligrams of plutonium.
- In November, Grote Reber publishes the first radio-contour maps of the universe.

1945

- Geneticist George Beadle and biochemist Edward Tatum formulate the one gene-one enzyme hypothesis.
- The Federation of American Scientists (FAS) is founded by atomic scientists committed to the peaceful resolution of international disputes.
- On July 16, in the Trinity Test, the first atomic bomb is tested at Alamogordo, New Mexico.
- On August 6, the first atomic bomb used in warfare, an American uranium bomb, is dropped on Hiroshima, Japan, killing more than fifty thousand.
- On August 9, Americans drop a plutonium atomic bomb on Nagasaki, Japan, killing more than forty thousand.

1946

- Engineers J. Presper Eckert, Jr., and John W. Mauchly complete the ENIAC (Electronic Numerical Integrator and Calculator), the first successful automatic electronic digital computer.
- Biochemist Seymour Stanley Cohen pioneers the use of radioactive labeling of microorganisms.
- Physicists Felix Bloch and Edward Purcell independently introduce the technique of nuclear magnetic resonance.

- Anthropologist Ruth Benedict publishes *The Chrysanthemum and the Sword,* an effort to explain Japanese culture to the West; her study was financed by the U.S. government during World War II.

- On January 24, the United Nations sets up an Atomic Energy Commission and proclaims its intention to restrict atomic energy to peaceful uses.

- On June 14, the Baruch Plan, calling for control of atomic power, is presented to the United Nations. The plan calls for the destruction of the U.S. stockpile of atomic weapons and UN-monitored on-site inspections of the atomic-research facilities of all member nations.

- In August, Albert Einstein and others found the Emergency Committee of Atomic Scientists to encourage peaceful uses of atomic energy.

- On August 1, the U.S. Atomic Energy Commission is established to provide civilian control over military and nonmilitary atomic-energy development.

1947

- Chemist Willard Libby develops a radiocarbon-dating technique using the decay rate of carbon-14 atoms.

- On October 14, the Bell X-1, piloted by Capt. Charles E. Yeager, becomes the world's first airplane to fly faster than the speed of sound.

- In December, Harry Truman creates the Interdepartmental Committee for Scientific Research and Development to coordinate federal science.

1948

- John Bardeen, W.H. Brattain, and William Shockley invent the point-contact transistor.

- George Gamow announces his "big bang" theory of the universe's origins.

- Chemist Karl Folkers isolates vitamin B12.

- On January 2, the University of Chicago, in cooperation with seven individual corporations, announces that it will engage in atomic research for industrial development.

- On June 3, the largest existing telescope, the 200-inch Hale telescope, is completed at Mount Palomar Observatory at the California Institute of Technology.

1949

- Anthropologist Margaret Mead publishes *Male and Female: A Study of the Sexes in a Changing World,* claiming that many aspects of Western culture result from child-rearing practices in the West.

- Biologists John Enders, Thomas Weller, and Frederick Robbins cultivate the poliovirus in vitro on human embryonic tissue.

- Maurice Wilkes builds EDSAC, the first working computer with a stored program.

- Richard Feynman delivers a paper, "Space-Time Approach in Quantum Electrodynamics," in which he introduces "Feynman diagrams" to calculate the probable path integrals for electromagnetic scattering of atomic particles.

- In January, the National Bureau of Standards announces the development of an atomic clock.

- On February 24, the first rocket with more than one stage is successfully launched.

- On March 2, U.S. Air Force Superfortress B-50, *Lucky Lady II,* completes the first nonstop flight around the world.

- In July, the Federation of American Scientists opposes loyalty oaths for scientists applying for U.S. Atomic Energy Commission fellowships. In response, the commission decides to curtail its fellowship program.

- In August, the American Association for the Advancement of Science denounces loyalty programs and security clearance requirements at the Department of Defense and the Atomic Energy Commission.

- In November, construction begins on the world's first breeder reactor.

Linus Pauling's Research Notebooks

Notebook

By: Linus Pauling

Date: 1940–1949

Source: Pauling, Linus. Research Notebook 14, 1940–1949. Linus Pauling Archives. Available at Oregon State University online at http://osulibrary.orst.edu/specialcollections/rnb/14/14-056.html; website home page http://osulibrary.orst.edu (accessed March 21, 2003).

About the Author: Linus Pauling (1901–1994) was born in Portland, Oregon. He graduated from Oregon State Agricultural College in 1922 and earned his Ph.D. at the California Institute of Technology in 1925. For two years thereafter he worked in Europe with first-rate scientists. In 1927 he joined the faculty at Cal Tech, where he became a professor in 1931. His publications from 1935 to 1947 laid down the foundations for modern chemistry. He won the Nobel Prize in chemistry in 1954 for his work on quantam mechanics' application to chemistry. Pauling was not only a very prolific scientist, but also an activist. He was one of the first scientists to speak out against nuclear weapons and war. For his political efforts, in 1962, he was awarded a second Nobel Prize, this time for peace. Pauling's long and very productive life spanned almost the entire 20th century. ∎

Introduction

In the 1940s there was a tremendous amount of research in the U.S. taking place on the molecules of life; proteins, DNA, sugars, and lipids. At this time scientists knew quite a lot about "what" specific biological molecules did. But, little was known about "how" they did what they did. This is where Pauling fixed his attention: How did organisms transfer hereditary characteristics? How did enzymes recognize and bind to certain substances (called substrates) and thereby catalyze reactions? How did antibodies recognize and bind specific antigens and thus fight infection?

Found within Linus Pauling's research notebooks are experimental observations detailing the nature of chemical bonds and the chemistry of biological molecules. Pauling started this type of recording in 1922 and continued doing so until his death. His notebook entries dur-

Linus Pauling, two-time Nobel prize winner, examines a molecular model in his laboratory in Pasadena, California. AP/WIDE WORLD PHOTOS. REPRODUCED BY PERMISSION.

ing the 1940s focused on the binding of antibodies to antigens. Antibodies are a part of the immune response. They are produced when humans (and other animals) are exposed to foreign substances like proteins, bacteria, or viruses. Antigen is the general term used to describe any foreign substance that causes an immune response. Pauling's research notebooks 14 through 17 describe the experiments he performed in order to understand what happens when antibodies bind to antigens. What Pauling found was that binding is accomplished through the shape and size of molecules in addition to ordinary chemical properties. Large biological molecules like antibodies fold into specific shapes that allow only one, or a few, antigens to bind them. This biological specificity explains how the antibody for the chicken pox virus recognizes and binds only to the chicken pox virus. Pauling also introduced the concept of complementariness to explain biological specificity. Complementary molecules match up together. Antibodies and their antigens, enzymes and their substrates, and the two strands of DNA all exhibit complementariness.

Significance

Linus Pauling's work during the 1940s on the nature of antibody and antigen binding established the concept

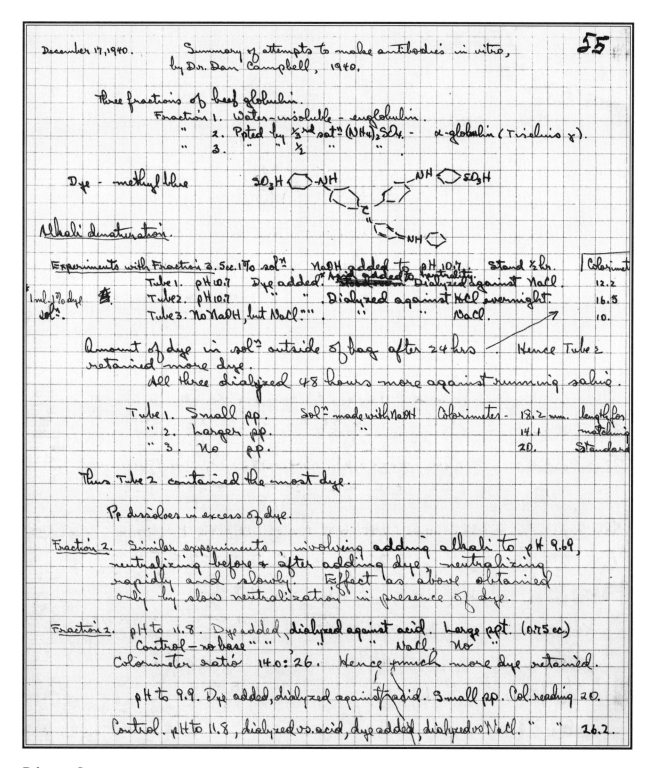

Primary Source

Linus Pauling's Research Notebooks [excerpt] (1 OF 3)

SYNOPSIS: The following excerpts from Pauling's research notebooks present unique access to the mind of this great scientist at work on a variety of issues. Linus Pauling's research notebook number 17, page 56, discusses the attempts to make antibodies in vitro. LINUS PAULING RESEARCH NOTEBOOKS, DECEMBER 1940: SUMMARY OF ATTEMPTS TO MAKE ANTIBODIES IN VITRO, BY DR. DAN CAMPBELL. FROM THE AVA HELEN AND LINUS PAULING PAPERS, SPECIAL COLLECTIONS, OREGON STATE UNIVERSITY.

Linus Pauling's Research Notebooks

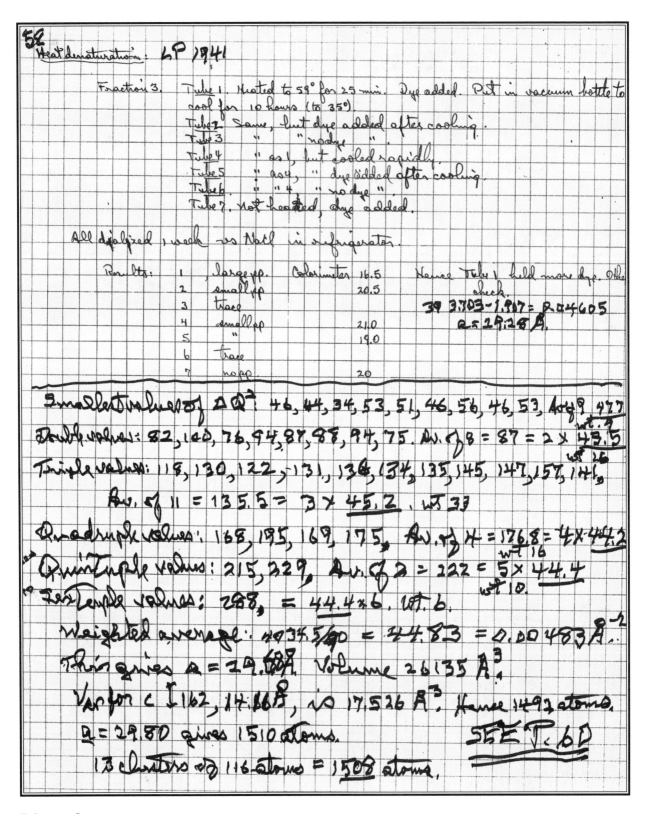

Primary Source

Linus Pauling's Research Notebooks [excerpt] (2 OF 3)
Linus Pauling's research notebook number 17, page 57, notes further attempts to make antibodies in vitro. LINUS PAULING RESEARCH NOTEBOOKS, DECEMBER 1940: SUMMARY OF ATTEMPTS TO MAKE ANTIBODIES IN VITRO, BY DR. DAN CAMPBELL. FROM THE AVA HELEN AND LINUS PAULING PAPERS, SPECIAL COLLECTIONS, OREGON STATE UNIVERSITY.

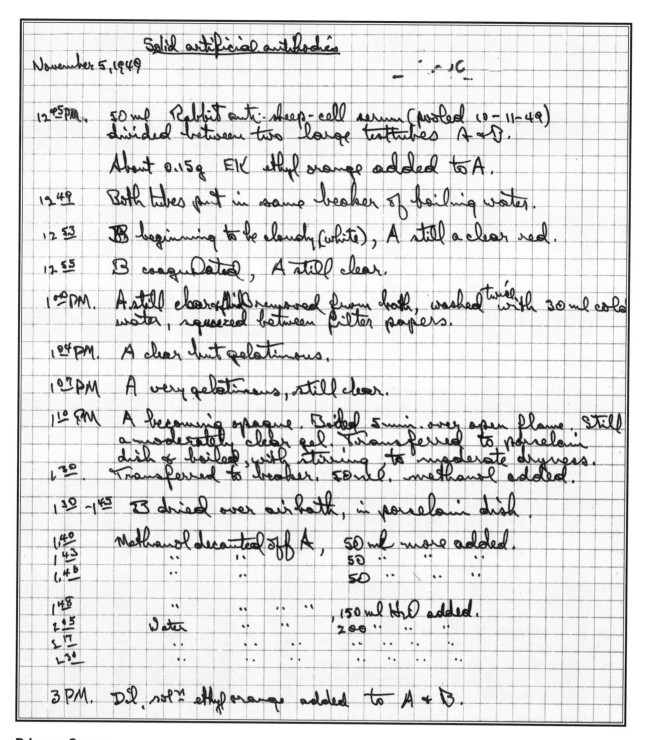

Primary Source

Linus Pauling's Research Notebooks [excerpt] **(3 OF 3)**

Linus Pauling's research notebook number 14, page 54, talks about solid, artificial antibodies. LINUS PAULING RESEARCH NOTE-BOOKS, NOVEMBER 5, 1949: "SOLID ARTIFICIAL ANTIBODIES". FROM THE AVA HELEN AND LINUS PAULING PAPERS, SPECIAL COLLECTIONS, OREGON STATE UNIVERSITY.

"Analogies between Antibodies and Simpler Chemical Substances" [excerpt]

I am convinced that it will be found in the future, as our understanding of physiological phenomena becomes deeper, that the shapes and sizes of molecules are of just as great significance in determining their physiological behavior as are their internal structure and ordinary chemical properties. I believe that the thorough investigation of the shapes and sizes of molecules will lead to great advances in fundamental biology and medicine; and because of this belief I am now turning my efforts in this direction. It seems clear that complementariness of the sort we have been considering must be involved in the autocatalytic activity (production of replicas) and heterocatalytic activity (production of other specific molecules) of the tens of thousands of genes that carry to us our inheritance from our ancestors.

And, moreover, I am convinced that progress in our attack against disease, in our better understanding of the human body, of bacteria, viruses, and other vectors of disease, and of their interactions with each other depends on a better understanding of intermolecular forces and interactions. "The long habit of living indisposeth us to dying";

and, as we have got better and better control over the infectious diseases, the degenerative diseases—cancer, cardiovascular disease—have become more and more important, and call more and more urgently for control: but we cannot yet attack these diseases in a straightforward way—we need leads, hints, which a better understanding of the phenomena of growth, development, and disease in terms of molecular structure would surely provide. I have hopes that it will be possible to carry on a program of research in molecular structure that will lead to significant contributions to biology and medicine.

Nearly sixty years ago Walt Whitman wrote about Life and Death:

The two old, simple problems ever intertwined,
Close home, elusive, present, baffled, grappled,
By each successive age insoluble, passed on
To ours today—and we pass on the same.

Let us resolve that as we pass on these problems to our following generation we shall make also our contribution toward their solution.

SOURCE: Pauling, Linus. "Analogies between Antibodies and Simpler Chemical Substances." Harrison Howe Memorial Lecture, Rochester, N.Y., February 1946. Available online at http://www.chem.rochester.edu/~rocacs /howe/pauling.htm; website home page: http://www.chem.rochester.edu (accessed March 31, 2003).

of the molecular basis of disease. During the first Harrison Howe Memorial Lecture in 1946, Pauling said, "I am convinced that progress in our attack against disease, in our better understanding of the human body, of bacteria, viruses, and other vectors of disease, and of their interactions with each other depends on a better understanding of intermolecular forces and interactions." Indeed Pauling's research on antibodies led to the understanding of the disease mechanism involved in Sickle Cell Anemia. Pauling's research into biological specificity (molecular recognition and binding) led to the discovery that hemoglobin in sickled red blood cells is misshapen and unable to function properly. This was the first time the cause of a disease was traced to a molecule. Linus termed this "molecular disease."

Pauling's work on complimentariness, chemical binding, and his discovery of the alpha helical structure in proteins, provided core principles in the field of molecular biology. James Watson and Francis Crick, who along with Maurice Wilkins received a Nobel Prize for determining the structure of DNA, give much of the credit for their discovery to Linus Pauling. The alpha helix, which Pauling discovered, is a key part of the structure of DNA. In 1954 Pauling won the Nobel Prize in Chemistry "for his research into the nature of the chemical bond

and its application to the elucidation of the structure of complex substances."

Further Resources

BOOKS

Hager, Thomas. *Force of Nature: The Life of Linus Pauling.* New York: Simon & Schuster, 1995.

Pauling, Linus. *General Chemistry.* (1947). New York: Dover, 1989.

Serafini, Anthony. *Linus Pauling: A Man and His Science.* Published by iUniverse.com, April 2000.

WEBSITES

Ava Helen and Linus Pauling Papers. Special Collections. Oregon State University. Available online at http://www.orst .edu/Dept/Special_Collections; website home page http:// www.orst.edu (accessed September 29, 2002).

Linus Pauling's Biography. Nobel e-Museum. Available online at http://www.nobel.se/chemistry/laureates/1954/pauling-bio .html; website home page http://www.nobel.se (accessed September 29, 2002).

"Scientist for the Ages." The Linus Pauling Institute. Available online at http://lpi.orst.edu (Accessed September 29, 2002).

"The Molecular Basis of Disease." The National Library of Medicine - Profiles in Science. Available online at http:// profiles.nlm.nih.gov/MM/Views/Exhibit/narrative/disease .html; website home page http://www.profiles.nlm.nih.gov (accessed August 11, 2002).

Atanasoff/Mauchly Correspondence, 1941

Letters

By: John V. Atanasoff and John W. Mauchly

Date: March–September 1941

Source: Atansoff, John V., and John W. Mauchly. Letters. March–September 1941. Reprinted in Mollenhoff, Clark R. *Atanasoff: Forgotten Father of the Computer.* Ames, Iowa: Iowa State University Press, 1988, 249–255.

About the Authors: John Vincent Atanasoff (1903–1995) was born near West Hamilton, New York. Mastering college algebra by the age of nine, Atanasoff eventually earned his Ph.D. in physics from Iowa State College (now University). In 1930, he joined the faculty staff at his alma mater, a position he held until 1952. He then established the Ordnance Engineering Corporation in Maryland, where he worked until his retirement in 1961.

John William Mauchly (1907–1980) was born in Cincinnati, Ohio, and received a Ph.D. in physics from Johns Hopkins University in 1932. In 1945, while a professor of physics at Ursinus College in Collegeville, Pennsylvania, Mauchly built the Electronic Numerical Integrator and Computer (ENIAC). ■

Introduction

While a graduate student during the 1920s, John Atanasoff studied helium's electronic structure, work that required weeks of laborious calculations. This drudgery left him longing for a machine that could do such calculations on its own. Those machines that already existed—the IBM "tabulator" and Monroe calculator—were excruciatingly slow and often inaccurate, so Atanasoff took it upon himself to develop a computer, a goal that he pursued as a physics professor at Iowa State College in Ames, Iowa.

With the help of graduate student and electronics wiz Clifford Berry (1917–1963), Atanasoff hit upon a design for the first digital computer. He decided to separate memory from computation, and made computation a function of a digital—rather than the more common but problematic analog—process. A digital computer assigns numbers to functions. The simplest digital process uses the binary system of "zero" and "one." Zero represents the cessation of flow of electricity to a computer component. Users know this as "off." One represents the flow of electricity to a component, which is when a computer is "on." Atanasoff coupled the idea of a binary system with electronic switches. Zero signaled a switch to turn off, whereas one signaled a switch to turn on. With this idea, humans no longer needed to flip switches, as had been the case with previous computers. Atanasoff's computer would perform this function on its own.

The difficulty with a binary system was that Atanasoff had to use a capacitor to represent zero and one.

A capacitor is the element that gives a computer its energy. When a capacitor holds no charge, it represents zero. When it holds a charge, it represent one. The problem with capacitors in those days is that they tended to lose their charge quickly, reverting to zero when what was needed was one. Atanasoff solved this dilemma by charging a capacitor at intervals, so it would not lose its charge.

Other problems plagued the project, as well, and while Atanasoff and Berry eventually overcame all these obstacles, it took years to do so. Finally, in 1939, the Atanasoff-Berry Computer (ABC) prototype was unveiled to the cries of an amazed university audience. With much encouragement, Atanasoff made efforts to obtain the necessary patents for the ABC, a process that took years and caused quite a controversy.

Significance

Shortly after introducing the ABC prototype, Atanasoff attended a lecture given by Dr. John W. Mauchly. Mauchly expressed great interest in Atanasoff's digital computer and asked to see the prototype. Atanasoff willingly agreed—a decision he would come to regret.

Unfortunately, Mauchly implemented many of Atanasoff's ideas in his design of the ENIAC, a digital computer that revolutionized the way information could be managed. As a result, Mauchly enjoyed popularity as the coinventor of the ENIAC. Even today, Mauchly is often hailed as the Father of the Computer, but those who work in the industry refer to Atanasoff as the Forgotten Father of the Computer.

Charges of piracy were eventually brought against Mauchly. But it wasn't until 1972 that Atanasoff was given the credit he deserved, when Judge Earl Richard Larson ruled that the ENIAC was "derived" from Atanasoff's ideas.

In building the first digital computer, Atanasoff and Berry laid the foundation for the modern computer. In 1944, Howard Aiken and a group of engineers at IBM built the Harvard Mark I, the successor to the ABC. Other models followed, with the transistor replacing the vacuum tube in the late 1950s. The transistor's small size, reliability, and low power consumption made it superior to the vacuum tube. In the late 1960s, computer engineers built the integrated circuit, a tiny silicon chip with hundreds of transistors, diodes, and resistors. The integrated circuit gave computers greater speed, memory, and reliability, and at lower cost. By the 1970s, engineers were able to pack thousands of transistors onto a chip smaller than a fingernail, and by the 1980s, a chip of only two square centimeters could hold three million transistors. Each advance brought better performance at lower prices. Today, the digital computer is the workhorse of home and office.

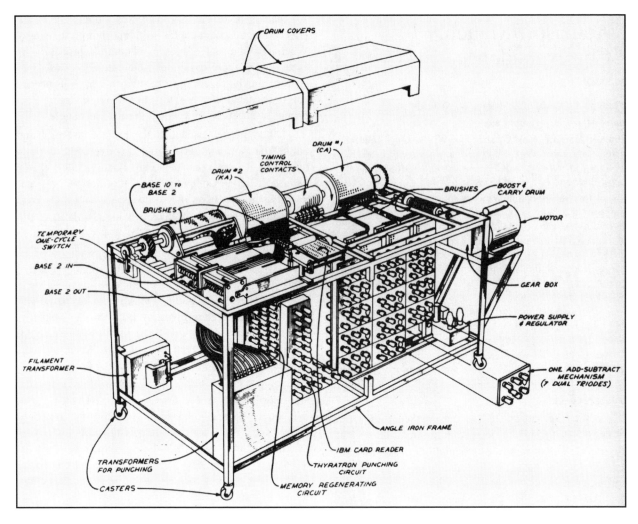

A drawing of the first digital computer, built by John Atanasoff and Clifford Berry. **REPRODUCED BY PERMISSION OF THE IOWA STATE UNIVERSITY LIBRARY/SPECIAL COLLECTIONS DEPARTMENT.**

Primary Source

Atanasoff/Mauchly Correspondence, 1941

SYNOPSIS: Frequent accounts report that John Atanasoff came up with his ideas for the first electronic digital computer over three Scotch-and-waters in an Iowa saloon. Whatever the origins, he unassumingly shared his ideas with John Mauchly, who integrated many of them into his ENIAC design. After the court hearings, Mauchly's patent was invalidated, but Atanasoff never received his. The digital computer belonged to everyone, which saves every computer company today from paying hundreds of thousands of dollars in licensing fees.

March 7, 1941

Dear Dr. Mauchly:

By all means, pay us a visit if you can arrange it. Just drop me a line letting me know when you will get here so I will be sure to be on hand. At present,

I am planning to attend the Washington meetings at the end of April. Several of the projects which I told you about are progressing satisfactorily. Pieces for the computing machine are coming off the production line and I have developed a theory of how graininess in photographic materials should be described and have also devised and constructed a machine which directly makes estimates of graininess according to these principals. We will try to have something here to interest you when you arrive if nothing more than a speech which you made.

Signed,
Dr. John V. Atanasoff

May 27, 1941

Dear Dr. Atansoff:

It was a disappointment to me, too, not to get in touch with you while in Washington. After leaving the message at the desk, I haunted the groups out on the grass in front of the East Building. Then when I again inquired at the desk I found that you had just collected the message and gone. Apparently you left the Bureau at once, so I went out to Urry's hoping to hear from you before we left. I fear that the message as you received it may not have contained the "dead-line" clause—that we were leaving about 8 o'clock.

Well, anyway, there is more than a little prospect of my making the trip, starting from here about the tenth of June. I have a passenger who will very likely pay for the gas, and that will help.

From your letters I have gathered that your national defense work is unconnected with the computing machine. This puzzles me, for as I understand it, rapid computation devices are involved in N.D. In a recent talk with Travis, of the E.E. School at U. of Pa. I asked him about this, and the matter seemed the same way to him. But if Caldwell has looked over your plans (I think you said that he was out there) and hasn't seen any N.D. possibilities, I suppose that means your computer is not considered adaptable to fire control devices, or that they have something even better. Travis (who goes into active duty with Navy this week) pointed out the advantages of lightness and mass-production for electronic computing methods, but said that when he was consulting with General Electronic over plans for the G. E. differential integraph they figured it would take about one-half million dollars to do the job electronically, and they would only spend 1/5 of that, so they built the mechanical type with polaroid torque-amplifiers.

I note that there is a physics colloquium at U. of Iowa June 12–14, and Sutton from Haverford is to be there. I wonder how he's travelling—maybe I could pick up another passenger!

It's too bad you couldn't stop when you were east, but try again—no doubt you will have to come east more often.

Sincerely yours,
J. W. Mauchly

May 31, 1941

Mr. J. W. Mauchly
Ursinus College
Collegeville, Pennsylvania

Dear Doctor Mauchly:

I think that it is an excellent idea for you to come west during the month of June or any other time for that matter. You might visit the Physics Colloquium at the University of Iowa if you wish. I generally do

not go because the discussions are mainly in the field of physics teaching. But you could either go back by Iowa City or stop on your way west. Or, if it proves more convenient, I could drive you over. We have plenty of room and will be delighted to have you stay with us while here.

As you may surmise, I am somewhat out of the beaten track of computing machine gossip, and so I am always interested in any details you can give me. The figures on the electronic differential integraph seem absolutely startling. During Dr. Caldwell's last visit here, I suddenly obtained an idea as to how the computing machine which we are building can be converted into an integraph. Its action would be analogous to numerical integration and not like that of the Bush Integraph which is, of course, an analogue machine, but it would be very rapid, and the steps in the numerical integration could be made arbitrarily small. It should therefore equal the Bush machine in speed and excel it in accuracy.

Progress on the construction of this machine is excellent in spite of the amount of time that defense work is taking, and I am still in a high state of enthusiasm about its ultimate success. I hope to see you within two or three weeks.

Very sincerely yours,
J. V. Atanasoff
Associate Professor, Math. and Physics
JVA:vb

June 22, 1941

Dear J.V.,

The trip back here was uneventful, except for the fact that I was carrying on a mental debate with myself on the question of whether to teach at Hazleton, or to learn something of U. of Pa. My natural avarice for knowledge vied with that for money, and won out, so after obtaining assurance from Marsh White at State College that they could find someone else to take the Hazleton work, I dropped that and prepared to become a student again.

I drove to Southbridge, Mass., Friday evening, and looked through the American Optical plant on Saturday morning. They seem quite serious in their intentions toward me, but no decision is to be made for several weeks.

On the way back east a lot of ideas came barging into my consciousness, but I haven't had time to sift them or organize them. They were on the subject of computing devices, of course. If any look promising, you may hear more later.

The first digital computer, built by John Atanasoff and Clifford Berry in 1941. REPRODUCED BY PERMISSION OF THE IOWA STATE UNIVERSITY LIBRARY/SPECIAL COLLECTIONS DEPARTMENT.

I do hope that your amplifier problem has been licked by some adequate design. The tubes that I ordered two weeks ago aren't here yet, so I couldn't try anything here even if I had time.

I forgot to ask what happens to Cliff Berry after he gets a master's degree—does he stay on for Ph.D. work?

Please give the enclosed note to your wife. We enjoyed our trip very much, and hope you can stop here some time.

Sincerely,
J. W. Mauchly

June 28, 1941

Dear Mr. Clayton,

Up to a few days ago I was in hope of making a trip to Massachusetts this June with the possibility of returning the Sundstrand machine which you

so kindly lent us. Now it appears that I can't do that, and within the week I shall properly pack the machine and forward it by express.

I know this must have inconvenienced you already, and I feel that we owe you a great deal for your loan.

Immediately after commencement here, I went out to Iowa State University to see the computing device which a friend of mine is constructing there. His machine, now nearing completion, is electronic in operation, and will solve within a very few minutes any system of linear equations involving no more than thirty variables. It can be adapted to do the job of the Bush differential analyzer more rapidly than the Bush machine does, and it costs a lot less.

My own computing devices use a different principle, more likely to fit small computing jobs.

All my time since coming back from Iowa has been taken up with an Emergency Defense Training

Course at the Univ. of Pa. I had a chance to teach for the summer in a defense course given to high school graduates, but turned that down in order to become a student myself. I am working in electrical engineering and electronics. Whether or not I am given a defense job involving electronics later on, the training will be helpful in connection with electronic computing devices.

I haven't had any chance to work on weather problems recently. I did hear Rossby talk at Iowa City—concerning the training of students for meteorology, etc. Let's hope your own work is getting along well.

Sincerely yours,
John W. Mauchly

September 30, 1941

Dear J.V.:

This is to let you know that I still have the same living quarters, but a different job. During the summer I looked around a bit while sounding out the Ursinus people as to promotions and assistance; I finally gave up the idea of taking an industrial job (or a navy job) and stayed in the ranks of teaching.

The Moore School of Electrical Engineering (Univ. of Pa.) is what I have joined up with, and they have me teaching circuit theory and measurements and machinery—but only 11 hours a week instead of the 33 that Ursinus had developed into.

As time goes on, I expect to get a first-hand knowledge of the operation of the differential analyzer—I have already spent a bit of time watching the process of setting up and operating the thing—and with more such background I hope I can outdo the analyzer electronically.

A number of different ideas have come to me recently: anent computing circuits—some of which are more or less hybrids, combining your methods with other things, and some of which are nothing like your machine. The question in my mind is this: Is there any objection, from your point of view, to my building some sort of computer which incorporates some of the features of your machine? For the time being, of course, I shall be lucky to find time and material to do more than merely make exploratory tests of some of my different ideas, with the hope of getting something very speedy, not too costly, etc.

Ultimately a second question might come up, of course, and that is, in the event that your present design were to hold the field against all challengers, and I got the Moore School interested in having something of the sort, would the way be open for us to build an *"Atanasoff Calculator"* (a la *Bush* analyzer) here?

I am occupying the office of Travis, the man who designed the analyzer here (duplicated at Alberdeen); I think I told you that he is now in the Navy, so I have no opportunity of benefiting by his rich experience.

I hope your defense efforts have been successful, but not so time-consuming as to stop progress on the computer. When you are East, arrange to see us. Perhaps you would like to look over the diff. analyzer, etc.

Convey my best regards to your family, and Cliff Berry and all the gang.

Sincerely yours,
John W. Mauchly

Further Resources

BOOKS

Burks, Alice, and Arthur Burks. *The First Electronic Computer: The Atanasoff Story.* Ann Arbor, Mich.: University of Michigan Press, 1988.

Mollenhoff, Clark R. *Atanasoff: Forgotten Father of the Computer.* Ames, Iowa: Iowa State University Press, 1988.

WEBSITES

"John Atanasoff." About.com—Inventors. Available online at http://inventors.about.com/library/inventors/blatanasoff_berry .htm; website home page: http://www.inventors.about.com (accessed December 13, 2002).

"John Vincent Atanasoff and the Birth of the Digital Computer." Iowa State University Department of Computer Science. Available online at http://www.cs.iastate.edu/jva /jva-archive.shtml; website home page: http://www.cs.iastate .edu (accessed December 13, 2002).

"John W. Mauchly and the Development of the ENIAC Computer: The John Atanasoff Controversy." University of Pennsylvania Library. Available online at http://www.library .upenn.edu/special/gallery/mauchly/jwm7.html; website home page: http://www.library.upenn.edu (accessed December 13, 2002).

"Reconstruction of the Atanasoff-Berry Computer (ABC): 60 Years of Digital Computing." Scalable Computing Laboratory, Iowa State University. Available online at http: //www.scl.ameslab.gov/ABC; website home page: http:// www.scl.ameslab.gov (accessed December 13, 2002).

Heredity and Environment
Report

By: Robert S. Woodworth
Date: 1941

Source: Woodworth, Robert S. *Heredity and Environment: A Critical Survey of Recently Published Materials on Twins and Foster Children.* New York: Social Science Research Council, 1941, 1–3.

About the Author: Robert S. Woodworth (1869–1962) became interested in psychology while taking philosophy courses at Amherst College in Massachusetts. As a graduate student at Harvard, he encountered William James's *Principles of Psychology,* which inspired him to study psychology in earnest, though he retained his interest in philosophy. Finally settling on psychology in 1903 (twelve years after graduation), Woodworth joined the faculty of Columbia University. His 1938 book, *Experimental Psychology,* was considered the "bible" in its field for many years. ■

Introduction

In 1941, Woodworth was asked by the Committee on Social Adjustment of the Social Science Research Council to weigh in on the "nature versus nurture" debate. Woodworth was an expert at asking the right question, and sifting through a large amount of information to find the answer. In *Heredity and Environment,* Woodworth reviewed a number of published reports on child development. His focus was to determine whether experimental investigation could settle the debate, which centers on the question: What is more important to human mental development, heredity or environment?

Woodworth was a firm believer in experimental psychology, where scientific research methods are used in the study of human behavior. The basic design of a scientific experiment consists of a control group and a sample group. The control and sample groups are exactly the same except for precisely one variable. In this way the *effect* of the variable can be observed in the outcome of the experiment.

The collection of reports Woodworth reviewed described studies involving either foster children or identical twins reared apart. These two situations were unique in that they afforded experimental psychologists rare ways to study human development within scientific experimental parameters. Unrelated children growing up in the same foster home have a different genetic make-up, but grow up in the same environment. This situation provides insight into the effect of genes on development. Twins provide an alternative set of circumstances. Identical twins growing up in different families have identical genetic traits but grow up in different environments. In this case the importance of environment on child development can be studied.

Woodworth didn't make any striking conclusions in his review. However, he did provide valuable observations and offered suggestions for future research to help clarify the issues concerning heredity versus environment. Included in Woodworth's observations was the finding that in practice there were serious difficulties in separating genetic factors from environmental factors when it comes to human intelligence and personality. Intelligence quotient (IQ) tests were, and still are, generally used to assess intelligence. But in the 1940s there was no way to directly determine an individual's genetic makeup.

Significance

Ever since the discovery of genes—the smallest units of inheritance, whereby parents pass traits to their offspring—society has debated the importance of genetics in intelligence, behavior, and personality. That genetics determine the physical characteristics of individuals is well-known. Hereditary traits such as hair, eye, and skin color, as well as some diseases like Cystic Fibrosis, are clearly linked to particular genes. However, when it comes to psychological characteristics such as intelligence, behavior, or personality, the role of genetics is less clear. Many people believe genes matter less in shaping an individual mentally than the *environment* in which the individual grows up, or develops. In the early twenty-first century, as well as in the 1940s when Robert S. Woodworth wrote, most scientists, including Woodworth, agree that both genes and environment are factors. Woodworth says, "To ask whether heredity or environment is more important to life is like asking whether fuel or oxygen is more necessary for making a fire."

In 1941, the Social Science Research Council, comprised of representatives from several important American scientific associations, such as the American Anthropological Association, the American Psychological Association, and the American Sociological Association, asked Woodworth to appraise published scientific research concerning nature versus nurture. *Heredity and Environment* was the result. Wordworth's conclusions assisted the Council to formulate its position in the debate.

Woodworth's review of the published material on twins and foster children is regarded as a significant report in the nature versus nurture debate. Woodworth's work was important in highlighting the importance of experimental investigation in psychology. His conclusions and suggestions for future work influenced many who came after him. He called for assessing *environments* based upon clearly established *environmental factors* known to affect development, such as economic or educational level of parents. The debate on heredity versus environment continues in the early twenty-first century, and has yet to be resolved.

Primary Source

Heredity and Environment: A Critical Survey of Recently Published Materials on Twins and Foster Children [excerpt]

SYNOPSIS: In this excerpt Woodworth explains the purpose and value of the report that he was asked to produce. In particular he explains why the question of heredity vs. environment is best addressed by critically examining the methods and findings of recent studies on identical twins reared apart and foster children.

Nothing is more certain, after a little consideration, than the statement that heredity and environment are coacting factors in the development of any living individual and that both are absolutely essential. If the individual's hereditary potencies could somehow be annulled he would immediately lose all physiological and mental characteristics and would remain simply a mass of dead matter. If he were somehow deprived of all environment, his hereditary potencies would have no scope for their activity and, once more, he would cease to live. To ask whether heredity or environment is more important to life is like asking whether fuel or oxygen is more necessary for making a fire. But when we ask whether the *differences* obtaining between human individuals or groups are due to their differing heredity or to differences in their present and previous environments, we have a genuine question and one of great social importance. In a broad sense both heredity and environment must be concerned in causing individuals to be different in ability and personality, but it is a real question whether to attach more importance to the one or the other and whether to look to eugenics or euthenics for aid in maintaining and improving the quality of the population.

Biologists, because of the very impressive advances in the science of genetics, are quite justifiably inclined to stress the importance of heredity in the human field. Sociologists and educators, dealing with environmental factors, are properly inclined to emphasize the importance of environment. Psychologists are more divided in their interests and it is perhaps in the field of this science that the controversy between hereditarians and environmentalists is most acute. The progress of investigation has however made it necessary for each party to recognize some merit in the claims of the other. Genetics is forced to admit that the genetic determination of such a human trait as intelligence is exceedingly complex and not easily to be controlled by eugenic measures. Educators and sociologists are forced to recognize the existence of large and obstinate individual differences in every important human trait. It would seem that the rapprochement between the two parties has gone far enough to enable them to join forces in investigation. In any competent study of the problem, at least with respect to human be-

Twins have always been of particular interest in studies regarding heredity and one's development. © H. ARMSTRONG ROBERTS/CORBIS. REPRODUCED BY PERMSSION.

ings, it is necessary to combine a sound knowledge of genetics with a full appreciation of the possibilities of learning and adjustment to the physical and social environment.

Because of the intricate interplay of heredity and environment in human behavior, it is easy to fall into the habit of interpreting all the differences among men in terms either of heredity or of environment. The same body of data will appear to one student as obviously resulting from the one cause, and to another student as quite clearly the result of the other. Musical ability runs in families—a clear instance of heredity to one student, of environmental influences to another. The investigator's task is to produce a body of data which is susceptible to only one interpretation. He wishes to find some situation in which either heredity or environment is uniform, so that the differences which appear there can be attributed to the factor which varies.

Two typical situations in which some separation of the factors occurs furnish the basis for the recent studies covered by the present review. Both are concerned with the development of children, especially their intellectual development. Concentration of effort on this phase of development is due largely to the relatively satisfactory measures available for the intelligence of children. One typical situation is afforded by the mental development of twins, and the other by that of foster children. In connection with the study of foster children, some of the work on children reared in institutional homes will receive brief mention.

The limitations of the review must be recognized. It does not aim to cover all the relevant studies but devotes itself mostly to a few of the recent investigations which have given rise to rather strong claims on one side or the other. The reviewer, from intensive and repeated scrutiny of the published reports, has endeavored to discover what can be accepted as definitely or probably proved, and what must be regarded as undecided pending further investigation.

Further Resources

BOOKS

Burlingham, Dorothy. *Twins: A Study of Three Pairs of Identical Twins.* London: Imago, 1952.

Ceci, Stephen, J. and Williams, Wendy, M., eds. *The Nature-Nurture Debate: The Essential Readings.* Malden, Mass.: Blackwell, 1999.

Woodworth, Robert. S. "Autobiography of Robert S. Woodworth." In *History of Psychology in Autobiography,* vol. 2. Carl Murchison, ed. Worcester, Mass.: Clark University Press, 1930, 359–380.

————. *Contemporary Schools of Psychology,* 3rd ed.. New York: Ronald Press, 1964.

————. *Experimental Psychology,* Rev. ed. New York: Holt, 1954.

————. *First Course In Psychology.* New York: Holt, 1951.

PERIODICALS

Thorndike, Edward L., and Robert S. Woodworth. "The Influence of Improvement in One Mental Function upon the Efficiency of Other Functions (I-II-III)." *Psychological Review* 8, 1901, 247–261, 384–395, 553–564.

WEBSITES

"Autobiography of Robert S. Woodworth ." *Classics in the History of Psychology.* Available online at http://psychclassics .asu.edu/Woodworth/murchison.htm; website home page: http://psychclassics.asu.edu/ (accessed October 19, 2002).

Minnesota Twin Family Study. Available online at http://www .psych.umn.edu/psylabs/mtfs/default.htm; website home page: http://www.psych.umn.edu/ (Accessed September 29, 2002).

Twins Studies—Abstracts. Available online at http://psych .fullerton.edu/nsegal/twins.html; website home page: http:// psych.fullerton.edu (accessed October 19, 2002).

"Feasibility of a Chain Reaction"
Report

By: Enrico Fermi

Date: November 26, 1942

Source: Fermi, Enrico. "Feasibility of a Chain Reaction." Report CP-383, November 26, 1942. In *Collected Papers, Volume II: United States 1939–1954.* Chicago: University of Chicago Press, 1965.

About the Author: Enrico Fermi (1901–1954) was born in Rome, Italy. As a student, he excelled in mathematics and physics. His academic achievements won him a scholarship at the University of Pisa, where he received his Ph.D. in physics in 1922. In 1927, he became professor of theoretical physics at the University of Rome. In 1938, Fermi won the Nobel Prize for his contributions to the knowledge of nuclear energy. That same year, he came to the United States and participated in the Manhattan Project to develop the atomic bomb. He was professor of physics at Columbia University from 1939 to 1942. By the time of his death, Fermi held more than fifteen patents, including that of the first nuclear reactor. ∎

Introduction

A plaque at the University of Chicago reads: "On December 2, 1942, man achieved here the first self-sustaining chain reaction and thereby initiated the controlled release of nuclear energy." This achievement was accomplished by the group of scientists and engineers involved in the Manhattan Project, a U.S. attempt to develop a nuclear bomb for World War II (1939–1945). The Germans attempted a similar undertaking across the Atlantic, but only the U.S. project succeeded.

The Manhattan Project was based on Enrico Fermi's work in nuclear fission, the fragmenting of atomic nuclei. In 1938, Fermi won the Nobel Prize in physics for his identification of new radioactive elements and his discovery of nuclear reactions affected by neutron bombardment. Immediately after he accepted the Nobel Prize, Fermi and his family emigrated to the United States from Italy. After Italy declared war on the United States, Fermi was considered an "enemy alien." Though he was the chief physicist and essential to the success of the Manhattan Project, Fermi was said to be only "a consultant."

"Feasibility of a Chain Reaction" was one of several reports written by Fermi documenting the progress of the Manhattan Project. In the report, dated November 26, 1942, Fermi discussed the factors that would provide a *self-sustaining* nuclear chain reaction. Fermi was an expert in a type of nuclear reaction in which the nucleus of the radioactive element uranium was fragmented, or fissioned, by neutron bombardment. This bombardment by neutrons resulted in the release of more neutrons, which

Scientists who took part in the building of the first atomic pile gather in 1946 on the fourth anniversary of the accomplishment. Among those gathered is Enrico Fermi, front row, left. © CORBIS. REPRODUCED BY PERMISSION.

in turn bombarded nearby uranium atoms, resulting in the release of more neutrons, and so on. Certain conditions needed to exist for the reaction to be self-sustaining, however. The most important of these factors was *coefficient k,* called the reproduction or multiplication factor because it referred to how fast the neutrons multiplied. In his report, Fermi noted that coefficient k must be kept constant for the reaction to proceed sustainably and at a slow, controllable rate. If coefficient k got too high, Fermi said, the reaction would proceed sustainably, but it would do so uncontrollably and with a huge explosive force.

On December 2, 1942, Fermi and his colleagues achieved a controlled nuclear chain reaction. However, the goal of the Manhattan Project was not the *controlled* release of nuclear energy, but an *explosive* reaction. For the atomic bomb, coefficient k was not to be kept constant, but to be sent as high as possible.

Significance

Though Fermi's work on nuclear fission—and, specifically, on coefficient k—initially resulted in the achievement of a controlled nuclear reaction, it also resulted in the ultimate goal of the Manhattan Project: the creation of an uncontrolled nuclear reaction, or an atomic bomb. On August 6, 1945, the United States dropped an atomic bomb on the Japanese city of Hiroshima. Three days later, a second was dropped on Nagasaki, essentially ending the war.

Fermi's work enabled humans to harness some of the vast power contained within atomic nuclei. Most of the scientists involved in the Manhattan Project believed that the United States needed to develop the atomic bomb before the Germans did. They also believed that the bomb would save lives by bringing the war to a swift end. However, they were sobered and aghast at seeing the actual destruction the bombs wrought.

The first experimental nuclear reaction was designed at the University of Chicago under the collaborative efforts of a large group of scientists. © CORBIS. REPRODUCED BY PERMISSION.

The United States and the rest of the world still live under the specter of nuclear menace. No atomic bombs have been dropped since World War II, but the threat of a nuclear war has never gone completely away. During the Cold War, Americans lived with the palpable threat of nuclear war as the Soviet Union and United States squared off. With the opening of the Iron Curtain, Russia is now more friend than foe, but the nuclear menace has simply changed hands. In the early twenty-first century, the biggest nuclear threat to the United States may come from countries such as North Korea.

The atomic bomb was not the only result of Fermi's work on nuclear fission and coefficient k. The energy contained within atomic nuclei can be harnessed for the production of electricity. If coefficient k is kept constant, as Fermi asserted, the nuclear chain reaction is controllable. At nuclear power plants across the nation, con-trolled nuclear reactions produce heat that is used to spin turbines and generate electricity. In 2002, about 15 percent of the electricity generated in the United States was provided by nuclear power.

Primary Source

"Feasibility of a Chain Reaction" [excerpt]

SYNOPSIS: In this excerpt from his November 26, 1942, report, Fermi discusses recent experiments that confirm the feasibility of a controlled nuclear chain reaction. Just six days later, on December 2, he and his colleagues would achieve such a reaction.

Will the Reaction Be Self-sustaining?

Since the early discussions on the possibilities to produce a chain reaction by making use of the neutrons emitted in the fission of uranium, it appeared that two essential factors determine whether the reaction will or will not be self-sustaining.

(a) One of them is the so-called reproduction factor k. This is defined as the average number of neutrons that are produced in one generation per neutron absorbed in a system of infinite large dimensions. It is clear that a system of sufficiently large size will be chain-reacting provided its reproduction factor is greater than 1. If the reproduction factor is less than 1, it is not possible to produce a chain-reaction by an increase of the dimensions.

(b) If the neutrons are generated in a system of finite size, some of the neutrons are lost by diffusion outside of the reacting mass. We express this factor in terms of a coefficient of retention l defined as the probability that a neutron produced inside the mass will not leak out.

It is clear that the leakage factor will increase with increasing dimensions of the system and will approach 1 when the dimensions become infinitely large. For a system of spherical shape the leakage factor is given approximately by the formula $l = \dfrac{1}{1 + \dfrac{A}{R^a}}$ where R is the radius and A is a constant.

For a uranium-graphite system A is of the order of 7000 cm^2.

The condition for the production of a self-sustaining chain reaction is that the total number of neutrons does not change. This is the case when the product of a reproduction factor and diffusion factor is equal to 1, i.e.:

$$kl = 1.$$

If kl is less than 1, the number of neutrons present in the system will gradually decrease. If kl is greater than 1, the number of neutrons present in the system will increase exponentially.

If the reproduction factor is larger than 1 by only a very small amount, the size of a chain-reacting system shall have to be very large so as to keep the loss of neutrons due to leakage very small.

If the reacting system has a spherical shape, one can find immediately from the two preceding formulas that the critical radius is given approximately by the expression $R = \sqrt{\dfrac{A}{k - 1}}$.

It follows from the preceding discussion that one of the primary tasks for the experimental production of a chain-reaction is to develop methods for mea-

suring the reproduction factor k for various arrangements. . . .

Will the Reaction Be Thermally Stable?

From the practical point of view of planning and constructing chain reacting units in which large amounts of energy can be released, it is important to know the effect of changes of temperature on the reactivity of the system. If the reactivity increases with increasing temperature, the system would be thermally unstable because an accidental rise of the temperature would increase the development of energy and consequently determine a further rise of temperature. If, instead, the reactivity decreases with increasing temperature, the system is thermally stable. . . .

Will the Reaction Be Controllable?

Since it is by no means certain that chain-reacting systems will be thermally stable, it is very important to develop methods for the control of the reaction capable of keeping the system operating at any required level of energy production. Most of the controlling devices that have been considered so far involve the use of substances having a strong neutron absorption that should be introduced inside the pile so as to reduce the number of neutrons available for the reaction. Such substances may be in the form of solid rods that can be pushed mechanically in suitable slots in the pile. Or they may be liquids that can fill up to a controlled level one or more pipes passing inside the pile. Or they may be gases which could be introduced at a variable pressure and would fill the empty spaces in the graphite conglomerate. Of these various possibilities, the only one that has been developed to a considerable extent is the use of solid rods.

Further Resources

BOOKS
de Latil, Pierre. *Enrico Fermi: The Man and His Theories.* New York: Paul S. Eriksson, 1966.

Fermi, Enrico. "Atomic Energy for Power." The George Westinghouse Centennial Forum: Science and Civilization—The Future of Atomic Energy (May 1946). In *Collected Papers.* 2 vols. Edoardo Amaldi et al., eds. Chicago: University of Chicago Press, 1962–1965, 550–557.

Segre, Emilio. *Enrico Fermi: Physicist.* Chicago: University of Chicago Press, 1970.

Weaver, Jefferson Hane, ed. *The World of Physics,* vol. 2. New York: Simon & Schuster, 1987.

WEBSITES
"Enrico Fermi." Time 100: Scientists and Thinkers. Available online at http://www.time.com/time/time100/scientist/profile

/fermi.html; website home page: http://www.time.com (accessed October 17, 2002).

"Enrico Fermi—Biography." Nobel e-Museum. Available online at http://www.nobel.se/physics/laureates/1938/fermi-bio .html; website home page: http://www.nobel.se (accessed October 17, 2002).

The Enrico Fermi Institute. Available online at http://efi .uchicago.edu (accessed October 17, 2002).

Fermi National Accelerator Laboratory. Available online at http://www.fnal.gov (accessed October 17, 2002).

"Race for the Superbomb." The American Experience. Available online at http://www.pbs.org/wgbh/amex/bomb/index .html; website home page: http://www.pbs.org (accessed October 17, 2002).

ENIAC Progress Report

ENIAC Progress Report

Report

By: Mauchly, John W., and J. Presper Eckert, Jr.
Date: 1942–1947
Source: *ENIAC Progress Report.* Document sent to Ballistic Research Lab, Aberdeen Proving Ground, MD, 1944.
About the Authors: John W. Mauchly (1907–1980) attended John Hopkins University on scholarships due to his outstanding academic achievements. Though initially interested in engineering, he received a doctorate degree in Physics, and obtained a professorship at Ursinus College, near Philadelphia. In 1941, he became affiliated at the Moore School of Electrical Engineering of the University of Pennsylvania. Here Mauchly was able to combine his interests in engineering and physics by working on the pioneering ENIAC (Electronic Intgrator and Computer) project, together with J. Presper Eckert Jr., with whom he would be associated for the rest of his life.
J. Presper Eckert Jr. (1919–1995) received a Master's degree in electrical engineering from the University of Pennsylvania in 1941. He was Chief Engineer at that university's Moore School of Electrical Engineering when John Mauchly wrote a preliminary report on the possible construction of a computer, which resulted in the ENIAC project. A founder of the Eckert-Mauchly Computer Corporation in 1946, Eckert became vice president of the Remington Rand Division of Sperry Rand Corporation in 1955. He served in that position until 1962, during which time the company became UNIVAC and then UNISYS. Among his many awards was the U.S. National Medal of Science in 1969.

"Computer Operators Work on the ENIAC"

Photograph

By: Anonymous
Date: ca. 1946

Source: "Computer Operators Work on the Eniac." ca. 1946. Corbis. Image no. BE056270. Available online at http://pro .corbis.com (accessed April 30, 2003).

"General View of the ENIAC"

Photograph

By: Anonymous
Date: April 1946
Source: "General View of the ENIAC." April 1946. Library of Congress. ■

Introduction

World War II (1939–1945) was the driving force behind many inventions in the 1940s. At the U.S. Army Ballistics Research Laboratory (BRL), much of the work centered on calculating machines that were used to produce firing tables for field artillery. Firing tables contained trajectories needed by gun crews to fire artillery shells accurately. Each trajectory (the path and landing location of the shell) was based on a series of complicated mathematical calculations that took into account factors such as the size of the gun, type of projectile, air temperature, wind speed, humidity, and wind direction.

The BRL sponsored many projects at the University of Pennsylvania Moore Electrical Engineering School. The Moore School had an analog computing device called the differential analyzer, which was able to perform the calculations needed for one trajectory in about thirty minutes. This was the quickest method available to the Army for producing the artillery firing tables.

One of the adjunct professors at the Moore School, John W. Mauchly was an avid meteorologist. While thinking about a device that could assist with weather prediction, he had come up with an idea for a different kind of computing machine. Unlike the analog differential analyzer, Mauchly's machine was based on digital signals. Analog machines represent data using measurable ranges whereas digital machines represent data with discrete (individually distinct) items.

In 1941 Mauchly met Presper P. Eckert, a brilliant engineer at the Moore School. Eckert, the engineer, and Mauchly, the theoretician eventually submitted a proposal to the U.S. Army to build the Electronic Numerical Integrator And Computer, or ENIAC. The ENIAC employed more than 18,000 vacuum tubes and many thousands of relays and resistors for operation. It used decimal arithmetic, which meant that it was based on a scale of ten and it incorporated a form of conditional branching, called logic. It was the first electronic computer.

The constant pressure for firing tables led the Army to accept Mauchly and Eckert's proposal. Every time the Army built a new gun, used a new artillery shell, or op-

Primary Source

"Computer Operators Work on the ENIAC"

SYNOPSIS: Frances Bilas (right) and Bett Jennings arrange the program settings on the Master Programmer, 1946.
© BETTMANN/CORBIS. REPRODUCED BY PERMISSION.

erated in a new geographic area, a fresh set of firing tables had to be produced. Theoretically, the ENIAC could calculate a trajectory in less than five minutes. On June 5, 1943, the Army officially contracted for the making of the ENIAC.

Significance

The Electronic Numerical Integrator And Computer, or the ENIAC, is considered the most important predecessor of the modern computer. Like many inventions, modern computers evolved over time based upon the efforts of several scientists. Other computing machines constructed around the same time include the Atanasoff-Berry Computer, (ABC), the Harvard Mark I, the Electronic Discrete Variable Calculator (EDVAC), the Electronic Delay Storage Automatic Computer (EDSAC), and the Automatic Computing Engine (ACE). However, the ENIAC was the first general purpose electronic digital computer; it, more than any other machine, pointed to the future.

That ENIAC was used for weather prediction was fitting, since this is what Mauchly had intended when he first conceptualized a digital computing machine. But the ENIAC wasn't used only for its intended purpose. The U.S. Army accepted John W. Mauchly and J. Presper Eckert's proposal for the ENIAC in order to speed up the production of artillery firing tables that were needed in World War II. It performed calculations used in the development of the hydrogen bomb, wind tunnel design, and weather forecasts. However, the ENIAC wasn't completed until 1946, after the war had ended.

The ENIAC caused the federal government to realize that high-speed computing could serve more than just military purposes. In 1946, the U.S. War Department issued a press release concerning the ENIAC. Titled "The Uses of Computers in Industry," it described the computer as a means of accelerating economic growth and establishing civilian industries after a devastating war. The ENIAC had convinced military scientists and tech-

Primary Source

"General View of the ENIAC"

SYNOPSIS: The ENIAC, an immense system, occupied a 30x50 foot room. THE LIBRARY OF CONGRESS.

nical experts of the value and practicality of electronic computation.

Primary Source

ENIAC Progress Report [excerpt]

SYNOPSIS: This excerpt discusses how the ENIAC was built and the controversy that surrounded it since its invention by John Mauchly and J. Presper Eckert, Jr.

In this report, submitted in accordance with the terms of Contract W-670-ORD-4926, some items will be found discussed in detail, and others of equal importance but briefly. This is a consequence of the fact that this report is a final report for the six-months' work ending December 31, 1943 and at the same time must have some of the characteristics of a progress report since the project, as anticipated by both the sponsors and the contractor, was well under way but not near completion at that date. A topic which might logically be expected to appear but which is not discussed is not a topic ignored, but rather one on which work had not progressed sufficiently up to December 31, 1943 to warrant detailed reporting.

The project was orginally undertaken as a result of consideration of ballistic calculations as carried out by the Army Ordnance Department. The ENIAC will, however, be an instrument of quite general character, composed of units which will perform the operations of addition, subtraction, multiplication, division, and function-remembering. Despite frequent references to possible applications in ballistics, the essential generality of the ENIAC should be kept in mind insofar as this report is concerned.

The primary objective of the development is to increase the *speed* of ballistic computations. The successful conclusion of the project would cut the time by a large factor, and would give an *accuracy* sufficient for all presently foreseen purposes. The ENIAC is being made as *flexible* as possible, and a large amount of attention has been given to *reliability* of operation.

It was hoped originally that counter circuits and other circuits of basic importance would be available from the work of others. Actually this has not been found to be the case, and a large amount of effort has been given over to the development of circuits of sufficient scope and reliability to be included in the ENIAC.

A second change from original plans has involved placing programming equipment with each

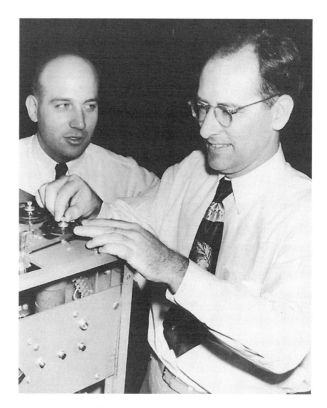

J. Presper Eckert (left) and Dr. John W. Mauchly work with a tape recording-transmitting machine. **AP/WIDE WORLD PHOTOS. REPRODUCED BY PERMISSION.**

unit; for example in an accumulator panel as now being built approximately 30 per cent of the equipment is for programming purposes. Programming is thus very appreciably decentralized.

No attempt has been made to make provision for setting up a problem automatically. This is for the sake of simplicity and because it is anticipated that the ENIAC will be used primarily for problems of a type in which one setup will be used many times before another problem is placed on the machine. Thus the units of the ENIAC will provide addition, subtraction, multiplication, division, and function-remembering devices, but the appropriate joining of these for carrying out a problem will be done by plugging in connections manually.

At the time the project was started, the means of recording the results were left in abeyance. This is primarily a question to be resolved by the sponsor, and plans were being made at the date of this report to decide the form in which results are desired. (Without output printers or other devices, the ENIAC will indicate results by signal lamps.)

In the month and a half following the date (December 31, 1943) of this report, final wiring diagrams and construction drawings have been prepared for most of the circuits not reported in detail here, and construction of complete panels has been begun.

Further Resources

BOOKS

Davis, Martin. *The Universal Computer: The Road from Leibniz to Turing.* New York: Norton, 2000.

Eckert, John Presper, and John Mauchly. "The Electronic Numerical Integrator and Computer" (ENIAC). US Patent Office. Patent # 3,120,606. Filed on June 26, 1947.

Freiberger, Paul, and Michael Swaine. *Fire in the Valley: The Making of the Personal Computer.* New York: McGraw-Hill, 2000.

Mauchly, John. "The Use of High Speed Vacuum Tube Devices for Calculating." Unpublished memo. University of Pennsylvania Library, ca. 1943.

Mauchly, John, and J. Presper Eckert, Jr. "A Progress Report on the EDVAC." Internal Document. University of Pennsylvania Library, September 30, 1945.

McCartney, Scott. *ENIAC: The Triumphs and Tragedies of the World's First Computer.* New York: Walker, 1999.

PERIODICALS

Weik, Martin H. "The ENIAC Story." *Ordnance: Journal of the American Ordnance Association,* January–February 1961, 9–23.

WEBSITES

"John W. Mauchly and the Development of the ENIAC Computer." Penn Special Collections, University of Pennsylvania Library. Available online at http://www.library.upenn.edu /special/gallery/mauchly/jwmintro.html; website home page: http://www.library.upenn.edu (accessed October 19, 2002).

"Presper Eckert and John Mauchly: The ENIAC and UNIVAC Computers." Available online at http://inventors.about.com /library/inventors/bleniac.htm#enac; website home page: http:// www./inventors.about.com (accessed October 19, 2002).

"Presper Eckert Interview." Smithsonian National Museum of American History. Computer History Collection. Available online at http://americanhistory.si.edu/csr/comphist/eckert .htm; website home page: http://americanhistory.si.edu (accessed October 19, 2002).

Radar Electronic Fundamentals

Reference work

By: Bureau of Ships, U.S. Navy

Date: June 1944

Source: Bureau of Ships, U.S. Navy. *Radar Electronic Fundamentals.* Washington, D.C.: U.S. Government Printing Office, 1944, 1–4. ■

Introduction

The use of the airplane during World War I (1914–1918) led military planners to seek a way of detecting planes before they could attack troops and materiel. In 1930 Lawrence Hyland, a staff officer at the U.S. Naval Research Laboratory, discovered that radio signals transmitted from the ground reflected back from airplanes to the ground, allowing troops to detect them while they were still miles away.

Another officer at the National Research Laboratory, Leo Young, modified Hyland's discovery by producing short bursts of radio waves at fixed intervals. Young conceived of high frequency radio waves clustered in short bursts and sweeping the sky in all directions. The reflection of waves from aircraft fixed their location, and the time required for the waves to return to the sender revealed the distance of aircraft from the sender. In the work of Hyland and Young lay the origin of what the U.S. Navy would call radio direction and ranging, or radar.

Significance

By the end of 1942 British and U.S. physicists had perfected radar. This excerpt from *Radar Electronic Fundamentals* defines radar, describes how it works, and lists its uses. It emphasizes the use of radar in detecting aircraft and the coordination of radar with anti-aircraft guns to shoot down enemy aircraft. Radar was effective not only from the ground, the author noted, but from ships and airplanes. Radar became the eyes of U.S. and British forces during World War II (1939–1945).

Radar was crucial to America's success during the war. The U.S. faced the challenge of fighting a two-front war—one theater in Europe and the other in the Pacific. The detection of enemy aircraft was important in both theaters, particularly in the Pacific, where U.S. and Japanese fleets fought one another with aircraft and never came within sight of one another.

During World War II, a Dr. Jewett, president of the National Academy of Sciences, called the conflict a "physicists' war," in contrast to World War I, which had been called the "chemists' war" (Bernhelm Booss and Jens Høyrup). In addition to the development of radar, the most spectacular achievement of the physicists was the development of the atomic bomb, which ended World War II when the U.S. Army Air Corps dropped two atomic bombs on Hiroshima and Nagasaki, Japan.

Thanks to these achievements, American physicists emerged from the war with unprecedented prestige. A poll in 1945 revealed that the American public had greater respect for physicists than for the members of any other profession. The prestige of physics led to a close relationship between the federal government and physicists after the war. A few years later, the rise of the Cold War led the federal government to fund military research at the physics laboratories of America's universities. Physics had become essential to the nation's defense.

Primary Source

Radar Electronic Fundamentals [excerpt]:
Reference work

SYNOPSIS: In this excerpt, the author defines radar, describes how it works, and lists its uses. The author emphasized the use of radar in detecting enemy aircraft and the coordination of radar with anti-aircraft guns to shoot down enemy aircraft. Radar was effective not only from the ground but from ships and aircraft. Illustrations accompanying the original text are reproduced here.

Introduction to Radar

1. Definition

Radar is a radio device which may be used to locate airplanes or ships in darkness, fog, or storm. Radar means *radio direction and ranging*. It is one of the greatest scientific developments which has emerged from World War II. Its development, like the development of every other great invention, was mothered by necessity, that is, off-setting an offensive weapon which first appeared in the last war— the airplane. The basic principles upon which its functioning depends are simple. Therefore, the seemingly complicated series of electrical events encountered in radar can be resolved into a logical series of functions.

2. Principles of Operations

a. Sound wave reflection

(1) The principle upon which radar operates is very similar to the principle of sound echoes, or wave reflection. If a person shouts toward a cliff, or some other sound-reflecting surface, he hears his shout "return" from the direction of the cliff. What actually takes place is that the sound waves, generated by the shout, travel through the air until they strike the cliff. They are then "bounced off" or reflected, some returning to the original spot where the person hears the echo. Some time elapses between the instant the sound originates and the time when echo is heard, since sound waves travel through air at approximately 1,100 feet per second. The farther the person is from the cliff, the longer this time interval will be. If a person is 2,200 feet from the cliff when he shouts, 4 seconds elapse before he hears the echo: 2 seconds for the sound waves to reach the cliff and 2 seconds for them to return.

(2) If a directional device is built to transmit and receive sound, the principles of echo and velocity of sound can be used to determine the direction, distance, and height of the cliff shown in figure 1. A

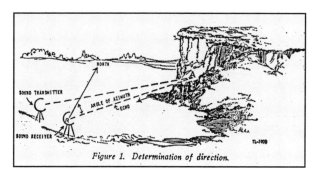

Figure 1. Determination of direction.

Figure one from *Radar Electronic Fundamentals,* an illustration of the method of determining the direction of an object. **RADAR ELECTRONIC FUNDAMENTALS. NAVSHIPS900,016. NAVY DEPT. BUREAU OF SHIPS. JUNE 1944**

source of pulsating sound, at the focus of a parabolic reflector, is so arranged that it throws a parallel beam of sound. The receiver is a highly directional microphone located inside a reflector to increase the directional effect. The microphone is connected through an amplifier to a log speaker. It is assumed that the distance between the transmitter and receiver is negligible compared with their distance from the cliff.

(3) To determine distance and direction, the transmitting and receiving apparatus is placed so that the line of travel of the transmitted sound beam and the received echo coincide. The apparatus is rotated until the maximum volume of echo is obtained. The distance to the cliff can then be determined by multiplying one–half of the elapsed time in seconds by the velocity of sound, 1,100 feet per second. This will be the distance along the line R–A. If the receiver has a circular scale which measures degrees of rotation and which has been properly oriented with a compass, the direction or azimuth of the cliff can be found. Thus, if the angle read on the scale is 45 degrees, the cliff is northeast from the receiver position.

(4) To determine height (fig. 2), the transmitter and receiver are elevated from the horizontal position while still pointing in the same direction. At first the echo is still heard but the elapsed time is increased slightly. As the angle of elevation is increased further, a point is found where the echo disappears. This is the angle at which the sound is passing over the top of the cliff and therefore is not reflected back to the receiver. The point at which the echo just disappears is that where the angle of elevation is such that the apparatus is pointed at *B*. If the receiver is equipped with a scale to read the angle of elevation, the height of the cliff *A–B*

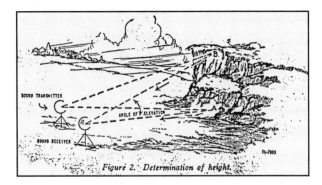

Figure two from *Radar Electronic Fundamentals,* an illustration of the method of determining the height of an object. **RADAR ELECTRONIC FUNDAMENTALS. NAVSHIPS900,016. NAVY DEPT. BUREAU OF SHIPS. JUNE 1944**

can be calculated from this angle and the distance *R–A.*

b. Radio wave reflection

(1) All radar sets work on a principle very much like that described for sound waves. In radar sets, however, a radio wave of an extremely high frequency is used instead of a sound wave (fig. 3) The energy sent out by a radar set is similar to that sent out by an ordinary radio transmitter. The radar set, however, has one outstanding difference in that it picks up its own signals. It transmits a short pulse, and receives its echoes, then transmits another pulse and receives its echoes. This out-and-back cycle is repeated from 60 to 4,000 times per second, depending upon the design of the set. If the outgoing wave is sent into clear space, no energy is reflected back to the receiver. The wave and the energy which it carries simply travel out into space and are lost for all practical purposes.

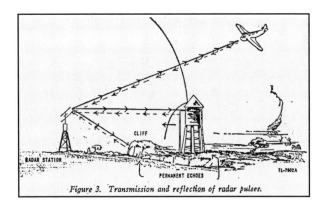

Figure 3. Transmission and reflection of radar pulses.

Figure three from *Radar Electronic Fundamentals,* an illustration of the transmission and reflection of Radar pulses. **RADAR ELECTRONIC FUNDAMENTALS. NAVSHIPS900,016. NAVY DEPT. BUREAU OF SHIPS. JUNE 1944**

(2) If, however, the wave strikes an object such as an airplane, a ship, a building, or a hill, some of the energy is sent back as a reflected wave. If the object is a good conductor of electricity and is large, compared to a quarter-wavelength of the transmitted energy, a strong echo is returned to the antenna. If the object is a poor conductor or is small, the reflected energy is small and the echo is weak.

(3) Radio waves of extremely high frequencies travel in straight lines at speed of approximately 186,000 miles per second as compared to 1,100 feet per second for sound waves. Accordingly, there will be an extremely short time interval between the sending of the pulse and the reception of its echo. It is possible, however, to measure the interval of elapsed time between the transmitted and received pulse with great accuracy—even to one ten-millionth of a second.

(4) The directional antennas employed by radar equipment transmit and receive the energy in a more or less sharply defined beam. Therefore, when a signal is picked up, the antenna can be rotated until the received signal is maximum. The direction of the target is then determined by the position of the antenna.

(5) The echoes received by the radar receiver appear as marks of light on a specially constructed instrument called the "oscilloscope," often called "scope" for short. This scope may be marked with a scale of miles, or degrees, or both. Hence, from the position of a signal echo on the scope, an observer can tell the range and direction of the corresponding target.

3. Uses Of Radar

a. General

Modern defense against aircraft attack requires that the presence, height, bearing, and range of hostile airplanes be make known long before the airplanes can be seen or heard. This knowledge must be available irrespective of atmospheric conditions; fog, clouds, or smoke during the day or night must not interfere with the detection of hostile aircraft. Radar has provided a source for such information, and at the same time has opened new fields for greatly improving traffic control and safety for both airplanes and ships.

b. Long-range reporting or search

Reporting is accomplished by fixed or shipborne stations constantly searching a specific area to warn

This large radar receiver array was used by the U.S. Air Force. **THE LIBRARY OF CONGRESS.**

of enemy attack. Information from such stations is recorded continuously. The data are used to guide interceptor craft toward an enemy target.

c. Gun laying or fire control

Radar sets capable of determining with a high degree of accuracy the range, bearing, and elevation of the enemy target when within firing range are used for the control of land-based defense equipment, such as searchlights, antiaircraft, batteries, and coastal batteries. Similar radar sets aboard ships are used for fire control, for antiaircraft secondary, and main batteries. In such applications the data must be formulated rapidly and accurately.

d. Airborne use

Portable equipment is used in patrol aircraft to search for the presence of enemy targets; and in combat aircraft to locate the target, and for fire control. The equipment may be designed for the detection of aircraft, surface vessels, or submarines. It may also be used as an aid to navigation to determine the course or position in relation to a home beacon station.

e. Identification

It is possible to use auxiliary equipment with radar to determine whether an echo has come from a friendly or enemy craft.

4. Historical Development

One of the first observations of "radio echoes" was made in the United States in 1922 by Dr. Albert H. Taylor of the Naval Research Laboratory. Dr. Taylor observed that a ship passing between a radio transmitter and receiver reflected some of the waves back toward the transmitter. Between 1922 and 1930 further tests proved the military value of this principle for the detection of surface vessels which were hidden by smoke, fog, or darkness. Further developments were conducted with carefully guarded secrecy. During this same period Dr. Breit and Dr. Tuve, of the Carnegie Institute, published reports on the reflection of pulse transmission from electrified layers in the upper atmosphere which forms the earth's ceiling. This led to the application of the principle to the detection of aircraft. Other countries carried on further experiments independently and with the utmost secrecy. By 1936, the United States Army was engaged in the development of a radar warning system for coastal frontiers. Between 1936 and 1940, the pulse system of transmission was further developed. By the end of 1940, mass production of radar equipment was under way. By September 1940, the British had developed radar to such a point that they were able to bring down great numbers of enemy airplanes with very little loss to themselves. Beginning in 1941, British-American cooperation in the development of radar has given the United Nations the best radar equipment in the world. However, our enemies have also made great strides in radar development. This was evidenced by the sinking of the British battle cruiser Hood by the German battleship Bismarck, by means of radar range finding, before the Hood could fire her second salvo.

Further Resources

BOOKS

Berkowitz, Raymond S., ed. *Modern Radar: Analysis, Evaluation, and System Design.* New York: Wiley, 1965.

Brookner, Eli, ed. *Aspects of Modern Radar.* Boston: Artech House, 1988.

Eaves, Jerry L., and Edward K. Reedy, eds. *Principles of Modern Radar.* New York: Van Nostrand Reinhold, 1987.

Page, Robert M. *The Origin of Radar.* Garden City, N.Y.: Anchor Books, 1962. Reprint, Westport, Conn.: Greenwood Press, 1979.

Skolnik, Merrill I. *Introduction to Radar Systems,* 3rd ed. Boston: McGraw-Hill, 2001.

Tzannes, Nicolaos S. *Communication and Radar Systems.* Englewood Cliffs, N.J.: Prentice-Hall, 1985.

PERIODICALS

Bell, John. "A Short History of Early Radar." *Electronics Australia,* July 1996, 20–25.

WEBSITES

Booss, Bernhelm, and Jens Høyrup. "On Mathematics and War." Available online at http://mmf.ruc.dk/~boos/mathwar/boos-hoyrup.pof; website home page: http://mmf.ruc.dk (accessed July 9, 2003).

"Invention of Radar." Available online at http://murray.newcastle.edu.au/users/staff/eemf/ELEC351/SProjects/Calligeros/Page1.htm#start; website home page: http://www.murray.newcastle.edu (accessed October 21, 2002).

"Radar Was an Accident." Available online at http://www.speedsite.com/~temps/January2.htm; website home page: http://www.speedsite.com (accessed October 21, 2002).

"World's Greatest Mathematical Calculator"

Press release

By: Harvard University

Date: August 7, 1944

Source: News Office, Harvard University. "World's Greatest Mathematical Calculator." August 7, 1944. Reprinted in Cohen, Bernard et al., *Makin' Numbers: Howard Aiken and the Computer.* Cambridge, Mass.: MIT Press, 1999. Appendix A, 249–252.

About the Author: Howard Aiken (1900–1973), born in Hoboken, New Jersey, received a bachelor's degree in electrical engineering from the University of Wisconsin in 1923. Following ten years of work as an engineer for public utilities, he enrolled at Harvard for graduate studies, where he earned his doctorate in physics in 1939. He then began a five-year project, working with engineers at the International Business Machines laboratory, to design and build a large-scale calculator. The machine they constructed is considered to mark the beginning of the computer era. Aiken retired from Harvard in 1961 and later held a business/consulting position for several years at the University of Miami, Florida. ∎

Introduction

The ideas that were the basis for the Mark I originated in 1937 and were based on Howard Aiken's scientific needs. Aiken, a graduate student in communication engineering at Harvard, routinely encountered difficult and tedious mathematical problems. He believed that such laborious calculations could be mechanized, and he eventually pitched his idea to Thomas Watson, chief executive officer of IBM.

Howard Aiken stands next to his early computer, which was created for IBM. © BETTMANN/CORBIS. REPRODUCED BY PERMISSION.

In 1939 IBM agreed to build a mechanized calculating machine based on Aiken's design. The Mark I was assembled by IBM engineers based on Aiken's specifications, and it was based on devices for the most part that were already a part of IBM's technical inventory, such as tape readers, decimal counters, and dial switches.

The Mark I was a complex machine with shafts and gears powered by an electric motor. It computed with discrete (separately distinct) numbers, and therefore was digital. The needs of war spurred the construction of many advanced computing machines. Yet very few of the new *digital* machines, which eventually evolved into modern computers, actually were used in the war. It was *analog* technology, such as Vannevar Bush's Differential Analyzer, that was actually the workhorse during World War II (1939–1945). However, the Mark I was actually one of the few digital machines that did get some use in the war effort.

The Harvard News Release concerning the Mark I created some controversy. The original Harvard News Release referring to the inventor of the Mark I mentioned only Howard Aiken, angering Thomas Watson of IBM. Subsequently, a revised news release was published, giving more credit to IBM.

Significance

The Mark I was an early entrant in computer history. It was one of several computing machines developed during this time. Others included the Atanasoff-Berry Computer (ABC), IBM's electronic multiplier, the ENIAC, the Electronic Discrete Variable Calculator (EDVAC), the Electronic Delay Storage Automatic Computer (EDSAC), and the Automatic Computing Engine (ACE).

The Harvard Mark I was the first of four large calculating machines designed by Howard Aiken. Mark II, Mark III, and Mark IV were based on the original Mark I. The Mark I was digital and represented an improvement over analog computing devices such as Vannevar Bush's Differential Analyzer. However, it was mechanically driven and could not perform logical operations.

The ENIAC, which came soon after the Mark I, was the first completely electronic digital computer and was at least a thousand times faster than the Mark I.

The significance of the Howard Aiken–designed Mark I in the history of the modern computer was not in its use of any new circuitry or its blazing computational speed. Rather, it is important because it demonstrated that machines could solve complicated mathematical problems without errors.

Primary Source

"World's Greatest Mathematical Calculator"
[excerpt]

> **SYNOPSIS:** This Harvard news release is about the Mark I invented by Howard Aiken with the assistance of IBM engineers. The terms of its "dedication" in 1944 presenting Aiken as the sole inventor caused a rift, with Aiken and Harvard on the one side and IBM on the other.

The world's greatest mathematical calculating machine, a revolutionary new electrical device of major importance to the war effort, will be presented today to Harvard University by the International Business Machines Corporation to be used by the Navy for the duration.

This apparatus will explore vast fields in pure mathematics and in all sciences previously barred by excessively intricate and time-consuming calculations, for it will automatically, rapidly, and accurately produce the answer of innumerable problems which have defied solution.

The ceremonies in University Hall today will include the presentation of the automatic sequence controlled calculator by Mr. Thomas J. Watson, president of International Business Machines Corporation, and its acceptance by President James B. Conant, of Harvard University. The formal transfer of the machine will be attended by high ranking Navy officers, state and university officials, executives and engineers of International Business Machines Corporation, and representative leaders of science and industry.

The machine is completely new in principle, unlike any calculator previously built. An algebraic superbrain employing a unique automatic sequence control, it will solve practically any known problem in applied mathematics. When a problem is presented to the sequence control in coded tape form it will carry out solutions accurate to 23 significant figures, consulting logarithmic and other functional tables, lying in the machine or coded on tapes. Its powers are not strictly limited since its use will sug-

gest further developments of the mechanisms incorporated.

In charge of the activity since the installation of the calculator in the Research Laboratory of Physics at Harvard is the inventor, Commander Howard H. Aiken, U.S.N.R. (B.S. University of Wisconsin '23, A.M. Harvard University '37, Ph.D. Harvard University '39) who worked out the theory which made the machine possible. Commander Aiken, now on leave as Associate Professor of Applied Mathematics in the Harvard Graduate School of Engineering, began his work on the device in 1935, when he joined the Harvard staff as Instructor in Physics and Communication Engineering.

Two years of research were required to develop the basic theory. Six years of design, construction, and testing were necessary to transform Commander Aiken's original conception into a completed machine. This work was carried on at the Engineering Laboratory of the International Business Machines Corporation at Endicott, New York, under the joint direction of Commander Aiken and Clair D. Lake. They were assisted in the detailed design of the machine by Frank E. Hamilton and Benjamin M. Durfee.

Commander Aiken was assisted by Ensign Robert V.D. Campbell, U.S.N.R., during the latter years of the construction of the machine. Commander Aiken having been detailed to other Naval duties, Ensign Campbell, then a civilian attached to Harvard University, carried on in a liaison and research capacity.

The machine is of light-weight, trim appearance: a steel frame, 51 feet long and 8 feet high, a few inches in depth, bearing an interlocking panel of small gears, counters, switches, and control circuits. There are 500 miles of wire, 3,000,000 wire connections, 3,500 multiple relays with 35,000 contacts, 2,225 counters, 1,484 ten-pole switches, and tiers of 72 adding machines, each with 23 significant numbers.

When in operation in the soundproofed Computation Laboratory, the calculator is so light and so finely geared that it makes no more noise than a few typewriters.

The new calculator is not designed for a specific purpose, but is a generalized machine that will do virtually any mathematical problem. Among the many problems treated are: 1. Computation and tabulation of functions. 2. Evaluation of integrals. 3. Solution of ordinary differential equations. 4. Solution of simultaneous linear algebraic equations. 5. Harmonic analysis. 6. Statistical analysis. . . .

When this calculator returns to civilian use and others like it are built, they will be of the greatest importance in astronomy in the solutions of dynamic equations of the solar system, never solved because of their intricacy and the enormous time and man-power requirements. . . .

It is already possible to visualize the peacetime functions of the calculator in pure and applied sciences. This machine is but the first step towards the establishment of a computation bureau which Commander Aiken hopes to establish for consultation by the research laboratories of science and industry.

Further Resources

BOOKS

Aiken, Howard. "The Automatic Sequence Controlled Calculator." Lecture 13, July 16, 1946. "Electro-Mechanical Tables of the Elementary Functions. Lecture 14, July 17, 1946. Moore School of Electrical Engineering. University of Pennsylvania. In *The Moore School Lectures.* Martin Campbell-Kelly and Michael. Williams, eds. Cambridge, Mass.: MIT Press, 1985.

Cohen, I. Bernard. *Howard Aiken: Portrait of a Computer Pioneer.* Cambridge, Mass.: MIT Press, 1999.

Cohen, I. Bernard, et al, eds. *Makin' Numbers: Howard Aiken and the Computer.* Cambridge, Mass.: MIT Press, 1999.

Davis, Martin. *The Universal Computer: The Road from Leibniz to Turing.* New York: Norton, 2000.

PERIODICALS

Aiken, Howard. "Trilinear Coordinates." *Journal of Applied Physics* 8, 1937, 470–72.

Aiken, Howard, and Grace Hooper. "The Automatic Sequence Controlled Calculator." *Electrical Engineering* 65, 1946, 391, 449–554.

WEBSITES

"Howard Hathaway Aiken." School of Mathematics and Statistics, University of St. Andrews, Scotland. Available online at http://www-groups.dcs.st-and.ac.uk/~history/Mathematicians/Aiken.html; website home page: http://www-maths.mcs.st-andrews.ac.uk/ (accessed October 20, 2002).

"Howard Aiken's Mark I (the IBM ASCC)." Maxfield & Montrose Interactive Inc. Available online at http://www.maxmon.com/1939ad.htm; website home page: http://www.maxmon.com (accessed October 20, 2002).

Hoyle, Michelle A. "History of Computing Science: The Harvard Mark I". Available online at http://www.eingang.org/Lecture/hmark1.html; website home page: http://www.eingang.org (accessed October 20, 2002).

"As We May Think"

Magazine article

By: Vannevar Bush
Date: July 1945

Source: Bush, Vannevar. "As We May Think." *Atlantic Monthly* 176, no. 1, July 1945, 641–649. Available online at http://www.theatlantic.com/unbound/flashbks/computer/bushf.htm; website home page: http://www.theatlantic.com (accessed March 20, 2003).

About the Author: Vannevar Bush (1890–1974) was born in Everett, Massachusetts. He received his M.S. degree from Tufts College in 1913, and earned Ph.D. degrees from both Harvard and MIT in 1916. Three years later he joined the MIT faculty and became professor of electrical engineering in 1923, vice president and dean of engineering in 1932, and president of the Carnegie Institution in Washington, D.C. in 1939. Among Vannevar Bush's many accomplishments and contributions to U.S. science and technology policy was the formation of the research partnerships that would develop the ARPANET, from which the Internet evolved. ∎

Introduction

World War II (1939–1945) was all but over—the Germans had surrendered and the Japanese were on the brink of surrendering—when "As We May Think" was published in *Atlantic Monthly*. Vannevar Bush, an electrical engineer, was the Director of the Office of Scientific Research and Development. He was responsible for coordinating scientists to help in the war effort. During the war, U.S. scientists literally stopped what they were doing to focus their attention on research that would help the United States defeat German and Japanese forces.

In his role as coordinator of the scientific effort during the war, Bush was impressed by the tremendous amount of research being conducted. The 1940s were very prolific for science. New discoveries, inventions, and scientific revelations were occurring regularly. Bush realized that awareness, access to, and organization of scientific information were crucial, as well as transmission of information between scientists. He noted that the tools available for managing information in 1945 were crudely inefficient, and would never be able to keep up with the huge amount of work being done. Bush feared that important discoveries might somehow get lost and go unrecognized in a sea of information.

In "As We May Think," Bush proposed, "a device in which an individual stores all his books, records, and communications, and which is mechanized so that it may be consulted with exceeding speed and flexibility." Bush called this device a "memex" short for "memory extension." Bush saw the memex as a way of "threading through the consequent maze to the momentarily important item." When the human mind thinks about one thing, many other things are usually tied to it. These other things are tied to still other things in a web of associations and facts. Out of this web there is one particular place or fact that one wants to find. One finds it by following the cascade or trail of associative thinking until ending up at the place or fact desired. To Bush the tools available for managing information needed to be like this. Hence, the title, "As We May Think." Bush's memex—a mechanical device that could store, and most importantly, *link* information—was, he envisioned, just such a device. Its essential feature, according to Bush, was associative indexing or the process of tying two (or more) pieces of information together.

Significance

Vannevar Bush's "As We May Think" is regarded as the conceptual beginning of the hypertext-based World Wide Web. The Web is simply a vast network consisting of linked information. Hypertext is the system that provides the links between the information. In a simple hypertext document, a word or phase might be bolded, underlined, or highlighted in some way. Selecting the highlighted word will take a web user to another document. The link between documents is called a hyperlink and it allows for navigating around the Web. Hypertext was the main concept that led to the invention of the World Wide Web.

It is useful to compare the Web and hypertext to Bush's memex. The memex would provide a trail to just the right piece of information. Associative indexing, which is the linking of two or more pieces of information, would form the trail. Thus, the memex provided a basic concept that was put into practice at the beginning of the evolution of the World Wide Web.

Primary Source

"As We May Think" [excerpt]

SYNOPSIS: In this excerpt, Bush explains why, in the aftermath of World War II, there was a need to mobilize the resources of science and technology, together with the creativity of scientists and engineers, for peaceful purposes. He sketches out a plan, including a proposal for a "memex," a precursor to hypertext, that was destined to be realized in what is now known as the Internet.

This has not been a scientist's war; it has been a war in which all have had a part. The scientists, burying their old professional competition in the demand of a common cause, have shared greatly and learned much. It has been exhilarating to work in effective partnership. Now, for many, this appears to be approaching an end. What are the scientists to do next?

For the biologists, and particularly for the medical scientists, there can be little indecision, for their war has hardly required them to leave the old paths. Many indeed have been able to carry on their war research in their familiar peacetime laboratories. Their objectives remain much the same.

It is the physicists who have been thrown most violently off stride, who have left academic pursuits for the making of strange destructive gadgets, who have had to devise new methods for their unanticipated assignments. They have done their part on the devices that made it possible to turn back the enemy, have worked in combined effort with the physicists of our allies. They have felt within themselves the stir of achievement. They have been part of a great team. Now, as peace approaches, one asks where they will find objectives worthy of their best.

Of what lasting benefit has been man's use of science and of the new instruments which his research brought into existence? . . .

There is a growing mountain of research. But there is increased evidence that we are being bogged down today as specialization extends. The investigator is staggered by the findings and conclusions of thousands of other workers—conclusions which he cannot find time to grasp, much less to remember, as they appear. Yet specialization becomes increasingly necessary for progress, and the effort to bridge between disciplines is correspondingly superficial.

Professionally our methods of transmitting and reviewing the results of research are generations old and by now are totally inadequate for their purpose. If the aggregate time spent in writing scholarly works and in reading them could be evaluated, the ratio between these amounts of time might well be startling. Those who conscientiously attempt to keep abreast of current thought, even in restricted fields, by close and continuous reading might well shy away from an examination calculated to show how much of the previous month's efforts could be produced on call. Mendel's concept of the laws of genetics was lost to the world for a generation because his publication did not reach the few who were capable of grasping and extending it; and this sort of catastrophe is undoubtedly being repeated all about us, as truly significant attainments become lost in the mass of the inconsequential.

The difficulty seems to be, not so much that we publish unduly in view of the extent and variety of present day interests, but rather that publication has been extended far beyond our present ability to make real use of the record. The summation of human experience is being expanded at a prodigious rate, and the means we use for threading through the consequent maze to the momentarily important item is the same as was used in the days of square-rigged ships.

Vannevar Bush works at an experiment in his laboratory. THE LIBRARY OF CONGRESS.

But there are signs of a change as new and powerful instrumentalities come into use. Photocells capable of seeing things in a physical sense, advanced photography which can record what is seen or even what is not, thermionic tubes capable of controlling potent forces under the guidance of less power than a mosquito uses to vibrate his wings, cathode ray tubes rendering visible an occurrence so brief that by comparison a microsecond is a long time, relay combinations which will carry out involved sequences of movements more reliably than any human operator and thousands of times as fast—there are plenty of mechanical aids with which to effect a transformation in scientific records. . . .

Consider a future device for individual use, which is a sort of mechanized private file and library. It needs a name, and, to coin one at random, "memex" will do. A memex is a device in which an individual stores all his books, records, and communications, and which is mechanized so that it may be consulted with exceeding speed and flexibility. It is an enlarged intimate supplement to his memory.

It consists of a desk, and while it can presumably be operated from a distance, it is primarily the piece of furniture at which he works. On the top are slanting translucent screens, on which material can be projected for convenient reading. There is a keyboard, and sets of buttons and levers. Otherwise it looks like an ordinary desk.

In one end is the stored material. The matter of bulk is well taken care of by improved microfilm. Only a small part of the interior of the memex is devoted to storage, the rest to mechanism. Yet if the user inserted 5000 pages of material a day it would take him hundreds of years to fill the repository, so he can be profligate and enter material freely.

Most of the memex contents are purchased on microfilm ready for insertion. Books of all sorts, pictures, current periodicals, newspapers, are thus obtained and dropped into place. Business correspondence takes the same path. And there is provision for direct entry. On the top of the memex is a transparent platen. On this are placed longhand notes, photographs, memoranda, all sorts of things. When one is in place, the depression of a lever causes it to be photographed onto the next blank space in a section of the memex film, dry photography being employed.

There is, of course, provision for consultation of the record by the usual scheme of indexing. If the user wishes to consult a certain book, he taps its code on the keyboard, and the title page of the book promptly appears before him, projected onto one of his viewing positions. Frequently-used codes are mnemonic, so that he seldom consults his code book; but when he does, a single tap of a key projects it for his use. Moreover, he has supplemental levers. On deflecting one of these levers to the right he runs through the book before him, each page in turn being projected at a speed which just allows a recognizing glance at each. If he deflects it further to the right, he steps through the book 10 pages at a time; still further at 100 pages at a time. Deflection to the left gives him the same control backwards.

A special button transfers him immediately to the first page of the index. Any given book of his library can thus be called up and consulted with far greater facility than if it were taken from a shelf. As he has several projection positions, he can leave one item in position while he calls up another. He can add marginal notes and comments, taking advantage of one possible type of dry photography, and it could even be arranged so that he can do this by a stylus scheme, such as is now employed in the telautograph seen in railroad waiting rooms, just as though he had the physical page before him.

All this is conventional, except for the projection forward of present-day mechanisms and gadgetry. It affords an immediate step, however, to associative indexing, the basic idea of which is a provision whereby any item may be caused at will to select immediately and automatically another. This is the essential feature of the memex. The process of tying two items together is the important thing.

When the user is building a trail, he names it, inserts the name in his code book, and taps it out on his keyboard. Before him are the two items to be joined, projected onto adjacent viewing positions. At the bottom of each there are a number of blank code spaces, and a pointer is set to indicate one of

these on each item. The user taps a single key, and the items are permanently joined. In each code space appears the code word. Out of view, but also in the code space, is inserted a set of dots for photocell viewing; and on each item these dots by their positions designate the index number of the other item.

Thereafter, at any time, when one of these items is in view, the other can be instantly recalled merely by tapping a button below the corresponding code space. Moreover, when numerous items have been thus joined together to form a trail, they can be reviewed in turn, rapidly or slowly, by deflecting a lever like that used for turning the pages of a book. It is exactly as though the physical items had been gathered together from widely separated sources and bound together to form a new book. It is more than this, for any item can be joined into numerous trails.

The owner of the memex, let us say, is interested in the origin and properties of the bow and arrow. Specifically he is studying why the short Turkish bow was apparently superior to the English long bow in the skirmishes of the Crusades. He has dozens of possibly pertinent books and articles in his memex. First he runs through an encyclopedia, finds an interesting but sketchy article, leaves it projected. Next, in a history, he finds another pertinent item, and ties the two together. Thus he goes, building a trail of many items. Occasionally he inserts a comment of his own, either linking it into the main trail or joining it by a side trail to a particular item. When it becomes evident that the elastic properties of available materials had a great deal to do with the bow, he branches off on a side trail which takes him through textbooks on elasticity and tables of physical constants. He inserts a page of longhand analysis of his own. Thus he builds a trail of his interest through the maze of materials available to him.

Further Resources

BOOKS

Bush, Vannevar. *Endless Horizons.* Introduction by Frank Jewett. Washington, D.C.: Public Affairs Press, 1946.

———. *Modern Arms and Free Men: A Discussion of the Role of Science in Preserving Democracy.* Westport, Conn.: Greenwood Press, 1985.

———. *Science Is Not Enough.* New York: Morrow, 1967.

———. *Science, The Endless Frontier: A Report to the President.* United States Office of Scientific Research and Development. Washington, D.C.: National Science Foundation, 1960.

Nyce, James M., and Paul Kahn, eds. *From Memex to Hypertext: Vannevar Bush and the Mind's Machine.* New York: Academic Press, 1991.

WEBSITES

"'As We May Think'—A Celebration of Vannevar Bush's 1945 Vision: An Examination of What Has Been Accomplished, and What Remains to Be Done—A Photographic Appreciation." Available online at http://www.eecs.mit.edu/AY95-96/events/bush/photos.html; website home page: http://www.eecs.mit.edu/ (accessed October 21, 2002).

"Events in the Life of Vannevar Bush—Timeline." Available online at http://www.cs.brown.edu/research/graphics/html/info/timeline.html; website home page: http://www.cs.brown.edu (accessed October 21, 2002).

Greenberg, Martin. "The Computers of Tomorrow." Available online at http://www.theatlantic.com/unbound/flashbks/computer/greenbf.htm; website home page: http://www.theatlantic.com/ (accessed October 21, 2002).

Landow, George Paul. "Vannevar Bush and the Memex." Available online at http://www.press.jhu.edu/press/books/landow/memex.html; website home page: http://www.press.jhu.edu (accessed July 9, 2003).

"Links to Vannevar Bush References." Austin Business Computers, Inc. Available online at http://www.ausbcomp.com/~bbott/wik/bushref.htm; website home page: http://www.ausbcomp.com/(accessed October 21, 2002).

Race: Science and Politics

Essay

By: Ruth Benedict

Date: 1945

Source: Benedict, Ruth. *Race: Science and Politics*. Rev. ed. New York: Viking Press, 1945, vii–viii, ix–xi.

About the Author: Born in New York, Ruth Fulton Benedict (1887–1948) began attending Vassar College at the age of seventeen. She graduated in 1909, and following a year of overseas travel, during which she considered various career choices, Benedict began graduate studies in the field of anthropology. Her instructors included Franz Boas and Edward Sapir, both of whom were prominent and influential anthropologists. Margaret Mead, who became a lifelong friend, was one of her students. Benedict obtained her Ph.D. from Columbia University in 1922 and remained there as a teacher until her death. ∎

Introduction

During World War II (1939–1945), the public perception about race was that there were biologically different types, or races, of people in the world. Associated with this notion of "difference" was the idea of superior and inferior, good and bad. Many times, so-called scientific facts were used to uphold this difference. This phenomenon came to be called "scientific racism."

Scientific racism was a prominent force during World War II. It was used by the Nazi regime in Germany to popularize the idea of a superior race and to justify the countless atrocities committed against Europe's Jewish population. Most Americans were repulsed by the Nazi claim of genetic superiority. At the same time, many of America's race troubles were making front-page news both in the United States and abroad. The country's sense of morality was threatened. Americans were uncomfortable, and most were compelled to reexamine their own racial attitudes. It was to this audience that Ruth Benedict spoke. Benedict, a teacher at New York's Columbia University, railed against scientific racism in her book *Race: Science and Politics*. The book, originally published in 1940, proved immensely popular, being reissued in 1943 and again in 1945.

The title of *Race: Science and Politics* is an apt one. In the book, Benedict presents two views of human differences. One is based on race. There are many facts that are known about human racial differences, and these, Benedict says, need to be presented objectively. Anthropologists, biologists, psychologists, and other scientists should have much to say on this view. The other view of human difference is based on racism. Race and racism, Benedict says, "are poles apart." Racism is based on social perceptions, not science. It uses race to justify and rationalize immoral acts and attitudes such as slavery or genocide.

Margaret Mead had said that Benedict wrote *Race: Science and Politics* as a service to mankind, as a way to contribute to the making of a better world. She believed that understanding of culture could increase understanding of life. She wanted to remove all handicaps based on race or sex and to build a world in which each human being could act with dignity.

Significance

Ruth Benedict's writings on race and culture had an immediate impact on anthropology in the 1940s. Benedict's work, along with that of Franz Boaz and Margaret Mead, helped to discredit the concept of scientific racism, the view that each race is essentially different from the other and that these differences are manifested in intellectual as well as physical characteristics. Their work played a major role in the shift from a racial view of human differences to a cultural view. This view was that human differences in intelligence or personality were not caused by racial differences, but by cultural ones. It's been said that Benedict's work, in particular, led to the study of *cultures* rather than culture.

The significance of Benedict's writings on race is also apparent in current anthropological tenets. The American Anthropological Association, in an official statement adopted in December 1994, said: "Differentiating species into biologically defined 'races' has proven meaningless and unscientific as a way of explaining variation (whether in intelligence or other traits)."

Ruth Benedict authored the 1940 book *Race: Science and Politics*. **THE LIBRARY OF CONGRESS.**

Primary Source

Race: Science and Politics [excerpt]

> **SYNOPSIS:** In this excerpt from the foreword to the 1945 edition of *Race: Science and Politics*, Ruth Benedict identifies some of the ways in which anthropologists, psychologists, and sociologists, among others, could make a contribution to the war (and postwar) effort by focusing on the issues of race and racism, and by exploding a few widely shared myths and misconceptions about race.

Today the United States is fighting alongside men of all races. On the Western and on the Eastern fronts there are Negro troops and Japanese troops fighting with the United Nations. We are fighting as allies with Mongoloid China and Negro Ethiopia. This war has aligned the nations without regard to race and this is as true in the Axis camp as among the United Nations.

Though this war has cut across all racial lines, it has not made race issues less conspicuous. Rather, race prejudice and all its works have been forced into the headlines. In part this has been due to the enemy nations who have recognized from the first that American race troubles make excellent pro-

paganda for them in their broadcasts to the Asiatics and the Africans. Early in the war Japan made great capital out of the Sojourner Truth riot in Detroit, using it to say to the Asiatics: "Will you trust this white man? He humiliates you. *Asia for the Asiatics.*" Germany, too, used race in her anti-American propaganda. She protested her righteousness in fighting the war as a "master race"; how could America object to her dogma when in her country Negroes even in the uniform of their country could be turned away from restaurants and from the movie houses?

Then, too, race has become headline stuff because Old Americans have had to re-examine their practices and attitudes in the light of our stated war aims, and because those minorities who have been discriminated against have raised their voices to call for what they feel to be decency and justice. Many Americans have realized for the first time that their nation has been guilty of grave injustices and slights, and they are criticizing actions which have gone unchallenged for decades. Their troubled consciences are good pleaders in the cause both of the minorities at home and of foreign nations overseas.

Postwar co-operation among the nations of the world also raises all the problems of interracial goodwill. No postwar pact can survive race war; how shall Asia and the Near East and Africa support the peace if they decide it was made for the benefit of a "white man's world"? Race prejudice is no longer a domestic issue. It threatens our success in winning the peace.

In this war procedures have been established which we have followed in our great emergencies. When we need new fuels, lighter metals or new plastics, when our natural rubber supply is cut off, we call in scientists and ask them to find out what is possible and what is impossible. The chemists tell us how to make metals lighter and how to produce synthetic rubber. They point out what Nature allows us to do if we will only do it. They point out what we have heedlessly wasted in our traditional processes. When it is our race prejudices which threaten the war effort we need the scientist just as much. We need to know what to do. . . .

These are scientific questions on which the anthropologist, the anatomist, the biologist, the psychologist and the sociologist have collected data for decades. They have answers, and the first section of this volume presents them. We do not need to proceed blindly about this race issue.

The second section is about the way race has been pressed into the service of politics. Modern nations have everywhere claimed that their race was biologically and perpetually superior to other races. As the Nazis put it, "A lower race needs less culture, less clothes, and less food." This is racism. It says: "I am better than you. No matter what I am or what I have done, I do not have to compare myself with you. I am better anyway. I belong to the superior race." Confusion between the facts of race and the claim of racism is universal in the modern world, and this volume is arranged to show that they are poles apart. They are different in their history, in their votaries, and in the data they make use of. Just as scientific knowledge of racial differences needs to be objectively presented, so too racism in the modern world is a subject for sober recording. It is a painful history but it is a necessary one for us to know. Men have sometimes learned from past errors.

In the final chapter I have written an anthropologist's answer to the question, "How can we stop this epidemic of racism?" Race attitudes are not something which can be legislated like taxes and rationing. These latter have to be attacked on a national front and rules and regulations laid down for everyone to conform to. Race prejudice has to be conquered on the local front in our schools, our churches, our factories, our cities, our rural districts. Improvements in hiring and firing, in housing, in educational and health facilities will come eventually only as they are locally supported. In race attitudes the behavior of the employer, the union member, the neighbor on our block, the waiter in the restaurant, the customer in the grocery store add up to the only total there is or can be. It is not a mere matter of complying with regulations or of supporting decisions of the higher-ups. On the race front each man and woman and child can help by every act of fair play and every bit of co-operation and courtesy. Whatever he does to improve race relations is not only a mark of his own democracy and Christianity and decency; it is also for his own self-interest and security. For the dominant race cannot have freedom for themselves unless they grant it without regard to race and color. As Booker T. Washington once said, "To keep a man in the ditch, you have to stay there with him."

At this moment when we are fighting shoulder to shoulder with all races and must gird ourselves to organize a postwar world, race is an issue we cannot dodge. We of the White race, we of the Nordic race, must make it clear that we do not want the kind of cheap and arrogant superiority the racists promise us. We must make it clear that we respect character and ability wherever we find them and con-

demn no people to servitude or lack of opportunity because of the color of their skin. Only so shall we have learned the right to be respected and only so will all races respect us. Without such a mutual respect we shall not build a better postwar world.

Further Resources

BOOKS

Benedict, Ruth. *The Chrysanthemum and the Sword: Patterns of Japanese Culture.* Boston: Houghton Mifflin, 1946.

———. *Patterns of Culture.* Boston: Houghton Mifflin, 1934.

———. *Zuni Mythology.* New York: AMS, 1935.

Caffrey, Margaret M. *Ruth Benedict: Stranger in This Land.* Austin, Tex.: University of Texas Press, 1989.

Mead, Margaret. *An Anthropologist at Work: Writings of Ruth Benedict.* Boston: Houghton Mifflin, 1959.

———. *Ruth Benedict.* New York: Columbia University Press, 1974.

Modell, Judith S. *Ruth Benedict: Patterns of a Life.* Philadelphia: University of Pennsylvania Press, 1983.

WEBSITES

Hochman, Susan K. "Ruth Fulton Benedict." Webster University. Available online at http://www.webster.edu/~woolflm/ruthbenedict.html; website home page: http://www.webster.edu (accessed October 17, 2002).

"Ruth Fulton Benedict Papers." Vassar College Libraries. Available online at http://library.vassar.edu/information/special-collections/benedict/benedict_register.html; website home page: http://library.vassar.edu (accessed October 17, 2002).

"Statement on 'Race' and Intelligence." American Anthropological Association. Available online at http://www.aaanet.org/stmts/race.htm; website home page: http://www.aaanet.org (accessed October 17, 2002).

"Three-Electrode Circuit Element Utilizing Semiconductive Materials"

Patent application, Diagram

By: John Bardeen and Walter Brattain

Date: 1948

Source: Bardeen, John, and Walter Brattain. "Three-Electrode Circuit Element Utilizing Semiconductive Materials." U.S. patent 2,524,035, 1948. Available in a search for patent 2,524,035 online at http://www.uspto.gov/patft/index.html; website home page: http://www.uspto.gov (accessed March 20, 2003).

About the Authors: John Bardeen (1908–1987) received his Ph.D. in mathematics and physics from Princeton University in 1936. After World War II, he obtained employment at Bell

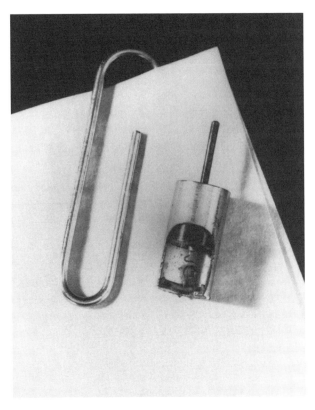

The transistor, at its invention, was smaller in size than your average paperclip. **THE LIBRARY OF CONGRESS.**

Telephone Labs, where he studied electron conduction properties in semiconductors. His work in that area led to his achievements on the point-contact transistor, as well as to the development of a theory of superconductivity and a theory that explained various properties of semiconductors. In addition to winning the Nobel Prize twice—the first person to do so—he was awarded the Presidential Medal of Freedom in 1977. Walter Brattain (1902–1987) was born in Amoy, China. He joined Bell Telephone Labs in 1929, where he conducted pioneering research on the surface properties of solids, especially the atomic structure of materials at their surfaces. He wrote extensively on solid state physics, which resulted in applications that replaced the vacuum tube. Brattain joined the National Academy of Sciences in 1959, and became Adjunct Professor at Whitman College in Walla Walla, Washington, in 1967. He held a number of patents. ∎

Introduction

It could arguably be said that every invention, innovation, or discovery of the 1940s was impacted by World War II (1939–1945). Therefore, it is no surprise that the war played a part in the invention of transistors—tiny solid-state devices that are used in radios, telecommunications equipment, televisions, and computers. John Bardeen, who invented transistors along with Walter Brattain and William Shockley, has said that the development of new and efficient techniques for the purifica-

tion of germanium and silicon had an enormous impact on the discovery of transistors. Germanium and silicon were the focus of government sponsored research into new materials for use in the war.

Bardeen, Brattain, and Shockley worked at Bell Telephone Laboratories where they were engaged in experimental work concerning semiconductors—various crystalline materials that are midway between insulators (poor carriers of electricity) and conductors (good carriers of electricity). During the war semiconductors composed of germanium and silicon were developed for use in point contact, or "cat's whisker," detectors for radar. After the war both fundamental and practical research into semiconductors continued, particularly at Bell Laboratories. Semiconductors were seen as a promising component in electronic devices, which in 1947 included several new advanced computing machines.

Transistors manipulate electric currents. Also called diodes, transistors can act as switches, using the voltage level to determine whether the switch is off or on. Additionally, transistors can function as amplifiers to strengthen weak signals. Finally, transistors are able to convert electrical current from AC (alternating current) into DC (direct current). Modern computers contain millions of transistors that function to switch a current off and on, without generating a lot of heat and with tiny amounts of power.

Significance

The transistor may well have had more impact on modern society than any other invention since the advent of electricity. Fittingly, transistors function in the manipulation of electricity and other electronic signals. The influence of television and computers in modern society owes much to the transistor invented by John Bardeen, Walter Brattain, and William Shockley.

The invention of the transistor was pivotal in bringing the modern computer into everyday life. The transistor allows computers to be used for a full spectrum of commercial and industrial uses by hugely decreasing their size and cost.

Before the transistor, vacuum tubes acted as switches, alternating between off and on, in electronic devices. However, vacuum tubes are relatively large (about the size of a light bulb), consume large amounts of energy (much of it wastefully expended in heat), and are very unreliable. By contrast, transistors are compact, use little electricity and radiate very little heat, are inexpensive to manufacture, and are very reliable. Accordingly, transistors replaced vacuum tubes in radios and television sets, and made possible such electronic devices as CD players, personal computers, and many others.

Bardeen, Brattain, and Shockley were awarded the Nobel Prize in Physics in 1956 for their invention of the

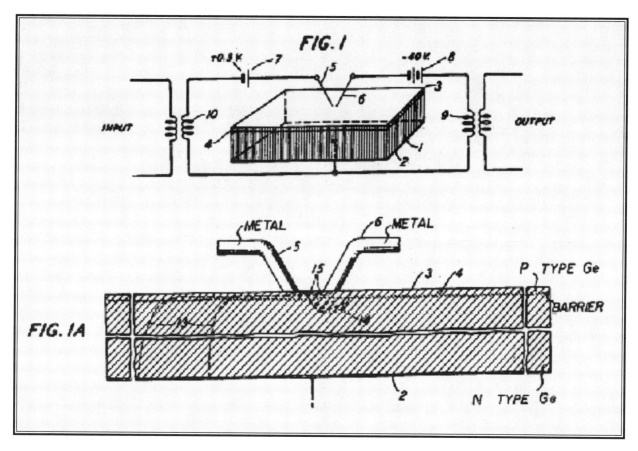

Primary Source

"Three-Electrode Circuit Element Utilizing Semiconductive Materials": Diagram

SYNOPSIS: The patent for the first transistor was filed by Bardeen and Brattain in 1948 and included this diagram. **PUBLIC DOMAIN.**

transistor, which along with semiconductors, is the focal point of a scientific discipline that emerged after World War II. Solid-state physics focuses on the conductive properties (the movement of electrons) of solid materials.

Primary Source

"Three-Electrode Circuit Element Utilizing Semiconductive Materials" [excerpt]: Patent application

> **SYNOPSIS:** This excerpted document discusses the design and patent for the first point-contact transistor using semiconductive materials, filed by Bardeen and Brattain in 1948. This was the culmination and convergence of research that they had undertaken since the 1930s. The accompanying diagram was included in Bardeen and Brattain's patent application.

This invention relates to a novel method of and means for translating electrical variations for such purposes as amplification, wave generation, and the like.

The principal object of the invention is to amplify or otherwise translate electric signals or variations by use of compact, simple, and rugged apparatus of novel type.

Another object is to provide a circuit element for use as an amplifier or the like which does not require a heated thermionic cathode for its operation, and which therefore is immediately operative when turned on. A related object is to provide such a circuit element which requires no evacuated or gas-filled envelope. . . .

The present invention in one form utilizes a block of semiconductor material on which three electrodes are placed. One of these, termed the collector, makes rectifier contact with the body of the block. The other, termed the emitter, preferably makes rectifier contact with the body of the block also. The third electrode, which may be designated the base electrode, preferably makes a low resistance contact with the body of the block.

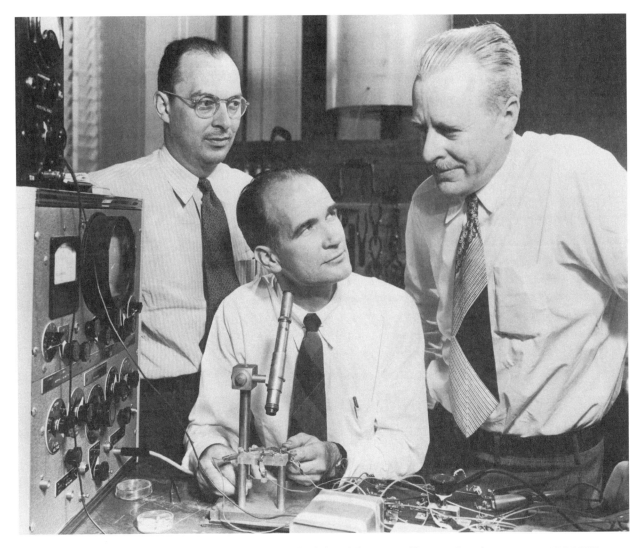

William Shockley (seated), John Bardeen, and Walter Brattain in a Bell Telephone Laboratory, working on an invention. © BETTMANN/CORBIS. REPRODUCED BY PERMISSION.

Further Resources

BOOKS

Bardeen, John. "Semiconductor Research Leading to the Point Contact Transistor." In *The World of Physics,* vol. 2. Jefferson H. Weaver, ed. New York: Simon and Schuster, 1987, 543–562.

Kursunoglu, Behram, and Arnold Perlmutter, eds. *Impact of Basic Research on Technology.* New York: Plenum Press, 1973.

Riordan, Michael, and Lillian Hoddeson. *Crystal Fire: The Birth of the Information Age.* New York: Norton, 1997.

Shockley, William. "Transistor Technology Evokes New Physics." In *The World of Physics,.* vol. 2. Jefferson H. Weaver, ed. New York: Simon & Schuster, 1987, 565–583.

WEBSITES

"The First Transistor, Nov. 17–Dec. 23, 1947." This Month in Physics History. American Physical Society. Available online at http://www.aps.org/apsnews/1100/110004.html; website home page: http://www.apps.org (accessed October 21, 2002).

"Transistor History." Lucent Technologies. Available online at http://www.lucent.com/minds/transistor; website home page: http://www.lucent.com/ (accessed October 21, 2002).

"Transistorized! The History of the Invention of the Transistor." Available online at http://www.pbs.org/transistor; website home page: http://www.pbs.org/ (accessed October 21, 2002).

Cybernetics

Nonfiction work

By: Norbert Wiener

Date: 1948

Source: Wiener, Norbert. *Cybernetics, or Control and Communication in the Animal and the Machine.* New York: Wiley and Sons, 1948, 1, 2, 3, 6, 8, 11.

About the Author: Born in Cambridge, Massachusetts, Norbert Wiener (1894–1964) studied at the University of Cambridge, England and the University of Göttingen, Germany. He joined the staff at the Massachusetts Institute of Technology in 1919 as an instructor in mathematics. During this time he was developing his interest in the parallels between feedback control in circuits and mental processes. This led to the creation of a new discipline which he called cybernetics, the study of control, communication, and organization. He propounded a new approach to the study of man in his technological environment, a science of man as component of an age of automation. He died in Stockholm. ∎

Introduction

Wiener's book, *Cybernetics, or Control and Communication in the Animal and the Machine,* resulted in part from Wiener's involvement in World War II (1939–1945). Wiener, like John von Neumann, John Mauchly, Presper Eckert, and Howard Aiken, was involved in the development of advanced machines for the war effort.

Wiener applied an interdisciplinary viewpoint to his wartime projects. Before the war, Wiener had been collaborating with Arturo Rosenblueth, a doctor at Harvard Medical School. They both believed that the overlap between different fields of science contained important concepts that were being overlooked. They supported the idea of tackling scientific challenges with a team of scientists having diverse backgrounds. Wiener and his collaborators applied mathematics, statistics, neurophysiology, and psychology to the development of machines needed for the war.

Cybernetics refers to the design of self-operating machines which receive, process, store, and send information, much like the brain, nerves, synapses, and other nervous system components do in animals. In 1948, Wiener and Rosenblueth coined the term cybernetics, and created a new field of science that comparatively studies *control and communication* functions in animals and machines. Cybernetics incorporates principles of physiology, mathematics, statistics, and electronics.

In *Cybernetics, or Control and Communication in the Animal and the Machine,* Wiener compares the inner workings of machines with the nervous system. For example, a photoelectric cell that senses light is like the eye. Nerve cells either at rest or firing, Wiener says, are like a machine's electrical relays, switching on and off. Wiener makes the point that self-operating machines contain sensory organs and the equivalent of a nervous system for the integration and transfer of information.

Significance

Norbert Wiener's book, *Cybernetics, or Control and Communication in the Animal and Machine* was the first

Norbert Wiener explains mathematical equations at the blackboard. **THE LIBRARY OF CONGRESS.**

cybernetics textbook. It provided the theoretical foundations for a new field of science: Cybernetics, the comparative study of animals and machines. Cybernetics has branched out into other science curricula such as bioengineering and biomechanics, as well as systems theory. It can be said that cybernetics has contributed to the development of computers, bionics, pacemakers, and prosthetics (artificial body parts).

Wiener's book provided basic concepts that contributed to the development of computers. In the introduction to his book, Wiener reveals part of a memo he had written to Vannevar Bush, who as the Director of the Office of Science and Research, was coordinating the scientific war effort. In the memo, Wiener illustrated some basic principles that he believed were prerequisites of advanced computing machines. Wiener suggested that an advanced computing machine should be electronic and not mechanical, be based on electric switches and the binary number scale, make logical decisions, be self-operating, and have a memory. The computers of the early twenty-first century utilize every one of Wiener's prerequisites.

Wiener was one of the first scientists to look at humans and other animals, especially their nervous systems, not in terms of biology, but in terms of information flow. Wiener believed that control and communication in any complex system was centered around the message itself, the information. Whether the system was biological, electrical, or mechanical was not as important.

Primary Source

Cybernetics [excerpt]

SYNOPSIS: In this excerpt from the introduction to his book, Wiener reveals the importance of interdisciplinary research for the establishment of a new field of science that he and his colleague termed "cybernetics."

This book represents the outcome, after more than a decade, of a program of work undertaken jointly with Dr. Arturo Rosenblueth, then of the Harvard Medical School, and now of the Instituto Nacional de Cardiologia of Mexico. . . .

There are fields of scientific work, as we shall see in the body of this book, which have been explored from the different sides of pure mathematics, statistics, electrical engineering, and neurophysiology; in which every single notion receives a separate name from each group, and in which important work has been triplicated or quadruplicated, while still other important work is delayed by the unavailability in one field of results that may have already become classical in the next field. . . .

Dr. Rosenblueth has always insisted that a proper exploration of these blank spaces on the map of science could only be made by a team of scientists, each a specialist in his own field, but each possessing a thoroughly sound and trained acquaintance with the fields of his neighbors; all in the habit of working together, of knowing one another's intellectual customs, and of recognizing the significance of a colleague's new suggestion before it has taken on a full formal expression. The mathematician need not have the skill to conduct a physiological experiment, but he must have the skill to understand one, to criticize one, and to suggest one. . . .

We had agreed on these matters long before we had chosen the field of our joint investigations and our respective parts in them. The deciding factor in this new step was the war. . . .

At any rate, I found myself engaged in a war project, in which Mr. Julian H. Bigelow and myself were partners in the investigation of the theory of prediction and of the construction of apparatus to embody these theories. . . .

On the communication engineering plane, it had already become clear to Mr. Bigelow and myself that the problems of control engineering and of communication engineering were inseparable, and that they centered not around the technique of electrical engineering but around the much more fundamental notion of the message, whether this should be transmitted by electrical, mechanical, or nervous means. . . .

Thus, as far back as four year ago, the group of scientists about Dr. Rosenblueth and myself had already become aware of the essential unity of the set of problems centering about communication, control, and statistical mechanics, whether in the machine or in living tissue. On the other hand, we were seriously hampered by the lack of unity of the literature concerning these problems, and by the absence of any common terminology, or even of a single name for the field. After much consideration, we have come to the conclusion that all the existing terminology has too heavy a bias to one side or another to serve the future development of the field as well as it should; and as happens so often to seientists, we have been forced to coin at least on artifical neo-Greek expression to fill the gap. We have decided to call the entire field of control and communication theory, whether in the machine or in the animal, by the name of *Cybernetics,* which we form from the Greek word for *steersman.*

Further Resources
BOOKS
Barr, Avon, Paul R.Cohen, and Edward A. Feigenbaum, eds. *Handbook of Artificial Intelligence,* vol. IV. Stanford, Calif.: HeurisTech Press, 1989.

Heims, Steve J. *John von Neumann and Norbert Wiener: From Mathematics to the Technologies of Life and Death.* Cambridge, Mass.: MIT Press, 1980.

Ilgauds, Hans Joachim. *Norbert Wiener.* Leipzig, Teubner, 1980.

Kurzweil, Raymond. *The Age of Intelligent Machines.* Cambridge, Mass.: MIT Press, 1990.

Masani, Pesi Rustom. *Norbert Wiener, 1894–1964.* Boston: Birkhäuser, 1990.

Wiener, Norbert. *Ex-Prodigy: My Childhood and Youth.* New York: Simon and Schuster, 1953.

———. *The Human Use of Human Beings: Cybernetics and Society.* NewYork: Da Capo Press, 1988.

PERIODICALS
Jerison, David, and Daniel Stroock. "Norbert Wiener." *Notices of the American Mathematical Society* 42, no. 4, April 1995, 430–438.

Mandrekar, V. "Mathematical Work of Norbert Wiener." *Notices of the American Mathematical Society* 42, no. 6, June 1995, 664–669.

Wiener, Norbert. *Bulletin of the American Mathematical Society* 72, 1966.

WEBSITES

"Foundations of Cybernetics." American Society of Cybernetics. Available online at http://www.asc-cybernetics.org /foundations/index.htm; website home page: http://www .asc-cybernetics.org/ (accessed October 21, 2002).

"Norbert Wiener." School of Mathematics and Statistics, University of St. Andrews, Scotland. Available online at http:// www-groups.dcs.st-and.ac.uk/~history/Mathematicians /Wiener_Norbert.html; websit home page: http://www-maths .mcs.st-andrews.ac.uk/ (accessed October 21, 2002).

"Norbert Wiener (1894–1964)." Jones Telecommunications & Multimedia Encyclopedia. Available online at http:// www.digitalcentury.com/encyclo/update/wiener.html; website home page: http://www.digitalcentury.com (accessed October 21, 2002). *Includes a biographical sketch and useful related links.*

"The General and Logical Theory of Automata"

Presentation

By: John von Neumann

Date: 1948

Source: Von Neumann, John. "The General and Logical Theory of Automata." Presented at the Hixon Symposium on September 20, 1948, at the California Institute of Technology. Reprinted in *The World of Physics: A Small Library of the Literature of Physics from Antiquity to the Present.* Jefferson Hane Weaver, ed. New York: Simon and Schuster, 1987, 606–607.

About the Author: John von Neumann (1903–1957) received early instruction in his native Budapest from Michael Fekete, publishing his first paper with Fekete at the age of 18. He went on to study in Berlin and Zurich, completing his Ph.D. in mathematics at the University of Budapest in 1926. One of the original six professors of mathematics at Princeton University's Institute for Advanced Studies (IAS), von Neumann played a large part in the design of the IAS computer. He also served on the Atomic Energy Commission before his premature death from cancer at the height of his career. ∎

Introduction

The latter part of the 1940s, after the end of World War II (1939–1945), was a thriving time for research into advanced computing machines. The war had provided the initial impetus for their development: the need for machines that could perform huge volumes of computations. However, most digital and electronic predecessors of the modern computer were constructed after the war had ended.

It was 1948 when von Neumann presented "The General and Logical Theory of Automata," at the California

Institute of Technology. The concepts he presented were an extension of his work on the Electronic Digital Variable Computer (EDVAC). The EDVAC was one in a line of computing machines that gradually evolved into the modern computer. It represented an improvement over its immediate predecessor, the ENIAC, in that it was based on a scale of two rather than a scale of ten. The EDVAC was also significant in that it was the first computer designed to embody the stored program concept (computer memory). The stored program was created to allow the EDVAC to be self-operating. Automata is plural for automaton, which means self-operating machine.

In "The General and Logical Theory of Automata," von Neumann discusses the relationship between an artificial logical system (a machine) and the nervous system of animals. In the winter of 1943–1944, von Neumann attended a meeting at Princeton University, the subject of which came to be called cybernetics. At the meeting mathematicians like von Neumann and Norbert Wiener, neurophysiologists such as Warren McCulloch, and engineers such as Goldstine discussed the common ideas present in neural (nerve) physiology and advanced computing machines. The influence of cybernetics is seen throughout von Neumann's work.

In this excerpt of von Neumann's presentation, he expands on the work of another computer pioneer and brilliant mathematician, Alan M. Turing. Both von Neumann and Turing compared computers with the human brain. They both believed that the brain is in essence a universal computer, continually executing logical computations at lightening-fast speed. An artificial, electronically constructed universal computer based upon the brain they termed a *formal neural network.*

Significance

It is hard to overestimate John von Neumann's contributions to the development of modern computers. His theories on logic and computer memory, which are reflected in "The General and Logical Theory of Automata," continue to be incorporated in the basic structure of computers in the early twenty-first century.

The modern computer has a distinct lineage. Starting with the ENIAC there was a gradual progression from a mechanical assembly to an electrical assembly, from the scale of ten to the scale of two, from a mechanical relay to an electrical relay, and from human-directed operation to automatically directed operation. Each new machine was an improvement over the earlier one.

The Electronic Discrete Variable Calculator (EDVAC) was constructed to overcome the deficiencies of the ENIAC. The ENIAC has been called the first universal computer. This means it could be programmed to perform a variety of applications. However, every time

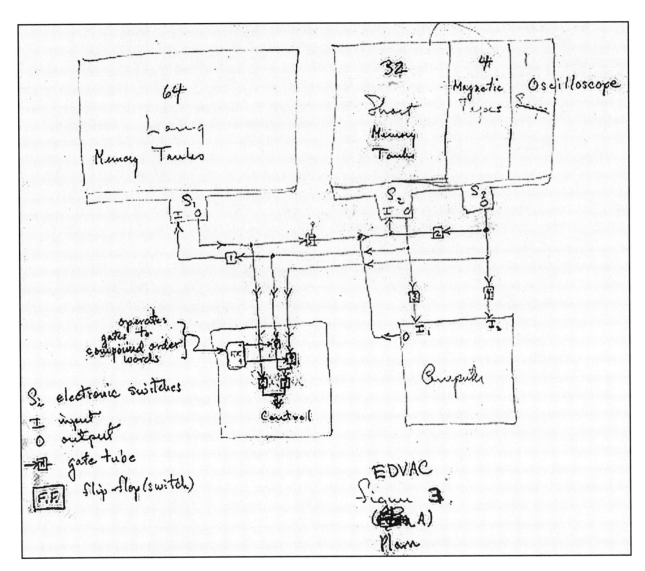

A blueprint for the EDVAC computer. JOHN W. MAUCHLY PAPERS, ANNENBERG RARE BOOK AND MANUSCRIPT LIBRARY, UNIVERSITY OF PENNSYLVANIA. REPRODUCED BY PERMISSION.

a new application was needed, a new program had to be installed. Installing a new program could take days, as it required a rearrangment of the entire machine. John von Neumann saw that a truly universal computer needed a *memory,* which would enable it to re-program, and therefore operate itself.

Von Neumann's concept of a "stored program," or memory, was one that could store both instructions and data. This architecture was designed into the EDVAC based on von Neumann's specifications. The stored program concept transformed computers by providing a means of self-operation, which ultimately led to a truly universal computer.

Many of the concepts John von Neumann set forth in "The General and Logical Theory of Automata" provide the basis for *nanotechnology,* a new field of science cen-

tered on the manufacture of extremely tiny technology. Nanotechnology is concerned with manipulating and producing molecular sized structures, often smaller than the eye can see. A key concept in nanotechnology is the creation of a technological organism that is able to reproduce and repair itself. This concept is clearly based on von Neumann's theories on artificial self-replicating systems.

Primary Source

"The General and Logical Theory of Automata" [excerpt]

> **SYNOPSIS:** In this excerpt, von Neumann describes the crucial concept of a "stored program," which is part of the "architecture" of almost all electronic digital computers in the early twenty-first century.

The EDVAC computer, 1948. JOHN W. MAUCHLY PAPERS, ANNENBERG RARE BOOK AND MANUSCRIPT LIBRARY, UNIVERSITY OF PENNSYLVANIA. REPRODUCED BY PERMISSION.

Broadening of the Program to Deal with Automata That Produce Automata

For the question which concerns me here, that of "self-reproduction" of automata, Turing's procedure is too narrow in one respect only. His automata are purely computing machines. Their output is a piece of tape with zeros and ones on it. What is needed for the construction to which I referred is an automaton whose output is other automata. There is, however, no difficulty in principle in dealing with this broader concept and in deriving from it the equivalent of Turing's result.

The Basic Definitions

As in the previous instance, it is again of primary importance to give a rigorous definition of what constitutes an automaton for the purpose of the investigation. First of all, we have to draw up a complete list of the elementary parts to be used. This list must contain not only a complete enumeration but also a complete operational definition of each elementary part. It is relatively easy to draw up such a list, that is, to write a catalogue of "machine parts" which is sufficiently inclusive to permit the construction of the wide variety of mechanisms here required, and which has the axiomatic rigor that is needed for this kind of consideration. The list need not be very long either. It can, of course, be made either arbitrarily long or arbitrarily short. It may be lengthened by including in it, as elementary parts, things which could be achieved by combinations of others. It can be made short—in fact, it can be made to consist of a single unit—by endowing each elementary part with a multiplicity of attributes and functions. Any statement on the number of elementary parts required will therefore represent a commonsense compromise, in which nothing too complicated is expected from any one elementary part, and no elementary part is made to perform several, obviously separate, functions. In this sense, it can be shown that about a dozen elementary parts suffice. The problem of self-reproduction can then be stated like this: Can one build an aggregate out of such elements in such a manner that if it is put into a reservoir, in which there float all these elements in large numbers, it will then begin to construct other aggregates, each of which will at the end turn out to be another automaton exactly like the original one? This is feasible, and the principle on which it can be based is closely related to Turing's principle outlined earlier.

Further Resources

BOOKS

Davis, Martin. *The Universal Computer: The Road from Leibniz to Turing.* New York: Norton, 2000.

Glodstine, Herman. *The Computer from Pascal to von Neumann.* Princeton: Princeton University Press, 1993.

von Neumann, John. *The Computer and The Brain,* 2nd ed. New Haven, Conn.: Yale University Press, 2000.

———, and Arthur W. Butts. *Theory of Self-Reproducing Automata.* Urbana, Ill.: University of Illinois Press, 1966.

———, and Oskar Morgenstern. *Theory of Games and Economic Behavior.* Princeton: Princeton University Press, 1944.

PERIODICALS

Aspray, William F. "Pioneer Day 82: History of the Stored Program Concept." *Annals of the History of Computing* 4, no.4, 1982, 358ff.

Stern, Nancy. "Von Neumann's Influence on Electronic Digital Computing." *Annals of the History of Computing* 2, no.4, 1980, 349–362.

von Neumann, John. "The Principles of Large-Scale Computing Machines." 1948. Reprinted in *Annals of the History of Computing* 3, no. 3, 1981, 263–273.

WEBSITES

Frietas, Robert A., Jr., and William P. Gilbreath, eds. "Advanced Automation for Space Missions: 5. Replicating Systems Concepts: Self-Replicating Lunar Factory and Demonstration." Available online at http://www.islandone.org/MMSG/aasm/chapter5.htm; website home page: http://www.islandone.org (accessed October 21, 2002).

"John von Neumann: Biography." Available online at http://ei.cs.vt.edu/~history/VonNeumann.html; website home page: http://www.ei.cs.vt.edu (accessed October 21, 2002).

Kim, Y.S. "John Von Neumann." Available online at http://www.physics.umd.edu/robot/neumann.html; website home page: http://www.physics.umd.ed (accessed October 21, 2002). *Provides links to information and images on von Newmann's colleagues, friends, and projects.*

"Self-Replication and Nanotechnology." Available online at http://www.zyvex.com/nanotech/selfRep.html; website home page: http://www.zyvex.com/nano/ (accessed October 21, 2002).

Draft Letter from Niels Bohr to Werner Heisenberg, ca. 1957

Letter

By: Niels Bohr

Date: ca. 1957

Source: Bohr, Niels. Draft Letter to Werner Heisenberg, ca. 1957. Niels Bohr Archive. Reprinted in *Naturens Verden* 84, no. 8–9, 2002. Available online at http://www.nbi.dk/NBA/papers/docs/d01tra.htm; website home page: http://www.nbi.dk/NBA/webpage.html (accessed March 20, 2003).

About the Author: Niels Bohr (1885–1962) received his physics doctorate at Copenhagen in 1911, then moved to England where he worked briefly with noted physicist J.J. Thomson at Cambridge's Cavendish Laboratory. He held a physics lectureship at Victoria University in Manchester, where he worked under Ernest Rutherford. Bohr was appointed Professor of Theoretical Physics at Copenhagen University in 1916. Four years later, the university established the Institute of Theoretical Physics, naming Bohr its director. He won the Nobel Prize in 1922 for his contributions to the knowledge of atomic structure. Toward the end of his life he developed an interest in molecular biology. ■

Introduction

Heisenberg, and another German, Carl von Weizsacker, were in Copenhagen to speak at a German cultural institute. It is clear from both Heisenberg and Bohr that Heisenberg was also concerned for the safety of his friend, and the speaking engagement may have been arranged only as a prop so that Heisenberg could meet with Bohr.

What the two men actually said to each other in September 1941 has been the subject of much speculation. As indicated in Bohr's draft letter, he and Heisenberg had ended up "as representatives of two sides engaged in mortal combat." What were Heisenberg's motives for meeting with Bohr? What were Heisenberg's feelings about using an atomic bomb? These questions are complicated and emotional and ultimately lead to broader questions for all scientists, such as What role does ethics play in science?

Significance

The Copenhagen meeting between Werner Heisenberg and Niels Bohr has come to symbolize the moral and ethical considerations inherent in science. Science can lead people to the loftiest of goals, such as cures for human diseases. However, science also has the potential to do great harm. Scientists are often in the middle, and must weigh the ethical consequences of their work.

Before World War II (1939–1945), Werner Heisenberg and Niels Bohr concerned themselves with the inner workings of atoms. However, due to the war, these scientists and others were forced to make decisions that not only directly affected their lives, but which had the potential to affect all of humanity.

It can be said that World War II was fought on an additional "front," one that can't be described in terms of geography. The battle between Germany and the United States to be the first to develop an atomic bomb was surely one of the most important battles within the war. Scientific discoveries are most often driven by a quest for knowledge, a quest to understand what is currently unknown. However, the consequences of Hitler having possession of an atomic bomb were the main driving force behind U.S. efforts to develop atomic weapons.

In 2002, more than sixty years after the Copenhagen meeting took place, a play written about that meeting garnered large audiences at college campuses across the United States. Playwright Michael Frayn's play *Copenhagen* is a fictional account of Heisenberg and Bohr's meeting. When the play was shown at the Massachusetts Institute of Technology (MIT), Werner Heisenberg's son, Jochen, a physics professor at the University of New Hampshire, was part of a symposium that discussed the ethical considerations faced by Heisenberg and other scientists during World War II. The play also stirred debate on ethical considerations for scientists in the early twenty-first century, such as those surrounding human cloning and stem cell research.

Primary Source

Draft Letter from Niels Bohr to Werner Heisenberg, ca. 1957 [excerpt]

SYNOPSIS: Niels Bohr wrote various letters to Werner Heisenberg during the period from 1957 until his death in 1962. However, his letters went unsent and remained private until the Bohr family released drafts of the letters in February 2002. The following draft letter seems to be in response to a book, by Robert Jungk, *Brighter Than a Thousand Suns,* which was published in the late 1950s. The Danish and English translations of Jungk's book included Heisenberg's recollections of a meeting between the two preeminent physicists in Copenhagen, Denmark, during the height of Nazi supremacy. The following draft letter written by Bohr was found after his death in the pages of his personal copy of the book.

Physicist Niels Bohr's meeting with friend and fellow scientist Werner Heisenberg has been the subject of much speculation, granted new light after the revelation of an unsent, draft letter written by Bohr to Heisenberg after their meeting. © **HULTON-DEUTSCH COLLECTION/ CORBIS. REPRODUCED BY PERMISSION.**

Dear Heisenberg,

I have seen a book, "Stærkere end tusind sole" ["Brighter than a thousand suns"] by Robert Jungk, recently published in Danish, and I think that I owe it to you to tell you that I am greatly amazed to see how much your memory has deceived you in your letter to the author of the book, excerpts of which are printed in the Danish edition.

Personally, I remember every word of our conversations, which took place on a background of extreme sorrow and tension for us here in Denmark. In particular, it made a strong impression both on Margrethe and me, and on everyone at the Institute that the two of you spoke to, that you and Weizsäcker expressed your definite conviction that Germany would win and that it was therefore quite foolish for us to maintain the hope of a different outcome of the war and to be reticent as regards all German offers of cooperation. I also remember quite clearly our conversation in my room at the Institute, where in vague terms you spoke in a manner that could only give me the firm impression that, under your leadership, everything was being done in Germany to develop atomic weapons and that you said that there was no need to talk about details since you were completely familiar with them and had spent the past two years working more or less exclusively on such preparations. I listened to this without speaking since [a] great matter for mankind was at issue in which, despite our personal friendship, we had to be regarded as representatives of two sides engaged in mortal combat. That my silence and gravity, as you write in the letter, could be taken as an expression of shock at your reports that it was possible to make an atomic bomb is a quite peculiar misunderstanding, which must be due to the great tension in your own mind. From the day three years earlier when I realized that slow neutrons could only cause fission in Uranium 235 and not 238, it was of course obvious to me that a bomb with certain effect could be produced by separating the uraniums. In June 1939 I had even given a public lecture in Birmingham about uranium fission, where I talked about the effects of such a bomb but of course added that the technical preparations would be so large that one did not know how soon they could be overcome. If anything in my behaviour could be interpreted as shock, it did not derive from such reports but rather from the news, as I had to understand it, that Germany was participating vigorously in a race to be the first with atomic weapons.

Besides, at the time I knew nothing about how far one had already come in England and America, which I learned only the following year when I was able to go to England after being informed that the German occupation force in Denmark had made preparations for my arrest.

All this is of course just a rendition of what I remember clearly from our conversations, which subsequently were naturally the subject of thorough discussions at the Institute and with other trusted friends in Denmark. It is quite another matter that, at that time and ever since, I have always had the definite impression that you and Weizsäcker had arranged the symposium at the German Institute, in which I did not take part myself as a matter of principle, and the visit to us in order to assure your-

selves that we suffered no harm and to try in every way to help us in our dangerous situation.

This letter is essentially just between the two of us, but because of the stir the book has already caused in Danish newspapers, I have thought it appropriate to relate the contents of the letter in confidence to the head of the Danish Foreign Office and to Ambassador Duckwitz.

Further Resources

BOOKS

Bohr, Aage. "The War Years and the Prospects Raised by the Atomic Weapons." In *Niels Bohr: His Life and Work as Seen by His Friends and Colleagues.* Stefan Rozenthal, ed. New York: Elsevier, 191–214.

Cassidy, David C. *Uncertainty: the Life and Science of Werner Heisenberg.* New York: Freeman, 1992.

Frayn, Michael. *Copenhagen.* New York: Anchor Books, 2000.

Heisenberg, Elisabeth. *Inner Exile: Recollections of a Life with Werner Heisenberg.* Boston: Birkhäuser, 1984.

Jungk, Robert. *Brighter Than a Thousand Suns: A Personal History of the Atomic Scientists.* New York: Harcourt Brace Jovanovich, 1958.

Powers, Thomas. *Heisenberg's War: The Secret History of the German Bomb.* New York: Knopf, 1993.

Ross, Paul Lawrence. *Heisenberg and the Nazi Atomic Bomb Project: A Study in German Culture.* Berkeley: University of California Press, 1998.

Szöllösi-Janze, Margit. *Science in the Third Reich.* New York: Berg, 2001.

PERIODICALS

Glanz, James. "New Twist on Physicist's Role in Nazi Bomb." *The New York Times,* February 7, 2002, A1, A8.

WEBSITES

Cassidy, David C. "A Historical Perspective on *Copenhagen* : What Was Werner Heisenberg Trying to Tell Niels Bohr During his Visit to Copenhagen in 1941, and What Did He Want From Bohr?" *Physics Today Online* July 2000. Available online at http://www.aip.org/pt/vol-53/iss-7/p28.html; website home page: http://www.aip.org (accessed October 18, 2002).

"Werner Heisenberg and the Uncertainty Principle." The American Physics Institute. Available online at http://www.aip.org/history/heisenberg/; website home page: http://www.aip.org (accessed October 18, 2002).

12

SPORTS

WILLIAM J. THOMPSON

Entries are arranged in chronological order by date of primary source. For entries with one primary source, the entry title is the same as the primary source title. Entries with more than one primary source have an overall entry title, followed by the titles of the primary sources.

Important Events in Sports, 1940–1949

1940

- On January 12, the University of Chicago announces the elimination of its football program, saying the sport is a handicap to education.

- On April 3, the Finnish education minister says Finland cannot host the Olympic Games in 1940; the games are canceled because of war and do not resume until 1948.

- On May 27, New York Yankee outfielder Joe DiMaggio receives the Golden Laurel as the outstanding U.S. athlete of 1939.

- On July 10, golfer Patty Berg signs a six-year pro contract.

- On July 13, the American Professional Football League forms with six teams.

- On September 8, the Baltimore Elite Giants defeat the New York Cubans 3-0 to win the Ruppert Memorial Cup, the highest achievement in Negro baseball.

- On October 8, the Cincinnati Reds defeat the Detroit Tigers 2-1, in the seventh game of the World Series.

- On November 5, baseball writers choose Hank Greenberg of Detroit as the American League player of the year.

1941

- On January 1, Morris Brown College of Atlanta defeats Wilberforce University, 19-3, in the first annual Steel Bowl (also called the Vulcan Bowl) at Birmingham, Alabama, before eight thousand fans to determine the national Negro college football title.

- On March 21, heavyweight boxing champion Joe Louis knocks out Abe Simon in the first round, the fifteenth "Bum of the Month" Louis has dispatched since winning the boxing title in 1937.

- On April 3, all eleven first-string players on the Boston University football team volunteer for service in the U.S. Naval Air Corps.

- On May 3, Whirlaway, ridden by Eddie Arcaro, sets a new Kentucky Derby course record of 2:01 for the 1¼-mile track.

- On May 7, Detroit Tigers star outfielder Hank Greenberg is inducted into the army.

- On June 7, Whirlaway wins the Belmont Stakes, becoming the first Triple Crown winner since War Admiral in 1937.

- On September 21, the Homestead (Pennsylvania) Grays defeat the New York Cuban Stars, 20-0 and 5-0, in a doubleheader at Yankee Stadium to win the Negro National Baseball League championship.

- On October 6, the New York Yankees win their ninth World Series, defeating the Brooklyn Dodgers four games to one.

- On December 15, because of the Japanese bombing of Pearl Harbor on December 7, the Rose Bowl is transferred to Durham, North Carolina, from Pasadena, California, to eliminate the chance of a Japanese bombing of the annual West Coast football classic.

- On December 17, a poll of sportswriters names Joe DiMaggio athlete of the year.

- On December 21, the Chicago Bears win the NFL championship for the second successive year by defeating the New York Giants, 37-9.

1942

- On January 10, the U.S. Golf Association cancels the open, the amateur, the women's amateur, and the amateur public championships for one year due to the war.

- On January 16, in his famous "green light letter" to the baseball commissioner, President Franklin D. Roosevelt expresses his hope that the war would not interrupt the 1942 season.

- On March 27, Army private and heavyweight champion Joe Louis knocks out Abe Simon in the sixth round in Madison Square Garden.

- On May 18, the New York police commissioner ends night baseball in the city for the war's duration because the glow from lights endangers shipping.

- On May 21, Boston Red Sox great Ted Williams joins the military.

- In July, a series of three all-star baseball games, which include players currently in the service, nets $171,000 for the Army and Navy Relief Funds and baseball's Bat and Ball Fund.

- On July 15, Whirlaway surpasses Seabiscuit as the top money-winning racehorse, capturing the Massachusetts Handicap at Suffolk Downs, setting a new track record of 1:48.20. The horse's lifetime earnings now top $454,336.

- In September, All-Army all-star teams challenge professional football teams in an eight-game exhibition designed to raise one million dollars for Army Relief.

- On September 29, the Kansas City Monarchs defeat the Homestead Grays to win the Negro World Series.

- On October 5, the Saint Louis Cardinals defeat the Yankees before 69,052 fans in Yankee Stadium to win the World Series in five games.

- On October 29, Branch Rickey becomes president and general manager of the Brooklyn Dodgers, replacing Larry MacPhail, who has entered the army.

- On December 5, Willie Mosconi regains the pocket billiard championship by winning nine of ten matches in national tournament play.

- On December 13, the Washington Redskins upset the Chicago Bears, 14-6, to win the NFL championship.

- On December 25, *Ring* magazine names Sugar Ray Robinson fighter of the year.

1943

- The All-American Girls Professional Baseball League is established.

- On January 13, Joe DiMaggio enlists in the Army.

- On January 17, New York baseball writers name Boston Red Sox outfielder Ted Williams player of the year.

- On April 6, the Cleveland Rams withdraw from the NFL for the remainder of the war.

- In July, still recovering from a serious automobile accident, golfer Patty Berg wins the Western Golf Open medal, then enlists in the marines.

- On October 11, the New York Yankees win the World Series, defeating the Saint Louis Cardinals four games to one.

- On November 23, Philadelphia Phillies owner William Cox is banned from baseball for betting on his own team.

- On December 26, the Chicago Bears beat the Washington Redskins, 41-12, to win the NFL championship.

1944

- On June 24, Olympic champion Babe Didrikson Zaharias wins the Women's Western Golf Open in Chicago.

- On October 9, the Saint Louis Cardinals win the sixth game of the World Series, 3-1, to defeat the Saint Louis Browns.

- On December 18, swimmer Ann Curtis and golfer Byron Nelson are named outstanding athletes of 1944 by an Associated Press poll. Curtis also wins the James E. Sullivan award as outstanding athlete of 1944 on January 4, 1945.

- On December 23, War Mobilization and Reconversion Director James F. Byrnes bans all horse racing effective January 3 to save labor and critical materials.

1945

- On January 26, a syndicate consisting of Larry MacPhail, Dan Topping, and Del Webb buys 96.88 percent of the New York Yankees and its minor-league properties for $2.8 million from the heirs of the late Colonel Jacob Ruppert.

- On February 8, Lt. Paul Brown agrees to coach the newly created Cleveland team of the All-American Football Conference, effective when he leaves the service.

- On February 21, the 1945 All-Star baseball game is canceled as a travel-conservation measure.

- On May 7, Branch Rickey announces the formation of the United Negro Baseball League with six teams.

- On May 9, the ban on horse racing is lifted. Santa Anita in Arcadia, California, and Jamaica in New York resume races within days.

- On June 23, Babe Didrikson Zaharias takes her third Western Women's Open Golf title with a victory over Dorothy Germain in Indianapolis.

- On October 10, the Detroit Tigers win the World Series over the Chicago Cubs four games to three.

- On October 23, Jackie Robinson becomes the first African American player admitted to organized professional baseball as he signs with Montreal of the International League, a Brooklyn Dodgers farm team.

- On November 12, the American League announces a record paid attendance for the 1945 season of 5,580,420.

- On December 16, the Cleveland Rams defeat the Washington Redskins, 15-14, in Cleveland to win the NFL championship.

- On December 21, golfers Byron Nelson and Babe Didrikson Zaharias are named male and female athletes of the year by an Associated Press poll.

1946

- The professional All-American Football Conference starts the 1946 season with an eight-club league.

- On January 10, the AAU and the NCAA enter into a formal partnership, agreeing for the first time to respect each other's rights, rules, and territories.

- On March 21, Kenny Washington becomes the first African American in the NFL since 1933, signing with the Los Angeles Rams.

- On June 19, in the first heavyweight fight ever televised, Joe Louis knocks out Billy Conn in eight rounds.

- On August 28, a meeting of American and National League owners results in an agreement to give players representation in creating rules and policies, to set a minimum salary, and to establish a pension fund.

- On October 13, the Saint Louis Cardinals defeat the Boston Red Sox four games to three to win the World Series.

- On November 1, the professional Basketball Association of America starts its first season.

- On December 3, Notre Dame is named the best college football team by an Associated Press sportswriters poll.

- On December 15, an attempted fix of the NFL title game between the Chicago Bears and the New York Giants is exposed.

- On December 23, Babe Didrikson Zaharias, winner of the 1946 women's golf championship, is chosen outstanding woman athlete of the year by an Associated Press poll of sportswriters.

- On December 27, Davis Cup tennis competition resumes after six years. The United States team wins the cup for the first time since 1938, defeating Australia, 5-0, in Melbourne.

- On December 29, *Ring* magazine names Tony Zale fighter of the year.

1947

- On January 1, a college football boom spawns a proliferation of New Year's Day bowl games, such as the Raisin Bowl, won by San Jose State, 20-0, over Utah State. Claude "Buddy" Young of Illinois is the first African American player to score a touchdown in Rose Bowl history. Illinois wins, 45-14, over UCLA.

- On January 31, the War Department rejects the requests of Felix "Doc" Blanchard, Glenn Davis, and Barney Poole for leave from the armed forces to play professional football.

- On April 9, Leo Durocher, manager of the Brooklyn Dodgers, is suspended for "unpleasant incidents detrimental to baseball"—associating with gamblers.

- On April 10, Jackie Robinson becomes the first African American player to play major league baseball in the twentieth century after the Dodgers purchase his Montreal contract.

- On April 22, the Basketball Association of America's first playoff championship is won by the Philadelphia Warriors over the Chicago Stags four games to one.

- On May 17, the United States regains the Walker Cup in golf competition in St. Andrews, Scotland.

- On May 30, Mauri Rose wins the thirty-first annual Indianapolis 500 racing classic in 4:17:52.17.

- On July 5, First baseman Larry Doby becomes first African American player in the American League, signing a contract with the Cleveland Indians.

- On August 14, Babe Didrikson Zaharias relinquishes her amateur status to accept three hundred thousand dollars for a series of golf movies.

- On September 12, Dodgers infielder Jackie Robinson is named baseball's rookie of the year by *The Sporting News*.

- From September 30 to October 6, the World Series is televised for the first time, with Gillette Safety Razor and Ford Motor paying sixty-five thousand dollars for joint sponsorship. The Yankees take their eleventh World Series title over the Brooklyn Dodgers four games to three. Major-league baseball draws a record attendance of 19.9 million fans for the season.

- On October 7, Larry MacPhail sells his share of the world-champion New York Yankees to partners Dan Topping and Del Webb for an estimated two million dollars.

- On December 13, the Missouri Valley Conference votes to ban all racial bias in athletics by September 1950.

1948

- On January 17, African American professional golfers Bill Spiller, Ted Rhodes, and Madison Gunter sue the Richmond (Virginia) Golf Club and the PGA for $105,000, charging they were barred from a Richmond golf tournament on racial grounds.

- On January 30, the fifth Winter Olympiad opens in Saint Moritz, Switzerland, with twenty-seven nations participating—the first Olympic games since 1936.

- In February, Dick Button becomes the first American to win a figure skating championship in the Olympics.

- On April 6, the U.S. Golf Association bars Babe Didrikson Zaharias from the National Golf Open, ruling that the tournament is restricted to men.

- On May 1, Eddie Arcaro rides Citation to victory in the seventy-fourth Kentucky Derby, winning $83,400.

- On May 10, the Basketball Association of America expands to twelve teams when four teams jump from the National Basketball League.

- On May 31, Mauri Rose wins his second straight Indianapolis 500 with an record average speed of 119.813 miles per hour, earning twenty-eight thousand dollars.

- On June 12, Citation wins the $117,300 Belmont Stakes to become the eighth horse to win racing's Triple Crown.

- On June 25, heavyweight champion Joe Louis knocks out Joe Walcott in the eleventh round for Louis's twenty-fifth and last title defense. He announces his retirement from boxing following the fight.

- On July 7, the Cleveland Indians sign Negro American League pitching star Satchel Paige, who started his career in 1925.

- From July to August, the 1948 summer Olympics, held in London, without the Soviet Union, draws 1.5 million spectators. The United States leads in gold medals with thirty-eight.

- On August 6, Bob Mathias wins his first Olympic decathlon at age seventeen with 7,139 points.

- On October 11, the Cleveland Indians win the World Series four games to two with a 4-3 victory over the Boston Braves.

- On November 30, the Negro National League dissolves, leaving the ten-team Negro American League the only segregated baseball association.

- On January 16, Marshall Teague wins the National Stock Car championship in a 100-mile race at Daytona Beach, Florida.

- On May 30, Bill Holland wins the Indianapolis 500, averaging 121.327 miles per hour.

- On June 22, Ezzard Charles wins the world heavyweight title left vacant by the retirement of Joe Louis in a fifteen-round decision over "Jersey" Joe Walcott; he later beats Gus Lesnevich, Pat Valentino, and Freddie Beshore to become the undisputed heavyweight champion.

- On July 5, the New York Giants sign their first African American players, outfielder Monte Irvin and infielder Hank Thompson, from Jersey City.

- On August 3, the Basketball Association of America and the National Basketball League merge to form the new National Basketball Association (NBA).

- On October 9, the New York Yankees win the World Series, defeating the Brooklyn Dodgers four games to one.

- On November 19, Jackie Robinson is named NL MVP for 1949 by the Baseball Writers Association, the first African American player to receive this honor.

- On December 9, the NFL and the All-American Conference end their four-year rivalry as they merge into a single National-American Football League.

- On December 26, *Ring* magazine names Ezzard Charles fighter of the year.

Athletes in the Military

Joe DiMaggio and "Pee Wee" Reese in Uniform; "Bob Feller Taking Military Oath"; "Nile Clarke Kinnick Jr. Holding Trophy"

Photographs

Date: December 6, 1939; December 11, 1941; July 8, 1944
Source: Joe DiMaggio and Harold "Pee Wee" Reese in uniform before a Central Pacific Service Championship game. July 8, 1944. AP/Wide World Photos. Available online at http://www.apwideworld.com (accessed March 19, 2003); "Bob Feller Taking Military Oath." December 11, 1941. Corbis. Image no. BE049915. Available online at http://pro.corbis.com (accessed March 19, 2003); "Clarke Kinnick Jr. Holding Trophy." December 6, 1939. Corbis. Image no. U894609INP. Available online at http://pro.corbis.com (accessed March 19, 2003).

Joe Louis in Uniform

Poster

By: Office for Emergency Management
Date: 1943
Source: "Joe Louis in Uniform." Office for Emergency Management, Office of War Information, Domestic Operations Branch, Bureau of Special Services. "Pvt. Joe Louis Says. . . ." 1943. National Archives, College Park, Md. Records of the Office of Government Reports. Record Group 44. Available online at http://arcweb.archives.gov/arc/arch_results _detail.jsp?&pg=3&si=0&nh=8&st=b; website home page: http://www.archives.gov (accessed March 19, 2003). ■

Introduction

In 1940, Congress narrowly passed legislation instituting the military draft in response to the war in Europe and Asia, and its growing threat to the United States. In spring 1941, baseball was affected by conscription when Philadelphia Phillies pitcher, Hugh Mulcahy, and Hank Greenberg, all-star first baseman of the Detroit Tigers, were drafted. Neither player sought a deferment, and exchanged baseball jerseys for military uniforms.

On December 7, 1941, Bob Feller, Cleveland Indians pitcher, drove from his Iowa home to baseball meetings in Chicago. Feller, at age twenty-three, was already considered baseball's best pitcher—a strikeout artist with a blazing fastball, whose best years were in front of him. While in his car, Feller learned of the Japanese attack on Pearl Harbor. When he arrived in Chicago, Feller contacted the Navy recruiting office about enlisting. Feller had been classified 3-C for the draft. He was his family's sole breadwinner, his father was ill with cancer, his mother did not work, and his sister was a teenager. On December 10, in a ceremony covered live on radio and recorded by newsreels because of his celebrity, Bob Feller enlisted in the Navy. Commander Gene Tunney, former heavyweight-boxing champion, who headed a naval physical fitness program, swore in Feller. When asked about his decision to enlist immediately after the Pearl Harbor attack, Feller later replied that "we needed some heroes right now. . . . at that point, we were losing the war."

Beginning in early 1942, college and professional sports in the United States were affected by the loss of athletes to the draft or enlistment. Baseball and professional football were greatly affected, although top-notch performers in every sport ended up in uniform. After Pearl Harbor, athletes, as well as the male population at large, signed up for classification with local draft boards. In baseball, sixty-one major leaguers were in uniform at the start of 1942; by 1943, 219; 470 by 1944—comprising sixty percent of 1941 starting players—and more than five hundred by early 1945. Baseball's biggest stars, in addition to Feller and Greenberg, were in military service by 1943: Joe DiMaggio, Ted Williams, and many others. In the National Football League, a total of 638 players, coaches, and team officials served, 355 as commissioned officers.

Of the hundreds of amateur and professional athletes who served in the armed forces during World War II, many never saw combat, being assigned to army and naval bases throughout the United States. Teams of all-stars representing military installations traveled to bases to play exhibition contests, with Norfolk Naval Training Station and Great Lakes Naval Training Station fielding strong baseball squads.

Many athletes, however, served in combat. Ted Williams flew bombing missions as a Marine Corps pilot (and later in Korea as well), and Yogi Berra was at Normandy on D-Day. Bob Feller, after a time pitching for the naval base team in Norfolk, decided he wanted to do more that just "hand out bats and balls and make ball fields out of coral reefs." Feller volunteered to take gunnery training, and he was assigned to the USS *Alabama*. He went to the North Atlantic to protect American shipping interests, and then to the South Pacific to provide

Primary Source

Athletes in Uniform: Joe DiMaggio and Harold "Pee Wee" Reese in uniform before a Central Pacific Service Championship game (1 OF 3)

SYNOPSIS: The Japanese attack at Pearl Harbor on December 7, 1941, brought the United States into World War II. The onset of war and the need for military manpower prompted American athletes such as Joe DiMaggio, Ted Williams, Bob Feller, Joe Louis, and Nile Kinnick to enlist. Athletes protected the country through military service in a time of national crisis. Some decorated veterans, such as Feller, returned to their professional careers. Tragically, other great athletes such as Kinnick, lost their lives in World War II. Here, Joe DiMaggio, of the New York Yankees, and Harold H. "Pee Wee" Reese, of the Brooklyn Dodgers, sign autographs for a military vice admiral and brigadier general. AP/WIDE WORLD PHOTOS/U.S. NAVY. REPRODUCED BY PERMISSION.

cover for carriers by firing at Japanese aircraft. African American athletes were in a unique position with regard to military service in World War II. Other than the army, the other service branches essentially shunned African Americans. The military remained racially segregated. Nonetheless, the African American press promoted the slogan, "Double V" for "victory over our enemies at home and our enemies on the battlefield." The most

prominent African American athlete in uniform was Joe Louis, the heavyweight-boxing champion. As a symbol of minority support for the war effort, Louis toured military bases in the United States and Great Britain, giving boxing exhibitions, joined by the young fighter Sugar Ray Robinson. Louis, Sugar Ray Robinson, Jackie Robinson and other black athletes had to fight the indignities of racism, both on base and off, as local customs

football players died, including Al Blozis, a 1943 all-star New York Giants tackle, who was killed in France in 1945.

Perhaps the most famous athlete to die in World War II was Nile Clarke Kinnick Jr., the 1939 Heisman Trophy winner from the University of Iowa, one of the most dominating football players of his time. A five-foot nine, 170-pound quarterback, Kinnick could run, pass, punt, and drop kick field goals. An A student in college, Kinnick turned down professional football offers to attend law school. After Pearl Harbor, Kinnick became a naval pilot. On June 2, 1943, Kinnick was lost at sea in the Caribbean, when his plane crashed during a training mission several miles from the aircraft carrier USS *Lexington*. After his death, Kinnick was elected to the College Football Hall of Fame, and the University of Iowa football stadium was named in his honor.

The war's impact changed the attitudes and outlook of many athletes. Entering military service as young men, they emerged after the war hardened by firsthand observations of war. Athletics was not mortal combat, nor the most important thing in life, rather a game and a means

Primary Source
Athletes in Uniform: "Bob Feller Taking Military Oath" (2 OF 3)
Cleveland Indians' starting pitcher Bob Feller is sworn into the Navy by Lieutenant Commander Gene Tunney on December 11, 1941. © BETTMANN/CORBIS. REPRODUCED BY PERMISSION.

and ordinances made no exceptions for African Americans in uniform.

Significance

A number of athletes were wounded in wartime military service, and, sadly, others did not come back at all, paying the ultimate price. Lou Brissie, a future major league pitcher, suffered severe shrapnel wounds. Bert Shepard, a young pitching prospect, lost his right leg after crashing his plane on a bombing mission, but he later appeared in one major league game. Cecil Travis, a star shortstop before the war, suffered frozen feet at the Battle of the Bulge, and he never regained his full abilities.

The number of men killed in combat or in training-related accidents was relatively small, but significant. Forty-one minor league baseball players were killed during the war, as well as two former big leaguers—Elmer Gideon, an outfielder for five games with the 1939 Washington Senators, was shot down in France; and Harry O'Neill, a catcher in one game with the 1939 Philadelphia Athletics, was killed at Iwo Jima in 1945. Twelve active professional

Primary Source
Athletes in Uniform: "Nile Clarke Kinnick Jr. Holding Trophy" (3 OF 3)
Nile Clarke Kinnick Jr. holds the Heisman Trophy in 1939. He died four years later when the Navy plane he was flying crashed in the Carribean Sea. © BETTMANN/CORBIS. REPRODUCED BY PERMISSION.

Pvt. Joe Louis says...

"We're going to do our part ...and we'll win because we're on God's side"

Primary Source

Athletes in Uniform, "Joe Louis in Uniform": Poster

SYNOPSIS: Heavyweight boxing champion Joe Louis served in the army during World War II. As with many famous athletes in military service, Louis's fame meant he was more useful as a symbol and spokesperson than as a combat soldier. His duties revolved around building and maintaining support for the war effort and boosting the morale of the troops, to which end Louis toured the country and appeared in posters, newsreels, and other media. Louis's loyal service in the military, at a time when it was still largely segregated and discrimination against African Americans was widely accepted in American society, made him all the more important as a symbol of American unity and determination. NATIONAL ARCHIVES. REPRODUCED BY PERMISSION.

to earn a living. As veterans, these athletes brought a more determined and serious approach to sports.

Many athletes kept in excellent shape during their military service and, for the most part, were able to resume their careers without a noticeable decline in their abilities. Others, however, because of age, the extended layoff, lack of conditioning, or injuries in battle, were never able to recapture fully their prior athletic prowess. Baseball players, such as DiMaggio, Williams, Feller, Reese, and others continued play at a high skill level, although the natural effects of age began to affect their play.

Further Resources

BOOKS

Baender, Paul, ed. *A Hero Perished: The Diary and Selected Letters of Nile Kinnick.* Iowa City: University of Iowa Press, 1991.

Gilbert, Bill. *They Also Served: Baseball and the Home Front, 1941–1945.* New York: Crown Publishers, 1992.

Goldstein, Richard. *Spartan Seasons: How Baseball Survived the Second World War.* New York: Macmillan, 1980.

Mead, William B. *Even the Browns.* Chicago: Contemporary Books, 1978.

Season of 1941: DiMaggio and Williams

My Turn at Bat: The Story of My Life

Autobiography

By: Ted Williams, with John Underwood

Date: 1969

Source: Williams, Ted, with John Underwood. *My Turn at Bat: The Story of My Life.* New York: Simon and Schuster, 1969, 81, 83, 85, 86.

About the Author: Ted Williams (1918–2002) was born in San Diego, California. Williams played his entire career with the Red Sox (1939–1960), hit 521 home runs, compiled a .344 career batting average, won two Triple Crowns, two MVP awards, and was selected to seventeen All-Star games. His brilliant career was interrupted for military service in World War II and Korea. Williams managed the Washington Senators and Texas Rangers after his playing career. Williams was elected to baseball's Hall of Fame in 1966.

Joe DiMaggio Hitting in His 56th Consecutive Game

Photograph

Date: July 16, 1941

Source: "Joe DiMaggio and Al Milnar During Cleveland Game." July 16, 1941. Corbis. Image no. U613188ACME.

Available online at http://pro.corbis.com (accessed March 19, 2003). ∎

Introduction

In 1941, Americans were worried about the war that was raging in Europe and Asia. The 1941 season provided baseball fans a glorious, if only temporary, diversion from world events. The highlights of the 1941 season were the fifty-six-game hitting streak by the New York Yankees' Joe DiMaggio, Ted Williams of the Boston Red Sox chasing .400, and a dramatic All-Star game.

When the season began, DiMaggio, at age twenty-six, was an established star with several World Series championships under his belt. Williams, at twenty-two, the brash "Kid" or "Splendid Splinter," was a star in the making. On May 15, 1941, the DiMaggio streak began. The Yankee centerfielder had been in a slump that dropped his batting average to .306. At that point, Williams was hitting well over .400. Williams matched DiMaggio's hitting streak for the first twenty-three games, batting a phenomenal .489 over that stretch, while DiMaggio hit a solid .374.

Both players were selected for the All-Star game at Detroit's Briggs Stadium in July. The American League trailed 5-3 in the bottom of the ninth, when Williams hit a three-run, game-winning home run. DiMaggio, whose hitting streak then stood at a major league record (forty-eight games), was the first to greet Williams as he crossed home plate.

The DiMaggio streak was front-page news despite events in Europe, where Hitler had launched an invasion of Russia. On July 16, DiMaggio extended the streak to fifty-six games in Cleveland. His batting average was at .375, while Williams dipped to .395, after being over .400 for much of the season.

On July 17, DiMaggio's hitting streak ended in Cleveland before a sellout crowd of 67,468. Indians' pitchers Al Smith and Jim Bagby kept DiMaggio hitless in three official at bats. On his first trip to the plate, Cleveland third baseman, Ken Keltner, robbed DiMaggio of a hit, fielding a hard line drive down the third baseline. DiMaggio walked in his next at bat, prompting boos from the huge crowd. DiMaggio hit another hard grounder to Keltner his third time up. DiMaggio's last chance to extend the streak was in the eighth inning. DiMaggio hit the ball sharply to Lou Boudreau at shortstop, who turned a double play. Cleveland rallied in the ninth inning to cut the Yankee lead to 4-3, but the game ended. The amazing DiMaggio streak was over.

When Williams returned to the Red Sox lineup on July 22 from a foot injury, the focus of the season shifted to his quest to hit .400. Williams's hitting was torrid during August (batting .466 between the 7th and the 21st of

Primary Source

Joe DiMaggio Hitting in His 56th Consecutive Game

SYNOPSIS: While Ted Williams was in the midst of his remarkable season at the plate, the New York Yankees' Joe DiMaggio achieved something even more extraordinary. Between May 15 and July 16, 1941, DiMaggio hit safely in fifty-six consecutive games. Sixty years later his record is still unequaled and seldom challenged. Over the fifty-six game stretch, DiMaggio batted .408 (91 hits in 223 at bats, with 15 home runs). © BETTMANN/CORBIS. REPRODUCED BY PERMISSION.

that month), before tailing off somewhat in September. His average stood at .400—officially .39955—on September 27, the day before season's end. Red Sox manager Joe Cronin suggested to Williams that he might want to sit out one or both games of the season-ending doubleheader against the Philadelphia Athletics. As Williams recalled years later, he did not think it was the proper choice. He responded by going four for five in the first game, including hitting his thirty-seventh home run. He was two for three in the second game. Williams's six-for-eight performance in the doubleheader raised his season average to .406.

Significance

The accomplishments of DiMaggio and Williams during 1941 had not been equaled as of 2003. No major league player has ever hit safely in as many consecutive games as DiMaggio, nor has any player hit .400 since Williams. The 1941 season was the last "normal" year in baseball until 1946, as the United States was plunged into World War II two months after the World Series ended. For four years, the war affected baseball dramatically, as

many of its most talented players—including DiMaggio and Williams—were either drafted or enlisted for military service.

Both DiMaggio and Williams resumed their baseball careers after the war. For DiMaggio, the postwar years saw a gradual decline of his many skills from age and injury. Unwilling to play at a lesser level, DiMaggio retired in 1951. He became a fixture at Yankee Old-Timers Games for decades, until his death in 1999. Williams remained one of baseball's top hitters. Enduring a second career interruption for military service in Korea, Williams retired in 1960. He dramatically ended his career with a home run in his final at bat.

Primary Source

My Turn at Bat: The Story of My Life [excerpt]

SYNOPSIS: In 1941, baseball's last season before America entered World War II, fans enjoyed two of what would become baseball's most legendary performances. One was that of Ted Williams. Over the course of the season, Williams hit for a batting av-

Ted Williams, Boston Red Sox outfielder, takes a swing on the way to a batting average of .406 for the season. © BETTMANN/CORBIS. REPRODUCED BY PERMISSION.

erage of .406. Williams was the first major leaguer to hit .400 since 1930, and first American League player to do so since 1923. As it turned out, he would be the last major league player in the twentieth century to top .400 for a season. In this excerpt, Williams recounts the last day of the season.

The .400 thing got bigger as the season went on because a lot of guys had hit .400 for two months and then tailed. And, truthfully, it got bigger to me with the years. I had to think then that I wasn't going to be the last to do it, or that I might even do it again myself. . . .

It came to the last day of the season, and by now I was down to .39955, which, according to the way they do it, rounds out to an even .400. We had a doubleheader left at Philadelphia. . . . In the last ten days of the season my average dropped almost a point a day. Now it was barely .400. The night before the game Cronin offered to take me out of the lineup to preserve the .400. . . .

I told Cronin I didn't want that. If I couldn't hit .400 all the way I didn't deserve it. It sure as hell meant something to me then, and Johnny Orlando, the clubhouse boy, always a guy who was there when

I needed him, must have walked ten miles with me the night before, talking it over and just walking around. . . .

. . . It turned up cold and miserable in Philadelphia. It had rained on Saturday and the game had been rescheduled as part of a Sunday doubleheader. They still had 10,000 people in Shibe Park, I suppose a lot of them just curious to see if The Kid really could hit .400. I have to say I felt good despite the cold. And I know just about everybody in the park was for me. As I came to bat for the first time that day, the Philadelphia catcher, Frankie Hayes, said, "Ted, Mr. Mack told us if we let up on you he'll run us out of baseball. I wish you all the luck in the world, but we're not giving you a damn thing."

Bill McGowan was the plate umpire, and I'll never forget it. Just as I stepped in, he called time and slowly walked around the plate, bent over and began dusting it off. Without looking up, he said, "To hit .400 a batter has got to be loose. He has got to be loose."

I guess I couldn't have been much looser. First time up I singled off Dick Fowler, a liner between first and second. Then I hit a home run, then I hit two more singles off Porter Vaughan, a left-hander who was new to me, and in the second game I hit one off the loudspeaker horn in right field for a double. For the day I wound up six for eight. I don't remember celebrating that night, but I probably went out and had a chocolate milk shake. During the winter Connie Mack had to replace the horn.

Further Resources

BOOKS

Allen, Maury. *Where Have You Gone, Joe DiMaggio: The Story of America's Last Hero.* New York: Dutton, 1975.

Cramer, Richard Ben. *Joe DiMaggio: The Hero's Life.* New York: Simon & Schuster, 2000.

Creamer, Robert. *Baseball in '41.* New York: Viking, 1991.

Linn, Ed. *Hitter: The Life and Turmoils of Ted Williams.* New York: Harcourt, Brace, and Company, 1993.

Seidel, Michael. *Streak: Joe DiMaggio and the Summer of '41.* New York: McGraw-Hill, 1988.

———. *Ted Williams: A Baseball Life.* Chicago: Contemporary Books, 1991.

PERIODICALS

"Batting Mark of .4057 for Williams." *The New York Times,* September 29, 1941.

Drebinger, John. "DiMaggio Streak Ended at 56 Games." *The New York Times,* July 18, 1941, 12.

Durso, Joseph. "Joe DiMaggio: Yankee Clipper Dies at 84." *The New York Times,* March 9, 1999, A1.

WEBSITES

"Joe DiMaggio." The National Baseball Hall of Fame and Museum. Available at http://www.baseballhalloffame.org/hofers_and_honorees/hofer_bios/dimaggio_joe.htm; website home page: http://www.baseballhalloffame.org (accessed February 28, 2003).

The Official Ted Williams Web Site. Available at http://www.tedwilliams.com (accessed February 28, 2003).

"Ted Williams." The National Baseball Hall of Fame and Museum. Available at http://www.baseballhalloffame.org/hofers_and_honorees/hofer_bios/williams_ted.htm; website home page http://www.baseballhalloffame.org (accessed February 28, 2003).

AUDIO AND VISUAL MEDIA

"Sixth Inning: The National Pastime, 1940–1950." Part 6 of *Baseball: A Film by Ken Burns*. PBS Home Video, 1994, VHS.

"73 to 0"

Magazine article

By: George Halas

Date: December 6, 1941

Source: Halas, George. "73 to 0." *Saturday Evening Post* 214, December 6, 1941.

About the Author: George Halas (1895–1983) was born in Chicago, Illinois, the son of immigrant parents. After graduating from the University of Illinois, Halas played semi-pro football, and baseball for the New York Yankees in 1919. In 1920 Halas was part of a group that met in Canton, Ohio, to establish what would become the National Football League (NFL). Halas represented the Decatur (Illinois) Staleys, sponsored by a corn products manufacturer. The Staleys became the Chicago Bears in 1922, and Halas would play for the Bears, coach them until 1967—winning more than three hundred games and eight NFL championships—and serve as the Bears' owner until his death. Halas was elected as a charter member of football's Hall of Fame in 1963. ■

Introduction

The Chicago Bears, known as "The Monsters of the Midway," were professional football's dominant team during the NFL's early years. Halas not only played for the Bears in the 1920s, but also coached the team and became its owner in 1921. As owner, Halas had a keen eye for talent and promotion. This led him to sign star players, including Harold "Red" Grange, legendary 1920s halfback, and Bronko Nagurski, bruising fullback of the 1930s. Both Grange and Nagurski are members of football's Hall of Fame.

Halas also was an innovator on the field, installing the "T Formation," an attacking scheme that placed the quarterback directly behind center, with a running back set to each side. This allowed the quarterback to direct the offense, by passing or handing off the ball. Most other teams used the "single wing," where a halfback took the snap from center and was a threat to run or pass the ball. The Bears did not perfect the T Formation at first, and Halas brought in Clark Shaughnessy, a college coach who had successfully installed the scheme, to make adjustments.

In 1940, the Bears had an excellent team featuring a number of outstanding performers, including quarterback Sid Luckman, linemen Clyde "Bulldog" Turner and Dan Fortmann, and backs George McAfee and Bill Osmanski. The other dominant NFL team in that era was the Washington Redskins. The Redskins' star player was quarterback "Slingin'" Sammy Baugh, who also played defensive back and punter. In the season's ninth week, the Redskins defeated the Bears 7-3. The often theatrical Redskin owner George Preston Marshall was never known as a gracious winner. After the game, Marshall stated that his team should be conceded the NFL championship.

The Bears and Redskins won their respective divisions and met again in the NFL championship game. During the week before the game, Halas again enlisted Shaughnessy, whose Stanford University team was bound for the Rose Bowl, to help with the Bears' preparations. The war of words between the two owners continued until the game started—as Halas later would recall with delight.

Sunday, December 8, 1940, was a mild day in Washington for the NFL title game. From the moment the Washington Redskins took the field at Griffith Stadium, they never had a chance. As *New York Times* columnist, Arthur Daley wrote, "The weather was perfect. So were the Bears." The 36,000 Redskin fans watched in horror as Bill Osmanski scored on a sixty-eight-yard touchdown run fifty-six seconds into the game. A photograph, showing four Redskin players in pursuit of Osmanski on the play, depicted the game's story line. The Bears started fast and never looked back. The score was 21-0 at the end of the first quarter, and 28-0 at the half. In the second half, the Bears never let up, tallying twenty-six third quarter points and nineteen in the fourth quarter. The final score was 73-0. The Bears scored eleven touchdowns, seven on offense and four on defense, including three interception returns for touchdowns. Halas used all thirty-three players on his roster against the overmatched Redskins.

Significance

The Bears' seventy-three points in the 1940 championship game remains the most points ever scored by one team in a professional football game, regular or postseason. The T Formation became the primary offensive formation in professional football. By the early 1950s, the single wing nearly had vanished, as the flying wedge, a rugby-like formation, had been abandoned in the 1890s.

Chicago Bears back Bill Osmanski is taken down by Washington Redskin Willie Wilkin after a short gain in the NFL championship game, December 8, 1940. © BETTMANN/CORBIS. REPRODUCED BY PERMISSION.

The Redskins were in shock afterward. Early in the game, Redskin end Charlie Malone dropped a sure touchdown pass from Sammy Baugh. Asked afterward whether Malone's catch would have made a difference, Baugh remarked, "Yeah, that would have made it 73 to 6."

In the years after the 73-0 debacle, the Chicago Bears and Washington Redskins remained bitter rivals. In 1941, the Bears went 10-1-0 and repeated as NFL champions, defeating the New York Giants in Chicago. The 1942 Bears won all eleven regular season games, extending the winning streak to eighteen games. They faced the Redskins for a chance to win a third consecutive title. Washington stunned the Bears 14-6, exacting a measure of revenge for the 1940 drubbing. In 1943, Chicago regained the title from the Redskins 42-21. After 1945, the Chicago Bears remained a championship contender, but never again put together a string of three championships in four years, as they had in the early 1940s. Halas coached the team until 1967, winning his last title in 1963. He owned the Bears until his death in 1983.

Primary Source

"73 to 0" [excerpt]

SYNOPSIS: On December 8, 1940, the Chicago Bears, coached by George Halas and led by quarterback Sid Luckman, defeated the Washington Redskins 73-0 in the most lopsided NFL championship game ever. Halas, one of the National Football League's founders, credited the victory to avenging a 7-3 loss to the Redskins earlier in the season, and the success of the T Formation offense.

And now the whistle blows for the championship game. The Bears were properly pitched. George Marshall had done a beautiful job as a human goad, our boys needed no fight talk. The starting line-up was wonderfully fast and young, averaging only twenty-three and two thirds years.

The Bears received the kickoff and Nolting brought the ball out to the twenty-four. At that point we put out a feeler. Our first four offensive plays—unless we were forced to punt—had long since been charted. On the initial play we sent our left end far out to the flank, and the Redskins's defensive right half went out to watch him. Then we sent the left halfback in motion far to his right. The Washington backer-up covered him. That was the tip-off we wanted. Flaherty had not changed his basic defense. We knew who was covering whom. That little item was all-important.

The first play was a quick opener in the line, with George McAfee carrying for seven yards. McAfee, a magnificent halfback, has a trick of running right up to the backers-up, then leaping sideways and dashing on, glory bound. On the second play we again sent the left end eighteen yards out on the flank. We sent the right halfback in motion, also out to the left. They were promptly covered by the two men whom we expected to cover them. With these two key defenders definitely out of the picture, Osmanski, who is a ten-second fullback, went outside tackle as though he had been shot out of a gun, and set sail for the goal line.

At one point Ed Justice and Charley Malone, of the Redskins, appeared to have a chance of driving him into the side line. But they were both suddenly upended by a tremendous block by George Wilson, our right end. It was a beautiful parlay. Osmanski crossed the goal line unmolested. . . .

I see no point in gloating over the eight touchdowns which followed. Except to add this, which throws additional light on the score:

Washington had used one particular pass into the flat which had worked successfully in the first game. Hampton Pool, our Bear end, was on the alert for it. Finally it came. Pool anticipated the play, intercepted the ball and ran it back for a touchdown. On another occasion, Bulldog Turner, Bear center, also watching for a certain Washington pass, guessed rightly, intercepted the ball and scored a touchdown. Even with a top-heavy score, would you have allowed yourself to be tackled? Or would you have scurried away to score a touchdown in a championship game?

. . . We had a 28 to 0 margin at the end of the first half. If Baugh should start to hit his targets in the second half, the twenty-eight points would not be an utterly safe margin. In the dressing room, therefore, I again mentioned to the boys that they had been tagged as a "first-half team." adding that we would start the second half from scratch, as though the score were 0 to 0.

I shall now make a confession. With a good start, the Bears began to resurrect plays out of the dim past—in fact they began to enjoy themselves. Each had the equivalent of $873.99 in his hands, the winning players' share. They even tried a screwy play we had used only once before—in an exhibition game at Peoria in the long, long ago. It was good for a long gain.

On the placements for the extra points after the first nine touchdowns, the balls were kicked into the stands and the spectators were allowed to keep them as souvenirs. After the tenth touchdown, however, the referee, Red Friesell, meekly approached the acting captain of the Bears.

"Would you mind awfully," he asked apologetically, "passing or running for the point after this touchdown? You see this is our last ball."

The Chicago Bears, 1940 National Champions, hoist their owner-coach George Halas after embarassing the Washington Redskins in the championship game, 73-0. © BETTMANN/CORBIS. REPRODUCED BY PERMISSION.

"Not at all," the captain replied airily. "It is a pleasure to be of some assistance to you. And after our next touchdown you can count on us to do the gentlemanly thing."

After the eleventh touchdown the Bears passed for the extra point, like the little gentlemen they are.

Further Resources

BOOKS

Halas, George, et al. *Halas By Halas: The Autobiography of George Halas.* New York: McGraw-Hill Book Company, 1979.

National Football League. *The First Fifty Years.* New York: Simon & Schuster, 1969.

Peterson, Robert W. *Pigskin: The Early Years of Pro Football.* New York: Oxford University Press, 1997.

Vass, George. *George Halas and the Chicago Bears.* Chicago: Henry Regnery Company, 1971.

PERIODICALS

Daley, Arthur J. "Bears Overwhelm Redskins By Record 73-0 Score." *The New York Times,* December 9, 1940.

Durso, Joseph. "George Halas, Football Pioneer, Dies." *The New York Times,* November 1, 1983.

WEBSITES

Carroll, Bob. "1940: The Triumph of the T." Professional Football Researchers Association. Available at http://www .footballresearch.com/articles/frpage.cfm?topic=t-1940;

website home page: http://www.footballresearch.com (accessed February 28, 2003).

Chicago Bears home page. Available at http://www.chicagobears.com (accessed February 28, 2003).

Letter to Kenesaw M. Landis

Letter

By: Franklin D. Roosevelt

Date: January 15, 1942

Source: Roosevelt, Franklin D. Letter to Kenesaw M. Landis, January 15, 1942. National Baseball Hall of Fame and Museum. Reproduced online at http://www.baseballhalloffame .org/education/primary%5Fsources/world%5Fwar%5Fii/letter %5F01%5Fsmall.htm; website home page: http://www .baseballhalloffame.org (accessed March 19, 2003).

About the Author: Franklin D. Roosevelt (1882–1945) was born at Hyde Park, New York. Educated at Harvard, Roosevelt was elected to the New York Senate in 1910, and served as assistant secretary of the navy from 1913 to 1920. After losing a bid for vice president in 1920, Roosevelt contracted polio, leaving his legs permanently paralyzed. Returning to politics, Roosevelt was elected governor of New York in 1928, and he defeated Herbert Hoover for the presidency in 1932. Roosevelt was reelected in 1936, 1940, and 1944. The only president to serve more than two terms, Roosevelt led the nation through the Great Depression and during World War II. ■

Introduction

The U.S. entry into World War II on December 8, 1941, guaranteed that the nation would never be the same. As in many areas of national life, the war greatly affected sports. Over 60 percent of 1941 starting major leaguers had joined the military by 1944. Baseball, along with other sports, continued operations for the duration of World War II. They filled major league rosters with 4-F's (persons physically or mentally unable to serve), teenagers, those over forty, and handicapped players. They also reduced the number of minor league teams— from ninety-three in 1940 to nine in 1943.

After Pearl Harbor, baseball was unsure whether to cancel the 1942 season. Baseball's commissioner, Judge Kenesaw Mountain Landis, wrote to President Franklin D. Roosevelt on January 14, 1942, to seek the president's opinion. Landis wrote: "Baseball is about to adopt schedules, sign players, make vast commitments, go to training camps. . . . What do you want us to do? If you believe we ought to close down for the duration of the war, we are ready to do so immediately. If you feel we

St. Louis Browns one-armed outfielder Pete Gray at Yankee Stadium, New York City, May 27, 1945. AP/WIDE WORLD PHOTOS. REPRODUCED BY PERMISSION.

ought to continue, we would be delighted to do so. We await your order."

Roosevelt's reply of January 15, which became known as the "Greenlight Letter," gave baseball and other sports encouragement to continue. FDR wrote that baseball would take minds off the war, even temporarily, and he encouraged expansion of night baseball. Roosevelt said that all able-bodied men should either serve in the military or in war-related jobs, and that older players might lower the quality of play, but not the popularity of baseball.

Baseball continued play for the duration of the war. Twilight games, rather than night games, were common. The mix of 4-F's, teenagers, and "graybeards" gave baseball a unique appearance during this era. On June 10, 1944, Joe Nuxhall became the youngest player—at fifteen years, ten months, and eleven days—to appear in a major league game. While the New York Yankees and St. Louis Cardinals remained strong even with its star players in the service, some traditionally weak franchises took advantage of manpower shortages to field winning teams.

In professional football, roster limits were cut from thirty-three to twenty-eight. Despite rosters of older players and those coaxed out of retirement, such as 1930s star Bronko Nagurski of the Chicago Bears, some teams were unable to field a complete squad. In 1943, the Pittsburgh Steelers and Philadelphia Eagles merged their rosters for

THE WHITE HOUSE
WASHINGTON

January 15, 1942.

My dear Judge:-

Thank you for yours of January fourteenth. As you will, of course, realize the final decision about the baseball season must rest with you and the Baseball Club owners -- so what I am going to say is solely a personal and not an official point of view.

I honestly feel that it would be best for the country to keep baseball going. There will be fewer people unemployed and everybody will work longer hours and harder than ever before.

And that means that they ought to have a chance for recreation and for taking their minds off their work even more than before.

Baseball provides a recreation which does not last over two hours or two hours and a half, and which can be got for very little cost. And, incidentally, I hope that night games can be extended because it gives an opportunity to the day shift to see a game occasionally.

As to the players themselves, I know you agree with me that individual players who are of active military or naval age should go, without question, into the services. Even if the actual quality of the teams is lowered by the greater use of older players, this will not dampen the popularity of the sport. Of course, if any individual has some particular aptitude in a trade or profession, he ought to serve the Government. That, however, is a matter which I know you can handle with complete justice.

Here is another way of looking at it -- if 300 teams use 5,000 or 6,000 players, these players are a definite recreational asset to at least 20,000,000 of their fellow citizens -- and that in my judgment is thoroughly worthwhile.

With every best wish,

Very sincerely yours,

Franklin D. Roosevelt

Hon. Kenesaw M. Landis,
333 North Michigan Avenue,
Chicago,
Illinois.

Primary Source

Franklin D. Roosevelt to Kenesaw M. Landis, January 15, 1942
SYNOPSIS: The loss of athletes to military service during World War II created manpower shortages in most sports, particularly baseball and professional football. President Franklin D. Roosevelt's "Greenlight" letter in January 1942 encouraged baseball to continue operations during the war. Teams were forced to use 4-F's, aged, and teenage players. In pro football, several teams merged temporarily to compensate for player shortages. NATIONAL BASEBALL HALL OF FAME, COOPERSTOWN, NEW YORK. REPRODUCED BY PERMISSION.

Pete Gray

Pete Gray was born Peter Wyshner in Nanticoke, Pennsylvania in 1915. At age six, his right arm was mangled in the spokes of a moving wagon, and it was amputated above the elbow. Determined to pursue his dream of being a ballplayer, Gray eventually played minor league baseball. After hitting .333 with sixty-eight steals with Memphis of the Southern Association in 1944, the St. Louis Browns contracted Gray for $20,000. Gray was an outfielder, and his fielding technique was to catch the ball, stick the glove under the stump of his right arm, draw the ball clear with his left hand, and throw it to the infield. At the plate, he hit with a thirty-five-ounce bat. In 1945, his only season, pitchers discovered Gray could not hit curveballs, and this took away his ability to bunt. As a result, Gray only hit .218. While he was popular with fans, many of his teammates believed him to be a liability who cost the team the pennant. The Browns released Gray, and he spent a couple seasons in the minors before retiring.

one season, and compiled a 5-4-1 record as the "Steagles"—the name fans gave them. In 1944, the Cleveland Rams suspended operations for one season, but came back to win the NFL title in 1945. That same year, the Steelers and Chicago Cardinals merged for one season to become "Card-Pitt," a woeful team. The team was nicknamed the "Carpets" because of their 0-10 record, and how their opponents "wiped their feet on them."

Significance

In the short run, the war provided an opportunity for youngsters to shine and gave older players a chance to rekindle past glory. Keeping baseball, along with other sports, going provided a boost in morale to millions of Americans, if only a brief respite from worries about family members in the service or their own well-being.

In many cases, those who returned from World War II to athletic competition had a new sense of purpose. The war highlighted the importance of sports to the United States and, in some respects, set the stage for the incredible changes that would occur after 1945, including the racial integration of baseball in 1947. The end of the Great Depression ushered in a new era in American history, and sports would play a new and expanded role in the post–World War II period.

Further Resources

BOOKS

Gilbert, Bill. *They Also Served: Baseball and the Home Front, 1941–1945.* New York: Crown Publishers, 1992.

Goldstein, Richard. *Spartan Seasons: How Baseball Survived the Second World War.* New York: Macmillan, 1980.

Lingeman, Richard. *Don't You Know There's a War On?* New York: G.P. Putnam's, 1970.

Mead, William B. *Even the Browns.* Chicago: Contemporary Books, 1978.

PERIODICALS

Goldstein, Richard. "Pete Gray, Major Leaguer with One Arm." *The New York Times,* July 2, 2002.

Infield, Tom. "When the Steagles Roamed on the Gridiron." *Philadelphia Inquirer,* October 26, 1993, D1.

Basketball's Big Men

Coach

Memoir

By: Ray Meyer, with Ray Sons
Date: 1987
Source: Meyer, Ray, with Ray Sons. *Coach.* Chicago: Contemporary Books, 1987, 41–42, 43, 44, 45, 46, 47, 48, 56.
About the Author: Ray Meyer (1913–) was born in Chicago, Illinois. Meyer attended the University of Notre Dame, where he was captain of the basketball team his last two seasons. After graduation, Meyer played Amateur Athletic Association (AAU) basketball and became the assistant coach at Notre Dame. In 1942, Meyer returned to Chicago to become the head coach at DePaul University. In forty-two seasons at DePaul, Meyer won 724 games, had thirty-seven winning seasons, and made thirteen National Collegiate Athletic Association (NCAA) tournament and seven National Invitation Tournament (NIT) appearances. After retirement, Meyer has worked as a broadcaster for DePaul basketball games. Meyer was inducted into basketball's Hall of Fame in 1979.

"Seven-Foot Trouble"

Magazine article

By: Bruce Drake, as told to Harold Keith
Date: February 19, 1944
Source: Drake, Bruce, as told to Harold Keith. "Seven-Foot Trouble." *Saturday Evening Post* 216, February 19, 1944, 16, 17, 88.
About the Author: Bruce Drake (1905–1983) was born in Gentry, Texas. After lettering in basketball, track, and football at the University of Oklahoma, Drake became head basketball coach at Oklahoma in 1938. In seventeen seasons as coach, Drake won two hundred games and made three NCAA tournament appearances with a passing, ball-control offense that earned his teams the nickname, "Roundball Runts." His personal crusade against goaltending began after Bob Kurland of archrival Oklahoma A&M blocked twenty-two shots

in a 1943 game. While at Oklahoma, Drake started and coached the golf and swimming teams. After leaving Oklahoma, Drake coached industrial league basketball for twenty seasons and conducted clinics around the world. He was elected to the basketball Hall of Fame in 1973. ■

Introduction

In the decades since basketball inventor Dr. James Naismith hung peach baskets at Springfield College in Massachusetts, basketball players had grown taller—as had the nation as a whole. Prior to World War II, few players taller than six-feet five made a significant impact on the game. With the ten-foot-high basket and lenient goaltending rules (allowing shots on its downward arc to be batted away), a talented tall player, especially those over six feet ten, could radically change the game. In the 1940s, two tall players—called "goons" by critics—entered college basketball and changed the game forever, Bob (Foothills) Kurland and George Mikan.

Bob Kurland was born in St. Louis, Missouri, in 1924. He grew to nearly seven-feet tall and enrolled at Oklahoma A&M University. Coach Henry Iba realized that Kurland might be a star in the making.

George Mikan, also born in 1924, grew up in Joliet, Illinois. A broken leg in high school prevented Mikan from playing basketball and kept him bedridden for eighteen months. Trying out for the basketball squad at the University of Notre Dame, the bespectacled, six-foot seven Mikan performed poorly. The Notre Dame coach told Mikan, "Basketball isn't your game." The coach suggested that if Mikan really wanted to play, he should enroll in a smaller school where he could be given special attention and more playing time. A witness to Mikan's sorry performance during the tryout was Ray Meyer, Notre Dame's assistant coach. Meyer soon would become head coach of DePaul University in Chicago. Within a year, Mikan grew to six-feet ten and enrolled at DePaul, where he and Meyer reunited. Mikan embarked on a vigorous basketball and conditioning program under Meyer's direction, and Mikan transformed himself from an awkward player into a dominating center.

Bob Kurland and George Mikan opposed each other several times during their collegiate careers. Two games were especially significant. In March 1944, the two "giants" of basketball squared off in the semi-finals of the National Invitational Tournament (NIT) at Madison Square Garden in New York. DePaul beat Oklahoma A&M 41-38. Kurland outscored Mikan fourteen to nine, as the DePaul star fouled out with more than fifteen minutes remaining in the game. Newspapers reported that over the course of the game, Kurland "batted out a half-dozen two pointers in his goaltending role." The second meeting between the stars was also at Madison Square Garden in March 1945. Oklahoma A&M, the NCAA champion, faced DePaul, the NIT winner, in a Red Cross benefit game. A&M won 52-44, as Kurland again outscored Mikan fourteen to nine. Mikan got into early foul trouble and was gone from the game less than fifteen minutes into the first half.

Significance

Bob Kurland and George Mikan had a lasting impact on the game of basketball. As a result of Kurland's knack for batting the ball off the rim and away from the basket, goaltending was outlawed in 1945. This ban came after rival Oklahoma's coach, Bruce Drake, wrote a nationally-circulated article calling for changes in the rule. As a result of the rule change, Kurland became a more complete player, particularly as an offensive threat. Kurland became a three-time all-American, led the Oklahoma Aggies to two NCAA championships, and scored fifty-eight points in his final college game. Kurland turned down an offer from the National Basketball League (later to merge into the National Basketball Association). He played, instead, for the Phillips (Petroleum) 66ers in Amateur Athletic Union (AAU) competition, while in management training with the firm. He refused to turn professional to remain eligible for Olympic competition, then only open to amateur athletes. Kurland won two gold medals as a member of the 1948 and 1952 United States Olympic basketball teams. Kurland was elected to basketball's Hall of Fame in 1961.

Mikan led the nation in scoring his last two seasons with DePaul, and he was twice named college basketball player of the year. He led the Blue Demons to the 1945 National Invitation Tournament (NIT) title. After graduation, Mikan signed with the National Basketball League. He joined the Minneapolis Lakers, who later merged into the NBA. Mikan led the Lakers to six league championships between 1947 and 1954, averaging more than twenty points a game. He became the professional game's first big star and gate attraction. In response to Mikan's scoring ability—between 1947 and 1951, he averaged over twenty-seven points per game—the NBA widened the foul lane from six to twelve feet and instituted the three-second violation. As a result of these rule changes, Mikan's scoring average dropped several points per game. Mikan was voted the "Game's Greatest Player" for the first half of the century, and he was elected to basketball's Hall of Fame in 1959.

As a result of Kurland and Mikan, big men became an important, and often dominant, part of basketball. Basketball—previously a game of shorter players passing, dribbling, and taking two-handed set shots—became a battle taking place above the rim. Taller players and those with superior leaping ability came to dominate the sport.

Primary Source

Coach [excerpt]

SYNOPSIS: Basketball in the 1940s saw the emergence of tall players as a dominant force in the game. Formerly a ball control, outside shooting contest, basketball became more of an inside-the-lane, above-the-rim game. George Mikan of DePaul University (and later the professional Minneapolis Lakers) is seen through the eyes of his legendary college coach, Ray Meyer, in this excerpt.

Mikan had enrolled at DePaul the September before my arrival, but had not played as a freshman. As he became a player, he made me a coach. It didn't come easily for either of us. After a few practices that spring, I dismissed the rest of the squad. George and I had a lot of work to do.

George was 6'8" and 215 pounds then and still growing. He grew to 6'10." That is not unusually large by today's standards, but he was a giant in his time. I knew the value of the big man in basketball. He gets more points by accident than a little guy on purpose.

Mikan was raw material with a little talent. His greatest asset was the desire to improve, which made him willing to listen and work. You can measure height and even talent, but not heart. Mikan showed me in the beginning he had the heart to be great. I realized he was going to come along real fast. It was going to take a lot of work, however. George needed help with his timing, coordination, quickness, and more.

For one thing, he didn't have a particularly good hook shot, which he needed if he was to play with his back to the basket as a pivot man must. To develop his righthanded hook, I would pass the ball in to him and have him shoot 100 times without dropping a towel held under his left arm. Then I'd have him shoot in the same manner with the left hand. George became an excellent shooter with the left, because he didn't have any bad habits to break with it, as he did with the right.

In an average training session, Mikan would take 200 to 300 shots with each hand. I was a slave driver, and he was a willing slave. I was young and full of energy and wanted him to be a great player.

Another thing that helped was "the Mikan Drill," which is probably still used by coaches. He would catch the ball with his left hand, turn around, and shoot with his right on the other side of the basket. As he landed on the floor, he caught the ball with his right hand as it came through the basket, raised it to his left hand, turned his body toward the basket, and put the ball in with his left hand. I'd make him do that 21 times with each hand.

Then I'd shoot the ball and make him jump up and bat it away from the rim to develop his timing. I would stand on the right side of the basket and pass the ball to the other side and make him tip it in from the left side with his left hand. Then I'd put him on the right side and make him tip it with his right. I would bounce the ball over the middle of the basket or off the backboard, and he would go up and tip it with either hand. If you can tip the ball with one hand, rather than two, you can reach about six inches higher.

I would also place a bench on the floor between Mikan and the basket to force him to jump over it as he moved to score. The higher you jump, the more time you get to shoot. The more time you get, the better you will shoot. . . .

I taught Mikan to protect his own shot by using the opposite arm as a stiff arm ahead of the shooting hand. That was an offensive foul, but he got away with it because he did it in such a way that it seemed a natural part of his shot. . . .

. . . To give George coordination and teach him to move his body with rhythm, I paid a coed to teach him to dance.

To help improve his hand and foot speed, I also made Mikan jump rope 10 minutes a day, using a speed rope with ball bearings at the grips. And I got the boxing coach to teach him to punch a light speed bag.

That took care of George's hands and feet, but his most dangerous weapons were his elbows. He once cracked the teeth of his own brother, Ed, in practice. He decked more than one opposing center with an elbow, and he had another elbow technique for aggressive opponents who were giving our guards a nasty time. He'd hold the ball in one hand away from the offending opponent. When the guy ran past him to reach it, George would stick out an elbow face high. Pow! . . .

George has trouble with his elbows today and says it is all my fault, because I taught him to use them to such effect.

While doing all of this, he somehow found time to get good grades in a prelaw curriculum, commute daily by bus from Joliet (an 80-mile round-trip), and tend bar in his family's restaurant in Joliet. Greatness didn't come to George by accident. He earned it. . . .

. . . Adolph Rupp, the "Baron of Basketball," brought his fine Kentucky team into the stadium a week after beating Notre Dame. . . . Kentucky had a pair of guards, . . . whose outside shots were an automatic two points from 25 feet or less, so I stationed Mikan under the basket to bat their shots away. He not only did that, but he would catch the ball and throw it back over their defense to set up baskets on the other end. We coasted to victory, 53-44. . . .

Two seasons later, such goaltending was outlawed. The era of the big man had arrived, and the rules had to be changed. . . .

Mikan improved from game to game, like a flower blooming. He was a great competitor. If we won by 30 points, he would be content with 5 or 6. In a close game, he would get 25 or 30. He would miss free throws early in a game but make them at the end with the game on the line. And I noticed a great change in Mikan's personality during that first season. Where he used to walk around the school halls with his shoulders slumped, as though he were ashamed of his height, he now seemed to be proud of his stature. He walked with shoulders back and head up. Where he had been quiet, now he was more outgoing. . . .

The Mikan Era ended March 9, 1946. . . .

In 1950, sportswriters and broadcasters voting in an Associated Press poll named George the greatest basketball player, college or pro, of the first half of this century. Nobody had ever dominated college basketball as Mikan did in his time. He had scored 1,870 points, and his rebounding was tremendous. On the defensive boards, he limited the other team to one shot. On offense, he would get us the second shot.

Primary Source

"Seven-Foot Trouble" [excerpt]

SYNOPSIS: Another player, seven-foot Bob Kurland of Oklahoma A&M University (and later the Amateur Athletic Union [AAU] and Olympic Games), was one of the first tall men to have a significant impact on basketball. In this excerpt he is seen through the eyes of an opposing coach.

In December, Oklahoma A. & M. came out at the West and, in full view of thousands of witnesses, began committing grand larceny on some of the most respectable basketball courts in the East. The second-story work was performed by Bob (Foothills) Kurland,

the Aggies' incredible seven-foot-one inch center, who climbs in the air like a cat burglar to snatch out opposing shots just as they are about to drop through the hoop. I am told Kurland took thirteen potential field goals from Westminster College in this fashion, to transform what might have been a decisive Westminster victory into a 41-39 overtime win for the Aggies. Against City College of New York he plucked out enough probables to insure the twelve point margin by which Oklahoma A. and M. ultimately triumphed. His deft aviation also beat Temple in Philadelphia.

Kurland's leaping larceny off the lip of the goal isn't new. The East, and every other section of the country, for that matter, has seen lots of it in recent years by other boys of monstrous height. Like many another conquest all over the country the last two seasons, these recent Aggie triumphs in the East were clear-cut cases of victory through goal tending, a practice which is entirely legal as the rules now stand, but one which, until recently, had never been extensively associated with basketball although Phog Allen. . . . Kansas, tells me that back in 1904 Herman Ber . . . a six-foot-seven-incher with the Sioux City, Iowa Y.M.C.A., was an accomplished goal shoplifter. There were so few of them in the old days that they were generally regarded as amusing and harmless fresh.

The Rise of the Goal Robber

The alarming thing is that in the last three years basketball coaches have begun searching out tall timber so industriously, and developing it so skillfully after they found it, that it is practically impossible beat a team whose giant raises his defensive umbrella over your goal, if that team has any assisting strengths at all. . . .

Even the coaches of these Gargantuan goalies generally don't like the practice, although, naturally, they will continue to take advantage of it until it is ruled against. "I know it smells," frankly admitted Hank Iba, the Oklahoma Aggie coach, at a weekly luncheon of the New York Metropolitan sports writers in December. "I hope Kurland is the cause of getting goal tending, and also the three-second rule, out of the game." Joe Lapchick, the cagey coach of St. John's' Harry Boykoff, once told me, "I'm for the big guy who can play basketball, but I'm against the big guy who only tends goal. Most big guys can score, but they are usually suckers on the defense if not allowed to tend goal. I used a goalie last year and I'll use one this year. But there should be positive legislation against it." . . .

George Mikan (99) of DePaul, and Bob Kurland (90) for Oklahoma A&M battle on the court at Chicago stadium, where Oklahoma A&M won 46-38.
© BETTMANN/CORBIS. REPRODUCED BY PERMISSION.

My friends will probably chuckle that this article was conceived out of my discouragement over having to try to stop Kurland, and they won't be far wrong. As a freshman, Big Bob took twenty-two of our shots out of the basket to beat us singlehanded at Stillwater last year, and we still have to face him for three more seasons, including this one.

However, I am consoled by the knowledge that I am not the only coach who is upset about goal tending. By last season it had become so widespread that the national rules committee received protests from coaches all over the nation, instead of just an occasional sectional yelp.

The Biggest Problem in Basketball

. . . Now the rules committee has decided to submit in its next annual questionnaire the proposal "to award a field goal when a defensive player touches a try-for-goal above the level of the basket after the ball has started its downward arc," which means it could go into the rule book by 1945. Meanwhile the proportion of excessively tall players is likely to increase, if anything, for the duration, since the military services generally turn down men of abnormal height.

The tall man has been a stormy issue in basketball for many years, but previously discussion centered around curbing him on the offense. After the 1937 season the rules committee largely eliminated the center jump, thus preventing a team with an altitudinous center from getting possession of the ball on the tip-off 65 to 70 per cent of the time. Following the 1939 season, it passed the three-second rule, making it illegal for a member of the offensive team to stand in the free-throw lane for more than three seconds, and thus preventing gigantic pivot men from taking as many swing shots at point-blank range as before. But to my mind, the defensive problem of goal tending is by far the greatest evil involving the tall player.

Any springy-legged youngster of even six feet four inches can jump up and intercept shots at the goal nowadays, and, moreover, is being carefully trained to do it. If the trend continues, it will ultimately become possible for two teams, each with a goal-tending specialist planted beneath the defensive hoop, to contend the full forty minutes without either side scoring a field goal. Basketball will turn into a low-scoring game like ice hockey, and I'll leave it to you how well the fans would like that. . . .

Basketball coaches have been demanding relief from the abnormally tall goal tender for five years without getting any favorable action from the national rules committee. However, back in 1939, the evil had reared its ugly head only in isolated spots and the committee had not yet had the opportunity of seeing for itself the goal tender at work. So the recommendation was shelved and the committee yawned.

But the matter instantly becomes very real to any coach who has to play a team employing a goal tender. Coaches don't like goal tenders, especially in the livery of an opponent, because they destroy the effects of good coaching. It is maddening to a coach on the bench to see his team set up a carefully rehearsed floor play—the pass, the screen, the feed to a man in the clear, and the shot from point-blank range—only to have a gigantic opposition player posted beneath the basket rise in the air like a pole vaulter to reach a foot above the rim and catch or deflect the ball before it can drop through. At such a time a coach feels as a golfer would if his opponent suddenly reached out his hand to intercept a perfect putt inches in front of the can.

A Ceiling for Big Boys

I believe either the proposed two-point penalty or Phog's twelve-foot goal would make for better basketball. Big men who are goal tenders and nothing else would have to learn some of the skills the average-sized player had to master before he could even step on the court. They would have to learn to guard man-for-man, gain defensive rebound positions, dribble well enough to come out from the backboard when they capture a rebound, play the post and handle the ball. Basketball thus would more nearly become a game for the majority and not for just a few.

I want to make it plain here that when I say big men I am not referring to the average big fellow who is already a reasonably competent guard, screener, dribbler, passer and shot, but who isn't tall enough to tend goal. Nor am I referring to the abnormally tall player who tends goal but is also enough of a basketball player to get by if goal tending were eliminated. The lad I'm talking about is the well-meaning but clumsy youngster who can do nothing but jump up and take an opponent's shot out of the ring. If the rules committee does follow its present plan of penalizing a goal tender for capturing a descending shot, I think the penalty will have to be a full two points. Should it be anything less, any team with a goal-tending center would be willing to deflect descending shots all night and take the penalty, rather than let field goals drop through. Nor do I believe that the rules committee should first suggest a period of experimentation, as is sometimes done with proposed new rules. What coach with a goal tender on his club is going to agree to abandon his specialty in a regularly scheduled game?

Further Resources

BOOKS

Bjarkman, Peter C. *Hoopla: A Century of College Basketball.* Indianapolis: Masters Press, 1996.

Hollander, Zander, ed. *The Modern Encyclopedia of Professional Basketball*, 2d ed., rev. New York: Doubleday, 1979.

Isaacs, Neil D. *All the Moves: A History of College Basketball.* Philadelphia: J.P. Lippincott Company, 1975.

Lake, John. "George Mikan." In Zander Hollander, ed. *Great American Athletes of the 20th Century.* New York: Random House, 1966.

McCallum, John D. *College Basketball, USA: Since 1892.* New York: Stein and Day, 1978.

PERIODICALS

Effrat, Louis. "Oklahoma Aggies Top DePaul, 52-44." *The New York Times*, March 30, 1945.

Frank, Stanley. "High Guy." *Colliers*, March 17, 1945, 32.

Army vs. Notre Dame

"Army and Irish Players Unhappy After Their Tie"

Newspaper article

By: Hugh Fullerton Jr. and Whitney Martin

Date: November 10, 1946

Source: Fullerton, Hugh, Jr., and Whitney Martin. "Army and Irish Players Unhappy After Their Tie." *Baltimore Sun,* November 10, 1946.

"Echoes From the Yankee Stadium"

Newspaper article

By: Arthur Daley

Date: November 10, 1946

Source: Daley, Arthur. "Echoes From the Yankee Stadium." *New York Times,* November 10, 1946.

About the Author: Arthur J. Daley (1904–1974) was born in New York City. A baseball player at Fordham University, Daley turned to writing and became sports editor of the college newspaper. After graduation, he joined *The New York Times* in 1926. Recognized early on as an outstanding sportswriter, Daley took over the "Sports of the *Times*" column in 1942 "until further notice." He wrote the column for nearly thirty years until his death. Covering all sports, including five Olympics, Daley was a well-prepared interviewer who predicted the rise of professional basketball and football as major spectator sports. He won the Pulitzer Prize in 1956—the first sportswriter to do so—and wrote five books and numerous magazine articles. ■

Introduction

In the 1940s, Army and Notre Dame had perhaps their greatest decade of football achievement. However, World War II impacted the programs in very different ways. For Army football, it was very advantageous—although there were questions about their recruiting and deferment practices. Under Earl "Red" Blaik, one of West Point's most successful coaches, the "Black Knights of the Hudson" marched to consecutive undefeated seasons in 1944 and 1945—outscoring opponents 504-35 and 412-46, respectively. Leading the national championship teams were running backs, Felix "Doc" Blanchard ("Mr. Inside") and Glenn ("Mr. Outside") Davis. Both were consensus All-Americans during their college careers. Blanchard won the Heisman Trophy in 1945, and Davis won it the next season.

In the immediate prewar years, Notre Dame Coach, Frank Leahy, returned the Fighting Irish to the glory days of Knute Rockne and the 1920s. However, the war years decimated the Notre Dame squad, as star players entered military service. Army crushed the Irish 59-0 in 1944 and

48-0 in 1945. With returning veterans and new recruits, Notre Dame had a score to settle with the Cadets. In 1946, Leahy also had two outstanding backfield players in Terry Brennan and Johnny Lujack.

The Army–Notre Dame game of November 9, 1946, was billed as one of the great epics in college football history. As sportswriter Grantland Rice wrote: "Two rocks of Gilbralter crashed on the turf of the Yankee Stadium this afternoon, and neither rock could budge the other." Over 74,000 spectators packed the stadium to its capacity. The crowd included generals Dwight D. Eisenhower and Omar Bradley, West Point graduates and heroes of World War II, as well as several members of President Harry S. Truman's cabinet. A reporter wrote that, "The stands were so jammed with Army and Navy brass that insignificant one or two star generals had to slink along back passageways." The processional march into the stadium by two thousand uniformed cadets, and the Fighting Irish marching band, belting out the Notre Dame fight song, added to the pageantry.

Early in the game, Army had advantage, but they were stopped inside Notre Dame territory by a tenacious Irish defense. In the second quarter, after stopping an Army drive, Notre Dame marched the length of the field to the Army four-yard line. There the Irish went for the touchdown, rather than a sure field goal, and were stopped by the stiffening Army defense. Despite impressive drives by each team, the game remained scoreless at halftime. In the third quarter, both teams failed to score, and each gave up the ball on a turnover. As the game rolled into the fourth quarter and shadows fell on Yankee Stadium, both teams made last ditch efforts to score. Late in the game, Doc Blanchard, carrying the ball for Army, broke into the clear, heading for an apparent touchdown. Johnny Lujack, defending for Notre Dame, raced across the field to make the game-saving tackle and preserve the scoreless tie. The game ended, and both teams were frustrated and dissatisfied with the result. In later years, some of the participants blamed the coaches for their cautious play-calling and offensive strategy. Arthur Daley, *The New York Times'* eminent sports columnist, aptly summed up game by concluding, "You might even call it: Much ado about nothing—to nothing."

Significance

For Army, the tie blemished an otherwise undefeated season, and it likely cost them a third consecutive national championship. Blanchard, Davis, and the other cadets graduated and fulfilled their military commitments. Blanchard never played professional football, becoming a career army officer. Davis played for several years with modest success in the National Football League. The Army program under Red Blaik would remain competitive into the 1950s, and produced Heisman

Arnold Tucker (17), Army star back, runs with the ball after the opening kickoff of the Army-Notre Dame game. November 9, 1946. © BETTMANN/ CORBIS. REPRODUCED BY PERMISSION.

winner, Pete Dawkins. But it would suffer a loss of prestige early in the 1950s, when a cheating scandal at West Point ravaged the football team. Blaik's son, the starting quarterback, was involved in the scandal.

Notre Dame, on the other hand, saw the tie with Army begin one of the great dynasties in college football history. They won the 1946, 1947, and 1949 national championships. Two players from that era, Johnny Lujack and Leon Hart, won the Heisman Trophy, and another, George Connor, would be elected to football's Hall of Fame. Terry Brennan, a running back in the 1946 game, later became the Fighting Irish head coach. Over the next half-century, Notre Dame became, arguably, the

most successful college football program in the nation, with several national championship teams, Heisman Trophy winners, many All-Americans, and a large and devoted fan base.

Primary Source

"Army and Irish Players Unhappy After Their Tie" [excerpt]

SYNOPSIS: Army and the University of Notre Dame, the two dominant college football programs of the 1940s, met on a cold afternoon, November 9, 1946, at Yankee Stadium in New York City. The epic

Army back Arnold Tucker (17), who had just intercepted a Notre Dame pass, is tackled by an unidentified Irish player during the 1946 game.
© BETTMANN/CORBIS. REPRODUCED BY PERMISSION.

struggle between the two college football power-houses, featured three future Heisman Trophy winners, Army's Felix "Doc" Blanchard and Glenn Davis, and Notre Dame's Johnny Lujack. The game, billed as "one for the ages," ended in a 0-0 tie.

There were no shouts of victory in the dressing rooms of Army and Notre Dame following their score-less tie at Yankee Stadium yesterday. Here are descriptions of the scenes that followed the struggle, in which neither of the two undefeated teams could beat the other:

Notre Dame

New York. November 9 (AP). The roar of 74,000 voices was heard faintly in the passageway under Yankee Stadium as a door opened and a "beaten" Notre Dame team filed into its dressing room.

It wasn't beaten, of course. The Irish had put up a whale of a battle to hold a fine Army team to a scoreless tie. But in every move, every attitude, the Irish looked like a dejected group of players.

They obviously had expected to win and were disappointed.

Later, after Coach Frank Leahy had kept the press and well-wishers waiting a half hour while he and his players took their showers and cooled off, Quarterback Johnny Lujack put it this way:

"I hope we didn't disappoint too many people. Here it was the football battle of the century, and we stunk it out."

Leahy More Conservative

Leahy, smiling and affable, was somewhat more conservative in his analysis.

"The boys are a little bit depressed," he said. "We really expected to win."

"I really was amazed at the display of fine defensive, football by both teams. I thought they both would score at least two or three touchdowns."

He put it mildly when he, said, "a little bit depressed." There was hardly a sound in the big locker room where the players were putting on their street clothes. Lujack and a few others answered questions in low tones, but there was none of the shouting and jubilance that goes with victory or even an unexpectedly good performance.

Hugh Fullerton, Jr.

Army

New York, Nov. 9 (AP) There was no elation, nor was there any dejection as Army's still unbeaten, but now tied, footballers trooped into their dressing room deep in the heart of Yankee Stadium after their bruising battle with Notre Dame.

Subdued might be the word. Their winning streak of 25 straight over a nearly three-year period had been snapped, and realization of this made them quiet and thoughtful as they hurriedly showered, donned heavy warmup suits and hurried to their bus.

Coach Earl (Red) Blaik, although still high on his Cadets, nevertheless showed his disappointment when someone suggested he should feel good about the game.

Battle Of Defenses Cited

"Why should I feel good?" he countered. Blaik termed the game a great battle of defenses, and said he maintains his opinion, to wit: that Army still is a great team.

Doc Blanchard and Glenn Davis, the famed touchdown twins, were pretty well bottled up by the stout Notre Dame defense, but Blaik said he was highly satisfied with their showing. The two Cadet stars were marked men all afternoon, with the comparatively unsung Arnold Tucker stealing much of the spotlight with his sparkling play.

Big Herman Hickman, Cadet line coach, obviously was proud of the way his pupils withstood the attack of the touted South Benders, and said that toward the finish the Cadet forwards were more than holding their own. It had been expected that Notre Dame might have an advantage up front due to superior replacements, but this did not hold true.

Whitney Martin

Primary Source

"Echoes from the Yankee Stadium" [excerpt]

SYNOPSIS: A famous sportswriter emphasizes the bittersweet quality of a tie.

No one scored any points. But nobody in the huge Yankee Stadium throng yesterday asked for his money back. The Army-Notre Dame game was a tense, exciting drama all the way. . . .

This bruising, rib-rattling struggle could have been waged until doomsday without ever determining a winner. That's how well matched the teams were with the final count—or lack of count—reflecting it perfectly.

The result almost brought back memories of a championship fencing match. Two contestants whack the daylights out of each other with blunt blades until the judge imperiously calls a halt. Then he discusses the play of blades with the jury at considerable length. Finally he takes a deep breath and, while an absolute silence settles over the gathering, intones: "Nothing done."

Further Resources

BOOKS

Beach, Jim, and Daniel Moore. *Army vs. Notre Dame: The Big Game, 1913–1947.* New York: Random House, 1948.

Blaik, Earl H., with Tim Cohane. *You Have to Pay the Price.* New York: Holt, Rinehart, and Winston, 1960.

Gildea, William, and Christopher Jennison. *The Fighting Irish.* Englewood Cliffs, N.J.: Prentice Hall, 1976.

PERIODICALS

Danzig, Allison. "Army, Notre Dame, Play to 0-0 Draw." *The New York Times,* November 10, 1946.

Rice, Grantland. "Defenses Control Play in Army-Irish Clash." *Baltimore Sun,* November 10, 1946.

"Jackie Robinson With Ben Chapman"

Photograph

Date: May 9, 1947

Source: "Jackie Robinson With Ben Chapman." May 9, 1947. Corbis. Image no. U834662ACME. Available online at http://pro.corbis.com (accessed April 16, 2003).

About the Athlete: Jackie Robinson (1919–1972) was born in Cairo, Georgia, grew up in Pasadena, California, and attended UCLA, lettering in baseball, basketball, football, and track. After serving in the army as a second lieutenant during

World War II and a season in the Negro Leagues, Robinson signed with the Brooklyn Dodgers. He played the 1946 season with Montreal, Brooklyn's top minor league team. In 1947, Robinson joined the Dodgers and played ten seasons with the team. After his playing career, Robinson remained active in business, politics, and a champion of civil rights causes until his death. ∎

Introduction

During World War II, African Americans had fought under the "Double V"—"victory over our enemies at home and our enemies on the battlefield abroad." Most sports in America, including baseball, remained for whites only at the end of the war. Barred from playing in the major and minor leagues, the only option for African Americans were the Negro Leagues. A major roadblock to entry for African Americans was baseball's commissioner, Judge Kenesaw Mountain Landis, who prevented their admission into professional baseball.

Branch Rickey, president and general manager of the Brooklyn Dodgers, believed that the time was right for lifting the ban on African Americans in the major leagues given Landis's death, in 1944, and the end of World War II, in 1945. Rickey undertook an extensive effort to find a suitable African American player to break the "color barrier" in baseball. Rickey sent his scouts out to search the Negro Leagues. In Jackie Robinson, Rickey found his man. Talented, well educated, exposed to integrated society, and possessing a spotless personal reputation, Robinson was just the man to shoulder the burden of being the first African American major leaguer. Rickey expected Robinson to take the abuse that would be heaped on him.

After leading the Montreal Royals, Brooklyn's top minor league club, to a championship and winning the league's batting title, Robinson joined the Dodgers in 1947. He was greeted by some teammates—especially those from the South—with a mixture of skepticism and barely concealed hostility. Robinson's excellent performance on the field in 1947 earned him National League Rookie of the Year honors. Robinson also won the respect and admiration of the other Dodger players (Rickey had traded most of the early malcontents), most notably the team captain, Harold "Pee Wee" Reese, star shortstop and Kentucky native.

Jackie Robinson faced many difficulties as he traveled to National League cities during his rookie season. Typical "bench jockeying" became racially motivated. Many ballplayers were from the South, where laws were in place prohibiting athletic competition between whites and African Americans. These players also feared social stigma from family and friends back home, if they played on the same field as an African American. Baseball executives, using threats of fan violence to hide personal

Primary Source

"Jackie Robinson With Ben Chapman"

SYNOPSIS: The ending of the color barrier in major league baseball occurred in 1946 when Branch Rickey, president and general manager of the Brooklyn Dodgers, signed Jackie Robinson, four-sport athlete at UCLA, army veteran, and Negro League player. After a year in Montreal, Brooklyn's top minor league team, Robinson joined the Dodgers in 1947, winning Rookie of the Year honors, and helping his team to the World Series. Here, Jackie Robinson poses with Ben Chapman, manager of the Philadelphia Phillies, before a game on May 9, 1947. Chapman, along with many other players and managers, was verbally abusive towards Robinson. Robinson played ten seasons with the Dodgers, retiring after the 1956 season. He was elected to baseball's Hall of Fame in 1962. © BETTMANN/CORBIS. REPRODUCED BY PERMISSION.

I Never Had It Made [excerpt]

Early in the season, the Philadelphia Phillies came to Ebbets Field for a three-game series. . . . Starting to the plate in the first inning, I could scarcely believe my ears. Almost as if it had been synchronized by some master conductor, hate poured forth from the Phillies dugout.

"Hey, nigger, why don't you go back to the cotton field where you belong?"

"They're waiting for you in the jungles, black boy!"

"Hey, snowflake, which one of those white boys' wives are you dating tonight?". . .

Those insults and taunts were only samples of the torrent of abuse which poured from the Phillies dugout that April day.

I have to admit that this day of all the unpleasant days in my life, brought me nearer to cracking up than I ever had been. Perhaps I should have become inured to this kind of garbage, but I was in New York City and unprepared to face the kind of barbarism from a northern team that I had to associate with in the Deep South. . . . I felt tortured and I tried to just play ball and ignore the insults. But it was really getting to me. . . .

For one wild and rage-crazed minute I thought, ". . . I have made every effort to work hard, to get myself into shape. My best is not enough for them." I thought what a glorious, cleansing thing it would be to let go. . . .

I had started the season as a lonely man, often feeling like a black Don Quixote tilting at a lot of white windmills. I ended it feeling like a member of a solid team. The Dodgers were a championship team because all of us had learned something. I had learned how to exercise self-control—to answer insults, violence, and injustice with silence—and I had learned how to earn the respect of my teammates. They had learned that it's not skin color but talent and ability that counts. Maybe even the bigots had learned that too.

SOURCE: Robinson, Jackie, with Alfred Duckett. *I Never Had It Made.* New York: G.P. Putnam's Sons, 1972, 70, 71, 81.

prejudice, pressured Rickey not to "bring the nigger" to their ballparks. This was the case with the Philadelphia Phillies general manager, Herb Pennock, and manager, Ben Chapman. Chapman, a Tennessee native, determined to make Robinson's life as miserable as possible if he dared to play in Philadelphia.

Significance

The abuse Robinson took from opposing players and managers united the Dodger team. Robinson's teammates knew that he was under strict orders from Rickey not to strike back or retaliate in any fashion. Eventually, after fulfilling his three-year pledge of silence, Robinson began speaking out and playing aggressively, more in keeping with his natural tendencies. Over the years, Robinson got into scrapes and verbal exchanges with umpires, as well as opposing players and managers.

In his ten-year career, Robinson became the acknowledged leader of the Dodgers. He led the team to six National League pennants, and a World Series title in 1955. He had a career .311 batting average, 137 home runs, and 197 stolen bases, including nineteen steals of home plate. Robinson won the 1949 Most Valuable Player award, as he led the league with a .342 average. As a gate attraction, Robinson was, perhaps, the most popular baseball player since Babe Ruth. He attracted many fans at ballparks around the country, especially African Americans.

The success Jackie Robinson attained in his 1947 rookie season with Brooklyn made it somewhat easier for other African American baseball players to join the major leagues, even if racial harmony was far from complete. Later in 1947, Cleveland Indians owner Bill Veeck signed Larry Doby, the American League's first African American player, and other major league clubs gradually followed suit. Robinson eventually would have fellow African Americans as teammates, including catcher Roy Campanella, and pitchers Joe Black and Don Newcombe. Within a few years, baseball, and especially the National League, would see outstanding African American players such as Willie Mays, Hank Aaron, and Frank Robinson, who, in 1975, became baseball's first African American manager. Each of these stars gave due credit to Jackie Robinson for blazing the trail for them to follow.

Jackie Robinson occupies a unique place in the history of American sport and society. A sportscaster once noted that while Robinson may not have been the best baseball player ever to put on a uniform, he may have been the most important.

Further Resources

BOOKS

Allen, Maury. *Jackie Robinson: A Life Remembered.* New York: Franklin Watts, 1987.

Falkner, David. *Great Time Coming: The Life of Jackie Robinson, from Baseball to Birmingham.* New York: Simon & Schuster, 1995.

Rampersad, Arnold. *Jackie Robinson: A Biography.* New York: Alfred A. Knopf, 1997.

Robinson, Rachel. *Jackie Robinson: An Intimate Portrait.* New York: Abrams, 1996.

Tygiel, Jules. *Baseball's Great Experiment: Jackie Robinson and His Legacy.* New York: Oxford University Press, 1983.

PERIODICALS

Anderson, Dave. "Jackie Robinson Dies." *The New York Times,* October 25, 1972.

WEBSITES

"By Popular Demand: Jackie Robinson and Other Baseball Highlights, 1860s–1960s." The Library of Congress. Available at http://memory.loc.gov/ammem/jrhtml/jrhome.html; website home page: http://memory.loc.gov (accessed March 1, 2003).

"Jackie Robinson." The National Baseball Hall of Fame and Museum. Available online at http://www.baseballhallof-fame.org/hofers_and_honorees/hofer_bios/robinson_jackie.htm (accessed March 1, 2003).

AUDIO AND VISUAL MEDIA

"Sixth Inning: The National Pastime, 1940–1950." Episode six of *Baseball: A Film by Ken Burns.* PBS Home Video, 1994, VHS.

"Babe Didrikson Takes Off Her Mask"

Magazine article

By: Pete Martin

Date: September 20, 1947

Source: Martin, Pete. "Babe Didrikson Takes Off Her Mask." *Saturday Evening Post* 220, September 20, 1947, 27. ∎

Introduction

Prior to the 1930s, little attention was paid to women's athletics in the United States. Olympic competition was open to women, but female athletes in most sports either labored in obscurity, or were criticized for their lack of femininity. Babe Didrikson's emergence onto the national sports stage in the 1930s was the result of both her incredible natural athletic skills and her talent for self-promotion.

Mildred Didrikson was born in 1911 in Port Arthur, Texas. Nicknamed "Babe" after Babe Ruth because of her childhood athletic prowess, she possessed an unlimited ambition to compete in sports. As Didrikson said in her autobiography, "Before I was in my teens, I knew exactly what I wanted to be when I grew up. My goal was to be the greatest athlete who ever lived." In the 1932 Summer Olympics in Los Angeles, Didrikson won gold medals in the javelin and 80-meter high hurdles.

Although Didrikson's Olympic performance was widely reported and praised, she had few money-making options. Since she needed to compete professionally for financial reasons, the Amateur Athletic Union (AAU) de-clared her ineligible for amateur track and field competition. Recognizing both the need to capitalize on her fame and to make money, Didrikson performed on stage in vaudeville, pitched and hit against major league baseball teams (on one occasion even striking out Joe DiMaggio), toured with the House of David baseball team, and barnstormed the country with her own traveling basketball squad. Babe took up tennis, and her coach, who had mentored women's champion, Alice Marble, said that Didrikson immediately could become a top court player. However, the AAU's ban on Didrikson effectively barred her from tennis competition, as only amateurs were eligible to participate in the sport's prestigious tournaments.

It was at golf that Babe Didrikson would achieve her lasting fame in American sports. Stories vary about how and when she began playing golf, although Didrikson, from the early 1930s, would go out on the links with various people, especially male sportswriter friends Grantland Rice and Paul Gallico. Encouraged by them and her former employer, Colonel M.J. McCombs of the Employers Casualty Company of Dallas, Didrikson took up golf full time. After winning two amateur tournaments in Texas, she was again declared professional. Didrikson signed a contract with a sporting goods firm and went on an exhibition tour. She competed against mostly male golfers, with great success.

In 1938, Babe married professional wrestler and promoter, George Zaharias. In 1943, after a three-year layoff from golf, Didrikson regained her amateur status. Her presence was immediately felt. From 1943 to 1947, Didrikson competed as an amateur and won forty tournaments, including fourteen consecutive in one stretch. In 1947, Didrikson, along with another star golfer, Patty Berg, cofounded the Ladies Professional Golfing Association (LPGA). As a professional, Didrikson's superior athletic skills and her flamboyance and showmanship won a large following for the women's tour, often outdrawing male players. As a professional, Didrikson won forty-two tournaments, and she was named female athlete of the year six times. In 1953, Babe was diagnosed with colon cancer, but she returned to the tour within three months. In 1954, she won the U.S. Women's Open by a record twelve strokes. Didrikson won two more tournaments in 1955, before the cancer recurred. She died in September 1956.

Significance

Babe Didrikson was, perhaps, the greatest female athlete in American history. Although talented in many sports, it was in track and field and golf that she achieved lasting fame. Didrikson's achievements were such that her obituary was on page one of *The New York Times.* Her many achievements were recognized in 1950, when the Associated Press named Didrikson the greatest woman athlete in the first half of the twentieth century. Didrikson won, in all her years of competition in various sports, 364 events and earned approximately one million dollars in prize money.

A great athlete who understood her marketing value, Babe Didrikson was not a feminist by later twentieth-century standards. Women athletes routinely had their femininity called into question. So Didrikson willingly conformed to society's standards of femininity, in dress, deportment, and desire for domesticity. Her marriage to Zaharias was publicly portrayed as harmonious, but the two were estranged in later years. Babe Didrikson was a great athlete who was a role model for women. But she was not an activist in the manner of Billie Jean King, who revolutionized both her own sport and women's athletics generally.

Primary Source

"Babe Didrikson Takes Off Her Mask" [excerpt]

SYNOPSIS: In the first half of the twentieth century, one female athlete towered above the rest. Mildred "Babe" Didrikson won two gold medals in track and field at the 1932 Olympics. In this article, author Pete Martin recounts his interview with Didrikson, and comments on her career accomplishments, her physical attributes, and her public persona.

The Mildred Didrikson Zaharias who came home this past summer, with the British Ladies' Amateur Champion golf crown, was a different person. The crown had mellowed the Babe. As an amateur, her first thought was no longer to put on a show for the customers. Her tournament manners were impeccable. She reserved her wisecracks, exuberance and trick-shot making until she had a match safely tucked away, which usually happened at the thirteenth or fourteenth hole.

Symptomatic of her new phase was the fact that she was making a mild effort to rid herself of her nickname. She realized that any attempt to persuade the public to call her anything but "the Babe" which they had called her familiarly for so many years was a hopeless undertaking. But when she hinted to me, "My friends call me Mildred," she put a significant emphasis on the word "friends." She is no longer given to unseemly braggadocio, but married life hasn't made her a shrinking violet . . . she suggested that I title this article "Marvelous Mildred."

She met George Zaharias, a wrestler, in 1938 at a Los Angeles golf tournament. As a publicity stunt, during the medal play she was teamed with George and a golf-playing minister from Occidental College.

Babe Didrikson follows through on a shot at the 1947 British Women's Open tournament. **AP/WIDE WORLD PHOTOS. REPRODUCED BY PERMISSION.**

Photographs were taken of the Babe perched on George's shoulder. Other photos were shot of him showing her how to use what she calls the "neck holt." She sees no reason for being coy about how much George means to her. "You can't tell a husband how much you love him after he's dead. It was his smile that got me," she told me. "While I was giving him the neck holt, he looked up and smiled at me and said, 'How about us going out. . . . ?'

"Everything I do, I do for George. He's the only thing I've got on my mind. I'd give up golf if he couldn't be with me. The first time we had been apart for more than three days was when I was in Scotland."

Babe is no longer button-breasted. The bust measurement of this ex-Texas girl, "born halfway between masculine flats and angles and the rubbery curves of femininity"—which was the way a sports writer described her in the 1930's—is now a Valkyrian forty inches. The bust measurement of Jane Russell, Hollywood's leading sweater-filler, is only thirty-eight and one half inches. Mildred Zaharias' waist is twenty-seven inches; her hips thirty-seven. She weighs 140. There is little resemblance to the so-called "muscle moll" of yesteryear. Her arms are no more muscular than those of any normally healthy woman, although her legs are still impressive columns of flesh and sinew.

Nor is her manner of dress as Spartan as it once was. Perfume, lipstick and fingernail polish lie on her dressing table. Style and class hang in her closets. "I go in more for fashion now," she admitted. "I don't stop at forty-five dollars for dresses any longer. I'll go up to two or three hundred for them if I have to." Such frills and fripperies are a far cry from the cotton union suits she once wore, and the make-up she defiantly *didn't* wear.

In the fifteen years between her emergence from Texas and her return from England, a sizable and peculiar body of legend has grown up around her. For the most part, such flights of fancy are due to inspired prose of overimaginative sports writers, although, in justice to the tribe, it must be admitted that, just doing what comes naturally to her, she has an irresistible legend-generating quality, and she has been known to give such legends a leg-up to help a friendly writer "get a good story." She belongs in a class with Amelia Bloomer, Annie Oakley, Carrie Nation, Belle Boyd, the Confederate spy, and Nellie Bly, and, like them, she has become a part of our national folklore.

It has been written that she wrestled, boxed and played football. She has never wrestled. Strictly speaking, she has never boxed or played football. When she put on the gloves to pose for a publicity picture with heavyweight contender Young Stribling, the chance for fact-embroidery was too much for one sports writer, who tapped out a story that the Babe had landed a haymaker on Stribling's nose, thereby fetching forth a cascade of gore.

The only time she donned a football suit was for a Grantland Rice movie sports short. She grinned when she told me, "The boys on the other team fell over themselves getting out of my way so I'd look good."

Those who have chronicled her career thus loosely have even gone in for fantasy about her personal life. A writer in a picture magazine recently offered what purported to be a nugget of Zaharias low-down. "Her middle name really is Babe," he wrote, meaning that she was christened "Mildred Babe Didrikson." She described the way she came to be known as "Babe" to me as follows: Her brothers and sisters called her "baby" when she was small. After a while her mother told the rest of the family, "Mildred's getting to be a big girl now; it's about time you all were calling her something else," so the family shortened "baby" to "Babe." When she grew older, her home-run slugging made people think of Babe Ruth. After that, "Babe" stuck.

Further Resources

BOOKS
Cayleff, Susan E. *Babe: The Life and Legend of Babe Didrikson Zaharias.* Urbana, Ill.: University of Illinois Press, 1995.

Johnson, William Oscar, and Nancy P. Williamson. *"Whatta-Gal:" The Babe Didrikson Story.* Boston: Little, Brown, 1977.

Zaharias, Babe Didrikson, as told to Harry Paxton. *This Life I've Led: An Autobiography.* New York: A.S. Barnes, 1955.

PERIODICALS
"Babe Zaharias Dies; Athlete Had Cancer." *The New York Times,* September 28, 1956, A1.

Hicks, Betty. "Foremothers: Babe Didrikson Zaharias." *Women Sports,* November–December 1975.

Sports and Television

"Fifty Mile Bleachers"
Magazine article

By: Edward P. Morgan

Date: September 27, 1947

Source: Morgan, Edward P. "Fifty Mile Bleachers: Television is Becoming Big Business at the Corner Bar and Grill." *Colliers* 120, September 27, 1947.

"Inside Sports: Things to Come"
Magazine article

By: Bill Fay

Date: February 19, 1949

Source: Fay, Bill. "Inside Sports: Things to Come." *Colliers* 123, February 19, 1949. ∎

Introduction

In the late afternoon of May 17, 1939, an event took place in New York City that would change the world of sport forever. With the flip of a switch at the RCA Building, a visual image appeared on a little silver screen. W2XBS broadcasted a Columbia-Princeton baseball game, marking the first sporting event shown on the new visual medium. Veteran radio announcer, Bill Stern, donned a toupee for the occasion. In 1939, during the months that followed, W2XBS broadcast several more sporting firsts: June 1, the first televised boxing match, between Max Baer and Lou Nova; August 9, the first tennis match; August 26, the first major league baseball game, between the Brooklyn Dodgers and Cincinnati Reds (with the legendary Walter "Red" Barber at the microphone); and October 22, the first professional football telecast, between the Brooklyn Dodgers and Philadelphia Eagles.

Soon television expanded its sports coverage, with basketball and horse racing competitions shown for the first time on the screen. World War II slowed the advance of television, but, after 1945, television again began covering athletics. This programming included two sports created especially for the small screen, professional wrestling and roller derby. "Pro" wrestling combined legitimate techniques with large doses of acting and slapstick, and it featured competitors with names like "Gorgeous George" and the "Masked Marvel." These overweight men threw each other into the ropes of boxing rings, body slammed and pummeled one another, and "hit" each other with metal chairs and other objects. There were female wrestlers, as well, who pulled each other's long hair and kicked and punched one another. Roller Derby was a sport consisting of men and women on "teams" such as the "Los Angeles Thunderbirds," skating around a banked track with padded railing, essential as the sport featured staged, violent collisions. Roller derby and pro wrestling helped popularize television and were a driving force in television's early years. These matches, complete with ringside or trackside announcers, frequently were broadcast on Friday evenings and weekends.

Television's impact on American sports would not be complete until after World War II. Sponsors recognized the opportunity afforded by television, and they were eager to jump on the bandwagon. The 1947 World Series, between the New York Yankees and the Brooklyn Dodgers, was broadcast on television for the first time by the NBC network, after the Gillette Razor Company and Ford Motor Company agreed to put up $65,000 for rights to advertise during the telecast.

Significance

The early years of television sports brought more questions than answers. For owners of professional sports franchises, sports promoters, athletic directors, and officials at all levels of sport, came the big question: How would televising sporting events impact attendance? Would people watch a weekday afternoon World Series game, a Saturday afternoon college football game, a Sunday afternoon pro football game, or a Friday night boxing match at the event itself, or would they go to the corner tavern with a television or to the neighbor's up the street, the first on the block to have the small screen?

Eventually every household in the United States had a television set, and the corner bar or lucky neighbor no longer had a monopoly on TV. With more televisions in circulation, and, as a means to preserve attendance at ballgames, baseball and football owners instituted "blackout rules," where home games would not be shown on local television. Televised football emerged after the broadcast of the 1958 National Football League (NFL) championship game between the Baltimore Colts and New York Giants, the first title game to go into overtime. The 1960s brought huge television contracts for the NFL, and its rival, the American Football League, which merged into the NFL in 1970. Football, as it turned out, was made for TV. Baseball would have network television contracts as well, but for various reasons, would have trouble keeping up with football in retaining the viewing public. Television enhanced the appeal of basketball, auto racing, golf, tennis, and the Olympic games. By the 1970s, it seemed that sports had never existed without television.

Primary Source

"Fifty Mile Bleachers: Television is Becoming Big Business at the Corner Bar and Grill" [excerpt]

SYNOPSIS: The presentation of sports in America changed forever in May 1939, when station W2XBS, transmitted to a few thousand homes in the New York City area, carried the first telecast of a sporting event. The telecast featured a Columbia-Princeton college baseball game. Within the next year, W2XBS had broadcast the first telecasts in major league baseball, boxing, tennis, and collegiate and professional football. Television's appearance in 1939 set the stage for the boom in sports broadcasting, beginning in the late 1940s after World War II.

"Sports will be to television what music was to radio," is the prediction of General John Reed Kilpatrick, president of Madison Square Garden. He looks forward with pardonable fervor to the day when Joe Louis and his successors, if any, will defend the heavyweight title before a "ringside" crowd of millions.

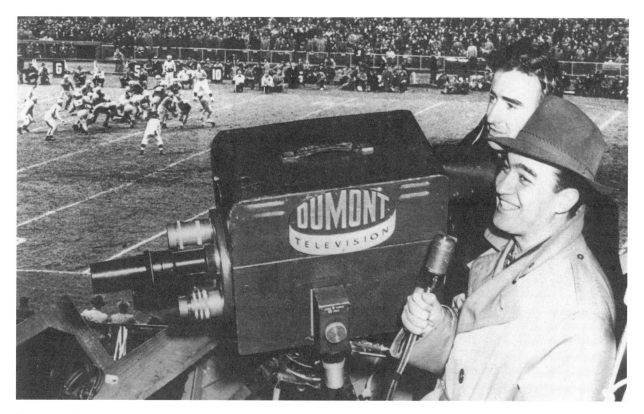

Sportscaster Mel Allen gives the play-by-play action for the Notre Dame–North Carolina football game on the DuMont Television Network. AP/WIDE WORLD PHOTOS. REPRODUCED BY PERMISSION.

They will view the bout on giant screens in special theaters all over the country, after such details as box-office percentages have been worked out with the promoters.

But what, in that event, will television do to sports? The question has ignited a major furor which most fans, busy with their beer and barside seats, have thus far overlooked.

Baseball Commissioner "Happy" Chandler's attitude has been to "wait and see" what television may mean to baseball. At least one broadcaster has approached him on the possibility of televising the coming World Series if one New York club is a contender, but, at this writing, no commitments had been made to anybody. If the classic develops into a subway siege between the Yanks and Brooklyn, all three New York television stations will press hard to get in on it.

The key to Chandler's consent in that event would be held, interestingly enough, by the Mutual Broadcasting System, which won't have a television outlet until sometime in 1948. Mutual and the Gillette Safety Razor Company have the radio-broadcasting rights to the Series through 1951, and Mutual has first refusal of television rights. Mutual officials have

said in private they would definitely not object to the '47 Series being televised; if they were asked they would probably recommend the assignment go, in New York, not to CBS or NBC but to WABD, operated by the Allen B. Du Mont Laboratories, Incorporated, which makes television equipment.

New Source of Revenue

Baseball magnates are both intrigued and puzzled by the potentialities of television. They smell fresh revenue. A good major-league ball club now realizes upward of $50,000 a season from radio and as television takes hold it will be another source of income although some of it will undoubtedly be at the expense of the radio account. "We probably can't expect to carry water on both shoulders," one National League official said. But what about gate receipts? It has been conjectured that fans prefer to watch a major-league game on television rather than a minor-league team on its home grounds and that this, in part, explains the box-office slump of the Newark Bears this season.

This might conceivable be classified as an invasion of a baseball club's "territorial rights" which are protected now in radio broadcasting by a complicated code. Under the rules, a Boston station, for instance, could not air a New York game without permission of the local Boston teams. There is no such code for television yet. President Ford Frick of the National League is chariman of a four-man committee studying the problem in that circuit and due to come up with recommendations in December. The American League is doing similar research through the major leagues' executive council.

Screwily enough, television may eventually cause the disappearance of billboards from ball parks. Last fall when the Ford Motor Company bought the CBS telecast of the Dodgers pro football games from Brooklyn, the agency handling the account ordered the scoreboard kept off the screen—because it carried an ad for a watch competing with a timepiece made by another of the agency's clients. Herbert Bayard Swope, Jr., red-haired young director of CBS sports telecasts, got that one overruled. In this case it was the agency, not the sponsor, which betrayed the hypersensitivity, but wherever possible the television cameras now avoid backgrounds extolling goods rivaling the sponsor's products.

What might be called the "Gee whiz" and "Wish you were here, friends," schools of sports announcing—and writing—are bound to be toned down too, in future, because television fans will indeed be there in all but the flesh, to see for themselves.

Although television may affect the gate at an individual event, many experts think it will stimulate sports attendance in the long haul, just as radio has done. Some pugilists and promoters, whose livelihood is ordinarily geared to gate percentages, have been peeved over exclusion from the television kitty. Some fighters are said to object to changing the color of their trunks so they can be more readily identified. (Black and purple, standard shades for boxers, are indistinguishable over television.)

General Kilpatrick, whose Garden encourages the televising of every event possible from the circus to a dog show, reacts to these minority protests something like this: Television revenue permits payment of higher percentages than fighters would otherwise get, and if they're any good on the screen they'll eventually attract a following to the money seats anyway.

To pessimists, Harry Markson, Promoter Mike Jacobs' press agent, likes to tell the following stock but avowedly veracious story: "Friend of mine in Flatbush, a real-estate dealer, used to kid the pants off me, saying fights were no good, that he'd never seen one in his life and never would. Then his old man

bought a television set and this guy sees his first bout. Since then, he's been to the Garden five times this summer."

Primary Source

"Inside Sports: Things to Come" [excerpt]

SYNOPSIS: In this excerpt from 1949, Bill Fay predicts the future impact of television on sports. How good a prophet was he?

During the next 10 years, television will boom all sports, but you may have a hard time recognizing your favorite sport on the video screens of 1959. Here's what's ahead:

Golf

Tournament committees ban view-obstructing galleries. Mobile television cameras report matches stroke by stroke. Prize money, swollen by television advertising receipts, skyrockets from $10,000 to $100,000 per tournament.

Baseball

Minor leagues, the financial victims of network big-league television, collapse and disappear. Major leagues expand to San Francisco and Los Angeles. Owners schedule all week games at night to accommodate maximum video audiences; raze unoccupied grandstands to enlarge parks and thus make home-run distances uniform. Players develop in sand lots and colleges, then jump to majors (as pro football headliners did in 1949).

Horse Racing

Bookies operate via television sets. Betting totals soar. The government legalizes handbooks and levies a 10 per cent tax on winning tickets. National budget finally balances.

Football

Colleges solve campus housing shortage by converting the empty stadiums into dormitories. Video audiences of 50,000,000 watch big games. The telescopic lens of the television camera gives every fan a 50-yard-line seat. New York, Chicago and other large population centers build weather-beating indoor fields designed for telecasts.

Basketball

Takes over officially as world's number one spectator sport—with enthusiastic support in South America, Europe and Far East.

Boxing

Big fights move from ball parks into television studios.

Minor Sports

Water polo, table tennis, squash, bowling, handball and other telegenic sports (previously overlooked because of limited spectator facilities) surpass wrestling, the original television wonder, in the audience polls.

Further Resources

BOOKS

Johnson, William O., Jr. *Super Spectator and the Electric Lilliputians.* Boston: Little, Brown, 1971.

Patton, Phil. *Razzle-Dazzle: The Curious Marriage of Television and Professional Football.* Garden City, N.Y.: Dial Press, 1984.

Powers, Ron. *Supertube: The Rise of Television Sports.* New York: Coward-McCann, 1984.

Rader, Benjamin G. *In Its Own Image: How Television Has Transformed Sports.* New York: Free Press, 1984.

Smith, Curt. *Voices of the Game.* New York: Simon & Schuster, 1992.

Fort Wayne Daisies: 1947 Yearbook

Program

By: Fort Wayne Daisies

Date: 1947

Source: *Fort Wayne Daisies: 1947 Yearbook.* Fort Wayne, Ind.: Sherman, White, 1947. Excerpts reprinted in Johnson-Noga, Aleene. "All-American Girls' Baseball League—Its History in Brief—1943 to 1946." *All-American Girls Professional Baseball League 1943–1954.* Available online at http://www.aagpbl.org/articles/arti_bh.html; website home page: http://www.aagpbl.org (accessed April 20, 2003).

About the Organization: The All-American Girls Professional Baseball League (AAGPBL) sponsored women's baseball from 1943 to 1954. Some of the best records of the league are found in the yearbooks of the individual teams. After its demise, the league was repeatedly honored for its contribution to American sports and women's athletics. In 1992, interest in the league was renewed when Penny Marshall directed a popular film based on the AAGPBL, *A League of Their Own,* starring Tom Hanks, Geena Davis, and Madonna. ∎

Introduction

World War II (1939–1945) brought many challenges besides that of military strategy. On the civilian home front, those who worked to support the troops and war-

time economy needed more than news updates about the fighting overseas: they needed escape. Entertainment was harder to find because many actors, musicians, and athletes were taking part in the war. The sport of baseball took a lesson from the world of manufacturing. When men left factory jobs to serve in the armed forces, women took their places. The AAGPBL applied the same idea to the sport of baseball. However, what began as stopgap wartime entertainment outlived the 1940s to provide a professional showcase for female athletes.

Chicago Cubs owner and chewing-gum magnate Philip K. Wrigley founded the league in 1943, recruiting women from the United States, Canada, and Cuba. In the league's twelve-year history, approximately 545 women played for its teams. Although the league began by using large, nearly softball-sized balls for underhand pitches, the game soon evolved to resemble conventional baseball with small, hard balls and overhand pitches. At first, some expressed concern that U.S. interest in baseball would wither when many of the men from major league baseball were called for military service. The AAGPBL, however, held to such a high level of competition that at the league's peak it drew more than a million fans to the ballparks. In fact, after World War II the league competed successfully with men's major league baseball for several years. Only after men's games became televised did interest in the AAGPBL—and efforts to promote its games—begin to wane. The league dissolved in 1954.

Significance

The AAGPBL provided much-needed escapist entertainment for a nation at war. Men, women, and children alike attended league games and followed favorite teams. Fears that World War II would be the death of sports, baseball, in particular, eroded as the AAGPBL actually renewed enthusiasm for America's pastime. The postwar success of men's major league baseball owed no small debt to the professionalism of the AAGPBL. But the AAGPBL had a second important impact. Even as it proved that women could be athletes and compete in supposedly male sports, the league also reinforced certain gender stereotypes. Teams had names such as "Chicks," "Daisies," and "Peaches"—not exactly words that put fear into competitors' hearts. League founder Philip K. Wrigley and later owner Arthur Meyerhoff insisted that the players exemplify the traditional image of "the highest ideals of womanhood"; team members therefore were required to wear lipstick and attend charm school classes. Wearing trousers even off the field was forbidden. Some of these requirements, such as wearing short skirts that interfered with sliding into bases, actually impeded the women's opportunities as athletes. While the AAGPBL was a breakthrough for women in America, it could not solve all issues of inequality at once.

Most importantly, the AAGPBL paved the way for later women's sports in the United States. Remarkable talents such as first baseman Dorothy Kamenshek, second baseman Sophie Kurys, and pitcher Jean Faut served as role models for future women athletes. Once the public had seen that women could play ball—and advertisers had seen that women's sports could sell—the development of permanent amateur and professional women's athletic programs from basketball to volleyball and beyond was just a matter of time.

Primary Source

Fort Wayne Daisies: 1947 Yearbook [excerpt]

SYNOPSIS: Team yearbooks such as this one were sold at games and gave the history of the league and team, introduced the players, and recorded the statistics of past seasons.

Already a buxom baby when it started its fourth year in 1946, girls' professional baseball has really grown up as a result of the season just completed and seems destined to stay and to continue its healthy growth as a solid sports attraction for the baseball public. Having been started in 1943 with four teams in mid-western communities, the All-American Girls' Baseball League came of age in 1946 with development of the wheel into eight full-fledged, community owned and operated, non-profit clubs in the cities of Racine and Kenosha, Wisconsin; Rockford and Peoria, Illinois; South Bend and Fort Wayne, Indiana; Grand Rapids and Muskegon, Michigan. . . .

The league opened its regular schedule of 112 games on May 22. South Bend won the Opening Day Attendance Trophy which was won by Racine in 1945, the first year of such competition, the Indiana City attracting upwards of 5,300 fans to its inaugural. Over 5,000 fans also saw the Grand Rapids Chicks open the season in their home city and crowds of 5,000 and upwards were common throughout the season, especially in these two cities.

The teams play a full season of baseball, with single games scheduled every night of the week and doubleheaders on Sundays and holidays. Only in Racine has any daytime ball been played and that team scheduled a limited number of Sunday doubleheaders in the afternoon. The special and exclusive All-American Girls' Baseball League ball, eleven inches in diameter, was used throughout the season. The bases were moved to a distance of 70 feet apart and the pitching distance from the mound to the plate was set at 43 feet. The league permits

Dorothy "Dottie" Schroeder, pitcher for the Fort Wayne Daisies. SCHROEDER, DOROTHY "DOTTIE," PHOTOGRAPH.

runners to lead off bases and steal at any time and rigidly enforces a half-balk rule, making the game wide open and replete with action and thrills.

For the first time in 1946, league pitching rules were relaxed sufficiently to allow for a limited sidearm pitch from an underhand delivery with certain restrictions and the season saw the rapid development of many pitchers as the adoption of the new style of pitching became general. A better and smaller ball, however, reacted to the benefit of the hitters and batting averages generally were on the up-trend.

To add to the general interest, there was a season long dog fight for top league honors, with Grand Rapids showing the way in the early weeks due to a record breaking start when the team won its first 13 games. In the late weeks, it was a battle between the Chicks, the Racine Belles and the South Bend Blue Sox for the pennant, with the Racine team finally clinching the flag on the second to the last day of the season for its second league championship in four years. The Belles were followed in the final standings by Grand Rapids, South Bend and the 1945 champion Rockford club in that order and these four teams qualified for the Shaughnessy play-off series which proves the climax of the All-American season. . . .

The players devote themselves one hundred per cent to playing ball during the season, without other occupation. They live in the cities of their home town team, usually in pairs or threesomes in private homes in the community and they become a part of the social and civic life of that community in which they play. Road trips involve two annual visits to each of the other cities in the circuit, each for a four-game series, at which time the visiting players stay at the best hotels in those communities. All travel expenses, including meal money for individual players on the road, are paid by the team, whereas living expenses in the home town city, usually quite nominal, are the individual responsibility of the player.

The game has had a great influence for the good in communities where it has operated so successfully for the past several years. Girls professional baseball has become an outstanding family attraction with men, women, boys and girls forming about an equal cross section of the average game attendance. In several of the communities, it has been the most successful sports venture to attract the general interest in many years and it has out-drawn any other sports venture in the history of some of these cities. The revenue from the operation in several of the league cities has already been turned to excellent purpose in helping promote and sustain other worthy youth recreation activities.

Further Resources

BOOKS

Berlage, Gai. *Women in Baseball: The Forgotten History.* Westport, Conn.: Praeger, 1994.

Gregorich, Barbara. *She's on First.* New York: Contemporary Books, 1987.

Macy, Sue. *A Whole New Ball Game: The Story of the All-American Girls Professional Baseball League.* New York: Holt, 1993. Reprinted New York: Puffin, 1995.

Madden, W.C. *The Women of the All-American Girls Professional Baseball League: A Biographical Dictionary.* Jefferson, N.C.: McFarland, 1997.

———. *The All-American Girls Professional Baseball League Record Book: Comprehensive Hitting, Fielding, and Pitching Statistics.* Jefferson, N.C.: McFarland, 2000.

Rader, Benjamin G. *Baseball: A History of America's Game.* Urbana, Ill.: University of Illinois Press, 1992.

Seymour, Harold. *Baseball.* Oxford, England: Oxford University Press, 1960.

Citation Wins the Belmont

Photograph

Date: June 12, 1948

Source: "Belmont Stakes." June 12, 1948. Corbis. Image no. IH136407. Available online at http://pro.corbis.com (accessed March 25, 2003). ∎

Introduction

Despite World War II, the 1940s were a golden age for thoroughbred horse racing. The decade saw four horses win racing's Triple Crown (Kentucky Derby, Preakness, and Belmont Stakes); Whirlaway in 1941, Count Fleet in 1943, Assault in 1946, and, perhaps the greatest of the group, Citation in 1948.

Citation was born in April 1945. Bred at Calumet Farm in Lexington, Kentucky, "Big Cy," as he was nicknamed, won eight of nine races as a two-year-old in 1947. As a result, Citation was voted the two-year-old colt of the year, earning $155,680 in prize money. Citation's only defeat as a two-year-old was to his stable mate, Bewitch. As a three-year-old, Citation had what many considered to be the greatest year ever by a thoroughbred. He won nineteen of twenty races, including sixteen in a row and the Triple Crown, and earned $709,470 in prize money. After winning the first two races of the season, Citation's jockey, Albert Snider, disappeared with two companions on a fishing trip in the Florida Keys. Snider's replacement was Eddie Arcaro, considered by many the greatest in racing history. Arcaro won 4,779 races in his career, including the Triple Crown triumphs of Whirlaway in 1941.

Arcaro's first ride on Big Cy at the Chesapeake Trial in Havre de Grace, Maryland, resulted in the colt's only defeat of 1948. Arcaro claimed that he was conserving Citation's strength for the Triple Crown races. During the race, another horse interfered with Citation, and Citation also was boxed in along the rail. This convinced Arcaro not to push his horse too hard on the muddy track. At the last warm up before the Kentucky Derby, the Derby Trial

Primary Source

Citation Wins the Belmont

SYNOPSIS: Despite World War II, the 1940s were a golden age for thoroughbred horse racing, as four three-year-old horses won the prestigious Triple Crown (Kentucky Derby, Preakness, and Belmont Stakes). Perhaps the greatest of the decade's Triple Crown winners was Citation, who won nineteen of twenty races as a three-year-old in 1948. Citation compiled thirty-two victories in forty-five career starts in his illustrious career. In this photo, Eddie Alcaro rides Citation around the last turn to victory in the Belmont Stakes on June 12, 1948. With this victory Citation won the Triple Crown. © BETTMANN/CORBIS. RE-PRODUCED BY PERMISSION.

on April 27, Citation romped to an easy victory. Prior to 1948, no horse had ever won both the Derby Trial and the Kentucky Derby.

On April 30, the day of the Kentucky Derby, it appeared Citation's main competition in the race was his stable mate, Coaltown, a good, but somewhat untested horse. The Kentucky Derby turned out to mean roses for Citation, as he outdistanced Coaltown to win by three and a half lengths. Next was the Preakness two weeks later in Baltimore, where Citation romped to a five-and-a-half-length victory. Arcaro commented after the Preakness that Citation was "the easiest horse I've ever handled. He does everything you ask him." With the Belmont Stakes three weeks away, the decision was made to race Citation at the

Citation races to an easy victory at the Preakness, winning the second leg of the Triple Crown. © BETTMANN/CORBIS. REPRODUCED BY PERMISSION.

Jersey Stakes to keep him in top shape. Although a risky decision, Citation brushed aside the field to win by eleven lengths. He was ready for his date with destiny. On June 12, 1948, Citation became horse racing's eighth Triple Crown winner, as he overpowered the Belmont Stakes field by eight lengths. Each race saw Big Cy increase his margin of victory. *The New York Times* commented that Citation's performance seemed to be "expending as much energy as a midweek workout."

Significance

However, Citation's golden third year was not finished, as he faced challenging older horses. Citation won all four of his remaining races and finished the year with a remarkable nineteen victories in twenty starts. In 1949, Citation developed a "hot spot" on his left foreankle that kept him out of action as a four-year-old, generally considered a horse's prime racing age.

After a year's layoff, Citation returned to racing in 1950, but won only two races. Racing observers noted, however, that all of the horses that defeated Big Cy needed to set personal bests to beat him. In 1951, as a six-year-old, Citation won his last race in July. Citation was retired to stud at Calumet Farm in Lexington. In his career, Citation won thirty-two races, finished second ten

times, and third place twice in forty-five starts—finishing out of the money (below third place) only once. Citation was a profitable horse, winning $1,085,760 in prize earnings—the first colt to earn over a million dollars in total purse money. Citation produced twelve prizewinners, but was generally considered a poor sire. Nonetheless, Citation's reputation had diminished little by the time of his death, at age twenty-five, in August 1970.

A legendary horse when he won the Triple Crown in 1948, Citation achieved almost mythical status over the years as no horse would win the Triple Crown for twenty-four years. In 1973, Secretariat, perhaps the greatest ever three-year-old thoroughbred, won the Triple Crown. Secretariat won the Belmont Stakes by a staggering thirty-one lengths. After Secretariat, two more thoroughbreds, Seattle Slew in 1977 and Affirmed in 1978, have won horse racing's Triple Crown.

Further Resources

BOOKS
Robertson, William H.P. *The History of Thoroughbred Racing in America.* New York: Bonanza Books, 1964.

Smith, Pohla. *Citation.* Lexington, Ky.: Eclipse Press, 2000.

Stoneridge, M.A. *Great Horses of Our Time.* Garden City, N.Y.: Doubleday, 1972.

PERIODICALS
"Citation is Dead at 25; Won Triple Crown in '48." *The New York Times,* August 12, 1970.

Linthicum, Jesse A. "Preakness Easily Won By Citation." *Baltimore Sun,* May 16, 1948.

Roach, James. "Citation, 1-5, Ties Record in Belmont." *The New York Times,* June 13, 1948.

_____. "Citation Outraces Coaltown in Derby." *The New York Times,* May 2, 1948.

WEBSITES
"Citation." Thoroughbred Champions. Available online at http://thoroughbredchampions.com/gallery/citation.htm; website home page: http://thoroughbredchampions.com (accessed March 2, 2003).

Bob Mathias Hurls the Discus in the Decathlon
Photograph

By: Associated Press
Date: August 6, 1948
Source: Associated Press. Bob Mathias Hurls the Discus in the Decathlon. August 6, 1948. AP/Wide World Photos. Available online at http://www.apwideworld.com (accessed March 25, 2003). ■

Introduction

The Summer Olympics resumed in 1948 in London, after being canceled in 1940 and 1944 because of World War II. The focal point of the Olympics was the track and field events, and no event held as much attention and fascination as the decathlon. The decathlon consists of ten events contested over two days: 100-meter dash, long jump, shot put, high jump, 400-meter run, 110-meter hurdles, discus, pole vault, javelin, and 1,500-meter run. In the competition, the athlete's performance is rated against a total score of 10,000 points. The decathlon winner was considered the "world's greatest athlete," given the need for both skill and versatility in excelling in the event.

Bob Mathias was born in 1930 in Tulare, California. At age eleven, Bob developed anemia, a shortage of red blood cells, and was treated by his physician father. In high school, Bob developed into an outstanding athlete, winning all-state honors in basketball, football, and track. In the spring of 1948, Mathias's performance in track and field events convinced his coach that the youngster had the potential to do extremely well in the decathlon, and, perhaps, even win the event at the 1952 Olympics.

After sending away for books on the decathlon, Mathias decided to try the event. With three weeks before his first scheduled competition, Mathias had never pole vaulted, thrown the javelin, long jumped, or run a distance race. Mathias won his first decathlon in Pasadena, California. He next competed in the U.S. Olympic Trials in Bloomfield, New Jersey, with the London games just six weeks away. At the Olympic Trials, Mathias defeated three-time national champion Irving "Moon" Mondschein, but Mathias was not considered a serious contender for the gold medal.

On August 5, 1948, a cold and misty morning in London, Bob Mathias entered Wembley Stadium for the first day of competition. With his parents and two brothers among the 70,000 spectators, Mathias hoped to win a bronze medal in the event. Mathias figured that he could aim for the gold in 1952. On the first day, Mathias finished third in the long jump, won the shot put, tied for first in the high jump, and after an extended weather delay, finished third in the 400-meter run. At the end of the first day's competition, Mathias was in third place with 3,848 points, only forty-nine behind the leader.

The weather on the second day was even worse. A cold, heavy rain fell, once again delaying the events. The decathletes were divided into two groups, with Mathias's group adversely affected by delays, while his main rivals competed first. For twelve hours, Mathias huddled under a blanket in the cold and rain, emerging only to compete. His only food was two box lunches. Mathias held his own in the 110-meter high hurdles. In the day's second event, the discus, Mathias threw the "wet platter" 145 meters.

But a subsequent throw by Mondschein slid along the wet grass and uprooted Mathias's spot marker. A careless judge picked up the marker, and embarrassed Olympic officials searched in the rain for more than an hour to find it. The officials threatened to disqualify Mathias if any American came down to the field to look for the marker. Finally, after failing to find the marker, Mathias was awarded a throw six meters less than the original toss. However, he still won the event.

Torrential rain fell during the afternoon. In the pole vault, Mathias passed up the chance to vault at a lower height to conserve his energy. Slippery pole (with a piece of white cloth on the end to detect it in the darkening stadium) and all, Mathias vaulted eleven feet five and three-quarters inches for a first place tie. By now, Mathias' two main rivals had finished, but he still had two events to go. With rain clouds hanging over the dimly lit and sparsely populated stadium, the javelin competition began at 10:15 P.M. Officials scurried around with flashlights. It was so dark that Mathias missed the take-off line completely on his first javelin attempt. Needing the aid of flashlights beaming on the foul line to continue, Mathias came through with a 165-meter throw. With one event to go, Mathias was in a great position to win the gold medal. All he needed was a six minute or better in the 1,500-meter run. Clinching victory, Mathias ran the 1,500 meters on the muddy track in five minutes, eleven seconds, overtaking Ignace Heinrich of France to capture the gold medal. As New York Times sportswriter Alison Danzig wrote, "Considering the miserable conditions under which they were scored, in rain, on a track covered with water, on jumping and vaulting runways that were slippery and a bit risky, in fading light, and finally under flashlights, it was an amazing achievement."

Significance

Arriving home, the seventeen-year-old Olympic champion was given a hero's welcome. Mathias met President Truman, was honored in a large parade in Tulare, and Mathias won the Sullivan Award as the nation's top amateur athlete of 1948. In 1952, Mathias went to Helsinki, Finland, seeking to reclaim the gold medal. The decathlon competition was billed as the world versus Bob Mathias—and the world lost. Mathias repeated his decathlon triumph with 7,887 points, bettered his own world record, and finished 912 points ahead of fellow American, Milt Campbell. In his career as a decathlete, Mathias never lost a competition. He was widely considered to be the favorite again in 1956, but he chose not to compete. After his athletic career ended, Mathias moved on to other pursuits. He was a movie and television actor, and served for eight years as a congressman from California. Later, he headed the U.S. Olympic Training Center in Colorado Springs, Colorado. Mathias was elected to the track and

Primary Source

Bob Mathias Hurls the Discus in the Decathlon

SYNOPSIS: The renewal of the Olympic Games in 1948, after an interruption of twelve years because of World War II, featured Bob Mathias, a seventeen-year-old high school senior from California, who won the ten-event decathlon with a final score of 7,139 just months after taking up the event. His nearest opponents had scores of 6,974 and 6,950. Mathias repeated his gold medal performance in the decathlon in 1952, before retiring undefeated in competition. AP/WIDE WORLD PHOTOS. REPRODUCED BY PERMISSION.

field Hall of Fame in 1973, and the U.S. Olympic Hall of Fame in 1983. Mathias lives in California.

Bob Mathias's impact on American sport was substantial. His back-to-back victories led to United States dominance in the decathlon for a generation, as Milt Campbell, Rafer Johnson, Bill Toomey, and Bruce Jenner all won gold medals in the event between 1956 and 1976. Mathias's feat of two consecutive decathlon gold medals has not been surpassed, and was not duplicated until Great Britain's Daley Thompson did so in 1984.

Further Resources

BOOKS

Katz, Fred. "Bob Mathias." In Hollander, Zander, ed. *Great American Athletes of the 20th Century.* New York: Random House, 1966, 87–89.

Kieran, John, and Arthur Daley. *The Story of the Olympic Games.* Philadelphia: J.P. Lippincott, 1965.

Tassin, Myron. *Bob Mathias: The Life of the Olympic Champion.* New York: St. Martin's Press, 1983.

Zarnowski, Frank. *The Decathlon: A Colorful History of Track and Field's Most Challenging Event.* Champaign, Ill.: Leisure Press, 1989.

PERIODICALS

"Mathias Wins Decathlon for U.S." *The New York Times,* August 7, 1948, A1.

Scott, Jim. "Mighty Mathias." *Sport,* August 1952, 38–39, 80–81.

"Strength of Ten." *Time,* July 21, 1952, 68–75.

Veeck—As in Wreck: The Autobiography of Bill Veeck
Autobiography

By: Bill Veeck, with Ed Linn
Date: 1962
Source: Veeck, Bill, with Ed Linn. *Veeck—As in Wreck: The Autobiography of Bill Veeck.* New York: G.P. Putnam's Sons, 1962, 173–175, 178, 179, 180.
About the Author: Bill Veeck (1914–1986) was born in Chicago, Illinois, and, as a young man, worked for the Chicago Cubs. In the early 1940s, Veeck bought the Milwaukee Brewers, then a minor league baseball team. Veeck served in the Marines in World War II, sustaining an injury requiring the amputation of his right leg. Veeck bought the Cleveland Indians in 1946, signed the American League's first African American player the next year, and won the World Series in 1948. After selling the Indians, Veeck bought the St. Louis Browns in 1951, and he sold them two years later. Later, Veeck owned the Chicago White Sox twice—in the late 1950s, winning a pennant, and again in the mid-1970s. He left baseball after selling the White Sox in 1980. ∎

Introduction

Most baseball owners wore coats and ties, were frugal with a dollar, paid little attention to fans, and treated their employees—specifically the players—in a high-handed fashion. Even so, they jealously protected the "traditions" of the game, and they disliked "mavericks" that rejected their conservative philosophy. Bill Veeck, who owned major league baseball teams from the 1940s to 1970s, was a maverick, in the worst possible sense, to baseball's "old guard." He treated the fans as guests, his players with respect and generous compensation, and used outrageous promotions to bend tradition and add fun to baseball. And he never wore a tie.

Bill Veeck was born into baseball. His father, William Veeck Sr. was the business manager of the Chicago Cubs. Outwardly a conservative man, the elder Veeck sought to make baseball games more fan-friendly. Treating fans with respect was a legacy the elder Veeck left to his son. Bill Jr. exhibited a rebel streak from childhood, and he was nearly expelled from Kenyon College.

When Veeck Sr. died, Bill left college, returned to Chicago, and worked for the Cubs. But Veeck had ambitions to own his own ball club. After World War II began, Veeck enlisted in the Marine Corps. He injured his right foot in an anti-aircraft gun accident, resulting in the amputation of his right leg. This required him to wear an artificial wooden prosthesis. In typical Veeck fashion, to facilitate his heavy smoking, he carved an ashtray in his leg.

Veeck bought the nearly-bankrupt Milwaukee Brewers, a minor league franchise, in 1944. The Brewers were a last place team with a deteriorating ballpark and low attendance. Within two years, Veeck turned the Brewers around on the field. They won consecutive American Association pennants and drastically increased attendance through a number of fan-friendly, and often outrageous, promotions. Veeck sold the Brewers in 1945. With baseball still in his blood, Veeck put together an ownership group that bought the Cleveland Indians in 1946 for $2.2 million. Veeck later claimed the deal that bought him the Indians was not his first attempt to buy a major league team. In his autobiography, *Veeck—As in Wreck,* Veeck claims to have made an offer for the Philadelphia Phillies in 1942. He planned to stock the team with Negro League players four years before Branch Rickey signed Jackie Robinson for the Brooklyn Dodgers. For many years, the Phillies–Negro League story was part of the Veeck mystique. However, in recent years, a number of baseball historians have presented solid evidence that Veeck may have invented the entire story. If the story was fabricated, it was unnecessary. Veeck's record as a civil rights advocate, both within and outside baseball, is well documented.

After buying the Indians, American League officials warned Veeck that "gags" of the type he used in Milwaukee would not be tolerated. Veeck responded by bringing baseball "clowns" to entertain at the ballpark, as well as staging a mock "funeral" when the Indians were eliminated from the pennant race. However, Veeck also instituted many fan-friendly innovations including restrooms for women and nurseries for their toddlers. In 1947, several months after Robinson debuted with the Dodgers, Veeck signed Larry Doby, a star player on the Newark Negro League club. Veeck compensated the team's owner for signing Doby, something Rickey did not do when signing Robinson. Attendance in Cleveland climbed to 2.6 million in 1948, then an all-time record. That year, the Indians won their first American League pennant and World Series championship in twenty-eight years.

Success in Cleveland did not last, and Veeck sold the Indians in 1949. Not out of baseball for long, Veeck bought the lowly St. Louis Browns, winner of one American League (AL) pennant in its fifty years of existence. With little hope in the short term of improving the team on the field, Veeck planned to improve attendance and compete with the National League Cardinals for the St. Louis baseball dollar. Veeck's outrageous promotions, including pregame cow milking contests, continued. On "Grandstand Managers Day," fans with "yes," "no," and other signs "voted" on managerial decisions, while the Browns manager sat in a rocking chair near the dugout. Perhaps Veeck's greatest "stunt" in his years as an owner occurred in August 1951. Veeck had Eddie Gaedel, a midget at three-foot seven, bat in an official league game against the Detroit Tigers. When Veeck died thirty-five years later, Gaedel's at bat was mentioned in the first sentence of his *New York Times* obituary. In 1953, with the Browns unable to win on the field or at the gate, Veeck attempted to move the team to Baltimore. The other owners, tired of his antics, forced him to sell the team. The Browns moved to Baltimore, under the new ownership, and became the Orioles.

Significance

Exiled from baseball for five years, Veeck returned in 1959, when he bought the Chicago White Sox. Veeck's ownership reaped immediate results. The White Sox won the 1959 American League pennant—their first since the Black Sox scandal in 1919—and attendance skyrocketed, aided by a new round of Veeck promotions, including an exploding scoreboard and a staged, mock "invasion" of Comiskey Park by "Martians." By 1961, Veeck's poor health forced him to sell the White Sox, and he left baseball. For the next fifteen years, Veeck wrote two books, as well as articles for newspapers and periodicals, and Veeck owned Suffolk Downs horse racing track in Massachusetts. Veeck played a behind-the-scenes role in racial

integration on Maryland's Eastern Shore, his "retirement" residence. In 1975, after attempting to buy other teams, Veeck returned to baseball. He repurchased the White Sox. Although attracting notice with the Sox's outrageous uniforms (featuring shorts) and an ill-fated mass record burning called "Disco Demolition Night," which quickly turned into a riot, Veeck's cash-strapped operation could not compete in the late 1970s baseball world of free agency and high salaries. In 1980, Veeck sold the White Sox and left baseball for good. In his last years, Veeck returned to Wrigley Field, the baseball home of his youth, as a fan, an image he always projected as an owner. Veeck died in 1986.

Almost every public relations gimmick and promotion used in baseball today can trace its origin to Bill Veeck. He had an important role in the integration of baseball, and later worked against the reserve clause—the right of an owner to bind a player to his team for life unless traded—and establish free agency. What is sometimes lost in the Veeck gags and gimmicks is that his teams were often successful on the field. As of 2003, the Cleveland Indians have not won a World Series since 1948, nor have the Chicago White Sox won another American League pennant since 1959. The Veeck promotional legacy is secure with his son, Mike, a minor league owner, who has created considerable controversy with his baseball operations.

Primary Source

Veeck—As in Wreck: The Autobiography of Bill Veeck [excerpt]

SYNOPSIS: The image of the aristocratic baseball owner was shattered by Bill Veeck, owner of the Cleveland Indians, St. Louis Browns and Chicago White Sox. Always casually attired, and always the consummate showman, Veeck had a social conscience. He signed Larry Doby, the first African American player to play in the American League, in 1948. Here Veeck discusses his encounters with prejudice and his attempt to hire Negro League players to the Philadelphia Phillies.

It Only Takes One Leg to Walk Away

When I signed Larry Doby, the first Negro player in the American League, we received 20,000 letters, most of them in violent and sometimes obscene protest. Over a period of time I answered all. In each answer, I included a paragraph congratulating them on being wise enough to have chosen parents so obviously to their liking. If everyone knew their precious secret, I told them, I was sure everyone would conform to the majority. Until that happy day, I wrote, I was sure they would agree that any man should be judged on his personal merit and allowed to exploit

Larry Doby (r) signs a contract to play for Bill Veeck's (l) Cleveland Indians on July 5, 1947. AP/WIDE WORLD PHOTOS. REPRODUCED BY PERMISSION.

his talents to the fullest, whether he happened to be black, green, or blue with pink dots.

I am afraid irony is lost on these people, but that's not the point I want to make here. A year later, I was a collector for what is now called the Combined Jewish Appeal. This time I got something close to 5,000 violent and sometimes obscene letters. In answering, something very interesting happened. The names began to have a familiar ring. I became curious enough to check our files and I found they were to an astonishing degree—about 95 percent—the same people. A year after that, I converted to Catholicism. About 2,000 anti-Catholics were concerned enough about my soul to write me violent and again often obscene letters. All but a handful of them were already in our anti-Negro and anti-Semitic files.

So I am one man who has documentary proof that prejudice is indivisible. The jackal, after all, doesn't care what kind of animal he sinks his teeth into.

I have always had a strong feeling for minority groups. The pat curbstone explanation would be that having lost a leg myself, I can very easily identify myself with the deprived. Right? Wrong. I had tried to buy the Philadelphia Phillies and stock it with Negro

players well before I went into the service. I think we live in a time when we psychoanalyze everybody's motives too much and that it is entirely possible to look at something which is ugly and say "This is ugly" without regard to conditioning, environment or social status. My only personal experience with discrimination is that I am a left-hander in a right-handed world, a subject on which I can become violent.

Thinking about it, it seems to me that all my life I have been fighting against the status quo, against the tyranny of the fossilized majority rule. I would suppose that whatever impels me to battle the old fossils of baseball also draws me to the side of the underdog. I would prefer to think of it as an essential decency. If someone wants to argue the point I won't object, although we'd have a better chance to be friends if he didn't.

Let me make it plain that my Philadelphia adventure was no idle dream. I had made my offer to Gerry Nugent, the president of the fast-sinking club, and he had expressed a willingness to accept it. As far as I knew I was the only bidder. The players were going to be assembled for me by Abe Saperstein and Doc Young, the sports editor of the Chicago *Defender,* two of the most knowledgeable men in the country on the subject of Negro baseball. With Satchel Paige, Roy Campanella, Luke Easter, Monte Irvin, and countless others in action and available, I had not the slightest doubt that in 1944, a war year, the Phils would have leaped from seventh place to the pennant.

I made one bad mistake. Out of my long respect for Judge Landis I felt he was entitled to prior notification of what I intended to do. I was aware of the risk I was taking although, to be honest, I could not see how he could stop me. The color line was a "gentleman's agreement" only. The only way the Commissioner could bar me from using Negroes would be to rule, officially and publicly, that they were "detrimental to baseball." With Negroes fighting in the war, such a ruling was unthinkable.

Judge Landis wasn't exactly shocked but he wasn't exactly overjoyed either. His first reaction, in fact, was that I was kidding him.

The next thing I knew I was informed that Nugent, being in bankruptcy, had turned the team back to the league and that I would therefore have to deal with the National League president, Ford Frick. Frick promptly informed me that the club had already been sold to William Cox, a lumber dealer, and that my agreement with Nugent was worthless. The Phillies were sold to Cox by Frick for about half what I had been willing to pay.

Word reached me soon enough that Frick was bragging all over the baseball world—strictly off the record, of course—about how he had stopped me from contaminating the league. That was my first direct encounter with Mr. Frick.

There is a suspicion, I suppose, that if I tried to buy the Phillies and stock it with Negro players, it was only because, showman that I am—promoter, con man, knave—I was grabbing for the quick and easy publicity and for the quick and easy way to rebuild a hopeless team. I am not going to suggest that I was innocent on either count.

On the other hand, I had no particular feeling about making it either an all-Negro team or not an all-Negro team. The one thing I did know was that I was not going to set up any quota system—a principle which cost me my original backer. As always, I was operating from a short bankroll. The most obvious backer, it seemed to me, was the CIO, which had just begun a campaign to organize Negro workers in the South.

The CIO was ready and eager to give me all the financing I needed. The money, in fact, was already escrowed when the CIO official I was dealing with

asked for my assurance that there would always be a mixed team on the field. (I don't like to duck names, but there was a promise from the beginning of the negotiations that his name would not enter into any of the publicity.) The only assurance I am willing to give anybody, ever, is that I will try to put the best possible team on the field.

I had another potential—and logical—backer, Phillies Cigars, who had already indicated a willingness to bankroll me. Ford Frick lowered the boom.

What offends me about prejudice, I think, is that it assumes a totally unwarranted superiority. For as long as I can remember I have felt vaguely uneasy when anybody tells me an anti-Negro or anti-Semitic or anti-Catholic joke. It only takes one leg, you know, to walk away. . . .

All this is background, a presentation of credentials to the signing of Larry Doby and Satchel Paige. When I came to Cleveland, I was almost sure I was going to sign a Negro player. We had four or five Negro friends sending us reports from the beginning. At the start of the 1947 season, I hired a Negro public relations man, Lou Jones, so that he could familiarize himself with the league ahead of time and serve as a companion and a buffer to the player we signed. I spoke to the Negro leaders of the city and told them I was going to hold them responsible for policing their own people in case of trouble. (There was nothing for them to be responsible for, of course. We never had one fight in Cleveland in which a Negro was involved.)

I moved slowly and carefully, perhaps even timidly. It is usually overlooked, but if Jackie Robinson was the ideal man to break the color line, Brooklyn was also the ideal place. I wasn't that sure about Cleveland. Being unsure, I wanted to narrow the target areas as much as possible; I wanted to force the critics to make their attacks on the basis of pure prejudice—if they dared—and not on other grounds. To give them no opportunity to accuse us of signing a Negro as a publicity gimmick, I had informed the scouts that I wasn't necessarily looking for the best player in the Negro leagues but for a young player with the best long-term potential. And I only wanted to sign one Negro because, despite those glowing credentials I have given myself, I felt that I had to be in a position to extricate the club fairly easily in case we ran into too many problems.

The player whose name kept floating to the top was Larry Doby, the second baseman of the Newark Eagles. Still moving with great caution, I told Rudie to have Bill Killifer follow Doby for a few games without leaking what he was doing. Rudie followed instructions so well that he didn't even leak word to Killifer. He just told Bill to go down to Atlanta over the weekend, scout Newark and call us back with a rundown of all their players. Bill, logically enough, arrived in Atlanta under the impression that he was supposed to scout the Newark team in the International League. Upon looking through the paper and seeing that Newark wasn't in town, he did what any sensible man would do at the end of a wild-goose chase. He got stiff.

By the time Rudie tracked him down two days later, the Newark Eagles were in New Orleans. Bill eventually turned in a favorable report on Doby, and I scouted him myself, back in Newark, just before we bought him.

I had always felt that Mr. Rickey had been wrong in taking Jackie Robinson from a Negro club without paying for him. Contract or no, the owner of a Negro club could not possibly refuse to let a player go to the major leagues. It meant too much to the whole race. For anyone to take advantage of that situation, particularly while talking about equal rights, was terribly unfair.

I offered Mrs. Effa Manley, the owner of the Newark club, $10,000 for Doby's contract, plus an additional $10,000 if he made our team. Effa was so pleased that she told me I could have the contract of her shortstop, who she thought was just as good, for $1,000. Our reports on the shortstop were good too. We had eliminated him because we thought he was too old. To show how smart I am, the shortstop was Monte Irvin. . . .

In his first day in uniform, July 3, 1947, Doby saw action as a pinch hitter and struck out. During that whole first year, he was a complete bust. The next year, however, when Tris Speaker and Bill McKechnie converted him into a center fielder, Larry began to hit and one of our weak positions suddenly became one of our strongest.

Some of the players who had not seemed overjoyed at having Larry on the team became increasingly fond of him as it became apparent that he was going to help them slice a cut of that World Series money. The economics of prejudice, as I have discovered many times, cuts both ways.

And when Doby hit a tremendous home run to put us ahead in the fourth game of the World Series, it could be observed that none of the 81,000 people who were on their feet cheering seemed at all concerned about—or even conscious of—his color.

Doby was as close to me as any player I have ever known, although it took awhile before he would stop in the office to talk over his troubles. I am extremely fond of Larry and of his wife, Helyn, and their children. After all that is said, I have to add, in all honesty, that he was not the best man we could have picked for the first Negro player in the league. I don't say that from the club's point of view, since we could not have won without him, but from his.

Larry had been an all-sports star in Paterson, New Jersey. A local hero. He had never come face-to-face with prejudice until he became a big-leaguer. Prejudice was something he knew existed, something which he had accommodated himself to in his youth if only in the knowledge that it was going to keep him out of organized baseball. He had not been bruised as a human being, though; he had not had his nose rubbed in it. It hit him late in life; it hit him at a time he thought he had it licked, and it hit him hard.

Further Resources

BOOKS

Eskenazi, Gerald. *Bill Veeck: A Baseball Legend.* New York: McGraw-Hill Book Company, 1988.

Moore, Joseph Thomas. *Pride Against Prejudice: The Biography of Larry Doby.* New York: Praeger, 1988.

Tygiel, Jules. *Baseball's Great Experiment: Jackie Robinson and His Legacy.* New York: Oxford University Press, 1983.

Veeck, Bill, with Ed Linn. *The Hustler's Handbook.* New York: G.P. Putnam's, 1965.

PERIODICALS

Durso, Joseph. "Bill Veeck, Baseball Innovator Dies." *The New York Times,* January 3, 1986.

Jordan, David M. et al. "Bill Veeck and the 1943 Sale of the Phillies: A Baseball Myth Exploded." *The National Pastime: A Review of Baseball History,* 1998.

Robinson and LaMotta

"In This Corner . . . !"

Eyewitness accounts

By: Peter Heller

Date: 1973

Source: Heller, Peter. *"In This Corner . . . !" Forty World Champions Tell Their Stories.* New York: Simon and Schuster, 1973, 278, 297.

About the Author: Peter Heller (1947–) published *In This Corner . . . Forty World Champions Tell Their Stories,* in 1973. His first book, it contained interviews with past boxing champions. Heller's 1989 biography, *Bad Intentions: The Mike Tyson Story,* was an early profile of the controversial heavyweight champion. A producer for ABC Sports, Heller lives in Putnam County, New York, and Boca Raton, Florida.

Sugar Ray: The Sugar Ray Robinson Story

Autobiography

By: Sugar Ray Robinson, with Dave Anderson

Date: 1970

Source: Robinson, Sugar Ray, with Dave Anderson. *Sugar Ray: The Sugar Ray Robinson Story.* New York: Viking, 1970, 101, 102, 108, 109.

About the Author: Sugar Ray Robinson (1921–1989) was born Walker Smith Jr. in Detroit, Michigan, and he moved to New York City, at twelve, with his mother. Smith won ninety fights as an amateur boxer under the name Ray Robinson (after having to borrow an Amateur Athletic Union (AAU) card one night from a Ray Robinson). Turning professional in 1940, he won his first forty fights and was given the nickname "Sugar Ray." Over a career lasting twenty-five years and more than two hundred bouts—174 victories, including a streak of ninety-one in a row—Robinson won six world titles, including welterweight, middleweight (five times), and light heavyweight championships. Considered by many to be the greatest boxer in history, Robinson was a businessman, actor, and head of a charitable organization until his death in 1989. ∎

Introduction

Boxing enjoyed a period of great prosperity in the 1940s. Individual fighters made their mark, and there were great rivalries that increased fan interest. These rivalries included Joe Louis–Billy Conn in the heavyweight division, Rocky Graziano–Tony Zale in the middleweight classification, and Sugar Ray Robinson–Jake LaMotta in the welterweight and middleweight divisions.

The six Robinson-LaMotta bouts between 1942–1951 matched men of the same age, but contrasting backgrounds, fighting styles, and personalities. At the time of their first fight on October 2, 1942, at Madison Square Garden in New York, Robinson was the better-known fighter, with more than one hundred amateur and professional victories. LaMotta was just beginning to gain notice, having turned pro the previous year. Despite LaMotta's twelve-pound weight advantage, Robinson won their first bout in a ten-round decision, extending his professional winning streak to thirty-six. On February 5, 1943, in Detroit, LaMotta, with a sixteen-pound weight advantage, dealt Robinson his first loss in forty professional fights and 130 fights overall. In the eighth round, LaMotta hammered Robinson with a right to the body and left to the head that drove Sugar Ray through the ropes and down onto the ring apron. Fortunately for Robinson, the bell ended the round before Robinson was counted out. The two fought again three weeks later in Detroit. Again outweighed by sixteen pounds, Robinson, who was about to enter the army, avenged his defeat with a unanimous, ten-round decision. But Sugar Ray's victory was not easy, as LaMotta floored Robinson with a left jab to the face. Robinson was down for an eight count before struggling to his feet to continue.

On February 24, 1945, Robinson and LaMotta fought for the fourth time, and again Sugar Ray won a ten-round unanimous decision. Robinson, fighting as a welterweight, weighed ten pounds less than the middleweight LaMotta. Robinson had fifty-four victories in fifty-five bouts. Seven months later, at Chicago's Comiskey Park, Robinson made it four out of five over LaMotta, in what was the closest judged fight of their rivalry. The referee gave the bout to Robinson by a close sixty-one to fifty-nine margin, while the two ring judges split their decisions. LaMotta, according to newspaper accounts, was the favorite of the Comiskey Park crowd, especially when Robinson fought cautiously in the last several rounds. The announcement of the twelve round split decision for Robinson prompted a loud chorus of boos.

The rivals would not fight again for more than five years. In the intervening time, Robinson won the welterweight title in 1946, while LaMotta won the middleweight title in 1949. Robinson added extra weight, and on February 14, 1951, in Chicago, the two rivals fought for the last time for the undisputed world middleweight championship. Weighing only five pounds less than LaMotta, Robinson dominated the fight, as he aggressively pummeled the "Bronx Bull" throughout. Finally, at two minutes, four seconds of the thirteenth round, the referee stopped the fight, as Robinson had LaMotta on the ropes, pounding away. A newspaper account said only "indomitable courage" by LaMotta kept him from collapsing to the canvas for the first time in his career. In his book *Raging Bull* (1970), LaMotta attributed the losses to the skill of Robinson: "Don't get me wrong— Ray is one fighter that I would never knock. I never minded saying he was the greatest. He was lucky in a couple of fights with me, but there's no question that he's one of the best."

Significance

Robinson retired from boxing in 1952, but returned three years later to regain the middleweight crown. He continued fighting and finally retired from the ring at age forty-four in 1965, no longer the dominant boxer he had been. LaMotta fought for several more years, never regaining the middleweight crown, before retiring in 1954.

The two fighters had distinctive boxing styles in the ring and personalities outside. Robinson was a finesse fighter, who danced around the ring, used evasion tactics to tire his opponent. LaMotta, on the other hand, was the

Sugar Ray Robinson catches Jake LaMotta with a long right to his head at Madison Square Garden on February 23, 1945. © BETTMANN/CORBIS. REPRODUCED BY PERMISSION.

"bull," a reflection of his street fighter background. He was relentless in pummeling opponents, as well as being bloodied himself from constant punches to the face and torso. Robinson was self-confident, almost cocky. He shrewdly managed his own career, driving a hard bargain in negotiating his fights. LaMotta never shed his tough guy persona. His career was overshadowed by accusations that he was a tool of mob interests. In 1947, LaMotta admitted to a U.S. Senate committee that he threw a fight, which led to his suspension from boxing for seven months.

Robinson moved to California after his boxing career ended, continued his career as an actor and entertainer, and established an inner-city youth program in 1969. His ring career inspired a later generation of boxers, notably Muhammad Ali, who was fond of telling Sugar Ray, "You are the king, the master, my idol." Robinson developed Alzheimer's disease and died in 1989.

Jake LaMotta's life on the edge continued after his boxing career ended. Operating a nightclub in Miami Beach, LaMotta's playboy lifestyle brought him crashing to earth. He was convicted of contributing to the delinquency of a minor and sentenced to a Florida prison chain gang. After his release from prison, LaMotta wrote his autobiography, but remained in hard times until 1981, when the movie *Raging Bull,* was released. It chronicled his life, and helped him recover financially.

Primary Source

"In This Corner . . . !" [excerpt]

SYNOPSIS: Sugar Ray Robinson and Jake "The Bronx Bull" LaMotta fought each other six times between 1942 and 1951. The following excerpts are from interviews with Peter Heller where they each describe what it was like to fight the other. The interview with

Sugar Ray Robinson was conducted on December 25, 1972; the interview with Jake LaMotta occurred in February 1970. Both took place in New York.

Sugar Ray Robinson

[Jake LaMotta and I fought] six times. We almost got married. Every time I put my name on that paper I knew what I was in for. That guy was one of the toughest guys, gee whiz! I want to tell you something. This guy, Jake LaMotta, you hit this guy, I didn't knock him out, you know. They stopped the fight. They stopped the fight on a technical knockout. This guy, you just hit him with everything and he'd just act like you're crazy. . . .

Jake LaMotta

I fought Sugar Ray so many times it's a wonder I don't have diabetes. I fought him six times. The first time I fought him he won a close decision from me. Second time I fought him I knocked him down, first time he was ever down, and I won the fight. The third time I fought him I had him down and out, the bell saved him, they dragged him back to his corner, and they gave him the fight by 1 point because he was going in the army the next day. The fourth time I fought him it was a close decision. The fifth time I fought him he was down and out, the bell saved him, they dragged him back to his corner and two out of three judges gave him the fight, total points I was ahead. See, all the fights I had with him were very close. That's why we fought six times. You don't fight six times unless it's very, very close. I had the style, and let me tell you something. He knew he was in a fight and I knew I was in a fight. I fought the greatest fighter of them all. It was a really, really tough fight. No foul blows or nothing. We stood there toe to toe and banged away. But most of the times I had to chase him, chase him. I had to be in superb condition, had to beat him to the punch all the time, keep on top of him, press him, press him, press, press, press, press. And the ultimate outcome was that the fights were very, very close.

Primary Source

Sugar Ray: The Sugar Ray Robinson Story [excerpt]

SYNOPSIS: Robinson's version of events seems slightly more generous to his opponent, but since he won all but one of the bouts, he did not need to be defensive.

In the days before the fight, George kept reminding me, "The matador and the bull. You are the matador, LaMotta is the bull. The matador will win if he has the finesse. The matador never wins if he acts like the bull." When the bell rang, I realized that I would have been safer in a bull ring than a boxing ring.

LaMotta had about ten pounds on me, and he knew how to use his weight. He forced me back, or moved me to the side. Despite his strength, I was doing fairly well. I was hitting him consistently, and around the middle of the fight I caught him with a good combination.

I had him along the ropes. He had his head down and I was really measuring him. For one of the few times in my career, my arms got weary from throwing so many punches. I stepped back for a breather. Jake had his head down and his gloves were up around his head, protecting himself. I thought, *man, he has to fall any moment now.* But not Jake, not the Bull. His head popped up and he let go a left hook that almost tore through my stomach. It hurt so much, I had tears in my eyes, like a little kid. I got the decision but I learned that Jake LaMotta was some animal.

Not many guys had gone the distance with me. The decision over Jake had been my thirty-sixth consecutive victory as a pro, with twenty-seven knockouts—too many knockouts, I soon discovered. . . .

Across the ring Jake LaMotta was glowering, his round head bobbing on his thick, squat shoulders.

"And in this corner," the announcer droned, turning toward me, "from New York City, Sugar Ray. . . ."

All around me in the Detroit Olympia, a roar went up—but suddenly, for the first time in my boxing career, I was unsure of myself. That moment when you're being introduced, man, that's a boxer's moment of truth. You're all by yourself then. It's too late for anybody to help you and what's worse, it's too late to help yourself. That's what worried me. Staring at the canvas and jiggling my body, I heard the applause from my pop and my other old friends in the Black Bottom neighborhood, but that rhythm wasn't flowing. I hadn't trained properly. My Army induction date had been set for three weeks from tomorrow, and I had been enjoying myself. But now, as I looked across at the Bronx Bull, I knew he would make me sorry.

You left all your strength with those girls you were chasing, I scolded myself.

Edna Mae had remained in New York, and I had discovered that there were pretty girls in Black Bottom, too.

Jake La Motta, left, knocks Sugar Ray Robinson through the ropes in the eighth round of their match in Detroit, Michigan, on February 5, 1943. AP/WIDE WORLD PHOTOS. REPRODUCED BY PERMISSION.

And those days you went bowling instead of to the gym, I thought.

In my previous fights, hearing my introduction always gave me confidence. To me, the ring was like home. I was the rabbit in the briar patch, because I was prepared. But this time, the rabbit had been trapped in the open, trapped by himself, and a bull, the Bronx Bull, was about to stomp him.

When I walked out at the bell, Jake stomped me with his first left hook. And he stomped me for ten rounds.

In the eighth round, he did something nobody had ever done to me before. He hit me with a right hand in my mid-section and when I doubled up, he let go a left hook to my jaw. For the first time in my career, I had no legs. I sagged through the ropes and onto the ring apron and sprawled there. In my daze, I could hear the referee, Sam Hennessy, counting, ". . . six . . . seven . . . eight . . ."

I made it back into the ring in time, but when the round ended, George scolded me.

"Well, Robinson," he growled, "maybe next time you will listen to me when I tell you you're not trainin' correctly. You wouldn't do anything I told you for this fight, and maybe now you'll believe me because now you're payin'."

I was not only paying in pain, I was paying in embarrassment, in front of my pop and my Black Bottom friends.

I survived the last two rounds, but at the final bell I knew the decision would be unanimous for Jake, and it was. When I heard the announcer's voice echo, "The winner, Jake LaMotta," I wept. After forty consecutive victories as a pro, I had lost. And as I sat there on my stool, with the boos burrowing inside my blue-and-white robe, I made a vow never to get into a ring unless I was in perfect condition, unless I could face my moment of truth.

Further Resources

BOOKS

LaMotta, Jake, with Joseph Carter and Peter Savage. *Raging Bull.* Englewood Cliffs, N.J.: Prentice-Hall, 1970.

Roberts, James B., and Alexander G. Skutt. *The Boxing Register: International Boxing Hall of Fame Official Record Book,* 2d ed. Ithaca, N.Y.: McBooks Press, 1999.

PERIODICALS

"18,000 See Robinson Outpoint LaMotta." *The New York Times,* February 24, 1945.

Anderson, Dave. "Sugar Ray Robinson, Boxing's 'Best' is Dead." *The New York Times,* April 13, 1989.

Nichols, Joseph C. "Robinson Takes Unanimous Decision Over LaMotta," *The New York Times,* October 3, 1942.

"Robinson Gains Award Over LaMotta." *The New York Times,* February 27, 1943.

"Robinson Knocks Out LaMotta in 13th Round." *The New York Times,* February 15, 1951.

"Robinson Outpoints LaMotta in Chicago." *The New York Times,* September 27, 1945.

"Robinson's Streak Ended By LaMotta." *The New York Times,* February 6, 1943.

AUDIO AND VISUAL MEDIA

Raging Bull. Original release, 1980. Directed by Martin Scorsese. 128 min. MGM/UA Video. VHS, DVD.

GENERAL RESOURCES

General

Adams, Michael C.C. *The Best War Ever: America and World War II.* Baltimore: Johns Hopkins University Press, 1994.

Blum, John Morton. *V Was For Victory: Politics and American Culture During World War II.* New York: Harcourt Brace Jovanovich, 1976.

Boyer, Paul S. *Promises to Keep: The United States since World War II.* Boston: Houghton Mifflin, 1998.

Buchanan, A. Russell. *The United States in World War II.* New York: Harper & Row, 1964.

Dear, I.C.B. *The Oxford Companion to the Second World War.* New York: Oxford University Press, 1995.

Diggins, John Patrick. *The Proud Decades: America in War and in Peace, 1941–1960.* New York: Norton, 1988.

Ellis, John. *World War II: A Statistical Survey.* New York: Facts on File, 1993.

Fried, Richard M. *Nightmare in Red: The McCarthy Era in Perspective.* New York: Oxford University Press, 1990.

Hodgson, Godfrey. *America in Our Time.* Garden City, N.Y.: Doubleday, 1976.

Keegan, John. *The Second World War.* New York: Viking, 1990.

Kennedy, David M. *Freedom from Fear: The American People in Depression and War, 1929–1945.* New York: Oxford University Press, 1999.

Nash, Gerald D. *The Crucial Era: The Great Depression and World War II, 1929–1945.* New York: St. Martin's Press, 1992.

O'Neill, William L. *A Democracy at War: America's Fight at Home and Abroad in World War II.* New York: Free Press, 1993.

Patterson, James T. *Grand Expectations: the United States, 1945–1974.* New York: Oxford University Press, 1996.

Perrett, Geoffrey. *Days of Sadness, Years of Triumph; the American People, 1939–1945.* New York: Coward, McCann, & Geoghegan, 1973.

Polenberg, Richard. *War and Society: The United States, 1941–1945.* Philadelphia: Lippincott, 1972.

Sherry, Michael S. *In the Shadow of War: The United States since the 1930's.* New Haven: Yale University Press, 1995.

Weinberg, Gerhard L. *A World at Arms: A Global History of World War II.* New York: Cambridge University Press, 1994.

Whitfield, Stephen J. *The Culture of the Cold War.* Baltimore: The Johns Hopkins University Press, 1991.

Websites

National Archives and Records Administration. "A People at War." Available online at http://www.archives.gov/exhibit _hall/a_people_at_war/a_people_at_war.html (accessed August 8, 2002).

The Arts

Arnason, H. Harvard. *History of Modern Art: Painting, Sculpture, Photography.* 3rd ed. Englewood Cliffs, N.J.: Prentice-Hall, 1986.

Ashton, Dore. *The New York School: A Cultural Reckoning.* New York: Viking, 1973.

Balliett, Whitney. *American Musicians: Fifty Portraits in Jazz.* New York: Oxford University Press, 1986.

Breslin, James E.B. *Mark Rothko: A Biography.* Chicago: University of Chicago Press, 1993.

Carpenter, Humphrey. *A Serious Character: The Life of Ezra Pound.* Boston: Houghton Mifflin, 1988.

Carr, Virginia. *The Lonely Hunter: A Biography of Carson McCullers.* New York: Doubleday, 1975.

Castleman, Riva, and Guy Davenport, eds. *Art of the Forties.* New York: Metropolitan Museum of Art, 1991.

Charters, Samuel B. and Leonard Kunstadt. *Jazz: A History of the New York Scene.* Garden City, N.Y.: Doubleday, 1962.

Coe, Jonathan. *Humphrey Bogart: Take It and Like It.* New York: Grove Weidenfeld, 1991.

Cripps, Thomas. *Making Movies Black: The Hollywood Message Movie from World War II to the Civil Rights Era.* New York: Oxford University Press, 1993.

Davis, Francis. *The History of the Blues.* New York: Hyperion, 1995.

De Antonio, Emile, and Mitch Tuchman. *Painters Painting: A Candid History of the Modern Art Scene, 1940–1970.* New York: Abbeville, 1984.

de Mille, Agnes. *America Dances.* New York: Macmillan, 1980.

———. *Martha: The Life and Work of Martha Graham.* New York: Random House, 1991.

Doherty, Thomas. *Projections of War.* New York: Columbia University Press, 1993.

Ellison, Curtis W. *Country Music Culture: From Hard Times to Heaven.* Jackson: University of Mississippi Press, 1995.

Erenberg, Lewis A. *Swingin' the Dream: Big Band Jazz and the Rebirth of American Culture.* Chicago: University of Chicago Press, 1998.

Frank, Rusty E. *Tap!: The Greatest Tap Dance Stars and Their Stories, 1900–1955.* New York: William Morris, 1990.

Frascina, Francis, ed. *Pollock and After: The Critical Debate.* New York: HarperCollins, 1985.

French, Warren, ed. *The Forties: Fiction, Poetry, Drama.* Deland, Fla.: Everett/Edwards, 1969.

Friedrich, Otto. *City of Nets: A Portrait of Hollywood in the 1940's.* New York: Harper & Row, 1986.

Gayle, Addison. *Richard Wright: Ordeal of a Native Son.* Garden City, N.Y.: Anchor/Doubleday, 1980.

Geldzahler, Henry. *New York Painting and Sculpture: 1940–1970.* New York: The Metropolitan Museum of Art, 1969.

Giddins, Gary. *Celebrating Bird: The Triumph of Charlie Parker.* New York: Beech Tree Books, 1987.

Gitler, Ira. *Jazz Masters of the Forties.* New York: Macmillan, 1966.

———. *Swing to Bop: An Oral History of The Transition in Jazz in the 1940s.* New York: Oxford University Press, 1985.

Graham, Martha. *Blood Memory.* New York: Doubleday, 1991.

Haslam, Gerald W. *Workin' Man Blues: Country Music in California.* Berkeley: University of California Press, 1999.

Hess, Thomas B. *Abstract Painting: Background and American Phase.* New York: Viking, 1951.

———. *Six Painters.* Houston, Tex.: Rice University Press, 1968.

Higham, Charles. *Orson Welles, the Rise and Fall of an American Genius.* New York: St. Martin's Press, 1985.

Hill, Constance Valis. *Brotherhood in Rhythm: The Jazz Dancing of the Nicholas Brothers.* New York: Oxford University Press, 2000.

Howlett, John. *Frank Sinatra.* London: Plexus, 1980.

Janson, H. W. *History of Art.* 5th ed. New York: Abrams, 1995.

Karl, Frederick R. *American Fictions, 1940–1980.* New York: Harper & Row, 1983.

Koppes, Clayton, and Gregory Black. *Hollywood Goes to War.* New York: Free Press, 1987.

Kramer, Hilton. *The Twilight of the Intellectuals: Culture and Politics in the Era of the Cold War.* Chicago : I.R. Dee, 1999.

Malone, Bill C. *Country Music, U.S.A.* Austin: University of Texas, 1985.

———. *Don't Get above Your Raisin': Country Music and the Southern Working Class.* Urbana: University of Illinois Press, 2002.

Mazo, Joseph H. *Prime Movers: The Makers of Modern Dance in America.* Princeton, N.J.: Princeton Book Company, 1977.

McDonagh, Don. *The Complete Guide to Modern Dance.* Garden City, N.Y.: Doubleday, 1976.

Moszynska, Anna. *Abstract Art.* New York: Thames & Hudson, 1990.

Naifeh, Steven, and Gregory White Smith. *Jackson Pollock: An American Saga.* New York: HarperCollins, 1991.

Porter, James A. *Modern Negro Art.* Washington, D.C.: Howard University Press, 1992.

Revill, David. *The Roaring Silence: John Cage, a Life.* New York: Arcade, 1992.

Rosenberg, Harold. *The Tradition of the New.* New York: Horizon, 1959.

Sandler, Irving. *The Triumph of American Painting: A History of Abstract Expressionism.* New York: Harper & Row, 1976.

Sanjek, Russell. *American Popular Music and Its Business Vol. III, From 1900 to 1984.* New York: Oxford University Press, 1988.

Shearer, Moira. *Balletmaster: A Dancer's View of George Balanchine.* London: Sidgwick & Jackson, 1986.

Silver, Alain, and Elizabeth Ward. *Film Noir: An Encyclopedic Reference to the American Style.* 3rd ed. Woodstock, N.Y.: Overlook Press, 1992.

Stodelle, Ernestine. *Deep Song: The Dance Story of Martha Graham.* New York: Schirmer, 1984.

Stowe, David. *Swing Changes: Big-Band Jazz in New Deal America.* Cambridge, Mass.: Harvard University Press, 1994.

Stravinsky, Vera, and Robert Craft. *Stravinsky in Pictures and Documents.* New York: Simon & Schuster, 1978.

Tawa, Nicholas E. *Serenading the Reluctant Eagle: American Musical Life, 1925–1945.* New York: Schirmer, 1984.

Tosches, Nick. *Country: Living Legends and Dying Metaphors in America's Biggest Music.* London: Secker & Warburg, 1985.

Trilling, Diana. *Reviewing the Forties.* New York: Harcourt Brace Jovanovich, 1978.

Truman, Maurice, ed. *The New York School: Abstract Expressionism in the 40s and 50s.* London: Thames & Hudson, 1970.

Tuska, Jon. *Dark Cinema: American Film Noir in Cultural Perspective.* Westport, Conn.: Greenwood Press, 1984.

Wilson, Edmund. *The Forties: From Notebooks and Diaries of the Period.* New York: Farrar, Straus & Giroux, 1983.

Wright, William. *Lillian Hellman: The Image, the Woman.* New York: Simon & Schuster, 1986.

Business and the Economy

Barber, William J. *Designs within Disorder: Franklin D. Roosevelt, the Economists, and the Shaping of American Economic Policy, 1933–1945.* New York: Cambridge University Press, 1997.

Eiler, Keith E. *Mobilizing America: Robert P. Patterson and the War Effort, 1940–1945.* Ithaca, N.Y.: Cornell University Press, 1997.

Catton, Bruce. *The Warlords of Washington.* New York: Harcourt Brace, 1948.

Lichtenstein, Nelson. *Labor's War at Home: the CIO in World War II.* New York: Cambridge University Press, 1982.

———. *The Most Dangerous Man in America: Walter Reuther and the Fate of American Labor.* New York: Basic Books, 1995.

Markusen, Ann R. *The Rise of the Gunbelt: The Military Remapping of Industrial America.* New York: Oxford University Press, 1991.

Milward, Alan S. *War, Economy, and Society, 1939–1945.* Berkeley: University of California Press, 1979.

Nash, Gerald D. *World War II and the West: Reshaping the Economy.* Lincoln: University of Nebraska Press, 1990.

Nelson, Donald M. *Arsenal of Democracy: The Story of American War Production.* New York: Harcourt Brace, 1946.

Overy, Richard. *Why the Allies Won.* New York: Norton, 1995.

Vatter, Harold G. *The U.S. Economy in World War II.* New York: Columbia University Press, 1985.

Websites

Library of Congress. "Rosie Pictures. Select Images Relating to American Women Workers during World War II." Available online at http://lcweb.loc.gov/rr/print/126_rosi.html (Accessed August 8, 2002).

Smithsonian National Museum of American History. "Produce for Victory: Posters on the American Homefront." Available online at http://www.americanhistory.si.edu/victory/index.htm (Accessed August 8, 2002).

Education

Berube, Maurice R. *American School Reform: Progressive, Equity, and Excellence Movements, 1883–1993.* Westport, Conn.: Praeger, 1994.

Cremin, Lawrence Arthur. *American Education, the Metropolitan Experience, 1876–1980.* New York: Harper & Row, 1988.

Cuban, Larry. *How Teachers Taught: Constancy and Change in American Classrooms, 1890–1990.* New York: Teachers College Press, 1993.

Cutler, William W. *Parents and Schools: The 150-year Struggle for Control in American Education.* Chicago: University of Chicago Press, 2000.

Fass, Paula S. *Outside in: Minorities and the Transformation of American Education.* New York: Oxford University Press, 1989.

Ravitch, Diane. *Left Back: A Century of Failed School Reforms.* New York: Simon & Schuster, 2000.

———. *The Troubled Crusade: American Education, 1945–1980.* New York: Basic Books, 1983.

Spring, Joel H. *The Sorting Machine Revisited: National Educational Policy since 1945.* New York: Longman, 1989.

Tyack, David B. *Public Schools in Hard Times: The Great Depression and Recent Years.* Cambridge, Mass.: Harvard University Press, 1984.

Tyack, David B., and Larry Cuban. *Tinkering toward Utopia: A Century of Public School Reform.* Cambridge, Mass.: Harvard University Press, 1995.

Zilversmit, Arthur. *Changing Schools: Progressive Education Theory and Practice, 1930–1960.* Chicago: University of Chicago Press, 1993.

Fashion and Design

Balmain, Pierre. *My Years and Seasons.* London: Cassell, 1964.

Batterberry, Michael, and Ariane Batterberry. *Mirror, Mirror: A Social History of Fashion.* New York: Holt, Rinehart & Winston, 1977.

The Changing American Woman: 200 Years of American Fashion. New York: Fairchild, 1976.

Ewing, Elizabeth. *History of Twentieth Century Fashion.* Totowa, N.J.: Barnes & Noble, 1986.

Gaines, Jane, and Charlotte Herzog. *Fabrications: Costume and the Female Body.* New York: Routledge, 1990.

Gutner, Howard. *Gowns by Adrian: The MGM Years, 1928–1941.* New York: Harry N. Abrams, 2001.

Hall, Carolyn. *The Forties in Vogue.* New York: Harmony Books, 1985.

Harrison, Martin. *Appearances: Fashion Photography since 1945.* New York: Rizzoli, 1991.

Hillier, Bevis. *The Decorative Arts of the Forties and Fifties Austerity Binge.* New York: C.N. Potter, 1975.

Kellogg, Ann T., et al. *In an Influential Fashion: An Encyclopedia of Nineteenth- and Twentieth-Century Fashion Designers and Retailers Who Transformed Dress.* Westport, Conn.: Greenwood Press, 2002.

Ley, Sandra. *Fashion for Everyone: The Story of Ready-to-Wear, 1870–1970s.* New York: Scribners, 1975.

Lloyd, Valerie. *The Art of Vogue Photographic Covers: Fifty Years of Fashion and Design.* New York: Harmony, 1986.

Lloyd. *McDowell's Directory of Twentieth Century Fashion.* Englewood Cliffs, N.J.: Prentice-Hall, 1985.

Martin, Richard, and Harold Koda. *Christian Dior.* New York: Metropolitan Museum of Art, 1996.

Olian, JoAnne, ed. *Everyday Fashions of the Forties as Pictured in Sears Catalogs.* New York: Dover Publications, Inc., 1992.

Steele, Valerie. *Fifty Years of Fashion: The New Look to Now.* New Haven, Conn.: Yale University Press, 1997.

Temko, Allan. *Eero Saarinen.* New York: G. Braziller, 1962.

Trahey, Jane, ed. *Harper's Bazaar: 100 Years of the American Female.* New York: Random House, 1967.

Wood, Barry James. *Show Windows: Seventy-five Years of the Art of Display.* New York: Congdon & Weed, 1982.

Yohannan, Kohle, and Nancy Nolf. *Claire McCardell: Redefining Modernism.* New York: Harry N. Abrams, 1998.

Government and Politics

Alperovitz, Gar. *Atomic Diplomacy: Hiroshima and Potsdam.* New York: Simon & Schuster, 1965.

Ambrose, Stephen E. *Rise to Globalism.* 7th rev. ed. New York: Penguin, 1993.

Brinkley, Alan. *The End of Reform: New Deal Liberalism in Recession and War.* New York: Alfred A. Knopf, 1995.

———. *Liberalism and its Discontents.* Cambridge, Mass.: Harvard University Press, 1998.

Cole, Wayne S. *Roosevelt and the Isolationists, 1932–1945.* Lincoln: University of Nebraska Press, 1983.

Culver, John C., and John Hyde. *American Dreamer: The Life and Times of Henry A. Wallace.* New York: Norton, 2000.

Dallek, Robert A. *Franklin D. Roosevelt and American Foreign Policy, 1932–1945.* New York: Oxford University Press, 1981.

Davis, Kenneth Sydney. *FDR, the War President, 1940–1943: A History.* New York: Random House, 2000.

Dickinson, Matthew J. *Bitter Harvest: FDR, Presidential Power, and the Growth of the Presidential Branch.* New York: Cambridge University Press, 1997.

Divine, Robert A. *Roosevelt and World War II.* Baltimore: Johns Hopkins University Press, 1969.

Donovan, Robert J. *Conflict and Crisis: The Presidency of Harry S. Truman, 1945–1948.* New York: Norton, 1977.

Dower, John. *War without Mercy: Race and Power in the Pacific War.* New York: Pantheon Books, 1986.

Feingold, Henry L. *The Politics of Rescue: The Roosevelt Administration and the Holocaust, 1938–1945.* Expanded and updated ed. New York: Holocaust Library, 1980.

Feis, Herbert. *Between War and Peace: The Potsdam Conference.* Princeton, N.J.: Princeton University Press, 1960.

———. *Churchill, Roosevelt, and Stalin: The War They Waged and the Peace They Sought.* Princeton, N.J.: Princeton University Press, 1957.

———. *The Atomic Bomb and the End of World War II.* Princeton, N.J.: Princeton University Press, 1961.

Fleming, Thomas J. *The New Dealers' War: Franklin D. Roosevelt and the War within World War II.* New York: Basic Books, 2001.

Freeland, Richard M. *The Truman Doctrine and the Origins of McCarthyism: Foreign Policy, Domestic Politics, and Internal Security, 1946–1948.* New York: Schocken, 1974.

Gaddis, John Lewis. *The Long Peace: Inquiries into the History of the Cold War.* New York: Oxford University Press, 1987.

———. *The United States and the Origins of the Cold War, 1941–1947.* New York: Columbia University Press, 1972.

Hamby, Alonzo L. *Beyond the New Deal: Harry S Truman and American Liberalism.* New York: Columbia University Press, 1973.

———. *Man of the People: A Life of Harry S Truman.* New York: Oxford University Press, 1998.

Heale, M. J. *Franklin D. Roosevelt: The New Deal and War.* New York: Routledge, 1999.

Hofstadter, Richard. *The American Political Tradition and the Men Who Made It.* New York: Knopf, 1948.

Hogan, Michael J. *The Marshall Plan: America, Britain, and the Reconstruction of Europe, 1947–1952.* New York: Cambridge University Press, 1987.

Kimball, Warren F. *The Juggler: Franklin Roosevelt as Wartime Statesman.* Princeton, N.J.: Princeton University Press, 1991.

Kryder, Daniel. *Divided Arsenal: Race and the American State during World War II.* New York: Cambridge University Press, 2000.

LaFeber, Walter. *America, Russia, and the Cold War, 1945–1996.* New York: McGraw-Hill, 1997.

Lawson, Steven F. *Running for Freedom: Civil Rights and Black Politics in America since 1941.* Philadelphia: Temple University Press, 1991.

Leffler, Melvyn P. *A Preponderance of Power: National Security, the Truman Administration, and the Cold War.* Stanford, Calif.: Stanford University Press, 1992.

Levine, Lawrence W. *The People and the President: America's Conversation with FDR.* Boston: Beacon Press, 2002.

McCormick, Thomas. *America's Half-Century: United States Foreign Policy in the Cold War.* Baltimore: Johns Hopkins University Press, 1989.

Perrett, Geoffrey. *Days of Sadness, Years of Triumph: The American People, 1939–1945.* Madison: University of Wisconsin Press, 1985.

Schlesinger, Arthur M., Jr. *The Age of Roosevelt.* 3 vols. Boston: Houghton Mifflin, 1956–1960.

Smith, Gaddis. *American Diplomacy during the Second World War.* New York: Wiley, 1965.

Sparrow, Bartholomew H. *From the Outside In: World War II and the American State.* Princeton, N.J.: Princeton University Press, 1996.

White, Graham J., and John Maze. *Henry A. Wallace: His Search for a New World Order.* Chapel Hill: University of North Carolina Press, 1995.

Wyman, David S. *The Abandonment of the Jews: America and the Holocaust, 1941–1945.* New York: Pantheon, 1984.

Yergin, Daniel. *Shattered Peace: The Origins of the Cold War and the National Security State.* Boston: Houghton Mifflin, 1977.

Zinn, Howard. *Postwar America, 1945–1971.* Indianapolis: Bobbs-Merrill, 1973.

Websites

Avalon Project at Yale Law School. "World War II Documents." Available online at http://www.yale.edu/lawweb /avalon/wwii/wwii.htmn (Accessed August 8, 2002).

Avalon Project at Yale Law School. "The Cold War." Available online at http://www.yale.edu/lawweb/avalon/coldwar .htm (Accessed August 8, 2002).

Harry S. Truman Presidential Museum and Library. "Harry S. Truman: The Presidential Years." Available online at http:// www.trumanlibrary.org/hst/index.html (Accessed August 8, 2002).

National Archives and Records Administration. "Powers of Persuasion: Poster Art from World War II." Available online at http://www.archives.gov/exhibit_hall/powers_of_persuasion/powers_of_persuasion_home.html (Accessed August 8, 2002).

Law and Justice

Armor, John C., and Peter Wright. *Manzanar.* New York: Times Books, 1988.

Belknap, Michal R. *Cold War Political Justice: The Smith Act, the Communist Party, and American Civil Liberties.* Westport, Conn.: Greenwood Press, 1977.

Bigel, Alan. *The Supreme Court on Emergency Powers, Foreign Affairs, and Protection of Civil Liberties.* Lanham, Md.: University Press of America, 1986.

Chin, Steven. *When Justice Failed: The Fred Korematsu Story.* Austin, Tex.: Raintree Steck-Vaughn, 1993.

Daniels, Roger. *Prisoners without Trial: Japanese Americans in World War II.* New York: Hill & Wang, 1993.

Dickson, Del, ed. *The Supreme Court in Conference (1940–1985): The Private Discussions Behind Nearly 300 Supreme Court Decisions.* New York: Oxford University Press, 2001.

Douglas, William O. *The Court Years, 1939–1975: The Autobiography of William O. Douglas.* New York: Random House, 1980.

Harrison, Maureen, and Steve Gilbert, eds. *Landmark Decisions of the United States Supreme Court II.* Beverly Hills: Excellent Books, 1992.

Hiss, Alger. *Recollections of a Life.* New York: Holt, 1988.

Houston, Jeanne Wakatsuki, and James D. Houston. *Farewell to Manzanar: A True Story of Japanese-American Experience during and after the World War II Internment.* Boston: Houghton Mifflin, 1973.

Irons, Peter H. *Justice at War: The Story of the Japanese Internment Cases.* Berkeley: University of California Press, 1983.

Kessler, Ronald. *The Bureau: The Secret History of the FBI.* New York: St. Martin's Press, 2002.

Kutler, Stanley I. *The American Inquisition: Justice and Injustice in the Cold War.* New York: Hill & Wang, 1982.

Palmer, Jan. *The Vinson Court Era: The Supreme Court's Votes: Data and Analysis.* New York: AMS Press, 1990.

Tateishi, John. *And Justice For All—An Oral History of the Japanese American Detention Camps.* New York: Random House, 1984.

Taylor, Telford. *The Anatomy of the Nuremberg Trials.* New York: Knopf, 1992.

tenBroek, Jacobus, et al. *Prejudice, War, and the Constitution.* Berkeley: University of California Press, 1970.

United States Department of Justice. *Justice Department Briefs in Crucial Civil Rights Cases, 1948–1968.* New York: Garland, 1991.

Urofsky, Melvin I. *Division and Discord: The Supreme Court under Stone and Vinson, 1941–1953.* Columbia: University of South Carolina Press, 1997.

Weinstein, Allen. *Perjury: The Hiss-Chambers Case.* New York: Random House, 1997.

Websites

Smithsonian National Museum of American History. "A More Perfect Union: Japanese Americans & the U.S. Constitution." Available online at http://americanhistory.si.edu/perfectunion /experience/index.html (Accessed August 8, 2002).

University of Washington Japanese American Exhibit and Access Project. "Camp Harmony Exhibit." Available online at http://www.lib.washington.edu/exhibits/harmony/Exhibit /default.htm (Accessed August 8, 2002).

Lifestyles and Social Trends

Anderson, Jervis. *A. Philip Randolph.* New York: Harcourt Brace, 1973.

Anderson, Karen. *Wartime Women: Sex Roles, Family Relations, and the Status of Women During World War II.* Westport, Conn.: Greenwood Press, 1981.

Bailey, Beth, and David Farber. *The First Strange Place: Race and Sex in World War II Hawaii.* Baltimore: Johns Hopkins University Press, 1994.

Berube, Allen. *Coming Out Under Fire: The History of Gay Men and Women in World War Two.* New York: Penguin Books, 1991.

Buchanan, A. Russell. *Black Americans in World War II.* Santa Barbara, Calif.: Clio, 1977.

Campbell, D'Ann. *Women at War with America: Private Lives in a Patriotic Era.* Cambridge, Mass.: Harvard University Press, 1984.

Chafe, William. *The American Woman: Her Changing Social, Economic, and Political Roles, 1920–1970.* New York: Oxford University Press, 1972.

Costello, John. *Virtue Under Fire: How World War II Changed Our Sexual and Social Attitudes.* Boston: Little, Brown, and Co., 1985.

Dalfiume, Richard M. *Desegregation of the U.S. Armed Forces.* Columbia: University of Missouri Press, 1969.

Erenberg, Lewis A., and Susan E. Hirsch. *The War in American Culture: Society and Consciousness during World War II.* Chicago: University of Chicago Press, 1996.

Graebner, William. *The Age of Doubt: American Thought and Culture in the 1940s.* Boston: Twayne, 1990.

Hartmann, Susan M. *The Home Front and Beyond: American Women in the 1940s.* Boston: Twayne, 1982.

Higonnet, Margaret Randolph, et al., eds. *Behind the Lines: Gender and the Two World Wars.* New Haven, Conn.: Yale University Press, 1987.

Jackson, Kenneth T. *Crabgrass Frontier: The Suburbanization of the United States.* New York: Oxford University Press, 1985.

Jones, Landon Y. , *Great Expectations: America and the Baby Boom Generation.* New York: Coward, McCann, & Geoghegan, 1980.

Kennett, Lee. *G.I.: The American Soldier in World War II.* New York: Charles Scribner's Sons, 1987.

Lemann, Nicholas. *Out of the Forties.* Washington, D.C.: Smithsonian Institution Press, 1998.

Lingeman, Richard. *Don't You Know There's War on? The American Home Front, 1941–1945.* New York: Putnam, 1970.

Litoff, Judy Barrett, and David C. Smith, eds. *We're in this War Too: World War II Letters from American Women in Uniform.* New York: Oxford University Press, 1994.

May, Elaine Tyler. *Homeward Bound: American Families in the Cold War Era.* New York: Basic Books, 1988.

Mazon, Mauricio. *The Zoot-Suit Riots: The Psychology of Symbolic Annihilation.* Austin: University of Texas Press, 1984.

McGuire, Phillip, ed. *Taps for a Jim Crow Army: Letters from Black Soldiers in World War II.* Santa Barbara, Calif.: ABC-CLIO, 1983.

Meyer, Leisa D. *Creating GI Jane: Sexuality and Power in the Women's Army Corps During World War II.* New York: Columbia University Press, 1996.

Meyerowitz, Joanne. *Not June Cleaver: Women and Gender in Postwar America, 1945–1960.* Philadelphia: Temple University Press, 1994.

Myrdal, Gunnar. *An American Dilemma: The Negro Problem and Modern Democracy.* New York: Harper & Row, 1944.

Pells, Richard H. *The Liberal Mind in a Conservative Age: American Intellectuals in the 1940s and 1950s.* New York: Harper & Row, 1985.

Skolnick, Arlene. *Embattled Paradise: The American Family in an Age of Uncertainty.* New York: Basic Books, 1991.

Sugrue, Thomas J. *The Origins of the Urban Crisis.* Princeton, N.J.: Princeton University Press, 1998.

Terkel, Studs. *"The Good War": An Oral History of World War II.* New York: Ballantine Books, 1984.

Tuttle, William M., Jr. *"Daddy's Gone to War": The Second World War in the Lives of America's Children.* New York: Oxford University Press, 1993.

White, Walter. *A Rising Wind.* Garden City, N.Y.: Doubleday, Doran, 1945.

Winkler, Allan M. *Home Front U.S.A.: America During World War II.* Arlington Heights, Ill.: Harlan Davidson, 1986.

Wynn, Neil. *The Afro-American and the Second World War.* London: P. Elek, 1976.

Websites

Hales, Peter Bacon. "Levittown: Documents of an Ideal Suburb." Available online at http://tigger.uic.edu/pbhales/Levittown .html (Accessed August 8, 2002).

Smithsonian National Museum of American History. "Produce for Victory: Posters on the American Homefront." Available online at http://www.americanhistory.si.edu/victory/index.htm (accessed August 8, 2002).

Media

Barnouw, Erik. *A History of Broadcasting in the United States, Vol. II, The Golden Web, 1933 to 1953.* New York: Oxford University Press, 1968.

———. *Tube of Plenty: The Evolution of American Television.* New York: Oxford University Press, 1975.

Benton, Mike. *The Comic Book in America: An Illustrated History.* Dallas: Taylor, 1989.

Castleman, Harry, and Walter J. Podrazik. *Watching TV: Four Decades of American Television.* New York: McGraw-Hill, 1982.

Douglas, Susan J. *Listening in: Radio and the American Imagination, from Amos 'n' Andy and Edward R. Murrow to Wolfman Jack and Howard Stern.* New York: Times Books, 1999.

Dunning, John. *Tune in Yesterday: The Ultimate Encyclopedia of Old-Time Radio 1925–1976.* Englewood Cliffs, N.J.: Prentice-Hall, 1976.

Herzstein, Robert Edwin. *Henry R. Luce: A Political Portrait of the Man Who Created the American Century.* New York: C. Scribner's Sons, 1994.

Honey, Maureen. *Creating Rosie the Riveter: Class, Gender, and Propaganda During World War II.* Amherst: University of Massachusetts Press, 1984.

Kisseloff, Jeff. *The Box: An Oral History of Television, 1920–1961.* New York: Viking, 1995.

Lichty, Laurence W., and Malachi Topping. *American Broadcasting: A Source Book on the History of Radio and Television.* New York: Hastings House, 1975.

MacDonald, J. Fred. *Don't Touch That Dial: Radio Programming in American Life from 1920 to 1960.* Chicago: G. K. Hall, 1979.

Maslowski, Peter. *Armed with Cameras: The American Military Photographers of World War II.* New York: The Free Press, 1993.

Roeder, George H., Jr. *The Censored War: American Visual Experience During World War II.* New Haven, Conn.: Yale University Press, 1993.

Samuel, Lawrence R. *Brought to You by: Postwar Television Advertising and the American Dream.* Austin: University of Texas Press, 2001.

Sterling, Christopher, ed. *The History of Broadcasting: Radio to Television.* 32 vols. New York: New York Times/Arno, 1972.

Tebbel, John William, and Mary Ellen Zuckerman. *The Magazine in America, 1741–1990.* New York: Oxford University Press, 1990.

Terrace, Vincent. *The Complete Encyclopedia of Television Programs: 1947–1979,* 2d ed. New York: Barnes, 1980.

Websites

"The Black Press: Soldiers Without Swords." Available online at http://www.pbs.org/blackpress (accessed August 8, 2002).

Smithsonian National Museum of American History. "July 1942: United We Stand." Available online at http://www.americanhistory.si.edu/1942/index.html (accessed August 8, 2002).

Medicine and Health

Adams, David P. *The Greatest Good to the Greatest Number: Penicillin Rationing on the American Home Front, 1940–1945.* New York: P. Lang, 1991.

Brandt, Allen M. *No Magic Bullet: A Social History of Venereal Disease in the United States Since 1880.* New York: Oxford University Press, 1987.

Cassedy, James H. *Medicine in America: A Short History.* Baltimore: Johns Hopkins University Press, 1991.

Companion Encyclopedia of the History of Medicine. London: Routledge, 1993.

Cowdrey, Albert E. *Fighting for Life: American Military Medicine in World War II.* New York: Free Press, 1994.

Cohn, Victor. *Sister Kenny: The Woman Who Challenged the Doctors.* Minneapolis: University of Minnesota Press, 1975.

Dolan, John Patrick. *Health and Society: A Documentary History of Medicine.* New York: Seabury, 1978.

Duke, Martin. *The Development of Medical Techniques and Treatments: From Leeches to Heart Surgery.* Madison, Conn.: International Universities Press, 1991.

Gathorne-Hardy, Jonathan. *Sex the Measure of All Things: A Life of Alfred C. Kinsey.* Bloomington: University of Indianapolis Press, 2000.

Gould, Tony. *A Summer Plague: Polio and its Survivors.* New Haven, Conn.: Yale University Press, 1995.

Herman, Ellen. *The Romance of American Psychology: Political Culture in the Age of Experts.* Berkeley: University of California Press, 1995.

Jones, James H. *Alfred C. Kinsey: A Public/Private Life.* New York: W.W. Norton, 1997.

Paul, John R. *A History of Poliomyelitis.* New Haven, Conn.: Yale University Press, 1971.

Reiser, Stanley Joel. *Medicine and the Reign of Technology.* New York: Cambridge University Press, 1978.

Sewell, Patricia W., ed. *Healers in World War II: Oral Histories of Medical Corps Personnel.* Jefferson, N.C.: McFarland, 2001.

Stevens, Rosemary. *American Medicine and the Public Interest.* New Haven, Conn.: Yale University Press, 1971.

Valenstein, Elliot S. *Great and Desperate Cures: The Rise and Decline of Psychosurgery and Other Radical Treatments for Mental Illness.* New York: Basic Books, 1986.

Religion

Ahlstrom, Sydney E. *A Religious History of the American People.* 2 vols. Garden City, N.Y.: Doubleday, 1975.

Beckwith, Bernham P. *The Decline of U.S. Religious Faith, 1912–1984.* Palo Alto, Calif.: Beckwith, 1985.

Brown, Charles C. *Niebuhr and His Age: Reinhold Niebuhr's Prophetic Role in the Twentieth Century.* Philadelphia: Trinity Press International, 1992.

Cavert, Samuel McCrea. *The American Churches in the Ecumenical Movement, 1900–1968.* New York: Association Press, 1968.

Cooney, John. *The American Pope: The Life and Times of Francis Cardinal Spellman.* New York: New York Times Books, 1984.

Drinan, Robert F. *Religion, the Courts, and Public Policy.* New York: McGraw-Hill, 1963.

Eighmy, John L. *Churches in Cultural Captivity: A History of the Social Attitudes of Southern Baptists.* Knoxville: University of Tennessee Press, 1987.

Feingold, Henry L. *The Jewish People in America, Vol. IV, A Time for Searching: Entering the Mainstream, 1920–1945.* Baltimore: Johns Hopkins University Press, 1992.

Hadden, Jeffrey K. *The Gathering Storm in the Churches.* Garden City, N.Y.: Doubleday, 1970.

Hennesey, James. *American Catholics: A History of the Roman Catholic Community in the United States.* New York: Oxford University Press, 1981.

Hertzberg, Arthur. *The Jews in America: Four Centuries of an Uneasy Encounter: A History.* New York: Simon & Schuster, 1989.

Hutchinson, William R. *The Modernist Impulse in American Protestantism.* Cambridge, Mass.: Harvard University Press, 1976.

Jones, Donald G., and Russell E. Richey, eds. *American Civil Religion.* San Francisco: Mellen Research University Press, 1990.

Long, Edward L. *The Christian Response to the Atomic Crisis.* Philadelphia: Westminster, 1950.

Marty, Martin E. *Modern American Religion, Vol. III, Under God, Indivisible, 1941–1960.* Chicago: University of Chicago Press, 1986.

Pfeiffer, Leo. *Church, State, and Freedom.* 2d ed. Boston: Beacon, 1967.

Richey, Russell E. *American Civil Religion.* New York: Harper & Row, 1974.

Silk, Mark. *Spiritual Politics: Religion and America since World War II.* New York: Simon & Schuster, 1988.

Stone, Ronald H. *Reinhold Niebuhr: Prophet to Politicians.* Nashville: Abingdon, 1972.

Tussman, Joseph, ed. *The Supreme Court on Church and State.* New York: Oxford University Press, 1962.

Walker, Brooks R. *Christian Fright Peddlers.* Garden City, N.Y.: Doubleday, 1964.

Wilson, Edmund. *The Dead Sea Scrolls, 1947–1969.* New York: Oxford University Press, 1969.

Wuthnow, Robert. *The Restructuring of American Religion: Society and Faith since World War II.* Princeton, N.J.: Princeton University Press, 1988.

Science and Technology

Allen, Garland. *Life Science in the Twentieth Century.* Cambridge: Cambridge University Press, 1978.

Boyer, Paul. *By the Bomb's Early Light: American Thought and Culture at the Dawn of the Nuclear Age.* New York: Pantheon, 1985.

Campbell-Kelly, Martin, and William Aspray. *Computer: A History of the Information Age.* New York: Basic Books, 1996.

Ceruzzi, Paul E. *A History of Modern Computing.* Cambridge, Mass.: MIT Press, 1998.

Compton, Arthur Holly. *Atomic Quest: A Personal Narrative.* New York: Oxford University Press, 1956.

Corn, Joseph J. *The Winged Gospel: America's Romance with Aviation, 1900–1950.* New York: Oxford University Press, 1983.

Degler, Carl N. *In Search of Human Nature: the Decline and Revival of Darwinism in American Social Thought.* New York: Oxford University Press, 1991.

Edwards, Paul N. *The Closed World: Computers and the Politics of Discourse in Cold War America.* Cambridge, Mass.: MIT Press, 1996.

Feingold, Henry L. *Science, Jews, and Secular Culture: Studies in Mid-Twentieth-Century American Intellectual History.* Princeton, N.J.: Princeton University Press, 1996.

Fermi, Laura. *Illustrious Immigrants: The Intellectual Migration from Europe.* Chicago: University of Chicago Press, 1968.

Fleming, Donald, and Bernard Bailyn, eds. *The Intellectual Migration.* Cambridge. Mass.: Harvard University Press, 1969.

Goldstein, Herman H. *The Computer from Pascal to von Neumann.* Princeton, N.J.: Princeton University Press, 1972.

Groves, Leslie R. *Now It Can Be Told: The Story of the Manhattan Project.* New York: Harper, 1962.

Haugelan, J. *Artificial Intelligence: The Very Idea.* Cambridge, Mass.: MIT Press, 1985.

Kass-Simon, G., and Patricia Farnes, eds. *Women of Science.* Bloomington: University of Indiana Press, 1990.

Keller, Evelyn Fox. *A Feeling for the Organism: The Life and Work of Barbara McClintock.* New York: Freeman, 1983.

Kevles, Daniel J. *In the Name of Eugenics: Genetics and the Uses of Human Heredity.* New York: Knopf, 1985.

———. *The Physicists: The History of a Scientific Community in Modern America.* New York: Knopf, 1978.

Mayr, Ernst, and William B. Provine. *The Evolutionary Synthesis: Perspectives on the Unification of Biology.* Cambridge, Mass.: Harvard University Press, 1980.

McGill, Frank. *Great Events From History II.* Science and Technology Series; Vol. III, 1931–1952 Pasadena, Calif.: Salem Press, 1991.

Metropolis, N., ed. *A History of Computing in the Twentieth Century.* New York: Academic Press, 1980.

Rhodes, Richard. *The Making of the Atomic Bomb.* New York: Simon and Schuster, 1986.

———. *Dark Sun: The Making of the Hydrogen Bomb.* New York: Simon & Schuster, 1995.

Riordan, Michael, and Lillian Hoddeson. *Crystal Fire: The Birth of the Information Age.* New York: Norton, 1997.

Simon, Herbert Alexander. *Sciences of the Artificial.* Cambridge, Mass.: MIT Press, 1969.

Thrachray, Arnold, Jeffrey Sturchio, P. Thomas Carroll, and Robert Bush. *Chemistry in America, 1876–1976.* Dordrecht, Holland: Reidel, 1985.

Wang, Jessica. *American Science in an Age of Anxiety: Scientists, Anticommunism, and the Cold War.* Chapel Hill, N.C.: University of North Carolina Press, 1999.

Sports

Alexander, Charles C. *Our Game: An American Baseball History.* New York: Holt, 1991.

Ashe, Arthur R., Jr. *A Hard Road to Glory: A History of the African-American Athlete Since 1946.* New York: Warner, 1988.

Baker, William J., and John M. Carrol, eds. *Sports in Modern America.* Saint Louis: River City, 1981.

Cady, Edwin H. *The Big Game: College Sports and American Life.* Knoxville: University of Tennessee Press, 1978.

Camper, Erich. *Encyclopedia of the Olympic Games.* New York: McGraw-Hill, 1972.

Durant, John. *Highlights of the Olympics.* New York: Hastings House, 1965.

Finoli, David. *For the Good of the Country: World War II Baseball in the Major and Minor Leagues.* Jefferson, N.C.: McFarland, 2002.

Gerber, Ellen W., Jan Feshlin, Pearl Berlin, and Waneen Wyrick. *The American Woman in Sport.* Reading, Mass.: Addison-Wesley, 1974.

Grimsley, Will. *Golf: Its History, People and Events.* Englewood Cliffs, N.J.: Prentice-Hall, 1966.

———. *Tennis: Its History, People and Events.* Englewood Cliffs, N.J.: Prentice-Hall, 1971.

Guttman, Allen. *A Whole New Ball Game: An Interpretation of American Sports.* Chapel Hill: University of North Carolina Press, 1988.

Harris, Dorothy V., ed. *Women and Sports.* University Park: Pennsylvania State University Press, 1972.

Hietala, Thomas R. *Fight of the Century: Jack Johnson, Joe Louis, and the Struggle for Racial Equality.* Armonk, N.Y.: M. E. Sharpe, 2002.

Isaacs, Neil D. *All the Moves: A History of College Basketball.* Philadelphia: Lippincott, 1975.

Kaye, Ivan N. *Good Clean Violence: A History of College Football.* Philadelphia: Lippincott, 1973.

Mandel, Richard D. *Sport: A Cultural History.* New York: Columbia University Press, 1984.

Olsen, Jack. *The Black Athlete: A Shameful Story.* New York: Time-Life Books, 1968.

Peterson, Robert W. *Only the Ball Was White.* Englewood Cliffs, N.J.: Prentice-Hall, 1970.

Rampersad, Arnold. *Jackie Robinson: A Biography.* New York: Knopf, 1997.

Smith, Leverett T., Jr. *The American Dream and the National Game.* Bowling Green, Ohio: Bowling Green University Popular Press, 1975.

Tygel, Jules. *Baseball's Great Experiment.* New York: Oxford University Press, 1983.

Voigt, David Q. *America Through Baseball.* Chicago: Nelson-Hall, 1976.

PRIMARY SOURCE TYPE INDEX

Primary source authors appear in parentheses. Page numbers in italics indicate images, and those followed by the letter t indicate tables.

Primary source authors appear in parentheses. Page numbers in italics indicate images, and those followed by the letter *t* indicate tables.

Primary source authors appear in parentheses. Page numbers in italics indicate images, and those followed by the letter *t* indicate tables.

Primary source authors appear in parentheses. Page numbers in italics indicate images, and those followed by the letter *t* indicate tables.

GENERAL INDEX

Page numbers in bold indicate primary sources; page numbers in italic indicate images; page numbers in bold italic indicate primary source images; page numbers followed by the letter t *indicate tables. Primary sources are indexed under the entry name with the author's name in parentheses. Primary sources are also indexed by title. All primary sources can be identified by bold page locators.*

A

Abstract art, 46–48

Academic freedom, 244–246

Address at the Dedication of the Thomas Jefferson Memorial, 178–181

   speech (Roosevelt), **180–181**

"Address by General George C. Marshall Secretary of State of the United States at Harvard University, June 5, 1947," 239–242

   speech (Marshall), **240–241**

Adult education, 120–123, *121*

Advertising

   education and, 131

   Montgomery Ward on labor strike, *76*

AFL (American Federation of Labor), 99–101

African American artists, 21–23

African American athletes, 554–555, 574–577

African American composers, 15–17

African American education

   Bethune-Cookman College curriculum, 119–120

   higher education goals, 144–148

   United Negro College Fund, 155–158

African American teachers

   Bethune, Mary McLeod, *117,* 117–120

   Patterson, Frederick D., 155–158, *156*

African American writers

   Ellison, Ralph, 30–31

   Wright, Richard, 30–34

African Americans

   abolition of restrictive covenants, 294–296

   desegregation of armed forces, 296–299

   Seventy-Five Years of Negro Progress Exposition, 312–314

   Tuskegee Airmen, *297, 298*

   voting rights in primary elections, 285–288

Agee, James, 38–42

   movie review, **39–42**

Agricultural commerce, 275–279

Aiken, Howard, 528–531, *529*

Aikin, Wilford M., 127–130

   speech, **128–130**

"The Aims of Music for Films," 6–9

   newspaper article (Copland), **6–9**

Air raid shelters, 319–321

All-American Girls Professional Baseball League, 327–331, 583–585

   guidebook, **329–331**

Allen, Mel, *581*

Allen, Raymond B., 244–246

   journal article, **244–246**

Allwright, Smith v. (1944), 285–288

Amazing Stories, 314–317

America First Committee, 360, *361*

"America Is Learning What to Eat," 427–430

   illustration *(The New York Times), 428*

   newspaper article (McCoy), **428–430**

"America Was Schoolmasters" (Coffin), **134–135**

American architecture, 185–190

American artists, 46–48

American composers

   Comden, Betty, *28*

   Copland, Aaron, 6–9, *7*

   Green, Adolph, *28*

American Council of Christian Churches, 467–469

   constitution, **468–469**

American Federation of Labor (AFL), 99–101

American Medical Association, 438–442

American Men in Three Wartime Posters, 170–174

   "Get Hot—Keep Moving" (Barclay), *173*

   "Keep 'Em Fighting" (Barclay), *172*

   "Man the Guns—Join the Navy" (Barclay), *171*

Page numbers in bold indicate primary sources; page numbers in italic indicate images;
page numbers in bold italic indicate primary source images; page numbers followed by the letter *t* indicate tables.

Page numbers in bold indicate primary sources; page numbers in italic indicate images; page numbers in bold italic indicate primary source images; page numbers followed by the letter *t* indicate tables.

Page numbers in bold indicate primary sources; page numbers in italic indicate images; page numbers in bold italic indicate primary source images; page numbers followed by the letter *t* indicate tables.

Page numbers in bold indicate primary sources; page numbers in italic indicate images;
page numbers in bold italic indicate primary source images; page numbers followed by the letter *t* indicate tables.

Page numbers in bold indicate primary sources; page numbers in italic indicate images;
page numbers in bold italic indicate primary source images; page numbers followed by the letter *t* indicate tables.

Page numbers in bold indicate primary sources; page numbers in italic indicate images; page numbers in bold italic indicate primary source images; page numbers followed by the letter *t* indicate tables.

Page numbers in bold indicate primary sources; page numbers in italic indicate images;
page numbers in bold italic indicate primary source images; page numbers followed by the letter *t* indicate tables.

Page numbers in bold indicate primary sources; page numbers in italic indicate images; page numbers in bold italic indicate primary source images; page numbers followed by the letter *t* indicate tables.

Page numbers in bold indicate primary sources; page numbers in italic indicate images; page numbers in bold italic indicate primary source images; page numbers followed by the letter *t* indicate tables.

Page numbers in bold indicate primary sources; page numbers in italic indicate images;
page numbers in bold italic indicate primary source images; page numbers followed by the letter *t* indicate tables.

Page numbers in bold indicate primary sources; page numbers in italic indicate images; page numbers in bold italic indicate primary source images; page numbers followed by the letter *t* indicate tables.

Page numbers in bold indicate primary sources; page numbers in italic indicate images; page numbers in bold italic indicate primary source images; page numbers followed by the letter *t* indicate tables.

Page numbers in bold indicate primary sources; page numbers in italic indicate images;
page numbers in bold italic indicate primary source images; page numbers followed by the letter *t* indicate tables.